Dictionary of AMERICAN IMMIGRATION HISTORY

edited by
Francesco Cordasco

The Scarecrow Press, Inc.
Metuchen, N.J., & London
1990

BOOKS BY FRANCESCO CORDASCO

Shaping of American Graduate
   Education (1960)
Educational Sociology (1965)
The School in the Social Order
   (1967)
Jacob Riis Revisited: Poverty
   and the Slum (1968)
Education in the Urban
   Community (1969)
Minorities and the American
   City (1970)
Italians in the United States
   (1972)
Puerto Ricans on the United
   States Mainland (1972)
Equality of Educational
   Opportunity (1973)
The Puerto Ricans (1973)
Italians: Social Backgrounds of
   an American Group (1974)

Bilingual Schooling in the
   United States (1976)
Immigrant Children in
   American Schools (1976)
The Black Hand: A Chapter in
   Ethnic Crime (1977)
Italian Mass Emigration (1980)
American Ethnic Groups: The
   European Heritage (1981)
The White Slave Trade and the
   Immigrants (1981)
The Puerto Rican Community
   and Its Children (3rd ed.,
   1982)
The Immigrant Woman in
   North America (1985)
The New American Immigration
   (1987)

British Library Cataloguing-in-Publication data available

Library of Congress Cataloging-in-Publication Data

Dictionary of American immigration history / edited by Francesco
Cordasco
     p.   cm.
   Includes bibliographical references.
   ISBN 0-8108-2241-5
   1. United States—Emigration and immigration—History—
Dictionaries. I. Cordasco, Francesco, 1920–
JV6450.D53   1990
325.73'03—dc20   89-37041

In memory of

GIOVANNI CORDASCO (1883–1953)

Intrepid voyager to the New World

Most immigrants said nothing that we can hear, though from time to time, in a letter or a fragment of a diary, in the record of a speech or a riot, they impress themselves on our minds. Their descendants, of course, cannot interpret them: they are merely surprised at their parents' or grandparents' preoccupation with worlds that are not their own. It is for the historian to employ such skill as he possesses to uncover individual stories and to detect patterns in the imperfect evidence. If he judges the effort worth making, it will be because he can feel respect and fascination when confronted by the hardships, the disillusion, the modest achievements of the millions who crossed the Atlantic. Fascination above all: for now and again, from the faceless crowd, there emerge, in Lewis Hine's photographs or the sketches of Jacob Epstein and Joseph Stella, features more striking, more noble even, than those of the generals and prelates, the politicians and magnates, of whom most history is told.

—Philip Taylor, *The Distant Magnet* (1971)

CONTENTS

PREFACE

"Dictionaries are like watches," Dr. Samuel Johnson, the lexicographer, said; "the best cannot be expected to go quite true, but the worst is better than none." There is little doubt that this *Dictionary of American Immigration History* has long been a desideration.

In the "Introduction" to the *Harvard Encyclopedia of American Ethnic Groups* (1980), the editors noted that Louis Adamic (1898–1951), the ethnic journalist and novelist, proposed a work which he believed "would excite all America about herself ... a great Encyclopedia of the Population of the United States, from the Indians down to the latest immigrant group [which would chronicle] in as great detail as possible, of what sort of human stuff America is made ... [which] might well revolutionize American writing and affect all thinking about the United States." Adamic believed that such a work "would be invaluable to thousands of ... school principals and teachers ... and to librarians and social workers. It would appeal not only to New Americans and their immigrant parents ... but to America as a whole." [*My America,* 1938]

The *Dictionary of American Immigration History* is designed as a reference compendium on most aspects of American immigration history. Since the writing of history is so much a matter of selection, anyone who compiles a work of this kind is bound to be guided, when it comes to deciding what should be included or omitted, by certain considerations which seem relevant to the compiler, but might not be so to other people, though none would argue with the overriding consideration of space limitations.

In its hundreds of entries, the *DAIH* includes data on most American ethnic groups, although how many there are and how they are to be identified or classified are matters on which there is no agreement. Cited are individuals important in the history of American immigration—as disparately contrasting, to name a few, as Senator William Dillingham, Henry Pratt Fairchild, Charles Loring Brace, Jacob Riis, and Jane Addams; notices of immigrant historical societies, mutual aid societies, immigrant-help groups, immigration legislation, and restrictionism; plus conceptual themes exploring *(inter alia)* ethnicity, ethnic studies, pluralism, assimilation, and related modalities. There are included, as well, the *disjecta membra* strewn across the historical landscape which fail to fall into definable categories.

Inevitably, difficulties have been encountered and, for the most part, regrettably left unresolved. A case in point: I had decided to include an entry on "Native Americans" and invited a number of scholars to contribute such an entry; none chose to do so. A distinguished Native American academician wrote: "It would probably be a mistake to include 'Native Americans.' This mistake would be political rather than scholarly. Indians object vehemently to being called immigrants, and [they] would get any scholar who wrote [the entry] in very hot water with native peoples. This is a complex issue. I assure you the omission will result in less flack than its inclusion."

Ostensibly, the *Dictionary* is not exhaustive (comprehensive, perhaps), and no such pretense is made. How vast the expanses of American immigration are, is suggested by my recent *The New American Immigration: Evolving Patterns of Legal and Illegal Emigration* (1987) and the huge literature it surveys.

Entries range in size from a paragraph to essays of several thousand words. Where appropriate, entries are followed by a short list of references. Contributors of entries were encouraged to develop individual entries in whatever conceptual and developmental modality they thought appropriate; only a uniformity of style (i.e., format) was proposed to achieve consistency in presentation. Entry format is illustrated in this brief sample entry:

> **PETROSINO, GIUSEPPE** (1860–1909). Italian-American legendary New York City detective who fought the dreaded *La Mano Nera* (the Black Hand) (*q.v.*), whose terror (criminal violence, extortion, etc.) dominated the Italian-American communities of the first two decades of this century. Petrosino was murdered in Palermo, Sicily, in 1909 when he was on assignment to investigate the Italian criminal connections with the American Black Hand.
>
> *References*
> Arrigo Petacco, *Joe Petrosino* (1974); Thomas M. Pitkin and Francesco Cordasco, *The Black Hand* (1977).
>
> *T.M.P.*

Kindly note: Entry title is in capital letters; references (if any) are captioned and subjoined; contributor's initials are appended to the entry. In many instances, entry title is followed by an additional explanatory legend identifying the specific intent/subject of the entry. An example:

> **JEWS, American Jewry and United States immigration policy.** During the period between 1880 and the 1950s, no public

issue inspired greater concern on the part of American Jews than
did the formation of United States immigration policy, particularly, policy from the onset of the vast eastern European migration
to the United States through the time of the reaffirmation of the
national origins system nearly four decades after it was first
adopted. Arranged chronologically, Jewish activity can be best
placed into a number of major episodes: (1) the early reaction to
the arrival of the eastern European Jews and the attempt to curb
their entry; (2) the response to the literacy test; (3) the response to
the quota legislation; (4) the effort to admit refugees from Nazism;
(5) the reaction to the displaced persons question; and (6) the effort
to modify the quota system during the 1950s.

Reference
Sheldon M. Neuringer, *American Jewry and the United States
Immigration Policy, 1881–1953* (1980).

F.C.

Cross-referencing has been extensively employed (using the convenient device of *q.v.* within entries), and, where needed, cross-refer-
ences appended to entries themselves. Also, individual cross-reference
entries have been used to facilitate convenient use.

Contributors are identified by initials appended to the entries. The
contributors can be identified by reference to the List of Contributors, in
which the listing is an alphabetical arrangement of initials rather than
surnames, the former system having been judged to afford greater
convenience.

A book, Walt Whitman has said, should "go as lightly as the bird
flies in the air or a fish swims in the sea." The *Dictionary of American
Immigration History* is heavily freighted with hundreds of entries and
bibliographical references; it could not have been otherwise. Reference
books, as a genre, are both portentous and ponderous.

Acknowledgments

The list of individuals to whom I owe thanks is too long to print.
Above all, my first indebtedness is to the many contributors who make
Dictionary of American Immigration History theirs as well as mine.
Their views, as expressed in the contributed entries, are their own. A
number of individuals who not only wrote entries, but afforded impor-
tant counsel, should be noted: Robert F. Harney, Multicultural History
Society of Ontario; Maldwyn A. Jones, University College, London;
Carleton C. Qualey, Immigration History Society; M. Mark Stolarik,
Balch Institute; Lydio F. Tomasi, Center for Migration Studies; and
Lubomyr R. Wynar, Center for the Study of Ethnic Publications. David
Nelson Alloway (1927–1987), a colleague and friend, would have

joined me in this venture had it not been for illness. His untimely death is a tragic loss to the academic community. The entries Professor Alloway managed to contribute to the *DAIH,* despite the debility of a harrowing illness, are a testimony to his courage. Theodore Besterman (1904–1976), with whom I was long associated, concluded the "Introduction" to his monumental *World Bibliography of Bibliographies* (4th ed., 5 vols., 1965–1966) with the plaintive valedictory of Hemacandra: "May the noble-minded scholars instead of cherishing ill feeling kindly correct whatever errors have been here committed through the dullness of my intellect in the way of wrong interpretations and misstatements." The sentiments are appropriate at any book's publication. They have a singular affinity with this *Dictionary* and its fortunes.

FRANCESCO CORDASCO

West New York, N.J.
March 1988

LIST OF CONTRIBUTORS

Initials appear at the end of each entry. Contributors can be identified by referring to this list. The listing is an alphabetical arrangement of initials rather than surnames.

A.A.	Alfred Aversa, Jr., Fairleigh Dickinson University
A.C.B.	August C. Bolino, Catholic University of America
A.J.M.	August J. Molnar, American Hungarian Foundation
A.L.W.	Allen L. Woll, Rutgers University
A.N.	Alixa Naff, Smithsonian Institution
A.R.	Andrew Rolle, Occidental College
A.S.	Alice Scourby, Long Island University
A.T.K.	Andrew T. Kopan, DePaul University
B.L.	Benjamin Lichtenberg, Caldwell College
C.C.	Charlotte Croman, City University of New York
C.E.C.	Carlos E. Cortès, University of California/Riverside
C.M.C.	Charles M. Carlton, University of Rochester
C.U.	Carmelo Urza, University of Nevada
D.A.	Dina Abramowicz, Yivo Institute for Jewish Research
D.B.	Dag Blanck, Augustana College
D.D.M.	Deborah Dash Moore, Vassar College
D.M.	Diane Matza, Syracuse University/Utica College
D.M.B.	Dorothy M. Balancio, Mercy College
D.M.J.	David Maldwyn Ellis, Hamilton College
D.M.R.	David M. Reimers, New York University
D.N.A.	David Nelson Alloway, Montclair State College
D.R.S.	Dale R. Steiner, California State University/Chico
D.W.H.	David W. Haines, Fulbright Scholar/Europe
E.P.N.	Eugene P. Nassar, Syracuse University/Utica College
F.C.	Francesco Cordasco, Montclair State College
F.J.C.	Frederick J. Conway, San Diego State University

F.K.	Frances Kraljic, City University of New York
F.M.P.	Felix Masud-Piloto, South Florida Community College
F.P.	Fortune Pope, The Pope Foundation
F.X.F.	Francis X. Femminella, State University of New York/Albany
G.B.	George Bernstein, Montclair State College
G.J.P.	George J. Prpic, John Carroll University
G.R.N.	George R. Nielsen, Concordia College
G.Y.O.	Gary Y. Okihiro, Santa Clara University
H.B.	Henry Bischoff, New Jersey History Consortium
H.C.C.	Helen C. Chapin, Hawaii Pacific College
H.C.N.	Humbert C. Nelli, University of Kentucky
H.L.F.	Henry L. Feingold, City University of New York
H.T.	Harold Takooshian, Fordham University
J.A.	John Andreozzi, Immigration History Research Center/University of Minnesota
J.A.H.	John A. Hostetler, Temple University
J.A.K.	John A. Kromkowski, National Center for Urban Ethnic Affairs
J.D.B.	John D. Buenker, University of Wisconsin/Parkside
J.F.M.	John F. McClymer, Assumption College
J.H.D.	James H. Dorman, University of Southwestern Louisiana
J.H.S.	Jason H. Silverman, Winthrop College
J.J.A.	John J. Appel, Michigan State University
J.M.B.	James M. Bergquist, Villanova University
J.M.G.	John Maxtone-Graham, Steamship Historical Society/University of Baltimore
J.M.M.	Joseph M. Murphy, Georgetown University
J.R.G.	Joan Rezner Gundersen, St. Olaf College
J.R.J.	John R. Jenswold, Augsburg College
J.S.P.	James S. Pula, State University of New York/Binghamton
K.C.	Kitty Calavita, Middlebury College
K.D.B.	Karel D. Bicha, Marquette University
L.A.R.	Louis A. Romano, West New York (New Jersey) Board of Education
L.F.T.	Lydio F. Tomasi, Center for Migration Studies/New York City
L.J.I.	Luciano J. Iorizzo, State University of New York/Oswego
L.J.R.	La Vern J. Rippley, St. Olaf College

L.P.   Leo Pap, State University of New York/New Paltz
L.P.D.   Linda Pegman Doezema, Houghton College
L.R.W.   Lubomyr R. Wynar, Kent State University
L.S.   Leo Schelbert, University of Illinois/Chicago
L.W.   Leslie Wilson, Montclair State College

M.A.J.   Maldwyn A. Jones, University College/London
M.A.O.   Michael A. Olivas, University of Houston
M.D.B.   Michael D. Behiels, University of Ottawa
M.M.   Margherita Marchione, Fairleigh Dickinson University
M.M.S.   M. Mark Stolarik, Balch Institute for Ethnic Studies

N.B.   Neil Betten, Florida State University
N.C.   Norman Coombs, Rochester Institute of Technology
N.V.M.   Nicholas V. Montalto, International Institute of New Jersey

P.K.   Peter Kivisto, Augustana College
P.M.H.   Philip M. Hosay, New York University
P.N.   Pellegrino Nazzaro, Rochester Institute of Technology
P.R.M.   Paul Robert Magocsi, University of Toronto
P.S.C.   Philip S. Cohen, Montclair State College
P.W.F.   P. William Filby, Maryland Historical Society

R.A.M.   Raymond A. Mohl, Florida Atlantic University
R.B.W.   Raymond B. Williams, Wabash College
R.M.M.   Randall M. Miller, St. Joseph's University
R.R.   Richard Renoff, Nassau Community College
R.S.S.   Richard S. Sorrell, Brookdale Community College
R.T.   Richard Tuerk, East Texas State University
R.U.P.   Remigio U. Pane, Rutgers University

S.C.   Sucheng Chan, University of California/Santa Cruz
S.C.M.   Stuart Creighton Miller, San Francisco State University
S.M.   Salvatore Mondello, Rochester Institute of Technology
S.M.M.   Sally M. Miller, University of the Pacific
S.P.M.   Seamus P. Metress, University of Toledo

T.J.C.   Thomas J. Curran, St. John's University
T.L.Z.   Theodore L. Zawistowski, Pennsylvania State University
T.M.P.   Thomas M. Pitkin, National Park Service
T.P.R.   Thomas P. Riggio, University of Connecticut

V.K.   Vitaut Kipel, New York Public Library

W.O.M.   Wendy Oxman-Michelli, Montclair State College
W.P.S.   Wallace P. Sillanpoa, University of Rhode Island
W.W.V.   William Wolkovich-Valkavicius, St. George's
           Rectory/Norwood, Massachusetts

INTRODUCTION

I

In 1978, the U.S. Congress passed a law providing for a worldwide immigration cap of 290,000 created by combining both hemispheres, with a preference system and 20,000-person per country limit. The reforms begun in 1965 were now complete. Why had reform been so strong a force in immigration policy by the mid-1960s? For some time it was clear that

> the overt racism of the national-origins admission system could not be sustained in a nation that was already multiracial and multicultural in its composition and that boasted to the world of these attributes. Thus, the movement in the 1950s and early 1960s to overhaul the U.S. immigration system gradually accumulated sufficient momentum to accomplish most of its goals. The capstone of this drive occurred on October 3, 1965, when President Lyndon Johnson signed into law the Immigration and Nationality Amendments of 1965, or the Hart-Celler Act. . . . The legislation was a lengthy series of amendments to the Immigration and Nationality Act of 1952, but in terms of its policy significance it has been called "the most far-reaching revision of immigration policy" since the imposition of the first numerical quotas in 1921. Since its passage, immigration to the United States has changed dramatically both quantitatively and qualitatively.[1]

II

For almost a century, American immigration policy was restrictionist. In the 1880s Congress began an active role in the administration and control of immigration, and this new role was evident in the passage of the Chinese Exclusion Act of 1882, which suspended entry of Chinese workers for ten years and barred all foreign-born Chinese from acquiring citizenship. In 1885, Congress enacted the Foran Act, which prohibited unskilled laborer recruitment with prepaid passage and advance contracting; in 1888, Congress ordered the deportation of all alien contract laborers within one year of entry.

Between 1890 and 1921, Congress attempted to impose literacy requirements to restrict immigration. Four literacy bills were debated in Congress between 1896 and 1917; the Congress passed three literacy acts, each of which received a presidential veto. In 1907, legislation established an Immigration Commission whose appointment President Theodore Roosevelt had long called for. The commission published its *Report* in 1911 in forty-one volumes, and Oscar Handlin called it "one of the most ambitious social science research projects in the nation's history up to then, barring only the censuses"; but the *Report* was restrictionist in its basic recommendations, and Briggs has succinctly characterized it as "neither impartial nor scientific." The commission spent over a million dollars, convened a staff of three hundred, and took over three years in its deliberations, but the

> commission found that the new immigrants differed significantly from the nation's older immigrants. It deemed the new immigrants to be "inferior" and to possess attributes that would make it difficult for them to assimilate. It argued that a slower rate of expansion—a rate that emphasized the ability of immigrants to adapt to their new surroundings—would be preferable to a rapid and uncontrolled rate, which imperiled the prevailing wages and employment opportunities of American citizens. Laced throughout the commissioner's argument were pseudo-scientific theories pertaining to "superior" and "inferior" persons. The mixture of economic and ethnic arguments in the commission's report plagued all efforts to discuss and to legislate immigration reform impartially since that time.[2]

In 1917, over a presidential veto, an Immigration Act was passed which required literacy for immigrants over sixteen years of age (in English, or any other language); and in 1921 the Johnson Act introduced a system of national quotas, determined as the percentage of the number of immigrants from the country in question at a designated census. The 1921 Act (which had been vetoed by President Woodrow Wilson earlier, but signed into law when Warren Harding took office) limited the annual number of immigrants of each admissible nationality to 3 percent of the foreign born of that nationality as recorded in the U.S. census of 1910, and set a limit on European immigration at 350,000.

When the Johnson Act expired in 1924, Congress passed the Johnson-Reed Act, which set national quotas at 2 percent of the 1890 population and also provided that as of July 1, 1927, the quota limit would be 150,000, allocated on the base of the estimated national-origins distribution of the continental U.S. population in 1920; postponed twice, this latter provision became effective in 1929. Between 1929 and 1968, quotas were determined by the "national origins" formula which

> provided that the annual quota equal one-sixth of one percent of the number of white inhabitants in the continental United States, less Western Hemisphere immigrants and their descendants. The annual quota for each nationality was then determined by the same ratio to 150,000 as the number of inhabitants of each nationality living in the continental United States in 1920 to the total inhabitants, although a minimum quota for any nationality was 100.[3]

Various other pieces of restrictionist legislation were passed by the Congress in the period following the Johnson-Reed Act of 1924, but the only piece of major immigration legislation passed was the McCarran-Walter Act (Immigration and Nationality Act) of 1952, which changed the formula for computing the annual quotas of any country to one-sixth of one percent of the numbers of persons of that national origin in the United States in 1920 as computed for the 1924 Quota Act.

> The McCarran-Walter Act basically reinforced the tough immigration restrictions of the 1920s, reaffirmed the national origins quotas, and added security provisions designed to make it almost impossible for suspected subversives to enter the United States.[4]

The McCarran-Walter Act, however,

> could not survive changes at home and abroad. At home the immigrants of the great wave from Eastern and Southern Europe, and their children growing to maturity, were becoming more and more effective politically, developing greater resources economically, becoming bolder in asserting their wishes against a weakening nativism. Abroad, crises that produced waves of refugees from Communism—in Hungary in 1957, in Cuba in 1960 and later— were also changing public opinion about immigration. Perhaps more potent in changing these attitudes were the fading fears of depression, as post-war prosperity continued, marred only by occasional recessions. Perhaps most potent was the radical change in American attitudes on race that accompanied the rise of the civil rights movement. The attempt to freeze the composition of the American people by favoring Northwestern Europe was increasingly seen as basically immoral and wrong.[5]

By 1965, it was clear that the national-origins system had to be changed.

III

The Hart-Celler Act of 1965 eliminated national origins as the basis for selection of immigrants to the United States. Instead, it established an annual limit of 170,000 aliens (and a per country quota of 20,000) who could enter the United States as immigrants. It set a ceiling of 120,000 on immigration from the Western Hemisphere, thus allowing (with the annual limit of 170,000 elsewhere) for the admission of 290,000 immigrants a year. Further, the act established a system whereby immigration visas would be distributed according to a seven-point preference list that favored close relatives of U.S. citizens and those with special occupational skills. The definition of refugees was broadened to include those who were victims of natural calamities, as well as the victims of religious and/or political persecution. Three categories of exclusion were established: (1) people with mental diseases or drug and alcohol addictions; (2) criminals, prostitutes, and those with contagious diseases; (3) subversives and some twenty other categories of aliens. Continuing immigration reforms included the passage of legislation for the admission and resettlement of refugees, mainly from the Soviet Union, Southeast Asia, and Cuba, e.g., the Indochinese Refugee Resettlement Program which allowed the admission of 200,000 Indochinese refugees. In 1980, the Refugee Act established an overall policy for the admission and resettlement of refugees. The Immigration Act of 1965 had unanticipated consequences.

> The people who were fighting for the bill were Jews, Italians, Greeks, Poles, who hoped their relatives, their fellow countrymen, and their co-religionists would have an easier time getting in, and the bill itself favored strongly the principle of family unification. . . . It turned out the chief beneficiaries of the new immigration regime were Asians and Latin Americans. Starting from a modest base, the numbers of Asian immigrants increased rapidly; and as they increased family reunification played a greater and greater role in enabling immigration and resulted in steadily larger numbers of immigrants from Hong Kong and Taiwan, the Philippines, Korea, and India. The disaster in Vietnam added Vietnamese, Cambodians, and Laotians. In the decade of the 1970s, astonishingly, the number of Asians in the United States doubled to three-and-a-half million.[6]

In 1984 the Asian and Mexican immigrants to the United States led all others, with Mexican immigrants in first place. The immigration reforms of 1965 had not foreseen these developments: if the intentions of the immigration reformers in 1965 had been the removal of discriminatory provisions in the earlier legislation against the countries of

Southern and Eastern Europe, the new immigration reforms benefited others. Europe's postwar prosperity generally discouraged large-scale emigration.

In the 1970s, continuing concerns over various immigration issues led to mounting criticisms and demands for reform. Illegal immigration was the paramount concern, but other related issues (e.g., the status of temporary foreign workers and refugee accommodation) continued to be controversial.

The intensity of the debate surrounding the "new immigration" is indicated in the somber observations of Raymond A. Mohl:

> The great surge of new immigrants and refugees since 1960, in particular, has yet to be placed in the larger context of immigration history. In many ways, the new immigration of the past few decades has been reshaping some of the major U.S. metropolitan areas. For instance, in 1983 *Time* magazine reported that the Los Angeles metropolitan area was home not only for over two million Mexican-Americans, but also for hundreds of thousands of other new immigrants. These included 200,000 Salvadorans, 200,000 Iranians, 175,000 Japanese, 150,000 Chinese, 150,000 Koreans, 150,000 Filipinos, 130,000 Arabs, and smaller but still sizeable concentrations of Israelis, Samoans, Colombians, Hondurans, Guatemalans, Cubans, Vietnamese, Pakistanis, and East Indians. Similarly, New York City has become a magnet for Asian, Caribbean, Hispanic, and other new immigrants and refugees. Huge concentrations of Haitians, Dominicans, Colombians, West Indians, and the like have created new ethnic neighborhoods in areas formerly populated by the Italians, Jews, Germans, Scandinavians, and Irish.[7]

In 1978, Congress established a Select Commission on Immigration and Refugee Policy to make a major study of immigration and recommend changes; the sixteen-member commission (including congressional representatives and senators, cabinet officials, and presidential appointees) was chaired by Father Theodore Hesburgh, then president of Notre Dame University; its work was directed by Professor Lawrence Fuchs of Brandeis University. The commission's *Report* was submitted to Congress in March 1981, and its recommendations were that the basic immigration system be kept intact, with more flexibility, adjustments in preferences, and increases in immigration to assist in easing backlogs in certain nations. Its recommendations on illegal (undocumented) aliens proved very controversial, but the *Report* became the basis for immigration reform legislation then pending in the Congress.

In 1984 different versions of the Simpson-Mazzoli Bill, entitled the Immigration Reform and Control Act of 1982, passed both houses of Congress. Its major provisions would impose civil and criminal penalties against employers who knowingly hire illegal aliens; require national identity cards for all legal aliens; grant permanent residence status to illegal aliens who could prove continuous residence in the United States since January 1, 1977, and temporary residence status to those who could prove continuous residence in the United States since January 1, 1980; and establish a new ceiling for the number of legal aliens who would be allowed to enter each year. On June 25, 1986 (with Congressman Peter Rodino, Chairman of the House Judiciary Committee taking a major role), for the third time in five years, the House Judiciary Committee approved a comprehensive bill to revise the nation's immigration laws and to curtail the influx of illegal aliens. The Senate passed a generally similar bill in September 1986 by a vote of 69 to 30, and the Reagan administration supported it. The House and Senate bills would have both prohibited employers from hiring illegal aliens. In addition, they offered legal status to many illegal aliens already in the United States. But the two measures differed in many important details.

The Senate bill would establish a new government program under which farmers could bring up to 350,000 aliens into the United States to harvest perishable fruit and vegetables. By contrast, the bill approved by the House Judiciary Committee would permit certain foreign workers to become residents of the United States, with most of the rights of citizens. Under the House bill, the attorney general would grant lawful permanent resident status to any illegal alien who could prove that he or she had been working in American agriculture for at least sixty days in the period from May 1, 1985, to May 1, 1986. The plan called for the admission of additional aliens if needed to work on farms in subsequent years; they, too, could qualify for permanent resident status. The Senate passed comprehensive immigration bills in 1982, 1983, and 1985. The House passed a bill in 1984 by a five-vote margin, but the measure died when the House and Senate could not work out their differences.

On October 9, 1986, in a dramatic reversal, the U.S. House of Representatives approved a comprehensive bill to overhaul the nation's immigration law and curtail the influx of illegal aliens. The vote was 230 to 166. The U.S. Senate had passed its version of the immigration bill by a vote of 69 to 30 in September 1985.

On October 14, 1986, House and Senate negotiators reached agreement, reconciling all differences between the Senate and House bills; and on October 17, 1986, as it moved toward adjournment, Congress gave final approval to the landmark immigration bill. By a vote of 63 to 24, the Senate agreed to the compromise bill, clearing the measure for action by President Reagan.

The Immigration Reform and Control Act of 1986 marks a historic change in American immigration policy. Under existing law, illegal aliens could be deported, but it was generally not illegal for employers to hire them. Under the new bill, employers who hired illegal aliens would be subject to civil penalties, with fines ranging from $250 to $10,000 for each such alien. The aliens bill, a product of nearly a decade of work in Congress, would make the biggest changes in immigration law in at least twenty years. The bill had broad bipartisan support. It was sponsored in the House by Representatives Peter W. Rodino, Jr., of New Jersey and Romano L. Mazzoli of Kentucky, both Democrats.

The number of illegal aliens in the United States is disputed. Jeffrey S. Passel, a demographer at the Census Bureau, has stated that the bureau estimated there were 2.5 million to 3.5 million illegal aliens who had their usual residence in the United States at the time of the last census in 1980. The bureau estimates that the number of illegal aliens has grown since then by 100,000 to 300,000 a year, so the total now probably stands at three million to five million. These figures do not include the thousands of illegal aliens who go back and forth across the border, working in the United States but returning to permanent residences in Mexico or other countries.

The Immigration Reform and Control Act of 1986 is a milestone in the history of American immigration policy. In Colonial times, immigration was generally encouraged. The first federal restriction on immigration was not adopted until 1875, when Congress barred the admission of prostitutes and convicted criminals. The new bill ranks in importance with the Quota Act of 1921, which established the first numerical restrictions on immigration, and the Immigration and Nationality Act of 1952 (the McCarran-Walter Act), which listed dozens of ideological and other reasons for excluding aliens. Under the new bill, aliens in the United States illegally could apply for legal status in the one-year period starting six months after the bill becomes law. Then, after eighteen months as lawful temporary residents, the aliens could apply for status as permanent residents, and after another five years they could apply for citizenship. If the illegal aliens did not seek legal status, they would remain subject to deportation. Members of Congress and lobbyists said that two factors added impetus to the drive for a comprehensive immigration bill. First, they said, liberals feared that any such bill adopted by the next Congress would be more restrictive and less generous to illegal aliens. In addition, the Reagan administration argued that the bill was needed to help combat drug smuggling. Immigration officials said that many illegal aliens and smugglers of aliens were involved in illicit drug traffic.

Main Provisions of the
Immigration Reform and Control Act
of 1986

• Employers would be forbidden to hire illegal aliens. The ban would apply to all employers, even those with just a few employees. For a first offense, the employer would be subject to a civil penalty of $250 to $2,000 for each illegal alien hired. For subsequent offenses, the employer would be subject to civil penalties as high as $10,000 for each.

• For a "pattern or practice" of violations, the employer would be subject to criminal penalties, up to a $3,000 fine and six months' imprisonment.

• Employers would have to ask all job applicants for documents, such as a passport or a birth certificate and a driver's license, to confirm that they were either citizens or aliens authorized to work in the United States. The employer is not required to check the authenticity of the document. The bill says that it does not authorize the issuance or use of national identification cards.

• The government would offer legal status to aliens who entered the United States illegally before January 1, 1982, and have resided here continuously since then. For five years, they would be ineligible for welfare, food stamps, and most other federal benefits, with some exceptions.

• The federal government will set aside $1 billion a year for four years to reimburse state governments for providing public assistance, health care and education to illegal aliens who gain legal status.

• Under a special program, illegal aliens who worked in American agriculture for at least ninety days in the period from May 1, 1985, to May 1, 1986, could become lawful temporary residents of the United States. After two years in that status, they could become permanent residents, eligible for American citizenship after five years more.

• If there is a shortage of seasonal farm workers, the government could admit additional aliens in the fiscal years 1990 through 1993. They would have to work in agriculture and, after three years as temporary residents, could become permanent residents.

• Immigration officers could not enter a farm without a search warrant or the owner's permission if they wanted to question a person believed to be an alien.

• Employers would be forbidden to discriminate against legal aliens because of their national origin or citizenship status. A new office would be established in the Justice Department to investigate complaints of such discrimination.

• States would generally have to verify, through records of the

Immigration and Naturalization Service, the legal status of aliens seeking welfare benefits, Medicaid, unemployment compensation, food stamps, housing assistance, or college aid under federal programs.
  • To improve enforcement, the Immigration and Naturalization Service would receive $422 million more in fiscal year 1987 and $419 million in FY 1988. The agency's budget in FY 1987 was $593.8 million, of which $379.7 million was for enforcement.

The bill also envisioned a 50 percent increase in Border Patrol personnel, although there was no guarantee that Congress would actually provide money for the increase, and Congress has as yet (1988) not done so. In 1987 the Border Patrol had 3,694 officers. President Ronald Reagan signed the Immigration Reform and Control Act of 1986 into law on November 6, 1986.

IV

Since its enactment, the Immigration Reform and Control Act of 1986 has had an uncertain success. The amnesty provisions for the registration of undocumented aliens have not worked well; enforcement of the act has proved increasingly difficult; congressional funding has not continued at anticipated levels; but, most critically, critics of the 1986 act have proposed major changes which would redefine who could legally immigrate to the United States.
A new immigration bill has been proposed by U.S. Senators Edward M. Kennedy (D: MA) and Alan K. Simpson (R: WY). This new bill, introduced in early 1988, would establish an overall limit on legal immigration of 590,000 people a year. That is about 80,000 above the current level. Under current law, certain types of immigrants are subject to a numerical limit, but other types, including immediate relatives of United States citizens, are not. Under the bill, a larger proportion of immigrants would be selected on the basis of occupational skills rather than family ties. The new proportion would be 20 percent, up from the current 10 percent. Kennedy said he expected the bill to facilitate immigration from countries in western Europe that he described as ''the older sources of immigration.'' Senator Kennedy, who is chairman of the Judiciary Subcommittee on Immigration, has taken a particular interest in the Irish. But other Europeans feel they, too, were placed at a disadvantage by a 1965 immigration law. The 1965 law abolished the use of national origins as a basis for issuing visas and setting quotas on immigrants.
The Kennedy-Simpson bill proposes that the Government would select 55,000 immigrants each year with a point system meant to identi-

fy aliens who could best contribute to the American economy. Points would be awarded on the basis of age, education, occupational training, work experience, and English language skills. Senator Kennedy said of the new bill: ''[It will] pick up where we left off in 1986''; and Senator Simpson observed that about 90 percent of legal immigrants qualified for visas because they had relatives in this country. ''Only 10 percent are admitted because they possess skills that are specifically needed by U.S. employers or skills that the Government has determined would well serve our society.'' Asia, Latin America, and the islands of the Caribbean account for little more than 70 percent of legal immigration to the United States. In supporting the Kennedy bill, Senator Alfonse M. D'Amato (R: NY) said: ''Family reunification is a goal we all support. But what about those who have no immediate relatives in the United States? The law shuts them out because they are from countries like Ireland or Italy, whose great days of immigration are long in the past. People from those countries do not have immediate relatives who are American citizens or permanent residents.''[8]

Family reunification would remain an overriding goal in immigration policy under the Kennedy bill; 470,000 visas would be issued each year to people with relatives in the United States. The bill would make more visas available to the spouses and young children of permanent resident aliens, but it would curtail eligibility for married brothers and sisters, in-laws, nieces and nephews of United States citizens. The bill would set aside 120,000 visas each year for immigrants selected for their talents. That group includes the 55,000 to be chosen through a point system. It also includes certain aliens eligible for preferences under current law: those who can show ''exceptional ability in the sciences or the arts'' or skills in short supply here. The proposed point system favors no specific nationality. It may help western Europeans. But State Department officials predicted that many well-educated, English-speaking citizens of China, India, and the Philippines would also score well and qualify for immigrant visas.

No progress has been made on the Kennedy-Simpson proposals, and its continuing consideration appears delayed by a complex of factors, among which and not unimportant is the 1988 Presidential election.

Notes

1. Vernon M. Briggs, Jr. *Immigration Policy and the American Labor Force.* (Baltimore: Johns Hopkins University Press, 1984), p. 61.
2. *Ibid.*, p. 37.
3. *Statistical Abstract of the United States, 1984.* 104th ed. (Wash-

ington, DC: U.S. Department of Commerce, Bureau of the Census, 1983), p. 104.

4. David M. Reimers. *Still the Golden Gate: The Third World Comes to America.* (New York: Columbia University Press, 1985), p. 20.
5. Nathan Glazer, ed. *Clamor at the Gates: The New American Immigration.* (San Francisco: Institute for Contemporary Studies, 1985), p. 6.
6. *Ibid.,* pp. 7–8.
7. *Immigration History Newsletter* 16 (May 1984), p. 1.
8. The observations of Senators D'Amato, Kennedy, and Simpson are reported in *The New York Times,* February 14, 1988, p. 46.

DICTIONARY OF AMERICAN IMMIGRATION HISTORY

ABBOTT, EDITH (1876–1957). Social reformer. Edith and Grace Abbott were born in Nebraska in the late 1870s. They were lifelong leaders in movements for social justice from the Progressive period through the New Deal. In their lives, the Abbott sisters were involved with issues concerning immigrants, mothers and infants, child labor, women's suffrage, and world peace. Grace is perhaps best known as the successor to Julia Lathrop (*q.v.*) in heading the U.S. Children's Bureau; Edith for her pioneering study *Women in Industry* (1909), and for her role in the development of the University of Chicago's School of Social Service and Administration. The Abbotts were also among that group of women who centered around Jane Addams (*q.v.*) and Hull House—a group that included Addams herself, Florence Kelley (*q.v.*), and Sophonisba P. Breckinridge (*q.v.*).

Reference
Lela B. Costin, *Two Sisters for Social Justice: A Biography of Grace and Edith Abbott* (1983).

F.C.

ABBOTT, GRACE (1878–1939). *See* Abbott, Edith.

ABU MADY, ELIAS. *See* Lebanese.

ACADIANS. The Acadians and their descendants are the original settlers of Acadia, the region encompassed presently by the maritime provinces of Canada. From a mere 2,000 at the time of the Treaty of Utrecht in 1713, the Acadian population (as per ethnic origin) grew to over 337,000 by 1981, composing 35.9 percent of the population of New Brunswick, 8.5 percent of Nova Scotia, and 12.2 percent of Prince Edward Island. Their survival and development as a distinct Acadian community has been marked by numerous trials and tribulations which served merely to harden their desire to survive and leave their mark on the world.

1

French-speaking Catholics, soon known as Acadians, first settled in Port Royal, Nova Scotia, in 1604. Hampered by the fact that they were on the border between two warring imperial powers as well as by internal disputes, the Acadians over a century and a half succeeded in putting down their roots throughout the entire region. They concentrated on farming the rich marshlands of the region, raising livestock and trading with whomever, French or English, could provide them with much-needed supplies and services.

When peninsular Nova Scotia came under the control of the British in 1713, the Acadians pursued aggressively a policy of neutrality so as not to be drawn into the imperial conflict. Their strategy worked quite effectively and their community expanded rapidly and prospered by supplying both the English and French agricultural needs. The French military leaders in Louisbourg sought incessantly to draw them once again under the French flag. The British commanders at Annapolis Royal, while distrusting the motives and ultimate objectives of these self-designated "neutral French," could do little until the 1750s to establish effective military security over the region. The British became increasingly eager to force the Acadians to swear the oath of loyalty and be available for military duty against the French.

The opportunity came at the outset of the Seven Years War, when in 1755 the British lieutenant-governor in Halifax, Col. Charles Lawrence, pressured by colonial commanders in Boston and in the Royal Navy, decided that the Acadians' refusal to take the oath warranted immediate deportation. Between 1755 and 1763, some 10,000 of the approximately 13,400 Acadian men, women, and children living in the region were rounded up and deported in ships to various British-American colonies, Great Britain, and France. A thriving, successful, self-reliant, and determined society was destroyed, it appeared to most observers, forever.

The call of kinship and the homeland proved to be far more powerful than anyone could have imagined. The ink was barely dry on the 1763 Treaty of Paris when hundreds upon hundreds of displaced Acadians began the long journey back from exile to rebuild their society. The task proved to be arduous and time consuming. Their former lands, fertile and productive, had been granted to New England Planters. Acadians settled along the French shore of southwestern Nova Scotia, on Cape Breton and Prince Edward islands where they made their living in the fishing industry. The Loyalist influx into New Brunswick, after 1784, forced Acadians to move yet again into the less fertile northeastern regions of the colony where they engaged in marginal farming, forestry, shipbuilding, and fishing.

It took Acadians three generations to reestablish the socioeconomic basis of their communal survival. Inspired, in part, by Henry Wadworth

Longfellow's famous poem "Evangeline" in 1847 and an account of their own past by the sympathetic French historian, Edme de Rameau de Saint Père in 1859, an Acadian national consciousness began to take shape. By the time of Confederation in 1867, thanks in large measure to the activities of clerical and petty-bourgeois élites, the Acadian community had acquired a college and a newspaper. Acadians also managed to elect four members to the provincial legislature in 1871. Throughout the 1880s a series of very successful national conferences were held during which the tenets of an Acadian nationalism were hammered out and national symbols were adopted—a flag (a tricolor with a star), and an anthem ("Ave Maris Stella")—and a national holiday, August 15, was chosen. The central themes of this Acadian nationalism were agriculture, colonization, the problems of emigration, education, journalism, and the Acadianization of the Catholic church.

The nationalist movement, aided by an expanded press, proved beneficial. Acadians acquired their first bishop in 1912 and a French-language parish in Moncton in 1914. More Acadian teachers were certified and better French-language texts were introduced into the curriculum. Yet, provincial funding for separate Catholic schools remained beyond the community's political reach. Nevertheless, the economic lot of the vast majority of Acadians remained dismal. Most families were forced to supplement the meager salaries they received in the forestry and fishing industries with marginal farming. The traditional élites sanctioned this state of affairs because it maintained relatively intact the traditional value system and social structure. On the positive side, the Catholic church's active colonization program helped to ensure that the rate of outmigration of Acadians remained consistently lower than for New Brunswick's Anglophones. Consequently, spurred on by a high birth rate, the Acadian proportion of the province's population rose steadily from 16 percent in 1861 to 28 percent in 1911, to 31 percent in 1921 and an all-time high of 38 percent by 1951. The Acadian community would henceforth become a political force capable of shaping not only its own sociocultural development but also that of the province as a whole.

Following the conscription crisis of World War I, the vast majority of Acadians switched their loyalty from the Conservative party. They, henceforth, voted overwhemingly for the Liberal party at both the provincial and federal levels. Acadian nationalism did not call for any significant change in the political structure of New Brunswick or Canada in order to accommodate Acadian aspirations. In the pre–social welfare state era, Acadian objectives were normally achieved at the local and regional levels, through municipal councils and school boards, church-sponsored and administered social welfare and educational institutions, and a myriad of other voluntary associations such as the cooperative movements and credit unions. The values espoused continued to be those of a rural, agricultural, traditional Catholic society.

Since the early 1960s the Acadian society has been undergoing a dramatic transition. This process was set into motion with the rapid urbanization and industrialization of that society after 1940. Between 1941 and 1971 the percentage of Acadians employed in the primary sector declined from 54 percent to 11 percent while those employed in the service sector went from 29 percent to 61 percent and in manufacturing from 11 percent to 28 percent. Outmigration to Quebec and other parts of Canada set in and the birth rate began to fall. Furthermore, the rate of assimilation, calculated on the basis of the divergence between ethnic origin and mother tongue, began to increase markedly in the 1960s. This modernization process was supported and accentuated by the Liberal regime of Louis J. Robichaud, the second Acadian to become premier of the province (1960–1970). Under Robichaud the province began the process of taking over full responsibility for the funding and administration of all levels of education, as well as social welfare and health services. The Catholic church was hardest hit as its leaders were forced to stand on the sidelines as state control and secularization became irreversible trends. In fact, secular leaders realized that they, too, stood to lose control over their own society if a new nationalist strategy were not adopted to meet the needs and aspirations of modern Acadians.

In fact, two divergent nationalist strategies emerged to contest the allegiance of Acadians. By the late 1960s, leaders of the Société Nationale des Acadiens (renamed Société des Acadiens du Nouveau Brunswick in 1973) and many other Acadian organizations were shaken out of their lethargy and began to elaborate a political strategy that would ensure Acadians equal access to employment opportunities in a rapidly expanding provincial civil service as well as in all other parapublic institutions of education, health, and social welfare. They demanded that these employment opportunities allow Acadians to function and obtain promotion while working most of the time in their own language. The Conservative administration of Richard Hatfield eventually responded to intensified political pressure from the Acadian community by making room for Acadians in public and parapublic institutions. New Brunswick became officially bilingual in 1977 and most Acadians eventually switched their political loyalty to the Conservative party.

Other Acadian nationalists, influenced by neonationalist and separatist developments in Quebec, rejected the bilingual option of limited power sharing. They came together in 1972 under the auspices of the Parti Acadien. For the radical nationalists the most effective solution to their problems was the creation of a democratic socialist society that would be annexed to a dynamic Québécois society on the verge of gaining its independence. Few Acadians supported this option—4 percent in 1974 and 12 percent in 1978. By the late 1970s, the majority of moderate neonationalists committed themselves to the achievement of a social democratic Acadian province within the Canadian federal system. In the interim, the application of linguistic duality to all public and parapublic institutions would ensure Acadians effective power sharing and lay the foundation for future developments. Underlying this political renaissance of Acadia has been a remarkable cultural renaissance symbolized by a rich array of poetry, theater, fiction, and song which has permeated, thanks to radio and television, every dimension of Acadian life and received international attention and acclaim. Acadians and the Acadian society have indeed come a long way from the humiliation and destruction created by the deportation of 1755–1763. Few ethnic minorities have had the opportunity to redress history with such a vengeance.

References
Andrew Hill Clark, *Acadia: The Geography of Early Nova Scotia to 1760* (1968); Bona Arsenault, *History of the Acadians* (1966); Dudley J. LeBlanc, *The Acadian Miracle* (1966); for the Acadians of Louisiana, see Sidney A. Marchand, *Acadian Exiles in the Golden Coast of Louisiana* (1943); Steven L. Del Sesto and Jon L. Gibson, eds., *The Culture of Acadians: Tradition and and Change in South Louisiana* (1975); also, generally, Edward Schriver, ed., *The French in New England, Acadia, and Quebec* (1972).

M.D.B.

ACT TO REPEAL THE CHINESE EXCLUSION ACTS, TO ESTABLISH QUOTAS, AND FOR OTHER PURPOSES (December 17, 1943). In May 1942 a Citizens Committee to Repeal the Exclusions Acts was formed, and in the following year Representative Warren Magnuson introduced a bill entitled ''An Act to Repeal the Chinese Exclusions Acts, to Establish Quotas, and for Other Purposes.'' The chief goal of this bill was to amend Section 303 of the Nationality Act of 1940—to add to the classes eligible for naturalization Chinese persons and persons of Chinese descent and to give them an annual quota of 105 immigrants. The House passed the bill on October 21, 1943, and the bill was reported without amendment by the Senate committee. Although a number of attempts were made to amend the bill, they were all rejected and the Senate passed the bill on November 26, 1943. The act ended more than sixty years of discriminatory policy toward Chinese immigration.

References
Jack Chen, *The Chinese of America* (1980); Hyung-Chan Kim, ed., *Dictionary of Asian American History* (1980).

D.N.A.

ACUTE REFUGEES. A refugee concept proposed by E. F. Kunz. According to Kunz, two separate patterns in the movement of refugees can be recognized: flight-arrival and associative. Included in the flight-arrival patterns are two models: the acute refugees and the anticipatory refugees. Acute refugees are defined as people who are compelled to move because of great political or other drastic changes. They move from one place to another in large numbers, their main purpose being to reach a place of safety where they will be allowed to stay. Soon after their arrival in a new place or country they begin to redefine their relationship to their native land, for they realize that they will probably not return to their homeland. This redefinition often serves as the first step toward changing status from refugees to exiles. *See also* Anticipatory Refugees.

Reference
E. F. Kunz, "The Refugees in Flight: Kinetic Models and Forms of Displacement," *International Migration Review* 7 (Summer 1973); 125–146.

D.N.A.

ADAMIC, LOUIS (1898–1951). Novelist and journalist. Adamic, born in Yugoslavia, was America's leading expert on Yugoslavia. Adamic was known for a literary innovation that was called the "New Journalism." He wrote mainly about two social phenomena, violence within the labor movement and the tendency of second-generation immigrants to reject their heritage while the third generation seeks to find its roots. Adamic won the John Anisfield Award in 1940 for his important contribution to the study of race relations. Adamic called for a new morality and spiritual regeneration in his writings. He may have been the most controversial figure of the American literary scene during the first half of the twentieth century. Adamic involved himself in politics and supported Tito in the latter part of his life, and became disgusted with United States policies. His violent death has remained a mystery. Adamic's chief works were *The Native's Return* (1934); *Dynamite: The Story of Class Violence in America* (1931); *Laughing in the Jungle: The Autobiography of an Immigrant in America* (1932); *The Native's Return: An American Immigrant Visits Yugoslavia and Discovers His Old Country* (1934); and *Grandsons: A Story of American Lives* (1935).

Reference
Rudolph Vecoli, "Louis Adamic and the Contemporary Search for Roots," *Ethnic Studies* 2 (1978).

C.C.

ADDAMS, JANE (1860–1935). Jane Addams was the most famous social settlement director in the country for four decades and probably

the most renowned woman of her generation. She was born in Cedarville, Illinois, the daughter of John Huy Addams, a prosperous miller,
banker, and politician, and the former Sarah Weber. In 1882, just after
her father's death, she received a B.A. from Rockford College as valedictorian of her class and attended the Medical College for Women in
Philadelphia for one year before she was forced to withdraw due to
illness. After a partially successful operation, she spent two years tour-
ing Europe and studying. Returning to London in 1888, she spent
several months at Toynbee House, a social settlement guided by the
tenets of Christian socialism. On September 18, 1889 she and her
friend, Ellen Gates Starr, opened the first social settlement in America
in a mansion at Polk and Halsted Streets in Chicago donated by Charles
J. Hull. She chose that neighborhood "precisely because it contained a
wide variety of immigrants." The Hull House charter proclaimed its
purpose "to provide a center for higher civic and social life; to institute
and maintain educational and philanthropic enterprises, and to investigate and improve conditions in the industrial districts of Chicago."

Over the next three decades, Hull House expanded to include
thirteen buildings, nearly seventy-five residents (mostly volunteers),
and a myriad of services for the immigrants of the Nineteenth Ward,
including playgrounds, preschool nurseries, a kindergarten, theater,
music lessons, a woman's club, working men's debating society, book
bindery, library, handicraft shops, coffee house, and an evening school
for the twenty-six ethnic groups of the neighborhood. It also included
the Jane Club, an apartment for single working girls, and a home and
dining hall for the residents. Perhaps most unique of all was its Labor
Museum, where European arts and crafts were displayed and immigrants gave demonstrations of their Old World skills. The settlement
also housed the Juvenile Protective and Visiting Nurses Association and
the Immigrant Protective League, formed in 1908, to protect new arrivals, regulate employment agencies, steamship agents, cabbies, ex-
pressmen, and banks, fight "white slavery," and interpret foreigners to
mainstream America.

As the Labor Museum attests, Addams believed that immigrants
brought many gifts to the United States which ought to be preserved
even while they were becoming "Americanized" in political and socioeconomic terms. Hence she and her colleagues encouraged people of
every nationality to stage festivals, pageants, plays, and dancing and
musical activities. She also believed that such efforts would prevent the
intergenerational conflict and self-hatred that destroyed so many immigrant families and show more sophisticated native Americans how to
cope with urban, industrial life. Finally she saw in her multiethnic
neighborhood a microcosm of the world of nations, one that could serve
as a model of peace and harmony.

To further aid her immigrant constituency, Addams and her colleague involved themselves in unionization drives and politics. They manned picket lines, provided food and comfort to strikers and organizers, and managed boycotts. At the ward level, Addams aided the Municipal Voters League in trying, unsuccessfully, to unseat alderman and ward boss Johnny Powers. Addams herself served a three-year term as neighborhood garbage inspector and two years (1905–7) as a member of the "radical" school board appointed by Mayor Edward F. Dunne. She and Florence Kelley (*q.v.*) were the primary lobbyists behind the Illinois Workshop and Factory Act of 1893 and the Child Labor Law of 1903. Over the years, Addams lobbied with appreciable success for a juvenile court, a model tenement housing code, public baths, recreational facilities, vocational schools, industrial education, medical inspection in the schools, and the suppression of cocaine and prostitution. On the national level, Addams served as vice-chairman of the national executive committee of the Progressive party in 1912, and was largely responsible for the platform sections on "Social and Industrial Justice" and "Immigration."

A highly regarded author, Addams did much to explain immigrants to mainstream America, in *Democracy and Social Ethics* (1902), "Why the Ward Boss Rules"(1898) and *Twenty Years at Hull House* (1910). Perhaps Addams's greatest profession of faith in immigrants was her staunch opposition to the rising tide of nativism and the concomitant push for immigration restriction. Her influence was largely instrumental in keeping the National Conference on Charities and Correction on the side of open immigration.

From 1914 on, Addams's energies were increasingly absorbed by the war in Europe and the resultant movement for peace and disarmament, through the Women's Peace Party, the First International Conference of Women, and the Second International Congress of Women at Zurich which created the Women's International League for Peace and Freedom. She was co-recipient of the Nobel Peace Prize in 1931. Addams died of cancer and was buried in Cedarville.

References
Allen F. Davis, *American Heroine: The Life and Legend of Jane Addams* (1973); Jane Addams, *Twenty Years at Hull House* (1910); John C. Farrell, *Beloved Lady: A History of Jane Addams' Ideas On Reform and Peace* (1967); Daniel Levine, *Jane Addams and the Liberal Tradition* (1971); Mary Jo Deegan, *Jane Addams and the Men of the Chicago School, 1892–1918* (1987).

J.D.B.

ADELSVEREIN. *See* Germans.

AFFIRMATIVE ACTION. The term "affirmative action" has come to mean many things to many persons, and the concept is one of the major civil rights achievements. Affirmative action requires more than mere nondiscrimination in employment and other distributive benefits. It is a program requiring good-faith efforts to provide equal employment opportunity. Acceptable plans include at least three components: an analysis of employment patterns to discover whether there is an under-utilization of women and minorities in the work force; goals and timetables to correct any deficiencies (for example, a disproportionate under-representation of minorities in management positions, relative to their availability in the potential hiring pool); and active, open advertising of vacancies to bring openings to the attention of a wide pool of applicants.

Affirmative action was established by Executive Order 11246, although subsequent executive orders and court cases have amended the original concept. It still retains the basic elements of fairness and thoroughness in employment, however, and can be a powerful tool for eliminating discrimination in the workplace. For immigrants, the "national origin" protections are most often legally invoked for protecting against discrimination based upon surname, language, accent, race and color, and alienage.

References

A. P. Sindler, *Bakke, Defunis, and Minority Admissions: The Quest for Equal Opportunity* (1979); S. H. Nahmod, *Civil Rights and Civil Liberties Litigation* (1979; annual supp.).

M.A.O.

AFRICAN COMMUNITIES LEAGUE. *See* Garvey, Marcus.

AFRICAN LODGE. *See* West Indian Immigrants.

AFRICAN METHODIST EPISCOPAL CHURCH. *See* Afro-Americans.

AFRO-AMERICANS. The only immigrant group that came to America involuntarily. For that reason, they often are not included in immigration discussions. Instead of anticipating a new life in a new home, they were faced with the prospect of lifelong drudgery as slaves in an alien culture. Instead of their being assimilated into America as productive members of society, slaves were excluded and prevented from developing their talents and abilities. Being black in a society that was largely white and being in bondage in a culture that was proud of its freedoms profoundly impacted on the Afro-American experience in contrast to that of all other immigrants.

The first twenty Africans to "settle" in America were traded at Jamestown by a Dutch pirate in 1619. As the first law permitting slavery was not passed till 1660, these early Afro-Americans were probably treated as indentured servants. This would seem to be confirmed by records showing black property owners in Virginia as early as 1640. However, slavery for blacks was certainly the standard long before the passage of legislation justifying it. The bulk of Afro-Americans came from West Africa by way of the triangular slave trade. Slave traders, usually based in Europe, traded European goods including guns for African slaves, and, when this was not possible, raided the coast and seized Africans forcibly. The slaves were traded in the Americas for sugar, tobacco, and other raw materials for European consumption. While the slave trade impoverished Africa of some of its best manpower, it provided an abundant source of cheap labor to America to rapidly accelerate its economic development.

The legal importation of slaves into the United States was ended by 1808, but occasional slave ships arrived until the eve of the Civil War. The end of the trade was supported by slave owners who feared that fresh African slaves would be more prone to revolution and violence than would blacks who were raised within the system. The concern to keep slaves docile and obedient led masters to do whatever they could to make Afro-Americans forget their African past. The use of their native language was discouraged as was any practice of African ways including African religion. Masters certainly became nervous when African religion included voodoo, as they had good reason to fear they might be its object. The Society for the Propagation of the Gospel came from England to Christianize both Indians and blacks. Masters feared that if their slaves became Christian brothers, they would have to free them, but soon the law proclaimed otherwise. Then, masters found that Christian teachings on obedience were helpful and gradually encouraged Christianization of slaves. Richard Allen was a slave preacher and was permitted to buy his freedom. After finding that the Methodist church prevented full participation by blacks, he began the African Methodist Episcopal church in Philadelphia in 1794. Shortly, independent black churches sprang up across the North among Baptists, Methodists, and other denominations, and, after the Civil War, blacks were able to form their own churches in the South as well. The black church has clearly been the major cultural institution for Afro-Americans and provided the center for their community development.

Music was the art form that best survived in the conditions of slavery because it required no physical artifacts. Masters encouraged singing to keep up slave spirits and assist in teamwork. Gradually, Afro-Americans blended techniques from both the European and African traditions to create a new music of their own. Work songs and spirituals were its early products. Later, after Emancipation, blues and jazz embodied elements such as polyrhythms, syncopation, and texture. Bessie Smith was a blues singer in the 1920s, and world-famous instrumentalists like Louis Armstrong and Duke Ellington made jazz popular around the world.

The American Colonization Society was founded in 1817 to send some Afro-Americans back to Africa, specifically to Liberia, and 15,000 blacks did return. Twelve thousand of them were slaves who received freedom on the grounds that they would return. The society was founded by prominent national leaders and funded by both federal and state governments. Monrovia, the capital of Liberia, was named after President Monroe. Richard Allen headed a meeting in Philadelphia to discuss this venture, and the vast majority of black leaders condemned it. They insisted that they wanted full rights as Americans and that they need not go back to Africa any more than Europeans had to return to their homes. Shortly before the Civil War, however, growing numbers of blacks were increasingly disillusioned with America, and several, including Henry Garnet, a prominent clergyman, and Martin Delany, an early black physician, talked openly about emigration. President Lincoln invited key black leaders to the White House and tried to gain their support for this idea. His plan was to settle them in Latin America. Most, including Frederick Douglass, vigorously rejected the proposal.

The slavery issue divided the North and South from the beginning of the Republic. The Constitution calculated a slave as three-fifths of a person in proportioning delegates to the House of Representatives. All of the northern states abolished slavery shortly after the Revolution. Some 5,000 blacks were members of the Continental Army and those who were slaves were granted freedom for participating. The power conflict between North and South had more to do with politics and economics than with slavery, but the increasing numbers of slaves who fled with the aid of the underground railway (a loosely organized system for helping fugitive slaves escape to Canada or to the Northern free states) made regional antagonisms even worse. Harriet Tubman was undoubtedly its most famous worker. Lincoln had promised not to abolish slavery because he believed it would split the Union, but this gesture did not prevent the Civil War. Finally, he did issue the Emancipation Proclamation as a military action. The proclamation only freed slaves belonging to masters who were in rebellion. Lincoln hoped to stir revolt behind the Confederate lines. However, it spelled the end of slavery in the United States, and this was legitimized with the Thirteenth Amendment in 1865.

During Reconstruction, 1866–1876, Afro-American ex-slaves found themselves thrown into an individualistic, competitive society with no real preparation. Douglass had said that Emancipation had freed the slaves but done nothing for the Negro. Southern blacks voted by the thousands and many were elected to state and local governments. Over thirty were elected as congressmen. White extremists formed the Ku Klux Klan to force blacks "back into their place." When President Hayes terminated Reconstruction, the traditional white power structure returned and inaugurated legal segregation and also, with a variety of legal maneuvers, removed blacks from the voting booths. R. Logan contends that the low point in Negro history was at the turn of the twentieth century. Between 1890 and 1910 over 200 blacks were lynched each year. Booker T. Washington, president and founder of Tuskegee Institute, emerged as a national Afro-American leader counseling conciliation of whites to earn their eventual support and respect. W. E. B. DuBois, a founder of both the Niagara movement and the National Association for the Advancement of Colored People, opposed him and urged a policy of self-assertion.

In the early twentieth century, Afro-Americans began migrating from the rural South to the urban North in ever-growing numbers. The mass production industries needed unskilled workers. While many jobs were filled by the expanding wave of European immigrants, blacks found new employment as well. A. Locke noted that these immigrants brought a "new Negro" into the American scene. For the first time, thousands of blacks were making basic decisions governing their own lives, and, he contended, this created a new mood of vitality and hope. Harlem became known as the culture capital of the Negro world. The Negro Renaissance catapulted black musicians, writers, and artists into national prominence. Langston Hughes and Richard Wright became well-known authors. However, the 1929 stock market crash and the following depression hit Afro-Americans harder than any other group. "Last hired, first fired" was the rule, and the hope and vigor ended in despair.

Blacks served in both World War I and II in large numbers. For many this was a consciousness-raising experience. Abroad, they found less prejudice than they knew at home. They were less willing to return as second-class citizens. In the Cold War, Russia took every opportunity to embarrass America because of its racism. Both whites and blacks were becoming more aware of the contradiction between American ideals and its racial practices. In 1954 the Supreme Court reversed its earlier "separate but equal" justification of segregation and declared separate black and white schools to be unconstitutional. The Rev. Dr. Martin Luther King, Jr. headed a mass movement during the following decade which resulted in the passage of two pieces of significant legislation. The Civil Rights Act of 1964 ended the system of legal segregation throughout the South, and the Voting Rights Act of 1965 resulted in thousands of blacks becoming registered to vote. In subsequent years, black elected officials increased greatly, including black mayors of several major cities.

During the 1960s and 1970s various levels of government established a variety of "affirmative action" policies aimed at including larger numbers of qualified blacks at higher levels in business and society. While it resulted in an expanding group of middle-class Afro-Americans, increasing numbers of whites expressed resentment at what they saw as "reverse racism." At the same time other blacks voiced a preference for creating a separate black society of their own. Marcus Garvey had popularized the concept half a century before. Black Muslims, beginning in the 1930s, also advocated separating from what they perceived as an evil white society. Stokely Carmichael moved the Student Nonviolent Coordinating Committee away from integration and toward a policy of "black power." Huey Newton and Bobby Seale formed the Black Panther Party which also strove to develop a strong black community that would not have to depend on "well-meaning" white sympathizers in order to further its cause.

In spite of the significant legal and economic gains, urban areas, in the 1980s, are becoming more heavily populated by poor blacks, and increasing numbers of whites have fled to suburbia. With the economic shift toward technological industries and the increase of the service sector, poor blacks are finding it harder to procure well-paying unskilled employment. It is debated how much of this problem results from continuing racial prejudice or whether it is primarily, now, an industrial class situation. Nevertheless, large numbers of Afro-Americans have not been able to assimilate into the American culture. Many still reside in mainly black neighborhoods and only a small, though growing, number have gained access to leadership roles in major institutions of the country. Not only do Afro-Americans differ from other immigrant groups by not having come to this country voluntarily, but they have had a greater difficulty in becoming full partners in their new land.

References
John Hope Franklin, *From Slavery to Freedom* (4th ed., 1974); Norman Coombs, *Black Experience in America* (1983); August Meier and Elliott Rudwick, *From Plantation to Ghetto* (3rd ed., 1976); C. Vann Woodward, *The Strange Career of Jim Crow* (3rd ed., 1974); Lawrence Levine, *Black Culture and Black Consciousness* (1977). A major repository of materials on black Americans is the Schomburg collection in New York City.

N.C.

AFROYIM v. RUSK (387 U.S. 253). *See* [Citizenship]: Determinations.

AIDAI. *See* Lithuanians.

AIR STUDY. *See* Bilingual Education.

ALBANIANS. Offspring of the ancient pre-Christian Illyrians, a pe-
rennially harassed ethnic community subjugated for centuries by more
powerful neighbors from all directions. The Albanian homeland is surrounded by the Adriatic Sea on the west, by Yugoslavia to the north and
east, and by Greece to the south. The worldwide count is an estimated
4.5 million Albanians. Immigrants to the United States and their progeny probably number some 70,000. Four centuries under Turkish rule
from the fifteenth century explain the 70 percent of at least nominally
Muslim adherents. The remainder are roughly 20 percent Orthodox and
10 percent Roman Catholic. The phenomenon of the ''crypto-Chris-
tian'' refers to one who externally accepts the Muslim religion for
whatever motives of privilege or benefit while continuing private allegiance to Christian tenets and practices.

Albanians in recognizable numbers began arriving in Boston
around the turn of this century. For the first decade, females were
hardly to be found among these immigrants as these newcomers hoped
to earn money and return to their native country. They became candy
dealers, fruit peddlers, and restaurant workers. Others moved farther
into Massachusetts to shoe factories in Natick, Worcester, and South-
bridge. Still others settled in places like Bridgeport, Connecticut;
Jamestown, New York; and Detroit. The Boston area has remained the
stronghold.

The Albanian nationalist movement produced independence for the
first time in 1912. For several decades, several factions vied for leadership. Since World War II, Albania has been under Communist rule.
Immigrants to this country played a major role in the nationalist
awakening, through agitation in the press and with financial aid. An
integral aspect of this awakening involved secession from the traditional
Greek Orthodox church, sparked by a controversial burial case in Hudson, Massachusetts, in 1907. Research has disproven the recent Albanian claim that Greek priests were refusing to bury Albanian nationalists. But it appears that the nationalist drive would have
precipitated an eventual separation of Albanian Christians from the
Greek church anyway. By spring of 1908, separatist Albanians welcomed Fan Noli as their first spiritual guide, ordained a priest in New
York City by a Russian Orthodox bishop. His subsequent elevation to
the rank of bishop and his political activities here and abroad made him
a controversial figure. The Albanians who broke ranks with the Greek
Orthodox hierarchy exist as an autonomous diocese, with some dozen
parishes, mostly in Massachusetts and the east coast. They have a
cathedral in south Boston. Two other Albanian parishes (Boston and
Chicago) function under Greek jurisdiction. The Bronx (New York) and
Detroit each have a Roman Catholic parish. Albanian Muslims tend to
worship in private. Meanwhile, for ethnic and political causes, Alba-

nians are inclined to unite. Despite their diaspora, they maintain ethnic awareness, especially through their nationally circulated, bilingual newspaper *Liria,* published in south Boston, and through annual banquets and outdoor festivals and tour groups to the homeland. Their "Free Albania" association serves as an umbrella to bind people of Albanian ancestry. *See also* Italian-Albanians.

References
The Albanian Struggle in the Old World and New (1939); Fiftieth Anniversary of the Albanian Orthodox Church in America, 1908–1958 (1958); Constantine A. Demo, The Albanians in America: The First Arrivals (1960); Robert N. Tochka, "The Development of the Boston Albanian Community, 1900–1920," honors paper, Boston College, 1978; Dennis Lazar, "Ethnic Continuity as It Applies to a Less Visible National Group: The Albanian Community of Boston, Massachusetts," Ph.D. dissertation, Rensselaer Polytechnic Institute, 1982.

W.W.V.

ALEXANDER, MOSES (1853–1924). Politician. Moses Alexander, Idaho's governor, 1914–18, was born in Obrigheim, Bavaria, in 1853. He emigrated to America in 1867. After a short stay in New York City he moved to Chillicothe, Missouri, where he became involved in the merchandising business, was elected to the city council, and was elected mayor of the city for two terms. Alexander was Idaho's war governor, and he demonstrated his patriotism in all his actions. In response to a call from President Wilson, he sent Idaho National Guardsmen to the Mexican border in 1916 and again mobilized the National Guard for service in the regular army during the world conflict. He directed Idaho's participation in the shipbuilding program, the raising of foodstuffs, and the funding of the war.

Reference
David L. Crowder. "Moses Alexander, Idaho's Jewish Governor, 1914–1918," Ph.D. dissertation, University of Utah, 1972.

B.L.

ALIEN ADJUSTMENT AND EMPLOYMENT ACT OF 1977. On August 4, 1977, President James Carter sent a message to the Congress outlining his initiatives for treating the growing undocumented alien problem in the United States. Subsequently, the administration forwarded to the Congress the legislative proposals requiring enactment if this presidential initiative is to succeed. As outlined in Attorney General Griffin B. Bell's letter of transmittal to Congress, the proposed legislation has three primary objectives: "(1) to adjust those undocumented aliens who have resided in the United States continuously prior to January 1, 1970 to lawful permanent residents; (2) to create a new five year temporary resident status for undocumented aliens who have resided in the United States continuously since January 1, 1977; and (3) to restrict employment opportunities for undocumented aliens in the United States.''

Reference
Michael G. Wenk, "The Alien Adjustment and Employment Act of 1977: A Summary," *International Migration Review* 11 (Winter 1977): 533–538.

                                                                        F.C.

ALIENS, constitutional rights upon arrest. Congress has delegated to the Immigration and Naturalization Service (INS) broad power to regulate the flow of aliens into the United States and to regulate their activities while in the United States. However, these powers are tempered by the constitutional rights of aliens which flow to them solely as a result of their presence in the United States. There is a delicate balance between the power of INS officers to interrogate and arrest without warrant under Section 287 of the Immigration and Nationality Act, and the right of the alien guaranteed by the Fourth Amendment to be free of any unreasonable searches or seizures. The Immigration and Naturalization Service is charged by law to prevent unlawful entries by aliens and to detect aliens who enter or remain in the United States unlawfully. The basic tool to perform this task is Section 287 of the Immigration and Naturalization Act which contains several subsections, the first of which states: Any officer or employee of the Immigration and Naturalization Service authorized under regulations prescribed by the attorney general shall have power without warrant (1) to interrogate any alien or person believed to be an alien as to his right to be or to remain in the United States. The key words in the section are contained in the phrase "alien or person *believed* to be an alien." There can be no lawful interrogation without a reasonable belief or suspicion that the person is an alien.

On June 24, 1975, the Supreme Court in the case of *United States* v. *Brignoni-Ponce* held that the Fourth Amendment does not allow a roving patrol or border patrol to stop a vehicle and question its occupants about their citizenship and immigration status when the only ground for suspicion was that the occupants appeared to be of Mexican ancestry. In 1973, the Supreme Court in the case of *Almeida-Sanchez* v. *the United States* (413 U.S. 266; 1973), held that the Fourth Amendment prohibited the use of roving patrols to search vehicles without a warrant or probable cause at points removed from the border and its functional equivalence. Under the rule enunciated in *Almeida-Sanchez*, it was necessary for the INS to demonstrate that either the search took place at the border or a functional equivalent thereof. Functional equivalency was determined by whether there was any access to the particular point where the stop took place that would have originated in the United States and not necessitated the automobile crossing the border.

References
Austin T. Fragomen, Jr., "Constitutional Rights of Aliens Upon Arrest," *International Migration Review* 7 (Spring 1973): 67–71, and "Rights of Aliens upon Arrest: Revisited," *International Migration Review* 9 (Fall 1975): 383–385.

F.C.

ALIENS, *Defense of the Alien,* ed. Lydio F. Tomasi. Proceedings of the Annual National Legal Conference on Immigration and Refugee Policy sponsored by the Center for Migration Studies from 1978 to the present. Papers contained in these proceedings are by a prominent roster of speakers including members of Congress, government representatives, national and international immigration and refugee specialists, lawyers, experienced voluntary agency representatives, social scientists, and other experts in the field. Among the various contemporary topics analyzed in these papers are immigration law and legal representation; the rights of aliens; the impact of immigration policy on U.S. population and the labor market; grounds of exclusion and deportation; the Select Commission on Immigration and Refugee Policy and the national interest; refugees and territorial asylum; implementation prospects of proposed immigration legislation; refugees and political asylum; international migration and foreign policy; immigration enforcement and effects on jobs and businesses; immigration and human rights; and refugees and asylees.

Reference
Lydio F. Tomasi, ed., *Defense of the Alien,* vols. 1–8 (New York: Center for Migration Studies, 1978–).

F.C.

ALIENS, deportable. Analysis of apprehension data was undertaken by the Immigration and Naturalization Service (INS) with the aid of the Bureau of the Census. The INS's form I-213, Record of Deportable Alien, is the basic data collection instrument administered to known illegal aliens. The aim of the study was to analyze data from a sample of I-213 forms to determine demographic and economic characteristics of illegal aliens apprehended in the interior of the United States in calendar year 1978. The importance of such an analysis is twofold: (1) to increase our knowledge of the illegal alien population, and (2) to examine the validity of the I-213 forms as a statistical data-gathering mechanism.

Reference
C. A. Davidson, "Characteristics of Deportable Aliens Located in the Interior of the United States," paper presented at Population Association of America Annual Meeting, Washington, D.C., March 26–28, 1981.

F.C.

ALIENS, net alien immigration to the United States. Net immigration is different from the number of arrivals. Many people come to the United States declaring their intention to settle. When they change their minds and leave to reside elsewhere, they are not counted. The Immigration and Naturalization Service has not collected statistics on emigration since 1957. Keely and Percy believe many of the published estimates to be too low.

Reference
Charles B. Keely and Ellen Percy, "Recent Net Alien Immigration to the U.S.: Its Impact on Population Growth and Native Fertility," *Demography* 15 (1978), 267–283.

F.C.

ALIENS, restating the rights of aliens. A restatement of the foreign relations law of aliens. Nafziger begins with a description and critique of Section 722 of Tentative Draft No. 4 of the Restatement of Foreign Relations Law of the United States (Revised), providing suggestions for revisions in order to reflect recent cases. Analysis focuses on the limited scope of Section 722, whose comments and notes largely exclude nonadjudicated interpretations of international law and international legal obligations to protect the rights of aliens.

Reference
James A. R. Nafziger, "Restating the Rights of Aliens," *Virginia Journal of International Law* 25 (Fall 1984), 125–141.

F.C.

ALIENS, Social Security benefits. A study (see *infra*) commissioned by the U.S. comptroller general examines the circumstances under which Social Security benefits are paid to alien retirees and dependents living abroad and discusses the characteristics of this beneficiary group. Also presents information concerning aliens who, while working in violation of the Immigration and Nationality Act, can earn Social Security credits.

Reference
U.S. General Accounting Office, *Issues Concerning Social Security Benefits Paid to Aliens,* Report to the Congress of the United States by the Comptroller General (General Accounting Office, 1983).

F.C.

ALLEN, HORACE N. *See* Koreans.

ALLEN, RICHARD. *See* Afro-Americans.

AL-MASIH HADDAD, ABD. *See* Lebanese.

ALMEIDA-SANCHEZ v. *UNITED STATES. See* Aliens, constitutional rights.

ALTGELD, JOHN PETER (1847–1902). Jurist, Illinois governor, reformer. John Peter Altgeld came from a German immigrant family and spent his early years in poverty. As a young Missouri lawyer he established himself as a politician comfortable with Grangerism and Jeffersonianism. In 1875 he went to Chicago where he was successful not only in law but also in real estate investment. But he did not forget the poverty of his early years and embarked on a lifetime of reformist activities, both in writing and politics. In 1884 he published his first work, *Our Penal Machinery and Its Victims* in which he denounced the system of law enforcement and prosecution. In 1886 he was elected judge of the Cook County Superior Court. On May 4, 1886, six months before Altgeld became judge, there was a mass rally in Chicago's Haymarket to protest police brutality and several thousand assembled peacefully to listen to talks by labor leaders. When about half of those present had left, Captain John Bromfield and his officers prepared to attack those still present, and a bomb was thrown. Eight Chicago labor leaders were brought to trial and all were found guilty. The so-called "Haymarket Trial" received international attention, and in the United States there was an hysterical reaction against the "anarchists," although there was at the same time considerable support for the workers. In 1892 Altgeld was elected the first Democratic governor of Illinois and the first foreign-born governor ever. In 1893 Altgeld pardoned those fortunate labor leaders who had not been hung. In the 1894 Pullman strike, Altgeld was sympathetic to the labor men who had been put in prison. One of the last acts of his reformist spirit was his political support for William Jennings Bryan in the 1896 presidential campaign.

Reference
Henry M. Christman, ed., *The Mind and Spirit of John Peter Altgeld: Selected Writings and Addresses* (1960).

G.B.

AMALGAMATED CLOTHING WORKERS. *See* Hillman, Sidney.

AMERASIANS. A class of refugees fathered by U.S. servicemen stationed in Vietnam during the Vietnam War (1964–1975). Most Amerasian children are unacceptable to the Americans and unwanted by the Vietnamese. Their distinctive Caucasian or black features mark them as descendants of U.S. servicemen. They are favored by both Washington and Hanoi for priority emigration. Since 1982 an average of 875 Amerasian children and their families have come to the United States. In 1986 only 579 Amerasian children arrived in the United States. An estimated 12,000 Amerasian children remain in Vietnam, with none migrating to the United States since the spring of 1986, when the Vietnamese stopped the process. Until 1983 most Amerasians left Vietnam under the United Nations–administered "Orderly Departure Program," which since 1979 had helped some 45,000 Vietnamese fleeing their homeland following the Communist takeover. In the early days, Amerasian children wishing to be airlifted out of Vietnam were required to prove their heritage either through birth certificates, parental acknowledgment, or an established pattern of contact between the child's mother and father. The weakness of the law requiring proof of American parentage caused U.S. lawmakers to set up an immigration category for Amerasian children which gave them a special refugee status. As of early 1986, 3,700 Amerasian children and 5,300 family members have emigrated to the United States.

Reference
Susan Katz, "Breaking the Emigration Deadlock," *Insight* 3 (Jan. 19, 1987): 32–33.

F.C.

AMERICAN ASSOCIATION FOR THE STUDY AND PREVENTION OF INFANT MORTALITY. The association, formed as a result of a conference held at New Haven in 1909, chose J. H. Mason Knox as its first president. Knox, who taught at Johns Hopkins University and directed Maryland's child health program, was one of the pioneers in the child health movement. At the meeting important addresses and papers were presented by such notables as Irving Fisher (Yale University), William Welch (Johns Hopkins), Abraham Jacobi, and John Fulton (then at Johns Hopkins, subsequently at Yale). There was at the conference a significant discussion of "Municipal, State and Federal Prevention of Infant Mortality." The association advocated establishment of a Federal Department of Health, within which there would be a Department of Child Hygiene. It issued an attack on the "League for Medical Freedom" which opposed public medical programs.

Reference
Transactions of the First Annual Meeting of the American Association for the Study and Prevention of Infant Mortality (1910; rpt. 1974).

F.C.

AMERICAN BAPTIST PUBLICATION SOCIETY. *See* Baptists and Immigrants.

AMERICAN BREEDERS' ASSOCIATION. Founded in 1903 by plant and animal breeders who wanted to keep informed about theoretical and new advances; by 1907, the association embraced eugenics (*q.v.*) with its emphasis on unalterable human inequalities. Charles B. Davenport (*q.v.*), a leading American eugenicist, was one of the leaders of the ABA who believed that the immigration problem was basically a biological one, and that admitting "degenerate breeding stock" was a desperate measure inevitably harmful to the nation.

Reference
Stephen Jay Gould, *The Mismeasure of Man* (1981).

F.C.

AMERICAN COLLEGE IN ROME. *See* O'Connell, Denis J.

AMERICAN COLONIZATION SOCIETY. *See* Afro-Americans.

AMERICAN IMMIGRATION COLLECTION (41 vols., New York: Arno Press/New York Times, 1969). Oscar Handlin, Carl Wittke, and John Appel served as advisory editors. A massive reprint program of basic materials on the history of American immigration. Also (series 2), Victor Greene, Oscar Handlin, and John Appel, advisory eds., *The American Immigration Collection* (33 vols., 1970).

F.C.

AMERICAN ITALIAN HISTORICAL ASSOCIATION (209 Flagg Place, Staten Island, New York, 10304). Founded in 1966, the AIHA is incorporated as a nonprofit organization and is tax exempt under state and federal law. With a membership of historians, educators, social scientists, and other interested persons, the AIHA seeks to create a better understanding of the American-Italian experience. Its members encourage American-Italian studies and collect, preserve, study, and popularize materials that illumine the American-Italian experience in the United States and Canada. Among its activities, the AIHA sponsors an annual national conference; publishes a national newsletter; presents an annual award for the best-written essay in American-Italian studies; and sponsors resource depositories for the collection and preservation of historical records.

F.C.

AMERICAN LABOR MUSEUM. The American Labor Museum, the nation's only labor museum, celebrates the history of the working people from its unique headquarters just outside Paterson, New Jersey, in Haledon's historic Botto House National Landmark. This is the first Italian-American home to be honored with a National Landmark designation. The museum was formed by prominent leaders from labor, corporate, historical, and local sectors who raised funds to purchase the Botto House as its headquarters in 1982. From this important labor history site, the museum conducts a vigorous program of seminars, topical tours, museum workshops, and publications about working people. The galleries, period rooms, and ethnic gardens of the Botto House National Landmark are available for group meetings, tours, and outings. A gift shop offers unique reproductions from the museum's collection and membership brings discounts on these, as well as free admission, a quarterly newsletter, and reduced fees to many museum-sponsored programs.

The museum headquarters, the Botto House National Landmark, captures a common heritage of those who find their roots in the history of the immigrant family during the first quarter of this century. Built in 1908 for Pietro and Maria Botto, immigrants from Italy, this site represents the lifestyle of a working-class family through restored period rooms and a garden complete with grape arbor, bocci court, and wine cellar. The property was declared a National Landmark in 1982 because of the role it played as a haven for free speech and assembly during a stirring chapter of American history, the 1913 Paterson Silk Strike. During this seven-month strike, crowds of 20,000 gathered around the front balcony of the Botto House to hear famous labor and social leaders of the day advocate the eight-hour day, minimum wage standards, and other worker benefits. The 1913 strike is considered to be a milestone in the reform of the American workplace.

References
John A. Herbst, *A Slice of the Earth: The Story of the American Labor Museum* (1983); John A. Herbst and Catherine Keene, *Life and Times in Silk City: A Photographic Essay of Paterson, New Jersey* (1984).

F.C.

AMERICAN LATVIAN ASSOCIATION. *See* Latvians.

AMERICAN PROTECTIVE ASSOCIATION. Expressions of anti-Catholicism appeared from time to time in the years following the Civil War. Suspicious anti-Catholics generally pointed to three developments as the basis for their fears: (1) the appearance of a so-called Catholic vote; (2) the continuing controversy over the public schools, which involved discussions of the teaching of morality and the use of tax money in support of nonpublic institutions; and (3) a so-called Catholic influence over organized labor. The Democratic party was usually regarded as subservient to Catholics, illustrated most often by references to the Irish-Democratic control of several large cities. President Ulysses S. Grant's action in recommending a constitutional amendment to forbid use of public money for any sectarian purpose gave to the Republicans a reputation for favoring the anti-Catholic position. Numerous nationalistic and patriotic societies were organized in this same period. Many of them included anti-Catholicism as one of the planks in their platforms. The American Protective Association, an oath-bound, secret, anti-Catholic organization with a membership open to both men and women, was organized on March 13, 1887, in Iowa. It was intended to have a nationwide appeal and to take an active part in politics.

Reference
Donald L. Kinzer, *An Episode in Anti-Catholicism: The American Protective Association* (1964).

F.C.

AMERICAN SLOVENIAN CATHOLIC UNION. *See* Slovenes.

AMERICAN SOUTH, efforts to attract immigrants. The unwillingness of the immigrant to come to the South can be explained by the divergence of wage rates between the North and South for this period. Wages, both on a nominal and real basis, were higher in the North than the South from 1860 to 1900. The thesis shows that a great deal of effort was put forth by the Southerners to turn the immigrants toward the South. All the southern states established immigration bureaus, advertised in Europe extensively, and sent agents to Europe to recruit settlers. Counties, cities, and private organizations and individuals also joined in the promotion effort of the South. Yet immigrants refrained from coming to the South in any large numbers throughout the period of the great migrations.

Reference
Henry M. Booker, "Efforts of the South to Attract Immigrants, 1860–1900," Ph.D. dissertation, University of Virginia, 1965.

F.C.

AMERICANIZATION MOVEMENT. Americanization as a movement, as an organized campaign to guarantee political loyalty and cultural conformity, was a phenomenon of the World War I years. At its height, between 1915 and 1921, more than thirty states, and hundreds of cities, adopted Americanization measures. Some of this legislation simply provided night classes in the public schools where immigrants could study English and civics. Other measures were more draconian, banning the use of foreign languages in public settings or prohibiting unnaturalized immigrants from holding particular jobs.

There was no federal Americanization legislation, but several federal agencies, especially the bureaus of Naturalization and Education and the wartime Committee on Public Information, nonetheless conducted aggressive campaigns. The Bureau of Naturalization, for example, developed its own textbook for use in the public schools, an action which the Bureau of Education regarded as entrenching upon its turf. Both agencies lobbied local superintendents of schools to adopt their particular curricular materials. Both tried to win the support of employers' associations. And neither would acknowledge the right of the other to play a major role in the movement. The Committee on Public Information, in keeping with its mandate to promote patriotism as well as disseminate information, commandeered the editorial pages of the foreign-language press for the duration of the war. It also sponsored its own ethnic associations, like the American Friends of German Democracy, and staged elaborate public demonstrations of immigrant loyalty. It organized scores of parades on the Fourth of July in 1918, for example, in which ethnic associations marched to show their patriotic devotion to the United States.

Active as local, state, and federal agencies were, the greatest impetus behind the Americanization crusade came from the more than one hundred private organizations, each of which created its own Americanization programs. These ranged from Henry Ford's on-the-job English and citizenship classes for his alien employees to the language classes sponsored by the United Mine Workers of America, and from the efforts of the General Federation of Women's Clubs to bring "fresh air" and "American" vegetables (instead of the "inevitable" cabbage) into immigrant homes to the sympathetic celebrations of ethnic heritages sponsored by the International Institutes of the Young Women's Christian Association. So rapidly did programs proliferate that, by April 1919, the Chicago *Daily Tribune* editorialized that "only an agile and determined immigrant possessed of overmastering devotion to the land of his birth can hope to escape Americanization by at least one of the many processes now being prepared for his special benefit. . . ."

What caused this extraordinary burst of activity? Americanization, after all, had been a process long before it became a movement. As noted by Julius Drachsler, a pioneer student of ethnicity and a professor of sociology at Smith College and the City College of New York, many immigrants showed an "almost pathetic willingness to fit as quickly and as inconspicuously as possible into the general life about them." This self-chosen conformism and the "steadily increasing rate of inter-marriage" were "irresistibly making for the amalgamation of the European peoples in this country." Americanization in this sense of the term happened independently of any efforts on the part of the native-born population. So why, to restate the question, should there have been a vast national effort to accomplish something which was already happening of its own accord?

The answer is World War I. War, Drachsler said, "crystalized the vague uneasiness" native-born Americans routinely felt about immigrants "into a neurotic dread." Further, the dread took a new and significant form. There had been moments of acute anxiety about immigrants before. What set the World War I years apart, and made the Americanization movement possible, was that, for the first time, the fear was that immigrants and their descendants would prove disloyal. That this fear was new can be seen in the forty-two volume *Report* of the Dillingham Immigration Commission (1911). This is a virtual compendium of prewar anti-immigrant sentiment and belief, and nowhere in these thousands of pages is there a hint of the concerns that would drive the Americanization movement.

The long period of official U.S. neutrality which followed the outbreak of war in Europe meant that various nationality groups would attempt to influence the Wilson administration. Anglophiles pressured the administration to support the Allies; Irish-Americans and German-Americans called upon it to live up to its promise to be neutral in thought as well as deed. Jewish groups also initially opposed any hint that the administration might favor the Allied powers both because Russia had the worst record of anti-Semitism of any European nation and because Zionists believed that the Ottoman Empire offered the best hope of them achieving a Jewish homeland in Palestine. Poles in the United States had reason to hope for the defeat of both Germany and the Austro-Hungarian Empire and of Russia.

Advocates of Anglo-American solidarity, including President Wilson and his most vociferous critic, Theodore Roosevelt, saw the efforts of these ethnic groups to shape U.S. foreign policy as virtual treason. Moreover, as radical journalist Randolph Bourne (*q.v.*) put it, the "discovery of diverse nationalistic feelings among our great alien population" hit "most people as an intense shock." They were forced to recognize "that assimilation in this country was proceeding on lines very different from those we had marked out for it." Immigrants, horrified believers in Anglo conformity discovered, expected to enter American society in their own ways and on their own terms. As the *Daily Jewish Courier* of Chicago made the case in 1916, "America has not, as yet, one tradition or one culture of her own. If immigrants would have left their spirit and culture behind, America would be without culture." Anglo conformists vehemently disagreed. What they saw, in the light of the war in Europe and the likelihood of eventual U.S. entry into it, was the danger of a "Balkanized" America unable to unite against its enemies.

This new perception of the immigrant as a potentially permanent cultural alien lay at the heart of the Americanization movement. Diversity had become, in Americanizers' eyes, disloyalty. Ethnicity had become treason. Woodrow Wilson, lecturing to an audience of newly naturalized citizens in 1915, stated that "a man who thinks of himself as belonging to a particular national group in America has not yet become an American. . . ."

Ethnic spokespeople decried, in the word of *Narod Polski,* "American chauvinists" who understood by Americanization "only one language, unity of thought and opinion, one sympathy and antipathy." Another Polish-language paper, *Dziennik Zwiazkowy,* protested that the Americanization movement had "in it not the smallest particle of the true American spirit, the spirit of freedom, the brightest virtue of which is the broadest possible tolerance." What was more, "the present war shows that the American 'melting pot' is entirely superfluous." Immigrants were proving their patriotism on the battlefield. "What more does America need, what more can it desire?"

The "more" that Americanizers desired was complete conformity to the customs, values, and practices of white Anglo-Saxon Protestants. Conformity extended to all matters no matter how insignificant. As John J. Mahoney, Massachusetts director of immigrant education, phrased it, "Everything that touches the immigrant's life is an instrumentality for his Americanization or the reverse." It is this mentality, what Theodore Roosevelt (*q.v.*) ringingly called "100 percent Americanism," which explains why Americanizers sought to discourage the use of cabbage as well as encourage the use of English. It explains why civics classes for immigrants placed as much stress on the importance of airing out one's bedding as on voting. William Sharlip and Albert A. Owens, authors of a standard manual, *Adult Immigrant Education: Its Scope, Content, and Methods,* explained the stress on "personal hygiene and home sanitation" in terms of the "clannish" proclivities of immigrants. They alleged that the newcomers considered only "the welfare of those belonging to their own particular group" while ignoring "the outsider and the community at large." It was "essential to break down all clannishness . . . and to stress the interdependence of individuals in the matter of good health and sanitation." In a real sense, for Americanizers, Americanism included "American" vegetables and an "American" way of cleaning one's teeth.

Clearly the task Americanizers set for themselves, the rooting out of all traces of the immigrants' Old World pasts, was an impossible one. This does not mean, however, that it had no important or lasting effects. When Theodore Roosevelt insisted during his 1916 campaign for the Republican presidential nomination that "every citizen of this country has got to be pro–United States first, last, and all the time, and not pro–anything else at all . . . ," he pioneered a demagogic use of loyalty which would appeal to subsequent generations of politicians seeking a popular issue. Further, Americanization reinforced an old tendency in American culture to identify radical political and economic ideas with foreigners. And so it contributed to the antiunion, anti-Socialist campaigns of the immediate postwar years.

Most of all, the Americanization movement ratified the equation of "100 percent Americanism" with Anglo conformity. Leonard Covello, (*q.v.*) one of the founders of Italo-American studies and a leading educator in New York City, succeeded in introducing the study of Italian into the curriculum of DeWitt Clinton High School in 1920. It was "perhaps the only Italian class in any public school in the country at that time" and he frequently found himself "accused of 'segregating' my students, and more than once by Italian-Americans themselves." "The war," he wrote in his autobiography, "had strengthened the idea of conformity. Americanization meant the casting off of everything that was 'alien,' especially the language and culture of national origin."

The Americanization movement had another, paradoxical effect. It strengthened the very ethnic consciousness it sought to extirpate. This was because Americanizers demanded that immigrants and their children publicly display their loyalty. This meant, for example, that the Treasury Department sponsored contests in major cities between nationality groups to see which would purchase the most war bonds. German-Americans, as one of their newspapers editorialized, had to "Subscribe and Talk About It." "All must purchase" the bonds "if they do not want to appear lukewarm or have their loyalty questioned." Similarly, a Polish-language paper urged its readers to consider "how great the benefit to the Polish cause will be if we buy bonds and indicate that it is Poles who are buying them!" The goal was to "prove that we are one of the most loyal national groups in America, despite the fact that we do not forsake our Polish nationality, but rather place emphasis on it everywhere and always."

Other Americanizing programs could have the same effect. The Chicago *Sunday Jewish Courier* hailed the Committee on Public Information–sponsored Fourth of July parade as "a most welcome opportunity for the Jews to display their patriotism for America." Since the committee wanted each group "to show their 'true colors,' " we "must celebrate this occasion as Jews."

Americanizers insisted upon these symbolic displays precisely because their fears of alien disloyalty could only be allayed by the massing of vast numbers of visibly loyal immigrants. But for them to be visibly immigrants they had to be seen celebrating the very ethnic ties Americanizers sought to suppress. It was an irony lost on almost everyone.

References
Frank V. Thompson, *Schooling of the Immigrant* (1920); William M. Leiserson, *Adjusting Immigrant and Industry* (1924); John Palmer Gavit, *Americans by Choice* (1922); A. Gerd Korman, *Industrialization, Immigrants and Americanizers: The View from Milwaukee, 1865–1924* (1967); Philip Gleason, "American Identity and Americanization," *Harvard Encyclopedia of American Ethnic Groups* (1980); John F. McClymer, "The Federal Government and the Americanization Movement, 1915–1924," *Prologue* (1978); John F. McClymer, "The Americanization Movement and the Education of the Foreign-Born Adult, 1914–1925," in Bernard J. Weiss, ed., *American Education and the European Immigrant* (1982); Robert A. Carlson, *The Americanization Syndrome: A Quest For Conformity* (1987).

J.F.M.

AMERICANIZATION STUDIES; THE ACCULTURATION OF IMMIGRANT GROUPS INTO AMERICAN SOCIETY. A series of individual studies commissioned by the Carnegie Corporation and published in 1920–21. The series was republished in 1971 with new introductions to each of the studies: vol. 1: *Schooling of the Immigrant,* by Frank V. Thompson, with a general introduction to the republished studies by William S. Bernard, and a new introduction by Clarence Senior; vol. 2: *America via the Neighborhood,* by John Daniels, with a new introduction by Florence G. Cassidy; vol. 3: *Old World Traits Transplanted,* by William I. Thomas, together with Robert E. Park and Herbert A. Miller, with a new introduction by Donald R. Young; vol. 4: *A Stake in the Land,* by Peter A. Speek, with a new introduction by Rabel J. Burdge and Everett M. Rogers; vol. 5: *Immigrant Health and the Community,* by Michael M. Davis, Jr., with a new introduction by Raymond F. O'Dowd; vol. 6: *New Homes for Old,* by Sophonisba P. Breckinridge, with a new introduction by William S. Bernard; vol. 7: *The Immigrant Press and Its Control,* by Robert E. Park, with a new introduction by Read Lewis; vol. 8: *Americans by Choice,* by John Palmer Gavit, with a new introduction by William S. Bernard; vol. 9: *The Immigrant's Day in Court,* by Kate Holladay Claghorn, with a new introduction by Ann S. Petluck; vol. 10: *Adjusting Immigrant and Industry,* by William M. Leiserson, with a new introduction by Gerd Korman.

Reference
Milton Gordon, "Americanization Studies" [Review], *Social Forces* 54 (Dec. 1975): 470–474.

F.C.

AMERIKA EESTI HEATEGEV SELTS. *See* Estonians.

AMERIKABREV (letters). *See* Norwegians.

AMERIKAI MAGYAR NEPSZAVA. *See* Hungarians.

AMERIKAI NEMZETOR. *See* Hungarians.

AMERIKAN TAUTI. *See* Finns.

AMERIKANSKI SLOVENAC. *See* Slovenes.

AMERIKAS VESTESNIS. *See* Latvians.

AMISH. *See* Mennonites.

AMORAL FAMILISM. A theory that proposes that "amoral famil-ism" in southern Italian society and family life is an ethos "which has been produced by three factors acting in combination: a high death rate, certain land tenure conditions, and the absence of the institution of the extended family." Advanced by Edward C. Banfield in his *The Moral Basis of a Backward Society* (1958). Reference should be made to Charlotte G. Chapman, *Milocca: A Sicilian Village* (1971), a study undertaken in 1928, written in 1935, and published in 1971 which does not use Banfield's conceptual approach; and to Feliks Gross, *Il Paese: Values and Social Change in an Italian Village* (1973).

F.C.

ANABAPTISTS. *See* Mennonites.

ANCIENT ORDER OF HIBERNIANS (AOH). A fraternal organiza-tion for Catholics of Irish birth and Irish descent founded in New York in 1836. The St. Patrick's Fraternal Society along with other immi-grants, many of whom were members of secret societies, met at St. James Church to found the order. The AOH defended the rights of Catholic immigrants in America and in general supported the struggle for independence in Ireland. It has survived several ideological splits throughout its history and today claims over 20,000 members with an equal number in the women's auxiliary. It remains active in the promo-tion of Irish history and culture today and publishes a monthly, *The National Hibernian Digest*. Its membership also continues to support the present struggle for freedom in northeast Ireland.

Reference
J. O'Dea, *History of the Ancient Order of Hibernians and Ladies Auxiliary*, 3 vols. (1923).

S.P.M.

ANDER, O. FRITIOF (1903–1978). Immigration historian. Ander obtained his education from Augustana in Rock Island in 1927, his doctorate from Illinois in 1930, and spent his entire professional career at his college alma mater for thirty-eight years thereafter. He was promoted early to full professorship in 1933 and served as departmental chairman from the next year until his retirement in 1968. He published works extensively and of high quality on Swedish, Swedish-American, and Illinois historical subjects. His published dissertation, *T. N. Hasselquist* (1931) is the standard biography of a leading Swedish-American clergyman; his *Cultural Heritage of the Swedish Immigrant* (1956) is his best-known immigrant work, and his *Building of Modern Sweden* (1958) was well received as a comprehensive survey of contemporary Sweden. His many credits attested to his high standards of scholarship; he was holder of Guggenheim, Fulbright, and American Philosophical Society awards, and was made Swedish Royal Knight of the North Star and fellow of the International Institute of Arts and Letters, both in 1961.

Reference
Victor Greene, "O. Fritiof Ander (1903–1978)," *Immigration History Newsletter* 10 Nov. 1978): 14.

D.N.A.

ANDERSON, RASMUS B[JORN] (1846–1936). Journalist, politician. Anderson rose to considerable prominence as educator, journalist, author, translator, agitator, and politician on the Norwegian immigrant scene in the Midwest. His career reflects the character and personality of the man himself, and the historical forces (European, American, and frontier) that influenced his career and views. His books and articles had immediate and lasting impacts upon his society.

Reference
Lloyd M. Hustvedt, *Pioneer Scholar: A Biography of Rasmus Bjorn Anderson* (1966).

F.C.

ANGEL ISLAND. Modeled after Ellis Island, these facilities in San Francisco Bay were used between 1910 and 1940 as a detention center almost exclusively for Chinese who had failed to convince immigration officials of the legitimacy of their claims of eligibility for entry into the

United States under its exclusion laws. Fraudulent papers were easily purchased to document that the bearer was returning from a trip back to China, or more often that he was related to an American citizen. Because almost all of the 175,000 Chinese who were shunted to Angel Island for further interrogation were teenaged males, they were labeled "paper sons." Equipped with "coaching books," they memorized incredible minutiae about the alleged family home in China, from the number of steps and windows to the location of the rice bin, names of neighbors, etc., which had to agree with the responses of the alleged relative. Such aids had to be jettisoned before arrival, and to avoid further coaching, they were allowed no visitors until after the cross-examination. For a fee, however, Chinese cooks would sometimes smuggle in additional details. Chinese interpreters were routinely rotated to prevent collusion. One interpreter conceded that approximately 90 percent of the detainees were illegal, although 75 percent were passed and allowed to land.

Those who failed were quickly deported unless they appealed the decision, which prolonged their stay for months, sometimes years. While waiting, many drew, painted, or carved on the walls moving poems expressing their frustration, hopes, despair, anger, boredom, and loneliness. Many such poems, some of which are exceptionally sophisticated, still survive and have been translated and published.

A riot in 1919, largely over food, but also over the prisonlike conditions, was quelled by federal troops. A self-governing association (Zizhui hui) was formed that year to orient newcomers. Membership fees were used to buy books and to construct recreational facilities. The center was closed in 1940 when the administration building, which also housed the smaller number of females, burned down. Today the island is a national park. *See also* Chinese, paper sons.

Reference
Him Mark Lai and Judy Yung, *Island: The History and Poetry of Angel Island* (1980).

S.C.M.

ANGOFF, CHARLES (1902–1979). Novelist and playwright. Angoff is best known for a series of autobiographical novels which chronicle Jewish life in America. A native of Minsk, Russia, he analyzed the relationship of American Jews to Israel. The son of a tailor, he graduated from Harvard, served variously as professor of English at Fairleigh Dickinson University, as editor of the *Literary Review*, and as research director of "Meet the Press" (1945–1955). He received the Ellis Island Award in 1977 for significant contributions to the United States. His most popularly acclaimed novel, *In the Morning Light* (1954), won the Daroff Memorial Fiction Award for the best Jewish novel. Other chief works are *The World of George Jean Nathan* (1952), *Winter Twilight* (1970), and *William Carlos Williams* (1974). Angoff's pseudonym was Richard W. Hinton.

Reference
J. T. Benton, *World of Charles Angoff: On the Occasion of His 75th Birthday* (1977).

C.C.

ANTICIPATORY REFUGEES. Sociological concept advanced by E. F. Kunz, who suggests that the movements of refugees can be divided into two separate patterns: the flight-arrival pattern and the associative pattern. The flight-arrival pattern is further divided into two types: the acute and the anticipatory. According to Kunz, anticipatory refugees are those who have actually prepared themselves to leave their home country. They are well informed, and many of them are well-to-do and well educated and tend to do well in their host society as they adjust satisfactorily to a new life. *See also* Acute Refugees.

References
E. F. Kunz, "The Refugee in Flight: Kinetic Models and Forms of Displacement," *International Migration Review* 7 (Summer 1973), and "Part II: The Analytic Framework," *International Migration Review* 15 (Spring–Summer 1981).

D.N.A.

ANTIN, MARY. (1881–1949). Novelist. Antin was a product of the mass emigration of Jews from Russia in 1894. The great wave of emigration that began in 1882 after the assassination of Czar Alexander II triggered pogroms in southern Russia and laws were passed expelling Jews from the Pale. Antin's most famous novel, *The Promised Land* (1912), was a best-selling autobiography depicting a young girl's spiritual journey from the Old World of the *shetl* in Russia to early twentieth-century America. Antin's family settled in the slums of Boston, which was the subject of *From Plotzk to Boston* (1899). Her themes were of patriotism, idealism, and complete assimilation. Antin married a Lutheran, but by 1918 was an ardent Zionist. She suffered a mental breakdown in 1918 and went from one institution to another searching for a spiritual direction and reawakening. Critics have compared her with the best writers of the immigrant experience such as Benjamin Franklin, Jacob Riis, and Booker T. Washington.

Reference
Oscar Handlin, "Foreword" to *The Promised Land* (1969).

C.C.

ANTI-SEMITISM. *See* [Jews]: Ideological Anti-Semitism.

AQUILAR FREE LIBRARY SOCIETY. *See* Educational Alliance.

ARAB AMERICAN INSTITUTE. *See* Arabs.

ARABS. Almost two million Americans are descended from Arab ancestors. This estimate may be too high or too low, but it is reasonable in
the absence of accurate statistical data. Perhaps two-thirds of these are
descendants of immigrants who migrated to the United States between
1880 and 1940; the rest came after World War II. Christians were the
overwhelming majority in the first wave; Muslims were more numerous
in the second.

Because the majority of the first wave originated in the Ottoman
province of Syria which included the autonomous *sanjak* of Mt.
Lebanon (with a relatively small number from Palestine), they called
themselves Syrian. Any reference to themselves as Arab was, like the
Syrian reference, cultural rather than nationalistic, since at the time of
their migration there was no independent Syria, and Arab nationalism
was an incipient idea. Nevertheless, these pioneer immigrants were
fiercely proud of their Arab heritage. The strongest identity factors were
more personal. The structure of Ottoman-Muslim society was such that
for centuries its members identified themselves by family, religion,
sect, and village or town of origin.

About 90 percent of the early, or pioneer, immigrants were Christians of Eastern rite sects from Mt. Lebanon, the pre–World War I
Christian stronghold of the Middle East. They were joined by a scattering of Lebanese Druze (a semi-Islamic sect) as well as by Christians and
Muslims from Syria proper.

Those who came were mainly poor but they were not destitute.
They were illiterate or semiliterate men, women, and children, most of
whom probably had never previously traveled further than the next
village. They were, on the whole, young, single, adventurous owners—
or sons and daughters of owners—of small disconnected plots of land.
Frequently, they had to supplement the family income through crafts
and trade. In short, they were farmer/tradesmen and farmer/artisans.
Although the economies of both Mt. Lebanon and Syria proper were not
sufficiently depressed to yield despair, neither were they brisk enough
to meet rising expectations. Poverty was common although not abject,
and life was difficult.

On the other hand, the post–World War II wave of Arabic-speaking immigrants contained a high percentage of skilled and professional,
politicized, and nationalistic young men and women, as well as refugees from war-torn regions on the eastern Mediterranean. The immigrants of the second wave, originating as they do from the twenty-one
independent nations known since the war as the Arab World, identify

themselves as Arabs. These, too, migrated to improve their economic status and seek better career opportunities.

Like millions of other immigrants to the United States, the Syrians (first-wave immigrants) came to an America that was industrializing and urbanizing in the last quarter of the nineteenth century. But unlike other immigrants, they were not drawn here by the promise of industrial jobs. Nor were they driven out of their country by economic oppression or by religious or political persecution. The pioneer Syrians who arrived before the turn of the century came solely to get rich quick and return to their villages to live and raise their children in an environment of economic comfort and security.

Mass emigration from the eastern Mediterranean to America was activated by rumors of streets paved with gold, by steamship agents, and particularly by glowing letters containing money orders from individuals who had gambled on the rumors of easy wealth in America. Sometimes these individuals, visiting their village, dazzled their countrymen by their three-piece suits, polished leather shoes, and gold watch fobs.

Syrians who migrated subsequently, for whatever reason—to avoid military conscription or Ottoman oppression during World War I, for example—came to the United States and other parts of the Western Hemisphere because the adventurous "gold-seeking" pioneers had opened the way. It was only while pursuing their get-rich-quick goal that they discovered the ideals of freedom, democracy, and equal opportunity and embraced them fervently.

Until 1899 Syrians, in official immigration records, were not distinguished from other ethnic subjects of the Ottoman Empire. Lumped together with Turks, Greeks, and Armenians from the empire under the classification "Turkey in Asia," their exact numbers are difficult to determine. Official records, however, show that a total of 115,838 Syrians and Palestinians immigrated between 1899 and 1940 in addition to several thousands who had previously been listed under "Turkey in Asia." They do not show, for example, those who entered from Canada, South and Central America, and the West Indies after years of residence there.

According to census records, there were, by 1940, 206,128 Americans of Syrian and Palestinian origin and descent living in every state of the Union and Alaska. This wide distribution was already a fact by 1910, the result of pack peddling, the primary occupation of Syrian immigrants. Women joined the migration from the beginning, and by the peak of Syrian immigration in 1913, wives, mothers, sisters, and daughters constituted about 32 percent of the migrants.

Of the majority listed as illiterate in the official immigration statistics, many may have learned at least the rudiments of Arabic in native and missionary schools. In the United States, they improved their literacy and taught others so that they could communicate with families left behind and read newspapers for information about the homeland as well as the new land.

A fundamental factor in the Syrian experience in the United States was pack peddling. It was not unique to Syrian immigrants. Other Mediterranean and Eastern European immigrants had used it as an expedient and initial immigrant occupation. Generally, these groups preferred the pushcart to the pack and the city to the country. None, however, except for the German Jewish immigrants of an earlier period, made the deep and broad identification with the trade as did the Syrians. Like these Jews, they used peddling as a stepping stone on the upward path toward personal success and middle-class status. As the Syrians—men, women, and children—practiced the trade, it initially involved notions cases full of rosaries, crosses, notions, and jewelry, but expanded to include backpacks containing practically everything that a farm wife or housebound pre–World War I town dweller needed or desired. Despite hardships on the road in all climates and its demands on their physical and psychological resources, Syrians usually preferred it to the drudgery of the factory and the isolation of American farm life.

Not only did they leave their villages to follow America's promise of quick wealth, but they pursued that promise on foot, by horse and buggy, and later by automobile to every quarter of the American continent. Peddling provided a first-hand, closeup introduction to American life, served as a window to new ideas and values, and raised expectations. Its other basic virtues were that it required no advanced training, capital, or language skills, and was a means of earning money immediately on arrival. Furthermore, it spared them the job uncertainty endemic to industrial labor, and its itinerancy precluded a ghetto mentality. It forced them to learn English quickly.

Peddling settlements centered around a supplier—a veteran peddler who attracted or recruited peddlers from his and nearby villages. The supplier sold them merchandise on credit and helped them, as any village leader was expected to do, for settlements were incomplete replicas of the village populated by relatives and fellow villagers. Settlements were also both the peddlers' base and their refuge. It was there that the peripatetic peddler came to rejuvenate his spirit after long and difficult periods on the road.

These immigrants had been accustomed to hardships in their homeland, but they never reckoned on what they would encounter on the road in America. Much of their pain, fear, frustration, and fatigue is preserved in a body of peddlers' anecdotes which tell of cold nights spent in barns or trees, of frozen skirts that cut into frozen ankles, of parched throats and relentless heat, of being mired in mud, robbed, beaten, killed, and lost, and of being chased by farmers with guns and barking dogs. When shared with fellow peddlers back at the settlement, these anecdotes were not only the source of much laughter, but they served as a psychological safety valve.

Almost from the beginning, the trend was toward permanent residence despite continued vows to return to the homeland. As experience washed away the mystery and uncertainty of living in the new land, early settlements began to mature into communities around ethnic institutions: Eastern rite sectarian churches; clubs based on religion, family, and village of origin; and the Arabic-language press in particular. Mosques were not built until the late 1920s. New York was the foremost business, cultural, and intellectual center for Syrians until well after 1948.

Peddling hastened acculturation and in the process contributed to its own obsolescence. Few mourned its passing. With acquired capital and new values, Syrians decided to settle permanently in the United States. The majority opened family businesses in cities and towns throughout the country. Dry goods and grocery stores were the most common, but Syrians engaged in businesses of all kinds. Failure was common but it was not daunting. Experiences on the road and in the settlements were open doors to assimilation; the ethnic forces to protect the immigrants against the irresistible pull of American life were too weak within the community. On the other hand, the advantages of acquiring an American veneer were not only economic but social; they enhanced one's prestige in the settlements as well as back home in the village. In addition, nationalistic feelings and ideologies, common deterrents to changing identities, were weak or absent in many Syrians and ambivalent in others. Not to be underestimated was the general satisfaction with what peddling Syrians found in America.

The Arabic-language press was one of the important factors in the remarkably rapid assimilation of the first-wave Syrian immigrants. From its inception in 1892, it interpreted American life for them as best it could and provided guidance. While it explained, it also idealized and oversimplified, presenting America, as a rule, in uncritical and glowing terms. In addition to social and cultural items, it advocated American patriotism and good citizenship.

Relying on their wits, Syrian peddlers persevered against hardships, saved enough money to pay debts, sent promised remittances back home, and paid for fares to bring relatives to America. Before World War I, a peddler could average $1,000 annually compared to the average annual American labor wage of about $650.

Syrian peddlers collectively performed a special economic function. As they roamed into the remote regions of the country, they took the products of small American industries into remote markets, altering

tastes and habits. Thus, they promoted commerce and encouraged production. At the same time, they contributed a minimum of about $60
million to the gross national product between 1899 and 1910. It was
inevitable that at about 1910, as Syrians outgrew the peddling trade as
an immigrant occupation, American society would outgrow their services because of innovative merchandising such as Montgomery Ward's
mail order house and the spread of department stores.

Although the Arabs of both waves of immigration were eager to
become American, they did not entirely shed their native values and
traditions. Foremost among these is the obligation to elevate and defend
family honor and status, which produced such traits as generosity,
hospitality, a competitive spirit, a strong work ethic, shrewdness, con-
servatism, and clannishness. On the other hand, the fear of bringing
shame and dishonor on the family restrained crime and the accepting of
welfare. Given the economic opportunities and system of values in the
United States, Syrians readily became success oriented and claim that
they have much in common with American culture.

In their eagerness to prosper in America, the early Syrian immigrants and their children assimilated rapidly and in the process they
neglected their own culture. The language declined and the youth married outside the group. If after World War II political and economic
events had not reactivated Arab immigration and an interest in Arab
culture, Syrian-Americans might have Americanized themselves out of
existence.

The second wave of Arabic-speaking immigrants was, in many
important ways, different from the first. Like the earlier immigrants, a
large percentage came to improve their economic status, but unlike
them they are not only educated but also politicized and nationalistic
because they had come from independent Arab states where most had
experienced disturbing political events in the homeland. Thousands,
like the stateless Palestinian refugees, were driven from their native
land by the creation of the State of Israel and by subsequent Arab-Israeli
conflicts. Since 1975, a second stream of refugees from Beirut and
southern Lebanon was precipitated by the Lebanese civil war and the
Israeli invasion of that region in 1978 and 1982. Most are Muslims, but
whether muslim or Christian, Saudi Arabian or Syrian, they call themselves Arabs and have inspired the Syrian-Americans to do the same.
And, most, like the pioneer Syrians, intended to return but did not.

Unlike the pioneers, these more recent arrivals came to a United
States that had filled its continent from border to border, experienced
two world wars, and had become the world's leading industrial, scientific, technological, and military power—one that preferred skilled and
educated professional immigrants to the unskilled masses. Many, if not
most, of the new immigrants entered with the education and skills

useful to postwar America. Of these, many are graduates of American universities. Thus, they have little difficulty adjusting to American life and finding the kind of work for which they were trained. Others came to join families.

Records of the United States Immigration and Naturalization Service show that about 200,000 Arabs migrated since the end of World War II. The largest groups are Palestinians arriving from Israel and from several other Arab and other countries to which they had spread since 1948; the poor peasants of southern Lebanon; Egyptians; and Yemenis. The countries of the Arabian Peninsula (other than the Yemen Arab Republic) and North Africa, west of Egypt, account for the fewest Arab Immigrants. Again, official immigration figures are misleading. They again do not show Arabs entering from countries other than their native homeland. Nor are the census figures more reliable since the ethnic question in them is blurred.

Wherever they settle in America, the new Arab immigrants find American-born Arabs. If they come to join Syrian-Americans, they find that the majority of them are scattered in suburbs. Some Palestinians, Egyptians, and Yemenis formed their own communities and attract countrymen to them. Professionals usually settle where they find employment and in a very short time, except for their Arab accents and features, one is hardly able to distinguish them from their American colleagues. Many, like the Yemenis, the southern Lebanese Muslim refugees, and some Palestinians who join the large Arab Dearborn community, benefit from the assistance of the descendants of Syrian-Americans who have established a center for economic, legal, and social services to facilitate the adjustment of these unsophisticated and unskilled immigrants. Their civil rights are defended against anti-Arab discrimination.

Because of the increase of Muslim immigrants from Arab and other countries, there has been a sharp increase in the number of mosques in the United States. Moreover, because Arabic is the language of Islam, it has been revived. Muslim religious teachers (*imams*), arriving from the Arab World to direct the mosques, try to restore the poor religious discipline and knowledge of long-Americanized Syrian Muslims. Many Christian churches, too, stirred by the ethnic feelings of their congregations, began to offer programs in Arabic language and culture but, like the efforts of earlier Syrian immigrants, with limited success. Leaders in both groups, hoping to promote a better understanding between the Americanized Syrian-Americans and new Arabs, began to sponsor events to instill a sense of common purpose and unity. While the children of Syrian-Americans are returning to their Arab roots, the children of new Arabs are attending American schools, watching American television, and joining American friends at American movies. In short, they are becoming American.

The Arabic press, which was in serious decline before World War II, has also been revived. Numerous Arabic and Arab-English newspapers and journals appeared, most with a limited life span and none with the national appeal of earlier ones—they tend to be local and narrow in outlook. While they, too, bring social and cultural news, they tend to emphasize politics stemming from the Arab-Israeli conflict and the economics of the developing countries of the Arab World, and reflect the political frustrations of much of the Arab population in the United States.

New Arabs are also inclined to form numerous clubs. Religious, family, and village societies continue to be popular and several new kinds have been formed locally and nationally. Some are based on nation of origin, some are cultural, and some are professional, such as the law and medical associations. Social or professional as their aims are, politics is never far below the surface despite the fact that purely political clubs which focus on the Palestinian problem and its related issues are scattered throughout the nation.

The Syrian-American clubs were slow to unite nationally and failed in their attempts to do so. The reason offered after the last attempt in the early 1950s was that the Syrians had become too Americanized to need an ethnic organization. This attitude was reversed after the 1967 Arab-Israeli war. The anti-Arab attitude in America which it generated aroused the Arab-Americans politically. They began to organize in order to raise the consciousness of apathetic Americans of Arab origin and descent, to influence American Middle East foreign policy, to counter the work of the Israeli lobby in the United States, and to inform American public opinion about Arab and Arab-American peoples and culture. The ultimate purpose was to reverse the anti-Arab attitude. These national organizations are the Association of Arab American University Graduates, formed in 1967; the National Association of Arab Americans, founded in 1972; the American Arab Anti-Discrimination Committee, organized in 1980; and the Arab American Institute, added in 1985. The relatively larger and broader memberships that these organizations enjoy indicate that they will continue to exist as long as the conditions which gave rise to them persist.

Syrian-Americans as a group did not find it necessary, before 1967, to gain influence in political parties or labor unions; the emphasis was on individual achievement. As early as the turn of the nineteenth century, scores of the pioneer generation had filtered to the top in business and finance. A large number of their immediate descendants continue to achieve in these fields. Some of them could even be called tycoons. More recently, however, the choice of careers has been in the professions. A great many Syrian-Americans have turned to law and medicine; others have turned to the sciences, engineering, public service, journalism, politics, education, and entertainment, among other endeavors. A sizable list of them have become national personalities.

That Arabs have a high rate of achievement in America should surprise no one. The descendants of the pioneers, driven toward success by the combination of their ethnic and American values, were already pursuing the American dream as Americans long before World War II. Many saw themselves as following in the footsteps of Horatio Alger. Most of the new Arabs arrived already equipped with skills and the will to succeed. If their list of public personalities is relatively short, it is because, on the one hand, they have been in the United States barely over a generation and, on the other hand, they are trying to achieve in an anti-Arab environment.

Reference
Alixa Naff, *Becoming American: The Early Arab Immigrant Experience* (1985).

A.N.

ARBERESH. *See* Italian-Albanians.

ARENA, THE. *See* Flower, B[enjamin] O[range].

ARESE, FRANCESCO (1805–1881). Italian nobleman, traveler. Count Arese's *A Trip to the Prairies and in the Interior of North America, 1837–1838* describes a trip up the Missouri River to what is now western Iowa, and into the Vermilion River country of present-day South Dakota, southwestern Minnesota, Wisconsin, and Michigan to Montreal and Quebec, in all a six-thousand-mile trip. His impressions helped shape European attitudes toward North America.

Reference
Count Francesco Arese, *A Trip to the Prairies and in the Interior of North America, 1837–1838*, trans. (from the original French) Arthur Evans (1934; rpt. 1975).

F.C.

ARIDA, NASEEB. *See* Lebanese.

[ARMENIANS]. *Armenian American Almanac,* ed. Hamo Vassilian (1985). A first comprehensive guide to Armenian institutions and organizations designed to help find the most current information on Armenian-American communities in the United States.

F.C.

ARMENIANS. This ancient people has lived for over 2,500 years in the Caucasus mountains and Eastern Anatolia. During World War I, the vast majority of Armenians were killed or uprooted from their lands. Today they number about seven million scattered around the world. After the Armenian SSR (with 3.4 million) and the rest of the Soviet Union (with 1.5 million), the largest community in the Armenian diaspora is in the United States, with some 800,000 citizens, whose numbers have grown steadily in recent decades through immigration.

Historical Background. The Armenian homeland is in the Caucasus mountains between modern-day Russia and Turkey. It is here, according to the Bible, that Noah's Ark landed, on the mountains of Ararat, within sight of the modern-day capital city of Erevan, which will mark its 2,770th anniversary in 1988.

Several features make Armenians ethnically distinct. They have their own language and alphabet (originally thirty-six characters plus two letters added in the twelfth century) that was invented by St. Mesrob Mashdotz in the beginning of the fifth century A.D. in order to translate the Bible into Armenian. The Armenian Apostolic church, an autocephalous church founded in A.D. 301, was the first national Christian church. According to the latest theory and linguistic evidence, the Armenians are indigenous to Eastern Anatolia and their language forms a distinct branch of the Indo-European language family. Through the centuries they have maintained their identity, though outnumbered and often subject to the hegemony of neighboring peoples—Hittites, Assyrians, Persians, Romans, Mongols, Turks, and Russians. Dispersed throughout the world, they are a distinct cultural group with their own cuisine, clothing, music, holidays, architecture, and customs.

Migration to the U.S.A. Like many other U.S. ethnic groups, the Armenians came to North America in response to events in their ancestral homeland. Three main phases can be distinguished in this migration:

1. In 1870 the Armenians in America numbered less than one hundred, being mostly enterprising students, businessmen, or adventurers who planned eventually to return to their homeland. Among the first Armenians in America was a certain "Martin, the Armenian" who in 1618 helped John Smith grow silkworms in the new Virginia Bay Colony. Another notable Armenian immigrant was the veterinarian/inventor Dr. Kristapor Seropian, who in the 1850s invented the green dye used in printing U.S. currency.

2. From 1890 to 1924, there was a great influx of Armenians into the United States, which came in two waves. From 1890 to 1914, before World War I, some 64,000 immigrants fled oppression and massacre in their homes in Ottoman Turkey, where they were a small but economically influential minority. After the war, some 30,771 sur-

vivors of the genocide entered until the imposition of the 1924 immigrant quota system, which drastically reduced the number permitted to enter the country. The majority of these newcomers settled in and around New York and Boston, receiving aid from those Armenians already established in the United States.

3. The new surge of immigration from the Middle East following World War II was accelerated by the rise of three potent forces—Islamic fundamentalism, nationalism, and socialism. One by one the largest and most prosperous Armenian communities in the Middle East fell victim to political upheaval—in Egypt (1952), Turkey (1955), Syria (1961), Iraq (1958), Iran (1978), and Lebanon (1975)—driving nearly half of their combined 700,000 Armenians toward Western Europe and North and South America. Because the U.S. Immigration and Naturalization Service has not recognized the Armenians as a nationality since 1931, it is not known how many Armenians have entered the United States from the Middle East. Estimates put their number at roughly 2,000 per year before the 1975 civil war in Lebanon, and roughly 10,000 annually since then. Between 1947 and 1979, one U.S.-based organization alone, ANCHA (the Armenian National Committee to aid Homeless Armenians), resettled from Communist and Muslim countries 25,000 Armenians which the U.S. State Department officially classified as political refugees.

In the United States today there are roughly 800,000 Armenians. In the 1980 census about 250,000 identified themselves as Armenian, when asked if they considered themselves ethnic Americans, and over 100,000 reported using the Armenian language at home. The single largest Armenian community in the United States is in California, with well over 250,000 in Fresno, San Francisco, and greater Los Angeles; noteworthy in this regard is the one-square-mile area in Hollywood which is home to 40,000 new immigrants. Other parts of the country with large numbers of Armenians are the mid-Atlantic states (175,000), New England (90,000), the Midwest (65,000), and Florida (10,000).

Institutions. As with other ethnic groups, the Armenian community is supported by hundreds of churches and organizations in the United States, national and local. While some Armenians practice Roman Catholicism and Protestantism, the vast majority of Armenians belong to the national church, the Armenian Apostolic (Orthodox) church, founded in A.D. 301 by St. Gregory the Illuminator. There are 150,000 Armenian Catholics worldwide, 30,000 of them in the North American Diocese, formed in 1981. The Armenian rite of the Roman Catholic church, which comprises five parishes, is attended by 3 percent of all North American Armenians. There are twenty-four Armenian Protestant churches, mostly evangelical. These denominations were started by

Western missionaries who visited Turkey in the 1800s and converted the Armenians from the national church to Protestanism. Approximately 7 percent of the Armenians in North America (50,000) are Protestant. The Armenian Apostolic church is the church of 90 percent of all Armenians in North America, with over 700,000 members and nearly one hundred churches. Disagreements over Soviet hegemony, among other issues, led to a division of the church into two parts—the diocese, which comprises fifty-seven churches, and the prelacy, which comprises thirty. While the parts are doctrinally identical and recognize the Catholicos of All Armenians in Etchmiadzin as the spiritual head of the church, the diocese falls directly under the jurisdiction of the Catholicos of All Armenians in Etchmiadzin in Soviet Armenia, whereas the prelacy falls under the jurisdiction of the Catholicos of the Great House of Cilicia in Lebanon. Many Armenians are unhappy with the division in the church and are working toward unity.

Aside from its churches, the Armenian-American community, particularly the first-generation immigrants, established hundreds of other organizations, local and national. These include about a dozen national newspapers, daily and weekly, which feature international news about Armenians; about fifty publishers and distributors of Armenian books; two dozen learned and professional societies; over twenty-five day schools, most of them formed in the 1970s; endowed chairs in Armenian Studies at U.S. universities (Columbia, Harvard, Michigan, Pennsylvania, U.C.L.A.); over one hundred local cultural organizations, supporting Armenian theater, dance, literature, the arts, youth activities, and social services; a half-dozen national philanthrophic and political organizations, most of which raise funds for social services and education for Armenians in need both inside and outside of the United States. This vibrant network of community organizations has served both as a vehicle for the perpetuation of the community in America and as an entry point for immigrants into American life.

Identity. As individuals, Armenian immigrants to the United States (and other countries) typically make an easy transition to life in their new land. Most are multilingual, English frequently being their second or third language. Most heads of families come as educated professionals, skilled craftsmen, or prosperous businessmen who are readily absorbed into the U.S. economy. In general they have come as part of a "chain migration," with some family members already in the United States who are ready and able to help them get established. The very active and diverse network of community organization also helps in overcoming the culture shock of living in a new country. And last, but not least, as a low-profile group, Armenians have been subject to little discrimination upon arrival and are in general respected as hard working and patriotic by Americans familiar with them.

References
Arra S. Avakian, *The Armenians in America* (1977); M. Vartan Malcom, *The Armenians in America* (1919); Robert Mirak, *Torn Between Two Lands* (1983); Harold Takooshian, "Armenian Immigration to the United States Today from the Middle East," *Journal of Armenian Studies* (1987); Hamo B. Vasilian, *Armenian-American Almanac* (1985).

H.T.

ASCH, SHOLEM (1880–1957). Novelist. Born in Poland, Asch was a prolific novelist who, early in his writing career, wrote entirely in Yiddish. Asch depicted a world of misery and decay. To Asch, belief in God was the world's only hope of salvation. His novels are a joyous affirmation of faith in God, a faith that redeems mortals from their worldly pain. The schism between Christians and Jews in Europe was upsetting to Asch and he actively tried to improve relations. For this, he was criticized by Jews during World War II for promoting further hatred of them. Asch's most controversial work, which focuses on the schism, is his biblical trilogy *The Nazarene* (1939), *The Apostle* (1943), and *Mary* (1949). Other chief works are *The Small Town* (1904) and a play, *God of Vengeance* (1918).

Reference
Encyclopedia of World Literature in the Twentieth Century (updated ed., 1967).

C.C.

ASIA PACIFIC TRIANGLE. Term used in the Immigration and Naturalization Act of 1952 (*q.v.*). Appears in Section 202(a) of the act, and defines a section of the world that includes the Asian continent and almost the entire Pacific Ocean. The area specified as the Asia Pacific Triangle includes all of the earth's surface between 60 degrees east and 165 degrees west longitude and from the North Pole south to 25 degrees south latitude. At the time the act was passed (1952) there were twenty independent nations within this triangle, and each was given a special quota of one hundred per year for entry into the United States.

D.N.A.

ASIAN IMMIGRANTS, and social services. Squires (*infra*) has studied recent Asian immigrants and the social service agencies providing support programs to them. Providers of services have assumed that problems of participation are based on unfamiliarity with their programs. A more fundamental cause is that the immigrants and the agencies have very different cultural expectations about appropriate mechanisms for providing social support. Effective delivery of care has required modification of the providers' model of individualized therapy to include social and cultural factors.

Reference

S. E. Squires, "Cultural Change: Asian Immigrants and Social Services in New England," paper presented at the American Anthropological Association 83d Meeting, Denver, Colorado, November 14–18, 1984.

F.C.

ASIAN INDIANS. The designation "Asian Indian" was used officially for the first time as a special minority category in the 1980 census to take account of the rapidly increasing population of immigrants with a heritage in India. Prior to the 1980 census, immigrants from India were classified as Caucasian; now they are classified as an ethnic minority within the "Asian or Pacific Islander" general classification. Restrictions in the immigration laws allowed only a few to enter from the Indian subcontinent prior to 1965, but a change in the law that year opened the doors to immigrants from India.

Early Migration. Although the first immigrants came from India in 1820, it was not until the beginning of the century that more than 275 persons came from India in a single decade. A significant movement from British Columbia into the west coast states began in 1907, following a serious anti-Oriental riot in Vancouver, and between 1907 and 1920 approximately 6,400 Indians entered, mostly Punjabi Sikh agricultural workers who made their way to California.

The restrictive Immigration Act of 1917 included India in the Asiatic Barred Zone and thereby made it virtually impossible for people from India to enter the country legally as permanent residents. Opportunity for citizenship was further restricted by a decision of the United States Supreme Court (*The United States* v. *Bhagat Sing Thind*), which ruled that Indian immigrants were not "free white persons" within the law and, therefore, were not eligible for citizenship. Some certificates already given were withdrawn. Not until 1946 did the Luce-Celler Bill remove India from the barred zone and make it possible for immigrants from India to become citizens. From 1820 to 1960 a total of only 13,607 persons immigrated legally from India, and an unrecorded number of these departed.

These early immigrants supported the Ghadar movement, which, from a headquarters in San Francisco, published literature and a newspaper (begun in 1913), raised funds, and enlisted "freedom fighters" to oppose the British in an uprising planned in the Punjab in 1915. The Ghadar movement continued in the United States after it was effectively banned in India, and the members in the United States were more militant than most of the nationalists in India. Mark Juergensmeyer notes that this was not simply a nationalist struggle; rather, the struggles against oppression in America and in India were fused into one struggle. He describes the "Ghadar syndrome" as "a militant nationalist movement created abroad by expatriates, for whom the movement is also an outlet for their economic and social frustrations, and a vehicle for their ethnic identities.'' The Ghadar movement was repressed during World War I, but it continued to publish a paper and agitate until the time India gained independence and the restrictive laws of the United States were changed. The headquarters of the Ghadar party in San Francisco was given to the Government of India, and the government donated a Ghadar Party Memorial Building on the site in 1974. These Punjabis and their descendants now form a prosperous and influential agricultural community in California.

The New Immigrants. The 1980 census recorded 387,223 Asian Indians, and estimates of current population range from a conservative 550,000 to 850,000. The change has been dramatic. More immigrants from India came in the single year of 1982 than came in all the years prior to 1960. Some immigrants in the 1960s were Indian graduate students who elected to remain in the United States because until 1972 it was easy for students to change their resident status. Now, even though India ranks seventh in the number of students from abroad in American colleges and universities, it is much more difficult for students to change their status to remain permanently.

Immigration policy selected from the Indian subcontinent the best educated, the professionals, those trained in scientific and technical fields, those who could make the most rapid adjustment to the new setting. They entered under preference categories for professional people and skilled workers. To those who know them well, ''Asian Indian'' implies well-educated, technically trained, energetic, and relatively prosperous; at least that describes most who entered prior to 1980; they may well be the most talented and easily acculturated of all immigrants to have come to the United States. It is common for Asian Indians to speak of their community as having two main occupation groups— doctors and engineers—because in the decade following the change in the law, doctors, nurses, engineers, and scientists were in great demand in the American economy, and many came from India. These very successful technocrats provide significant financial support and leadership for Asian Indian organizations.

The consequence of this selection process is a group of highly educated and successful new immigrants. The median household income of Asian Indians reported in the 1980 census ranked second highest among ethnic groups at $25,644, when the median household income for the entire country was $16,841. They quickly established themselves in the professional class and moved into affluent suburbs, so the Asian Indians are not found in ghettos. Moreover, Asian Indians are scattered in metropolitan areas and towns across the country. The states with the largest Asian Indian population in the 1980 census were New

York and New Jersey, California, Illinois, and Texas. In the census listing of place of residence of minority groups, out of 370 urbanized areas of 50,000 or more, only 3 did not have a number of Asian Indians, and of some 680 towns and cities, only 20 did not include some Asian Indians. Thus, although some Indian shopping areas with Indian food stores, restaurants, and clothing and appliance stores are located in areas that have become known as "Little India," the Asian Indian population is scattered throughout metropolitan areas and across the country. Urban organizations and religious institutions serve a dispersed population of Asian Indians.

The success of the majority should not, however, hide the difficulties faced by some Asian Indians who have been unable to gain certification in the professions equal to their Indian credentials. Many are underemployed. The downturn of the American economy in the early 1980s led to layoffs from high-paying jobs and created unemployment even among those who were certified, and some Asian Indians are among "the educated poor." There were 3,176 families of those who immigrated from India between 1970 and 1979 whose income for 1979 was below the poverty level. Many of the more recent immigrants are employed in unskilled jobs.

As earlier immigrants have now become citizens and are eligible to bring members of their families to the United States, most immigrants from India since 1980 have entered under preference categories for family reunification. It is no longer easy for physicians, engineers, and those in many of the other technical occupations to get labor certification and immigrant status, and in 1982 only 2,208 of the 16,964 persons from India were admitted under the preference categories for professionals and skilled workers. The rest come to join their families. Few of these immigrants have the high level of attainment that marked immigrants of the previous two decades, and some tensions exist within the Asian Indian community as a result. The complaint is made that many families have encouraged nonprofessional members to come who are ill prepared to be successful. The most recent immigrants join relatives and friends, but they face the frustrations of wanting to succeed like those who came before them and to have the material benefits and status that characterize the earlier immigrants, while having fewer skills and being relegated to the least well-paid menial jobs.

The designation of Asian Indians as a distinct minority group in the census conferred special legal rights on the individuals as members of a group eligible for various forms of affirmative action. The decision of the Small Business Administration, for example, to grant minority status and to make Asian Indians eligible for the agency's programs to promote minority entrepreneurship is potentially of great value for the more recent immigrants.

Some reverse migration exists, but it is very small in spite of the fact that most came with the intention of returning to India after they completed their studies or after they had earned enough for a secure future. Many forces join to cause them to stay. Those who are successful have attained a standard of living and professional satisfaction difficult to duplicate in India, and those who have not been successful do not have the resources necessary to return and establish themselves in family and career without considerable embarrassment. Moreover, their American children are strong and permanent ties to the United States A common joke among Asian Indians who meet each other after a prolonged period is: "I see that you're still earning your passage back to India."

Ethnicity. The single designation "Asian Indian" masks great diversity, and all-India organizations and festivals attempt to unite into one new ethnic group persons from many countries, linguistic and cultural regions, and religions. A person is an Asian Indian only in the United States.

Although most Asian Indians came directly to the United States from India, many have never lived in the Indian subcontinent, but entered the United States after long residence in other countries. Independence of the East African countries—Kenya, Tanzania, and Uganda—and the subsequent explusion of Asians from Uganda in 1972 caused a vast migration, and some East African Asians made their way to the United States. Others entered after a period of residence in other African countries, Burma, Great Britain, or Canada. All Asian Indians have ancestoral ties in the Indian subcontinent, but not all have lived there. English is an "all-India language," and virtually all the immigrants are fluent in English, except for a few new brides and elderly parents.

All of the major regional-linguistic groups of India are represented among immigrants. The ten Indo-European languages of north and west India and the four Dravidian languages of the south are the basis of divisions into cultural-linguistic regions. The southern region includes four major subcultures in four states: Tamil Nadu, where Tamil is the principal language; Kerala, where the language is Malayalam; Mysore, where the language is Kannada; and Andhra Pradesh, where Telugu is spoken. The ten languages of the north and west are Hindi, Gujarati, Punjabi, Bengali, Rajasthani, Marathi, Kashmiri, Assamese, Bihari, and Oriya. These ten languages and cultures shade into one another. Census statistics are not available for various regional-linguistic groups in the United States, but the best estimates are that approximately 40 percent are Gujaratis and 20 percent are Punjabis. Other regional-linguistic groups are represented, with Bengalis, Tamils, Telugu, and

Malayalees in significant numbers. Organizations based on regional-linguistic ties, such as the Gujarat Samaj and the Tamil Sangam, as well as regional caste groupings, such as the Patidar Samaj, are present in most metropolitan areas. Hence, Asian Indians have the potential to create personal and group identities based on a number of ethnic or minority designations, depending on which elements they decide to emphasize. So, to the majority of the population the new immigrant may be an Asian Indian, while to others from India he may be a Malayalee or a Sindhi. Other subgroups related to caste, religion, profession, or political allegiance may create significant boundaries and elements of identity to be activated in particular social situations.

In the 1960s the Asian Indian community was relatively small, even in major urban areas, and members tended to form inclusive primary groups for all Indians, and even included some Pakistanis. As the Asian Indian community grew, it could support many subgroups, so gatherings and organizations developed for the various regional-linguistic groups. Organizations such as the Gujarati Samaj merely reflect the refraction of the community into language-based subgroups for social and cultural affairs. Some leaders think it is inevitable that future generations, who will have lost the ability to communicate in the regional languages or to appreciate regional customs and symbols, will adopt the general designation ''Asian Indian'' as an ethnic as well as a legal minority designation, and they try to prepare their children for that future.

It is difficult for immigrant parents to establish the regional-linguistic identity for their children, and they express concern and some anxiety regarding the appropriate socialization of their children. Parents who express an intention to return to India give as the reason a desire to save their children from peer pressures in American society. The arrival of children at school age and then the early teens is a major impetus for many parents to attend to those ethnic and religious institutions that are surrogates for the extended family. Nevertheless, the second generation is losing contact with Indian languages and cultures, and few of the children are fluent in written or spoken forms of an Indian language. A dialectic is present that is in part between the generations but that is also between all-India identification and institutions and regional-linguistic identification and institutions. It is too early to predict the results of this dialectic.

Religions. Immigrants are religious, by all counts more religious as a group than they were before they emigrated, because religion is one of the important markers of identity which helps them preserve individual self-awareness and cohesion as a group. All of the major religions present in the Indian subcontinent are in evidence among the immigrants—Hindu, Muslim, Sikh, Jain, Christian, Parsi, even Jewish, and many of their subsects and denominations—and these are in the process of adaptation to the new setting.

Variation exists among the ways immigrants use religions for emphasis on national and ethnic identity, and three patterns can be distinguished. In the first, the religious affiliation is portrayed as identical with regional-linguistic identity. So, some elements of Sikh rhetoric identify Sikh religion with Punjabi identity and demand unified support of Sikh and Punjabi nationalism. In the second, elements of religious symbolism are supportive of regional-linguistic ethnic identity, and religious gatherings are the primary loci for use of Indian languages and cuisines outside the home. Thus the Durga Puja, which is a religious ceremony, is the most important celebration for Bengalis, and it incorporates many elements of Bengali cultural and artistic tradition along with the religious. Sectarian forms of Hinduism and Christianity, such as Swaminarayan Hinduism of Gujarat and St. Thomas Christianity of Kerala, are intimately connected with the language and culture of particular regions of India, and the two faces of ethnic identity and religious affiliation support each other. A third pattern is found in those religions that stress a universality that transcends boundaries of language, region, or nation. Some Christians, Muslims, Jews, and Parsis form religious organizations that encompass immigrants of the same religion from several other countries and cultures. Thus, Asian Indians are building Hindu temples of many types, Muslim mosques and *jamat khanas,* Sikh *gurdwaras,* Jain temples, and Christian churches which are transforming the American religious landscape.

Asian Indians are a prime example of the ''new ethnics'' who are part of the ''brain drain'' from the Third World to western industrialized countries. They established themselves rapidly in the professions and in a fairly narrow economic class of the modern technocratic elite, but they reflect all of the regional, cultural, and religious divisions of the Indian subcontinent. The community grows rapidly through continued immigration from several countries and through births in a relatively young population, and social, economic, and religious adaptation in a new society continues apace. It seems likely that Asian Indians will number over one million in the 1990 census and will certainly continue to be an important cultural and religious force in the society.

References

Mark Juergensmeyer and N. Gerald Barrier, eds., *Sikh Studies* (1979); Parmatma Saran, *The Asian Indian Experience in the United States* (1985); Parmatma Saran and Edwin Eames, eds., *The New Ethnics: Asian Indians in the United States* (1980); A. Thomas and T. M. Thomas, *Kerala Immigrants in America* (1984); Raymond B. Williams, *Religions of Immigrants from India and Pakistan: New Threads in the American Tapestry* (1988).

R.B.W.

ASIANS, immigration and naturalization trends. Asks (*infra*) whom we have integrated within America culturally, socially, civically, and in terms of national identification. Focuses on selected demographic characteristics of Asians (Middle Easterners, Far Easterners, and Indians)—the regional group that went from 5 percent of all new citizens in fiscal year 1951 to 39 percent in 1978.

Reference
E. H. Barkan, "Whom Shall We Integrate? A Comparative Analysis of the Immigration and Naturalization Trends of Asians Before and After the 1965 Immigration Act (1951–1978)," *Journal of American Ethnic History* 3 (1983): 29–57.

F.C.

ASIATIC EXCLUSION LEAGUE. Organized in 1905; claimed over 100,000 members largely opposed to Japanese and Oriental immigration. Allied with the Japanese and Korean Exclusion League, whose activities resulted in the San Francisco school board issuing an order in 1906 segregating all Chinese, Japanese, and Korean children in the public schools. Protest by the Japanese government forced President Theodore Roosevelt to intervene.

References
Robert A. Divine, *American Immigration Policy* (1957; rpt. 1972); Roy L. Garis, *Immigration Restriction* (1927).

F.C.

ASSEMBLY CENTERS. Temporary detention camps established by the Wartime Civil Control Administration (WCCA) on March 11, 1942. John L. DeWitt, commanding general of the Western Defense Command, established the WCCA, with Colonel Karl R. Bendetsen as its director, to carry out the evacuation of Japanese-Americans.

Reference
Hyung-Chang Kim, ed., *Dictionary of Asian American History* (1986); Michi Weglyn, *Years of Infamy* (1976).

D.N.A.

ASSIMILATION. A key concept for students of immigration, assimilation has been used not only as an heuristic tool for understanding the immigrant experience in the United States but also as a vehicle for maintaining and fostering a particular ideology. The term is used in the social sciences in its bioecological sense of adaptation of individuals and groups; that is, physiologically, it refers to the process of converting (food) into a substance suitable for absorption by the body. When applied analogously, it refers first to the modification of the individual and collective activity of the immigrants as they adjust to the new cultural environment, and second to the degree of the immigrants' relative change, conformity, and absorption into the host culture and/or society. In this latter sense it is viewed as a culmination of a process that begins with contact and moves through toleration, accommodation, and acculturation.

The colonization of the Americas over the past five hundred years began as an invasive settlement by culturally diverse migrants in the lands of equally culturally diverse autochthons (native peoples). The immigrants and natives interacted; overall it was the natives that had to alter their lives for the aliens, but the migrants had to adjust also, to the land and to the people they found here. Those immigrants that followed had to adapt to the ones that came before.

United States society, particularly during the past two centuries, expected more from its newcomers than just accommodation and acculturation. It anticipated that the immigrants would learn about the American life-styles (acculturation) and adjust their behavior patterns to fit in (accommodation). But more than that, it demanded that they shed all trace of their former culture and eventually conform entirely to the dominant Anglo-American culture. This has been referred to as the homogenization of immigrants in America; it is an important part of the notion of the "melting pot" which was idealized in the United States largely as a result of pervasive economic and geopolitical forces from the earliest days of the new nation.

The first settlements of the Spanish, Portuguese, Dutch, French, English, and Africans were to a very great extent impelled or forced migrations and, on arrival, these people had to come to grips with the difficult untamed physical environment. Their settlements were charted by European powers, and they remained socially separated. By the middle of the nineteenth century, the population increased both in number and in diversity. Scots, Welsh, Irish from both the north and south of Ireland, and English made up the population from the British Isles. There were Germans from both the north and south of Germany. One could also find Norwegians, Swedes, and some Danes. In addition, there were Dutch, French, Swiss, and Italians, mainly from the north. A large population of Africans, originally brought to these shores as indentured servants or as slaves in the seventeenth century, were freed and migrated and settled throughout the United States and the territories. All of the major religious groups found in Europe were present. As diverse as these people were, they built a nation. By the twentieth century, the great migration of peoples from eastern and southern Europe took place and the cultural makeup of the nation was even more markedly variegated.

The unity of the nation required cohesion between these groups and, for a variety of reasons, economic factors probably being the most salient, cultural homogeneity was thought to be the necessary agent. The melting pot notion had been used to describe American unity by early travelers and visitors from Europe who wrote about the United States. But for many working people whose jobs and salaries were threatened by the influx and importation of what was perceived of (by both employers and workers) as cheap, hard-working labor, and certain intellectuals, "melting pot" meant that immigrants ought to be required to "melt" culturally and lose all trace of "foreignness." Early nineteenth-century advocates of public schools saw this transforming of aliens into Americans as the proper role of the schools and the settlement houses. The nativist movements of that century portrayed the immigrants' foreignness as politically dangerous for the nation.

These movements called for the "Americanization" of all newcomers, by which they meant the imposition of Anglo life-styles upon them. The melting pot notion of Israel Zangwill differed somewhat from this Anglo-conformity kind of melting in that what was envisioned was the cultural "melting together" of both the host and the newcomer in the formation of a new and superior culture. Strong feelings centered around the immigrant question in the early days of the twentieth century. Once raised, the arguments for and against each kind of "melting pot" had proponents on either side, and the real complexity of the issue began to be recognized. New explanatory concepts were developed as new dimensions of assimilation were discovered. The idea began to be proclaimed that culturally diverse people could live together, make a nation, and at the same time each people could retain its own culture. This was called "cultural pluralism" by John Dewey and Horace Kallen and it represented an alternative to both the Anglo-conformity and the "melting pot" notions. Emotions ran high on these issues, sparked by xenophobia, by economic threats, and by ethnocentrism. Religious bigotry and racial prejudice were becoming embedded in the American character. The heightened demand for Anglo conformity was disguised under the pseudo-patriotic invocation of "Americanization"; and it was resisted in part because of the immigrants' physical, social, cultural, and psychological inability to conform, and in part because of their philosophical and ideological convictions. They were supported in their endurance by some American intellectuals who believed that a democracy implies the right of citizens to retain cultural differences and distinctions, and that "American" did not refer necessarily to a fixed Anglo cultural style. Nevertheless, the influential clamoring of the dominant group led eventually to the passage of such restrictive immigration legislation as the Chinese Exclusion Act and the National Quota

Act which were to alleviate the "problems" caused by the presence of
too many "unassimilable," that is, southern and eastern European and
Asian, peoples in the country.

The concept of assimilation was used to refer, first, to the degree
or the extent to which immigrants and/or their progeny conformed to
the Anglo cultural forms (cultural assimilation) and, second, to the
degree or extent to which immigrants and/or their progeny entered into
and became an integral part of the new society (structural assimilation).
Since the early decades of the twentieth century, social scientists have
recognized that assimilation takes place as a result of the social processes in which the migrant and host groups engage. Cooperation,
competition, and conflict may be said to be prerequisite to assimilation.
Theorists have, over time, linked the study of assimilation to the study
of American ethnicity. Ethnicity refers to those social, cultural, and
psychological qualities and characteristics that are held in common by a
group of individuals who share a sense of peoplehood. Fundamental to
the notion of ethnicity is people consciously or unconsciously sharing a
real or fictitious "ideology" made up of a real or putative common
ancestry, memories of a shared historical past, etc. There may be a
common language or dialect, a common place of origin, a common
territory, a unique way of life, a set of religious doctrines or dogmas,
kinship relations, common phenotypical features, a consciousness of
kind, or any combination of these. When the research focus is moved
off the "group" and centers on the "individual-in-group," the Erikso-
nian notion of ego-identity has heuristic importance. An individual's
ethnicity resides in the ego-identity (in the form of ethnic ideological
themes), internalized even beyond levels of consciousness, passed on
through generations by socialization and incorporation processes.

American culture may be characterized as being essentially a multiethnic culture. Using equilibrium or functionalist perspectives, sociologists have equated assimilation and Anglo conformity or the melting pot idea, wherein the immigrant subordinate ethnic status group is
seen as moving toward the dominant ethnic status group. Some sociologists and historians have placed assimilation in opposition to cultural pluralism, viewing them as mutually exclusive possibilities. From
a conflict perspective (that is, from a dialectical point of view), assimilation is akin to "integration" in recognizing the cultural and structural
assimilation that occurs both in Anglo conformity and in the melting pot
idea, on the one hand, and also in pluralism, on the other. The dominant
ethnic group generates its opposite—estranged intruders—by territorial
behavior toward the immigrant. The members of the subordinate ethnic
group, aware of the freedom that is the promise of America, refuse to
accept this social, economic, and cultural subordination imposed upon

them and instead learn the survival techniques of the marketplace. Out of the contradiction comes conflict which is resolved in a dynamic synthesis. A cultural and then structural integration takes place that changes not only the persons involved, nor even only their respective groups, but the whole society. The immigrant subordinates move toward the dominants; and the dominants move toward the subordinates. The heat of the conflict impacts and integrates the two groups in a way such that while there is real assimilation, there remains cultural heterogeneity.

References
Francis X. Femminella, "The Ethnic Ideological Themes of Italian Americans," in R. N. Juliani, ed., *The Family and Community Life of Italian Americans* (1983); Milton M. Gordon, *Assimilation in American Life* (1964); Gerard A. Postiglione, *Ethnicity and American Social Theory* (1983).

F.X.F.

ASSOCIATION FOR IMPROVING THE CONDITION OF THE POOR (AICP). *See* Community Service Society.

ATTERDAG COLLEGE. One of the Danish Folk High Schools established in the United States. Atterdag College was located in the Danish colony of Solvang, California, and classes were held there from 1914 until 1937. The experiences of Atterdag College serve as an example that the Folk High School as an educational institution did not, or could not, adapt to the American milieu. With some accommodation the Danish Folk High Schools might have survived as a part of the educational scene in America.

Reference
Gloria Houston, "The Origins, Development and Significance of Atterdag College—A Danish Folk High School in America," Ph.D. dissertation, University of California, Los Angeles, 1971 (DA 32:3653-A).

F.C.

AUGUSTANA SYNOD. *See* Swedes.

AUGSBURG COLLEGE (Minneapolis). *See* Norwegians.

AUSTRALIA, alien legalization programs. Australia, proportionately, accepts more immigrants than the United States and, consequently, immigrants and immigration policy carry a greater impact there than in the United States. Although Australia's location limits its experience with undocumented migrants, there have been enough of them to cause Australia to conduct three alien legalization programs in 1973, 1976, and 1980. Australia's small-scale programs, by U.S. standards, provide some useful lessons to the United States.

Reference
David S. North, "Down Under Amnesties: Background, Programs and Comparative Insights," *International Migration Review* 18 (Fall 1984): 524–540.

F.C.

AUTOCEPHALOUS ORTHODOX CHURCH. *See* Byelorussians.

AYRES, LEONARD PORTER (1879–1946). Economist. Ayres was on the staff of the Russell Sage Foundation (1908–1917), and was a pioneer in the application of statistical methods to educational and social research. He is the author of *Laggards in Our Schools* (1909), a survey on retardation, covering more than fifty city school systems. This is an in-depth study of New York City, with an analysis of records of 20,000 children from fifteen schools, noting that 23 percent of all students were at least a year behind expected grade level for their age; it also studies the relationship between nationality and retardation.

F.C.

BAHAMIANS. Little has been written of Bahamian immigration to the United States, but a distinctive Bahamian presence had been established in south Florida, especially in Key West, by the mid-nineteenth century. Early in the twentieth century, a new wave of black immigrants from the Bahamas settled in Miami, then a rapidly growing tourist town. By 1920, some 4,815 black immigrants from the Bahamas composed 52 percent of all Miami's blacks and 16.3 percent of the city's entire population. At that time, Miami had a larger population of black immigrants than any other city in the United States except New York.

Bahamians had been coming to Florida's lower east coast long before the building of Miami in the 1890s. In the early nineteenth century, when Florida was isolated and undeveloped, the area was frequented by Bahamian fishermen, shipwreck salvagers, and Indian traders who, according to one Bahamian writer, regarded Florida "much as another island of the Bahamas." Plantation agriculture was never very successful in the Bahamas, and most islanders earned a livelihood from the sea or from subsistence agriculture. Meager economic prospects at home stimulated a migratory urge that was common among all the islands of the Caribbean—"livelihood migration," involving temporary labor elsewhere and a later return to the home island. By the 1830s, for example, black and white Bahamians had begun a migration to the Florida Keys, where they worked in fishing, sponging, and turtling. Bahamians composed about a third of Key West's population in 1890, and a large majority of Key West blacks can trace their ancestry to Bahamian origins. By the late nineteenth century, Bahamian blacks were also working all over Central America as stevedores for American and German shipping lines, as canal laborers in Panama, and as contract laborers in the lumber trade, on banana and coffee plantations, and building roads and railroads.

The building up of Miami after 1896 created new opportunities for Bahamian migrant workers, who were attracted to the city for the same reasons that European immigrants poured into the industrial cities of the Northeast and Midwest at the turn of the century—better jobs and higher wages. The building boom in Miami made jobs plentiful, and pilgrims returning home enticed others to follow with exaggerated tales of their fame and fortune in the "promised land." The introduction of regular steamship service between Miami and Nassau by the early twentieth century made the trip to Florida cheap and convenient for Bahamians. According to Bahamian population studies, ten to twelve thousand Bahamians left the islands for Florida between 1900 and 1920—about one-fifth of the entire population of the Bahamas.

In Florida, the Bahamian newcomers found work in building construction, as railroad laborers, and as stevedores on the Miami docks. The emergence of Miami as a tourist center in the early twentieth century provided job opportunities for Bahamian women, especially as maids, cooks, and laundry and service workers in the city's new hotels and restaurants. Large numbers of Bahamians worked in the citrus industry and as field hands in south Florida agriculture. Many of the Bahamians came as migrant laborers during the harvest season, returning to the islands each summer. In the years before effective federal regulation of immigration, Bahamian blacks moved easily and often between south Florida and the islands.

As the migration process continued, increasing numbers of Bahamians became permanent residents in south Florida. A Florida state census of 1915 reported 6,718 black immigrants in four south Florida counties. By 1930, over 5,500 foreign-born blacks, virtually all Bahamians, lived in Miami alone. As agriculture expanded along Florida's Atlantic coast, Bahamians responded to new work opportunities. As a result, by 1945 the Florida state census could report more foreign-born blacks living in Palm Beach County (5,597) than in Dade County (4,609).

Actually, these census figures, taken at static moments in time, disguise the full dimensions of the Bahamian labor migration. During the 1930s, annual statistics in the *Bahamas Blue Book* demonstrate that emigrants from the islands surpassed 10,000 in most years. In the single year 1937, almost 14,000 Bahamians left the islands—more than 20 percent of the total Bahamian population. Almost the same number returned to the islands in 1937, suggesting the dual nature of the migratory flow. This Bahamian migration continued uninterrupted despite the restrictive immigration legislation of the 1920s, since British West Indians were included under the large and generally unfilled annual quota accorded to Great Britain.

The massive outflow of Bahamian migrants to Florida, as well as consequent labor shortages, caused official concern in Nassau. For thousands of Bahamians from the 1890s to the 1940s, however, the widespread perception of economic opportunity in Florida was too strong to resist. But the Bahamians routinely encountered segregation and white racism in Florida. Racial confrontations involving Bahamian blacks and white policemen in Key West, Miami, and Jacksonville were not uncommon. The Bahamas governor and the British Foreign Office often protested police brutality and other forms of racial discrimination directed against Bahamians in Florida, generally without result.

Bahamians in Miami established flourishing ethnic communities in Coconut Grove and "Colored Town" (now known as Overtown), the two major black neighborhoods in early twentieth-century Miami. They built or bought houses, established businesses, and laid the foundations for churches and a vibrant organizational life. The permanence and stability of their neighborhoods, along with strong links to the islands, contributed to cultural maintenance and a strong sense of nationality.

From Miami's earliest days in the 1890s, the Bahamian presence made the city's black population distinctively different from that in most southern cities. The Bahamians had an impact on cultural patterns, food ways, and dress and other customs. Bahamian drum rhythms, dance and song traditions, and folk culture had a powerful impact on native black communities in South Florida. Although nominally Anglican in religion, the Afro-Caribbean cult of *obeah* remained strong among Florida Bahamians. To both Key West and Miami, the Bahamians brought a distinctive architectural style typified by two-story wooden frame houses, with wide, two-tiered, balustraded porches designed to take advantage of ocean breezes. Following British and Bahamian traditions, Florida Bahamians regularly celebrated Guy Fawkes Day and other holidays.

Unfettered Bahamian migration ended with World War II, when the agricultural labor supply came under governmental regulation. But enough Bahamians had settled permanently in south Florida in earlier decades to sustain the growth of cohesive communities held together by a strong sense of nationality and cultural distinctiveness. To this day, some sections of black Miami and Key West have retained the indelible atmosphere of the Bahamas.

References
The Florida Negro Collection at the University of South Florida; Raymond A. Mohl, "Black Immigrants: Bahamians in Early Twentieth-Century Miami," *Florida Historical Quarterly* 65 (Jan. 1987): 271–297; Ira De A. Reid, *The Negro Immigrant: His Background, Characteristics, and Social Adjustment, 1899–1937* (1939).

R.A.M.

BAKER, S[ARA] JOSEPHINE (1873–1945). Physician, public health administrator. Baker organized and directed the New York City Bureau of Child Hygiene, the first tax-supported agency in the United States concerned exclusively with improving child health. For forty years she took part in the fight to reduce the staggering rate of infant and maternal mortality in the immigrant communities and lived to see that hope being realized. As commissioner of health she instituted reforms (e.g., the strict licensing of midwives whose patients were overwhelmingly immigrant women; foster mother care for foundlings) that significantly reduced infant mortality.

Reference
S. Josephine Baker, *Fighting for Life* (1939; rpt. 1974).

F.C.

THE BALCH INSTITUTE FOR ETHNIC STUDIES. Founded in 1971 by the Orphan's Court of Philadelphia, acting on behalf of trusts established by the Balch family a half-century earlier. The institute is located one block from Independence Hall in Philadelphia and is housed in a six-story library/museum complex which was constructed in 1976. It is supported by the Balch family endowments, by annual stipends from the City of Philadelphia and the Commonwealth of Pennsylvania, and by donations from members and private individuals and organizations. The institute is nearing the successful completion of a $1 million capital fund campaign, supported by a matching grant from the National Endowment for the Humanities, to increase its endowment and enhance programs.

The Balch Institute's mission, defined by the court, is to document and interpret American immigration history and ethnic life. The institute supports a research library, an ethnographic museum, and a recently expanded education program and conducts cooperative programs with a number of other organizations. Major interinstitutional programs include the Temple University–Balch Institute Center for Immigration Research, which is currently computer indexing ship passenger manifests for the port of New York for the period 1847–1896; and the Philadelphia Jewish Archives Center at the Balch Institute. The Jewish Archives, which was founded in 1972, recently moved to the institute and is now administered as part of the Balch Library. Institute programs are closely related and their activities are mutually supportive.

The Balch Institute Library, beginning from a zero base at the time of the institute's founding in 1971, has acquired a collection of over 50,000 volumes, 1,200 linear feet of archival records, 5,000 reels of microfilm, 12,000 photographs, and smaller holdings of sheet music, audio recordings, and ephemera. The Philadelphia Jewish Archives Center at the Balch Institute increases the library's archival resources by approximately an additional 1,500 linear feet. The library's holdings and its collecting policy reflect the breadth of the institute's mission, as well as an ongoing effort to define its role in ethnic studies and its relationship to other repositories. Beginning with a collecting program that was broad and exploratory, the library acquired a diverse accumulation of holdings in the first five years, consisting of a national print collection and archival materials which centered on Philadelphia and New York but spread across the mid-Atlantic region. Chronologically, the collection extended from the early colonial period to the present, and it included materials for approximately seventy ethnic groups.

In recent years the Balch Library has endeavored to strengthen its program and to define its role in ethnic studies and immigration history in terms of its existing holdings, its organizational strengths and weaknesses, the programs of other repositories, and identifiable needs in the field. In practice this has meant placing a high priority on establishing intellectual control over its collections and reporting them to national catalogues and information data bases, developing a professional staff with skills in managing multiethnic collections and in multilanguage processing and cataloguing (supported by a large corps of volunteer translators), working cooperatively with other ethnic libraries and archives, and refining its collecting policy to distinguish between print and nonprint material and active and passive collecting.

During the past five years the library has undertaken four major projects to preserve and establish intellectual control over its holdings. In 1980–81 twenty-nine newspaper titles were microfilmed, most from the Balch Library collection, but including titles or issues from the New York Public Library, the Center for Research Libraries, and other repositories. During 1981–82 the library processed its backlog of manuscript collections. Both of these projects were supported by grants from the National Endowment for the Humanities. In 1982 the first three-year stage of a six-year project, supported by the Pew Memorial Trust, to catalogue all holdings, current and retrospective, was begun. And during 1984 the library developed a visual access catalogue to its photograph collection and implemented needed photo conservation work.

The library collects material on all American ethnic groups for the period 1789 forward. It does not acquire materials published in the country of origin except for those that directly relate to emigration. Collection development, except for the purchase of current monographs, took a back seat to processing and cataloguing in the late 1970s and early 1980s. Active collecting resumed with the acquisition of the Ethnic Heritage Studies Clearinghouse Collection in 1982 and the implementation in late 1983 of a two-year project, supported by the National Endowment for the Humanities, to survey and access primary source materials in the anthracite region of northeastern Pennsylvania. The Ethnic Heritage Collection and the Anthracite Region Project, the one a national cumulation of ethnic curriculum material and the other a regional archives project, reflect the library's two-tiered collecting policy, national and regional respectively, for print and archival material.

References
R. Joseph Anderson, *Building a Multi-Ethnic Collection: The Research Library of the Balch Institute for Ethnic Studies* (1985); M. Mark Stolarik, "The Balch Institute for Ethnic Studies," *Ethnic Forum* 1 (Sept. 1981): 43–45.

F.C.

BALTAKIS, PAULIUS. *See* Lithuanians.

BAMBACE, ANGELA (1898–1975). Labor activist, union officer, community leader. Born of Italian immigrant parents in Brazil, Bambace and her family finally settled in East Harlem, New York City. Scarpaci states:

> This account of her life relies heavily then on oral testimony, on conversations with Angela Bambace, her friends, and her relatives. Such sources obviously include only those who have survived, and so important opinions like those of her husband, Romolo Camponeschi, will never be recorded. Her friend and companion, the Italian American anarchist, Luigi Quintilliano, her associates from the Italian anti-fascist and labor movement, Carlo Tresca [*q.v.*], Luigi Antonini and Frank Bellanca knew her well but left almost no account of their shared struggle.

Reference
Jean A. Scarpaci, "Angela Bambace and the International Ladies Garment Workers Union: The Search for an Elusive Activist," in George E. Pozzetta, ed., *Pane e Lavoro: The Italian American Working Class* (1980), pp. 99–118.

F.C.

BANCROFT NATURALIZATION TREATIES (1868–1910). The Bancroft Naturalization Treaties were a group of related agreements between the United States and the five German states (North German Confederation, Bavaria, Baden, Württemberg, and Hesse) that subsequently united to form the German Reich. No single unifying treaty between the United States and the Reich was ever negotiated, nor was any agreement ever reached that would have formally extended the provisions of the original treaties to Alsace-Lorraine, the territory annexed to the Reich after its formation. A complex set of peculiar and transitory circumstances led both the United States and the original German partner states to sign the agreements.

Reference

Luciana R. Meyer, "German-American Migration and the Bancroft Naturalization Treaties, 1868–1910," Ph.D. dissertation, City University of New York, 1970 (DA 31:1731-A).

F.C.

BANDELIER, ADOLPH. *See* Swiss.

BANGO. Copper disc distributed to each plantation worker in Hawaii for the purpose of identification. On paydays, plantation police would check each worker's bango before the paycheck, which was sealed in an envelope, was given to the right person. The origin of the term may be related to the Japanese word for number.

D.N.A.

BAPTISTS AND IMMIGRANTS. Itinerant Baptist missionaries, familiar figures in America as early as the late eighteenth century, increased in number during the nineteenth century. This occurred because American Baptists in that century committed themselves to assisting and converting the immigrants from Europe, Asia, and Latin America by organizing mission departments for immigrants within the American Baptist Home Mission Society, the Woman's American Baptist Home Mission Society, the American Baptist Publication Society, and other denominational organizations. Baptist foreign mission societies complemented home mission departments, encouraging missionaries to work not only among immigrants in the United States but also among their compatriots overseas. Preference for a mobile ministry operating within an international network of churches and mission societies placed the Baptists in the forefront of Christian efforts to assist immigrant communities.

The first Baptist mission for the Chinese of California was organized in Sacramento in 1854 by J. K. Shuck, who was also the first American Baptist missionary in China. During his seven years of work among the Chinese immigrants, he established a church and baptized sixteen Chinese, including Wong Mui, who returned to China to serve as pastor of a Baptist church in Canton. Wong Mui achieved such fame that he became known as "the Luther of the Chinese Christians." By 1915 the Chinatown of San Francisco had "one of the largest mission schools for Chinese boys and girls belonging to any denomination in the world outside of China." The early Baptist activities among the Chinese and later the Mexican immigrants eventually resulted in the establishment of large ethnic churches in San Francisco, including the First Chinese South and the First Spanish churches, with memberships of 187 and 185 respectively in 1974.

American Baptists were even more successful in reaching German and Scandinavian immigrants, establishing precedents for later Baptist evangelization among the immigrants from southern and eastern Europe. The Baptist Germans and Swedes established powerful foreign-speaking churches in cooperation with the Home Mission Society and won the right to train their own ministers. Bilingual ministers traveled to Germany and Sweden, where they organized Baptist congregations with close ethnic ties to the American German and Swedish churches. These ties remained so strong that immediately after World War II German-American Baptists through the Baptist World Alliance sent aid to the German displaced persons in the camps and assisted many displaced persons to come to the United States.

Anders Wiberg was a prototypical Swedish-American leader of the nineteenth century who helped forge close links between the American and European brethren. Converted to the Baptist faith in Copenhagen, he migrated to New York City, where the Baptist Mariner's Church employed him as a colporteur and missionary for work among the Norwegians, Danes, and Swedes. Ordained to the Baptist ministry in 1853, he traveled throughout the Midwest, preaching and aiding in the organization of Swedish-speaking churches. After returning to the northeast, he was employed by the Baptist Publication Society as a colporteur and writer. Wiberg returned to Sweden in 1855 to assist and establish churches. Eight years later this peripatetic evangelist was back in the United States.

F. O. Nilsson was another prominent Swedish missionary who helped to win the respect of native American Baptists for his minority group and who helped to forge strong ties between the Swedish and Swedish-American Baptists. Nilsson emerged as the chief pioneer and founder of Swedish Baptist churches in Minnesota, the major area of Swedish Baptist concentration. When the parishioners of the Twenty-Fifth Street Church in New York City decided to send a missionary to Sweden, Nilsson became their choice. After assisting and establishing churches in his native land, he returned to his work in Minnesota. By 1939 the Swedish Baptist General Conference, established in 1879, ranked among the largest of the fourteen Baptist national conferences in the United States.

German-American Baptists were as influential as their Swedish brethren; unlike the Swedes, they were more interested in assisting and assimilating other Baptist minorities. Under the leadership of August Rauschenbusch, the German department at the Rochester Theological Seminary in New York was established to train bilingual ministers. German Baptist leaders built national churches, sponsored German-language publications, and maintained ethnic schools, hospitals, and orphanages. Rauschenbusch's son Walter became a celebrated spokesman for the Social Gospel movement, a church movement aimed at helping the poorer classes in America. German-American ministers assimilated the French Baptists of New York City and the Czech Baptists of Chicago by welcoming them into their German churches.

Some Baptist leaders disapproved of the multiethnic composition of the brethren. In 1917 the editors of a Baptist newspaper wrote: "We do not want to be melted up with the Chinese and Japanese or even with the Russians. We do not wish to be melted at all. We want to preserve American ideals." But German American ministers like Henry C. Gleiss and Dan L. Schultz of Pittsburgh were preserving American ideals by defending the rights of immigrant steel and coal workers from southern and eastern Europe. At the same time, Italian-American Baptists, led by Antonio Mangano and Angelo DiDomenica, were emulating the earlier-arriving Germans and Swedes by establishing a department to train Italian ministers, by supporting their own publications, and by organizing Italian churches in Italy and America; like other ethnic Baptists, Italian national churches gave way to bilingual churches before becoming American congregations of mixed ethnic background.

To a majority of America's Baptists, ethnic Baptists are Baptists first and ethnics second. This was certainly evident during World War II, when American Baptists denounced the government's program of incarcerating Japanese-American Baptists in detention camps. In 1973 the Reverend Jitsuo Morikawa, who ministered to his people in the camps, wrote: "When historical events suddenly made us unwanted people to be avoided, it really wasn't the universities, the liberal press, the intellectuals, and the artists, not even the Supreme Court which came to our support: it was the Church, and among the churches the American Baptists and the Quakers were the first to lay their commitment on the line without waiting to see what others would do." That commitment had firm historical foundations.

References

Lawrence B. Davis, *Immigrants, Baptists, and the Protestant Mind* (1973); Salvatore Mondello, "Baptist Churches and Italian-Americans," *Foundations* 16 (July–Sept. 1973): 222–238; Salvatore Mondello, "The Integration of Japanese Baptists in American Society," *Foundations* 20 (July–Sept. 1977): 254–263.

S.M.

BARON DE HIRSCH FUND. In 1890, the Baron Maurice de Hirsch, a wealthy French philanthropist, established the Baron de Hirsch Fund in the United States to aid Jewish immigrants. Administered by prominent Jews (Jacob Schiff, Oscar Strauss, Jesse Seligman, Mayer Sulzberger, and others), the fund maintained schools to teach trades, and English and civics; provided agricultural implements and loans for those who wished to settle on the land; encouraged Jewish immigrants to reside outside of the congested slums of the cities; and conducted programs of general relief and protection.

Reference
Samuel Joseph, *History of the Baron de Hirsch Fund: The Americanization of the Jewish Immigrant* (1935; rpt. 1976).

F.C.

BARONI, GENO C. (1930–1984). Roman Catholic priest; Catholic coordinator for the 1963 Civil Rights March on Washington, D.C.; director of the U.S. Catholic Conference Task Force on Urban Problems; president of The National Center for Urban Ethnic Affairs (*q.v.*); assistant secretary, U.S. Department of Housing and Urban Development; counselor to the archbishop of Washington, D.C., James Hickey.

During the 1960s Baroni was the founder of scores of organizations in Washington, D.C. that shaped the civil rights movement; the V Street Ecumenical Center; Capitol Head Start; the Urban Rehab Corporation; the Sursum Corda Housing Corporation; the first community-based federal credit union; the Midtown Montessori; the Opportunities Industrialization Center; the Interreligious Committee on Race; and the D.C. Urban Coalition. As a consultant to federal agencies and a respected advocate on Capitol Hill, Baroni was among the foremost activist priests who proposed and achieved a new era and method of religious participation in American public affairs. Starting with the creation of the USCC Campaign for Human Development and the Call to Action, and continuing his contributing works on the bishops' pastorals in housing, crime, racism, ethnic pluralism, nuclear weapons, and the economy, as well as his participation in NETWORK, the Catholic Committee on Urban Ministry and Catholic Charities Ministry, Baroni prompted new departures for the church that focused on community or neighborhood rather than doctrinal discussions or worship. His wit and humor made this point: "it's not enough for us to gather around the altar as a way to heaven, when the neighborhood around the church is going to hell." During this period, *The Afro-American* offered these praises: "Geno's one of the few relevant white men in the sixties."

In the 1970s Baroni became the guiding force behind the neighborhood movement, and with support from the Ford Foundation found-

ed the National Center for Urban Ethnic Affairs (NCUEA) which pioneered a host of social inventions and policy critiques that fashioned a
new approach to urban policy. Baroni argued that "people don't live in
cities; they live in neighborhoods. Neighborhoods. Neighborhoods are
the building blocks of cities. If neighborhoods dies, cities die. There's
never been a Federal policy that respected neighborhoods. We destroyed neighborhoods in order to save them"; and "the government
cannot do it for people and neither can the private sector. People must
do things for themselves and make judgments about what's best for their
neighborhoods"; "my goal is to encourage equal partnership among
neighborhood groups, government, and the private sector in urban revitalization"; "I used to think I wanted to save the world. Then I got to
Washington, and thought I'd save the city. Now I'd settle for one
neighborhood."

In addition, Baroni founded the Bicentennial Ethnic/Racial Coalition which offered the clearest voice to the new ethnicity/ethnic renewal
of the 1960s and 1970s. His support for the legitimacy of immigrant
populations and respect for cultural diversity and their unequal access to
power emerged from his youth as an immigrant son in Acosta, Pennsylvania. Baroni once recalled, "You've got to understand coal mines.
Very ecumenical. The Episcopalians owned them. The Lutherans,
Methodists, and Presbyterians were the bosses. And the Hunkies, Italians, Poles, Slavs, and Hillbillies dug the coal." And what Baroni
found in his 1960–1970s tours of older industrial cities made the case
for new approaches: "For 27 years I had been taught to melt or else.
And I discovered there wasn't a melting pot. We were very pluralistic.
America is still looking for a sense of identity"; "If cities are not to end
up black, brown, and broke, we have to form new coalitions. What are
the convergent issues between groups—redlining, drug abuse, employment—around which both black and ethnic communities can co-
alesce"; "Two experiences we haven't really digested very well—
one's the slavery experience; and the other's the immigrant experience."

Msgr. Baroni founded the National Italian American Foundation
and in various ways sought to open the doors to public power for the
ignored and neglected residents of urban ethnic neighborhoods. He
discovered and nurtured hundreds of persons whose neighborhood-
based experiences proved to be the tonic need for an administrative state
that was paralyzed by cultural, economic, and social contradictions.
Baroni, the brilliant, witty storyteller, often told his audiences of his
most important contribution to urban policy: "In a basement a bunch of
neighborhood people began to figure out that this big bank had taken
money out of their neighborhood. When people wanted to borrow money, they couldn't—redlining. It took six years to get the Home Mortgage Disclosure Act passed. It did not come from the Federal Home

Loan Bank Board, nor the Executive Branch. This issue came from a community to the national level.''

J.A.K.

BARRETT, KATE WALLER (1858–1925). *See* Crittenton, Charles Nelson.

BARRY, LEONORA KEARNEY (1849–1930). Labor leader; born in County Cork, Ireland. Barry emigrated during the potato famine and settled in New York. She married Patrick Barry but was later widowed and left with three small children. During her work in a hosiery factory in Amsterdam, New York, she became concerned with the brutal working conditions of the day. In 1884 she joined the Knights of Labor and in 1886 was one of sixteen women delegates to the Knights of Labor General Assembly. She was elected to the post of investigator of women's work and traveled throughout the United States. Her work was responsible for the passage of the first factory inspection act in Pennsylvania in 1889 which became a model for other states. After retirement she took up the cause of women's suffrage.

S.P.M.

BARTHOLDI, AUGUSTE FREDERICK (1834–1904). French sculptor of the Statue of Liberty who already had a number of monuments and statues to his credit when (in 1865) the French jurist Eduoard Laboulaye, who had written a three-volume history of the United States, proposed a monument for the one hundredth anniversary of the American Revolution (1876) commemorating the alliance of France with the American Colonies during the American Revolution. The statue would be paid for by the French people and the Americans would furnish the site and the pedestal. In 1871 Bartholdi came to the United States to propose the project and find the site. President Grant liked both the sketch Bartholdi had made and his choice of Bedloe Island for the site. On October 28, 1886 one million Americans watched President Cleveland inaugurate the monument: Liberty Enlightening the World. The name was changed to the Statue of Liberty and the island became Liberty Island. In 1965 Ellis Island, the entrance point of millions of immigrants, became part of the Statue of Liberty monument. The second bicentennial of Bartholdi's monument was watched on television by millions of people here and abroad as a symbol of the American dream.

Reference
Leslie Allen, *Liberty: The Statue and the American Dream* (1985).

R.U.P.

BASEL FOREIGN MISSIONS SOCIETY. The occasion of the Basel Mission's work in America was provided by religiously destitute German immigrants who appealed for ministers to serve among them. In conformity with its principle the Basel Mission, having accepted this challenge, aimed at extending the Christian gospel and not at transplanting German traits and mores upon American soil. It differed, therefore, from some German missionary efforts in the New World that were directed toward the preservation of racial ties with the German nation.

Reference
David G. Gelzer, "Mission to America: Being a History of the Work of the Basel Foreign Missions Society in America," Ph.D. dissertation, Yale University, 1952 (DA 28: 3253A).

F.C.

BASQUES. The Basque country is located where the corner of southwestern France and northern Spain touches the Bay of Biscay. The international border dividing the Basque country at the Bidasoa River was established in 1512, giving rise to the modern distinction of the French and Spanish Basque country. Three languages are spoken: Basque, French, and Spanish. This area occupies about 20,600 square kilometers, with some 2.7 million inhabitants. Most of the land area and inhabitants are situated on the Spanish side. A varied ecology encompassing coasts, plains, and Pyreneean mountain terrain have created diverse ways of life which include farming, livestock, fishing, commerce, and industry.

Despite this internal geographical, political, linguistic, and social diversity, the Basques find unity in their perception of themselves as a distinct and even unique people. This appreciation is founded upon the Basque language: a unique, non–Indo-European language, unrelated to Spanish and French; a distinct physical type and serological profile unlike that of their neighbors; and an unknown origin which baffles historians and philologists. All of these factors have produced a distinct Basque culture.

Emigration. The Basques have historically demonstrated a penchant toward migration, perhaps motivated by the inheritance customs of the society. In traditional rural society, farms were inherited by only one son or daughter, usually the oldest. If, then, a family had nine children, one inherited the farm and other eight would marry into another farm or find some other means of livelihood. As a result, many of the younger children were likely to explore the opportunities afforded by emigration. Basques constituted an important part of the Roman legion's defense of the Rhine and of the Hadrian Wall in England. During the Middle Ages, they engaged in widespread commerce in the

Atlantic and Mediterranean, and Basque vessels were routinely fishing in Labrador by the first half of the sixteenth century.

However, the true explosion of Basque emigration came with the discovery of America. Having already developed large ships with which to hunt for whales and engage in trade, Basque men of the sea were well positioned to become a major force in Spain's vastly expanded shipping requirements, as well as the colonization process itself. Basque vessels and crew made a significant contribution to Christopher Columbus's expedition and constituted 80 percent of all Spanish shipping to the New World between 1520 and 1580.

At this time, the rule of the Spanish monarch over the Basque country was indirect. That is, the Basques maintained a number of rights not available to the citizenry of Spain, including universal nobility. In the less imperially conscious Spanish Empire, then, they were able to assume major roles in the hierarchy of the developing American colonies. This factor contributed to the success they enjoyed in the New World.

Furthermore, perhaps as a response to the inheritance customs mentioned above, Basques have traditionally joined the Church in large numbers, oftentimes attaining important positions. Thus, as hand-maidens of Catholic Spain's proselytizing zeal, Basques frequently spearheaded church-dominated colonization efforts.

During the first half of the nineteenth century, Basque immigration in the Americas increased dramatically as thousands of refugees were displaced by war and social upheaval on both sides of the Bidasoa. The French Basque country was rocked by the French Revolution, while the Spanish side was affected during much of the century by the Carlist wars. Most of the Spanish emigrated to Argentina, Chile, Uruguay, and Mexico, where the educated were able to secure positions in the urban centers and where the peasant farmer immigrants headed for the uninhabited fringes as pioneering settlers. The goal of most of these peasant farmer immigrants was to work hard for a few years, save their money, and return to their village to buy a farm or start a small business. Thus they were motivated to sacrifice and to take risks in order to accumulate money quickly. For many this opportunity was afforded by establishing sheep bands on the vast unclaimed pampas of Argentina and Uruguay. Here, one man and his dogs could quickly establish an operation and turn a profit quickly without the need for capital investment and labor.

Immigration to the U.S. Basques were present in the Spanish colonization of the American Southwest and California, although little continuity from that period has carried over into the American era.

Modern Basque immigration began with the California gold rush. As was noted above, during the first half of the nineteenth century there were thousands of Basques trying to make their fortunes in South America. When news of the gold strike reached them, many opted to seek their fortune in California. Traveling by ship from southern South America, they landed in San Francisco and headed for the gold fields. As can be expected, many quickly became disillusioned with mining and, exploring other entrepreneurial opportunities, discovered conditions not unlike those they had left in Argentina. That is, there were large unclaimed expanses of range and an ever-growing demand for food as a result of a population growing exponentially.

Consequently, Basques reconstituted the open range itinerant sheep-raising model developed in Argentina and adapted it to the particular conditions of California. Here, they usually grazed the sheep on the valley floors during the winter lambing season and in the mountains during the summer. The first generation of Basque sheepmen sent back to the Old World for kinsmen to work as herders in their expanding operations. These, in turn, would commonly take their wages in sheep, enabling them to establish their own band in a few years. It was an ever-expanding process which created greater demand for herders and for increased Basque emigration to the United States. As the central valley became overstocked, newcomers were forced to the fringes of civilization. Thus the Basque itinerant herder became ubiquitous throughout the American West by the end of the nineteenth century. Along the way, Basques became a cornerstone of the sheep industry in the United States.

However, the very nature of the sheep industry caused considerable resentment. First, Basques had to compete with established ranchers for the open or public range; this often developed into the classical confrontation of cattlemen versus sheepmen. Later, they also encountered opposition from the growing environmentalist movement which believed that the public range was being damaged by overgrazing from these ever-moving bands of sheep.

The Basque itinerant operators were technically correct in assuming that they had access to the public domain but, as a group, they were hated and virtually without political power. Few were American citizens or spoke the language, and the very nature of their work and short-term aspirations in the United States made it unlikely that they could mount an effective defense to growing political pressures. Over a period of time, fragmented legislation began to create a national forest system which curtailed access to the open range.

The issue of the itinerant sheep operator was definitively resolved in 1934 with the promulgation of the Taylor Grazing Act. This legislation brought public land under the jurisdiction of the Bureau of Land Management. Uncontrolled access to the public range was ended, and with it the operations of many Basque sheepmen. Most sold out and returned to Europe. Others, however, became citizens, bought a ranch, and qualified for their own grazing allotment. Still others moved to town and began small businesses.

Ironically, two decades later, it was the established ranchers themselves who, responding to a labor crisis in the industry, established the Western Range Association for the purpose of recruiting primarily Basque herders from Europe. In this way several hundred Basques came to the United States with visa restrictions which precluded any possibility of attaining permanent residence. These laws were later liberalized but, by the 1970s, it was largely a moot issue, for the economy of the Basque country had greatly improved and few young men were attracted to the spartan lifestyle and low wages of the herder occupation.

Institutions. A number of factors made it difficult for the Basques in the United States to form associations. First, the anti-itinerant sentiment, combined with the low social esteem associated with the sheepherding occupation, was not conducive toward the creation of high-profile public institutions. Second, the nature of the industry meant that Basques were scattered lightly over much of the American West, thus handicapping the development of ethnic associations. Finally, most were sojourners, single males or married men with families in Europe, planning to return home with their savings as soon as possible.

Nonetheless, one widespread ethnic institution was the Basque hotel or boarding house, usually run by a married ex-herder who was somewhat conversant in English. The boarding house provided the herder with a permanent address, lodging when not working, and a place to socialize with his own kind. Furthermore, the owner of the boarding house would frequently help the herder establish bank accounts or arrange to send his savings to Europe, and translate for him when visiting the doctor, shopping, or dealing with the U.S. immigration authorities.

The boarding house served also as a social center for the local Basque-American population and was the site for weddings, baptisms, dances, wakes, and handball competition. The elderly herder who did not wish to return to Europe would often become a permanent boarder.

Over the last three decades, Basques have demonstrated greater willingness to display ethnic pride. This could be attributed, in part, to the fading image of the disliked itinerant herder. Basque-Americans are now engaged in many different occupations and professions, and have developed a group reputation for being dependable, hard-working, and honest citizens. Furthermore, there are now many second-, third-, and fourth-generation Basque-Americans and they too have been caught up in the "roots" phenomenon.

The 1980 census places the number of Basques in the United States at approximately 50,000, with the greatest concentrations in California, Idaho, and Nevada.

Today, there are some twenty Basque clubs in the West and two on the east coast. Several of them have their own buildings, complete with bar and banquet facilities and handball courts. Many clubs have dance groups which perform publicly and each organizes local Basque picnics and dances. These clubs are linked through an overarching organization called the North American Basque Organizations or NABO. NABO coordinates club activities and sponsors an annual music camp, handball competitions, and *mus* card game tournaments.

There are two journals in the United States dedicated to basque topics and, since 1967, the University of Nevada (Reno) has developed a Basque Studies Program with a large collection of Basque-related materials. The University of Nevada Press also publishes a very successful Basque Book Series. In 1982, a consortium of American universities established study-abroad programs located in both the French and the Spanish Basque country.

It can be said, then, that Basques in the United States have emerged from the privacy of the sheep camps and the boarding houses to become part of the American melting pot while successfully maintaining their identity through organized ethnic institutions.

References
Robert Clark, *The Basques: The Franco Years and Beyond* (1980); William Douglass, "The Vanishing Basque Sheepherder," *American West* 17 (1980); William Douglass and Jon Bilbao, *Amerikanuak: Basques in the New World* (1975); William Douglass and Richard Lane, *Basque Sheepherders of the American West: A Photographic Documentary* (1985); Rodney Gallop, *A Book of the Basques* (1930); Robert Laxalt, *Sweet Promised Land* (1957); Robert Laxalt, "Basque Sheepherders: Lonely Sentinels of the American West," *National Geographic* 129 (1966).

C.U.

BECK, VILHELM. *See* Danes.

BELAFONTE, HARRY. *See* West Indian Immigrants.

BELLEVUE HOSPITAL VISITING COMMITTEE. *See* Schuyler, Louisa Lee.

BELLOW, SAUL. *See* Immigrant Novel.

BELTRAMI, GIACOMO CONSTANTINO (1779–1855). Italian traveler, adventurer. A political exile of the Napoleonic Wars, Beltrami arrived in America in 1823. He joined a governmental topographical expedition headed by Major Stephen H. Long (1784–1864) to explore the region west of Lake Superior. His chief work was *A Pilgrimage in*

Europe and America Leading to the Discovery of the Sources of the Mississippi and Blood River, with a Description of the Whole Course of the Former and of the Ohio (1828).

Reference
Andrew F. Rolle, *The Immigrant Upraised: Italian Adventurers and Colonists in an Expanding America* (1968).

F.C.

BENDETSEN, KARL R. *See* Assembly Centers.

BENJAMIN FRANKLIN HIGH SCHOOL (New York City). *See* Covello, Leonard.

BENNETT LAW (1889). In 1889 Wisconsin placed upon its statute books the Bennett Law, an apparently innocuous piece of legislation that provided that all the children of the state be taught the common branches of education in the English language. Over this law there arose, in 1890, a bitter and acrimonious social debate that resulted in a political catastrophe for the long-seated Republican party. Prior to 1890 Wisconsin school law applied mainly to the public institutions only, but the Bennett Law extended state supervision to the parochial schools by requiring them to offer the common branches of English. To the friends of the parochial school, and to the leaders of *Deutschtum* (Germandom), the law appeared to be an entering wedge of state domination over the church school, the church itself, and over German culture and language. To a lesser degree, nationality groups other than the Germans—such as the Scandinavians—entertained similar fears, but the main burden of the battle fell to the Germans, both Catholic and Lutheran. These parties believed their fundamental rights of freedom of conscience and parental control of their children to be violated by an overweening and paternalistic state. The Bennett Law was but one facet of the general school crisis of the 1890s. The cultural-religious-state conflicts that centered on this particular school controversy only reflected some of the numerous collisions that unsettled American society at that time. Few educational problems, as such, were solved by the Wisconsin battle royal, but the congeries of social forces operating upon the school were dramatically displayed for the benefit of the entire nation.

Reference
Robert J. Ulrich, "The Bennett Law of 1889: Education and Politics in Wisconsin," Ph.D. dissertation, University of Wisconsin, 1965 (DA 26:3145).

F.C.

BERKMAN, ALEXANDER. *See* Goldman, Emma.

BERNARDY, AMY A[LLEMAND] (1879–1959). College teacher and writer. A graduate of the University of Florence, Amy Bernardy came to the United States at the end of the nineteenth century as part of the diaspora of professional Italians and taught Italian at Smith College, in Northhampton, Massachussets (1902–9). She socialized with the Boston elite and her fellow Italian professionals in the Circolo Italiano-Americano (founded in 1902) and in the Società Dante Alighieri, where she was a frequent lecturer. She traveled extensively throughout the United States and observed and learned first hand the vicissitudes of the Italian immigrants not only in Boston and New England, but also in New York, Chicago, New Orleans, and the Far West. Upon her return to Italy she devoted her talents to disseminating her knowledge of the Italian experience in the United States by means of lectures, articles, and books. Her two book-length articles on the conditions of Italian women and children in the United States appeared in the *Bollettino dell'Emigrazione* (1909,1911). Two of her books are: *America vissuta* (Life in America, 1911) and *Italia randagia attraverso gli Stati Uniti* (An Italian Wandering Across the United States, 1913).

Reference
Anna Maria Martellone, *Una Little Italy nell'Atene d'America: La communità italiana di Boston dal 1880 al 1920* (1973).

R.U.P.

BETTINA, TEXAS (German immigrant communal settlement). *See* Von Herff, Ferdinand.

BETTS, LILLIAN W[ILLIAMS] (d. 1938). Social reformer; sympathetic observer of immigrant life in New York City. See her "The School Child Out of School Hours," *Outlook* 75 (Sept. 1903): 209–216; *The Leaven in a Great City* (1903); and "Italians in New York," *Settlement Studies* 1, no. 3 (1908).

F.C.

BIELARUS. *See* Byelorussians.

BIEN. *See* Danes.

BIKUBEN. *See* Danes.

BILINGUAL EDUCATION. In its *bicultural* orientations, bilingual education is directly related to the black civil rights movement and the new affirmations of identity and proclamations of ethnic pride by Mexican-Americans, Puerto Ricans, Cubans, and by the progeny of earlier European immigrants—Italians, Greeks, Jews, Poles, Slavs, and others. In a prescient foreword to Kloss' *The American Bilingual Tradition,* Mackey observes:

> The popular image of the United States as a nation united by one language and one culture has always been illusory. It was an ideal engendered by the now outmoded values of nineteenth-century nationalism. Although the American melting pot has indeed fused millions of second- and third-generation immigrant families into unilingual English-speaking Americans, unmelted or partially melted millions have also survived whose isolation or regional dominance has permitted them to maintain their ethnic identity in their new and spacious land.

Some 5 million youngsters in the United States come from homes in which the generally spoken language is other than English. Estimates based on samplings in various states suggest that there are an estimated 3.6 million pupils in the country who need bilingual education to enable them to manage the regular school curriculum. Bilingual education is best defined as academic instruction in two languages, i.e., the child's native language and English. Particular approaches used vary considerably, but most bilingual practice in the United States is *transitional.* Use of the child's native language as a medium of instruction will enable the student to learn cognitive skills and prevent academic retardation. English taught as a second language will, in time, move the student to an English-language proficiency and end the need for instruction in the native language. Continuing attention to the child's heritage and culture (i.e., *bicultural* education) will build self-esteem, stimulating both comprehension and motivation.

Bilingual education is a promising pedagogical tool, but it is not without controversy. The passionate debate that accompanies the controversy derives from a complex set of factors. The implementation of bilingual programs is perceived as poor, and this charge is not easily rebutted. There have been few evaluation studies of bilingual programs, and many programs were hastily undertaken without regard to the adequacy of staff training, the diagnosis of children's language needs, and appropriate curricular materials. Popular support for bilingual education has been lacking. In the past, public education has served as the chief vehicle for the assimilation of immigrant children into the mainstream of American society; English had always been the sole language of instruction in the schools. The use of native languages in bilingual education programs in the schools reversed what was perceived as a national policy. To this there was (and continues to be) serious resentment by the progeny of earlier immigrants, who see the new policy of bilingual education as the first step toward the official recognition of multilingualism extending from the schools across all public institutions of American society.

The most dynamic element in the controversy surrounding bilingual education, however, is the popular perception that it is a stratagem for ethnic employment related to the social, political, and economic aspirations of Hispanic minorities. Pifer of the Carnegie Corporation of New York has, in his *Bilingual Education and the Hispanic Challenge,* addressed this issue directly:

> The programs have been strongly promoted by Hispanic organizations, and the educational, political, and administrative leadership for bilingual education has been mainly Hispanic. Indeed, bilingual education, as a vehicle for heightening respect and recognition of native languages and culture, for fighting discrimination against non–English-speaking groups, and for obtaining jobs and political leverage, has become the preeminent civil rights issue within Hispanic communities. This development, coupled with the fact that Hispanics, through natural increase and immigration, are growing rapidly in numbers, has made the issue more visible and politicized than it might otherwise have been. Bilingual education is no longer regarded strictly as an educational measure but also as a strategy for realizing the social, political, and economic aspirations of Hispanic peoples.

Given this background, bilingual education cannot be considered without reference to larger frames in which it has evolved, and it remains vulnerable to political criticism, with the continuing need to justify itself educationally. In *Language, Ethnicity and the Schools,* Epstein, critical of bilingual education, proposes a set of policy alternatives for bilingual-bicultural education. However, Epstein's strictures should be evaluated alongside the views expressed by Gaarder in his *Bilingual Schooling and the Survival of Spanish in the United States;* in the dimensional overviews afforded in *Case Studies in Bilingual Education,* edited by Spolsky and Cooper, and in their companion volume, *Frontiers of Bilingual Education;* and in Cordasco, *Bilingualism and the Bilingual Child: Challenges and Problems.*

Actually, bilingual education is not new in the United States and, in a nation as diverse in origins as ours, it should not be surprising. English has not always been the only language used in American schools. School laws in the 1800s in Ohio (1839), Wisconsin (1846), Colorado (1867), Oregon (1872), Maryland (1874), and Minnesota (1877) dealt directly with the language issue in the curriculum either as a medium of instruction or as a subject to be taught.

German immigrants (whose progeny make up the largest ethnic group in America) established German-English bilingual schools in Cincinnati, Indianapolis, Hoboken, Cleveland, and many other cities. These were public schools, and German was not only taught as a subject, it was used as a medium of instruction. Between 1880 and 1917, these schools flourished; they were eagerly supported by a powerful and socially stratified German community. Only the political tensions of World War I ended their history. The rationale given by German immigrants to support the use of the German languages in the schools of the nineteenth century is essentially that given to justify the existence of modern "maintenance" programs in bilingual education. The German immigrants argued that German was important as an international language, its use in the schools made sense for children from German-speaking families, and it was also enriching for children from English-speaking families. Covello (*q.v.*) advanced much the same views in recommending the use of Italian for Italian-speaking children in the New York City schools during the period of heavy Italian immigration (c. 1880–1920), and he outlined a program in his massive *The Social Background of the Italo-American School Child.* The German experience in American schools is extensively documented in Viereck's (*q.v.*) *German Instruction in American Schools,* which includes a wealth of material on the German bilingual public school systems in Cincinnati, Baltimore, Indianapolis, Cleveland, and other American cities. Viereck's report was originally published in *The Annual Report (1900–1901) of the United States Commissioner of Education;* it also appeared in a German edition, *Zwei Jahrhunderte der Unterricht in den Vereinigten Staaten.* It has been reprinted in *Bilingual-Bicultural Education in the United States.*

In Louisiana, French was used as the medium of instruction, and in New Mexico, Spanish was used. These were limited efforts and largely early- and mid-nineteenth-century phenomena, but they confirm a bilingual tradition in America. In New York City, at different times and with differing commitments, the public schools taught children in Chinese, Italian, Greek, Yiddish, and French. In a real sense, present-day efforts in bilingual education are a rediscovery of a respected and traditional American educational practice.

Legislation: State and Federal Roles. The modern revival of public bilingual education in the United States did not originate in the area of foreign-language teaching. It evolved within the context of minority rights that in various forms defined the critical social issues of the 1960s. As part of the social awareness inherent in President Johnson's war on poverty, it was felt that ethnic poverty, exacerbated by unilingual teaching in English, seriously impaired the educational opportunities of non–English-speaking children. Since education was a basic right, it was argued that the schools had an obligation to use the native languages of non–English-speaking children as the medium of instruction.

It was in the context of evolving equity-oriented legislation that the Bilingual Education Act of 1968 was passed by the Congress as Title VII of the amended Elementary and Secondary Education Act which had been enacted in 1965. The political support for the Bilingual Education Act came out of the large Mexican-American community of the Southwest, and its sponsor was Senator Ralph Yarborough of Texas, who was eventually joined by other supporters in Congress.

The aims of Title VII were modest. The act provided funds for the planning and implementation of programs "designed to meet the special needs of children of limited English-speaking ability in schools having a high concentration of such children from families . . . with incomes below $3,000 per year." Geffert's *The Current Status of U.S. Bilingual Education Legislation* provides a complete overview of federal, state, and other "American" legislation in effect as of April 15, 1975, and updates Kloss's *Laws and Legal Documents Relating to Problems of Bilingual Education in the United States,* which was published in 1971. Developments since Geffert's 1975 work can be traced in Thernstrom's "Language: Issues and Legislation" in the *Harvard Encyclopedia of American Ethnic Groups.*

The Bilingual Education Act was renewed in 1974 and again in 1978 and in 1983, with continuing further change across the 1980s. Federal support has ranged from $7.5 million in 1969, supporting 76 projects reaching about 26,000 children to $107 million, supporting some 575 projects, and reaching some 315,000 children.

Bilingual education has been strengthened by the decision in *Lau* v. *Nichols* (*q.v.*), in which the U.S. Supreme Court ruled that children with a limited English-speaking ability were entitled to some sort of remedial instruction. The Court held that "under these state-imposed standards there is no equality of treatment merely by providing students with the same facilities, textbooks, teachers, and curriculum; for students who do not understand English are effectively foreclosed from any meaningful education." *Lau* v. *Nichols* was a class action suit filed on behalf of some 1,800 non–English-speaking Chinese students against the San Francisco Unified School District. The intricacies of the *Lau* decision and its effect on the 1974 bilingual amendments were studied by Schneider in *Revolution, Reaction or Reform: The 1974 Bilingual Education Act.*

In 1971, Massachusetts was the first state to legislate the establishment of transitional bilingual programs; until that time no state had mandatory bilingual education legislation. By 1978, ten states had enacted similar bilingual education statutes, but not without considerable

struggle and with continuing controversy. A vivid and painstaking account of the struggle in New York City by the Puerto Rican community
on behalf of its children is chronicled in Santiago's *A Community's
Struggle for Equal Educational Opportunity: Aspira v. Board of Education.*

English as a Second Language. English as a Second Language
(ESL or more properly TESOL, i.e., "Teaching English to Speakers of
Other Languages") is not, technically, bilingual education. In the
United States, ESL has become an ancillary component of *transitional*
bilingual programs. ESL is related to Americanization and immigrant
naturalization programs in which English acquisition remained an integral part. As such, ESL is part of a tradition which, unfortunately, had
as some of its major objectives the eradication of cultural differences,
language suppression, and an ethnocentricism essentially inimical to
immigrant aspirations. The structural/functional (S/F) approach is the
position (if not explicit, almost always tacitly assumed) of the ESL
advocates in the ESL versus bilingual education controversy. Clearly, it
is the position of the United States government. Structural/functional
theorists focus on the homeostatic or balancing mechanisms by which
societies maintain a "uniform state." In such a paradigm, ESL is an
integral component of bilingual education programs.

Evaluation, Tests, and Measurements. In a very real sense, evaluation techniques have been enhanced by the sharpened perspectives of
sociolinguistics, which probes the interrelationships between language
and social behavior and in which a recurring theme is the importance of
the social, linguistic, and psychological context to the effective understanding of speech and writing.

In 1976 the United States General Accounting Office (GAO) issued its *Bilingual Education: An Unmet Need,* a report to Congress. The
study maintained that the United States Office of Education (USOE)
had made little progress in identifying effective means of providing
bilingual education instruction, in training bilingual education teachers,
and in developing suitable teaching materials. A damaging evaluation,
commissioned by the USOE, extending over four years and examining
the progress of 11,500 Hispanic students, was published in 1978. The
evaluation was done by the American Institutes of Research (AIR) and
submitted under the title *Evaluation of the Impact of ESEA Title VII
Spanish/English Bilingual Education Program: An Overview of Study
and Findings.* It concluded that most of the children did not need to
learn English; those who were being taught it were in fact not acquiring
it; with few exceptions the programs aimed at linguistic and cultural
maintenance; and to the degree that children were already alienated
from school, they remained so. The Center for Applied Linguistics
published a *Response to the AIR Study,* but the AIR evaluation forced

the reorientation of bilingual programs, as reflected in the renewed but amended Bilingual Education Act of 1978. The 1978 amended act placed a ceiling of 40 percent on the number of English-speaking children who could be included in the programs; placed a new stress on parental involvement; instructed local schools to use personnel proficient in both the language of instruction and English; and described eligible participants as children with limited English proficiency (as opposed to limited English-speaking ability), thus expanding the meaning of linguistic deficiency to include reading and writing. These 1978 modifications have not succeeded in quieting the controversy that continues to surround bilingual education.

The Bilingual Education Act and its future are uncertain. However, it would be a mistake, whatever the future of the act, to believe that bilingual education will disappear. A variety of other federal and state legislative acts fund bilingual education. Ten states have made bilingual education mandatory, and sixteen others have enacted legislation that generally authorizes the development of bilingual programs. Bilingual components are parts of important and influential federal acts, among which are the Emergency School Aid Act, the Vocational Education Act, the Adult Education Act, and the Higher Education Act. The *Lau* remedies entangle judicial decisions and regulatory guidelines which make even more complex any efforts to end, or even curtail, bilingual education programs. And there is little doubt that academicians are unaware of the perilous state in which American bilingualism finds itself, as is attested in the recent judicious overview of all aspects of bilingual practice in Alatis, *Current Issues in Bilingual Education.*

At this juncture, the most salutary view may well have been voiced by Pifer:

> What is needed now, is a determined effort by all concerned to improve bilingual education programs in the schools through more sympathetic administration and community support, more and better trained teachers, and a sustained, sophisticated, and well-financed research effort to find out where these programs are succeeding and where they are failing and why.

References

American Institutes of Research, *Evaluation of the Impact of ESEA Title VII Spanish/English Bilingual Education Program: An Overview of Study and Findings* (1978); Francesco Cordasco, "Bilingual Education: Overview and Inventory," *Education Forum* (Spring 1983): 321–334; Francesco Cordasco, *Bilingual Schooling in the United States: A Sourcebook for Educational Personnel* (1976); Francesco Cordasco, ed., *Bilingualism and the Bilingual Child: Challenges and Problems* (1978); Leonard Covello, *The Social Background of the Italo-American School Child: A Study of the Southern Italian Mores and Their Effect on the School Situation in Italy and America,* ed. Francesco Cordasco (1972); A. Bruce Gaarder, *Bilingual Schooling and the Survival of Spanish in the United*

States (1977); Hannah N. Geffert et al., *The Current Status of U.S. Bilingual Education Legislation* (1975); Kenji Hakuta, *Mirror of Language: The Debate on Bilingualism* (1986); Heinz Kloss, *The American Bilingual Tradition* (1977); Heinz Kloss, *Laws and Legal Documents Relating to Problems of Bilingual Education in the United States* (1971); Alan Pifer, *Bilingual Education and the Hispanic Challenge* (1980); Isaura S. Santiago, *A Community's Struggle for Equal Educational Opportunity: Aspira vs. Board of Education* (1978); Susan G. Schneider, *Revolution, Reaction or Reform: The 1974 Bilingual Education Act* (1976); Bernard Spolsky and Robert L. Cooper, eds., *Case Studies in Bilingual Education* (1978); Abigail M. Thernstrom, "Language: Issues and Legislation," in *Harvard Encyclopedia of American Ethnic Groups,* ed. Stephen Thernstrom (1980); Louis Viereck, *German Instruction in American Schools* (1978); U.S. General Accounting Office, *Bilingual Education: An Unmet Need* (1976).

F.C.

BILINGUAL/BICULTURAL EDUCATION: A PRIVILEGE OR A RIGHT? A REPORT (1974.) This document is the result of a two-year investigation by the Illinois Advisory Committee to the U.S. Commission on Civil Rights on the educational experiences of Hispanics in Illinois. The report is an extraordinarily detailed text on the major failings in Illinois to meet the educational needs of the non–English-speaking child. The Illinois Advisory Committee prepared the report as a set of recommendations to implement Illinois Public Act 78-727 which required that bilingual education be offered to language minority students. The committee's recommendations are valuable for the articulation of a national policy in bilingual-bicultural education, and are largely congruent with the recommendations for bilingual-bicultural education made by the parent commission in its study of Mexican-American educational needs in the five southwestern states of Arizona, California, Colorado, New Mexico, and Texas.

F.C.

BINET, ALFRED (1857–1911). *See* Goddard, Henry H.

BINTEL BRIEF. A letters column ("Bundle of Letters") in the [New York] *Jewish Daily Forward* (*q.v.*) in which readers (many of them women) described their problems and sought advice from the editor. The "Bintel Brief" became an important institution of immigrant life, and its range of themes was very wide. As a genre, it has survived to the present.

Reference
Issac Metzker. *A Bintel Brief: Sixty Years of Letters from the Lower East Side to the Jewish Daily Forward* (1971).

F.C.

BIRKBECK, MORRIS. *See* English.

BISHOP HILL (Illinois). A Swedish religious utopian and communal colony in Henry County, Illinois, founded in 1846 and dissolved in 1861.

During the period 1846–1854 between 1,200 and 1,500 Swedes emigrated mainly from the provinces of Hälsingland, Västmanland, and Uppland in north-central Sweden and formed the colony of Bishop Hill on the prairies in Henry County, Illinois. The reasons behind the emigration were primarily religious. In the 1840s the lay preacher and self-appointed "prophet" Erik Jansson emerged as the charismatic head of a religious revival movement in Sweden, directed against the Lutheran state church. A series of confrontations with the secular and ecclesiastical authorities forced Jansson and his followers to emigrate to the United States, beginning in 1846. That year, Jansson founded the utopian colony Bishop Hill in Illinois. It was based on his theological beliefs, which were perfectionist in character and postulated that his followers were a chosen people and thus lived a sin-free life. Jansson was the strong man in the colony and served as its spiritual as well as secular leader.

Life in the colony was communal and strongly shaped by Jansson's religious ideas with religious services sometimes held three times a day. The colony's land and property were collectively owned, labor was communal, and men and women lived in separate buildings. Like many other American utopian colonies, Bishop Hill was economically successful, and by 1858 a total of 14,000 acres of land were under cultivation. In addition, a number of profitable industries were started, such as textiles, blacksmithing, wagon making, furniture, lumber, and milling. Several impressive buildings were also erected, among them a colony church that was completed only three years after the first colonists' arrival, and a big brick building with ninety-six rooms and a large dining room. "Big Brick" was at the time of its completion the largest brick structure west of Chicago.

The colony was officially dissolved in 1861. This was due to the economic crises of the late 1850s, which hit the colony hard, but also to the declining faith in the new leadership of the colony which had taken over when Erik Jansson was assassinated in 1851 by a disgruntled colonist. The communally owned property was divided among the remaining settlers in Bishop Hill and the Janssonist religious beliefs abandoned.

Today Bishop Hill counts some two hundred inhabitants, the great majority of whom are fourth- or fifth-generation descendants of the original settlers. Since the mid-1960s there has been a renewed interest in the history of Bishop Hill. Annual Swedish-American festivals are held and an historic preservation society has with financial assistance from both Sweden and the United States restored many of the original buildings to their original state. In 1984, Bishop Hill was designated a National Historic Landmark by the Department of the Interior.

References
Paul Elmen, *Wheat Flour Messiah: Eric Jansson of Bishop Hill* (1976); Olov Isaksson and Sören Hallgren, *Bishop Hill: A Utopia on the Prairie* (1969); Michael Mikkelsen, *The Bishop Hill Colony: A Religious Communistic Settlement in Henry County, Illinois* (1892; rpt. 1972).

D.B.

"BLACK BLUES." *See* Jazz.

BLACK HAND *(La Mano Nera).* As Italian immigration rose spectacularly at the turn of the century, extortion—usually by threatening letter—became a common practice in the Italian colonies of New York and other American cities. Italian ex-convicts followed their honest compatriots to the United States, resuming their customary practices. These included counterfeiting, kidnapping, and extortion. They often found willing accomplices among the youth of the poor and crowded Italian slum settlements. Extortion letters commonly were signed with the names of Old World criminal societies, notably the Mafia of Sicily and the Camorra of Naples. The usual threat for noncompliance with a demand for money was dynamiting or shooting. Such threats often were implemented.

Beginning in 1903 and following a case in Brooklyn in which the threatening letters were signed "La Mano Nera," the term Black Hand—or Mano Nera—generally supplanted the others. The term, and the symbol of a black hand as a threat, seem to have originated in Spain, where an alleged anarchist society using them was broken up in 1882. Italian extortionists had taken over the society. In the Brooklyn case, a reporter gave the Black Hand dramatic coverage in the *New York Herald,* and other journals followed suit. Italian newspapers adopted it, preferring it to the old labels, especially "Mafia," which for years had been applied to Italian crime and sometimes to Italians generally. The belief in an actual and powerful Black Hand society of criminals, fostered by both the press and the criminals themselves, came to have wide currency among both Italians and native Americans. The Black Hand label soon was applied to almost any crime of violence in Italian neighborhoods in New York, Chicago, and other cities. Its use spread rapidly to the mining towns of Pennsylvania and other states, to labor camps in upstate New York, and to most communities where Italians were found in numbers. American police, often Irish, found Italian crime hard to combat. Witnesses could not be found, failed to show up in court, or declined to testify effectively for the prosecution. The American police and press generally attributed this to the code of *omertà,* or refusal to cooperate with law enforcement agencies, a supposedly universal Italian tradition. Actually, such reticence among most Italians was little more than sheer terror.

Although American police were generally ineffective in combating such crime, often deliberately ignoring it, Italian detectives—notably Joseph Petrosino (*q.v.*) of the New York City force—were more successful. In 1909 Petrosino was sent to Italy and Sicily to arrange cooperation with the Italian police and other agencies in curbing the Black Hand. Italian law forbade the issuance of passports to ex-convicts, and American law forbade their admittance to the United States; but numbers of them were coming to America by one means or another. Petrosino was assassinated in Palermo; and Italian crime in New York and other American cities, which had been curbed to some extent, resumed an upward curve and soon reached new heights. The growing belief that Italians, particularly those of southern Italy, were a criminal race, was strengthened. This belief eventually was translated into law in the form of the discriminatory quota immigration laws.

The Secret Service, with its basic mission of combating counterfeiting, was for years the only federal agency that took part in fighting Italian crime. It had considerable success over the years, most notably in breaking up the Lupo-Morello gang of New York in 1910. This gang had operated for a long time and had contacts extending from Palermo—where it kept in touch with Mafia chiefs—to New Orleans and Chicago. It engaged extensively in extortion, kidnapping, murder, and other crimes as well as in counterfeiting. At about the same time, the postal authorities began bringing Black Hand cases before the federal courts on charges of mail fraud. In Chicago, the post office seems to have been for years the only agency that curbed the Black Hand to any extent.

In both New York and Chicago, municipal corruption extending deeply into their own forces greatly hampered the efforts of police administrators in all crime control. In both cities the Italian communities attempted to organize to protect themselves against the Black Hand, but these efforts were largely ineffectual. In New York the reform administration of Mayor John Purroy Mitchel (1914–17), with Arthur Woods as police commissioner, set out to destroy the Black Hand and criminal gangs in general. These gangs—largely Irish, Jewish, Italian, and often ethnically mixed—had flourished under previous administrations. They often actually controlled municipal elections through dirty work at the polls, under the guidance and protection of corrupt politicians. The efforts of the Mitchel administration, involving the use of authoritarian methods, were for a time quite successful but were aborted largely with the coming of Prohibition. Black Handers and gangsters of varied ethnic origin turned eagerly to bootlegging, with its often spectacular profits. The Black Hand, as a symbol, as a technique, and as a supposed organization, soon disappeared. Chicago became most notorious in the gangland wars that resulted from competition for control of the illicit alcohol supply, but New York suffered almost equally. Corruption, under the gangster profits from bootlegging, grew worse than ever. Law enforcement throughout the country was affected disastrously. Italians were prominent in bootlegging and gang warfare; but the term "Black Hand," along with "Mafia" and "Camorra," dropped almost entirely out of currency. Gangsters of all ethnic origins were designated as just that or as "hoodlums" or "mobsters," though crime movies tended to depict them as Italians.

Reference
Thomas Monroe Pitkin and Francesco Cordasco, *The Black Hand* (1977).

T.M.P.

BLACK MUSLIMS. *See* Afro-Americans.

BLACK PANTHERS. *See* West Indian Immigrants; Afro-Americans.

BLACK STAR STEAMSHIP LINE. *See* United Negro Improvement Association.

BLEGEN, THEODORE C. (1891–1969). Norwegian-American historian, educator, and administrator. Born in Minneapolis of Norwegian parents, Blegen became the primary American historian of Norwegian immigration in the twentieth century. In his long career he taught at Hamline College and the University of Minnesota, and served as superintendent of the Minnesota Historical Society (1931–39) and dean of graduate studies at the University of Minnesota (1940–1960). As first editor of the Norwegian-American Historical Association (*q.v.*), 1925–1960, Blegen was responsible for preparing forty-one volumes on various aspects of Norwegian migration and immigrant life. Throughout his career, he wrote, edited, or translated several works on Norwegian immigration and Minnesota history. Major works include: *Norwegian Migration to America, 1825–1860* (1931); *Norwegian Migration to America: The American Transition* (1940); *Norwegian Emigrant Songs and Ballads* (with Martin B. Ruud, 1939); *Land of Their Choice: The Immigrants Write Home* (1955).

Reference
John T. Flanagan, *Theodore C. Blegen: A Memoir* (1977).

J.J.

BLUMER, ABRAHAM. *See* Swiss.

B'NAI B'RITH. The first Jewish fraternal society founded in 1843 in New York City as the Independent Order of B'nai B'rith by twelve German Jewish immigrants, it is the oldest continuously existing Jewish organization in the United States. The name, in German (*Bundes Bruder*) and Hebrew (*B'nai B'rith*) refers to the "sons of the covenant," or Jews. Originally established as a mutual aid fraternal group, B'nai B'rith rapidly spread throughout the United States, attracting members by its insurance features, sociability, charitable activities, and educational programs. In the 1880s the first international lodges were founded in Germany and Austria-Hungary and later throughout Europe and in Palestine. As the immigrant members became financially secure, B'nai B'rith poured more energy into supporting orphan asylums, old age homes, and libraries. The mass immigration of eastern European Jews to the United States at the turn of the century prompted B'nai B'rith involvement in political and reform activities. In 1903 the order helped establish the Industrial Removal Organization to assist Jewish immigrants to leave New York City and settle in the West and South. The Leo Frank case in Atlanta and increasing prejudice and discrimination against Jews spurred the creation in 1913 of the Anti-Defamation League of B'nai B'rith to fight anti-Semitic stereotypes on the stage and screen and in the press. The ADL subsequently became the most important agency of B'nai B'rith and increasingly assumed a broader mandate to fight all forms of racial and religious prejudice in the United States. During the interwar decades, as the membership came to be largely native born, B'nai B'rith established two influential programs for youth: Hillel, a religious and educational organization for Jews on college campuses (1923) and AZA, a fraternity for teenage Jewish boys (1924). AZA later became the basis for the B'nai B'rith Youth Organization (1942), which included girls. During World War II B'nai B'rith with its 100,000 members provided crucial leadership to unite American Jewish organizations in their response to the Holocaust. After the war, B'nai B'rith maintained its leadership position through both the organization and ADL. It supported Israel in the American political arena, publicized the plight of Soviet Jews, participated in Jewish-Christian dialogues, and developed new programs in adult Jewish education to complement its youth activities and an international council to coordinate its worldwide branches. With over 200,000 members, largely middle class and concentrated in small cities, B'nai B'rith is one of the largest mass membership organizations in the American Jewish community and bears scant resemblance today to its origins as an immigrant fraternal order.

References
Edward E. Grusd, *B'nai B'rith: The Story of a Covenant* (1966); Deborah Dash Moore, *B'nai B'rith and the Challenge of Ethnic Leadership* (1981).

D.D.M.

BOARD OF SPECIAL ENQUIRY. *See* Ellis Island.

BOHEMIANS. *See* Czechs.

BOK, EDWARD. *See* Immigrant Autobiographies.

BOLLETTINO DELL'EMIGRAZIONE. *See* The Italian Commissariat of Emigration.

BØNDER (peasant landowners). *See* Norwegians.

BOODY, BERTHA M. (1877–1951). Psychologist; author of *A Psychological Study of Immigrant Children at Ellis Island* (1926), a psychological survey of immigrant children testing the charge of innate inferiority of recent nationalities. The author, a professional psychologist, stationed herself at Ellis Island in the years of heaviest migration, 1922 and 1923, to examine incoming children. The book includes a review of procedures at Ellis Island, literature on immigrant testing, and application of conclusions to the Immigration Law of 1924; it concludes that

> the smaller number of immigrants arriving, the more careful selection at the source, the lower quotas for races which have come to this country in the last few years, in numbers impossible of assimilation, the opportunity for more intensive physical and mental examination on arrival, and for greater leisure in getting the facts necessary to determine the fitness of the individual, all give promise of the establishment of improved conditions throughout the country.

F.C.

BOSTON PILOT. Immigrant Irish newspaper. The *Pilot,* an integral part of Irish-American life in nineteenth-century America, adds a significant dimension to the knowledge of the immigrant's world. Irish opposition to abolitionism and support of the Union in the Civil War becomes more intelligible when placed in context. The *Pilot* provides the historian with a rich source of material on the Irish reaction to nativism, politics, reform, the Negro, and attitudes toward other immigrant ethnic groups. Always interested in the working class, the paper became a militant champion of labor's demands during the last quarter of the nineteenth century.

Reference
Francis R. Walsh, "The Boston *Pilot:* A Newspaper for the Irish Immigrant," Ph.D. dissertation, Boston University, 1968 (DA 29:2201-A).

F.C.

BOTTO HOUSE NATIONAL LANDMARK. *See* American Labor Museum.

BOUQUET, HENRI. *See* Swiss.

BOURNE, RANDOLPH S[ILLIMAN] (1886–1918). Essayist, social reformer. Bourne wrote a number of books on progressive education that were sympathetic to the educational needs of immigrant children, e.g., *The Gary Schools* (1916) and *Education and Living* (1917), both of which reflect the influence of John Dewey. Bourne supported the unit school (a single building housing all grades from kindergarten through high school) concept advanced by William A. Wirt (*q.v.*), which Bourne saw as the ideal realization of John Dewey's philosophy of democratic education. A controversy surrounded the implementation of the Gary concept in New York City between 1914 and 1918. See Murray and Adeline Levine, "The Gary Schools: A Socio-Historical Analysis of the Process of Change," *California Elementary Administrator* (Spring 1970), which serves as an introduction to an annotated edition of Bourne's *The Gary Schools* (1970).

References
J. A. Moreau, *Randolph Silliman Bourne* (1966); and Bourne's *History of A Literary Radical,* ed. Van Wyck Brooks (1920).

F.C.

BOZNIA. *See* Croatians.

BRACE, CHARLES LORING (1826–1890). Social reformer. A founder of the [New York City] Children's Aid Society (*q.v.*), he remained an active officer of the society for some forty years. Brace studied for the ministry, and in the late 1840s he worked as a missionary among the "squalid poor" of New York City, largely immigrant Irish. He described these as "classes with inherited pauperism and crime" and recorded his efforts with them in his major work: *The Dangerous Classes of New York and Twenty Years Among Them* (3d ed., 1880).

Consistent with the current spirit of individualism, Brace disliked the idea of institutional care for children. "The best of all Asylums for the outcast child," he asserted, "is the *farmer's home.*" One of the major purposes of the Children's Aid Society, which he organized in 1853, was to procure foster homes in rural districts for New York's vagrant boys and girls. Promoting emigration, however, was not the sole aim of the society, but rather the final step in what Brace called the program of "moral disinfection." The first step was the assignment of a visitor or paid agent to a given neighborhood. It was his duty to learn all he could about the area, and to make himself acquainted with the children and their problems. The next move was to conduct informal religious exercises for boys of the neighborhood. In time, if circumstances warranted and resources were available, the society established a free reading room, an industrial school (for children who were "too poor, too ragged, and undisciplined for the public schools"), and lodging houses for newsboys and other homeless working children. Eventually, through vacation and convalescent homes, and a sick children's mission employing twelve doctors and four nurses to visit sick children in their homes, the original program was significantly broadened.

References
Emma Brace, *The Life of Charles Loring Brace* (1894); Robert H. Bremner, *From the Depths* (1956); Francesco Cordasco, "Charles Loring Brace and the Dangerous Classes: Historical Analogues of the Urban Black Poor," *Journal of Human Relations* 20 (3d quarter, 1972): 379–386.

D.N.A.

BRACERO PROGRAM. Foreign labor programs are not new to the United States. There have been several such programs in the past, and there are several ongoing at the present. Thus, if experience is a form of education, lessons can be learned from looking at both the past and the present before any evaluation is offered concerning the merits and demerits of similar undertakings for the future.

The First Bracero Program. It is ironic that, only months after the United States enacted the most restrictive immigration legislation in history—the Immigration Act of 1917—the first foreign labor program was initiated. In response to strong pressure from the large agricultural employers of the Southwest, Congress included in this very restrictive legislation a provision that would allow entry of "temporary" workers who were "otherwise inadmissible." The statute allowed the secretary of labor to exempt such persons (Mexicans in this instance) from the head tax required of each immigrant and from the ban on any immigrants over age sixteen who could not read. In May 1917, such an order was issued for the creation of a "temporary" farm worker program. Later it was expanded to allow some Mexican workers to be employed in nonfarm work. When the program was announced, so were a number of governing rules and regulations. Ostensibly, these rules were designed to protect both citizen workers and Mexican workers, as well as to ensure that the Mexicans returned to Mexico after their work was completed. But, as has been the historic pattern, "these elaborate rules were unenforced."

The "temporary" worker program was enacted during the period of World War I. It was partly justified as being in the national defense. This program, which Kiser and Kiser refer to as "the first bracero program," was extended until 1922, well after the war had ended in 1918. It was terminated because its rationale as a national defense policy could no longer be maintained; because organized labor contended that the program undermined the economic welfare of citizen workers; and because many people believed that there were no labor shortages but only greedy employers who wished to secure economic gains from being able to secure cheap and compliant workers. During its life span, 76,862 Mexican workers were admitted to the United States, of which only 34,922 returned to Mexico.

The Second Bracero Program. With the advent of World War II, the military requirements of the United States and its related manufacturing needs led to assertions that another labor shortage existed in the agricultural sector. The growers of the Southwest had foreseen these developments before the Pearl Harbor attack in 1941. They made two fateful decisions: first, the pool of cheap labor in Mexico was to be tapped to fill the labor deficit; second, the federal government was again to be the vehicle of deliverance.

The initial requests of U.S. growers for the establishment of a contract labor program were denied by the federal government in 1941. By mid-1942, however, the U.S. government had come to favor the program, but the government of Mexico balked at the prospect of a formal intergovernment agreement. The unregulated hiring of Mexican citizens by foreign nations is prohibited by Article 123 of the Mexican Constitution of 1917. Moreover, in the 1940s the Mexican economy was flourishing; Mexican workers justifiably feared that they would be drafted; there were bitter memories of the "repatriation drive" of the 1930s; and there was knowledge of the discriminatory treatment accorded people of Mexican ancestry throughout the Southwest at the time.

Negotiations between the two governments, however, resulted in a formal agreement in August 1942. The Mexican Labor Program, better known as the bracero program, was launched. Mexican workers were to be afforded numerous protections with respect to housing, transportation, food, medical needs, and wage rates. Initiated through appropriations for Public Law 45, the program was extended by subsequent enactment until 1947. Braceros were limited exclusively to agricultural work; any bracero who was found holding a job in any other industry was subject to immediate deportation. When the agreement ended on December 31, 1947, the program was continued informally and without regulation until 1951. In that year, under the guise of another war-related labor shortage, the bracero program was revived by Public Law 78. This program continued to function until it was unilaterally terminated by the United States on December 31, 1964.

The bracero program demonstrated precisely how border policies can adversely affect citizen workers in the United States—especially, in this case, the Chicanos who composed the bulk of the southwestern agricultural labor force. Agricultural employment in the Southwest was removed from competition with the nonagricultural sector. At the program's peak, almost half a million braceros were working in the agricultural labor market of the Southwest. The availability of Mexican workers significantly depressed existing wage levels in some regions, modulated wage increases that would have occurred in their absence in all other regions, and sharply compressed the duration of the employment many citizen farm workers could find. Citizen farm workers simply could not compete with braceros. The fact that braceros were captive workers who were totally subject to the unilateral demands of employers made them especially appealing to many employers. The bracero program was a significant factor in the rapid exodus of rural Chicanos between 1950 and 1970 to urban labor markets, where they were poorly prepared to find employment and housing.

A lasting effect of the second bracero program was its exposure of hundreds of thousands of penniless Mexican workers to the wide array of economic opportunities, as well as the higher wages and benefits, that were available in the United States economy. It is not surprising that both paralleling the bracero years and immediately following the program's termination in 1964 there has been an accelerated growth in the number of illegal immigrants. Many thousands of these illegal aliens were former braceros, who had been attracted to the Mexican border towns from the rural interior of central and northern Mexico by the existence of the contact labor program. To this degree, there is an element of truth to the proposition that the United States itself has created the illegal alien problem. By the same token, however, it is grossly simplistic to conclude that the problem would not eventually have surfaced in the absence of the bracero program. The vast economic differences between the two national economies are simply too great.

References
Vernon M. Briggs, Jr., "Foreign Labor Programs as an Alternative to Illegal Immigration: A Dissenting View," in Peter G. Brown and Henry Shue, eds., *The Border That Joins: Mexican Migrants and U.S. Responsibility* (1983), pp. 223–245 (from which the

entry is drawn with permission); Richard B. Craig, *The Bracero Program* (1971); Maria Herrera-Sobel, *The Bracero Experience: Elite Lore Versus Folklore* (1979); R. C. McElroy and E. E. Gavett, *Termination of the Bracero Program: Some Effects on Farm Labor and Migrant Housing Needs,* Agricultural Economic Report No. 77 (U.S. Department of Agriculture, Economic Research Service, 1965).

F.C.

BRAIN DRAIN. One of the many factors which have added a stimulus to the immigration of Brain Drain personnel into the United States has been the enactment of the Immigration and Nationality Act of 1965. In place of the national quotas, the new immigration laws have substituted a series of "preference categories," each of which has set numerical limitations. The one most pertinent from the Brain Drain point of view is the "third preference" category, which "consists of qualified immigrants who are members of the professions or who, because of their exceptional ability in the sciences or the arts, will substantially benefit the national economy, the cultural interests or the welfare of the United States."

Grubel believes that the brain drain problem has been exaggerated. Only India and the Philippines appear to be affected by it and both overproduce professionals in some areas. Suggests that return migration statistics would show that the loss is not so important. A voluntary contribution by skilled workers who choose to leave underdeveloped countries would take care of the problem.

Bhagwati places the blame on the United States but notes that Canada too has begun to emphasize skills in evaluating prospective immigrants. Sees the elimination of racial quotas as resulting in an increased flow of skill and expertise. In "Taxing the Brain Drain" (*Challenge,* XIX, 1976, 34-38) proposes an income tax on the earnings of people who leave poorer countries to live and work in richer ones. The funds so raised would go to the home countries.

References
T. L. Bernard, "United States Immigration Laws and the Brain Drain," *International Migration,* 8 (1970); Jagdish N. Bhagwati, "The Brain Drain," *International Social Science Journal,* 28 (1976): 691–729; Herbert C. Grubel, "Reflections on the Present State of the Brain Drain and a Suggested Remedy," *Minerva,* 14 (1976): 209–224.

F.C.

BRIDGE. *See* Danes.

BRIZGYS, VINCAS. *See* Lithuanians.

BRONCK, JONAS. *See* Danes.

BROOKS, CHARLES ALVIN (1871–1931). Baptist administrator; executive secretary of the Cleveland Baptist Association, 1907–14. Superintendent of city missions and foreign-speaking work for the [Baptist] Home Mission Society from 1914 to his death. In 1916, Brooks edited *The Church and the Foreigner,* a manual of methods for Protestant missionaries to the immigrants; and in 1922 he wrote a history of the Baptist home mission efforts among immigrants, *Through the Second Gate.* "More than any other individual, this energetic and humane clergyman helped to steer his denomination away from . . . bigotry and prejudice" (Davis, 168).

Reference
Lawrence B. Davis, *Immigrants, Baptists, and the Protestant Mind in America* (1973).

F.C.

BROZ-TITO, JOSIP. *See* Croatians.

BRUMIDI, CONSTANTINO (1805–1880). Born in Rome, July 26, 1805, of an Italian mother and a Greek father. At an early age, having demonstrated extraordinary talent in the art of painting, he was admitted to the Accademia di San Luca in Rome. At the academy, Brumidi studied painting under Vincenzo Camuccini and Filippo Agricola and sculpture and modeling under Antonio Canova and Berthel Thorwaldsen. In 1840, Brumidi was commissioned, with other artists, to do the restoration of the eleventh bay of the third loggia of the Vatican. Brumidi and his collaborators worked on three frescoes symbolizing *Senectus Mala* (Wicked Old Age), *Senectus Bona* (Good Old Age), and the Coat of Arms of Gregory XVI.

From 1842 to 1844, Brumidi decorated the family chapel of the Torlonia Palace in Rome. There is reason to believe that this artistic achievement in the Torlonia Chapel might have convinced Brumidi of his ability in producing art, in the technique of the fresco of considerable size, and that in virtue of this successful achievement, he undertook in 1865 the execution of the *Apotheosis of George Washington,* which adorns the canopy of the dome of the Capitol Rotunda in Washington, D.C.

In February 1851, Brumidi and a large group of persons were arrested on warrants by the Tribunal of the Sagra Consulta of Rome on charges of grand larceny, aggravated assault, and kidnapping, allegedly committed against churches, convents, and monks of the City of Rome during the period of the Roman Republic of 1849. On March 20, 1852, following a series of written petitions to the pope, in which the artist reiterated his full innocence of any wrongdoing, Pius IX granted Brumidi full and unconditional pardon and ordered his immediate release. On September 18, 1852, Constantino Brumidi arrived in New York City, seeking a continuation of his artistic career in the United States. From 1855 to 1880, the year of his death, Brumidi worked relentlessly in the decoration of the interior of the nation's Capitol. In 1855, Captain Montgomery Meigs gave Brumidi the opportunity to execute frescoes for the House Committee on Agriculture.

In 1863, Brumidi was given the commission to fresco the concave canopy of the dome of the Rotunda. The execution was unveiled in 1866 and was hailed as magnificent work of art: "The grandest and the most imposing that has ever been executed in the world." Indeed, the fresco remains the focal point of the Rotunda. There is little doubt that in the *Apotheosis of Washington* Brumidi reached the highest degree of neoclassical expression and execution. While the artist was striving for the grandiose, he also achieved superior pictorial effect and symmetry in an ensemble of motifs and colors. From 1859 to 1860, Brumidi decorated the President's Room in the Senate Extension.

Almost simultaneously with this execution, Brumidi decorated the rooms of the Committee on Military Affairs, now the Senate Appropriations Committee Rooms, with scenes and events of the Revolutionary period. Brumidi also decorated the Senate Reception Room. His last major artwork and fresco in the Capitol was the frieze of the Rotunda. The frieze, "a belt nine feet wide which circles the Rotunda 58 feet from the floor," was frescoed by Brumidi with the technique of imitation high-relief (*altorilievo*). While working on the frieze in October 1879, Brumidi fell from the scaffolding, barely missing death. The artist never fully recuperated and died in February 1880.

Reference
Myrtle Chene Murdock, *Constantino Brumidi: Michelangelo of the United States Capitol* (1965).

P.N.

BRUNNER, FRANZ VON SALES. *See* Swiss.

BUKOVIANS. *See* Romanians.

BUKOVINA. *See* Ukrainians.

BULGARIANS. Located on the eastern periphery of Europe, the geopolitical importance of Bulgaria has historically made it a target for outside colonizers. It is significant that the period leading up to the mass migration of Bulgarians to America was a time when five centuries of rule by the Ottoman Turks was coming to an end, culminating in the liberation of the country in 1878 (made possible by the intervention of Russian troops) and the establishment of a republic in 1908. Though industrialization began in the latter years of the nineteenth century, Bulgaria remained an economically underdeveloped country with a fragile political system and a precarious relationship with regional neighbors. The inability of the new republic to incorporate the contested region of Macedonia into its borders led to an irredentism that fueled conflict with Turkey, which included a major, unsuccessful, Macedonian uprising in 1903.

In this context, Bulgarians began to migrate to the United States during the first decade of the twentieth century, prompted by economic and, especially in the case of Macedonians, political factors. A majority of the Bulgarian immigrants were from Macedonia. Given the fact that official statistics lumped Bulgarians with Serbs and Montenegrins, precise estimates of the number of Bulgarians emigrating between 1900 and 1924 are impossible to obtain, though it is probable that the actual number is somewhere between 50,000 and 70,000. After 1924, the number was reduced to a trickle, though after World War II and the Communist victory in Bulgaria, several thousand anti-Communists became political exiles.

During the main period of mass migration, the immigrant population was composed overwhelmingly of males. Over 90 percent of them were unskilled laborers (including farm laborers) and over a third were illiterate. Most of the immigrants were, at least officially, Eastern Orthodox, though some joined various Protestant churches, in part due to Protestant missionary efforts in Bulgaria in the nineteenth century. They exhibited a markedly high rate of reemigration, in no small part because of the decision of many to participate in the Balkan Wars of 1912 and 1913.

These immigrants gravitated to burgeoning industrial centers. While some located on the East Coast, especially in Philadelphia, most headed for the Midwest. Major cities of settlement include Cleveland, Detroit, Gary, Indianapolis, Minneapolis/St. Paul, Pittsburgh, St. Louis, and Youngstown. They also settled in mining and lumbering regions in the upper Midwest and the West. A major enclave was established in southern Illinois, with Granite City coming to constitute a focus of cultural life for the Bulgarian-American community and the home of its most important newspaper, *Naroden glas* (National Herald), until it ceased to publish in 1950.

As with many other ethnic groups, the first significant ethnic institutions to emerge were the boarding house and the coffeehouse. Shortly thereafter, various fraternal and mutual aid societies were created, with the two most important national organizations being the Bulgarian People's Union and the Macedonian Political Organization.

The Bulgarian Orthodox Church appeared during this time as well. In terms of affiliations outside of the ethnic community, a sector of the ethnic group was drawn to various left-wing political and labor organizations. They established a language federation in the Socialist party in 1910, and in the second decade of the century were attracted to the Industrial Workers of the World (IWW). Involvement with this latter organization was related to Bulgarian-American participation in major labor battles, including strikes in Ludlow, Colorado, in 1913 and on Minnesota's Mesabi Range in 1916. The attraction of leftist politics continued into World War II, leading to repression in the Cold War period and conflict with newly arriving anti-Communist Bulgarians.

The post–World War II period was one of decline for the ethnic community. Ethnic institutions and newspapers eroded, exogamous marriages increased, and contact with the homeland decreased. While efforts have been made to preserve aspects of the ethnic heritage, they have met with only limited success.

References
Nikolay Altankov, *The Bulgarian-Americans* (1979); Emily Balch, *Our Slavic Fellow Citizens* (1910); Stanley Evans, *A Short History of Bulgaria* (1960); George Prpic, *South Slavic Immigration in America* (1978); Joseph Roucek, "The American-Bulgarians," *Orientator* (1937).

P.K.

BURBA, ALEKSANDRAS. *See* Lithuanians.

BYELORUSSIANS. The Byelorussians are little known under this name, which came into use in the English language in approximately 1945, at the time the Byelorussian Soviet Socialist Republic became one of the charter members of the United Nations and has been a member ever since. Byelorussians are better known as White Russians, or White Ruthenians. Byelorussia is located in Eastern Europe, bordered by Poland in the west, Russian in the east, the Ukraine in the south, and Lithuania and Latvia in the north. Minsk, the capital of Byelorussia, lies on the railroad route between Moscow and Warsaw. The majority of the Byelorussians, a Slavic people, live in the Byelorussian S.S.R. and the Bialystok region of Poland.

Historical Background. The confusion in identifying Byelorussians has historical roots. The Byelorussian territory formed the core of the state known as the Commonwealth of the Grand Duchy of Lithuania, from the thirteenth to the eighteenth centuries, and the people were known as and called themselves "Licviny," loosely translated as "Lithuanians." The Byelorussians came under strong Polish cultural influence during the seventeenth and eighteenth centuries, and those Byelorussians who were of the Roman Catholic faith, i.e., about one-fourth of the population, were simply considered to be Poles. During the last quarter of the eighteenth century, the entire Byelorussian territory was occupied by the Russian Empire, and the unprecedented process of Russification, the uprooting of any and all characteristics of Byelorussian separateness, began: the territory was stripped of any specific ethnic name and became officially "The North Western Territory"; the term "Licviny" became applicable to present-day Lithuanians only; all Byelorussians of Eastern Orthodox faith were labeled as "Russians"; the use of the Byelorussian language was outlawed and schooling for the local urban population was reduced to a minimum, and there were almost no schools in the countryside. As a result of these policies, the Byelorussian territory became one of the poorest regions of the Russian Empire with its population living under medieval conditions.

Mass Emigration. The exodus of the Jewish population from the Byelorussian territory in the nineteenth century gave the Byelorussians the idea of emigrating to America also. The Byelorussian emigration began during the last decade of the nineteenth century and reached its peak around 1910–13. The Soviet Byelorussian demographers estimate that between 500,000 and 700,000 Byelorussians emigrated to America. During the process of emigration/immigration, neither the Russian authorities nor the American Immigration and Naturalization Service considered Byelorussians as a separate ethnic group. Religion was used as the determining criterion: Byelorussians of Eastern Orthodox faith were considered Russians, and those of the Roman Catholic religion were considered Poles. The Byelorussian immigrants themselves did not dare to contradict any official terminology, nor did they care. Their only desire was to get to the "gold-paved" streets of the new world. If ever asked about their true ethnicity, they invented the term "locals" (*tutejshy,* in Byelorussian).

The Byelorussian immigrants came from the following regions and cities: Minsk, Pinsk, Vilna, Grodno, Mogilev, Vitebsk, Smolensk, Gomel, Polotsk, Brest, and Bialystok. About 98 percent of them were peasants, almost all illiterate; however, they came with the desire to work at any job, make money, and then to go back to the old country "to buy a piece of land." Almost all of them settled in the Northeast, in New Jersey, New York, Connecticut, and Massachusetts, and the industrial cities of the Midwest. Ironically, about 80 percent of them remained permanently in this country.

Post–World War I and World War II Immigration. Regardless of the degree of oppression, the Byelorussians were able to proclaim their independence on March 25, 1918. This was short-lived, unfortunately, and was crushed by the rising Soviet Empire which proclaimed their own Soviet Byelorussian Republic in 1919. Although the national situation for the Byelorussians changed after 1918 with the establishment of

Byelorussian schools, the rehabilitation of the language, and the development of national cadres of intelligentsia, life under the Soviets or the Polish government (part of Byelorussia came under Poland according to the Riga Treaty in 1921) was not a panacea, and thousands of Byelorussians fled the country at every opportunity. During the period from 1920 to the post–World War II years, about 100,000 Byuelorussians came to the United States.

Organizations: Church and Church-Related Groups. At the time that the masses of Byelorussian immigrants were coming to the United States, the majority of them joined the Russian Orthodox church, because about 90 percent of them were Eastern Orthodox, and the Byelorussian people have strong religious feelings. The brotherhoods of the people from Minsk, Vilna, Grodno, and other regions were most commonly church-related groups. The church hall was, as a rule, the center of social activities such as weddings, christenings, and celebrations for patron saints. A typical characteristic of Byelorussians was and still is that all activities are celebrated in song. As a matter of fact, the Byelorussian people have songs appropriate for any and all occasions, seasons and even types of food, especially potatoes. Unfortunately for the Byelorussians, however, the Russian Orthodox church was under strict and totalitarian control by the Russian government and it espoused Russian imperial theories. Thus, any manifestation of separateness was intolerable. Therefore these uneducated masses, the majority of them deeply religious, were totally controlled by the Church. The descendants of these Byelorussian peasants were brainwashed into believing they were Russians. It was not until the late 1940s that the Byelorussians in the United States began to organize their own parishes, mostly under the jurisdiction of the Byelorussian Autocephalous Orthodox church. Some groups, however, chose to establish parishes under the jurisdiction of the Greek Patriarchate. Byelorussian churches function presently in New Jersey, New York, Michigan, Ohio, Illinois, and California. There is also one Byelorussian Roman Catholic church in Chicago.

Secular Organizations. A Byelorussian fraternal insurance society was established in Michigan in 1913. It was short-lived and was dissolved before very long. A White Russian Press Bureau, organized in New York City in 1921, was active for a few years and published a bulletin. A more lasting organization, the Whiteruthenian-American National Association, was established in Chicago in the mid-twenties and was active for many years. In 1926, the Chicago group published the first Byelorussian newspaper in the United States, *The Whiteruthenian Tribune.* It was obvious that the chief concern of early Byelorussian leaders in the United States was to convince the masses to quit the Russian-controlled churches. Although it did not happen overnight, the idea of forming purely Byelorussian organizations began to take hold.

Many Byelorussian organizations began to form after World War II with the new wave of immigrants. These were national societies, youth groups, cultural and sports clubs, and scholarly groups. The Byelorussians built numerous recreational centers and national homes. The group publishes twelve to fifteen journals in the Byelorussian language. Almost all groups are associated with two umbrella organizations: the Byelorussian American Association, with chapters in about ten states, and the Byelorussian Congress Committee; both are headquartered in New York City. The Byelorussian American Association publishes a monthly newspaper, *Bielarus*. This newspaper, mostly in Byelorussian, but occasionally with an English-language page, basically reflects the concerns and activities of the group. Although Americanization is progressing very rapidly, the group maintains intensive contacts with the homeland, which are even stronger among the descendants of the early Byelorussian immigrants. Presently, the major preoccupations of the Byelorussian-American community are the restoration of the Byelorussian heritage in America, moral support to the home country in the struggle against Russification, and concern about the effects of the Chernobyl disaster on Byelorussia.

References
Vitaut Kipel, *Byelorussian Americans and Their Communities of Cleveland* (1982); Ivan Lubachko, *Belorussia Under Soviet Rule, 1917–1957* (1972); N. P. Vakar, *Belorussia: The Making of a Nation* (1956).

V.K.

BYGDELAG. Immigrant societies composed of Norwegians from a particular region (or *bygd*) in Norway. The first *bygdelag* was founded in Minneapolis in 1899 by 890 persons from Valdres. At its peak, the *bygdelag* movement consisted of fifty societies with a total of 75,000 members. In reaction to both American industrialism and Norwegian high culture, the *bygdelag* celebrated the rural origins of Norwegian-Americans. Their major activity was the sponsoring of an annual reunion, or *stevne*. Other activities included promoting folk art, music, and dialects, and publishing yearbooks and other publications. In 1914 a coordinating body of the groups (Bygdelagenes Fellesraad) was founded, which played a major role in the festivities marking the centennial of the Norwegian constitution (1914) and the hundredth anniversary of the beginning of organized Norwegian immigration (1925).

Reference
Odd S. Lovoll, *A Folk Epic: The Bygdelag in America* (1975).

J.J.

BYZANTINE RUTHENIAN CHURCHES. *See* Carpatho-Rusyns.

CABRINI, [MOTHER] FRANCES XAVIER (1850–1917). Prioress of her foundation, the Institute of the Missionary Sisters of the Sacred Heart. Cabrini was sent to the United States by Pope Leo XIII to help Italian immigrants. She was canonized in 1946. Archival material is located in the Cabriniana Room, Cabrini College (Philadelphia, Pennsylvania).

References
Pietro Di Donato, *Immigrant Saint: Life of Mother Cabrini* (1960); Sergio C. Lorit, *Frances Cabrini* (1970).

F.C.

CAHAN, ABRAHAM (1860–1951). Journalist, born in Vilnius, Lithuania. Cahan emigrated to New York City in 1882. He helped found the *Jewish Daily Forward* (*q.v.*), and served as editor in chief after 1902; he was active in the Socialist party and the unionization of workers in the garment trades. His writings in English include: *Yekl: A Tale of the New York Ghetto* (1896); *The Imported Bride and Other Stories* (1898); and *The Rise of David Levinsky* (1917). His autobiography (in Yiddish), *Blatter von mein Leben* (5 vols., 1926–1931), is an invaluable resource in immigrant history.

> There were, in reality, four Abraham Cahans. As American author, he is a minor but interesting figure—a pioneer realist who wrote our best Jewish-American novel. As Yiddish editor and journalist, he introduced to Yiddish journalism the sure-fire—if not always creditable—circulation-building techniques of American journalism. A natural outcome of his dual role as American author and Yiddish journalist was his contribution to understanding between the two worlds he straddled, explaining the Jewish immigrant to his American audience and Americanizing his Jewish audience. As a socialist, he helped shape the Socialist Party in America through founding, with others, the Social Democratic Party and his repeated support of Eugene Debs. To the extent that many socialist principles were eventually adopted by the major American political parties, Abraham Cahan's legacy forms a portion of the climate of our own time (Pollock).

Reference
Theodore M. Pollock, "The Solitary Clarinetist: A Critical Biography of Abraham Cahan, 1860–1917," Ph.D. dissertation, Columbia University, 1959.

B.L.

CALIFORNIA ORIENTAL EXCLUSION LEAGUE. Established in September 1919 as a result of a meeting held by Asian exclusionists in the office of State Controller John S. Chambers. The league, founded with Senator J. M. Inman as its president, proposed a five-point program: cancellation of the Gentlemen's Agreement; the exclusion of "picture-brides"; the exclusion of Japanese as immigrants; the denial of citizenship to Asians; and the passage of a constitutional amendment limiting U.S. citizenship to children born of both parents who were eligible for U.S. citizenship.

D.N.A.

CAMBRIAN. *See* Welsh.

CAMINETTI, ANTHONY (1854–1923). Congressman; U.S. commissioner of immigration, 1913–1921. Appointed by President Woodrow Wilson as U.S. commissioner of immigration in 1913, a fact not unrelated to the heavy flow of Italian immigration at the time. Caminetti was a restrictionist, and called for the total exclusion of Asians.

D.N.A.

CAMPANILISMO. Italian regionalism, local patriotism, parochialism. In many Italian communities, there is a civic tower called the *campanile*. It contains the bells and perhaps a chiming clock that are symbols of the community. The word *campanilismo* has often come to serve as a synonym for parochialism. It is the historical and social emphasis on the village, the local culture and mores. It has sometimes been contrasted with some larger identity, often the nation. In the history of modern Italy the conflict between local and national interests has often been interpreted as a divisive one, but one that stubbornly persisted. At least in theory, *campanilismo* has been interpreted positively as providing rootedness for people, emphasizing the identification with family and local traditions that needed to be preserved. When seen negatively, it was believed to be a principal obstacle to a successful national identity and an obstacle to various kinds of progress. When millions of Italians emigrated to the United States they brought with them their keen love of the local region of origin, often establishing a host of organizations and support groups which were heavily flavored with the habits and associations of their *paese,* their local homeland in Italy.

Reference
Sydel Silverman, *Three Bells of Civilization: The Life of an Italian Hill Town* (1975).

G.B.

CANADA, American and Canadian immigration policies and trends. Despite a common emphasis on labor needs and the desirability of reuniting families, the two countries differ in the importance they place on immigration's economic contribution. Canada gives preference to job preparation while the United States assigns most of its numerical limit to family members. The United States limits its immigration, letting people in if they fit into a permitted category. Canada uses immigration as an important part of its economic programs, raising and lowering the limits as conditions change. While Canada's immigration policy and administration are relatively centralized, the United States assigns responsibilities to several offices and agencies.

Reference
Monica Boyd, "Immigration Policies and Trends: A Comparison of Canada and the United States," *Demography* 13 (1976): 83–104.

F.C.

CANADA, Green Paper on immigration policy.

The Canadian government's Green Paper on immigration policy was finally tabled in the House of Commons on February 3rd of this year by the Minister of Manpower and Immigration, the Honorable Robert Andras. As in Britain, Canadian governments produce green papers in order to initiate a national discussion on particular issues, and white papers when they wish to make specific policy proposals, often leading to legislation. According to tradition, therefore, this document has been presented as a discussion paper and does not make policy recommendations (Hawkins).

References
Freda Hawkins, "Canada's Green Paper on Immigration Policy," *International Migration Review* 9 (Summer 1975): 237–249, and *Canada and Immigration* (1972).

F.C.

CANADA, illegal immigrants. Immigration policies and their management in a country like Canada have long been an interesting and instructive study for other countries. With borders naturally protected by great distance from almost all migrant routes; with a long, undefended border with the United States and a further 3,000 kilometers to its border on the south; with a parliamentary system capable of comparatively rapid legislative and administrative responses to problems; and with a relatively small legal, and even smaller illegal population, Canada has historically "experimented" with novel, often quite creative, immigration policies and programs to both encourage and control the increases in its population.

Reference
W. G. Robinson, "Illegal Immigrants in Canada: Recent Developments," *International Migration Review* 18 (Fall 1984): 474–485.

F.C.

CANADA, immigration policy and the American farmer. The last three decades of the nineteenth century witnessed a rapid decline in agricultural opportunity in the Midwest and Plains states. The long agricultural depression of 1873–1896 dispossessed many farmers, while the rapid increase in land prices after 1896 and the scarcity of virgin land put farm ownership out of the reach of many farmers. For many rural residents of the Midwest and Plains states life on the farm was synonymous with a heavy mortgage burden or permanent tenant status. To improve their economic position farmers resorted to economic organization, political protest, and migration to marginal areas to the Southwest, the Great Basin, and the cutover portion of the Lake states. Many abandoned the farm for the city. Others chose a final alternative: migration to the vast, unexploited Canadian prairie region.

Reference
Karel D. Bicha, "Canadian Immigration Policy and the American Farmer, 1896–1914," Ph.D. dissertation, University of Minnesota, 1963.

F.C.

CANARY ISLANDERS. Natives of the Islas Canarias, a group of seven islands off Spanish Sahara, in the Atlantic Ocean. These islands constitute two provinces of Spain. The greatest proportion of Spanish emigrants to the United States originated in the Canary Islands, as well as in Galicia, Asturias, Catalonia, the Basque provinces, New Castille, and Andalusia. Like other Spaniards (*q.v.*) in the United States, there is little evidence that Canary Islanders have ever worked to maintain a separate ethnic identity or community.

Reference
J. J. Parsons, "The Migration of Canary Islanders to the Americas: An Unbroken Current Since Columbus," *Americas* 39 (April 1983): 447–481.

F.C.

CAREY, MATTHEW (1760–1839). Political economist, publisher. Carey was born in Dublin, Ireland and emigrated to Philadelphia because of his antigovernment writing. He had a long career as a writer and publisher. He is chiefly remembered for his economic scholarship which helped shape early American economic theory. He worked hard to protect the indigent, especially the poor, the immigrants, and the aged. Carey published the first *Encyclopedia Americana* in 1829 as well as the first American edition of the Douay version of the Bible.

S.P.M.

CARIBBEAN IMMIGRANTS, transitional networks. Caribbean immigration, as a component of the "new immigration" to the United

States, may be distinguished by kinship and friendship networks that transcend national boundaries. Such networks affect the patterns of migration by recruiting new immigrants, maintaining close ties with the country of origin, and sustaining cultural persistence. Findings were made during fieldwork among black immigrants from Trinidad to Los Angeles. Multicultural and multiracial facets of the "new immigration" present a formidable challenge to social scientists of the assimilation school.

Reference
C. Ho, "Transnational Networks Among Caribbean Immigrants in the United States," paper presented at the American Anthropological Association 83d Annual Meeting, Denver, Colorado, November 14–18, 1984.

F.C.

CARIBBEAN MIGRANT WORKERS, in Florida sugar cane industry. A major study reports the findings of a study of a labor program that has, for the last thirty-nine years, brought workers from the Commonwealth Caribbean (known as the British West Indies prior to independence) to south Florida to harvest sugar cane. The eight to nine thousand men in this work force currently constitute the largest legal foreign migrant labor program in the United States.

Reference
T. L. McCoy and C. H. Wood, *Caribbean Workers in the Florida Sugar Cane Industry* (University of Florida: Center for Latin American Studies, December 1982).

F.C.

CARIBBEAN MIGRATION. Is emigration from the Caribbean area to the United States an essential escape valve, releasing destabilizing population pressures and permitting space for economic development? Or do the talented, skilled, and professional people exit, reducing the possibilities for development? In answering these questions, the contributors to this volume (*infra*) offer an in-depth analysis of the unexplored relationship between two crucial phenomena shaping the region: migration and development. The contributors break new ground in challenging old assumptions that underlie current policies, offering new proposals that aim to multiply the benefits of migration to Caribbean development while reducing the costs. They examine the impact of various development strategies on migration and suggest projects and strategies that could reduce the pressures of migration. Finally, they assess the impact of U.S. immigration policies on Caribbean economic development and U.S.-Caribbean relations and offer proposals to modify policies.

Reference
Robert A. Pastor, ed., *Migration and Development in the Caribbean: The Unexplored Connection* (1985).

F.C.

CARIBBEAN MIGRATION, policies and people.

Throughout the twentieth century, the United States has feared that political instability in the Caribbean could be exploited by adversaries. The best way to address the causes of instability is to contribute to the region's social, economic, and political development. Therefore, the U.S. and the nations of the Caribbean share a compelling interest in the region's development. The dramatic increase in legal and illegal immigration to the U.S. from the Caribbean in the last two decades has offered an additional human reason for U.S. interest in the region. This migration has also created a new source of dependence and vulnerability for the region. Curtailment of the migration would undoubtedly affect the region, and if the effect were social and political instability, then the U.S. would also share those consequences. Conversely, policies that take migration into account offer the opportunity to enhance development and social-political stability (Pastor).

Reference
Robert A. Pastor, "Migration and Development in the Caribbean: Relating Policies and People," *International Migration Review* 19 (Spring 1985): 144–151.

F.C.

CARIBBEAN REFUGEES, *Caribbean Refugee Crisis: Cuban and Haitians,* hearing before the Committee on the Judiciary, U.S. Senate, 96th Congress, 2d Session, May 12, 1980. It includes the testimony of Bishop Edward A. McCarthy of Miami; Msgr. Walsh of Miami's Catholic Charities; Donald Hohl of U.S.C.C. Migration and Refugee Services; and Ambassador Victor Palmieri, the U.S. coordinator for refugee affairs and spokesman for the Haitian refugees in Miami. Appendix 1: "Report on the Status of Human Rights in Haiti"; Appendix 2: "Violations of Human Rights in Haiti—1980," by the Lawyers' Committee for International Human Rights; Appendix 3: "Report of Department of State Study Team on Haitian Refugees, June 19, 1979."

F.C.

CARMICHAEL, STOKELY. *See* West Indian Immigrants.

CARPATHO-RUSYNS. The Carpatho-Rusyns are a little-known group, even though the golden-domed cupolas of their churches are

familiar to many Americans who travel across the urban landscape of
the northeast and north-central states. Part of the reason for their unfamiliarity is that Carpatho-Rusyns never had their own state; the other
part is that they have frequently been claimed to belong to other Slavic-
American groups, whether Russian, Slovak, or Ukrainian. Generally,
they have referred to themselves as Rusyns, Ruthenians, Carpatho-
Russians, Uhro-Rusyns, or by the regional term Lemko.

Carpatho-Rusyns derive from the hills and valleys of the north-
central ranges of the Carpathian Mountains in the geographic heart of
Europe. Until 1918, this territory was ruled by the Austro-Hungarian
Empire (divided into the Hungarian Kingdom and Austrian province of
Galicia); then during the interwar years by Czechoslovakia and Poland;
and since 1945 by the Soviet Union (the Transcarpathian oblast of the
Ukrainian S.S.R.) and Poland. This area has since medieval times been
a border region between several political entities, between the linguistic
spheres of the East Slavs and West Slavs, and between the religious
realms of the Eastern Orthodox and Western Catholic churches. Although the Carpatho-Rusyns are East Slavs who speak East Slavic dialects and who traditionally have used the Cyrillic alphabet in their
writings, they have been strongly influenced by long-term contacts with
neighboring West Slavs (Slovaks and Poles) and Hungarians, which has
had a marked influence on their language and world view.

The Carpatho-Rusyn homeland with its hilly landscape and for-
ested mountains could support at best a limited number of small-scale
farmers and shepherds. With no industry to absorb and support the
population increase in the second half of the nineteenth century, Carpatho-Rusyns began to emigrate to the New World. From the 1880s to
1914, between 125,000 and 150,000 Carpatho-Rusyns emigrated to the
United States. This was the first and only major wave of migration;
since that time, only about 20,000 arrived during the interwar years and
at most a few thousand more since World War II. It is estimated that
today there are about 650,000 Americans who have one or more Carpatho-Rusyn forbears.

Driven from their homeland for economic reasons, the pre-World
War I immigrants included a high percentage of males who desired to
work for a few years in the mines and mills of the northeastern industrial
belt and then return home. In fact, it was not uncommon during the two
decades before 1914 to find individuals who migrated to and from the
United States several times, with the result that in some years there were
as many or more returnees than arrivals. The disruptions of World War I
during the five-year period 1914–18 changed the last of the "temporary" immigrants into permanent settlers, so that the immediate postwar
years witnessed the arrival of many women and children to join their
husbands in America.

The settlement pattern of the early years set the tone for the Carpatho-Rusyn presence in the United States ever since. The first destination was the coal-mining region of eastern Pennsylvania, then the steel mills and associated industrial works in the Pittsburgh area. These two regions attracted the highest proportion of Rusyn-Americans (54 percent by 1920), others going for the most part to northern New Jersey (Passaic, Paterson, Rahway, New Brunswick), New York (New York City, Yonkers, Binghamton), southern Connecticut (Bridgeport), and Ohio (Cleveland and Youngstown), Indiana (Gary), and Michigan (Detroit). All these areas remain today the focal point for Carpatho-Rusyn community and organizational life, although like the rest of the American population many individuals, especially retirees, have begun in the last two decades to move into the Sun Belt states of Florida and California.

Carpatho-Rusyn culture had always been strongly influenced by religion; thus it is not surprising that the church became, and in large measure still remains, the focal point of Carpatho-Rusyn life in America. The Carpatho-Rusyns are Eastern Christians, whose very name, *Rus'/rus'kyi*, was historically synonymous with all Orthodox East Slavs, whose Christian tradition goes back to the Byzantine Empire and its missionaries.

As a result of their geographical origins along the borderland of Catholic and Orthodox Europe, the Carpatho-Rusyns belong to two Eastern Christian traditions—Greek Catholic (Byzantine Ruthenian Catholic) and Orthodox. In the course of the seventeenth and eighteenth centuries, all Orthodox Carpatho-Rusyns had become Greek Catholics, who initially were distinguished from the Orthodox only by their recognition of the pope instead of the ecumenical patriarch as the head of the church. This meant that distinctly "Eastern rite" practices such as a married clergy, the liturgy in Church Slavonic, and the Julian calendar (about two weeks "behind" the western Gregorian calendar) were retained. When the earliest Carpatho-Rusyn immigrants arrived in the United States, they began to establish Greek Catholic parishes and to construct churches already in the 1880s, but they were from the very outset opposed by the American Catholic hierarchy which was "scandalized" by the "strange" traditions—especially the married clergy—of these East Slavs.

In essence, the clash between Greek Catholic practices of the Eastern rite and Roman Catholic norms was to determine the whole course of Carpatho-Rusyn history in America. In response to the Roman Catholic challenge, some Rusyn Greek Catholics "returned" to the ancestral faith and converted to Orthodoxy. The most famous of these was the Reverend Alexis Toth, who because of his Orthodox proselytizing efforts in the years after 1892 became known as the "father of Russian

Orthodoxy in America.'' On the other hand, other Rusyn Greek Catholics tried to resist the American Catholic pressure until the 1930s, when a new Carpatho-Rusyn Orthodox church was founded. At the same time, the remaining Greek Catholics in the Byzantine Ruthenian church gave up most of their traditional Eastern practices.

Today, Carpatho-Rusyns are found primarily in three churches. Two of them have traditionally been associated with the Carpatho-Rusyns: the Byzantine Ruthenian Catholic church, with its seat in Pittsburgh and four dioceses; and the American Carpatho-Russian Orthodox Greek Catholic church, with its seat in Johnstown, Pennsylvania. There is also a very high percentage (some estimate half) of Carpatho-Rusyns in the Orthodox Church in America (formerly the Russian Orthodox church—the Metropolia), with its seat in New York City.

The effort to preserve distinct religious and cultural traditions in a foreign land was also in part the motivation for the creation of secular societies, the most important of which were brotherhoods or fraternals. Although all were run by laymen, they were often closely associated with the church. The oldest and largest fraternal still in existence today is the Greek Catholic Union (Sojedinenije), founded in 1892 in Wilkes Barre, Pennsylvania and later transferred to the Pittsburgh area. The basic objectives of this and other fraternals were twofold: to provide basic insurance coverage against work accidents and deaths and to preserve the Carpatho-Rusyn cultural and religious heritage. The latter objective was carried out through publishing newspapers, like the long-running and influential *Amerikansky Russky Viestnik/Greek Catholic Messenger* (1892–present); through sponsoring cultural, social, and sports events; and by attempting to influence church affairs whenever it seemed that traditional Eastern rite practices were being threatened. In the end, each of what quickly became rival churches, whether Byzantine Ruthenian Catholic or Orthodox, had its own secular fraternal society.

In the course of the various and repeated attempts to defend Eastern rite religious practices, Carpatho-Rusyn spokesmen were also forced to address the issue of ethnic or national identity. Whereas some felt that Carpatho-Rusyns formed a distinct East Slavic nationality, others argued that they were simply a regional group that should be identified and associated with Russians, Slovaks, or Ukrainians. Each of these orientations has existed from the earliest days of the immigration, although today the largest churches (Byzantine Catholic, Carpatho-Russian Orthodox), fraternals (the Greek Catholic Union, Prosvita), and cultural organizations (the Carpatho-Rusyn Research Center) support by their activity and/or by their very existence the idea that in the United States the Carpatho-Rusyns form a distinct Slavic group.

For a group of Americans that derives primarily from immigrants who came before 1914 and who cannot associate their ancestral heritage with an existing state, it has been rather difficult to sustain a distinct Carpatho-Rusyn identity in the United States. As the decades have passed and as travel to the homeland especially since World War II has been difficult or at times impossible because of the restrictions of the Communist states which rule the Carpatho-Rusyn lands, knowledge of the language and memories of the traditional heritage have faded or disappeared.

In recent decades, however, an increasing number of American-born third-, fourth-, and even fifth-generation Carpatho-Rusyns have established dance groups, folk festivals, culture courses, and scholarly conferences and publications which have clearly revived the Carpatho-Rusyn community. Most of this activity began under the impact of the "roots fever" in the 1970s, and it continues today through emphasis on the distinctiveness of Carpatho-Rusyns as a group in the United States. Therefore, despite the developments in the European homeland, where Carpatho-Rusyns have become assimilated (with Ukrainians or Slovaks) or physically dispersed (as among the Lemkos in Poland), it seems that the group in the United States, with its newfound sense of identity, is destined to survive for the foreseeable future.

References
Paul Robert Magocsi, *Our People: Carpatho-Rusyns and Their Descendants in North America* (1984); Paul R. Magocsi, "Carpatho-Rusyns," in *Harvard Encyclopedia of American Ethnic Groups* (1980), pp. 200–210; Richard Renoff and Stephen Reynolds, eds., *Proceedings of the Conference on Carpatho-Ruthenian Immigration* (1975); Alex Simirenko, *Pilgrims, Colonists, and Frontiersmen: An Ethnic Community in Transition* (1964); Walter C. Warzeski, *Byzantine Rite Rusins in Carpatho-Ruthenia and America* (1971).

P.R.M.

CARPATINA. *See* Romanians.

CASA ITALIANA (Columbia University). The Casa Italiana of Columbia University traces its beginnings to the year 1914 when a group of Italian-American students formed an Italian Club in Columbia College with the aim of collecting "a modern Italian library." In April 1920, twenty-five students formed a Circolo Italiano, headed by Peter Riccio, to raise funds and collect books. Columbia president Nicholas Murray Butler encouraged the students with the offer of a facility on West 117th Street for Italian studies and cultural activities. Judge John Freschi, and eventually other prominent Italian-Americans, joined the administration and students in the effort to raise funds for the erection of the Casa.

In 1923, an Institute of Italian Culture was formed under the chairmanship of Professor John L. Gerig, and an executive committee was assigned responsibility for building the Casa. In the next four years, the Italian House Fund Committee, including Professor Riccio and the noted scholar Dino Bigongiari, launched a major fund drive. Joseph Paterno offered to back the construction of the Casa on university-donated land. The university gave the plot at the corner of Amsterdam Avenue and 117th Street. McKim, Mead and White, the architects who planned the Columbia campus, donated their services at cost, and Dr. Charles V. Paterno pledged a library of 20,000 volumes. Mr. Anthony Campagna joined the Committee for Building and Construction. By late 1925, $65,000 had been raised. Two years later, because of the combined efforts of the administration, students, faculty, and donors, with voluntary work by Italian-American skilled laborers, the Italian Renaissance palazzo was formally opened. President Nicholas M. Butler, Senator Guglielmo Marconi, Professor Dino Bigongiari, and the donors celebrated the dedication of the Casa Italiana of Columbia University on October 12, 1927. Since its establishment, the Casa Italiana has been a center for the study and appreciation of Italian culture in the United States, not only of Italy's art, music, and literature, but also its history, politics, and economics. The Casa offers Italians in America and Americans interested in Italy a focus for their common interests.

References
Casa Italiana Newsletter (irregular); *Casa Italiana, Columbia University, Fortieth Anniversary Souvenir* (1967); *Casa Italiana, Columbia University, Fiftieth Anniversary Souvenir* (1977); Giuseppe Prezzolini, *The Case of the Casa Italiana* (1976).

F.C.

CASA ITALIANA EDUCATIONAL BUREAU (Columbia University). Founded in 1932 and directed by Leonard Covello (1887–1982) (*q.v.*), during its short-lived existence (1932–35). Leonard Covello organized the Casa Italiana Educational Bureau in May 1932. Housed in two small rooms at the Casa Italiana, its financial support derived from the Federal Writers' Project which had been set up by the United States government as part of the Works Progress Administration: as such it was a small part of that chapter in American sociopolitical history which saw needy writers, actors, artists, and musicians put to work, as WPA head Harry Hopkins remarked, "because they've got to eat just like other people." The CIEB was, of course, a very small part of the WPA and its Federal Writers' Project; additional support came from the Italian government which contributed $3,000, and a benefit held on the transatlantic liner, Rex, raised another $6,000—in all, very modest support for what Leonard Covello planned. If financial support from the Italian-American community was expected to be small (the economic depression and the plight of Italian-Americans in the 1930s explain this), an anticipated difficulty arose in the hostility in academic communities to the Casa Italiana, which was considered to be under Fascist domination. (Covello notes: "There was hesitation in assigning personnel to the Casa because it was considered a Fascist stronghold.") Leonard Covello, nonetheless, proceeded undaunted.

The purposes of the CIEB were very ambitiously proposed. They may be listed under three categories: (1) The bureau was to be a *fact-finding* organization. Its purpose was to gather and present social and educational facts for all agencies and individuals to whom such information may be of interest and value; (2) the bureau was to serve as a medium for *centralization of efforts* directed toward the social and cultural advancement of Italian-Americans; (3) the bureau was to formulate and initiate a *promotional* program of educational and social activities. To this end it was to concern itself with the establishment and guidance of similar organizations throughout the United States. Almost from its initiation, the CIEB undertook a number of projects "in laying a sound foundation for the larger aspects of its work." It began a campaign "for the diffusion of the Italian language by utilizing educational elements in the Italian communities, as well as those elements in American life that show a desire to cooperate in this movement." It defined a number of reference and research areas and began the accumulation of data: (1) a study of the Italian population in New York City; (2) a study of the disintegrative and disruptive forces in the Italian-American communities of New York City (e.g., retardation, truancy, and juvenile delinquency); (3) a study of the Italian language press in the United States; and (4) "a comprehensive list of reference material as well as a bibliography on immigration and problems created by the immigrant in America with special reference to the Italian group." And it organized a speakers' group that would "concern itself with Italian-American educational problems and . . . be at the service of any cultural or educational organization."

This comprehensive program was never implemented. Although the CIEB was involved in a multiplicity of efforts that touched the Italian communities of New York City and its environs in many ways (e.g., the involvement of Italians in the work of the Folk Festival Council of New York City), its main objectives were not achieved. In all, it published thirteen bulletins (1932–35) which were of uneven quality, but each of which was significant in attesting a seriousness of purpose:

[No. 1]   Mario E. Cosenza, *Eleventh Annual Report*. Italiana Teachers Association [1931–32].

[No. 2]   Peter M. Riccio, *Why English Speaking People Should Study Italian.*

[No. 3]   Rachel Davis-DuBois, *Some Contributions of Italy and Her Sons to Civilization and American Life.*

[No. 4]   Leonard Covello, *The Casa Italiana Educational Bureau— Its Purpose and Program.*

[No. 5]   Henry Grattan Doyle, *The Importance of the Study of the Italian Language.*

[No. 6]   Leonard Covello, *The Italians in America. A Brief Survey of a Sociological Research Program of Italo-American Communities with Population Maps and Tables.*

[No. 7]   William B. Shedd, *Italian Population in New York City.*

[No. 8]   John D'Alesandre, *Occupational Trends of Italians in New York City, 1916–1931.*

[No. 9]   Giuseppe Prezzolini, *A Program of Cultural Activities for Italian Clubs or Societies.*

[No. 10]   Marie Lipari, *The Padrone System: An Aspect of American Economic History.*

[No. 11]   Leonard Covello, *Language Usage in Italian Families.*

[No. 12]   Genoeffa Nizzardini, *Infant Mortality for Manhattan, Brooklyn, Bronx.*

[No. 13]   Genoeffa Nizzardini, *Health Among Italians in New York City.*

The bulletins were not all published under the imprint of the CIEB; straitened financial circumstances forced the publication of a number of them in the *Italy-America Monthly* and in *Atlantica;* those published under the bureau's imprint were done in short print runs, and are very rare in their original form. The support Covello had hoped for from Italian communities never materialized. He sadly noted: ''The Italian communities, I regret to say, never understood educational programs of this character. Their allegiance and their interest and involvement were with the political leaders and such things as educational research and educational programs even for the propaganda for the Italian language never had any financial support.'' For Covello, the absence of support was not unanticipated; he had been involved over the years in a number of organizations whose objectives encompassed strengthening Italian-American communities, encouraging Italian-language instruction, improving the education of Italian children, and generally enhancing the position of Italian-Americans in American society: all of these efforts had, at best, limited success.

When the WPA program terminated, the CIEB came to an end; with no staff, and the support of the Casa Italiana (if only for modest facilities) wavering, the bureau could not have continued. Covello did not give up at first. He rented a storefront on 108th Street in East Harlem, created an Italian-American Educational Bureau (and an Hispanic, i.e., Puerto Rican, educational bureau), and carried the files of the CIEB along with him. In 1942, he rented a whole floor over the National City Bank at 1st Avenue and 116th Street in East Harlem for what he called the East Harlem Educational and Research Bureau, "paid for rent, personnel, etc., for two years and then simply had to quit. The collection went to the Sanitation Department for old paper." The collection included fifty-four transfer files of carefully catalogued materials—an irretrievable loss: in Covello's words, "It was hard for me to give up what I thought was the record of the strivings of our people to make their way in the new world—but financial support never materialized."

The CIEB was a unique undertaking; it proposed a number of functions, but it primarily sought to provide Italian-American communities with help in understanding and meeting needs (and at a time when these communities were most vulnerable); the bureau's other purposes were subordinated to this role. With the dispersal of Italians and the disappearance of the Italian-American urban ghettoes of the 1930s, the CIEB (as Covello visualized it) would have little meaning today. However, in a very real sense, the bureau initiated the sociohistorical study of the Italian-American experience on a systematic basis, and, despite its limited success, its pioneering efforts remain important. More to the point, there is no evidence that the sociohistorical investigations that Covello proposed are being systematically pursued elsewhere under any auspices; and the archives/collections of materials that chronicle the Italian-American experience are only now being assembled. Leonard Covello's bureau was, ostensibly, related to its time; yet much of what it proposed has still to be achieved. And the CIEB's true significance may be recognition of that fact.

Reference

Francesco Cordasco, "Leonard Covello and the Casa Italiana Educational Bureau," in Francesco Cordasco, *Studies in Italian American Social History* (1975), pp. 1–9.

F.C.

CASTIGLIONI, LUIGI (1757–1832). Italian nobleman, traveler, scientist. One of the very few Italians to make the arduous journey to America and to produce a detailed day-to-day account of his findings, Castiglioni in his *Viaggio negli Stati Uniti dell'America Settentionale fatto negli anni 1785, 1786 e 1787* (1790) reveals a rare systematic compendium of information drawn from both observation and secondary sources on the topography, history, institutions, agriculture, and industry of the individual states from Massachusetts to Georgia and

Canada. Woven throughout his text are first-hand descriptions of some of the growing country's major cities—New York, Boston, Philadelphia—and sketches of some of its key figures, including Washington, Franklin, Jefferson, John Jay, Ethan Allen, and John Paul Jones. A trained botanist, and to some extent a biologist and agronomist, Castiglioni had a keen eye for natural surroundings he found. As an attempt to report everything about the emergent new nation—its natural features, flora and fauna, primitive and early colonial history, events of the recent war, and the state of contemporary society—the work is a rare and honest rendition of the intellectual posture of natural science in the eighteenth century. Soon after its publication in Milan, a copy was transmitted by Castiglioni to the American Philosophical Society through Benjamin Rush. In addition to the accounts of his travels, Castiglioni provided "Botanical Observations."

Reference
Luigi Castiglioni's Viaggio: Travels in the United States of North America, 1785–1787, trans. and ed. Antonio Pace, with natural history commentary by Joseph and Nesta Ewan (1982).

F.C.

CASTLE GARDEN. *See* Ellis Island.

CATHER, WILLA SIBERT (1876–1947). Novelist, short story writer. Cather moved with her family from Virginia to Nebraska as a child where she was immensely influenced by "the land." Cather believed in the possibility of a society esthetically and ethically worthy of the land. Although Cather is not an "ethnic novelist," her *My Antonia* (1918), and its Bohemian heroine, represents a society both esthetically and ethically worthy of the land through the creative energy of European immigrants with their rich cultural tradition.

References
J. L. Woodress, *Willa Cather* (1970); Sharon O'Brien, *Willa Cather* (1987).

F.C.

CATHOLIC CENTRAL UNION. *See* Czechs.

CATHOLIC CHURCH, and European immigrants, 1870–1924. The growth of the American Catholic church in the nineteenth century, resulting from increased European immigration, greatly concerned American Catholic leaders. This concern intensified, especially after the 1880s, when the accommodation of hundreds of thousands of new immigrants from southern and eastern Europe confronted the predominantly Gaelic-American hierarchy. As the Catholic population of the country doubled between 1880 and 1900, and reached nearly twenty million by the 1920s, the problem became more pressing. Because American Catholic bishops did not generally promulgate joint policies, procedures for incorporating immigrants remained the province of the individual bishop. Linkh argues that the church leaders during these years rejected the idea of hasty "Americanization" of the immigrant and opted instead for gradual assimilation into a "melting pot with an extremely low flame," a theory similar in many respects to cultural pluralism. Church leaders, considering the newcomer's language and culture essential for the preservation of his faith, were reluctant to encourage rapid "Americanization" lest the immigrant be lost to the church.

Reference
Richard M. Linkh, *American Catholicism and the European Immigrant, 1900–1924* (1975).

F.C.

CATHOLIC COLONIZATION BUREAU. *See* Ireland, John.

CATHOLIC SOCIETIES, Federation of Catholic Societies. Catholic societies existed in the United States as early as the 1830s, but the notion of federating societies into a national organization suggested itself only after Pope Pius IX founded the Catholic Union of Belgium in 1871. Struck by the pope's words, a New York group drafted a constitution for local unions with the aim of forming a national Catholic union comprised of the individual sections. One unit in the formation of a successful union was the Catholic Society. Although the efforts failed, the notion of a federative movement lingered. It cropped up during the preparation of the First Catholic Congress in 1889 in Baltimore and again before the Second Catholic Congress in 1893. Catholic societies received much attention in the papers at both congresses. However, it was Martin Griffin who made a first suggestion for a federation of Catholic societies, which was finally attempted on the diocesan level in Pittsburgh in 1890.

Reference
Mary F. Gorman, "Federation of Catholic Societies in the United States, 1870–1920," Ph.D. dissertation, Notre Dame University, 1962 (DA 23: 614).

F.C.

CATHOLIC WOMEN'S ALLIANCE. *See* Lithuanians.

CATHOLIC WORKERS ALLIANCE. *See* Lithuanians.

CATHOLIC WORKMAN. *See* Czechs.

CELLER, EMANUEL (1888–1981). United States congressman; senior member, House of Representatives, from 1965 until retirement in 1972; ranking minority member, then chairman, of the House Judiciary Committee. Celler supported labor, immigrants, civil rights, international cooperation, and Zionism. He was an active proponent of antitrust legislation; he sponsored the Federal Kidnapping Act and wiretapping and antilynching legislation. He supported the Civil Rights Act of 1957, which was the first comprehensive civil rights legislation in eighty-two years, and helped guide the 1964 Civil Rights Act through Congress.

B.L.

CENTER FOR MIGRATION STUDIES (Brooklyn College, City University of New York). Organized to "assist scholars in the social sciences, education, humanities, and related fields in the collection, preservation, and analysis of primary and secondary materials for the study of the migration processes." An Archives of Migration "will solicit manuscripts, photographs and taped autobiographies and interviews with significant persons involved in various aspects of migration."

F.C.

CENTER FOR MIGRATION STUDIES (209 Flagg Place, Staten Island, New York, New York 10304). A specialized library on migration and a card catalogue of books, articles, and dissertations on migration, it is particularly strong (at the present time, the most comprehensive) in its collection of Italian-American materials. Publishes *The International Migration Review,* a scientific journal studying sociological, demographic, historical, and legislative aspects of migration. Maintains connections with Centro Studi Emigrazione (Via Dondolo 58, Roma, Italia), a center staffed by the Society of St. Charles, a religious order that has ministered to migrants since 1887 and publishes *Studi Emigrazione.*

Reference
Olha Della Cava (Center for Migration Studies), comp., *A Guide to the Archives* 1 (1974); 2 (1977).

F.C.

CENTER FOR THE STUDY OF ETHNIC PUBLICATIONS IN THE UNITED STATES. In March 1971, the Program for the Study of Ethnic Publications in the United States was established at Kent State University as a result of a proposal submitted by Professor Lubomyr R.

Wynar. The center's initial research program focused on the study of ethnic periodicals and newspapers in the United States, including their historical development, typology, and current trends. Later the tasks of the center were expanded to encompass three broad areas: (1) research; (2) curriculum development; and (3) cooperation with institutions, archives, libraries, and ethnic organizations.

During 1971 and 1972 the first comprehensive national survey of ethnic newspapers and periodicals was conducted covering forty-three ethnic groups. This project resulted in the publication of the *Encyclopedic Directory of Ethnic Newspapers and Periodicals in the United States* by L. R. Wynar (1972) which was selected by the American Library Association as one of the "Best Reference Books" for 1972. A second revised edition was published in 1977. During the years 1973 through 1975 another comprehensive study was conducted pertaining to ethnic organizations in the United States. This survey resulted in the publication of *Encyclopedic Directory of Ethnic Organizations in the United States* (1975). In 1977 the center conducted the first major survey of ethnic cultural institutions in the United States (archives, libraries, and museums) suggested by the U.S. Office of Education. As a result of this study the *Guide to Ethnic Museums, Libraries and Archives* by L. Wynar and L. Buttlar was published by the center in 1978. Within this area the center also conducted a survey of Slavic cultural institutions that culminated in the publication of *Slavic Ethnic Libraries, Museums and Archives in the United States* (1980). In 1986 the center published the *Guide to the American Ethnic Press: Slavic and East European Slavic Periodicals.*

Another important accomplishment of the center in promoting ethnic studies in the United States was the launching of a new periodical, *Ethnic Forum: Journal of Ethnic Studies and Ethnic Bibliography,* in 1980. The journal publishes research materials pertaining to ethnic history, education, sociology, ethnic bibliography, and other relevant ethnic disciplines.

The center was instrumental in the development of a special graduate curriculum at Kent State University introducing in 1976 two graduate library science courses, "Ethnic Collections and Publications" and 'Library Services to Ethnic Communities." Also, in cooperation with the center, the graduate library school also offers individual investigations and practica in the area of ethnic studies. In this respect, this is the most comprehensive and unique graduate library science ethnic curriculum in the United States.

During the last fifteen years, the center for the Study of Ethnic Publications has made impressive advances in the field of ethnic studies, especially in the area of the ethnic press, ethnic cultural institutions, and university curricula.

References
Grzegorz Babinski, "Centrum Badania Publikacji Etnicznyuch przy Kent State University in Kent, Ohio, USA" (1980); L. R. Wynar, "Center for the Study of Ethnic Publications. The First Decade: 1971–1981," *Ethnic Forum* 1 (Sept. 1981); Lubomyr R. Wynar, *Guide to American Ethnic Press: Slavic and East European Slavic Periodicals* (1986); Lubomyr R. Wynar, "The Study of Ethnic Press in the United States," *UNESCO Journal of Information Science, Librarianship and Archives Administration* 1 (Jan.–March 1979).

L.R.W.

CENTRAL AMERICAN REFUGEES, *Central American Refugees: Regional Conditions and Prospects and Potential Impact on the United States,* report to the Congress of the United States by the comptroller general of the United States (July 20, 1984). Discusses the policies and extent of assistance given to Central American refugees by the UN high commissioner for refugees and other international organizations; refugees' living conditions and prospects in asylum countries; and U.S. and asylum government policies toward refugees. It also examines (1) the link between assistance and asylum opportunities available to refugees in the region and the possible future migration of refugees to the United States and (2) the potential impact of such migration.

F.C.

CENTRAL AMERICANS. The Sandinista revolution, the Salvadoran civil war, political repression, and economic depression are the leading factors for the migration of hundreds of thousands of Central American refugees to the United States in the 1970s and 1980s. Although the factors are varied and complex, the U.S. government, in determining refugee status for Central Americans, often dismisses the political causes and usually denies asylum to people with legitimate claims of having been persecuted in their native countries. Denial, specially in the case of Salvadorans, usually means deportation, and reprisals against the individual when he/she returns home.

The refugee status question/controversy can be traced back to the post–World War II period, when the U.S. government designed a refugee policy that favored those "fleeing Communist repression" (Refugee Relief Act, 1953). In relation to Latin America, the policy worked well through the 1960s and 1970s, when the overwhelming majority of refugees from the area came from Communist Cuba. By the 1980s, however, most Latin American refugees were coming from Central America, and they were not fleeing "Communist repression," but right-wing military dictatorships supported by the United States.

The Refugee Act of 1980 defined refugees as people who were "unable and unwilling" to return to their homeland because of political, racial, religious, or other persecution. Applicants, however, had to prove a "clear probability" that they would be killed, tortured, or persecuted if they returned to their home country. Thus, those who failed to prove a well-founded fear of persecution were classified as economic refugees and returned home.

While the law affected refugees from all parts of the world, it had a particularly adverse effect on Central Americans due to the complexity of their situation: (1) Although they claim to be fleeing political repression and violence—and most Salvadorans and Guatemalans are—they are also emigrating from extremely poor countries. Thus the U.S. Immigration and Naturalization Service usually rules against political asylum. Nicaraguans, however, present a particularly difficult problem for the INS because although the Reagan administration supports the anti-Sandinista forces ("contras"), Nicaragua is not a Communist country. (2) Refugees from El Salvador and Guatemala claim to be escaping violence at the hands of governments supported by the United States. For the United States to admit large numbers of political refugees from these countries would mean at least an embarrassment to U.S. foreign policy. (3) In Central America, politics and economics cannot be separated, since the former strongly affects the latter.

Central American migration to the United States is a relatively new phenomenon. Before the current political turmoil in El Salvador, Guatemala, and Nicaragua, citizens of those countries as well as other Central Americans tended to migrate within the region, usually to Mexico and Costa Rica. Prolonged political violence in Central America, and the establishment of a large Latin community in Miami since the 1960s, has made the United States a viable alternative to those Central Americans trying to start a new life away from the violence and repression of home.

Causes for the Migration. The main cause for Central American migration to the United States in the 1970s and 1980s is political. This is particularly true in the cases of El Salvador, Guatemala, and Nicaragua. Political unrest, however, is not limited to those countries; Costa Rica, Honduras, and Panama are already feeling the effects of the wars in El Salvador and Nicaragua. Honduras has, since 1983, become the United States military nerve center in the region by hosting continuous training exercises and war games near the Nicaraguan border. In Panama, growing opposition to the military's influence in the government has resulted in sporadic violence and economic boycots. Costa Rica, traditionally the most stable and peaceful Central American nation, and the only one without a standing army, does not share the political unrest of her neighbors, but a weak economy and a ballooning foreign debt pose equally serious threats to her stability.

In El Salvador, a civil war between the military-dominated govern-

ment and leftist rebels has claimed the lives of more than 65,000 civilians since 1979. Human rights organizations attribute most of the deaths
to the government's security forces as well as government-linked death
squads and paramilitary groups.

The Salvadoran civil war shows no sign of ending anytime soon
and has already caused the displacement of more than 2 million of the
nation's population of 5 million. Inside the country more than 1 million
people, mostly orphaned children, war widows, and the elderly, live in
refugee camps. Another half-million have escaped political violence by
migrating to Mexico, Nicaragua, and Honduras, while an estimated
700,000 have made their way to the United States.

In Nicaragua, the Sandinista revolution, in one way or another, is
the main cause for the hundreds of thousands of Nicaraguan refugees
who now live, legally or illegally, in Honduras, Costa Rica, Panama,
and the United States. Beginning with the revolution's triumph in 1979,
thousands of deposed-dictator Anastasio Somoza's national guardsmen
fled to Honduras and Costa Rica to escape Sandinista justice. The
guardsmen were followed out of the country by members of the upper
class who would be adversely affected by the new social order. Many in
that group immigrated directly to the United States.

In addition to the immediate migration triggered by the revolution,
the anti-Sandinista war, supported and financed by the United States
since 1981, has produced a new wave of immigrants, many of whom,
like the Cubans in the 1960s and 1970s, have gone to Miami to await
political changes in their homeland. The fact that there is no end in sight
for the war makes life all the more difficult and uncertain for the 75,000
Nicaraguans (most of whom are illegal) presently living in Miami.

In Guatemala, since the CIA-backed overthrow of Jacobo Ar-
benz's government in 1954, the military regimes have been responsible
for the death of more than 50,000 civilians. Government-sponsored
terror reached such an alarming proportion in 1977 that Amnesty International listed the Guatemalan government as one of the most repressive
regimes in the world. During that period repression was particularly
brutal against the Amerindians, which represent over 50 percent of the
population and have historically been isolated from the "mainstream"
Guatemalan society.

Government terror forced hundreds of thousands to flee to neighboring Mexico and Honduras, while tens of thousands made the much
longer and dangerous trek through Mexico and into the United States,
illegally. The election of a civilian government in 1984 has reduced
government-sponsored terror considerably, and as a result reduced the
number of refugees. For the thousands who made it to "el Norte,"
however, the future remains uncertain: their legal status is still in limbo
and the political situation at home is far from stable.

The United States and Central America. Guided by geopolitical and economic interests, the United States plays an active role in the Central American conflicts. Hoping to quell the Salvadoran revolution and to stop the Sandinistas, the United States, has, in the past eight years, provided more than $3 billion in economic and military aid to El Salvador and Honduras. In addition, the Reagan administration has gradually resumed military aid to the Guatemalan government, which was cut off in 1977 when Amnesty International declared it one of the most repressive regimes in the world. Finally, the administration, with congressional approval, supports the efforts of the rebel forces trying to overthrow the Nicaraguan government.

The Sanctuary Movement. Outraged and horrified by the INS's almost systematic and arbitrary deportation of Central Americans (over 50,000 Salvadorans deported in 1981), people of faith throughout the United States have taken it upon themselves to offer sanctuary to Central Americans fleeing terror at home, but denied entry to the United States. The sanctuary movement, a network of approximately 250 churches, synagogues, and Quaker meeting houses, has since 1982 provided transportation, shelter, and protection for hundreds of Central Americans who would have otherwise been deported to an almost certain death at home.

Sanctuary workers, estimated at about 100,000, are committed to circumventing and violating what they consider unfair and arbitrary laws. Saving the lives of Central Americans and providing them with sanctuary is, in the eyes of the movement's activists, both legal and moral.

The Future. In 1986 the U.S. Congress approved the Immigration Reform and Control Act, a law designed to reduce, and eventually eliminate, illegal aliens by offering amnesty from prosecution and legal status to most illegals already in the country. The law also calls for heavy fines against employers who knowingly employ illegals. The guiding logic of the law is, of course, to discourage illegal immigration. It is obviously too early to measure the effects of the law, but most experts believe that the law will do little to stem the tide of illegal immigrants from Central America. Political unrest, military repression, and economic depression will continue to push people out of Central America and into the fabled land of "el Norte."

References
Renato Camarda, *Forced to Move: Salvadoran Refugees in Honduras* (1985); Elizabeth G. Ferris, *The Central American Refugees* (1987); Renny Golden and Michael McConnell, *Sanctuary: The New Underground Railroad* (1986); Lester D. Langley, *Central America: The Real Stakes* (1985); Gary MacEoin, ed., *Sanctuary: A Resource Guide for Understanding and Participating in the Central American Refugees' Struggle* (1985); Felix Masud-Piloto, *With Open Arms: The Political Dynamics of the Migration from Revolutionary Cuba* (1987).

F.R.M.-P.

CENTRAL-VEREIN. The German Roman Catholic Central-Verein was founded in 1855 and still exists at the present time. It began as a national federation of local benevolent societies; at first it confined its activities closely to mutual insurance but gradually broadened its interest to include education and other matters affecting the German-American Catholic population. In the 1880s and 1890s the Central-Verein became involved in controversies with the American Catholic church and developed attitudes that persisted into the twentieth century.

Reference
John P. Gleason, *The Central-Verein, 1900–1917: A Chapter in the History of the German-American Catholics* (1968).

F.C.

CENTRO STUDI EMIGRAZIONE (Via Dondolo 58, Roma, Italia). The center is staffed by the Society of St. Charles, a religious order ministering to migrants since 1887, which publishes *Studi Emigrazione,* a trimestral review with materials on all phases of immigration. The center's library holdings are particularly rich in immigration history. See Centro Studi Emigrazione, *Catalogo della Biblioteca* (Parte 1, 1972; Parte 2, 1980).

F.C.

CHARITABLE IRISH SOCIETY. The oldest Irish organization in the United States; founded in Boston in 1753. Its major purpose was to assist needy Irish emigrants. It was founded by successful Irish Protestants and until 1760 banned Catholics from holding office. The society has survived the ups and downs of Irish-American and Irish politics and still exists today.

Reference
C. T. Curke, *The Silver Key* (1973).

S.P.M.

CHARITY ORGANIZATION SOCIETY (COS). *See* Community Service Society.

CHARITY REFORMERS AND THE IMMIGRANT POOR. By the 1830s the growth of New York's poor population already challenged the sympathies of contemporary observers and their belief in a democratic society where all had equal opportunity. A group of social reformers, old-stock Americans with roots in New England, attempted to meet this challenge through charity work. Their ideological goal was to make the urban poor self-reliant members of a cohesive community, united by a common commitment to social values. The manner in which they sought to achieve this goal and their willingness to strive for it depended on their diagnosis of the causes of poverty. These causes fell into three broad categories: moral, environmental, and hereditarian. During the Civil War charity workers gradually turned against the poor. Although still intent on making New York into a cohesive community, reformers began to believe that dependent persons suffered from hereditary diseases that made them incapable of becoming an integral and productive part of this community. This hostile attitude was rooted in the anti-Irish nativism of charity workers. As the Irish made rapid social advances and assumed political control of the city, reformers, filled with resentment, stereotyped them as a people incapable of self-support. They considered them a permanent class of hereditary paupers. Their pessimistic view of the Irish widened to include all of the poor when the economic depression of 1873 and a large influx of poor immigrants created a tremendous burden of poverty that strained to their utmost limits the capabilities of private charity. By the end of the 1880s the charity movement declined in importance as a vehicle for molding New York into a cohesive community. Another economic depression and more impoverished immigrants sustained a hereditarian diagnosis of poverty.

When viewed alongside the settlement movement, the failure of the older charity reform movement to maintain its vitality was in large part the failure of its leaders to escape their vision of what constituted a desirable community. Wedded to the belief that the good urban community was a homogeneous collective of shared values rooted in the Protestant American experience, these charity reformers could never accept a pluralistic community structure, seemingly fragmented into ethnically and religiously divided self-sustaining subcommunities. The city's heterogeneity had reignited their interest in the poor, but only to heighten their awareness of the deep divisions that separated the people of the city and of the impossibility of achieving their goal of a culturally homogeneous urban community. This pessimistic appraisal of progress toward this goal, together with the reformers' inability to reduce the number of dependent poor in the city, sustained a hereditarian diagnosis of poverty that undercut their desire to help the poor. They thus withdrew from organized charity, leaving their places to the professional social worker.

Reference
Philip M. Hosay, *The Challenge of Urban Poverty: Charity Reformers in New York City, 1835–1890* (1980).

P.M.H.

CHARLESTON, SOUTH CAROLINA: AS PORT OF ENTRY.
See Immigrants in the Old South.

CHETNICKS. *See* Serbs.

CHICAGO COMMONS. *See* Taylor, Graham.

CHICAGO VICE COMMISSION. In its report, *The Social Evil in Chicago* (1911), the Chicago Vice Commission offered a number of recommendations to eliminate prostitution which were eventually adopted, not only in Chicago, but in many other cities. The attempt to eliminate prostitution focused on the immigrant girl who investigators revealed was the prime victim of prostitution. The leaders in this reform movement to protect the immigrant were women who wanted to make modern urban America safe not only for the defenseless immigrant, but for all women.

Reference
Egan Feldman, "Prostitution: The Alien Woman and the Progressive Imagination, 1910–1915," *American Quarterly* 19 (1967): 192–206.

                                                                    F.C.

CHICANOS. *See* Mexicans.

CHILD, LYDIA MARIA [FRANCES] (1802–1888). English traveler. Describes her impressions of ethnic New York City in her *Letters from New York* (1843) which includes *The Jews, Fear of Public Opinion,* and *Anecdotes of the Irish*. See also her *Good Wives* (1833); and *The History of the Condition of Women in Various Ages and Nations* (1835).

                                                                    F.C.

CHILDREN'S AID SOCIETY (New York City). A voluntary, non-sectarian agency serving thousands of New York City children and their families yearly with a network of services, including: neighborhood centers; camps; mental health, foster care, medical, and dental services; and education and recreation programs. Founded in 1853 by Charles Loring Brace (*q.v.*), the society initially cared for the orphaned and destitute (mostly immigrant) children who roamed the streets of New York by operating lodging houses and industrial schools and by placing children in homes in the West. It has pioneered in child care through: the placement of children in foster homes as members of families; free hot lunches; a visiting nurse service; a school nurse service; free dental clinics; and free nurseries for children of working mothers. The society set a new trend for child care in the middle decades of the nineteenth century. The CAS was the first group to formulate an alternative to orphan asylums and reformatories for indigent children, and the story of their placing-out procedures (Rev. Charles Loring Brace, during his tenure, placed some 90,000 children with western farm families) is of crucial importance to social history.

References
Winifred Bell, *Aid to Dependent Children* (1965); *Children's Aid Society of New York: Its History, Plans, and Results* (1893); *The Crusade for Children: A Review of Child Life in New York During Seventy-Five Years, 1853–1928* (1928); Walter Trattner, *Crusade for the Children* (1970); also, *Annual Reports,* Children's Aid Society (Feb. 1854–)—the early reports have been gathered and published as [Children's Aid Society], *Children's Aid Society Annual Reports, 1–10. February 1854–February 1863* (1971).

F.C.

CHINESE. Today there are more than a million Americans of Chinese ancestry whose history in the United States has been one of travail as well as triumph. Americans began interacting with China and its people when the clipper ship *The Empress of China* set sail from Boston in 1784. In the ensuring years, a few Chinese sailors, artisans, entertainers, and merchants visited North America, but significant numbers of Chinese landed on the pacific coast only after the gold rush to California began in 1848.

Immigration. Chinese immigration can be divided into four periods: 1848–1882, 1882–1943, 1943–1965, and 1965 to the present.

Unrestricted Immigration, 1848–1882. There were about 500 Chinese in California when the 1850 federal census was taken, but it was not until 1852, when over 20,000 aspiring Chinese gold miners passed through the Customs House in San Francisco, that mass immigration began. Over the next three decades, some 322,000 Chinese (including reentrants) came to the United States for whom San Francisco was the chief port of entry. About half of them eventually returned to their homeland, while an unknown number died in the New World. An additional 55,000 went to Hawaii, an independent kingdom until 1893. Five years after the monarchy was overthrown, the islands were annexed by the United States and American laws concerning Chinese became applicable there. Only about 5 percent of the immigrants were women. Before the mid-1870s most of them worked as prostitutes, but as prostitution was wiped out, an increasing share of the female population consisted of wives and daughters.

Very little information is available on the socioeconomic origins of the Chinese who came during the period of unrestricted entry. Some of the earliest arrivals were merchants and artisans, but the vast majority were peasants and laborers, almost all of whom came from a small number of districts in the single province of Guangdong in southeastern China. A handful of the earliest emigrants to Hawaii were "sugar masters" skilled in the manufacture of sugar from cane juice.

The estimated maximum number of Chinese in the United States in the nineteenth century was 130,000 in the early 1880s. Until the turn of the century, the majority of them resided in California. In the 1860s, Chinese began moving out of that state in two directions: northward to the Pacific Northwest and Alaska and eastward first to the other western states and eventually to East Coast metropolises, particularly Boston, New York, and Washington, D.C. A small number had also appeared in Chicago by 1900. Both movements were initially stimulated by the discovery of precious metals in Nevada, Oregon, Washington, Idaho, Montana, British Columbia, and Alaska, and as far east as the Black Hills of South Dakota. Laying the tracks for a number of railroads also took Chinese to places such as Texas and Alabama, where they might not have traveled otherwise. Beginning in the mid-1870s, an increasing number also left the Pacific coast as anti-Chinese sentiments and activities became rampant in that region.

Exclusion, 1882–1943. The free entry of Chinese ended in 1882, when the United States Congress passed the Chinese Exclusion Law, which barred the entry of Chinese laborers for ten years. Whereas in earlier periods the United States had restricted the immigration of certain kinds of individuals, such as the insane, paupers, or prostitutes, the Chinese were the first people to be excluded solely on the basis of their race. When the first exclusion law expired, others were enacted, so that, with the exception of certain "exempted classes," Chinese were kept out of the United States until 1943, when the laws were rescinded by Congress as a gesture of good will toward China, our ally during World War II.

During the sixty-one-year exclusion period, only merchants, students, diplomats, and temporary visitors, who numbered several thousand a year, could land in the country. Virtually no Chinese women were allowed to come (until the U.S. Supreme Court handed down a ruling in 1900 to enable wives of merchants to enter), so the slow increase of the female population came almost entirely from the birth of girls on American soil. Although the majority of those who arrived continued to come from Guangdong, a small number (mainly students) from other provinces of China also began to appear.

Entry Under Special Legislation, 1943–1965. Lifting the bar against Chinese immigration in 1943 was at best a symbolic gesture, for the Chinese were given an annual quota of only 105 persons. Moreover, all of those who were ethnically Chinese, regardless of where they were born or which countries claimed them as citizens, were charged against the Chinese quota, whereas the same rule did not apply to immigrants of other national backgrounds.

In this period, far more Chinese entered under special legislation than under the meager quota alloted them. The two largest groups were war brides and political refugees. An estimated 13,000 Chinese-Americans (including some who were not even U.S. citizens) had served in various branches of the U.S. armed forces during World War II. Several thousand of these who married Chinese women petitioned for their wives' entry when the War Brides Act of 1945 was amended in 1947 to include Chinese women. More than 6,000 came in the next few years. Small as this group was, its coming had profound social significance, for virtually overnight, the number of Chinese women in the United States increased by 30 percent, and Chinese-American communities had a baby boom of their own.

After a Communist government came into power on the Chinese mainland in 1949, approximately 5,000 Chinese—most of them highly educated intellectuals and former government officials—were granted political asylum in the United States. Other refugees (almost all from the same elite background) followed, cumulatively numbering some 15,000 persons by 1967. Because the war brides and the refugees came from many different areas of China, for the first time in the 1950s a significant number of Chinese-Americans spoke dialects other than the ones found in Guangdong Province.

Immigration Since 1965. One of the reforms undertaken by Congress during the presidency of Lyndon Johnson was the enactment of new legislation that removed "national origins" as the basis for setting immigration quotas. The new law allowed a maximum of 20,000 persons from any country to enter under the quota each year (with a ceiling of 170,000 from each hemisphere) beginning in 1968. In addition, certain individuals, such as unmarried minor children of American citizens, could enter on a nonquota basis. The main objectives were to reunite families and to encourage the influx of people with certain kinds of skills and, to a smaller extent, with capital to invest. Asian immigrants were thus finally put on the same footing as people from other lands.

In late 1986, the immigration law was extensively revised, after five years of national debate. Its impact on Asian immigration has been less noticeable than on Latin American, particularly Mexican, immigration. However, the amnesty provision that allows aliens who have resided in the United States unlawfully since before 1981 to obtain legal temporary resident status has affected a small number of Asians.

In the last two decades, between 20,000 and 30,000 Chinese have arrived every year, so that Chinese-Americans now count as the largest group of Asian-Americans. Today, Chinese immigrants originate from many different places: Taiwan, Hong Kong, the People's Republic of China, and various Southeast Asian as well as Latin American countries. More than half of the post-1965 immigrants have been women, children, or older family members. A large percentage (more than 25 percent in some years) bring with them higher degrees and professional and technical training, which helps to account for the "successful minority" image of the Chinese in recent years—an image that tells only a small part of the story, since large numbers of Chinese-Americans remain underemployed and inadequately served by social service agencies.

Employment and Discrimination. In each of the four periods of immigration, since the bulk of the immigrants came from different socioeconomic backgrounds and the opportunities open to them also varied in different periods in the localities where they settled, they fitted into American society in divergent ways according to region and time period. During the nineteenth century, the Chinese earned a living in three kinds of regional economies: mining, agriculture, and urban employment. A different pattern of employment was found in each.

In mining regions, the vast majority of Chinese (up to 90 percent in some counties) dug gold for a living. As gold deposits became exhausted, many turned to common labor and domestic service for survival. Merchants usually made up about 3 to 5 percent of the Chinese population in these areas, domestic servants and cooks 5 to 10 percent, laundrymen up to 3 percent, and artisans and professionals under 2 percent.

In the agricultural areas, 30 to 40 percent of the Chinese earned a living as truck gardeners, farmers, and farm workers. Another 30 percent worked as nonagricultural laborers, about 12 to 20 percent as cooks and servants, a little over 10 percent as laundrymen, under 3 percent as merchants, and 2 to 3 percent as artisans and professionals.

In urban centers such as San Francisco, Sacramento, Seattle, New York, and Boston, the Chinese were distributed over a broader range of jobs. They worked as cooks, domestic servants, common laborers, and factory hands. Factory workers making garments, boots and shoes, cigars, woolen textiles, and other light household goods constituted almost 30 percent of the gainfully employed Chinese in 1880 in San Francisco, the major manufacturing center west of the Rocky Mountains. Merchants and laundrymen each made up 10 or more percent of the Chinese population, with laundrymen being especially numerous in the East Coast cities. In the early years, fishermen and prostitutes also formed important components in San Francisco.

The Chinese were, of course, best known for building the western half of the first transcontinental railroad. Between 1867 and 1869, the

Central Pacific Railroad Company kept 12,000 or more Chinese on its payroll. In addition, Chinese also helped build the other three transcontinental railroads and many branch lines throughout the trans-Mississippi West.

In Hawaii in the early years, the bulk of the Chinese worked on sugar cane plantations. They also grew rice, taro, pineapples, vegetables, and other crops. Many who moved to Honolulu became merchants, so that by the 1880s, more than 30 percent of the stores in that city were owned by Chinese. Among second-generation Chinese-Hawaiians, a larger percentage became managers, administrators, craftsmen, and entrepreneurial workers than did their counterparts on the mainland.

Though the Chinese immigrants managed to earn a living in the United States, they had to do so against tremendous odds. Not only did they have to function in a society with a different culture, social structure, and language, but they also faced severe discrimination in many areas of life. Economically, while the Foreign Miners' Tax, the poll tax, and other discriminatory levies took away a significant portion of their earnings, laundry ordinances and restrictions against the type of fishing nets they favored were used to drive them out of those occupations. What the law could not accomplish, violence, boycotts of their products, and barring them from membership in labor unions did. By the 1890s, Chinese were no longer found in manufacturing industries and only a few artisans and skilled craftsmen still plied their trades within the confines of Chinatowns. In the 1920s, Chinese were prohibited by law from engaging in more than two dozen occupations in New York State.

Chinese were made politically impotent when they were not allowed to testify in court, to become naturalized citizens, or to vote. Their upward social mobility was retarded when their children were sent to segregated schools in San Francisco and in a number of communities in the Sacramento Delta, and their residence was increasingly confined to ghettos. Antimiscegenation laws prevented them from marrying white women, while immigration restrictions forbade Chinese women from entering the country. Consequently, as prostitution disappeared, the aging men who chose to remain in the United States were forced to live in celibacy.

After Chinese exclusion went into effect, the Chinese population declined in number and became increasingly urbanized in both residential location and in employment. The stereotype of Chinese running mainly laundries and restaurants originated in this period, for an increasing number of them eked out a living in this manner. As an American-born second generation grew to adulthood in the early decades of the twentieth century, persons of Chinese ancestry began to be employed in low-grade white-collar occupations. However, many of the college-educated youngsters could not find jobs commensurate with their training until World War II, when the need for engineers and scientists was so great that nonwhites with the requisite skills were finally employed in technical and professional jobs.

The well-educated postwar refugees also increased the strength of the emerging Chinese-American middle class. They, along with Chinese-American veterans and their war brides, led the slow exodus out of the Chinatowns and into the suburbs, although discrimination in housing was a barrier that Chinese-Americans had to fight a long though quiet battle to overcome. School segregation statutes were also allowed to lapse without much fanfare.

Post-1965 immigration brought Chinese from many different class backgrounds. Today, the Chinese-American population is bimodally distributed in terms of education, income, and occupational status: a highly visible minority with educational attainment and income levels surpassing those of white Americans coexists with a virtually invisible majority who still suffer from language, economic, and social discrimination. The latter are employed either in the Chinatown enclaves or mostly in service jobs in the larger economy. Many are poorly housed in crowded Chinatowns in big cities.

Community, Culture, and Politics. Since so few Chinese women immigrated, most of the Chinese in America lived in households rather than in families. To perform some of the major functions that clans and families took responsibility for in China, the immigrants established many community organizations, including separate associations for people from each of the major emigrant districts, for individuals with the same family names, and for those in the same occupations, as well as secret societies in which sworn brotherhood was the basis for membership. These associations provided mutual aid, temporary lodgings, and news of employment opportunities. They also exercised social control over their members by collecting debts, issuing exit permits, and adjudicating internecine quarrels.

To deal with the outside world—which became increasingly hostile from the late 1870s onward—the largest district associations, known as *huiguan,* formally coalesced into the Consolidated Chinese Benevolent Association in 1882. (An informal confederation had existed before that date.) White Americans dubbed this organization the Chinese Six Companies, even though it often had more than six component units.

In the early years, merchants dominated these organizations, but after a Chinese ambassador was posted in Washington, D.C. and a consul general in San Francisco in 1879, the Chinese government played an increasingly active role in guiding and controlling them.

Between 1882 and 1925, their directors were usually scholars imported from China. The CCBA in San Francisco has for a century been the most important umbrella organization, but other CCBAs were also established in cities with sizable Chinese populations: New York (established 1883), Honolulu (1884), Victoria, Canada (1884), Lima, Peru (1885), and Portland (c. 1887). These organizations and family associations held sway over American Chinatowns until the early 1960s.

Imported Cantonese opera troupes, temples dedicated to a variety of deities (Chinese folk religion being an amalgam of Confucianist, Taoist, Buddhist, and folk beliefs and practices), cemeteries, Chinese-language schools, newspapers, literary groups, and particularly the celebration of Chinese holidays, all kept selected aspects of Chinese culture alive. Public school teachers and Protestant missionaries, meanwhile, worked hard to acculturate the Chinese.

Organizations serving the interests of the American-born generation—such as the Chinese American Citizens Alliance and various cultural and recreational clubs, some of which were branches of American organizations such as the YMCA, YWCA, and the Boy Scouts—emerged in the early decades of the twentieth century. As kinship and locality became less important organizing principles, more and more groups founded on nonethnic criteria appeared. Today, there are hundreds of professional, business, recreational, political, and civic organizations among Chinese-Americans across the nation.

Though Chinese were not allowed to participate in American electoral politics until they acquired the right of naturalization in 1943, they had nevertheless engaged in various forms of political activity, including strikes, lawsuits, and involvement in homeland politics before that date. In the last two decades, they have also participated in American politics.

Though American employers created antagonism toward Chinese workers by using them as scabs, there are also records of Chinese going on strike. In 1867, some 2,000 railroad workers tunneling through solid granite in the Sierra Nevada Mountains struck for higher wages and better working conditions. In the 1880s, Chinese farm workers went on strike in the Santa Clara Valley and in Kern County. In 1938, Chinese women garment workers organized their own union and struck against a Chinese-owned chain store.

Though Western-style law was not yet practiced in China, time after time, Chinese in America hired expensive and prominent lawyers to challenge discriminatory laws. Although they lost most of the cases, they did win a few. In *Yick Wo* v. *Hopkins* (1886), they won the right to operate laundries in wooden buildings; in *United States* v. *Wong Kim Ark* (1898), American-born Chinese retained their right to U.S. citizenship; while in *United States* v. *Gue Lim* (1900), Chinese merchants won the right to bring their wives and children into the United States.

At the turn of the century, Chinese political reformers such as Kang Youwei and Liang Qichao and revolutionaries such as Sun Yat-sen visited Chinese-American communities, where thousands supported the causes they espoused. In 1905, Chinese-Americans provided both financial support and leadership for a boycott of American goods by students, merchants, and patriots in China, who were protesting against the permanent exclusion of Chinese laborers and the maltreatment of even those who had the legal right to enter the United States. In the 1930s, they picketed ships loading American scrap iron destined for Japan, in opposition to Japanese military aggression in China.

In the 1960s, Chinese-Americans began to participate in the American electoral process as well as protest politics. Hiram Fong, a wealthy businessman from Hawaii, was elected as the first Chinese-American U.S. senator in 1959. Today, March Fong Eu serves as California's secretary of state and S. B. Woo as the lieutenant governor of Delaware. Other Chinese-Americans serve on school boards, in the judiciary, and various local, state, and federal political bodies. Younger and more radical Chinese-Americans participated in the movement against the war in Vietnam, in the civil rights movement, and in efforts to establish ethnic studies programs on university and college campuses.

These activities to secure their rightful place in American society, together with their gradual acculturation and laudable academic achievements, have turned Chinese-Americans into the highly visible ethnic group they are today.

References
Sucheng Chan, *This Bittersweet Soil: The Chinese in California Agriculture, 1860–1910* (1986); Clarence E. Glick, *Sojourners and Settlers: Chinese Migrants in Hawaii* (1980); and Peter C. Kwong, *The New Chinatown* (1988); Sandy Lydon, *Chinese Gold: The Chinese in the Monterey Bay Region* (1985); Shih-shan Henry Tsai, *The Chinese Experience in America* (1986).

S.C.

CHINESE, gangs of [New York City] Chinatown. Before 1965 the city's Chinese population had been fairly stable. Then it began to climb rapidly, putting great pressure on the small area known as Chinatown to provide housing, schools, and recreation facilities. The Fifth Precinct of the New York City Police Department, covering Chinatown, reported fewer than ten arrests a year of young people before 1966. By 1977 that figure grew to two hundred.

Reference
Berkely Rice, "New Gangs of Chinatown," *Psychology Today* 10 (1977): 60–69.

F.C.

CHINESE, name change and acculturation. A study of social life of 262 Chinese students at the University of Minnesota in 1967 shows that 36.2 percent of these students anglicized their names. The change of a person's name is theorized to be a symbolic representation of his identity change. The study reveals that those students who changed their names displayed significantly more out-group–oriented attitudes and behaviors than those who did not change their names.

Reference
T. S. Kang, "Name Change and Acculturation: Chinese Students on an American Campus," *Pacific Sociological Review* 14 (Oct. 1971): 403–412.

F.C.

CHINESE, paper sons (slot cases). Paper sons were fabricated by those who wanted to sell fraudulent certificates to Chinese willing to pay their entry into the United States. Paper sons were Chinese who would come to the United States as sons born abroad of Chinese fathers, who were citizens of the United States and therefore were allowed to bring their sons under the legal provisions made on February 1, 1855. This law existed until 1934, when it was changed to require that the citizen-father be a resident of the United States for at least ten years before the birth of the children, who then could claim derivative citizenship. This privilege of Chinese who were citizens of the United States was abused in fabricating sons who were legal only on paper. The U.S. government responded to this scheme by creating blood tests of "paper sons" to determine whether they were real children of their fathers as they claimed. *See also* Angel Island.

D.N.A.

CHINESE EXCLUSION LAW. *See* Chinese.

CHINESE IMMIGRANTS, adaptations and impacts.

Over half a million people of Chinese ancestry now live in the United States. This number represents more than a 300 percent increase in the last twenty-five years. One of the major factors that has contributed to this dramatic growth is the influx of immigrants from Taiwan and Hong Kong in recent years. In fact, approximately 50 percent of the Chinese-Americans today are immigrants who came to the United States after the implementation of the 1965 immigration law. Some obvious questions readily come into mind when a demographic change of such magnitude has occurred. How are the immigrants adapting to their new environment? What is the response of the established members of the Chinese-American community to the new immigrants? The purpose of this note is to call attention to these issues which arose from an exploratory study in Los Angeles and San Francisco. Specifically, it seeks to point out the need to investigate the effect of migration patterns on adaptation, the effect of community organization on adaptation and the impact of immigrants on the social economic life of Chinatown (Hong).

Reference
Lawrence K. Hong, "Recent Immigrants in the Chinese-American Community: Issues of Adaptations and Impacts," *International Migration Review* 10 (Winter 1978): 509–514.

F.C.

CHINESE PRESBYTERIAN MISSION HOME. *See* Donaldina Cameron Home.

CHINMOK-HOE. *See* Koreans.

CHISHOLM, SHIRLEY. *See* West Indian Immigrants.

CHURCH WORLD SERVICE, IMMIGRATION AND REFUGEE PROGRAM. *See* Refugees, Church World Service.

CIRCOLO ITALIANO. *See* Covello, Leonard.

[CITIZENS' ASSOCIATION OF NEW YORK]. Report of the Council of Hygiene and Public Health of the Citizens' Association of New York Upon the Sanitary Conditions of the City (1866; rpt. 1974). Provides one of the most detailed descriptions of the physical condition of an American city in the mid-nineteenth century and the conditions under which immigrants lived. The Citizens' Association, a group of prominent New Yorkers who aimed to work for "municipal reform and public improvement," conducted this study as a result of mob violence in slum and immigrant areas in the summer of 1863. Results of the study indicated that New York City's high mortality rate (the highest in the country and higher even than London's and Liverpool's) was related to overcrowding and lack of proper ventilation and sunshine in slum areas. Topography, drainage and sewage, conditions of streets, number and type of houses, courts and alleys, brothels, saloons, stores and markets, stables, churches and schools, the character of the population, the condition of sanitation and amount of sickness in tenement houses, and the source of preventable disease in each district of the city are detailed in the report. The report had its effect; shortly after its publication, New York City organized a Board of Health and passed a tenement house law.

F.C.

CITIZENSHIP Determinations. Some ten years after *Perez* v. *Brownell* (356 U.S. 44), a majority of the Supreme Court, in *Afroyim* v. *Rusk* (387 U.S. 253), decided that the minority in *Perez* was right after all. But in holding that a U.S. citizen (at least a citizen "born or naturalized in the United States") has "a constitutional right to remain a citizen in a free country unless he voluntarily relinquishes that citizenship," the Court provided little in the way of guidance for determining what constitutes voluntary relinquishment. This task was left to the administering agencies—the Department of State and the Department of Justice. And there were widely differing views within and between those departments as to what *Afroyim* meant.

Reference
Frederick Smith, Jr., "The Department of State and U.S. Consular Officers Abroad in Citizenship Determinations," *International Migration Review* 5 (Winter 1971): 436–446.

                                                                F.C.

CITIZENSHIP, illegal aliens in American polity. Schuck and Smith take as their point of departure a situation they consider anomalous if not absurd—that under current law children born in the United States to illegal aliens are decreed citizens. To explain and respond to this odd situation, they trace the history of doctrines of citizenship in the United States well back into its English common-law antecedents. They identify two strands of thought and practice on citizenship—one based on ascriptive principles that supports a birthright standard, and one based on consensualist principles that supports a standard more sensitive to the wishes of potential citizens and to the community. The authors trace these two strands through American history and law, arguing that the two have coexisted in uneasy combinations, but that the time has come to move toward a more consistent legal standard, one based on the consensualist viewpoint.

Reference
Peter H. Schuck and Roger M. Smith, *Citizenship Without Consent: Illegal Aliens in the American Polity* (1985).

                                                                F.C.

CLAN NA GAEL. An Irish-American revolutionary organization founded in New York City in 1867 by former Fenians. It was a nonsectarian secret society that advocated the use of armed force to secure Irish freedom. The clan has been involved in all phases of the Irish struggle from the Irish National Land League of the 1880s to the Easter Uprising of 1916 and on to the present situation in northeast Ireland. During the Land War, the clan operated a front group in the United States, the Irish National Land League of America, that publicized the case against landlordism and raised large amounts of money to help evicted peasants. Beginning in 1916 the Friends of Irish Freedom, another clan front group, raised large sums of money for use in the struggle against British rule in Ireland. Although the Clan na Gael today is small compared to other Irish groups, it was the most important Irish Nationalist organization in American history.

References
S. Cronin, ed., *The McGarrity Papers* (1972); J. Devoy, *Recollections of an Irish Rebel* (1929); L. O'Broin, *Revolutionary Underground: The Story of the Irish Republican Brotherhood 1858–1924* (1976).

S.P.M.

CLOPPER, EDWARD N. (1879–1953). Administrator, child welfare reformer. Clopper was a longtime secretary of the National Child Labor Committee which was organized in 1904 "to investigate child labor [for the most part, immigrant progeny], report the facts and promote protective legislation." He conducted many of the committee's early child studies, and his *Child Labor in City Streets* (1912; rpt. 1974) draws parallels between children's street work and other problems, compares the extent of children's street labor in the United States to comparable work in Europe, and discusses the regulation of street trading here and abroad. Chief work: *Society and the Child* (1929).

F.C.

COLOMBIAN EMIGRATION, quantitative extent. An important enquiry (*infra*) which has two objectives. One is to provide a brief overview of quantitative estimates of Colombian emigration, including formal attempts to estimate the volume of net emigration. The second objective is to update the existing estimates with more recent data (in a highly speculative fashion). The goals of the note are modest; there is an attempt to summarize existing evidence while providing a brief discussion of how the estimates were prepared. Some of the estimates discussed involve a very laborious methodology impossible to summarize in a few paragraphs. The ultimate goal of the exercise is to derive a "plausible" estimate of the extent of Colombian net emigration in 1980, although no claim is made that this estimate is correct or final. A more definitive estimate will not be available until after the careful and detail evaluation of the 1980 round of censuses, although even these data will fail to yield answers to many questions related to the volume of Colombian emigration.

Reference
Sergio Diaz Briquets and Melinda J. Frederick, "Columbian Emigration: A Research

Note on Its Probable Quantitative Extent," *International Migration Review* 18 (Spring 1984): 99–110.

F.C.

COLORADO: 1903 AND 1913–14 LABOR STRIKES. *See* Jones, Mary Harris.

COLORADO COAL STRIKE (1913–14). On September 23, 1913, nine thousand coal miners of southern Colorado launched one of the most bitter strikes in American history. Striking for recognition of the United Mine Workers' Union, the miners were convinced that their political and social freedom, as well as their economic welfare, had for too long rested upon an industrial despotism—a despotism that was not always benevolent and seldom very wholesome. The strikers included immigrant workers.

Reference
George S. McGovern, "The Colorado Coal Strike, 1913–1914," Ph.D. dissertation, Northwestern University, 1953 (DA 13: 1166).

F.C.

COLORADO FUEL AND IRON COMPANY WORKS. *See* Ludlow Massacre.

COLORADO RURAL LEGAL SERVICES. *See* Guatemalan Refugees.

COMMISSION ON POPULATION GROWTH. *See* Immigration Recommendations, Commission on Population Growth.

COMMITTEE FOR IMMIGRANTS IN AMERICA (New York City). *See* Kellor, Frances.

COMMITTEE ON PUBLIC INFORMATION. *See* Americanization Movement.

COMMITTEE ON WOMEN'S WORK (New York City). *See* Van Kleek, Mary.

COMMONS, JOHN ROGERS (1862–1945). Labor historian, founder of international economics, and formulator of labor legislation. Professor of political economy at the University of Wisconsin, 1904–1932. Principal works: (ed.), *Documentary History of American Industrial Society* (10 vols., 1910–11) and *Races and Immigrants in America*

(1907; rev. ed. 1920), in which he rejected the egalitarian idealism of the Progressivism (*q.v.*) of the early twentieth century and sought to isolate and classify racial characteristics among industrial groups and to evaluate their effect on the organizational life of trade unions and sections of the economy. Commons dogmatically established categories of "inferiority" and "superiority," and called for immigration restriction, fearing an immigrant "degraded peasantry" which would cause class divisions and endanger free institutions.

References
Roy L. Garis, *Immigration Restriction* (1927); John Higham, *Strangers in the Land: Patterns of American Nativism, 1860–1925. Corrected and with a new Preface* (1973).

F.C.

COMMUNITY SERVICE SOCIETY (New York City). A nonprofit, nonsectarian social agency whose origins in New York City go back to 1843; it is devoted to the improvement of family and community. The society's published reports and archives constitute an invaluable resource on the immigrant poor of New York City from the society's earliest efforts down to the present. The CSS was the successor to the Association for Improving the Condition of the Poor (AICP) founded in 1843, and the Charity Organization Society (COS) founded in 1882. The CSS was formed in 1939 by the union of the AICP and the COS.

Reference
Lilian Brandt, *Growth and Development of the A.I.C.P. and C.O.S.: A Preliminary and Exploratory Review* (1942).

F.C.

COMPULSORY EDUCATION ACT (New York City). *See* Immigrant Children in the Schools.

CONFERENCE ON THE CARE OF DEPENDENT CHILDREN (1909). Convened by President Theodore Roosevelt, this conference brought together practically every leading social reformer of the Progressive period. Their proposals for treating an estimated 168,000 (mostly immigrant) needy and institutionalized children helped to revolutionize practices, and indicated that, for the first time, poverty would not be reason enough to break up a family.

Reference
[Conference on the Care of Dependent Children], *Proceedings of the Conference on the Care of Dependent Children, Held at Washington, D.C., January 25, 1909,* 60th Congress, 2d Session, Senate Document No. 721 (Rpt. 1971).

F.C.

CONGREGATION SHEARITH ISRAEL (New York City). *See* Noah, Mordecai M[anuel].

CONSAG, FERNANDO. *See* Croatians.

CONSOLIDATED CHINESE BENEVOLENT ASSOCIATION. *See* Chinese.

CONSTITUTIONAL SOCIETY OF 1784. *See* Mazzei, Philip.

CONSUMERS' LEAGUE OF OHIO (1909–1937). The league progressed from voluntary, private efforts to political action in the fields of immigrant child and women's labor. The wartime emergency actually furthered these causes in Ohio, and the league continued to press for advances in these areas in the 1920s and 1930s.

Reference
Dennis Irven Harrison, "The Consumers' League of Ohio: Women and Reform, 1909–1937," Ph.D. dissertation, Case Western Reserve University, 1975.

F.C.

CONTESSA ENTELLINA. *See* Italian-Albanians.

COOK, JAMES. *See* Hawaiians.

COOLIE TRADE. The selling and buying of Chinese laborers who were shipped from China to many parts of the world to be employed in raising coffee, sugar, and other agricultural crops. Scholars equate the coolie trade with the slave trade of Chinese laborers. The coolie trade as a means of sending Chinese laborers abroad should be separated from the contract labor system through which Chinese obtained their entry into Hawaii, the U.S. mainland, and other parts of the world.

The Western powers began to have labor shortage problems as native populations in their colonies either refused to cooperate with them or were wiped out. The labor shortage problem was exacerbated in 1862 when the slave trade was banned internationally. Westerners then looked to China as a source of cheap labor. The coolie trade was a means of replacing black slave laborers with Chinese.

As early as 1810 Chinese laborers were shipped to the Western Hemisphere. The large-scale migration of Chinese to the Western Hemisphere occurred in the late 1840s, as a result of the discovery of gold in California in 1848 and the need for cheap labor in South America. Chinese laborers who were drawn to California were voluntary immigrants who came as contract laborers and acquired their passage to

California on credit to be paid off through their hard labor. A minority of them worked in gold mines; the majority of them held domestic or menial jobs.

The coolie trade, the business of selling and buying Chinese laborers who very often were deceived into signing work contracts that made them no better than slaves, began in 1847, when the first shipment of Chinese laborers to Peru left Macao. Macao served as a center of Chinese immigration to Southeast Asia, and subsequently in the next twenty-nine years, Cuba imported 150,000 and Peru 74,000 Chinese coolies. The business of buying and selling Chinese laborers began to draw the attention of American officials in both China and Washington, D.C. American authorities were embarrassed by the participation of American ships in transporting Chinese laborers, and Congress passed a law prohibiting the participation of American ships and citizens in the coolie trade in February 1862. However, American ships continued to engage in the trade even after this law was passed. The coolie trade continued until the early 1870s, when Yung Wing was appointed to investigate the coolie traffic; he presented data delineating the abuse of Chinese laborers to the Peruvian commissioner. The Ch'ing government banned the coolie traffic, and the Portuguese authorities in Macao also outlawed it in 1874.

References
Robert L. Irick, *Ch'ing Policy Toward the Coolie Trade, 1847–1878;* Hyung-Chan Kim, *Dictionary of Asian American History* (1986).

D.N.A.

COOLIE TRADE, Act to Prohibit the Coolie Trade by American Citizens in American Vessels (1862). Passed by the Congress February 19, 1862, and signed by President Abraham Lincoln. It ended the "coolie trade." *See* Coolie Trade.

Reference
Robert L. Irick, *Ch'ing Policy Toward the Coolie Trade, 1847–1878* (1982).

D.N.A.

COOTE, WILLIAM. *See* White Slave Trade.

CORNISH. Immigrants to the United States from Cornwall, the eighty-mile long peninsula and most southwestern county of England.

Emigration out of Cornwall began as early as the 1830s, with settlement in the United States largely in the Upper Mississippi Valley where Cornishmen followed traditional occupations in mining, agriculture, and fishing. The devastating collapse of the copper-mining industry in Cornwall in the 1860s caused large-scale emigration overseas, principally to the United States and Australia. In American immigration records, Cornish migrants were classified as English or British. Given this, and extensive re-migration, it is difficult to estimate the number of Cornish and their descendants in the United States. Intermarriage with other English-speaking peoples resulted in a further loss of Cornish identity. Estimates of the number of Cornish Americans range from 100,000 (before World War I) to some quarter million in the 1980s.

In some old mining areas (*e.g.*, Grass Valley, California, and Butte City, Montana) there is still a distinctly Cornish population, but continuing exhaustion of the copper and iron deposits of the Lake Superior region has significantly reduced the predominantly Cornish population in this region.

References
A. L. Rowse, *The Cousin Jacks: The Cornish in America* (1969); John Rowe, *The Hard-Rock Men: Cornish Immigrants and the North American Mining Frontier* (1974); Shirley Ewart, *Cornish Mining Families of Grass Valley, California* (1987).

F.C.

CORSI, EDWARD (1896–1965). Lawyer, government official. Corsi served as a member of the staff of Haarlem House (*q.v.*), and as its director. In 1931 he was appointed commissioner of immigration at Ellis Island (*q.v.*) by President Herbert Hoover, and in 1933 was appointed commissioner of immigration and naturalization by President Franklin D. Roosevelt. During World War II, Corsi served as chairman of the Alien Enemy Hearing Board, Southern District of New York; and in 1954–55, he served as special assistant to the U.S. secretary of state for refugee and migration problems. Chief writings: *In the Shadow of Liberty: The Chronicle of Ellis Island* (1935); *Pathways to the New World* (1940); *Paths to the New World: American Immigration, Yesterday, Today and Tomorrow* (1953).

Reference
Robert Thibault, comp., *Edward Corsi: Inventory of His Papers, Syracuse University Library* (1969).

F.C.

COSTA RICANS. *See* Central Americans.

COUNTS, GEORGE S[YLVESTER] (1889–1974). Educator, social reformer; professor at Teachers College, Columbia University; president of the American Federation of Teachers, 1939–1942. His primary interest was in the reformation of the education of the immigrant child.

Chief works: *The Social Composition of Board of Education* (1927), which deals with the socioeconomic stratification of social class representation on boards, and the exclusion of laboring classes; *The American Road to Culture* (1930); *The Prospects of American Democracy* (1938); *The Challenge of Soviet Education* (1957); and *Education and the Foundations of Human Freedom* (1962).

Reference
Gerald L. Gutek, *The Educational Theory of George S. Counts* (1971).

F.C.

COVELLO, LEONARD (1887–1982). Educator. Leonard Covello was born on November 26, 1887 in Avigliano (Potenza) Italy, and brought in 1895 to the United States by his emigrating parents, who settled in East Harlem. Leonard Covello's life (and the forces that influenced it) are inextricably linked to East Harlem, an immigrant enclave located in the northeast sector of Manhattan Island, New York City (the 1930 census indicated a total of 89,000 first- and second-generation Italians living in East Harlem). It was here that he went to school (P.S. 83 and Morris High School), and here that he was to spend nearly a quarter-century (1934–1956) as principal of Benjamin Franklin High School. Following graduation from Columbia College (B.S., 1911), Leonard Covello served as a teacher of French and Spanish at De Witt Clinton High School (his teaching began as early as 1913), and from 1926 to 1934 he served at De Witt Clinton as chairman of the Department of Italian. It was from De Witt Clinton in 1934 that he went on to the principalship of Benjamin Franklin High School. As early as 1930 he had matriculated for the Ph.D. at New York University, and he achieved the degree in 1944 (educational sociology); his thesis was *The Social Background of the Italo-American School Child* (1967; 1972), the massive sociocultural chronicle that had taken over a decade to write. Between 1929 and 1942, Covello taught as an adjunct professor at New York University where his course "The Social Background and Educational Problems of the Italian Family in America" represented the earliest systematic enquiry (at the university level) of Italian family mores in the United States.

Leonard Covello touched the life of the Italian community in New York City in a variety of ways: there was virtually no activity organized by Italians in which Dr. Covello did not participate. As early as 1910, he (with John Shedd) organized the Lincoln Club of Little Italy in East Harlem. At De Witt Clinton High School, a Circolo Italiano was established as early as 1914 under Dr. Covello's sponsorship; and he participated in the work of the Italian League for Social Service (organized in 1915), and the Young Men's Italian Educational League (organized in

1916), energetically ambitious early efforts to improve the lot of Italian-Americans. From its inception in 1912, Dr. Covello served as vice-president of the Italian Teachers Association [New York City], a major force in stimulating Italian-language study; and he was the guiding force behind the Italian Parents Association (organized in 1927) which afforded a bridge between the schools and the Italian community. It was Dr. Covello's strategic deployment of the influence of the Order Sons of Italy which helped lead in 1922 to the New York City Board of Education granting parity to Italian with other modern languages in the city schools. And there were continuing involvements and participations: in the work of the Italian Educational League; the Italy-America Society; the Casa Italiana Educational Bureau; and the Istituto di Cultura Italiana (later, the Casa Italiana of Columbia University); and it was Dr. Covello who provided the major impetus for the founding of the American Italian Historical Association in the mid-1960s (whose operating expenses he assumed for several years in a lonely vigil passed in an East Harlem brownstone, as though awaiting the Italian community, long since gone, to be reborn).

In a somewhat belated tribute, Columbia University conferred its "Medal for Distinguished Service" on Dr. Covello. Although the laconic commendation studiously avoided the use of words like "immigrant" or "Italian," the tenor of its message was clear—the university was honoring a distinguished alumnus whose professional life had been spent in the service of the immigrant poor:

> Declared by generations of his professional peers to be one of New York City's greatest educators, having demonstrated a quarter of a century ago that a large urban high school can serve its whole community; a man who throughout his career as teacher, principal and consultant has demonstrated the vitality of our great ideal of equal, excellent, integrated education for people of all races, creeds and conditions: For your tireless and continuing efforts to bring schools and communities together in the service of all children and youth, Teachers College [Columbia University] confers upon you its Medal for Distinguished Service.

In 1972, Leonard Covello accepted an invitation from Danilo Dolci, the Sicilian social reformer, to serve as a consultant to Dolci's Center for Study and Action in western Sicily, where the center is waging a militant crusade against disease, unemployment, hunger, illiteracy, and violence. Leonard Covello died in Messina, Sicily, on August 19, 1982.

References
Francesco Cordasco, ed., *Studies in Italian American Social History: Essays in Honor of*

Leonard Covello (1975); Leonard Covello, *The Heart Is The Teacher* (1958; rpt. 1970); Robert Peebles, *Leonard Covello* (1978); *Register of Leonard Covello Papers, 1907–1974*, Balch Institute, Philadelphia, 1982.

F.C.

CREDINTA. *See* Romanians.

CREOLES. In its original and most prevalent usage, the term "Creole" refers to a person of European ancestry born in a New World colony of Spain, Portugal, or France. Over time, however, the word came to take on a great variety of variant and subsidiary meanings, such that a single, precise definition is impossible to construct. One close student of the concept has noted that the term "Creole" has "assumed an incalculable number of meanings" (Oudaka, 3) depending on the circumstances of its use and the intent of the user. It is thus a slippery concept, and often misunderstood.

Etymology. The word "Creole" derived from the Latin "Creare" ("to create or originate"), and came into popular use in Spanish ("Criollo") and in Portuguese ("Crioulo") at the outset of the seventeenth century with the meaning noted above. When the French joined the quest for colonial possessions in the New World the term "Creole" came to be used in its French form, carrying the same meaning. But by the mid-seventeenth century the word began to take on a variety of subsidiary implications. For example, in that "Creoles" were by definition distinct from indigenous native colonial populations, the implication developed that such persons were socially superior within the resident colonial social order. Another subsidiary implication suggested that "Creole" referred to *any* population element that was not endemic to the colony, e.g., that persons of African ancestry born in the colonies were also "Creoles," as were colonial populations of genetically mixed ancestry, regardless of provenance. This implication was commonly accepted by the early eighteenth century. Finally, the term took on a set of meanings associated with the *cultures* of societies dominated by "Creole" populations (of whatever sort), such that the notion of "Creole societies" emerged, and the terminology came into common use. Within such societies, Creole populations tended to identify themselves and to be identified by others as specific ethnic populations, manifesting identifiable cultures. At the same time, the adjectival usage of the word "Creole" was expanded to include various products or culture elements associated with ethnic Creoles, including their *languages*, which were produced primarily by way of linguistic blending of European and African language elements within a colonial setting. In this sense, "Creole" was used to refer to a language proper (e.g., "Haitian Creole") as well as to the people speaking the language. Similarly, the distinctive cuisine that developed in a Creole society, normally a blend of European and colonial forms of food preparation, was frequently termed "Creole." Finally, New World colonial *products* were often identified as "Creole" (e.g., "Creole cane," "Creole oranges"). By the late eighteenth century, then, the term had come to mean many different things depending on the context in which it was used.

Colonial Louisiana. French colonization of the northern Gulf of Mexico (beginning in 1699) produced yet another New World Creole population, one that would ultimately come to form an ethnic group within the United States. The initial usage of the term in French Colonial Louisiana was similar to the earlier European usages, i.e., the self-defined French "Creole" element perceived itself as genetically European, culturally distinctive, and patently of higher social status than other resident colonial population elements. During the years of Spanish control in Louisiana (1763–1802), French-speaking whites of Spanish ancestry also came to be included in the self-styled European Creole population of the colony. But in the later eighteenth century, Creole had come to be applied to the genetically mixed, French-speaking Afro-European population that also saw itself as a distinctive, relatively high-status group, at least within the black population. This was especially true in the New Orleans area, though several enclaves of such "Creoles of color" settled in outlying rural communities as well.

Creoles in the United States. When the United States purchased Louisiana in 1803, the white Creoles still constituted a self-aware, distinctive group, whose members saw themselves as the social and political leaders of the region, even as the Anglo-American population increased in numbers, wealth, and ultimately power in the nineteenth century. The "Creoles of color," however, also continued to manifest their own version of Creole culture, and throughout the nineteenth century miscegenation among the various French-speaking peoples yielded additional genetic blending within this Creole element. Ironically, while many genetically mixed people thus termed themselves "Creole," white Creoles continued to insist that "Creoles" by definition had to be genetically "pure" Caucasians of European descent. In the United States, then, as elsewhere, the term referred to several different groups as well as to their ethnic cultures, and thus continued to be situationally defined.

Creoles Today. While the Louisiana Creoles (of all sorts) constitute the major Creole populations of the United States, the tendency over the years was toward greater acculturation to American norms. American cultural hegemony had come to prevail by the mid-nineteenth century, and the Creoles continued to blend into the generalized American population, leaving only vestigial shadows of their former distinctive cultures. This was especially true of the white Creoles. Though they remained Roman Catholic, most white Creoles began to use English as their primary language, and other distinctive cultural elements gave way to the acculturation process as well. Creole cuisine, however, featuring the use of tomatoes, okra, green peppers, and onions in spicy combinations with seafood and rice, persisted in Louisiana and the southern Gulf. And among the "Creoles of color" (they normally referred to themselves simply as "Creoles"), group identity has also persisted. The French language ("Creole French") has been maintained, as have certain other distinctive cultural elements. Prominent among these survivals is a musical form ("Zydeco") that combines elements of jazz, blues, and Cajun French music in a characteristically "Creole" blend. Beyond this, there is little that remains of the Creole cultures that once were so prominent in the region. Even so, the Louisiana Creoles represent historically significant populations that contributed substantially to the development of the distinctive culture of Louisiana and the southern American Gulf today.

References
George W. Cable, *The Creoles of Louisiana* (1885); Virginia R. Dominguez, *White by Definition: Social Classification in Creole Louisiana* (1986); Dell Hymes, ed., *Pidginization and Creolization of Languages* (1971); Gary B. Mills, *The Forgotten People: Cane River's Creoles of Color* (1977); Larbi Oukada, *Louisiana French: An Annotated Bibliography* (1979).

J.H.D.

CRÈVECOEUR, MICHEL-GUILLAUME JEAN DE (1735–1813). Essayist, traveler. Crèvecoeur, born in Normandy in 1735, is the source of much of our knowledge of the British colonies in North America in the eighteenth century. He went to New York in 1759 and became a naturalized American citizen in 1765, having acquired a farm near Chester, New York. He also served under Montcalm and saw something of the Great Lakes and the outlying country. Crèvecoeur tells of frontier and farm; the life of Nantucket fishermen and their wives; the life of the Middle Colonies. Far removed from the fashionable cities of London and Paris, he must not, however, be thought of as an unlettered and unfeeling colonial. Simply and expressively, he transmits in *Letters from an American Farmer* (1782) his pictures of the early America and, with its story of an energetic people bent on rapid growth, his account of the pioneer age caught the imagination of countless contemporaries; it is a record that is still invaluable today:

> The *Letters* has been valued chiefly as a document in social history, while its irony and subtleties, its stature as a work of art, have been overlooked. Only in the last decade has there been a serious effort to revise the traditional estimate. A convincing case has

begun to emerge for reading the *Letters* as a novel in epistolary form, with James the American Farmer as protagonist instead of simply the author's transparent persona. One important consequence of such a reappraisal is that if correct it establishes Crèvecoeur as the first novelist to write in America. (Gilmore, xix)

References
J. Hector St. John de Crèvecoeur, *Letters From an American Farmer*, with an Introduction by Michael T. Gilmore (1971); Thomas Philbrick, *St. John de Crevecoeur* (1970).

F.C.

CRITTENTON, CHARLES NELSON (1833–1909). Philanthropist. In 1883, Crittenton founded the Florence Crittenton Mission in New York City for the rescue of prostitutes and wayward girls, many of whom were immigrant women. Under the leadership of Kate Waller Barrett (1858–1925), Crittenton's assistant and successor as president of the National Mission, the homes became refuges for expectant unwed mothers. By 1933 there were sixty-five Florence Crittenton Homes located across the country.

Reference
Otto Wilson, *Fifty Years' Work with Girls, 1883–1933: A Story of the Florence Crittenton Homes* (1933; rpt. 1974).

F.C.

CROATIANS. A South Slavic people, the Croatians inhabit the western parts of the Balkan Peninsula in southeast Europe. They have lived since the 600s along the Adriatic Sea from the vicinity of Trieste (in the north) almost to the borders of Albania (in the south).

First under their dukes, and after 925 under their kings, the Croatians had their own independent state, with a strong army and navy. They were able to repulse all foreign invasions. Croatia was located at the crossroads of the East (with Byzantine and Near Eastern influences) and the West (with Roman-Latin influences). Following the fall of their medieval state, Croatia joined in 1102 in union with Hungary. The Croatian Bosnian state existed until 1463. Then the Ottoman Turks gradually occupied Bosnia, Herzegovina, and large sections of western and northern Croatia. In the early 1500s the Croatian Diet elected the Habsburgs as rulers of Croatia. Preserving all the time the vestiges of their statehood the Croatians remained under the Habsburg rule until 1918.

During their rule and incessant warfare the Turks deported from Croatian lands about two million people as slaves and prisoners of war. Due to the Turkish, Venetian, and other invasions Croatia was partitioned into the following parts which were ruled by the Turks until

1878: Croatia proper (with Sriem or Syrmium); Dalmatia, Istria (in the Adriatic region); and Bosnia-Herzegovina.

Many Croatian settlements are also located in adjacent areas: Baranja, Baćka (former southern Hungary), and Sanjak, east of Bosnia-Herzegovina. Numerous settlements have existed since the early 1500s in western parts of Hungary, eastern Austria (Burgenland), Lower Austria, Slovakia, and as far south as southern Italy.

In December 1918, following the destruction of Austria-Hungary, the Croatian lands were forcibly absorbed by the Serbian-dominated South Slavic State (known as Yugoslavia since 1929). From April 1941 until May 1945, during the turbulent times of World War II, the Independent State of Croatia existed. The Communist forces, led by Josip Broz-Tito, with the help of Western Allies, finally crushed the Croatian resistance. In May 1945 the Croatian lands were incorporated in a Communist Yugoslavia, officially known as the Socialist Federal Republic of Yugoslavia.

During centuries of warfare, in two world wars, and after the tragic spring of 1945, hundreds of thousands perished. In addition, many lost their lives as soldiers in foreign armies.

The flight and migrations, caused by wars and foreign invasions, had been going on since the 1400s. The Adriatic Sea connected Croatia with the entire world. As excellent sailors the Croatians, on the ships of the ancient Republic of Dubrovnik (Ragusa), and from other Adriatic ports, had navigated to the shores of Spanish America and other parts of the world ever since the early 1500s. All these overseas and overland migrations made Croatia a typical nation of emigrants. From the 1500s to the end of the 1800s many of them arrived as immigrants on the Atlantic and Pacific shores of South and North America. While thousands of Croatian Christians entered foreign services in various European countries, many thousands of Croatian Muslims spread the glory of the Ottoman Empire.

In the Americas well over a million Croatians have settled during the past four centuries. The mass immigration, mostly of peasants, to the United States took place from the 1890s until 1914. After 1945 close to 100,000 entered the United States; over 25,000 immigrated to Canada; some 15,000 found home in Argentina; several thousands were dispersed in various Latin American countries, while thousands of Croatian Muslims found refuge in the Middle East. A high percentage of post–World War II immigrants were refugees, political exiles, and "displaced persons."

In the exodus of the 1950s–1970s over 700,000 left Croatia for several Western European countries, Australia, and other parts of the world. More than 100,000 emigrated to the countries of the Middle East (Croatian Muslims). All these migrations were caused by grave political and economic conditions in Croatia. Whole regions became depopulated. In foreign lands the old Croatian diaspora continued and by the new influx was revived and expanded. Today almost every third Croatian lives abroad.

On account of Eastern and Western influences the Croatians belong to three major religions. Close to 70 percent are members of the Roman Catholic church; about 20 percent profess Islam (mostly in Bosnia-Herzegovina); and some 10 percent are Eastern Orthodox. In modern times thousands of Croatians have belonged to various Protestant denominations and Judaism.

Historical and ethnic Croatian lands constitute an area of approximately 111,000 square kilometers or 43,000 square miles (this is about the size of Pennsylvania). Not included here are Croatian ethnic territories in Bačka and Sanjak. There are in present Yugoslavia over 6.5 million Croatians (Catholic, Muslim, and others). Among 1.2 million "Yugoslavs" counted in the 1981 census a considerable number of people are of Croatian nationality. The same census reveals the fact that there were about 100,000 fewer Croatians than in 1971, which is a result of exodus to foreign lands.

Over 1.5 million Croatian immigrants and their descendants live in the United States, with over 100,000 in Canada, some 200,000 in Argentina, and some 50,000 scattered in several Latin American countries.

These sturdy, hard-working, adventurous, and enterprising people have contributed to their new homelands their skills, intelligence, talents, blood, and in thousands of instances their lives; in southern and western parts of the United States the Croatians have been doing this for the past hundred and fifty years. The greatest contributors were the anonymous immigrants: sailors, fishermen, laborers, ranchers, fruit growers, men of various trades and skills.

Rev. Fernando Consag (Konšćak), S.J., who died in Baja California in 1759, opened the road for the conquest of California by his explorations and maps. Today the most successful and wealthiest American Croatians live in large numbers in California.

The largest Croatian settlements are in Pittsburgh, New York, Cleveland, Chicago, Los Angeles, and San Francisco. A majority of the Croatians live in the East, Midwest, and West; however, thousands are scattered all over the country, including Alaska. Their heavy concentrations are in centers with heavy industry, steel, iron, construction, and mining.

Nikola Tesla (1856–1943), the electrical genius and the greatest inventor of our time, helped lay the foundations of an industrialized modern America. It can be said that since his arrival in 1884 the Croatians have come a long way.

Captain Anthony Lucas (Lučić) (1853–1921) struck oil at Spindletop, Texas in January of 1901. He ushered in a new era in the huge American oil industry. In other industries his countrymen worked and died by the hundreds. The Croatian contribution in steel is epitomized by the saga of Joe Magarac, the steelman, now a part of American folklore.

Ivan Meštrović (1883–1962), the internationally famous sculptor, was the greatest Croatian contribution to fine arts of America. Maxo Vanka (1890–1963) will forever be remembered for his tremendous murals in a Croatian church in Millvale, Pennsylvania. And there have been other sculptors and painters along with these that contributed their genius and talent to the operatic arts, music, and ballet.

America was also enriched by the contribution of thousands of Croatian scholars, teachers, librarians, scientists, engineers, architects, shipbuilders, mechanics, skilled industrial workers, priests, fruit growers, wine makers, and members of other occupations, trades, and professions. Thousands of highly educated and professional people have arrived here since 1950. They established themselves successfully and have made a real impact on this country, its progress, and civilization.

During the past 130 years the Croatians formed virtually hundreds of societies and fraternal, cultural, and political organizations and clubs. The Croatian Fraternal Union, founded in 1894, is the largest organization. In existence are several hundreds of national homes, halls, centers, and recreational facilities, approximately sixty Catholic churches, parishes, rectories, and convents, along with about twenty parochial schools. In addition, some 250 different newspapers, periodicals, almanacs, and magazines have emerged since 1884, when the first paper appeared. About two dozen exist today.

The Croatians have created a whole literature of their own both in Croatian and English. Folklore, folk arts, and ethnic studies have been stimulated by the continual influx of new immigrants and new trends in ethnicity and multiculturalism. There are presently more tamburitza, singing, dancing, and folklore groups than ever before. The Cultural Junior Federation of the CFU has been staging huge annual festivals with singing, dancing and music by many hundreds of youngsters in beautiful national costumes. Croatian folk arts are indeed thriving as proved by many concerts, festivals, and exhibits.

In politics too, the Croatians are now making their impact. The first governor of Alaska was Mike Stepovich; a late congressman of Alaska was Nick Begich. The present governor of Minnesota is Rudy Perpich.

Among scholarly organizations are: the Croatian Academy of America (now thirty years old) and the Association for Croatian Studies. One of the more recently formed political organizations is the Croatian National Congress.

References
Gerald G. Govorchin, *Americans from Yugoslavia* (1961); George J. Prpic, *Croatian Immigrants in America* (1971), *Croatian Publications Abroad After 1939: A Bibliography* (1969), *Croatia and Croatians: An Annotated and Selected Bibliography in English* (1972), and *South Slavic Immigration in America* (1978).

G.J.P.

CUBAN AND MEXICAN IMMIGRANTS, data from longitudinal survey. This volume presents research data from a longitudinal survey of legally admitted Cuban and Mexican adult males. Waves of the survey were conducted in 1973, 1976, and 1979. As important as the data are, however, this volume's significance also lies in its carefully crafted inferences drawn from competing theoretical perspectives. It draws on a variety of labor market, ethnic relations, and immigration theories to develop testable hypotheses, and notes significant theoretical gaps. Immigrants, as opposed to ethnic groups, are included in most theories only through analogical reasoning: in dual market theories, immigrants are more like secondary workers. In middleman theories, they are less like native-born minorities. In split labor market theories, they are more like some groups and less like others. In assimilation theories, they are less like, on their way to becoming more like, the native born. The authors exploit contradictions and conflicting predictions to generate their hypotheses.

Reference
Alejandro Portes and Robert L. Bach, *Latin Journey: Cuban and Mexican Immigrants in the United States* (1983).

F.C.

CUBAN EXILES, refugee migration. Pedraza-Bailey provides a portrait of Cuba's exiles that encompasses all their waves of migration, while utilizing the Cuban exodus to shed light on the broader phenomenon of refugee migration. She argues that to understand the changing social characteristics of the exiles over twenty years of migration, we need to understand the changing phases of the Cuban revolution. Utilizing the Cuban exodus as data, she uses Egon F. Kunz's theoretical framework for refugee migration to shed light on the refugees' varying experiences, while also using the actual Cuban refugee experience to react to Kunz's abstract model.

Reference
Silvia Pedraza-Bailey, "Cuba's Exiles: Portrait of a Refugee Migration," *International Migration Review* 19 (Spring 1985): 4–34.

F.C.

CUBAN EXILES, rise of ethnicity. Portes traces the evolution of perceptions of social distance and discrimination by the host society among members of a recently arrived foreign minority. Determinants of these perceptions suggested by three alternative hypotheses in this area are reviewed and their effects compared empirically. Data from a longitudinal study of adult male Cuban exiles interviewed at the time of arrival in the United States and again three and six years later are presented. The results suggest a significant rise in perceptions of social distance and discrimination from low initial levels and a consistent association of such perceptions with variables suggested by the ethnic resilience perspective.

Reference
Alejandro Portes, "The Rise of Ethnicity: Determinants of Ethnic Perceptions Among Cuban Exiles in Miami," *American Sociological Review* 49 (June 1984): 383–397.

F.C.

CUBAN REFUGEES, administrative developments. Fragomen:

> On September 16, 1976, the Immigration and Naturalization Service announced that Cuban refugees in the United States may become permanent resident aliens without having to wait for visa numbers to become available under the Western Hemisphere quotas. Cuban refugees who in the past were paroled into the United States are now eligible to apply for adjustment of status after maintaining parole status for a minimum of two years, subject to the numerical limitation of 120,000 persons per year for natives of the Western Hemisphere. This results in delays of approximately two and one-half years and expends 30,000 to 40,000 of the 120,000 members available to qualify immigrants from the Western Hemisphere per year. Henceforth, Cuban refugees will be able to adjust status in the United States outside the Western Hemisphere numerical limitation.

Reference
Austin T. Fragomen, Jr., "Administrative Developments [regarding Cuban Refugees]," *International Migration Review* 10 (Winter 1976): 527–529.

F.C.

CUBAN REFUGEES. Michael G. Wenk, "Adjustment and Assimilation: The Cuban Refugee Experience," *International Migration Review*

3 (Fall 1968): 38–49. Study for the U.S. Catholic Conference. Questionnaires were sent to diocesan resettlement directors and directors of special Cuban refugee committees asking that they contact five Cuban families in their area at random and submit questionnaires to them concerning their experiences with the Cuban refugee program, as well as their own adjustment to life as families. Questions concerned "family mode of living, employment, income, educational status and current schooling, their reasons for coming to the United States and evidences of success or problems in adjustment."

F.C.

CUBANS. The Cuban Revolution of 1959 and its consequences have had a dramatic impact on American immigration in the second half of the twentieth century. The revolution ended the long regime of Fulgencio Batista and brought Fidel Castro to power. Most Cubans at first welcomed the new revolutionary government, but the implementation of socialist policies soon turned Cuban elites, professionals, and the urban middle class against the new Cuban order. As a result, a great human exodus began, one that brought considerably more than 800,000 Cubans to United States between 1959 and 1980. Despite federal government efforts to relocate Cuban exiles throughout the United States, most eventually settled in south Florida, particularly Miami. By the early 1970s, Miami had become the world's second largest Cuban city, smaller only than Havana.

The massive immigration of Cuban exiles since 1959 has diverted attention from earlier Cuban migration patterns. Actually, Florida had been providing a place of refuge for Cuban exiles since the late nineteenth century. In 1868, at the beginning of Cuba's Ten Years War, Cuban political exiles began migrating in large numbers to nearby Key West. Some 2,000 Cubans had settled in Florida's southernmost city by 1870, and by the mid-1880s more than 5,500 Cubans had come to Key West, where the mostly working-class newcomers established a thriving cigar industry. A similar Cuban influx to Tampa took place in the 1880s, as a second cigar-making center emerged; Tampa had almost 2,500 Cuban-born residents in 1890 and over 5,000 by 1930. A third center of Cuban emigrés grew in late nineteenth-century New York City, where Jose Martí provided exile leadership in the establishment of the Partido Revolucionario Cubano, representing a political union of Cubans in New York and Florida.

A new Cuban exile community began to emerge in Miami in the wake of the Cuban Revolution of 1933. Over 1,100 Cuban-born immigrants lived in Miami by 1940, a colony which gradually grew over the next two decades. Militant anti-Batista exiles were active in New York and Miami in the 1950s, including Fidel Castro himself. Even before the success of Castro's revolution in 1959, a concentrated area of Cuban settlement had begun to take shape in Miami's central city, and the neighborhood was already being called "Little Havana." Thus, the exiles who flowed out of Cuba in such astonishing numbers during the 1960s and 1970s were only the latest in a long line of Cubans who sought refuge in Florida and the United States. The existence of a Cuban community in nearby Miami attracted the newest exiles, and the city's nearness to Cuba made it the ideal place to wait out the Castro regime or organize for its overthrow.

The Cuban exiles came to the United States in several waves over two decades, an erratic migration flow dictated by the state of U.S.-Cuban relations at any particular time. This relationship also determined the form of the exile movement. At various times, the Cubans have arrived in Florida by boatlift, airlift, or travel through third countries.

The first great wave of Cuban exiles came to the United States by commercial aircraft between January 1959 and October 1962. Some 215,000 Cubans arrived during this period. As exiles from a Communist nation, they were granted special "parolee" status outside the regular immigration quota. The Cuban Missile Crisis in October 1962 ended this early Cuban exodus, and over the next three years only about 30,000 Cubans left the island, either by travel to third countries or in small boats and rafts. An agreement between the two nations at the end of 1965 led to an orderly resumption of Cuban exile migration. Over the next eight years, a second great wave of over 340,000 Cubans arrived in Miami by way of an airlift—two daily "freedom flights" from Cuba that brought in 3,000 to 4,000 newcomers each month.

Castro ended the airlift abruptly in 1973, and Cuban emigration drastically declined. By the end of the 1970s, only a few thousand Cubans were arriving in the United States each year, mostly as escapees in small boats or by travel to third countries such as Mexico and Spain. But in 1980, when most thought the large-scale migration of Cubans to the United States was over for good, Castro opened the exile gates once again. The Mariel boatlift of May to September 1980 brought 125,000 new Cuban exiles to Florida. This massive third wave of Cuban newcomers created controversy because Castro had loaded up the "freedom flotilla" with thousands of criminals and other "undesirables." Mariel Cubans with relatives in Florida, about half of the total number, quickly were absorbed into Miami's Cuban community. Federal officials dispersed the rest to special camps in Wisconsin, Arkansas, and Pennsylvania, but once released, most of them drifted back to Miami.

The great exodus of Cubans reflected growing disenchantment with the outcome of the Cuban Revolution. Revolutionary goals led to the expropriation of property and the redistribution of wealth. The rural poor and the urban working classes benefited from the new social policies, but established elites felt betrayed. The earliest exiles were ideological opponents of Castro; later exiles were more likely to have been initial supporters whose revolutionary zeal had been eroded by pragmatic experience in the new Cuba. More recent exiles may have been pulled more by economic opportunity in America than pushed by political or social conditions in Cuba. The early period of Cuban migration to the United States uprooted an entire business and professional class, while later refugees tended to be more similar demographically to the Cuban population as a whole. Whatever the reasons for leaving the homeland, becoming an exile usually involved a wrenching personal or family decision.

Federal policy opened the gates to the anti-Communist Cuban exiles, who entered the United States without immigration quotas or restrictions. Most of these Cuban newcomers entered the United States through Miami, which became one of the nation's chief immigration ports after 1959. Beginning in 1960, the federal government's Cuban Refugee Program (CRP) handled the actual processing and resettlement of the Cuban exiles in Miami. After initial security screening by the Immigration and Naturalization Service, the CRP's Cuban Refugee Emergency Center provided the exiles with a variety of social services, educational programs, job training and placement, and medical assistance. By 1973, more than $1 billion had been spent by the federal government to assist Cuban resettlement in the United States. The center also coordinated private aid from numerous religious and voluntary agencies. The Catholic Diocese of Miami, in particular, played an important part in Cuban refugee settlement.

One important goal of the CRP was to resettle the Cubans throughout the United States. It was believed that such a dispersal would not only relieve the economic and social burden on Miami but also speed the assimilation of the Cubans. Within two days of their arrival in Miami, tens of thousands of Cubans "were on their way to somewhere else," one journalist wrote in 1966. But Miami had a magnetic pull for the Cuban exiles, and a large portion of those resettled elsewhere eventually returned to their original port of entry.

By the 1980s, more than 60 percent of all the Cubans in the United States resided in the Miami metropolitan area. Other large residential concentrations of Cubans have emerged as well: about 50,000 in Union City and West New York, New Jersey; over 90,000 in New York City; some 30,000 in Los Angeles; and almost 25,000 in Chicago. Smaller communities of a few thousand Cubans can be found in a dozen other cities, ranging from Dallas and New Orleans to Boston and Washington. But Miami remains the preeminent center of Cuban exile life in the United States, and no other immigrant group in American history has remained so heavily concentrated in a single city.

Given the professional and business backgrounds of the early Castro-era exiles, the enormous amount of resettlement assistance, and their concentration in a single city, it is not really surprising that the Cubans have adjusted well and prospered in their new home. They have created a thriving ethnic community in Miami's Little Havana, in Hialeah, and in other sections of the Miami metropolitan area. After an initial period of adjustment, the entrepreneurial Cubans pursued the American dream of economic success with a vengeance. Numerous studies have demonstrated the rapid upward socioeconomic mobility of the early waves of Cuban exiles. In Miami they created an "enclave" economy of 25,000 businesses, ranging from retail stores, service stations, small factories, and restaurants to banks, construction companies, auto dealerships, and fishing fleets. It is also evident that the enclave economy has provided jobs for a steady succession of Cuban newcomers and contributed in important ways to Spanish-language maintenance. The Cuban presence has been largely responsible for the recent emergence of Miami as an important center of international banking, trade, and tourism.

Cubans who settled elsewhere in the United States generally have not formed distinct residential communities based on nationality. The chief exception is the Cuban community in Union City and West New York, New Jersey, where over 50,000 Cubans established another exile enclave. The New Jersey Cubans are more distinctly working class than those in Florida, but their community is residentially stable, economically prosperous, and culturally vibrant. There are some differences between the New Jersey and Florida Cuban communities, but it is even more clear that the Cubans as a group are distinctly different from other Hispanics in the United States. Despite the leveling tendency of Cuban emigration over time, the statistical evidence suggests that the Cubans have more education, better jobs, higher incomes, and lower fertility rates than the Hispanic population generally.

The massive immigration of Cubans since 1959 has had a dramatic effect on the character of politics in the south Florida area. When the Cubans first came to Miami in the 1960s, they came as exiles rather than refugees. Almost universally, they hoped to depose Fidel Castro and return to their homeland. By the early 1960s, almost 200 anti-Castro exile organizations had been established. Thus, for many years Castro and Cuba were more important to Miami's newcomers than local political issues. Because they planned to return, few became naturalized citizens at first. But by the 1970s, the hope of return had been abandoned by most. As the Cuban exiles increasingly came to view south

Florida as a permanent place of settlement, they put down roots and became citizens and voters.

Exile politics remains powerful in every Cuban community, but recent years have witnessed an important shift from exile politics to ethnic politics, particularly in south Florida. Local politics in the Miami area is now organized primarily around issues of race and ethnicity. Elections since the mid-1970s, especially on the local level, have demonstrated the growing power of the Cuban vote. By 1987, Hispanics totaled well over 50 percent of Miami's registered voters, controlled the nonpartisan city commission, and held many of the city's major administrative positions and a growing portion of municipal jobs. A Cuban-born mayor, Xavier Suarez, was elected in 1985.

At the level of partisan politics, the Cubans have permanently altered the political landscape in Florida. Traditionally, Florida was an integral part of the one-party Democratic South, but this is no longer true. The Cubans blamed the Democrats for the failure of the Bay of Pigs invasion in 1961, and the Republican party has been the beneficiary. The hard-line, anti-Castro positions of Republican presidents from Nixon to Reagan have earned solid Cuban political support in the United States. The trend is clear: increasing numbers of Cubans are becoming citizens and voters; they register and vote heavily for Republican state and national candidates. The Miami Cubans, especially, have become new players in the old game of ethnic politics. To a certain extent, the same is true for the New Jersey Cuban community, where Cuban-American Robert Menendez was elected mayor of Union City in 1986.

Scholars of the Cuban immigration experience have differed over the degree to which these newcomers have assimilated to the American mainstream. Some have argued that the Cubans have assimilated more rapidly than other groups in American history. Such studies may be far more assimilationist in orientation than present evidence warrants. To be sure, the Cubans have adjusted to life in the United States, and they have been successful economically and politically—more so than other immigrant groups at a similar stage of the adjustment/assimilation process.

But adjustment is not the same as assimilation, and Cuban Miami especially remains an active and vibrant ethnic community. The social and cultural landscape of Cuban life in the United States has been shaped by the language and religion of the homeland, as well as by Old Country family, food, and cultural patterns. The predominance of Cubans and other Hispanics in the city, along with new patterns of Latin American trade and tourism, has aided Spanish-language maintenance. Moreover, because Spanish is used extensively in such "high domains" as government and business, as well as in such "low domains" as the family, the language has remained instrumentally valuable. A recent political controversy over bilingualism in south Florida seems to have heightened Cuban cultural consciousness and the sense that the language should be preserved.

Beyond language, the Cubans have maintained their culture to an enormous degree in other ways. The Roman Catholic religion has remained as an important ingredient in Cuban-American culture. Cuban religious fervor, however, is not directed so much toward the organized church as expressed in devotions to saints and the Virgin Mary. Afro-Indian religious beliefs grafted onto Catholicism in Cuba persist in the personalized religious practices among Cubans in Miami and elsewhere. A similar pattern can be found in adherence to *santería (q.v.)*, a cult religion of Afro-Cuban origins. With its elaborate system of ceremony and ritual, magic and medicine, the practice of *santería* has surged in recent years, perhaps because of the massive wave of new Cuban exiles or perhaps because *santería* serves as a link to the Cuban past. Adherents of both Catholicism and *santería* often express their devotion by erecting yard shrines, thousands of which adorn front yards throughout the Miami area.

Similarly, Cubans in the United States have held tenaciously to their Old Country cuisine; over 1,100 Cuban groceries and restaurants in the Miami area insure its preservation. An active Cuban literary, artistic, and musical heritage prevails in south Florida and other Cuban centers. Festivals, carnivals, and parades celebrating Cuban nationality are a common event in Little Havana. The organizational life of the Cubans remains strong, with many group activities structured along the lines of old-country municipalities. Of the 126 *municipios,* or townships, in pre-Castro Cuba, some 114 are represented by exile organizations, most of which sponsor a wide range of cultural and social programs. And finally, the reality of the Castro regime, only a few hundred miles away, has kept the anti-Communist issue alive and strengthened the self-consciousness of the Cuban community. The reality of continued Hispanic migration to Miami, the possibility of future Cuban boatlifts, and the potential of future Latin American revolutions to produce new Hispanic exile communities—these suggest that pluralism will prevail in Cuban Miami, at least for the short-term future, and possibly a lot longer than that.

The Cuban exile migration to the United States is surely one of the most unique chapters in the history of American immigration. And by most measures, it would seem that the Cuban exile story has been a huge success; it clearly demonstrates how newcomers seize opportunity in America. The Mariel boatlift of 1980, with its attendant problems, represented a temporary setback, but it seems likely that most of the newest Cuban exiles will ultimately share the positive experiences of those who came in the earlier waves of Cuban immigration to the United States.

References

Thomas D. Boswell and James R. Curtis, *The Cuban American Experience* (1984); José Llanes, *Cuban Americans: Masters of Survival* (1982); Lyn MacCorkle, *Cubans in the United States: A Bibliography for Research in the Social and Behavioral Sciences* (1984); Raymond A. Mohl, "Cubans in Miami: A Preliminary Bibliography," *Immigration History Newsletter* 16 (May 1984): 1–10; Felix R. Masud-Piloto, *With Open Arms: Cuban Migration to the United States* (1988); Alejandro Portes and Robert L. Bach, *Latin Journey: Cuban and Mexican Immigrants in the United States* (1985).

R.A.M.

CUBBERLEY, ELLWOOD PATTERSON (1868–1941). Educator; author of *Changing Conceptions of Education* (1909), a typical tract of the period for the view that to Americanize was to Anglicize. Cubberley viewed southern and eastern Europeans as "illiterate, docile, lacking in self-reliance and initiative, and not possessing the Anglo-Teutonic conceptions of law, order, and government." Cubberley was professor of education at Stanford University for many years and exerted great influence through his many books, e.g., *Public Education in the United States* (1919).

Reference

Lawrence A. Cremin, *The Wonderful World of Ellwood Patterson Cubberley: An Essay on the Historiography of American Education* (1965).

F.C.

CULTURAL PLURALISM. An antiassimilationist theory to prevent the disappearance of America's disparate ethnic groups into the "melting pot," or their cultural transformation through Anglo conformity. Instead, ethnicity would be preserved in a larger cultural mosaic. Although the term was not coined until early in the twentieth century by Horace Kallen (*q.v.*), the idea is much older, implicit at least in John Adams' "wonderful mixture of nations," Thomas Paine's "composite nation," Timothy Dwight's "cultural federalism," Herman Melville's "ethnographic panorama," and Walt Whitman's "nation of nations." Parochial schools, Jewish *schulehs,* and Indian reservations are a few institutionalized reflections of this pluralism.

Kallen wrote and taught in an era of aggressive Anglo conformity which seemed to convert the "melting pot" into a steaming cauldron designed to scrub away immigrant traits. This began with the "Americanization" programs of the Progressives, was enhanced by patriotic excesses during two world wars and the hysterical association of dangerous radicalism with foreign ways between those wars, and finally ended with the ill-advised "termination" policy to speed the entrance of Indian tribes into America's cultural mainstream. Kallen insisted that the right to one's "psycho-physical inheritance" was "inalienable." As he explained it, one might change his clothing, politics, religion, language, or wives, but not his grandfathers. Following his Harvard mentor, William James, Kallen rejected the popular notion that one was superior to many: one nation, one culture, one God (he rejected the orthodox faith of his rabbi father, calling himself a "Hebraist," rather than a "Judaist"). Many diverse, separate cultures would maintain a sense of *gemeinschaften* in a profoundly *gesellschaft* world, he reasoned, and "a federation or commonwealth of national cultures" would mirror the political union. He used an orchestral metaphor of many diverse instruments blending to create a beautiful, harmonious symphony of "cultural freedom."

Only after World War II did Kallen's idea begin to take hold, and then largely among immigration historians, with reservations. Ethnic groups were not equal, and the educational and economic opportunities for improvement often lay outside the ghetto. These scholars feared that a strict, permanent pluralism would merely crystallize that inequality. Theirs was a "soft" pluralism that would stress the crucial contributions made by ethnic minorities in building America, too often ignored or discounted in older histories. By setting the record straight, they hoped to lower prejudice in general and remove the ethnic biases in America's restrictive immigration laws.

When the country became "unglued" in the 1960s, a Black Power racist strategy embraced a harder pluralism, a strict and permanent segregation. Black nationalism has a long history in America, and was more recently advocated by Marcus Garvey, and then by the Muslims. Other self-appointed ethnic leaders followed suit, and this "hard" pluralism was quickly endorsed by many scholars, even sanctified as the "correct" view, beyond the pale of criticism. As Moses Rischin observed:

> Cultural pluralism became virtually a climate of opinion and a mystical formula for harmonizing all our diversities in a world consciously or unconsciously bent on their dissolution. Despite its patent inadequacies as a theory of group relations even for American Jews, and perhaps just because of its imprecision, the philosophy and rhetoric of cultural pluralism continues in varying degrees to inform American society at every turn.

Some institutionalized changes followed the trend. Racially segregated dormitories were organized on some campuses, and programs in black studies proliferated, invariably separated from the academic mainstream. Similar programs for Asian and Hispanic groups followed. The very term "minority" was appropriated by "people of color," a coup supported by governmental programs that deny minority status to Jews, Italians, and all white minorities. The scholarship produced by hyperethnic programs has been shoddy for the most part. All too often, particularly in black and Hispanic programs, flagrant advocacy, angry, raw propaganda, and a strident anti-intellectualism replaced any pretense to objective scholarship. Kallen's "symphony" became discordant, a cacaphonous celebration of prejudices, new and old. As John Hope Franklin complained, "the universities wouldn't have dared hire whites with such poor qualifications as some of the people hired to teach black studies." Like Franklin, leading minority scholars have avoided ethnically specialized programs, preferring appointments in regular departments. Minority students have also opted for more traditional majors. Of almost 2,000 black undergraduates attending San Francisco State University between 1978 and 1980, for example, only seventeen majored in black studies. That university's School of Ethnic Studies, the nation's oldest, has since its inception consistently housed almost twice as many instructors than it has majors. Of close to 500 university programs in black studies a decade ago, less than half still survive. One legacy, the small but healthy black theater, thrives, although it has become much more conservative to appeal to a middle-class audience, black and white.

Marxist scholars had always been uncomfortable with this "new," or "hard" pluralism because of its divisive challenge to the "solidarity" of the working class. "Old," or "soft" pluralists, among them some of the nation's most distinguished immigration historians and minority scholars, joined their Marxist colleagues in breaching the ideological consensus protecting pluralism. Ultimately, this heated controversy has to be settled by impersonal social forces, many of which seem destined to undermine a pluralistic solution for America. First and foremost, the less than enthusiastic support for such programs by members of ethnic groups suggests that such a solution may not be as popular as its proponents claim. Prejudice and discrimination probably constitute a sine qua non for pluralism by producing a siege mentality that enhances group solidarity and discourages exogamy. It is doubtful that Jewish ethnicity could have survived the diaspora without anti-Semitism. Kallen acknowledged as much, and this explains why ethnic radicals simply refuse to concede that there has been any improvement in this area in recent years, and often resort to prejudices and discrimination of their own. Unless the mass media and public schools become ethnically specialized, both will continue to weaken pluralism. The dramatic increase in opportunity for higher education via public universities, or scholarships exclusively for minorities at more prestigious private ones, creates more upward social mobility with its attendant middle-class acculturation, often confused with and denounced as Anglo conformity by ethnic radicals. This also results in greater geographic mobility, which dissipates the ghetto so essential to pluralism. A younger mobile generation is more prone to structural assimilation and to intermarriage, particularly in a society that has become increasingly secular, ecumenical, and egalitarian. Statistics on intermarriage indicate that this is already occurring at an accelerating rate. This will weaken ethnic identities in future generations. Already close to half of America is so ethnically diluted that cultural pluralism cannot have much meaning for it. In fact, this poses a problem in verifying claimed identities for affirmative action quotas. Is one-half, one-quarter, or one-eighth sufficient to establish membership in a particular ethnic group? The Cherokees accept one-sixteenth. The governmental instructions promulgated to solve this conundrum often read like the Nuremberg Laws, or like ones that might have emanated from Pretoria rather than Washington. Finally, Kallen had used peaceful Switzerland for his model of pluralism at its best, but today we have too many negative examples of mindless bloodshed in "Balkanized" nations: Ulster, Sri Lanka, Lebanon, India, and virtually every nation that emerged from colonialism with ancient ethnic enmities still smoldering. This adds the question of desirability to the one of viability for a solution that would fragment, really "tribalize" America.

Essentially, cultural pluralism is a romantic concept, rooted in sentimental visions of an earlier America of unrestricted immigration, when New York was the world in microcosm with its ethnic quarters, Italian, Chinese, Armenian, German, a medieval Hasidic *shtetl,* and its colorful celebrations, the West Indian Day parade and the Jan Hus theater. Nostalgically remembered are the rich exchanges of exotic foods, costumes, and dances in elaborate street fairs, while conveniently forgotten are the warring adolescent ethnic gangs. Much of this still remains, but it is being evaporated with each successive generation and little replenishment in sight with restrictive immigration laws. Eventually, America's ethnic panorama could be replaced with a duller homogenization, but how to stop this process is problematic and the major weakness of the theory. People vote with their feet, and while an enforced institutionalized cultural pluralism might be democratic for the group, it would not necessarily be so for the individual, which is what America is all about.

References

Nathan Glazer and Daniel P. Moynihan, eds., *Ethnicity: Theory and Experience* (1975); John Higham, *Send These to Me: Jews and Other Immigrants in Urban America* (1975); Horace Kallen, *Culture and Democracy* (1924); Orlando Patterson, *Ethnic Chauvinism: The Reactionary Impulse* (1977); Moses Rischin, "The Jews and Pluralism: Toward an

American Freedom Symphony," in Gladys Rosen, ed., *Jewish Life in America in Historical Perspectives* (1980); Howard Stein and Robert F. Hill, eds., *The Ethnic Imperative: Examining the New White Ethnic Movement* (1977); Stephen Steinberg, *The Ethnic Myth* (1980).

S.C.M.

CURTIS, HENRY STODDARD (1870–1954). Educator. Curtis was an advocate of the play movement and the philosophy that "proper development of play and social guidance in connection with various institutions, especially with children . . . can do more to correct the evils of institutional life than any other single agency." He was secretary of the Playground Association. Chief works: *Education Through Play* (1915), and *Practical Conduct of Play* (1916).

F.C.

CZECH-SLAVIC BENEVOLENT SOCIETY. *See* Czechs.

CZECHS. Historically resident in Bohemia and Moravia—the western half of contemporary Czechoslovakia—the Czechs are the westernmost of the Slavic peoples. From the ninth century to 1620 they maintained a precarious independence as a nation-state, a Slavic island in a German sea. As a consequence of the religious reforms initiated by Jan Hus (d. 1415), the Bohemian kingdom became the first Protestant nation in Europe. In the first phase of the Thirty Years War, however, the Habsburgs crushed Bohemian independence, drove the nobility into exile, commenced a systematic Germanization policy, and recatholicized the population. The Czechs languished as a people, and until 1918 existed only as constituents of the multinational Habsburg state.

A "national revival" occurred in nineteenth-century Bohemia, and in the aftermath of the 1848 Prague uprising the Habsburgs abolished serfdom, clearing the way for the emigration of many Czech-speaking people. Between 1848 and 1914 more than 300,000 Czechs, largely from the poorer areas of southern Bohemia and eastern Moravia, left for the United States, migrating primarily in family units. As the earliest of the Slavs to enter the United States in sizable numbers, the Czechs were the only Slavic immigrants able to enter agriculture on a significant scale. In the early 1850s enclaves of Czech farmers appeared in eastern Wisconsin, and later in the decade Czech farming colonies were established in eastern Iowa, central Minnesota, and central Texas. The Texas settlements were largely the creation of Moravians, and they formed from the outset a distinctive and largely independent part of the Czech-American population. Immigrants from Bohemia dominated the settlements in the northern states, and in the late 1860s and the 1870s many of the early immigrants initiated a secondary migration to eastern Nebraska and, to a lesser extent, north-central Kansas. After 1889, moreover, a number of Nebraska, Kansas, and Texas Czechs migrated again to establish farms in the newly opened Oklahoma Territory.

Simultaneously, but especially after 1870, other Czechs began to concentrate in New York, Cleveland, and Chicago, and smaller colonies grew up in St. Louis, St. Paul, Baltimore, and Omaha. In the 1880s Chicago emerged as the dominant urban Czech community, and by 1900 Chicago contained more Czech-speaking people than all of the other urban centers combined. The Chicago colony was in fact so large that its residents could live, work, and secure all of the ordinary services in a Czech milieu. Clearly, by the 1890s, the arriving immigrants were largely urban oriented, reflecting a distinctly non-Slavic level of occupational skill. Tailors, shoemakers, carpenters, masons, and professional musicians were predominant among the skilled immigrants.

The "national life" of the Czech-Americans flourished until 1920, but the inevitable erosion of both ethnic consciousness and institutional vitality began in the 1920s. Two subsequent additions to the Czech stock—a migration of political refugees in the aftermath of the Communist accession to power in 1948 in Czechoslovakia, and a smaller migration of similar people who arrived after the Soviet invasion of 1968— failed to arrest the decline. The latter groups largely consisted of an elite of professional people and government officials. They have little in common with the descendants of the pre-1914 immigrants, and surprisingly little in common with each other.

From the outset the most obvious characteristics of Czechs in the United States have been divisiveness and the absence of a sense of community. The first division was religious, for more than half of the pre-1914 immigrants parted company with Catholicism and established a vital, institutionally complex "freethought" movement. Freethinkers controlled the early ethnic institutions—the press, the emerging fraternal societies, and *Sokol,* the Czech equivalent of the German *Turnverein.* The Catholics created parallel institutions, and Czech-American life proceeded on a dual track. For example, the first fraternal organization, the Czech-Slavic Benevolent Society (CSPS), founded in 1854, and its offspring, the Western Bohemian Fraternal Association (ZCBJ), founded in 1896, were militantly secular. The Catholic fraternals, Catholic Central Union (1877), and Catholic Workman (1891) reflected a similar exclusiveness.

The fractured nature of Czech America was equally apparent in the Czech-language press, for most of the 326 newspapers and periodicals which appeared before 1911 represented one of the rival religious positions. But the press situation was even more complex—a result of political divisiveness. Many immigrants embraced anarchist or Socialist causes in the 1870s and 1880s, and after 1900 Czechs formed one of the largest of the "foreign language federations" in the Socialist Party of America. The political radicals produced a spate of intransigent papers of their own, reflecting an obvious split in the freethinker camp from which the radicals obviously were drawn. Between 1900 and 1920 Chicago's Czechs supported four daily newspapers—*Svornost* (Harmony), *Narod* (The Nation), *Spravedlnost* (Justice), and *Denni Hlasatel* (Daily Herald). They represented, respectively, the interests of the freethinkers, the Catholics, the Socialists, and those prudent enough to observe a scrupulous neutrality. Not surprisingly, only *Hlasatel* has survived, but it no longer appears on a daily basis.

Czech-Americans have never created a domestically oriented institution with which all members of the group might comfortably affiliate. Czech-Americans have participated in the ethnic revival which began in the 1960s in the United States, but they have done so in their traditionally particularistic manner. Profound examples of this are Nebraska Czechs, Inc., Oklahoma Czechs, Inc., and the Czech American Heritage Society (Velehrad), which in spite of the nomenclature, is an organization of Chicago Catholics. Archival repositories have been established at Illinois Benedictine College at Lisle; Southern Illinois University, Edwardsville; the University of Chicago; and the University of Nebraska–Lincoln. The work of dedicated members of the academic community, not ethnic group pressure, underlies the creation of these archives. Obviously there is no real Czech-American historical society.

References

Josef J. Barton, "Religion and Cultural Change in Czech Immigrant Communities, 1850–1920," in Randall M. Miller and Thomas Marzik, eds., *Immigrants and Religion in Urban America* (1977), pp. 3–24; Karel D. Bicha, "Karel Jonas of Racine: First Czech in America," *Wisconsin Magazine of History* 63 (Winter 1979–1980): 122–140; Joseph Chada, *The Czechs in the United States* (1981); Bruce M. Graver, "Czech American Freethinkers on the Great Plains, 1871–1914," in Frederick C. Luebke, ed., *Ethnicity on the Great Plains* (1980), pp. 147–169; Vera Laska, *The Czechs in America, 1633–1977: A Chronology and Fact Book* (1978).

K.D.B.

DABOVIC, SEBASTIAN. *See* Montenegrins.

DAIGNAULT, ELPHÈGE. *See* French: Sentinelle Affair.

DALMATIA. *See* Croatians.

DALMATIANS. *See* Croatians.

DANA COLLEGE. *See* Danes.

DANES. Even though Danes traveled to the United States throughout American history, the heaviest period of migration took place during the last half of the nineteenth century. The peak year for the migration was 1882 when 11,618 migrated, and the decade of the 1880s was the heaviest ten-year period when 88,000 crossed the Atlantic. Between 1820, when the United States began to count the immigrants, and 1980, 370,000 Danes journeyed to this country.

Danish Migration by Decades

1821–1830	189
1831–1840	1,063
1841–1850	539
1851–1860	3,749
1861–1870	17,094
1871–1880	31,770
1881–1890	88,132
1891–1900	50,231
1901–1910	65,285
1911–1920	41,983
1921–1930	32,430
1931–1940	2,559
1941–1950	5,393
1951–1960	13,706
1961–1970	11,771
1971–1980	4,500

Colonial Migration. Because of geographic proximity and a common maritime tradition, Denmark and Holland for centuries had enjoyed commercial exchange. Many Danes served on Dutch ships, and others worked as laborers in Dutch enterprises or as domestics in Dutch homes. When the Dutch established and developed the colony of New Netherland, Danes participated. The Borough of the Bronx, for example, is named after Jonas Bronck who migrated in 1639 and purchased 500 acres of land from the Indians. Danes fit into the Dutch system and even changed their names so that Jorgen Thomsen from Ribe became Jurian Thomassen van Ripen. Nevertheless the Danes retained some of their heritage and in 1704, after the British gained control and permitted more religious diversity, the Danes in New York constructed a Lutheran church.

Later in the 1730s and 1740s Danes were attracted to colonial America through the work of the Moravian Brethren. This religious movement, heavily pietistic and ecumenical, became active in a missionary program, especially to aboriginal groups. Some Danes, who joined the fellowship in Europe, were among the Moravians who settled at Bethlehem, Pennsylvania. As in the case of New Netherland, their number was small and in Pennsylvania they became part of the German community.

A decade earlier the founder and leader of the Moravian Brethren, Nicholas Louis Count von Zinzendorf, learned about conditions of the slaves in the Danish West Indies (Virgin Islands) and sent missionaries to the islands. Although the early missionaries were Germans and not Danes, the connection between the Danish West Indies and the colonies was consolidated, and Danes from the Indies came to the English colonies to receive an education, to carry on trade and commerce, or to take up residence. More Danes became citizens in 1917 when United States purchased the Virgin Islands from Denmark.

The Mormons. The Church of Jesus Christ of Latter-Day Saints began its mission to Denmark in 1850 when the leadership appointed Peter Hansen to the task. Using Hansen's translation of the Book of Mormon, the missionaries converted 300 Danes within the first year. Although the Danish constitution granted religious liberty, the missionaries had to overcome the harassment of the populace and denouncements from the Lutheran clergy. Retaining a base of converts in Denmark to promote the faith, other newly converted Mormons migrated to the Zion in Utah. This has been called a shepherded migration in that the leaders arranged for transportation of the groups by ship, rail, handcart, and wagon. Converts began arriving in the Territory of Utah in 1852, and from 1860 to 1880 Utah was one of the top two states or territories with a Danish population. By the end of the century approximately 17,000 had migrated. Numerous Danes never arrived at Utah, however, but dropped out at settlements in Iowa and Nebraska. Others became disenchanted and returned to the Midwest. Mormon policy encouraged assimilation and already on ship the Danes learned English. Nevertheless, the Danes maintained some ethnic identity and there was a sufficient number of Danes to support a Danish newspaper, *Bikuben* (The Beehive), which was published from 1876 to 1935.

Denmark. Shortly before the onset of the major migration, Denmark suffered some critical reverses that greatly reduced its power and international prestige. Caught between the large powers during the Napoleonic era, Denmark lost most of its navy to the British and witnessed the destructions of sections of Copenhagen as well. Then, following the termination of hostilities, Norway was taken away and placed under Swedish rule. These disasters were followed by financial problems when the national bank declared itself bankrupt and the government was forced to create a new currency. The countryside suffered additionally when the price for grain fell. To compound it all, Denmark experienced the dislocation associated with industrialization.

Slesvig. An impetus for migration took place in 1864 when Prussia and Austria went to war with Denmark over the sovereignty of the duchies of Slesvig and Holstein. Denmark suffered a decisive defeat at Dybbøl and was forced to relinquish the limited control it had over the provinces. When the 150,000 Danish-minded people, located primarily in northern Slesvig, were confronted with the Prussian administration, military service, and the German language, many considered migration to Denmark or the United States. By the end of the nineteenth century, 60,000 people from Slesvig left the area.

Motives. The primary motives for emigration prior to the massive migration of the 1880s had been religious, as illustrated by the Mormons and Moravians, and politicocultural in the case of the Slesvig Danes. The motives that influenced most of the immigrants in the latter half of the century were economic and social. The underlying factor in this situation was the population explosion common to nineteenth-century Europe. The agricultural economy could not absorb the expanding population, so Danes migrated to the cities for work in the factories. But even there unemployment was a problem along with low pay and undesirable living conditions. Return to the countryside was not reasonable, so migration to America, with its expanding economy, seemed a desirable alternative.

Settlement Patterns. Although there were Danish communities and concentrations, Danes generally scattered throughout the United States. While Norwegians settled more closely together, so that in 1890 51 percent were located in two states, only 22 percent of the Danes were concentrated in two states.

The predominant portion of Danes settled in the Midwest and occupied an area west of Chicago and Racine through southern Wisconsin, Minnesota, Iowa, and Nebraska. Outside of this region in Michigan there were Danish concentrations along the eastern shore of Lake Michigan and in Montcalm County, in the central part of the state. In addition to the large number of Danes in southern Wisconsin, many Danes lived in Polk County, in the northwestern part of the state.

Racine, in 1900, claimed to have the greatest concentration of Danes in proportion to the population, outside of Denmark. Danes went to Racine to work for implement and farm equipment factories. To this day they celebrate their Danish heritage with an annual Kringle Festival.

Chicago possessed the greatest number of Danes in the United States, with a Danish population in 1900 of more than 10,000 Danes. At that time most Danes lived in an area east and south of Humboldt Park, and the strip of businesses on North Avenue between Western and California avenues was referred to as the "Danish Broadway." The Chicago Danes supported various clubs such as Dania, several newspapers, singing and theatrical societies, and even a circle of intellectuals, successful businessmen, and artists. Included in this group were such men as Louis Pio, a Socialist, Emil Dreier, a businessman, and Carl Rohl-Smith, a sculptor. For a time the Danes staged an annual celebration of the Danish constitution at an amusement park that attracted as many as 10,000 people, and financed the statue of Hans Christian Andersen placed in Lincoln Park. Max Henius, a prominent Danish spokesman of the Danes in Chicago, was a promoter for the creation of Denmark's Rebild Hills National Park.

The Danish settlement in the western Iowa counties of Shelby and Audubon is considered to be the largest rural concentration of Danes. Elk Horn, which boasts a Danish windmill, has now been selected as the location for the Danish Immigrant Museum. The Danish Immigrant Archives are housed at nearby Grand View College in Des Moines.

The Danes also went west with the settlement of the Plains states. Nebraska, for example, contained two major Danish concentrations. One was in Omaha and the counties to the north and west, and the other was along the Platte River in the central part of the state. Omaha became the home of the Danish Brotherhood, a fraternal organization and insurance company, and for a time, *Den Danske Pioneer,* a Danish newspaper presently being published in Hoffman Estates, Illinois.

Immigration to the Plains states was also encouraged by the Danish Church and by the Danish Folk Society (Dansk Folkesamfund), which was founded in 1887 by leaders of the Church. One way in which the church could support the Danish language and culture was to establish colonies of Danes. Two of these colonies (Tyler, founded by the church; and Askov, founded by the society) were major communities in Minnesota. From Minnesota and Iowa Danes migrated westward into the Dakotas and shortly after the turn of the century crossed the border into Montana.

The Danish community in Texas, Danevang, was another project of the Danish Folk Society. In 1894 the society purchased 25,000 acres in Wharton County and then advertised among the Midwest Danes, 600 miles away. Nature dealt blows to the young colony when storms damaged property and disease killed some horses, but the settlers also created some problems for themselves by trying to grow the crops of the Midwest. Soon they adopted southern crops such as cotton, and the settlement prospered.

Danes who settled on the East Coast stopped in such towns as Falmouth, Maine; Bridgeport and New Haven, Connecticut; and Troy, New York and New York City. The most significant concentration was at Perth Amboy, New Jersey, where Danes owned and worked in the terra-cotta factories. Just as in Chicago, the Danes of the East Coast organized clubs and societies and kept track of each other through the newspaper *Nordlyset* (The Northern Light). Since 1940 New York has been the state with the second largest number of Danes in the United States.

On the West Coast, California is the state that since 1920 has had the largest number of Danes when it nudged out Iowa. Danes had been present already in the days when California was part of Mexico and men such as Peter Lassen held land in the northern part of the region. Following the gold rush, San Francisco became a major Danish community, and its newspaper *Bien* (The Bee)—still in print but published now in Los Angeles—began its publication. Danes contributed to the raisin industry in Fresno, to the poultry and egg production at Petaluma, and to the dairying and agriculture in Humboldt County to the north. Although Los Angeles contains numerous Danes, Solvang, near Santa Barbara, is best known for being a Danish town and attracts more than two million tourists each year.

Other Danish communities on the west coast are in Portland, Seattle, Tacoma, and Enumclaw, Washington. The Oregon town of Junction City is the home of *The Bridge,* the journal of the Danish American Heritage Society.

Danish-American Institutions. The Lutheran church, which was the state church of Denmark, was an institution that was present in a modified form in America. While the church in Denmark provided a broad umbrella for various religious views, there was division in the church in America. One wing of the church looked to N. F. S. Grundtvig for direction. An ardent nationalist, gifted hymnist, and founder of the Danish Folk High School movement, Grundtvig placed greater emphasis on the creeds than on the Bible itself. The Bible, he maintained, only contained the word of God, but was not itself God's word. He gave up the Bible as the basis for faith and instead substituted the living and confessing church. In America the Grundtvigian branch of the church was called the Danish Evangelical Lutheran Church in America (Danish church), and established seminaries first at West Denmark, Wisconsin, and later at Grand View College, Des Moines, Iowa. It also fostered the Danish Folk High Schools which Grundtvig had established in Denmark. Instead of administering exams and granting diplomas these schools hoped to inspire the spirit and enrich the life of young people of college age. While practical subjects such as mathematics and grammar were part of the course of study, there was an emphasis on Danish history and culture.

Another branch of the church was influenced by the views of Vilhelm Beck and an organization called the Church Society for Inner Mission. In contrast to Grundtvig's views, Beck emphasized a life of piety and held the view that the Bible was indeed God's word and must therefore be accepted as such. This branch of the church initially joined with like-minded Norwegians in forming a Lutheran denomination, but later separated and eventually formed the United Evangelical Lutheran church. Trinity Seminary and Dana College at Blair, Nebraska were its institutions. The Danish language and culture was not as great a concern for this denomination as it was for the Danish church, so there was more rapid assimilation and an earlier use of the English language within its congregations.

Both denominations established colonies in Minnesota, Texas, North Dakota, and West Coast states, and actively recruited Danes from Denmark and the older settlements in the United States. Even though Lutheran congregations were present in United States, only a small percent of the Danes were affiliated. In 1920 the Danish church had a membership of 21,000, while the United church was larger, with 26,000. Estimates of the percentage of Danes in either of these denominations vary from 8 to 35 percent. Many Danes joined the Lutheran congregations of the Norwegians, Germans, and Swedes, others joined the Danish Baptists, Methodists, and Seventh-Day Adventists, and many did not join any church. With the 1987 merger of various Lutheran bodies into the Evangelical Lutheran Church in America, both branches of Danish Lutheranism have united into one denomination.

Assimilation and Retention. Of all the ethnic groups, the Danes have been among the most rapid assimilators. While assimilation was well underway before the turn of the century because of the immigrants' own desire for it, the greatest pressure on the Danes came during the time of World War I. The Jacob A. Riis League, named after a Dane who Americanized rapidly, was formed to promote American patriotism among Danish-Americans. Statistics also illustrate the rapid assimilation. In 1911, for example, 97 percent of Danes spoke English, compared to 53 percent for other ethnic groups. In 1930, 75 percent of Danes had been naturalized—a greater percentage than for any other group. Danes frequently married into other ethnic groups. In Chicago, 27 percent of Danes found spouses from other groups, while only 19 percent of Swedes and 8 percent of Norwegians did so.

Nevertheless, many Danes have retained their heritage and ties to the homeland. Organizations and societies survive. Families continue to celebrate Danish festivals and religious holidays, such as Christmas, in the Danish way. And beginning in the 1970s, great efforts have been made to recapture the history of the Danish migrants to the United States.

References
Kristian Hvidt, *Danes Go West: A Book About the Emigration to America* (1976); Enok Mortensen, *The Danish Lutheran Church in America: A History and Heritage of the*

American Evangelical Lutheran Church (1967); George R. Nielsen, *The Danish Americans* (1981); Erik Helmer Pedersen, *Drømmen om Amerika* (1985).

G.R.N.

DANSK FOLKESAMFUND. *See* Danes.

DA PONTE, LORENZO (1749–1838). Opera librettist; advocate of Italian culture. Lorenzo Da Ponte is probably best known as the librettist for several of Mozart's operas—*Le Nozze di Figaro, Don Giovanni,* and *Cosi fan tutte.* He also acquired a reputation as a librettist for other composers such as Martini, and was something of a poet. When his collaboration with Mozart was at an end he sought other opportunities and seemed to find some in London. But his financial reverses in that city inspired him to leave for America rather than risk debtor's prison, and he spent the years 1805–1838 in the New World. In the search for an income he spent some of his time tutoring enthusiastic young men in the Italian language and literature, and finally was given recognition of a modest kind by being offered the position of professor of Italian literature at Columbia University in 1825. However, he was not paid a salary for that post, although it was the first in Columbia's history. He was dependent on students' fees, and since there were no students who registered for his courses, he received no money. Columbia University, however, benefited from Da Ponte's presence in another way. He was desperately in need of money for himself and his family and so he sold hundreds of Italian-language works from his own library to the institution. The last six years of his life were terribly bitter and he desperately fought a battle for survival. He became involved in efforts to establish Italian opera in New York, but was unsuccessful. He had managed to have an Italian opera house built and get singers to perform for a time, but his financial partner, Riva-Finoli, disappeared and two years after the start of this late venture, the opera house burned down. Da Ponte, the librettist of Mozart, died in poverty on August 17, 1838.

Reference
Joseph Louis Russo, *Lorenzo Da Ponte: Poet and Adventurer* (1966; original ed. 1922).

G.B.

DARBINKAS. *See* Lithuanians.

DAVENPORT, CHARLES B[ENEDICT] (1866–1944). Biologist. Davenport taught at Harvard University and University of Chicago, and was the director of the Eugenics Record Office at Cold Spring Harbor, New York, and a supporter of the eugenics movement. Davenport lamented "that the best of that grand old New England stock is dying out through failure to reproduce," and he believed that "environment could never modify an immigrant's germ plasm and that only a rigid selection of the best immigrant stock could improve rather than pollute endless generations to come." Mrs. Edward Henry Harriman, the wife of the railroad magnate, financed the Eugenics Record Office, pouring over a half-million dollars into the agency, whose main task was the compilation of an index of the American population, and furnishing advice on eugenical problems.

References
John Higham, *Strangers in the Land* (1973); Oscar Riddle, "Charles Benedict Davenport," National Academy of Sciences, *Biographical Memoirs,* 25 (1949): 75–91.

F.C.

DAVIS, MICHAEL M[ARKS] (b. 1879). Medical administrator; director of the Boston Dispensary. Davis was the author of *Immigrant Health and the Community* (1920), which was part of the Carnegie Corporation–sponsored "Americanization Studies: The Acculturation of Immigrant Groups Into American Society" (*q.v.*). Davis studied the health problems of immigrants in urban environments, and made recommendations for improving health standards as an important element in effective Americanization.

F.C.

DeCOCK, HENDRICK. *See* Dutch.

DeFOREST, ROBERT W[EEKS] (1848–1931). Social reformer. President of the Russell Sage Foundation (*q.v.*) and of the Charity Organization Society of New York (*q.v.*), DeForest was also chairman of the [New York] State Tenement House Commission, and co-editor (with Lawrence Veiller [*q.v.*]), of *The Tenement House Problem: Including the Report of the New York State Tenement House Commission of 1900* (2 vols., 1903; rpt. 1974). Prior to the passage in 1901 of the building law recommended in the report around which this book is centered, conditions in New York City's tenements (largely immigrant) were the worst in the country. The tenements were overcrowded, unventilated, unlighted, unsanitary, and were fire and health hazards. The report detailed the conditions found in the tenements and recommended a building law that set new standards for light, air, and sanitation in all new tenements and required landlords to make improvements in existing buildings. DeForest for many years was regarded as the "First Citizen of New York" for his humanitarian activities. After passage of the new building law, DeForest was appointed the first commissioner of the New York City Tenement House Department with responsibility for enforcing the new building law.

Reference
Roy Lubove, *The Progressives and the Slums: Tenement House Reform in New York City, 1890–1917* (1962).

F.C.

DEL VAYO, J. ALVAREZ. *See* Spaniards.

DE NAVARRO, JOSE FRANCISCO. *See* Spaniards.

DEN DANSKE PIONEER. *See* Danes.

DENNI HLASATEL. *See* Czechs.

DE ONATE, JUAN. *See* Spaniards.

DEPORTATION OF ALIENS. The problem of deportation of aliens is the problem of reconciliation of two competing concepts. One concept is based on the idea that the power to deport arises from the same source as the power to exclude aliens: namely, the inherent authority of a sovereign nation to protect itself from the presence of undesirable aliens. This principle was expounded in 1892 in *Fong Yue Ting* v. *United States,* the landmark decision of the Supreme Court. A corollary of this concept is the principle that deportation is a civil proceeding. Thus, the constitutional principles, guarantees, and remedies applicable to criminal proceedings do not prevail. The second concept is based on the idea that aliens enjoy certain residual rights under the Constitution that may not be denied them without affording them the same guarantees as those available to citizens.

References
Marion T. Bennett, *American Immigration Policies* (1963); Robert J. Frye, "Deportation of Aliens: A Study in Civil Liberties," Ph.D. dissertation, University of Florida, 1959 (DA 20:2876); John Higham, *Send These to Me: Jews and Other Immigrants in Urban America* (1975).

F.C.

DER DEUTSCHE PIONIER. *See* Immigrant Historical Societies.

DE SMET, PIERRE JEAN. *See* Immigrants in the West.

DEUTSCHER RECHTS SCHUTZ VEREIN. *See* Legal Aid Society.

DEVOY, JOHN (1842–1928). Publisher, journalist, and revolutionary; born in County Kildare, Ireland, and exiled to the United States in 1871. Devoy founded the Clan na Gael, the successor to the Fenian Brotherhood. He worked closely with Michael Davitt to engineer the Land War in Ireland in the 1880s and later collaborated with the organizers of the Easter Uprising of 1916. He founded and served as editor of the *Gaelic American* newspaper, which advocated Irish freedom as well as labor reform in America. His memoirs were published as *Recollections of an Irish Rebel*.

Reference
J. Devoy, *Recollections of an Irish Rebel* (1929).

S.P.M.

DI DONATO, PIETRO. *See* Immigrant Novel.

DILLINGHAM, WILLIAM PAUL (1843–1923). Lawyer, politician. Dillingham was governor of Vermont from 1888 to 1890, and a U.S. senator (R–Vermont) from 1900 to 1923. A moderate restrictionist on immigration policy, Dillingham was chairman of the U.S. Immigration Commission (*q.v.*) from 1907 to 1911, which was established by legislation (at the request of President Theodore Roosevelt) to study the immigration question. Dillingham was the architect of the temporary Quota Law of 1921 (*q.v.*), which limited immigration from any Eastern Hemisphere country to 3 percent of the foreign-born persons from that country living in the United States in 1910.

F.C.

DIRVA. *See* Lithuanians.

DISPLACED PERSONS ACT OF 1948. Passed by the U.S. Senate on June 2, 1948, and by the House on June 11, 1948. President Harry S. Truman signed it into law on June 25, 1948. The bill was the result of concern about displaced persons (DPs) in Europe during World War II. It was estimated that the war had displaced 6 million people in Europe. One million were resettled in various parts of the world, and the United States admitted 2,551 DPs from Europe in 1945. However, a long-term solution was lacking, and so President Truman urged Congress to turn its attention to the problems of DPs. In its final form, the bill allowed the admission into the United States of up to 205,000 DPs for a period of two years. The original act affected only Europeans, but an amendment added to the 1948 act on June 16, 1950, allowed the Chinese already in America to remain in the United States. Many Chinese were reluctant to return to a China controlled by Communists. As many as 15,000 Chinese in America were allowed to adjust their status.

References
Robert A. Divine, *American Immigration Policy, 1924–1952* (1957); E. P. Hutchinson, *Legislative History of American Immigration Policy, 1798–1965* (1981).

D.N.A.

DIVISION OF INDUSTRIAL STUDIES (New York City). *See* Van Kleek, Mary.

DJORDJEVIC, LEPOSAVA. *See* Serbs.

DOMINICANS. Migrants from the Dominican Republic are one of the largest Hispanic groups in the United States. There are probably 500,000 and possibly as many as 800,000 Dominicans in the United States. The greatest concentration of Dominicans is in the New York City area, where they are the fastest-growing Hispanic group. Significant Dominican communities can also be found in Connecticut, Massachusetts, and Rhode Island, as well as in Puerto Rico. In spite of their numbers, Dominicans in the United States are a somewhat invisible minority, and there is relatively little information available about them compared to larger Hispanic groups.

Background. The history of the Dominican Republic differs from that of its Hispanic neighbors, Cuba and Puerto Rico, with consequences for its patterns of migration to the United States. The site of the earliest Spanish colony in the Americas, the Dominican Republic became independent of foreign domination in 1844, more than fifty years before the Spanish-American War in which Cuba became independent and Puerto Rico was taken over by the United States. Relations between the United States and the Dominican Republic have been difficult, with United States armed forces invading the country in 1916 (occupying it until 1924) and again in 1965.

From 1930 to 1961, the Dominican Republic was controlled by the dictator Rafael Trujillo. After Trujillo's assassination, the Dominican Republic underwent several years of political instability, followed by a period of electoral politics. From the late 1960s, the Dominican government encouraged the growth of foreign investments and the development of export-oriented agricultural and manufacturing industries.

The economic expansion of the post-Trujillo period greatly increased the labor force in manufacturing, as well as urban middle and lower-middle classes oriented toward consumption. However, the very nature of the export-oriented economy was unstable, dependent on foreign capital and fluctuating markets. The Dominican economy has been unable to sustain its new middle class, whose employment opportunities and purchasing power declined drastically from the late 1970s. These developments have led to an urban population with material aspirations but little means of attaining them, and an increasingly impoverished rural population forced to compete for employment. This situation has proved a strong motivating factor for migration northward.

Patterns of Migration to the United States. In contrast to their Puerto Rican neighbors, Dominicans are not U.S. citizens free to enter the United States and its dependencies without a visa. Unlike Cubans, they cannot easily claim refugee status, with its attendant support services and other advantages. Unlike Mexicans, they cannot walk across the international border. Immigration for Dominicans is costly and encumbered with restrictions.

Settlement in the United States occurs in a number of ways. Between 1961 and 1981, more than 255,000 Dominicans legally immigrated in the United States. An unknown number have entered the United States legally on temporary visas, but stayed beyond their authorized period. Some migrants have entered the United States with false visas and others have traveled to neighboring Puerto Rico by boat to enter United States territory without any official documents; once in Puerto Rico, undetected air travel to the United States mainland is not difficult.

The fact that a significant number of Dominicans are undocumented has made it difficult to estimate the Dominican population residing in the United States. Recent research has estimated that less than one-fifth of the U.S. Dominican population is undocumented at any given time, though one-third may have been undocumented at one point, before regularizing their status.

Most Dominicans who migrate to the United States do so explicitly for economic reasons. They seek to improve their own economic status and that of their kin at home. Remittances to family members in the Dominican Republic have become an important part of the country's economy. Most Dominicans also intend to accumulate savings to finance a return to secure middle-class status in the Dominican Republic. For these reasons, many Dominican immigrants view their stay in the United States as impermanent and instrumental. For many families, even for children born in the United States, "home" is defined as the Dominican Republic.

Immigration is a household enterprise for Dominicans in the United States, almost all of whom live with kin. The high rate of women immigrants, more than half in most surveys, reflects this trend. Immigration follows kin lines, with family members in the United States arranging travel, residence, and employment for relatives leaving home. Dominican definitions of family structure often conflict with

United States immigration regulations. Thus viable family groups in Dominican terms often include undocumented residents in the view of the U.S. Immigration and Naturalization Service. Households often function as corporate groups, pooling income and sharing expenses. Households with extended family members increase the number of working adults able to contribute income. Nevertheless, at least a third of the Dominican households in New York are headed by women.

Class Background and Occupational Status. In striking contrast to popular stereotypes, Dominican emigration is largely a middle-class phenomenon, with many leaving skilled but poorly paid jobs at home to take unskilled but better-paid jobs in the United States. A study of undocumented Dominicans in the New York area indicated that they tend to be even more urban, middle-class, and educated than legal Dominican residents. Lower-class Dominicans are no less eager to emigrate, but are unable to afford the costs of documents and air travel.

The rates of participation of both Dominican men and women in the United States labor force are high. Virtually all adult immigrants have worked at some point during their stay in the United States. Most Dominicans work as operatives in the manufacturing sector, with the garment industry as the single largest employer, especially of Dominican women.

The garment industry has also provided a niche for a few Dominican entrepreneurs, who own small, marginal, and sometimes clandestine manufacturing firms. These firms assemble specialty items on contract from larger companies in the industry. The ability to organize a cheap and flexible labor force is essential to respond to the volatile fashion market. With their kin-based and hometown networks, the Dominican entrepreneurs are able to mobilize just such a labor force. The relationship of management to labor in such firms is usually paternalistic, with little or no unionizing activity and few efforts to improve working conditions.

The participation of Dominicans in the garment industry should not be exaggerated, however. Only about one-fourth of the male Dominican labor force is in the garment industry; furthermore, as much as one-half of Dominican men work outside of manufacturing as a whole. Even among Dominican women the majority work in industries other than garment manufacturing.

Adaptation to the United States. Dominican men and women have adapted differently to their lives in the United States. The fact that most Dominican women in the United States are employed has had a profound impact on their familial roles. For the first time, many Dominican women are contributing substantially to the income of their households. This position has enabled them to negotiate new roles and authority at home. These women now participate in decisions about the disposition of household income and receive the cooperation of men in performing household tasks.

These changes have made many Dominican women more satisfied with their positions as wives and mothers in the United States than they were, or could be, in the Dominican Republic. Some Dominican women have become reluctant to return to the Dominican Republic, where employment opportunities are fewer and traditional household roles more difficult to alter. Thus newfound roles in the United States have altered Dominican women's attitudes toward the purpose of their migration and toward returning to the Dominican Republic. On the other hand, for many men, the original intent, to accumulate sufficient savings to invest in a middle-class life at home, remains unchanged.

Some Dominican immigrants have achieved their economic goals and returned home to retire or establish small businesses. Nevertheless, their numbers are still few and for most Dominican immigrants there is a tension between the dream of returning home and the greater economic opportunities in the United States. These tensions can be expected to increase as a new generation of Dominicans comes to age in the United States and as economic possibilities in the Dominican Republic decline. Thus Dominicans face new challenges as a Hispanic minority in the United States.

References
David Bray, "The Dominican Exodus: Origins, Problems, Solutions," in *The Caribbean Exodus* (1987); Sherri Grasmuck, "Immigration, Ethnic Stratification, and Native Working Class Discipline: Comparisons of Documented and Undocumented Dominicans," *International Migration Review* (1984); Douglas T. Gurak and Mary M. Kritz, "Hispanic Immigration to the Northeast in the 1970s," *Migration Today* (1985); Glenn Hendricks, *The Dominican Diaspora* (1974); Patricia Pessar, "The Role of Gender in Dominican Settlement in the United States," *Women and Change in Latin America* (1986).

F.J.C.

DOMINICANS, Dominicans and Colombians in New York City. There are differences between two parts of what many New Yorkers perceive as the Hispanic community. Dominicans are predominantly rural, while the Colombians are urban. Rural Colombians prefer to go to Venezuela, Ecuador, and Panama. In New York, both groups form voluntary associations, but of different kinds. The Dominicans have more clubs (thirty-six compared to sixteen for the Colombians) and feature recreation as a larger part of their program. The Colombian associations come from the elite and tend to use their groups to gain political objectives for the community.

Reference
Saskia Sassen-Koob, "Formal and Informal Associations: Dominicans and Colombians in New York," *International Migration Review* 13 (1979): 314–332.

F.C.

DOMINICANS, family networks and U.S. immigration policy. One of the major objectives of the 1965 immigration law was the reunification of families, that is, of parents, spouses, siblings, and children. The law neglects godparents, godchildren, aunts, nephews, and "assumed relatives" who, under Dominican traditions, are important. In order to reunite Dominican-defined families after one member has immigrated to the United States, a whole arsenal of subterfuges is employed. If the United States' policy were more open to the realities of "family" in the Dominican Republic, fewer people would need to resort to illegal means to immigrate.

Reference
Vivian Garrison and Carol I. Weiss, "Dominican Family Networks and United States Immigration Policy: A Case Study," *International Migration Review* 13 (1979): 264–283.

F.C.

DOMINICANS, household and workplace of Dominican women in United States. There is an interdependence between the household and workplace in the lives of Dominican immigrant women. Ethnographic research documents that while women's participation in wage work contributes to an improvement in domestic social relations, these household-level changes do not in turn stimulate modifications in female workers' consciousness and demands for improved working conditions. Paradoxically, the beliefs about immigration and work that are rooted in the family, and the immigration goals that are realized through household cooperation, militate against working-class identification and organized resistance in the workplace.

Reference
Patricia R. Pessar, "The Linkage Between the Household and Workplace of Dominican Women in the U.S.," *International Migration Review* 18 (Winter 1984): 1188–1211.

F.C.

DOMINICANS, households in international migration. Pessar (*infra*) states that an

> analysis of the role of the household in migration necessitates a theoretical framework that encompasses both variables. This study of Dominican migration contributes to this goal by exploring sev-

eral propositions. Principal among these is the claim that the structure within which Dominican migration occurs is capital's requirement for a continuous stream of cheap, vulnerable labor and the need of households to reproduce themselves at an historically and culturally prescribed level of maintenance. The article's emphasis on household strategies clarifies several important issues, such as variation in the rates of migration among groups in the same peripheral area, the increased impoverishment of nonmigrant members of sending communities, and the intensified dependency of emigrant households on the core economy.

Reference

Patricia R. Pessar, "The Role of Households in International Migration and the Case of U.S.-Bound Migration from the Dominican Republic," *International Migration Review* 16 (Summer 1982): 342–361.

F.C.

DOMINICANS, international migration. The Dominican Republic represents a microcosm of all the major migration patterns: substantial emigration and immigration, sizable return migration, and persistent internal rural-urban migration. The impacts of these various types of migration are related and have a significant influence on the development process. This study (*infra*) analyzes the causes of these migrations as well as the costs and benefits in terms of the individual migrants and the country as a whole. Finally, it investigates the implications of migration for development planning in the Dominican Republic. A major conclusion of the study is that the migration issue is not an area distinct from the various development focuses but rather cuts across and is related to many of the program areas in which the government is involved.

Reference

Thomas K. Morrison, "International Migration in the Dominican Republic: Implications for Developing Planning," *International Migration Review* 16 (Winter 1982): 819–836.

F.C.

DOMINICANS, multiple migratory experiences of Dominican women. Gonzalez:

An analysis of sex as a discriminatory factor in the migratory process leads to a consideration of the larger implications of Dominican migration in relation to the political economy of the Caribbean. It is suggested that prostitution, domestic service, and— more recently—work in the United States garment industry, are among the few avenues open to lower-class Dominican women seeking to improve their situations. Regardless of her social class, however, a Dominican woman's residence in the United States offers her opportunities not available at home. The extensive out-migration from the Dominican Republic can be seen as being related to the increasing urban unemployment rate and to the decreasing availability of land for small agricultural pursuits.

Reference
Nancie L. Gonzalez, "Multiple Migratory Experiences of Dominican Women," *Anthropological Quarterly* 49 (1976): 36–44.

F.C.

DOMINICANS, in New York City. Glenn Hendricks describes the social processes triggered by the migration and consequent culture contact of the population from Sabana de Corona, Dominican Republic, in New York City, through the variables of the cultural experience in the sending society, the legal and social mechanisms involved in the process of entering the United States, and the socioeconomic niche they have come to occupy in the receiving society. He assumes that the experience of these immigrants is "proto-typical" of a fairly sizable number of the current immigrating population of New York City, and shows that technology, "both in modes of transportation and communication, makes an understanding of the sending society an essential element in any attempt to explicate immigrant behavior."

References
Glenn Hendricks, *The Dominican Diaspora: From the Dominican Republic to New York City. Villagers in Transition* (1974); Also: Nancy Foner, *New Immigrants in New York City* (1987).

F.C.

DONALDINA CAMERON HOME. Originally called the Chinese Presbyterian Mission Home, founded by Margaret Culbertson in 1873 in San Francisco's Chinatown. The home was used as a center for aiding and educating Chinese slave girls and prostitutes so that they could earn a living. The building that housed the home was destroyed during the San Francisco earthquake in 1906, but it was again opened in 1907. Donaldina Cameron came to work at this home for Chinese girls in trouble in April 1895 and continued there until she died in 1968. In recognition of her lifetime devotion to the welfare of the Chinese community in San Francisco, the home was renamed the Donaldina Cameron Home on June 7, 1942, and is still used as a Chinese community center.

D.N.A.

DONGJI-HOE. *See* Koreans.

DOUGLAS, DAVID (1799–1834). Botanist, explorer. The most extraordinary and most prolifically successful botanist of all time, Douglas traveled between 1823 and 1834 all over the North American continent on behalf of the Royal Horticultural Society of London. His name is perhaps best remembered for the Douglas fir, the greatest tree in lumber, but among his hundreds of other discoveries are California poppies, lupins, evening primroses, and the only peony to be found in the Western Hemisphere. His passion for plants led him to forsake his native Scotland for the widely differing worlds of sophisticated London, provincial New York, pastoral California, and the primitive American northwest. He shot the rapids of the Columbia River, braved onrushing grizzly bears and Indian arrows, climbed peaks in the Rockies, fell in love with a Chinook princess, and finally, when only thirty-five, found death in mystifying circumstances in a cattle pit in Hawaii.

Reference
William Norwood, *Traveller in a Vanished Land: The Life and Times of David Douglas* (1973).

                                                                                    F.C.

DOUGLASS, FREDERICK (1817–1895). Born Frederick Augustus Washington Bailey as a slave in Maryland in 1817, Douglass escaped to the North in 1838 when he changed his name to prevent his recapture. He was self-educated and became a famous orator and author in the abolitionist cause. After publishing his autobiography in 1845, he spent two years in England, again to avoid being returned to slavery. There he gained funds to purchase his freedom and to begin his own abolitionist paper, the *North Star,* which he published for years in Rochester, New York. Although he was a committed Christian and disliked violence, he came to believe that violence would be necessary to end slavery, and he was approached by John Brown for support. He questioned Brown's plan, but did help raise funds and aided in finding men who did go south with Brown. When Lincoln called him to the White House to get his support for a plan to emigrate blacks to Latin America, Douglass used his influence to oppose the idea. He did, however, help recruit blacks for the Union army. After the war he was disappointed that the government did not do more to help ex-slaves to start new lives, and complained that Emancipation "freed the slave and did nothing for the Negro." He continued to oppose racism in the years until his death in 1895. He was U.S. minister to Haiti and marshal of the District of Washington. For most of the century, he was the leading spokesman for Afro-Americans in the United States. He is buried in Rochester, New York, his chosen home.

References
Frederick Douglass, *My Bondage and My Freedom* (1962); P. S. Foner, ed., *Life and Writings of Frederick Douglass*, 4 vols. (1950–55).

                                                                    N.C.

DRACHSLER, JULIUS. *See* Americanization Movement.

DRAUGAS. *See* Lithuanians.

DREISER, THEODORE [HERMAN ALBERT] (1871–1945). Novelist, poet, playwright, social critic. Dreiser was born in Terre Haute, Indiana, the ninth living child of Sarah Schnänäb and Johann Paul Dreiser, who emigrated from Germany in 1844. In his autobiography *Dawn* (New York, 1931), Dreiser depicts his German-speaking, Roman Catholic, lower-middle-class family and gives a detailed account of the economic, social, and psychological pressures facing many nineteenth-century immigrant families. *Dawn* describes the typical bilingual and bicultural experiences of first- and second-generation Americans: the foreign-born father who fails to understand his children's American ways and loses his paternal authority; the second generation's rebellion against Old World religious and moral values; the role of the public school system in the Americanization process; the isolated, beleaguered mother who attempts to mediate between traditional customs and the emotional needs of her children. Dreiser first gave fictional form to these themes in *Jennie Gerhardt* (New York, 1911). Based on the life of one of his sisters, the novel tells the story of a German-American girl compelled by economic forces to abandon her immigrant family life for the larger American world of her lover, the son of an wealthy Irish immigrant.

In addition to the Germans, Dreiser dealt extensively and sympathetically with other immigrant groups in industrial America. A partial selection includes the Lower East Side Jews in *The Hand of the Potter* (New York, 1918); the studies of southern and eastern European immigrants in *The Color of a Great City* (New York, 1923); short stories like "St. Columba and the River," and "Old Rogaum and His Theresa;" biographical sketches such as "The Mighty Rourke" and "Culhane, the Solid Man" in *Twelve Men* (New York, 1919) and "Bridget Mullanphy" and "Ida Hauchawout" in *A Gallery of Women* (New York, 1929); pictures of immigrant life in his memoirs, notably *A Book About Myself* (New York, 1922) and *A Hoosier Holiday* (New York, 1916), the latter of which contains an elaborate defense of immigrants against the anti-immigration legislation of the early 1900s. Even *The Financier* (New York, 1912) and *The Titan* (New York, 1914), novels centering on an Anglo-American businessman, feature many immigrant characters. In addition, Dreiser's book about his European travels, *A Traveler at Forty* (New York, 1913), highlights his ambivalent sense of social identity, especially in the chapters on Germany and his visit to his father's hometown of Mayen.

During World War I, conservative critics pointed to Dreiser's German heritage in their attack on his writing. By the 1920s he had recovered sufficiently to write his masterpiece, *An American Tragedy* (New York, 1925), as well as *Dreiser Looks at Russia* (New York, 1928), a product of his stay in the U.S.S.R. in 1927–28. Always a critic of American consumer culture, in the 1930s Dreiser moved further to the left politically when he became a social activist and abandoned fiction for book-length critiques of capitalism like *Tragic America* (New York, 1931) and *America Is Worth Saving* (New York, 1941). Before his death he joined the American Communist party.

References
Richard Lingeman, *Theodore Dreiser: At the Gates of the City, 1871–1907* (1986); Thomas P. Riggio, ed., *The Dreiser-Mencken Letters, 1907–1945* (1986); W. A. Swanberg, *Dreiser* (1965).

T.P.R.

DUBOIS, W. E. B. *See* Afro-Americans.

DUFOUR, JEAN JACQUES. *See* Swiss.

DUNKERS. *See* Germans; German Baptist Brethren.

DUNNE, FINLEY PETER (1867–1936). Writer and humorist. Dunne's chief creation was a comic character named Martin Dooley, who was a Chicago Irish-American saloon keeper. Known for his political satire, Dunne exerted a great influence on national thought through Mr. Dooley. Mr. Dooley stood for the blunt honesty, patriotism, and democratic politics of the Irish-American Sixth Ward on Chicago's South Side, although Dooley's fictional town was "Bridgeport," a community which represented the values and customs of the working-class immigrant Irish. Mr. Dooley became the Irish-American "Everyman" moralizing on the disparity between American democratic principles and common, if corrupt, American practices. Dunne began his career as a journalist and by the age of twenty-five was in charge of the editorial page of the *Chicago Evening Times*. His chief works were *Mr. Dooley in Peace and War* (1892); *Mr. Dooley in the Hearts of his Countrymen* (1899); *Mr. Dooley's Philosophy* (1900); *Mr. Dooley's Opinion* (1901); and *Observations of Mr. Dooley* (1902). Dunne produced Mr. Dooley essays until 1926, while having resumed a journalistic career.

Reference
Charles Fanning, *Finley Peter Dunne and Mr. Dooley: The Chicago Years* (1978).

                                                                    C.C.

DUTCH. From the start of their immigration to America in the early seventeenth century, the Netherlanders have been an accepted and welcomed immigrant group in North America. Their immigration, although continuous since that time, has varied in rate and rationale. They have been considered an easily assimilable people, being socially and culturally compatible with America's "native stock." Although viewed as easily integrated into American society, they have demonstrated a clustering pattern of settlement, and a social organization that is bound formally and informally with religious, familial, and ethnic associations. Undoubtedly, both their acceptance and their clannishness (a strong support system) have contributed to their tendency to avoid some of the social adjustment problems of some of the other immigrant groups.

Spanning more than three and a half centuries, the Netherlanders' participation in American immigration has closely paralleled the broader American immigration scene, and has been described as occurring in three phases: the *commercial* migration of the colonial era, the *free* or *great* migration of the nineteenth and early twentieth centuries, and the *planned* migration which followed World War II.

Dutch-Americans have never been a large immigrant group. At the end of the Dutch colonial era, when the English took control of the Dutch North American colony (1664), it is thought that the population of the colony was about 10,000 and that approximately 30 percent were non-Dutch. During the great migration which began in the mid-nineteenth century, it is estimated that about 250,000 Dutch immigrated to the United States. Between 1945 and 1965 approximately 80,000 Dutchmen, including Dutch nationals from Indonesia, entered the United States.

Not unlike most ethnic groups, the large majority of the immigrants, particularly of the first two phases, have been described as "mingegoeden": people of small means. The seventeenth-century Dutch colony, New Netherland, attracted the unemployed, the poverty stricken, tenant farmers, a few religious refugees, very few families, and many who hoped to become wealthy quickly. The great migration almost two centuries later brought families of farmers, peasants, and others with rural skills. In contrast, the post–World War II immigration brought more skilled workers, professionals, and technicians.

The Commercial Migration. The Dutch presence in North America was established by Henry Hudson's explorations in 1609, and was primarily a commercial venture. Hudson, hired by the Dutch East India

Company, was looking for a northwest passage to the Far East. Although unsuccessful, his "discovery" generated some interest among Dutch entrepreneurs to develop trade with the North American Indians. Trading posts were established on the Hudson River, and in the early 1620s the Dutch West India Company was granted a monopoly in the Dutch trade business which included New Netherland, the colony along the Hudson. New Netherland was never a primary concern of the company; establishing a colony was secondary to the company's interest in fur trading.

Most individuals and families base migration decisions on both "push" and "pull" factors. Conditions during this period in Dutch history seemed to lack both. New Netherland was reportedly uncleared land, primarily wilderness and given to Indian hostilities. The company established a feudal land system (the large tracts of land were initially held only by major company stockholders) and other economic restrictions, particularly concerning trade. During this period, Holland was enjoying its "Golden Age." Industry and trading were expanding in the homeland and unemployment was not a major problem. The conditions of even the peasant population compared favorably with those in many other parts of Europe. There was, moreover, a lack of religious persecution in the Netherlands at this time. During this period of time, other European nations welcomed Dutch immigrants; some actually attempted to attract them because of their farming and trade skills. Thus, if a Hollander was interested in emigration there were opportunities nearer his home, without three thousand miles of ocean to cross and a wilderness with which to contend.

These conditions combined to minimize seventeenth-century Dutch migration to the New World. This failure of the Dutch to populate the colony, together with the overriding interest in trade rather than farms and settlements, is often cited as the reason for the loss of New Netherland to the English in 1664. Since the Dutch West India Company was interested in quick and substantial profits, fur trading was more appealing than the slow and painful process of colonization. Remigration was common during this time. Many came hoping to make a profit and return to the Netherlands more economically and socially prominent. Either because they secured their profits, or because of discouragement in their ventures, they returned home. The demoralizing effect of conflicts with the Indians and the hardships of wilderness living also caused hundreds of colonists to return to Holland.

Although the colony was not very successful, by 1664, when New Netherland fell to the English, the Dutch had become firmly rooted in numerous small settlements, mostly along the Hudson River and on western Long Island. The largest of these settlements was New Amsterdam (later named New York City).

Throughout the eighteenth and early nineteenth centuries Dutch immigration to this area was merely a trickle: clergymen for the Dutch Reformed churches; merchants; and working-class families. Several small groups of Dutch Quakers and Mennonites joined William Penn's colony in Pennsylvania. Also immigrating in the latter part of the seventeenth century was a small group of Dutch Labadists (a quietist sect established by Jean de Labadie.) Because of discrimination in the Netherlands, a missionary zeal, and poverty, this group established a utopian community in Maryland.

Although initially few in number, the original Dutch colonists began to multiply, primarily by producing large families. Within this now English-owned colony, the Dutch frequently achieved successful positions in business and political circles. Many became the elite in the growing communities in New York and New Jersey. As land became scarce they moved north and then west. Although separated by years and miles from their homeland and their Dutch culture, they continued their ethnic traditions through their clannishness, the establishment of Dutch Reformed churches with clergy imported from the Netherlands, and their persistence in the use of the Dutch language in their homes, churches, and social relations.

After more than two centuries, the Old Dutch in the United States had generally become well established and prosperous. This, plus retention of their Dutch cultural and religious identity, were great assets to a new wave of Dutch immigration which reached its first peak in 1847. The Old Dutch welcomed the new immigrants and helped to establish them.

Great Migration. Although there was little interest among the Dutch to immigrate to the United States during the colonial and early national years, this began to change in the 1840s. It was during this time that emigration from European countries in general assumed mass proportions. The number of emigrants peaked in 1847 and 1854. An economic depression (beginning in 1857) and the American Civil War (1861 to 1865) temporarily halted the flow into the United States. Dutch interest in the United States increased again after the war and peaked again in the 1880s. There was no mass exodus from the Netherlands during any of this period. The approximately 250,000 Dutch immigrants who came to the United States at this time were only a small fraction of Holland's total population; and compared to the total number of Europeans who immigrated at this time, the number of Dutch immigrants was very small.

Unlike the commercial venture of the colonial immigration, the great immigration has been described as a free movement: primarily a voluntary response to the conditions in the Netherlands in the mid-1800s. Beginning in the 1830s, the immigration was sporadic and consisted of individuals and single families. Since the mid-1700s the Netherlands had experienced a significant growth in its population, and by the early 1800s pressures from this growth brought some who were seeking to better themselves economically. By the mid-1840s the individual immigration changed to a group movement of congregations, neighborhoods, and kinship groups.

Historians cite mainly religious and economic reasons for this group phase of Dutch migration: pietistic reaction against the Dutch Reformed (state) church and a failure of the potato crop.

King William I of the Netherlands and his Church Reorganization Law of 1816 attempted to centralize the administration of the Dutch Reformed church. In so doing, there was a loss of local autonomy in the church; key officials in the church were now appointed by the state, ecclesiastical bodies and committees became more closely supervised, the training of ministers came under stricter state control and, in the opinion of many, rationalist influences began to dominate the church. Protests were instigated by several ministers in the 1830s. The so-called Secession of 1834 was lead by the Rev. Hendrick De Cock, followed closely by Revs. H. P. Scholte and A. C. Van Raalte. By 1835, sixteen congregations had seceded. Persecution and discrimination, both official and social, became the lot of the Seceders. Coupled with a declining economic situation in the Netherlands, conditions encouraged emigration. The United States became the destination and Van Raalte and Scholte organized and led the first two large groups of Seceders to leave the Netherlands in 1846 and 1847. Scholte and his congregation settled in Iowa, and Van Raalte's group chose Michigan. Several other congregations followed to these areas. Once these communities were established, the letters home to friends and relatives encouraged others to follow. More communities of Dutchmen were founded in Iowa and Michigan, but also in New Jersey, the Chicago area, and Wisconsin.

By 1848, religious persecution in the Netherlands had all but disappeared with the adoption of a new, more liberal constitution. For many Seceders this change came too late, because the decision to emigrate was already firmly implanted. Although the Seceders were the largest number of initial Dutch immigrants in this nineteenth-century movement, they were not the majority of those Dutch who came to the United States prior to World War I.

Economic reasons motivated most of those who emigrated. Suffering from the aftereffects of the Napoleonic era, rising birth rates, heavy taxes, high unemployment, and an agricultural crisis, the Dutch economy appeared to fuel the movement. The rural, agricultural provinces were most affected, because of periodic flooding and plant and livestock diseases. The potato disease and subsequent famine of 1845 and 1846 caused serious food shortages and a dramatic increase in emigrant numbers. The majority of these were farmers and rural artisans, coming from the hard-hit agricultural areas of the Netherlands. For the most, the United States attracted them because of reports received from those already established in America that it was possible to own one's own farm and be an independent farmer (a high-status position in the Netherlands.)

This too, was a movement of groups. Most often the group or association sent a small number in advance to make contacts and locate settlement sites. Americans of Dutch descent, many of whom dated back to the colonial era, were instrumental in aiding the new arrivals. Some of the old established Dutch Reformed churches of New York created immigrant aid societies which provided housing, food, information, employment, and money. Whether Seceder, Catholic, nonseceding Protestant, or nonbeliever, most of these immigrants exhibited the characteristic clannishness by creating communities or settling near already established Dutch settlements.

Dutch immigration to the United States slowed down considerably in the late 1850s due to some improvement in homeland economic conditions, and the new constitutional protection for religious dissenters. Also, on the other side of the Atlantic, the U.S. economic panic of 1857, the subsequent depression, and the outbreak of the Civil War discouraged immigration. After the Civil War the character and composition of Dutch immigration was altered. The movement became one of individuals and individual families rather than congregations, associations, and neighborhoods. This pattern has been called "chain" or "follower" migration and its cause is traced to the correspondence between family and friends, between homeland and adopted country. The reasons for emigration had shifted: "pull" factors outweighed "push" factors. There was less of a need to move, and more of a desire to come to the United States where there were, reportedly, better economic opportunities: cheap farmland, urban jobs available through contacts with family and friends, and no class system to inhibit educational and career opportunities for the children.

The chain migration persisted until approximately 1930, waning during periods of war and economic depression. Another depression in the mid-1890s, World War I, the Great Depression, and World War II all served to inhibit immigration. An agricultural crisis in Holland in the 1880s brought almost 75,000 people to the United States before 1893. Another 75,000 came between 1900 and 1914, and about 35,000 between 1920 and 1930. The United States immigration quota laws greatly reduced Dutch movement to the States. First exercised in 1921 and revised in 1924, the quota allowed only 3,136 Dutch to enter annually. Waiting lists resulted.

Planned Migration. Post–World War II immigration has been

called a planned migration. Between 1945 and 1965 approximately 80,000 Dutch settled in the United States. The depression and war severely damaged the economy of the Netherlands. A high birth rate, damage from Nazi occupation, bombing and plundering by occupying armies, mass killing and deportation of a major portion of the labor force, destruction of many acres of farmland by the inundation of salt water, destruction and deterioration of industrial facilities, and the loss of the Indonesian colony all left the Netherlands government in a position of not being able to provide for its population. Thus, the Dutch government instituted an emigration policy which encouraged movement to other countries. The plan included financial subsidies to defray transportation costs, vocational training to enhance chances for admission into other countries, language courses, information programs, assistance with job applications, and other services. The Netherlands Emigration Service used the media to promote emigration and spent approximately 218 million guilders in two decades of sponsoring emigration.

Surveys done during this time by the Netherlands' commissioner for emigration indicated that prospective emigrants preferred the United States for relocation. The chain migration concept was still a significant factor. The decision to leave was being encouraged by the homeland conditions, but the choice of destination was being influenced by family and friends who were reporting success in their adopted country.

Because of the restrictive U.S. quota system less than 100,000 of the over one million post–World War II Dutch emigrants were allowed to settle in the United States. Since the quota was based on the principle of national origin represented in the population before 1920, and because the Dutch immigration prior to 1920 had never been comparatively large in numbers, the Dutch found themselves discriminated against in this matter of entry into the United States. The Dutch government was able to negotiate agreements with Canada, Australia, South Africa, New Zealand, and others.

As in the other periods of Dutch immigration, earlier arrivals organized themselves to assist postwar immigrants. The Dutch Reformed churches (the Christian Reformed church and the Reformed Church in America) helped, as did the Christian Seaman's Home and Immigration Bureau in Hoboken, New Jersey, which disbanded in 1962 when mass air travel became more popular than the Holland-American Line (ocean travel).

The already established Dutch-American communities received most of these new arrivals. Southern California communities were the most favored, followed by those in Michigan, New York, New Jersey, Illinois, Washington, Florida, and Iowa. An occupational shift in the composition of the Dutch immigrants caused these new arrivals to settle

in more urban areas rather than the rural midwestern Dutch communities. As the postwar immigration continued, less farmers and rural
laborers arrived, and an increasing number of skilled laborers, industrial
workers, professionals, and technicians sought new opportunities in the
States. One percent of the Dutch immigrants were farmers in the
mid-1960s, compared with 48 percent in 1948. Most were orthodox
Calvinists (similar to the tradition of the Seceders) and Catholics.

In the late 1960s the U.S. Congress replaced the national origins
quota system with a needed skills quota system. Since 1968 only about
1,500 Dutchmen are permitted entry each year. But because of the
1970s' economic prosperity in the Netherlands, the demand to emigrate
has declined.

Prior to World War II, comparatively few Dutch immigrants re-
emigrated. It is estimated that their numbers are as low as 13 to 15
percent. Recent surveys show even smaller percentages of post-1945
Dutch arrivals who claim to be dissatisfied with their new situation, or
who wish to return for other reasons. Despite the fact that mass air
travel makes reemigration more feasible, few Dutch immigrants return
to the Netherlands. The most frequent reasons given for wishing to
return are family ties and Holland's social welfare benefits for the sick,
aged, and unemployed.

For the majority, immigration was a rational decision accompanied
by a well-thought-out plan and the intent to stay. Most were not desperate and therefore could assess goals and alternatives. Also, the majority
had contacts who were already established in the States, and most were
received into communities where cultural, religious, and familial bonds
could ease the transition. It is estimated that there are currently four
million people of Dutch descent in the United States; the Dutch rank
about eighteenth in size among American ethnic groups.

References
Gerald F. DeJong, *The Dutch in America, 1609–1974* (1975); Henry S. Lucas,
*Netherlanders in America: Dutch Immigration to the United States and Canada, 1789–
1950* (1955); Robert P. Swierenga, ed., *The Dutch in America: Immigration, Settlement,
and Cultural Change* (1985); Jacob Van Hinte, *Netherlanders in America: a Study of
Emigration and Settlement in the Nineteenth and Twentieth Centuries in the United States
of America* (1928; trans. 1985); Bertus H. Wabeke, *Dutch Emigration to North America,
1624–1860: A Short Story* (1944).

L.P.D.

DUTCH NORTH GERMAN MENNONITES. *See* Mennonites.

DUTCH Reformed Church of America: Americanization. The
Dutch Reformed church became an American institution through the
sporadic stages of a process that was protracted over more than two

centuries. This gradual transformation was the result both of a novel environment and of cultural interaction. It began slowly during the brief tenure of the Dutch, was vastly forwarded under the British, and achieved its final form in the early years of the American republic. Through all its permutations the church displayed the stamina and tenacity characteristic of bonds arising from religioethnic sources.

Reference
John P. Luidens, "The Americanization of the Dutch Reformed Church," Ph.D. dissertation, University of Oklahoma, 1969.

F.C.

DUTCH Reformed Church in America: ecumenical and unionist tendencies. The Reformed Church in America is the current name for the Netherlands-originated, Calvinist-bred church planted in New Amsterdam in 1628. Prior to 1850 it had Americanized slowly and consequently grown rather slowly too. Preponderantly a sectional church located in the states of New York and New Jersey, it still bore some traces of previous factionalism. The Reformed Church in America has evidenced a consistent willingness to cooperate and even to attempt union with other denominations, but, owing largely to the one union it did achieve in 1850, it probably will never unite again. Nevertheless, the idea of a union has refused to die and since 1962 the church has been negotiating with the Southern Presbyterians. Whatever the outcome of this approach it is unlikely that the church can long maintain both its current distinct identity and its present degree of unity.

Reference
Ernest H. Post, "A Century of Ecumenical and Unionist Tendencies in the Reformed Church in America: 1850–1950," Ph.D. dissertation, Michigan State University, 1966.

F.C.

DUVALIER, FRANÇOIS. *See* Haitians.

DUVALIER, JEAN-CLAUDE. *See* Haitians.

EAST HARLEM, NEW YORK CITY.

East Harlem [New York City] is an interesting area. Most minority groups have lived there at one time or another; however, the ideal melting pot never melted substantially. The immediate scope of this paper is to trace the movement of the largest ethnic groups through this area from 1900 to 1960. These groups are Italians, Jews, Puerto Ricans, and Negroes. The aim of this paper is to document and establish probable reasons for the change in East

Harlem from a "Little Italy" to a so-called Spanish Harlem, and eventually to an extension of Negro Harlem. East Harlem housed during the 1920's the largest Italian immigrant community in the United States. We will attempt to explain and trace the growth of the Italian population and its replacement by Puerto Ricans and Negroes, with some notice of the Jewish subcommunity which slowly withdrew from the area. (Cordasco and Galatioto)

Reference
Francesco Cordasco and Rocco G. Galatioto, "Ethnic Displacement in the Interstitial Community: The East Harlem Experience," *Phylon: The Atlantic University Review of Race & Culture* 31 (Fall 1970): 302–312.

F.C.

EAST SLAVS. *See* Slavs.

ECHO Z POLSKI. *See* Poles.

EDGEWATER CRECHE. A fresh air resort in Edgewater, New Jersey for immigrant city children from New York City. Founded in 1890 under religious auspices "to provide summer season fresh air day resorts near the City of New York for . . . poor children."

Reference
Francesco Cordasco, "Summer Camp Education for Underprivileged Children," *School and Society* 93 (Summer 1965): 299–300.

F.C.

EDUCATIONAL ALLIANCE. The Alliance was a consolidation of efforts (e.g., of the Hebrew Free School Association, the Young Men's Hebrew Association, and the Aquilar Free Library Society) by German Jews (earlier immigrants) to aid Eastern European Jews in New York City. A major source of help to the new immigrants, the Alliance *Reports* (1893–) are a rich source for immigrant life.

Reference
S. P. Rudens, "A Half-Century of Community Service: The Story of the New York Educational Alliance," *American Jewish Year Book* (1944): 73–86.

F.C.

EGYPTIANS. *See* Arabs.

EIDGENOSSENSCHAFT (oath-association). *See* Swiss.

EIDSVOLD CONSTITUTION. *See* Norwegians.

EIRE-IRELAND. *See* Irish American Cultural Institute.

EISTEDDFOD. *See* Welsh.

EJIDO SYSTEM. In Mexico, this is the communal ownership and operation of land by the peasantry, a system largely destroyed by the regime of Porfirio Diaz (1830–1915) in the enforcement of provisions in the Constitution of 1857 that forbade civil corporations from owning land. The *Ejido* was restored in the Constitution of 1917.

Reference
David Ronfeldt, *Atencingo: The Politics of Agrarian Struggle in a Mexican Ejido* (1973).

F.C.

EL ANTI-FASCISTA. *See* Spaniards.

ELLING'S SYNOD. *See* Norwegians.

ELLIS ISLAND. The United States Immigration Station (1892–1954). It has been called "the Gateway," "the Golden Door," and "the Island of Hope and the Island of Tears." Situated in the Narrows, between Brooklyn and Staten Island, it is north of the Statue of Liberty and is now part of the Statue of Liberty National Monument. Originally 3.3 acres, the island was expanded by landfills in 1890, 1913, 1920, and 1934, to its present size of 27.5 acres.

Ellis Island was opened as an immigration station on January 1, 1892. Before then, it was used as an oyster-shucking place and as a storage depot for powder magazines. Its immigration history relates to the passage of the Immigration Act of 1882, which excluded "any convict, lunatic, idiot, or any person unable to take care of himself or herself without becoming a public charge." Until Ellis Island opened, immigrants were processed at Castle Garden on lower Manhattan Island. But concern for crowding, crime, and lack of supervision brought the immigration process under federal control. Ellis Island was chosen as the place to process newcomers, because it was difficult to escape from an island.

The original buildings of Georgia pine burned in June 1897. The new stone structures, completed in 1900, were impressive. The main building (the Great Hall) was built in the French Renaissance style. It was 338 feet long, 168 feet wide, and 100 feet high, with four turrets. The first floor contained the baggage room, administrative offices, a railroad room, and a wide stairway that led up to the Registry Room—where the actual inspection took place.

In 1904, the ferry boat "Ellis Island" was completed with a capacity of 600 persons. It was used eighteen hours per day to take immigrants from Ellis Island to the Battery. When the island closed, the "Ellis Island" was left in the ferry slip, where it sank on August 11, 1968.

Most persons who passed through Ellis Island came steerage class. From the ship, they were taken to the ferry landing by barge or tug and from there to the baggage room. They were processed in groups of thirty, corresponding to the number on the manifest sheet that had been completed by the ship's captain. At the top of the steps began the physical examination. Those with problems were given tags or letters on their lapels: L for lung problem, H for heart disease, and X for mental deficiencies. If they survived this part, the next stop was the Registry Section, and as many as thirty-three questions. Name? Age? Height? How did you pay for your passage? Do you have relatives here? Do you have promise of a job? Where born? Last residence?

For those who passed inspection, this whole process took only forty-five minutes. For them, final arrangements were made at the currency exchange and the railroad ticket office. But approximately 2 percent were detained and many of these were deported, after an appearance before the Board of Special Enquiry.

The peak period of Ellis Island immigration was 1900 to 1920, with 1,004,756 being received in 1907. Other peak years were 1905, 1910, and 1914. Between 1914 and 1918, Ellis Island immigration fell from 878,052 to 28,867. On July 30, 1916 German saboteurs damaged the immigration station severely, causing the evacuation of 600 occupants. When the United States entered the war, crews of German ships were held at Ellis Island. Several other factors stemmed the massive tide of immigration. The literacy test was adopted in 1917, over President Wilson's veto, and during World War I there was the "Big Red Scare." In 1919, thousands of suspected aliens were interned at Ellis Island, and later deported. Finally, in 1921, a quota system was introduced which favored northern and western Europeans. Immigration was further restricted in 1924 under the National Origins Act.

By 1930, Ellis Island served mainly as a detention and deportation station. In the Great Depression, many foreigners voluntarily sought deportation to escape the worsening economic times. In 1933, there were 4,488 incoming aliens at Ellis Island and 7,037 leaving the United States from there.

Under the New Deal's Public Works Administration, Ellis Island was expanded for the last time by landfill. A new administration building was constructed and other areas improved. When World War II erupted in Europe, these new, never-used facilities were assigned to the U.S. Coast Guard to train and house recruits to patrol the waters under the Neutrality Act of 1935.

Between 1946 and 1949 Ellis Island was nearly vacant, but the passage of the McCarran-Walter Act, over President Truman's veto, created a brief flurry of activity on the island, since all incoming aliens had to be screened for membership in Communist and Fascist organizations.

On November 9, 1954, Ellis Island was vacated and declared excess federal property. The General Services Administration made three attempts to sell the island by sealed bids. None of twenty-one bids was deemed suitable. Finally, President Johnson, on May 11, 1965 issued Proclamation 3656 adding Ellis Island to the Statue of Liberty National Monument.

In 1968, the National Park Service completed a Master Plan for Ellis Island. It called for the retention of the main building and removal of most other structures. It was not acted on because of growing public opposition to the demolition of these important historical buildings. As the nation's bicentennial approached, patriotic fever mounted. The National Park Service met with representatives of ethnic groups who wanted to restore Ellis Island. Thus was born the Restore Ellis Island Committee (which was succeeded by the Ellis Island Restoration Commission). It not only saved Ellis Island, but it was responsible for opening up the island on May 30, 1976 for the bicentennial celebration and in subsequent summers.

Consistent with the Reagan administration's plan "to privatize" the public sector, the National Park Service sent out, in 1981, a request for proposals (RFP) to lease the southern two-thirds of Ellis Island. A year later on May 18, 1982, Secretary James Watt announced the creation of the Statue of Liberty/Ellis Island Centennial Commission. The centennial of the Statue of Liberty was celebrated in July 1986 and the Ellis Island centennial will be celebrated in 1992. Lee Iacocca, president of the Chrysler Corporation, was made chairman of the Centennial Commission and the Ellis Island Foundation, which was to raise the funds for restoration of the national monument. As of July 1987, the foundation had raised approximately $230 million, more than half of which was spent restoring the Statue of Liberty.

References
August C. Bolino, *The Ellis Island Source Book* (1985); Thomas Kessner, *The Golden Door* (1977); Ann Novotny, *Strangers at the Door* (1971); Thomas Pitkin, *Keepers of the Gate* (1975); Harlan D. Unrau, *Statue of Liberty/Ellis Island* (1984).

A.C.B.

ELLWOOD, CHARLES A. (1873–1946). Social Gospel leader. Sociologist at the University of Missouri and at Duke University. In his early career, Ellwood strongly opposed the "new immigration," arguing the biological inferiority of the immigrants. In 1915, he broke with the assumptions of eugenics, and criticized racial interpretations of human behavior. His chief work is *An Introduction to Social Psychology* (1917), in which he examined cultural and social phenomena from a cultural, not a psychological, perspective; however, he still thought of cultural development in terms of steps of cultural evolution, after the fashion of British anthropology, largely because he could reconcile that with his progressive ideological commitments to liberal Protestantism and civic reform.

Reference
Arthur L. Tracy, "The Social Gospel, 'New' Immigration and American Culture: An Analysis of the Attitudes of Charles Ellwood, Shailer Mathews and Graham Taylor Toward the 'New' Immigration," Ph.D. dissertation, American University, 1975 (DA 36: 5476-A).

F.C.

ELY, RICHARD THEODORE (1854–1943). Economist, social reformer. Ely was a founder of the American Economic Association, and an early leader of Christian socialism in America. He advocated public control of resources, the development of labor unions, and prohibition of child labor. He was a friend and advocate of many of the Progressive reformers, e.g., Florence Kelley (*q.v.*), and joined them in their fight against slums, factory conditions, and exploitation of immigrants. Ely favored immigration restriction. His autobiography is *Ground Under Our Feet* (1938).

References
J. R. Everett, *Religion in Economics* (1946); B. G. Rader, *The Academic Mind and Reform* (1966).

F.C.

EMANCIPATION PROCLAMATION. *See* Afro-Americans.

EMMET, THOMAS ADDIS (1828–1919). Physician, Irish patriot. Emmet was an associate of the gynecological surgeon J. Marion Sims, with whom he was in practice at the New York City Woman's Hospital. He was the author of *Principles and Practice of Gynaecology* (1879; 3d ed. 1884), a pioneering work. Emmet was an advocate of Irish Home Rule, and was president of the Irish National Federation of America. He was the author of *Ireland Under English Rule* (1903).

Reference
Thomas Addis Emmet, *Incidents of My Life* (1911).

F.C.

ENGLAND, JOHN (1786–1842). Bishop. Born in Cork, Ireland, England was sent to the United States in 1820 to work in the diocese of Charleston, South Carolina. In 1822 he founded the first Catholic newspaper in the United States, the *The U.S. Catholic Miscellany*. He worked hard to upgrade the Catholic clergy and built local seminaries to train home-grown talent.

References
P. Carey, *John England and Irish-American Catholicism, 1815–1842* (1975); P. Carey, *An Immigrant Bishop* (1982).

S.P.M.

ENGLISH. Except for Native Americans (the so-called Indians), the English were the earliest group to contribute to the peopling of that part of North America which was to become the United States. English immigrants inaugurated the era of permanent European settlement in the early seventeenth century, when they founded the colonies of Virginia, Maryland, Plymouth, and Massachusetts Bay, and for almost a century thereafter they heavily outnumbered arrivals from elsewhere. In all, some 500,000 English people may have left their homeland for the New World between 1630 and 1700, more than half of them during the middle third of the century. After 1700, because of the large influx of Germans, Scotch-Irish, and other groups into the colonies, the English contribution was relatively less important, but emigration from England remained sizable and continuous, except in times of war. At the time of the Revolution people of English birth or descent still constituted about half the colonial population and, moreover, were everywhere in the ascendant. During the era of mass immigration that began in 1815 England contributed a steadily declining proportion to the aggregate flow. Even so, prodigious numbers of English immigrants have continued to enter the United States. Precisely how many is unknown because United States immigration statistics do not distinguish between arrivals from England and those from Wales and Scotland, but it seems certain that the English made up the great majority of the 5,040,000 immigrants who arrived in the United States from Great Britain between 1820 and 1985.

Colonial Period. Historians have sometimes drawn an exaggerated contrast between the first settlers in the Chesapeake and those in New England, particularly in respect of their motives for leaving England. Nevertheless, there were significant differences between them. The small band who took the lead in planting Virginia were predominantly young men, unaccompanied by women or children. Virtually none had an aristocratic background but some came from the squirearchy or from yeoman stock, or were the sons of substantial merchants. What attracted them to Jamestown was the prospect of quick wealth. They were accompanied by a motley group of adventurers and undesirables whose idleness exacerbated the problems of the settlement. By contrast the great migration to Massachusetts Bay involved much larger numbers: 2,000 in the year 1630 alone and 20,000 more in the succeeding decade. Most of them were fairly well-to-do and well educated, and they generally brought their families with them. The fact that a sizable proportion came from the Puritan strongholds of East Anglia and the West Country, and that they included whole congregations along with their ministers, would seem to confirm the traditional view that religion was the mainspring of the movement. But while it is undeniable that religion was a major motive for some, especially the leaders, the degree of religious persecution has been exaggerated. In any case, economic factors such as rising prices, a depression in the cloth trade, and a succession of bad harvests contributed to the movement.

With the outbreak of the English Civil War in the 1640s emigration to New England virtually ceased and remained insignificant for the rest of the century. But despite the fact that emigration was officially frowned upon after 1660, there was a steady flow to the Chesapeake colonies, a majority of them indentured servants who received free passage across the Atlantic by entering into an agreement or indenture to enter into unpaid service for a term of years. On average an estimated 2,000–2,500 indentured servants reached Virginia and Maryland from England each year from 1635 to 1705. Controversy surrounds their social and occupational characteristics. Some historians have argued that they were drawn predominantly from the middle class. But recent inquiries have suggested that they represented a much wider spectrum of English society and included substantial numbers of laborers and servants as well as farmers and craftsmen.

Although after 1700 or so black slaves were increasingly preferred to white indentured labor in the Chesapeake colonies, substantial numbers of English servants continued to be imported into all the colonies south of New England. It has been estimated that of all the English immigrants to colonial America before 1776, between one-half and two-thirds arrived as bound laborers. In the eighteenth century a much larger proportion consisted of convicted felons. In 1717 Parliament created the new legal punishment of transportation for capital and other serious offenses, and contractors began to carry out regular shipments from the jails. Between then and the Revolution well over 30,000 convicts were transported to America, chiefly to Virginia and Maryland, colonial objections notwithstanding. Having been sold into servitude for periods of seven years or longer, transported felons toiled in conditions not very different from those of black slavery.

Despite being officially discouraged after 1660, emigration remained substantial and in the early 1770s reached levels that prompted a government inquiry. This revealed that from December 1773 to April 1775, over 6,000 emigrants sailed from English ports to the colonies, three-quarters to Virginia and Maryland, and nearly all the rest to Pennsylvania. Just over 60 percent were indentured servants or redemptioners; the rest paid their own fares. Whether free or not, most were young men, traveling alone. A majority were people of some substance: craftsmen, tradesmen, or independent farmers. Very few were unskilled laborers. One group, consisting largely of young men with some skill, came from London and surrounding counties, the others were chiefly north of England farmers and tradesmen.

Mass Migration. In the forty years after American independence immigration from England, as from elsewhere, was extremely limited. The British government placed obstacles in the path of emigration: it tightened the laws forbidding the departure of skilled artisans and limited the numbers that could be carried on emigrant ships. In any case war repeatedly disrupted transatlantic communication. Only when peace returned in 1815 and the expansion of commerce in subsequent decades opened an era of cheap transatlantic travel did English emigration assume sizable proportions. Until 1850 or so English arrivals were heavily outnumbered by those from Ireland and Germany, but by the 1880s equaled or even surpassed them. The nineteenth-century English exodus occurred in three great waves, each more powerful than its predecessor. The first, beginning soon after 1815, gathered momentum steadily and reached an annual rate of 30,000 or so in the 1840s and early 1850s; the second attained an annual level of perhaps 60,000 in about 1870, at which point English immigration for the first time exceeded the Irish; the third came in the 1880s and early 1890s, when all-time peaks of 80,000 and more were achieved annually. In all English immigrants may have accounted for about one-seventh of all arrivals from Europe in the century after 1815.

A variety of agencies, among them labor unions, Poor Law authorities, individual philanthropists and entrepreneurs, and charitable organizations, were active in encouraging and assisting departures from England. Colonization schemes abounded, beginning with Morris Birkbeck's English Settlement in pioneer Illinois in 1818 and continuing through the English rural colonies planted in the trans-Mississippi West in the 1870s and 1880s by American railroads, English land speculators, and the Salvation Army. There was also a rash of communitarian experiments like Robert Owen's New Harmony society, established in Indiana in 1825. A much larger-scale and also more successful communitarian effort was the emigration, stimulated by Mormon missionaries and carried out under close church supervision, of some 50,000 English converts bound for the Great Salt Lake Valley. But although organized and assisted migration has attracted much scholarly attention, it accounted for only about 9 percent of British departures between 1815 and 1914. The movement from England was predominantly one of self-financing and self-directed individuals and families.

During the first half of the nineteenth century, a majority of English emigrants probably came from rural rather than urban areas. And while these were years of agricultural depression and distress, the rural exodus was made up of independent farmers rather than of farm laborers. Uncertainty about the future rather than the pressure of absolute want provided the stimulus. The really poor did not emigrate because they lacked the means. Similar considerations explained the outflow from industrial areas, which was particularly heavy at times of cyclical unemployment such as in 1827 and 1841–42. Those leaving were not so much displaced handicraftsmen as the possessors of industrial skills such as workers in cotton and woollen operatives, potters, coal miners, tin miners, and iron and steel workers. During the latter half of the century the character of English immigration changed. As well as being more numerous, immigrants now included relatively fewer farmers and skilled industrial workers and far more unskilled laborers. Whereas economic depression in England had determined rates of departure up to 1850, the lure of a surging American economy did so thereafter. By the 1880s the bulk of the immigrants were unskilled urban dwellers, many of them traveling alone rather than in the family groups of earlier decades. Moreover, now that the steamship had made the United States more accessible, temporary and transient migration became more common: large numbers of building workers, for example, emigrated regularly each spring, only to return home in the fall.

The decline of immigration that set in after the 1893 depression turned out to be permanent. There were henceforth fewer opportunities for Englishmen in the United States. The frontier was closed, changes in American industrial technology reduced the demand for skills, and the unskilled labor market was preempted by southern and eastern Europeans. After 1900 the United States ceased to be what it had been for nearly three centuries: the favored destination of English emigrants. The great majority went instead to Canada, Australia, and New Zealand. The generous quota England was assigned under the national origins system in operation between 1929 and 1969 proved to be far greater than the number of applicants. England did contribute significantly to the "brain drain" of the 1970s and 1980s, when skilled and professional people—doctors, nurses, engineers, technicians, teachers, secretaries, and so on—accounted for perhaps half of English arrivals. Nonetheless, the English-born share in the American population has continued to decline both relatively and absolutely.

Distribution. Throughout the past two centuries English immigrants have shown a marked preference for the most urban and industrialized sections of the United States. For much of the nineteenth century they were heavily concentrated in the mid-Atlantic states and in New England, though a substantial proportion located in the newer industrial states of the Midwest, particularly Illinois, Wisconsin, and Ohio. From the 1790s onward English immigrants were heavily represented in American manufacturing and mining, and some historians contend that English technological expertise was a key factor in each of the basic American industries, especially during the formative stage. However that may be, skilled artisans certainly gravitated to the American centers of their crafts. Thus Lancashire and Yorkshire textile workers congregated in Massachusetts mill towns like Lawrence, Lowell, and Fall River; Macclesfield silk workers in Paterson, New Jersey; Staffordshire potters in East Liverpool, Ohio; and coal miners and steelworkers in the industrial counties of Pennsylvania, Ohio, and Illinois. But occupation did not always determine location: some English industrial workers took up farming in America, especially before 1850. The lure of cheap land remained strong enough to ensure that, throughout the nineteenth century, about 20 percent of English arrivals became farmers, generally on the advancing frontier where newly opened, unimproved land was available. In the twentieth century, as English immigration has become more specialized and highly qualified, the tendency to concentrate in cities, especially the larger ones, has become more marked. In 1980, the highly urbanized states of Massachusetts, California, and New York contained 40 percent of the English born.

Identity. Because they were culturally more akin to Americans than any other group, faced no language barrier and, moreover, were relatively well-to-do, English immigrants made comparatively easy social and economic adjustments. For the most part accepted as equals, they felt less need than other immigrants for distinctive institutions to maintain their identity and preserve their distinctive heritage. Thus the English made no effort to establish their own churches: there was no point in doing so when every English religious denomination had its American counterpart and every English newcomer could worship in his own tongue. Again, when American newspapers were readily comprehensible and, in addition, dealt with matters of more immediate concern to immigrants, the few papers catering exclusively for the English did not circulate widely or last long. Attempts in the 1880s to establish English political clubs so as to counter the Irish influence were equally unsuccessful. Working-class immigrants did frequently transplant the clubs, fraternal lodges, benefit societies, and trade unions they had known at home, but since these institutions were essentially class based it was impossible for them to remain ethnically exclusive. Residential patterns and rates of intermarriage confirm the view that English immigrants were more readily assimilated than other groups. They did not feel compelled, as others did, to cluster together for mutual support in distinct residential areas, and their high standing enabled even the first generation to intermarry freely with native-born Americans. Yet naturalization statistics suggest that it would be wrong to conclude that group consciousness was entirely lacking among English immigrants. They were in fact more reluctant than any other group to seek American citizenship. Although they generally felt themselves to be at home in America, they clung to old loyalties and hesitated before foreswearing allegiance to the land of their birth. Even so, they found it difficult to think of themselves as immigrants. Moreover their children, unlike those of other immigrants, found that what they retained of their Old World heritage was no obstacle to their being accepted completely as Americans.

References
Rowland T. Berthoff, *British Immigrants in Industrial America* (1953); Bernard Bailyn, *Voyagers to the West: Emigration from Britain to America on the Eve of the Revolution* (1986); Dudley Baines, *Migration in a Mature Economy: Emigration and Internal Migration in England and Wales, 1861–1900* (1985); C. J. Erickson, *Invisible Immigrants: The Adaptation of English and Scottish Immigrants in Nineteenth-Century America* (1972); Maldwyn A. Jones, "The Background to Emigration from Great Britain in the Nineteenth Century," *Perspectives in American History* 7 (1973):3–92.

M.A.J.

ENGLISH AS A SECOND LANGUAGE. *See* Bilingual Education.

EPSTEIN, NOEL. *See* Bilingual Education.

ESTONIANS. Ethnically and linguistically different from their Latvian neighbors, Estonians are a small Baltic group of Finno-Ugric origin, whose established history dates from the thirteenth century. Estonia borders on the Gulf of Finland on the north, Russia on the east, Latvia on the South, and the Baltic Sea to the west. The ancient Estonian language is akin to Finnish and Hungarian. In religious tradition, Estonians have been principally Lutheran, with a minority of Eastern Orthodox faith, and a tiny group of Roman Catholics. For several centuries, Estonians suffered invasions from various neighboring enemies, including the Teutonic Knights of the Sword. Estonia came under total Swedish control in 1645, and was ceded to Russia in 1721 after the Great Northern War. During the European nationalist movement of the nineteenth century, hope for a separate country arose. Estonia became a nation-state for the first time, declaring independence on February 24, 1918. For this reason, prior U.S. immigration records are hazy. Estonian estimates of emigrants range from 70,000 to several hundred thousand.

A variety of ship-jumping fishermen and sailors, farmers, and professionals in the later nineteenth century, and political refugees after the 1905 revolt in Czarist Russia, made up the immigrant influx. Some came through Crimea and sections of Russia, entering the United States via the Pacific coast. Estonians were scattered about in rural regions such as: Eureka, California; Snohomish, Washington; Dundee and Rose Lodge, Oregon; Irma and Gleason, Wisconsin; and Moorcroft, Wyoming. Clusters settled in San Francisco and New York City. At the call of the Lutheran Missouri Synod, the Rev. Hans Rebane came to New York in 1896 to serve Estonians and Latvians. The next year he founded the first Estonian newspaper here. Other firsts included: a Lutheran Estonian parish at Fort Pierre, South Dakota (1897); the publication of an Estonian book, and the start of a fraternal benefit society (''Amerika Eesti Heategev Selts'') in New York (1898). Other relatively small churches, societies, and publications appeared subsequently from time to time. Estonians have often collaborated with Latvians and Lithuanians in political matters affecting their homelands. Like their Baltic neighbors, Estonians experienced a fresh wave of arrivals displaced by World War II. The fate of the three Baltic groups has been quite similar to this day under the Soviets.

References

Tönu Parming, ''American Ethnic Statistics: An Evaluation Based on Estonian Immigration to the United States,'' paper presented at the 5th Conference on Baltic Studies in Scandinavia at Stockholm, Sweden, June 14–17, 1979; E. Pennar, A. Parming, and E. Rebane, *The Estonians in America, 1627–1975* (1975); ''Estonia,'' in *Encyclopedia Lituanica*, vol. 6 (1978); E. Uustalu, *The History of Estonian People* (1952).

W.W.V.

ETHNIC FAMILIES. *Ethnic Families in America: Patterns and Variations* (Charles H. Mindel and Robert W. Habenstein, eds., 1976). This collection is designed to fill a gap in the literature on ethnic and other minority group family styles in America. Most of the contributors are members of the group about which they are writing. In addition to brief introductory and concluding chapters by the editors, the volume consists of fifteen original essays, of which only two appear in other books. Of the four sections of the book, the first, ''Early Ethnic Minorities,'' contains essays by Helena Z. Lopata on the Polish; Harry H. L. Kitano and Akemi Kikumura on the Japanese; Francis X. Femminella and Jill S. Quanagno on the Italians; Ellen Horgan Biddle on Irish Catholics; and Lucy Jen Huang on the Chinese. The second section, ''Recent and Continuing Ethnic Minorities,'' contains essays by Abdo A. Elkholy on the Arabs; George A. Kourvetaris on the Greeks; and Joseph P. Fitzpatrick on Puerto Ricans. The third section, ''Historically Subjugated but Volatile Ethnic Minorities,'' includes essays by Robert Staples on blacks; John N. Price on North American Indians, and David Alverez and Frank Bean on Mexicans. The concluding section, "Socioreligious Ethnic Minorities," is comprised of essays by Gertrude Enders Huntington on the Amish; Laurence French on the French; Bernard Farber, Charles H. Mindel, and Bernard Lazerwitz on the Jews; and Bruce L. Campbell and Eugene E. Campbell on the Mormons.

F.C.

ETHNIC FORUM: JOURNAL OF ETHNIC STUDIES AND ETHNIC BIBLIOGRAPHY (1980–; semiannual). *Ethnic Forum* was initially started as a cooperative venture between the Center for the Study of Ethnic Publications at Kent State University and the Intercollegiate Academic Council on Ethnic Studies in Ohio. The founder and the editor of the *Journal* is Dr. Lubomyr R. Wynar of Kent State University. The *Journal* provides a forum for the discussion and evaluation of various trends in ethnic studies, ethnic curricula within educational institutions, various aspects of the ethnic press, ethnic historiography, and ethnobibliography, library services to ethnic communities, and other relevant topics. Special sections are devoted to reviewing both print and nonprint ethnic materials. Address: *Ethnic Forum,* Center for the Study of Ethnic Publications, Kent State University, Kent, Ohio 44242. *See also* Center for the Study of Ethnic Publications in the United States.

L.R.W.

ETHNIC GROUPS. *Harvard Encyclopedia of American Ethnic Groups* (Stephan Thernstrom, ed., 1980). A guide to the history, culture, and distinctive characteristics of the more than one hundred ethnic groups who live in the United States. Each ethnic group is described in detail. The origins, history, and present situation of the familiar as well as the virtually unknown are presented. Not only the immigrants and refugees who came voluntarily, but also those already in the New World when the first Europeans arrived, those whose ancestors came involuntarily as slaves, and those who became part of the American population as a result of conquest or purchase and subsequent annexation are included. The group entries are at the heart of the book, but it contains, in addition, a series of thematic essays that illuminate the key facets of ethnicity. Some of these are comparative, some philosophical, and some historical; others focus on current policy issues or relate ethnicity to major subjects such as education, religion, and literature. American identity and Americanization, immigration policy and experience, and prejudice and discrimination in U.S. history are discussed at length. Several essays probe the complex interplay between assimilation and pluralism—perhaps the central theme in American history—and the complications of race and religion.

F.C.

ETHNIC STUDIES. "Ethnic Studies" is a rubric for courses or programs of academic study in the curricula of American colleges, universities, and high schools that chronicle the experience of a broad variety of groups, including blacks, Hispanics, American Indians, Asians, and white ethnics (postimmigrant generations principally from southeastern Europe, especially Poles, Italians, Greeks, and Slovaks). Ethnic studies programs may vary from those concerned with a particular group, such as black studies or Chicano studies, while others, sometimes called multiethnic or cross-cultural studies, may focus comparatively on several groups. However, ethnic studies as used in this entry do not include or refer to higher education programs in international studies, such as Latin American studies or Russian studies.

History. Starting in the late 1960s, ethnic studies programs began to appear in the offerings of colleges and universities. Precipitated by the events of the civil rights movement, starting in 1954 with the momentous Supreme Court decision on desegregation, leaders of various ethnic communities sought to mobilize the sentiments of their constituencies. Their efforts took a variety of forms, including reviving old ethnically oriented fraternal organizations and founding new ones, organizing consciousness-raising rallies, publishing ethnically focused magazines, and urging ethnic academics to turn their talents to writing about the "ethnic" experience and to develop formal courses of study which focused on that experience.

Giving impetus to this latter effort was the passage of the federal government's Ethnic Heritage Program, part of the Educational Amendments of 1972, which provided funds for the development of academic programs on the history, cultures, and traditions of various ethnic groups.

Black scholars took the lead in developing such courses and quickly established them as legitimate areas of academic concentration that led to degrees in black studies. Following the success of early black studies programs, scholars from other ethnic groups lobbied for the inclusion of courses in the curricula of academic institutions which offered ethnic students the opportunity to learn about their heritage.

By 1972 a survey of over 200 American higher education institutions by Bengelsdorf (1972) showed that ethnic studies programs included such groups as Asian-Americans, blacks, Chicanos, American Indians, white ethnics (Armenian-Americans, French-Americans,

Greek-Americans, Hungarian-Americans, Irish-Americans, Italian-Americans, Jewish-Americans, and Polish-Americans); multiethnic studies programs also existed. Bengelsdorf concluded her survey with the prediction that: "By almost every measure used—number of courses offered, survey data, comments and predictions of most experts, general societal conditions—it can be concluded that Ethnic Studies is a continuing and growing field in higher education."

Goals. Rationales by advocates and scholars of ethnic studies range from thinly veiled claims of academic universality to an unabashed insistence that schools at all levels have an obligation to provide curricula opportunities that help students understand the unique experiences of their own ethnic group origins as well as the experiences of all the ethnic groups that constitute America. A pervasive contention underlying many early ethnic studies programs was that, until the 1960s, American culture was studied as though ethnic groups did not exist. Thus, the thrust of such programs, consciously or unconsciously, was to correct this "neglect" by ignoring the reality of American culture and highlighting the reality of ethnic groups.

Content. Syllabi of early ethnic studies courses contained materials that focused on the specific ethnic groups rather than on the common elements of all ethnic groups. Typically such courses traced the origins of the group, described its traditions, identified and eulogized its heroes, and attempted to demonstrate the persistence of ethnic residues in the lives of ethnic Americans. Much of both the popular and scholarly literature upon which these courses were based was subjective and historically episodic; often it was calculated to cast the ethnic experience in heroic terms. Its authors staunchly defended their subjectivity and hyperbole on the grounds that only they as "insiders" could comprehend the importance and meaning of ethnicity. Anything written by "outsiders" was either suspect or dismissed as irrelevant. Despite the recency and unevenness of this literature, extensive bibliographies of articles, books, and periodicals exist for every major ethnic group.

Trends. By the 1980s ethnic studies had undergone several major transformations and began showing signs of achieving a more mature status as a scholarly and educational enterprise.

Cordianni and Tipple (1980) argue that the basic reason for these changes is the shift from the "melting pot" image of America toward a recognition of the persistence of ethnic differences among contemporary Americans. This recognition, often termed the "new cultural pluralism," has, in turn, led to new directions in ethnic studies. These include the adoption of social science concepts to systematize ethnic studies, the shift from courses devoted exclusively to a single ethnic group toward those with a comparative, multiethnic approach, and the increase in the number of state laws that have mandated the inclusion of multiethnic courses in the curriculum.

References
James A. Banks, *Teaching Strategies for Ethnic Studies* (1979); Winnie Bengelsdorf, *Ethnic Studies in Higher Education: State of the Art and Bibliography* (1972); Anthony V. Cordianni and Bruce E. Tipple, "Conceptual Changes in Ethnic Studies," *Viewpoints in Teaching and Learning* (1980); and Howard F. Stein and Robert Hall, *The Ethnic Imperative: Examining the New White Ethnic Movement* (1977).

A.A.

ETHNIC STUDIES, irony of. Passi argues that ethnic studies in America have been "ironic" in that they have ignored the persistence of ethnic consciousness in American society and instead have sought to demonstrate the process by which white ethnic communities have been, or are being, absorbed into a homogeneous American culture. This, in turn, results from deeply rooted assumptions about American society which center on the belief that in the New World men were freed from the history, traditions, and institutions of the Old World to recover the ancient freedoms of the "natural" man. This view shaped the interpretation of American nationality from Crèvecoeur to Frederick Jason Turner. Urbanization, industrialization, and mass immigration in the late nineteenth century, in the minds of many American intellectuals, seemed to preclude the possibility of further assimilation of immigrants and threatened to shatter the presumed homogeneity of American culture. Professional social scientists in the emerging universities, however, offered a new synthesis which would make the traditional view of American society compatible with urbanization and industrialization. Drawn largely from the rural and small-town, old-stock, Protestant middle class, these professional academics did not challenge the normative assumption that the society ought to be culturally homogeneous. As new members were recruited into the academic profession, many of them from ethnic backgrounds, the assimilationist position remained unchallenged. This resulted in part from the fact that the concept of assimilation tended to rationalize the upward mobility of ethnic Americans, and in part because the socialization process in the universities compelled students to adopt the intellectual framework of the profession.

Reference
Michael M. Passi, "Mandarins and Immigrants: The Irony of Ethnic Studies in America Since Turner," Ph.D. dissertation, University of Minnesota, 1972.

F.C.

ETHNIC STUDIES HERITAGE ACT (June 23, 1972). 20 U.S.C. 900, P.L. 92-318, Sec. 504(a), 86 Stat. 346, 347. Statement of policy:

> In recognition of the heterogeneous composition of the Nation and of the fact that in a multiethnic society a greater understanding of

the contributions of one's own heritage and those of one's fellow citizens can contribute to a more harmonious, patriotic, and committed populace, and in recognition of the principle that all persons in the educational institutions of the Nation should have an opportunity to learn about the differing and unique contributions to the national heritage made by each ethnic group, it is the purpose of this title to provide assistance designed to afford to students opportunities to learn about the nature of their own cultural heritage, and to study the contributions of the cultural heritages of the other ethnic groups of the Nation.

Further:

The Commissioner is authorized to make grants to, and contracts with, public and private nonprofit educational agencies, institutions, and organizations to assist them in planning, developing, and establishing, and operating ethnic heritage studies programs, as provided in this title. . . . Each program assisted under this title shall: (1) develop curriculum materials for use in elementary or secondary schools or institutions of higher education relating to the history, geography, society, economy, literature, art, music, drama, language, and general culture of the group or groups with which the program is concerned, and the contributions of that ethnic group or groups to the American heritage; or (2) disseminate curriculum materials to permit their use in elementary or secondary schools or institutions of higher education throughout the Nation; or (3) provide training for persons using, or preparing to use, curriculum materials developed under this title; and (4) cooperate with persons and organizations with a special interest in the ethnic group or groups with which the program is concerned to assist them in promoting, encouraging, developing, or producing programs or other activities which relate to the history, culture, or traditions of that ethnic group or groups. . . . There is hereby established a National Advisory Council on Ethnic Heritage Studies consisting of fifteen members appointed by the Secretary who shall be appointed, serve, and be compensated as provided in part D of the General Provisions Act.

In 1981, ESHA grants were incorporated into the Educational Block Grants, and since consolidation ESHA monies and grants have had diminishing effect.

F.C.

ETHNICITY. In a general sense the term "ethnicity" designates the state, character, and/or quality of belonging to an ethnic group. Such a definition, however, implies a precision of usage that does not in fact prevail in the literature of immigration/ethnic studies. Despite the fact of its widespread use, the term is still problematic, and warrants further elaboration in any meaningful effort to encompass the protean qualities characteristic of its usage.

Etymology. As it is currently employed, the concept of ethnicity is of relatively recent vintage. It appeared first in some of the sociological literature of the 1940s and gained general acceptance only in the 1970s, the decade in which ethnic studies proliferated in the United States. Within a short time the term began to evince troublesome conceptual difficulties, largely the result of scholarly disagreement on precisely what "ethnicity" actually encompassed. There was general agreement that it somehow referred to manifest values and other qualities associated with an ethnic group, but in that the precise nature of the ethnic group was also open to controversy, the correlative concept "ethnicity" lost any semblance of precision. Despite the conceptual imprecision, however, the term continued to be used.

Ethnic Groups and Boundaries. Clarification of this confusion necessitated determining the nature of the ethnic group itself. Was such a group an historically derived collectivity sharing certain manifest features (i.e., language, religion, dress style, cuisine, music, lore, and the like) distinctive to its subculture? Or was it essentially an "ascriptive" group, the features of which were ascribed to it (accurately or otherwise) by its members and/or by those who perceived it from the outside? Did its manifest cultural content constitute its definitive quality, or was it rather a group that existed by virtue of its ascribed differences from other groups with which it came into contact? Was such a group an objective reality, primordial in origin and existential in character? Or was it a subjective, relative phenomenon, maintained out of sociopolitical convenience and the psychological need for group and individual identity? It was in the heat of the debate over such questions that the anthropologist Frederick Barth offered a solution to the dilemma. In a seminal essay published in 1969, he argued that for the terms "ethnic group" and "ethnicity" to have any analytic value, the "critical focus of investigation" should be on "the ethnic *boundary* that defines the group, not the cultural stuff that it encloses" (Barth, 14). It was thus the boundaries separating groups, as marked by ascribed cultural qualities, that determined the group's existence and nature. Ethnic groups were, indeed, ascriptive groups, and the ascriptive process provided the essential boundary markers distinguishing one group of ascriptively defined people from the various others with which they came into contact. Barth thus provided students of ethnic phenomena with an essentially new approach to the analysis of ethnic groups. And while not all of the conceptual problems were immediately resolved, the Barthian model came generally to prevail in the field of ethnic studies.

Ethnicity as Affect. With boundaries and boundary maintenance thus established as the "critical focus of investigation" of ethnic groups, there remained but to reexamine the concept of "ethnicity." While the term obviously pertained to the state of belonging to an ethnic group, was there not a further implication that suggested the way an individual member of an ethnic group *felt* about being a part of the group? As the term came to be employed, did it not carry an *affective* connotation? The answer would seem to be yes. Indeed, there is a likelihood that ethnicity should be viewed primarily as an affective phenomenon; a way of feeling about oneself as a member of an ethnic group. In this sense, ethnicity constitutes a significant ingredient in individual identity formation and contributes substantially to the maintenance of the individual's sense of self. While the precise nature of the manifest ethnic culture may thus never be clearly established, and cultural content may constantly be changing and reshaping itself, the individual's associations with, and perceptions and memories of, such ethnic cultural elements evoke emotional responses. "Ethnicity" thus suggests the measure of individual attachment to the group and its ways. It may be primordial/existential or circumstantial/subjective (or both) but it remains primarily a personal phenomenon relating to one's attitude and feeling toward the group and its cultural ways.

Functional Ethnicity: The Larger Dimension. In that ethnicity can be such an important ingredient in identity-formation and group maintenance, it has historically served as a major means whereby humans divide themselves into groups deeply committed to their own "kind." Ethnicity and ethnocentrism would seem to be linked in human group dynamics, and together they have served as a fragmenting force among the world's populations. They also have been the source of considerable friction among those populations even as they have (reciprocally) provided individual and group identity and personal self-esteem. Such dilemmas are common to the human experience. Benign forms of ethnicity can and do exist, but when group ethnocentrism takes on aggressive qualities it can easily turn malignant, and many have died as a result of such malignancies. Nonetheless, ethnicity has been and is a dominant force in human social dynamics, and is almost certain to remain so for the foreseeable future.

References
Frederick Barth, *Ethnic Groups and Boundaries* (1969); George A. DeVos and Lola Romanucci-Ross, eds., *Ethnic Identity* (1975); Nathan Glazer and Daniel P. Moynihan, eds., *Ethnicity: Theory and Experience* (1975); Orlando Patterson, *Ethnic Chauvinism: The Reactionary Impulse* (1978); Werner Sollors, *Beyond Ethnicity* (1986).

J.H.D.

ETS, MARIE HALL. *Rosa: The Life of an Italian Immigrant* (1970). Narrative by a social worker at the Chicago Commons (World

War I and after) of the life of an Italian immigrant peasant woman, assembled out of stories told by Rosa of her early life and experiences.

F.C.

ETTOR, JOSEPH. *See* Arturo M. Giovannitti.

EUGENICS. Eugenics was seen by one of its early twentieth-century leaders, Charles B. Davenport, to be the "science of the improvement of the human race by better breeding." Many eugenicists thought that people's characters, minds, and physiques were rooted chiefly in heredity and concluded that it was imperative to weaken what they considered to be the effect of the "unfit" on the biological and consequently the social history of humanity. They thought that reforms in the environment were largely useful and that, for example, the social class structure of society was an accurate reflection of innate abilities, and that those near the bottom of the social system were there not because of inadequacies of the social system but of their own inherent weaknesses. The eugenicists believed that in eugenics they had discovered the scientific foundation for believing that the "best" families, class, and race should rule and breed.

When eugenicists viewed human history and society they were deeply troubled. They believed, for example, that the decline and fall of Rome was due not to a complex set of political, economic, and social conditions but to the genetic composition of the population. Rome had been inundated by immigrants from the far corners of the empire and these masses had a "poorer hereditary quality." In the Middle Ages, it was argued, those with the best genes had been killed off. In the American colonies the inferior types had settled in the hills of Tennessee and Kentucky while those with more admirable genes had gone to Virginia and New England.

Coming up to their own time—the turn of the century—they believed they saw ominous developments in the United States. They assumed that the native stock was far superior to the immigrant stock. Accompanying the influx of "inferiors" was a decline, thought eugenicists, in the birth rate of the highly talented, and an alarming growth in insanity, crime, and feeble-mindedness.

Eugenicists were determined to convince Americans of the urgent necessity of giving the greatest attention to what they perceived as America's greatest danger. Their concern was expressed in various kinds of organizational work and publications. The Committee of Eugenics of the American Breeders' Association and the Eugenics Record Office were both run by Charles B. Davenport. The latter institution was intended to be a "clearing house" for two hundred "eugenics field officers." The Eugenics Committee of the United States of America had an Immigration Subcommittee which was responsible for trying to make clear the danger to America of allowing the immigration to America of "racially" harmful groups.

The activities of eugenicists were by no means limited to stemming the tide of immigration. The eugenicists threw the net of their concern widely into the sea of dangers. In the early twentieth century some states passed eugenic marriage laws to forbid marriage to a variety of persons seen as biologically and socially harmful to society. The syphilitic, alcoholic, epileptic, and feeble-minded were among those covered. There were also efforts in the direction of asexualization and sterilization. Dr. Harry Sharp, a physician at the Indiana Reformatory, angrily asked in 1902 whether we should "permit idiots, imbeciles and degenerate criminals to continue the pollution of the race. . . ?" Eugenicists went after criminals of various kinds, and those suffering from a wide variety of sicknesses. All such people were often literally seen as dangers to the existence of civilization.

Eugenicist concerns were also expressed in the halls of Congress. If on the one hand, there was peril among the indigenous population, there was also fear that many immigrants entering the country were bringing the genes of inferior stock, and that they would contribute to still further degeneration of the society. The views that those of Anglo-Saxon societies were the most promising candidates for entering America were held by many Americans. Albert Johnson, the chairman of the House Committee on Immigration and Naturalization, was a congressional leader favoring the significant reduction of immigration from eastern and southern European countries. His efforts and those of his allies inside and outside Congress led to the passage of the Immigration Restriction Act of 1924, a decision that may be considered one of the political triumphs of the eugenicist movement.

During roughly the first third of the twentieth century, eugenics was one of the powerful pseudo-sciences that gained a grip on the American imagination. It was, however, challenged, even during its heyday, by geneticists and other scientists who publicly stated that it did not possess the rigorousness of scientific research. Still others argued that its premises had no place in a democratic society. By the late thirties it had lost much of its appeal, although it must be said that there were still advocates, some of whom looked with keen favor at the eugenicist policies of Hitler's Germany.

References
Mark H. Haller, *Eugenics: Hereditarian Attitudes in American Thought* (1960); Kenneth M. Ludmerer, *Genetics and American Society: A Historical Appraisal* (1972).

G.B.

EUGENICS RECORD OFFICE. *See* Davenport, Charles Benedict.

EXECUTIVE ORDER 11246. *See* Affirmative Action.

FAIRCHILD, HENRY PRATT (1880–1956). Sociologist and cultural historian. Fairchild is the author of a major scholarly study, *Greek Immigration to the United States* (1911), dealing with the conditions, causes, and sources of emigration from Greece, Greeks in the United States, and the effects of the emigration on Greece. Fairchild was an opponent of unrestricted immigration based on a seeming prejudice against European immigrants and what he viewed as the incapacity of the nation to absorb them. His restrictionist views are presented in a wide range of articles (e.g., "Restriction of Immigration," *American Journal of Sociology* 17 [March 1912]: 637–646) and books, chief of which are *Immigrant Backgrounds* (1922); *The Melting Pot Mistake* (1926); and *Race and Nationality as Factors in American Life* (1948).

F.C.

FARRELL, JAMES T. (1904–1975). Novelist. In his *Gas House McGinty* (1933), Farrell, born in Chicago's South Side to immigrant Irish laborers, portrays an urban Irish ghetto full of weak-willed people who become victims of their illusions born out of their physical and spiritual poverty. Farrell's criticism and depiction of the social costs of living in a class society reached its zenith in *Studs Lonigan* (1935). Early in his career Farrell became a leader of the anti-Stalinist literary left in the United States, speaking out for artistic freedom of thought. Later in life, he became a liberal anti-Communist. Farrell was considered a leader of twentieth-century critical realism, defending the principles of Marxist literary theory. His main contribution was a sympathetic treatment of the Irish-American experience. Farrell's chief works were *Young Lonigan: A Boyhood in Chicago Streets* (1932) and *Studs Lonigan: A Trilogy* (1935).

Farrell won a Guggenheim Fellowship in 1936 and a Book of the Month Club Fellowship Award for *Studs Lonigan* in 1937; he was elected to the National Institute of Arts and Letters in 1941, received the Newberry Literary Fellowship in 1949, and accepted the Emerson-Thoreau Award from the American Academy of Arts and Sciences in 1969.

Reference
Alan Wald, *James T. Farrell: The Revolutionary Socialist Years* (1978).

C.C.

FELBER, ANSELMA. *See* Swiss.

FELICIAN SISTERS. *See* Poles, Felician Sisters.

FENIAN BROTHERHOOD. The American wing of the Irish Republican Brotherhood (IRB). It was founded in New York on St. Patrick's Day, 1858, and was a secret society dedicated to the destruction of British rule in Ireland. The American Civil War was to be its recruitment and training ground, and indeed many soldiers were sworn into the Fenians. After the war the movement was infiltrated by spies and suffered from serious internal disputes. Several ill-fated invasions of Canada and the military failure of the Fenian rising in Ireland in 1867 contributed to the demise of the organization.

References
W. D'Arcy, *The Fenian Movement in the United States 1858–1886* (1947); W. S. Neidhardt, *Fenianism in North America* (1975).

S.P.M.

FILIPINO REPATRIATION ACT OF 1935. Passed in the midst of the Great Depression in order to send back to the Philippines those Filipino residents in America who were willing to go home at the U.S. government's expense. During the first year of operation, a total of 533 Filipinos were sent back to their native land, at an average cost of $116 per person. By the end of the program in December 1940, a total of 2,190 Filipinos had been repatriated to the Philippines.

Reference
Casiano Coloma, *A Study of Filipino Repatriation Movement* (1974).

D.N.A.

FILIPINOS. Americans of Filipino ancestry today number over one million and vie with Chinese-Americans as the largest group of Asian-Americans. However, because more Filipinos than Chinese are immigrating each year, by 1990 they will very likely be the most numerous.

Immigration from the Philippines into the United States in the last eight decades has been tied closely to the political relations between the two countries. By the terms of the Treaty of Paris, which ended the Spanish-American War in 1899, Spain ceded the Philippines—its colony for 333 years—to the United States for U.S. $25 million. But because Filipino revolutionaries were in the midst of trying to overthrow Spanish colonial rule, not all Filipinos readily accepted their new masters. After three years of guerrilla warfare between American and Filipino forces, military rule was replaced by a civilian government, installed on July 4, 1902, but sporadic mopping-up campaigns continued until the end of the decade.

Since there was considerable sentiment in the United States against the acquisition of the Philippines, those who supported the move had to justify it in lofty terms. They argued that the United States would keep its new insular territory—the word "colony" was eschewed—only until Americans had "tutored" Filipinos in the art of self-government. Accordingly, the colonial administration set up an American-style public education system and recruited thousands of school teachers to help promote the "benevolent assimilation" of America's "little brown brothers." Then, starting in 1903, hundreds of Filipino students (called *pensionados*) were sent on government scholarships to attend universities in the United States. True immigration did not begin, however, until the Hawaiian Sugar Planters' Association (HSPA) sent Albert Judd to the Philippines to recruit laborers in 1906.

Immigration. Filipino immigration can be divided into four periods: 1906–1934, 1934–1946, 1946–1965, and 1965–present.

Recruited Immigration, 1906–1934. Judd managed to secure only 15 Filipinos for the first shipment to Hawaii. In 1907, he persuaded another 150 to go. Given these poor results, the HSPA ceased its efforts in 1908, but it started up again the following year, bringing over 600 to Hawaii. By this time, Japanese laborers could no longer come because the United States and Japan had entered into a "Gentlemen's Agreement" to stop the influx. Since Filipinos were classified as "nationals" of the United States who traveled on U.S. passports, though they did not enjoy any of the other rights of citizenship, their entry was not affected by laws or informal agreements barring immigration from Asia, so the HSPA concentrated its recruitment efforts in the Philippines and in Puerto Rico, which had also been ceded to the United States by the Treaty of Paris. But due to the higher cost of passage from Puerto Rico, it never became a major source of labor supply.

Most of the early batches of Filipinos sent to Hawaii came from Tagalog- and Cebuano-speaking regions in the vicinity of Manila and Cebu City, but beginning in 1915, the HSPA's agents focused on the Ilocano-speaking areas along the northwestern coast of Luzon. Only then did the numbers of immigrants soar because the Ilocano provinces were less fertile and their people had a longer tradition of outmigration. In the 1910s, 29,000 entered Hawaii, about 4,000 of whom returned home, and 2,000 proceeded to the mainland. In the 1920s, 74,000 landed in Hawaii, 26,000 went home, and 13,000 sailed to the continent. Between 1930 and 1935, almost 15,000 came but 31,000 returned home—a reflection of conditions during the Great Depression. For the entire period, among the 119,000 laborers, who were called *sakada,* there were about 9,000 women and 6,000 children.

Few Filipinos traveled directly to the mainland until the mid-1920s. Besides the *pensionados,* a small number of other students came at their own expense. The 1910 U.S. census of population counted only a little over 400 Filipinos in the United States and Alaska, while the 1920 census showed a total of 5,600 on the continent. By 1930, however, an additional 45,000 had arrived. These "first-wave" Filipinos to the mainland called themselves *Pinoys* and *Pinays.*

Virtual Exclusion, 1934–1946. The increasing visibility of Filipino workers elicited negative reactions. In the early 1930s, efforts were made to repatriate them but only slightly over 2,000 accepted the offer of free passage home. Anti-Filipino leaders who wished to exclude them realized that they could not do so until the political status of Filipinos was changed. Thus, a strange coalition developed between individuals who supported independence for the Philippines and others who wanted to keep Filipinos out of the United States. Their goals were realized when the 1934 Tydings-McDuffie Act simultaneously made the Philippines a Commonwealth—with the promise of full independence by 1946—and limited Filipino immigration to 50 persons a year. The HSPA, however, managed to slip in a clause that would grant Hawaii a waiver to import Filipino workers should an emergency need arise in the future.

Limited Immigration, 1946–1965. Filipino immigration after World War II resulted from the role that Filipinos had played during the war. Japan had invaded the Philippines on December 8, 1941, seven hours after its bombers destroyed the American naval base at Pearl Harbor. In the next four months, 15,000 American and 65,000 Filipino soldiers fought side by side as they retreated to Bataan, which fell in April 1942, and Corregidor Island, which fell the first week in May. Both American and Filipino soldiers were then forced on a "death march" to concentration camps.

Meanwhile, Filipinos in the United States volunteered for service by the thousands. The Selective Service decided that Filipino nationals could be reclassified as United States citizens for the purpose of drafting them. So many volunteered that they had to be sworn in at mass naturalization ceremonies. Altogether, 12,000 Filipinos in the United States served in the First and Second Filipino Infantry Regiments during the war. About 1,000 of them became reconnaissance officers who were taken by submarine to the waters off the Philippines and slipped ashore to prepare the way for General Douglas MacArthur's landing at Leyte in 1944. Several thousand others served in the U.S. Navy, which had employed Filipino stewards since the turn of the century.

New reports of the wartime bravery of Filipinos helped to change the negative image that the American public had held of them in earlier years. In 1946, the Philippines became independent and the Luce-Celler

Act granted Filipinos the right of naturalization as well as a token annual immigration quota of 100. In 1946, due to a labor shortage in Hawaii's plantations, the HSPA invoked its right to bring in Filipinos, and 6,000 men, 446 women, and 915 children came.

Far more Filipinos entered the United States as war brides of Filipino-American veterans or as wives of American military personnel between 1946 and 1965, however. Even after the Philippines became independent, the United States continued to maintain military installations there, and some servicemen and officers married Filipinos. Of the 22,000 Filipinos who came to the United States during this period, the vast majority were women who entered as dependents.

Post-1965 Immigration. On October 3, 1965, President Lyndon Johnson signed into law an immigration bill that removed "national origins" as the basis of the quota system of immigration. One of the countries that has sent large numbers of emigrants to the United States since the law went into full effect in 1968 has been the Philippines. An average of 30,000 Filipinos have arrived every year; in one or two years, as many as 40,000 have entered. This is more than the maximum annual number of 20,000 allowed from each country because spouses and unmarried minor children can enter on a nonquota basis. Filipinos have also used the fifth preference (whereby citizens or resident aliens may sponsor their siblings) more extensively than any other immigrant group. Initially women outnumbered men, but at present about two-thirds of the immigrants each year are male.

More than one-quarter of the newcomers have professional, technical, or managerial backgrounds. Medical and health professionals—particularly nurses—have been especially prominent. Some observers have characterized their departure from their homeland as a "brain drain." So many educated people have emigrated because the Philippines has the second highest number of college graduates per capita in the world—next only to the United States. Yet its economy is not sufficiently developed to absorb all the highly trained people its educational institutions produce. Thus, large numbers of professionals emigrate in search of better opportunities not only in the United States but also elsewhere, such as the Middle East. The influx of professionals reached a peak in the early 1970s, but it has slackened since 1976, after an amendment to the 1965 law was passed to downgrade the third preference for skilled manpower to sixth place. Now most come under family reunification criteria.

The urge to emigrate will remain strong among Filipinos because their country has one of the highest population growth rates in the world (2.7 percent in 1980, down from 3.5 percent in 1970). Its gross national product, however, is not keeping pace with population growth and is in fact declining. The income disparity between the rich and the poor has been widening, while martial law—which Ferdinand Marcos declared in 1972 to allow himself to remain in office as his second and final presidential term permitted by the then-existing Constitution neared its end—made the political situation in the country very volatile. Marcos was forced out of office in 1986, but it remains to be seen whether President Corazon Aquino and those who support her will be able to carry out the changes that are needed to insure stability.

Employment, Discrimination, Resistance, and Social Organization. Like the Chinese, Japanese, and Korean immigrants who preceded them, Filipinos also worked initially in the sugar plantations of Hawaii and the fields and orchards of the Pacific coast states. However, they were concentrated in farm work even more heavily than the other three groups. By the mid-1920s, the majority of Hawaiian plantation laborers were Filipinos, while a few years later, Filipinos and Mexicans constituted the bulk of the migrant farm laborers in the western United States.

Those who resided in urban areas earned a living as houseboys, waiters, dishwashers, and bellhops. During the summers, several thousand joined the salmon-packing crews in British Columbia and Alaska. A small number in the Chicago area were employed as Pullman car porters. The most widely dispersed group of Filipinos worked for the U.S. Navy and were located at major ports along the Atlantic, Gulf of Mexico, and Pacific coasts.

Compared to the other Asian immigrant groups, relatively few Filipinos went into business because not many had experience in it, since Spanish colonial policy had relegated retail trade to the Chinese— a pattern that persisted under American rule—and of those who became storekeepers in the villages and small towns, the majority were women, but relatively few of the latter emigrated before World War II. The very small number of Filipinos in the United States who had their own businesses ran barbershops, newsstands, and cigar and candy stalls. Filipinos tended to patronize Chinese-owned outfits, especially gambling joints.

Discrimination against Filipinos in the labor and housing markets was blatant. Signs stating "No Filipinos and dogs allowed" were quite commonplace along the Pacific coast. Anti-Filipino forces were especially eager to eliminate certain features of the *Pinoys'* social life: because such a large proportion of the *Pinoys* were single, whenever they had money to spend, they frequented so-called "taxi dance halls" that employed white women who charged them ten cents a dance. The social interaction across racial lines aroused the ire of many whites.

Hostility on occasion led to violent outbreaks. In late October 1929, some white men attending a festival at Exeter, California, threw objects at a number of Filipinos who were with white women. A Filipino then stabbed one of the white men. Infuriated, a mob of 300 marched to a nearby ranch whose owner had employed Filipino farm workers and burned the barn.

Early in January of the following year, the Monterey (California) Chamber of Commerce passed an anti-Filipino resolution. Ten days later, when a new taxi dance hall opened near Watsonville, a town in the Monterey Bay area, 200 armed whites roamed the streets looking for Filipinos to harass. A few days after that, vigilantes raided the dance hall. Then on the evening of January 22, about 500 men destroyed buildings that housed Filipinos, beat up several of them, and killed Fermin Tober, who was hiding in a bunkhouse at Murphy's ranch. Tober's body was shipped back to Manila where it lay in state for two days before it was buried. The bullet that killed Tober, declared an orator at the funeral service, "was not aimed at him particularly; its principal target was the heart of our race."

In August 1930, dynamite was thrown into a camp in Reedley, California, where 100 Filipino farm workers slept. Sporadic violence also greeted Filipinos in Imperial, Lake, Sonoma, and Stanislaus counties in California in the next few years.

Despite such intimidation and the offer of the U.S. government to pay the passage home of any Filipino willing to repatriate, Filipinos remained in the country and continued to associate with white women. So the courts moved to outlaw interracial marriages. Initially, in *Roldan* v. *Los Angeles County* (1933), the courts had ruled that existing anti-miscegenation statutes did not apply to Filipinos even though the California attorney general had instructed county clerks to treat them as "Mongolians," who, like blacks, were barred from marrying whites. But the California state legislature soon amended Section 60 of the Civil Code to read: "All marriages of white persons with Negroes, Mongolians, members of the Malay race, or mulattos are illegal and void." Since Filipinos are Malayo-Polynesians, they could no longer marry whites.

Filipino immigrants dealt with the harsh conditions they faced by organizing themselves. In 1919, Pablo Manlapit founded the Filipino Federation of Labor in Hawaii and began to organize Filipino plantation workers. Some 3,000 of them subsequently participated in the multiracial strike of 1920. They struck again in 1924 on twenty-three plantations, during which sixteen Filipinos and four policemen were killed. In 1937, Antonio Fagel led 3,500 workers in a strike against the Puunene plantation. When the International Longshoremen's and Warehousemen's Union began organizing in Hawaii in 1934, Filipinos were among the most ardent participants, even though the Filipino Federation of America, a religious fraternal organization under the leadership of Hilario Moncado, opposed all union membership.

In the early 1930s also, many who worked in the salmon canneries of Alaska became active members of the Cannery Workers and Farm Laborers Union chartered by the American Federation of Labor. This organization broke with the AF of L and became Local 7 of the United Cannery, Agricultural, Packing and Allied Workers of America in 1937. It then went through several incarnations, affiliating first with the Congress of Industrial Organizations and later with the International Longshoremen's and Warehousemen's Union.

In California, Filipino farm workers under the leadership of the Filipino Labor Union struck against Salinas lettuce growers in 1934, and another 6,000 organized by the Filipino Agricultural Laborers' Association (FALA) struck against asparagus growers in the San Joaquin Delta in 1939. FALA also won contracts for brussels sprouts pickers in San Mateo County, celery cutters in San Joaquin County, and garlic harvesters in San Benito County. In 1940, when it claimed 30,000 members, it affiliated with the AF of L. Thus, when Filipino farm workers in the Agricultural Workers Organizing Committee (AWOC) under Larry Itliong struck against California grape growers in 1965, they were perpetuating a long tradition of labor militance. In 1967, AWOC joined together with Mexican-American farm workers led by Cesar Chavez to form the United Farm Workers of America.

Filipinos also found fellowship through several nonlabor organizations. The two most important were the Caballeros de Dimas-Alang (Dimas-Alang was the *nom de plume* of Jose Rizal, the national hero of the Philippines) and the Legionarios del Trabajo. The first had been established in Manila in 1906 to advocate independence for the Philippines and a branch was set up in San Francisco in 1921 to promote the ideas of Rizal and another nationalist leader, Apolinario Mabini. The latter, organized in Manila in 1916 in the wake of a strike against the Manila Electric Company, set up a branch in San Francisco in 1924. In the American context, both organizations functioned primarily as fraternal lodges with accompanying women's auxiliaries. Clubs of fellow provincials and townspeople also sprang up whose members gathered each year to honor the patron saints of their localities. Finally, churches—Catholic and Protestant—provided social as well as spiritual sustenance.

The more recent immigrants are quite a different lot and the social organization of contemporary Filipino-American communities reflects their different status. Although fraternal orders and similar organizations still exist, professional and trade associations have assumed far more importance. Many have been formed to deal with the obstacles that Filipino professionals face in the United States today. Lawyers, for example, usually must attend certified law schools in the United States before they can hope to pass the bar. Physicians who may have practiced independently for years before emigration must serve as interns and residents before they can qualify for licensing. A California law prohibits foreign optometrists from taking state licensing examinations. Before 1970, foreign-trained nurses could work so long as they came in under student visas or as exchange visitors, but since 1970 they have had to pass examinations before they can get hired. Filipino accountants in California are granted licenses only on a case-by-case basis. In terms of visibility, these professionals and their struggles have overshadowed the still large number of aging plantation laborers and farm workers who continue to live under poor conditions and who are ill served by social service agencies.

As their numbers increase, Filipino-Americans are also beginning to flex their political muscles. Some of the first ones who ran for public office successfully were women: Dolores Sibonga was the first Filipino elected to the Seattle city council; Thelma Garcia Buchholdt served four terms in the Alaska state legislature; and Connie Chun of the Hawaii state assembly has expressed ambitions for higher office. Men are also becoming active: Monty Manibog served as mayor of Monterey Park, California; Ernie Sana has just announced his candidacy for the Daly City (California) city council. In the very near future, Filipino-Americans, who are already the largest group of Asian-Americans in California, will no doubt claim their place in the political arena and will use the power they thus gain to erase whatever social and economic discrimination that their compatriots still experience.

References
Ruben R. Alcantara, *Sakada: Filipino Adaptation in Hawaii* (1981); Edwin B. Almirol, *Ethnic Identity and Social Negotiation: A Study of a Filipino Community in California* (1985); Fred Cordova, *Filipinos: Forgotten Asian Americans, A Pictorial Essay, 1763–1963* (1983); Bruno Lasker, *Filipino Immigration* (1931; rpt. 1969); and Jesse Quinsaat, ed., *Letters in Exile: An Introductory Reader on the History of Filipinos in America* (1976).

S.C.

FILIPINOS, migrations abroad.

Migratory movements have always been present as an underlying element of continuity in Philippine history. From the earliest colonizations (Yengoyan 1967), to the major frontier movements of the twentieth century, long-distance migration—often permanent, frequently disruptive socially, but generally positive in its motivation—has been the recurrent theme. One such pattern of frontier movements is the focus of this essay: the migration of Filipinos across the borders of their nation to places beyond. The purpose of this article is to place the facts of Filipino migration to the United States, the most important foreign destination, in demographic perspective. This is accomplished by setting forth the statistical evidence in two general areas: 1) the basic demography of Filipinos in the Philippines (emphasizing, of course, marked patterns of internal migration and redistribution); 2) the changing social and demographic structure of the Filipino population in the United States. (Smith)

Reference
Peter C. Smith, "The Social Demography of Filipino Migrations Abroad," *International Migration Review* 10 (Fall 1976): 307–353.

F.C.

FILIPINOS, Pensionado Act of 1903. Approved by the Philippine Commission on August 26, 1903, under the Taft administration. The act, which went into operation in November of that year, enabled young Filipinos to come to America for their training and education at various institutions of higher learning at government expense. The first 100 students were selected from 20,000 applicants, and they were placed in American homes to learn about life in the United States. Their fields of study were education, engineering, agriculture, and medicine. By 1907 there were 183 Filipinos enrolled in forty-seven schools and colleges. At the end of their education in 1910, all *pensionados* returned to assume important positions in the Philippine Islands under American control.

D.N.A.

FILIPPINI RELIGIOUS TEACHERS. Founded in 1692 by Saint Lucy Filippini and Cardinal Marcantonio Barbarigo in Montefiascone, Italy. Since 1910, through teaching and social work, the Religious Teachers Filippini have brought hope to a vast number of Italian immigrants. Commissioned by Pope Pius X, five sisters arrived in Saint Joachim Paris, Trenton, New Jersey, to care for the spiritual and educational needs of immigrants. Like all pioneers, they encountered many difficulties. With Bishop Thomas Joseph Walsh's encouragement, the struggling community prospered. Under the dynamic leadership of Mother Ninetta Jonata, an American mother house and novitiate was established when a group of young sisters from Italy joined them in 1921. To compete with other teachers, they attended American colleges and universities and soon taught the Italian immigrants that the most effective way to give themselves and their children dignity in the American social environment was through education. Not only did they help preserve the customs and traditions of the Italian community, but they also directed church choirs and plays, visited homes and local hospitals, and conducted catechetical classes for those unable to attend their schools.

The Religious Teachers Filippini presently work in Italy, England, Brazil, Switzerland, Ireland, Ethiopia, and India. In the United States they staff fifty-five schools and missions in fifteen dioceses and three archdioceses and are actively engaged in a variety of apostolic works. Among their accomplishments as educators, they were the first to seek and obtain approval from the Department of Education in New Jersey for the teaching of Italian to be placed on the same level as other foreign languages. As part of the teaching profession, the Religious Teachers of Saint Lucy Filippini have inspired numberless students who have distinguished themselves as doctors, lawyers, businessmen, political leaders, religious, clergymen, and teachers.

Reference
Margherita Marchione, *From the Land of the Etruscans* (1986).

M.M.

FINNISH EVANGELICAL LUTHERAN CHURCH. *See* Finns.

FINNISH PEOPLE'S REPUBLIC. *See* Nuorteva, Santeri.

FINNS. Though a relatively small immigrant group, because of their unique settlement patterns and their distinctive political proclivities, the Finns had a significant impact on certain regions of the United States. They were fewer in numbers than their Norwegian and Swedish counterparts and they arrived later, at a period in American history characterized by rapid industrialization. A small number of Finns arrived in North America as early as the 1630s, playing a role in the establishment of the short-lived Swedish colony along the Delaware River. In addition, Finns were in evidence in Russian-governed Alaska and in California during the gold rush. However, mass immigration did not begin until 1870, with the peak period of migration occurring between 1900 and 1915.

Migratory Push and Pull Factors. Due in part to Finland's geographical remoteness and in part to the lateness with which industrialization occurred, mass migration did not begin prior to the Civil War. However, after labor recruiters succeeded in bringing Finns, along with Norwegians and Swedes, to the Upper Peninsula of Michigan to work in the copper mines during the war, Finns began to arrive in substantial numbers. Between 1870 and 1920, 350,000 Finns left their homeland destined for the United States. During this time, but more importantly after the enactment of immigration restriction legislation in 1924, Canada played an important role as receiving country. Approximately one-ninth of the total population of the country emigrated during this fifty-year period.

Emigration was fundamentally a result of the disruptive consequences associated with the industrialization and urbanization of Finland. Several push factors contributed to the willingness to migrate. Population pressures increased due to a rapidly rising birth rate. The agricultural economy and the lumber industry suffered serious crises, making it impossible for a growing sector of the landless rural population to survive economically. Emigration resulted, rather than internal migration, because of the inability of urban industrial centers to absorb this incipient working class. Finally, in addition to these demographic and economic factors, political considerations became prominent due to the Russification campaign of Czar Nicholas II (a province of Sweden for several centuries, Finland had become a Grand Duchy of Russia in 1809). One of the elements of this campaign that served as a stimulus to migration was the decree requiring mandatory military conscription in the Russian army.

Though the Finnish upper class and the hierarchy of the Lutheran state church roundly condemned emigrants, *Amerikan tauti* (American fever) spread, aided by the emergence of a well-developed transportation system and by the process of chain migration that began once a small contingent of Finns had gained a foothold in America. Those who arrived early influenced others through their letters and frequently provided money and prepaid tickets to family members and friends still in the homeland.

Finns settled in three major regions of the United States: the Northeast, the upper Midwest, and the Pacific Northwest. The western Great Lakes region, which includes Michigan's Upper Peninsula, eastern Minnesota, and northern Wisconsin, was the locale that constantly attracted a majority of emigrating Finns. The area was more male-dominated than the other regions, and young workers found employment among the ranks of unskilled laborers in copper and iron mines, in the lumber industry, and on the docks. Many, sometimes after an initial stint in an industrial setting, acquired small farms. The Finns tended to settle in smaller cities rather than major urban complexes, thereby enhancing their numerical impact on the settlement communities. Thus, they chose Calumet over Detroit, Duluth over Minneapolis, Rockford over Chicago, and Ashtabula over Cleveland. By 1920, 52 percent of Finns in America resided in this area.

At the same time, 25 percent of the ethnic group resided in western states, including the largest concentrations in Washington, Oregon, and California, and with smaller settlements in Colorado, Wyoming, Utah, Montana, Nevada, and Idaho. They were often engaged in the same primary extractive industries as their counterparts were in the Midwest. Farming was not as extensively pursued, but in some places commercial fishing was a major source of employment. Finns settled in large numbers in the small towns, such as Eureka rather than San Francisco, and

Astoria rather than Portland. Indeed, Astoria earned the appellation "the Helsinki of the West."

In the East, Finns settled primarily in Massachusetts and New York. In the latter case, while there were rural settlements such as that in Spencer, New York City proved to be a magnet. Two ethnic enclaves developed, one in the Red Hook section of Brooklyn and the other in Harlem. This was an anomaly to the general locational pattern, as can be seen when observing the situation in Massachusetts. There Finns preferred such locales as Worcester, Fitchburg, Gardner, Maynard, Cape Ann, and Lanesville to Boston. At least 80 percent of Finns in the state resided in urban environs. Occupational patterns were more varied, with many finding employment in granite quarries and in the textile industry.

Ethnic Institutions. In the earliest period of ethnic group life in America, the boardinghouse and the saloon served as important, if makeshift, institutions. However, very rapidly new institutions were created, abetted by the organizational activities of varied and disparate ethnic entrepreneurs and leaders. During the first three decades of the twentieth century, the Finnish-American community was composed of four types of institution, each with a number of distinct and often oppositional variants: churches, mutual aid societies, radical political organizations, and consumer cooperatives. Linked to these efforts, newspapers served a vital function and the number rapidly proliferated, due in no small part to the high literacy rate among the Finnish immigrants.

Approximately 25 percent of the immigrant generation affiliated with various churches. Though some opted for Methodism, Unitarianism, or Congregationalism, most remained Lutheran. However, within the ranks of Lutherans, various antagonistic strains developed, the differences often based on conflicting views about the appropriateness of establishing an arm of the Finnish state church in America. In 1890 the Finnish Evangelical Lutheran church (or Suomi Synod) was established by leaders who perceived it to be the "true daughter" of the homeland church. Eight years afterwards the synod was challenged by the Finnish American National church and by various sectarian groups that referred to themselves as Apostolic Lutherans or Laestadians.

While a variety of mutual aid societies was established, perhaps the most important were the temperance societies which sprang up around the country as testimony to the fact that alcoholism was a serious social problem for Finns. Among the other societies to emerge, the Knights and Ladies of Kaleva should be singled out as one of the most influential and enduring.

Finnish immigrants constituted perhaps the most politically radical ethnic group in America. It is estimated that between one-fourth and one-third of Finnish-Americans participated in the institutional network forged by radicals. Between 1906 and 1914, the Finnish Socialist Federation was the largest of the Socialist party's foreign-language federations. After 1914 Finns converted in droves to industrial unionism and they became the dominant ethnic group in the Industrial Workers of the World (IWW). During the 1920s, the so-called "Red Decade," Finns shifted toward communism, coming to constitute nearly 45 percent of the Workers' (Communist) party.

Finally, Finns played an important role in creating consumer cooperatives in the country. Though based on the Rochdale model, radicals politicized the cooperative movement, viewing it as an important training ground for the future leaders in the socialist commonwealth. These locally based coops were quite often very successful business enterprises.

From Immigrants to Ethnics. By the 1930s, and at an accelerated pace in the postwar period, far-reaching changes in the institutional structure of the ethnic community occurred. This resulted in the steady erosion of members from mutual aid societies, cooperatives, and radical political organizations and the progressive Americanization of the churches. Temperance societies were increasingly perceived to be old-fashioned and parochial by Finnish-Americans whose mores included the acceptance of social drinking. The insurance programs of the mutual aid societies were forced to compete with giant corporations. Similarly, cooperatives were unable to compete successfully with supermarket chains, especially since younger Finns were not inclined to exhibit loyalty to distinctly ethnic enterprises. Radicalism declined due to a combination of factors, including internecine political strife, the flight of several thousand Finnish-Americans to Soviet Karelia in the 1930s, the changing class structure of the United States, the prosperity of the 1950s, and political repression. In the case of churches, the Suomi Synod merged with the Lutheran Church in America in 1963 and the smaller National church merged with Missouri Synod Lutherans the following year. Only the sectarian Apostolic groups remain as ethnic churches.

Linked to these changes has been the steady decline in language loyalty and the steady increase in exogamous marriages. Nonetheless, since the 1960s there has been an expansion of interest in the history of the ethnic community by largely assimilated third- and fourth-generation Finns. This interest tends largely to be a manifestation of symbolic ethnicity, where feeling ethnic does not have any behavioral consequences.

References
A. William Hoglund, *Finnish Immigrants in America, 1880–1920* (1960); Ralph Jalkanen, ed., *The Finns in North America* (1969); Eino Jutikkala, *A History of Finland*

(1962); Michael Karni and Douglas Ollila, eds., *For the Common Good* (1977); Reino Kero, *Migration from Finland to North America in the Years Between the United States Civil War and the First World War* (1974); Peter Kivisto, *Immigrant Socialists in the United States: The Case of Finns and the Left* (1984); Carl Ross, *The Finn Factor in American Labor, Culture, and Society* (1977).

P.K.

FINNS, radicalism in the Western Great Lakes Region. Approximately 25–30 percent of the Finnish immigrants after 1900 were radicals. They were either radicalized before they left Finland or quickly converted to radicalism once they arrived in America, helped to that position by a strong corps of immigrant agitators among them. After 1913 there was no solidarity among them. At that time the Finnish Socialist Federation was split in the Midwest. Approximately 3,000 members thought joining the IWW (instead of remaining in the Socialist party) would more clearly reflect their position. This action caused much trouble in the Midwest. Despite the factionalized character of the Finnish radicals, however, it must be recognized that their radicalism was due in large part to the failure of American life to give them what they immigrated for. At their peak the Finns claimed 17,000 card-carrying members of radical movements and an undetermined number of unofficial supporters.

Reference
Michael G. Karni, "*Yhteishyva*—or, For the Common Good: Finnish Radicalism in the Western Great Lakes Region, 1900–1940," Ph.D. dissertation, University of Minnesota, 1975.

F.C.

FINNS, spatial patterns in America. The unique concentrations of Finnish immigrants in the United States have attracted much attention and considerable speculation as to the reason why multitudes decided to settle in the same towns or farming settlements, or at least in the same general area. The assertions that the Finns have settled those areas of the United States that most "looked like Finland" and are "most similar to Finland" have been repeated often enough to be accepted as a general truth. Kaups examines the environmentalist material bearing upon the problem. Also, the location and concentrations of Finnish immigrants in the United States is reevaluated in spatial and temporal perspectives. The cross-sectional method of historical geography is employed. A series of choropleth maps on national, regional, and local scales depict the changing spatial patterns of the Finnish immigrants in the United States (1880–1920).

Reference
Matti E. Kaups, "Suuri Laansi—Or the Finnish Discovery of America," Ph.D. dissertation, University of Minnesota, 1966.

F.C.

FINNS, working-class radicalism. Finnish immigrants to Midwest mining communities have had a major impact upon the development of radical political and labor movements in the western Great Lakes region. Gedicks explores a number of questions about Finnish-American participation in these radical movements. He traces the origins of Finnish-American radicalism in the initial penetration of the Finnish countryside by capitalist agriculture. In opposition to the explanation advanced by the "social disease of industrialism" theorists, he argues that it is the emergence of capitalist forms of social relations, rather than the breakdown of precapitalist forms of social relations, that accounts for radical predispositions among Finnish immigrants. This hypothesis is tested with data on the agrarian origins of Finnish and Swedish immigrants and their differing political responses in Michigan and Minnesota mining communities.

Reference
Albert J. Gedicks, "Working Class Radicalism Among Finnish Immigrants in Minnesota and Michigan Mining Communities," Ph.D. dissertation, University of Wisconsin, Madison, 1979.

F.C.

FIRST CATHOLIC SLOVAK UNION. *See* Slovaks.

FLOWER, B[ENJAMIN] O[RANGE] (1858–1918). Social reformer, editor. Flower served to alter the condition of immigrant poor by rousing the conscience of the nation. He sincerely believed that once a "plain bald statement of facts" had been submitted to public judgment, nothing could stand in the way of reform. *The Arena,* edited by Flower, was primarily a journal of social reform advocacy. As editor of *The Menace,* Flower was virulently anti-Catholic. His chief work was *Civilization's Inferno; Or, Studies in the Social Cellar* (1893).

F.C.

FLYNN, ELIZABETH GURLEY (1890–1964). Communist, social activist among unskilled, unorganized, mostly immigrant workers.

Reference
Elizabeth Gurley Flynn, *I Speak My Own Piece: Autobiography of "The Rebel Girl"* (1955; rpt. 1973).

F.C.

FOERSTER, ROBERT F[RANZ] (1883–1941). Economist; professor of economics, Princeton University. Foerster's primary interest was the economic context in which immigration was to be studied; as he observed: "It is assumed in most of our writings upon immigration that the causes of emigration may be glossed over, the situation of emigrants in other lands ignored, the policy of the country of emigration passed by, and so forth." Foerster's *The Italian Emigration of Our Times* (1919; rpt. 1968) is a vast storehouse of information on the mass Italian migrations between 1876 and 1919 to all parts of the world. Chapters 17–20 (pp. 320–411) are devoted to the experience in the United States. See also Foerster's *Racial Problem Involved in Immigration from Latin America* (1925).

Reference
Francesco Cordasco, *Italian Mass Emigration* (1980).

F.C.

FOLKS, HOMER (1867–1963). Public health crusader, child welfare worker, welfare administrator. Folks was a pioneer in policy development for the care of needy delinquent and orphan children. His long services (1893–1947) as executive secretary of the New York State Charities Aid Association (SCAA) (*q.v.*) brought him into continuing association with the immigrant poor and their children. Folks believed that, for the most part, delinquency and dependency among the poor and their children were the results of family disintegration caused by poverty rooted in social and economic conditions, a view not generally held at the time. Chief works: *The Care of Destitute, Neglected and Delinquent Children* (1902); *The Human Costs of the War* (1920); *Public Health and Welfare* (1958).

Reference
Walter I. Trattner, *Homer Folks: Pioneer in Social Welfare* (1968).

F.C.

FORCED MIGRATIONS. Teitelbaum:

> The mass expulsion of hundreds of thousands of people can no longer be viewed as the aberrational behavior of mad political leaders. To the contrary, such actions have become quite deliberate instruments of both domestic and foreign policy for various sovereign nations. In the past decade alone, literally millions have been coerced—often by their own governments—to flee their homes, sometimes onto the high seas in unseaworthy boats. Obvious examples include those of Vietnam, Uganda, and Cuba, discussed in greater detail below, but other expulsions have also occurred or loom as future possibilities. . . . Whatever approach

is taken, it seems clear enough from the experiences of the past decade that mass expulsions of citizens pose serious threats to peaceful relations among the state involved, and to the human rights of the victims. The prospects for future state actions of this type are disturbingly real, and as such the matter deserves attention at the highest levels of governments and international institutions.

Reference
Michael S. Teitelbaum, "Forced Migration: The Tragedy of Mass Expulsions," in Nathan Glazer, ed., *Clamor at the Gates: The New American Immigration* (1985), pp. 261–283.

F.C.

FORD, HENRY. *See* Americanization Movement.

FORD, PATRICK (1837–1913). Journalist. In his *Irish World* (New York), Patrick Ford, a native of County Galway, Ireland, not only attacked British tyranny in Ireland, but also condemned American capitalism and Irish landlordism as twin exploiters of the Irish poor on both sides of the Atlantic Ocean. Ford's attack on the landlord system in Ireland was a prelude to the New Departure strategy in Irish nationalism which eventually led to peasant proprietorship in Ireland and the emergence of Charles Stuart Parnell as commander over the forces of Irish nationalism. In the mid-1880s, industrial violence in the United States persuaded Ford to retreat from an economic radicalism inspired by Henry George to more moderate and pragmatic social and economic positions. He stopped his assaults on Catholic clericalism and abandoned anticapitalism. Instead he advised Irish-Americans to improve their conditions in America by embracing middle-class habits of ambition and thrift.

Reference
James Paul Rodechko, *Patrick Ford and His Search for America: A Case Study of Irish-American Journalism, 1870–1913* (1976).

F.C.

FOREIGN-BORN EMIGRATION FROM THE UNITED STATES. The study of emigration of foreign-born persons by age and sex for 1960 to 1970 by census counts of the foreign-body population, adjusted life table survival rates, and annual statistics on alien immigration published by the Immigration and Naturalization Service suggests that more than one million foreign-born persons left the United States between 1960 and 1970. "This has important implications for U.S. immigration policy and for net immigration policy and for net immigration data used to estimate the population of the United States."

Reference
Robert Warren and Jennifer M. Peck, "Foreign-Born Emigration from the United States: 1960 to 1970," *Demography* 17 (Feb. 1980): 71–84.

F.C.

FRANCO-AMERICANS. *See* French.

FREE ALBANIA ASSOCIATION. *See* Albanians.

FRENCH, Americanization of French Louisiana. Newton traces the relations between the "old" population and the "new" population to 1960 and explains the process of absorption of the former by the latter. Newton explains the use of certain terms. He shows that the population of Louisiana in 1803 was mainly French in derivation and character. This population was variously termed "old," "ancient," "native," "French," and "Creole," and by these terms it was meant to exclude the few Anglo-Americans who were then in Louisiana. A Creole was properly one born in Louisiana of French or Spanish parentage or remoter descent, and in no sense did it imply a mixture with Negro or Indian blood. Often the term assimilated to itself in usage all persons of French descent, whether born in Louisiana, France, or elsewhere, but Newton has usually employed the word "French" rather than "Creole" when these latter were included. Only occasionally is "Creole" used to signify anything native to Louisiana, such as Creole cane, Creole eggs, or Creole cotton; and then such usage seems to have been derived from the fact that such things were produced in the land of the Creoles. The part of Louisiana's population that came from the other states or territories of the United States or were descended from such immigrants are referred to as "new," "American," or "Anglo-American." Though Newton recognizes that, strictly speaking, the French and Anglo-Americans are not separate races, common usage would seem to justify the employment of the word "race" or "racial" in this study when reference is made to the peculiar attitudes of these two groups.

Reference
Lewis W. Newton, *The Americanization of French Louisiana: A Study of the Process of Adjustment Between the French and the Anglo-American Population of Louisiana* (1980).

F.C.

FRENCH, The Sentinelle Affair, 1924–1929. The Sentinelle affair involved a group of Franco-Americans (French Canadian immigrants and their descendants) in New England, most notably in Woonsocket, Rhode Island, who in the years following World War I became increasingly disturbed about the state of their ethnic and religious survival in the United States. Led by Elphège Daignault, they decided militantly to defend their nationality's rights. These Franco-American militants identified the Irish hierarchy of the Catholic church as the principal enemy. They felt that the church wanted forcibly to "Americanize" Franco-Americans by limiting the teaching of native language and customs in their parochial schools and by centralizing diocesan activities, which would threaten the autonomy of individual Franco-American parishes.

Reference

Richard S. Sorrell, "The Sentinelle Affair (1924–1929) and Militant *Survivance:* The Franco-American Experience in Woonsocket, Rhode Island," Ph.D. dissertation, State University of New York, Buffalo, 1975.

F.C.

FRENCH (CANADIANS). Many Americans think of French and French Canadian as synonymous, an error which neither nationality appreciates. The more than six million people of French ancestry who live in Canada, primarily in the province of Quebec, are of course descendants of the few thousand souls from France who settled in the colony of New France prior to the English Conquest in 1763. However, there has been little population flow between France and Canada since that time, and French Canadians are proud of their more than two centuries of survival as a nationality distinct from the French.

The term "Franco-American" includes both French and French Canadian immigrants to the United States, but emigration from French Canada has been much greater than from France. Since colonial times more than 700,000 people have emigrated from France to the United States; many of these were Protestant Huguenots who arrived before 1790, and almost all have been assimilated into American society to a greater degree than have French Canadians. The total number of French Canadian immigrants to America is about 1.5 million, twice as high as the French figure, and most of the French Canadians are more recent arrivals, from after the Civil War. About half a million came during each of the two greatest periods of immigration, 1865–1890 and 1905–1929. The total number of Franco-Americans today with Canadian ancestry is in excess of two million, if all generations are included.

When an American thinks of French influences in his country, the first image that comes to mind is that of New Orleans and Louisiana. For the real center of Franco-Americana, however, one must look to New England where approximately three-quarters of those of French Canadian descent settled (henceforth "Franco-American" and "Franco" shall refer only to those of Canadian origin). Francos have long been one of the most regionally concentrated ethnic groups in the United States, but the casual tourist to New England may be unaware of this. Unlike many other nationalities, French Canadians did not gravitate en masse to the largest cities, in this case Boston, Providence, or Hartford. The true "Little Canadas" of New England are to be found in the smaller cities (Woonsocket, Rhode Island; Lewiston, Maine; Manchester, New Hampshire; Fall River and Lowell, Massachusetts) which form a large semicircle around Boston, and which were dependent upon textiles and shoes for their industrial livelihood in the decades between the Civil War and World War I.

La survivance has for centuries been the raison d'être for French Canadians living in Quebec. This term refers to their belief, dating back to the English Conquest of 1763, that they have a divine mission to preserve their national "race" and religion against Anglo-Saxon inroads. Such national survival was traditionally seen as hinging on two triads: devotion to church, family, and the land were the means by which a loyal French Canadian would maintain *la foi* (Roman Catholicism), *la langue,* and *les moeurs* (traditional customs) of his homeland.

The urban-industrial environment of New England was far removed from the traditional peasant culture of nineteenth-century rural-agricultural Quebec. However, the Franco-American elite (priests, doctors, lawyers) strenuously attempted to preserve these triads of *la survivance* among the masses of Franco-American factory workers. During their period of greatest migration (from the Civil War until the Great Depression), this struggle to resist assimilation was largely successful, primarily due to three factors.

(1) Franco-Americans can be grouped with Mexicans and Puerto Ricans under the category of "commuting (im)migrants," groups whose proximity to respective homelands slowed their acculturation into American society. Only a few hundred land miles from Quebec, Franco-Americans in New England could easily renew contacts with their homeland which would fortify their desire to maintain *la survivance*.

(2) Concentrated mainly in the smaller cities of New England mentioned previously, where they often constituted from one-fourth to over one-half of the total population, Franco-Americans were neither as dispersed nor as dwarfed as immigrant groups who were more widely distributed throughout the entire country or were living in large metropolises. Such demographic preponderance led to the development of a strong ethnic community life which fostered *la survivance*.

(3) Quebec was not only geographically close to Franco-Americans: the struggle for *la survivance* in the Quebec homeland, with its nationalistic and religious ramifications, was the core of a living experience central to the existence of the emigrant elite, who inherited the

French Canadian sense of history as destiny (*Je me souviens*—"I remember"; *Notre Maître, le passé*—"Our Master, the past"). As a minority group in a country that they no longer controlled after 1763, Quebec's French Canadians had developed a sense of aloneness and an introspective obsession with group solidarity and national survival.

Thus, those Franco-Americans who emigrated from Quebec had a sense of being a minority, hence an ethnic group, even *before* they arrived in the United States. This may explain much of their success at ethnic survival after they immigrated, a survival that seemed secure as late as the 1920s. The ultimate irony, however, is that the Franco-American elite believed that they were clinging to traditions developed in the Quebec homeland; yet, even when *la survivance* was strong, all of these traditions and the institutions that emerged to support them (national parishes and parochial schools within the American Catholic church, fraternal and mutual benefit societies, a French-language press) were being altered by the differences between the situation of French Canadians in Quebec and that of Franco-Americans in New England.

Could *la survivance* ever be as successful in New England as it was in Quebec? The answer is no, since New England was not Quebec and therefore *la survivance à la* the motherland was not transferable. In America there was a tradition of separation of church and state, and of no established religions, which meant that Catholicism could never play as dominant a role in Franco-American life as it did in Quebec. In addition, Francos did not control the hierarchy of the Catholic church in America, as did their brethren in French Canada. The Irish-American hierarchy of the American Catholic church supported an assimilationist position, and ultimately triumphed over the Franco-American view which fused ethnic identity and religion (*Qui perd sa langue, perd sa foi*).

The guarantees French Canadians had won from their British rulers and English Canadian co-citizens, which protected their religion, language, laws, and customs in Quebec, could never be gained anew in the United States. There, Francos were merely one of many nationalities in a polyglot country, while in Canada they were recognized either as one of two founding nationalities, or at the least a special minority entitled to distinctive rights and privileges. Finally, Franco-Americans could never numerically dominate New England, not even its mill towns, to the degree that French Canadians dominated the province of Quebec, where they constituted four-fifths of the population. Without this demographic solidarity, assimilationist inroads were inevitable.

These inroads became dramatically evident in the years after 1930. Emigration from Quebec fell off drastically. Class concerns loomed larger than ethnicity during the Great Depression. World War II gave most Americans a common purpose, and members of all nationalities who served in the war gained new horizons beyond ethnic neighborhoods. An upsurge in prosperity and suburban living followed the war. The new accessibility of the American ideal of the middle class, coupled with occupational and residential mobility, meant a further breaking down of old ethnic identities. Franco-American youths began to show apathy toward aspects of their heritage, such as the French language and conservative Catholic values. This trend went hand in hand with declining attendance in national parishes and parochial schools, which were facing mounting financial problems.

Some of these assimilationist trends seem to have been reversed in the 1970s and 1980s, as a new generation of Franco-Americans, caught up in the neo-ethnic revival, takes a greater interest in its ethnic past. Franco-American linguistic and historical centers (most notably the French Institute of Assumption College in Worcester, Massachusetts) have recently emerged in New England as part of this ethnic renaissance, and these centers are working hard to promote bilingualism and ethnic historical awareness among younger Franco-Americans. Nevertheless, this new generation is far more distant from its heritage as a result of more than half a century of inexorable acculturation. To most Franco-Americans of today, their history is at best an interesting subject of study, and no longer destiny. *La survivance* is alive in Quebec, but is moribund in New England.

References
Gerard J. Brault, *The French-Canadian Heritage in New England* (1986); Jacques Ducharme, *The Shadow of the Trees: The Story of French Canadians in New England* (1943); Mason Wade, *The French Canadians, 1760–1967* (1968); Madeleine Giguère, ed., *A Franco-American Overview*, vols. 3 and 4: *New England* (parts 1 and 2) (1981); Robert Rumilly, *Histoire des Franco-Américains* (1958).

R.S.

FRUMKIN, BORIS. *See Jews, America, and Immigration.*

GADSDEN PURCHASE. *See Mexicans.*

GAELIC AMERICAN. *See Devoy, John.*

GAJ, LJUDEVIT. *See Yugoslavs.*

GALARZA, ERNESTO. *See Immigrant Autobiographies.*

GALLATIN, ALBERT. *See Swiss.*

GALVESTON, TEXAS: AS PORT OF ENTRY. *See* Immigrants in the Old South.

GAMORAN, EMANUEL (1895–1962). Educator. Gamoran served as the director of education of the Union of American Hebrew Congregations (UAHC) from 1923 to 1958. The creation of rich Jewish experiences for the Jewish child was the major objective of Emanuel Gamoran's philosophy of education. He believed that this could only be achieved in the Jewish school. In the context of the American situation Gamoran viewed the Jewish school as the primary means of helping the immigrant Jew adjust from the ghetto environment of Eastern Europe to the modern industrial society of the United States, without the loss of Jewish heritage.

Reference
Robert J. Wechman, "Emanuel Gamoran: Pioneer in Jewish Religious Education," Ph.D. dissertation, Syracuse University, 1970 (DA 31-5583-A).

F.C.

GARDEN STATE IMMIGRATION HISTORY CONSORTIUM. This consortium is composed of faculty members from eighteen New Jersey public and private colleges and universities plus professionals from several museums and libraries in the state. The purpose of this group is to do research and to develop and disseminate curriculum materials and public programs to further knowledge about immigration and ethnic life, particularly in New Jersey. The group had its origins when eight faculty members who had been Ellis Island fellows at Rutgers University decided in 1985 to continue their work on improving knowledge and teaching about immigration history. The consortium has had important funding from New Jersey's Department of Higher Education. Its numbers expanded particularly through a 1986 workshop for thirty college faculty members and through ongoing seminars and conferences.

The consortium members have produced photo exhibits on workmen of the "new" and "old" immigration and on immigrant and ethnic foods and the food merchants; a computer simulation on decisionmaking by turn-of-the-century immigrants from Italy and Russia; a television film on Cubans in Hudson County; a study of Anguillans in Perth Amboy; a teaching module of immigrant and ethnic New Jerseyans in fiction; a walking tour of Dublin, a two-hundred-year-old ethnic neighborhood in Paterson; an exhibit on immigrant life in Trenton in the early 1900s as seen in newspaper accounts; a study of American immigration as part of world immigration through maps; studies on immigration history as family history and immigration, women, and labor history as seen in selected primary documents related to the 1913 Paterson strike; and a demographic study of West Indians in New Jersey. These materials have been discussed in continuing teacher workshops and in presentations at conferences nationally. Much of the consortium's material is available in "Teaching Immigration History," a special October 1987 issue of *The Social Studies*.

The consortium has its office at Ramapo College of New Jersey, Mahwah, New Jersey 07430.

H.B.

GARLAND FUND. *See* NAACP.

GARVEY, MARCUS (1887–1940). Businessman, activist, and writer. Born and raised in Jamaica, West Indies, Garvey was one of the first Afro-American leaders to view race and racism in an international context. Based on extensive travels throughout the Caribbean, Central and South America, and England, he came to the conclusion that the problems of blacks worldwide required immediate attention. On August 1, 1914, he formed the UNIA (Universal Negro Improvement and Conservation Association and African Communities League). This organization was designed to "establish a universal confraternity among the race."

In 1916, Garvey brought his movement to America. From this date until his deportation on charges of mail fraud in 1927, he built one of the largest mass movements of people of African descent. Although he borrowed heavily from the ideologists of self-help spokesmen like Booker T. Washington, Garvey's program was overtly nationalistic. The UNIA developed community-owned businesses, from bakeries to laundries to a steamship line. It supported an African Orthodox church, published several newspapers, and sponsored international UNIA conferences. However, Garvey's greatest contribution was the development of black pride and unity. He promoted numerous parades with Black Cross Nurses; founded African Legions and various auxiliaries; held UNIA meetings in "Liberty Halls" throughout the nation; and bestowed hundreds of Afro-American people with ranks of nobility.

While in the United States Garvey established his headquarters in New York City. It was here that he had his largest following, and it was from this base that his message spread across the nation. By the mid-1920s the UNIA had more than 700 branches in thirty-eight states and over one million members. Chief works: *Philosophy and Opinions of Marcus Garvey*, ed. Amy Jacques Garvey; *More Philosophy and Opinions of Marcus Garvey*, ed. E.U. Essien-Udom and Amy Jacques Garvey; and his weekly newspaper, the *Negro World* (1918–1923).

References
John Henrik Clarke and Amy Jacques Garvey, eds., *Marcus Garvey and the Vision of Africa* (1974); E. David Cronin, *Black Moses: The Story of Marcus Garvey and the UNIA* (1969); Amy Jacques Garvey, ed., *Philosophy and Opinions of Marcus Garvey* (1974); Robert Hill, ed., *The Marcus Garvey and UNIA Papers*, vols. 1 and 2 (1983); Tony Martin, *Race First: The Ideological and Organizational Struggles of Marcus Garvey and the UNIA* (1976); Robert A. Hill and Barbara Blair, eds., *Marcus Garvey: Life and Lessons* (1987).

L.W.

GARY PLAN. *See* Wirt, William.

GEISSENER   AUSWANDERUNGSGESELLSCHAFT.   *See* Germans.

GENTLEMEN'S AGREEMENT. On October 11, 1906, the San Francisco Board of Education passed a resolution excluding Chinese, Japanese, and Korean children from its public schools. The Japanese government protested, charging that the San Francisco board's action violated the Treaty of Commerce and Navigation between the United States and Japan, signed on November 22, 1894. President Theodore Roosevelt (*q.v.*) intervened and, through his efforts, the San Francisco Board of Education rescinded its segregation order in 1907. In 1908, President Roosevelt and Secretary of State Elihu Root negotiated the "Gentleman's Agreement" with Japanese Foreign Minister Hayashi Tadasu. As part of the agreement, the Japanese government agreed not to issue passports to Japanese laborers who wanted to go to the United States. Excepted from the agreement were previous residents of the United States who had returned to Japan, and the wives, children, and parents of Japanese residents in the United States. The Gentlemen's Agreement also closed Japanese immigration to the United States through Mexico, Canada, and Hawaii. The details of the agreement were formalized in February 1908. Its text is not spelled out in a single document; it derives from a series of letters exchanged by the United States and Japan over a year's time. The agreement placated Californians who opposed the immigration of Japanese laborers. The agreement lasted until 1924, when it was abrogated with the statutory exclusion of Japanese immigration provided in the Immigration Act of 1924 (*q.v.*). Japanese exclusion provisions were not repealed until 1952.

References
Thomas A. Bailey, *Theodore Roosevelt and the Japanese-American Crisis* (1934); Vernon M. Briggs, Jr., *Immigration Policy and the American Labor Force* (1984).

D.N.A.

GERMAN AMERICAN BUND. 1936–1941. Organized in March 1936 at a convention in Buffalo, New York, the Nazi-inspired German American Bund began its short and stormy existence by seeking to unite the entire German-American community under its direction. The Bund had been preceded by numerous Nazi splinter groups and an organization known as the Friends of the New Germany. The chief distinction between the Bund and its predecessors was the requirement that only American citizens could hold leadership positions in the organization. The Bund also tried to be more circumspect in its relations with Nazi agencies in Germany.

Reference
Leland V. Bell, "Anatomy of a Hate Movement: The German American Bund, 1936–1941," Ph.D. dissertation, West Virginia University, 1968 (DA 30:645A).

F.C.

GERMANS. For three centuries immigrants from the territory delineated from 1870 to 1945 as the German nation have been pouring into the United States. Beginning with the first organized group migration from Krefeld in the Rhineland to Germantown (now incorporated into Philadelphia) in 1883, Germans have kept coming, many to acquire freedom of religion, others for economic opportunities or simply for adventure. Large-scale immigration started in 1709 when some 13,000 from the Palatinate in southwestern Germany left the overpopulated, economically depressed region for England, many of whom reached the Mohawk Valley of New York soon thereafter. Others—Swiss Mennonites, Baptist Dunkers, Schwenkfelders, Moravian Brethren, and similar separatist groups came in subsequent decades to William Penn's land of religious freedom, as well as to Maryland, the Carolinas, and New Jersey. By the close of the colonial period about 100,000 Germans had come to the United States and by 1790 an estimated 8.6 percent of the United States population was of German descent. Pennsylvania was the center of colonial German life, with perhaps 33 percent of its population German.

Wars always inhibit the free movement of people. Consequently immigration slowed both during the French and Indian War (the Seven Years War in Europe, 1756–1763) and again during the Revolutionary War (1775–1781), although at least 5,000 German mercenary soldiers brought to America by the British deserted in order to remain in the United States.

During all of the colonial period, religion was central in the German settlements. Missionaries were sent from the German homeland, especially the Moravians who founded cities with biblical names like

Bethlehem and Nazareth in Pennsylvania. Like the Moravians, Pietistic Lutherans and Reformed church ministers established congregations that supported private German-language school systems. When Pennsylvania initiated public schools in 1834, the Germans struggled for decades in this and many other states to retain their German ethnicity under the guise of preserving their faith, but without ultimate success. Because the Germans were too small as a percentage of the total population in all of the colonies except Pennsylvania, only in this state was assimilation successfully resisted. Because the Pennsylvania Germans were too distant from the homeland and yet large enough in their own right to maintain German culture, their language gradually evolved into a new German dialect known today as "Pennsylvania Dutch." However, even in Pennsylvania the pressures for absorption into American society were so strong that only Mennonite (sometimes called Amish) groups have successfully maintained their language and culture.

Following the American Revolution, immigration was slow due largely to the turmoil caused by the Napoleonic Wars in Europe which culminated with the emperor's defeat in 1815. The disastrous economic and political dislocation that Napoleon effected triggered a century of heavy immigration from Germany to the United States. Between 1820 (when exact statistics were first kept) and 1980 nearly 7 million Germans have immigrated to the United States (15 percent of all U.S. immigrants during the period), more than from any other country. The next highest nation in supplying immigrants was Italy with 5,300,000 (10.9 percent of the total), of whom, however, great numbers remigrated to their homeland. In third place is Great Britain with 4,900,000 (10 percent), followed by Ireland with 4,725,000 (9.7 percent), and Austria-Hungary with 4,315,000 (8.9 percent). Since many Austro-Hungarians, Swiss, Luxembourgers, and Germans from the Russian empire spoke German as their mother tongue, it is estimated that about 10 million German-speaking immigrants reached American shores. In the 1880s there were an estimated 12 million mother tongue speakers of German in the United States. The entire population of the United States in 1900 was a mere 76 million; some 15.8 percent of them spoke German. The next largest percentage spoke Italian. Unquestionably these statistics alone help us to understand why there was a vicious eruption of xenophobic anti-Germanism in the United States during World War I. Fears are not easily rationalized and the size of the "alien" population within the United States was indeed large.

Immigration from Germany around 1817 brought some 20,000 from southwestern Germany. For the next three decades the annual influx increased until peaking at 215,000 in the single year of 1854, the result of the revolutions of 1848 in Germany and the subsequent crop failures. Another period of sustained high German immigration occurred in the seven years following the Civil War. The third and highest wave of German immigrants peaked in 1882 when in a single year 250,000 Germans arrived in the United States. By this time however, immigration was coming not from the southwestern rural areas of Germany but from the northern and industrialized cities and especially from northeastern Germany. Between the years 1830 and 1900 Germans accounted for 27 percent of all new arrivals, a figure that rises considerably if we include the German-speakers who came from Austria, Switzerland, and the German-speaking areas of Russia. Between 1930 and 1960 the Germans contributed 18 percent of all the immigrants to the United States. Today, however, that percentage has dropped below 3 percent.

Always the flow of German immigrants was conditioned by the interaction of situations in the homeland and in the United States—the "push and pull" factor. Immigration to the United States was repeatedly determined by revolutionary and civil wars in the United States. Crop failures abroad also affected the movement. Like the Irish, the Germans suffered potato famines from 1845 to 1855. Economic recessions (called "panics") in the United States periodically lessened the pull; these occurred in 1837, 1873, 1893, and of course in 1929 when the recession became a depression. Such economic downturns often slowed the influx but they simultaneously built up pools so that the years of heavy German immigration can be charted with reference either to a war on one of the two continents or an economic collapse, each of which inevitably yielded to a recovery and a new wave of immigration.

Beyond push and pull factors conscious efforts were made to foster German immigration. Sometimes churches organized group migrations such as the Old Lutherans who refused to accept the unification by Prussia of the Lutheran and the Reformed churches in 1837. Some came to Missouri to found the Lutheran Synod. Others moved to the Milwaukee area from which the Wisconsin Synod derives. Other groups were the Harmonists of Pennsylvania and Indiana; the Amana Colonies in Iowa and such others as the Catholic St. Nazianz, Wisconsin group; and the many religious communities of monks and nuns who left Germany during Bismarck's *Kulturkampf,* an effort during which (1873–1880) the state tried to dismember Catholic educational and cultural organizations in Germany.

Other organized efforts to aid German immigration were the many German-language guidebooks printed to explain the United States and the opportunities it offered. Frequently these were published by societies established by governmental units such as the Geissener Auswanderungsgesellschaft; the Adelsverein, which targeted people toward Texas; or the Nationalverein für deutsche Auswanderung und Ansiedlung. The latter national society was particularly helpful in arranging transportation, supplying information, assisting with legal problems of inheritance and property transfer, handling banking arrangements for emigrants, and targeting departures to link up with existing German communities in the United States.

Soon government units in the United States recognized the value of soliciting German immigrants. After 1840 it became known that Germans who came to the United States were not destitute but small farmers, artisans, and cottage manufacturers interspersed lavishly with professionals—doctors, merchants, manufacturers—who collectively represented significant economic opportunity for the receiving lands. As a result the states in the American Midwest from 1850 to 1890 operated immigration bureaus to attract German immigrants for their pocket money and the activity they would bring to the state's economy. Operating in close tandem with official state offices were railroad agencies, some of which hired their staff members from state bureaus and generally cooperated to induce ever more immigrants to settle in a given territory. The Northern Pacific and Burlington railroads were particularly energetic in recruiting German immigrants to settle on their lands.

The churches also operated indirect agencies of immigration in the form of organizations for the protection of the immigrants such as the Catholic St. Raphaelsverein. Protestant missionary aid societies, especially the one at Neuendettelsau in Bavaria, were equally active. Catholics also benefited financially from the Leopoldinen-Stiftung in Austria and the Ludwig Missionsverein of Munich. There were also hundreds, perhaps thousands of mutual aid organizations that operated within religious organizations either at the parish level or in the diocese. Many aided the immigrant before departure, protected him from swindlers along the way, and helped him secure employment once in the United States. Railroads also offered the services of immigration houses along their lines and provided reduced or free transportation if their land grants were being acquired. The greatest aid came from private societies, families who frequently supplied "prepaid" tickets, and the personal support that the immigrant needed in leaving his homeland.

The geographic distribution of the Germans in the United States followed closely the pattern that had been established in early colonial times. Basically that means that the Germans expanded westward from Pennsylvania. Naturally the bounds of the German westward movement fanned out to include northern cities like St. Paul and a more southern extreme like St. Louis. Although there were settlements of Germans in New Orleans, Georgia, and the Carolinas, the real home of the Germans was in the Midwest, especially in the states of Ohio, Illinois, southern Michigan, Wisconsin, Minnesota, Iowa, Missouri, Nebraska, the Dakotas, and Kansas. A strong but isolated pocket developed and remains in central Texas. There are large colonies on the West Coast, in New York City, and in Florida. New York has always had more German-born residents than any other state, followed by Illinois, Ohio, Wisconsin, and Pennsylvania. Wisconsin, however, has always been the state with the largest proportion of its population from Germany. In 1920 German-Americans were well over three times more numerous in Wisconsin than their share of the national population would suggest. Minnesota followed and all of the states mentioned above, except Kansas, had more Germans in 1920 than called for by the national average.

German settlers on the frontier often were not fresh from the Old Country but westward movers from a previous American experience. Cincinnati drew Germans from Pennsylvania; Chicago attracted them from New York and Buffalo; Milwaukee Germans often came from Chicago or Detroit. In turn, Wisconsin residents from the 1850s blazed trails to Minnesota, and eventually to the Dakotas. Some from Illinois and Iowa moved on to Nebraska and Kansas. Only the Germans from Russia came directly to the Great Plains, in part because it was the only land available to them when they arrived from rural Black Sea and Volga German territories, and in part because they were especially well experienced to cope with the arid farming conditions demanded for success on the Great Plains. Also, among the Germans from Russia, who settled on the Great Plains, migration chains from older communities to new ones created a leapfrog pattern.

Settlements large enough to support a German church usually expanded over time and solidified the territory, intensifying the German character of the vicinity. Religion was always an important catalyst for the success and permanence of a German community. Seldom did German rural settlements dominate a large region, although in Wisconsin in 1910 there were at least ten contiguous counties with populations above 35 percent first- and second-generation German. Minnesota, Iowa, Nebraska, and Texas each had one county with a similar concentration.

Between 1850 and 1950 Germans concentrated in several cities of the North. New York City had the largest number of German born in 1900 (324,000), followed by Chicago (203,700), Philadelphia (73,000), Milwaukee (69,000), St. Louis (60,000), Buffalo (50,000), Cleveland (44,000), and Detroit (42,700). Germans who settled in the cities claimed to be skilled craftsmen, bakers, carpenters, brewers, and the like, though many were also merchants, musicians, and common laborers. Compared to American workers as a whole, they were overrepresented in industry, manufacturing, the mechanical trades, and mining. Butchering, brewing, baking, cigar making, cabinetmaking, and tailoring were particularly characteristic of German city workers. They were underrepresented, however, among doctors, lawyers, clerks, teachers, and factory laborers. German women were a smaller portion of the work force than other immigrant women. German women who did take employment were nurses, hotel keepers, bakers, tailors, and laundresses. Germans generally were not in the top management of the nation's corporations. In the 1970s the median family income for Americans of German descent was higher than the national median, though lower than that for Russians, Poles, Italians, the British, and Irish. Second-generation German-Americans in the 1970 census also reported a lower median number of school years completed and a smaller proportion of professional occupations than the average for second-generation Americans. Spectacular success seems to have favored the exceptional few who had technical skills of one kind or another: Jacob Astor in fur trading, Claus Spreckels in sugar, Frederick Weyerhaeuser in lumber, Henry Villard (Hilgard) in railroading, John A. Roebling in engineering and bridge building, and Wernher von Braun in rocketry.

The Germans have not been notable for their presence in higher elective political office in the United States. Certainly they failed to produce officeholders commensurate with their large numbers. To this day, an enumeration of the greats begins and ends with Carl Schurz, the liberal forty-eighter who supported Lincoln, and then became a Missouri senator and subsequently secretary of the interior under President Rutherford Hayes. Dwight Eisenhower scarcely qualifies as a German-American. German-born Henry Kissinger certainly was an exception to the rule. Still, the Germans occasionally voted as a bloc, notably in opposition to temperance, women's suffrage, and of course participation in World War I, wherever such votes were held. Usually they opposed uniform public schools mostly because that meant a failure of the cherished German-language private schools.

After the debacle of two world wars in which the fatherland was on the opposing side, German-Americans are understandably subdued and assimilated. A few local organizations like the Steuben Society of New York and the German-American National Congress, founded in 1958 in Chicago, claim several thousand members and a bit of political influence. Smaller units like the American Historical Society of Germans from Russia (Lincoln), the Germans from Russia Heritage Society (Bismarck), or the Society for German American Studies provide services for researchers. A few ethnic traditions persist in the folkways of the nation. The wedding dance continues, as does the feast at the home of the deceased after his funeral. But the flower-bedecked processions for Corpus Christi, the Kirmes (feast of a patron saint), and Epiphany house visits have faded. The harvest feast has been revived more as a copy of the Munich Octoberfest of today (a grand, outdoor beer party) than as a vestige of its former thanksgiving celebration. *Sängerfeste* (singing competitions) are rare, *Schützenfeste* (shooting competitions) have vanished, shotguns on New Year's eve are silent, and St. Nicholas no longer visits children on December 6. The second Christmas and second Easter have gone the way of the pre-Lenten carnivals and masked balls.

German ethnicity in the United States today, despite the once enormous size of this group, has adopted for itself the nostalgic image attributed to it by the popular media. Curiously, the Germans, including those of recent arrival, seem content with the stereotype of men attired in *Lederhosen,* women in *Dirndls,* both tilting a heavy mug of beer. The German language is gone and with it authentic German culture. Not infrequently a still solidly German rural community high school offers Spanish if any foreign language at all. On the other hand there is a genuine upsurge of pride in ancestry that may in the long run perpetuate scattered bits of German ethnicity in the United States. The old adage that economic power willy nilly brings political power seems to apply to Germany since 1950. Americans of German descent are pleased with West Germany's new prominence. Even East Germany enjoys an economic and technological prestige unknown elsewhere in the Soviet bloc. While German-American culture as it existed before the world wars will surely not revive, a more mature satisfaction with the German heritage is on the upswing among Americans of German descent.

References

Albert B. Faust, *The German Element in the United States* (1927); Günter Moltmann, ed., *Germans to America: 300 Years of Immigration, 1683–1983* (1983); Richard O'Connor, *The German Americans* (1968); LaVern J. Rippley, *The German Americans* (1976); Arthur R. Schultz, *German-American Relations and German Culture in America: A Subject Bibliography, 1941–1980,* 2 vols. (1985); Frank Trommler and Joseph McVeigh, eds., *America and the Germans: An Assessment of a Three-Hundred-Year History,* 2 vols. (1985); Klaus Wust and Heinz Moos, eds., *Three Hundred Years of German Immigrants in North America, 1683–1983* (1983).

L.J.R.

GERMANS, American Friends of German Democracy. *See* Americanization Movement.

GERMANS, Americanization of German Lutherans, 1683–1829. The economic, political, ecclesiastical, physical, and psychological conditions existent in Germany between 1618 and 1776 moved a large number of German Lutherans to emigrate to America between 1683 and 1776 and conditioned the emigrants toward a readiness to acclimatize themselves in America. The long, arduous, costly, and dangerous journey to America served both as a guarantee of the permanent settlement of the German Lutherans in America and as a deterrent to any return to Germany. The unorganized condition in which these German Lutherans arrived in America and the absence of a German colony to which they could resort made them dependent upon and subject to the prevalent English culture in which they found themselves. The indenture system, the obligatory oaths of allegiance to the British Crown, and the exigencies of frontier life afforded a condition of malleability that facilitated their adjustment to the new culture in which they found themselves. The ecclesiastical disorganization of the German Lutherans, marked by a lack of pastors and congregational organization, prepared the way for Heinrich Melchior Muhlenberg (1711–1787), who by his personal life, organizational policies, and ecclesiastical and political attitudes led them to a high degree of accommodation to and participation in the life and culture of the American colonies.

Reference
Richard C. Wolf, "The Americanization of the German Lutherans, 1683 to 1829," Ph.D. dissertation, Yale University, 1947.

F.C.

GERMANS, the Central-Verein. The German Roman Catholic Central-Verein was founded in 1855 and still exists at the present time. Its organization began as a national federation of local benevolent societies; at first it confined its activities closely to mutual insurance, but gradually broadened its interest to include education and other matters affecting the German-American Catholic population. In the 1880s and 1890s the Central-Verein became involved in controversies with the American Catholic church and developed attitudes that persisted into the twentieth century.

Reference
John P. Gleason, *The Conservative Reformers: German-American Catholics and the Social Order* (1968).

F.C.

GERMANS, in Cincinnati. There is an assumption that American navitism of the World War I era had destroyed or at least given the coup de grace to German culture in America. As it turned out, the German community, at least in Cincinnati, was moribund before the war had even begun in Europe. Therefore, if it died during the war, its death was of its own making; the war served only to heighten its agony. In this sense, nativism, upon reaching its full strength at the war's end, had found only a dead or dying horse to flog. Further, should one think in terms of nativism applying the coup de grace with Prohibition and influenza as its accessories, it should be seriously questioned whether it was not really the other way around. In the case of Cincinnati decay was manifested primarily by two major symptoms: one physical, the other sociopsychological, with, of course, considerable interaction. The community's physical disintegration showed itself not only biologically in the decrease of new blood coming from Germany, but also geographically in its members being spread increasingly thin over an ever-expanding metropolitan area.

Reference
Guido A. Dobbert, *The Disintegration of an Immigrant Community: The Cincinnati Germans, 1870–1920* (1980); Don H. Tolzmann, *The Cincinnati Germans After the Great War* (1987).

F.C.

GERMANS, Evangelical Lutheran Church. The General Council of the Evangelical Lutheran Church in North America, of which this dissertation is a history, existed from 1867 until it merged with two other Lutheran bodies to form the United Lutheran Church in America in 1918. Origins of the General Council are related to a large extent to the confessional issue among some of America's Lutherans, and particularly to the involvement of the Ministerium of Pennsylvania in that issue. Some Lutherans had been advocating an accommodation of the sixteenth-century Lutheran Confessions to the nineteenth-century American scene. Others believed that the only churches justified in using the name "Lutheran" were those that subscribed to the doctrines of the Reformation as they were originally given.

Reference
William A. Good, "A History of the General Council of the Evangelical Lutheran Church in North America," Ph.D. dissertation, Yale University, 1967.

F.C.

GERMANS, German Baptist Brethren (Dunkers). Eller has described the settlement and frontier accommodation of the German Baptist Brethren (Dunkers) in three geographic areas of the western Ohio Valley. These areas are the Green River country in western Kentucky, Union County in southern Illinois, and along the White River in Orange and Lawrence counties, Indiana. The congregations formed in these areas may be considered representative of Brethren activity in the western Ohio Valley between 1790 and 1850. The Dunkers were a Pietist and Anabaptist background sect whose trans-Allegheny frontier experience has not been adequately studied, for its impact either on the Brethren in the later nineteenth century or on wider Protestant development. Because the Brethren left few church records, extensive use has been made of various federal, state, and county records to plot migration patterns and congregational activity.

Reference
David B. Eller, "The Brethren in the Western Ohio Valley, 1790–1850: German Baptist Settlement and Frontier Accommodation," Ph.D. dissertation, University of Miami, 1976.

F.C.

GERMANS, immigration to Minnesota. Massman's study reviews the causes of emigration and government attitudes, with emphasis on their interrelationship to fluctuations in German emigration. It deals intensively with the promotional efforts and techniques utilized by settlers, missionaries, colonization groups, Minnesota's government, and railroads to attract German settlers to Minnesota. Attention also is focused on the hazards encountered and the efforts to protect the immigrants on their journey from Europe to Minnesota. The final chapters analyze the growth of German settlements in Minnesota, their ratio to their total population and to other national groups, and distribution patterns. German social, religious, and educational activities are discussed briefly in terms of their influence on the problems of population growth and distribution patterns.

Reference
John C. Massman, "German Immigration to Minnesota, 1850–1890," Ph.D. dissertation, University of Minnesota, 1966.

F.C.

GERMANS, Lutheran Church and Predestination controversy. In the 1870s and especially 1880s a fiercely fought predestination controversy raged in the Lutheran synods in America that lasted into the 1930s. Although it was limited to the Lutheran church, the controversy spread to Germany, Australia, and New Zealand. In the main it was a conflict between the Missouri Synod under the leadership of C. F. W. Walther on the one hand, and Gottfried Fritschel of the Iowa Synod, F. A. Schmidt of the Norwegian Synod, and Matthias Loy and Friedrich W. Stellhorn of the Joint Synod of Ohio on the other.

Reference
Hans R. Haug, "The Predestination Controversy in the Lutheran Church in North America," Ph.D. dissertation, Temple University, 1968.

F.C.

GERMANS, Lutheran Church, Missouri Synod. The Lutheran church–Missouri Synod is a conservative Lutheran denomination organized by German immigrants in 1847. It grew to be the largest of the original immigrant Lutheran groups, expanding from the Midwest to both coasts. The synod retained, however, both a remarkably monolithic structure and a distinctly German character well into the twentieth century. By World War I German was still the language of most worship services and religious instruction. Such usage indicated the general lack of Americanization within the synod. The Missouri Synod was not completely Americanized by 1929, but it had changed remarkably since 1917, and gave every indication of having established the base for future growth among American, rather than immigrant, denominations.

Reference
Alan N. Graebner, "The Acculturation of an Immigration Church: The Lutheran Church–Missouri Synod, 1917–1929," Ph.D. dissertation, Columbia University, 1965.

F.C.

GERMANS, Lutheran College choirs. The Lutheran church had its origin in America in the seventeenth century but did not become a denomination of significance until the eighteenth. The arrival of many German immigrants during the eighteenth century and the strong leadership of Henry Melchior Muhlenberg (*q.v.*) during this period created an organization of Lutheran churches into a synod that gave status to this denomination. During the last half of the nineteenth century Lutheran colleges in the Midwest began to include music in the curriculum. Glee clubs were the earliest type of choral organization that became established at these schools. Oratorio societies were organized at several colleges of Swedish background. Choral unions were popular at colleges founded by Norwegians and Danes.

Reference
Paul E. Neve, "The Contribution of the Lutheran College Choirs to Music in America," Ph.D. dissertation, Union Theological Seminary, 1967.

F.C.

GERMANS, Lutheran Parochial schools. The Lutheran parochial school movement began in the earliest colonial days and was carried on in the eastern colonies and states by several regional Lutheran synods and reached the high point of development in 1830, after which it declined steadily and ceased altogether by 1890. The second movement began with the arrival of the Saxon Lutherans in Missouri in 1839 and the formation of the Missouri Synod in 1847. The Missouri Synod school system flourished and continues to the present day. Damm has attempted to ascertain just why the schools of the older Lutheran bodies declined during the very decades of the nineteenth century when the Missouri Synod was active in establishing schools. The factors that contributed to the school's growth and decline are discussed and viewed against the larger background of the doctrinal issues at stake in these two Lutheran groups.

Reference
John S. Damm, "The Growth and Decline of Lutheran Parochial Schools in the United States, 1638–1962," Ph.D. dissertation, Columbia University (Teachers College), 1963.

F.C.

GERMANS, in Milwaukee, 1836–1860. Within ten years of its 1836 founding, immigrants constituted a majority of Milwaukee's population; by 1860 Germans alone headed over half its households. Given such numerical dominance in a new and not yet industrialized city of the mid-nineteenth-century frontier, what kind of initial accommodation could be expected of a relatively skilled immigrant population such as the Germans? Conzen hypothesizes that Milwaukee's frontier situation, as well as the size, character, and timing of its German immigration, would have permitted the development of a particularly independent ethnic community in the first generation of immigrant settlement. Such a community would then in theory ease the adjustment trauma and economic integration of its individual members while encouraging only limited acculturation and minimal structural assimilation into any kind of "American" life—a situation in which the Germans were neither ghetto residents in the classic sense of the term nor yet participants in a "melting pot" society.

Reference
Kathleen Conzen, *Immigrant Milwaukee, 1836–1860* (1979).

F.C.

GERMANS, in Nebraska, 1880–1900. Largely a lower-middle-class people, the Germans formed a significant part of Nebraska's population ever since territorial organization. The majority were farmers, although artisans and shopkeepers were also common among them. Mostly Protestant in religion, they often settled in rural ethnoreligious ghettos where the pressures to conform to group standards were strong and where opportunities for interpersonal contacts with native Americans were minimal.

Reference
Frederick C. Luebke, *Immigrants and Politics: The Germans of Nebraska, 1880–1900* (1969).

F.C.

GERMANS, and nineteenth-century Texas agriculture. Many striking similarities exist between the farming systems established by the Germans and the Southerners, as well as some clear differences. Certain European practices were successfully transplanted to the new homeland. In the more subtle aspects of farming—intensity, productivity, locational stability, and land tenure—major and persistent differences were detected. The Germans put more into the land in terms of labor and capital, and more out of it in value of production, and were more likely to own their land than the native Southerners. In addition, the Germans devoted more attention to small grains, white potatoes, market gardening, tobacco, and wine making than did the Southerners, and they were less likely to own slaves.

Reference
Terry G. Jordan, *German Seed in Texas Soil: Immigrant Farmers in Nineteenth Century Texas* (1966).

F.C.

GERMANS, in St. Louis, 1850–1920. Historians of German immigration to the United States have recorded the deeds and contributions of that ethnic group to American life. Their study of the German community with relation to its assimilation into the host society has led them to conclude that the German ethnic group was progressing toward assimilation until World War I forced them into a self-awareness of their nationality; that the ethnic community was not becoming assimilated until World War I broke the hyphen in "German-American"; and that the wealthy German-Americans abandoned the community, resulting in a resurgence of ethnic self-consciousness on the part of the less economically and socially mobile members of the group. These conclusions were based on the predication of the existence of a close-knit German ethnic community, and, essentially, were the experiences of the St. Louis German community.

Reference
Audrey L. Olson, *St. Louis Germans, 1850–1920* (1980).

F.C.

GERMANS, *Westliche Post* of St. Louis. The *Westliche Post* was a daily newspaper published in the German language in St. Louis, Missouri, from September 27, 1857, to June 14, 1938. Although primarily serving the German immigrants, who were numerous in St. Louis during the latter half of the nineteenth century, the *Westliche Post* played an active part in the affairs of St. Louis and Missouri, as it guided the political direction of German-Americans to some extent.

References
Sally M. Miller, ed., *The Ethnic Press in the United States* (1987); Harvey Saalberg, "The Westliche Post of St. Louis: A Daily Newspaper for German-Americans, 1857–1938," Ph.D. dissertation, University of Missouri, Columbia, 1967.

F.C.

GERMANS, wishing in and shooting in the New Year. The German-American custom of wishing in and shooting in the New Year is as follows. A group of men ("shooters") make the rounds of homes, where they practice a ceremony for householders, prominent people, and eligible girls, consisting of playing musical and noise-making instruments, wishing, singing, and shooting, and are then served refreshments in return.

Reference
Walter L. Robbins, "The German-American Custom of Wishing in and Shooting in the New Year," Ph.D. dissertation, University of North Carolina, 1969.

F.C.

GERMER, ADOLPH (1881–1966). Labor leader. Adolph Germer spent more than sixty years in the labor movement among immigrant workers. Successively active in the United Mine Workers, the Socialist party, and the CIO, Germer never reached the pinnacles of union power. Germer's active years illuminated in microcosm the transformation of trade unions from a peripheral element in the nation's life to a powerful block. Specifically, his career reflected the declining importance of ideology in the unions, the labor movement's quest for equilibrium, and the implications of that search.

Reference
Lorin L. Cary, "Adolph Germer: From Labor Agitator to Labor Professional," Ph.D. dissertation, University of Wisconsin, 1968 (DA 29: 4416-A).

F.C.

GHADAR MOVEMENT. *See* Asian Indians.

GIBRAN, KAHLIL. *See* Lebanese.

GINZBURG, SHIMON. *See, Jews, America, and Immigration.*

GIOVANNITTI, ARTURO MASSIMO (1884–1959). Poet and political activist. Born in the Molise region of Italy, Giovannitti emigrated when seventeen years old to pursue theological studies at McGill University that led to his ordination as a Protestant evangelical minister. The young minister served briefly in a small Pennsylvania mining community, but by 1906 he had abandoned his post, moved to New York, and quickly became a prominent figure among the city's left and Bohemian communities. An ardent labor activist all his life, Giovannitti was a steadfast member of New York's Federazione Socialista Italiana, serving first as editor (1909) and then as general director (1911) of the federation's newspaper, *Il proletario*. Giovannitti nurtured strong personal and political ties to the Industrial Workers of the World (IWW) (the "Wobblies"), and traveled extensively throughout the United States urging support of the IWW's call for industrial unionism. It was at this time that Giovannitti became a fast friend of the Italian-American IWW organizer Joseph Ettor.

At the urging of IWW leadership, Giovannitti and Ettor were called to direct the great 1912 textile strike—the "Bread and Roses" strike—in Lawrence, Massachusetts. In Lawrence, Giovannitti and Ettor were joined by IWW leaders Elizabeth Gurley Flynn (*q.v.*) and "Big" Bill Haywood, as well as by Socialist Eugene Debs. On January 29, a young Italian-American striker, Annie LoPizzo, was shot and killed in a confrontation with police. Giovannitti and Ettor, together with another Italian-American striker, were charged with the death. (Many students of the strike today concur that the murder was carried out by an *agent provocateur,* probably in the mill owners' pay.) The three men awaited trial for ten months in jail, and when the trial did take place in Salem, all three were acquitted. From the outset, a defense committee had organized an international mobilization to free the three.

While awaiting trial, Giovannitti wrote what is perhaps his best-known poem in English, "The Walker." The poem was originally published in the *Atlantic Monthly,* and was immediately translated into the world's major tongues including Chinese, Japanese, and Esperanto. After Lawrence, Giovannitti continued to write poetry (in English and in his native Italian). Many of his English-language poems were first published by *The Masses* and, after 1918, by *The Liberator.* Also after Lawrence, Giovannitti was for a time editor of *Il fucco,* a literary and political journal of the Italian-American left published in New York. The verse published while in jail was collected and published in 1914 under the title *Arrows in the Gale,* with a foreword by Helen Keller. *The Collected Works of Arturo Giovannitti* were published after the poet's death with an introduction by Norman Thomas. Though not complete, the 1962 volume does contain a great deal of Giovannitti's major English-language poetry. Giovannitti's antiwar play, *As It Was in the Beginning,* enjoyed a successful run on Broadway in 1917.

Giovannitti's political activism ran concurrently with his literary production. After his work for the WWI, he served a term as general secretary of the Italian Chamber of Labor, and then of the Italian Labor Education Bureau, a post he held into the 1940s. Earlier, in 1923, Giovannitti helped form and served as secretary to the Anti-Fascist Alliance of North America (*q.v.*) that sought to combat pro-Fascist and pro-Mussolini propaganda directed at the Italian-American community in particular and public opinion in general. In 1957, Giovannitti published a collection of his Italian poems entitled *Quando canta il Gallo,* and he was busily engaged in editing his English poems at the time of his death (he had been bedridden for years with a paralysis of the legs).

Once hailed as "the Bard of the Proletariat," Giovannitti composed verse whose underlying themes display a sustained rebellion against the inequities wrought by American capitalism, and a passion for social justice. His "protest" poetry is tempered, at the same time, by a haunting lyricism and a "Latin" celebration of sensual delight, joyous camaraderie, and humor amid the seriousness of political struggle. In "The Nuptials of Death," Giovannitti's hushed intensity could be compared to the quiet desperations of an Emily Dickinson, while in those poems of a more homely demotics, the presence of Whitman can be felt. The sarcasm of his invective verse attains an incisiveness to be surpassed only later in the poetry of an Allen Ginsberg or of an Amiri Baraka. This range is all the more remarkable when considering that English for Giovannitti was an acquired tongue.

References
Mario DeClampis, "Arturo Massimo Giovannitti poeta giornalista drammaturgo per la causa dei lavoratori," *La Parola del Popolo* (July–August 1974); Wallace P. Sillanpoa, "The Poetry and Politics of Arturo Giovannitti," paper delivered at the 18th Annual Conference of the American Italian Historical Association, Providence, Rhode Island, November 8–9, 1985; Joseph Tusiani, "La poesia inglese di Arturo Giovannitti," *La Parola del Popolo* (Chicago) (Nov.–Dec. 1978).

W.P.S.

GIRARD COLLEGE, PHILADELPHIA. Founded in Philadelphia in 1831 as a privately endowed free boarding school for white, indigent, fatherless boys between the ages of six and eighteen. Overwhelmingly, the boys it served were the progeny of the Irish and Italian immigrant poor. Girard College is of particular interest to the historian of education because it was founded in that period of United States history when formal, carefully structured, and organized instruction of a practical nature was almost nonexistent for a major portion of the citizenry and for the lower classes. The school was founded by the testament of Stephen Girard (1750–1831) and opened on January 1, 1848. It maintains and educates free of charge as many boys as the income from the endowment will permit. Civil rights legislation has led to the admission of blacks and females.

References
G. A. Herrick, *Stephen Girard* (1923); Louis A. Romano, *Manual and Industrial Education at Girard College* (1980).

L.A.R.

GIRARD, STEPHEN (1750–1831). *See* Girard College.

GLASS, MONTAGUE. *See* Immigrant Novel.

GODDARD, HENRY H[ERBERT] (b. 1866). Eugenicist; director of research at the Vineland (N.J.) Training School for Feeble-Minded Girls and Boys. Goddard popularized the work of the French psychologist Alfred Binet (1857–1911) in America, and applied his tests (scales for measuring intelligence).

> He agreed with Binet that the tests worked best in identifying people just below the normal range—Goddard's newly christened morons. But the resemblance between Binet and Goddard ends there. Binet refused to define his scores as "intelligence," and wished to identify in order to help. Goddard regarded the scores as a measure of a single, innate entity. He wished to identify in order to recognize limits, segregate and curtail breeding to prevent further deterioration of an endangered American stock threatened by immigration from without and by prolific reproduction of its feeble-minded within. (Stephen Jay Gould)

Goddard's chief works were: *The Kallikak Family: A Study in the Heredity of Feeblemindedness* (1912), in which, it appears, Goddard falsified both photographs and data; *School Training of Defective Children* (1914); and *Human Efficiency and Levels of Intelligence* (1920). In a study for the United States Public Health Service at Ellis Island in 1912, Goddard reported that, based upon his examination of "the great mass of average immigrants, 83 percent of Jews, 80 percent of Hungarians, 79 percent of Italians, and 87 percent of Russians were feeble-minded." See "The Binet Tests in Relation to Immigration," *Journal of Psychoasthenics* 18 (1913): 105–117.

Reference
Stephen Jay Gould, *The Mismeasure of Man* (1981).

F.C.

GOLD, MICHAEL. *See* Immigrant Novel.

GOLDMAN, EMMA (1869–1940). Anarchist, feminist. Born in Kovno, now Lithuania, Goldman moved with her family to Koenigsberg, Prussia, where she gained a preliminary education despite her resistance to discipline. She rapidly became a political radical and dissident, and immigrated to the United States to gain freedom from her family. For a brief spell she lived and worked in Rochester, New York, but her emotional reaction to the murder of the Haymarket strikers sent her on a new course. She moved to New York City where she became acquainted with the leading anarchist personalities, and was associated with Alexander Berkman in publishing the anarchist paper *Mother Earth*. She was deported in 1919 to Russia. Chief writings: *Anarchism and Other Essays* (1911); *My Disillusionment with Russia* (1921); and her autobiography, *Living My Life* (2 vols., 1931; rpt. 1970).

References
Richard Drinnon, *Rebel in Paradise: A Biography of Emma Goldman* (1976); Emma Goldman, *Living My Life,* ed. Richard Drinnon and Anna Maria Drinnon (1977); Alice Wexler, *Emma Goldman: An Intimate Life* (1984).

                                                                  F.C.

GOLDMARK, JOSEPHINE (1867–1950). Labor and legislative reformer. Chairperson of the National Consumers' League's legal division, an organization founded in 1899 to obtain better working conditions for immigrant and poor women. Chief work: with Louis D. Brandeis, *Women in Industry* (1907; rpt. 1971).

                                                                  F.C.

GRAND CARNIOLAN SLOVENIAN CATHOLIC UNION. *See* Slovenes.

GRANT, ANNE McVICAR (b. 1755). Grant came to America at a young age and settled, with her mother, at Claverack on the Hudson. She learned the Dutch language and became interested in the social life and customs of the New York area. *Memoirs* consists of early recollections of Margarita Schuyler of Albany, descriptions of the manners and customs of the descendants of the early Dutch settlers, historical sketches of New York, and tales about the Indians of New York.

Reference
Anne McVicar Grant, *Memoirs of an American Lady, with Sketches of Manners and Scenery in America, as They Existed Previous to the Revolution* (1808; rpt. 1970).

                                                                  F.C.

GRANT, MADISON (1865–1937). Racist, eugenicist, nativist. Grant was one of the leading exponents of the notion that there were "racial" traits that were fixed immutably in groups through heredity, and that they could not be altered or significantly influenced by environmental factors. He saw the "long-skulled" Nordics as the race most favored through nature's generosity. They possessed what he believed were *racial* characteristics such as "love of organization, of law and military efficiency." A nation's strength in war and civilization were to be measured by the degree to which it had the good fortune to have Nordic qualities. He warned that America should do its utmost to avoid contamination by lesser breeds and pressed for restrictions on immigration to prevent "ethnic horrors" from taking place in the future. Grant was among those who believed that his dislike of immigrants from southern and eastern Europe was based on scientific findings and were not simply expressions of prejudice. Grant's animosity was generously distributed among many different ethnic groups, but his anti-Semitism was perhaps the most vehement and determined. Among Grant's published works were: *The Passing of the Great Race* (1916) and *The Conquest of a Continent* (1933).

References
John Higham, *Strangers in the Land: Patterns of America Nativism* (1973 ed.); Kenneth M. Ludmerer, *Genetics and American Society. A Historical Appraisal* (1972).

G.B.

GRATZ, REBECCA (1781–1869). Social reformer. One of five children of the distinguished mercantile family of Philadelphia, Rebecca Gratz is known in Jewish history as a founder of the Philadelphia Orphan Society (1815) and the Jewish Sunday School movement (1838). In literary history she holds an equally honored place as the prototype of Rebecca in Sir Walter Scott's *Ivanhoe*. Gratz served as secretary of the Philadelphia Orphan Society for forty years.

References
Rollin G. Osterweis, *Rebecca Gratz* (1935); David Philipson, ed., *Letters of Rebecca Gratz* (1929; rpt. 1975).

F.C.

GREEK CATHOLIC MESSENGER. *See* Carpatho-Rusyns.

GREEK CATHOLIC UNION. *See* Carpatho-Rusyns.

GREEKS. The initial Greek presence in America can be traced to 1766 when some 400 Greeks were brought as indentured laborers to Florida by a Scottish entrepreneur who had secured a British land grant. The colony was named New Smyrna after the birthplace of his Greek wife. The Greeks, not knowing that they were brought here as indentured servants, were compelled to work under insufferable conditions. Instead of opportunity, they encountered starvation and malaria. By 1777, those who survived fled to St. Augustine where they prospered as merchants and established a place of worship which was recently designated a shrine to their memory by the Greek Orthodox Archdiocese of America. The total population at that time was extremely small so that they were gradually absorbed into the larger community of St. Augustine. During the Greek War of Independence (1821–1829) against four centuries of rule by the Ottoman Turks, Greece had gained the support and sympathy of many American philhellenes. They were instrumental in bringing young, orphaned boys to the United States. Most of these youngsters became prominent professionals in their adopted country; one, Lucas Militiades Miller, was elected to the Wisconsin legislature in 1853 and in 1891 became the first American of Greek descent to be elected to the United States Congress.

In addition to these young immigrants, another group emigrated during the same period. They were the merchants who established their import-export businesses in American cities. It was they who established the first Greek Orthodox Church in America in the city of New Orleans in 1864. But, in terms of numbers, it was neither the orphaned of the War of Independence nor the merchants who established a network of Greek institutions and community life. This was to be left to the poor and uneducated peasant farmers who left the villages of Greeks seeking economic betterment.

Mass Immigration. The vast influx of Greek immigrants began in the 1880s and coincided with America's era of industrial expansion. It is estimated that approximately 500,000—nine out of ten males—arrived in the United States. The motive behind emigration was economic. Four centuries of Ottoman rule had a paralyzing effect on the Greek people and their country. The patient peasants pushing their wooden ploughs behind small, bony oxen and the women grinding their cereal between primitive millstones were as typical of 1821 as of 1453. In 1879, almost fifty years after the War of Independence, about 82 percent of the Greek population lived in rural areas trying to eke out a living in a barren and arid land of which two-thirds was mountainous. Chronic crop failures and the pressing need to provide dowries, without which daughters could not marry, forced both fathers and brothers to emigrate.

Despite the presence of regional variations, Greek rural life shared the same fundamental value system: the people were all members of the Greek Orthodox church, and they all shared in an agricultural economy in which the role and status of each member was clearly defined. The basic unit was the family, with strong patriarchal control and deeply binding extended kinship relationships. Lineal relationships were strong, and the need to defend family honor inhered in a code strong enough to support vendetta claims of individual family members. Protecting the patrimony of which the daughter was a part lay completely in the hands of the family, which ideally functioned as an integrated unit for its own integrity and enhancement. Loyalty was turned inward to the family and to a specific locale. Patriarchy was an accepted fact for the immigrant who came to American shores during the first half of this century; departure from the homeland in no way challenged the essential values of Greek life. It was the economic motive that propelled Greeks to leave; they saw themselves as sojourners who would return to their homeland once they had sufficient capital.

Having arrived on Ellis Island the new immigrant would seek out a relative who had preceded him or head for a job promised him by a labor agent in Greece before his departure. If neither of these options were available to him, he would seek a place where some of his fellow villagers could be found. The immigrant pattern shows that Greeks either went to large northern cities, mainly New York and Chicago where they worked as peddlers, bootblacks, dishwashers, or busboys, or went west to work in the mines of Utah and Colorado, or on railroad gangs. Many headed for the New England mill towns to work in textile and shoe factories and others went south to Tarpon Springs where they developed the sponge industry.

While the Greeks came to the United States as unskilled laborers, it became evident by the 1920s that they had a talent for entrepreneurship; their business acumen was to be demonstrated in such areas as restaurants, confectionary shops, retail and wholesale produce, shoeshine parlors, dry cleaning stores, and the fur industry. Business represented a firm step in upward mobility for those who had initially engaged in menial jobs. As early as 1909 the *American Journal of Sociology* noted that "during the short time he has been in Chicago, the Greek has established himself as a shrewd businessman. On Halsted Street they are saying, 'It takes a Greek to beat a Jew.' "

When a number of Greeks settled in an area they organized a "community" which included all of the Greeks in the area with an executive committee to administer to the community's needs. The first step of the "community" was to build a church around which collective ethnic life could be sustained. Greek Orthodoxy is so firmly entrenched in Greek life that it is taken for granted. It is the embodiment of religious, social, cultural, and historical continuity; it is the locus of collective identity and ethnic survival. The Greek Orthodox Church in America grew out of the immigrant experience; it was not instituted by either the ecclesiastical authorities in Athens or Constantinople (Istanbul). The communal network with the church at its center included Greek-language schools; Sunday schools; fraternal organizations representing the different regions of origin of Greece; and ethnic newspapers which represented both conservative and radical views and always reported on the political events of Greece. By the 1920s it was the presence of Greek women in America that made it possible to think of America as a permanent home. Family life now evolved along the closely knit pattern of the homeland, enveloping the Greek language, Orthodoxy, and cultural traditions. With the zeal of pioneers, Greek women stabilized family life and made possible the growth of Greek-American communities.

During these early years the immigrants were young and ambitious as they moved from the ranks of manual labor to becoming proprietors. Their children were still young and tractable; they spoke Greek at home, attended Greek-language schools where they learned about the grandeur of classical Greece, the oppression of Greeks under Ottoman rule, and Greek Independence. Greek parents of the first generation were determined that their children would exceed them, not succeed them—and education was the means by which to do it. For the Greek, manual labor was demeaning; it diminished one's self-respect and dignity. According to a 1975 census report among twenty-four second-generation ethnic groups, Greeks trailed only Jews in income, and they ranked first in educational attainment and enjoyed earnings 31.5 percent higher than the native white population. The data also show that 82 percent of native-born Greek males completed four years of college or more. Greek parents had high expectations for their sons. The same report reveals that only 20 percent of native-born Greek females completed four years of college or more, reflecting the absence of egalitarianism in Greek life and the persistence of traditional attitudes.

Studies of Greek mobility patterns tend to highlight the conventional occupations pursued and the successes achieved vis à vis the Horatio Alger route. They tend to ignore the self-motivated individuals intent upon success outside the mainstream in the world of the arts, where a number of them became highly respected artists and writers. It is true that few Greeks went into the arts. Traditional patterns may have had something to do with that. Greek rural life was and remains market oriented. Buying and selling, even for the modestly comfortable peasant farmer, depended on how skillfully the male head of the household made his deals. His reputation and prestige was based on his success. This was an orientation that augured well for urban commercial life. The arts were alien and perhaps a threat to the insularity and reciprocal relations embedded within the Greek family. Many Greek-Americans have achieved prominent political positions in the United States, but this is a sphere congenial to traditional attitudes and values.

Not unlike other ethnic groups in the United States, the Greeks were excluded from full participation in its social system; they were held in low esteem, more often than not, and were subject to physical violence, suspicion, and contempt. Insulating themselves against the disruptive forces of the larger society, their ethnic communities were reinforced. However, in the early decades they were not without internal disruptive forces, tied as they were to the political events of Greece. Political ideologies tore them and the church apart. As the years passed the immigrants became more preoccupied with America's economic destiny. The restrictive immigration law of 1924, the Great Depression, the founding of a Greek Orthodox Seminary in 1937 to provide education for American-born Greeks to enter the clergy, the passing of time, and the dimming of Old World memories all signified the primacy of acculturation for the Greek-American community in the United States. Greece's role as an ally in World War II enhanced the country in the eyes of the world; American patriotism and pride for the Greeks now merged the two worlds.

New Immigrants. The question of how many Greek-Americans there are cannot be answered with any precision. The question of ethnic identity itself is problematic; determining place of origin and ethnicity and computing fractions of Greece ancestry resulting from mixed marriages complicate the picture. The 1980 census data report a figure of 990,000, but spokespersons for the Greek-American community regard the number as underrepresentative, maintaining that their calculation of somewhere between 2 to 3 million is a more realistic one.

Between 1957 and 1969, 1,066 scientists left Greece for the United states. The 1950s and 1960s introduced a new category of arrivals significantly different from their predecessors and from the majority of new emigrés. They were educated, had lived through Greece's devastating civil war (1946–1949), and many came with a very liberal political ideology. They were instrumental in infusing Greek-American communities with a sensitivity to Hellenic history, Hellenic consciousness, and Hellenic studies. The year 1965 was a turning point for Greek immigration. From 1966 through 1977 an estimated 150,000 emigrated to this country. Compared with the first wave of Greek immigration at the century's turn, the new arrivals seemed to be better educated and more urbane, with both men and women emigrating. The males tend to be blue-collar workers whose wives also enter the blue-collar labor force—a pattern shunned by earlier immigrants whose wives generally stayed in the home. Recent arrivals have also gone into the food business, coffee shops, diners, pizza parlors, and souvlaki restaurants.

Tensions exist between the newcomer and the older immigrant and second-generation Greek-Americans, who see recent arrivals as undoing the gains that have been made. The language question is a case in point: recent immigrants view the Greek language as central to their ethnic identity; it is the symbol around which a group constructs its social organization and preserves its uniqueness. Despite the fact that language erosion has taken place across generational lines, the new immigrants blame the church's assimilationist trend. In 1970, the Greek Orthodox church approved the use of English for Greek in the liturgy; it saw this as the only realistic action that would be taken in the light of the fact that a new generation of American-born Greeks was emerging without a competent knowledge of the Greek language. It was a genuine effort to reconcile Hellenism with the demands of American society. But the recent immigrants view the introduction of English in the church as part of a conspiracy to "de-Hellenize" it. The language issue is a critical one in the light of the fact that mixed marriages within the church exceed 70 percent; this fact, coupled with a decline in language proficiency by the third generation, makes it a top-priority issue for the Greek-American community. There can be no Greek-American community without the church; it is the focal point from which Greek-Americans have derived a sense of community and identity that no other institution has been able to provide. Clearly, ethnic identity is extremely difficult to pinpoint. The concept is a fluid one and changes along a continuum of such variables as generation, education, occupation, and class. The first generation viewed nationality, language, and religion as part and parcel of their identity. Ethnicity for the second generation was still identified with language (albeit in a truncated form), religion, and tradition, but was modified in conjunction with the American ethos of success and upward mobility. The third generation still identifies with the church but there is a greater identification with the broader cultural values of the Greek community, i.e., music, the folk dance, and Greek cuisine. For the majority of new immigrants, identification is rooted in language, Greek nationalism, and the church. If they do not find a totally Greek-language church, they build one. An unestimated number of Greek churches, not affiliated with the Greek Archdiocese of North and South America, have already been founded in the New York metropolitan area. Like their early counterparts the recent immigrants expect a Hellenized church, and continuity of experience within the church. If the Greek language and Greek values are not the focal points of the established church, then other avenues for maintaining self-esteem are sought. In time, the children of the new immigrants may react against the ethnic church their parents hold on to so tenaciously, and if so, a new ethnic identity will evolve—such is the chameleon quality of ethnicity.

The Greek-American community is not a homogeneous one. There has been no singular American experience in which all Greeks participated collectively. The challenge of the cities, the coal mines, the tanneries, the textile mills, and the vagaries of small businesses produced varying degrees of assimilation and intergroup antagonism. And yet, to be sure, all Greek-Americans share a common ground, bound as they are by religions and traditional values that were transposed to the United States to produce the prototype of the Greek-American. But one must tread cautiously lest the prototype blur the ever-present diversity that makes up the Greek experience in America.

References
Charles C. Moskos, *Greek Americans: Struggle and Success* (1980); John Papajohn and John Spiegel, *Transactions in Families* (1975); Theodore Saloutos, *The Greeks in the*

United States (1964); Alice Scourby, *Third Generation Greek Americans: A Study of Religious Attitudes* (1980); Alice Scourby, *Greek American Community in Transition* (1982); Alice Scourby, *Greek Americans* (1984); Evangelos C. Vlachos, *The Assimilation of Greeks in the United States* (1968).

A.S.

GREENWICH HOUSE (New York City). *See* Simkhovitch, Mary Kingsbury.

GRIFFIN, MARTIN IGNATIUS JOSEPH (1842–1911). *See* Catholic Societies, Federation of Catholic Societies.

GROSE, HOWARD B. (1851–1939). Religious journalist. Grose served as a correspondent for the *Chicago Tribune,* and moved into the world of Baptist periodicals with an appointment to the editorial staff of the *Baptist Examiner* in 1879. In 1896 (after teaching at the University of South Dakota and Chicago University), Grose became associate editor of the *Watchman,* and in 1904 editor of the *Baptist Home Mission Monthly.* During his editorship, the *Monthly* gave top priority in its paper to the new immigration and its implications for Protestants. Grose showed "a remarkable degree of sympathy and objectivity" in his descriptions of European immigrants and these sentiments were reflected in his books *The Incoming Millions* (1906) and *Aliens or Americans?* (1906).

> A complete environmentalist, [Grose] made his chief center of attack the circumstances in which immigrants lived. Both books called attention to the pathos and heartbreak of life in a tenement—the absence of light and fresh air for children, the unsanitary conditions, the neighborhood saloons—all allowed to exist because of corruption and the indifference of men who failed to respond to their consciences. (Davis, 146)

Reference
Lawrence B. Davis, *Immigrants, Baptists, and the Protestant Mind in America* (1973).

F.C.

GRUNDTVIG, N. F. S. *See* Danes.

GUAMANIANS. In 1950 the United States Congress enacted the Organic Act of Guam, conferring U.S. citizenship on the inhabitants of the Territory of Guam. Henceforth, Guamanians were free to enter the United States without restriction. Since they have not been identified as a separate ethnic or racial group in United States census data collections, no accurate census data on Guamanian migrants in the United

States exists. It is estimated that some 20,000 Guamanians are in the Los Angeles area.

Reference
Faye Untalan Munōz, *An Exploratory Study of Island Migration: Chamorrow of Guam* (1979).

D.N.A.

GUATEMALAN REFUGEES, an overview. There are an estimated 55,000 Guatemalan refugees in the United States and more coming. Based on interviews (*infra*) with refugees and with advocates for the refugees, as well as a review of relevant literature, Brintnall presents an overview of the Guatemalan refugee situation in the United States, including the underground railroad, church sanctuary, the threat of deportation, living conditions, and social organizations. He also examines the question of emerging ethnic relations in the new context of U.S. society.

Reference
D. Brintnall, "Guatemalan Refugees in the United States: An Overview," paper presented at the American Anthropological Association 83d Annual Meeting, Denver, Colorado, November 14–18, 1984.

F.C.

GUATEMALAN REFUGEES, deportation. U.S. policy does not grant the legal status of refugees to Guatemalans who have left Guatemala in fear of government violence. Instead, Guatemalans are treated as undocumented aliens, and the danger of deportation is real. Based on recent legal experience in dealing with Guatemalan cases in Colorado, Wheeler outlines the major legal issues and describes the processes by which the Colorado Rural Legal Services has succeeded in saving Guatemalan refugees from deportation.

Reference
C. Wheeler, "Legal Issues and Processes in Preventing the Deportation of Guatemalan Refugees," paper presented at the American Anthropological Association 83d Annual Meeting, Denver, Colorado, November 14–18, 1984.

F.C.

GUATEMALANS. *See* Central Americans.

GUATEMALANS, migrant workers in Florida. An estimated 55,000 (1984) Guatemalan refugees have entered the United States illegally. Based on Composeco's experiences as a Guatemalan Indian and his work with Guatemalan refugees in the United States, he lays out (*infra*) a framework for understanding the immigration of Guatemalans to the United States via Mexico, and then within the United States from centers in the Southwest to Florida, where work is available. He focuses on the conditions of the Guatemalan refugee migrant laborers in Florida, including their relations with other Hispanic groups and other migrant laborers, and on the dangers of capture and deportation by the Immigration and Naturalization Service.

Reference
J. Composeco, "Guatemalans as Migrant Laborers in Florida," paper presented at the American Anthropological Association 83d Annual Meeting, Denver, Colorado, November 14–18, 1984.

F.C.

GUEST WORKER PROGRAMS, in agriculture. In dealing with the problem of illegal immigration from Mexico, neither a policy of strictly policing the border nor a policy of opening the border seems acceptable. An alternative is to permit temporary migration by Mexican guest workers. Morgan and Gardner (*infra*) assess the possible consequences of this policy by analyzing the earlier experience with the bracero program under Public Law 78 in the 1950s and 1960s. Using an econometric model of the supply of and demand for farm labor in the seven states that received almost all the braceros, they estimate that the bracero program on average reduced farm wages by about 8 percent and imposed losses of about $140 million per year on U.S. farm workers. The estimated gains to U.S. employers and consumers of farm products sum to about $185 million per year, for a net gain to the U.S. population of about $45 million per year. The effects of the braceros on other aspects of social welfare and on illegal immigration are also discussed. They conclude that the more pessimistic warnings about the ill effects of a guest worker program are unsupported by the U.S. experience with the bracero program.

Reference
Larry C. Morgan and Bruce L. Gardner, "Potential for a U.S. Guest-Worker Program in Agriculture: Lessons from the Braceros," in Barry R. Chiswick, ed., *The Gateway: U.S. Immigration Issues and Policies* (1982), pp. 361–411.

F.C.

GUEST WORKER PROGRAMS, United States policy. Reubens considers the implications of a temporary worker program by examining the social and economic effects of previous guest worker programs in the United States and Western Europe from the perspective of both sending and receiving societies. Attention is paid to the efficacy of these programs in promoting temporary versus long-term immigration of foreign workers as well as their developmental impact on sending countries.

Reference
E. P. Reubens, "Guestworker Programs: Evidence from Europe and the United States and Some Implications for U.S. Policy," paper presented at the Population Association of America Annual Meeting, Washington, D.C., March 26–28, 1981.

F.C.

GÜLDIN, SAMUEL. *See* Swiss.

GYMANFA GANU. *See* Welsh.

H-2 PROGRAMS. *See* Temporary Foreign Workers, Policies.

HAARLEM HOUSE. *See* Ruddy, Anna C[hristian].

HADASSAH. Founded in 1912 by Henrietta Szold (*q.v.*) as the women's affiliate of the American Zionist movement. Hadassah has done considerable work in Israel in medical services, child welfare, and refugee aid. In the United States, its activities are mainly educational and charitable.

Reference
Marlin Levin, *Hadassah* (1973).

F.C.

HAITIAN COMMUNITY CENTER. *See* Haitians.

HAITIAN IMMIGRANTS, oral histories. Oral histories (*infra*) of upwardly mobile Haitian immigrants in western New York are examined in terms of two models of how immigrants construe personal agency and social identity. The social action model presents actors as making instrumental use of religious affiliations, kin networks, and status markers to move across social boundaries. The second model grounds action in culturally constituted "primordial attachments" to place, family, and sacred beings; action is expressive or ritually participatory. Both models have antecedents in Haitian culture and both have adaptive functions for immigrants to America.

Reference
R. Chierici and S. Roark-Calnek, "Two Models for the Construction of Experience Among Haitian Immigrants," paper presented at the American Anthropological Association 83d Annual Meeting, Denver, Colorado, November 14–18, 1984.

F.C.

HAITIAN MIGRANTS, and background imperialism. Plummer discusses "the structure of North American domination in the Caribbean, and the intensifying crisis imperialism has engendered as it seeks to block genuine transformation in the area." Haiti, Haitian migration, and U.S. policy in this area are discussed.

Reference
G. Plummer, "Haitian Migrants and Background Imperialism," *Race and Class* 26 (Spring 1985): 35–44.

F.C.

HAITIAN REFUGEE CENTER. *See* Haitians.

HAITIAN REFUGEES, in South Florida. Based on a random sample survey of recently arrived Haitians, participant observation, and intensive interviewing, this research (*infra*) examines the following areas: (1) individual background characteristics of Haitian immigrants; (2) their arrival and early resettlement experiences; (3) their education and knowledge of English and information about the United States; (4) current employment status and occupation; (5) income and use of public assistance; (6) predictors of employment, occupation, and income; and (7) beliefs and orientations. These results are presented after a discussion of the methodology of the study and the context of out-migration from Haiti.

Reference
Alex Stepick and Alejandro Portes, "Flight Into Despair: A Profile of Recent Haitian Refugees in South Florida," *International Migration Review* 20 (Summer 1983): 329–350.

F.C.

HAITIAN REFUGEES, plight of.

While the number of Haitians entering the United States in recent years has been a major cause of concern, it pales into insignificance when compared with the total number of refugees who have entered this country during the last decade. With 124,789 Cubans coming to this country during the Mariel boat lift and 600,424 Southeast Asians arriving in the United States since 1975, the 40,023 boat people from Haiti constitute only a small percentage of the total refugee population of this country. Although conceding the truth of the above, some government officials insist that the Haitian boat people are not refugees, but instead are illegal aliens. However, even when considering aliens who have come to this country without acceptable documents, Haitians constitute only an insignificant percentage. While the number of such aliens is not known, the INS estimated that there were between three and five million in the United States in 1979. In appraising the impact upon this country of Haitian boat people, Professor Virginia Dominguez observed: "By comparison to the millions of Mexicans who reside in the United States at any given point without proper documentation, this flow is totally insignificant. Even if it is compared to the number of Haitians who reside in the New York metropolitan area illegally . . . the entry of Haitian boat people is insignificant." (Miller)

Reference
Jake C. Miller, *The Plight of Haitian Refugees* (1984).

F.C.

HAITIANS. Few recent immigrant groups to the United States have captured as much national attention as the Haitian boat people who have been washing up on Florida beaches in small, homemade boats since the 1970s. In 1980 alone, at least 13,000 and possibly as many as 25,000 Haitians arrived in Florida, while many others died at sea or drowned as their boats foundered in turbulent waters within sight of their destination. Escaping political repression and the poverty of the Western Hemisphere's poorest nation, the Haitian newcomers shared with other immigrant peoples the search for political freedom and economic opportunity in the United States. But because the Haitians were black immigrants, and because their petitions for political asylum were routinely rejected by American immigration officials, they were treated quite differently from Cuban or Nicaraguan refugees who were arriving in Florida at the same time.

The Haitian immigration to the United States is a relatively recent phenomenon. Like many other Caribbean Islanders, Haitians traditionally demonstrated strong labor migration patterns, especially to Cuba and the Dominican Republic early in the twentieth century. United States marines occupied Haiti between 1915 and 1934, and Americans remained in financial control of the country until 1946—an occupation that served to establish an economic and cultural orientation toward the United States among the Haitian elite, but did not trigger any great migration. About 500 Haitians had settled in New York City by the late 1930s, and the Miami Haitian colony totaled only 239 by 1960.

The rise of François Duvalier to power in Haiti in 1957 stimulated the first sizable Haitian migration to the United States. Haitian political exiles, professionals, wealthy merchants, and big landowners sought to escape the brutality of the Duvalier dictatorship, which was characterized by terror, repression, and exploitation of the people. Although there were some divisions among these exiles, they generally shared a preference for French culture and language. They adhered to Catholicism rather than lower-class voodooism, and they tended to be light-skinned mulattos rather than blacks. By the 1960s, these early exiles increasingly were being joined by the urban middle class of shop-keepers, teachers, and skilled workers. During the 1960s, Haitian im-migrants to the United States created new communities in Boston, Phil-adelphia, Chicago, Washington, Miami, and especially New York City. Other Haitians were attracted to Canada during this period, particularly Montreal, by the prevalence of French language and culture.

By the mid-1960s, some 80 percent of Haiti's engineers, lawyers, physicians, teachers, and other professionals had been driven out of the country by "Papa Doc" Duvalier's ruthless personal rule. The business and professional elites who came in the early wave of Haitian immi-grants generally entered the United States legally and they came by airplane. After the rule changes introduced by the Immigration and Nationality Act of 1965, Haitians increasingly arrived in the United States on tourist or commercial visas, overstayed their time, and be-came illegal immigrants and undocumented workers. In addition, as people of more modest means joined the wealthy and the well educated in the flight from poverty and repression, they were forced to leave in clandestine fashion by small boat to the Bahamas or south Florida. As early as 1965, according to the Immigration and Naturalization Service (INS), Haitians were being smuggled into Florida by boat from the Bahamas.

Political repression and economic deprivation intensified in Haiti in the early 1970s, especially after Jean-Claude "Baby Doc" Duvalier assumed control of the government when his father died in 1971. As a result, a new exodus began from Haiti of the urban lower classes and the rural poor—a migration that strengthened substantially during the dec-ade and into the 1980s. These new migrants were different from their predecessors; they were black rather than mulatto, they spoke Creole rather than French, and they identified with the Afro-Haitian peasant culture and folk religion rather than the Catholicism and French culture of the upper classes. Most of these Haitian newcomers arrived in the United States by small boat, either directly to south Florida or by way of the Bahamas, where tens of thousands of Haitians have temporarily settled.

The number of Haitian immigrants to the United States is a matter of some dispute. One recent estimate suggests that about 600,000 Hait-ians have come to the United States since the beginning of the Duvalier regime in 1957. Another careful estimate places the number of Haitians and Haitian-Americans (the American born of Haitian descent) cur-rently in the United States at 800,000. It is generally agreed that the largest number of Haitians and Haitian-Americans live in New York City—some 400,000 to 450,000. In south Florida, at least 60,000

Haitians had settled in Miami by the mid-1980s, while another 40,000 or more lived just to the north in Broward and Palm Beach counties. But these statistics are imprecise and probably much too low, because of the enormous number of illegal and uncounted Haitian immigrants. Conveying a sense of this imprecision, the U.S. State Department estimated 100,000 to 300,000 illegal Haitians in the country in 1980.

The recent Haitian newcomers have received a less than enthusiastic welcome in the United States. It has been difficult to ignore the double standard in American immigration policy—one that welcomed mostly white refugees from Cuban communism, for example, but rejected black immigrants from Haiti who also claimed to be political exiles from a totalitarian government. The INS has refused to accept Haitian appeals for political asylum. The Haitians, the INS has argued, are seeking economic opportunity in America and not fleeing political persecution. Thus, the thousands of Haitians who arrived in Florida in 1980 and after were officially "detained" by the INS in the Krome Refugee Camp west of Miami and, for a time, at another camp in Puerto Rico. By contrast, the Cuban "Marielitos" without criminal records went free immediately.

Since the Haitian boat people were considered illegal immigrants by the INS, it became official policy to deport them as soon as possible. Beginning in the 1970s, many Haitians were pressured or coerced into accepting immediate "voluntary" return to Haiti. For those who claimed political asylum, however, immigration law conveyed the right to deportation hearings, an option increasingly chosen by Haitian newcomers. By the end of 1981, almost 40,000 Haitian refugees were awaiting exclusion or deportation hearings.

Several thousand Haitian detainees ended up in the squalid and depressing Krome Refugee Camp, some for as long as eighteen months. The Krome Camp became a symbol of hopelessness and despair for thousands of Haitians. Demonstrations by Haitian supporters focused public attention on the Krome situation, while legal action by the Haitian Refugee Center, a private Miami advocacy organization, forced the issue into the federal courts. In 1982, a federal judge ruled the INS detention policy illegal and released all Haitian detainees pending individual deportation hearings.

However, as a deterrent to further Haitian immigration, the Reagan administration in 1981 initiated an "interdiction" policy to halt the flow of boat people at sea near Haiti. Haitians seized at sea by the U.S. Coast Guard get shipboard INS hearings, followed by immediate return to the Haitian mainland. This interdiction policy remains in effect, and it has reduced dramatically the number of Haitian boat people arriving in south Florida. Nevertheless, some Haitians continue to drift up on Florida beaches in small, overcrowded, barely seaworthy boats after a dangerous, 800-mile voyage in the open seas. Since 1975, at least 40,000 black boat people have completed this perilous trip. Immigration experts report that at least an equal number have died at sea.

In the United States, the Haitian newcomers have been confronted with the traditional immigrant task of adjustment and accommodation. The Haitians bear the dual stigma of being both foreign and black. Thus, it is not surprising that they have had difficulty entering the mainstream of American life. Nevertheless, like other immigrant groups before them, they have succeeded in establishing new ethnic communities with important institutional and cultural attributes.

In New York City, Haitian immigrants live in distinct sections of Manhattan, Brooklyn, and Queens. The Upper West Side of Manhattan seems to function as an initial staging area, from which Haitians later move to other parts of the city as they acquire financial savings and perceive alternative housing choices. Haitian restaurants, groceries, shops, and other evidences of institutional life flourish in these neighborhoods. However, the Haitians are handicapped in the city's labor market by poor language and job skills, compounded in a large number of cases by their status as illegal or undocumented aliens. Thus, New York's Haitians tend to work primarily in marginal jobs as unskilled factory and service workers. The Haitian adjustment process has been aided by the Catholic church and by several social agencies, such as the Haitian Community Center established in Brooklyn in 1969.

Haitian group political life in New York City has been strong since the beginning of the Duvalier regime. Major Haitian exile organizations emerged after 1957, although they remained badly divided among themselves for many years. Haitians also began to participate in New York City's traditional ethnic politics as early as 1968, particularly within the structure of the Democratic party. Political organization among Haitians in New York encouraged a sense of ethnic identity and ultimately led to a more widespread associational community life based on the common Haitian origin.

It is also quite clear that the racist bias of American society has encouraged New York Haitians to use their ethnicity in the adjustment and adaptation process, as well as to protect individual and group interests. Thus, as with earlier white immigrants, family, religion, language, culture, and traditional values and beliefs have not only been transplanted but strengthened by the migration process. As a result, Haitians find themselves divided from native American blacks by language and tradition, even though both groups suffer from racial bias. As Michel Laguerre, who has written extensively on the Haitians, put it: "Haitian newcomers often feel segregated from whites by their color, and cut off from American blacks by their culture."

The Haitians in Miami have also begun to build a new ethnic

community, despite their problems with the INS. The Haitian immigrants to Florida have settled heavily in the Edison–Little River section of Miami. One of the city's oldest neighborhoods where white residents were already fleeing, Edison–Little River attracted the Haitians because of cheap housing and nearby job opportunities in warehousing, light manufacturing, and the garment industry. Now known as Little Haiti, the community is well over 40 percent Haitian, with most of the rest of the residents American blacks.

Researchers are just beginning to sketch out the full dimensions of Haitian community life in Miami. Like earlier immigrants, the Haitians came to Miami through the process of chain migration. A study of the 1980 Haitian entrants, for example, revealed that 88 percent knew someone in the United States before arrival—usually brothers, sisters, or cousins. The Miami Haitians are relatively young, overwhelmingly male, and at least one generation removed from rural peasantry. One study noted that women made up only 25 percent of the Haitian community in Miami, but because they were in their prime child-bearing years, the size of the Haitian community could easily double within two decades even without replenishment through new immigration. These newcomers were mostly semiskilled rather than unskilled workers in Haiti, and they had achieved some education—averaging 7.6 years of schooling—before arrival in Florida. In the United States, as a group they have continued to seek education, with one study reporting almost half of all Miami Haitians enrolled in some sort of school or educational program. Generally, they have picked up English, and Spanish too, remarkably well.

The Haitian boat people, it has been argued, are "positively selected"—that is, they are risk takers who are ambitious and willing to work hard and take chances in the struggle to get ahead. Despite this strong work ethic, the Florida Haitians have high rates of unemployment and underemployment. They have established a growing entrepreneurial sector in Little Haiti, although it tends to consist almost entirely of small retail and service businesses or other kinds of informal enterprises, all generally marginally profitable. The Haitians lack the self-sufficient enclave economy the Cubans have created in Miami's Little Havana. They work mainly in low-paying service and labor jobs, where they compete with American blacks and other Third World immigrants. Several thousand Haitians have found work as cane cutters in rural south Florida's sugar industry, and other thousands have joined the migrant farm worker stream that ranges up and down the eastern seabord. Racial discrimination in the labor market has hindered their upward economic mobility. Other adjustment problems in Little Haiti include overcrowded housing, inadequate health care, and a poor level of social services. Regardless of problems and handicaps, survey researchers report that the Haitians have a high degree of satisfaction with life in the United States, and few have expressed much interest in returning to their home country.

Premigration Haitian culture remains a powerful ingredient of community life in south Florida. Haitian dress, food, music, and art are prevalent in Little Haiti, and frequent festivals and celebrations convey the homeland flavor. The extended family structure serves important functions, ranging from facilitating the chain migration process to providing job recruitment for newcomers. Haitian Catholic parishes in Miami, with French- and Creole-speaking priests and nuns, provide a form of religious continuity; so also do some thirty storefront Protestant churches in Little Haiti. Like the Cubans, the Haitians have mixed organized religion with folk religion of African origins. Haitian voodoo includes a melange of music, magic, ceremony, ritual, natural medicine, and animal sacrifice. An indelible part of Haitian culture, the informal voodoo rites are commonly practiced even by those belonging to organized churches.

The Florida Haitians have also maintained their identity through political organization. Numerous exile groups organized in Miami with the avowed aim of toppling the Duvalier regime. One such group, the Haitian National People's Party, actually conducted an ill-fated invasion of the island in 1982, but there is little evidence that Miami Haitians played any role in the events leading to Jean-Claude Duvalier's flight to France in 1986. The anti-Duvalier exile politics that marked the Haitian community in Miami has now been defused, but the direction of the Haitian Revolution continues to be a matter of concern. Inevitably, the growing Haitian population in Miami will become increasingly interested in local issues. Miami already has 4,500 Haitian voters, and there could be as many as 10,000 by the end of the 1980s. A shift to ethnic politics for these new Caribbean immigrants may not be far off.

The Haitian migration of the past several decades is part of a larger movement of Third World peoples to the United States. The Haitians have been pushed by poverty and political repression and pulled by the opportunities they perceive in the United States. In Miami and New York, especially, the Haitians are pursuing the old immigrant dream, building ethnic communities, and gradually adjusting to life in the new land.

References
Michel S. Laguerre, *American Odyssey: Haitians in New York City* (1984); Raymond A. Mohl, ''The New Haitian Immigration: A Preliminary Bibliography,'' *Immigration History Newsletter* 17 (May 1985): 1–8; David Nicholls, *Haiti in Caribbean Context: Ethnicity, Economy and Revolt* (1985); Alex Stepick, *Haitian Refugees in the U.S.* (1982); Jake C. Miller, *The Plight of Haitian Refugees* (1984).

R.A.M.

HAITIANS, emigration in the early twentieth century. Standard migration theories see receiving countries as the dynamic agents that pull migrants to them. These theories, while useful for explaining many cases, appear inadequate for the case of labor migration from Haiti to Cuba and the Dominican Republic in the early twentieth century. This history offers an alternative theoretical framework for explaining this migration flow. It is argued that the prime cause of migration from Haiti is the situation in the sending country.

Reference
Glenn Perusek, "Haitian Emigration in the Early Twentieth Century," *International Migration Review* 18 (Spring 1984): 4–18.

                                                                    F.C.

HAITIANS, language and identity. Of the some 300,000 Haitians living and working in the New York City area, most have arrived after 1968. Since only 2 to 5 percent of the people in Haiti speak French, most of the New York Haitians speak Creole. These two languages are mutually unintelligible. Since French-speaking people generally hold high status in Haiti, the language difference mirrors and reinforces class distinctions. In New York, language differences continue to divide Haitians in even more complex subgroupings.

Reference
Susan H. Buchanan, "Language and Identity: Haitians in New York City," *International Migration Review* 13 (1979): 298–313.

                                                                    F.C.

HAITIANS, migration of. Haitian ethnicity has intensified as a result of the migration experience. As Laguerre puts it, "The racist structure of American society compels them to use ethnicity in their adaptation process." More specifically, the Haitians have used ethnicity "in a tactical manner to maintain and protect individual and group interests." Thus, as with earlier white immigrants, family, religion, language, culture, and traditional values and beliefs have not only been transplanted but strengthened by the migration process. Some 800,000 Haitians and American-born Haitian children reside in the United States as of 1984. Perhaps 450,000 of these live in New York City and another 90,000 or so in south Florida. The Haitian migration first took on sizable proportions after 1957, when François Duvalier came to power. The brutal Duvalier regime made exiles of many from the urban elite and professional classes. During the 1960s, these Haitian immigrants created new communities in New York, Montreal, Boston, Philadelphia, Washington, and Miami. The Haitian exodus swelled in the 1970s after the installation of Jean-Claude Duvalier as president-for-life, but now the exiles included the urban working class and the rural peasantry.

Reference
Michel S. Laguerre, *American Odyssey: Haitians in New York City* (1984).

F.C.

HAITIANS, in New York City. An overview (*infra*) of "the silent minority" in New York City, looking into their distrust of any government and their fear for relatives left in Haiti. Haitian culture and characteristics are explored through discussions of a recent Haitian Cultural Festival at the American Museum of Natural History and interviews with various Haitian immigrants. Discusses the policy of immigration officers in New York who are arresting Haitians and the problems of housing, jobs, and language that most Haitians face.

Reference
Jarvis Anderson, "A Reporter at Large: The Haitians of New York," *New Yorker* (March 31, 1975): 50–75.

F.C.

HAITIANS, in Philadelphia. Given their noneligibility (as a group) for "refugee" status, Haitian entrants have had little or no recourse to federal funds and organizations for aid. They rely on individuals and themselves for help in coping in and with U.S. institutional and social systems. Preliminary research shows that among the Haitians themselves, there is no unified support system. There is a difficulty in their joining together, which is exacerbated by the subconscious manifestation of the social stratification that exists in Haiti. Studying the entrants' social networking patterns reveals what they do to live not only among native-born and other U.S. residents, but also among each other.

Reference
N. C. Francis, "Haitian Entrant Relocation in Philadelphia," paper presented at the American Anthropological Association 83d Meeting, Denver, Colorado, November 14–18, 1984.

F.C.

HALDIMAND, FRÉDÉRIC. *See* Swiss.

HALL, PRESCOTT F[ARNSWORTH] (1868–1920). Lawyer and lobbyist; advocate of immigration restriction. A founder of the Immigration Restriction League (*q.v.*) and sometime chairman who influenced Congressman Albert Johnson (*q.v.*) in immigration legislative reform, Hall supported the new science of eugenics and chaired a committee on immigration for the American Breeders' Association (*q.v.*). Hall characterized the "fatuous belief in universal suffrage" and the "lust for equality" as forms of paranoia. Chief writings: *Immigration and the Educational Test* (1897); *Selection of Immigration* (1904); *Immigration and Its Effect on the U.S.* (1906).

Reference
[Mrs. Prescott Farnsworth Hall], *Immigration and Other Interests of Prescott Farnsworth Hall* (1922).

F.C.

HALL, PRINCE. *See* West Indian Immigrants.

HAMILTON, ALICE (1869–1970). Physician and educator; founder of industrial toxicology, co-worker of Jane Addams (*q.v.*), and first woman professor at Harvard. Alice Hamilton's life spanned the Victorian and Vietnam War eras. Her *Autobiography* is valuable for the description of industrial areas (and their hazards) in which immigrants formed the majority of workers.

References
Alice Hamilton, *Exploring the Dangerous Trades. The Autobiography of Alice Hamilton, M.D.* (1943); Barbara Sicherman, *Alice Hamilton: A Life in Letters* (1984).

F.C.

HANSEN, MARCUS LEE (1892–1938). An historian, Hansen taught at the University of Illinois. He spent considerable time in Europe collecting materials for a history of immigration. His *The Atlantic Migration 1607–1860* (1940), the first volume of a projected trilogy, earned him (posthumously) the 1941 Pulitzer Prize for history. Other works were: *Old Fort Snelling, 1819–1858* (1918); *Welfare Campaigns in Iowa* (1920); *German Schemes of Colonization Before 1860* (1924); *The Immigrant in American History* (1941); and the influential *The Problem of the Third Generation Immigrant* (1938), an historical interpretation of migration with special reference to the problems confronting the historian in the study of the third-generation immigrant. Those of the third generation develop a spontaneous and almost irresistible impulse to interest themselves in their common heritage. Hansen was concerned with how to direct this impulse toward a dignified contribution to the development of the receiving country.

References
Eugene L. Bender and George Kagiwada, "Hansen's Law of 'Third Generation Return' and the Study of American Religio-Ethnic Groups," *Phylon* 29 (Winter 1968): 360–370;

Marcus Lee Hansen, *The Problem of the Third Generation Immigrant,* a republication of the 1937 address with an Introduction by Peter Kivisto and Oscar Handlin (1987).

P.K.

HANUS, PAUL (1855–1941). *See* [New York City]: New York City Board of Estimate and Apportionment. . . . *Report of Committee on School Inquiry.*

HAOLE. Hawaiian term for white Americans or Caucasians. It originally meant "foreigners." Natives are called *kanaka.*

Reference
Andrew W. Lind, *Hawaii's People* (1980).

D.N.A.

HAPGOOD, HUTCHINS (1869–1944). Journalist, student, and observer of immigrant life. His *The Spirit of the Ghetto: Studies of the Jewish Quarter of New York* (1902; rpt. 1966) is a sympathetic report on scholars, rabbis, women, poets, the stage, literature, art, the press, and idiosyncratic types whom Hapgood called "odd characters." *The Spirit of the Ghetto* included drawings by Sir Jacob Epstein (1880–1959), then a young immigrant in New York City.

Reference
Moses Rischin, ed., *Hutchins Hapgood, the Spirit of the Ghetto* (1965).

F.C.

HARASZTHY, AGOSTON. *See* Hungarians.

HARDY, MARY [MCDOWELL] DUFFUS (1825–1891). Traveler. Lady Duffus Hardy describes her trip through urban and rural regions of nineteenth-century America with vignettes of immigrant life in her *Through Cities and Prairie Lands: Sketches of an American Tour* (1881).

F.C.

HARRIGAN, EDWARD (1845–1911). Playwright, actor, producer. Author of thirty-nine plays, and many variety sketches. His characters and his subject matter were drawn chiefly from the immigrant Irish and Germans, and the native New York blacks, as well as the newly arriving Italians, Slavic Jews, and Chinese. For these people, Harrigan's rancor comedies and simple melodramas became, in effect, a kind of school for integration into the mainstream of life in their newly adopted homeland. Chief plays: *The Mulligan Guards* (1873); *Cordelia's Aspirations* (1883); and *Dan's Tribulations* (1884).

Reference

Warren T. Burns, "The Plays of Edward Green Harrigan: The Theatre of Intercultural Communication," Ph.D. dissertation, Pennsylvania State University, 1969 (DA 30: 3130-A).

F.C.

HAUGE, HANS NILSEN. *See* Norwegians.

HAWAII, ethnic Caucasians in Hawaii. All groups in Hawaii, including the Caucasian or *haole* (the old Hawaiian word for foreigner), are minorities. The current population is: 27 percent Caucasian, 39.9 percent Asian (including Filipino), 17.2 percent Hawaiian and part Hawaiian, and 15.9 percent others. The level of persistence of ethnic or non-Anglo Caucasian identity today is tied to that group's immigration to and reception in Hawaii for over two hundred years.

Foreigners from all over the globe quickly followed the British explorers of 1778 who opened Hawaii to the world. By 1828, persons from thirty-three different countries resided in the Hawaiian Kingdom. Anglo Caucasians with American ties, however, rose to political and economic power soon after their arrival in 1820. By the mid-1850s, a burgeoning capitalistic sugar industry required an ever-increasing amount of cheap labor. The government set up a Bureau of Immigration in 1864. In the next 100 years, planters' agents and government officials sought nonwhite male workers in South China, Japan, the Philippines, Korea, and far-flung Pacific Islands. Wanting a "balanced" population to offset the large numbers of imported Asians, they also turned to the recruitment of families. Russians from Mongolia and Siberia; blacks from the United States; Puerto Ricans; and Europeans from the Madeira and Azores Islands, Germany, Norway, Austria-Hungary, Spain, and Italy. Assisted immigration from 1852 to 1946 brought in 400,000 people. Workers came under an independent monarchy (up to 1893), a republic (1894–1898), and a U.S. territory (1900–1959). Their status ranged from that of indentured contract to free wage laborers. Independent immigration added French, Belgians, Jews, Greeks, and others to the population.

The Anglo Caucasian *haole* elite controlled Hawaii until statehood (1959) as a Republican stronghold and a feudal plantation. Although a multiethnic society developed over two hundred years, and although in the last thirty years the small elite has been forced to share power with Japanese-Americans and a resurgent ethnic Hawaiian political movement, Caucasians still represent power and wealth to the non-Caucasians who are more than 70 percent of the population. Some non-Anglo or ethnic Caucasians, forming a middle class, have accepted the dominant group's values and ethos, including racial and political biases. Others have not done so—in the 1890s, for example, they formed alliances with Europeans and native Hawaiians to oppose the annexation of Hawaii by the United States. They still reject the idea that *haoles* form a single identity.

Portuguese. Among the most ethnically conscious are the Portuguese. Mariners reached Hawaii in the early nineteenth century. Portuguese were also the first assisted Europeans to be recruited for the plantations. Between 1878 and 1913, 16,200 Portuguese from the Azores and Madeira Islands were shipped in as families to "Terra Nova" (the new land) and established their own communities. The men were given supervisory (and lesser paid) positions on the plantations and were used as buffers between the *haole* managerial class and the non-Caucasian laborers. Along with the Spanish and Puerto Ricans, they were counted separately from "other Caucasians." They were a politically significant group with their own language newspapers and Roman Catholic and Pentecostal churches through the Territorial years.

Separate categories were dropped in the 1940 U.S. census. Many Portuguese have disappeared into the general Caucasian population or have intermarried, particularly with ethnic Hawaiians. But the Hawaii state census reports approximately 26,400 Portuguese claiming single ancestry today. Many live in rural (formerly plantation) areas. They are successful ranchers and farmers, are active in business and the professions, and maintain civic associations and clubs, which sponsored the Portuguese centennial in 1978. Once economically and socially discriminated against, they are today proud of their heritage.

Galicians. Illustrative of the record of mistreatment and exploitation of assisted labor, some 365 Galicians from Austria-Hungary (present-day Poland and the Ukrainian S.S.R.) were recruited in Europe and shipped to Hawaii in 1897–98. Their three-year contracts called for wages of $15 per month. Bitter about their terms of employment, they struck, were arrested, and jailed. Management drove many off the plantations; others fled, more than half to California. As an example of surviving ethnicity, however, a small "Ukrainian" settlement that descended from those who stayed exists today in a country town on the island of Hawaii, with its own Roman Catholic church, decorated homes and clothing, and folk customs.

Puerto Ricans. After 1900 Hawaii became subject to U.S. laws that did not permit Asians to become naturalized citizens. Puerto Ricans were considered desirable because they could be "Americanized." Ironically, although Puerto Rico and Hawaii were now U.S. possessions, Puerto Ricans were not enabled to vote in Hawaii until 1917.

Between 1900 and 1920, 6,000 were recruited from San Juan and
Ponce. The 1900 contingent was shipped across the continental United
States in what appeared to be sealed railroad cars, leading to charges of
slavelike conditions and causing mass desertions. Those who embarked
from California were sent almost at random to Kauai, Maui, Oahu, and
Hawaii. Puerto Rican movement off the plantations was quite rapid. By
the 1950s, more than 40 percent of all Puerto Ricans were living in the
urban center of Honolulu.

Although predominantly Spanish, the Puerto Ricans are racially
and culturally mixed—an estimated 75 percent over the years have
married non–Puerto Ricans. Yet there is ethnic survival. During the
1930s they formed the popular Puerto Rican Baseball League and also
burial and self-help associations. Active organizations today include the
Kohala Puerto Rican Social Club and the United Puerto Rican Association of Hawaii. Their Roman Catholic and Pentecostal churches remain
strong, and there are sporadic efforts to preserve the Spanish language,
customs, and food. Previously disconnected from their motherland,
they have recently made contact through travel to the homeland and
through Puerto Rican military personnel stationed in Hawaii. There are
7,082 single-ancestry and another 14,997 part Puerto Ricans residing in
Hawaii today.

Jews. Not recruited as labor, Jews began to arrive in Hawaii in the
1850s. Principally from Europe (Germany, England, Austria-Hungary,
Russia), they set up major mercantile establishments in the Hawaiian
Kingdom. They were coffee and sugar planters and agents, wholesale
and retail clothing merchants, auctioneers, and professionals. Their
business activities were directly or indirectly responsible for 400 to 500
Jews residing in Hawaii by the time of U.S. annexation. The first public
Jewish services were held in 1898; the first Hebrew congregation was
formed in 1901. While Hawaii does not contain the degree of anti-
Semitism Jews have met with elsewhere in the United States, Hawaii's
Jews are still keenly aware of their history of persecution and pain.
Today the Jews participate in general business and government activities, but they support Orthodox, Conservative, Reform, and unaffili-
ated congregations on the major islands. The *Hawaii Jewish News* is an
effective information outlet for foreign and domestic concerns and community events. An estimated 4,500 Jews live in Hawaii, approximately
80 percent of them in Honolulu. Among the Caucasian ethnics, they
form one of the most visible ethnically identifiable groups.

Italians and Greeks. These groups were among early independent
travelers to Hawaii. A colorful and charismatic Celso Caesar Moreno
briefly captured the confidence of King Kalakaua, in the 1880s, whose
government sponsored the education and training of 12 young Hawaiian
men in Italy under Moreno's direction. At the turn of the century, the

Italian government refused to permit recruitment, and the Hawaiian Sugar Planters' Association (HSPA) hired an agent in New York to recruit southern Italian immigrant men among the newly arrived. Only 84 actually arrived in Hawaii, and their stay was brief. Independent inmigration has resulted in an estimated 5,300 Italian-Americans, including the Honolulu city mayor, residing in the fiftieth state. Italian assimilation is fairly well developed, but there is an active Sons of Italy Aloha Lodge. By contrast, Greek ethnicity is quite pronounced. Unassisted, it was highly successful and led to a permanent community of 3,000 (*see* Greeks).

Norwegians and other Scandinavians. These are among the more assimilated groups. In 1881, 615 Norwegian men, women, and children from Drammen were imported, the adults as indentured servants with three-year contracts. Claiming harsh treatment and broken promises, their well-publicized situation led the king of Norway and Sweden to send a representative to Hawaii to investigate.

Scandinavians have also migrated on their own. In the nineteenth century they became substantial landholders and prominent in business. While the laboring people were initially treated as outsiders by the *haole* elite, Scandinavians and northern Europeans in general came to be accepted, adopted the elite's values, and assimilated. Today, there is limited interest in ethnicity among Scandinavians who sponsor a joint association that holds yearly celebrations.

Germans. Necessity explains the deliberate twentieth-century assimilation of Germans. They were more clearly identifiable in earlier years. German sailors arrived with the whaling trade in the 1800s. Merchants and traders soon followed and met with marked success in the islands' expanding economy. Claus Spreckels was the most famous nineteenth-century German in Hawaii—a poor immigrant boy who rose to be a sugar baron, shipping tycoon, and banker in the 1880s to King Kalakaua.

Between 1881 and 1890, 1,300 men, women, and children were recruited from northwest Germany for plantations on three islands. In 1882, they established a German-language school on Kauai, and, in 1893, a Lutheran church. At the outbreak of America's entry into World War I, the Germans were the subjects of violent attacks. Their schools and churches were forced to disband. Residents changed their personal and business names (Hackfeld's to American Factors, for example, and its retail outlet to Liberty House). World War II hastened assimilation and the destruction of the German community. Today there are 22,000 Germans of single ancestry in Hawaii, including 700 aliens. Some Germans maintain informal and not too visible connections of friendship, family assistance, and a shared language and customs.

Russians and Spanish. Russian exploring vessels visited Hawaii as early as 1804. Through the nineteenth century, individual Russian set-tlers achieved prominence, like Dr. Nicholas Russel, Senate president of Hawaii's first Territorial legislature. Assisted immigration of planta-tion workers occurred when 2,248 Russians from Manchuria were brought in between 1909 and 1912. This costly ($16,903 for transporta-tion and agents' fees for 200 people) and largely unsuccessful recruit-ment resulted in the workers quickly leaving the plantations and Hawaii. Little evidence remains of their presence.

The same is true of the Spanish. There are interesting (but spec-ulative) claims that Spanish and Portuguese ships made contact with Hawaii in the sixteenth century, two hundred years before the British. During the years of the Hawaiian Kingdom, individual Spaniards rose to prominence—one, Francisco de Paula Marin, of obscure origins, became physician to King Kamehameha I. In 1907, 2,250 Spaniards were recruited from Malaga and were distributed on plantations on several islands. They quickly deserted their unrewarding jobs, and most left for the mainland.

References
Edward D. Beechert, *Working in Hawaii: A Labor History* (1985); Eleanor Davis, *Norwegian Labor in Hawaii: The Norse Immigrants* (1962); John Henry Felix and Peter F. Senecal, eds., *The Portuguese in Hawaii* (1978); Lawrence H. Fuchs, *Hawaii Pono: A Social History* (1961); Eleanor C. Nordyke, *The Peopling of Hawaii* (1977); Niklaus Schweitzer, *Hawaii and the German Speaking People* (1982); *Social Process in Hawaii* 29 (1982); *The State of Hawaii Data Book 1986: A Statistical Abstract* (1986); Ronald Takaki, *Pau Hana: Plantation Life and Labor in Hawaii 1835–1920* (1983).

                                                                    H.G.C.

HAWAII, Greeks. Greek seafarers found their way to the Pacific with Captain George Vancouver's voyages in the 1790s, and with whalers and trading vessels in the early 1800s. Settlement began in 1878. Sever-al Greek men who had migrated from Greece to the Portugal-held Atlantic islands of Madeira and the Azores were among the Portuguese recruited for sugar plantation labor. These men married Portuguese or Hawaiian women, and their families eventually blended into Hawaii's multiethnic or "local" culture.

An ethnic Greek colony took root in 1884 with the arrival of men from Sparta. Part of the out-migration from Greece in the last third of the nineteenth century, these men first set up fresh produce importing and exporting businesses and restaurants in California, then expanded their enterprises to the Hawaiian Kingdom (and Australia). Chain mi-gration accounted for about thirty residents, most of whom were relat-ed, before the United States annexed Hawaii in 1898. During the tur-bulent last years of the monarchy the men were all royalist sympathizers. Several fought in a counterrevolution aimed at restoring the Hawaiian queen to her throne and suffered jail and economic losses when that effort failed.

After Hawaii became part of the United States, the men traveled to Greece or to mainland American cities for wives, then returned and established family life on the islands of Hawaii and Oahu. By 1941, two hundred men, women, and children functioned as a closely knit community that celebrated and kept alive traditional Greek customs. Greek-run businesses included restaurants, cafes, and two major hotels, the latter owned by George Lycurgus, locally famous as "Uncle George." Lycurgus's colorful life spanned Hawaiian history from kingdom to republic to territory to statehood (he lived to be 101).

The small colony was replenished after World War II by new in-migration from Greece and from the mainland United States. Greeks today have successfully entered into all phases of Hawaii's multicultural life; they own cabarets, restaurants, and specialty shops; they are doctors, teachers, architects, and engineers; they serve in the military; and they are employed by the federal and state governments. Yet they retain their distinctiveness. Island Greeks extend help and support to each other and maintain their religion, language, and customs. They return to Greece to visit relatives and, in turn, are visited by them. The Greek Orthodox church, established in Honolulu in 1965, provides a cultural center for the present community which numbers about three thousand.

References
Helen Geracimos Chapin, "From Sparta to Spencer Street: Greek Women in Hawaii," *Hawaiian Journal of History* 13 (1979); Helen G. Chapin, "The 'Queen's Greek Artillery Fire': Greek Royalists in the Hawaiian Revolution and Counterrevolution," *Hawaiian Journal of History* 15 (1981).

H.G.C.

HAWAIIAN SUGAR PLANTERS' ASSOCIATION. *See* Puerto Ricans in Hawaii.

HAWAIIANS. The history of the Hawaiians is rooted in immigration. Hawaii's native people centuries ago migrated thousands of miles over an uncharted ocean to establish themselves in an unknown place. They developed a society that flourished in isolation until they were invaded by waves of nonnative immigrants. In an attempt to survive, they formed a centralized monarchy. Descendants of American immigrants in alliance with U.S. agents, however, overwhelmed them and turned their independent country into a territory of the United States. Hawaiians officially became Americans in 1898 when their homeland was annexed. In 1959 Hawaii became the fiftieth state. Today, the results of over two hundred years of immigration have contributed to the possibility that Hawaiians may be absorbed into extinction. Population problems remain among their most pressing political, economic, social, and cultural concerns. Their ethnic tenacity, however, is noteworthy.

Early Migrations. The Hawaiian Islands were probably the last large land mass in the Pacific to be inhabited.by a human population. Some 25 million years ago, a volcanic chain of islands began building up from the ocean floor. Perhaps 5 million years ago the islands broke the ocean's surface to form the Hawaiian archipelago, a 2,000-mile-long range of undersea mountains, except where they peak above the water to expose eight large islands and more than a hundred smaller islands, shoals, and reefs. Over millions of years, plant and animal life, carried by trade winds, ocean currents, and migrating birds, became established.

The eight major islands are, northwest to southeast, Niihau (privately owned), Kauai, Oahu, Molokai, Maui, Lanai, uninhabited Kahoolawe, and Hawaii. The archipelago lies 2,400 miles west of the next closest continental land (California) and extends 1,523 miles. With a land area of 6,450 square miles, it ranks forty-seventh in size among the states. Volcanic eruptions still occur on the easternmost island of Hawaii and are slowly increasing the state's land area.

The Hawaiians as a geographical race are Polynesians. A subdivision of Oceania, Polynesia, which means "many islands," forms a vast watery triangle. Hawaii is the triangle's northernmost tip, New Zealand its southwestern, and Easter Island its southeastern boundary. Polynesia was originally settled by waves of migrations stemming from south Asia. About 3,000 years ago the Polynesians became isolated in a home group of islands in the southern Pacific, with common traits of physique, culture, and language. The triangle contains, among hundreds of other islands, Samoa, the Cook Islands, Tonga, the Society Islands of French Polynesia (which includes Tahiti), and the Marquesas.

From approximately 190 A.D. up to the 1200s, perhaps warfare or food shortages, the spirit of adventure, or a combination of factors sent migrants northward in two major waves. Archeological, anthropological, botanical, and linguistic studies have determined that the race that was to become Hawaiian migrated first from the Marquesas and then from the Society Islands. There was also through branching migration a connection with the New Zealand Maori.

The Polynesian seafaring pioneers covered enormous distances of open ocean in sturdy double-hulled canoes. Master navigators charted the voyages by the rising and setting sun and stars, the winds, ocean swells and currents, flights of birds, and cloud formations. No written population figures exist, but it is thought that several hundred men, women, and children, with domestic animals and provisions, made the initial voyages, and that repeat round trips were conducted. The settlers called the islands Havaiki after the ancient mythological homeland of their gods.

For unknown reasons, the voyages ceased. During the next five centuries, and in virtual isolation except for possibly a few shipwrecked or wandering seamen, the Hawaiian population, free from most infectious diseases, increased and thrived in a complex Stone Age culture. A subsistence economy, based on agriculture and fishing, supported a cooperative and familial society that valued group affiliation over individual assertion and material possessions. The material present and the spiritual world were part of a seamless universe. In intimate relationship with the land and ocean, the Hawaiians achieved a balance with their biological and ecological environment and fashioned a society rich in meaning for themselves.

The Arrival of Foreigners. The English explorer Captain James Cook, on January 18, 1778, while in search of a northern sea passage from the Pacific to the Atlantic, accidentally found the Hawaiians. His landing permanently altered their civilization. Cook's officers estimated the Hawaiian population to be between 242,000 and 500,000—a wide variation which still haunts population studies because of its political implications: the larger the original population, the more catastrophic its decline. The generally accepted figure is 300,000. Cook described the islanders as frank, cheerful, and friendly, and he was impressed by the affection women and men showed toward children. He recognized their remarkable good health and attempted, without success, to prevent his crew, many of whom carried venereal diseases, from going on shore or visitors from coming on board. On his return voyage in 1779, he lost his life in an altercation with Hawaiians, but international interest had been awakened and the fatal impact made. With no natural immunities to the diseases of Westerners or Asians, the Hawaiians rapidly fell prey to a series of epidemics: syphilis, gonorrhea, dysentery, measles, mumps, smallpox, influenza, cholera, and leprosy.

A group that was to have a powerful effect on the lives of the Hawaiians arrived in 1820. Hawaii was contended for by various European powers (the French, Russians, and British), but the arrival of American Protestant missionaries from New England was decisive in that it coincided with the rise of the United States as an imperialistic Pacific power. Furthermore, just prior to permanent American settlement, Kamahameha I died. A politically astute and powerful warrior, he unified the islands under one rule in 1810. In 1819, the old religious system based on *kapu* (tabu, or taboo), that preserved natural and social order, fell—a culmination of decades of foreigners disregarding the system. The nonliterate culture, with its nature-based religion, dependent on land tenure and communal sharing, was rapidly displaced by a competitive culture that promoted Christianity, American-style government and laws, land ownership, and private property. Hawaii became the arena for intense value conflicts and radical change, with its native inhabitants on the losing end of the struggle. An American-led revolution deposed Queen Liliuokalani in 1893, and a Hawaii-led counter-revolution, which attempted to restore her to the throne, failed.

Later Immigration and Out-Migration. Since contact, four major themes relating to immigration have dominated Hawaiian history: the depopulation of the native inhabitants, the immigration of foreign labor, intermarriage among the various racial groups, and the out-migration of Hawaiians.

Regarding the first, the native population, from 1778 to 1820, fell by more than 50 percent. King Kamehameha IV stated at midcentury: "The decrease of our population is a subject in comparison with which all others sink into insignificance." By 1900, there were fewer than 30,000 Hawaiians; in 1987 there are only about 6,000 pure Hawaiians—less than 1 percent of the population.

Part-Hawaiians are now officially designated as ethnic Hawaiians, except by the State Health Department which still counts them separately. They number approximately 170,000 or about 19 percent of the 1986 total resident population of 1,062,300 (Hawaii is thirty-ninth among the states in population). Caucasians are currently 25 percent, while Asians, including Filipinos, are 42 percent. Other groups combine to make up the rest.

The development of a part-Hawaiian group is an outgrowth of the second population pattern, the in-migration of foreign labor. A Masters and Servants Act in 1850 opened the way for the importation of contract laborers. This was aimed at offsetting the soaring mortality of Hawaiians and a plummeting labor supply. A centralized capitalistic sugar industry came to dominate the islands' economy until after statehood and promoted worldwide labor recruitment. The in-migration of first the Chinese in 1852, then the Portuguese in 1879, and the Japanese in 1868 and 1885, led to drastic changes in the composition of the people. After 1900, plantation labor immigrants included Puerto Ricans, Spanish, Russians, Koreans, and Filipinos. Because Hawaii now fell under American laws, the restrictive immigration policies after 1924 stopped all contract labor importation except for supplementary groups of Filipinos in 1931 and in 1946. In 95 years, 400,000 nonnatives entered Hawaii.

Prior to World War II, the *haole* (Caucasians) were a small minority with enormous power. In effect, a tiny *haole* oligarchy ruled the islands as a feudal plantation colony. Just before World War II, however, there was a large influx of working-class Caucasians, needed for the buildup of Hawaii's military and civilian defense forces. From the 1950s on, the oligarchy was forced to share its power. Effective in breaking their control was the rise of labor unions and the demand by Japanese immigrants' descendants, who had fought bravely for America in the war, for equal opportunity.

Today, a new type of in-migration is greatly accelerated by air travel. Southeast Asians, Polynesians from Samoa and Tonga, Caucasians from mainland states, and others continue to arrive. A burgeoning (from 1.1 million visitors in 1967 to 5.6 million in 1986) tourist industry has replaced sugar and pineapple as the primary economic base. With its accompanying highrises, freeways, luxurious resort hotels, and golf courses, tourism relies upon local low-paid labor in a high cost of living state and has been called "the new plantation." In second economic place is the defense industry.

The third factor, the intermarriage of Hawaiians with other races, stems in part, then, from in-migration of labor. In addition, historically their culture has been welcoming and inclusive. Hawaiians have intermingled with all races, but particularly with Caucasians, Filipinos, and Chinese, and to a lesser extent with Japanese. A noted population expert fears that by the end of the twenty-first century the Hawaiian race may have merged beyond recognition.

This type of projection, when coupled with statistics that show Hawaiians on the lowest rungs of the socioeconomic system, is discouraging. They are at highest risk for many major medical diseases, like cancer and heart disease, and are dramatically overrepresented in prisons, on welfare rolls, and in their use of social assistance agencies. They have the largest percentage of high school dropouts, substance abuse cases, and incidents of domestic violence. This has all led to what Hawaiians have called "an endless list of statistical despair" and has contributed to their feeling that they are powerless strangers in their own land. Furthermore, the best part of their culture, encompassing the spirit of friendliness and hospitality, the *luau* or communal feast, music, the hula, has been heavily commercialized and exploited.

The final factor in migration is the out-migration of Hawaiians. This began soon after contact by Cook. The islands became a regular stop for merchant and whaling vessels needing fresh water and provisions. Known for their excellent ability on the ocean, Hawaiian men were actively recruited as additions to crews. Some women shipped out, too. Hawaiians found work and homes in America and other countries. Small communities were established in the Pacific Northwest where Hawaiians worked in the fur, lumber, and fishing trades. There is an "Owhyee River" in Washington state and a "Kanaka Village" near Vancouver, British Columbia (Owhyee is a corruption of "Hawaii," and Kanaka is Polynesian for a man of aboriginal blood). After the gold rush of 1848–49, California became a favored destination.

Out-migration statistics in the nineteenth century are speculative. From an estimated 200 in 1823, the numbers increased to 4,000 in 1850, which represents 5 percent of the total Hawaiian population at that time and 22 percent of all Hawaiian males eighteen years and older.

During the years 1845–47 alone, nearly 2,000 Hawaiians enlisted as seamen on foreign ships. In 1850 and again in 1864, Hawaiian monarchs unsuccessfully attempted to make the emigration of young men illegal.

Statistics of out-migration in the twentieth century are also unreliable because of a highly mobile military population. There are many Hawaiians in the military, and civilians have also emigrated for economic reasons. The 1980 census reveals 31.4 percent of all Hawaiians in the United States to be on the mainland. The greatest number, 23,086, resides in California. There are from 3,000 to 1,000 each in Oregon, Texas, New York, Florida, and Illinois, and fewer than 1,000 each in other states. Vermont, with 18, has the fewest number of Hawaiian residents.

Recent Developments. While the forecast for Hawaiians may seem gloomy, there have been positive movements in recent years. Seeking self-determination, Hawaiians are challenging basic assumptions underlying the rampant promotion of international tourism. Like Native Americans and Native Alaskans, Hawaiians are pressing claims against the state and federal governments for reparations for lands appropriated at the time of annexation and for equitable land and water distribution. Activists are demanding an end to the U.S. Navy's use of the island of Kahoolawe as a bombing target. They wish to preserve ancient religious sites there and elsewhere from destruction. Today, there is a State Office of Hawaiian Affairs (OHA), and Hawaii is led for the first time since annexation by an elected Hawaiian governor.

Most encouraging is the resurgence of pride in heritage and a heightened consciousness of Hawaiian culture. Modern Hawaiians have recreated the ancient canoe and navigating culture. In 1976, the Hokule'a, a reconstructed double-hulled canoe, made a 5,000-mile round trip voyage to Tahiti, a stunning achievement utilizing only traditional Polynesian noninstrument navigation. This has been a catalyst for additional voyages, the most recent a two-year epic journey of 13,000 miles that followed the ancient ocean routes through the Polynesian triangle. There is a revival, too, of the language and a renaissance of authentic music, dance, arts, and crafts. Hawaiian studies have been reintroduced into the schools.

Hawaii's immigration history remains unique among all the states. The majority of its population has its roots in the Pacific islands and Asia instead of in Europe and Africa. It is the only state in the union in which all ethnic groups are minorities. Because in-migration continues at such a heavy rate and threatens its fragile environment and its native people, Hawaii has taken the lead in considering the formulation of an official population policy. While there are constitutional restrictions and other practical considerations, Hawaii and Hawaiians are attempting to manage migration-related problems which have faced them for more than two hundred years.

References
Peter Bellwood, *The Polynesians: Prehistory of an Island People* (1978); Peter Henry Buck, *Vikings of the Pacific* (1959); Gavan Daws, *Shoal of Time: A History of the Hawaiian Islands* (1968); Janice K. Duncan, *Minority Without a Champion: Kanakas on the Pacific Coast, 1788–1850* (1972); Ben R. Finney, *Hokule'a: The Way to Tahiti* (1979); Lawrence H. Fuchs, *Hawaii Pono: A Social History* (1961); Irving Goldman, *Ancient Polynesian Society* (1970); Jack Golson, *Man in the Pacific Islands* (1972); Edward Joesting, *Hawaii: An Uncommon History* (1972); George Hu'eu Sanford Kanahele, *Kū Kanaka, Stand Tall: A Search for Hawaiian Values* (1986); Noel Kent, *Hawaii: Islands Under the Influence* (1983); Ralph S. Kuykendall, *The Hawaiian Kingdom*, 3 vols. (1938, 1953, 1967); Ralph S. Kuykendall and A. Grove Day, *Hawaii: A History from Polynesian Kingdom to American State* (1961); Liliuokalani, *Hawaii's Story by Hawaii's Queen* (1898, 1964); Eleanor C. Nordyke, *The Peopling of Hawaii* (1977); Douglas L. Oliver, *The Pacific Islands* (1961); Robert S. Schmitt, *Demographic Statistics of Hawaii 1778–1965* (1968); *The State of Hawaii Data Book 1986: A Statistical Abstract* (1986).

H.G.C.

HEBREW FREE SCHOOL ASSOCIATION. *See* Educational Alliance.

HEBREW IMMIGRANT AID SOCIETY [HIAS]. The Hebrew Immigrant Aid Society and the Hebrew Sheltering House Association merged in 1909 to aid and meet the needs of Jewish immigrants from eastern Europe to the United States. In 1954, the Joint Distribution Committee, the United Service for New Americans, and HIAS formed a single international migration agency.

Reference
N. Wischnitzer, *Vistas to Freedom: The History of HIAS* (1956).

B.L.

HEBREW SHELTERING SOCIETY (Hevra Hachnosas Orchim). Founded in New York City in 1890 to feed, lodge, and clothe indigent Jewish immigrants and to help in finding employment. In 1909 it united with the Hebrew Immigrant Aid Society (*q.v.*).

F.C.

HELLENIC STUDIES. *See* Greeks.

"HELSINKI OF THE WEST." *See* Finns.

HENDERSON, CHARLES R[ICHMOND] (1848–1915). Baptist clergyman; sociologist. Served as university chaplain and professor of sociology, University of Chicago, 1892–1915. Henderson made continuing efforts to meet the needs of the immigrant poor. He was a major force in the social justice movement in the Progressive era. Chief works: *Introduction to the Study of the Dependent, Defective and Delinquent Classes* (1893); *Social Settlements* (1899); *Major Methods of Charity* (1904); *A Reasonable Social Policy* (1909).

F.C.

HENRY, ALICE (1857–1943). Journalist, labor leader. For many years Henry was editor of the publications of the Women's Trade Union League (*q.v.*) which was founded, with President Samuel Gompers' blessing, at the 1903 convention of the AF of L. For a quarter of a century the WTUL championed working women on the job and in the union. In *Women and the Labor Movement* (1923; rpt. 1971), Alice Henry inventoried the strength and position of women workers in the early twenties. She surveyed the variety of union policies for the female worker and her position in the ranks of union leadership, and pointed out the indications of discrimination. Fascinating chapters (*infra*) trace the work of women in primitive, colonial, and machine age times; other chapters focus on protective legislation for women and the minimum wage.

Reference
Robin Miller Jacoby, "The Women's Trade Union League and American Feminism," *Feminist Studies* 3 (1975); 126–140.

F.C.

HENRY STREET SETTLEMENT HOUSE. *See* Wald, Lillian.

HERBST, JOHANNES (1735–1812). Bishop, musician. Emigrated to America in 1786 from Germany. A Moravian bishop, Herbst was the composer of "geistliche lieder" and anthems. His collection of manuscripts is a major source of Moravian music studies.

Reference
Joan Ormsby Falconer, "Bishop Johannes Herbst (1735–1812), an American-Moravian Musician, Collector and Composer," Ph.D. dissertation, Columbia University, 1969 (DA 32: 6475-A).

F.C.

HERZEGOVINA. *See* Croatians.

HIAS. *See* Hebrew Immigrant Aid Society.

HILLMAN, BESSIE ABRAMOWITZ (1895–1970). Union Organizer. Played a leading role in the Chicago garment strike of 1910.
Together with her husband, Sidney Hillman (*q.v.*), she became a founder of the Amalgamated Clothing Workers of America, and later was a
prominent union organizer.

Reference
Jane Julianelli, "Bessie Hillman: Up from the Sweatshop!" *Ms.* 1 (May 1973): 16–20.

F.C.

HILLMAN, SIDNEY (1887–1946). Labor leader. Participated in successful clothing workers' strike (1910) in Chicago. In 1914 he began a
long tenure as president of the Amalgamated Clothing Workers of
America. Hillman was one of the founders of the Congress of Industrial
Organization (CIO). Essentially opposed to labor schism, Hillman was
a moderate in a period of intense labor struggle in which immigrants
assumed a major role.

Reference
Matthew Josephson, *Sidney Hillman* (1952).

F.C.

HINE, LEWIS W[ICKES] (1874–1940). Photographer, social reformer. Hine began his career in photography in 1908 while teaching at
the Ethical Culture School in New York City. A vast portfolio of photographs taken over the years (1908–1914) for the National Child Labor
Committee helped bring about legislative reforms. Hine was a member
of the Pittsburgh Survey (*q.v.*) staff, contributing to the survey's *Report*
an assembly of photographs delineating the horrors of industrial life. He
prepared a photographic study of tenement home work, largely done by
immigrant women and children, for the New York State Factory Investigating Commission, and for the Russell Sage Foundation (*q.v.*), Hine
photographed New York City slum children.

> Hine persevered in his photographic investigations through good
> times and bad, mainly the latter as far as his personal fortunes were
> concerned, until his death in 1940. His pictures recorded vital
> aspects of changing social conditions in the United States from
> before the panic of 1907 until near the close of the New Deal.
> Through them it is possible to follow immigrants from their arrival
> at Ellis Island to the homes and jobs they eventually found or made
> for themselves in America. His photographs show the circum-

stances in which 2,000,000 American children at the start of the century labored in textile mills, coal mines, glass factories, canneries, in their homes, and on the streets. Hine's camera revealed the arduousness of the twelve-hour day in the steel mills and the dangers to which men, women, and children were equally subjected in their work. He provided graphic evidence that was used effectively by social workers and humanitarian reformers in their attempts to awaken the public to the incongruous contrast between ostentatious wealth and desperate poverty in democratic America. Charles Edward Russell called Hine's child-labor photographs "witnesses against ourselves"; for they exhibited faces and bodies that testified to the ugly towns, squalid houses, unwholesome meals, monotonous tasks, and vicious recreations that made up many of the children's whole existence. But Hine also chronicled the gradual improvement of conditions in many areas as, for example, the change for the better accomplished at Ellis Island between 1905 and 1926; and his camera recorded the progress made by and as a result of the activities of public and private welfare agencies. (Bremner, 197)

References
Robert H. Bremner, *From the Depths: The Discovery of Poverty in the United States* (1964); Judith M. Gutman, *Lewis Hine* (1967); and see the large collection of Hine photographs (particularly those taken at Ellis Island) in the George Eastman House Collection, Rochester, New York.

F.C.

THE HISPANIC RESEARCH CENTER (HRC). A research institution dedicated to promoting a humanistic and scientific understanding of the mental health needs and experiences of the Hispanic population in the United States and Puerto Rico. Through research the HRC seeks to improve the general welfare of the entire Hispanic community, including Puerto Ricans, Cubans, Dominicans, and all other Latin American groups living in the United States. The HRC was established at Fordham University (New York City) in 1977 under Research Grant 1RO1-MH30569-01 from the National Institute of Mental Health, Center for Minority Group Mental Health Programs.

F.C.

HISPANICS, changing the face of America. With relatively high fertility rates and growing legal and illegal immigration, the U.S. Hispanic population increased by some 265 percent, from an estimated 4 million in 1950 to 14.6 million (and 6.4 percent of the total population) counted in the 1980 census. By 2020 they could number some 47 million and displace blacks as the largest U.S. minority if immigration were to continue at the recent estimated level of one million a year (legal plus illegal, Hispanics plus all others). Self-identified as persons who trace their heritage to Spanish-speaking countries, Hispanics consist of Mexican-Americans (60 percent of the total), still concentrated in the Southwest; Puerto Ricans, living mainly in New York and New Jersey; Cubans, headquartered in Florida; and the second largest, most scattered "other Hispanic" group from some sixteen other Latin American countries and Spain, plus some Mexican-Americans established for many generations in the U.S. Southwest. Fully 88 percent of Hispanics, compared to 75 percent of the general population, live in metropolitan areas. Except for Cubans, Hispanics are younger than the U.S. average (a median of twenty-three years versus the general median of thirty in 1980) and have higher fertility rates (an estimated 2.5 versus 1.8 births per woman), though their life expectancy may now equal that of all U.S. whites. They are also more likely to be divorced or separated and live in female-headed families. Hispanic occupational status and educational attainment will lag far behind the U.S. average, unemployment is 40–50 percent higher, and Hispanic families average 70 percent of the median income and 2.7 times the poverty rate of all U.S. white families. But younger Hispanics and Cubans in particular are beginning to catch up, as is likely also for future generations of U.S. Hispanics. However, with their common language and large numbers (including a large, if unknown, number of "undocumented" aliens), assimilation into the U.S. "melting pot" may take longer for Hispanics than it did for other immigrant ethnic groups before them.

Reference
C. Davis et al., "U.S. Hispanics: Changing the Face of America," *Population Bulletin* 38 (June 1983): 1–44.

F.C.

HISPANICS, earnings. The relationship between market segmentation and the work earnings of native and foreign-born Hispanic origin workers is discussed (*infra*). The book assesses how earnings differentials among four Spanish birthplace groups are shaped by the differential allocation of native and immigrant workers to core and periphery labor market sectors and the differential evaluation of worker characteristics according to market sector. The analysis found

> sectoral location to be important in stratifying and differentiating native and foreign born. Results show that it is inappropriate to study income inequality only in terms of individual worker characteristics. This is because both nativity and market sector interact with individual worker characteristics and labor market characteristics in determining earnings.

Reference
M. Tienda and L. J. Neidert, *Segmented Markets and Earnings Inequality of Native and Immigrant Hispanics in the United States* (1980).

                                                                    F.C.

HISPANICS, labor supply of male Hispanic immigrants in the United States. Studies have begun the systematic analysis of the labor market characteristics of Hispanics in the United States. Research has focused on two related issues: (1) how the immigration and assimilation experience affects Hispanic earnings; and (2) the measurement of wage differentials between Hispanics and non-Hispanics. The main findings are that the earnings of (some) Hispanic immigrants rise rapidly after immigration; and that the wage differential between Hispanics and non-Hispanic whites is generally due to differences in observable skill characteristics.

Reference
George J. Borjas, "The Labor Supply of Male Hispanic Immigrants in the United States," *International Migration Review* 17 (Winter 1983–84): 653–671.

                                                                    F.C.

HISPANICS, miscounting the Spanish origin population in the United States. Hutchison's purpose is threefold: (1) to identify the discrepancies in the 1970 census figures; (2) to suggest alternative strategies for correcting the original figures and briefly report on an estimate of the possible "correct" figures for 1970; and (3) to summarize briefly the implications of the corrected figures for past and present research. It will be seen that the revised figures lower the total Spanish origin population for 1970 by nearly 1 million persons, but in so doing they increase the relative importance of the other (Mexican, Puerto Rican, and Cuban) groups. In addition, the lower base figure resulting from the corrections makes the rate of growth for the Spanish origin population in the 1970–1980 decade even greater than has previously been thought.

Reference
R. Hutchison, "Miscounting the Spanish Origin Population in the United States: Corrections to the 1970 Census and Their Implications," *International Migration* 22 (1984): 73–89.

                                                                    F.C.

HISPANICS, in New York City. Archdiocesan Survey. Summarizes (*infra*) the two-volume report, "Hispanics in New York: Religious, Cultural and Social Experiences" (Archdiocese of New York: Office of Pastoral Research, 1982). The three-year study based on in-depth interviews with a sample of 1,000 subjects confirms the achievements of past pastoral effects and identifies new resources and challenges for the Church. Three other components to the study: (1) a demographic profile, (2) some case studies to provide a more concrete illustration of the religious experience of Hispanics, and (3) a series of background papers.

Reference
Joseph P. Fitzpatrick, "Hispanics in New York: An Archdiocesan Survey," *America* 148 (March 1983): 185–188.

F.C.

HISPANICS, Puerto Rican and Non–Puerto Rican Hispanics. Using the 1980 census' Summary Tape Files 2 and 4 and the Public Use Microdata Samples provides a comprehensive look at the demographic and socioeconomic characteristics of Puerto Ricans and "other Hispanics," those non–Puerto Rican immigrants exclusive of Cubans and Mexicans, in New York City. Results show wide differences in socioeconomic status of the groups, closely related to basic disparities in fertility, labor force participation, and, most of all, family structure and composition. Moreover, an examination of the two largest "other Hispanic" subgroups, Colombians and Dominicans, revealed differences that were, in many instances, wider than those between Puerto Ricans and all "other Hispanics."

Reference
E. S. Mann and J. Salvo, "Characteristics of New Hispanic Immigrants to New York City: A Comparison of Puerto Rican and Non–Puerto Rican Hispanics," paper presented at the Population Association of America Annual Meeting, Minneapolis, Minnesota, May 3–5, 1984.

F.C.

HISTORIANS AND IMMIGRANTS. *American Historians and European Immigrants, 1875–1925* (Edward N. Saveth, 1948; rpt., 1965). The development of racism in America with special references to immigrants. Ideas of racial superiority that were developed in the nineteenth century are traced in the writings of Theodore Roosevelt, Woodrow Wilson, and twentieth-century historians. Bibliographies include (1) writings by historians; (2) writings about historians; and (3) general references. See also Saveth, "Race and Nationalism in American Historiography: The Late Nineteenth Century," *Political Science Quarterly* 64 (Sept. 1939): 421–441.

F.C.

HITZ, JOHN. *See* North American Grütli-Bund.

HMONG REFUGEES, self-reliance. Theory suggests that the process by which traditional societies become more self-reliant involves entrepreneurship in experimenting with different ways to move from known to unknown forms of economic activity. Innovative projects in the United States indicate that Hmong refugees are in the midst of such a movement. Progress to date has been slow and difficult, but the very fact that the projects exist and that participants in many of them are learning how to improve performance provides a basis for cautious optimism about self-reliance outcomes.

Reference
Simon Fass, "Innovations in the Struggle for Self-Reliance: The Hmong Experience in the United States," *International Migration Review* 20 (Summer 1986): 351–380.

F.C.

HMONG REFUGEES, social tension and public ethnic identity. The public identity of the Hmong from Laos has changed in America vis-à-vis their public identity in Laos. In the United States the Hmong have experienced significant loss of control over basic areas of their lives as compared with their circumstances before U.S. military involvement in Southeast Asia. These changes in public identity involve perceptions of Hmong occupational competence, economic productivity, the importance of patrilineality, access and use of medical curing, and distinctive features of material culture. The consequences of these changes are reflected in interactions within the Hmong community.

Reference
M. G. Hurlich and N. D. Donnelly, "Social Tension and the Development of a Public Ethnic Identity: Hmong Refugees from Laos," paper presented at the American Anthropological Association 83d Annual Meeting, Denver, Colorado, November 14–18, 1984.

F.C.

HMONGS. Major ethnic group in southern China, Vietnam, Laos, and Thailand today. The Hmongs' original homeland was in Central Asia, but they gradually migrated southward until they settled in the mountains of southern China. Driven away by the Chinese, they moved southward once more. From the beginning of the nineteenth century to the present, more than half a million Hmongs have fled from southern China, although 2.5 million Hmongs still live in China. Before the Vietnam disaster in 1975, there were an estimated 50,000 Hmongs in Thailand, 225,000 in Vietnam, and 350,000 in Laos. Some 50,000 of these came to America as refugees in the mid-1970s. The Hmongs did not choose to become refugees; they were displaced from their homeland because of foreign invaders. During World War II they fought against the Japanese, and after the war they sided with the Royal Lao in opposition to the Pathet Lao. The two sides fought from 1955 to 1975. It is estimated that about 30,000 Hmongs died in the conflict and that as many as 120,000 Hmong tribesmen became war refugees as of 1974.

D.N.A.

HOAN, DANIEL W. (1881–1961). Politician. The son of German immigrants, Hoan served as city attorney of Milwaukee (1910–16) and as mayor of that city (1916–1940). Hoan was a major influence in the German immigrant community of Milwaukee. Throughout his career he was a member of the Socialist party and was the party's most successful candidate. He is generally recognized as the leader in establishing Milwaukee's reputation for good government.

Reference
Floyd J. Stachowski, "The Political Career of Daniel Webster Hoan," Ph.D. dissertation, Northwestern University, 1966 (DA 27: 2124A).

F.C.

HODUR, REV. FRANCISZEK. *See* Polish National Catholic Church.

HOLLAND, JOHN PHILIP (1841–1914). Teacher, inventor. Holland was born in Lisdonvarna, County Clare, Ireland, and fled that country for political reasons. He taught school and experimented with the development of the submarine in Paterson, New Jersey. As the father of the submarine he became more appreciated after the World War I successes of German submarines.

S.P.M.

HOLT, L[UTHER] EMMETT (1855–1924). Physician. Superintendent of the Babies Hospital of New York and professor of diseases of children at the College of Physicians and Surgeons, New York City. A pioneer in the children's health field and immigrant infant care, he was the author of some of the most widely read literature on pediatrics during his lifetime. Published in 1894, his book *The Care and Feeding of Children* was known virtually throughout the world. It was translated into Spanish, Russian, and Chinese. In the foreword to this volume, one of his students recalled: "his word was law, not only to physicians, but to countless parents faced with the responsibility of bringing up children. He dominated pediatrics."

Reference
R. L. Duffus and L. Emmett Holt, Jr., *L. Emmett Holt: Pioneer of a Children's Century* (1940; rpt. 1974).

F.C.

HONDURANS. *See* Central Americans.

HOWE, FREDERICK C. (1867–1940). Municipal reformer. Served as commissioner of immigration (appointed by President Woodrow Wilson) at the Port of New York (Ellis Island [*q.v.*]) from 1914–19, a controversial tenure during the period of the wartime interlude in immigration to the United States, and the period of the "Red" scare. Chief works: *The Modern City and Its Problems* (1915); *The Confessions of a Reformer* (1925).

References
Thomas Monroe Pitkin, *Keepers of the Gate: A History of Ellis Island* (1975); Robert A. Huff, "Frederick C. Howe: Progressive," Ph.D. dissertation, University of Rochester, 1967.

F.C.

HUA-CH'IAO. Chinese term referring to all ethnic Chinese living abroad, regardless of their citizenship. The word *hua-ch'iao* is placed after the name of the country where the Chinese live. The Chinese living in Hawaii, for example, are called Hawaii *hua-ch'iao*.

D.N.A.

HUGHES, JOHN (1797–1864). Archbishop born in County Tyrone, Ireland; emigrated to the Baltimore area in 1817. St. Elizabeth Ann Seton encouraged him to become a priest. In 1837 he was appointed coadjudicator of New York under Bishop John DuBois. He developed the parochial school system and founded what was to become Fordham University. He founded over one hundred churches and many hospitals. In October 1850 he became the first archbishop of New York and while in that position built St. Patrick's Cathedral. He was nicknamed "Dagger John" because of his tough-minded approach to threats from nativists and other enemies; he played a charismatic role as the leader of Irish immigrants in the politics of his time.

References
R. Shaw, *Dagger John: The Unquiet Life and Times of Archbishop John Hughes of New York* (1977); J. R. Hassard, *Life of Most Reverend John Hughes First Archbishop of New York* (1866).

S.P.M.

HUGHES, LANGSTON. *See* Afro-Americans.

HUGUENOTS. Following the Reformation, French Catholics and Protestants (Huguenots) struggled for control of the state and monarchy.

Strong support for Protestantism among the French nobility complicated the struggle. In 1598 a tenuous peace was restored when the Protestant Henry of Navarre converted to Catholicism and ascended the throne. To quell Protestant fears he issued the Edict of Nantes promising freedom of worship to existing Protestant congregations in fortified towns without Catholic bishops. Peace, however, was illusory, for the French government soon considered the Protestant enclaves a threat to the newly emerging national state. Occasionally resorting to outright violence (such as the destruction of Rochelle) but more often applying new discriminatory regulations and a strict reading of the original edict, the French government pursued a policy of attrition until 1675.

In 1675 Louis XIV ordered troops into heavily Protestant Poitou to "preserve" Catholicism. The troops "dragooned" half of the province's 100,000 Protestants into converting to Catholicism following a period of murder, rape, and plunder. For the next ten years troops ravaged Protestant areas of France. Then on October 22, 1685 Louis XIV revoked the Edict of Nantes, ordering Protestant ministers to emigrate or convert, but requiring laity to remain and convert. Many fled nonetheless.

All through the years of civil war and truce, small numbers of Huguenots had left France for other parts of Europe and the New World. France's earliest attempts at New World settlement were led by Huguenots. The sixteenth-century colony on the St. John's River in Florida (St. Augustine) was crushed by Spain, and others along the Carolina coast and in the bay of Rio de Janeiro also failed. The revocation of the Edict of Nantes sent a wave of refugees rolling over Europe. Historians have estimated their numbers as ranging from a low of 131,000 to over 2 million. Large numbers settled in Holland, Prussia, and the British Isles. Huguenots who joined the army of William of Orange swelled the number of refugees in Britain after 1689.

The English colonies had long welcomed Huguenot settlers; thus, from 1680 to 1700 successive waves of Huguenots settled in the colonies, especially South Carolina, Virginia, New York, and Massachusetts. Some historians have claimed that between 10,000 and 15,000 refugees settled in the British colonies. However, a recent study by Jon Butler argues that only about 1,500 refugees arrived by 1700. This estimate underestimates the total Huguenot emigration by excluding the Virginia settlement at Manakin and later emigrants to the middle colonies from the refugee communities in Germany.

In the colonies, the immigrants created separate French-language congregations and communities. Everywhere, however, these communities were cut off from cultural reinvigoration brought by later immigrants or renewed contact with their homeland. The European bases for the immigration were themselves communities in exile. Although the

Huguenot refugees maintained ties between their scattered communities, they lacked an accessible cultural homeland. The remnants of Protestantism in France were too weak and disorganized to provide even symbolic focus. Although later immigrants did arrive from Switzerland and France, only in New York did these immigrants bring new life to existing Huguenot institutions.

The Huguenot presence was strongest in South Carolina, where they settled in five locations: Charleston, Craven County (St. James Santee Parish); the Orange Quarter (St. Denis Parish); and two settlements in Berkley County (St. John's Parish and St. James Goose Creek Parish). The new Huguenot arrivals were soon drawn into South Carolina politics and provided crucial votes when the assembly passed the act of establishment for the Church of England in 1706. South Carolina Huguenots included a number of skilled craftsmen, but they quickly moved to farming and a number became substantial slave owners. By 1720 some of the refugees (such as Isaac Mazyck and Gabriel Manigault) were accepted as part of the South Carolina elite.

Huguenots in New York followed a pattern similar to that in South Carolina. Congregations at New Rochelle and Staten Island were largely rural, while those who settled in New York City practiced a great variety of trades. Over half of all the Huguenot refugees in 1706 were farmers, most with small holdings. In New York City the refugee community included the very poor and the very wealthy. City poor rolls listed a number of Huguenot names, especially after 1730 when poor relief through the French churches broke down. A few families, especially the DeLanceys and Jays, became part of the wealthy governing elite of the colony. Here too, the Huguenots held a disproportionate share of slaves.

The Manakin Colony in Virginia provides a contrast to the South Carolinian experience. While there were small Huguenot settlements in Norfolk and Stafford counties, the bulk of Virginia Huguenots arrived in an organized expedition led by the Marquis de la Muce and Charles Sailley. Virginia officials directed them to an abandoned Indian town on the frontier and set aside two grants of 5,000 acres each for the refugees. The desperate poverty of the first several years encouraged some settlers to scatter. Following community bickering and the withdrawal of families to North Carolina in 1707 and South Carolina in 1712, the remainder settled down as small-scale wheat and tobacco farmers. The group never became a political force in colonial Virginia, although descendants of the refugees would be a factor in Virginia's Great Awakening and frontier settlement.

The Huguenot settlements in New England were less stable than those of South Carolina and Virginia. Initial settlements in Narragansett County, Rhode Island, and Oxford, Massachusetts lasted less than a decade due to economic problems, bickering over religion, and Indian attack. The settlers dispersed to other Huguenot colonies. Most of the Naragansett settlers went to New York, and the Oxford ones to Boston. The Huguenots in Boston found material success and intermarried with English families. The French congregation disbanded in 1748 but Huguenot descendants continued to be prominent in the community.

One notable trend throughout the British Empire was the transformation of independent Huguenot congregations into French-language parishes of the Anglican church. Only the colonial congregations at Charleston and New York City remained independent throughout the colonial period. Anglicans encouraged the conformity of French congregations by incorporating French congregations into the Church of England parish structure, providing salary support to ministers who conformed, and by sending reordained Huguenot clergy to parishes near French communities. In return, clergy of Huguenot background were a visible presence in the Anglican church. In the 1730s, for example, four French-background clergy served regular parishes in Virginia.

The road to Anglican conformity was not entirely smooth. Several congregations (in both Virginia and South Carolina), influenced by minister Claude Phillipe de Richebourg, tried to return to Huguenot practices. Only in St. Denis Parish, South Carolina, was resistance disorderly. Beginning in 1713, the protests led to religious radicalism influenced by the so-called French prophets in England. The matter ended in disaster when a magistrate was killed trying to arrest members of the Dutartre family for bigamy. Elsewhere, the 1711 decision of New Rochelle Huguenots to conform to the Church of England led dissidents to withdraw. For the next half-century they maintained an independent congregation.

Huguenot immigrants found a ready acceptance in their new communities. Historians have often commented on their rapid assimilation. Such judgments are based on Huguenot intermarriage, adaptation to colonial economies, and conformity to the established churches. Certainly the lack of a steady supply of qualified ministers, and factional disputes within congregations, helped to encourage Huguenots to join other churches. However, it was not until the 1750s and 1760s, three-quarters of a century after the major immigration to the colonies began and a half-century after the last large wave arrived, that the communities faltered.

In other ways the decades of the 1720s and 1730s forshadowed the undermining of the congregations. Young adults coming of age were second- and third-generation refugees. Exogamous marriages became noticeable after 1720. Pressures for English-language services began about the same time, although the parishes all continued at least some French-language services until midcentury. The years 1720–1740 saw Huguenot craftspeople in New York start drawing apprentices from the whole community, and the Manakin community in Virginia switch from wheat to tobacco culture using slave labor. Huguenot distinctiveness was clearly on the decline. By the time of the Revolution, Huguenots lived comfortably within the emerging American culture while retaining oral traditions and relics of a refugee past.

Midcentury saw the disbandment of the independent congregation at New Rochelle and Boston and the merger of St. Denis Parish in South Carolina with its Anglican neighbor. The Huguenot parish of King William in Virginia stopped keeping separate records after 1750, and the departure of New York City's Huguenot minister in 1763 led to quarrels and the closing of the church thirteen years later. It was second-, third-, and fourth-generation Huguenots who witnessed these erosions. The immigrant generation was dead or elderly. By the American Revolution the surviving Huguenot churches were maintained more as memorials to an historic past than as centers of an ethnic community.

References
Charles Baird, *History of the Huguenot Emigration to America*, 2 vols. (1885); Jon Butler, *The Huguenots in America: A Refugee People in New World Society* (1983); Robert Crewdson, "The Manakin Experiment: A French Protestant Colony in the New World," *Historical Magazine of the Protestant Episcopal Church* 55 (Sept. 1986); Joan R. Gundersen, "The Double Bonds of Race and Sex: Black and White Women in a Colonial Virginia Parish," *The Journal of Southern History* 52 (Aug. 1986); Arthur Hirsch, *The Huguenots of Colonial South Carolina* (1928); Roger Howell, Jr., "'The Vocation of the Lord': Aspects of the Huguenot Contribution to the English-Speaking World," *Anglican and Episcopal History* 51 (June 1987); David Konig, "A New Look at the Essex 'French': Ethnic Frictions and Community Tensions in Seventeenth Century Essex County, Massachusetts," *Essex Institute Historical Collections* 110 (1974); Leslie Tobias, "Manakin Town: The Development and Demise of a French Protestant Refugee Community in Colonial Virginia, 1700–1750," M.A. thesis, College of William and Mary, 1982.

J.R.G.

HUIGUAN. *See* Chinese.

HULL HOUSE, CHICAGO. Founded by Jane Addams (*q.v.*) in 1899, based on the university settlements begun in England by Samuel Barnett. Hull House served as a community center for the neighborhood poor (overwhelmingly immigrant), and as a potent force for social reform activities. It became a model for numerous other settlements established in the United States, with some one hundred settlement houses operating in American cities by World War I. *See* Settlement House Movement.

Reference
Allen F. Davis, *Spearheads for Reform: The Social Settlements and the Progressive Movement* (1967).

D.N.A.

HULL HOUSE BULLETIN (1896–1910). Published monthly. Invaluable source material for the Chicago settlement movement. *See* Addams, Jane.

F.C.

[HULL HOUSE]. *Hull House Maps and Papers* (1895). A massive survey of the Chicago neighborhood block by block, house by house, to determine nationality and income, and modeled on Charles Booth's *Labour and Life of the People of London* (1889; 3d ed., 17 vols., 1902–3). Largely the work of Florence Kelley (*q.v.*) and the economist Richard T. Ely (*q.v.*). *See* Addams, Jane.

F.C.

HUNGARIANS. The 1980 U.S. census counted Hungarian ancestry for 1,776,902 persons, who reported at least one specific ancestry group. Of that number 772,223 reported Hungarian as a single ancestry and 1,049,679 reported multiple ancestry. The following states had major population figures for Hungarian ancestry: New York, 244,672; Ohio, 243,232; Pennsylvania, 203,285; New Jersey, 168,500; California, 164,903; Michigan, 126,819; Florida, 89,587; Illinois, 84,642; Connecticut, 53,451; and Indiana, 44,312. Those states that counted 20,000–40,000 in the Hungarian ancestry group were Wisconsin, Texas, Maryland, Virginia, and Massachusetts. Over 70 percent of the Hungarian-American population lives in the Northeast and North Central regions.

Background. In east central Europe Hungary dates its European history from 896. Its people have considered themselves an integral part of Western Europe. At the end of World War I Hungary lost two-thirds of its territory and population. Present-day Hungary has a population of 10.7 million. Its capital city, Budapest, has been called the "Queen of the Danube." The Hungarians, or Magyar people, speak a language that linguistically belongs to the Uralic language family. In Europe, its linguistic relatives are the Finns, Estonians, and Lapps, who all belong to the Finno-Ugric group of the Uralic language family.

Mass Migration. From Hungary mass migration to the United States began in 1880 and was interrupted in 1914 by the outbreak of World War I. During that period a multinational immigrant population arrived from Hungary including Hungarians (Magyars), Slovaks, Germans, Rusyns, Slovenes, Croats and other ethnic groups. Over two-thirds of these arrivals at Ellis Island declared themselves non-Magyars.

The population of Hungary was also divided along religious lines. Some 60 percent were Catholics of the Latin or Roman rite. One-sixth of the Catholics were Byzantine, or Greek Catholics, and observed the

Eastern rite traditions. About 25 percent of the population of Hungary was Protestant, and most were Calvinists belonging to the Reformed Church of Hungary. The other Protestants included Lutherans and in a smaller number Unitarians and Baptists. About 5 percent of the population were Jews. The remaining 10 percent belonged to Eastern Orthodox churches, although almost none of the Orthodox were Magyars. A greater proportion of migration tended to come from those areas of Hungary that included more Protestants.

After a time the United States immigration records and statistics limited the term "Hungarian" to Magyar-speaking people of Hungary and their descendants. Most of these were ethnic Magyars; however, they also included Jews, Slavs, and others who had assimilated into the dominant Magyar culture of Hungary. By 1899 one in every four emigrants who left Hungary spoke Magyar. By 1902 the proportion was one in three. In 1903 the Magyars were the largest single group of emigrants from Hungary.

In 1878 to 1889 women totaled 40 percent of the emigrants from Hungary. In 1907 it was 28 percent, but by 1913 more women (53.8 percent) were emigrating than men. The majority of the emigrants were in their prime productive years. During the period 1905–7, 61.5 percent were between twenty and forty years old. A significant group (23.2 percent) were under twenty.

Emigration traffic of over two million people between 1880 and 1910 resulted in a net population loss of only 886,176 persons in Hungary. This net figure was possible because of the traffic of repeated trips to the United States; every fourth emigrant made the trip to America and back home at least twice. Such mobility reflected nonpermanent emigration and was a positive response to temporary job opportunities offered. The agrarian population joined the earlier pioneers of craftsmen, storekeepers, and village artisans to produce the mass emigration by which means the emigrant sought to better his lot in Hungary. Mass emigration developed especially in those areas where emigration was already a tradition, while in some areas of Hungary emigration was almost nonexistent. Only a few returned to Hungary among those who stayed ten to fifteen years; however, of those who did return, their savings were turned into a new house, land was bought for cultivation, and debts were paid. This transfer of funds may be referred to as a private, nongovernmental American economic foreign aid.

Early Travelers. Hungarians had traveled to the New World soon after its discovery. One leader of George Washington's cavalry was Colonel Commandant Michael Kovats (1724–1779), who died in the Battle of Charleston against the British. After the Revolution Hungarian travelers came to write about the New Land. They were followed by merchants, naturalists, and explorers. Among these was Agoston Haraszthy (1829–1869), who first settled in Wisconsin with his family and then traveled West where he came to be known as the "Father of California Wine."

The first major Hungarian emigré group to come to the United States were the followers of Governor Louis Kossuth. They fled Hungary in 1849 after the failure of the War of Independence. Kossuth himself came in 1851–52 for six months and spoke before the Joint Houses of Congress. Kossuth's followers settled mainly on the East Coast, although they founded a short-lived town of New Buda in Iowa. During the Civil War some 800 officers and veterans of the Hungarian War of Independence joined the Union Army and distinguished themselves as Lincoln's Hungarian heroes.

Settlements and Their Composition. Between 1899 and 1914, the peak years of emigration, 458,000 Magyar-speaking immigrants came to the United States. Most were under thirty years of age and two-thirds of them were men. Nearly 89 percent were literate, even though the literacy rate in Hungary was merely 59 percent. These immigrants found employment in coal mines and in the steel industry in western Pennsylvania, eastern Ohio, West Virginia, northern and southern Illinois, and Indiana. Earlier Hungarian immigrants had settled in New York, New Jersey, and Connecticut. Before 1899 New York City and Cleveland were Hungarian centers. Other settlements followed in Pittsburgh; Chicago; Bridgeport, Connecticut; Trenton, New Brunswick, and Passaic, New Jersey; South Bend; Youngstown; Toledo; Detroit; and St. Louis.

In Hungary by the late nineteenth century Jews identified closely with the Magyar-speaking Hungarians. When they came to America, Hungarian Jews tended to isolate themselves from the rest of the American Jewish population. Moreover, they came to stay in America. In many towns and cities Hungarian Jews had preceded the Hungarian mass migration. They began arriving in the 1850s and 1860s and then established Magyar-speaking synagogues in such major Hungarian centers as New York, Cleveland, Pittsburgh, Chicago, Detroit, St. Louis, Bridgeport, and New Brunswick, New Jersey. In time, being prone to assimilate, these congregations did not preserve their Hungarian character much beyond the founding generation. Then, in the 1930s, when conditions in Hungary, including restrictions faced in higher education, forced many Hungarian Jews to emigrate and settle in America, a new Magyar-speaking Jewish congregation was founded in New York City.

Before Christian churches began to be formally organized in the 1890s, benefit societies were founded to provide some modicum of financial security on a self-help basis in the event of illness or injury on the job. The first of these Hungarian societies was established in Newark, New Jersey in 1882. By 1910 over a thousand such societies, both small and large, served the needs of Hungarian immigrants. In 1886 thirteen miners in Hazelton, Pennsylvania, founded the antecedent organization of the William Penn Association, which at present is the largest Hungarian established fraternal organization. Other social and cultural organizations followed as glee clubs and cultural societies. Professional and literary associations were founded before and after World War I. In 1906 the American Hungarian Federation was established as an umbrella organization. At that time, it also sought to advance the independence of Hungary from Austria. Since 1906 it has continued to represent the interests of Hungarian-Americans and their organizations.

As churches were established in the 1890s, they served as centers of the immigrant community's social life also. Through these activities the parishioners and their children retained contact with their ethnic tradition and their native language. Lay participation and direction of the local church's affairs increased in contrast to what was possible in the Old Country.

The Protestant Hungarians were the first to organize congregations. The stricter hierarchy of the Roman Catholic church and its energetic insistence on assimilation placed the Hungarian Catholic parishes in an extremely difficult position. Still, some larger Roman Catholic parishes had Hungarian day schools. Protestant "Hungarian schools" were conducted in the form of Sunday schools and summer schools. These continued through the 1940s. Then a renaissance of interest in language and culture blossomed after 1956 and the event of the revolt in Hungary.

More than 200 Hungarian language newspapers, dailies, weeklies, and biweeklies were published for shorter and longer periods in the United States. The successful newspaper the *Amerikai Nemzetör* (American National Guardian) appeared from 1884 to 1895. It served as a model for the two largest and most influential dailies (published in Cleveland and New York City, respectively), the *Szabadság* (Liberty) and *Amerikai Magyar Népszava* (American Hungarian People's Voice). Presently, these are published as weeklies. Among the numerous short-lived Socialist-Communist papers of Hungarian America from 1895 on, *Új Elöre* (New Forward) became the third largest daily from 1927 to 1937.

After World War I the immigrant Hungarian-American found a hostile environment in America, because Hungary had been on the losing side. The introduction of the quota system by the United States to end the mass migration of "undesirable" peoples of Hungary and other lands further conditioned the immigrant and his family. Then World War II again drew Hungary into the whirlpool of diplomacy with the Axis Powers; the Holocaust; and finally defeat. All of this deeply colored the self-image of Hungarian-Americans. It was the event of 1956 in Hungary that brightened that image and recreated it.

Becoming an American. World War II hastened the process of the adoption of American ways. Thousands of young Hungarian-American men served in the United States armed forces. With their return to their communities they found rapid changes had taken place; the communities were decentralizing and following the urban population spread to the suburbs, a process that had been slowed down during the war years.

Earlier, during the interwar years, Hungarian-American miners and their families moved to new industrial centers like Detroit and Cleveland. The Depression years of the 1930s forced change upon Hungarian-American families and their organizations. By the late 1930s and 1940s an equilibrium had developed in Hungarian-American communities. An increasing segment of the second generation was seeking higher education and social mobility. There was a recognition of the contributions made to American life by noted Hungarian-born scientists, musicians, businessmen, artists, and educators, working in fields as diverse as atomic research and Hollywood's motion picture industry.

Postwar Immigration. Between 1920 and 1945 under 100,000 Hungarians emigrated to the United States from Hungary and the ceded territories. Most arrived in the early 1920s because in 1924 the Immigration Restriction Act closed the door to unlimited immigration. Hungarians had an annual quota of 473 persons; therefore, they now emigrated to Canada and South America with the hope of eventually reaching the United States. Although in the early 1920s some 32,000 Hungarians chose repatriation to Hungary, the vast majority of the Hungarian immigrant population now made the decision to remain permanently. By World War I only 15 percent of the Hungarian immigrants had become United States citizens. By 1930 this number reached 55.7 percent.

In 1945, with the cessation of hostilities in Europe, refugees from Central Europe included about half a million Hungarians. Many were repatriated but some 120,000 chose to remain in refugee camps, and another 40,000 joined them between 1946 and 1950. This represented a major political emigration. Of these a total of 26,532 came to the United States under the Displaced Persons Act. Known generally as DPs, they represented a world view, a society and life, that came to an end in 1945. Besides their significant political differences, there was a cultural and generational gap between the postwar immigrant and the earlier immigrant.

Then, during October–November of 1956, Hungarians fought to free their land of occupation by Soviet troops and establish a neutral government. With the defeat of the Hungarian Revolution over 200,000

Hungarians left the country. Between 1956 and 1960 another 47,643 Hungarians settled in the United States. The immigrants of 1945 and 1947 were middle-aged, and many had families; the 1956 immigrants generally were young, single, and still studying or at the beginning of their professional careers. Over two-thirds of them were males. This new group of Hungarians found American industry and universities extremely hospitable. By making the most of such opportunities their American assimilation was rapid as was their success professionally and financially, which far exceeded that of the earlier immigrants from 1945 and 1947.

Segmented Community Life. Since World War II we have witnessed the distilling of the Hungarian-American community into three distinct and often separate groups. The first includes the early immigrants and some of their descendants of several generations. Many of the old immigrants continue to live in the ethnic neighborhoods, while members of the subsequent generations live in the suburbs, or where their employment has taken them. They are fully a part of the American scene, but many retain ties to Hungarian-American institutions. The second group consists of the 1945 and 1947 immigrants, and a large group of the 1956 immigrants. They are tied by their common way of life and by mutual political views; however, this segment tends to consider itself separate from the old-timers. The third group is an amalgam of the 1956 immigrants and the second generation of the 1945 immigrants, who are professionally successful and mostly live where their work takes them. At present, it is the second group, which with some members of the second and third generation of the old-timers, provides most of the leadership and body of the Hungarian-American communities.

References

Paul Böarody, "Hungarian Immigrants in North America," *Immigration History Newsletter* (1976); John Kosa, "A Century of Hungarian Emigration 1850–1950," *American Slavic and East European Review* (1957); August J. Molnar, "Hungarian," in *The New Jersey Ethnic Experience* (1977); Julianna Puskás, *From Hungary to the United States 1880–1914,* (1982); Steven Bela Vardy, *The Hungarian Americans* (1985); Edmund Vasvary, *Lincoln's Hungarian Heroes* (1939).

A.J.M.

HUNGARIANS, The Hungarian Reformed Church. The Hungarian Reformed Church in America is the only autonomous Hungarian Reformed denomination in the United States, but the majority of Hungarian Reformed congregations in America are affiliated with other denominational bodies. All of these churches originated from the Reformed Church of Hungary, one of the oldest and largest church bodies of the Calvinistic Reformation in Europe, which preserved its unity since Reformation times without schisms and church divisions.

Reference
Aladar Komjathy, "The Hungarian Reformed Church in America: An Effort to Preserve a Denominational Heritage," Ph.D. dissertation, Princeton Theological Seminary, 1962.

F.C.

HUNGSA-DAN. *See* Koreans.

HUNTER, ROBERT (1874–1942). Social reformer; chairman of the Child Labor Committee in New York City which succeeded in enacting a statewide child labor law, greatly reducing the exploitation of immigrant children. His *Poverty* (1904; rpt. 1970) was "the most comprehensive as well as the most controversial treatment of the subject yet attempted in the United States" (Bremner, 151). As the first general statistical survey of America's poor, *Poverty* asserted that no fewer than 10 million persons in the United States lived in poverty, even in prosperous times. Although Hunter's figure was attacked as too high or at best an unscientific estimate, *Poverty* "was a plea for recognition of the nation's obligation to ascertain how well or badly its people fared. . . . neglect even to inquire into the amount of distress in the state struck him as symptomatic of the 'grossest moral insensitiveness' on the part of the society" (Bremner, 152).

Reference
Robert H. Bremner, *From the Depths: The Discovery of Poverty in the United States* (1964).

F.C.

HURST, FANNIE (1889–1968). Novelist and short story writer. Hurst, the daughter of American-born Jews of German descent, is mainly noted for escapist literature that was popular during the Depression. Her novels were variations on the theme of rags to riches from a woman's point of view. Critics have said that Hurst's novels and stories are realistic portraits of the beliefs of her readers. Hurst treated her heroine's problems sympathetically. These problems were central to her theme, which was that no matter how much a woman may have achieved she is nothing without a man. Hurst's chief works were *Back Street* (1931) and *Imitation of Life* (1933).

Reference
Saturday Review (Oct. 1937).

C.C.

HUSMENN (cotters). *See* Norwegians.

IL PROGRESSO ITALO AMERICANO. *See* Pope, Generoso.

ILLEGAL ALIENS, counting the uncountable. Keely reviews attempts to estimate the number of undocumented aliens in the United States, concluding that these estimates have been weak. Estimates were based more on budget needs and organizational dynamics than on concern for reliable counts and proper estimation techniques. He suggests that serious problems may result from policies based on inaccurate estimates.

Reference
Charles B. Keely, "Counting the Uncountable: Estimates of Undocumented Aliens in the United States," *Population and Development Review* 3 (Dec. 1977): 473–481.

F.C.

ILLEGAL ALIENS, cultural pluralism and American unity. Assuming that over time the descendants of undocumented workers now in the United States will behave substantially like descendants of those who immigrate legally, some have concluded that the long-term impact of illegal migration barely will be noticeable provided that it is reduced substantially in the future. The process of acculturation will work in the same way for both groups as it has for other ethnic groups in the past, given comparable levels of education and length of family residence in the United States. As to the illegal migration of Spanish-speaking workers, it has been hypothesized that the behavior of their descendants will not differ from the descendants of other immigrants, legal or illegal, in ways that disrupt fundamental patterns of American political unity and cultural pluralism.

Reference
Lawrence H. Fuchs, "Cultural Pluralism and the Future of American Unity: The Impact of Illegal Aliens," *International Migration Review* 18 (Fall 1984): 800–813.

F.C.

ILLEGAL ALIENS, employment prohibition laws.

Most countries reported that employer sanction laws have helped to deter illegal alien employment. For example, five of the eight countries and Hong Kong reported that these laws were a moderate or great deterrent against illegal alien employment. This group included Germany and France which reported in 1982 that their laws were not an effective deterrent. The three countries that reported their laws were less of a deterrent (Italy, Canada, and

Spain) acknowledged that various problems with the enforcement of these laws had lessened their effectiveness. Nevertheless, Hong Kong and six of the eight countries reported that if they had not enacted employer sanction laws, the problem of aliens working illegally would be greater than it is. Two countries (Italy and Canada) reported the problem would be about the same as it is. From 1981 through September 1985, the estimated number of aliens working illegally reportedly decreased in Hong Kong and one country, remained about the same in three countries, and increased in four countries (Italy, Canada, France, and Spain). All respondents reported that little or no discrimination against citizens or legal aliens has resulted from employer sanction laws. (U.S. General Accounting Office)

Reference
U.S. General Accounting Office, *Illegal Aliens: Information on Selected Countries' Employment Prohibition Laws* (1985).

F.C.

ILLEGAL ALIENS, illegal alien problem in the United States. Chapman reports that

in the United States there are an estimated eight million illegal aliens, nearly all of whom have entered the nation in search of employment. Although nationals of Mexico make up a large number, aliens illegally in the United States come from many countries of the world. Many are in metropolitan centers, holding jobs in industry and service. The practical solution to the problem is legislation to reduce job opportunities for illegal aliens by making it unlawful to employ them. In the absence of such legislation, with populations growing rapidly in Latin America, the number entering will continue to increase.

Reference
Leonard F. Chapman, Jr., "The Scope and Impact of the Illegal Alien Problem in the United States," paper presented at the Population Association of America Annual Meeting, Montreal, Canada, April 29–May 1, 1976.

F.C.

ILLEGAL ALIENS, Texas School Case. The "Texas school case" arose over an attempt to deny undocumented immigrant children (irregular status migrants) access to public education. The appended reference (*infra*) reviews and evaluates the case and the social, political, and educational issues pertinent to it, and further provides social and demographic data from a sample of parents of undocumented children while analyzing the international ramifications of the case.

Reference
"Research on Undocumented Immigrants and Public Policy: A Study of the Texas School Case," *International Migration Review* 18 (Fall 1984): 505–523.

F.C.

ILLEGAL ALIENS. U.S. General Accounting Office, *Illegal Aliens: Limited Research Suggest Illegal Aliens May Displace Native Workers* (1986). A synthesis and assessment of fifty-one studies dealing with the effects of illegal aliens on the U.S. Labor market which addresses the following question: Do illegal alien workers displace native or legal workers? The major finding of this report is that illegal alien workers appear to displace native or legal workers. However, "this finding is a qualified one, because the research we used to reach it was limited and suffered from important methodological weaknesses. The information that would allow a conclusive answer to this question is not presently available."

F.C.

ILLEGAL ALIENS, in the United States labor market. The objectives of North and Houstoun's study (*infra*) were to

> gather heretofore unavailable data on the characteristics and labor-market experiences of illegal aliens in the U.S. work force, to present those data within the context of current information on illegal immigration, and to examine the resulting policy implications, with special reference to the question of the role and impact of illegals in the U.S. labor market. With the financial support and intellectual encouragement of the Office of Manpower Research and Development, of the Department of Labor, and the cooperation of the Immigration and Naturalization Service (INS), of the Department of Justice, 793 apprehended illegal aliens who had worked at least two weeks in the U.S. were interviewed in 19 sites across the nation. In addition, with the assistance of the Catholic Migration Service and the law firm of Fried, Fragomen, and del Rey, supplemental interviews were conducted of 51 unapprehended illegals working in two of those sites. In order to achieve as high a level of cooperation and honesty as possible, a common procedure used with such surveys has been followed; all interviews were voluntary, and neither the name nor the address of any who responded were recorded.

Reference
David S. North and Marion F. Houstoun, *The Characteristics and Role of Illegal Aliens in the U.S. Labor Market: An Exploratory Study* (1976).

F.C.

ILLEGAL IMMIGRANTS, estimates counted in 1980 census by state. Estimates have been made of the number of undocumented aliens counted in the 1980 census for each state and the District of Columbia. The estimates, which indicate that 2.06 million undocumented aliens were counted in the 1980 census, are not based on individual records but are aggregate estimates derived by a residual technique. The census count of aliens (modified somewhat to account for deficiencies in the data) is compared with estimates of the legally resident alien population based on data collected by the Immigration and Naturalization Service in January 1980. The final estimates represent concessions to the state level of national estimates developed by Woodrow and Passel (1984). Estimates have been developed for each of the states for selected countries of birth, and for age, sex, and period of entry categories.

Reference
Jeffrey S. Passel and Karen A. Woodrow, "Geographic Distribution of Undocumented Immigrants: Estimates of Undocumented Aliens Counted in the 1980 Census by State," *International Migration Review* 18 (Fall 1984): 642–671.

F.C.

ILLEGAL IMMIGRANTS, government records. North examines governmental records to secure data on the intersection between illegal immigrants and the U.S. labor market and various income transfer programs. Illegal immigrants are likely to pay taxes and are paid below-average wages. Findings contradict the assumptions that illegal immigrants rarely seek income transfer payments and stay in the U.S. labor market only briefly.

Reference
David S. North, *Governmental Records: What They Tell Us About the Role of Illegal Immigrants in the Labor Market and in Income Transfer Programs* (1981).

F.C.

ILLEGAL IMMIGRANTS, number of illegal residents in the United States. There are no reliable estimates of the numbers of illegal residents in the country or of the net volume of illegal immigration to the United States in any recent past period. Several analytic studies now available are subject to major limitations. On the basis of studies conducted by others, it is estimated that

> the total number of illegal residents in the United States for some recent years, such as 1978, is almost certainly below 6.0 million, and may be substantially less, possibly only 3.5 to 5.0 million. . . . The Mexican component of the illegal resident population is almost certainly less than 3.0 million, and may be substantially less, possibly only 1.5 to 2.5 million.

Reference
U.S. Department of Commerce, Bureau of the Census, *Preliminary Review of Existing Studies of the Number of Illegal Residents in the United States,* paper presented by Jacob S. Siegal et al. for the Research Staff of the Select Commission on Immigration and Refugee Policy (1980).

F.C.

ILLEGAL IMMIGRANTS, size of illegal alien population. Reviews have been made of the previous estimation attempts, the problems attending the use of alternative estimation methods, and the options for acquiring improved policymaking information in the illegal alien area. Estimates of the resident illegal alien population range from 1 million to 12 million, with the most widely accepted range being 3.5 to 6 million. The most frequently cited estimate of the number who enter illegally each year is 500,000. The General Accounting Office found no single previous estimate of either the national illegal alien population or its annual flow to be both valid and reliable. Current estimates stem from incomplete or questionable data bases or untested or demonstrably incorrect assumptions or are restricted to a subgroup of the illegal alien population.

Reference
U.S. General Accounting Office, *Problems and Options in Estimating the Size of the Illegal Alien Population,* report to the chairman of the Subcommittee on Immigration and Refugee Policy of the Committee on the Judiciary United States Senate (1982).

F.C.

ILLEGAL IMMIGRANTS, in Texas. Impact on Social Services. A survey conducted of undocumented aliens and providers of public services showed that the state of Texas receives more from taxes paid by undocumented persons than it costs the state to provide them with public services, such as education, health care, correctional facilities, and welfare. The same survey showed that six cities in the state (Austin, Dallas, El Paso, Houston, McAllen, and San Antonio) together expended more to provide services to undocumented aliens than they received in taxes. The survey concentrated on undocumented persons not detained by the immigration authorities and found that this group constituted a population distinct from those in detention centers in that the former exhibited normal characteristics of settled families while the latter were predominantly the familiar young, single, and peripatetic male.

Reference
Sidney Weintraub, "Illegal Immigrants in Texas: Impact on Social Services and Related Considerations," *International Migration Review* 18 (Fall 1984): 733–747.

F.C.

ILLEGAL IMMIGRATION, the colonization of the American labor market. A major report (*infra*) (1) finds that the ready availability of illegal alien workers in major industries and geographical regions is having far-reaching and often unanticipated consequences for patterns of investment, employment, and business competition in the United States; (2) documents the displacement of American workers by illegal immigrants in agriculture, food processing, services, and construction, analyzing the processes of network recruiting and subcontracting that lead ultimately to the exclusion of American citizens and legal residents from many workplaces; and (3) concludes that our acquiescence in illegal immigration has become a selective labor subsidy that has contributed in the last two decades to distorted investment decisions, slower growth, and the proliferation of low-skill, low-productivity jobs in the American labor market.

References
Philip L. Martin, *Illegal Immigration and the Colonization of the American Labor Market,* (Center for Immigration Studies, 1986); see also Philip L. Martin, *Guest-Worker Programs: Lessons from Europe,* report prepared for the Bureau of International Labor Affairs, U.S. Department of Labor (1980).

F.C.

ILLEGAL IMMIGRATION, consequences. Downes predicts that the United States will become increasingly Spanish-speaking because of the unrestrained influx of illegal immigrants. He suggests two possible outcomes: either through peaceful transition the country becomes entirely and officially Spanish-speaking, or violence occurs between the two language groups and the Spanish-speaking Southwest breaks off to form a separate country.

Reference
Richard Downes, "Future Consequences of Illegal Immigration," *Futurist* 11 (1977): 125–127.

F.C.

ILLEGAL IMMIGRATION, impact on U.S. labor market. After briefly reviewing the historical role of immigrant labor in this country, Flores (1) treats as a working hypothesis the observation that unfavorable economic conditions and not individuals such as undocumented workers cause unemployment; and (2) examines the positive economic impact of undocumented workers' employment. Flores concludes that

> undocumented immigrants play a vital role in the overall scheme of production and in the most recent societal trend of production reorganization. In production plans as a whole, immigrants filter into the labor market at jobs that are, for the most part, unattractive

to the domestic labor force. In terms of production reorganization, mobile and fiscally weighty corporate capital flies from areas of worker strength to areas where cheap labor is available.

Reference
Estevan T. Flores, "The Impact of Undocumented Migration on the U.S. Labor Market," *Houston Journal of International Law* 5 (Spring 1983): 287–321.

F.C.

ILLEGAL IMMIGRATION, and the labor force. Martinez traces the long record of Spanish-speaking workers in the Southwest since 1848. During the Depression of the 1930s illegal Mexican migrants were deported and legal ones encouraged to repatriate. Martinez sees the latest attention on illegal immigration as one more example in a long history of using Mexican workers as an elastic labor supply to be sent home when not needed.

Reference
Vilma S. Martinez, "Illegal Immigration and the Labor Force," *American Behavioral Scientist* 19 (1976): 335–350.

F.C.

ILLEGAL IMMIGRATION, methods of analysis. A major barrier to the discussion of the scope and impact of illegal immigration on the American economy has been the inadequacy of existing data. Although data problems are not unique to this topic, the limited availability of macro-data on the size of the annual flows and of the accumulated stock of individuals, as well as of micro-data on their influences on selected labor markets, has been effectively used to forestall policy reform efforts.

Reference
Vernon M. Briggs, Jr., "Methods of Analysis of Illegal Immigration Into the United States," *International Migration Review* 18 (Fall 1984): 623–641.

F.C.

IMAMS. *See* Arabs.

IMMIGRANT AUTOBIOGRAPHIES. Immigrant autobiographies do not detail the lives of ordinary immigrants. Their authors, having acquired sufficient means, confidence, and literary skills to emerge from the anonymous mass of newcomers to America, are clearly exceptional. Nonetheless, immigrants who present their life stories usually claim to speak for their voiceless counterparts, and in a very real sense they do: the experiences that they recount are often representative of what many have undergone.

Although eighteenth- and nineteenth-century immigrants occasionally published autobiographies—Venture Smith's *A Narrative of the Life and Adventures of Venture* (1798), for example—it was not until the early twentieth century that immigrant autobiography emerged as a distinct genre. As immigration reached record levels and changed in ethnic composition, it became the object of increasingly unfavorable comment and inspired efforts at restriction. Those attacks in turn produced a wealth of immigrant autobiographies characterized both by a certain sense of urgency and by a unity of purpose. "With the unprecedented way in which the American public has turned its attention to the all-important question of the assimilation of the immigrant, it became increasingly clear to me that I owed it to my adopted country to give [my] story to the public," Constantine Panunzio explained in introducing *The Soul of an Immigrant* (1928).

Immigrant writers often appealed to the conscience of Americans and their sense of fair play. Mary Antin (*The Promised Land,* 1912) urged "my American friend" to be more tolerant of the immigrants "too absorbed in their honest affairs to notice the looks of suspicion which you cast at them, the repugnance with which you shrink from their touch." Panunzio reminded his readers that their forebears had, after all, been immigrants too: "We all 'came over' sometime."

But these authors did not rely merely on pleas for consideration. Sometimes they tried to preempt the debate by declaring their devotion to the United States. "I love Thee, America," insisted Panunzio. "I am of Thee; Thou art mine." Indeed, the autobiographers asserted that the immigrants' unique perspective guarantees a *greater* appreciation of America than that exhibited by natives. "A foreign-born citizen of the United States," observed Michael Pupin (*From Immigrant to Inventor,* 1923), "has many occasions to sing praises of the virtues of this country which the native-born citizen has not." Echoing Pupin, Edward Bok (*The Americanization of Edward Bok,* 1920), mused "I wonder whether, after all, the foreign-born does not make in some sense a better American."

In recounting their own successful lives the autobiographers implicitly revealed their common belief that immigrants contributed something more tangible to America than simple loyalty. This point was stated explicitly as well. Immigrants, according to Antin, furnished "your armies of workers, thinkers, and leaders." In *Laughing in the Jungle* (1932) Louis Adamic characterized as "immense" the immigrants' "contributions as workers to the current material greatness and power of the United States."

Since immigrant autobiographers were united in their purpose of establishing the place of immigrants in American life, it is not surprising that they utilized common thematic devices to do so. Their works are quintessential American success stories that could well have come from the pen of Horatio Alger. The very title of Pupin's book, *From Immigrant to Inventor,* echoes the Alger theme of "from rags to riches." "When I landed at Castle Garden forty-eight years ago," Pupin began, "I had only five cents in my pocket." And such poverty was always conquered by the same means—hard work. "He began to work, and to work hard, almost from the day he set foot on American soil," Bok noted of himself. Antin similarly characterized her life as "striving against the odds of foreign birth and poverty, and winning."

Immigrant authors acknowledged, however, that their efforts might well have been wasted anywhere else. Antin wrote of the "abundant opportunity" America afforded; Bok termed it "the most priceless gift that any nation can offer," adding that "here a man can go as far as his abilities will carry him." This portrayal of the United States as *The Promised Land*—the title of Antin's autobiography—is indicative of another element common to the genre: the concept of two different worlds. In contrast to the opportunity available in the New World, the Old World was bleak, confining, repressive. "In Blato," Adamic recalled of his native village, "no one ate white bread or soup or meat, except on Sundays and holidays, and only few then." Antin described pogroms in which Russia's Jews "were attacked . . . with knives and clubs and scythes and axes."

The differences between the worlds are personified by the immigrants who, in their own telling at least, existed in both, but belonged to neither. Their autobiographies describe a search for identity that is nearly epic in proportion and typically unfulfilled until the final chapter. Jacob Riis asserted early on that "thirty years in the land of my children's birth . . . left me as much of a Dane as ever," although the title of his account, *The Making of an American* (1924), foretold the last-page revelation, a chance encounter with the American flag abroad that convinced him he "had become an American in truth." Panunzio's closing chapter, titled "My Final Choice," detailed a similar experience. Back in Italy as World War I concluded, he happened to glimpse "the Stars and Stripes waving gloriously in the last radiant beam of light," and his confusion was resolved. "I knew where my heart lay," he reported.

Following the passage of restrictive immigration laws in the early 1920s, immigrant autobiographies tended to take on a more aggressive tone in claiming a place for immigrants in the United States. "If the present standards had prevailed forty-eight years ago," Pupin observed, "I should have been deported. There are, however, certain things which a young immigrant may bring to this country that are more precious than any of the things which the present immigration laws prescribe." The intangible qualities to which Pupin referred could well inspire "a possible spiritual and intellectual flowering of America," according to Adamic, who characterized "the early American stock" as "emotionally, spiritually, and intellectually flat. For generations the old stock [has] been pickled in the sour juice of Puritanism."

The ethnic pride evident in Adamic's remark became a major concern in later immigrant autobiographies, whose authors insisted that such feelings enhance rather than inhibit Americanization. Ernesto Galarza noted in *Barrio Boy* (1971) that "being a proud American . . . did not mean feeling ashamed of being a Mexican." In *The Heart Is the Teacher* (1958) Leonard Covello described his rebellion against, and reform of, an educational system that made children "Americans by learning how to be ashamed of [their] parents."

Clearly, immigrants who wrote their autobiographies did more than merely record their life stories. They attempted, through the medium of a distinct literary form, to convey positive messages about the United States and the people who were drawn to it from abroad.

References
Titles as cited in text; see also William Boelhower, *Immigrant Autobiography in the United States* (1982).

                                                        D.R.S.

IMMIGRANT CHILDREN IN THE SCHOOLS. The immigrant child was the child of his own immigrant subcommunity within the American city in which his parents had settled. In this immigrant subcommunity (or "ghetto," which carries with it a pejorative connotation), the child was securely related to an organized social life which largely duplicated the customs and mores that his parents had transplanted to America. It was the school that introduced him to a different world, and it was the school that saw its role essentially as one of enforced assimilation. Cubberley, the educational historian, makes this vividly clear:

> Everywhere these people [immigrants] tend to settle in groups or settlements and to set up their own national manners, customs and observances. Our task is to *break up* their groups and settlements, to assimilate or amalgamate these people as a part of the American race, and to implant in their children, so far as can be done, the Anglo-Saxon conception of righteousness, law, order, and popular government, and to awaken in them reverence for our democratic institutions and for those things which we as people hold to be of abiding worth.

By 1911, 57.5 percent of the children in the public schools of thirty-seven of the largest American cities were of foreign-born parentage; in the parochial schools of twenty-four of these thirty-seven cities, the children of foreign-born parents constituted 63.5 percent of the total registration. To the immigrant child the public elementary school was the first step away from his past, a means by which he could learn to assume the characteristics necessary for the long climb upward. And by 1911 almost 50 percent of the students in secondary schools were of foreign-born parentage. In American cities the major educational challenge and responsibility was the immigrant child.

The situation in New York City was not atypical. Serious deficiencies existed in the adequacy of available school facilities. In 1890, it was estimated that in New York City some 10,000 children who were within the legal ages for school attendance were without actual school accommodations, and this figure was undoubtedly conservative. The passage of the Compulsory Education Act in 1895, stipulating that all children between the ages of eight and sixteen years attend school (with certain exceptions as to employment, etc.) exacerbated the situation in New York City, and because of the lack of accommodations, the Compulsory Education Act was virtually inoperative. The expansion of secondary education (three new high schools were opened in 1897) imposed the need for vast curriculum changes in the upper grades of the elementary school, with a concomitant awareness of the need for the expansion of manual training schools. When the Consolidation Act (January 1, 1898) created a greater New York, bringing together the boroughs, the schools in Manhattan and the Bronx were divided into primary and grammar departments with separate classes for boys and girls, with the elementary schools consisting of seven grades. In the other boroughs the elementary school was organized into eight grades. The first New York City superintendent of schools, William H. Maxwell (q.v.), addressed himself to the major problems of the expansion of facilities, the opening of more kindergartens, the uniformity of an eight-year elementary school, and the establishment of manual training schools; and to the problems of urbanization and mounting school enrollments (some 20,000 to 40,000 new students had to be accommodated each year) was added the increasingly heavy immigration.

It was against the background of these problems that the immigrant child presented himself to the New York City public schools. By 1900, approximately 80 percent of the New York City population was either foreign born or of foreign parentage, and by 1910 a significant shift in the birthplace of the majority of the immigrants from the north to the south of Europe had occurred. For the schools, the non–English-speaking child presented still another dimension to overwhelming problems. *The Third Biennial School Census* in 1906 showed that 17 percent of the entire public school enrollment was foreign born (113,740), and although there was some controversy about the accuracy of the figures (particularly over whether the figures reflected cases of truancy and the number of children working illegally), the enormity of the problems presented to the schools was dramatically underscored. The children of the more recent immigrants constituted the bulk of elementary and intermediate enrollments, while the children of earlier immigrants were generally in higher grades. More symptomatic than any other factor of the general malaise of the schools was the pervasive phenomenon of the overage pupil who was classed under the rubric of "retardation," with all of its negative connotations. The Immigration Commission of 1911 found that the percentage of "retardation" for the New York City elementary school pupils was 36.4, with the maximum retardation (48.8 percent) in the fifth grade. The commission observed:

> Thus in the third grade the pupils range in age from 5 to 18 years. In similar manner pupils of the age of 14 years are found in every grade from the first of the elementary schools to the last of the high schools. It will, however, be noted that in spite of this divergence the great body of the pupils of a given grade are of certain definite ages, the older and younger pupils being in each case much less numerically represented. It may, therefore, be assumed that there is an appropriate age for each grade. This assumption is the cardinal point in current educational discussion in regard to retardation. If it were assumed that there is a normal age for each grade, then the pupils can be divided into two classes—those who are of normal age or less and those who are above normal age. The latter, or overage pupils, are designated as "retarded."

Although the Immigration Commission concluded that the "races" that had most recently arrived in the United States (and in which a foreign language was used in the home) had a higher percentage of retardation, it cautioned against deriving from these data less mental ability, but rather ascribed the retardation to environmental and external circumstances that would be corrected within a generation. That the educational system was inadequate to the problems presented is unquestioned. In the main, there was a slow shift from concern with the problems of physical facilities and of congestion to the more important concerns of the needs of immigrant children; the problems of their maladjustment or "retardation"; the particular needs of ethnic groups; the preservation of the many cultures that the children brought to the schools; and the articulation of a learning situation that was fashioned out of new curricula and understandings.

Regarding the effort to respond to the immigrant child, it is important to note at the outset that no overall programs were developed to aid any particular immigrant group. Although there was little agreement as to what Americanization was, the schools were committed to Americanize (and to Anglicize) their charges. Ellwood P. Cubberley's *Changing Conceptions of Education* (1909), which Lawrence A. Cremin characterizes as "a typical progressive tract of the era," saw the new immigrants as "illiterate, docile, lacking in self-reliance and initiative, and not possessing the Anglo-teutonic conceptions of law, order, and government"; and the school's role was (in Cubberley's view) "to assimilate and amalgamate." What efforts were made to respond to the needs of immigrant children were improvised, most often directly in answer to specific problems; almost never was any attempt made to give the school and its program a community orientation. The children literally left at the door of the school their language, their cultural identities, and their immigrant subcommunity origins. The child's parents had virtually no role in the school; and the New York City experience was not atypical in its leaving the immigrant child to the discretion of the individual superintendent, principal, or teacher. In New York City no citywide system or policy was developed to meet the special needs presented by the immigrant child. Instead, largely left to the management of district superintendents, constructs and programs evolved along the broad lines of individual promotion; English instruction for foreigners; the provision of special classes; and, in some instances, of special schools.

Julia Richman (*q.v.*), district superintendent in New York School Districts 2 and 3, was particularly responsive to the needs of immigrant children. She experimented with a new system of individual promotion (in essence, graded patterns of instruction geared to individual needs), and her writings show a growing awareness of the need for community liaison and support. As early as 1903, other district superintendents (in Division I, embracing Manhattan south of 14th Street) were experimenting with a syllabus of instruction for teaching English to children who did not know the language. Certain superintendents instituted special classes for immigrant children (extending from one month to a whole year) for basic instruction in English which would bring them to grade level. And the most ambitious of the constructs devised was the large-scale introduction of special classes by Julia Richman throughout the school districts under her governance. These efforts by Julia Richman are worthy of special note.

In 1903, Richman conducted an investigation in her school districts to determine why so many children who applied to leave school were not at fifth-grade level (legally, children could leave school by age fourteen); and she maintained that the clearest indication of the failure of the schools was in the fact that large numbers of children desiring to leave school for employment at age fourteen were not at fifth-grade level. Students who were fourteen and had completed grade five or its equivalent were eligible for work certification. Richman found that pupils who were not progressing could be classified as follows: (1) foreign-born children who had lived longer than one year in the city who were unwisely classified and too slowly promoted; (2) children who were turned away from school or kept for years on waiting lists in the days when principals had that privilege; (3) children "run out of school" for misconduct when records were kept less carefully than at present; (4) children excluded because of contagion in the days when medical personnel and nurses were not able to control this situation; (5) children who had been neglected in classes where substitutes were placed in charge of afternoon part-time classes; (6) disorderly children; (7) truants; (8) defectives (mental or physical); and (9) children whose individual needs were overlooked when promotions were made. On the basis of these findings, Richman received permission from the Board of Superintendents to form special classes for these children in which a simplified and individualized course of study was to be used. Only the absolute essentials demanded by the compulsory attendance law were to be taught. By September 30, 1904, some 18 special classes had been instituted in School Districts 2 and 3; and a significant reversal was made in the earlier practice of placing the immigrant child, whatever his age, in the lowest or next-lowest grade. And by the end of the 1904–5 school year, some 250 special classes (principally for non–English-speaking children) were in operation.

As children acquired a competency in English, they were transferred to appropriate grades. Generally, an overall improvement was noted, with continuing difficulties only with those students who were highly transient and for whom the continuity of instruction was interrupted. Yet even these difficulties were minimized by special efforts and adaptations. Further refinements of the special class concept led to the definition of three categories of placement: Grade C for foreign-born children who did not speak English; Grade D for those pupils who were approaching age fourteen, could not finish elementary school, and wished to obtain work certificates; and Grade E for those pupils who hoped to graduate but needed special help to enter the seventh grade. There is little doubt that the special classes were an effective force in meeting the needs of the immigrant child; and a not inconsiderable number of native-born children received needed help as well.

Although the special classes gave principals and teachers considerable latitude in dealing with the problems of immigrant children, no effort was made to change the basic course of study in the regular classes to which these children eventually moved. Out of mounting criticism that the New York City school curriculum was inflexible, and not geared to the wide variety of needs exhibited by children, came recommendations for industrial education, vast curricular reforms (largely unmet), and the creation of schools for incorrigible boys (the forerunner of the present-day "600" schools). The emphasis on industrial education was a continuing reiteration of the need for manual education; a private manual training school had been established in New York City in 1887, and the city's Baron de Hirsch School (1891) trained boys for the mechanical and building trades. The emphasis on manual and trade education (no matter how inadequately met) may have been the surest symptom of a school system that found the children of immigrants uneducable along traditional lines.

That the public schools in New York City were unable or unwilling to meet the challenge of immigrant children is readily apparent in the paucity of the concepts and programs that were fashioned; in the few educational reformers (e.g., Julia Richman) who responded constructively to the multitude of challenges; in the continuing criticism of the schools by a host of lay reformers; and in the variety of nonschool agencies that were created to meet the very real problems that the schools ignored. Most of the social reformers directed their criticisms to the schools, and of these Jacob A. Riis (q.v.), Robert Hunter (q.v.), and John Spargo (q.v.) are but a few whose writings are valuable chronicles of the deficiencies of the schools; and despite its intricate involvements, the Public Education Association of New York City formulated a conception of the public school as "a legatee institution" whose responsibility (as the PEA saw it) was the entire problem of child life. Thus, central in the community mosaic of the urban settlement house was the provision for all those identities that poor youth sought and were denied in the schools.

The schools reflected the attitudes prevalent at the time of the great immigrations which, in essence, held that the immigrant was a one-generation problem. Assimilation was an educational process, and if immigrant children got a "good" education, the parents would be assimilated with them. In the process, parents and community were neglected, if not ignored. There is some doubt that the school acted as the main device through which the child was assimilated, and if so, it did its job poorly. Certainly, the schools did not ameliorate the plight of the immigrant parent. If anything, they provided little opportunity for the immigrant parent to obtain information about what the aims and objectives of the schools were, and in this respect schools and parents were in continuing conflict. If New York City was typical, the urban schools provided no systemwide policy that dealt with the educational needs of immigrant children; and where programs were fashioned to meet these needs, there was no attempt made to differentiate between immigrant groups (e.g., the experience of Italian and Jewish children in New York City strongly documents this failure). Instead, children were lumped under the rubrics "native-born" or "foreign-born." One cannot discount the dysfunctional programs, rampant discrimination, and authoritarian prejudice that existed in the schools and attribute the general patterns of failure to immigrant children or their parents. The blame for the failure lies almost wholly within the school and the dominant society which shaped its programs and articulated its cultural ideals.

Leonard Covello (*q.v.*), who spent half a century in New York City schools as a teacher and an administrator, and was himself an immigrant child in its schools, observed:

> Of no little importance was the fact that the Americanization programs were directed only toward people of foreign stock, without giving any consideration to the necessity of involving *all* Americans, regardless of the time of their arrival in the United States. But, above all, the early Americanization policies, by and large, denied or neglected the strength of, and the values in, the foreign culture of immigrant groups. The concept of Americanization was based upon the assumption that foreigners and foreign ideas and ways were a threat to American political, economic, and social stability and security. The infiltration of foreign culture, it was feared, would eventually bring about a deterioration of the American "way of life." Programs were designed, therefore, to suppress or eliminate all that was conceived of as "foreign" and to impose upon the immigrant a cultural uniformity with an American pattern. (Cordasco *infra*)

References
Selma C. Berrol, *Immigrants at School, New York City, 1898–1914* (1978); Stephen F. Brumberg, *Going to America, Going to School* (1986); Francesco Cordasco, *Immigrant Children in American Schools* (1976).

F.C.

IMMIGRANT HANDBOOKS. A very varied and rich genre of instructional pamphlets, guidebooks, and related ephemera intended as aids to emigrating nationals. Many are propaganda pamphlets with widely varying levels of objectivity. They appeared under many different auspices, e.g., religious groups, governmental agencies (including individual states), emigration societies, and companies recruiting immigrant labor. The genre has generally been neglected, despite its importance for the historian of immigration, but this neglect may be due to the scarcity of extant copies. Guidebooks for Italian emigrants (a particularly prolific literature, given the size and duration of Italian emigration to all parts of the world) deal with the same basic information: (1) before departure: basic information, required documents, tickets; (2) the departure: problems at the port of embarkation, the voyage; (3) the arrival: American immigration laws, adapting to American life, agencies offering assistance to immigrants; and (4) an Italian-English vocabulary of commonly used words and expressions.

Sample Immigrant Handbooks:

Gottfried Duden, *Bericht über eine Reise nach den westlichen Staaten Nordamerikas* (1829).

Evan Jones, *The Emigrants' Friend* (1880).

Roberto Marzo, *Guida dell'emigrante negli Stati Uniti del Nord America* (1892).

Edward S. Ellis [New Jersey Immigration Commission], *Guida per gl'immigranti italiani negli Stati Uniti* (1906).

Johan R. Reierson, *Pathfinder for Norwegian Emigrants* (1844).

[Union Pacific Railroad], *The Resources and Attractions of Idaho* (1893).

Immigrant handbook literature continued to be written well into the twentieth century, largely subsiding with the end of the mass immigration to the United States and the imposition of immigration restriction quotas (*q.v.*) in the mid-1920s.

References
Luigi Monga, "Handbooks for Italian Emigrants to the United States: A Bibliographical Survey," *Resources for American Literary Study* 6 (Fall 1976): 209–221; Carl B. Schmidt, "Reminiscence of Foreign Immigration Work for Kansas," *Kansas Historical Collections* 9 (1905–6): 405–497.

F.C.

IMMIGRANT HISTORICAL SOCIETIES. The earliest such societies were founded from the 1880s to the first decades of the present century, before the cessation of mass migration in the 1920s, to modify and offset the Anglo-American–oriented historical narratives and interpretations common in books, articles, and speeches of that time. Organized largely by first- and second-generation Swedes (1888), Scotch-Irish (1889), Jews (1892), Irish (1897), and Germans (1901) in the United States, these groups wished to document and publicize the positive participation of their group in the settlement and development of the nation in order to reduce the then prevalent Anglo-American, Protestant emphasis of American history, occasionally coupled with expression of disdain for recently arrived, non–Anglo-Saxon immigrants from southern and eastern Europe and Asia. In retrospect, spokesmen and writers for immigrant historical societies were among the first to challenge the Anglo-Protestant brand of American history, which was not decisively revised and widely abandoned until the 1960s.

Many professional historians associate these national organizations, especially the Scotch-Irish Society of America and the American Irish Historical Society, with filiopietistic excesses and with exploiting the past for the purpose of self-glorification. This charge is justified when applied to the contents of the ten volumes of *Proceedings of the Scotch-Irish Society*. The thirty-two volumes of *The Journal of the American Irish Historical Society* are less suspect, but also reflect the society members' desire to refute slanders against the Irish, vindicate the honor of Irish-Americans, and confound the ranks of the Scotch-Irish. My definition of immigrant historical societies excludes, somewhat arbitrarily, regional and local North American societies organized by first-generation immigrants for collecting and recording ancestral traditions and memories—organizations that often achieved high standards of historical and literary merit in their publications, i.e., *Der Deutsche Pionier*, published during the 1880s in Cincinnati, Ohio. I also exclude early American state and local bodies like the Massachusetts Historical Society, founded in 1791. Though they emphasized English antecedents, pride in common ancestry, and the achievements of immigrant forebears, the society's members preferred to speak about colonists and pioneers rather than immigrants when recalling their ancestors' experiences. ("Emigrant" was the common term in the eighteenth century to describe those who *left* a foreign country to settle in North America. It was gradually replaced by "immigrant"—sometimes by "refugee"—to emphasize the *coming* here. But the distinction breaks down when applied to actual groups of people: some colonists were driven by poverty and persecution; some immigrants came not in flight but with a vision of a better life in the New World.)

Besides rejecting claims for the superiority of Anglo-Saxon (and, sometimes, Germanic) moral and political principles, immigrant historical societies stressed the contributions of their ethnic groups to the nation in times of peace and war. This now somewhat shopworn concept of "contributions" almost invariably accentuated the positive, the Irish, Jew, or German as valiant fighter, selfless financier, or self-made merchant prince, and omitted the negative, immigrants as criminals, prostitutes, union organizers (a dirty word in the 1890s), rebels, or radicals.

Of course, this record of immigrant "contributions" was compiled at a time when reputable social scientists, historians, and public figures seriously discussed the "worth" of various national, racial, and religious groups for American society and its future. Thus the discovery of a Catholic Irishman who suffered with Washington's army at Valley Forge, or, better yet, accompanied Columbus on his first voyage, of a Jewish tailor turned Indian fighter, or another German who bled in General Siegel's army corps, meant not merely an addition to a more ecumenical, less Anglo-Protestant version of American history, but an asset in the ongoing debate over immigrant restriction and the ideal proportions for composite citizenships in "melting pot" America.

Older regional or state American historical societies sometimes included hereditary qualifications for membership. The immigrant historical societies also had ethnic and religious preferences. Some were eager to counter the lumping of their better-established, more assimilated members and compatriots with less well-off (considered by some Americans as less desirable) newcomers related to them by ties of geography, language, or religion but with variant, often clashing religious and political convictions and social mores. For instance, historians of the Scotch-Irish Society of America stressed that there were "Irish and Irish," by which they meant the "green" or "Pope's Irish," a distinctly less responsible, less valuable element than the "orange," Protestant worthies called Scotch-Irish. Americanized German Jews who organized the American Jewish Historical Society were upset when classed with "foreign," Yiddish-speaking eastern European Jews arriving in ever larger numbers in the 1890s. The American Irish Historical Society, responding to the virulent anti-Catholicism of the 1890s (just as the organization of the American Jewish Historical Society had reacted to the rising tide of anti-Semitism), overlooked no opportunity to smite the (Protestant) Scotch-Irish and other detractors of their Irish "race."

Another, more numerous and diverse category of immigrant historical societies drew support primarily, though not exclusively, from professional, college-educated teachers and scholars. Emerging after World War II, they were frequently affiliated with colleges and universities or were directed from academic institutions, adopted higher standards of historiography and a less parochial approach to the writing and research they promoted. Some, among them the Center for Migration Studies, the Immigration History Society, the Immigration History Research Center, and the Balch Institute for Ethnic Studies, though focused primarily on immigration studies, also serve a membership with interests ranging over a number of immigrant groups and promote lectures and exhibits of migration and ethnic and minority life. With the exception of the Norwegian-American Historical Association, founded in 1925, these associations date largely from the 1960s and following decades. They arose at a time when conferences, college courses, university ethnic studies departments, new books, new reference tools, and new historical and sociological journals devoted to ethnic studies proliferated as the result of a profound reorientation in the larger society involving issues of race, ethnicity, and minority rights.

The turmoil, which eventually redirected the teaching and writing of American history in schools and colleges, stemmed from the civil rights and Black Power movements and their repercussions among other ethnic groups. It was also fueled by the entry into higher education faculties of the children and grandchildren of "new" immigrants: Jews,

Slavs, Italians, Asians, and Hispanics, and other hitherto excluded minorities, many of them the first members of their families to attend college, sometimes with the aid of the G.I. Bill of Rights. Further, it was energized by the infusion of funds from public sources and private foundations. In 1973 Congress authorized the Ethnic Heritage Studies program (*q.v.*) of the U.S. Office of Education, thus putting a government stamp of approval on what critics of the "melting pot" concept called "the new ethnic pluralism." For the first time, many "ethnics" now questioned openly the tacitly accepted Anglo conformity philosophy that had governed most discussions of American citizenship. In art, politics, and education, the meaning of American nationality and community was probed; forgotten or suppressed aspects of the immigrant heritage were examined and found not wanting, indeed worth reviving or recalling. It was a good time for launching many-sided inquiries into the nature, origin, and persistence of the immigrant experience; to respond to public and private invitations to support ethnically oriented research projects and research "centers" at colleges and universities; and to form ethnic historical societies for the exploration of the migration process and immigrant or ethnic history in a wider, comparative perspective or focused on a single group. Among such new institutions were the Center for Migration Studies on Staten Island, New York; the Immigration History Research Center at the University of Minnesota; the Balch Institute for Ethnic Studies in Philadelphia; and the Asian Studies Center at the University of California, Los Angeles. Additionally, numerous smaller centers concerned themselves with the history and sociology of a single ethnic and immigrant group: the Basque Studies Center at the University of Nevada, Reno; the Slovenian Research Center at Kent State University, Ohio; the American Jewish Archives in Cincinnati, Ohio; and the Finnish-American Historical Archives at Suomi College, Hancock, Michigan.

Surviving organizations from the first immigrant historical societies organized before World War I took on new life. The American Jewish Historical Society uncrated its library from storage and found a permanent home on the campus of Brandeis University. (The German-American and Scotch-Irish societies were defunct; the American Irish Historical Society, functioning largely as a social club, maintained a building and library in New York City.) New organizations to explain and record ethnic and immigrant history, sociology, and culture were created, too many to supply names and descriptions of all.

The Immigration History Society, founded in 1965, with a membership of over 700 (approximately a third of them institutions) from various disciplines and countries, distributes a semiannual *Newsletter,* sponsors the *Journal of American Ethnic History,* and organizes program sessions at meetings of learned societies. The Polish American

Historical Association emerged in 1942; the Kosciusko Foundation and the Polish American Society, headquartered at the Polish Seminary in Orchard Lake, Michigan, chronicled the Polish American experience. Irish and Irish-American studies are served by activities of an American Committee for Irish Studies, in existence for more than a decade. Similar organizations serve the interests of Italian-Americans, German-Americans, and other nationality or ethnic groups. Across our northern border, the Canadian Ethnic Studies Association and the Multicultural History Society of Ontario pursue active research and publication programs. In addition to the German-American Studies Association and its yearbook, there are newsletters from organizations like the Slovak Studies Association and the Swiss American Historical Society. Many, though not all such organizations and their publications, may be found in the *Dictionary of Historical Societies.*

The earliest immigrant historical societies organized by Germans, Scotch-Irish, and Jews between 1889 and 1901 declined because of waning ethnic consciousness and the consequent dwindling of financial support from ethnic elites, the antiforeign climate of World War I, and the emergence of specialized ethnic and religious antidefamation, propaganda, and defense agencies. Another contributing factor, the increasing professionalization of historical scholarship, paradoxically aided in the eventual creation of new immigrant and ethnic societies with less strident claims, and in the revitalization of surviving older ones. Like third parties in politics, these first immigrant historical associations disappeared or were transformed from maverick bodies into mainstream organizations once their less extravagant claims were absorbed by the corpus of American history. Their historiography was deservedly suspect for uncritical claims, partiality, and bombast. Yet their records and proceedings remain instructive not merely for what they tell us about their groups' American experiences, but for what they reveal about their organizers' and members' anxieties, their preferences for sentimental rather than intellectual arguments, their partiality for using nationality and religion as true yardsticks of "worth," and their eagerness to create a pantheon of ethnic heroes closely integrated with the commanding figures and icons of American colonial and early republican history.

Despite their championship of environment over heredity, writers for their publications strengthened the notion of separate racial and ethnic identity for various immigrant groups by associating their "contributions" with "race" qualities. Unwittingly, they repeated and probably reinforced the emphasis of school and "public" history to favor the white soldier, politician, and self-made man over the laborer, nonconformist, rebel, radical, and farmer—or the woman and "colored" Americans of various hues.

Finally, a few remarks about the applicability of "Hansen's Law" to the founding of immigrant historical societies. In 1937, Marcus Lee Hansen, a prominent historian of immigration of his era, delivered before the Swedish Augustana Historical Society, a gathering of laymen, not historians, interested in the preservation of Swedish-American identity and traditions, an address entitled "The Problem of the Third Generation Immigrant." He told his listeners that their desire to support a historical society proved "that what the second generation wished to forget, the third (the immigrants' grandchildren) wishes to remember." This tendency, he added, might be illustrated by examples from the experiences of various groups.

After Hansen's untimely death in 1938, this generalization was elevated to "Hansen's Law" by academic specialists in immigrant and ethnic studies. As a schematic formula for explaining the founding of immigrant societies, "Hansen's Law" has been found wanting by several investigators who tested the validity of the evidence he cited. Founders of the earliest immigrant societies were prompted by a variety of motives, among which insecurity ("status anxiety") and the desire to put their group in the best possible light in the face of alleged or real denigration by other historians, played at least as large, perhaps a more decisive role, than the desire to remember and perpetuate memories of the parents' and grandparents' past and their ethnic heritage.

If a third-generation "return" to the ethnicity rejected by the second generation does not account for the founding of the early immigrant historical societies, impulses leading to the formation of later immigrant historical societies are equally problematical. Neither historians nor social scientists agree on what the "new," "symbolic," or "emergent" ethnicity represents and portends. Nevertheless, Hansen's work remains valuable for its sensitivity to the conflicts arising between immigrants and their children and the variability of what we have come to call ethnicity, in all of its shadings, according to the circumstances surrounding and conditioning its expression. This insightful observation, whether elevated to a historical "law" or not, surely also applies to a consideration of immigrant historical societies.

References
John J. Appel, *Immigrant Historical Societies in the United States, 1880–1950* (1980); John D. Buenker and N. C. Burckel, *Immigration and Ethnicity, a Guide to Information Sources* (1977); Marcus Lee Hansen, *The Problem of the Third Generation Immigrant,* a republication of the 1937 address with Introductions by Peter Kivisto and Oscar Handlin (Swenson Swedish Immigrant Research Center, Augustana College, Rock Island, Illinois, 1987); Donna McDonald, comp., *Dictionary of Historical Societies and Agencies in the U.S.A. and Canada* (American Association of State and Local History, 1975).

J.J.A.

IMMIGRANT IMAGES IN AMERICAN FILM AND TELEVISION. Motion pictures emerged as a mass medium when immigrants were coming to America's major cities in great numbers after the turn of the century. As immigration became a force that changed America's social and political life, it also became a prime topic for Hollywood films from the silent era to the present. Two additional factors increased the movies' interest in the new waves of immigration. First, immigrants constituted a major proportion of the audience for new films which were initially aimed at working-class viewers. Additionally, many of the movie makers—directors, screenwriters, producers, and actors and actresses—came from immigrant backgrounds during the early years of the cinema. With the Jews and the Irish most strongly represented in this new entertainment business, these film makers often presented rememberances of their own heritage on the silver screen. Nonetheless, care must be exercised as one evaluates the veracity of the images of the immigrant experience presented in Hollywood films. Were they realistic images of the American historical experience or were they dream constructs of immigrant film makers seeking to assimilate into American society?

The early silent films seemed to exult in the ethnicity of the immigrant groups presented. The ghetto life of the Italian, Jew, or Irish was presented with almost anthropological care, as the wider world of American culture remained almost a foreign culture. This celebration of immigrant life faded in the 1920s, as the theme of assimilation began to dominate. The prime goal of many of these films became the ultimate assimilation of immigrants into American society via intermarriage or the shedding of old ways and traditions. This can be seen vividly in the 1927 film *The Jazz Singer,* which bridged the worlds of silence and sound in motion picture history. Although the young Al Jolson comes from several generations of Jewish cantors, he seeks to make his living in the new world as a "jazz singer" who will ultimately become a Broadway star. He breaks with his father's way of life, and becomes a new New Yorker who will soon marry a (non-Jewish) showgirl. The passions and excitement of the new urban life are so attractive that the familial reconciliation of the final scene hardly negates the assimilationist message. Similarly, in films that appeared in the 1930s, the struggle for success (of particular importance during the Depression years) often dictated the shedding of one's ethnic identity.

The dilution of the American ethnic heritage on film continued in a curious fashion during World War II. Ethnic identifications were rampant in war films, as soldiers were given names which clearly signaled their heritage. Nonetheless, these immigrant name-tags paled before a more important goal—that of American unity during wartime. No matter what one's ethnic heritage, all were primarily Americans. A person's background therefore mattered little in the face of the Nazi threat. Ironically, the precise ethnic identifications symbolized a triumph of assimilation.

It is therefore something of a surprise that Hollywood films begin to change their treatment of immigrants by the 1960s to assume a more sympathetic view of the immigrant past. Independent film makers have contributed to this trend in such films as Joan Micklin Silver's *Hester Street* (1975), a study of Jewish immigrant life on New York's Lower East Side, and Wayne Wang's *Chan Is Missing* (1982) and *Dim Sum: A Little Bit of Heart* (1984), which viewed Asian-American life in San Francisco. Major studies have also manifested a new sympathy to America's immigrant past. The careful portrayal of the Italian immigrant experience in *The Godfather, Part II* (1974) suggests that one of the reasons for Michael Corleone's failure as Don is that he had forgotten his ethnic roots. Additionally, Italian-American director Francis Ford Coppola gave an insider's sympathy to Italian-American life in both *Godfather* films that probably could not have been attained by another director.

Television has also partaken of this newfound respect and sympathy for the immigrant past. It might also be argued that television helped to fuel the interest in America's ethnic past with ABC-television's broadcasting of *Roots* (1977) and *Roots, the Next Generations* (1979).

Despite the newfound interest in America's immigrant heritage in both motion pictures and television, the media still has difficulty with the problem of stereotyping ethnic and racial groups. While Hollywood has presented exemplary achievements in recent years, it has occasionally allowed long-standing derogatory ethnic images to mar recent advances.

References
Patricia Erens, *The Jew in American Cinema* (1984); Randall Miller, ed., *The Kaleidoscopic Lens: How Hollywood Views Ethnic Groups* (1980); Allen Woll, *The Latin Image in American Film* (1980); Allen Woll and Randall Miller, *Ethnic and Racial Images in American Film and Television: Historical Essays and Bibliography* (1987).

A.L.W.

IMMIGRANT LANGUAGES. America has been a polylingual society since the first generation of European settlements in the early seventeenth century. Although the dominant language became English, there were already Portuguese, Spanish, German, Dutch, Swedish, French, and other European tongues before the midcentury point had been reached. With the establishment of English imperial power extending over the Atlantic coastline and inland, English became the most commonly spoken language, but some of the others spread at the same time. The complex colonial experience created the foundation for a cultural situation that would continue to bedevil Americans and immigrant new-comers of later generations. It was undeniable that English was lin-guistically dominant in the society as a whole and was the language of political power. Yet other languages would continue to assert them-selves in a variety of ways.

During the eighteenth and even more clearly during the nineteenth century there existed the problem of what the relationship should be between the immigrant languages and the principal language. What—if anything—should be the role of American governments in determining the situation of immigrant languages in the new land? The continual influx of newcomers from many societies assured the continuation of a polylingual tradition within a predominantly English-speaking society.

The new tides of cultures and languages inspired three basic reac-tions, at least from the mid-nineteenth century on. Some thought Amer-ica was sufficiently flexible to accommodate itself to many tongues, and that variety would not threaten the basic social cohesion. Cultural plu-ralism and its companion, linguistic pluralism, were thought to enrich our society. This view was held by people who, by and large, opted for the predominance of English. A second view held that the tide of foreign tongues and cultures should be stemmed and that it was neces-sary to cut off the immigration from societies that seemed profoundly different from America. There was also a third group that wanted to make some temporary accommodation to newcomers linguistically and otherwise, but with the firm conviction that almost total assimilation should be the goal. Transformations in political, cultural, economic, and demographic life played a profound role in helping to determine which of the approaches would entice the public mind.

Many European languages that appeared in the first half of the seventeenth century—primarily those of Northern Europe—would con-tinue to be heard as the immigrants that spoke them came to America's shores in increasing numbers. But there were also massive linguistic shifts. For example, between 1890 and 1914 4.5 million Italians came, and from 1880 to 1914 1.9 million predominantly Yiddish-speaking Jews arrived. Many other new groups appeared in impressive numbers as well. In the mid-twentieth century there was a very large influx of Spanish-speaking immigrants, particularly from Mexico, Puerto Rico, Cuba and the Dominican Republic. By the late 1970s, it was clear that new waves of Asian immigrants were reaching America, bringing with them Chinese, Japanese, Korean, and an assortment of South Central Asian tongues.

Although it might be possible to make broad generalizations about the reception given to these many languages and cultures beginning in the seventeenth century, it is important to be aware that in the interplay between languages and cultures, the earlier residents and the newcomers did not fit one pattern. There were significant differences as well as broad similarities.

Germans, for example, introduced their language, culture, and skills here as early as 1639 when masons and stoneworkers were brought to Boston to help that small urban community expand. It is important to highlight this event because it points to the inadequacy of looking at linguistic relationships without paying attention to the skills, education, culture, politics, and economic situation of all concerned. In 1743 the first German-language Bible was printed, while in 1754 the Schwenkfelders established what was probably the first German-language Sunday school, Die Kindlehr. Certain basic patterns were established in the eighteenth-century German communities which continued during the nineteenth century, though with significant variations. Between 1845 and 1860 approximately a million and a quarter German immigrants came. Such an influx led to the establishment of German-language theaters and more than two hundred German language papers, most of which faded away by the early twentieth century. Many cities established either German-language schools or schools were German was the language of instruction for some grades. These efforts were perhaps at their strongest in the period from 1865 to 1890.

When Italians came to the United States in massive numbers, they also developed their own newspapers of various political persuasions, and had theatrical groups and supportive associations. But many Italians suffered from a paltry formal education in their *paesi*. Identification with the group was reinforced through home, neighborhood, and church. But even that determination, willed by the group and compelled by circumstances, crumbled in the course of time and Italians began to move into the American mainstream. That brought with it, as it did for Germans earlier, a weakening of the original language and the identification of success with the conquest of English.

The experiences of the Germans and the Italians, as well as that of the Hispanic groups arriving later, all occurred in the context of American society. All the groups made adjustments in the long run, but at the same time there continues to be debate about the social, cultural, and sometimes legal situation of the immigrant languages. Problems of linguistic assimilation, independence, and accommodation remain features of American life.

References
Charles A. Ferguson and Shirley Brice Heath, eds., *Language in the U.S.A.* (1981); Joshua A. Fishman, ed., *Language Loyalty in the United States: The Maintenance and Perpetuation of Non-English Mother Tongues by American Ethnic and Religious Groups* (1966); Heinz Kloss, *The American Bilingual Tradition* (1977).

G.B.

THE IMMIGRANT NOVEL. There is no agreed-upon definition of the immigrant novel. Simply to say that it is about an immigrant or immigrants is clearly unsatisfactory. Even to say that it is about an immigrant or immigrants and by an immigrant is unsatisfactory, since such a novel may not be about the immigrant as an immigrant. Also, a novel can easily be about immigrants as immigrants and not be by an immigrant. *Herzog* (1964) by Canadian-born Saul Bellow illustrates some of the problems of definition. Bellow moved with his family to the United States while he was still a child. Moses Herzog, the title character and protagonist of the novel, was also born in Canada and made the same migration. He even reminisces about his Canadian childhood. But neither he nor the author indicates that his problems or motivations stem from his immigrant status. He hardly ever even thinks of himself as an immigrant. Thus, *Herzog* cannot justly be classified as an immigrant novel. On the other hand, *Christ in Concrete* (1939) by American-born Pietro Di Donato and *Jews Without Money* (1930) by American-born Michael Gold are directly concerned with the immigrant experience and can be much more easily classified as immigrant novels than can *Herzog*.

For a work to be considered an immigrant novel, at least some of the central characters must be conscious of their position as immigrants (or the narrator must be conscious of their status as immigrants) and that status must have something to do with their roles in the novel. In some cases, the immigrant novel simply treats the problems the immigrant has adjusting to his new environment, problems sometimes presented merely for the sake of humor. In these novels, the implied point of view is often that New World ways are good and Old Country ways, if not bad, are at least humorous. An example is *Potash and Perlmutter* (1910), by English-born Montague Glass, a book that delighted many readers but outraged others because of the way it belittles the business practices and Yiddish accents of its title characters.

Often contrast, usually involving New World and Old, is central to the immigrant novel. Sometimes the contrast involves the New World alone in terms of what the immigrant thinks of it before arriving and what he or she thinks of it after living there for a while. In European-American immigrant novels, the Book of Exodus usually provides a structuring metaphor as well as a background against which life in the New World in measured. America becomes a kind of promised land in the mind of the immigrant-to-be. The novel then usually involves an account of the protagonist's disillusionment as he or she discovers that the streets in America are not really paved with gold, one must often live at least initially in a crowded ghetto or an undeveloped rural area, and one must work extremely hard for long hours to earn a bare living. Even long hours of work cannot guard against the caprices of nature and man, as the Hansas discover in *Giants in the Earth* (1927), by Norwegian-born O. E. Rolvaag. After the original disillusionment occurs, the protagonist often discovers that America is a kind of promised land after all, in which one can achieve a measure of success, usually material, not possible in the Old World. Still, as David Levinsky in *The Rise of David Levinsky,* by Lithuanian-born Abraham Cahan ultimately discovers, that success sometimes has too high a price attached. Levinsky, who becomes a millionaire in the garment trade, seriously wonders whether he was not better off as a poor yeshiva student back in Antomir in Russia or even as a greenhorn desirous of getting a university education than as a rich and powerful garment manufacturer.

Whereas Levinsky tries to discard his European background and the customs that go with it, the characters in other immigrant novels, such as those in Di Donato's *Christ in Concrete,* try to retain Old World customs in the face of what appear as dehumanizing tendencies in the New World. Di Donato's immigrants work as bricklayers on skyscrapers. His ultimate symbol of dehumanization is the embedding of Geremio in concrete. Still, largely through retaining folk customs, Di Donato's immigrants and their children refuse to surrender to the dehumanization that American technology seems to demand.

Often, the immigrants' problems in novels arise as a result not only of different customs in Old World and New but also—often especially—of different languages. Usually, the immigrant is faced with the need to adapt to a new way of life and learn a new language simultaneously. And most people who immigrate as adults more or less fail at both. Thus, central to many immigrant novels is a generation gap in which children born in America or who come here at a very young age are ashamed of their parents who speak heavily accented English and cannot comfortably assume "American" ways. Sometimes the children find themselves embarrassed when they first leave home and discover that they do not speak, act, or dress the way American-born children do. In *Take All to Nebraska* (1936), Sophus Keith Winther, born in Denmark, describes Hans Grimsen's chagrin when, on his first day of school, the teacher asks if anyone can recite a poem. Hans begins to recite one in Danish. He immediately learns that only English is appropriate for use in school. Along with this knowledge comes a sense of the inferiority of his native tongue and customs as viewed by his schoolmates and teacher. From here it is a small step to a sense of his own and his family's inferiority. Thus, an overriding passion in many immigrant novels is for the immigrant to become Americanized as soon as possible. Often, the immigrant discovers many years later that he or she did not have to discard Old World languages and customs and that they are not in any way inferior to those of families that have lived in America for generations.

Even embarrassment of the sort Hans suffers does not usually dim the immigrants' ability to love America. Again, in *Take All to Nebraska,* the Grimsen children become thoroughly Americanized, and the parents, in spite of numerous problems—including ethnic prejudice, the death of a daughter, failed crops, and even marital infidelity—decide that there is no returning to Denmark. At the end of the novel, Peter, Hans' father, decides to take out citizenship papers, and Meta, Hans' mother, vows that she will improve her ability to speak English.

Thus, for a novel to be considered an immigrant novel, it must in some way display a consciousness of the status of some of the central characters as immigrants. That status may be treated straightforwardly and seriously, ironically, or even humorously. Nonetheless, it must be one of the central concerns of the novel.

References
William Q. Boelhower, "The Immigrant Novel as Genre," *MELUS* 8 (Spring 1981): 3–13; David M. Fine, *The City, the Immigrant and American Fiction, 1880–1920* (1977); Marcus Klein, *Foreigners: The Making of American Literature, 1900–1940* (1981).

R.T.

THE IMMIGRANT PRESS. Starting in the eighteenth century, the press evolved as a key institution in virtually every immigrant group to establish itself in North America. As significant in the development of community life as the church, the school, and the fraternal society, the press has been a spontaneous development inherent to the growth of the various groups. While it was Benjamin Franklin himself who initiated the genre, with his short-lived *Philadelphische Zeitung* (Philadelphia News) in 1732, the immigrant press actually emerged from within the group rather than from outside. Thus, a more appropriate date for the debut of the immigrant press is 1739 with Christopher Sauer's *Der Hochdeutsch Pennsylvanische Geschichts-Screiber* (High German Pennsylvania Annalist).

In these two-and-a-half centuries the press has been a constant presence on the immigrant scene. It developed elaborately among some groups, such as the Germans, Jews, and Italians, so that dozens of dailies, weeklies, and monthlies appeared wherever the groups resided in the United States. The German-American press numbered perhaps 5,000 newspapers and periodicals over the centuries. Among other smaller groups, a limited but noticeable number of newspapers were published. The greatest number of individual titles appeared between the 1880s and 1920, with the peak year, 1917, witnessing over 1,300 such publications. However, statistics are unreliable in this area because directories were never comprehensive in their non–English-language newspaper compilations. Moreover, the changing of titles, the mergers of individual publications, and the duplicating of titles by new papers created great confusion. Sociologist Robert E. Park, the first student of the subject, suggested that any figures are misleading, since for every 100 newspapers initiated, about 93 ceased publication. Additionally, the numbers who read a single copy of such a paper can never be known.

The functions of the press have been several. Most fundamentally, the role of the newspapers was traditionally informational and educational to the extent that the press served as a school for adults who were novices at the habit of newspaper reading. The newspapers carried news of the country of origin, of the activities of their compatriots elsewhere in the United States, and of the local immigrant community as well. It also reinforced a group's values, folk ways, and heritage, helping its readers to define themselves in the new environment. It sometimes promoted a particular dialect of the Old World tongue into a national language or even gave written form to a language for the first time. Gradually the press helped to acclimatize newcomers to mainstream society as, indeed, the press itself experienced adjustments. Finally, it promoted the political and economic interests of the group in its pages and policies. In content, papers contained news; editorials; features such as social events and women's columns; serialized classics and poetry from ethnic literature; and advertisements and classifieds. Special Sunday editions were published as in the English-language press. Small publications, because of their meager resources, often simply reproduced news and features from influential dailies. In general, the immigrant press was slow to adapt to the technological changes that occurred in the newspaper world in the late nineteenth and early twentieth centuries, usually because of limited capital.

The ebb and flow in the microcosm of the immigrant press was determined by immigration patterns. The newspapers for the first century and more tended to be transient, often one-person operations in which an emigŕe intellectual, a cleric, or an incipient entrepreneur sought to reach out to his group. Such individuals gathered and reported the news, handled business matters, and oversaw production. Papers in that understaffed and undercapitalized environment found it almost impossible to establish themselves on a solid basis. When they succeeded it was because at least an embryonic community existed that the newspaper could help shape. A sufficient population base, adequately clustered, and a level of literacy were essential factors. In this pioneering period of immigrant journalism, a handful of papers succeeded in sinking roots to the extent that they are still publishing today. These include the German *Staats-Zeitung* (Public News) and the English-language Irish *Pilot,* both dating from the 1830s, and *Den Danske Pioneer* (The Danish Pioneer) and the *Svenska Amerikanaren* (The Swedish American), each of which was established in the 1870s. At least eight papers have published for a century, and in the next few years several more will mark their centennials, while others will attain a ninth decade. As examples, the Swedish-language Finnish *Norden* (The North), formerly called the *Finska Amerikanaren* (The Finnish American); the Jewish *Forverts* (Forward); *Slovak V Amerike* (The Slovak in America); *Svoboda* (Liberty), a Ukrainian daily; and *Young China* are all in these categories. Many of these newspapers have circulated also in the country of origin and, in some instances, especially where a sojourner mentality exists, focus to a large extent on issues of the home country more than on those facing the group in the United States.

Near the end of the nineteenth century, a new phase began. On the one hand, the existing immigrant newspapers transcended their adolescent years and were more sophisticated, increasingly better staffed, and more integrated into American journalistic practices and U.S. public issues. Some of the journalists themselves even "jumped" to the American newspaper world, most notably Joseph Pulitzer, a German immigrant reporter in St. Louis. On the other hand, the microcosm of the immigrant press experienced an explosion with the coming of new groups, all of whom, like their predecessors, needed voices of their own. Accordingly, an estimated 800 immigrant papers were published in the 1880s and the figure expanded to nearly 1,200 in 1900. In the second decade of the twentieth century, circulation figures were claimed of one million for the German-language press, nearly that number for the Yiddish and the Polish press each, three-quarters of a million for the Italian, and one-half million for the Swedish. International events such as wars, revolutions, and pogroms brought new readers and refugee intellectual writers to the papers, while World War I itself and the mass hysteria and national origins legislation which followed undercut the foundations and, indeed, the growth potential of the immigrant press. Further, aging first-generation readers and their American-born children represented a shrinking base for the foreign-language papers. By 1930 it became clear that a new phase or era had arrived for the immigrant press whereby readership declined and newspapers merged or ceased publication. Papers numbered about 1,000, reduced from the 1,300 of 1917. It seemed apparent that the foreign-language press had only a limited future.

However, a quarter-century later a new period of growth began. A complex of factors emerged that created a revived role for immigrant newspapers and periodicals. First of all, a new flexibility developed in American immigration policy after World War II in which a variety of groups in relatively limited numbers were allowed to enter the country. Secondly, the 1965 termination of the quota legislation and the implementation of a more open policy unlocked the gates again so that the

1970s saw more immigrants arrive in the United States than in any decade since the beginning of the century. Many of the newcomers were of groups that had never been represented in the United States or in only very minuscule numbers. These Koreans, Indians, Pakistanis, Central Americans, Southeast Asians, and others bore the same informational needs as immigrants in earlier generations. Third, newcomers of groups long established in the United States—Greeks, Poles, Portuguese, Chinese, etc.—as fresh immigrants had different perspectives and needs than their predecessors and required their own media. Fourth, the revival of ethnic consciousness over the last two decades, in part stimulated by the black civil rights movement, led individuals of the third or fourth generation to explore questions of identity and issues of group pride and, thus, to establish ethnic publications. All of these factors have led to the expansion of the immigrant press. Simultaneously, that press has become an ethnic press because it meets the needs not so exclusively of newcomers but more typically of Americans of specific backgrounds who wish to live within an ethnic context. In general, the great bulk of papers of this genre publishing in late twentieth-century America are in fact ethnic newspapers.

Scholars since Park have tried to categorize immigrant newspapers and periodicals in different ways, such as ideologically, but these efforts have been unsuccessful. The most straightforward approach is to divide the press among general circulation organs and special interest publications. General circulation papers have been those that aimed to circulate as widely as possible within a certain group. Special interest papers have been aimed at reaching a particular component of the group. Examples of the latter are religious, labor, women's, children's, recreational, literary, and other types of sheets. As to longevity, the publications of the fraternal organizations have tended to endure the longest because they were built on the resources of and membership lists of community organizations. In the course of time, with the toll taken by the process of assimilation, the press often tried to publish sections or columns in English (dubbed "mixed publications" by Joshua A. Fishman) or to convert entirely to the English language in order to claim the loyalty of the second generation and beyond.

The immigrant press is one of the most crucial primary sources for an understanding of the immigrant experience as it has mirrored the lives and concerns of its people. In fact, its significance cannot be underestimated. Ironically, the press had remained a relatively little-studied phenomenon until recently. Indeed, while studies of the immigrant press have now begun to appear, the work of content analysis, central to an in-depth consideration of the press, can only be seen as in its infancy. The mining of this rich resource and, further, the preservation of complete runs of immigrant newspapers in archives, are the major tasks now being undertaken by interested scholars, archivists, and students.

References
Joshua A. Fishman et al., ed., *Language Loyalty in the United States: The Maintenance and Perpetuation of Non-English Mother Tongues by American Ethnic and Religious Groups* (1966); Sally M. Miller. ed., *The Ethnic Press in the United States: A Historical Analysis and Handbook* (1987); Robert E. Park, *The Immigrant Press and Its Control* (1922; rpt. 1970).

S.M.M.

IMMIGRANT PRESS, and the Civil War Union Army. The immigrant press generally supported the Union cause, but with reservations. Immigrant journals that had supported Douglas in 1860 criticized Lincoln's handling of the war and the recruitment of immigrants in Europe and Canada; radical Republican German papers supported Fremont over Lincoln in 1864 and criticized Union army treatment of some Germans; and conservative Republican journals never criticized Lincoln or the army but devoted space to the achievements of immigrant soldiers in the war.

Reference
John C. Bodger, "The Immigrant Press and the Union Army," Ph.D. dissertation, Columbia University, 1951.

F.C.

IMMIGRANT PROTECTIVE LEAGUE. *See* Progressive Reformers and the Immigrants.

IMMIGRANT WOMEN. Immigrant (ethnic) women are individuals who emigrated to America from another culture, as well as the next few generations of females who identify with some of the distinct customs, traditions, and beliefs of their immigrant relatives' country of origin. The United States census officially considers the great-grandchildren of the immigrants as "American" with no other national designation. However, to truly understand the ethnic women there must be a consideration of gender, generation, and power issues.

Ethnicity. "Ethnic" originally was a term used to indicate belonging to a nation, especially a pagan one. Currently it is used to denote membership of a distinct people possessing its own customary ways or culture. Ethnicity is broader than nationality and includes characteristics such as a common language, common customs, beliefs, and cultural traditions. The Italians, the Jews, the Irish, the Germans, the Polish, the French, the Russians, the Spanish, the Greeks, the Gypsies, the Congo pygmies, the Japanese, the Mexicans, and even the Tropianders are some ethnic groups in our society.

Women. It is widely recognized that there is a paucity of records and documentation in the field of women's research. A researcher's efforts are further handicapped by the sexist bias in the material that exists. This biased orientation to the available literature reflects the dominant views of the urban, white, Western, heterosexual, privileged-class males. There were missing voices and misunderstood images. So, when defining ethnic women, attention must be paid to how they were described or not described in history, and how they are defined today. America is a society of strangers. Understanding the waves of immigration, with everyone equally considered, is critical if there is to be a real analysis of our social history. The immigrant generation is the first generation of ethnic Americans; the children of the immigrants are the second generation of ethnic Americans; and the third generation are the grandchildren of the immigrants.

Recently, feminist writers, historians, psychologists, and sociologists began to undertake a systematic approach to the problems associated with women's role in American life and in history. In fact, until the 1960s, there were no studies focusing on mother/daughter relationships. There were studies on husband/wife, father/son, father/daughter, and mother/son relationships. It seems that studying one not-so-significant person, a woman, was enough. However, to study two insignificant people, that is, two women (one young), would really be a waste. Ethnic women should be defined with the richness of their relationships with their mothers, grandmothers, daughters, and other relevant individuals that make up their biographies. In order to define ethnic women in America one must consider gender in an intergenerational analysis. The vantage point should place women at the center; their experiences should be taken seriously and valued. It is not enough to merely add an extra category called "women." Gender is not merely a variable that can be thrown into a pool of information; gender cannot be just added and stirred into a smooth, blended mixture. There is a depth, a complexity, and a pervasive dimension to the true place women, ethnic women, had in history.

Specifically, it is important to use that investigator's eye when looking at the work of ethnic women. The ethnic woman's work was for many immigrants voluntary or "unpaid labor." Nevertheless, this work should be seen as a contribution to the family, the community, and the society. There is also women's invisible work, work not noticed unless it is undone. The true analysis of ethnic women requires a different perspective, an expanded consideration of certain issues, and overlapping information. An illustration: the southern Italian and eastern European Jewish women arrived on these shores in large numbers during the mass migration period, between 1880 and the mid-1920s. These ethnic women were helpmates and partners to their husbands. Over time, the changing American culture, with such things as child labor laws, expanded the definition of the child. The second-generation ethnic women (daughters of the immigrants) evolved into an expanded definition of the mother role for their daughters. Some of the ethnic women's characteristics were altered as they were passed down the generations; others were and are preserved, mummified and unwrapped at appropriate times designated by tradition or custom.

The ethnic American subculture combines traditions, values, and beliefs from the Old Country with the contemporary culture in the context of the opportunity structure as experienced by the particular ethnic group. In a study of ethnicity, a population can be divided by country of origin, emigration date, and settlement location. Traditions and customs vary less within each population than they do within the country as a whole. Ethnic women must be looked at with a detective's eye because there are great variations. Power is another theme that should be considered in studying ethnic women. This means that sisters, daughters, nieces, wives, mothers, and workers all experience family, community, and society differently. Women are gendered. When discussing power there must be an understanding of its relationship to social category. To be a subordinate is to be locked into that category. To be dominant is to be allowed to be an individual and forget that you have a category. This is also how privilege works.

Established knowledge about ethnic women, along with its controlling male perspective, is important to understand because men are able to write about and concentrate on themselves as individuals. Men are free to write and express their individuality without concern for their gender category, since they are not subordinate. However, ethnic women must be concerned about being a ''female'' with all its stereotypes; then they can be concerned about being ethnic. Therefore, to accurately define ethnic women, there are assumptions that must be questioned; the seemingly familiar is problematized. Specifically, the focus of the analysis is on: gender, ethnic identity, differences of power, invisible work, the core of generational transference, the dimensions of intimacy, and self-esteem factors. Ethnic women are varied, complex, and significant contributors to the American society, past and present. The common thread that is woven through the wide range of their differences is the social category into which society (the old and the new) has placed them as women.

References
Edith Blicksilver, ''The Ethnic American Woman Anthologized,'' *California English* 18

Immigrant Women   347

(Nov.–Dec. 1982): 12–24; Francesco Cordasco, *The Immigrant Woman in North America* (1985); Maxine S. Seller, ed., *Immigrant Women* (1981).

D.M.B.

IMMIGRANT WOMEN, in the U.S. labor force. In the decades between 1890 and 1910 immigrant women from Europe and Canada composed one-fourth of the white female labor force of the United States. Immigrant women, as a whole, were found chiefly in three kinds of "women's work" in these decades: domestic service, textile work, and the needle trades. Clustering by ethnic (or nativity) groups within these work areas was very marked. Distinctions existed between the work roles of English, Irish, German, and Scandinavian immigrant women (the "old" immigration), and those of Italian, Russian, Polish, and Slavic immigrant women (the "new" immigration); most of the former were engaged as domestic workers, and the latter were in manufacturing. Dickinson concludes that

> the menial role of the immigrant women workers between 1890 and 1910 served to advance the women of other nativity classes both in the labor force itself, and outside, for it is probable that without the presence of the immigrant women workers in the kitchens, nurseries, textile mills, and clothing factors, the turn-of-the-century leisure class of women volunteers in church, community, and suffrage work might not have been possible.

Reference
Joan Y. Dickinson, *The Role of the Immigrant Women in the U.S. Labor Force 1890–1910* (1980).

F.C.

IMMIGRANT WORKERS, labor scarcity or social control. Recent analyses of the economic role of immigrant workers from Mexico in U.S. labor markets have been advanced from two divergent interpretations—a labor scarcity argument and a social control thesis. Jenkins analyzes the two perspectives, finding little evidence to support the labor scarcity argument. Immigrant workers are instead argued to be tied to social control functions in the peripheral sectors of the U.S. economy. Details from the historical experience of farm workers in southwestern agriculture are drawn upon to illustrate the argument.

Reference
J. Craig Jenkins, "The Demand for Immigrant Workers: Labor Scarcity or Social Control?" *International Migration Review* 12 (Winter 1978): 514–535.

F.C.

IMMIGRANTS IN AMERICA REVIEW. Monthly journal (vols. 1–2, March 1915–July 1916) published in New York City by the Committee for Immigrants in America, and edited by Frances Kellor (*q.v.*). Although short-lived, the journal is an important repository of materials on immigrants in a critical period of evolving immigration reform and the Americanization movement.

F.C.

IMMIGRANTS, and the American labor market. A study prepared for the Manpower Administration, U.S. Department of Labor, based primarily on an examination of documents filed by 5,000 working-age immigrants who entered the nation during fiscal year 1970. Visa applications, filed prior to entry, and alien address reports, filed in January 1972, were tabulated and compared. In addition, interviews were conducted with some of the immigrants, with employers of immigrants, and with other knowledgeable people. The principal findings of the study were that immigrants made a substantial, but uneven, impact on the labor market, that this impact is greater than previously supposed, and that immigrants are closer to the American norm, in demographic terms, than they were fifty and sixty years ago. The study also examines the adjustments made by immigrants as they come to terms with the U.S. labor market.

Reference
David S. North and W. G. Weissert, *Immigrants and the American Labor Market* (1973).

F.C.

IMMIGRANTS, and the American West. Until recently, this has been a vaguely researched topic. The standard image is of an Anglo-American West, with few cosmopolitan elements present. Yet its ranches, mining towns, and lumber camps once teamed with immigrants. In 1870 nearly three out of ten westerners were foreign-born. In that year 60 percent of Arizona's population was born abroad, while more than half of the men aged twenty-one and over in Utah, Nevada, Arizona, Idaho, and California were foreign born. In 1870 also, California's Irish constituted one in four of that state's residents while San Francisco and other urban centers had flourishing "Chinatowns."

Historians have usually focused attention upon the immigrant's trip across the ocean or his settlement along the eastern seaboard rather than in the interior. To move westward was a chancy endeavor, but restless immigrants of the sort that could never be content in a crowded urban environment took the gamble. To pass beyond the squalor of the eastern cities toward the West's open prairies and mountains was finally to separate oneself from Europe. To a degree, such thinking may have been escapism. Critics of immigration in the homeland thought that abandoning one's native soil was an illusionistic opiate, for the call of virgin lands acted like a magnet.

Many immigrants had farm backgrounds. From 1860 to 1900, when they swelled the growth of America's cities by almost 36 million persons, agricultural workers also helped increase its farm population by 9 million in only forty years. In 1901 an observer noted the character of this immigration: "Our immigrants as a whole are a peasant population, used to the open, with the simple habits of life. . . . Practically all the immigration from Austria-Hungary . . . is from the country, as is also the immigration from Italy."

The move beyond the confining steel and concrete skyline of the eastern city was complicated. To reach farm country not only required money, which the newly arrived immigrant did not have, but involved traveling great distances in a totally unfamiliar land. Out west they did encounter an acculturation usually based upon less friction than that faced by the eastern city immigrant or in the midwestern urban centers of Chicago or Kansas City. As viniculturists, cotton growers, hostelers, miners, or restaurateurs, most immigrants were accepted quite readily as members of a society new to them and to Americans as well.

Yet most western histories say next to nothing about the foreign population, which is indirect evidence either of rapid assimilation or lingering discrimination. Because most foreigners were, in fact, assimilated quite rapidly west of the Mississippi River, loss of national identification has been the rule rather than the exception. This was not the case in the large eastern cities. Oscar Handlin's and other immigration studies have focused attention upon the relatively slow acculturation of the Italian in Boston, New York, or Philadelphia. Yet standing in contrast to the once popular notion that immigrants were unassimilable is their virtual "disappearance" out west. Acculturation proceeded so rapidly that the story of western immigrants can be constructed only with great difficulty.

Neither the West nor the South were favorite destinations for America's "New Immigrants" who poured into the country after 1880; both attracted only half as many foreigners as New York City alone. In the Far West the number of immigrants reached no more than 5.6 percent of the total white population. But, in centers like San Francisco, Denver, or Kansas City the population percentages were markedly higher. In San Francisco during 1880, out of a population of 233,959 persons, 104,244 had been born abroad. By 1900, with a foreign-born population of close to 40 percent, San Francisco (along with New York and Chicago) was a major cosmopolitan center. It has remained so to this day, peopled by more Italians than any other foreign group, and it also bore the name of their fellow countryman, Francis of Assisi. Not only was there a thick European resident population, but also a sizable Chinese and Japanese representation. The city's "Chinatown," "Japantown," and "Little Italy" (on North Beach) still retain this individuality. After the California gold rush, thousands of Oriental males poured into the state to work on the railroads. Their seemingly strange ways and willingness to labor for low wages led "Anglos" to discriminate against them. Eventually, however, fine Cantonese cooking helped to make San Francisco's Grant Street ghetto a mecca for tourists in the same way that the city's Columbus Avenue attracted lovers of Italian food. It is still quite possible to pick up a crab cocktail (caught by Sicilians or Chinese) at Fishermen's Wharf, then to dine on sweet and sour pork, bamboo shoots, and water chestnuts in "Chinatown," and to finish one's meal with Italian zabaglione and capuccino on Columbus Avenue.

Outside the cities as well, the immigrant pattern was readily discernible. The Plains states saw a sprinkling of Scandinavians, Germans, and other nationalities among its ranches and towns. One can hardly think of Wisconsin without its Danish dairymen or of Saint Louis as devoid of its German brewers; and Minnesota's mining camps were never bereft of Norwegians and Swedes. Willa Cather has described charmingly Nebraska's "French farm country" in her *O Pioneers* (New York, 1913) while Mari Sandoz has left us a graphic picture of her crusty immigrant father in *Old Jules* (Boston, 1935). In the midst of Montana one would hardly have expected to find Italian priests who were assigned as missionaries among the Bitteroot Indians and other tribes in the 1840s by the Belgian Jesuit Pierre Jean De Smet.

Both the Italians and the French, however, flourished best in a Mediterranean environment, such as the wine-growing regions of California's Napa and Sonoma valleys. Armenian fig and date growers were attracted to the state's warmer Imperial and great Central valleys. Millions of Mexican-Americans, of course, settled in that state and throughout the southwestern states of New Mexico, Arizona, and Texas. In fact, Hispanics were the first European explorers and settlers of the farthest West. Today Los Angeles has the largest Mexican (Chicano) population outside Mexico City.

In Utah the Mormon religious experiment attracted all nationalities, with heavy recruiting of northern Europeans by missionaries sent abroad in search of immigrants. Nearby Nevada had the largest percentage of foreign born (including many Basque sheepherders) for two decades after the Civil War—long before the mass immigration of the late nineteenth century. From the 1880s onward the westward push of the transcontinental railroads encouraged migration into the rich farm valleys of the Pacific slope. Railroad construction workers also settled in lumber and mining camps at track's end. The foreign residents of Omaha, Denver, Reno, and Sacramento reached their destinations via the railroads, which (like the Mormons) promoted foreign immigration.

Meanwhile the Oregon and Washington coasts attracted Norwegian and Swedish seamen as well as Portuguese and Sicilian fishermen, while the northwestern lumber industry utilized immigrants of every nationality in its camps, sometimes as company "shills," or strikebreakers against the radical Industrial Workers of the World. In competition with unionized laborers, tensions between nationalities arose as foreigners competed for jobs. At the Ludlow Massacre in Colorado (1914), Italian immigrants furnished a convenient scapegoat for contending opponents, with catastrophic results.

Western settlement had a different effect on immigrants than did acculturation elsewhere. With certain notable exceptions (the Chinese in gold rush California and the Japanese during World War II), the Caucasian immigrant record was generally a successful one. While immigrants encountered prejudice and discrimination, they often refound themselves in a tradition-free setting. In short, the immigrant on the western land was as "upraised" as he was "uprooted." With a drama of its own, his record deserves at least some of the attention given to those clichéd symbols of the American West, the cowboys, outlaws, and Indians.

References

Gunther Barth, *Bitter Strength: A History of the Chinese in the United States, 1850–1870* (1964); Kenneth O. Bjork, *West of the Great Divide: Norwegian Migration to the Pacific Coast, 1847–1893* (1958); Lawrence Cardoso, *Mexican Emigration to the United States* (1980); Roger Daniels, *The Politics of Prejudice: The Anti-Japanese Movement in California . . .*(1962); Frederick Luebke, "Ethnic Minority Groups in the American West," in Michael Malone, ed., *Historians and the American West* (1983), pp. 387–413; Bernard Marinbach, *Galveston, Ellis Island of the West* (1983); William Mulder, *Homeward to Zion: The Mormon Migration from Scandinavia* (1957); Moses Rischin, "Beyond the Great Divide: Immigration and the Last Frontier," *Journal of American History* 55 (June 1968): 42–53; Andrew Rolle, *The Immigrant Upraised: Italian Adventurers and Colonists in an Expanding America* (1968); Wilbur S. Shepperson. *Restless Strangers: Nevada's Immigrants and Their Interpreters* (1970).

A.R.

IMMIGRANTS, and crime. In 1911, Senator William D. Dillingham (*q.v.*), chairman of the Federal Immigration Commission (1908–1911), transmitted to the 61st Congress of the United States the forty-two volumes that contained the final reports of the commission. Volume 36 dealt with the subject of immigration and crime. The scope of the reports was to inform the Congress and the American public of the cumulative evidence that had resulted from the inquiry of the commission. The results fell into four categories: (1) the amount of crime by the

American born and all immigrants together; (2) crime and the American-born children of immigrants; (3) Crime, races, and nationalities; and (4) crime and the aliens.

Since the commission could not undertake a thorough investigation to determine the *amount* of crime committed in the United States, due to the inadequacies of the census statistics, the investigation concentrated on the *nature* and the *character* of crime committed in the country. From the data gathered, the commission concluded: (1) That immigration had a "marked effect" upon the *nature* of crime committed in the nation. Consequently, offenses against persons (homicide, assault, rape, abduction, and kidnapping), offenses against public policy (drunkenness, disorderly conduct, and vagrancy), and offenses against chastity (prostitution) had increased. Also, offenses of pecuniary gains (extortion, blackmail, and fencing) had increased; (2) That more of these offenses were committed by Americans than by immigrants; (3) That the "marked effect" of the nature of crime had to be interpreted to mean that American-born children of immigrants were more prone to delinquency than their foreign-born parents and that the criminality of the children of immigrants was largely a product of the city and its environment; and (4) That the majority of the juvenile delinquents were found in the North Atlantic states, where immigrants represented a larger proportion of the population than any other section of the country.

Changes in the *character* of crime were linked to immigrants of different nationalities. The French were reported to commit a higher percentage of offenses against chastity (prostitution) than any other nationality. The Greeks had the highest percentage of violations against city ordinances. The Italians had the highest percentage of the aggregate offenses of violence against the person. These offenses were identified as "distinct" manifestations of Italian criminality and violent behavior. The Italians were reported to excel in the crimes of homicide, rape, kidnapping, abduction, blackmail, and extortion. The Russians, in particular the Russian Jews, excelled in the crimes of pecuniary gains, such as forgery, larceny, robbery, fencing, and pocket-picking.

When the commission analyzed all the aggregate offenses and the distribution ratio among the different nationalities in the cities of New York and Chicago, the results were: *Homicide:* in both cities the Italians showed the highest frequency. *Violent assault:* in New York City the Italians had the highest rate. In Chicago the Slavonians and the Lithuanians had higher rates than the Italians. *Abduction and kidnapping:* in New York City, the Italians had the highest rate. In Chicago, the Greeks slightly exceeded the Italians. *Blackmail and extortion:* In both cities, the Italians largely exceeded all other nationalities. *Burglary:* in both cities, the American-born offenders exceeded all other nationalities.

Larceny and fencing: in New York City, the American-born offenders exceeded the Russians and the English. In Chicago, the Russians were rated first, followed by the American-born offenders. *Robbery:* the American-born offenders had the highest rate in both cities, followed by the Russians. *Vagrancy:* in New York City, the English had the highest rate. In Chicago, the American-born offenders equaled the English. *Prostitution:* in New York City, the French and the Germans exceeded the Russians. In Chicago, the French and the Russians stood out prominently. *Violations of city ordinances:* in New York City, the Italians ranked first, followed by the Russians. In Chicago, the Greeks exceeded all other nationalities. For the issue of *aliens and crime,* the commission used the data compiled by the Bureau of Immigration and Naturalization in 1908. The figures provided a general landscape of the criminality of aliens in the United States. In 1908, there were 12,853 aliens incarcerated. Nearly 50 percent of those in custody belonged to four nationalities: Italians (southern Italians), Irish, Polish, and Germans. Altogether, the four nationalities represented 47.2 percent of all aliens incarcerated. Nearly 25 percent of them had been arrested and sentenced within three years after their arrival in the United States.

Given the importance of the task of the Dillingham Commission and the magnitude of the work, all available sources, data, and evidence were carefully examined. However, the commission concluded that no satisfactory evidence had been produced "to show that immigration has resulted in an increase in crime *disproportionate to the increase in adult population*" (italics added). After three years of work and forty-two volumes, the essence of the commission's findings was that no *direct nexus* between immigration and crime could be established; also, neither ethnic diversities nor physical traits or geographical or regional characteristics constituted *sufficient or necessary* causes of crime in this country. Consequently, the commission favored only a reduction of the immigration of unskilled workers and endorsed the literacy test.

Thus, the national policy of the United States favored still unlimited and unrestricted immigration from Europe. However, pressured by the Immigration Restriction League and by the American Federation of Labor, among others, Congress passed the literacy test. The bills were vetoed by Presidents Taft (1913) and Wilson (1915 and 1917).

Notwithstanding the Dillingham Commission findings, the racists and the eugenicists rumbled their new brand of antiforeignism. If the crime connection had not worked, why not try something different. So, the Grants, the Stoddards, the Goulds, and the Roberts issued a warning to the American people: Beware of the process of mongrelization. By 1920, the eugenicists had become so convincing in their arguments that Dr. Harry H. Laughlin (*q.v.*), staff member of the Eugenics Record Office of the Carnegie Institution of Washington, D.C., was appointed by the House Committee on Immigration and Naturalization as its eugenics expert and agent. During his appearances before the House committee (1920–28), Laughlin stated repeatedly that the time had arrived to introduce eugenic standards to test the qualities of the immigrants. The implementation of the standards would determine desirables and undesirables. Laughlin considered degeneracies and hereditary handicaps inherent in the blood. Laughlin was severely criticized for his generalizations by H. S. Jennings (*The Survey,* December 1923), J. M. Gilliam (*The American Journal of Sociology,* July 1924), and C. Kelsey (*The Annals,* May 1926). They denounced the methods used by the geneticist as unfounded, biased, logically unsound, and "clearly designed to place the recent and current immigrant in as unfair a light as possible." Before long, however, the House committee, strongly impressed by the geneticist's arguments, sponsored a bill aimed at reducing the quotas from 3 to 2 percent. A strong recovery of the American economy in 1923 "threw restrictionists on the defensive." But only temporarily. The Johnson-Reed Act, signed by President Coolidge on May 26, 1924, supported the policy of immigration restriction. It prohibited Japanese immigration and required European immigrants to apply for an entry "visa" to the United States. Eventually, the Johnson-Reed Act "kept America more American" but did not solve the problem of crime and criminality in the country.

In June 1931, George W. Wickersham, chairman of the National Commission on Law Observance and Enforcement, sent President Herbert Hoover the tenth report of the commission, entitled *Crime and the Foreign Born.* The report concentrated on the following issues: (1) criminal statistics and their accuracy; (2) crime and criminal justice in relation to the foreign born; and (3) the history of American public opinion with regard to immigration. As for the accuracy of the criminal statistics, the report revealed that the absence of accepted definitions of crimes at a national level "rendered comparisons of the records of different parts of the country, or of the same part of the country in different years, misleading and unreliable." Furthermore, the report denounced the existing statistics as "wholly wanting" and as being used by the American people to formulate opinions about immigrants built upon assumptions and unsupported evidence. What were supposed to be "incontestable criminal statistics" assembled by police stations revealed appalling irregularities and negligence. The report disclosed that in many cities the police recorded the nationality of a person according to his surname and not on proven identity. The owner of a fruit stand was automatically recorded as Italian or Greek "no matter what his name or nationality." More importantly, if the parents of a person were known to be "foreigners" that person was recorded as a foreigner even though born in the United States.

The issue of crime and criminal justice in relation to the foreign born revealed unequivocally that the differences of race, religion, language, habit, and trait were used to assume other negative characteristics. When a member of an ethnic group was found guilty of criminal or antisocial conduct, "the majority of Americans too quickly assumes such conduct to be characteristic of the group as a whole." The commission's report firmly established that in proportion to their numerical percentage, the foreign born committed fewer crimes than the native born. The perception that immigrants committed more crime than natives was absolutely false and "at variance with the facts."

The history of public opinion, from colonial to modern times, suggested that "misunderstanding and misjudgment" of immigration brought about a constant outcry of "America for Americans." The paradox, outlined in the report, was that each time the outcry was raised, those who manifested it were or included the descendants of a prior generation of immigrants against whom the same outcry had been raised or addressed.

How did American social scientists and/or criminologists perceive immigrants and crime? In a chapter on "Crime in Relation to Race and Nativity" (*Principles of Criminology*, 1947), Edwin H. Sutherland wrote: "The relation of immigration to crime in the United States is a problem of first-rate importance from the point of view of a theory of criminality." Sutherland affirmed that criminality among immigrants could be theorized in terms of *heritage* and in terms of *culture conflict*. He stated that the effect of the culture conflict on the immigrants was intensified by certain conditions: (1) the parents brought with them "heritages regarding behavior, law and punishment which, even when not resulting in lawlessness in their countries," easily led to lawlessness in America; (2) the parents were not able to direct the behavior of their children's conflict in standards and behavior; (3) the immigrants arrived in America with an expectation that American democracy would remove all barriers to allow class mobility; and (4) the country had no sufficient organizations (courts, police, and private support) to successfully confront the criminals. To support his theory, Sutherland, among others, analyzed the criminal behavior of Italian immigrants. He concluded that the criminogenic tendency to commit violent crimes against the person manifested by the Italians in this country was "a matter of tradition." His contention was that some groups "bring with them" special codes of violence in which "killing is a common practice." Hermann Mannheim, the distinguished German criminologist, pointed out in 1956 that the culture conflict theory was an expediency that "provided a welcome ready made opportunity to blame the immigrant for the increasing American crime rate" (*Comparative Criminology*, vol. 2, 1956)

Ever since social scientists and/or criminologists have developed theories on crime and criminality, no single theory has been able to explain crime and criminal behavior in one component. Such theories as differential association, anomie, social alienation, and reference group theory have been used to explain the career criminal, the professional criminal, and the white-collar criminal, among others., Modern positivism, cultural dimension, economic determinism, social disorganization, culture conflict, and group conflict theories have referred to a high incidence of crime, among others. And the subculture and delinquency, delinquency and opportunity, and lower-class culture theories have been used to explain delinquent behavior. The existence of so many theories represents the ultimate proof that when Americans contended that they had discovered an intricate web of correlation among the immigrants' heritage, background, race, nationality, culture, and crime and deviance in America, they were missing the core of crime.

References
Emory S. Bogardus, *Essentials of Americanization* (1923); Emory S. Bogardus, *Social Problems and Social Processes,* selected papers from the Proceedings of the American Sociological Society (1933); Hermann Mannheim, *Comparative Criminology* (1965); National Commission on Law Observance and Enforcement, *Report on Crime and Foreign Born* (1931); *Reports of the Immigration Commission: Immigration and Crime,* 61st Congress, 3d Session, Senate, Doc. No. 750 (1911); Stephen Schafer, *Theories in Criminology* (1969); Edwin H. Sutherland, *Principles of Criminology* (1939); Edwin H. Sutherland and Donald R. Cressey, *Criminology* (1978); Marvin E. Wolfgang, ed., *Crime and Culture, Essays in Honor of Thorsten Sellin* (1968).

P.N.

IMMIGRANTS, economic progress. On the basis of assumptions regarding the international transferability of skills and the favorable self-selection of migrants, hypotheses have been generated regarding the progress of economic migrants and refugees in comparison with the native born. These hypotheses are found to be consistent with data from the United States (by racial and ethnic groups) and other countries. Data on males from the 1970 census indicate that, although economic migrants initially have an earnings disadvantage in comparison with the native born, their earnings rise sharply with postimmigration labor market experience and, for those who have been in the United States for eleven to fifteen years, they reach earnings equality with native-born men of the same ethnic group and the same demographic characteristics. Economic migrants in the United States for more than fifteen years tend to have higher earnings than the native born. Refugees have lower earnings than economic migrants or the native born with the same characteristics, but the large differential shortly after immigration narrows with the duration of residence. The earnings of refugees approach but do not overtake those of the native born. The sons of immigrants are found to earn 5 to 10 percent more than the sons of native-born parents with the same demographic characteristics.

Reference

Barry R. Chiswick, "The Economic Progress of Immigrants: Some Apparently Universal Patterns" in Barry R. Chiswick, ed., *The Gateway: U.S. Immigration Issues and Policies* (1982), pp. 119–158.

F.C.

IMMIGRANTS, effects of immigrants on natives' incomes. Estimates have been made (*infra*) of the composite impact in each year following the immigrants' entry, as well as a present-value estimate of the entire stream of positive and negative effects in various years. Three most important elements govern. The first is the capital-dilution effect, where a new approach is sketched to estimate the proportion of the returns to capital captured by immigrants who arrive without capital. The second is the social security transfer effect, that is, the current benefits to the native population of the immigrants' social security tax contributions. Third, there is the impact on productivity of economies of scale, the sum of learning by doing, the creation of new knowledge, and other aspects of economies of scale. The life-cycle saving-and-transfer process has a positive effect on the income of natives and is of the same order of magnitude as the estimates of the capital-dilution effect. Assessing the effect of immigrants on productivity, together with other effects, requires a dynamic macro-model; a simple one is simulated in the research (*infra*). The results indicate that within a few years the productivity effect comes to dominate and thereafter dwarfs the capital-dilution and saving-and-transfer effects. Seen as an investment, the study estimates that immigrants yield a high return to the native population.

Reference

Julian L. Simon, "The Overall Effects of Immigrants on Natives' Incomes," in Barry R. Chiswick, ed., *The Gateway: U.S. Immigration Issues and Policies* (1982), pp. 314–338.

F.C.

IMMIGRANTS, immigrant-inequality trade-offs. Williamson (*infra*) applies a multisectoral general-equilibrium two-factor (labor and land-capital) model to the period 1839–1966. This confirms that immigration did indeed tend to increase income inequality among the native population as well as among the labor force augmented by the immigrants. Demand forces, however, appear to have been far more important than immigrants in driving America over the increasing inequality part of the Kuznets curve after the 1830s. Williamson believes that the timing of the immigration quotas correlates well with American experience with immigrant-absorptive capacity; political pressure in support of quotas and their subsequent enactment were a consequence of decreases in the elasticity of the demand for labor and in the supply of native labor that implied that immigration had a substantial depressing effect on wages.

Reference
Jeffrey G. Williamson, "Immigrant-Inequality Trade-Offs in the Promised Land: Income Distribution and Absorptive Capacity Prior to the Quotas," in Barry R. Chiswick, ed., *The Gateway: U.S. Immigration Issues and Policies* (1982), pp. 251–288.

F.C.

IMMIGRANTS, immigration and religioethnic groups. The sociological concept of "social disorganization" has been elaborated by W. I. Thomas, especially in his *Polish Peasant* volumes. Thomas argued that the trauma of immigration destroyed the old agricultural values of the Polish peasant and provided him with no new set of values with which to cope with the demands of urban industrial life in the United States. The result was a collapse of the intimate social structures that make life possible and success achievable. Thomas believes that the social disorganization theory, sometimes drastically oversimplified, has had enormous impact on both policymakers and educated Americans. A consideration of the history of the Polish-Americans whom Thomas described suggests that he may well have confused the pathology of a minority with the culture of the majority of the group. Using data from the General Social Surveys and other sources, Greeley shows that Polish-Americans rapidly acculturated into American life, achieving educational, occupational, and income parity in a relatively brief period of time without necessarily shedding many of their Polish cultural characteristics. Greeley believes that the success of Polish-Americans and other European Catholics raises serious questions about the claims that other "disorganized" groups cannot be successful in American life. Some preliminary data on several ethnic groups presented by Greeley from another analysis indicate that there may be many different roads to economic success. Some immigrants first acquire high income and then high levels of schooling, while others seem to use large investments in schooling as a path to high incomes.

Reference
Andrew M. Greeley, "Immigration and Religio-Ethnic Groups: A Sociological Reappraisal," in Barry R. Chiswick, ed., *The Gateway: U.S. Immigration Issues and Policies* (1982), pp. 159–192.

F.C.

IMMIGRANTS, and labor. Immigration to the United States can be conceptualized as the movement of a labor force. While other factors, such as the pursuit of religious or political freedom, have often been involved, the mass migrations of the nineteenth and twentieth centuries have been primarily motivated by economics. Most obviously, migrants from poor countries have been attracted to job opportunities in the United States. Equally important, U.S. policies historically have encouraged immigration as a way to increase the supply of labor.

In 1791, Alexander Hamilton told Congress that it must actively pursue immigration if the U.S. economy were to develop and compete with Europe. In particular, he argued that immigration would increase the size of the work force, thereby reducing wages and bringing down the cost of American goods. To this end, the federal government, the states, and private employers engaged in immigration recruitment efforts throughout the nineteenth century.

Skilled workers were recruited from England in the early part of the century for the purpose of setting up and supervising production in the fledgling factories of the eastern seaboard. While American entrepreneurs relied on the industrial skills of these British craftsmen, the scarcity of the supply and the fact that they had already been versed in union principles made them "peculiarly difficult to deal with," as one employer put it (Earl, 1877:111).

A resolution presented itself beginning in the 1840s, in the form of mechanization coupled with the influx of hundreds of thousands of unskilled immigrants from northern Europe. Between 1845 and 1854, more than 3 million immigrants landed in the United States, which at that time had a population of only 20 million. More than half of this flow consisted of Irish immigrants who had been driven from their homeland by the potato rot and widespread famine. In earlier years, impoverished Irish had fled to the industrial centers of England, but increasingly they were brought across the Atlantic by reports of high wages and opportunities in the newly industrializing United States.

In the decades between the Civil War and the turn of the century, both industrialization and immigration increased steadily, fueling each other. The primary source of immigration moved south and east, as the Irish and Germans were replaced by Italians, Poles, and eastern European Jews. Nonetheless, the central place of these new immigrants in the emerging industrial economy of the United States paralleled that of the Irish at midcentury.

In the last four decades of the nineteenth century, 25 million immigrants entered the United States, most of whom remained in the large cities and joined the industrial work force. By 1880, more than 70 percent of the populations in each of the largest cities were immigrants or their children. Furthermore, the foreign born made up the bulk of the industrial labor force.

As Alexander Hamilton had predicted, this large influx of unskilled immigrants from Europe not only increased the actual and potential supply of labor, but reduced wages in those industries in which immigrants predominated. In some cases, for example in textiles and in the iron and steel industries, the wage reductions were the consequence of increased mechanization and the de-skilling of the work force which a plentiful supply of unskilled labor permitted. In other cases, the reductions were the direct consequence of an oversupply of labor. The building up of a surplus work force via immigration was sometimes a deliberate strategy. In the early 1880s, for example, the Lehigh Coal Company and the Philadelphia and Reading railroads brought to their region hundreds of recently arrived immigrants and put them up in company barracks, to be used as a bargaining chip when wage reductions were to be implemented.

Immigrant workers were also used as a way to erode the power of labor unions, which by the 1880s were a significant ingredient in the balance of power between workers and their employers. Desperate, usually unversed in industrial relations, and often unable to communicate with the predominantly English-speaking strikers, recently arrived immigrants seemed to offer employers the perfect solution to the increased rate and intensity of strike activity. Mine workers were particularly hard hit by this strategy. Between 1872 and 1875, fourteen major strikes backed by the Miners National Association were broken by the introduction of Swedish, Italian, and German immigrant workers. In the early 1880s, Slavic, Hungarian, and Italian immigrants were imported from New York and other ports of entry to break almost every strike in the bituminous coal regions of Pennsylvania and Ohio. In New York City, when freight workers went out on strike, they were easily replaced with immigrants from the labor exchanges that lined the streets of New York across from the Castle Garden depot where the immigrants landed.

The benefits of European immigration were frequently extolled by employers and policymakers. Andrew Carnegie (1886:35) referred to immigration as "a golden stream which flows into the country each year." *The New York Journal of Commerce* in 1892 put it bluntly: "Men, like cows, are expensive to raise and a gift of either should be gladly received. And a man can be put to more valuable use than a cow." The U.S. Industrial Commission (1901:313–314) explained that "the fact that machinery and the division of labor opens a place for the unskilled immigrants makes it possible not only to get the advantages of machinery, but also to get the advantages of cheap labor." The editor of the *Engineering and Mining Journal* (1880:335) noted approvingly that

"Castle Garden, with its hosts of immigrants, appears to be solving the labor question."

The appreciation of immigration was not unanimous, however. As domestic workers watched the de-skilling of their work and the erosion of their bargaining power, many of them reacted with alarm. In the early period, violent anti-immigrant protests were common. American and foreign-born workers battled repeatedly on the railroads and in the textile mills in the 1840s. Striking weavers in Kensington, Pennsylvania rioted in the streets in the early 1840s, setting fire to the work and homes of strike-breaking immigrant weavers.

Anti-immigrant protests took less violent forms also. "Native American" political parties were organized, such as the Know-Nothing party, which reached its peak in the mid-1850s and which had as a central campaign plank the restriction of immigration. Nativist newspapers such as *The Boston Eagle* and the New York *American Republican* emphasized the need to protect the American working class from "foreign labor competition." Petition after petition piled up in Congress in the 1840s and 1850s demanding that immigration be restricted, none of which were acted upon.

By the 1880s, labor unions in the United States had assumed unprecedented proportions. The Knights of Labor, a national labor organization that embraced skilled and unskilled labor, domestic workers and immigrants, blacks and whites, men and women, had attracted close to a million members by 1886. The successful Gould strike of 1885 is perhaps the most notable indication of the Knights of Labor's strength, as they took on Jay Gould, one of the most powerful "robber barons" of the period, and won.

While the Knights of Labor were not anti-*immigrant,* they pressed for the restriction of immigration to protect their bargaining power. In 1885, Congress, feeling pressured to respond to the increasingly powerful labor lobby, passed the Anti-Alien Contract Labor Law, which barred those with prearranged work contracts from landing. Although introduced as the "salvation of American labor," the law prohibited foreign contract labor at a time when few employers resorted to prearranged contracts, and ultimately excluded only a handful of skilled craftsmen.

U.S. immigration policy in the nineteenth century, in recognition of the central role of immigrants in the emerging capitalist economy, was for all intents and purposes an open-door policy. Until 1875, there were no restrictions of any kind on aspiring immigrants. By the end of the century, a number of so-called selective measures had been imposed, aimed at barring the diseased, convicts, prostitutes, contract laborers, and those deemed likely to become a "public charge." In addition, a law in 1882 barred all Chinese immigration. In the early years of the twentieth century, ''anarchists'' were added to the list of those excluded. Nonetheless, these selective measures (not counting the Chinese exclusions, the effect of which is difficult to quantify) combined to exclude fewer than 1 percent of the total annual flow through the first years of the twentieth century. In part, this was because the restrictions had been written carefully so as not to cut down significantly on the ''golden stream''; in part, it was because it was the attitude of the immigration inspectors, who had almost unlimited discretion in enforcing the regulations, that it was important not to interrupt the steady supply of immigrant labor to American industries.

By the second decade of the twentieth century, a number of developments caused policymakers and employers to reconsider the advantages of an unlimited supply of immigrant workers from Europe. In the first place, the American Federation of Labor, with its focus on skilled craftsmen, replaced the more inclusive Knights of Labor as the most powerful American labor union. As immigrant workers were excluded from mainstream unions, they formed more marginal and often more militant unions of their own. The early twentieth century thus saw a subtle yet pronounced reversal, as more secure and conservative skilled domestic workers were increasingly reluctant to join strikes, while immigrant workers with little to lose provided the backbone of the more militant labor movement, sometimes having their strikes broken by domestic workers.

In addition, a minority of new immigrants from Europe were joining socialist and anarchist political organizations. While the fear of the radical potential of the new immigrants was probably exaggerated by alarmed policymakers, nonetheless the socialist political parties and organizations of the early twentieth century did count disproportionate numbers of new immigrants among their members.

Finally, racist theories of immigrants' genetic inferiority were increasing in popularity and garnered pseudo-scientific support at this time. Immigrants from southern and eastern Europe were pronounced racially inferior, ''feeble-minded,'' and in general predisposed to lives of poverty, criminality, and radicalism. In other words, the new European immigrants from southern and eastern Europe—deemed genetically inferior—were getting a reputation as troublemakers, increasingly forming the vanguard of strikes, enlisting in radical political organizations, and of course more often than not remaining in the United States to become permanent members of society.

It was in this context that Mexican migration gained momentum. The Dillingham Commission of 1911, which issued a forty-two-volume report on immigration, responded to the concerns over European immigrants, and suggested that Mexican labor might be a viable substitute. In fact, the commission argued, Mexican workers would constitute a preferable labor source, given the vicinity of Mexico, the expectation that Mexicans—as compared to Europeans—would be less likely to remain to become citizens, and the greater flexibility that this provided.

Initially, the overwhelming majority of Mexican immigrants to the United States were legally admitted. In fact, the most significant restrictions of the period explicitly exempted Mexicans from their orbit, in recognition of their importance as a back-door source of labor. When the literacy test requirement was passed in 1917, Mexicans were singled out for exemption from the requirement for the duration of World War I. As the war came to a close, Secretary of Labor Wilson and Immigration Commissioner Caminetti agreed to extend the Mexican exemption, in response to warnings from southwestern growers that the success of their harvests depended on a plentiful supply of Mexican workers. When the quota restrictions of 1921 and 1924 dramatically reduced European immigration, once again Mexico—along with other Western Hemisphere countries—was exempt.

In part as a result of these policies and employers' recruitment efforts, legal immigration from Mexico went from 11,000 a year in 1915 to 51,000 a year by 1920. Although most of the Mexican migrants were initially employed in southwestern agriculture, as World War I and later the restrictions of the 1920s cut down on the flow of Europeans, industries as far north as Chicago drew increasing numbers of Mexicans into their work force.

From 1942 to 1964, Mexican contract laborers, called braceros, were imported to work temporarily in U.S. agriculture through a series of bilateral agreements between the United States and Mexico. It was during the bracero period that illegal migration from Mexico substantially increased. Indeed, U.S. policies seemed to encourage the illegal flow. For example, the agreement of 1949 gave preference for employment to illegal Mexican workers apprehended in the United States over new braceros brought from Mexico. The U.S. Border Patrol sometimes took the apprehended aliens to the Mexican border, had them step to the Mexican side, and brought them back as legal braceros. In other cases, undocumented workers were "paroled" directly to employers. The Presidential Commission on Migratory Labor estimated in 1951 that from 1947 to 1949, more than 142,000 undocumented Mexican workers were legalized in this way, at a time when only 74,000 new braceros came from Mexico. By the end of the bracero programs in 1964, 5 million new braceros had been admitted and another 5 million illegal Mexican workers had been apprehended in the United States.

A congressional decision in 1952 had the effect of making employers immune to any risk involved in employing illegal aliens. The McCarran-Walter Act of 1952 made it illegal to "harbor, transport, and conceal illegal entrants." However, the Texas Proviso, named after the

Texas growers to whom it was a concession, excluded employment from the category of harboring. This amendment, as implemented by the Immigration and Naturalization Service, constituted a virtual carte blanche for the employment of undocumented workers.

Nurtured by economic imbalances between the United States and Mexico, recruitment schemes, and U.S. policies, a relationship of symbiosis between Mexican immigrants and U.S. employers had become well entrenched by the mid-twentieth century. However, the attitude of U.S. policymakers toward Mexican workers has not been unequivocal. Expulsions and roundups of Mexican workers and their families during the Great Depression of the 1930s and again during ''Operation Wetback'' in 1954 reflect the ambivalence of policymakers toward the Mexican work force. These roundups are indicative of more than ambivalence, however; they reveal the long-held view of Mexican labor as *flexible,* to be welcomed during periods of high demand and deported when the demand has waned.

The decades following the bracero period have been characterized by increased international migration, both documented and undocumented. The contemporary period has also witnessed the increased incorporation of Mexican and other migrants into sectors outside of agriculture. It has been estimated that in the early 1980s, approximately 85 percent of undocumented Mexican workers are employed in urban sectors of the economy.

Expressions of a concern to restrict illegal immigration have accompanied these increases in undocumented immigration and the increased visibility of undocumented workers in urban areas. Beginning in the early 1970s, Congress began considering ''employer sanctions'' legislation which would make it illegal to knowingly employ undocumented workers and would essentially close the Texas Proviso loophole. The Immigration Reform and Control Act of 1986 includes such an employer sanctions provision as its centerpiece.

Opponents of employer sanctions, in addition to their concern over its potential to unleash discrimination against those who look ''foreign,'' have argued that undocumented workers are critical to certain sectors of the U.S. economy, such as agriculture, food processing, the garment industry, construction, building maintenance, etc. Others have pointed to the difficulties of enforcing such a law, as it requires that prosecutors can prove that employers were privy to their workers' undocumented status. Certainly, reversing the long-standing pattern of undocumented migration and employment presents a significant challenge for any single piece of legislation. The task is compounded by the ongoing economic imbalances between Mexico and the United States and the economic reality of employers' dependence on this source of labor.

References
Kitty Calavita, *U.S. Immigration Law and the Control of Labor, 1820–1924* (1984);
Andrew Carnegie, *Triumphant Democracy, or Fifty Years March of the Republic* (1886);
H. H. Earl, *A Centennial History of Fall River* (1877); *Engineering and Mining Journal*
(1880); Phillip Foner, *History of the Labor Movement in the United States*, vols. 1 and 2
(1955, 1962); Manuel Garcia y Griego, *The Importation of Mexican Contract Laborers to
the United States, 1942–1964: Antecedents, Operation and Legacy* (1981); Herbert Gutman, *Work, Culture and Society in Industrializing America: Essays in American Working-
Class and Social History* (1976); *The New York Journal of Commerce* (1892); U.S.
Congress, House Industrial Commission, *Reports of the Industrial Commission* (1901);
Gwendolyn Mink, *Old Labor and New Immigrants* (1987); Thomas R. Bailey, *Immigrant
and Native Workers* (1987).

K.C.

IMMIGRANTS IN THE OLD SOUTH. Looking at the southern region as a whole, immigration seemed to have made little impression
before the Civil War, and even less during it. During the antebellum
period the South lacked immigrants and, so, ordered its world in terms
of race rather than ethnicity. According to the 1860 federal census, the
total foreign-born population of the eleven states that would make up
the Confederacy was negligible. The percentage of foreign born in
Alabama stood at 1.28 percent of the total population, in Georgia at
1.10 percent, in South Carolina at 1.42 percent, and in Virginia at 2.19
percent. Only Texas, with 7.19 percent, and Louisiana, with 11.44
percent, had foreign-born populations of more than 2.5 percent of their
total populations in 1860.

It had not always been so. During the eighteenth century the back-
country areas of Virginia, the Carolinas, and Georgia had swollen with
Germans, Scotch-Irish, and other European immigrants traveling down
the Great Wagon Road from Pennsylvania. Various religious colonies
also sprouted across the tidewater area. For instance, German Salz-
burgers established Ebenezer in Georgia,; German Moravians settled in
Georgia and North Carolina; and French Huguenots sought refuge in
South Carolina. The multiethnic South did not last, however, for during
and after the American Revolution immigration to the South flagged.
By 1820 the children and grandchildren of the earlier immigrants
largely had been absorbed into the great white southern mass, with only
the abundant Celtic surnames of many southern families echoing a once
rich immigrant past. Pockets of Germans in the Shenandoah retained
their German culture, but elsewhere the South had been transformed
from a multiethnic society into a biracial one.

When the great wave of immigration broke over America during
the 1830s and after, the South felt the impact much less than did the
North. The main Atlantic shipping lines that European immigrants used
to reach America favored northern ports. The North's expanding indus-

trial economy clamored for workers, and the liberal credit policies of land companies in the midwestern states lured immigrants there. Southern agricultural development did not require large numbers of foreign workers, and southern soil and climate did not suit the skills or constitutions of northern European immigrants. Slavery also made the South less appealing to prospective settlers. Finally, the growing southern sense of regional identity, rooted in agrarian beliefs and the mythology of a white *herrenvolk* democracy, scorned immigrants as dangerous in their cultural diversity, economic poverty, and political unreliability. The absence of immigrants, like the presence of slavery, distinguished the South from the North, and white southerners wore their homogeneity proudly. At midcentury only 5 percent of the free southern population had been born outside the United States, while one Northerner in seven was foreign born. By 1860 the margin had widened further.

Looking at the whole South, however, distorts the peculiar nature of immigration to the Old South. Various immigrant strains entered the region and came to define the social and cultural landscape of particular locales. During the 1820s and 1830s, especially, various German colonization societies attempted, with mixed success, to settle immigrants in Texas and Missouri. Pockets of German settlers cropped up in those states, and survived well into the twentieth century. Despite failures among the colonization companies, most dramatically of the Adelsverein project, good reports of land and liberty emanated from Germans in Texas and Missouri and persuaded others in Europe to follow them there. Germans clustered in the "German belt" of south-central Texas, where by force of numbers and fact of geographic isolation they reconstructed much of their Old World culture—much, but not all. In Texas, as in Missouri and in the Shenandoah, the settlers adapted to local building materials, livestock preferences, soils, crops, and marketing needs, even as they cultivated distinctive Texas-German, Missouri-German, and Shenandoah-German dialects, housing styles, crafts, and customs. Similarly, one hundred Upper Silesian Polish families in 1854 walked from Galveston to settle Panna Maria in south-central Texas, establishing what became the oldest Polish Catholic parish in the United States; they and their descendants lived in relative seclusion for almost a century and created a Texas Polonia of sorts. The Germans and Poles, like other groups of immigrants living in isolated circumstances in Alabama, Tennessee, and North Carolina, did not alter the balance of southern political power; indeed, rural immigrants largely avoided politics, turning inward to their own institutions and conceding to the host culture its insistence on slavery and a conservative social order. As such, they remained unnoticed by both contemporaries and historians.

Immigration had a major impact on southern urban life. Indeed, immigrants made southern cities less southern in the late antebellum period and more like northern ones. Immigration was the principal reason that southern cities grew substantially in population during the 1840s and 1850s. Immigrants came directly to the South via such port cities as New Orleans, Galveston, Mobile, Savannah, and Charleston. During the 1850s New Orleans became the nation's second leading port of entry for immigrants, and, indeed, between 1847 and 1857 roughly 350,000 immigrants disembarked there. Despite the extra length, and sometimes expense, of the journey from the principal European sending ports of Liverpool, Le Havre, Bremen, and Hamburg to New Orleans, many immigrants chose the Crescent City to gain ready access to the Mississippi River system connecting them with midwestern destinations. Probably few of the immigrants, especially the Germans and Irish who made up the vast majority of immigrants entering the South during the 1840s and 1850s, expected to stay in the region, but poverty, disease, and circumstance forced many of them to remain in New Orleans or in River cities along the journey northward. Thus, the mid-South gained a large and impoverished immigrant population by default—a fact that explained in part the more volatile immigrant-related politics in such cities as New Orleans, Memphis, and Louisville, as compared to eastern seacoast cities which also had large immigrant populations. Immigrants also traveled southward from northern communities, in search of jobs or in efforts to reunite with family members in southern cities. A regular traffic of seasonal migration developed between New York and Charleston, for example, as Irish immigrants sought employment in seasonal trades.

During the 1850s southern cities became immigrant cities. In 1860 40 percent of New Orleans' total population was foreign born, as compared to only 36 percent in Boston. In St. Louis 60 percent of the total population was foreign born, a higher proportion than that in New York, Chicago, or Milwaukee. More revealing in terms of the social and political dynamics of southern cities, however, was the high percentage of immigrants in the adult white population. Until the massive immigrant tide of the 1840s and 1850s, southern cities had been getting darker in population. Immigration restored white numerical majorities in such cities as Charleston and New Orleans. Immigrants accounted for almost all the increase in the urban white population during this period. Representative figures include: in New Orleans in 1860 immigrants constituted 70 percent of the adult (eighteen years or older), white, male urban population; in Charleston, the figures were 45 percent in 1850 and 49 percent in 1860; in Savannah they were 37 percent in 1850 and 51 percent in 1860; and in Memphis, they were 35 percent in 1850 and 49 percent in 1860. Even inland cities recorded significant infusions of immigrants (e.g., in Augusta immigrants made up 35 percent of the adult, white, male population in 1860, and in Richmond they constituted 34 percent of that cohort in 1860). Even including blacks and counting total population, the immigrant presence was conspicuous. In Louisville, for example, they made up 34 percent of the total population in 1860, in Mobile 24 percent, and in Natchez 25 percent.

In the major cities immigrants clustered in the poorer districts. In Memphis Irish crowded into "the Pinch" and Happy Hollow" along the riverfront; in Richmond the topography created isolated pockets of Irish, German, and blacks along Shockoe Creek and the James River, near factories and wharves; in Charleston, Irish immigrants lived by the city's warehouses and docks in what Frederick Law Olmsted called "packing filth, and squalor" equal to anything he had seen in Europe; in Savannah, Irish immigrants huddled in "squalid, cheerless negro huts" along the city's outskirts where rents were cheapest; and in New Orleans, Germans made Carrollton a German preserve. Population distribution varied according to place, however, and southern cities were so small in geographic and population size that physical and cultural isolation was not possible.

The immigrant influence was vitiated by the transiency of immigrants and the fact that immigration virtually ended with the Civil War. No significant immigration to southern cities would occur again until southern Italians appeared in New Orleans late in the century. Immigrant-based institutions founded in the eighteenth century had admitted persons regardless of ethnic background and had long metamorphosed into social clubs for the upper classes. The newer immigrant arrivals of the 1840s and 1850s lacked the standing to enter established "ethnic" institutions and had no resources to build their own. Save for their churches, they seemed not have been directed toward organizational activities. Only in New Orleans (among the French and the Germans) did an ethnic press and associational life prosper. French immigrants moved easily in the native French Creole culture. New Orleans sustained a German theater, musical societies, and beer gardens, but even there the Germans were so divided among themselves by class, region of origin, religion, and interest that the German influence remained largely inwardly directed rather than affecting the city culture as a whole. Within the churches immigrants battled for local control in appointing pastors, insisting on preaching in their native tongues, and in pushing particular rituals and devotional practices. The Catholic church, especially, felt the force of competing immigrant groups; ethnic differences were grafted onto issues of lay trusteeism and Germans demanded German preachers and parishes and, in New Orleans, French-speaking Catholics refused to yield their liberal Catholicism to the more austere Irish.

The heavy immigration of the 1840s and 1850s fundamentally altered the size, composition, and character of the working classes of southern cities. Indeed, by 1860 foreign-born workers were the principal source of free labor in all important southern river and port cities. The presence of large numbers of immigrant workers considerably eroded the already precarious economic position of free blacks in several cities. The increased labor pool gave employers an advantage in contracting for work, undermining the wage structure and other understandings black workers and white employers had established over time. Immigrants drove free blacks out of occupations as diverse as drayage, smithing, and fitting ships and into manual labor. Slave owners fought off demands by white workers to enforce municipal regulations against hiring out slaves in trades, but even slaves did not escape competition from immigrant workers. It was not wholly coincidental that as urban slavery declined, the immigrant working class increased. The agricultural flush times of the 1850s drew slaves away from cities to the countryside, leaving most urban craft trades to immigrants. Immigration, then, left blacks in a dangerously weakened economic position by 1860, less in control of skilled occupations and more tied to agricultural and manual labor.

The immigrants' poverty forced them to mix with blacks, sometimes violently, and made them suspect in native-born white southerners' eyes. The disproportionately male composition of the immigrants added to the social danger the immigrants posed to urban order—a fact southern politicians noted with apprehension. Southern cities beefed up police forces, ironically often by hiring immigrants, to control immigrant and black behavior. Nativism emerged in the 1850s, directed especially against Irish Catholics, who were accused of rowdyism, drunkenness, and consorting with blacks, even as they fought them for jobs and place. Weaned on a vigorous anti-Catholicism, the evangelical Protestant majority in the South feared the Catholic presence growing in the region. Already suspicious of urban culture, the rural southern white majority recoiled from the increasingly foreign nature of southern cities. Epidemic diseases, especially yellow fever, which raged throughout the antebellum period, afflicted southern cities first and immigrants most of all (because of the miserable sanitary conditions where they lived and worked, their inability to escape when epidemics began, and their lack of acclimation), further confirming in southern minds that immigrants threatened the region. Election riots involving Irish immigrants in Louisville and New Orleans in the mid-1850s fueled nativism. Amid the sectional crisis of the 1850s, defenders of southern institutions declaimed the order and virtue of southern society and institutions; the presence of immigrants bringing to southern cities all the social, political, and cultural ills of northern society was a danger southern apologists scarcely could ignore. Nativism did not consume southern cities during the 1850s because it was too diffuse, varying according to locale, and because most immigrants remained apolitical or at least overtly supportive of slavery and white dominance. Urban politicians acknowledged the immigrant presence by adding Irish and German names to election ballots, but immigrants were as yet too unorganized to claim effective political power.

Still, immigration forced southerners to grapple with the reality of cultural and social diversity, even as defenders of the South were constructing the myth of a monolithic, agrarian South. The master class resolved the dilemma by denying the existence of immigrants in the Old South, and subsequent southern architects of the Lost Cause were even more strident in insisting on the Anglo-Saxon purity of the white South. Thus, the immigrants in the Old South were lost in memory and to history.

References
Ira Berlin and Herbert G. Gutman, "Natives and Immigrants, Free Men and Slaves: Urban Workingmen in the Antebellum American South," *American Historical Review* 88 (1983): 1175–1200; Nathan M. Kaganoff and Melvin I. Urofsky, eds., *"Turn to the South": Essays on Southern Jewry* (1979); Ella Lonn, *Foreigners in the Confederacy* (1940); Randall M. Miller, "The Enemy Within: Some Effects of Foreign Immigrants on Antebellum Southern Cities," *Southern Studies* 24 (1985): 30–53; Randall M. Miller, "Immigrants in the Old South," *Immigration History Newsletter* 10 (Nov. 1978): 8–14; Randall M. Miller and Jon L. Wakelyn, eds., *Catholics in the Old South* (1983); John F. Nau, *The German People of New Orleans* (1958); Earl F. Niehaus, *The Irish in New Orleans, 1800–1860*; Klaus Wust, *The Virginia Germans* (1978).

R.M.M.

IMMIGRANTS, and organized benevolence. In the years between 1815 and 1865 the leaders of eight national benevolent societies tried, from their offices in Boston, Philadelphia, and New York, to mold the vigorous, growing immigrant nation. Lay people and clergy of several Protestant denominations, but mostly Presbyterians and Congregationalists, formed the American Education Society to subsidize poor ministerial students; the American Home Missionary Society to subsidize indigent pastors; the American Bible Society to publish and circulate the Holy Writ; the American Sunday School Union to issue religious and moral works for children; and the American Tract Society to guide adults. To stop wars, liquor drinking, and slavery they founded the American Peace Society, the American Society for the Promotion of Temperance, and the American Antislavery Society. At first the leaders attempted to persuade other men and women to be good by ministerial preaching and by millions of books and tracts distributed by thousands of agents and auxiliary societies. But a combination of failure and impatience produced political action. These self-styled stewards of the Lord demanded laws to stop wars, Sabbath profanation, liquor selling, and slavery's expansion. They tried to get Bibles and other religious books into common schools. And because all of the leaders feared the political and religious power of Catholics and other immigrants, they called for discriminatory ordinances against them.

Reference
Clifford S. Griffin, "Organized Benevolence in the United States, 1815–1865," Ph.D. dissertation, University of Wisconsin, Madison, 1957.

F.C.

IMMIGRANTS, supply of immigrants to the United States. This study (*infra*) adopts a short-run perspective by analyzing a cross section of international migration flows to the United States from as many origin countries as the available data allow. It develops and estimates a model to explain the international distribution of emigration from each of several countries of origin around the world to the receiving countries. A major conclusion emerging from this analysis is that observed emigration from many countries to the United States is substantially less than is predicted by the model, suggesting that U.S. immigration law is a binding constraint. If entry barriers were removed, Western Hemisphere nations appear most likely to supply the United States with large increases in immigrants. The study examines immigration to the United States from the perspective of the United States; that is, using U.S. data on immigration, it analyzes migration to the United States from various countries of origin. The model includes variables designed to capture the influences of differential economic advantage and variables intended to reflect the costs of transferring skills to the United States from abroad (as measured by the similarity of occupational structure). Distance and the earnings differentials appear to be important factors affecting the rate of migration from various countries to the United States. Another factor increasing the rate of immigration is a higher level of economic development in the sending country. Similarly, the availability of social security for the aged in the countries of origin discourages migration by the aged. Finally, the ability of prospective immigrants to transfer their occupational knowledge from their native country to the U.S. labor market is also an important influence on U.S. immigration rates.

Reference
Michael J. Greenwood and John M. McDowell, "The Supply of Immigrants to the United States," in Barry R. Chiswick, ed., *The Gateway: U.S. Immigration Issues and Policies* (1982), pp. 54–85.

F.C.

IMMIGRANTS' PROTECTIVE LEAGUE OF CHICAGO. Largely founded in 1908 as the result of the efforts in behalf of immigrants by Jane

Addams (*q.v.*) and Grace Abbott (*q.v.*). The league proved a failure because it never attracted nearly enough support to achieve broad governmental programs for immigrants. Nevertheless, it was "a serious attempt to deal with the 'immigration problem' in an imaginative, enlightened and humane way."

Reference
Henry B. Leonard, "The Immigrants' Protective League of Chicago, 1908–1921," *Journal of the Illinois State Historical Society* 66 (1973): 271–284.

F.C.

IMMIGRATION ACT OF 1924 (43 Stat. 153). The Immigration Act, or Johnson Bill, of 1924 marked the culmination of a crusade to restrict permanently the entry of central and southeastern Europeans into the United States. After a long legislative battle congressional forces successfully mustered sufficient support to stem the ingress of Italians, Poles, Slavs, and Jews, who, they believed, had inundated the country. Moreover, the measure prohibited Japanese immigration by abrogating the Gentlemen's Agreement (*q.v.*) which subsequently produced a major diplomatic crisis. Opponents of restriction charged that the act was un-American and discriminatory and that its basis rested on the anthropological theory of Nordic superiority. Proponents, on the other hand, hailed the new law as "the longest step forward ever taken in stabilizing the economic and political future" of the country and as representing "the greatest piece of constructive legislation which has come out of Washington in a generation."

References
Robert A. Devine, *American Immigration Policy, 1924–1952* (1957; rpt. 1972); Peter H. Wang, "Legislating 'Normalcy': The Immigration Act of 1924," Ph.D. dissertation, University of California, Riverside, 1971 (DA 32: 2626A).

F.C.

IMMIGRATION ACT OF 1965. David M. Reimers (who has called the Immigration Act of 1965 "a cautious reform") reminds us that

> Eradicating discrimination against Third World countries was not the focal point of those who disapproved of American immigration policies. Rather, critics urged a number of reforms, several of which would have benefited potential migrants from Third World nations, but the center of their critique was the national origins system embedded in the McCarran-Walter Act. Both Harry S. Truman and Dwight D. Eisenhower criticized policies established by the McCarran-Walter Act. In his veto message Truman declared, "The basis of this quota system was false and unworthy in 1924. It is even worse now. At the present time, this quota system

keeps out the very people we want to bring in. It is incredible to me that, in this year of 1952, we should again be enacting into law such a slur on the patriotism, the capacity, and the decency of a large part of our citizenry.'' (Reimers, 63)

By 1965, it was clear that the national origins system had to be changed:

In addition to the fact that the prevailing immigration system had been rendered obsolete, it is also true that the nation's attitudes toward race and ethnic background had changed dramatically by the early 1960s. The Civil Rights movement, which had begun in earnest in 1957 with the Montgomery, Alabama, bus boycott, had culminated in the passage of the Civil Rights Act of 1964 and the Voting Rights Act of 1965. Thus, it has been observed: ''The 1965 immigration legislation was as much a product of the mid-sixties and the heavily Democratic 89th Congress which produced major civil rights legislation as the 1952 Act was product of the Cold War period of the early 1950s.'' Just as overt racism could no longer be tolerated in the way citizens treated their fellow citizens, neither could it be sanctioned in the laws that governed the way in which noncitizens were considered for immigrant status. (Briggs, 62)

The Hart-Celler Act of 1965 eliminated national origins as the basis for selection of immigrants to the United States. Instead, it established an annual limit of 170,000 aliens (and a per country quota of 20,000) who could enter the United States as immigrants. It set a ceiling of 120,000 on immigration from the Western Hemisphere, thus allowing (with the annual limit of 170,000 elsewhere) for the admission of 290,000 immigrants a year. The act, further, established a system whereby immigration visas would be distributed according to a seven-point preference list that favored close relatives of U.S. citizens and those with special occupational skills. The definition of refugees was broadened to include those who were victims of natural calamities, as well as the victims of religious and/or political persecution. Three categories of exclusion were established: (1) people with mental disease and drug and alcohol addicts; (2) criminals, prostitutes, and those with contagious diseases; and (3) subversives and some twenty other categories of aliens. Continuing immigration reforms included the passage of legislation for the admission and resettlement of refugees, mainly from the Soviet Union, Southeast Asia, and Cuba, e.g., the Indochinese Refugee Resettlement Program which allowed the admission of 200,000 Indochinese refugees. In 1980, the Refugee Act established an overall policy for the admission and resettlement of refugees.

The Immigration Act of 1965 had unanticipated consequences:

> The United States was giving itself the moral satisfaction of pass-
> ing a nondiscriminatory immigration act that it expected would in
> no substantial way change the sources or volume of American
> immigration. The people who were fighting for the bill were Jews,
> Italians, Greeks, Poles, who hoped their relatives, their fellow
> countrymen, and their co-religionists would have an easier time
> getting in, and the bill itself favored strongly the principle of
> family unification. But the prophets were wrong. It turned out the
> chief beneficiaries of the new immigration regime were Asians and
> Latin Americans. Starting from a modest base, the number of
> Asian immigrants increased rapidly; and as they increased family
> reunification played a greater and greater role in enabling immi-
> gration and resulted in steadily larger numbers of immigrants from
> Hong Kong and Taiwan, the Philippines, Korea, and India. The
> disaster in Vietnam added Vietnamese, Cambodians, and Lao-
> tians. In the decade of the 1970s, astonishingly, the number of
> Asians in the United States doubled to three-and-a-half million. It
> will undoubtedly double again in the course of the 1980s. In 1984
> six out of the first seven countries, by size of number of immi-
> grants sent to the United States, were Asian. But the first was
> Mexico. And that, too, was not foreseen by the reformers of 1965.
> Thus a bill that had been expected to remove discrimination
> against the countries of southern and Eastern Europe, that had
> been passed by the political weight of immigrants from those
> countries and their children and grandchildren who had become
> warp and woof of the United States, benefited others and was
> taken advantage of by others. For Europe, too, was benefiting
> from post-war prosperity. There was no longer any strong demand
> from Europe to enter the United States. Europe's standards of
> living approached and in some countries surpassed that of the
> United States, its social benefits certainly surpassed that of the
> United States, class boundaries there were increasingly a thing of
> the past, and educational opportunities expanded and abounded.
> What need for the United States? (Glazer, 7–8)

References
Vernon M. Briggs, Jr., *Immigration Policy and the American Labor Force* (1984);
Francesco Cordasco, *The New American Immigration* (1987); Nathan Glazer, ed.,
Clamor at the Gates: The New American Immigration (1985); David M. Reimers, *Still the
Golden Door: The Third World Comes to America* (1985).

F.C.

IMMIGRATION, American Immigration and Ethnic History. In
the study of the history of immigration and ethnicity scholars very often
write about their own ethnic groups. That pattern has led to an over-
emphasis on the new immigrants of the early twentieth century, a lim-

itation of focus to the experiences of the first and second generations of individual immigrant groups, and a disinterest in immigration and ethnicity as processes. Efforts to produce comparative studies of various kinds and to use survey data as a source of primary information about later generations may help correct those shortcomings.

Reference

Thomas J. Archdeacon, "Problems and Possibilities in the Study of American Immigration and Ethnic History," *International Migration Review* 19 (Spring 1985): 112–134.

F.C.

IMMIGRATION AND NATIONALITY ACT OF 1952. *See* McCarran-Walter Act of 1952.

IMMIGRATION AND NATIONALITY ACT OF 1952, Section 245. Aliens who wish to immigrate to the U.S. generally must request a permanent visa from a consular office abroad. Sometimes an alien in the United States under a temporary visa desires to immigrate. To eliminate the inconvenience of leaving the United States to apply for a permanent visa, Section 245 allows qualified aliens to remain within the United States and request an adjustment of status. This procedure has been abused, and has been corrected in the Immigration Reform and Control Act of 1986 (*q.v.*).

Reference

Tamara K. Fogg, "Adjustment of Status Under Section 245 of the Immigration and Nationality Act," *San Diego Law Review* 20 (1983): 165–189.

F.C.

IMMIGRATION AND NATIONALITY ACT OF 1981. The Immigration and Nationality Act Amendments of 1981 (Pub. L. No. 97–116). During the past session of the 97th Congress, the bill, which was referred to as the "efficiency bill," passed the House by a voice vote on October 13, 1981 and was received in the Senate on October 14, 1981. Its purpose is to improve the efficiency of the Immigration and Naturalization Service, to provide clarification of certain provisions of the Immigration and Nationality Act, and in some cases to eliminate the need for Congress to consider private immigration bills. With the exception of a few provisions relating to students, foreign medical students, and the retention of fees by naturalization courts, the new law went into effect December 29, 1981.

Reference

Austin T. Fragomen, Jr., "Immigration and Nationality Act of 1981," *International Migration Review* 16 (Spring 1982): 206–222.

F.C.

IMMIGRATION, capital value and relative wage effects.
Schachter's study presents an estimate of the capital value of net immigration into the United States from 1870 to 1930. This was done by valuing an immigrant as a productive asset with earnings over time. In addition, this dissertation also presents evidence on the relative wage effects of immigration from 1870 to 1910. The capital value of net immigration into the United States from 1870 to 1930 is found to be equal to $109.7 billion. This figure was obtained on the basis of the occupations that immigrants adopted after settling in the United States. These occupations were derived from decennial census data on the occupations of the foreign-born population of the United States. If we take into account the maximum effect of skill upgrading of the occupational distribution of immigrants that took place after they entered the United States, then the capital value of net immigration from 1870 to 1930 is reduced by 15.2 percent to $93 billion. An examination of the occupational distribution of both the foreign-born population and immigrants shows that, contrary to the widely held belief, the "old immigration," i.e., immigration from northern and western Europe, was less skilled than the "new immigration," i.e., immigration from eastern and southern Europe.

Reference
Joseph Schachter, "Capital Value and Relative Wage Effects of Immigration into the United States, 1870–1930," Ph.D. dissertation, City University of New York, 1969.

F.C.

IMMIGRATION, decline of internationalism in the American working-class movement. Because the impact of immigration was felt most directly by the working class, it was inevitable that the working-class movement itself developed perspectives on immigration—perspectives that took into account the sectional interests of American workers. In broad outline, the perspectives that emerged closely paralleled the level of trade union development: During the early years of the "old" immigration the trade-union movement was characterized by the predominance of preindustrial craft unions. These unions—represented by the National Labor Union and later by the Knights of Labor—considered only one aspect of immigration, imported contract labor, to be a problem. They neither felt threatened by nor opposed free immigration, and their perspective was moderately internationalist.

Reference
Charles R. Leinenweber, "Immigration and the Decline of Internationalism in the American Working Class Movement, 1864–1919," Ph.D. dissertation, University of California, Berkeley, 1969.

F.C.

IMMIGRATION, economic aspects. Thomas Muller states:

> On balance, the economic benefits of immigration, based on our knowledge so far, tend to exceed private and in some areas public costs. However, serious research on the impact of recent immigration has merely begun. Further analysis may show that as a result of structural changes in the nation's economy, the effects of immigration are less positive than current information suggests. More likely are future findings showing that from an economic perspective immigrants are a plus to the nation. This should lead to a more thorough assessment of such noneconomic issues as social integration, language, and the environment.

Reference
Thomas Muller, "Economic Aspects of Immigration," in Nathan Glazer, ed., *Clamor at the Gates: The New American Immigration* (1985), pp. 109–133.

F.C.

IMMIGRATION, economic perspective. An effective American immigration policy has been complicated by the diversity of political interests and the absence of reliable statistics to determine the magnitude of the impact on the American economy. Estimates of the number of illegal aliens in the United States range from one to twelve million. While political biases and complexities and data inadequacies complicate our analysis, some generalizations seem to be confirmed by worldwide experience.

Reference
F. Ray Marshall, "Immigration: An International Economic Perspective," *International Migration Review* 18 (Fall 1984): 593–612.

F.C.

IMMIGRATION, ethnic stratification and native workers. A number of notions regarding the functions served by international labor immigration, especially the undocumented population, have been studied. Comparisons of the working conditions of documented and undocumented Dominicans in New York City have been made. Although the two groups resemble one another in terms of organization and industrial sector of employment, the organization of their respective firms is markedly different. It has been concluded that one of the most important functions served by the illegal alien population is political and resides in its controllability by employers in the secondary labor market and, consequently, operates to discipline the native labor force.

Reference
Sherri Grasmuck, "Immigration, Ethnic Stratification, and Native Working Class Disci-

pline: Comparisons of Documented and Undocumented Dominicans," *International Migration Review* 18 (Fall 1984): 692–713.

F.C.

IMMIGRATION, gainful workers into the United States, 1870–1930. This study (*q.v.*) presents socioeconomic occupational groupings of the foreign-born gainful workers of the United States at each census from 1870 through 1930. The series is then used to estimate the net immigration of gainful workers into the United States during each of the six decades from 1870 to 1930, cross-classified by occupational group and sex. Three conclusions are drawn from the above series. First, the socioeconomic position of the foreign-born population of the United States remained relatively stable from 1870 to 1910 but then increased appreciably from 1910 to 1930. Second, although most of the contribution that immigration made to the United States labor force was in the form of semiskilled and unskilled workers, the relative importance of professional, clerical, and skilled workers increased almost continuously from 1870 to 1930. Third, the "new immigration" was actually more skilled than the "old immigration."

Reference
J. Schachter, "Net Immigration of Gainful Workers Into the United States, 1870–1930," *Demography* 9 (Feb. 1972): 87–105.

F.C.

IMMIGRATION HISTORY RESEARCH CENTER, University of Minnesota (826 Berry Street, St. Paul, Minnesota 55114). An international center for the collection and preservation of the historical records of immigrants who came to the United States and Canada. See Rudolph J. Vecoli, "The Immigrant Studies Collection of the University of Minnesota," *American Archivist* 32 (April 1969): 139–145.

F.C.

IMMIGRATION, impact on level and distribution of economic well-being. Immigration tends to raise the income of the native population but to change the distribution of this income. The different impacts of high-skilled and low-skilled immigrants are considered. A dynamic element is introduced when the model allows for changing impacts as the relative skills of immigrants increase with their duration of residence. When an income transfer system (welfare, social services, and social overhead capital financed prior to the immigration) is introduced, income redistribution programs can make all native-born groups at least as affluent as before the migration. This cannot occur, however, if the immigrants themselves are substantial net recipients of these transfers. It could not occur, for example, if the immigrants were low-skilled workers and had access to the income transfer system equal to that of native-born, low-skilled workers. An immigrant tax (large visa fee or immigrant income tax surcharge) that captures some of the economic rent that visa recipients receive would raise the aggregate income of the native population and increase the annual number of visas that the United States would be willing to issue. Such a scheme would still provide opportunities for refugee and family reunification migration.

Reference
Barry R. Chiswick, "The Impact of Immigration on the Level and Distribution of Economic Well-Being," in Barry R. Chiswick, ed., *The Gateway: U.S. Immigration Issues and Policies* (1982), pp. 289–313.

F.C.

IMMIGRATION, impact on United States population size. During the nineteenth and much of the twentieth century, natural increase accounted for a substantial portion of all population growth. Recently, the contribution of net immigration has increased considerably. If both legal and illegal entries are included, close to half of all growth can now be attributed to net immigration. This is even greater than the impact of immigration on U.S. population growth in the late nineteenth century and first decade of this century, when waves of European immigrants arriving in the United States in search of a new life totaled as high as one million in some years.

Reference
Leon F. Bouvier, *The Impact of Immigration on U.S. Population Size* (1981).

F.C.

IMMIGRATION LAW, enforcing immigration law. Harwood (*infra*) states:

> When he declared that America had "lost control over its borders," the Reagan administration's Attorney General, William French Smith, was merely stating a truism familiar to all. References to the "revolving door" at our southern border or, more generally, to the "immigration crisis" have become stock cliches. They refer to a breakdown in immigration enforcement that began during the late 1960s, accelerated during the 1970s, and continues to the present time. Although the number of illegal aliens living in the U.S. is not known, a conservative estimate of from three to six million is accepted by most scholars. Estimates of the net annual influx of illegal immigrants coming to the U.S. range from

200,000 to 500,000. Whether the level of illegal immigration constitutes a "social problem" for our society is hotly disputed by scholars. Economists and policy analysts can be found on both sides of the fence. What is not in dispute is that the Immigration and Naturalization Service (INS) can no longer effectively deter illegal immigration.

Reference
Edwin Harwood, "How Should We Enforce Immigration Law," in Nathan Glazer, ed., *Clamor at the Gates: The New American Immigration* (1985), pp. 73–91.

F.C.

IMMIGRATION LAW, occupational preferences. Provisions limit skilled immigration but fail (because of illegal immigrants) to limit unskilled immigration effectively. A number of conceivable economic rationales for such provisions can be identified, and the relevance of each rationale explored. "Aggregate output" rationales viewing immigration as a way of maximizing an objective such as national output or per capita income are relevant, while rationales focusing on special conditions in specific occupations (labor shortages, monopoly elements, etc.) are not a useful basis for a general immigration policy. The U.S. use of immigration to ameliorate the so-called doctor shortage is an example. Broad policy implications of the aggregate output rationale can be explored, with simple models. Optimal immigration levels do exist and vary with the precise policy objective. The current system's ability to apply an aggregate output rationale effectively has been investigated. Sources of difficulty include the inability to set numerical limits on immigration by occupation group and the lack of incentives for selecting "high-quality" potential immigrants. Finally, there is the issue of who gets the "economic rents" generated by the nonprice rationing system. There is at present no mechanism for the native population to capture some of these economic rents and probably a substantial proportion of these rents not retained by the immigrants is received by immigration lawyers or otherwise dissipated in misallocations of resources designed to increase the probability of receiving a visa.

Reference
Robert S. Goldfarb, "Occupational Preferences in the U.S. Immigration Law: An Economic Analysis," in Barry R. Chiswick, ed., *The Gateway: U.S. Immigration Issues and Policies* (1982), pp. 412–448.

F.C.

IMMIGRATION LAW OF 1965, effects. Changes in immigration law have affected the characteristics of immigrants coming to the United States. Changes in immigration policy contained in the 1965

Immigration Act, which amended the McCarran-Walter Act of 1952, concerned the abolition of the quota system, preference system, and labor clearances for certain classes of immigrants. Keely (1975 *infra*) traces the effects of these policy changes on two controversial characteristics of immigrants, their country of origin and their occupational levels. The law led to clear changes in the origins of immigrants: southern European, Asian, and Caribbean immigrants make up a larger proportion of immigrants than previously. Although the volume of immigration increased, the distribution of occupational groups shifted to some extent, especially the professional level from Asian countries. In addition to setting a higher numerical limit (290,000 rather than 150,000) the new law increased the number of groups exempted from the ceilings. By repealing the national origins system, the law opened up immigration to countries where the interest was greater. Under the old law, many nations of northern Europe did not fill their yearly quota, but under the new law, countries of Southeast Asia regularly did. Different pooling provisions had an impact, because they permitted unused categories to be picked up by people lower on the preference list. The 1965 law did not just swell numbers, it also changed the occupational composition. The blue-collar segment increased slightly while that of farm-related occupations declined.

References
Charles B. Keely, "Effects of the Immigration Act of 1965 on Selected Population Characteristics of Immigrants to the United States," *Demography* 8 (May 1971): 157–169; also, Charles B. Keely, "Effects of U.S. Immigration Law on Manpower Characteristics of Immigrants," *Demography* 12 (1975): 179–191.

F.C.

IMMIGRATION LAW OF 1965, labor certification. Keely (*infra*) writes that:

> The amendments to the Immigration and Nationality Act signed into law on October 3, 1965 were aimed at major reform in the immigration policy of the United States. The 1965 Act contained three major policy changes—phasing out the national origins quota system, emphasizing family reunion as a basis for granting an immigrant visa preference, and introducing a system of individual labor certification for certain classes of immigrants. These three changes acting in concert could be expected to bring about significant modifications in the national origin, use of preferences, and levels of skill of immigrants. During debate on the bill in Congress there were projections for these changes, but no one was really sure what the changes would bring. The purpose of this paper is to document any changes in the occupational skill levels of immigrants after the 1965 Act took effect and to explain how

the provisions of the 1965 Act affected the labor characteristics of immigrants.

Reference
Charles B. Keely, ''Measuring the Effect of Labor Certification,'' *International Migration Review* 4 (Spring 1970): 87–92.

F.C.

IMMIGRATION LAWS, U.S. Congress, House and Senate, Committees on the Judiciary, Select Commission on Immigration and Refugee Policy, *Semiannual Report to Congress* **(1980).** This report outlined some of the initial efforts of the commission to review U.S. immigration laws and policies and provided background information on the formation, functioning, and goals of the commission.

F.C.

IMMIGRATION, legal status and the labor market impact of immigration. Theoretical analysis suggests that the influence of legal status on market wage rates and on minimum wage enforcement is weak and that to the extent that there is an effect, it depends on particular institutional arrangements. Although data are not adequate for a definite measurement of these effects, those data that are available support this conclusion. It does appear that the presence of undocumented as opposed to resident aliens can weaken union organizing efforts.

Reference
Thomas Bailey, ''The Influence of Legal Status on the Labor Market Impact of Immigration,'' *International Migration Review* 19 (Summer 1985): 220–238.

F.C.

IMMIGRATION, legislation control. Regarding the present controversy over immigration reform in the United States, Portes points out two gaps between the intention of policymakers and daily events in the rest of society: (1) the gap between present immigration law and its implementation; and (2) the gap separating current policy debates and the structure of economic and social forces deemed in need of ''reform.''

Reference
Alejandro Portes, ''Of Borders and States: A Skeptical Note on the Legislation Control of Immigration,'' paper presented at the Fourth Annual Earl Warren Memorial Symposium, ''America's New Immigration Law,'' University of California, San Diego, November 19–20, 1982.

F.C.

IMMIGRATION LEGISLATION. The Constitution gave the federal government the power to regulate immigration, but for nearly a century Congress took little interest in immigration policy. During the 1790s, Federalist legislators did pass an alien act granting the president the right to deport immigrants he deemed dangerous, even in peacetime, but President John Adams did not use the law and it lapsed when Thomas Jefferson became president in 1801. Congress had originally set the residency requirement for naturalization for white immigrants at two years. The Federalists raised this to fourteen years in 1798, but it became five years after 1800, and it remains that today.

From 1800 until the late nineteenth century Congress passed no legislation restricting the flow of immigration and for the most part contented itself with merely counting newcomers, a policy begun in 1820. As immigration from Ireland, Great Britain, and Germany grew after 1830, however, several states with large ports serving as entries for immigration passed laws to control it. New York, Pennsylvania, Maryland, and Massachusetts taxed shipmasters and developed health standards for the newcomers. Those states eager for new settlers established immigration bureaus to recruit immigrants either abroad or when they landed.

As the numbers of immigrants grew and as state activities and regulations mounted, the United States Supreme Court in an 1875 decision declared state regulation unconstitutional. Now it was up to the federal government to concern itself with immigration.

Between the Civil War and World War I Congress enacted a number of restrictions on immigration, and after 1917 severely cut the flow of newcomers. While the Civil War raged Congress passed a law to permit employers to contract laborers abroad, but in 1885 the lawmakers repealed this law.

Other restrictions took several forms and were the product of growing concern over immigration and especially the ethnic or racial background of those entering. On the West Coast Chinese laborers began to emigrate to the United States when news of the 1849 California gold rush reached China. Most Chinese worked in the mining areas of the West, then helped build the transcontinental railroads and finally settled in the nation's emerging Chinatowns. They were clearly not welcome, especially in California, where they were most visible. Working men and others attacked Chinese immigrants violently and urged that legislation be passed to restrict their economic activities and entry to the United States. A good deal of the hostility directed toward the Chinese was racist inspired. Angry whites insisted that the Chinese were a degraded race that should be barred from coming to American shores. After much debate, Congress passed the first major law to restrict an ethnic group from emigrating to America: the Chinese Exclusion Act of 1882 which virtually banned Chinese immigration to America.

The legislators also began excluding individuals they deemed undesirable. Excluded were convicts, lunatics, idiots, persons likely to become a public charge, and prostitutes. In 1891 Congress established a permanent bureau to deal with immigration, and in the 1890s Ellis Island opened and became the gateway for the majority of newcomers entering the United States. In 1903, following the assassination of President William McKinley by a U.S.-born anarchist, Congress barred the immigration of anarchists. Most Japanese immigrants were excluded by the "Gentlemen's Agreement" between the United States and Japan (1907–8). Other Asians, such as Indians, were barred in a 1917 congressional act.

While the post–Civil War restrictions excluded Asians, they scarcely affected the European flow. Many old-stock Americans believed that the growing number of newcomers from southern and eastern Europe, such as Jews, Greeks, Slavs, and Italians, were undesirable and inferior and that they should not be allowed to migrate to the United States in large numbers. In the early twentieth century the numbers passed the one million mark five times.

Schemes to exclude southern and eastern Europeans included a literacy test, a requirement that persons over sixteen years of age be literate in some language. Congress agreed to require this test several times, only to have presidents veto it. Finally, on the eve of World War I, Congress passed a literacy test bill over the veto of President Woodrow Wilson.

Immigration slumped during the war, but at the end of the war it rose again and many Americans were alarmed at the possibility of a new surge of immigration. The literacy test had not cut the flow and they wanted more drastic action. Amid ethnic and racial tensions and a considerable amount of bigotry, Congress passed severe immigration restrictions in the 1920s. In several laws, the lawmakers used quotas to curtail immigration, especially from southeastern Europe. Finally in 1924 the Johnson-Reed Immigration Act was passed which established the national origins system. This law excluded virtually all Asians and limited the number of Europeans to approximately 150,000. European nations were given quotas based on their proportion of the white population in 1920. Thus, Great Britain, Germany, and Ireland received two-thirds of the numbers and countries like Italy, Russia, and Greece were granted small quotas. Italy's was under 6,000 and Greece's only 308. The result was precisely what Congress wanted.

The immigration laws were tightly enforced during the Great Depression, and few refugees from Hitler's Germany managed to escape to America during the war. The legislators had placed no numerical limits on the Western Hemisphere, but allowed provisions such as banning those likely to become a public charge to regulate the flow from Mexico and elsewhere in the Western Hemisphere. During the Great Depression, tens of thousands of Mexicans were deported by local authorities and the federal government.

While nativism triumphed in the 1920s and 1930s, after World War II legislative policy began to change to permit substantial increases in immigration. In passing the McCarran-Walter Immigration Act of 1952, Congress did reaffirm the national origins system. But that law granted Asian nations small quotas, a practice begun in 1943 when Congress repealed the Chinese Exclusion Act. Moreover, other post–World War II refugee legislation undercut the national origins system.

In 1948 and again in 1950, Congress passed "displaced persons" acts to permit almost 400,000 refugees to migrate to America, many of them outside the quotas. In 1953 the legislators passed the Refugee Relief Act which opened the door for another 200,000 immigrants. Other laws in the 1950s admitted Hungarian and Chinese refugees. Moreover, President Dwight Eisenhower began a new policy of the president admitting refugees to settle here.

Finally in 1965 Congress passed a new immigration law which abolished the old national origins system. It gave each Eastern Hemisphere nation a quota of 20,000, excluding immediate family members, and established a preference system based upon family unification, economic skills needed in the United States, and refugee status. The Western Hemisphere for the first time had a ceiling, of 120,000, but no preference system. By 1968, further refinements constructed a worldwide policy based on the preference system of 1965 and a ceiling of 290,000, excluding immediate family members.

While trying to establish a uniform system, the legislators had to deal with the growing number of refugees. Hundreds of thousands of Cubans, Indochinese, and others entered by administrative action and special congressional law. Congress responded by passing the 1980 Refugee Act. This law set the "normal flow" of refugees at 50,000, but permitted the president to admit more if he deemed it in the national interest to do so.

These laws deal with legal immigration, but the legislators also had to confront the growing problem of illegal or undocumented immigrants. Desperate poverty and poor economic conditions drove millions to seek a better life in the United States, even if they could not satisfy immigration requirements; hence the number of illegal immigrants grew, though no one knew how many were here in the early 1980s. Faced with pressures for eliminating illegal immigration, Congress passed the Immigration Reform and Control Act of 1986. This law prohibited employers from knowingly hiring illegal immigrants and granted amnesty to those who had been living in the United States without proper documents since 1982. The legislation also provided for the admission of temporary agricultural workers if they were needed and allowed illegal workers in agriculture to become regular immigrants. The provision for the admission of temporary farm workers was not new because such workers, called braceros, had been allowed to work in the United States from World War II until the program was halted in 1964.

How this new law would work was not clear. Moreover, many private groups and persons in Congress worried about the growing number of refugees from Central America and elsewhere who were living without legal documents, but as of 1987 the legislators could not agree on a new refugee law.

References
Marion Bennett, *American Immigration Policies: A History* (1963); Leonard Dinnerstein and David M. Reimers, *Ethnic Americans: A History of Immigration* (1987); Robert Divine, *American Immigration Policy, 1924–1952* (1957); Roy Garis, *Immigration Restriction* (1928); John Higham, *Strangers in the Land: Patterns of American Nativism, 1860–1925* (1955); Edward Hutchinson, *Legislative History of American Immigration Policy, 1790–1965* (1981).

D.M.R.

IMMIGRATION LEGISLATIVE HISTORY. *Legislative History of American Immigration Policy, 1798–1965* (E. P. Hutchinson, 1981). This volume is to be a reference source on congressional attitudes toward immigration from 1798 to 1965. It presents a chronological account of all bills dealing with aliens that were brought before the Congress and provides summaries of the discussion surrounding them and their final disposition. An immense amount of material is covered. The scope requires that discussions be limited; rather than being definitive, the book serves as a useful guide to anyone seeking to identify the major areas of congressional concern. Prior to the second half of the nineteenth century, policy governing immigration was primarily in the hands of the states. State law determined the restrictions governing alien entry into the United States. The area where federal policy first impinged on immigrants related to naturalization. Uniform national policies for acquiring citizenship long preceded congressional regulation of the flow of foreigners into the country. There was also a body of national law governing the conditions of travel for immigrants, generally known as "steerage legislation." The problem of state versus federal jurisdiction was not resolved until 1882 when national responsibility for immigration law was clearly established. The federal government then embarked on an elaborate system of regulation. Criminals and those likely to become public charges were among the excludable classes since colonial days. The latter part of the nineteenth century saw the expansion of this category to include mental defectives, prostitutes, polygamists, and others deemed morally unfit. Race became a basis for exclusion during this period as did political beliefs thought to be subversive. The latter has remained a constant in immigration law since that time. The regulation of immigration led to restriction in the period following World War I. Ceilings on immigration appeared in the 1920s along with the national quota system that remained until 1965. By 1929, Congress had developed a quite highly evolved legislation structure for the regulation and numerical restriction of immigration, supplemented with the selective exclusion of certain classes of aliens and provisions for the deportation of aliens considered undesirable.

F.C.

IMMIGRATION POLICY, and employment trends. Briggs:

> The absence of any serious effort to forge an immigration policy based upon labor market considerations means that immigration policy today functions as a "wild card" among the nation's array of key labor market policies. Unlike all other elements of economic policy (*e.g.*, fiscal policy, monetary policy, employment and training policy, education policy, and anti-discrimination policy) where attempts are made by policymakers to orchestrate the diverse policy elements into a harmony of action to accomplish particular objectives, immigration policy has been allowed to meander aimlessly. This is a situation that no sensible nation can allow to continue.

Reference
Vernon M. Briggs, Jr., "Employment Trends and Contemporary Immigration Policy," in Nathan Glazer, ed., *Clamor at the Gates: The New American Immigration* (1985), pp. 135–160.

F.C.

IMMIGRATION POLICY, and the American labor force. Since the late 1970s and early 1980s, the United States has been in the midst of the largest influx of immigrants in its history. During this period, argues Vernon Briggs, political considerations have dominated contemporary immigration policy, with little concern for their labor market implications. Briggs (*infra*) charts the evolution of U.S. immigration policies toward all types of immigrants—legal immigrants, illegal immigrants, refugees, nonimmigrant workers, border commuters—and analyzes the impact of these policies upon American labor practices. He calls for a comprehensive policy reform and proposes a number of alternative options, including the establishment of immigration ceilings that are flexible and responsive to the nation's employment trends and a return to occupational preferences as the basis for allowing immigrants to enter the country. "The real issue, which is the thesis of this work, is that the immigration policy of the United States has been allowed to function without regard to its economic consequences."

Reference
Vernon M. Briggs, Jr., *Immigration Policy and the American Labor Force* (1985).

F.C.

IMMIGRATION POLICY, recent developments. Reimers (*infra*) reviews the post–World War II liberalization of the restrictive immigration legislation of the 1920s. He shows how struggles over the Displaced Persons Law of 1948, the Immigration and Nationality (McCarran-Walter) Act of 1952, and the various special laws of the 1950s and early 1960s led to the 1965 amendments that abolished the national origins quota system and the severe restrictions on Asians and substituted a preference system. The new law, while still selective, emphasized family unification, with a smaller role for occupational requirements and refugee status. The Refugee Act of 1980, which increased the number of visas for refugees and introduced other changes to facilitate refugee resettlement, was immediately shown to be inadequate by the "unscheduled" influx of 120,000 Cuban refugees. Congress amended the law several times, most recently in 1980, to provide for a uniform worldwide system of 320,000 immigrants subject annually to numerical limitation, in addition to visas for immediate relatives of U.S. citizens, who are not subject to numerical limitation (now about 125,000 per year), and "conditional" admission of refugees over and above this limit. The changes in the law in 1965 were accompanied by a gradual increase in immigration and shifting patterns of immigration. After World War II, southern and eastern Europeans began to replace northern and western Europeans, and both in turn gave way, after 1965, to immigration from the Third World. Immigration policy responded to economic forces and fears, foreign policy (especially the cold war), and ethnic politics. Arguments about race and ethnicity gave way to Cold War arguments and family concerns. The old-line restrictionist groups, like the veterans and patriotic organizations, took a back seat to the growing influence of ethnic and religious agencies and the executive branch in shaping immigration policy. Economic interest groups were more vociferous in discussions about the bracero program (1942–1964) and the illegal alien issue.

Reference
David M. Reimers, "Recent Immigration Policy: An Analysis," in Barry R. Chiswick, ed., *The Gateway: U.S. Immigration Issues and Policies* (1982), pp. 13–53.

F.C.

IMMIGRATION, Politics of Immigration Reform. The United States is the target for international migration, more now than ever. Population growth and economic stagnation in the Third World are increasing the pressures for out-migration, and current immigration law is wholly incapable of responding to the ever-increasing flow of illegal immigrants. Border apprehensions of illegal aliens in the United States were up 40 percent during 1983, and total apprehensions reached 1.25 million by the year's end. Recent public opinion polls have disclosed that an overwhelming majority of the American public demands immigration reform, and yet we as a nation have been distinctly unwilling or unable to respond to this clear public sentiment. Simpson discusses the politics of the issue: the current "Simpson-Mazzoli" Immigration Reform and Control Act, previous immigration legislation, current counterproposals for U.S. immigration policy, and the political realities of immigration reform.

Reference
Alan K. Simpson, "The Politics of Immigration Reform," *International Migration Review* 18 (Fall 1984): 486–504.

F.C.

IMMIGRATION RECOMMENDATIONS, Commission on Population Growth. An evaluation of the Commission on Population Growth's report indicates that: (1) there seems to have been some confusion between net civilian immigration and alien immigration due to dropping the word "civilian" in the commission's interim report; (2) there is a large group of nonimmigrants who are not accounted for in the "net civilian immigration" category; (3) the 400,000 figure as the input of immigrants to population growth is inappropriate; and (4) to focus on the percentage contributed by net civilian increase to population growth may not be the most appropriate course when natural increase is declining. The analysis concludes that eliminating alien immigration seems impossible and, from the point of view of national needs and foreign policies, undesirable at present.

According to Keely (April 1972),

the single word that best characterizes the handling of the topic of immigration by the Commission on Population Growth and the American Future is surprise. The commission and its staff were left floundering when they realized the possible impact of current levels of immigration on population growth: The *Interim Report* of the Commission, issued in March, 1971, stated: "Right now about 80 percent of our annual population growth results from natural increase—the amount by which births exceed deaths. About 20 percent of our current growth is due to net immigration; the number has been averaging about 400,000 annually. Historically speaking, that is not many. In the years just before World War I, the figures ran to twice that, at a time when the United States had less than half the number of people it has now. Even so, the long-term effects of immigration are large. This is partly because most immigrants enter the country in young adulthood, at an age when their childbearing is at its peak. If the average family (including immigrants) had two children, and immigration continued at 400,000 per year, the survivors and descendants of immigrants in the next 30 years would number 16 million in the year 2000, and would have accounted for one-fourth of the total population increase during that period. Over the next 100 years immigrants and their descendants would account for nearly half of the increase in population from 204 to 340 million. (Commission on Population Growth and the American Future, *Interim Report,* 1971, 8–9) . . .

References
Charles B. Keely, "Immigration Policy and Population Growth," paper presented at the Population Association of America Annual Meeting, April 1972, Toronto, Ontario; also, Charles B. Keely, "Immigration Recommendations of the Commission on Population Growth and the American Future," *International Migration Review* 6 (Fall 1972): 290–294.

F.C.

IMMIGRATION, reform: an economic necessity. McLennan and Lovell (*infra*) state that "if immigration is not increased, the American labor force will in all possibility not be sufficient by the end of the century to maintain the present level of social benefits afforded our elderly population." They point out that "in 19 years the ratio of elderly to overall population will be 1 to 5 (in 1965 it was 1 in 10). Since those now working are paying the pensions of those retired, working immigrants could help pay the pensions" and recommend that "in increasing the numbers of legal immigrants preference be given to specific skilled workers and professionals by increasing the temporary worker program. Control must come through the workplace and welfare system by means of a national identification system."

Reference
K. McLennan and M. Lovell, Jr., "Immigration Reform: An Economic Necessity," *The Journal of the Institute for Socioeconomic Studies* 6 (Summer 1981): 38–52.

F.C.

IMMIGRATION REFORM AND CONTROL ACT OF 1986. In the 1970s, continuing concerns over various immigration issues led to mounting criticisms and demands for reform. Illegal immigration was the paramount concern, but other related issues (e.g., the status of temporary foreign workers and refugee accommodation) were also concerns that continued to be controversial.

The intensity of the debate surrounding the "new immigration" is indicated in the somber observations of Raymond A. Mohl:

> Indeed, the twentieth century remains a great uncharted wilderness for immigration and ethnic historians. The great surge of new immigrants and refugees since 1960, in particular, has yet to be placed in the larger context of immigration history. In many ways, the new immigration of the past few decades has been reshaping some of the major U.S. metropolitan areas.

As the *New York Times* observed in 1981, "Immigrants are coming to New York City from virtually every country on the globe, creating a city more diverse in race, language and ethnicity than it was at the turn of the century when immigrants from Europe poured through Ellis Island." Reflecting this new surge of immigration, the foreign born made up about 25 percent of New York City's population in 1980. The incredible dimensions of this new immigrant flood are just beginning to be sketched out. According to a careful study by Douglas S. Massey, net immigration to the United States during the 1970s totaled more than 7 million persons—a figure surpassing the previous record high of about 6.3 million during the first decade of the twentieth century. Some specialists estimate that at the present rate, 35 million additional immigrants and refugees will come to the United States by the year 2000. It is not too early for ethnic historians to begin studying this late twentieth-century immigration.

In 1978, Congress established the Select Commission on Immigration and Refugee Policy to make a major study of immigration and recommend changes; the sixteen-member commission (including congressional representatives and senators, cabinet officials, and presidential appointees) was chaired by Father Theodore Hesburgh, former president of Notre Dame University; its work was directed by Professor Lawrence Fuchs of Brandeis University. The commission's *Report* was submitted to the Congress in March 1981; its recommendations were that the basic immigration system be kept intact, with more flexibility, adjustments in preferences, and increases in immigration to assist in easing backlogs in certain nations. Its recommendations on illegal (undocumented) aliens proved very controversial, but it became the basis for immigration reform legislation pending in the Congress.

In speaking of the commission and its *Report*, Father Hesburgh noted (*New York Times*, March 20, 1986):

> The essential recommendation was that America ought to open the front door of legal immigration a bit wider while shutting the back door of illegal immigration. While maintaining a generous policy toward those in an impoverished world who wish to come here, we cannot accommodate everyone and must regain control of our borders. To face this moral dilemma, I undertook my role as commission chairman by asking: Why should immigration be a problem? Why not let down the barriers and let people move freely? After our two years of study, the question answered itself. It is not enough to sympathize with the aspirations and plight of illegal aliens. We must also consider the consequences of not controlling our borders. . . . Under present law, it is illegal for an undocumented alien to be in this country, but it is not illegal to hire one. It was also the commission's strong, compassionate opinion that aliens who have been law-abiding residents for a reasonably long time should be granted the opportunity to legalize their status. Alternatives are limited. Failure to act quickly and responsibly to control the flow of illegal immigrants will lead to drastic solutions no one wants. No responsible proponent of reform wants immigration stopped. Controlled, legal immigration can continue to be beneficial to the nation.

In 1984 different versions of the Simpson-Mazzoli Bill, entitled the Immigration Reform and Control Act of 1982, passed both houses of the Congress. Its major provisions proposed civil and criminal penalties against employers who knowingly hired illegal aliens; required national identity cards for all legal aliens; granted permanent residence status to illegal aliens who could prove continuous residence in the United States since January 1, 1977, and temporary residence status to those who could prove continuous residence in the United States since January 1, 1980; it also established a new ceiling for the number of legal aliens who would be allowed to enter each year. Before it could be sent to the president for approval or veto, an agreement on key issues had to be reached by a joint committee of the House and the Senate. On June 25, 1986 (with Congressman Peter Rodino, chairman of the House Judiciary Committee taking a major role), for the third time in five years, the House Judiciary Committee approved a comprehensive bill to revise the nation's immigration laws and to curtail the influx of illegal aliens. The Senate had passed a generally similar bill by a vote of 69 to 30, and the Reagan administration supported it. The House and Senate bills both prohibited employers from hiring illegal aliens. In addition, they offered legal status to many illegal aliens already in the United

States. But the two measures differed in many important details. For example, the Senate bill would have established a new government program under which farmers could bring up to 350,000 aliens into the United States to harvest perishable fruit and vegetables. The workers could stay for up to nine months in any one year. By contrast, the bill approved by the House Judiciary Committee would have permitted certain foreign workers to become permanent residents of the United States, with most of the rights of citizens. Under the House bill, the attorney general would grant lawful permanent resident status to any illegal alien who could prove that he had been working in American agriculture for at least sixty days in the period from May 1, 1985, to May 1, 1986. The plan called for the admission of additional aliens if they were needed to work on farms in subsequent years; they, too, could qualify for permanent resident status. The Senate passed comprehensive immigration bills in 1982, 1983, and 1985. The House passed a bill in 1984 by a five-vote margin, but the measure died when the House and Senate could not work out their differences.

On October 9, 1986, in a dramatic reversal, the U.S. House of Representatives approved a comprehensive bill to overhaul the nation's immigration law and curtail the influx of illegal aliens. The vote was 230 to 166. Voting for the bill were 168 Democrats and 62 Republicans. Sixty-one Democrats and 105 Republicans voted against it. The U.S. Senate passed its version of the immigration bill by a vote of 69 to 30 in September 1985. On October 14, 1986, House and Senate negotiators reached agreement, reconciling all differences between the Senate and House bills; and on October 17, 1986, Congress gave final approval to the landmark immigration bill as it moved toward adjournment. By a vote of 63 to 24, the Senate agreed to the compromise bill, clearing the measure for action by President Reagan. The chief sponsor of the legislation, Senator Alan K. Simpson (R–Wyoming), said President Reagan "awaits this bill and has agreed to sign it." President Reagan proposed similar legislation in 1981 to tighten control of the borders and to curtail the influx of illegal aliens.

The Immigration Reform and Control Act of 1986 marks an historic change in American immigration policy. Under current law, illegal aliens may be deported, but it is generally not illegal for employers to hire them. Under the new bill, employers who hired illegal aliens would be subject to civil penalties ranging from $250 to $10,000 for each such alien. The aliens bill, a product of nearly a decade of work in Congress, would make the biggest changes in immigration law in at least twenty years. Senator Phil Gramm (R–Texas), led the opposition. He denounced the bill's amnesty for illegal aliens. In addition, he said it was "outrageous" that under one section, illegal aliens who had done only ninety days of agricultural work in this country could eventually become permanent residents. "I want to do what the founding fathers envisioned the Senate would do," Senator Gramm said. "I want to have a real debate on this." The provisions granting legal status to foreign agricultural workers were drafted by Representative Charles E. Schumer (D–Brooklyn). They were adopted by the House and accepted by a House-Senate conference committee. The provisions were part of a delicately balanced compromise that revived the bill after it was pronounced dead just three weeks ago. The bill had broad bipartisan support. It was sponsored in the House by Representatives Peter W. Rodino, Jr., of New Jersey and Romano L. Mazzoli of Kentucky, both Democrats.

The number of illegal aliens in the United States is disputed. Jeffrey S. Passel, a demographer at the Census Bureau, has stated that the bureau estimated that there were 2.5 million to 3.5 million illegal aliens who had their usual residence in the United States at the time of the last census in 1980. The bureau estimates that the number of illegal aliens has grown since then by 100,000 to 300,000 a year, so the total now probably stands at three million to five million. These figures do not include the thousands of illegal aliens who go back and forth across the border, working in the United States but returning to permanent residences in Mexico or other countries.

The Immigration Reform and Control Act of 1986 is a milestone in the history of American immigration policy. In Colonial times, immigration was generally encouraged. The first federal restriction on immigration was not adopted until 1875, when Congress barred the admission of prostitutes and convicted criminals. The new bill ranks in importance with the Quota Act of 1921, which established the first numerical restrictions on immigration, and the Immigration and Nationality Act of 1952, the McCarran-Walter Act, which listed dozens of ideological and other reasons for excluding aliens. Under the bill, aliens illegally in the United States could apply for legal status in the one-year period starting six months after the bill becomes law. Then, after eighteen months as lawful temporary residents, the aliens could apply for status as permanent residents, and after another five years they could apply for citizenship. If the illegal aliens did not seek legal status, they would remain subject to deportation. Members of Congress and lobbyists said that two factors added impetus to the drive for a comprehensive immigration bill this year. First, they said, liberals feared that any such bill adopted by the next Congress would be more restrictive and less generous to illegal aliens. In addition, in the last few months, the Reagan administration has argued that the bill was needed to help combat drug smuggling. Immigration officials said that many illegal aliens and smugglers of aliens were involved in illicit drug traffic.

*Main Provisions of the Immigration Reform
and Control Act of 1986.*

- Employers would be forbidden to hire illegal aliens. The ban would apply to all employers, even those with just a few employees. For a first offense, the employer would be subject to a civil penalty of $250 to $2,000 for each illegal alien hired. For subsequent offenses, the employer would be subject to civil penalties as high as $10,000 for each.

- For a "pattern or practice" of violations, the employer would be subject to criminal penalties, up to a $3,000 fine and six months imprisonment.

- Employers would have to ask all job applicants for documents, such as a passport or a birth certificate and driver's license, to confirm that they were either citizens or aliens authorized to work in the United States. The employer is not required to check the authenticity of the documents. The bill says it does not authorize issuance or use of national identification cards.

- The government would offer legal status to aliens who entered the United States illegally before January 1, 1982, and have resided here continuously since then. For five years, they would be ineligible for welfare, food stamps, and most other federal benefits, with some exceptions.

- The federal government will set aside $1 billion a year for four years to reimburse state governments for providing public assistance, health care, and education to illegal aliens who gain legal status.

- Under a special program, illegal aliens who worked in American agriculture for at least ninety days in the period from May 1, 1985, to May 1, 1986 could become lawful temporary residents of the United States. After two years in that status, they could become permanent residents, eligible for American citizenship after five years more.

- If there is a shortage of seasonal farm workers, the government could admit additional aliens in the fiscal years 1990 through 1993. They would have to work in agriculture and, after three years as temporary residents, could become permanent residents.

- Immigration officers could not enter a farm without a search warrant or the owner's permission if they wanted to question a person believed to be an alien.

- Employers would be forbidden to discriminate against legal aliens because of their national origin or citizenship status. A new office would be established in the Justice Department to investigate complaints of such discrimination.

- States would generally have to verify, through records of the Immigration and Naturalization Service, the legal status of aliens seeking welfare benefits, Medicaid, unemployment compensation, food stamps, housing assistance, or college aid under federal programs.

• To improve enforcement, the Immigration and Naturalization Service would receive $422 million more in the current fiscal year and $419 million extra next year. The agency's budget last year was $593.8 million, of which $379.7 million was for enforcement.

The bill also envisions a 50 percent increase in Border Patrol personnel, although there is no guarantee that Congress would actually provide money for the increase. At present, the Border Patrol has 3,694 officers.

References

Francesco Cordasco, *The New American Immigration* (1987); Raymond A. Mohl, "Cubans in Miami," *Immigration History Newsletter* 16 (May 1984): 1–10; U.S. Congress, House and Senate, Select Commission on Immigration and Refugee Policy, *U.S. Immigration Policy and the National Interest* (1981).

F. C.

IMMIGRATION RESTRICTION. For almost a century, American immigration policy was restrictionist. In the 1880s Congress began an active role in the administration and control of immigration, and this new role was evident in the passage of the Chinese Exclusion Act of 1882 which suspended the entry of Chinese workers for ten years and barred all foreign-born Chinese from acquiring citizenship. In 1885, Congress enacted the Foran Act which prohibited unskilled laborer recruitment with prepaid passage and advance contracting, and in 1888 Congress ordered the deportation of all alien contract laborers within one year of entry.

Between 1890 and 1921 (a period Vernon M. Briggs, Jr., has called the "era of screening without a numerical ceiling") Congress attempted to impose literacy requirements to restrict immigration. Four literacy bills were debated in Congress between 1896 and 1917; Congress passed three literacy acts, each of which met with a presidential veto. In 1907, legislation established the Immigration Commission, whose appointment President Theodore Roosevelt had called for. The commission was chaired by Senator William P. Dillingham (R–Vermont). The commission published its *Report* in 1911 in forty-one volumes, and Oscar Handlin called it "one of the most ambitious social science research projects in the nation's history up to then, barring only the censuses"; but the *Report* was restrictionist in its basic recommendations, and Vernon M. Briggs, Jr. has succinctly characterized it as "neither impartial nor scientific." The commission had spent over a million dollars, had convened a staff of three hundred, and taken over three years in its deliberations, but (as Briggs further observes):

> The Dillingham commission found that the new immigrants differed significantly from the nation's older immigrants. It deemed the new immigrants to be "inferior" and to possess attributes that would make it difficult for them to assimilate. It argued that a slower rate of expansion—a rate that emphasized the ability of immigrants to adapt to their new surroundings—would be preferable to a rapid and uncontrolled rate, which imperiled the prevailing wages and employment opportunities of American citizens. Laced throughout the commission's argument were pseudo-scientific theories pertaining to "superior" and "inferior" persons. The mixture of economic and ethnic arguments in the commission's report has plagued all efforts to discuss and to legislate immigration reform impartially since that time. (Briggs, 31)

In 1917, over a presidential veto, an immigration act was passed that required literacy of immigrants over sixteen years of age (in English, or any other language); and in 1921 the Johnson Act introduced a system of national quotas, determined as the percentage of the number of immigrants from the country in question at a designated census. The 1921 act (which had been vetoed by President Woodrow Wilson earlier but was signed into law when Warren Harding took office) limited the annual number of immigrants of each admissible nationality to three percent of the foreign born of that nationality as recorded in the U.S. census of 1910, and limited European immigration to 350,000.

When the Johnson Act expired in 1924, Congress passed the Johnson-Reed Act, which set national quotas at two percent of the 1890 population, and also provided that as of July 1, 1927, the quota limit would be 150,000, allocated on the base of the estimated national origins distribution of the continental U.S. population in 1920; postponed twice, this latter provision became effective in 1929, and

> between 1929 and 1968, quotas were determined by the "national origins" formula which provided that the annual quota equal one-sixth of one percent of the number of white inhabitants in the continental United States, less Western Hemisphere immigrants and their descendants. The annual quota for each nationality was then determined by the same ratio to 150,000 as the number of inhabitants of each nationality living in the continental United States in 1920 to the total inhabitants, although a minimum quota for any nationality was 100. (*Statistical Abstracts of the United States*, 1984)

Various other pieces of restrictionist legislation were passed by Congress in the period following the Johnson-Reed Act of 1924; the only piece of major immigration legislation passed was the McCarran-Walter Act (Immigration and Nationality Act) of 1952 which changed the formula for computing the annual quotas of any country to one-sixth of one percent of the numbers of persons of that national origin in the United States in 1920 as computed for the 1924 Quota Act. As Reimers notes:

> The McCarran-Walter Act basically reinforced the tough immigration restrictions of the 1920s. That law reaffirmed the national origins quotas and added security provisions designed to make it almost impossible for suspected subversives to enter the United States. Liberals generally saw the 1952 immigration act as containing unduly harsh security provisions and as racist because of its inclusion of national origins quotas that gave the vast bulk of immigrant slots to the peoples of northern and western Europe. President Truman agreed with the liberal position and vetoed the bill, but Congress overrode his veto by a vote of 278 to 113 in the House and 57 to 26 in the Senate. (Reimers, 20)

The McCarran-Walter Act, however,

> could not long survive changes at home and abroad. At home the immigrants of the great wave from Eastern and Southern Europe, and their children growing to maturity, were becoming more and more effective politically, developing greater resources economically, becoming bolder in asserting their wishes against a weakening nativism. Abroad, crises that produced waves of refugees from Communism—in Hungary in 1957, in Cuba in 1960 and later—were also changing public opinion about immigration. Perhaps more potent in changing these attitudes was the fading of fears of depression, as post-war prosperity continued, marred only by occasional recessions. Perhaps most potent was the radical change in American attitudes on race that accompanied the rise of the civil rights movement. The attempt to freeze the composition of the American people by favoring Northwestern Europe was increasingly seen as basically immoral and wrong. (Glazer, 6)

References
Vernon M. Briggs, *Immigration Policy and the American Labor Force* (1984); Robert A. Divine, *American Immigration Policy, 1924–1952* (1957; rpt. 1972); Roy L. Garis, *Immigration Restriction* (1927); Nathan Glazer, *Clamor at the Gates: The New American Immigration* (1985); David M. Reimers, *Still the Golden Door: The Third World Comes to America* (1985).

                                                                    F.C.

IMMIGRATION RESTRICTION LEAGUE. The immigration policy of the United States shifted noticeably in the last quarter of the nineteenth century. From an open-door policy, the national government began to erect barriers. Several recommendations surfaced: a head tax, limitations on immigrants of dubious moral character, the exclusion of the Chinese, and a demand for greater federal supervision of immigration.

By far the most radical proposal was advanced by Edward W. Bemis, a progressive economist from New England. In 1887, he recommended that the federal government should prohibit the admission of all male adults who could not read or write their own language. The idea languished until the young Boston congressman Henry Cabot Lodge became a prominent supporter of the idea.

Several factors aided Lodge's efforts: (1) the outbreak of cholera in 1892 aboard immigrant vessels coming to American ports, especially New York, heightened Americans' fears; and (2) the depression of 1893 intensified Americans' economic hysteria. Finally, the newly created Immigration Restriction League of Boston embraced the idea and became its most enthusiastic proponent.

Who organized the league? The league was established in 1894 in the Boston law office of Charles Warren (he later became a noted constitutional historian and a chair was endowed in his name at Harvard University). The founders were all from prominent Boston families and all had attended Harvard College in the 1880s. Two young men dominated the League from its inception: Prescott Farnsworth Hall and Robert De Courcy Ward.

Hall, who came from a wealthy Boston merchant family, had been graduated from Harvard College and the Harvard Law School. In 1894, at the age of twenty-six, he began the practice of law. He was always plagued by ill health but, as John Higham noted, "his mind was sharp and arrogant and proud." He served officially as secretary but was the recognized leader of the group.

His right-hand man and a Harvard classmate was Robert De Courcy Ward. Ward's father had served as an American consul in Dresden, Germany (1868–1872) and then in Switzerland, where he died in 1873. The family went to England for a time, then returned to Boston in 1874. Ward graduated from Harvard with a B.A. *summa cum laude* in 1885 and in 1893 received an M.A. from Harvard. He became an instructor in meteorology in 1895, then an instructor in climatology in 1896; by 1910, he became the first professor of climatology in the United States. He wrote a number of well-received monographs and textbooks on climatology.

For almost two decades Ward and Hall worked in tandem on the efforts to pass the literacy test. They enjoyed the support of a number of other wealthy Bostonians who were willing to provide financial support to the group, including the wealthy Boston merchant Samuel Billings Capen, who served as president of the American Board of Commissioners for Foreign Missions, and Robert Treat Paine, Jr. who had ties to the Cushing and Cabot families. The popular historian, John Fiske, served as honorary president of the Immigration Restriction League.

The league enjoyed the support of a large number of prominent social scientists who became vice-presidents of the organization or endorsed its efforts at restricting immigration from southern and eastern Europe. They included the sociologist Franklin Henry Giddings and his Columbia University colleague Richmond Mayo-Smith. The leading nativist sociologist of the period was undoubtedly Edward A. Ross. General Francis A. Walker, president of the Massachusetts Institute of Technology and former superintendent of the 1870 census, provided the premise for the league's work. He noted in 1891 that immigrants were changing the character of America's population. Native Americans' birth rates declined, while the newer immigrants' increased. The cause, according to Walker, was the economic competition of cheap foreign labor: native Americans limited their families' sizes in order to maintain their standard of living.

The league's history passed through a number of stages. Initially it had intended to become a national organization. By 1895, it had fifty-three members in fourteen states; but Hall and Ward decided to restrict the size of the group and emphasize its lobbying role for the literary test.

As a pressure group the league presented its message to the media. In its first six months, it forwarded almost 40,000 pamphlets and documents to the newspapers. It contacted the various boards of charity throughout the country as well as the more than 3,000 chambers of commerce in the nation. It asked for their support of the literacy test. By 1900, over 150,000 pamphlets had been distributed.

The league insisted that it was not anti-Catholic or anti-Semitic. It came close to success in 1895. Lodge, now a United States senator, introduced the literacy test proposal to the Senate, and Samuel McCall, another Boston Republican, introduced the measure in the House of Representatives. Both houses passed the measure, but differences existed and the matter was sent to a conference committee. The league's lobbying efforts appeared to be on the verge of success. The conference committee, however, released a bill with anti-Semitic overtones. The original bills called for the exclusion of those who could not read or write English or some other language. The conference bill would deny admission to all who could not read or write English or the language of their native or resident country. The bill appeared to be aimed at excluding Yiddish-speaking Jews. Hall and Ward wanted to admit only those who could read and write English. The bill caused a furor. A second conference committee presented a version with the "some other language" reinstated. The bill passed both houses, but was vetoed by the four presidents over the next twenty years.

The IRL continued to push for the passage of the literacy test. In the legislative session 1897–98, Lodge again introduced the legislation, but the outbreak of the Spanish-American War suspended discussion of the bill. With the end of the war and the outbreak of antianarchism and antiradical rhetoric as a result of the assassination of President McKinley in 1901, the IRL was able to raise some $6,000 from wealthy Bostonians. It hired Charles D. Edgerton, formerly with the United States Industrial Commission, as assistant secretary of the league. He remained in Washington, D.C., his function being to lobby for the literacy test.

Between 1901 and 1903, the league again came close to success. It won the support of the American Federation of Labor as well as the Junior Order of Mechanics. But despite this support, opposition to the measure had grown. Some business groups wanted open immigration and both political parties were attempting to win the support of the naturalized voters. And in 1898, the Immigrant Protective League was organized, and adamantly opposed the literacy test.

In 1904, therefore, the IRL suspended its activities since it was unable to influence either the Democratic or Republican party platforms. But in 1905, Ward spoke before a group of social workers who were interested in immigration restrictions. Both he and Hall were convinced—sincerely convinced—that the future of the nation was in peril with the continued influx of the "racially impure."

In 1906, therefore, their arguments shifted: they called for support of the new genetic principals that stressed control of racial developments. Ward and Hall became members of the American Breeders' Association. A committee on immigration was established within the group with Hall as chairman and Ward as secretary. Lodge and his son-in-law Congressman Augustus P. Gardiner appended the literacy test to Senator William Dillingham's immigration bill which called for an increase in the head tax from two to five dollars. Their efforts were nullified by Speaker of the House "Uncle" Joe Cannon. Hall was disappointed by the Immigration Act of 1907. It did not include the literacy test.

However, the act did establish the Dillingham Commission, with a definite proleague bias which gave the IRL renewed hope. After three years of study and the expenditure of one million dollars, the *Reports* recommended the literacy test. In the congressional session of 1911–12, both houses passed the literacy test, and after the conference committee ironed out the differences between the bills it was sent to President William Howard Taft. He promptly vetoed the measure as un-American.

Hall and Ward persisted. Their course was buttressed by the recession of 1913–14, the outbreak of World War I, and ethnic Americans' call for support of their homelands. These efforts of naturalized Americans seemed to conflict with America's neutrality. It called into question the patriotism of the naturalized citizens. Thus on 1915, the literacy test again passed both houses of Congress. It, too, was vetoed by President Woodrow Wilson.

But the loyalty issue of the naturalized Americans gave both Hall and Ward renewed hope. They persisted. The process of Americanization, with its emphasis on "one hundred percent Americanism," and restriction walked hand in hand, at least in the minds of Hall and Ward. The bill was again introduced in the 1916–17 legislative session; it passed, and was vetoed by Wilson. But on February 1, 1917 both houses overrode the veto. This bill became law.

The IRL held a victory dinner at the prestigious Boston Union Club. Hall's health continued to decline. He died in 1921. Ward lived on to see the failure of the literacy test as a restriction tool. The quota legislation of the 1920s was more effective. The most effective restrictive event, of course, was the worldwide recession of 1929–1939.

References
Thomas J. Curran, *Xenophobia and Immigration, 1820–1930* (1975); John Higham, *Strangers in the Land: Patterns of American Nativism* (1955); Barbara Miller Solomon, *Ancestors and Immigrants; A Changing New England Tradition* (1956); Joseph H. Taylor, "The Restriction of European Immigration, 1890–1924," Ph.D dissertation, University of California, 1936) (Taylor provides a précis of his work in "The Immigration Restriction League (1894–1924)," *Midwest Journal* [Summer 1949]).

T.J.C.

IMMIGRATION RESTRICTIONISM. The old restrictionism of the 1920s and 1950s came from the political right, but the new restrictionism of the 1970s and 1980s comes from a centrist or even liberal position. To be successful, restrictionism is changing its course. Restriction of immigration is defended on two grounds. First is that of population stabilization. With new concerns about energy use, the question of population stabilization has changed from whether or not to advocate it to whom. Since the change is imminent, limiting immigration could and should take place within a framework of tolerance and a climate of pluralism. The second argument centers on the effect of immigration on the labor market; it is argued that illegal immigration encourages a two-class society. People in the bottom sector suffer from inadequate protection on the job and from poor pay.

References
Otis L. Graham, *Illegal Immigration and the New Reform Movement* (1980), and "Illegal Immigration and the New Restrictionism," *Center Magazine* 12 (1979): 54–64.

F.C.

IMMIGRATION STATISTICS, National Research Council Report. Sponsored by the National Research Council, the report is the result of an intensive two-year study of immigration information by the Panel on Immigration Statistics. Policy decisions without adequate factual information are major concerns of the research panel and staff. Report sections include the perspective and recommendations of the panel; an historical view of U.S. immigration policy; a call for reliable and complete information; and a concern for improved cooperation and coordination among the many agencies involved. Panel recommendations are stratified by the major agencies and data sources used.

Reference
Daniel B. Levine, ed., *Immigration Statistics: A Story of Neglect* (Panel on Immigration Statistics, National Research Council, 1985).

F.C.

IMMIGRATION STATISTICS, United States population growth, 1790–1970. It is estimated that net immigration to the United States in the first twenty federal censuses amounted to 35.5 million persons. By 1970 that number had produced about 98 million of the total population. Making predictions for the future involves the current picture, so complicated by variables, that the past has little relevance for it.

Reference
Gibson Campbell, "The Contribution of Immigration to the U.S. Population Growth, 1790–1970," *International Migration Review* 9 (1975): 157–177.

F.C.

INDOCHINA MIGRATION AND REFUGEE ASSISTANCE ACT OF 1975 (Public Law 94-23). Passed by Congress on May 23, 1975 amending the Migration and Refugee Assistance Act of 1962 (MRAA-1962), which authorized the president of the United States to continue membership in the Intergovernmental Committee for European Migration. The president was empowered to assist the movement of refugees and to enhance the economic progress of developing nations by providing selected manpower and money. The United States was to pay its dues for its involvement in the Intergovernmental Committee. In addition, funds were to be appropriated for the high commissioner of the United Nations for refugee assistance, and funds were to be appropriated whenever the president decided it would be in the interests of the security of the United States to help certain refugee groups. In addition, the president was empowered to assist refugees in the United States, but he was responsible for defining a refugee as being a person who had left his or her country in the Western Hemisphere because of persecution or fear of persecution on account of race, color, religion, or political opinion and could not return for the same reasons.

The Indochina Migration and Refugee Assistance Act was passed by Congress to redefine the term "refugee" to include people from Vietnam, Laos, and Kampuchea, because MRAA-1962 was applicable only to people in the Western Hemisphere. The law made $455 million available for administering, accommodating, and settling Indochinese refugees.

Reference
William T. Liu, *Transition to Nowhere: Vietnamese Refugees in America* (1979).

D.N.A.

INDOCHINESE MUTUAL ASSISTANCE DIVISION OF THE DEPARTMENT OF HEALTH, EDUCATION AND WELFARE. Established on July 12, 1976, in order to provide technical assistance and liaison channels for more than one hundred self-help associations found among Indochinese refugees throughout the country.

D.N.A.

INDOCHINESE REFUGEE PANEL. *Report of the Indochinese Refugee Panel, April 1986* (Washington, D.C.: United States Department of State, 1986). The five-member commission headed by former Iowa governor Robert D. Ray proposed revising policies governing the immigration of Southeast Asians to give preference to "genuine refugees" and to require many relatives of the nearly 800,000 Indochinese already in the United States to follow regular procedures to obtain visas. It also recommended that the two-tier approach be adopted after current procedures are phased out over a two-year transition period. The report recommended further steps to encourage the nations of Southeast Asia to continue to provide "first asylum" to Indochinese refugees and advised that the United States reverse a four-year moratorium on accepting refugees without ties to former Indochinese governments or to this country, and "resume processing of cases of special concern."

The commission endorsed United States government efforts to encourage Vietnam to return to full operation a program initiated in 1979 under which, the report said, 100,000 persons have been granted exit visas and 40,000 persons have come to the United States. The report noted that 154,000 refugees from Cambodia, Laos, and Vietnam remain in camps in Southeast Asia, and estimated that another 250,000 displaced Cambodians and Vietnamese are encamped on the Thai-Cambodian border. It urged U.S. support of steps to ensure the safety of the border camps and expedited processing of immigrant visa applications by Cambodian camp residents. It endorsed screening programs for Laotian refugees in Thailand, intended to ensure the safety of those desiring to return to Laos.

F.C.

INDOCHINESE REFUGEES, adaptation and assimilation. After a brief discussion of international migration, forced migration, and governmental policy regarding refugees, the research (*infra*) provides a short historical and cultural snapshot of the Lao, Hmong, Cambodians, and Vietnamese, and then turns to federal and state resettlement policy. An account of how the first and second waves of refugees were processed is coupled with a description of federal refugee legislation and funding and the use of voluntary agencies and sponsorships to resettle the refugees. Since the refugees have tended to settle or resettle in selected states such as California and Texas, the construct discusses these states' policies, agencies, programs, and funding for refugees.

Reference
Paul J. Strand and Woodrow Jones, Jr., *Indochinese Refugees in America: Problems of Adaptation and Assimilation* (1984).

F.C.

INDOCHINESE REFUGEES, American policy. Surki examines American policy toward Indochinese refugees and possible changes in current programs, and concludes that

> there are no easy alternatives to current American programs. A reduction in the American intake by itself would increase the burden on other countries—notably the first asylum states in Southeast Asia, probably jeopardize the welfare of existing refugees, and conflict with the notion that America has a commitment to aid people wishing to leave communist countries. Other alternatives to limit the flow of refugees involve a radical change in U.S. policy toward Indochina.

Reference
A. Surki, *Indochinese Refugees: The Impact on First Asylum Countries and Implications for American Policy*, study prepared for the use of the Joint Economic Committee of the Congress of the United States (1980).

F.C.

INDOCHINESE REFUGEES, evolution of United States policy. This study (*infra*) reports that

> In the weeks prior to the collapse of the South Vietnamese government on April 30, 1975, elaborate plans were made whereby large numbers of Vietnamese would be evacuated when the United

States withdrew its personnel from that country. This group consisted of close family members of U.S. citizens, individuals (and their families) who had worked for the U.S. government or U.S. firms conducting business there and certain special cases ("high risk") whose lives would be endangered if they remained behind. Unfortunately, due to a variety of circumstances including the sudden demise of that government, very few of those selected were able to get out during the air-sea evacuation. In all, a total of nearly 130,000 evacuees were taken to temporary haven on Guam and Wake Island and later transferred to the processing centers located in California, Arkansas, Pennsylvania, and Florida. The resettlement process was undertaken following the traditional pattern by which the voluntary agencies were to find homes and jobs for the refugees with limited financial assistance from the government. The program of clearing the camps terminated on December 20, 1975 but the resettlement of these refugees still continues.

Reference
Donald G. Hohl, "The Indochinese Refugee: The Evolution of United States Policy," *International Migration Review* 12 (Spring 1978): 128–132.

F.C.

INDOCHINESE REFUGEES, fertility and adaptation. Levels of fertility among Indochinese refugees in the United States are explored in the context of a highly compressed demographic transition implicit in the move from high-fertility Southeast Asian societies to a low-fertility resettlement region. A theoretical model is developed to explain the effect on refugee fertility of social background characteristics, migratory history, and patterns of adaptation to a different economic and cultural environment, controlling for marital history and length of residence in the United States. Multiple regression techniques are used to test the model which was found to account for nearly half of the variation in refugee fertility levels in the United States. Fertility is much higher for all Indochinese ethnic groups than it is for American women; the number of children in refugee families is, in turn, a major determinant of welfare dependency. Adjustments for rates of natural increase indicate a total 1985 Indochinese population of over one million, making it one of the largest Asian-origin populations in the United States. This remarkable phenomenon has occurred in less than a decade. The implications of these findings for public policy are discussed, focusing on family planning, maternal and child health needs, and the attainment of refugee economic self-sufficiency.

Reference
Ruben G. Rumbaut and John R. Weeks, "Fertility and Adaptation: Indochinese Refugees in the United States," *International Migration Review* 20 (Summer 1986): 428–465.

F.C.

INDOCHINESE REFUGEES, [U.S.] General Accounting Office.
Greater Emphasis on Early Employment and Better Monitoring Needed in Indochinese Refugee Resettlement Program (Gaithersburg, Maryland: U.S. General Accounting Office, 1983). Reviews Indochinese refugee resettlement programs authorized by the Refugee Act of 1980, concentrating on the initial resettlement services provided by voluntary agencies under the State Department's Auspices and social services funded by the Department of Health and Human Services.

F.C.

INDOCHINESE WOMEN,*One Year After Arrival: The Adjustment of Indochinese Women in the United States,* 1979–1980 (Ingrid Walter, 1981). This volume addresses the adjustment of Indochinese women refugees who arrived in the United States in the month of September 1979 under the sponsorship of the Lutheran Immigration and Refugee Service (LIRS). It reviews their situation one year after arrival as seen through their own eyes and through the eyes of Americans in the community who accepted them as new neighbors, and considers their resettlement from the family, social, emotional, English-language, and economic standpoints, and looks at them with respect to differences in their ethnicity, age groups, and geographical locations: i.e., western, central, and eastern United States. In order to provide a framework to explain how and why in late 1980 they were residing in these various locations, Walter begins with an examination of the U.S. refugee resettlement program, the role of voluntary agencies, and factors, such as secondary migration, that may enhance or delay the adjustment of refugees.

F.C.

INDUSTRIAL EDUCATION MOVEMENT (1906–1917). The industrial education movement sought not to add vocational courses to existing curricula but rather to transform the entire school system from traditional general education to industrial education. While the passage of the Smith-Hughes Act (1917) marked its defeat, the movement still left many educators feeling that mass education along academic lines was inappropriate for most (in the cities, overwhelmingly immigrant) public school children.

Reference
Sol Cohen, "The Industrial Education Movement, 1906–1917," *American Quarterly* 20 (1968): 95–110.

F.C.

INDUSTRIAL WORKERS OF THE WORLD (IWW). *See* Syndicalism.

INTERNATIONAL ANTI-FASCIST LEAGUE. *See* North American Anti-Fascist Alliance.

INTERNATIONAL FUR WORKERS' UNION. *See* London, Meyer.

INTERNATIONAL INSTITUTE MOVEMENT. The International Institutes were immigrant service agencies set up by the Young Women's Christian Association (YWCA) during the second decade of the twentieth century. As "service bureaus for foreign-born women and girls," the institutes were viewed as an extension of the YWCA's program of service to factory and commercial employees and their families.

The first institute, begun as an experiment of the newly organized National Board of the YWCA, was established in New York City in 1910. The transfer of the fledgling enterprise to the jurisdiction of the YWCA of Metropolitan New York in 1912 signaled a readiness to implement the program nationally. In rapid succession, institutes were established in Trenton (1912), Lawrence (1913), and Los Angeles (1914). By 1917, the year when the first national conference of the International Institutes was held in Pittsburgh, there were eight fully organized institutes in operation.

With the help of funds from the War Work Council of the YWCA, the institute movement underwent rapid expansion during World War 1. The war created a sharper awareness of the social transformations that had occurred in America over the previous half-century of large-scale immigration. The responses of an "international people" to an "international conflict" were complex and far from uniform. A program that would affirm the self-worth of immigrant peoples and at the same time foster their rapid integration into the larger society was viewed as helpful to the larger war effort. The Department for Work with Foreign-Born Women (after 1924 called the Department of Immigration and Foreign Communities) was established in 1917. A year later, there were twenty-three people working out of the department's office in New York City. The results of their efforts on the local level were impressive. By the end of the war, some sixty-two institutes were in operation. When subsidies from the War Work Council were discontinued after the war, the number of institutes declined to roughly fifty. This number remained fairly constant through most of the 1920s.

The institutes were considered "branches" of local associations, but unlike regular branches elsewhere, they were not generally set up as neighborhood centers, but rather as citywide outreach programs with a select clientele. Most institutes occupied quarters separate from the central association, either in rented space or a building of their own, and were governed by separate "committees of management." For associations in smaller cities (with populations of less that 75,000) Foreign Communities Departments (later called Nationality Communities Departments) operating out of the main association building were set up.

The chief architect of the institute movement was a creative and dynamic woman by the name of Edith Terry Bremer. Educated at the University of Chicago and a veteran of the University of Chicago Settlement, Bremer was recruited by the National Board of the YWCA in 1910 to develop a comprehensive program of service to immigrant women and girls. Bremer believed that the program should be built upon certain "large and basic principles," the most important of which was recognition of the importance of the immigrant community in the life of the immigrant girl; "the community," wrote Bremer, "must be understood, sympathized with, and dealt with *as a part of treating the individual*." Bremer cautioned against the danger of isolating the individual from the community and thereby straining relations between the generations; it was imperative, she argued, to maintain the "integrity" and "unity" of the immigrant family during the process of acculturation.

Consistent with Bremer's belief in the importance of community was her formula for staffing the International Institutes. Bremer realized that only those individuals rooted in the cultures of the immigrants and fluent in their languages could render effective service to immigrant women. Thus, she insisted that the institutes turn to those communities to recruit, and if necessary train, indigenous personnel. These individuals became known as "nationality secretaries." As a result of this policy, carefully implemented by each agency, the International Institutes became, in Bremer's words, "possessed by the people they served." In 1928, more than half of all employed staff members in International Institutes across the country were recruited from the nationality groups. Bremer was also insistent upon the importance of providing a "complete program" for the immigrant girl, not just English classes, but all the activities of a regular local YWCA adapted to the needs and interests of the foreign born.

The institutes specialized in the manifold problems of transplanted peoples: helping to reunite families, to obtain visas and citizenship papers, to teach English, to counsel those who had run afoul of the law, to supply interpreters, and to find jobs for immigrants. The existence of a national network of immigrant service agencies with central direction and national support services increased the effectiveness of each local agency. The institutes also tried to influence public opinion and national policy on immigration. During the 1920s, institute leaders fought for reform of American immigration laws to permit the entry on a nonquota basis of "separated" members of families. During the 1930s, institute leaders condemned the arbitrary and unreasonable use of the deportation penalty. In 1940, the National Institute of Immigrant Welfare (see below) circulated a petition calling for an end to the "baseless fears and mass suspicions" caused by the presence of millions of aliens from Axis countries in the United States.

In performing their larger role in the community, institute workers considered "group work" to be a major responsibility. Each institute organized various educational, recreational, and dramatic clubs along nationality lines. At the Boston institute, clubs such as the "South Boston Armenian Women's Club," and the "Italian Girls Club" were organized during the 1920s. Most of the institutes also offered their facilities to outside ethnic organizations in need of meeting space; as a result, many of the institutes became multiethnic community centers. One of the more controversial policies adopted by the institutes was the encouragement they gave to ethnic identification among the children of the immigrants. A report issued in 1930 by the Commission on the Study of Second Generation Youth of the National Conference of International Institutes urged institute leaders to inculcate a "sense of continuity" with the past. Young people were brought together at the institutes to study the history, language, and literature of their parents' native lands. One could, for example, study Arabic at the Boston institute, Italian at the Brooklyn institute, Greek at the McKeesport institute, and Czech at the Trenton institute. Many institutes put on pageants and plays based upon Old World themes using members of the second generation; some of these productions were performed in the languages of the immigrants. The institutes also encouraged or sponsored the first communitywide, multiethnic folk festivals during the 1920s. Among the earliest of these were the "Old World Folk Festival of Early Spring" organized by the McKeesport International Institute in May of 1922 and the "Pageant of Peace Among the Nations" organized by the Butler, Pennsylvania YWCA that same month. Many current "Festivals of Nations," which have become great civic celebrations in cities such as Duluth, Milwaukee, St. Paul, and Toledo, were initiated by the institutes during the 1920s and 1930s. Many are still sponsored by International Institutes.

Some commentators have seen the work of the institutes as "pioneering" in nature and as an "early" and "unique" example of "cultural pluralism." While few would quarrel that the institutes represented a humane and enlightened approach to the problem of immigrant adjustment to an industrial society, the institute movement reflected a variety of viewpoints on the question of long-term cultural retention. Some proponents of cultural pluralism, many drawn from the ranks of the immigrant communities, found a home within the institutes. So also did proponents of "cultural democracy," a phrase coined by Julius

Drachsler in 1920, who believed in the conservation of immigrant cultural values for the purpose of enriching an emerging cosmopolitan core culture. So also did advocates of "scientific" Americanization, who realized that assimilation was a multigenerational phenomenon and that coercive approaches to assimilation would probably create problems worse than the disunity they were designed to correct.

Over time, the institutes came to possess a broader mission and clientele and evolved into multipurpose organizations characterized by an enlightened philosophy of group relations and a high level of acceptance within ethnic communities. Most institutes "emerged" from the YWCA and became independent organizations during the 1930s. Other institutes, especially those in smaller cities, failed to survive the Depression years. A new national organization, called the National Institute of Immigrant Welfare (NIIW) was established in New York City in 1934 to coordinate the work of the newly independent local agencies. In 1943, NIIW changed its name to the American Federation of International Institutes (AFII).

The program and services of the national organization as well as its local affiliates adapted to changing circumstances and community need after 1934. As thousands of immigrants rushed to avoid being stigmatized as "enemy aliens" during World War II, the process of naturalization consumed a great deal of staff time. The upheavals of World War II and its aftermath left millions of people homeless and stateless. AFII agitated on behalf of these "displaced persons" and, with workers overseas, assisted in the resettlement of thousands of them in the United States. Often persons of professional status and educational background, the "DPs" required services somewhat different from those provided an earlier generation of immigrants. As the civil rights movement gained strength and momentum, many institutes engaged in efforts to promote interracial understanding and cooperation.

A series of mergers and new affiliations strengthened the institute movement in later years. In 1958, AFII merged with the Common Council for American Unity, an organization that specialized in using print media to educate the foreign born about American life and to educate the American born about immigrant problems and contributions. The merged organization became known as the American Council for Nationalities Service (ACNS). The national organization later incorporated the United States Committee for Refugees and the American Branch of International Social Service. Other organizations that had not been part of the YWCA but which espoused similar goals, such as the Immigrants' Protective League of Chicago, affiliated with the International Institute network of agencies. Of the current thirty-five member agencies, twenty-four are offspring of the YWCA.

Reference
Nicholas V. Montalto, *A History of the International Education Movement, 1924–1941* (1982).

N.V.M.

INTERNATIONAL LADIES' GARMENT WORKERS' UNION.
At the turn of the century, the women's garment workers, mostly women and immigrants, and their industry seemed the least likely to develop a permanent union. Yet within the first decade these same garment workers were involved in two historic strikes—the shirtwaist makers' walkout in 1909 and the cloakmakers' revolt in 1910—that established the ILGWU as a continuing union, and its growing power was demonstrated in the convulsive strikes in the women's trades in 1913. A pioneering trade agreement, known as the Protocol (1910–16), was in effect in many branches of the industry, indicating the evolving power of the ILGWU.

References
Hyman Berman, "Era of the Protocol: A Chapter in the History of the International Ladies' Garment Workers Union, 1910–1916," Ph.D. dissertation, Columbia University, 1956 (DA 16:1245); Louis Levine (Louis Lorin, pseudonym), *The Women's Garment Workers: A History of the International Ladies' Garment Workers Union* (1924; rpt. 1974); Roger D. Waldinger, *Through the Eye of the Needle: Immigrants and Enterprise in New York's Garment Trade* (1986).

F.C.

IRELAND, JOHN (1838–1918). Roman Catholic archbishop. Ireland emigrated from Ireland in 1849 with his family, settling in St. Paul, Minnesota. He was ordained in 1861; became pastor of St. Paul's Cathedral in 1867; was consecrated coadjutor-bishop of St. Paul's in 1875; succeeded to the See in 1884; and was named archbishop in 1888. An advocate of western settlement by immigrants, Ireland encouraged them to move out of Eastern city slums with aid from his Catholic Colonization Bureau. He opposed native-language retention by immigrants (particularly Germans), and the appointment of bishops on ethnic and racial grounds. He was a friend of Presidents William McKinley and Theodore Roosevelt. An advocate of state support and inspection of Catholic schools, Ireland was an energetic spokesman for liberal American Catholicism.

References
J. H. Moynihan, *Archbishop John Ireland* (1953); Thomas E. Wangler, "The Ecclesiology of Archbishop John Ireland," Ph.D. dissertation, Marquette University, 1969 (DA 31:1885–A).

F.C.

IRISH. The Irish diaspora has been one of the most extensive movements of people in world history. Ten times more people of Irish ancestry live in the United States than in Ireland itself. Ireland was Britain's first colony and its history has been one of political and economic exploitation. Irish people left Ireland for the United States for a variety of reasons, including religious persecution, starvation, political oppression, and economic underdevelopment. However, the causes, extent, and composition of emigration differed markedly during different historic periods.

Stages of Emigration. It is useful to survey Irish emigration utilizing a five-stage model. The five stages consist of (1) the colonial period prior to 1815; (2) the prefamine period from 1815 to 1845; (3) the famine years, 1845–1855; (4) the postfamine years from 1855 to the 1920s; and (5) the postindependence years from the 1920s to the present.

During the colonial period Irish emigration was dominated by artisans, small shopkeepers, and small farmers from an Ulster Protestant background. However, the number of Catholics, contrary to the traditional view, was considerable, consisting of possibly 40 percent of the total Irish migration. About 400,000 to 500,000 came during this period, including a substantial number of Irish indentured servants brought here after the seventeenth-century Cromwellian War. Commercial restrictions on Irish economic development and religious persecution of both dissenters and Catholics were the primary causes of emigration. This wave of immigrants settled mainly in the mid-Atlantic states of Pennsylvania, Maryland, Virginia, and Delaware, and the southeastern states of Georgia, North Carolina, and South Carolina.

The prefamine emigration began at the conclusion of the Napoleonic Wars. The end of hostilities resulted in a partial loss of English markets for Irish agricultural products and further restrictions on Irish industrialization leading to greatly diminished economic opportunities. At the same time a shift from tillage to grazing encouraged estate clearance by the eviction of small farmers and peasants. At this time more and more American ships were carrying raw materials to England and thus on the return voyage could offer cheaper passage to America. Instead of returning empty the ship captains could use the emigrants as paying ballast. Agrarian secret societies were also beginning to use violence and intimidation to deal with oppressive landlords and their agents as well as resisting the tithes payable to the Anglican church.

A combination of these factors started a major push which led to about 1,500,000 going to America. At first many of these emigrants were Protestant dissenters from Ulster, but later Catholics from the south came to dominate. They settled in the eastern cities, especially

Philadelphia and New York, and later extended inland first along the canals and then the railroads. But significant portions did locate in agrarian settings and attempt to make a living as farmers.

The period most associated in the popular mind with Irish emigration is the famine years. From 1845 to 1855 about 1.5 million people came to the United States, largely from the west and southwest of Ireland. A massive failure of the potato crop due to a fungus, *Phytophora Infestans,* combined with British inaction and the colonial socioeconomic structure to produce massive death, destitution, and emigration. The emigrants left hurriedly and by any means they could, including overcrowded unseaworthy "coffin ships." These ships were characterized by a death rate similar to that of the slave ships from Africa. This group was the most destitute yet, the most aggressively Irish and Catholic of all the emigrant waves. They too settled in the eastern port cities as well as places like Akron, Toledo, St. Paul, and St. Louis along the inland transportation routes.

During the postfamine years from 1855 to the 1920s, emigration became an institutionalized part of Irish life. Over 2.5 million came to America and settled largely in the previously settled areas. Emigration during this period was generally the result of deteriorating economic conditions and increased political repression. Evictions began to increase and agrarian violence and disobedience intensified. These emigrants came largely from the economically impoverished areas of west and extreme southwest Ireland. It was this group that sent back massive amounts of money to Ireland in order to improve the conditions of those left behind or to pay for further emigration of relatives.

From the conclusion of the Anglo-Irish War and the partition of Ireland into two units to the present, the emigration pattern has been one of spurts and lulls. Shortly after the founding of the Irish Free State, emigration slowed dramatically. However, emigration from the six northeastern counties still under British control continued, especially among nationalists. The nature of the partitioned statelet with respect to employment, housing, and civil rights encouraged differentially greater nationalist emigration from the northeast. Recently emigration, legal and illegal, especially among the young, has increased again from the Republic of Ireland due to the disastrous economic situation there.

The arrival of the Irish in America throughout history has been characterized by much prejudice and exploitation. The Irish were viewed with suspicion by Anglo-Americans since the majority were poor, anti-English, and Catholic. They were subjected to high rents and crowded, unsanitary living conditions. From the famine until the mid-twentieth century a "No Irish Need Apply" attitude was commonplace.

Though largely a rural, peasant people the Irish urbanized in the United States. The urbanization of the Irish peasant was the result of

many different factors. Farming was a symbol of oppression characterized by poverty, rack rents, eviction, starvation, and foreign masters.
Furthermore, the farming technology of Ireland was unsuitable for
farming in the great American West and most of the Irish lacked the
finances to buy land, tools, and seed. However, the city offered opportunities of two types; one was unskilled jobs; the other a chance to
develop political power in numbers. In the urban ghettos there was
safety from hostile nativist attitudes toward emigrants as well as less
religious discrimination than in the predominantly Protestant rural
areas. Nativist reactions included anti-Irish riots, job and housing discrimination, and even anti-Irish political parties such as the Native
American party and the Know-Nothings.

The major institutional impacts of the Irish in America were in the
areas of politics, labor, and religion. It is in the area of politics, especially big city politics, that the Irish have achieved the most recognition. However, an often neglected political fact is the significant part
played by the Irish in the success of the American Revolution. The Irish
who came to America were familiar with techniques of representative
government and the manipulation of the democratic process, especially
those who emigrated after Daniel O'Connell's Catholic Emancipation
struggle. They knew how to organize rallies, prepare and deliver political oratory, and employ the art of pamphleteering.

The Irish aggressively used their experience to seize political
power. By the 1850s they had gained much local and neighborhood
power and from the 1860s to the 1890s gained control of many of the
big cities such as New York, Buffalo, Philadelphia, St. Louis, San
Francisco, and Kansas City. As machine politics declined during the
Depression the Irish became active participants in the New Deal and
remained the bulwark of the Democratic party until the nomination of
George McGovern.

Irish big city politics was based on a pragmatic view of what
people want. The Irish did not expect their leaders to be saints, so to
them some degree of corruption was inevitable. They differentially
conceptualized graft at the top, which helped a few, and graft at the
bottom, where it worked for everyone. Loyalty and responsiveness to
the needs of one's constituents were more important than honesty. It
was loyalty in the face of personal setbacks that held the organization
together. If you stand by your own and wait your turn you will be
rewarded eventually. To the Irish, self-righteousness would not win
elections, since most people are not ideologues. The machine politics of
the Irish has been criticized as being corrupt and in opposition to social
progress. But the machines were in reality more successful as reformers
than most liberals and may have created the climate for later social
programs by the establishment of the Democratic party's power base.

The reason for the success of the Irish in politics was multifactoral. In addition to their familiarity with the Anglo-American democratic system, their Catholicism served as an ethnic organizing force while the ghetto institutions such as saloons, social clubs, and athletic clubs were used for political organizing. Further, politics, unlike most of the professions, was open to self-made individuals with little formal training. Finally, many of the Irish exhibited a gregarious verbal nature that lent itself well to political campaigning.

In the field of labor many historians have portrayed the Irish influence as conservative or reactionary. But this stereotype is not supported by an examination of the labor movement. It was the Irish and their descendants who first attempted to organize the miners, longshoremen, and iron workers. In fact, the Irish and Irish-Americans provided much of the labor movement's early leadership such as Mike Quill and T. V. Powderly. Radical Unionism never really flourished in the United States due to state repression and fragmentation of the working class, but the Irish were important in two of the most radical unions, the IWW and the Western Federation of Miners. By the early years of the twentieth century Irish-Americans politically controlled a majority of the unions in the United States.

The Irish had an enormous effect on the nature of the American Catholic church. For the emigrants the church was a source of identity and psychic support, and its priests often helped fight the system. The Irish were not interested in accommodation with their old enemies, the Anglo-Saxons, and thus stirred up nativistic animosities that resulted in convent burnings and physical attacks on their neighborhoods. The great numbers of Irish Catholics, with their demand for an Irish clergy, simply overwhelmed the early church. The church in America changed from a predominantly quiet, subdued rural institution to an aggressively Irish and urban one.

By 1879 a conflict developed within the church between the liberals, led by Bishops Ireland, Gibbons, Keane, O'Connell, and Spaulding, and the conservatives, led by Bishops McQuaid and Corrigan. The liberals viewed the church as an agent for Americanization, stressed the "melting pot" concept, and supported the public school system and social justice. Conservatives felt that it was necessary to preserve Catholic ethnic identity and loyalty, stressed parochial education, and supported capitalism against labor unions and other calls for social justice. The controversy was carried all the way to Rome and in 1899 the liberals were censured, leading to a long period of caution among church liberals.

Irish church leaders created the parochial school system as well as most of the Catholic colleges and universities. However, these schools Americanized the students and their Catholicity replaced their Irishness.

Charges of inferiority of the parochial schools have not been supported by the facts, either historically or contemporaneously. The schools were important in the transition from immigrant status and greatly aided social and occupational mobility. Irish Catholics today send a higher percentage to college than any other ethnic group, excluding Jewish Americans.

Many Irish immigrants exhibited support for the long struggle of the independence of Ireland. From the early 1800s the Irish immigrants supported a variety of political movements to free their homeland from British domination. They contributed their money, time, and political influence to the repeal movement, the Fenians, the Young Irelanders, the Land League, the Sinn Fein party, and the Irish Republican Army (IRA). They organized American support groups such as the Fenian Brotherhood, Clan na Gael, Friends of Irish Freedom, and Irish Northern Aid.

Irish emigration to the United States established the base for a very large Irish-American population. In the 1980 census over 40 million people claimed Irish ancestry. But Irish America is extremely variable with respect to its identification with its Irishness. The identification can be one of name only, or limited to a gaudy, comic, superficial "St. Patrick's Day Irish" image. However, for a significant number it involves participation in Irish cultural activities such as dance, music, theater, courses and lectures, and Gaelic sports, while for others it involves active participation in the struggle for freedom and social justice in northeast Ireland today.

References

Clark, Dennis, *Hibernia America: The Irish and Regional Cultures* (1986); Doyle, David N., *America and Ireland 1776–1976* (1980); Fallows, Marjorie R., *Irish-Americans: Identity and Assimilation* (1979); Greeley, Andrew M., *The Irish-Americans Rise to Money and Power* (1980); McCaffrey, Lawrence J., *The Irish Diaspora in America* (1976); Metress, Seamus P., *The Irish-American Experience* (1981); Wittke, Carl, *The Irish in America* (1956).

S.P.M.

IRISH AMERICAN CULTURAL INSTITUTE. An Irish cultural organization founded in 1962 to foster an appreciation of Irish history and culture. It is based in St. Paul, Minnesota, with members in all fifty states and local chapters in many major cities. Since 1965 it has published an excellent quarterly journal, *Eire-Ireland: A Journal of Irish Studies*. The institute sponsors American tours for Irish craftsmen, authors, and scholars as well as programs for American high school students to study in Ireland. The institute also includes a mail order service for Irish books and media.

S.P.M.

IRISH, Irish-American Press. In the nineteenth-century, there evolved the two roles of Irish-American journalism: keeping the Irish Irish and making them American. American Irish ethnic journalists tried to construct bridges between the Irish "retrospect" and the American "prospect." Refugees from Irish famine and revolution in the late 1840s made the Irish-American press contentious and divisive. Irish-American newspapers debated Old Country issues—clerical versus anticlerical Catholicism, constitutional versus physical-force nationalism. After 1870 the press debates stopped, and journalists participated in a common effort to use Irish Catholicism and nationalism as instruments to forge Irish-American unity and progress within the American environment. This strategy was enhanced by the domination of Parnell's constitutional Home Rule movement over the direction of Irish nationalism. According to Joyce, John Boyle O'Reilly's *Boston Pilot* (*q.v.*) symbolized the Irish-American press effort to keep Irish America emotionally Irish while at the same time adjusting it to the goals, values, and tastes of the general American society.

Reference
William L. Joyce, *Editors and Ethnicity: A History of the Irish-American Press, 1848–1883* (1976).

F.C.

THE IRISH EMIGRANT'S GUIDE FOR THE UNITED STATES (1851). *See* O'Hanlon, John.

IRISH, emigration, marriage, and fertility. There is a belief that the word "Irish" is a synonym for "unique" in the field of population studies. While all other European nations increased in population during the last century, the population of Ireland decreased at every census except one between 1841 and 1961. The proportions of persons postponing marriage or remaining permanently single are higher among the Irish than among the people of any other European nation, yet the married Irish have Europe's highest rate of fertility. Kennedy attempts to distinguish those elements of emigration, marriage, and fertility that are indeed peculiar to Ireland from those that Ireland shares, to a greater or lesser extent, with other countries.

Reference
Robert E. Kennedy, *Irish Emigration, Marriage, and Fertility* (1973).

F.C.

IRISH, *Erin's Daughters in America: Irish Immigrant Women in the Nineteenth Century* (Hasia R. Diner, 1983). Described here are thousands of Irish women who saw in America the chance to utilize the

energy, ambition, and ability that would otherwise have remained sti-
fled by the poverty and social inflexibility of their native land. *Erin's
Daughters in America* follows these women from an Ireland devastated
by the Great Famine of the 1840s to their new homes in the United
States. Diner explores their postimmigration family life, their work and
education, their battles against poverty, alcoholism, and mental illness,
and the network of formal and informal ethnic organizations that developed to help them adjust to a different way of life. Diner also discusses
the stress that the immigrant women's newly found social and economic
independence put on already frail relationships with Irish men. In terms
of marriage, work, educational achievement, and upward mobility,
Irish women were very different from—and much more successful
than—other female immigrants. Diner describes that success in detail,
but her primary emphasis is on the qualities that enabled Irish women to
prosper in a new and challenging world. The origins of those qualities,
she argues, can be found only in Ireland, in a cultural tradition that the
immigrant women could neither live within nor leave behind them.

F.C.

IRISH NORTHERN AID. An organization founded in 1970 in New
York by Irish emigrants who sought to aid the embattled people of
northeast Ireland. The organization, better known as Noraid, has been
subject to much government scrutiny and its membership has been
harassed by government agents. Its major objectives are public education on the situation in northeast Ireland and fund raising to aid the
families of Irish political prisoners. It is a nonsectarian, activist organization that stretches from coast to coast, and the most effective voice of
Irish nationalism in the United States.

Reference
Dennis Clark, *Irish Blood* (1977).

S.P.M.

IRISH REPUBLICAN BROTHERHOOD. *See* Fenian Brotherhood.

IRISH WORLD. *See* Ford, Patrick.

ISLAND OF HOPE. *See* Ellis Island.

ISLAND OF TEARS. *See* Ellis Island.

ISSEI. Japanese term that means the first generation of immigrants
from Japan. The term is made up of two Japanese words: "first," or
"one," and "generation." When referring to the second generation,

the American-born children of Issei, the Japanese word *Ni,* which means second, replaces the first word of the above term to become *Nisei.* The third generation, the children of *Nisei,* is called *Sansei;* the first word of the term, *san,* means third or three.

Reference
John W. Connor, *Tradition and Change in Three Generations of Japanese Americans* (1977).

D.N.A.

ISTITUTO ITALIANO DI CULTURA (New York City). Founded in 1959, the Istituto Italiano di Cultura of New York is the Italian government's cultural agency in the United States. Its task is the strengthening of cultural ties between Italy and the country where it is located. The main lines of its activity are the following: (1) general and cultural information; (2) promotion of the Italian language; (3) promotion of Italian books; (4) assistance, particularly in the audio-visual field, to teachers of Italian language and literature; (5) promotion and organization of cultural events of Italian interest; (6) study of the problems involved in cultural relations between Italy and the United States and the promotion of cultural enterprises useful to both countries; and (7) assistance to American and Italian scholars.

F.C.

ISTRIA. *See* Croatians.

ISTRO-ROMANIANS. *See* Romanians.

ITALIAN-ALBANIANS. The Albanians, whose homeland lies on the eastern coast of the Adriatic Sea and the mountainous hinterland, also reside in a diaspora in many countries including Italy. Italian-Albanians commenced migrating to Calabria and Sicily during the Turkish occupation of their land during the sixteenth century. Most were Christians of the Byzantine rite from southern Albania who over the centuries would merge with the Italo-Greek Catholics. The Byzantine rite, with the liturgy (since 1968) celebrated in Albanian, continues to be a distinguishing characteristic. Unlike most Byzantine Christians in Albania and elsewhere who are Eastern Orthodox, the Italian-Albanians accept papal primacy. Their ecclesiastical centers are the eparchies of Lungro, Calabria (near Cosenza), and Piana degli Albanesi, Sicily (near Palermo).

Migration to the USA. Beginning around 1880 Italian-Albanians migrated to America as part of the economically motivated migration from the *Mezzogiorno.* Chain migration accelerated this movement and certain Old World villages declined in population, especially in young males. A conservative estimate is that 50,000 settled in America from 1880 to 1924 and, while no official statistics are available, they probably number over 100,000 at present.

Settlement Patterns. Italian-Albanians settled in Italian-American neighborhoods and not Albanian-American neighborhoods such as those of Boston and its surrounding towns. New York's Little Italy around Mulberry Street contained the largest settlement. Settlements were also reported in Chicago, Detroit, Philadelphia, St. Louis, Bayonne, Elizabeth, Jersey City, and Newark, New Jersey as well as New Orleans, Bensonhurst (Brooklyn), Inwood, and Oceanside, New York. Since World War II Italian-Albanians have been part of the suburban exodus.

Economic and Political Activities. Most immigrant men became laborers. Studies are scarce but a local study of Inwood, Long Island found that 11 percent of foreign-born males were entrepreneurs in 1900 with the most popular pursuits being junk dealing and businesses servicing their own people, such as boarding houses and groceries. Interviews with older individuals revealed that females contributed much to running family-owned businesses, yet the 1900 and 1910 U.S. censuses listed them as having no occupation. On Long Island several Italian-Albanians have been very successful in Republican politics and in New Orleans an Italo-Albanian Democrat was mayor during the 1960s. The proportion of white-collar workers has increased as part of the structural mobility of recent decades.

Identity. Language and religion are the chief boundary-maintaining mechanisms. Italian-Albanians speak Arbëresh, which is a branch of the southern Albanian Tosk dialect. Many of the first and second generation have been trilingual, knowing Arbëresh, English, and a southern Italian dialect. Byzantine rite Catholicism was brought to America, but most immigrants joined Latin rite parishes due to a shortage of Byzantine priests. Others came from villages that were already Latinized.

Rev. Ciro Pinnola, a native of Mezzoiuso, Sicily, founded Our Lady of Grace Greek Catholic Church on New York's Broome Street in 1906, the only officially Italo-Albanian church ever in America. Liturgy was celebrated in Greek according to the Byzantine rite. The chapel was later relocated in a storefront on Stanton Street, where poverty and sparse attendance hindered it. The parish ceased to exist with Father Pinnola's death in 1946.

Both Byzantine and Latin rite Italian-Albanians venerate Our Lady of Good Counsel. Mary's icon is said to have been brought from Albania to Italy during the fifteenth century exodus and Italian-Albanians consider the cult their own. An annual *festa* and procession is held each May at Our Lady of Good Counsel Parish, Inwood, Long Island. New Orleans Italian-Albanians also venerate St. Nicholas of Myra, and such

Latin rite cults as the Sacred Heart and St. Anthony have been adopted by Byzantine Catholics.

Present State. No church organization officially exists for Byzantine rite Italian-Albanians. A few attend St. Michael's Byzantine Church in Manhattan's Little Italy, where the pastor is sympathetic. A small number attend other Byzantine rite churches but most are Latin rite Catholics or indifferent to religion. Historically, Eastern rite Catholics have been generally treated harshly or ignored by the American Roman Catholic hierarchy so it is questionable whether the situation will change.

Societies attempting to maintain ethnic identity include: the Contessa Entellina of New Orleans; the Stella Albanese of Long Island; and Our Lady of Grace Society of Staten Island, which publishes a bimonthly newsletter.

Some language maintenance and much ethnic consciousness persist among older second-generation members. Despite parental opposition, many married Italian-Americans, having been Italianized in their neighborhoods. If marital assimilation is indicative, the third and fourth generations are in what sociologist Richard Alba calls the "twilight of ethnicity." Some Byzantine Catholic priests and lay persons are pursuing a cultural renaissance, and so the situation remains in flux.

References

Francis Dessart, "The Albanian Ethnic Groups in the World: A Historical and Cultural Essay on the Albanian Colonies in Italy," *East European Quarterly* 15, no. 4 (1981): 469–484; Gerard B. Donnelly, S. J., "Manhattan's Eastern Catholics: The Italo-Greek-Albanians," *America* 54, no. 25 (March 28, 1936): 589–596; Richard Renoff, Angela D. Danzi, and Joseph A. Varacalli, "The Italian-Albanian-American Community of Inwood, New York," paper read at the 19th Annual Conference of The American Italian Historical Association, November 14, 1986, Philadelphia; Andrew S. Shipman, "Greek Catholics in America," *The Catholic Encyclopedia* (1913), 6:744–752.

R.R.

ITALIAN CHAMBER OF LABOR (New York). *See* North American Anti-Fascist Alliance.

ITALIAN COMMISSARIAT OF EMIGRATION. Until 1888 Italy was without a general emigration law. The great exodus or *Völkerwanderung* of the Italians could not be ignored, and in 1888 a general emigration law was enacted, essentially restrictive in its intent. The law proved ineffective. Inevitably, Italian emigration received special bureaucratic attention and recognition in the law enacted by the parliament on January 31, 1901, a comprehensive emigration law almost paternal in character. Grazia Dore succinctly noted: "The emigrants were placed under state tutelage, under a commissariat to which was entrusted the supervision over cargo, over the embarkation operation, the voyages and recruitment." The Italian Commissariat of Emigration (R. Commissariato dell'Emigrazione) represented "the most elaborate creation" of the 1901 law. Foerster understood its centrifugal importance, and clearly recognized that the commissariat was both the pulsating heart and the body of the 1901 law: "It is the center of all the public protective institutions, and stands in a definite relationship with the private as well. . . . The Commissioner-General is a member of the Emigration Council, a broadly representative organization of twelve persons who meet in at least two sessions a year to discuss the larger problems that call for action." Actually, the commissariat was a component of the larger framework afforded by the Ministry of Foreign Affairs (Ministero degli Affari Esteri), from which it derived its authority.

The law of 1901 (and subsequent legislation) gave to the commissariat a multiplicity of authorizations which had been formerly assumed by other agencies, and the law empowered the commissariat in a variety of other jurisdictions hitherto ambiguously defined or nonexistent. The commissariat was empowered

> to grant licenses, fix the cost of tickets, oversee the ports of embarkation, establish and maintain hostels for the emigrants, furnish information, inspect emigrants on departure, grant permits to recruit workers for European countries (emigration agencies having been abolished by the law of 1901), ensure protection of emigrants on board ships through the medium of traveling commissioners, prepare international agreements on emigration and labor, and give aid and protection to emigrants in foreign countries. Carriers were required to lodge emigrants in case of delay in departure, to meet safety and hygienic standards for transporting both expatriates and repatriates, and to restore transportation costs to migrants rejected by immigration authorities provided it could be proved that the legal requirements were known to the undertaking before departure. Other legislation, likewise reflecting former abuses, prohibited propaganda or false representations, all-to-often responsible for consular repatriation for which, in some instances, carriers were made to pay the cost. To finance social assistance for emigrants, the Italian government established an Emigration Fund from taxes on railroad tickets and emigrants' passports, fees from recruiting and transport licenses, and fines for infringements of emigration laws.

The success of the commissariat was, in no small part, due to the men who were appointed commissioners-general of emigration, who were extraordinarily able, imaginative, and innovative, of whom Luigi Bodio and Giuseppe De Michelis are representative. The suppression of the commissariat in 1927 (and its replacement by the General Direction of Italians Abroad) was dictated by changing political patterns. This bureaucratic change emphasized the shift, under Fascist auspices, from a policy of encouragement to one of obstruction of emigration. No longer did Italian workers going abroad benefit from quick delivery of passports and reduced railway fares; instead, the latter advantage was offered to returning laborers. The Emigration Fund was abolished, punishment for clandestine emigration was increased, and emigrants were forbidden to export more than 10,000 lire. Abroad, the ardent propaganda activities of Fascist consular officials discouraged denationalization and assimilation of Italian subjects, thus producing unfavorable reaction not only in foreign circles, but to some extent among Italian immigrants.

In no area was the success of the commissariat more manifest than in its officially sponsored publications which offered assistance to emigrants, made available information vitally necessary for the comprehension of migration, and attempted analyses of a phenomenon that so critically affected the nation's destiny. The official publications fall into five categories: (1) the law and jurisprudence of emigration; (2) emigration and the immigrant colonies; (3) periodicals; (4) administrative and regulatory guides; and (5) informational and useful compendia. Each of the categories (and the series of publications that each includes) is an important repository out of which the shape and form of Italian emigration emerge. The publications attest the seriousness of the commissariat's endeavors, and the high purpose of its efforts. Of all the publications, none is more important than the *Bollettino dell'Emigrazione,* which was issued by the commissariat during its lifetime, and whose numbers constitute for the period 1902–1927 an unparalleled resource for the study of the twin dynamics of world emigration and immigration.

The *Bollettino* began publication in 1902 and continued, except for 1918, uninterrupted publication through 1927. Although termed "pubblicazione mensile," its periodicity is irregular. Each of its numbers includes articles, notes, and monographs on all phases of emigration: in a larger sense, the *Bollettini* are repositories of invaluable data which chronicle Italian emigration to all parts of the world, and which delineate the Italian experience outside Italy; and for the quarter-century in which they appear, the *Bollettini* are a contemporary record of the evolving debate that surrounds emigration.

Admittedly, the *Bollettino* is primarily a chronicle of Italian emigration to all parts of the world: but in the very process of chronicling the vast migrations of Italians, the *Bollettino* provides concomitant chronicles of Italian life abroad—in the greater Europe, in the Americas, in Australasia, and in Africa; and in the twin role of emigrant and immigrant, the Italian voyager touches the life of the country to which he goes in ways as profound as his departure affects his native Italy. Foerster speaks eloquently to this point:

One honor indeed Italy enjoys upon which little or no stress has been laid. Her blood makes its contribution to the great world races. Her sons die, but their sons live on. As generations of plants succeed one another, there is here an immortality of race stock. The Italian blood will count in the remotest future of Europe and North Africa, of South and North America, and in some important countries it will count for a great deal. What the natural historian of emigration here sees is no barren distinction to Italy. But, also, what he sees fails to send a thrill through the heart of the patriot in the Mediterranean, who beholds only the price that has inevitably to be paid political and cultural discontinuity and sacrifice.

The *Bollettino,* then, is indispensable to the scholar who wishes to understand the "future of Europe and North Africa, of South and North America," a future that prophetically has shown Foerster to be correct: certainly, the progeny of Italians has "in some important countries . . . count[ed] for a great deal."

The magnitude of the *Bollettino* is staggering. In all, 345 fascicles (i.e., numbers) were published, comprehending a total of over 36,000 pages. Some years (aggregating multiple fascicles) include several thousand pages (e.g., 1908, whose 24 fascicles include 2,671 pages; and 1910, whose 18 fascicles include 2,809 pages), and many of the fascicles are, in themselves, comprehensive monographs delineating in considerable detail themes of compelling importance. Nothing is truly comparable to Adolfo Rossi's (*q.v.*) study of Italians in the United States (no. 16, 1904); of inestimable value are the ubiquitous Adolfo Rossi's plaintive accounts of Italian immigrants in San Paolo, Brasil (no. 7, 1902), and of an inhospitable South Africa's exploitive responses to immigrant workers (no. 9, 1903). There is pathos in Amy Bernardy's (*q.v.*) sad portraits of Italian immigrant women and children in the urban ethnic enclaves of the United States (no. 1, 1909; no. 1, 1911); and largely unused are the sombre accounts of Alfonso Lomonaco of the travail and death of Italian immigrant workers in the building of the Panama Canal (no. 2, 1909). No adequate history of Argentina is possible without recourse to the multi-faceted monographs that explore the history of Italians in that nation written for the *Bollettino* by Umberto Tomezzoli (nos. 16 and 17, 1907; no. 3, 1908); Giuseppe Capra's study of Italians in Australia (no. 8, 1910) has been little used, and Giacomo Pertile's comprehensive overview of the Italian presence in Germany on the eve of World War I (nos. 11 and 12, 1914) is essential for an understanding of a Europe which was to disappear across the landscape of an insatiably destructive political struggle. The tragedy of endemic disease and the hazards of migration are poignantly delineated in Gennaro Candido's clinically harrowing account of the ravages of tuberculosis (no. 14, 1914).

In the thousands of notes, articles, reviews, legislative debates, regulatory codifications, and miscellanea which the *Bollettino* incorporates, there lies an evolving chronicle of human migration which touches the national sovereignties of four continents: in a unique way, the exodus of Italians is inextricably linked to the fortunes of other nations. The *Bollettino* is the key to "a great migration," and it affirms in its multitudinous archives the truth of Foerster's *obiter dicta:* "Those who compose a great migration may be never so ordinary; en masse they arrest attention."

References

Francesco Cordasco, *Italian Mass Emigration* (1980); Grazia Dore, "Some Social and Historical Aspects of Italian Emigration to America," *Journal of Social History* 2 (Winter 1968): 95–122; Robert F. Foerster, *The Italian Emigration of Our Time* (1919; rpt. 1968).

F.C.

ITALIAN EDUCATIONAL LEAGUE. *See* Covello, Leonard.

ITALIAN IMMIGRANTS IN LOUISIANA'S SUGAR PARISHES. In the late nineteenth century, a chronic labor shortage in the Louisiana sugar plantations led the state of Louisiana and prominent planters to initiate a movement to import foreign workers. After attempts to use Chinese and Scandinavian laborers failed, attention focused on Italian workers. Evolving patterns of immigration from Sicily to the southern United States created a large Italian community in Louisiana (the largest ethnic group in the state), but official census figures did not reflect the impact of immigrant workers in the sugar parishes. Each year at harvest time, thousands of Italians traveled from Sicily, Chicago, New York, St. Louis, and New Orleans to the sugar plantations, remaining in the cane fields from October through March, when they retraced their steps (estimates of this migration range from a conservative 16,000 to an unlikely 80,000). In her important study, Scarpaci deals with the phenomena of immigration from Sicily to Louisiana, Italian immigrants in agriculture, Italian relations with American black workers (and attempts to replace blacks with Italian immigrants), and the continuing efforts to recruit Italian laborers. In a larger sense, her study is a sociohistorical study of the Louisiana immigrant community and its evolving relationships with the native dominant white American community.

Reference

Jean Ann Scarpaci, *Italian Immigrants in Louisiana's Sugar Parishes: Recruitment, Labor Conditions, and Community Relations, 1880–1910* (1980).

F.C.

ITALIAN LANGUAGE SERVICE BUREAU. *See* Italian Teachers Association.

ITALIAN LEAGUE FOR SOCIAL SERVICE. *See* Covello, Leonard.

ITALIAN PARENTS ASSOCIATION. *See* Covello, Leonard.

ITALIAN TEACHERS ASSOCIATION (New York City). The history of Italian-language instruction in the United States is a significant aspect of the Italian-American past (and an important part of the present), since language maintenance by any community is an expression of the cultural ethos that defines that community, and must be regarded as one of the major forces that preserve and strengthen a culture. How important language maintenance is for the ethnic community has been shown in the studies by Joshua A. Fishman, particularly in his monumental *Language Loyalty in the United States* (1966).

In the archives of the history of Italian-language instruction in the United States, no documents are more important than the *Annual Reports* of the Italian Teachers Association. The association was organized in 1912; its activities were suspended at the outbreak of World War I, but were reactivated in 1921; and the association continued to function until 1939, after which date (its *Annual Reports* no longer published), it slipped into a chapter affiliation with the American Association of Teachers of Italian, itself an affiliate of the larger Modern Language Association. In a strict sense, the Italian Teachers Association functioned as a viable entity between 1912 and 1939, and may be regarded only as a remote progenitor of the contemporary New York City Italian Teachers Association.

Sociologically, the *Annual Reports* constitute a *unique* repository of data on Italian-language instruction in the United States for the period they cover, and they represent an important archives for the social/cultural history of Italians in America. Their periodicity and bibliographical history require explanation. The *Annual Reports* were presented to the association in September of each year. The *First Annual Report* was printed as part 2 of the *Tenth Annual Report;* the *Second Annual Report* (published originally in an outsize form) was published as part 3 of the *Thirteenth Annual Report;* and the *Eleventh Annual Report* was published as Casa Italiana Educational Bureau (*q.v.*) Pamphlet No. 1. The *Annual Reports* (1921/1922–1938/39) include sixteen numbers in all (or eighteen, since the *Second* is incorporated as part of the *Thirteenth* and the *First* is incorporated as part of the *Tenth*).

The association fought for and achieved parity for the Italian language in the New York City public schools; it projected a bibliographical register (whose entries directly intruded into the social history of Italians in the United States); and it brought into being (however short-lived) an Italian Language Service Bureau which was to serve as a clearinghouse "for all matters pertaining to the study and teaching of the Italian language in the United States." That the association failed in the achievement of these larger social goals can be attributed to a number of factors, chief among which was the insensitivity in modern language instruction to the study of sociohistorical contemporary contexts (the Italian-American community was, in the process, almost completely neglected by the teachers of Italian), and it might be cogently argued that the seeds of the declination of modern language instruction in an ethnically diverse United States were sown in this ethnocultural insensitivity and neglect.

Reference
Francesco Cordasco, *The Italian Community and Its Language in the United States: The Annual Reports of the Italian Teachers Association* (1975).

                                                                         F.C.

ITALIANS. The term "Italians" is vague and may be ambiguous; here it refers to those people who originated in the European "boot," the peninsula that extends southward from the southern slopes of the Alps to the islands of Sicily and Sardinia. *Italia* was the name given to the peninsula by the Romans. Almost 6 million people came to the United States from Italy since records were kept here. There are now between 12 and 16 million Italian-Americans in the United States, according to the U.S. Bureau of the Census. Many Italian-American leaders question this figure, asserting that, based upon their surveys, there are between 20 and 25 million.

Ancient Origins. The human inhabitation of the peninsula during the middle Paleolithic age is still a matter of conjecture and study; but the evidence of human presence through the Mesolithic and Neolithic ages is clearly documented. In various places, particularly in Sicily, successive civilizations can be deciphered; and Copper, Bronze, and Iron age artifacts are extant and preserved. In 1978, archaeologists uncovered in the city of Isernia (Molise), the remains of an ancient encampment of prehistoric man dating from more than 730,000 years ago. A little further south there is evidence of troglodytism (cave dwelling) from prehistoric, ancient, medieval, and even Baroque periods. The twentieth-century inhabitation of *Sassi* (stone houses) is a form of troglodytism.

The peninsula has been at the crossroads of civilizations from the north of Europe to Africa and from the west of Europe to Asia. This is reflected in the makeup of the Italians, who are Aesernian and Sicanian, Elimian and Siculian, Ligurian and Samnian, Phoenician and Sabine, Etruscan and Roman, Cathaginian and Greek, Visigoth and Vandal, Ostrogoth and Longobard, Arab and Byzantine, Norman and Swabian, Angevin and Spanish.

The unification of the southern part of Italy under the Normans was accompanied by the introduction of feudalism there, at the very time of the collapse of feudalism and the development of communes and city-states in central and northern Italy. This tenth-century difference between southern and northern Italy became magnified from the late thirteenth to the late nineteenth centuries, with the establishment of the great states in the north (the Duchy of Milan, the Republic of Venice, the Republic of Genoa, and the Duchy of Sabaudo) and in central Italy (the Papal States [Rome], and the Republic of Florence); while in the *Mezzogiorno* (the south), there were the Kingdoms of Naples and Sicily, dominated from the beginning by competing foreign powers.

"New World" Contacts. The earliest (fifteenth century) known connections of Italians with the Americas were those of the explorers, most of whom came under the aegis of non-Italian regimes. Columbus, Cabot, Vespucci, Verrazzano, Da Nizza, Pigafetta, and others less well known all attest to the initial ties between Italians and the "New World." The contribution of the early cartographers, such as the Arabic-Sicilian, Idrisi, Andrea Banco, etc., while not a direct contact, should be noted.

Many Italians were involved in religious proselytizing and missionary colonizing particularly in the West and Southwest. Many others, such as Antonelli, Tonti, Vigo, De Lieto (Duluth), Tagliaferro, and Beltrami, continued the tradition of exploration and discovery and established settlements in and about the Americas. Italians were involved in the creation of the United States. Phillip Mazzei (*q.v.*), Carlo Bellini, and William Paca are among the more famous, but additionally, a number of Italians are named in the regimental lists of officers of the Continental Army. Similarly, there were Italians in the War of 1812, the Texas War for Independence, and in the Mexican War of 1848–1850.

Old and New Migrations. Italians began coming to North America in the sixteenth century and continue to the present. But there are important differences between the earlier and later migrations. One important difference is that most of the Italians of the early period (before 1880) came from northern Italy. While there were peasant farmers among them, many of this group were doctors, artists and composers, intellectuals and teachers, merchants and architects; many were trained craftsmen: stonecutters, silk makers, winemakers, etc.—in general they were people with a more cosmopolitan perspective than the later migrants.

Another important difference was that, except for the Piedmontese Waldensians, who came and established a half-dozen communities in the seventy-five years between 1657 and 1732, most of these immigrants came on individual initiative and were not part of a group or mass movement. Finally, these Italians were more readily accepted by the receiving society for two probable reasons: (1) the dominant class of colonial America consisted of Enlightenment personages, many of whom read and spoke Italian and regarded Italians and Italian culture highly; and (2) since most were identified individually by their regional citizenship, they did not organize themselves and were not seen as a monolithic, economically threatening, or overbearing national group. The later migration (post-1880) may be characterized as a mass movement of peasants and poor workers from southern Italy. Except for some political escapees and intellectuals, these immigrants were to a large extent uneducated and illiterate. Although Italians settled in all parts of this country, the vast majority came to and remained in the industrial cities of the Northeast. Their neighbors were working-class and poor Americans, who were menaced by this arrival of new economic competition.

The Italians were able to find a mediating introduction to the society in the form of compatriots who had migrated earlier and could speak English; these *padroni,* as they are called, assisted the immigrant in his letter writing, banking, legal matters, government dealings, and most importantly, since they had contacts for employment, they were able to find work for the immigrant. Good *padroni* helped the immigrant integrate into the society; evil ones used their positions to exploit. Southern Italian immigrants were not readily accepted by the northern Italians who transferred their disdain for southern Italians from Italy to America.

Life in Italy. Italian society in the nineteenth and early twentieth centuries was characterized by a rigid stratification based upon the estate system commonly found in Europe. The aristocrats, landed rich, and wealthy merchants were not the Italians that immigrated to America. Rather it was the *contadino,* the peasant agricultural worker, that came, particularly in the later migrations. Italy was, in the large, an agricultural society with little industry. What industrialization there was could be found mainly in the North. Throughout the country, and particularly in the South, the peasants did not own their own land but worked on the large farms of others. Sometimes small parcels were purchased or more often rented so that the family could generate some cash. The *contadini* were engaged in grape, olive, and citrus fruit growing; in olive oil and wine making; in growing wheat, corn, and rice; in fishing and hunting; in raising livestock for milk and meat; in making cheese and preserving meats; and in the service occupations and crafts that met the needs of the populace.

They lived in cities and especially in villages but in the South they rarely lived in isolated farmhouses on the land, as is the norm in America. Instead, they worked in the fields by day, then returned to their homes in the village in the evening. Often they went home for their principal meal at midday, resting and then going back to the fields later. During the harvest when they had to work until dark, they might remain in the fields, taking refuge in a farm shack that was used to harbor the farm tools. These shacks could sometimes be quite elaborate, built of stone, and large enough to give shelter to a horse or two, as well as to the men working together in the field.

The major focus of their lives is centered around the family. In Italy the family is patrilineal, in the sense that children are given their father's family name, but bilineal in that there are strong ties to both parents' families. While the Italian family could appear to be patriarchal, a hidden matriarchy has been recognized, wherein the father's public authority role is modified by the mother's roles as interpreter of the law and regulator of the household. Usually her power is subtle and covert, hidden even from family members who are accustomed to the immediacy of the father's will, though this may be no more than a public statement of the mother's wish. On a day-to-day basis, for example, fathers may discipline their children, regulate family social engagements, etc.; customarily this is all done on mothers' advice.

Each nuclear family (husband, wife, and their children living in one household) is closely tied to related nuclear families, forming the extended family. For Italians, family is the major motivating force moderating life. It is the standard against which one measures one's aspirations and achievements. While there are many sources of this cohesion, the economic reality of families working together on a small piece of heavily mortgaged property, or in a cottage industry, with the father providing organizational leadership, is the most powerful adhesive. Individuals in Italian society do not feel themselves to be constrained by the family, but are enhanced by it. Success acquired singly is family success; failure by oneself is family failure. The aims and goals of the family collectivity are internalized and personalized in each member, and individuals' needs are the responsibility of all, even over generations.

Although all the major religions are represented in Italy, most Italians are Catholic; and this religion has an important role in the life of the Italians. The disengagement of the pope from temporal sovereignty over Italians in the mid-nineteenth century created or restored a filial affection on their part for their spiritual pastor. A strong anticlerical sentiment persisted, though, as peasants perceived so many of their priests as allies of the rich.

The piety of Italians is concrete; their religion is personal; they are devoted to the saints and especially to Mary, the mother of Jesus, under her many local titles, who intercedes in their behalf. By sponsoring someone into the religion, a godparent-godchild relationship is established that binds the sponsor and sponsored in a profound familial relationship. Godparents are honored to be chosen for the role; children are taught to love their godparents as they love their own parents. Religious feasts are the occasion of the most important annual celebrations, and this is accomplished through family gatherings and the *festa*.

Italian education in the nineteenth century was largely denied to the peasant classes. In the North some few years of schooling was available, particularly in the cities, but southern farmhands rarely found it possible to have their children educated; illiteracy was the norm for 90 percent of southern Italians. In spite of this, education was very much valued, and educated people were highly respected and envied, though, since they were the exploiters of the poor, they were distrusted. For future priests and the wealthier Italian, and for all, later, in the period beginning after World War I, education was mandatory.

For the peasant in southern Italy, education was a family affair, where morals and life values were taught both by word of mouth, usually with proverbs, and paradigmatically, by the example of the parents and older members of the family. Character formation was integrated into the instruction that fathers gave their sons and mothers gave their daughters as vocational preparation. The oral-aural learning style of the family is characteristic of all levels of Italian learning, including the university level.

Italy was in a state of political turmoil from the time of the breakup of the Holy Roman Empire in 1806. Ninety percent of *Italia* was under foreign domination; and revolutionary movements calling for freedom and independence and redistribution of land fired the minds of many. The operatic creations of Giuseppe Verdi brought this patriotic fervor to the people. Eventually there was the successful reunification (*risorgimento*) which began in 1861, establishing a constitutional monarchy. Some land reform, giving parcels to peasants, was instituted. Even then, there was little real participation in government on the part of most of the people. Regional differences in linguistic dialects, dress, foods, and folkloric traditions continued.

Migration to the U.S.A. The chain migration of millions of Italians to the United States was accompanied by a return of about half of them to Italy. There were more men than women, more single men than married ones, more southern than northern Italians who came. Although all of the regions of Italy sent migrants, Sicily sent more than any other and Molise, proportionate to its size, sent the most. Wives and children followed when husbands obtained employment and sent for them. The underlying motivation for emigration was economic; people were pushed by poverty. But not all of the poor decided to emigrate; other social, psychological, and cultural elements entered into the decision. They fled the land; and they were attracted by the promise that if they worked hard they would succeed and be able to afford a better life for themselves and their children. They were a doing and future-oriented people who sought to overcome their plight.

Life in America. Institutions began to be established to meet the needs of the immigrants; and "Little Italys"—immigrant communities—sprang up in the cities where most of the Italians settled. Churches were established, stores specializing in the foods of Italians opened, benevolent and fraternal associations were organized, family restaurants were set up, and the Italian-language press was instituted. Over many generations, these people whose origins are in the peninsula began to diminish their village and regional attachments and to think of themselves as having a connection to one another. They started to see themselves as Italian-Americans.

Although many returned to Italy, many who remained turned back to working on the land here and succeeded in agribusiness. Others remained in the cities and took the jobs that native-born Americans did not want. Skilled and unskilled, they worked in heavy industry, in the garment factories, and in construction; they served each other and the rest of the society in the menial tasks of sanitation and in service jobs like barbering that were available to them. Many left the cities by choice or by contract and worked in the coal and iron mines; others reestablished their old ways by joining the fishing fleets on both coasts.

Italian immigrants adjusted to this new society; but not without a struggle, and not without great personal and psychological cost. The prejudice they experienced is well documented. The conflict that was engendered by those who felt that Italians were usurping their employment opportunities and residential enclaves was bitter and often violent. The anti-Italian stereotypes that were developed in the first years of this century remain to the present. The most iniquitous of these is the perception that Italian-Americans are more disposed than others to criminal behavior. The Commission on Social Justice of the fraternal order of the Sons of Italy and the National Italian American Foundation are important organizations that seek to combat these stereotypes in the media and wherever they appear.

The cost of adaptation to life in America, for some, was life itself. For others it was a permanent psychic debilitation in the form of an "immigrant psychosis" that has never been officially established and so is called dementia, or schizophrenia, or identity disorder. Improperly diagnosed, it was never treated. But the alienation and profound personality disruption was there and affected more individuals and their families than is known.

Like metal tried in fire, the immigrants were tempered in the furnace of migration, with its uprootedness, disappointment, and radical change. Those that endured exerted enormous energy and sacrifice in their determination, and over the generations they succeeded. They

saw their children educated. They watched their children acquire material security, and they joined them in rejecting the old subjugation.

The immigrants' progeny are found in all walks of life in the
United States. In 1987, an Italian-American was appointed to the Supreme Court, the highest court of the land. While by that year there had
still not been an Italian-American president or vice-president, there
have been members of: presidential cabinets; the U.S. Senate and
House of Representatives; and various state legislatures. Italian-Americans have been state governors and lieutenant-governors, ambassadors,
and high-ranking civil servants. In addition, they have succeeded as
venture and managerial entrepreneurs, entertainers, physicians, lawyers, scientists, and artists. Some have failed, and some whose immigrant parents amassed great wealth became poor.

The generations that were born in the United States coped with
feelings of pride and shame over their heritage. Some denied their
ancestry, others minimized it, and others overemphasized it. Italian-
Americans, more than many other ethnic groups in America, have
married out.

In short, Italian-Americans, by any measure, are integrated into
the American society. They have contributed to every aspect of its
development, and they have profited from it.

References
Dino Cinel, *From Italy to San Francisco: The Immigrant Experience* (1982); Francesco
Cordasco, *The Italians: Social Backgrounds of an American Group* (1974); Leonard
Covello, *The Social Background of the Italo-American School Child* (1972); Luciano J.
Iorizzo, *The Italian Americans* (1971); Joseph Lopreato, *Italian Americans* (1970);
Proceedings of the American Italian Historical Association (1968–1989); Lydio F. Toma-
si, ed., *Italian Americans: New Perspectives in Italian Immigration and Ethnicity* (1985).

F.X.F.

ITALIANS, *Italian American Periodical Press, 1836–1980: A Comprehensive Bibliography* (Pietro Russo; forthcoming from the Center for
Migration Studies of New York). The result of twenty years of research
by Pietro Russo, director of the Institute of American Studies at the
University of Florence, the *Italian American Periodical Press*
represents the main result of a computerized archival program of Italian-
American bibliography initiated in 1965 in cooperation with the Centro
di Calcolo of the University of Florence and the major American research centers and libraries. This comprehensive catalogue includes
2,344 periodical press and serial publications that appeared in the
United States from 1836 to 1980: newspapers, journals, bulletins, and
other serials that (1) are all or in part Italian; (2) are published by
Italians or their descendants with an interest in things Italian-American;
(3) are substantially about Italian-American communities; (4) have reg-

ular sections or articles on Italian-Americans; and (5) deal basically with Italy or relationships between Italy and the United States. Place of publication, frequency, and other pertinent annotations accompany each title included in this catalogue.

F.C.

ITALIANS, Italian immigrant women and the garment industry, 1880–1950. Furio (*infra*) examines four questions on American immigration and labor history: (1) What was the impact of immigration on Italian women? (2) What were the factors that determined whether or not Italian women joined and remained members of the garment unions at various time periods? (3) How did the union affect Italian immigrant women? and (4) What contributions did these women, in turn, make to the American labor movement? Immigration was the answer to the economic necessities of the Italian peasants. While immigrant women experienced social and economic problems in their efforts to adapt to their new environment, the longest and often most wrenching adjustments had to be made in cultural transplantation and amalgamation; therein the crisis of immigration was truly evident. In southern Italian society, sociocultural forces and the personalities of the individual members in that society interacted with each other. Each made demands of the individual. The behavior of Italian women was, in many ways, an expression of the sanctions that operated within that culture. Preindustrial or peasant values persisted when the family unit emigrated to an industrial society. One of these values was familialism. Values of the dominant American culture entered into the social consciousness of these women, though at a slower rate than for men. Thus, factors that determined whether or not Italian women joined and remained union members, for instance, varied according to time periods. This study shows that unions were a tripartite force in the assimilation of Italian women to American society. Evidence has also shown that Italian women engaged in labor struggles through most of the twentieth century. "Italianness" and "rebelness" were not necessarily dichotomous qualities, but often appeared side by side in women unionists.

Reference
Columba M. Furio, "Immigrant Women and Industry: A Case Study. The Italian Immigrant Women and the Garment Industry, 1880–1950," Ph.D. dissertation, New York University, 1979.

F.C.

ITALIANS, *Little Italies in North America* (Robert F. Harney and J. V. Scarpaci, eds., 1981). The essays in this volume were originally prepared for a conference that took place in the spring of 1979 under the auspices of the University of Toronto's Ethnic and Immigration Studies Program and the Multicultural History Society of Ontario. The American Little Italies discussed were those of Chicago; New York; Philadelphia; Baltimore; the canal town of Oswego in upstate New York; Tampa; New Orleans; and St. Louis. For Canada, Little Italies in Toronto, Montreal, and Thunder Bay were described. The cities were chosen to show some of the variety of settlement in the United States and Canada as well as to contrast the Italian-Canadian and Italian-American experiences. The editors were interested in seeing if they "could limn more precisely the ways in which such variables as the size of each Italian colony, the predominant paesi of origin of the settlers in each, and the magnitude and nature—in ethnic groups—and the attitude toward immigrants of the host city or regional ecosystem, affected immigrant settlements and the subsequent Italian ethnoculture."

F.C.

ITALIANS, as reported in American periodical press, 1880–1920. The reaction of the American periodical press, from 1880 to 1920, to the Italian immigrants in urban America in this period can be measured. At any given moment the quantity of periodical literature on the Italian newcomers was in direct proportion to the physical dimensions of the influx. Since most of the Italian immigrants arrived in the first two decades of the twentieth century, awareness of their coming as reflected in periodicals is largely confined to the years between 1900 and 1920. Magazine opinion of the Italian immigrants was generally unfavorable. This aversion toward the Italian migration found expression in comments on the causes of the migration. The poverty of the Italian peasantry was viewed in the periodical press as a compelling reason for the exodus. The majority of magazine writers argued that the presumed misery in southern Italy was caused primarily by numerous agricultural problems, demographic pressures, and burdensome taxes. Moreover, it was generally believed that the southern Italians also emigrated to take advantage of economic opportunities, especially those resulting from the expansion of industry and urban services in America. The motivation of their migration was criticized as being primarily economic rather than political or idealistic. Furthermore, fears were expressed that their alleged backward way of life and poor working standards, which had supposedly impelled the exodus, might be transplanted to the American scene.

Reference
Salvatore A. Mondello, *The Italian Immigrant in Urban America, 1880–1920, as Reported in the Contemporary Periodical Press* (1980).

F.C.

ITALY-AMERICA SOCIETY. *See* Covello, Leonard.

JANSSON, ERIK. *See* Bishop Hill.

JAPANESE. Today Japanese-Americans number over 800,000 and rank behind Chinese-Americans and Filipino-Americans as the third largest group of Asian-Americans. Early contacts between Japan and the United States came in the form of several shipwrecked Japanese sailors and fishermen who were rescued and brought to Hawaii and the United States during the first half of the nineteenth century; the Treaty of Kanagawa that was signed between the two countries in 1854; a Japanese mission that visited the United States in 1860; and some 200 Japanese laborers who were smuggled out of the country to work in Hawaii and California in 1868 and 1869, respectively.

Immigration. Japanese immigration into Hawaii and the United States can be divided into six periods: 1885–1894, 1894–1908, 1908–1924, 1924–1952, 1952–1965, and 1965–present.

Government-Sponsored Emigration to Hawaii, 1885–1894. Sugarcane began to be cultivated on a commercial scale in Hawaii in the 1840s, and its production soared after the Reciprocity Treaty was signed in 1876 between Hawaii—at that time an independent kingdom—and the United States, which allowed sugar to enter the American market duty free. As cane acreage expanded, plantation owners needed an increasingly large labor force which had to be recruited from various places around the world, because the native Hawaiians, many of whom had died from disease and whose traditional society and means of livelihood had been disrupted, were not numerous enough to meet the demand for workers. Initially, Chinese filled the need, but because they had a tendency to leave the plantations after their contracts expired, the planters began to look for other sources of labor.

They turned to Japan, relying on Robert Irwin, an American businessman in Yokohama, to serve as their agent. Irwin, who knew Kaoru Inoue, the foreign minister, and Masuda Takashi, an official of the Mitsui Bussan, one of the largest financial groups in Japan, successfully negotiated a "convention," which spelled out the conditions under which Japanese could be recruited to work in Hawaii. Originally, the laborers were to receive free steerage passage, free lodgings, wages of nine dollars a month for men and six dollars a month for women, and food and medical attention when needed. They were to work ten hours a day in the fields or twelve hours a day in the mills, twenty-six days a month, for three years. However, the cost of passage was soon shifted onto the laborers themselves, and the planters often reneged on their obligation to provide a sufficient number of interpreters and doctors.

Between 1885 and 1894, almost 30,000 traveled under these terms to Hawaii, of whom 8,000 returned to their homeland. Three-quarters of them were young tenant farmers and farm laborers from several prefectures in southwestern Japan bordering the Inland Sea: Hiroshima, Yamaguchi, Kumamoto, Fukuoka, Wakayama, Nagasaki, and Okayama. Relatively few women emigrated because the plantation owners had specified that no more than one-quarter of the workers could be female, all of whom came as wives and daughters of the men.

Company-Sponsored Emigration to Hawaii, 1894–1908. Emigration under the Irwin convention ended because the Hawaiian government became disenchanted with Irwin at the same time that private emigration companies in Japan expressed a desire to take over what the Japanese government itself had done. Between 1891 and 1908, fifty-one companies operated for varying lengths of time to recruit people—their agents sometimes going from village to village—and to help aspiring emigrants get the necessary passports, visas, permits, and medical examinations, all for a fee. Approximately 125,000 Japanese left their country for Hawaii under the auspices of these companies, of whom 72,000 eventually returned home.

Immigration Into the United States Before 1908. Unlike the contract laborers who went to Hawaii, Japanese who entered the continental United States came on their own and consequently had more diverse socioeconomic origins. Between 1880 and 1907, not counting diplomats, tourists, and government-sponsored students, the Japanese government issued passports to more than 15,000 self-supported students, almost 16,000 merchants, 7,000 farmers and fishermen, almost 3,000 craftsmen, almost 16,000 laborers, and over 15,000 other persons destined for the continental United States.

The above figures undercount the total number of Japanese entering the United States in those years, however, because after the United States annexed Hawaii in 1898, federal laws—including one that prohibited the immigration of contract laborers—became applicable there after June 1900, and freed from their contracts thousands of Japanese plantation workers who left for the mainland in search of better wages and working conditions. But arrivals from Hawaii ended after 1907, when President Theodore Roosevelt signed Executive Order 589 to forbid Japanese in Hawaii, Mexico, and Canada to remigrate to the United States. He also negotiated the Gentlemen's Agreement with Japan, which agreed to stop issuing passports to laborers, and direct immigration from that country was greatly reduced also.

Limited Immigration, 1908–1924. Even after the Gentlemen's Agreement went into effect, about 48,000 Japanese entered Hawaii and 120,000 the Pacific Coast between 1908 and 1924. However, 86 percent of the former and 93 percent of the latter ultimately returned to Japan.

Those who stayed became the immigrant generation, whose members called themselves *Issei*. They often summoned younger relatives, referred to as *Yobiyose,* to join them in America. About two-thirds of the *Yobiyose* were female, and almost 60 percent of the women were "picture brides," whose marriages had been arranged by go-betweens using photographs in ceremonies at which the grooms were absent. Approximately 20,000 Japanese women traveled to Hawaii and about 28,000 to the United States between 1908 and 1920, when their influx ended because the Japanese government, in response to the outcry against their presence in the western United States, stopped issuing passports to them. As women came, children were born. By 1920, of the 109,000 persons of Japanese ancestry in Hawaii, 60,000 were *Issei* and 49,000 *Nisei* (American-born second generation); among the 111,000 in the continental United States, 81,000 were *Issei* and 30,000 *Nisei*.

Exclusion, 1924–1952. Japanese immigration ended when Congress passed the Immigration and Naturalization Act of 1924, which set an annual immigration quota for each nationality group equal to 2 percent of the total number of that group residing in the United States in 1890. Moreover, "aliens ineligible to citizenship" were barred altogether. Since the U.S. Supreme Court had ruled in *Ozawa* v. *The United States* (1922) that Japanese were ineligible for naturalization, immigration from Japan ended. Exclusion lasted for three decades.

Token and Nonquota Immigration, 1952–1965. In 1952 Japan, which the United States had vanquished in World War II and which American armed forces had occupied since the war ended, was given a token annual quota of 185 immigrants under the Walter-McCarran Act. A far larger number of Japanese entered the United States during this period, however, outside of the quota system. Beginning in the early 1950s, 4,000 to 6,000 Japanese women married to American military personnel came in each year as the latter's dependents. They constituted more than 80 percent of the immigrants from Japan in the 1950s and 1960s.

Immigration Since 1965. The removal of "national origins" as the basis of American immigration legislation in 1965 led to a resurgence of Asian immigration. However, Japan, alone among the Asian countries that had sent emigrants to the United States before the 1960s, has not supplied a large number of immigrants. Fewer than 5,000 Japanese per year have come to settle in the last two decades. The immigrants have been outnumbered by students and employees of Japanese multinational corporations who come in on temporary visas.

Settlement, Discrimination, and Resistance Before World War II.
Virtually all of the Japanese who went to Hawaii first worked as plantation laborers, while farm labor and domestic service served as the main
entry-level occupations for those who went to the mainland. In the
Pacific Northwest and the Rocky Mountain states, several thousand
worked for lumbering, mining, and railroad companies. Many also
fished up and down the Pacific Coast.

At the turn of the century, almost 30,000 Japanese made up two-
thirds of the plantation labor force in Hawaii. Such numerical dominance gave them a measure of power, which they quickly learned to use
by striking for higher wages and better working and living conditions.
They protested against the cruelty of the *lunas* (plantation foremen) and
the exploitation of emigration companies, banks, and plantation
owners, participating in dozens of walkouts and work stoppages in
1890, 1891, 1892, 1894, 1900, 1903, 1904, and 1905. Then, in May
1909, the first organized strike occurred, when more than 7,000 Japanese struck at all the plantations on the island of Oahu. The planters
broke the strike after a month by bringing in strikebreakers, evicting the
strikers from the plantation-owned bunkhouses, and arresting the leaders. Though the workers lost, the scale and degree of organization of
this event are historically significant.

The largest strike took place in 1920, when Filipino and Japanese
from dozens of plantations on several islands acted together to demand
higher wages. Plantation owners evicted an estimated 12,000 people
from their homes and brought in over 2,000 strikebreakers. Though the
demand for higher wages and union recognition was not met, some
concessions regarding living conditions were made. Both the 1909 and
1920 strikes received support from the larger Japanese community:
merchants and townspeople offered emergency shelter and food, while
newspapers served as channels of communication.

On the mainland, the Japanese were concentrated in California,
where during the first decade of the twentieth century, two-thirds of
those living in the rural areas worked as farm laborers. The number of
Japanese farm workers in the state stabilized around 16,000 after the
Gentlemen's Agreement cut off the influx of laborers. Unlike their
Hawaiian counterparts who lived in company housing on plantations,
farm workers along the Pacific Coast usually led a migratory existence,
which impeded their ability to organize. However, they still engaged in
enough strikes—usually right before a harvest—to antagonize growers,
who called them "cocky little brown men."

By 1913, 6,000 Japanese in California had become tenant farmers;
in 1917, that number had increased to 8,000. Smaller numbers of tenants also appeared in the other western states. Their tendency to move
up the agricultural ladder elicited a hostile reaction, which materialized

in the form of an Alien Land Law passed in California in 1913 that forbade "aliens ineligible to citizenship" (i.e., all Asian immigrants) to purchase land or to lease it for more than three years.

But the *Issei* managed to continue to farm because the law was not strictly enforced, and they bought land in the names of their *Nisei* children, who were American citizens. However, amendments enacted in 1920 and 1923 closed many of the loopholes. Similar laws were passed in Washington, Oregon, Idaho, Nevada, Arizona, New Mexico, Texas, and several other states.

Issei farmers defended their right to earn a living in court. Although they filed relatively few suits against the 1913 Alien Land Law of California, they repeatedly challenged the more stringent 1920, 1923, and 1927 laws in the same state and the 1921 and 1923 laws in Washington. Four landmark decisions of the U.S. Supreme Court in 1923 greatly diminished the ability of the Japanese to farm. *Terrace* v. *Thompson* and *Porterfield* v. *Webb* upheld the constitutionality of the California and Washington laws which prohibited leasing land to Japanese immigrants; *Webb* v. *O'Brien* banned sharecropping; and *Frick* v. *Webb* outlawed Japanese ownership of stock in corporations that owned land.

Perhaps because Japanese farm workers did not disappear even after the laws were passed, white mobs threatened them with violence and tried to drive them out of various localities. In California, townspeople evicted them from Turlock and Livingston in 1921; Delano, Porterville, and Los Angeles in 1922; Hopland and again Los Angeles in 1924; and Woodlake in 1926. In Oregon, Japanese were ousted from Toledo in 1925.

In spite of these strenuous efforts to remove them from the land, almost 70 percent of the Japanese immigrant population, including many Japanese urban dwellers who distributed the crops that the farmers grew, depended on agriculture for survival. In the late 1910s, *Issei* produced 50 to 90 percent of many of the truck and field crops in California. In Los Angeles, they controlled the most important wholesale produce market, while retail grocers distributed fresh fruit and vegetables to a growing urban population. In Seattle, they were important members of the Pike Street Market. Meanwhile, Japanese nurserymen and gardeners catered to the landscaping needs of homeowners.

In cities large and small, younger immigrants combined domestic service with schooling. Known as "school boys," they cleaned houses and prepared meals for white families who provided them with room and board and a flexible enough work schedule to allow them to attend school for part of the day. The presence of these "school boys" almost caused a diplomatic crisis between Japan and the United States when the

San Francisco School Board attempted to segregate ninety-three of them in 1906. Tokyo protested, so Washington, D.C. investigated. A compromise was reached whereby San Francisco agreed to let Japanese students attend the white public schools in exchange for efforts by the federal government to restrict immigration, which it did through the 1907 Executive Order and the Gentlemen's Agreement.

The most prominent urban *Issei* were merchants, many of whom supplied ethnic foods and other familiar wares to their compatriots. Others sold curios and artwork to white customers. Some ran boarding houses, pool halls, public bath houses, barbershops, restaurants, and brothels. Their establishments formed the nuclei of *Nihonmachi* (Japantowns) in Seattle, San Francisco, Sacramento, Fresno, Los Angeles, and smaller cities throughout the western United States. Men who staffed Japanese-language schools, Buddhist temples, Christian churches, newspapers, and the Japanese consulates also provided leadership.

Issei communities were very well organized. People from the same prefectures formed *kenjinkai;* individuals in the same occupations or professions established trade associations; those interested in various forms of recreation joined martial arts clubs, literary societies, and amateur theater groups; while the devout worshipped and socialized in a variety of Buddhist and Christian churches. The most important communitywide organization was the Japanese Association of America, whose leaders spoke on behalf of all Japanese-Americans vis-à-vis the outside world. When the *Nisei* started to come of age in the 1920s and 1930s, they formed organizations of their own, the most important of which was the Japanese American Citizens' League (JACL).

Internment During World War II. Community life was traumatically disrupted in the wake of Japan's bombing of the American naval installation at Pearl Harbor on December 7, 1941. Within weeks, some 2,000 *Issei* leaders were rounded up by the Federal Bureau of Investigation and confined in camps. Journalists, pressure groups, the congressional delegations from the Pacific Coast states, and John L. DeWitt, commander of the Western Defense Command, all called for the removal of persons of Japanese ancestry from the Pacific Coast. Despite the lack of any evidence that persons of Japanese ancestry were engaged in espionage or sabotage, those who favored removing and detaining them justified doing so on the basis of "military necessity" and "protective custody."

On February 19, 1942, President Franklin Roosevelt signed Executive Order 9066, authorizing the secretary of war or any military commander designated by him to establish military areas and to exclude therefrom any and all persons. The next day, Secretary of War Henry L. Stimson authorized DeWitt to carry out the evacuation of 112,000 persons of Japanese ancestry, two-thirds of them American citizens and among whom more than half were minors. In March, DeWitt proclaimed the western half of Washington, Oregon, and California and the southern third of Arizona as military areas and set up the Wartime Civil Control Administration to carry out the evacuation, while Roosevelt signed Executive Order 9102 to create a War Relocation Authority (WRA) to administer the relocation centers and Public Law 503 to make it a federal offense to violate any order of the military commanders implementing Executive Order 9066.

Between March and October, persons of Japanese ancestry were moved into temporary assembly centers. People were allowed to take only what they could carry, having to store, abandon, or sell at a loss most of their possessions. Between May and November, they were moved again into more permanent relocation centers, ten of which had been hastily constructed in desolate inland locations: Tule Lake and Manzanar in California, Minidoka in Idaho, Topaz in Utah, Poston and Gila River in Arizona, Heart Mountain in Wyoming, Granada in Colorado, and Rohwer and Jerome in Arkansas. However, persons of Japanese ancestry in Hawaii, with the exception of almost 1,000 community leaders and 2,000 fishermen, were not evacuated or interned, first because they composed 40 percent of the labor force and confining them would have disrupted the local economy severely, and second because the commanding general there said it was not necessary to do so.

In the ten mainland relocation centers, entire families were cramped into "apartments" measuring no larger than 10 by 20 feet within barracks; people slept on mattresses filled with straw, ate army ration in mess halls, and relieved themselves on toilets installed in a row with no partitions. The camps were enclosed by barbed wire and guarded by armed soldiers and searchlights mounted on observation towers. Those who were employed by the WRA received token wages of only $12 to $19 a month, regardless of their education, work experience, or what tasks they performed. Only English-speaking *Nisei* were allowed to serve as block leaders.

Initially there was relatively little protest, because *Issei* leaders had been arrested; the average age of the *Nisei* was only nineteen; and the JACL had urged cooperation. A handful of individuals, however, did challenge the evacuation order, but the U.S. Supreme Court ruled in *Hirabayashi* v. *The United States* (1943), *Yasui* v. *The United States* (1943), and *Korematsu* v. *The United States* (1944) that the evacuation was constitutional. In a fourth case, *Endo* v. *The United States,* the high court decided that the plaintiff could not be detained without individual charges against her but affirmed the government's right to take the actions that it did.

In the camps, protests erupted at Poston, Manzanar, Tule Lake, and Heart Mountain over a variety of issues: the deplorable living

conditions, WRA policies, the killing of several internees, rivalry between pro-American *Nisei* and anti-American *Kibei* (*Nisei* who had
received all or part of their education in Japan), the decision of the U.S.
army to recruit *Nisei* after sifting out the "loyal" from the "disloyal"
through a poorly worded questionnaire, and draft resistance. "Dis-
loyals" were moved to Tule Lake, which became a "segregation center" for the remainder of the war.

People could leave the camps only under certain programs: farm
workers left temporarily to harvest crops; college students promised
admission by midwestern and eastern universities left to continue their
education; a small number with guaranteed employment in those same
sections of the country also departed; and men who passed their phys-
icals joined the army. Altogether, 33,000 *Nisei,* about half from Hawaii
and the other half from the mainland, served in the army during World
War II. The best-known units were the 442d Regimental Combat Team,
the most decorated unit of its size, and the 100th Infantry Battalion,
both of which served in Europe. Less well known were 6,000 graduates
of the Military Intelligence Service Language School, 3,700 of whom
served in Asia before the war ended. *Nisei* casualties numbered almost
10,000 (including 900 dead): they had indeed proven their loyalty in
blood.

Postwar Developments. Despite this valiant record, when Japanese-Americans returned to the Pacific Coast after the war ended, they
often encountered hostility. Their property stolen, vandalized, or otherwise lost, the social foundations of their communities destroyed, and
many of the older *Issei* broken in health and spirit, most had to begin
life anew. But their recovery has been spectacular.

Today, Japanese-American men earn higher median incomes and
have more years of schooling than their white counterparts, though
women's earnings still lag far behind. They have entered politics in
larger numbers than any other Asian-American group, and are ably
represented in Congress by Senators Daniel Inouye and Spark Matsunaga of Hawaii and Congressmen Norman Mineta and Robert Matsui
of California. A host of others serve in the judiciary, on school boards,
and in many units of state and local government.

In 1979, the first "redress and reparations" bill was introduced in
Congress. In 1980, Congress established the Commission on Wartime
Relocation and Internment of Civilians, which, after hearing testimony
from 750 witnesses over twenty days in cities across the country and
studying voluminous documents, declared that the internment was a
"grave injustice" that resulted from "race prejudice, war hysteria and
a failure of political leadership." In 1983, based on evidence that the
federal government had suppressed evidence in documents submitted to
the U.S. Supreme Court forty years ago, and using a rare procedure

known as writ of error *coram nobis,* attorneys for Fred Korematsu succeeded in getting his conviction "vacated." A similar judgment was won by the attorneys for Min Yasui the following year, but in neither instance did the judges pursue allegations of government misconduct. However, in June 1985, the judge presiding over the reopened Gordon Hirabayashi case conducted a full evidentiary hearing and in February 1986 decided that the U.S. government had engaged in misconduct. The latter has appealed, and as of this writing (September 1987) the outcome is still pending. On September 17, 1987, the House of Representatives voted 243 to 141 to issue an official apology to Japanese-Americans for the wrong done them, to compensate each of 60,000 still-living internees with $20,000 apiece, and to allocate $50,000 for an educational fund.

References
Commission on Wartime Relocation and Internment of Civilians, *Personal Justice Denied* (1982); Roger Daniels, *The Politics of Prejudice: The Anti-Japanese Movement in California and the Struggle for Japanese Exclusion* (1962); Yamato Ichihashi, *Japanese in the United States* (1932); John Modell, *The Economics and Politics of Racial Accommodation: The Japanese of Los Angeles, 1900–1942* (1977); and Alan Takeo Moriyama, *Imingaisha: Japanese Emigration Companies and Hawaii* (1985).

S.C.

JAPANESE-AMERICAN PROJECT (University of California, Los Angeles, California 90024). The largest collection of manuscripts, memorabilia, and other materials of the Japanese-American community. See Jyji Ichioka, *A Buried Past: An Annotated Bibliography of the Japanese-American Research Project Collection* (Berkeley: University of California Press, 1974).

F.C.

JAPANESE-AMERICANS IN HAWAII. According to the 1980 census, Japanese-Americans numbered about 240,000 or 33.5 percent of Hawaii's 965,000 people. They are the second-largest ethnic group in the islands (second only to whites) and the largest Asian ethnic group by a wide margin. Japanese-Americans in Hawaii have been reviled and extolled, depicted as a threat and held up as a model of success. The reality, of course, is much more complicated.

Like most of the early immigrants to Hawaii, Japanese were drawn to the islands because of the sugar industry. The first group of 148 Japanese, called the *Gannen Mono* (or "First-Year People"), arrived in Hawaii in 1868. These were recruited to work on the sugar plantations by an envoy of the Hawaiian Kingdom who described the men as: "mere laborers who had been picked out of the streets of Yokohama,

sick, exhausted, and filthy, and without clothing to cover decency.''
Conditions on the plantations were dreadful, Japanese workers complained and refused to work, and planters viewed them as undesirable.

It was not until 1884 that the government of Japan agreed to terms
permitting Japanese contract labor to Hawaii, and in 1885, 682 men,
164 women, and 102 children arrived in Honolulu as the vanguard of
the *kanyaku imin* (or contract immigrants) who formed the nucleus of
the present-day Japanese-American community. By 1900, the Japanese
in Hawaii numbered 47,508 men and 13,603 women, or nearly 40
percent of the total population. Most of these labored on the sugar
plantations for ten hours a day, twenty-six days per month, for a
monthly salary of $12.50 for men and $7.50 for women.

Folk songs similar to the blues, called *hole hole bushi,* were sung
by workers as they labored under the hot tropical sun.

> My husband cuts the cane,
> I do the *hole hole* [stripping cane leaves].
> By sweat and tears
> We get by.

> Wonderful Hawaii, or so I heard.
> One look and it seems like Hell.
> The manager's the Devil and
> His *lunas* [overseers] are demons.

Given those conditions, it is no surprise that Japanese workers took
collective action to better their lot. In 1900 alone, there were twenty-
five recorded strikes involving about 8,000 laborers. The largest and
most far-reaching plantation strikes by Japanese workers took place in
1909 and 1920. About 7,000 laborers joined in the "Great Japanese
Strike" of 1909, costing the planters an estimated $2 million, and over
13,000 Japanese men, women, and children were directly affected by
the strike of 1920, resulting in plantation losses of $12 million.

The 1920 strike in particular was seen as a conspiracy by Japanese
for the control of Hawaii's industry and overthrow of American rule
(the United States annexed the Hawaiian Kingdom in 1898, making it
an American territory). Henceforth, two paths were trod. The first
sought to "Americanize" the Japanese, especially the *Nisei* (Japanese
born in Hawaii), through eliminating Japanese agencies of culture such
as the language schools and promoting Christianity and patriotism. The
second, led by the military, secretly planned martial law and the internment of Japanese leaders to ensure domestic tranquility in the anticipated war with Japan.

The Japanese attack on Pearl Harbor in 1941 triggered the implementation of these plans, resulting in the suspension of democratic rule

and the internment of 1,250 leaders of the Japanese community in Hawaii. Despite this cloud of suspicion, no act of espionage or sabotage by resident Japanese was ever proven, and the Japanese joined volunteer labor battalions, purchased war bonds, and contributed to the blood bank and Red Cross. Most prominently, Hawaii's Japanese served with great distinction in the segregated all-Japanese units of the U.S. army's 100th Battalion and 442d Regimental Combat Team in the European theater. Of Hawaii's war casualties, at a time when Japanese-Americans constituted less than 40 percent of the population, 80 percent of those killed and 88 percent of those wounded were Japanese-Americans.

After the war, Japanese-Americans pursued equality—paid for in blood—through education and politics. Japanese-Americans steadily moved away from labor to the professions until in 1980, 12.2 percent of all Japanese were engaged in professional occupations. Japanese-American involvement in electoral politics was pivotal in effecting a revolution of sorts in the installation of the Democratic over the previously dominant Republican party in the islands. George R. Ariyoshi became the first Japanese-American governor of a state when he was elected in 1974 (Hawaii became a state in 1959), and Hawaii's Daniel K. Inouye and Spark M. Matsunaga are the first Japanese-Americans to sit in the U.S. Senate.

Despite those gains, Japanese-Americans continue to be underrepresented in managerial positions, and Hawaii's economy continues to be dominated by whites. At the same time, Japanese culture, once depicted as alien and anti-American, now permeates much of island life, and the Japanese-American community, once seen as a contagion requiring containment, now occupies a central position in Hawaii's multiethnic society.

References
Dorothy Ochiai Hazama and Jane Okamoto Komeiji, *Okage Sama De: The Japanese in Hawai'i, 1885–1985* (1986); Roland Kotani, *The Japanese in Hawaii: A Century of Struggle* (1985); Franklin Odo and Kazuko Sinoto, *A Pictorial History of the Japanese in Hawai'i, 1885–1924* (1985); Dennis M. Ogawa, ed., *Kodomo no tame ni: For the Sake of the Children* (1978); Ernest K. Wakukawa, *A History of the Japanese People in Hawaii* (1938).

G.Y.O.

JAPANESE AND KOREAN EXCLUSION LEAGUE. *See* Asiatic Exclusion League.

JAPANESE, experiences in Canada and United States. An examination of the similarities and differences in the experiences of Japanese immigrants who settled in the United States and Canada from the 1860s to the 1970s concludes that Japanese immigrants and their descendants experienced the same kinds of problems whether they settled in the northwest part of the United States or in British Columbia. Differences that were encountered depended more on the size of the Japanese communities than on institutional differences between the countries.

Reference
Roger Daniels, "The Japanese Experience in North America: An Essay in Comparative Racism," *Canadian Ethnic Studies/Études Ethniques du Canada* 9 (1977): 91–100.

F.C.

JAZZ. A music form created by its Afro-American community, jazz combines both the African and European musical traditions into a new American musical style. Negro spirituals, slave work songs, black blues, and ragtime, all were creations of the Afro-Americans. They made use of many African musical techniques such as complex polyrhythms, syncopation, and rough vocal textures, and adapted the call and response of African vocal music. African music utilized a pentatonic rather than a diatonic scale, and in jazz this results in the third, fifth, and seventh notes in the scale being flattened. Most African art did not carry over to America because slaves were allowed few possessions. However, music does not require any artifacts, and it can be produced by the human voice and the use of hands and feet for rhythmic effect.

In Louisiana, the blacks were not completely segregated by the French, who taught them the use of European instruments and developed a rich musical tradition. When America gained Louisiana and these blacks were segregated, it had the effect of merging this European tradition with the African music of other blacks. Where these two streams merged, particularly in New Orleans, a new music was created. Jazz proper emerged at the turn of the twentieth century, and King Oliver, Louis Armstrong, and Jellyroll Morton were some of the men who helped shaped its beginnings. The first jazz recording was made by a white band, the Old Dixieland Jazz Band, in 1917. The jazz of such white musicians tended to be more structured and "sweet." Big band swing became common by the 1930s, and also more formalized and less improvised. Benny Goodman, the Dorsey brothers and, later, Glenn Miller were nationally prominent. After World War II, black musicians like Charlie Parker and Dizzy Gillespie felt that jazz was becoming insipid; Beebop was developed by black musicians primarily as an attempt to return to a more improvised style reflecting the blues roots. Rock 'n roll, the popular music that began in the 1950s and spread around the world, is also rooted in blues and jazz.

Reference
Leroi Jones, *Blues People* (1976).

N.C.

JENKS, JEREMIAH W[HIPPLE] (1856–1929). An economist and academician, Jenks taught at Cornell, Indiana, and New York universities. He served as a presidentially appointed member of the U.S. Immigration Commission (*q.v.*) from 1907 to 1911; this commission was convened by Congress to "make a full inquiry [of] the subject of immigration." The commission published its *Report* (41 vols.) in 1911, and Jenks was a major influence in its restrictionist views. Jenks (with W. Jett Lauck) was the author of *The Immigration Problem* (1912; 6th ed., 1926), essentially a summary of the U.S. Immigration Commission *Report*.

F.C.

JEWISH DAILY FORWARD (FORVERTS). The most widely read Jewish periodical in the United States. Founded in 1897, it soon grew to a circulation of a quarter of a million, with regional editions by 1920. With Abraham Cahan (*q.v.*) as editor, it helped to Americanize several generations of immigrants with its English lessons and advice columns. It was also a leader in developing socialism and the labor movement in America. The last remaining Yiddish daily, the *Forward* became a weekly in 1983.

Reference
Robert Singerman, "The American Jewish Press, 1823–1983," *American Jewish History* 73 (June 1984): 422–444.

B.L.

JEWISH PUBLICATION SOCIETY OF AMERICA. Founded in Philadelphia in 1888, the society has published and continues publication of Judaica and related materials, including the authoritative *American Jewish Yearbook* (1899–).

Reference
J. Bloch, *Of Making Many Books* (1953).

B.L.

JEWISH SUNDAY SCHOOL MOVEMENT. *See* Gratz, Rebecca.

JEWS. The most central fact of the American Jewish experience is the three waves of immigration that shaped its character and sustained it demographically for over three centuries. The periodization of American Jewish history is based on these immigration waves.

The Sephardic Immigration. The first wave is generally called the Sephardic immigration, and it refers to those Jews who trace their ancestry, directly or indirectly, to the Iberian peninsula. *Sephard* means "Spanish" in Hebrew, but documents usually speak of Sephards as Portuguese Jews, since the first contingent of settlers stemmed from Recife, Brazil. They were compelled to leave that country when Brazil was retaken by the Portuguese in 1654. Later these original settlers were supplemented by others from other areas of the Sephardic world, including especially, settlement in the Caribbean and on the Spanish-American mainland. Some of the earliest synagogues established during the Colonial period received financial help from these more established Caribbean communities. But for the most part the early Jewish settlers were compelled to worship privately in their homes. Public worship for Jews was forbidden. Under the governorship of Peter Stuyvesant, Jews were not welcome in New Amsterdam. Religious freedom was obtained only gradually and not confirmed until the Republic was established, and then not fully in all states until 1890.

The Sephardic community was a small one. The best estimate is that by 1780 it had reached less than 3,000 persons out of a total U.S. population of approximately 2,800,000. Moreover, as early as 1750 the numerical majority may no longer have been Sephardic but Ashkenazik, the Hebrew word for Jews steming from eastern and central Europe. But the Sephardic cultural dominance continued until after 1820 despite this group's declining proportion of the total Jewish population. Thereafter the remnants amalgamated with the second wave of immigrants from central Europe.

In the diverse religious landscape of colonial America Jews were not very conspicuous. Small in number, they neither shook nor quaked nor feared an imminent Armaggedon. Yet they also lived in a century that was passionately Christian and in a society that was a seething cauldron of religious hatreds, and exacted a price from nonbelievers. Their early economic activity was severely restricted. It required intercession from the directors of the East India Company to wrest even minimal economic freedom. Yet Sephardic Jewry was especially well equipped to negotiate these man-made shoals. Some had reconverted from the Christian faith they had been compelled to assume and were very generally more experienced in living in a Christian world. Although extremely loyal to their faith they were less separatist and more cosmopolitan than the later arrivals.

What distinguished them as much as religion was their commercial activity. In a society that was overwhelmingly agrarian and rural, they cast their lot with the city. They played pioneering roles in new areas of economic activity. They effectively utilized industrial and commercial "secrets" which had been in the Jewish sphere for centuries; these "secrets" involved the making of castille soap; wig making; the trade in precious stones; and the distilling of rum. They began to play a bridging role between the core economy and the periphery. They were among the first to exploit the Indian trade, especially in furs, and their connections with the Jewish communities of the Caribbean allowed them to partake in the risky but lucrative ocean commerce. They also played some role in the slave trade. Within a century what had been a poor and dependent community produced a commercial elite and became generally prosperous and highly regarded.

The German-Jewish Immigration. By 1820, driven out of central Europe by the excesses of the restoration period after the fall of Napoleon, a new group of Jewish immigrants, primarily from the German principalities, made their debut. They came in several waves and it is estimated that between 1820 and 1880 perhaps as many as 250,000 settled in America. The absence of accurate records does not permit precise estimates. But the increase in the number of Jewish congregations, from six in 1825 to seventy-seven in 1860, gives some idea of the increase in absolute numbers (In actual fact, though, the Jewish community was growing proportionately smaller, since the numerical increase of other immigrant groups was rising faster).

First to come were young, poor immigrant males from the small towns of Bavaria and the Rhineland. Later, they were followed by more established immigrants. The Jewish migration was part of a larger German migration, and was often, in fact, indistinguishable from these immigrants. Jews migrated with them, shared the hardships of the ocean voyage, lived in their communities, belonged to their *singvereins* and even their churches, and often adopted German culture as their own, including the political preference for the newly established Republican party which opposed the extension of slavery.

Rustic, unskilled, and poorly instructed, but arriving at the historical juncture when the West cried out for enterprising settlers, German Jewish immigrants, unlike their Sephardic forbears and their eastern European successors, settled in new towns, often of the trans-Mississippi West. Sometimes, as resident merchants, they were the founders of such towns. Many became peddlers, which had the advantage of support from the existing Jewish merchandizing network as well as the possibility of rapid capital formation. That was requisite if the perennial hope of the peddler of becoming a "merchant prince" was ever to be realized. The local Jewish merchant, needing to increase his trade volume, staked the peddler to merchandize. It was an internal credit network that proved remarkably well suited to the new immigrant's situation. Yet peddling was a hard business and only a handful actually succeeded in making the fabled jump from peddler to department store owner. Fewer still moved from that to commercial banking. The success odyssey of German Jews in America has been somewhat overstated. But there was frequent middling commercial success, and it stemmed again in good part from the pioneering role these Jews played in new areas of the economy as well as merchandizing. Such middle-sized industries as clothing manufacture, the shoe industry, Great Lakes fishing, mining, publishing, cattle exporting, meat packing, and all manner of export-import trading received a disproportionate input of Jewish capital and energy in their early stages of development. A separate Jewish banking nexus developed when Yankee banking houses rejected the representation by Jews on their boards of directors that their capital investments warranted. This nexus endured for one generation. Today there are no banking houses that are exclusively Jewish in capital or personnel.

Although much of the cultural and commercial energy of the German Jewish immigration was expended within the German-American immigrant community, German Jews also contributed considerably to the development of the American Jewish community of the nineteenth century. The remarkable organizational structure of American Jewry which continues to differentiate it from other ethnic Americans was largely established by these Jews who possessed a special cultural talent for building organizations. The most important such organizations were for defense and community relations. German Jewish activity was also noteworthy in the area of organized philanthropy, which remains today the envy of other ethnic groups. German Jewish settlers in America also innovated in the area of religious observance and ritual. Feeling that the strictures of the traditional observance had lost relevance in the New World, they attempted to modernize the faith so that it might better accommodate to the free American society. The result was the development of a new branch of Judaism known as the Reform movement.

The Eastern Jewish Immigration. The last and largest wave of Jewish immigration stemmed from eastern Europe, Russia, Poland, the Austro-Hungarian empire (especially the easternmost province of Galicia), and Romania. There had always been a trickle of such "new" immigrants during the Sephardic and German-Jewish period. Some researchers note that eastern Jews may actually have been the numerical majority as early as 1850 when the first large eastern European religious congregation was established in New York City. But they began to arrive in numbers after 1881. By 1924, when this immigration tapered off as a consequence of the restrictive immigration laws of 1921 and 1924, as many as 2.4 million Jewish immigrants may have settled here. About 71 percent came from Russia, 18.6 percent from the Austro-Hungarian Empire, and the remainder from Romania and other countries. Sixty-seven percent of the males were skilled workers in as many as thirty-five different trades. Most American Jews alive today trace their family roots to this wave of immigration which for the first time in their American experience gave Jews a conspicuous presence in American society and culture. Arriving when the transition to a complex industrial society based on urban living was fully under way, these immigrants faced a more complex problem of adjustment than did earlier waves. Moreover, there was already a well-established Jewish community with its own interest in reshaping the newcomers. The difficulty encountered by Jews in adjusting to each other at times appeared to be greater than that of adjusting to the host culture.

Again, most of the earliest arrivals of this wave were relatively young. Observers of later arrivals note that Jewish immigrants who again were part of a much larger wave of "new" immigrants from eastern and southern Europe were more likely to arrive with families and less likely to return to the "old home" which had after all not welcomed them. They also arrived with less money, which makes their rapid social mobility the more remarkable. Their settling in urban enclaves (ghettos) in the larger cities of the eastern seaboard, where they generated a distinct Jewish culture including a press, theater, and a labor movement, disturbed the now well-established German Jews. They attempted by several methods to disperse the new immigrants to the interior of the country where it was believed that they would more quickly adapt to American ways. One such dispersal was the Galveston movement, which brought about 10,000 eastern Jews through that port by 1914.

But it proved difficult to reshape that human clay by their would-be betters. In time the eastern Jews Americanized on their own terms and when they finally did move west it was the opportunity for business which drew them. The division between "uptown," the better-established German Jews and "downtown," the new arrivals from eastern Europe, pervaded every facet of American Jewish life, religion, culture, political behavior, and basic assumptions about how life should be lived. It did not fully disappear until after World War II. But these intragroup tensions did not disturb the ties of kinship and religion that continued to bind all Jews together in a shared communalism.

If the eastern Jewish immigrants were different in the way they defined their Jewish identity from their German Jewish brethren, they nevertheless had a similar need to establish themselves. The success story of the first two waves was repeated in different terms by the third. The release of pent-up energy and talent for achievement was awesome. It was as if a steel spring, for centuries confined by the walls of the European ghetto, had been released in the free atmosphere of America. The commercial elite produced by the eastern immigrants differed from that of the Sephardic and German Jews in that it did not remain commercial, but in the second generation made rapid inroads into the independent professions, medicine, law, accounting, and the professoriate. After World War II a common pattern was to combine a professional skill with traditional business acumen. The group thus formed is sometimes called "egghead millionaires." Such college-trained professionals played pioneering roles in developing new industries such as plastics, air conditioning, microchips, and all types of consulting. For the first time too a sizable number of Jews were proletarianized, working in Jewish-owned industries such as the garment industry. It was in this class that the Jewish labor movement was anchored; and in scale and activity it surpassed that of the German- and Finnish-Americans. Yet their tenure as workers lasted only one generation.

Immigration Codas. Those who predicted that with the arrival of the eastern Jews the cycles of Jewish immigration would come to an end could not foresee the rise of National Socialism in Germany with its special animus directed against Jews. It caused a sharp deterioration in the security of European Jewry and a new imperative to find a haven in the United States. Because official statistics do not classify immigrants according to religion we can only estimate how many Jews entered the United States between 1933 and 1945; between 110,000 and 130,000 seems a fair estimate. They came first from Germany and then from other areas of Europe that felt the Nazi lash. However, this was only a fraction of those who actually sought refuge here during the 1930s and 1940s. The restrictionist immigration law that made no distinctions between refugees in dire need of haven and normal immigrants was harshly administered during this period, so that only in 1939 was the full quota from Europe utilized. The State Department did issue 3,268 special visas to rescue prominent artists and scientists, many of whom were Jewish. Also, many of the Jewish physicists who contributed to the Manhattan Project, which first produced the atomic bomb, were Jewish. Generally, however, the Roosevelt administration was, for political and other reasons, unwilling to risk opening the gates wider, even though it possessed ample evidence of the rich human resources in the refugee stream. We will never know how many additional Einsteins, Kissingers, Szilards, and thousands of other highly skilled immigrants were lost because of their failure to gain entry. The accelerated development of Gestalt psychology, theoretical physics, art history, marketing research, architecture, and dozens of other fields in which America is supreme today was, in some measure, based on imported intellectual capital carried disproportionately by Jewish refugees. This smaller wave of involuntary immigration is referred to as a "coda." It was followed after the war by the arrival of additional codas composed of Holocaust survivors (DPs), and during the 1950s there were additional codas from Hungary and Latin America. The most recent supplement comes from the Soviet Union and Israel. It is difficult to estimate how many Jewish immigrants found a haven here after World War II; 250,000 may be too generous an estimate. In the interim the Jewish community has become practiced in helping such immigrants "get on their feet." For the most part they have repeated the highly successful accommodation of the three major waves of immigration.

Motivation. Although the pushes and pulls behind Jewish immigration share much in common with other waves of immigration, they are distinguished by the fact that the Jewish condition in countries of emigration gives them a more urgent flavor. Undoubtedly the image of America that had taken strong hold in the European underclass of which the Jews were part contributed greatly to their choosing America as the preferred community of settlement. Only Palestine witnessed a small counterflow. Also, the fact that a Jewish community already existed here and lived in relatively benevolent circumstances undoubtedly influenced the second two waves of immigration. An axiom of Jewish immigration might be that prior immigration facilitates present emigration. Like other groups, Jews migrated along a chain of waystations composed of relatives, friends and, by the third wave, organizations that facilitated the uprooting and rerooting process. Without such agencies in place the decision to move could not have been made so readily. Undoubtedly too, potential Jewish immigrants possessed the necessary "how to" information gleaned from their press and from the Jewish version of the "America letter." The Jewish dispersion itself was thus an important accelerant of new immigration.

There were for each wave primary reasons that made immigration a realistic option: the Sephardic immigrants had to leave reconquered Brazil because the reinstitution of the inquisition posed a threat to their lives; the German Jewish immigrants faced special onerous taxes, lack of access to craft guilds, severely restricted opportunities for commerce, limited prospects of marriage and family, and growing hostility from the host community; the eastern Jewish immigrants faced a similar hostility which in the second half of the nineteenth century increasingly took the form of murderous pogroms coupled with hostile government policies which were designed to contract their economic base of operation. The immigration began in earnest when extreme impoverization was already underway. Similarly, the German and central European Jews of the 1930s were fleeing for their lives. The same is true of the other codas of immigration after World War II, except for the immigration from Israel. Within that larger rationale there were the myriad of individual reasons why someone took the dire decision to try life anew elsewhere. In a sense it would not be wrong to say that there were as many reasons for immigration as there were immigrants.

Yet from a Jewish historical perspective immigration has comparatively greater weight than for other groups who have some claim to territorial space. For Jews immigration is a recurring phenomenon which has become part of their historical condition. That history began with the Exodus, which when purged of its mythical properties, is the first in a series of migrations that punctuate the Jewish historical experience. Anti-Semitism, the oldest and most sustained pathological hatred known to civilization, impinges directly on the Jewish condition. It often becomes difficult to determine whether Jews have left their homes voluntarily or conditions have been made so intolerable that they have been forced to leave. The familiar image of the "wandering Jew," which has been linked to the historical character of the Jew, is in fact accurate; Jews have been perennial refugees. Immigration shapes the Jew's historical experience and his occupational profile; he develops portable skills such as an expertise in medicine or the trade in precious stones. His drive to root himself is related to the need to "catch up," and to do that he must learn how the new host community operates. This may be what is behind the fabled ability of the Jew to adapt to alien societies while retaining his own religious culture

This characteristic also creates a distinctive interdependence between Jewish communities. In the American Jewish experience, for example, survival as a distinct people is based squarely on immigration. The Sephardic community would undoubtedly have vanished from the historical stage without the timely arrival of the Jewish immigration from central Europe, and these, too, would not have been able to sustain a distinct Jewish community without the eastern Jewish immigrants. It is this phenomenon that lends an element of uncertainty to the viability of American Jewry after the Holocaust. The question of survival which so exercises American Jews today is related to the fact that there no longer exists a Jewish community that can furnish the biological supplement and cultural enrichment that has in the past assured its continuance.

References
S. Birmingham, *Our Crowd* (1967); "Centennial of Eastern European Jewish Immigration," *American Jewish History* 71 (Dec. 1981); H. L. Feingold, *Zion in America: The Jewish Experience from Colonial Times to the Present* (1982); E. E. Hirschler, ed., *Jews From Germany in the United States* (1945); I. Howe, *World of Our Fathers* (1976); Ronald Sanders, *Shores of Refuge: A Hundred Years of Jewish Emigration* (1988); R. Sanders, *The Downtown Jews* (1969); M. Wischnitzer, *To Dwell in Safety: The Story of Jewish Migration Since 1900* (1948).

H.L.F.

JEWS, American Jewry, attitudes toward Eastern European Jewish immigration. Two million Eastern European Jews immigrated to the United States between 1881 and 1914. The significance of Jewish immigration in this period can be seen from the fact that the entire Jewish population of this country prior to World War I totaled approximately three million. The stream of eastern European Jewish immigration to the United States began prior to 1881, but sharply increased in the 1880s because of political events in the Russian Empire and Romania, and economic dislocation throughout eastern Europe. Jewish immigration to America practically came to a standstill after 1914. American Jewry, consisting largely of German Jewish immigrants and their children, in the 1880s and 1890s feared and tried to discourage eastern European Jewish immigration. By 1914, though, the American Jewish community considered their coreligionists welcome additions to the population. Despite the increase of nativism and anti-Semitism between 1881 and 1914, the overwhelming majority of Jews seeking these shores were granted admission. American Jewry by 1914 not only expended significant sums of money for domestic charities but also collected funds for overseas relief. The period of mass Jewish immigration to the United States coincided with an increase of nativism which was aimed at curtailing all immigration from eastern and southern Europe.

Reference
Myron Berman, *The Attitude of American Jewry Towards East European Jewish Immigration, 1881–1914* (1980).

F.C.

JEWS, American Jewry and United States immigration policy. During the period between 1880 and the 1950s, no public issue inspired greater concern on the part of American Jews than did the formation of United States immigration policy, particularly policy from the onset of the vast eastern European migration to the United States through the time of the reaffirmation of the national origins system nearly four decades after it was first adopted. Arranged chronologically, Jewish activity can be best placed into a number of major episodes: (1) the early reaction to the arrival of the eastern European Jews and the attempt to curb their entry; (2) the response to the literacy test; (3) the response to the quota legislation; (4) the effort to admit refugees from Nazism; (5) the reaction to the displaced persons question; and (6) the effort to modify the quota system during the 1950s.

Reference
Sheldon M. Neuringer, *American Jewry and United States Immigration Policy, 1881–1953* (1980).

F.C.

JEWS, Conservative Judaism. The ethnic church category constitutes a suitable frame of reference with which to analyze the development of

Conservative Judaism, one of the three divisions in American Jewish religious life. Due to certain factors special to the Jewish tradition, and aggravated by a very high rate of social mobility among the group, certain needs were so accentuated in the Jewish community as to require a greater degree of adjustment on the part of the Orthodox synagogue than this institution was able to make. Distinguished by a pervasive interest in group survival, Jews who shared a similar class position, degree of acculturation, and common background in the Judaism of eastern Europe established "Conservative" synagogues—chiefly during the second and third decades of the twentieth century—which brought into harmony their newly achieved status with patterns of Jewish worship.

Reference
Marshall Sklare, *Conservative Judaism: A Sociological Analysis* (rev. ed., 1972).

F.C.

JEWS, *Daily Jewish Courier*. *See* Americanization Movement.

JEWS, ideological anti-Semitism. Historians looking at the problem of American anti-Semitism have had to deal with the perplexing question of causation. Unlike the Europeanists, who have chronicled and analyzed centuries of Jewish oppression on the Continent as a chapter in the long and intricate story (which has often been antilibertarian) of European religious, political, and economic development, American historians have had the unenviable task of reconciling anti-Jewish prejudice with what is generally interpreted to be a basically democratic society. They have been able to do so by deflating the scope and intensity of anti-Jewish manifestations in America and by emphasizing the social and economic roots of prejudice, which are essentially transient, rather than the ideological and religious factors, which may indeed be permanent.

Reference
Michael N. Dobkowski, "Ideological Anti-Semitism in America, 1877–1927," Ph.D. dissertation, New York University, 1976; Susan S. Cohen, ed., *Antisemitism: An Annotated Bibliography* (1987).

B.L.

JEWS, *Jews, America, and Immigration: A Socialist Perspective* (Boris Frumkin and Shimon Ginzburg, 1907; rpt. 1980). This was originally a report to the International Socialist Congress written in 1907 concerning the recent immigrant Jewish workers in the United States. The authors were Marxist Socialists active in the Jewish Bund. They believed that the Jews had traded the tyranny of the czar for abuse by the great industrialists who ran the factories and sweatshops with more concern for their machines than their employees. Frumkin and Ginzburg could not understand why the American labor movement was not attracted to socialism to end its exploitation. The forces at work during this formative period of the Jewish community and its labor unions, including the restrictionist policy of immigration by the United States government, are illuminated in this historical document through the issue of emigration and immigration from the Socialist point of view.

F.C.

JEWS, Kehillah. The assembly or community of Jewish localities started in early Jerusalem and Babylonia and developed during the Middle Ages into almost self-governing communities with powers of management and taxation wherever Jews lived in Europe. From 1580 to 1764, the Kehillah dictated the public and religious life of the community, including meetings, ceremonies, and education.

In 1908, a Reform rabbi, Judah Leon Magnes (1877–1948), of New York's Temple Emmanuel, started a Kehillah in the United States. It included Reform, Conservative, and Orthodox organizations and dealt with education, labor relations, charity, and crime control. Internal controversies caused its demise in 1922.

Reference
Nathan S. Goren, *New York Jews and the Quest for Community: The Kehillah Experiment, 1908–1922* (1970).

B.L.

JEWS, Leo Frank case. The Leo Frank case highlights the problems of a society in transition. At the beginning of the twentieth century rural Georgians migrated to Atlanta to enjoy the heralded advantages of industrialization. To their chagrin they found harsh working conditions and squalid living quarters. Southern traditions, which glorified the Anglo-Saxon Protestant heritage, and the bitter memories of the Lost Cause, complicated the newcomers' reactions to urban life. Unable to retaliate against the industrialists whose colossal indifference caused them many hardships, the new urbanites vented their pent-up aggressions upon blacks and other vulnerable ethnic groups. It is against this background that the Frank case is to be understood.

Reference
Leonard Dinnerstein, *The Leo Frank Case* (1968).

B.L.

JEWS, Max Weinreich Center for Advanced Jewish Studies. *See* Yivo Institute for Jewish Research.

JEWS, Orthodoxy in Milwaukee. Polsky has studied the interaction between a sacred religious system and the pattern of an American secular society. Jewish Orthodoxy was separated into three component elements: its organization, with the synagogue as the primary institutional structure; its membership; and its role in the Jewish community. Jewish Orthodoxy, having at its source the rich sacred accumulated heritage of two thousand years, balanced to some extent the secularizing tendencies of the American social system. The American Jewish community will continue its unique development without a significant traditional Jewish Orthodox movement in its midst; this will result in an acceleration of the process of secularization of Jewish religious traditions and raise new problems and challenges for the survival of Judaism in America.

Reference
Howard W. Polsky, "The Great Defense: A Study of Jewish Orthodoxy in Milwaukee," Ph.D. dissertation, University of Wisconsin, Madison, 1957.

F.C.

JEWS, Reconstructionism and Jewish education. Reconstructionism is the name of a movement in American Jewish life initiated by Dr. Mordecai M. Kaplan and developed by him and many colleagues and disciples. It is critical of all of the existing major theories of Jewish life because of their failure to come to grips, philosophically and educationally, with the twofold challenge of modern democratic nationalism and modern naturalism. Reconstructionism aims to effect a creative adjustment of Jewish life to these new conditions of the modern world; it is a Jewish religious movement that seeks to integrate the patterns of democracy, the naturalistic outlook, the organismic point of view in psychology, and the method and intellectual mood of pragmatism.

Reference
Michael Alper, "Reconstruction and Jewish Education—The Implications of Reconstructionism for Jewish Education in the United States," Ph.D. dissertation, Columbia University (Teachers College), 1954.

B.L.

JEWS IN THE SOUTH. Although they have never composed more than a tiny percent of the total population of the South, Jews have been a significant ethnic minority in the region for over 240 years. From approximately the middle of the seventeenth century to the first quarter of the nineteenth century the first wave of Jewish immigrants entered the South. Mostly Sephardic, these Jews migrated primarily to the southern coastal colonies and established their first congregations in Richmond (Beth Shalom); Charleston (Beth Elohim); and Savannah (Mickve Israel). Indeed, southern Jewish history is said to have begun in 1733 with the arrival of forty Spanish-Portuguese and German Jewish refugees in Savannah. While Jewish names appearing in southern records predate this event, it is generally acknowledged that the Savannah immigrants constituted the first Jewish community in the South.

Interestingly, at this time half of the major Jewish settlements in America existed in the South, and Jews in the colonial South established many of the patterns and practices that eventually would be followed by the American Jewry as a whole.

Christian opposition to the Jews in Savannah, however, resulted in the Jewish community there being a short-lived one. With greater tolerance found somewhat up the coast in Charleston, South Carolina, many of the Savannah Jews had relocated by 1740. In Charleston, the Jews not only prospered but they assimilated as well, assuming many of the attitudes and ideologies of their Christian neighbors. So successful were the Jews in Charleston that by century's end they composed one of the largest antebellum Jewish communities in America.

In Charleston, as elsewhere in the "urban" South, Jews were able to establish shops or achieve reasonable success as peddlers. From there, many expanded their businesses while others prospered as merchants, financiers, artisans, and professionals. Today, such establishments as Riches in Atlanta, Neiman-Marcus in Dallas, and Thalheimers in Richmond vividly illustrate the entrepreneurial success and business acumen of Jewish immigrants in the South.

Certainly in the nineteenth century, though, one key ingredient to the success of Jews in the South was their adoption of the popular and prevailing notions articulated by the planter aristocracy. Like their white Christian counterparts, the Jews espoused the doctrine of states' rights, nullification, and secession. Although few owned plantations, some particularly affluent Jews owned slaves, and most countenanced the "peculiar institution." In fact, Rabbi David Einhorn of Baltimore, one of the leaders of the radical wing of the American Jewish Reform movement, was about the only prominent southern Jewish proponent of abolition.

Of course, the acceptance of the planter mentality was virtually the only choice for most white southerners—slave owners or not—in the antebellum South. For an immigrant minority seeking acceptance it was an imperative. And, with the exception of North Carolina, where full political equality was denied them until 1868, Jews enjoyed equal treatment throughout the South at this time. Nevertheless, the overwhelmingly agrarian nature of the southern economy dissuaded large groups of Jews from emigrating into the region and on the eve of the Civil War their numbers totaled less than 15,000.

Small numbers notwithstanding, Jews participated actively in the politics of the antebellum South. In 1845, David L. Yulee of Florida became the first Jew elected to the United States Senate. Of all southern Jews of the antebellum period, the most prominent surely was Judah P. Benjamin, who served as a U.S. senator from Louisiana and was, arguably, the most powerful member of President Jefferson Davis's Confederate war cabinet, first as attorney general, then secretary of war, and finally secretary of state.

During the Civil War southern Jews actively and enthusiastically endorsed the Confederacy either by their enlistment or through their financial contributions. But as the war wound down and the collapse of the Confederacy seemed imminent, anti-Semitism surfaced as a defeated people sought scapegoats. Following the peace at Appomattox, however, the enmity toward Jews subsided and Jews and Christians alike attempted to reconstruct the world around them.

During this period, and until approximately 1870, a small but steady stream of Jews, mostly from Germany, emigrated to the South. While the Jewish population in the coastal communities remained relatively constant during this time, the migration of Jews along the Gulf Coast and inland increased. Jewish communities were established along with congregations, Hebrew schools, and cemeteries, as well as benevolent, aid, and relief societies in such burgeoning southern urban areas as Atlanta, Dallas, Houston, Miami, and the District of Columbia. As they joined in the building of the New South, Jewish businessmen, peddlers, and merchants enjoyed moderate, albeit anxious, success.

Frustration and anger, though, precipitated in part by economic and political instability, often manifested itself in virulent white supremacist, anti-Catholic, and anti-Semitic behavior in the New South. The most flagrant example of the latter occurred in Georgia in 1915 with the brutal lynching of Leo Frank, a young Jew questionably convicted of murder by a prejudiced jury. This event was endemic of a renaissance, of sorts, of southern anti-Semitism. By the time of Frank's death, most Jews had been, or soon would be, relegated by such groups as the Ku Klux Klan to social and political pariahs.

The rampant xenophobia following World War I and the subsequent tightening of immigration laws in the 1920s successfully cut off the flow of eastern European Jews to the United States. The net effect of this on the antipathy directed toward southern Jews was, at best, negligible. However, forced continually to rely exclusively upon themselves for solace and succor, the southern Jewry at this time tended to form more cohesive, though still subtle, ethnic communities.

Ironically, anti-Jewish feelings in the South were exacerbated with the arrival of the modern civil rights movement in the post–World War II era. During the 1950s and 1960s, Jews again became targets of violence and vigilantism. And, although southern Jews were extremely timorous, when compared to their northern counterparts, in protesting and agitating for reform, their temples and their synagogues were none-theless attacked and firebombed frequently.

The 1970s and 1980s, for the most part, ushered in a new period of tolerance and acceptance in the South. Recognizing the region's favorable climate and economic opportunities, many northern Jews relocated to south of the Mason-Dixon Line. Some 785,000 Jews now live in the South, and are about 4 percent of the total regional population. They worship in over 200 temples and synagogues in the major urban areas throughout the region as well as in many smaller communities.

References
Myron Berman, *Richmond's Jewry: Shabbot in Shockoe, 1769–1976* (1979); Leonard Dinnerstein and Mary Dale Palsson, eds., *Jews in the South* (1973); Nathan M. Kaganoff and Melvin I. Urofsky, eds., *"Turn to the South": Essays on Southern Jewry* (1979); Bertram W. Korn, *The Early Jews of New Orleans* (1969); Jason H. Silverman, *Beyond the Melting Pot in Dixie: Immigration and Ethnicity in Southern History* (1989).

J.H.S.

JEWS, and World War I reactions in Yiddish Press. Having arrived in this country with the "new" immigration, the Yiddish-speaking element remained closely attached to Jewish communities in Russia, Poland, Galicia, Hungary, and Romania. Jewish immigrant wartime reactions must be measured in the light of the rejection of the conditions of their former life (which was the basis of the migration), and the desire to see the political, economic, and social emancipation of the eastern European Jewish community. The origins of Jewish nationalist and Socialist strivings, which played an important role in immigrant war attitudes, stemmed from this drive for emancipation, political or otherwise.

Reference
Joseph Rappaport, "Jewish Immigrants and World War I: A Study of American Yiddish Press Reactions," Ph.D. dissertation, Columbia University, 1951.

F.C.

JEWS, Zionist leadership and organization. Zionist ideology underwent changes during the first three decades of the twentieth century. Starting in eastern Europe as a nationalist ideology that asserted that the Jews were and should remain a separate political and cultural entity, Zionism was transformed in the United States into Palestinianism, a belief that all Jews should help in the building up of Palestine as a national Jewish home.

Reference
Ynoathan Shapiro, *Leadership of the American Zionist Organization, 1897–1930* (1971).

F.C.

JIBARO. The Puerto Rican *jíbaro* is an idealized folk hero with a distinct ethnic, social, and cultural inheritance and unique religion, family pattern, and attitudes. The *jíbaros* are a vanishing social class. The extensive sugarcane monoculture, established in the early twentieth century, drew many of the *jíbaros* from the hill towns and turned them into landless, wage-earning proletariats. It is the *jíbaros* who constituted the mass in the early migrations to the U.S. mainland following World War II.

Reference
José Rosario, *The Development of the Puerto Rican Jíbaro and His Present Attitude Towards Society* (1935; rpt. 1975).

F.C.

JOHNSON, ALBERT (1869–1957). A politician and journalist, Johnson served as a Republican congressman from Washington state for nine succeeding terms from 1913 to 1933. He supported a permanent immigration restriction policy in Congress; a close associate of prominent restrictionists, e.g., Prescott F. Hall (*q.v.*) and Madison Grant (*q.v.*), Johnson enlisted the cooperation of the leading eugenicist Harry H. Laughlin (*q.v.*) in providing "scientific" support for restrictionism. Johnson acknowledged these influences on his immigration policy in a speech in the House in 1922:

> In concluding I want to commend to all those interested in the racial and political aspects of the question two epoch-making books by Lothrop Stoddard entitled *The Rising Tide of Color* and *The Revolt Against Civilization,* [and] an equally important book by Madison Grant entitled *The Passing of the Great Race.* (*Congressional Record,* 1922, p. 12065)

As chairman of the House Immigration Committee, Johnson was a major influence in the enactment of the Emergency Quota Law in May 1921 (42 U.S. Statutes at Large) which provided "that the number of aliens of any nationality who may be admitted under the immigration laws to the United States in any fiscal year shall be limited to three (3) per cent of the number of foreign-born persons of such nationality resident in the United States census of 1910." This measure reduced the "new" (southern and eastern European immigration) to 20 percent of its 1914 total. The Immigration Act of 1924 (the Johnson-Reed Act, popularly known as the National Origins Act, 43 U.S. Statutes at Large) incorporated the principles enunciated in the Immigration Act of 1921, but was far more restrictive in its qualitative and quantitative aspects. For Albert Johnson, the 1924 act was a personal triumph. *See* Immigration Legislation.

References
Roy L. Garis, *Immigration Restriction* (1927); Barbara M. Solomon, *Ancestors and Immigrants* (1956); John Higham, *Strangers in the Land* (1973).

F.C.

JONES, MARY HARRIS (1830–1930). Socialist, labor leader. An Irish immigrant, Jones was familiarly known as "Mother Jones." No coherent or consistent philosophy guided her work; she was, rather, a "benevolent fanatic." Nevertheless, Mother Jones was "a folk heroine whose inspiration reached down to those people who were unimportant in name or wealth or title but all-important in numbers." A major force in the American labor movement, her *Autobiography* (1925) is a chronicle of her strike activity. Jones offers few insights into her personal life, but rather presents a picture of the famed agitator as she liked to be recognized—she narrates many adventures, including the 1903 march of the mill children and the great strikes (largely by immigrant workers) in Colorado in 1903 and 1913–14.

References
Dale Fetherling, *Mother Jones, the Miners' Angel: A Portrait* (1974); Mary Jones, *The Autobiography of Mother Jones,* ed. Mary Field Parton, Foreword by Clarence Darrow, Introduction by Fred Thompson (1925; rpt. 1971); Priscilla Long, *Mother Jones: Woman Organizer* (1976).

F.C.

JUNIOR ORDER OF UNITED AMERICAN MECHANICS. Secret fraternal order of American workingmen whose origins go back to the nativism (*q.v.*) of the 1840s. Its primary concern was immigrant competition, not unlike that of the Order of United American Mechanics and the Patriotic Order Sons of America. The *JOUAM* was anti-radical and anti-Catholic and vituperative in its denunciation of immigrants and immigration policy.

Reference
Roy L. Garis, *Immigration Restriction* (1927).

F.C.

KALEVA, KNIGHTS AND LADIES OF. *See* Finns.

KALLEN, HORACE M[EYER] (b. 1882). A major critic of the Americanization movement and an advocate of the philosophy of cultural pluralism. Kallen's chief works are: *Culture and Democracy in the United States* (1924); and *Cultural Pluralism and the American Idea*

(1956), which includes his elaboration of the concept of cultural pluralism, a series of critiques by other scholars, and a rejoinder by Kallen. *See also* Cultural Pluralism.

Reference
Fred H. Mathews, "The Revolt Against Americanism: Cultural Pluralism and Cultural Relativism as an Ideology of Liberation," *Canadian Review of American Studies* 1 (1970): 4–31.

F.C.

THE KALLIKAK FAMILY. *See* Goddard, Henry H.

KAMEHAMEHA I, IV. *See* Hawaiians.

KAPLAN, MORDECAI M. *See* [Jews]: Reconstructionism and Jewish Education.

KAPOCIUS, JUOZAS. *See* Lithuanians.

KELLEY, FLORENCE (1859–1932). Social worker and reformer. Kelley was for a time resident at Hull House (*q.v.*) in Chicago. From 1899 she served as director of the National Consumer's League (*q.v.*), whose main efforts were directed at industrial reform through consumer activity. She was a close associate of Josephine Goldmark (*q.v.*), the labor investigator and social reformer. Her chief works are: *Ethical Gains Through Legislation* (1905); and *Our Toiling Children* (1889). Kelley was a major force in the campaign against the evils of industrialism and especially against child labor. See also Kelley's "Child Labor," *Frank Leslie's Illustrated Weekly* (Feb. 1890); and "The Sweating System," in *Hull House Maps and Papers* (1895). Particularly important is her *Modern Industry in Relation to the Family, Health, Education, and Morality* (1914); and a series of autobiographical sketches in *The Survey:* "My Philadelphia" (Oct. 1, 1926); "When Co-education Was Young" (Feb. 1, 1927); "My Novitiate" (April 1, 1927); and "I Go to Work" (June 1, 1927).

References
Dorothy R. Blumberg, *Florence Kelley: The Making of a Social Pioneer* (1966); Josephine Goldmark, *Impatient Crusader: Florence Kelley's Life Story* (1953).

D.N.A.

KELLOGG, PAUL U[NDERWOOD] (b. 1879). Social reformer; a major figure in the Progressive movement and director of the massive *Pittsburgh Survey* (*q.v.*) to whose influence Jane Addams (*q.v.*) attributed the "veritable zeal for reform" that agitated the United States between 1909 and 1914, the years of the growing immigrant presence. Kellogg was an untiring advocate of preventing destitution through the adoption of public insurance against the main causes of poverty—accidents, illness, premature death, old age, and unemployment.

Reference
Robert H. Bremner, *From the Depths* (1964).

F.C.

KELLOR, FRANCES ALICE (1873–1947). Kellor, a social reformer, was a younger contemporary of Jane Addams (*q.v.*), Lillian Wald (*q.v.*), and Florence Kelley (*q.v.*), and was both a lawyer and a University of Chicago–trained sociologist. Operating out of Hull House in Chicago and the Rivington Street College Settlement House in New York, she helped to lead the Progressive attack on the problems of the new immigrant and blacks. Her efforts to halt the exploitation of household workers in New York culminated in 1906, when she founded the National League for the Protection of Colored Women, one of three organizations that consolidated in 1911 to form the National Urban League of today. Her chief works are: *Out of Work* (1915) and *Immigration and the Future* (1920).

References
John Higham, *Strangers in the Land* (1973); William J. Maxwell, "Frances Kellor in the Progressive Era: A Case Study in the Professionalization of Reform," Ph.D. dissertation, Columbia University (Teachers College), 1968 (DA 29: 3561-A).

F.C.

KELLY, MYRA (1876–1910). Short story writer and novelist. Many of her short stories recount her experiences as a schoolteacher with New York City Lower East Side Jewish immigrant children. Chief publications: *Little Citizens: The Humours of School Life* (1904); *Wards of Liberty* (1907); and *Little Aliens* (1910).

Reference
David M. Fine, *The City, The Immigrant and American Fiction, 1885–1917* (1977).

F.C.

KING, MARTIN LUTHER, JR. (1929–1968). Born in Atlanta, Georgia, in 1929; assassinated in Memphis, Tennessee in 1968. King was the leading black spokesman and philosopher for the nonviolent civil rights movement which led to the end of legal segregation throughout the southern United States. King received a bachelor's degree from Morehouse College, a divinity degree from Crozer Theological Seminary, and a doctorate from Boston University, where he also met his future wife, Coretta Scott. He was an active clergyman and the founder of the Southern Christian Leadership Conference. His philosophy was based on the teachings of Jesus and Mahatma Gandhi. He taught that humankind had one Father and that integration was therefore a logical necessity. He believed that nonviolent resistance must be developed as the only moral way to change society, and that suffering and love were powerful tools with which to combat evil.

Starting in Montgomery, Alabama in 1955, King led a number of protest demonstrations against segregation which resulted in his being jailed on more than one occasion. In 1963, before the Lincoln Memorial, he delivered his famous "I Have a Dream" speech, which looked forward to an integrated and loving society. In 1966, younger black leaders began to break away from his leadership; the Black Power movement advocated building a separate black movement, which King continued to believe would be counterproductive. However, in his last years he began to speak out against the Vietnam War and to condemn black poverty. These themes made him even more controversial than before. In April 1968, he was supporting a strike by garbage workers when he was shot by a white ex-convict, James Earl Ray. Besides being an eloquent orator, King was an accomplished author of many books. The movements for civil rights for women and immigrant groups were inspired by his work. The nonviolent branch of the antiwar movement was also indebted to his philosophy and tactics.

References
L. G. Davis, *Martin Luther King* (1973); Coretta King, *My Life with Martin Luther King* (1969); C. E. Lincoln, *Martin Luther King* (1970).

N.C.

KITTREDGE, MABEL H[YDE] (1867–1943). Social reformer; settlement house worker with special interest in immigrant poor. Author of *Practical Homemaking* (1914); and *The Home and Its Management* (1917). See also Kittredge's "Experiments with School Lunches in New York City," *Journal of Home Economics* 1 (June 1910): 174–177; "Housekeeping Centers in Settlements and Public Schools," *The Survey* 30 (April 1913): 188–192; and "The Needs of the Immigrant," *Journal of Home Economics* 5 (Oct. 1913): 308–317.

F.C.

KLOSS, HEINZ (1904–1987). For more than a half-century Kloss wrote about the sociology of language and linguistic minorities all over the world. Born at Halle, Kloss was employed from 1927 to 1945 at the Deutsches Ausland-Institute in Stuttgart, Germany. Kloss twice visited the United States (1930–31 and 1936–37) for research purposes. Durng the first trip he studied especially the Pennsylvania Dutch; during he second, at the invitation of the Carl Schurz Memorial Foundation in Philadelphia, he compiled his report on *Research Possibilities in the German-American Field* which, however, was not published until 1980 (Hamburg: Buske). In 1974 Elwert (Marburg) published his *Atlas of German-American Settlements,* work for which was begun in the 1930s and continued when he served as coordinator of American reeducation efforts (1947–1952) and as section chief at the reconstituted Institut für Auslands Beziehungen in Stuttgart (1953–59). Between 1959 and 1970 he directed research at the Institute for Nationalities and Languages in Kiel, which later moved to Marburg. Thereafter Kloss was a visiting professor at Laval University in Quebec (1968–1980) and employed at the Institute für Deutsche Sprache in Mannheim (1971–76). A 1976 Festschrift for Kloss (Hamburg) includes a bibliography listing 366 published articles and books. Since that date he published additional items including his books *The American Bilingual Tradition* (1977), *The Written Languages of the World* (vol. 1: *The Americas,* 1978) and *Deutsch als Müttersprache in den Vereinigten Staaten* (1985).

L.J.R.

KNIGHTS OF LITHUANIA. *See* Lithuanians.

KNIGHTS OF ST. CRISPIN. A tradition-bound union of shoemakers (largely German immigrants) which originated in Milwaukee. From 1867 through the ensuing decade it was a thriving organization of more than 50,000 members (larger than any other union of the day) concerned with basic trade union issues. Nevertheless, though it represented the industry, the Knights jealously guarded their skills. Gradually they began to close the ranks of their industry to outsiders, teaching their crafts only to sons of members. By 1878, the Knights of St. Crispin had ceased to exist.

Reference
Don D. Lescohier, *Knights of St. Crispin, 1867–1874* (1910; rpt., 1974).

F.C.

KOREAN IMMIGRANTS, adhesive sociocultural adaptation in the United States. Adhesive adaptation is conceptualized as a particular mode of adaptation in which certain aspects of the new culture and social relations with members of the host society are added on to the immigrants' traditional culture and social networks, without replacing or modifying any significant part of the old. In light of this conceptual framework, various patterns of Korean immigrants' adaptation in the United States are examined (*infra*). For data collection, 615 Korean immigrants in the Los Angeles area were interviewed in 1979. Findings indicate that the immigrants' strong and pervasive ethnic attachment is unaffected by their length of residence in the United States, their socioeconomic status, or their cultural and social assimilation rates. The adhesive mode of adaptation is thus empirically confirmed by this study. Theoretical and practical implications of this adhesive adaptation are discussed in the conclusion.

Reference
Won Moo Hurh and Kwang Chung Kim, "Adhesive Sociocultural Adaptation of Korean Immigrants in the U.S.: An Alternative Strategy of Minority Adaptation," *International Migration Review* 18 (Summer 1984): 188–216.

F.C.

KOREANS. Most of the over 600,000 persons of Korean ancestry in the United States today arrived only in the last two decades, although there are also some third- and fourth-generation Korean-Americans whose forebears came at the turn of the century. In 1882, the United States gained entry into Korea with the Treaty of Chemulpo. American Protestant missionaries and businessmen played key roles in promoting Korean emigration.

Immigration. Korean immigration into the United States can be divided into four periods: 1902–5; 1905–1952; 1952–1965; and 1965–present.

Recruited Emigration to Hawaii, 1902–1905. At the beginning of the twentieth century, sugar plantation owners in Hawaii turned to Korea as a possible source of labor because, by then, Japanese workers, who constituted two-thirds of the total plantation labor force in the islands, had become militant and were engaging in work stoppages and spontaneous strikes. In 1902, the Hawaiian Sugar Planters' Association (HSPA) met with Horace N. Allen, an American medical missionary who had proselytized in Korea since 1884, when he stopped in Hawaii on his way back to Korea from a visit to the United States. Allen had become quite involved in Korean affairs, having gained the confidence of Emperor Kojong, whom he served as personal physician. Desiring a more formal role in Korea's politics, he managed, with the help of George Nash, a friend of President William McKinley, to get himself appointed as the United States minister to Korea. Nash was the stepfather of David Deshler, an American businessman in Korea, with whom Allen subsequently entered into a partnership to recruit Koreans for Hawaii's plantations.

Several steps had to be taken before emigration could begin. First, Allen persuaded the Korean monarch to set up a bureau of emigration. The emperor agreed to do so because famine had stalked several northern provinces in 1902, and he thought that emigration might provide some relief. Meanwhile, Deshler opened a bank, in which the HSPA was the sole depositor. The Deshler Bank lent money to aspiring emigrants for their passage as well as for the $50 which they had to show upon arrival in order to meet the requirements of American law which prohibited the importation of contract labor. Few Koreans responded to the recruitment efforts, however, until the Reverend George Heber Jones persuaded members of his congregation that life for them as Christians would be more pleasant in Hawaii, a Christian land. About half of the first shipment that left in December 1902 were members of Jones' church. Another missionary, Homer Hulbert, who published the *Korea Review,* also urged Koreans to emigrate in the pages of his magazine. As a result of the active role that missionaries played, an estimated 40 percent of the over 7,000 Koreans who eventually landed in Hawaii were converts to Protestant Christianity.

The emigrants originated from scattered locations and diverse socioeconomic backgrounds. Although there is no definitive information on exactly where they came from or what occupations they had followed prior to departure, most were probably laborers, former soldiers, peasants, and artisans from the area around Inchon and Suwon. They traveled on ships owned by Deshler to Kobe, Japan, where they were medically examined before they set sail for Hawaii. More than 600 of the emigrants were women and more than 500 were children—figures that indicate that quite a large proportion probably intended to settle overseas. Eventually, about 1,000 returned to Korea while another 1,000 or so remigrated to the United States mainland to join the small number of Koreans—mostly merchants and students—who had gone there directly.

Restricted Emigration, 1905–1952. Emigration ended suddenly in 1905, when the Japanese government, which had declared Korea its protectorate following Japan's victory over Russia in the Russo-Japanese War of 1904–5, closed the emigration office and banned further departures. Japan wanted to protect Japanese workers in Hawaii by denying the sugar planters access to Koreans who were used as strikebreakers. At the same time, it also wished to keep Koreans at home to facilitate its efforts to develop the Korean economy, especially after it annexed Korea outright in 1910.

Under Japanese colonial rule, which lasted until 1945, the only Koreans who emigrated to the United States were some 1,000 "picture brides"—women whose marriages had been arranged through the use of photographs. About 900 joined husbands in Hawaii, while slightly more than 100 did so in the continental United States. About 500 students, many of them anti-Japanese political activists, also managed to enter the country. Some came without passports by way of China or

Europe, in search of political asylum. The vast majority of both the picture brides and the expatriates arrived before 1924. Students coming after that date were not allowed to remain in the United States after they completed their studies, as Congress had passed a law in 1924 that greatly restricted immigration from eastern and southern Europe and barred Asian immigration altogether.

The Immigration of American Dependents, 1952–1965. With Japan's defeat, which ended World War II, Korea regained its independence, but the country was partitioned at the thirty-eighth parallel between a northern Communist government and a southern regime aligned with the United States. A civil war broke out in 1950. American troops fought on behalf of the south while the People's Republic of China aided the north. After a truce was declared, the United States by agreement continued to station up to 39,000 military personnel in South Korea. Some of them married Korean women, more than 1,000 of whom entered the United States as American dependents every year. (Korean wives of American servicemen coming to the United States totaled more than 28,000 between 1950 and 1975.) In addition, thousands of children, many of mixed American and Korean parentage, were adopted by American families in this period, so that 90 percent of all Korean immigrants in the 1950s and early 1960 were women and children. (To date, some 50,000 Korean children have been adopted by American families.) In the same period, too, some 10,000 students came for higher education and about 70 percent of them later managed to adjust their status to that of resident alien.

Post-1965 Immigration. In 1965, Congress abolished "national origins" as the basis of American immigration legislation, finally putting Asian nations on the same footing as European ones. The new law was fully implemented after 1968, and beginning in the early 1970s, more than 20,000 (and in some years over 30,000) Koreans have been arriving each year. (Although the ceiling from each country is 20,000, spouses and unmarried minor children can enter outside of the quota.) While the 1970 census counted only 71,000 persons of Korean ancestry, by 1980 they numbered 355,000, and they were estimated at more than 540,000 in mid-1985.

Before 1976, some 45 percent of the immigrants had entered under professional and nonfamily preferences, so that the number of individuals with professional, technical, managerial, and business backgrounds who came in search of better economic opportunities and a more secure political environment was very large. However, after Congress amended the 1965 law in 1976 to downgrade professional immigrants from the third to the sixth preference, only 6 to 7 percent of Korean immigrants in the last decade have been highly trained personnel. Instead, over 90 percent now enter under kinship criteria: 57 percent as immediate family members, 19 percent as adopted children, and 18 percent as spouses in international marriages—the last category including people who marry Koreans already in the United States.

Korean emigration has been so vigorous because the population of the Republic of Korea (South Korea) has increased from 25 million in 1960 to 38 million in 1980, despite a government-sponsored program of birth control which reduced the birth rate from 2.9 to 1.6 in the same two decades. The Republic of Korea today has the third-highest population density in the world. Moreover, due to the maldistribution of land, more and more landless rural dwellers have been migrating to Seoul, the capital, in search of work, increasing that city's population from 1.6 million in 1962 to over 10 million today, creating a density that now averages 36,000 inhabitants per square mile, compared to New York City's 23,000. Seoul and other large urban centers have not been able to provide employment for this flood of internal migrants. Although the Republic of Korea has experienced what some observers have called an economic miracle, its economy is heavily geared to exporting labor-intensive light manufactured goods. Since 30 percent of all Korean exports go to the United States, and more than 20 percent to Japan, Korea is greatly affected by fluctuations in the world capitalist economy, which means that its lowly paid, nonunionized workers lead a precarious existence. Finally, Koreans are also leaving because life is restrictive under the political system that exists in their country and some fear another war between the north and south. An estimated 50 percent of the immigrants originally came from the north—people who had migrated south as refugees from communism when the country was partitioned and who have not satisfactorily reestablished themselves because they do not have the proper "connections" to get good jobs in the government or elsewhere.

To ease this state of affairs, the South Korean government has actively promoted emigration, to the extent of setting up special training programs to enable people to acquire specific skills desired by the United States so that they can gain entry into the latter country—the destination of over 80 percent of all contemporary Korean emigrants. The United States is so popular because the significant American military, economic, and cultural presence in Korea since the early 1950s has created a desire on the part of many Koreans—particularly members of the middle class—for an American pattern of consumption, even if they may disapprove of other aspects of the American lifestyle, such as premarital sex, divorce, and the reluctance of children to care for their elderly parents.

Employment, Social Organization, and Political Activities. Before the 1960s, Hawaii had the largest concentration of Korean-Americans, most of whose ancestors had worked in the sugar plantations. However, quite early on, as soon as they finished their terms, those who stayed in the islands migrated to Honolulu or the mainland, where they opened small stores, bath houses, or boarding houses. Their children studied hard and those in Hawaii found white-collar and professional employment, so that by the time immigration was renewed, the second- and third-generation Korean Americans in the fiftieth state were by and large members of the middle class.

On the mainland before the 1960s, Koreans lived primarily in California, but small numbers also scattered to the other western states. In the beginning, most toiled in the fields as migrant farm workers. Some worked as domestic servants, cooks, common laborers, and railroad section hands. The more ambitious and fortunate became tenant farmers, the most successful of whom grew rice in the northern Sacramento Valley of California during the rice boom of the late 1910s and early 1920s. Kim Jong-lim (also spelled Kim Chong-nim), who farmed more than 2,000 acres in Willows, California, was known as the Korean rice king, while Charles Kim (Kim Ho) and Harry Kim (Kim Hyung-soon) established the Kim Brothers Company in Reedley, California, where they managed six farms totaling 500 acres. They became famous for developing several varieties of hybrid fruit, including the nectarine. Other large acreages were farmed by Koreans in Utah and Colorado who grew sugar beets on contract. Those in cities depended on running produce stands and other small businesses for survival.

In contrast, the recent arrivals have been overwhelmingly urban settlers. Korean immigrants have dispersed themselves more widely than other Asian immigrant groups, but the majority of them are residing in towns and cities, where those with capital to invest have opened retail stores, especially groceries selling fresh produce, in the inner cities of many American metropolises, often revitalizing them. More than half of these proprietors are college graduates who went into business because they could not pass the U.S. licensing examinations required to practice their professions. In some black neighborhoods, Koreans have replaced Jewish merchants, and a familiar pattern of tension has developed between the customers and this newest group of entrepreneurs.

Like the Chinese and Japanese immigrants who preceded them, Koreans also quickly organized themselves. On the Hawaiian plantations, they formed *tonghoe* (village councils) in each locality with ten or more Korean families. Each year, the adult males selected a *tongjang* (head of the council), a sergeant-at-arms, and a few policemen to carry out the rules they established. However, outside of the plantations and on a larger scale, unlike the Chinese and Japanese, who formed community associations based on kinship, regional ties, or common dialects spoken, Koreans organized on the basis of religion and politics.

Within half a year after their arrival in Hawaii, they held the first Korean-language church service when the Methodists set up the Korean Evangelical Society. Other Korean Christians in the islands formed the Korean Episcopal church in 1905. In Los Angeles in 1904, Korean Christians started worshipping together at a mission school; the following year, individuals in San Francisco established the Korean Methodist church. A secessionist independent Korean Christian church appeared in 1917. These and other churches have always played a central role in not only the religious but also the social and political life of Korean immigrants. Today, there are over eighty Korean churches in Los Angeles alone, where perhaps as many as 200,000 persons of Korean ancestry now live.

Even more important than the churches have been nationalist-oriented political organizations, dedicated to the liberation of Korea from Japanese colonial rule. The three most prominent expatriate leaders were Ahn Chang-ho (1878–1939), Park Yong-man (1881–1928), and Syngman Rhee (1875–1965), each of whom proposed a different strategy to achieve the common end they all desired.

Ahn came to San Francisco in 1899, where he set up the Chinmok-hoe (Friendship Society), the first social organization among Koreans in California. He believed that the Korean people had first to "regenerate" themselves if they were to regain independence, so he encouraged the immigrants to clean and beautify their homes and to engage in honorable labor. In 1913, he founded the Hungsa-dan (Corps for the Advancement of Individuals). In 1919, when a provisional Korean government-in-exile was established in Shanghai, Ahn went there to serve as its secretary of the interior and then as the secretary of labor. He was arrested by the Japanese secret police in 1935 and died in 1938 shortly after being released from jail. His followers, however, kept the Hungsa-dan active long after his death.

Park Yong-man, on the other hand, thought that military means were necessary to liberate Korea. He came to the United States in 1904, and after graduating from the University of Nebraska in 1909 he set up a Korean Youth Military Academy in Nebraska where he trained some two dozen cadets. He then established four other military academies in California, Kansas, and Wyoming, as well as an airplane pilot training program in Willows, California—the last endeavor financed by Kim Jong-lim. In 1912, the different groups of cadets were consolidated into a single Korean National Brigade, with over 300 members commanded by Park and headquartered at the Ahumanu Plantation on the island of Oahu in Hawaii. Park served briefly as minister of foreign affairs in Shanghai, but resigned when Syngman Rhee, with whom he had long had strong disagreements, appeared to serve as president. He went to Manchuria to provide military training to Korean exiles there and was assassinated in 1928. After his death, his military corps soor disintegrated.

Syngman Rhee came to the United States in 1905 and became the first Korean to obtain a Ph.D. from an American university (Princeton, 1910). He believed the best course to follow was to cultivate American public opinion and to influence the powerful nations to exert pressure or Japan. Although he became the president of the provisional government in Shanghai, he did not live there long; he returned to the United States where he founded the Korean Christian church, the Dongji-hoe (Comrade Society), and a magazine, the *Pacific Weekly,* to advance his own viewpoint. He became president of the Republic of Korea in 1948, holding office until ousted by student demonstrators in 1960, whereupon he retired to Hawaii.

The conflict among the three leaders generated intense factionalism among the Korean immigrants in both Hawaii and the mainland. Moreover, contributing so much of their meager savings to the support of these leaders meant that Korean immigrants could not advance their individual welfare. However, the nationalist struggle was something they fervently believed in. To acquire greater political power, they formed the Korean National Association in 1909 to defend the rights and promote the interests of all their compatriots. While these political associations continued to exist for some years after Korea regained its independence, they finally folded, having lost their raison d'être.

Today, the largest community group is the Korean Association of Southern California. Dozens of alumni associations are also active, while Christian churches, many of which have only small congregations of several dozen persons, continue to provide a framework for social life. Some of these churches have also served as centers of resistance to the interference of the Korean Central Intelligence Agency in the life of the immigrant communities.

Although Korean-Americans have not yet become very active in local, state, and national politics, a few have entered the political arena. Alfred Song won a seat in the California state assembly in 1962 and one in the state senate in 1966; Gene Roh became a member of the school board in the Berkeley Unified School District in 1973; and Herbert Choy of Hawaii was appointed to the United States Court of Appeals for the Ninth Circuit in 1975. Meanwhile, in the cultural realm, pianist Francis Whang and novelist Richard Kim have won international acclaim. The accomplishments of such individuals, along with the excellent academic performance of Korean-American youngsters, help to compensate for the economic hardships and social discrimination that many Korean immigrants still face today.

References
Bong-youn Choy, *Koreans in America* (1979); Won Moo Hurh and Kwang Chung Kim, *Korean Immigrants in America: A Structural Analysis of Ethnic Confinement and Adhesive Adaptation* (1984); Hyung-chan Kim, ed., *The Korean Diaspora: Historical and Sociological Studies of Korean Immigration and Assimilation in North America* (1977); Illsoo Kim, *New Urban Immigrants: The Korean Community in New York* (1981); Eui-Young Yu et al., eds., *Koreans in Los Angeles: Prospects and Promises* (1982).

S.C.

KOREANS, class and ethnicity. Most of the research done on the topics of immigration and ethnicity overlooks the importance of understanding the class background of the immigrant population. The predominantly middle-class background of Korean immigrants in America serves as a significant factor in the formation and maintenance of their ethnic identity. The process in which Korean immigrants align their socioeconomic existence with the American capitalist system is analyzed by Kim in terms of the interplay between class background and ethnic identity, and the emergence of conflicting class interests within the ethnic group, are also explored.

References
Hyung-Chan Kim, "Class and Ethnicity: Korean Immigrants in America," paper presented at the American Anthropological Association 83d Annual Meeting, Denver, Colorado, November 14–18, 1984; Hyung-Chan Kim, "Some Aspects of Social Demography of Korean Americans," *International Migration Review* 8 (Spring 1974): 23–42.

F.C.

KOREANS, ethnic resources utilization. A high proportion of Korean immigrants are engaged in self-employed small business in the United States. In light of their business proliferation, this study has empirically investigated Korean immigrant entrepreneurs' ethnic resources utilization. Findings indicate that the Korean entrepreneurs rely heavily on their ethnic resources for both business preparation and operation. While such ethnic resources utilization facilitates the immigrants' business entry and gives them competitive advantage, the same mechanism poses serious problems; there is intraethnic business competition, and many feel themselves in the precarious position of a middle-man minority. The implications of these findings are discussed and suggestions are made for future research.

Reference
Kwang Chung Kim, "Ethnic Resources Utilization of Korean Immigrant Entrepreneurs in the Chicago Minority Area," *International Migration Review* 19 (Spring 1985): 82–111.

F.C.

KOREANS, in Los Angeles. Light (*infra*), concludes that

> as the underutilized capital of immigrants has risen, a function of their middle- and upper-middle-class social origins, their motives and capability for entrepreneurship have also risen. Even if the path of small business owners is harder now, contemporary immigrants are better prepared for entrepreneurship than were the unskilled, uneducated immigrants of the prewar epoch. Therefore, new immigrants surmount business hurdles that still obstruct the social mobility of low status blacks, whites, and Hispanics. When the *Wall Street Journal* wondered why Cubans in Miami could open numerous businesses whereas blacks in Miami could not, the newspaper concluded that the question unfairly ignored the money, Latin American import-export connections, and bourgeois social origin of at least a substantial minority of Miami's Cubans. This conclusion underscores the hazard of assuming that intergroup differences in rates of entrepreneurship reflect only ethnic resources. Ethnic resources do affect entrepreneurship, but before their effect can be identified in empirical cases one must discount intergroup differences in class resources.

Reference
Ivan Light, "Immigrant Entrepreneurs in America: Koreans in Los Angeles," in Nathan Glazer, ed., *Clamor at the Gates: The New American Immigration* (1985), pp. 161–178.

F.C.

KOREANS, in New York City. Across the 1970s the number of Koreans in the United States increased five times—from about 70,000 in 1970 to 355,000 in 1980. The majority of this rapidly increasing immigration group is concentrated in major metropolitan areas, such as Los Angeles, New York, and Chicago. Some 80,000 Korean immigrants have settled in the New York metropolitan region. Unlike the early immigrants who were largely uneducated laborers from rural Korea in the beginning of the twentieth century, a majority of the recent Korean immigrants are highly educated urban middle-class people. Kim's general theoretical framework for his book is thus the modern pattern of urban-to-urban migration in contrast to the traditional model of rural-to-urban migration.

Reference
Illsoo Kim, *New Urban Immigrants: The Korean Community in New York* (1981).

F.C.

KOSCIUSZKO, THADDEUS. *See* Poles.

KOSSUTH, LOUIS. *See* Hungarians.

KOVATS, MICHAEL. *See* Hungarians.

KRIZANIC, JURAJ. *See* Yugoslavs.

KU KLUX KLAN. Also known by its abbreviation "KKK." Largely a phenomenon of the American South of the Reconstruction, the KKK was at that time a terrorist organization that harassed blacks and attempted to circumvent the civil rights guaranteed to ex-slaves in federal legislation and the Constitution. Its terrorist practices have included lynching, arson, and assaults on blacks. Federal legislation provided protection in the early 1870s (Ku Klux Klan Act, 1871; Force Acts, 1870) and the movement declined. It was revived after World War I as an anti-Catholic and anti-Semitic as well as anti-black organization. The movement is characterized by donning of white cloaks and masks, secret meetings, the strange titles of its officers (e.g., Grand Kleagle), and the burning of crosses.

Reference
David M. Chalmers, *Hooded Americanism: The History of the Ku Klux Klan* (3d ed., 1986).

F.C.

LABADISTS. *See* Dutch.

LA GUARDIA, FIORELLO HENRY (1882–1947). Lawyer, congressman (1917–19, 1923–1933), and mayor of New York City (1934–1945). Born in Greenwich Village of immigrant parents, La Guardia spent his youth in the American frontier, first in North Dakota and then in Prescot, Arizona. In 1898 the La Guardias returned to Europe and Fiorello, at eighteen, got a job at the American Consulate in Budapest processing visas and passport applications. In 1903 he was promoted to consular agent in Fiume where he processed 90,000 emigrants a year who were leaving for the United States. To help immigrants avoid rejection at Ellis Island, he instituted a practice of medical examination before departure. In 1906 he returned to Greenwich Village where he attended law school in the evenings, and was appointed as a translator for Italian, German, and Croatian by the United States Immigration Service at Ellis island. In 1910 he passed the bar exam and opened a law office dealing only with immigration problems. He helped to organize the Amalgamated Clothing Workers of America, which consisted mainly of Jewish and Italian immigrants. In Congress he fought against passing the National Origins Bill (1924) and for labor reform legislation such as the Railways Labor Act, and sponsored the Norris–La Guardia

Act (1932) which prohibited injunctions in labor disputes. From 1934 to 1945 La Guardia was mayor of New York City and in 1946 he served the world as director of the United Nations Relief and Rehabilitation Administration in charge of feeding and resurrecting the war-ravaged countries of Europe, Africa, and Asia.

Reference
Lawrence Elliott, *Little Flower: The Life and Times of Fiorello La Guardia* (1983).

R.U.P.

LA GUARDIA MEMORIAL HOUSE. *See* Ruddy, Anna C[hristian].

LAISVE. *See* Lithuanians.

LAMBERT, CATHOLINA (1834–1923). *See* Passaic County, New Jersey, Historical Society.

LANGUAGE LOYALTY IN THE UNITED STATES: THE MAINTENANCE AND PERPETUATION OF NON-ENGLISH MOTHER TONGUES BY AMERICAN ETHNIC AND RELIGIOUS GROUPS (Joshua A. Fishman, et al., 1966; rpt. 1978). *Language Loyalty in the United States* is an invaluable repository of formal language-maintenance resources and institutions in American society. Fishman and his colleagues define the framework of their investigations in very broad terms: the study of language loyalty in the United States encompasses American ethnic historiography; the twin processes of de-ethnization and Americanization and the concomitant conflicts in the enforced acculturation that accompanies assimilation; and the history of immigrant language maintenance. Comprehensive in its coverage, with special attention to German, French, Spanish, and Ukrainian groups, *Language Loyalty in the United States* is a basic document for the "study of the self-maintenance efforts, rationales, and accomplishments of non–English-speaking immigrants on American shores." In the introduction, Einar Haugen observes: "Joshua Fishman has done us all a great service in building up a more positive image of the immigrant in this book. He has brought to light a facet of the immigrant's life in this country which has remained unknown and unheralded even by most historians of immigration, let alone historians of America."

F.C.

LAPOLLA, GARIBALDI M[ARTO] (1888–1954). Novelist. Beginning in the 1890s the section of New York City's Harlem that fronts the

East River witnessed an influx of immigrants from Sicily and southern Italy who crowded into the brownstones that had been built by earlier German and Irish immigrants. The Italian immigrants would, in turn, be largely supplanted by Puerto Ricans after World War II, but for a sixty-year period East Harlem was one of the best-known Italian-American communities.

Lapolla arrived in East Harlem with his parents in 1890, grew up there, and attended public schools. He later graduated from Columbia University and in 1910 began his lifelong career as a teacher and school administrator. A versatile and dynamic man, Lapolla had a wide variety of interests and accomplishments. In addition to his career as a teacher and school principal, he published three high school textbooks and two books on Italian-American cooking, served as an instructor at a number of New York City–area colleges and universities, and was an accomplished amateur artist.

Lapolla is best known, however, for his three novels on life in Italian Harlem: *Fire in the Flesh* (1931); *Miss Rollins in Love* (1932); and *The Grand Gennaro* (1935). Lapolla was one of the earliest Italian-American novelists to achieve literary distinction, and all three of the novels describe the economic conditions, social conflicts, and cultural dissonance that confronted Italian immigrants. The bulk of the Lapolla papers (1905–1954, 3 linear feet) have been deposited in the Balch Institute of Philadelphia and consist of unpublished literary manuscripts, including drafts of four novels, seven short stories, three plays, and a large number of poems. The papers also include literary notebooks as well as correspondence and other materials. The papers represent a valuable source both on a major Italian-American novelist and on Italian Harlem.

Reference
Rose Basile Green, *The Italian American Novel* (1974).

F.C.

LATHROP, JULIA CLIFFORD (1858–1932). Social worker and administrator. Lathrop was associated with Jane Addams (*q.v.*) at Hull House, Chicago. She was the first woman member of the Illinois Board of Public Charities (1893–1909). She was actively involved in improving the conditions of the immigrant poor, and in social improvements including mental hygiene, the establishment of juvenile courts, and the fight for women's suffrage. In 1912 she was appointed chief of the federal Children's Bureau which she headed until 1927. Lathrop was a major force in the regulation of child labor, in providing aid to working mothers, and in the promotion of welfare regulation.

Reference
Jane Addams, *Julia Clifford Lathrop* (1935).

F.C.

LATVIANS. From a land between Estonia and Lithuania, with the Baltic Sea on the west and Russia on the east, Latvians are akin to Lithuanians in Indo-European ancestry and language. Latvians emerged on the European scene in the twelfth century via contacts with German traders. After a century of warfare, Germans held Latvian and Estonian lands as Livonia until 1561. (The Polish-Lithuanian Commonwealth also held a portion of Latvia.) Swedes ruled Latvia from 1621 to 1710; eventually Czarist Russia reigned from 1795 until November 18, 1918, when Latvians declared independence for the first time.

Roughly three-fourths of Latvians are Lutheran; about 20 percent are Roman Catholics, mostly in the south; and the rest are Orthodox Jews and Baptists. The statistics of their emigration to the United States are incomplete; the 1930 federal census recorded some 20,000 native-born Latvians. A relatively large wave of émigrés came after World War II. In 1970 an estimated 100,000 of Latvian stock lived in the United States.

Prior to World War II, modest numbers of Latvians arrived in the United States. There is evidence of a scattering in California and the Midwest around the 1850s. The recognizable influx, though, dates from 1888 in Boston, with a carpenter—Jacob Sieberg, the "Father of Latvians." In the United States, he formed the first Protestant congregation and a benefit society; edited a newspaper, *Amerikas Vestesnis* [American Herald]; and authored several books. Soon other colonies appeared in Philadelphia, New York City, and Chicago. By 1907 there were seven Lutheran parishes as a result of the far-flung missionary work of Pastor Hans Rebane. By 1908, several thousand Latvians had settled in Wisconsin; 6,000 were reported in Massachusetts. More than a few short-lived publications served to unite the dispersed immigrants of whom many were semiskilled or professionals. Boston and Philadelphia served as cultural centers. Latvians have been highly successful in the arts: literature, painting, and music. Émigrés in the United States have offered financial and moral support to their homeland, while some one-fifth returned to Latvia around 1923. The fate of Latvians has been similar to that of Lithuanians and Estonians, all under Soviet rule since the end of World War II. Latvians here have been very vigorous in maintaining concern for the homeland and for ethnic preservation, e.g., through the American Latvian Association, founded in 1951; an active press; and numerous concerts and other cultural events.

References

Karliks, Streips, *The Latvians in America 1640–1973* (1974); "Latvians," in *Encyclopedia Lituanica* vol. 3 (1973); William Wolkovich-Valkavičius, "Immigrant Population Patterns of Finns, Estonians, Latvians, and Lithuanians in the U.S. Federal Census of 1930," *Lituanus* (Spring 1983).

W.W.V.

LAU v. NICHOLS (414 U.S. 563 [1974]). This was a landmark case in bilingual education; it was brought by Kinney Kinmon Lau and his guardians, on behalf of 1,800 children of non–English-speaking ability, against Alan H. Nichols, chancellor of the San Francisco Public Schools, for the purpose of "seeking relief against alleged unequal education opportunities resulting from the officials' failure to establish a program to rectify the students' language problem."

The case was first argued before the District Court of California. The lower court in San Francisco was very sympathetic but unresponsive. In the language of the court, "Yes, these children do have a problem, but it is one that should be addressed to the legislature, not the courts." The court ruled that, as long as these children received the same education made available under the same terms and conditions to the other tens of thousands of children in San Francisco, the program was adequate. The court did admit, and the judge recognized, that some children probably were not learning, but conceded that, in the court's judgment, this was a social and legislative problem, not a legal one. The court decided against Lau and the class of plaintiffs and dismissed the case.

Lau was appealed to the United States Court of Appeals for the Ninth Circuit; the Ninth Circuit affirmed the decision of the lower court. It found that "there was no violation of the equal protection clause of the Fourteenth Amendment or of Section 601 of the Civil Rights Act of 1964," and added: "Every student brings to the starting line of his educational career, different advantages and disadvantages caused in part by social, economic and cultural background, created and continued completely apart from any contribution by the school system." The case was finally appealed to the Supreme Court of the United States, which agreed to hear the case "because of the public importance of the question." The case was argued before the Supreme Court on December 10, 1973.

With the permission of both parties and the Court, a key figure entered the case as *amicus curiae*. This was Stanley Pottinger, who appeared as a representative of the United States government. Pottinger, then assistant attorney general, played an influential role in the ultimate presentation of the case. As a spokesman for the government, he supported the argument that Lau had rights based on the Office of Civil Rights regulations of May 25, 1970, which governed the use of federal funds under Title VI of the Civil Rights Act of 1964. These guidelines were cited by Justice William O. Douglas in the Supreme Court's decision to reverse the lower courts. He stated:

> It seems obvious that the Chinese-speaking minority receives fewer benefits than the English-speaking majority from respondents' school system which denies them a meaningful opportunity to participate in the educational program—all earmarks of the discrimination banned by the regulations. In 1970 HEW issued clarifying guidelines, 35 Fed. Reg. 11595, which include the following: Where inability to speak and understand the English language excludes national origin–minority group children from effective participation in the educational program offered by a school district, the district must take affirmative steps to rectify the language deficiency in order to open its instructional program to these students.

In reversing the decision, the Supreme Court added: "Basic English skills are at the very core of what these public schools teach. Imposition of a requirement that, before a child can effectively participate in the educational program he must already have acquired those basic skills, is to make a mockery of public education." The Supreme Court reasoned that "it is not the issue that you cause the problem. . . . School districts throughout the country have an affirmative obligation to start providing education that's geared to the needs and abilities of the child."

The Supreme Court's unanimous decision in *Lau* was particularly important because the Supreme Court had sidestepped the equal protection issue. The decision essentially supported the authority of the HEW argument based on guidelines and regulations of the HEW. In skirting the constitutional argument for equal protection under the law, the Court relied solely on statute:

> We do not reach the Equal Protection Clause argument which has been advanced but rely solely on Section 601 of the Civil Rights Act of 1964 (42 USCS Section 2000d) to reverse the Court of Appeals. That section bans discrimination on the ground of race, color, or national origin, in "any program or activity receiving Federal financing assistance." Discrimination is barred which has that *effect* even though no purposeful design is present.

References
Francesco Cordasco, *Bilingual Schooling in the United States* (1976); B. Stein, *Sink or Swim: The Politics of Bilingual Education* (1986); Herbert Teitelbaum and Richard J.

Hiller, "Bilingual Education: The Legal Mandate," *Harvard Educational Review* 47 (May 1977): 138–170.

F.C.

LAUGHLIN, HARRY H[AMILTON] (1880–1953). Eugenicist propagandist; protegé of Charles B. Davenport (*q.v.*). Laughlin supervised the Eugenics Record Office at Cold Spring Harbor, Long Island, New York, which Davenport had established in 1910 to study the hereditary traits of the American population. As an immigration restrictionist, Laughlin tied eugenics and the Nordic theory of racial superiority together. As its "expert eugenics agent," Laughlin testified before the House Committee on Immigration and Naturalization "on the bad breeding stock that was entering the country and spoiling its inborn national qualities." Chief writings: *Eugenical Sterilization in the United States* (1926); *American History in Terms of Human Migration* (1928); *Legal Status of Eugenical Sterilization* (1930); and *Immigration and Conquest* (1939).

References
Frances J. Hassencahl, "Harry H. Laughlin, 'Expert Eugenics Agent' for the House Committee on Immigration and Naturalization, 1921–1931," Ph.D. dissertation, Case Western Reserve University, 1970 (DA 32: 576-A); Hamilton Cravens, *The Triumph of Evolution* (1978).

F.C.

LAWRENCE, MASSACHUSETTS. Scene of the 1912 textile strike in which immigrants were decisively involved. Directed by the International Workers of the World (IWW), the 1912 strike was a protest against the oppressive conditions in the Lawrence textile mills. The context in which the Lawrence strike took place explains much of the violence and bitterness of the contest. Several issues were involved at once: the millhands were fighting their employers; the unskilled clashed with skilled workers; southern and eastern Europeans, living in the worst housing and unrepresented in the city government, were asserting their rights to equality with the English-speaking elements; the IWW and the American Federation of Labor, representing, respectively, revolutionary and conservative policies, challenged each other to war. In each of these ways the Lawrence strike represented the coming of age of the newer immigrant population.

References
Donald B. Cole, *Immigrant City, Lawrence, Massachusetts, 1845–1921* (1963); Edwin Fenton, *Immigrants and Unions* (1975).

F.C.

LAZARUS, EMMA (1849–1884). Poet and essayist. Lazarus was a spokesperson for Judaism, best expressed in *Songs of a Semite* (1882). Her sonnet about the Statue of Liberty, entitled "The New Colossus," was engraved on the statue's pedestal.

Reference
H.E. Jacob, *The World of Emma Lazarus* (1949).

B.L.

LEAGUE OF UNITED LATIN AMERICAN CITIZENS (LULAC). *See* Mexicans.

LEBANESE. The geographic Mount Lebanon range (some one hundred miles long, running north-south), celebrated for its beauty and its majestic cedars in the Bible, has been home to Canaanites, Phoenicians, Christians, Druze, and others seeking sanctuary or simply a bracing mountain existence throughout the 5,000 years of its recorded history. During the 400 years of Turkish Ottomon rule of the Near East (1516–1919), the inhabitants of Mount Lebanon, largely Christian and Druze, enjoyed a great deal of autonomy, though technically they were part of the Turkish province of Greater Syria. This autonomy continued under the French Mandate between World War I and II, until the formation of the State of Greater Lebanon in 1943, which included not only the mountain but also the largely Muslim coastal cities and the inland agricultural plain, the Bekaa.

It is important to note that the Lebanese have a loyalty, in Mount Lebanon as in the coastal cities and the plain, first of all to family, albeit a very widely extended family, and to friends of the family, then to their religious sect, and then to their village, and hardly at all to their region or nation-state. Clarity is needed therefore in any immigration history of the Lebanese in defining just what group of immigrant Lebanese one is treating.

Immigration, which began as a trickle in the 1870s, grew steadily in the 1880s and 1890s; the major wave of 1900–1914 was cut off by World War 1, and its brief revival ended with the Immigration Act of 1924. The distinguished Lebanese-American historian Philip K. Hitti estimated in 1924 that there were approximately 200,000 "Syrians" in America, of which, he explains, 95 percent are Christian and from Mount Lebanon. The three largest Christian groups among the immigrants from Lebanon in 1924, according to Hitti, were the Maronites (90,000), the Melchites (10,000)—both groups were affiliated with Rome, as "Eastern rite" Catholics—and the Greek Orthodox (85,000), which group has had a subsequent split in America into administrative loyalties to Antiochian and Russian Orthodoxy. Hitti estimated some

8,000 Muslims (both Sunni and Shiite) and 1,000 Druze in America in 1924. These proportions among the immigrant groups from Lebanon have perhaps not changed much in the immigration wave since World War II, although the terms of the Immigration and Nationalities Act of 1965 have caused a larger percentage of students and professionals to be among the immigrants. Estimates of the present number of people of Lebanese ancestry in America vary from one to one and a half million.

The earlier immigrants came primarily to better their economic status and that of the families they left behind in Lebanon. The Lebanese have been aggressive, independent-minded, mercantile people since the time of the Phoenicians, and they found in America the earlier tradition of the Yankee and Jewish peddler to be congenial to their temperament. Peddling networks based on family, village of origin, and/or religious affiliation were set up all over America, with suppliers of dry goods in the major cities sending weekly or monthly shipments by train to smaller merchants in smaller towns, who would then supply the peddler and perhaps his entire family, as they set off to walk the back roads of America. By this process the Lebanese immigrant put down roots in every corner of America, often becoming himself one of several dry goods merchants in a given small town. By the time of World War I, the Lebanese immigrant-as-entrepreneur had largely moved from peddling to small business; a very great number, especially in the Northeast and Midwest, had taken work in the factories; some throughout the United States entered truck farming. Between the two wars there was a gradual shift from dry goods to groceries as the favored small business, and one usually could find at least one corner in any village in America with a Lebanese grocery. Many of these small enterprises grew into large stores or several stores, and sometimes into interstate produce businesses.

The enormous respect for education among the Lebanese, coupled in the 1920s with growing means, caused a new professional group of doctors, lawyers, and teachers to emerge in the 1930s from the sons of the Lebanese businessmen. The aftermath of World War II saw the education of the Lebanese factory workers' sons (aided mightily by the G.I. Bill), and, finally, in the succeeding decades, the education of their daughters.

The pre–World War I immigration was largely of sturdy mountaineers who had had little opportunity for education beyond a church-run grade school in Lebanon. Social and cultural life in America centered around the home and garden, the church, the local provisions store or bakery, the *Ah'we* or coffeeshop, and the local (later, regional) clubhouse. A vigorous and numerous Lebanese-Arabic press sprang up in America at the turn of the century to aid and inform the immigrant, each paper usually organized to serve a sectarian or other subgroup interest. These early newspapers rendered the immigrant great service in the assimilation process, and also provided a cultural and intellectual context for a literary and cultural efflorescence in the Boston–New York City area in the first three decades of this century, a movement that greatly influenced the world of Arabic literature in general. The most famous name is that of the Lebanese emigré, Kahlil Gibran, but includes also Mikhail Naimy, Amin Rihani, Naseeb Arida, Elias Abu Mady, Abd al-Masih Haddad, and others. The Lebanese-born Congregationalist minister, Abraham Mitrie Rihbany of Boston, did much in his writings during this period to acquaint Americans with the cultural heritage of the Lebanese, and the Mokarzel brothers, Salloum and Naoum, attempted in their editorials, articles, newspapers, and magazines (especially the English-language *The Syrian World,* 1926–1932), to raise the consciousness of their heritage of the Lebanese themselves.

A final word on that heritage. At its best it comprises a vision of life that personalizes nature and God in terms of the Lebanese family, its garden, and its mountain village. The father ideally rules the family, but only in the context of the worship of the mother. Grandparents have the double respect of parents and of age. Dogs, vegetables, fruit trees, and all natural phenomena are seen in terms of brothers, sisters, and cousins. God is seen as village patriarch, as neighborhood visitor, even at times as village jokester. One weeds the garden and prunes the vine out of love of the lettuce leaf and the grape. It is a vision that tells much about the Lebanese character, its likely joys and inevitable sorrows in the adopted homeland, which could only partly assimilate that vision.

References

Sameer and Nabeel Abraham, *Arabs in the New World* (1983); Abdo Elkholy, *The Arab Moslems in the United States* (1966); Jean and Kahlil Gibran, *Kahlil Gibran: His Life and Work* (1981); Philip K. Hitti, *Lebanon in History* (1967) and *The Syrians in America* (1924); Eric J. Hooglund, *Crossing the Waters: Arabic-Speaking Immigrants to the U.S. before 1940* (1987); Louise S. Houghton, "The Syrians in the United States," *Survey* 26, no. 27 (1911); Philip and Joseph Kayal, *The Syrian-Lebanese in America* (1975); Lucius H. Miller, *Our Syrian Population* (1904); Salloum Mokarzel, *The Syrian Business Directory* (1908); John Moses, *The Lebanese in America* (1987); Alixa Naff, *Becoming American: The Early Arab Immigrant Experience* (1985); Eugene Paul Nassar, *Wind of the Land* (1979); Abraham M. Rihbany, *A Far Journey* (1914); Edward Wakim, *The Lebanese and Syrians in America* (1974); Adele Younis, *The Coming of the Arabic-Speaking People to the United States* (1961); Eric Hooglund, ed., *Taking Root: Arab-American Community Studies* (1985).

E.P.N.

LEESER, ISAAC (1806–1868). Educator. A major figure in the mid-nineteenth century in establishing institutions of Jewish learning in the United States, Leeser was the leading Jew of his time. He had the responsibility of guiding and informing the Jewish community of Philadelphia and indeed the nation as to what direction they should take. He was a strong traditionalist and a firm adherent of the Orthodox position, and urged American Jews to pursue a traditionalist path. The institutions he created were intended to foster Judaism in America and to guarantee a future for the Jewish people as a thriving religious and cultural group.

Reference
Milton Feierstein, "Isaac Leeser (1806–1868): Founder of Jewish Education in the United States," Ph.D. dissertation, State University of New York, Buffalo, 1971 (DA 32: 2499A).

F.C.

LEGAL AID SOCIETY. Founded in 1894 in New York City; a nonsectarian legal aid society whose origins go back to the Deutscher Rechts Schutz Verein, which was founded in 1876 by German immigrants.

F.C.

LEMKO. *See* Carpatho-Rusyns.

LENPI, GERTRUD. *See* Swiss.

LEO FRANK CASE. *See* [Jews]: Leo Frank Case.

LEOPOLDINEN-STIFTUNG. *See* Germans.

LETCHWORTH, WILLIAM P[RYOR] (1823–1910). Administrator, philanthropist. Letchworth served as commissioner of the New York State Board of Charities and became a major influence in the improvement of care for immigrant dependent and delinquent children, epileptics, and the insane poor.

Reference
William P. Letchworth, *Homes of Homeless Children: A Report on Orphan Asylums and Other Institutions for the Care of Children* (1903; rpt. 1974).

F.C.

LEWISOHN, LUDWIG (1882–1955). Literary and drama critic, novelist, and essayist. In his novel *The Island Within* (1928) Lewisohn, a native of Germany, focused on his belief that a Jew cannot truly assimilate without becoming spiritually impoverished. In 1932, *Expressions in America* was published, containing essays on Melville, Whitman, and James. In 1934, Lewisohn, who had become a Methodist while a teenager in Charleston, South Carolina, became an ardent Zionist. Between 1943 and 1948 he was the editor of *New Palestine*, a Zionist magazine. Lewisohn was recognized for his work in literary and dramatic criticism and as a proponent for a return to our historic roots. Lewisohn was awarded an LL.D. in 1914 by the College of Charleston.

Reference
David Singer, "Ludwig Lewisohn: The Making of an Anti-Communist," *American Quarterly* 23 (Dec. 1971).

C.C.

LIBERIA. *See* Afro-Americans.

LICVINY. *See* Byelorussians.

LILIENTHAL, META (1876–1947). Journalist, Socialist. Lilienthal produced pamphlets, scores of leaflets and short essays, and edited a women's page in the *New Yorker Volkszeitung* and a "Votes for Women" column in the *New York Call*. Her autobiography does not focus on her political accomplishments; it relates her childhood memories of New York City. Lilienthal provides scattered insights into the German immigrant radical milieu of the late nineteenth century, for her parents were ardent Socialists and prominent activists in the Socialist Labor party. Lilienthal's parents emigrated from Germany in 1861.

Reference
Meta Lilienthal, *Dear Remembered World: Childhood Memories of an Old New Yorker* (1947).

F.C.

LILIUOKALANI, QUEEN. *See* Hawaiians.

LIMITED-VISA PROGRAMS. *See* Temporary Foreign Workers, Policies.

LIRIA. *See* Albanians.

LITHUANIAN PRIESTS LEAGUE. *See* Lithuanians.

LITHUANIANS. Baltic people, a branch of the Indo-European family, Lithuanians migrated to the United States chiefly from their homeland on the Baltic coast in the north of east-central Europe. No certain statistics for these immigrants are possible. Estimates range from several hundred thousand to half a million. Some 80 percent are Roman Catholic; there are small minorities of Lutherans, Calvinists, and Russian Orthodox. One of the largest European settlements of Jews has composed the remainder of Lithuanian nationals.

Migration. The majority of Lithuanians came to the United States during the influx of 1868–1914 and the 1948–1951 wave of emgiré "displaced persons" after World War II, with the heaviest flow at the turn of the century. On immigration and census records, the earliest newcomers, having lived under the czar and also strong Polish influence, identified themselves as coming from Russia or Poland. Thus the insoluble problem of an accurate count. As the nationalist movement stirred in the homeland from the late 1880s, this revival enjoyed an effective counterpart in the United States. Accordingly, most Lithuanians here gradually, though not always amicably, severed their Polish ties in joint fraternal-benefit societies and churches. Typical of other eastern Europeans under czarist rule, Lithuanians emigrated mostly for economic survival or betterment, to avoid Russian military conscription, and to elude government harassment because of nationalist activities.

Demography. Though the Lithuanian immigrants were nearly all villagers, they brought few transferable agricultural skills and little money to allow settlement in rural areas. They encountered recruiters, from Pennsylvania coal mines and railroads, on the docks in New York City and other ports of entry. As a result, Lithuanians first resided in a string of anthracite towns, especially in the area of Scranton and Wilkes-Barre. Conditions of climate and labor were so opposite the idyllic surroundings of Lithuania that more than a few eventually trekked westward to Pittsburgh, Cleveland, Gary, and Chicago to work in steel mills and stockyards; others shifted to New England and its mills, producing paper, shoes, brass, and hardware goods. Nimble of hand, more than a few took up tailoring in Boston, Brooklyn, and Baltimore. Soon others traveled directly to these later colonies of the 1890s. Few ventured beyond the Mississippi River, and the largest single concentration was located in metropolitan Chicago. The New York–New Jersey–Pennsylvania area, the Cleveland-Pittsburgh region, and New England accounted for the bulk of the remainder.

Social Life. Not unlike other immigrant neighbors, Lithuanians promptly started sick-death benefit societies. As soon as a handful settled in a given community, they formed these associations under the patronage of a saint or medieval hero. In time, the immigrants started a variety of associations such as choruses, theater ensembles, military units, and citizens' clubs. Their organizations also reflected ideological differences among churchgoers, nonpartisan nationalists, and Free-thinkers. Fr. Aleksandras Burba of Plymouth, Pennsylvania and Fr. Juozas Žebris of Waterbury and New Britain, Connecticut were the leading priest-nationalists. A maverick Freethinker layman, the physician Jonas Šliūpas was the single most influential person in attacking religion and separating it from Lithuanianism. In 1886 he began an ill-fated national alliance, quickly superseded by a religion-oriented network, aimed at creating a nationwide body among Lithuanians. Within a decade, tension grew between clerical leaders and liberals over the relevance of religion in the organization. The alliance broke up at the 1901 convention, resulting in the Roman Catholic and National versions. Freethinkers (1900) and Socialists (1905) established their own nationwide union of local lodges.

Religious Revival. After several decades of growing Socialist and atheistic influence, the Catholic community responded with a countermovement. In 1909 the Lithuanian Priests League revived under Fr. Antanas Staniukynas. The association promptly launched a daily newspaper, *Draugas.* Other signs of this religious renewal quickly followed. In 1913, a layman—Mykolas Norkūnas—at Lawrence, Massachusetts founded the nationwide Knights of Lithuania on an ethnic-religious basis. In 1915, the [Catholic] Workers Alliance started in Boston, and the same year the [Catholic] Women's Alliance began in Chicago.

Communications. Lithuanians have made considerable use of the printed word to preserve their heritage. There is a rich history of publications, especially newspapers of every stripe. The first paper began in 1879, but lasted only a few months. The longest continuously publishing newspaper has been *Vienybė Lietuvninkų* (later simply *Vienybė*), dating from 1886. Unique to such a small ethnic group is *Draugas,* the Catholic nationwide daily of Chicago, begun in 1909 and still in print. Several weeklies, semimonthlies, or monthlies continue to appear, such as the Catholic *Darbininkas* of Brooklyn, the nationalist *Dirva* of Cleveland, and the Socialist (more recently nonpartisan) *Naujienos* of Chicago. There are two Communist papers: *Laisvė* of Brooklyn, and *Vilnis* of Chicago. *Aidai* is the principal Catholic cultural journal. English-language publications include the scholarly *Lituanus,* and newsletters of a popular nature such as *Bridges* of Brooklyn, and *The Observer* of Chicago. Juozas Kapočius of Boston has published two major reference works: the thirty-six-volume general *Lietuvių Enciklopedija* in Lithuanian (1953–1969, 1986), and the six-volume specialized *Encyclopedia Lituanica* in English (1970–78).

A popular method of ethnic maintenance has been the Lithuanian weekly radio broadcast, airing mostly on Sundays. Each region has had such a program, e.g., in the Boston area there have been the Minkus radio hour from 1931 to 1987; the "Liberty Bell" broadcast of Petras Viščinis, since 1954; the Worcester broadcast of Edward Meilus; and Jack Stukas' "Memories of Lithuania" in metropolitan New York–New Jersey.

Marriage Patterns. Marriage with people of other ethnic back-grounds, let alone different religions, was severely criticized for a long time among Lithuanians. Even to this day a few regard such unions as a form of ethnic suicide, in view of the Lithuanian plight under the Soviets. Among the early immigrants, the percentage of inmarriage was extremely high, second only to that of Jews; with the second-generation Lithuanians the percentage drops to about half. Proximity to other eth-nics and education account for the notable change.

Religious Life. Invariably the basic aim of the first associations was to found an ethnic parish, where immigrants could hear the gospel and sermons in the native language, and have a place to socialize. The oldest churches date from the 1880s in Pennsylvania, and from the 1890s in New England, Chicago, and elsewhere. As many as 130 such parishes were established from the 1880s through the 1920s. At first they were staffed by clergy from the homeland. Another wave came along, made up of men who began studies for the priesthood in the homeland, and then completed their preparation in U.S. seminaries. Others, as well as second-generation Lithuanians, pursued their entire seminary education in this country. One priest of Lithuanian descent, Charles Salatka, has become archbishop of Oklahoma City. An exiled emigré of World War II, Bishop Vincas Brizgys, resides in Chicago. While Roman Catholics function under their local bishops, there is a bishop, Paulius Baltakis, O.F.M., designated by the pope in 1984 for the pastoral care of Lithuanians all over the free world. Baltakis enjoys no jurisdiction over any one diocese, but does wield moral authority as the Lithuanian religious leader.

In the 1890s, a church movement to separate from the local bishop and from Rome arose among Poles, influencing Lithuanians. For sever-al decades a few dozen Lithuanian short-lived separatist congregations appeared. At this writing, two such independent parishes survive in Scranton, Pennsylvania and in Lawrence, Massachusetts.

The Homeland. Lithuanian immigrants here have always offered substantial aid to their birthplace. Literature was smuggled into Lithu-ania in the 1890s during a czarist press ban (1864–1904) on Lithuanian printing in its Latin alphabet. U.S immigrants helped greatly in sponsor-ing a successful exhibit at the Paris World Exposition of 1900. During World War I, various national committees with fund-raising branches organized on behalf of the homeland. By decree of President Wilson, November 1, 1916 was declared a fund-raising day in the nation for Lithuanian War Victims. After the armistice, a million signatures were delivered to President Harding, asking for *de jure* recognition of inde-pendent Lithuania, eventually granted by the United States in 1922. During the period of Lithuanian independence, 1918–1940, yearly tourists' visits were common. Lithuanian-Americans, during and after World War II, sent money, clothing, and supplies to refugees scattered about Europe, especially in German displaced persons camps. Since then, several major political bodies have kept alive hopes for a restored independent homeland, severed from the U.S.S.R.

References
Encyclopedia Lituanica (6 vols., 1970–1978); Victor R. Greene, *For God and Country: The Rise of Polish and Lithuanian Ethnic Consciousness in America, 1860–1910* (1975); Antanas Kučas, *Lithuanians in America* (1975); *Lituanus* (scholarly quarterly, 6621 S. Troy, Chicago 60629-2913); William Wolkovich-Valkavičius, *Lithuanian Pioneer Priest of New England: The Life, Struggles, and Tragic Death of Rev. Joseph Žebris, 1860–1915* (1980).

W.W.V.

LITTLE FALLS, NEW YORK, TEXTILE STRIKE. Led by Socialists and Wobblies, this was one in a series of strikes led by recent immigrants from southern and eastern Europe. Lasting for three months, from October 9, 1912, until January 4, 1913, the Little Falls strike involved over 1,300 unskilled workers, of whom an estimated 70 percent were women. Although the strikers gained wage increases and forced a major investigation of labor conditions in their city, their IWW local soon collapsed, and many of its most active leaders faced imprisonment for their strike activities.

Reference
Robert E. Snyder, "Women, Wobblies, and Workers' Rights: The 1912 Textile Strike in Little Falls, New York," *New York History* 60 (Jan. 1979): 29–57.

F.C.

LITUANUS. See Lithuanians.

LODGE, HENRY CABOT (1850–1924). U.S. senator. Lodge studied law at Harvard Law School, from which he graduated in 1874, and the following year he was admitted to the Boston bar. Lodge received his Ph.D. in 1876 and wrote a number of books, including *Life and Letters of George Cabot* (1878) and *Historical and Political Essays* (1892). In 1886 Lodge was elected to Congress, where he served until 1893. In that year he was elected to the Senate, where he served until his death on November 9, 1924. An uncompromising restrictionist, Lodge was a major force in the passage of the 1924 Immigration Act.

Reference
William C. Widenor, *Henry Cabot Lodge* (1980).

D.N.A.

LOMONACO, ALFONSO (d. 1932). Physician. A medical officer on Italian immigrant ships to America, his observations are valuable contemporary accounts of immigrant voyagers. In his *Da Palermo a New Orleans* (1897:45), e.g., he describes several immigrant youth:

> Vi ha un giovane alto, robusto, dagli occhi neri, naso aquilino e baffi folti appuntati; un giovane bellissimo, un vero tipo da bravo e seduttore di villaggio. Mi si dice che la sua famiglia, di cui pare sia l'unico superstite, abbia goduta un'êra di triste celebrità in New-Orléans. Suo padre fu un tempo il terrore della colonia italiana di quella città; esso teneva tutti sotto di se dispoticamente, maneggiava il coltello come se nulla fosse, finché gli altri, stanchi di sopportare la sua feroce tirannia, congiurarono di disfarsene una notte, quando era per rientrare in casa, lo freddarono con una pugnalata. . . . Dal colorito bruno arsiccio, magra, con un'espressione assai dura dei suoi lineamenti possiede però degli occhi neri voluttuosi che temperano l'asprezza della sua fisionomia, co'quali, quando le piace, lancia delle occhiate incendiarie. Dal fare altero e sprezzante, trova tutto male e niente la piace; tutto e *schifiusu* dinnanzi agli occhi suoi e al suo palato. Se vi ha qualcuno che strepita e reclama, con voce da principessa sdegnata, offesa nei suoi gusti o contrariata nei suoi ordini, se può essere sicuri che e lei, donna Rosina. . . .

Lomonaco also wrote extensive accounts of the Italian emigration to Chile (in the *Bollettino del'Emigrazione,* no. 1, 1905; no. 7, 1906; no. 14, 1906) and ''Il Canale di Panama e il lavoro italiano'' (*Bollettino dell'Emigrazione,* no. 2, 1909).

Reference
Francesco Cordasco, *Italian Mass Emigration* (1980).

F.C.

LONDON, MEYER (1871–1926). Born in the Russian-Polish province of Suwalki, London moved with his family to New York in 1891. He studied law at night and was admitted to the New York bar in 1898. His practice never became lucrative, but he found fulfillment in the trade union movement and in the Socialist party. London played an important role in the formative years of the International Ladies' Garment Workers' Union (*q.v.*) and the International Fur Workers' Union. He served these unions as legal counsel, adviser, and spokesman in negotiation. In 1910 he led the ILGWU during its great organizational strike and played a similar role two years later with the IFWU. Deploring violence, London believed that political activity and educational propaganda were the best means for advancing the cause of the labor movement.

Reference
Gordon J. Goldberg, "Meyer London: A Political Biography," Ph.D. dissertation, Lehigh University, 1971 (DA 32: 356A).

F.C.

LOS ANGELES, CALIFORNIA, as the New Ellis Island. Los Angeles is America's new melting pot. More than 90,000 foreign immigrants settled there during 1982, and since 1970, more than 2 million, mostly Hispanics, Asians, and Middle Easterners.

Reference
K. Anderson, "The New Ellis Island," *Time* (June 13, 1983): 18–26.

F.C.

LOWELL, JOSEPHINE SHAW (1843–1905). Reformer, philanthropist. Lowell was the first woman appointed to the New York State Board of Charities; she was also founder of the Charity Organization Society and an organizer of the Consumers' League. Lowell's *Public Relief and Private Charity* (1884; rpt. 1971) is a leading statement of post–Civil War attitudes toward poverty. The book points in particular to the effects of social Darwinism on philanthropy, and in general to the thinking that promoted the Charity Organization Society. The appeal of these ideas was so widespread that not even the Progressive reformers could altogether escape them.

Reference
William Rhinelander Stewart, *The Philanthropic Work of Josephine Shaw Lowell* (1911).

F.C.

LUCAS, ANTHONY. *See* Croatians.

LUDLOW MASSACRE. A tragic altercation growing out of attempts to unionize the Rockefeller-owned Colorado Fuel and Iron Company Works at Trinidad and Pueblo, Colorado:

> On April 20, 1914, at Ludlow, Colorado, . . . in a tent colony established at that mining camp, the Italians participated in a heated demonstration over wages, hours and working conditions. A pitched battle with the mine operators followed, with the state militia called out to quell the outbreak. Troopers raked immigrant and non-immigrant strikers with machine-gun fire and burned the Ludlow tent camp to the ground. Two Italian women and thirteen children were burned to death. President Woodrow Wilson inter-

ceded with a proposal to end the strike, and eventually the state of Colorado paid the Italians damages for the incident, thereby accepting partial responsibility for the deaths caused. (Rolle, 171)

Reference
Andrew Rolle, *The Immigrant Upraised* (1968); Giovanni Perilli, *Colorado and the Italians in Colorado* (1922).

F.C.

LUDWIG MISSIONSVEREIN. *See* Germans.

LUMINATORUL. *See* Romanians.

LUPO-MORELLO GANG (New York City). *See* Black Hand.

LUSATIA. *See* Wends.

LUSATIAN SLAVS. *See* Slavs.

LUTHER COLLEGE (Decorah, Iowa). *See* Norwegians.

LUTHERAN IMMIGRATION AND REFUGEE SERVICE [LIRS]. *See* Indochinese Women.

McCARRAN-WALTER ACT OF 1952. More properly known as the Immigration and Nationality Act of 1952. The act of 1952 codified existing policy, reaffirming the national-origins quota system and the general restrictive nature of the law. World War II and the Cold War created a number of conditions that seemed to necessitate a comprehensive reconsideration of this policy. The policy was broadened, on the one hand, by legislation granting small quotas to Orientals, admitting war brides and fiancées of American servicemen, and admitting "displaced persons" from Europe. On the other hand, postwar frustrations and Cold War anxieties intensified and were projected against "subversive" and "foreign" elements in the form of internal security legislation. This legislation strengthened immigration and nationality policy by giving officials more authority in excluding and deporting "undesirable" aliens.

References
Marius A. Dimmitt, "The Enactment of the McCarran-Walter Act of 1952," Ph.D. dissertation, University of Kansas, 1970 (DA 31: 5980-A); Richard R. Hofstetter, ed., *United States Immigration Policy* (1984).

F.C.

McCONE, SELMA J. *See Toveritar.*

MACEDO-ROMANIANS. *See* Romanians.

McGARRITY, JOSEPH (1874–1940). Businessman and revolutionary. McGarrity was born in Carrickmore, county Tyrone, Ireland and emigrated to Philadelphia in 1890 at age sixteen. He eventually became a wealthy businessman and devoted most of his time and money to the cause of Irish freedom. He was a major leader of Clan na Gael and advisor to Roger Casemont, Padraig Pearse, and Eamon DeValera. He helped fund the Easter Uprising of 1916 and later raised $8.5 million for the new Irish Republican government during the Anglo-Irish War. Even after the civil war and partition he continued to support forces that sought to unite the six counties to the rest of Ireland. His extensive papers are housed at Villanova University.

References
S. Cronin, ed., *The McGarrity Papers* (1972); M. V. Tarpaey, *The Role of Joseph McGarrity in the Struggle for Irish Independence* (1970).

S.P.M.

McKAY, CLAUDE (1890–1948). McKay was born in Jamaica in 1890 and died in Chicago in 1948. He was a poet, novelist, and short story writer. As a young boy, he was influenced by his older, free-thinking brother who was a teacher near Montego Bay. He moved to Kingston to learn a trade in his teen years, and then came to America to study agriculture at Tuskegee but rebelled against its strict regimentation. However, with a small inheritance, he moved to Harlem to devote his energies to writing. McKay became one of the leading poets of the Harlem Renaissance. His best-known poem is "If We Must Die," which expresses a defiance against aggression. While it was a black protest expression, it was quoted by Winston Churchill to inspire the British in the face of German attack. Although his black protest writing made him famous, the theme of much of his poetry was nostalgia for his youth in the tropics. His novels depict the conflict between educated white society and the "noble savage" of either Africa or the urban ghetto. This may well express his own inner conflict. Between 1923 and 1934, he traveled and lived in Russia, France, Spain, and other countries. He never joined the Communist party, but he did support a broad number of liberal and socialist causes. In 1943 he suffered a stroke. In 1944 he converted to Catholicism and became quite conservative in his views. His poetry, for which he is best remembered, was written in classic sonnet format. Although a leading figure in the Negro Renaissance, he never indulged in its experimentation with form or made much use of American negro folk material.

Reference
James Richard Giles, *Claude McKay* (1978).

N.C.

McLEOD, CHRISTIAN. *See* Ruddy, Anna C[hristian].

MAGNES, JUDAH L[EON]. *See* Jews: Kehillah.

MAGYARS. *See* Hungarians.

MAHONEY, JOHN J. *See* Americanization Movement.

MAINZER ADELSVEREIN. *See* Von Herff, Ferdinand.

MAKEMIE, FRANCIS (1658–1708). Makemie was born in Donegal, Ireland and emigrated to America in 1683. He founded the Presbyterian church in America, and in 1706 was elected the first moderator of the American Presbyterians.

S.P.M.

MALCOLM X. *See* West Indian Immigrants.

MALKIEL, THERESA SERBER (1874–1949). An organizer in the Jewish labor movement in the 1890s and a prominent activist and propagandist in the New York Socialist party after the turn of the century. Born in Bar, Russia, Malkiel immigrated to the United States in 1891 and soon after entered the infant cloakmakers' industry.

Reference
Sally M. Miller, "From Sweatshop Worker to Labor Leader: Theresa Malkiel, a Case Study," *American Jewish History* 68 (Dec. 1978): 189–205.

F.C.

MANGANO, ANTONIO (1869–1951). Baptist minister, and a leading Italian Protestant minister working among Italian immigrants. In 1904, Mangano was appointed general missionary for the Baptist Home Mission Society and was charged with the responsibility of coordinating comprehensive evangelical work among Italian immigrants. His chief works are: *Religious Work Among Italians in America* (1917); and *Sons of Italy* (1917; rpt. 1972).

References
Lawrence B. Davis, *Immigrants, Baptists, and the Protestant Mind in America* (1973);
Salvatore Mondello, "Baptist Churches and Italian Americans," *Foundations: A Baptist Journal of History and Theology* 16 (July–Sept. 1973): 222–238.

F.C.

MARCANTONIO, VITO (1902–1954). Lawyer, congressman (1934–36, 1938–1950). Born in East Harlem of an Italian-born mother and a native-born father, Marcantonio lived there all his life and represented that neighborhood in the United States Congress for fourteen years. De Witt Clinton High School's principal, Leonard Covello (*q.v.*), became his Italian teacher and lifelong friend and mentor. At the school's graduation in 1921 he shared the platform with the main speaker, Fiorello La Guardia (*q.v.*), who was so impressed with the young man that he became his political mentor. Marcantonio was elected to Congress representing East Harlem, La Guardia's old district, and like him worked incessantly for those he represented. He continued his collaboration with Leonard Covello and Mayor La Guardia in improving the lot of the East Harlem Italians, and did the same for the Puerto Ricans and blacks who were his constituents. In Congress he supported most of the New Deal legislation and fought against the repression of aliens and immigration restrictions.

Reference
Annette T. Rubinstein, ed., *Vito Marcantionio: Debates, Speeches and Writings* (1956, 1973).

R.U.P.

MARIEL BOATLIFT REFUGEES, work attitudes. Data concerning experienced job characteristics were collected from 135 Cuban boatlift refugees using structured and semistructured interview questions in March 1981, about eleven months after the Mariel boatlift began. Respondents described task characteristics, good performance contingencies, and work satisfactions related to their last job in Cuba. Comparing this data with parallel data for a representative sample of U.S. employees and Mexican-Americans indicates both a few differences and several notable similarities. The data concerning satisfaction and good performance contingencies imply that while refugees may be frustrated by the lack of economic rewards for good performance in the United States, they may be particularly pleased with other, noneconomic, aspects of work.

Reference
M. F. Peterson, "Work Attitudes of Mariel Boatlift Refugees," *Cuban Studies* 14 (Summer 1984): 1–20.

F.C.

MARSHALL, LOUIS (1856–1929). Lawyer, Jewish communal leader. Anti-Semitism in the form of social discrimination and as part of a broader nativism affected the American Jewish community during the early decades of the twentieth century. The initiative in defending Jewish rights was taken by the American Jewish Committee, whose president from 1912 to 1929 was Louis Marshall. A distinguished lawyer, Marshall functioned primarily as spokesman for the wealthy, confident, German Jewish elite. His ideology consisted of an amalgam of Americanism, reverence for the law, and firm loyalty to Judaism. Usually conservative on economic issues, he was a consistent advocate of civil liberties for all. He did not regard American anti-Semitism as a fundamental problem but was determined to prevent its expression in overt form. Marshall's tactics generally emphasized the traditional methods of rational argument, quiet intercession, and dignified application of pressure, but his effectiveness was strengthened by his political influence and by the implied power of Jewish voters. His leadership was increasingly questioned by the rising eastern European immigrants, but most Jews and non-Jews acknowledged him as the champion of Jewish rights.

Reference
Morton Rosenstock, *Louis Marshall and the Defense of Jewish Rights in the United States* (1965).

F.C.

IL MARTELLO (THE HAMMER). *See* Tresca, Carlo.

MATTSON, HELMI. *See Toveritar*.

MAXWELL, WILLIAM H. (1852–1920). Educator. A Scotch-Irish immigrant, Maxwell served as New York City superintendent of schools from 1898 (when the greater city of New York was chartered) until 1918. "An autocrat committed to egalitarian goals," Maxwell was a major force during the period when the immigrant child presence was at its height in New York City schools. Chief work: *A Quarter Century of Public School Development* (1912).

References
Samuel Abelow, *Dr. William H. Maxwell* (1930); Selma C. Berrol, "William H. Maxwell and a New Educational New York," *History of Education Quarterly* 8 (Summer 1968): 215–228.

F.C.

MAZZEI, PHILIP (1730–1816). Patriot, diplomat, writer. A versatile, enterprising, perceptive man from Tuscany, Italy, Mazzei participated in such world-shaking events as the American and French revolutions and the short-lived Polish constitutional reform in 1791. He founded "The Constitutional Society of 1784" to make available to legislators the opinions of the best minds concerning a new Constitution. In 1788 he published in Paris a four-volume history of the American colonies. His *Memoirs* are a rich eighteenth-century source book and commentary on his friendship with the first five presidents of the United States, as well as with other prominent figures of the Enlightenment. Both a transmitter of European ideas to the Americans and a bearer of American ideas across the Atlantic, Philip Mazzei may also be considered the first Italian immigrant to promote economic and political relations between the United States and Italy.

References
Philip Mazzei, *My Life and Wanderings*, trans. S. Eugene Scalia, ed. Margherita Marchione (1980); Philip Mazzei, *Selected Writings and Correspondence*, ed. Margherita Marchione (1983).

M.M.

MAZZUCHELLI, REV. SAMUEL (1806–1864). Dominican missionary. Born of a patrician Milano, Italy, family, he early volunteered for missionary work in America. His first "parish" stretched north from Detroit to Lake Superior, west beyond the Mississippi, and south almost to St. Louis. In 1835 Mazzuchelli came to the lead region from the Green Bay–Mackinac frontier. One year later he addressed the opening session of the territorial legislature. Soon he was establishing schools and preparing teachers for the children of the settlers. In 1847 he formed Wisconsin's first teaching sisterhood, the Sinsinawa Dominican Sisters. At Benton he founded the St. Clara Academy and taught science with the earliest laboratory instruments. To the Irish miners this American from Italy was "Father Matthew Kelly." To settlers of many creeds he was civic leader and friend, builder of the city of man and the city of God. At his death in 1864 Father Mazzuchelli was interred in the cemetery of St. Patrick's Church in Benton, one of the twenty churches he designed and built in the upper Mississippi Valley.

Reference
Luca Beltrami, *Padre Samuele Mazzuchelli* (1928); Edward Marolla, *Mazzuchelli of Wisconsin* (1981).

F.C.

MEAGHER, THOMAS FRANCIS (1823–1867). Soldier and politician, Meagher was the epitome of the romantic revolutionary. In 1848, he was one of the leaders of the Young Ireland revolution. After its failure, the British government sent him to Tasmania as a political prisoner. Escaping in 1852, Meagher came to the United States and settled in New York City. Meagher's American career included roles as journalist, lawyer, soldier, and politician. Meagher was the darling of the New York Irish. He led the famed Irish Brigade into combat during the Civil War; after hostilities ceased, President Andrew Johnson appointed Meagher governor of the Montana Territory, but shortly after accepting his new position, he drowned in the Missouri River.

Reference
Robert G. Athearn, *Thomas Francis Meagher: An Irish Revolutionary in America* (1949; rpt. 1976).

F.C.

MEGLENO-ROMANIANS. *See* Romanians.

MEIR, GOLDA [MABOVITCH] (1898–1978). Zionist. Born in Kiev, Russia in 1898, Golda (Mabovitch) Meir migrated with her family to the United States in 1906. She served as Israel's prime minister from 1969 to 1974. Before migrating to Palestine in 1921, Golda Meir was a schoolteacher in Milwaukee and early involved herself in the Zionist labor movement.

References
Peggy Mann, *Golda Meir* (1971); Golda Meir, *My Life* (1975).

F.C.

"MELTING POT." An idea suggesting the amalgamation of diverse ethnic and cultural groups in America. Historical attention paid to the melting pot idea has never been systematic. Usual references to it mention Jean de Crèvecoeur (*q.v.*) and Israel Zangwill (*q.v.*) and indicate that America seemed to be a melting pot of nationalities. The primary concepts and forces that fostered the melting pot included a Christian emphasis on the unity of mankind; an asylum image of America; the identification of America with natural rights and freedoms that regenerated men (refugees from European despotism); a desire for population that would build an economy; and an optimistic belief in the American future. All of these emphasized possible contributions of immigrants rather than a critical attitude toward their origins. The melting pot idea emerged as the most widely held answer to America's problem of creating a unity and a nationality out of diversity while preserving freedom of choice.

Reference
Richard C. Harper, *The Course of the Melting Pot Idea to 1910* (1980).

F.C.

MELUS. Society for the Study of the Multi-Ethnic Literature of the United States (University of Houston, Clear Lake, Houston, Texas 77058-1058). Founded in 1973, MELUS endeavors to expand the definition of American literature through the study and teaching of Afro-American, American Indian, Asian and Pacific American, Hispanic, and ethnically specific European-American literary works, their authors, and their cultural contexts. It publishes a quarterly journal, *MELUS*. MELUS has contributed strongly to American literary studies by presenting sessions in the conventions of such scholarly organizations as the MLA and its regional organizations, the CEA, NWSA, PAPC, and PCA (Popular Culture Association). Theoretical papers at MELUS sessions and in the MELUS journal point to a new, more broadly conceived American literature.

F.C.

MENACE, THE. *See* Flower, B[enjamin] O[range].

MENGARINI, GREGORY (1811–1886). Jesuit missionary. Before the mid-nineteenth century the star of empire had coursed across the continent, leading American settlers to the Pacific shore. Among the vanguard of the pioneer caravan that followed close upon the heels of the fur trapper was a significant minority who came in response to the repeated request for Blackrobes made during the 1830s by Indian tribes of the interior plateau, particularly the Flatheads. Among these missionaries was a young Roman Jesuit, Gregory Mengarini, whose *Memoirs* are a valuable chronicle of his experiences among the Flatheads. Mengarini later founded the University of Santa Clara in California.

Reference
Gloria R. Lothrop, "Father Gregory Mengarini, an Italian Jesuit Missionary in the Transmontane West: His Life and Memoir," Ph.D. dissertation, University of Southern California, 1970.

F.C.

MENNONITES. The Mennonites are direct descendants of the Anabaptist movement (originating about 1525), and their history is characterized by periods of severe persecution and subsequent migrations. In respect to immigration to North America we do well to distinguish between Mennonites from two geographic areas—those of Swiss and German background and the Dutch–North German groups.

The Swiss–South German Mennonites (including some from France, Germany, and Galicia-Volhynia) came directly to North America. This movement began in 1683 with the first permanent settlement at Germantown, Philadelphia, and it continued for about 200 years. This migration had great significance for the future of the Mennonites, even though it was a minor part of the great Atlantic migration from western Europe to America. This migration falls into six successive waves: (1) Lower Rhine to Germantown, 1683–1705, 100 persons; (2) Palatinate and Switzerland to Eastern Pennsylvania, 1701–1756, 3,000–5,000 persons, mostly Mennonite, possibly 300 Amish; (3) Alsatian, Bavarian and Hessian Amish to Ohio, Ontario, Indiana, and Illinois, 1815–1860, possibly 3,000 persons; (4) Swiss Mennonites to Ohio and Indiana, 1830–1860, possibly 500 persons; (5) Palatinate Mennonites to Ohio, Indiana, and Illinois, possibly 300 persons; and (6) Galician and Volhynian Mennonites to Kansas and South Dakota, 1875–1880, about 400 persons. (Of groups 3, 4, and 5 some continued to come after the Civil War [1861–65] until toward the end of the nineteenth century.) A total of possibly 8,000 persons crossed the Atlantic in the two centuries of migration. A considerable relocation to southern Ontario from eastern Pennsylvania took place in 1785–1840, accompanied by a southward movement to Maryland and Virginia. A movement westward (also from Virginia) across the Alleghenies into western Pennsylvania and Ohio, and finally from Ohio and Ontario to Indiana and northern Illinois took place in 1800–1860. An Amish movement westward into Ohio, Indiana, and Iowa (some to central Illinois) took place in 1800–1860. Some Amish from Illinois and Ontario reached Iowa and Nebraska in 1845–1880. Mennonites from Pennsylvania and Virginia reached Missouri and Kansas in 1865–1890, and some went into North Dakota, Oregon, and Alberta in 1890–1920. Some Amish reached Oregon from Ohio and Missouri, and also Iowa and Nebraska in 1880–1910.

Dutch–North German Mennonite Migration. When Anabaptism established itself in the Low Countries under the most adverse conditions, migration to other countries was often the only chance for survival. The Anabaptists from Flanders went to the Northern provinces of the Low Countries. On the other hand, German East Friesland became the haven of religious refugees from the Low Countries as a whole.

As early as 1530 Anabaptists found their way to the Vistula Delta, and the migration to this area continued for a long time. From here the Mennonites moved into Poland and Marienburg. Until the middle of the eighteenth century the surplus population was absorbed in new settlements along the Vistula. All migration had been on a scale involving small groups. From now on organized large-scale migration of Mennonites of Dutch background became common.

When Catherine the Great issued her Manifesto in 1763 inviting farmers from Western countries to settle in the Ukraine, the Mennonites of Prussia and Danzig were attracted. The approximate number that emigrated to Russia in 1787–1870 was 1,907 families, with a total of some 8,000 persons. Of this number about 400 families settled at Chortiza, some 1,049 at Molotschna, some 438 at Samara, and 20 families were reported to have gone to Vilna.

While the migration eastward was still in progress the Mennonites of Russia and Prussia were seeking a place where they could find complete exemption from military service, which they were in danger of losing in Prussia and Russia. In 1873–1884 some 18,000 Mennonites and 1,200 Hutterites left Russia to settle in the United States and Canada. The chief reasons for this mass migration were their unwillingness to accept a compulsory military service and their objections to a Russianization program inaugurated by the Russian government.

An even larger migration of Mennonites from Russia occurred after World War I, when in 1922–1930 some 25,000 Mennonites went to Canada. Many of the Low German–speaking Mennonites who came to Canada later migrated to Mexico, Brazil, Paraguay, Belize, and Bolivia. Some returned again to North America, and it is estimated that presently about 45,000 Mennonites in Latin America have a Canadian background. The reason for the mass migration from Russia was the threat of a complete disintegration of the religious, cultural, and economic way of life of the Mennonites. During the German occupation of the Ukraine in 1941–43 some 35,000 were evacuated by the German army to settle in the Vistula area where they had come from some 150 years earlier. Because of the outcome of the war nearly two-thirds of them were forcibly repatriated by the Russian army in 1945–46, while some 12,000 found their way to Canada and South America.

After the Revolution mass exiles and concentrations in slave labor camps contributed to the dispersion of the Mennonites. Large numbers were sent to northern European Russia and to Asiatic Russia. During the invasion of the Ukraine by the Germans in 1941 many Mennonite settlements were dissolved, the total population having been sent to Asiatic Russia by the Soviet government.

All the Mennonites of Prussia and Poland fled in 1945 when the Russian army approached. Some were interned for some time in Denmark, while the others escaped to West Germany, where many of them established new homes. A large number of the Danzig and Prussian and some of the Galician Mennonites migrated to Uruguay and Canada in 1948–1952.

The migrations across the Atlantic had as a major motive the search for religious toleration and freedom from military service, as well as economic stability.

The Dutch Mennonites rendered significant financial aid to the Swiss and Palatinate Mennonites in their migration to Pennsylvania in the first half of the eighteenth century. It is doubtful if many could have succeeded in the move without this help, since most of the Swiss were poor, and the Palatines had suffered heavily from the French invasions and the heavy taxes and economic restrictions of Palatine rulers.

The Amish, an offshoot of the Swiss Mennonites in 1693, came to America in two peak periods of immigration, one in the eighteenth century (1727–1770) and the other in the nineteenth century (1815–1860). Several Dutch and German Mennonite groups had settled in North America before the Amish came to Pennsylvania.

All Anabaptist Mennonite groups in Europe had encountered conditions that forced them to migrate. Although they were highly valued as skillful and productive farmers within German-speaking countries, they were not given legal religious status. They moved from frontier to frontier. Although some Palatine lords provided farming opportunities for the Mennonites, the area was politically unstable. Situated as it was between major countries at war, the Palatinate area was a battlefield that played havoc with the lives and possessions of the people in the area.

The several linguistically and culturally diverse Mennonite groups cooperate today in a worldwide service to aid migration and resettlement through a single organization, the Mennonite Central Committee (MCC). Organized in 1920 during the Bolshevik Revolution in Russia to help the famine-stricken people, this organization continues to respond to victims of disaster, persecution, and migration. Following major periods of war in the twentieth century, the Mennonites have helped many refugees to find new homes. Assisting their own and other uprooted people to find new lands and technical skills has drawn the worldwide Mennonite brotherhood closer together.

References

John J. Ruth, *Maintaining the Right Fellowship* (1986); C. Henry Smith, *The Mennonite Immigration to Pennsylvania* (1929); C. Henry Smith, *The Coming of the Russian Mennonites* (1927); J. C. Wenger, *The Mennonite Church in America* (1966); S. C. Yoder, *For Conscience's Sake* (1940); Delbert Gratz, *Bernese Anabaptists* (1953).

J.A.H.

MENNONITES, in Kansas, 1870–1940. The Mennonites who were brought to central Kansas by the railroads in the 1870s inherited a dualistic Anabaptist conception of the church and world that discouraged political involvement and forbade participation in warfare. Statistics of voting, naturalization, and office holding show that many Mennonites avoided political involvement through 1940, but also that a minority were involved in politics from the beginning in party votes not widely divergent from a non-Mennonite norm. Most of the central Kansas Mennonites emigrated from Russia or Europe in search of isolation and cultural autonomy, but they settled without guarantees of the preconditions of a closed settlement and exemption from national military service. Their trust in America was rewarded through the assistance of the railroads, the growth of prosperous farming communities, and an extended period of national peace, which postponed the potentially disruptive question of military conscription.

Reference
James C. Juhnke, "The Political Acculturation of the Kansas Mennonites, 1870–1940," Ph.D. dissertation, Indiana University, 1968.

F.C.

MESTROVIC, IVAN. *See* Croatians.

MEXICAN AMERICAN EDUCATION STUDY (United States Commission on Civil Rights, 1971–73). In the proliferating literature on Mexican-Americans and the Chicano heritage, none is more important than the detailed *Reports* which constitute the *Mexican American Education Study* published by the United States Commission on Civil Rights in 1971–73. The bilingual and bicultural educational needs of Mexican-Americans are the twin themes that are recurrent in the *Reports,* which were published under the following titles: (1) *Ethnic Isolation of Mexican Americans in the Public Schools of the Southwest;* (2) *The Unfinished Education: Outcomes for Minorities in the Five Southwestern States;* (3) *The Excluded Student: Educational Practices Affecting Mexican Americans in the Southwest;* (4) *Mexican American Education in Texas: A Function of Wealth;* and (5) *Teachers and Students: Differences in Teacher Interaction with Mexican American and Anglo Students.*

F.C.

MEXICAN IMMIGRATION, critical evaluation. Cardenas offers a critical evaluation of the "methodological and practical problems associated with data collected and utilized by the Immigration and Naturalization Service on the migration of Mexicans into the United States, focusing on the difficult issues surrounding the data about the flow of illegal aliens." He suggsts that "the data of the INS are collected, analyzed, and utilized in accordance with the social and political goals of the agency. If one accepts this orientation, then social scientists must examine alternative sources of data in order to interpret the data of the INS and to provide data to policy makers that suggest alternative ways to estimate the amount and the potential impact of Mexican immigration into the United States."

Reference
Gilberto Cardenas, "Public Data on Mexican Immigration into the United States: A

Critical Evaluation,'' in W. B. Littrell and G. Sjoberg, eds., *Current Issues in Social Policy* (1976); pp. 127–144.

F.C.

MEXICANS. Mexican-Americans (Chicanos) are only partially an immigrant ethnic group. They are also partially a conquered and annexed ethnic group. This dual origin has provided a uniqueness to the historical experience of Mexican-Americans.

Conquest and Annexation. In contrast to most other U.S. ethnic groups, which began when immigrants came to this country, Mexican-Americans came into existence when the United States came to them. This occurred in three stages. In 1845, the United States annexed Texas (the Lone Star Republic), which a decade earlier had won its independence from Mexico. In 1848, after being defeated in the 1846–48 U.S.-Mexican War, Mexico ceded to the United States much of its northern territory, including most of current California, Arizona, and New Mexico, in the Treaty of Guadalupe Hidalgo. Finally, in 1854, the United States bought the southern sliver of what is today New Mexico and Arizona via the Gadsden Purchase.

In this manner, the United States acquired approximately one-half of Mexico's territory and some 80,000 Mexicans, most of whom remained as the first Mexican-Americans. Like American Indian civilizations, these annexed Mexican-Americans had their own language, culture, traditions, and deep, historically rooted attachment to this land, in some cases stretching back to Juan de Oñate's 1598 New Mexico settlement expedition. Many contemporary Chicanos can trace their ancestry to these annexed Mexicans.

Immigration. The second and far larger group of Mexican-Americans consists of immigrants and their descendants. Immigration from Mexico has proceeded nearly continuously since 1848, with the 2,000-mile common border serving more as an avenue than an obstacle. Immigration was of modest size during the second half of the nineteenth century, but has been of major proportions throughout the twentieth century. The one major exception occurred during the Great Depression of the 1930s, which witnessed the century's only net out-migration of Mexicans. During that decade, some 500,000 Mexicans and Mexican-Americans were deported or moved voluntarily to Mexico as part of the governmental Repatriation Program.

Mexican immigrants have fallen into three categories: immigrants with permanent visas; undocumented immigrants; and legal temporary immigrants, such as those with work permits under the bracero program (1942–47, 1951–1964). While Mexicans have immigrated for a variety of reasons, including escape from political turbulence (particularly during the 1910–1920 Mexican Revolution), most have come for better economic opportunities. While many have remained here, others have stayed only temporarily, remitting funds to Mexico to support their families, saving money to build a better life back home, and ultimately returning to Mexico.

Life in the United States. For annexed Mexican-Americans, particularly those with wealth and social standing, becoming American occasionally led to increased prosperity and mainstream acceptance. But for most, annexation brought a cruel period of adjustment: massive loss of land, often through legal or financial chicanery; rapidly declining political status in the face of Anglo-American westward migration; relegation to the lower rungs of the socioeconomic ladder; and various forms of societal discrimination. Immigrants have encountered an even more difficult situation. Not only have they confronted the problems faced by annexed Mexican-Americans, particularly discrimination and economic marginalization, but they have also experienced the generic immigrant traumas of dislocation from their homeland.

Since annexation, Mexican-Americans have struggled to overcome these obstacles and obtain their full rights as Americans. They have been actively involved in the labor movement, leading and participating in agricultural and industrial strikes. They have challenged segregated schools, restrictive housing covenants, political gerrymandering, and segregation in theaters, restaurants, and public swimming pools. Mexican-Americans have been elected as governors of New Mexico and Arizona, as well as mayors of such cities as San Antonio and Denver. However, while making inroads into all aspects of American life, Chicanos continue to suffer from slow economic and occupational progress, low educational attainment, and political underrepresentation.

Probably the most dramatic recent phenomenon in Mexican-American history has been the Chicano movement, which began during the 1960s. It involved a more aggressive effort by Mexican-Americans to influence their own destinies. The movement included the organization of agricultural workers through the United Farm Workers led by César Chávez, challenges against various types of segregation, efforts to increase the Chicano presence within the Catholic church hierarchy, and demands for greater educational opportunity, including the development of bilingual education.

Mexican-American Culture and Society. While becoming acculturated to American life, Mexican-Americans have also developed their own social and cultural traditions. Faced historically with residential segregation and wishing to live near those who shared their language and culture, Chicanos built their own communities, generally known as *barrios* or *colonias*. These communities created a wide range of specialized services, ranging from Mexican grocery stores to Mexican-

American private schools. Beginning in the 1850s, Mexican-American newspapers have provided a force for community consolidation and an outlet for cultural expression.

Particularly with the twentieth-century growth of Chicano communities, Mexican-American organizations have flourished. *Mutualistas* (mutual aid societies) have provided a social, cultural, legal, and financial support system for Mexican immigrants and U.S.-born Mexican-Americans. Chicanos have not only joined general American labor organizations, but they have also formed their own unions. Mexican-American organizations have developed at both the community and national levels, such as the League of United Latin American Citizens (LULAC) and the American G.I. Forum veterans' organization. Chicanos have also joined with other Hispanics to create national professional organizations, such as Image, the U.S. Hispanic Chamber of Commerce, and the National Association of Latino Elected and Appointed Officials.

Mexican-Americans have been culturally active. Chicano novelists, poets, and playwrights have explored myriad themes, including the Mexican-American experience, using English, Spanish, and interlinguality (integrating English and Spanish). Chicanos have become active on stage, in television, and in motion pictures, with Chicano film makers having made such films a *El Norte* and *La Bamba,* dealing with the Hispanic experience in the United States. While Chicano artists and musicians have proven themselves in mainstream genres and styles, they have also used traditional Mexican forms of expression, such as murals that adorn barrio walls and the guitar-and-voice-based *corrido.*

Chicanos have also received constant cultural invigoration from neighboring Mexico. The common border has contributed to ease of migration, maintenance of family ties, continuity of cultural infusion, and inevitably of linguistic reinforcement. Mexican publications become accessible almost immediately, Mexican movies are being shown at increasing numbers of American theaters, and Spanish-language radio and television stations in the United States make heavy use of Mexican music and dramatic programs.

Mexican-Americans Today. The 1980 census reported 8.7 million persons of Mexican descent in the United States, an admitted undercount, particularly omitting undocumented Mexicans. Ninety percent of Mexican-Americans live in the Southwest, but they can now be found throughout the nation. While Chicanos were the most rural major American ethnic group in 1940, they had become 80 percent urban by 1970. About 75 percent of Mexican-Americans were born in the United States, but although English is the primary language of Chicanos, three-fourths also speak some Spanish.

High immigration and birth rates (compared to the national average) make Chicanos one of the fastest-growing ethnic groups in the United States, although the long-range impact of the 1986 Immigration Reform and Control Act is yet to be determined. Moreover, Mexican-Americans are forging links with other Hispanic groups, like Puerto Ricans and Cuban-Americans, in areas of common interest and concern. Given these factors, it is almost inevitable that Chicanos, along with other Hispanics, will play an increasingly significant role in the future of the United States.

References
Rodolfo Acuña, *Occupied America: A History of Chicanos* (1981); Carlos E. Cortés, "Mexicans," in *Harvard Encyclopedia of American Ethnic Groups* (1980); Leo Grebler, Joan W. Moore, and Ralph C. Guzmán, *The Mexican American People: The Nation's Second Largest Minority* (1970); Alfredo Mirandé, *The Chicano Experience: An Alternative Perspective* (1985).

C.E.C.

MEXICANS, border economy. Although examining regional development issues on both sides of the border in their respective contexts, Hansen (*infra*) devotes primary attention to the U.S. side. He analyzes the border economy in terms of the historical role of Mexican labor in the Southwest and finds that Mexican labor, whether legal or undocumented, has been a valuable asset in the growth and development of the economy of the Southwest. Special consideration is also given to the social and economic status of Mexican-Americans, and evidence is presented suggesting that the prospects of this historically disadvantaged minority have been improving. This study represents a synthesis of much of the existing secondary literature on immigration and extensive primary research. Major attention is given to a wide range of border theories, to the significance of the new international division of labor, and to European guest worker experiences, all of which have relevance to the Mexico-U.S. borderlands.

Reference
Niles M. Hansen, *The Border Economy: Regional Development in the Southwest* (1981).

F.C.

MEXICANS, channelization of Mexican nationals. Guttierrez has analyzed the migration process of Mexican nationals to the San Luis Valley of Colorado and identifies the characteristics of the migrating individuals. Specific objectives related to the primary purpose are: (1) to describe areas of origin of this illegal migrant population; (2) to evaluate the validity of the channelization concept for the migration of undocumented Mexicans from specific areas of origin to the San Luis Valley; and (3) to identify various social, economic, and personal characteristics of this migrant population. He demonstrates that the Mexican migration stream to the San Luis Valley of Colorado is different, possessing unique characteristics that distinguish it from streams to Texas, to the West Coast, and to the Midwest and Plains. The study's hypotheses are that (1) the San Luis Valley migration stream differs from other major migration streams in the source areas and routes taken by the migrating Mexicans; and (2) information channels and communication links are the major elements involved in this channelized migration.

Reference
Phillip R. Guttierrez, "The Channelization of Mexican Nationals to the San Luis Valley of Colorado," in Richard C. Jones, ed., *Patterns of Undocumented Migration: Mexico and the United States* (1984), pp. 184–198.

F.C.

MEXICANS, curbing illegal immigration from Mexico. Cuello (*infra*) has this to say on the subject:

> The Congressional formula for curbing illegal immigration is to legalize an undetermined percentage of the undocumented aliens already residing in the U.S., while at the same time beefing up the forces of the Border Patrol. What Congress ignores is that Mexican immigration, legal or illegal, has interwoven itself into the fabric of American society for 100 years. Patterns of behavior and mutual dependency have been deeply ingrained in both Mexican and American societies that will not be broken—they can only be modified, redirected, or channeled. The legalization proposed will serve only to open up a can of worms. It assumes most illegals are homogeneously intent on staying here and can prove continuous residency for three to five years. Some will be tempted, but will not have the documentation. Others will obtain forgeries. Many may reject the offer. Any arbitrary data will break up an undetermined number of families and communities. Most important, the flow of new illegals will not be stopped.

Reference
José Cuello, "Curbing Illegal Immigration from Mexico: Obstacles to a Successful Legislative Solution," *USA Today* 114 (March 1986): 10–14.

F.C.

MEXICANS, determinants of earnings. Controversy has arisen concerning whether the earnings of undocumented Mexican workers are lower than those of legal Mexican immigrant workers, holding constant other relevant characteristics. Data have been obtained from two systematic samples of Los Angeles County birth certificates in which either the mother or the father of the baby was reported to be of Mexican origin and in which the mother was either born in or outside the United States. Multivariate analyses were conducted with three dependent variables: (1) the natural log of annual earnings in hundreds of dollars in 1979; (2) total hours worked in 1979; and (3) the natural log of the average hourly wage in dollars in 1979. For both fathers and mothers it was found that being a legal rather than an undocumented immigrant had a statistically significant positive impact on the hourly wage. Findings concerning the impact of other independent variables on the hourly wage and other dependent variables have also been reported.

Reference
D. M. Heer and D. Falasco, "Determinants of Earnings Among Three Groups of Mexican-Americans: Undocumented Immigrants, Legal Immigrants and the Native Born," paper presented at the Population Association of America Annual Meeting, Minneapolis, May 3–5, 1984.

F.C.

MEXICANS, future migration patterns. Efforts to anticipate and account for future migration patterns hinge on an examination of the potential for the supply, demand, and replacement of labor. In Mexico, the projected number of males entering the labor force will be about 48 percent larger in the 1980s than in the 1970s and entrants will outnumber departures by a labor force replacement ratio of 407 to 100—a fifty-year high. Fertility declined significantly in Mexico in the 1970s, and the number of new entrants to the labor force in the 1980s will decline; the replacement ratio is projected to be about 330 to 100—a decrease of 19 percent. It seems very unlikely, even allowing for renewed rapid growth in Mexico's economy, that new job opportunities can be created to accommodate such an enormous influx to the job market. Accommodations may be made more difficult because of increasing expectations of workers.

Reference
Benjamin S. Bradshaw and W. Parker Frisbie, "Potential Labor Force Supply and Replacement in Mexico and the States of the Mexican Cession and Taxes: 1980–2000," *International Migration Review* 17 (Fall 1983): 394–409.

F.C.

MEXICANS, illegal alien workers. The flow of illegal immigration has been considered a continuation of the bracero program, augmented by other factors. When the program ended, the needs on both sides of the border did not. Mexico's spiraling population growth and the United States' need for labor in the late 1960s, when the market was tight, encouraged the continuation of the flow of workers north. The 1965 law added its own impetus by including the work certification provision.

Part of the responsibility for large illegal immigration has been placed on the Immigration and Naturalization Service, which has very little power or incentive to enforce the law, particularly because it lacks the support of other institutions. Penalties for hiring illegal immigrants are so light as to be ineffective.

Reference
Walter A. Fogel, "Illegal Alien Workers in the United States," *Industrial Relations* 16 (1977): 243–263.

F.C.

MEXICANS, illegal immigration. Although overlooked for decades, illegal immigration into the American Southwest from Mexico has now reached levels where considerable public interest has been evoked. Furthermore, the current scale and magnitude of illegal crossings induces a set of socioeconomic problems which beset the whole American Southwest. Concern for this topic can initiate public action involving domestic labor, which may result in the formulation of ameliorative policies dealing with labor force questions, migrant treatment, and citizenship status. Dagodag reviews basic regional problems associated with illegal Mexican aliens. Through the use of a case study focusing on California, he generates a profile of illegal immigrants examined from several perspectives, both spatial and aspatial.

Reference
W. Tim Dagodag, "Illegal Mexican Immigration to California from Western Mexico," in Richard C. Jones, ed., *Patterns of Undocumented Migration: Mexico and the United States* (1984): 61–73.

F.C.

MEXICANS, illegal Mexican laborers and the American economy. A tertiary labor market has been created, and is maintained, in an effort to provide American entrepreneurs with a never ending source of cheap labor. At the practical level examples of their economic contributions to the U.S. economy are the persistent and pervasive "wage differentials" that exist in the U.S. market, in the garment and restaurant industries, motels and hotels, hospitals and convalescent homes, landscape and construction, agriculture and horticulture, etc., where heavy concentrations of undocumented workers are commonplace. Issues to be addressed are the type of social services that are utilized by undocumented aliens and the various taxes that are paid to the American economy as a result of their participation in the tertiary labor market.

Reference
J. L. Gonzales, Jr., "The Contribution of Undocumented Mexican Laborers to the

American Economy,'' paper presented at the Western Social Science Meeting, San Diego, California, April 27, 1984.

F.C.

MEXICANS, immigrants and the United States. What are the effects of immigration by people of Mexican origin on the economic, educational, social, political, and linguistic systems of the United States? To answer this question, authors of the conference papers presented (*infra*) use a comparative method to provide objective information about the Mexican-American presence in the United States during the 1980s. Contents: ''Who Are the Mexican-Americans? A Note on Comparability''; ''Assimilation in the United States: The Mexican-Americans''; ''Conflict and Accommodation: Mexican-Americans in the Cosmopolis''; ''Ethnicity and Stratification: Mexican-Americans and the European *Gastarbeiter* in Comparative Perspective''; ''Transborder People''; ''Migration Theory and Practice''; ''Political Distinctiveness of the Mexican-Americans''; ''Mexican-American Political Mobilization and the Loyalty Question''; ''Political Mobilization in the Mexican-American Community''; ''Language Policies: Patterns of Retention and Maintenance''; ''National Language Profile of the Mexican-Origin Population in the United States''; ''Ethnic Revival in the United States: Implications for the Mexican-American Community''; and ''Conclusions: Through a Comparative Prism Darkly.''

Reference
Walter Connor, ed., *Mexican-Americans in Comparative Perspective* (1985).

F.C.

MEXICANS, labor market projections for the United States and Mexico. The supply of labor in the United States is projected on the basis of current demographic data, and the demand for labor necessary to meet planned or projected levels of output in selected years is then calculated. The results of comparing the supply and demand for labor in the two countries are sensitive to the particular parameters used, considering the wide range of predictions concerning sustainable rates of growth of output and productivity in both countries.

Reference
C. W. Reynolds, ''Labor Market Projections for the United States and Mexico and Their Relevance to Current Migration Controversies,'' in C. Vásquez and M. Garcia y Griego, eds., *Mexican-U.S. Relations: Conflict and Convergence* (Los Angeles: University of California, Chicano Studies Research Center, 1983), pp. 325–369.

F.C.

MEXICANS, labor mobility. Roberts (*infra*) examines the economic factors that affect labor allocation of rural landholding households in four areas of Mexico. The original research was considerably narrower, focusing on the "push factors" causing illegal migration to the United States. However, it soon became apparent that restricting the analysis to U.S. migration would make it impossible to distinguish between factors that cause members of households to work off-farm in general, and those that condition this wage labor to take various forms, such as local labor, circular or permanent migration within Mexico, or migration to the United States. At its broadest level, this is a study of the relationship between rural development and labor mobility. There are a number of interesting theoretical issues involved, especially those raised by the emerging literature on circulation and on peasant household decision making. This study, however, will keep the issue of undocumented migration as its central theme. Its conclusions challenge the assumption of an inverse relationship between rural economic development and undocumented migration. There are important implications for the effectiveness of development programs in slowing the long-term outflow of rural migrants. This study also sheds light on the suitability of a guest worker program as an "interim" solution to the current insufficiency of job opportunities in Mexico and high levels of illegal migration to the United States.

Reference
Kenneth D. Roberts, "Agricultural Development and Labor Mobility: A Study of Four Mexican Subregions," in Richard C. Jones, ed., *Patterns of Undocumented Migration: Mexico and the United States* (1984), pp. 74–92.

F.C.

MEXICANS, macro-patterns of undocumented migration. Approximately 100,000 to 300,000 people annually come to the United States, constituting between 3 and 10 percent of the total U.S. population growth. It is also clear that the typical migrant is young, male, and usually unskilled in nonagricultural work. He is poor, but not among the poorest from his village. He usually (in 60 percent of the cases) comes from a small town or rural area in Mexico, but is usually (in 70 percent of the cases) destined for an urban area in the United States. He seldom makes a planned, discretionary move, but is driven by episodic economic necessity at the origin and thus is most properly referred to as an "economic refugee." He spends six months to a year in the United States before returning to Mexico, and makes four or five such trips in a lifetime. Therefore, he is a temporary as opposed to a permanent migrant. Finally, while sending home one-third of his earnings on the average, he makes few claims on local social services and is quite pleased to work at wages below the legal minimum. Because of his limited participation in skilled occupations, his high productivity in unskilled work, his temporary status, his scant demand on social services, and his acceptance of low wages, the undocumented Mexican's impact on the host society may well be positive or at least neutral.

Reference
Richard C. Jones, ed., *patterns of Undocumented Migration. Mexico and the United States* (1984).

F.C.

MEXICANS, Mexican-American politics. Skerry (*infra*) concludes:

> For while there may be certain sociological similarities between Mexicans and the classic American ethnic groups, there are important differences. I have already mentioned the unique situation of the Mexican in the American Southwest. It is also significant that Mexican Americans today are dealing with a political and social system vastly different from that confronting European immigrants several generations ago. Mexican American politicians today, for example, lack the patronage resources that earlier ethnic politicians used to lure their countrymen into the political arena. Then, too, Mexican Americans are raising questions about ethnic politics and cultural pluralism at a time when the old rules and understandings are challenged and changing.

Reference
Peter Skerry, "The Ambiguity of Mexican American Politics," in Nathan Glazer, ed., *Clamor at the Gates: The New American Immigration* (1985), pp. 241–257.

F.C.

MEXICANS, Mexican migrants and United States responsibility. Hundreds of thousands of Mexican citizens now travel illegally back and forth across the 1,945-mile border stretching from the Pacific Ocean to the Gulf of Mexico, leaving home to seek work. U.S. treatment of these Mexican migrants has taken on enormous importance for both national governments and, of course, for the Mexican workers themselves and those Americans who may resist or welcome their coming. One of the most prominent suggestions for a U.S. response to the current illegal flow is to legitimize it through the creation of temporary worker programs. Are temporary worker programs desirable or feasible? How many workers should be permitted to come, and for how long? What benefits and protections should temporary workers be granted? What corresponding obligations should they incur? Controversial questions raised by proposed U.S.-Mexican temporary worker programs are examined (*infra*) in light of historical precedents, current labor patterns and conditions in both countries, and philosophical analyses of human rights and international obligations. Multidisciplinary experts drawn from Mexico, the United States, and Europe consider recent proposals against a background of seemingly similar programs, such as the bracero program earlier in this century and the European *Gastarbeiter* experience.

Reference
Peter G. Brown and Henry Shue, eds., *The Border That Joins: Mexican Migrants and U.S. Responsibility* (1983).

F.C.

MEXICANS, Mexican women. Ruiz presents both a statistical profile of Mexican women workers and a narrative examination of their relationship with trade unions. Using the 1980 census, as well as other materials, Ruiz compares occupational distribution, median incomes, and educational levels of Chicanas with those of Anglo, black, and American Indian women. Comparison of the median earnings of ethnic and Anglo women with those of Mexican and Anglo men reveals significant gender disparities. These cross-cultural and cross-gender perspectives illuminate the socioeconomic vulnerability of Chicana workers in particular and women in general. An analysis of obstacles facing female Hispanic industrial operatives illustrates their economic precariousness.

Reference
V. Ruiz, "Working for Wages: Mexican Women in the Southwest, 1930–1980" (Tucson, Arizona: Southwest Institute for Research on Women, The University of Arizona, Working Paper No. 19, 1984).

F.C.

MEXICANS, migration and rural development. United States migration policies and enforcement practices have adapted to the changing labor supply-demand situation. In the twenty years after World War II, Mexican immigrants were desired principally as field laborers in agriculture. The contract labor system of 1942–1964, the bracero program, and the deportation drive of 1954 (Operation Wetback) made it difficult for nonimmigrant Mexicans to find nonagricultural work. Operation Wetback cleared the undocumented migrants from the cities, forcing those interested in U.S. work to come as contract laborers in agriculture. By the late 1960s, however, as the demand for Mexican workers spread from agriculture to urban employment, immigration law enforcement could not keep up with events. Social security cards were easily obtained by undocumented workers until recently. The ebb and flow of hundreds of thousands of Mexicans across the border occurs largely outside the purview of U.S. immigration law.

Reference
Richard Mines, ''Network Migration and Mexican Rural Development: A Case Study,'' in Richard C. Jones, ed., *Patterns of Undocumented Migration: Mexico and the United States* (1984), pp. 136–155.

F.C.

MEXICANS, migration to the United States. In spite of the progress made in the identification and quantification of the socioeconomic characteristics of the Mexicans migrating to the United States, and in spite of the fact that there is a general consensus among the scientific community of both countries that the research findings of the last ten years have destroyed many of the myths surrounding this migratory phenomenon, there still exists an enormous gap between the consensus of the researchers of the phenomenon and public opinion reflected in the mass communication media of both countries.

Reference
Jorge Bustamente, ''The Mexicans Are Coming: From Ideology to Labor Relations,'' *International Migration Review* 17 (Summer 1983): 323–341.

F.C.

MEXICANS, *Nortēnos*. *Norteños* (citizens of northern Mexico) are said to be *pachos* (''bleached'') by their exposure to the United States. Does this bleaching extend to psychological constructs? Two studies were performed (see *infra*), one using managers from Guadalajara, Chihuahua, Texas, and Chicago. The study measured the needs for achievement, for affiliation, and for power. The second study used business owners, founders, and managers from Mexico City and Chihuahua and assessed the internal-external locus of control and traditional family ideology. The results showed that *norteños* were psychologically unique, but were not uniformly more similar to businessmen in the United States than to businessmen in the interior of Mexico. On each psychological construct the borderlands businessmen scored in the direction that would be most associated with business success. It appears that the borderlands businessmen, living on the border between two cultures, adopt those psychological characteristics from both cultures that are most associated with business success.

Reference
D. Cockrum and J. M. Redondo, ''Norteños as Pachos: A Psychological Phenomenon?'' paper presented at the Western Social Science Association 26th Annual Meeting, San Diego, California, April 28, 1984.

F.C.

MEXICANS, occupational and spatial mobility of undocumented migrants. Recent research on the spatial mobility of undocumented aliens to and within the United States has shown that over time they have dispersed northward. Research has not revealed much at all about the successive moves of individual migrants. The most popular conception is of undocumented migrants rooted to particular geographic localities year after year, by reason of kinship ties, fear of apprehension, lack of awareness of new opportunities, poverty, and the problems associated with adapting to new surroundings. This article shows that this impression is erroneous. Not only do migrants exhibit substantial geographic mobility, but it is of a highly organized nature. Furthermore, there is significant upward occupational mobility as well. Subsequent mobility levels off, however, once the migrant reaches the urban sector, despite the fact that undocumented aliens continue to travel long distances to undertake new jobs.

Reference
Richard C. Jones, et al., "Occupational and Spatial Mobility of Undocumented Migrants from Dolores Hidalgo, Guanajuato," in Richard C. Jones, ed., *Patterns of Undocumented Migration: Mexico and the United States* (1984), pp. 159–182.

F.C.

MEXICANS, Rand Corporation study. This study was undertaken to assess the current situation of Mexican immigrants in California and project future possibilities. It constructs a demographic profile of the immigrants, examines their economic effects on the state, and describes their socioeconomic integration into California society. To unify and interpret the extensive and varied data on which the study is based, it develops models of both the immigration and integration processes, and then uses these models to project future immigration flows.

Reference
K. F. McCarthy and R. B. Valdez, *Current and Future Effects of Mexican Immigration in California* (Santa Monica, California: The Rand Corporation, Executive Summary, November 1985).

F.C.

MEXICANS, rural development in Mexico and recent migration to the United States. Despite the much-heralded Green Revolution and the considerable expenditure of money and effort on agrarian reform and agricultural development by the Mexican government since 1920, hundreds of thousands of Mexicans have continued to migrate to the United States; 70 percent originate in just six states. This sending region, the states of Durango, Guanajuato, Jalisco, Michoacán, San Louis Potosi, and Zacatecas, has played this role during much of the twentieth century. The Mexican Revolution benefited the region by little, and subsequent

governmental agricultural policy decisions exacerbated rather than ameliorated conditions in the region. Agrarian reform created minifundios;
irrigation works were built elsewhere, income redistribution favored
others, and credit was too scarce or too dear. The Green Revolution
bypassed the ordinary farmer, for its technological and fiscal requirements were beyond his means. Predictably, residents of the region have
been "pushed" out of their homelands into large Mexican cities, especially on the border with the United States, or into the United States,
sometimes after a sojourn in such border cities as Tijuana.

Reference
Harry E. Cross and James A. Sandos, *Across the Border: Rural Development in Mexico
and Recent Migration to the United States* (1981).

F.C.

**MEXICANS, rural exodus in Mexico and Mexican migration to the
United States.** In the 1950s, labor conditions in the United States attracted Mexican migrants, mostly from rural areas, in sharply fluctuating patterns of active recruitment, laissez-faire, or repatriation. Because
these two movements have varied simultaneously and because they are
interrelated, it has been assumed that the rural exodus in Mexico generally explains the flow of migrants across the border to the United States.
They must, however, be analyzed instead as two distinct movements.
Data show that most of the migrants created by the prevailing conditions
in Mexican rural villages settle within Mexico, and that only specific
types of migrants are attracted over the border.

Reference
Lourdes Arizpe, "The Rural Exodus in Mexico, and Mexican Migration to the United
States," *International Migration Review* 15 (Winter 1981): 626–649.

F.C.

MEXICANS, source regions of illegal Mexican immigration. Most
illegal Mexicans come from the west-central section of Mexico, which
also furnished labor for the bracero program that employed 400,000
Mexicans in the United States each year from 1943 to 1964. Young
mestizo men from this rural area continue to respond to historical patterns of legal recruitment as well as to illegal smugglers.

Reference
W. Tim Dagodag, "Source Regions and Compositions of Illegal Mexican Immigration to
California," *International Migration Review* 9 (1975): 499–511.

F.C.

MEXICANS, temporary migration to the United States. Wiest analyzes migration from a single rural community in northern Michoacan in

terms of recent theoretical developments that for general purposes may be referred to as dependency theory. The first treats the explanation of migration and its effects, and deals briefly with the essential elements of the ''dependency'' approach; he argues for attention to long-term structural features of social systems based in the production process which involves all humans. The specific context of migration dealt with in this essay is then treated. This provides some sense of history of the process as well as the peculiarities of the case discussed. The main part of the essay details several specific impacts of migration that perpetuate and increase external dependency. Various elements of this increased dependency are discussed.

Reference
Raymond E. Wiest, ''External Dependency and the Perpetuation of Temporary Migration to the United States,'' in Richard C. Jones, ed., *Patterns of Undocumented Migration: Mexico and the United States* (1984), pp. 110–135.

F.C.

MEXICANS, twentieth-century migration to the United States. Contemporary migration from Mexico is quite different from migration in the 1920s and 1950s, two decades with high rates of immigration from Mexico. Mexico's population is 70 million, compared with 25 million in 1950 and 16 million in 1920. Thus, the number of potential immigrants is much larger. Similarly, the Mexican-American population of the United States is 8 to 10 million compared with under 3 million in 1950. The larger Mexican population of the United States provides a cultural and knowledge environment that facilitates additional migration. Fogel (*infra*) argues that the current migration is not very sensitive to shifts in the demand for labor in the United States but, more than in the past, is driven by population and labor force growth in Mexico. The analysis of the data on Mexican migration is consistent with this conclusion, although the available data do not permit definitive results. These findings have important implications for the United States because Mexican immigrants have much lower earnings than other immigrants and their offspring fail to catch up with other native-born white Americans. The current large migration from Mexico amounts to a rapid enlargement of a disadvantaged group.

Reference
Walter Fogel, ''Twentieth-Century Mexican Migration to the United States,'' in Barry R. Chiswick, ed., *The Gateway: U.S. Immigration Issues and Policies* (1982), pp. 193–221.

F.C.

MEXICANS, undocumented Mexicans. Warren and Passel estimated (1984) that nearly two-thirds of Mexican-born noncitizens entering the

U.S. during 1975–1980 and included in the 1980 census are undocumented immigrants. This study (*infra*) used the 1980 Public Use Microfiles to delineate four Mexican origin immigrant status groups—post-1975 Mexican-born noncitizens, pre-1975 Mexican-born noncitizens, self-reported naturalized citizens, and native-born Mexican-Americans. The pattern of sociodemographic differences among these groups provides support for the idea that the first two categories contain a substantial fraction of undocumented immigrants. These two groups (especially the first) reveal characteristics that one would logically associate with undocumented immigrants—age concentration (in young adult years), high sex ratios, low education and income levels, and lack of English proficiency.

Reference

Frank D. Bean et al., ''The Sociodemographic Characteristics of Mexican Immigrant Status Groups: Implications for Studying Undocumented Mexicans,'' *International Migration Review* 18 (Fall 1984): 672–691.

F.C.

MEXICANS, undocumented workers. Researchers are finding that the Mexican undocumented worker population is more heterogeneous than once assumed. In the past, *campesinos*—male farmhands—filled the ranks of undocumented workers. While Mexico's agricultural workers continue to venture north in search of employment, illegal migration is expanding throughout Mexico's social structure. Today's Mexican economic refugees are both urban dwellers and *campesinos,* both men and women. The diversity of adaptation to working and living in the United States parallels the heterogeneity of the undocumented worker population. There is the well-researched pattern of the migrant farm worker whose stay in the United States is limited to the harvest season. While many migrants move from state to state, others return each year from Mexico to the same U.S. agricultural center. Another pattern is common in the twin cities of the *fronteras* or border region. Here Mexicans work in the United States and routinely, often daily, commute back to Mexico. Permanent settlement in the United States is yet another pattern. The most committed of these permanent settlers will probably stay in the United States as long as gainful economic opportunities are available for them.

Reference

Reynaldo Baca and Dexter Bryan, ''Mexican Undocumented Workers in the Binational Community: A Research Note,'' *International Migration Review* 15 (Winter 1981): 737–748.

F.C.

MIAMI REPORT, *The Miami Report. Recommendations on United States Policy Toward Latin America and the Caribbean* (Coral Gables, Florida, 1983). This report represents the Miami community's call for response to an economic and political crisis. Its recommendations for U.S. policy on immigration are the following: (1) Support principles protecting the rights of potential immigrants and those seeking asylum; (2) Assert these principles by diplomatic means and in international organizations; (3) Enact legislation to grant residence status of undocumented aliens now in the United States; (4) Impose sanctions on those employing undocumented immigrants, while protecting the rights of U.S. citizens and lawfully admitted immigrants; (5) Establish control over the borders of the United States with due respect for the human rights of persons intercepted; and (6) Establish a reasonable, regulated, and orderly migration process for the surplus populations in the Caribbean Basin, including the establishment of special quotas.

F.C.

MID-EUROPEAN UNION. *See* Miller, Herbert A.

MIGRANT LABOR, and industrial societies. Michael Priore seeks simultaneously to provide a coherent theoretical analysis of labor migrations in industrial societies and to demonstrate the inadequacy of conventional economic theory in accounting for structural features of the labor market in such societies. He deals with the specificity of labor migration as a social phenomenon while pointing the way toward its integration into a more general macrosociology of industrial societies. He draws from a wide range of empirical cases concerning North America and Western Europe, some of which are founded on the author's own previous research on both continents. He is more concerned with analysis and interpretation than with description, and the study is therefore addressed mainly to readers already familiar with the literature surveying contemporary migratory trends as well as with the policy and theoretical controversies surrounding them.

Reference
Michael J. Priore, *Birds of Passage: Migrant Labor and Industrial Societies* (1979).

F.C.

MIGRATION, and employment. Preliminary investigation confirms a previous observation that the employment rate of migrants is generally lower than that of nonmigrants. Further analysis suggests that this does not mean that migration has no effect on employment; the two appear to be strongly related: "Migration enables some unemployed and initially disadvantageous persons to improve their employment status, making it more nearly comparable, though not equal to that of the general population'' (Li).

Reference
W. L. Li, ''A Note on Migration and Employment,'' *Demography* 13 (Nov. 1976): 565– 570.

F.C.

MIGRATION, economics of labor migration. Mueller views migration as a choice made in each time period among alternative destinations, with the origin as one destination. The characteristics of the individual and the various potential destinations enter the decision regarding the optimal destination. Multinominal logit (MNL) procedures are used to estimate the equations. Mueller defines a migrant as a worker who changed county of employment in 1969. The data are from the Social Security Administration's Longitudinal Employer-Employee Data file (LEED) which contains work histories from 1957 to 1969 for persons in covered employment. The file includes information on the employee's age, sex and race, as well as the location (county), industry, and wages for each job.

Reference
Charles F. Mueller, *The Economics of Labor Migration: A Behavioral Analysis* (1982).

F.C.

MIGRATION, international migration and taxation. This subject comprises two main issues. The first is the question of the appropriate exercise of income tax jurisdiction, whether it ought to be on the basis of citizenship, as in the United States and the Philippines, or on the basis of residence, as in the European countries and most less-developed countries. This question arises from the theoretical and policy discussions of the proposal to tax the ''brain drain,'' or emigration of skilled labor. The sending countries could impose the tax on their emigrants. Such a tax would require a change in U.S. policy only insofar as the sending countries seek bilateral treaties for a sharing of tax information to facilitate their enforcement. The second issue is one of sharing revenue in proportion to the taxes paid by the immigrants. Under such a scheme, the receiving countries, for example, the United States, would share the tax revenues raised in the normal course of events from immigrants with the countries of origin.

Reference
Jagdish N. Bhagwati, ''Taxation and International Migration: Recent Policy Issues,'' in

Barry R. Chiswick, ed., *The Gateway: U.S. Immigration Issues and Policies* (1982), pp. 36–103.

F.C.

MIGRATION, irregular. Three basic obstacles thwart all attempts to reduce irregular migration. The first, rather well known and analyzed, underscores the dependency of all regulation of migratory flows on the system of economic and political relations between developed and developing countries. The second obstacle resides in the persistence and growth of subsequent dependent irregular migration. This obstacle also reveals the relative autonomy of population movements compared with the employment situation in the labor market. The third, generally ignored obstacle, is the role played by migration itself, particularly the discriminatory status of foreign workers in the labor market, in producing irregular migration.

Reference
Yann Moulier-Boutang and Jean Pierre Garson, "Major Obstacles to Control of Irregular Migrations: Prerequisites to Policy," *International Migration Review* 18 (Fall 1984): 579–592.

F.C.

MIGRATION, patterns since World War II. Governmental policies are important in determining postwar migration patterns in Europe and North America. Nations have routinely regulated both the exit of nationals—by expulsion and by forcible retention—and the entrance of immigrants. Political and economic considerations have helped to define such policies, sometimes complementing each other and sometimes contradicting. In the United States between about 1920 and 1965, for example, economic interests dictated free entry of labor while political considerations encouraged the restriction of immigration on the grounds of national security. A compromise resulted from this conflict: entry became more difficult for Asians and southern and eastern Europeans, while Western Hemisphere immigration remained almost unregulated, providing a loophole that permitted the entry of Mexican and French Canadian laborers.

Reference
Aristide Zolberg, "Migration Patterns Since World War II in Europe and the Americas," *Immigration History Newsletter* 9 (May 1977): 1–2.

F.C.

MIGRATORY LABOR, Commission on Migratory Labor (1951). *See* Operation Wetback.

MILL CHILDREN: 1903 MARCH. *See* Jones, Mary Harris.

MILLER, HERBERT A[DOLPHUS] (1875–1951). Professor of sociology at Oberlin College, and a student of Czechs and other small national groupings in Central Europe. As a result of his interest in immigration problems, and his admiration of the Slavs, Miller became the principal organizer and guiding spirit of the Mid-European Union which sought a solution to the conflicting territorial aspirations of Central European nationalities. Miller's chief work is *Races, Nations and Classes* (1924). He is the author, also (with Robert E. Park [*q.v.*]), of *Old World Traits Transplanted* (1921; rpt. 1971). A contributor to the work was W.I. Thomas (*q.v.*), the Chicago sociologist. The work was a counterthrust to the arguments favoring compulsory Americanization, and was part of "Americanization Studies: The Acculturation of Immigrant Groups Into American Society," commissioned by the Carnegie Corporation (*q.v.*).

F.C.

MINERS NATIONAL ASSOCIATION. *See* Siney, John.

MINNESOTA, and the competition for immigrants. Despite the fact that their campaigns have received only scant attention, territorial and state immigration agencies actively promoted immigration to the West for three-quarters of a century following the Civil War. Minnesota was among the first to accept the responsibility of promoting settlement, with the appointment of an immigration commissioner in 1855. Although this position existed for only two years, the state resumed promotion in 1864. It continued its immigration program until 1927, when the board was permanently abolished. Between 1864 and 1927 Minnesota spent over $550,000 to promote the settlement of its lands. The methods used by Minnesota to attract immigrants included the employment of honorary and salaried agents, displays at fairs and exhibits, advertising in American and foreign newspapers, and the publication and distribution of more than 3 million pieces of promotional literature.

Reference
Peter J. Bistuben, "Minnesota and the Competition for Immigrants," Ph.D. dissertation, University of Oklahoma, 1964.

F.C.

MITCHEL, JOHN PURROY (1879–1919). Lawyer, politician. Mitchel was elected mayor of New York City on a fusion ticket in 1913. The Mitchel administration (1914–17) was a reform administration and fought political corruption and crime, particularly in immigrant neighborhoods. It waged a relentless campaign against Black Hand crime in Italian immigrant communities (*see* Black Hand).

Reference
Edwin R. Lewinson, *John Purroy Mitchel, The Boy Mayor of New York* (1965).

T.M.P.

MITROVICH, STEPHEN N. *See* Montenegrins.

MOBILE, ALABAMA: AS PORT OF ENTRY. *See* Immigrants in the Old South.

MODJESKA, HELENA (1840–1909). Actress, Polish nationalist. Modjeska was both a famous actress in her homeland and an activist in the cause of Polish nationalism. In 1876 she joined a group of Polish immigrants who formed a cooperative farm in the Santa Ana valley of California. Modjeska devotes a small portion of her memoirs to her encounter with communal living. By January 1877 the farm began to ail and Modjeska, to provide the needed funds, resumed her acting career. She learned English and conducted a successful tour of the eastern United States, but by the summer of 1878 the colony had disbanded.

Reference
Helena Modjeska, *Memories and Impressions of Helena Modjeska: An Autobiography* (1910).

F.C.

MOLEK, MARY (1909–1982). Museum curator, archivist. Molek was a member of the Yugoslav Socialist Federation in the 1930s and 1940s and a leading contributor to its newspaper, *Prosveta* (Chicago), edited by her husband, Ivan Molek. Her autobiography *Immigrant Woman* (1976) portrays Slovenian-American working-class life in the first decades of the twentieth century.

F.C.

MOLLY MAGUIRES. Long a symbol for industrial violence, the Molly Maguires was an Irish-Catholic secret society ''conceived in treason and dedicated to lawlessness.'' The Mollies were members of the Ancient Order of Hibernians who had rebelled against their English landlords in Ireland, and now rebelled against English mine owners in America. For a decade its members terrorized the coal fields of eastern Pennsylvania until the antilabor head of the Philadelphia and Reading Railroad (operator of most of the mines) arranged for the Pinkerton Detective Agency to send one of its ablest operatives (McParlan) into the coal fields. McParlan won his way into the organization, enjoyed the confidence of the men, became a Molly leader, and planned and led in the execution of some of their outrageous exploits. As a result the authorities were able to arrest, convict, and hang many Mollies in 1875.

Reference
J. Walter Coleman, *The Molly Maguire Riots: Industrial Conflict in the Pennsylvania Coal Region* (1936; rpt., 1974).

F.C.

MONTENEGRINS. When Emily G. Balch in her standard work *Our Slavic Fellow Citizens* introduced the almost completely unknown South Slavs to the Americans, she barely mentioned the Montenegrins. They are the smallest of South Slavic peoples. Their rocky homeland, north of Albania and near the southern Adriatic, is Montenegro (Crna Gora), meaning literally [the country of] "the Black Mountains." Alfred Lord Tennyson calls it in his sonnet the "smallest among peoples . . . rough rock-throne of Freedom" whose warriors were "beating back the swarm of Turkish Islam for five hundred years." American publisher W. Jovanovich (whose father was a Montenegrin immigrant) remarked in his introduction to the book *The Land Without Justice* (dealing with Montenegro) by Milovan Djilas, a native of Montenegro and the leading dissident in Yugoslavia: "The legend of Montenegro rests on history. One who values a man's courage and a nation's freedom will recognize that the history of Montenegro, in the daring and suffering of its people, generation after generation, is unequaled in Europe."

Its people, a mixture of Croatians, Serbs, Albanians, and descendants of Romans are—like Albanians—divided in clans and are (since the 1500s) predominantly Eastern Orthodox in religion. Originally called Dioclea, then Zeta, Montenegro was partly overrun by Turks. The tallest race in Europe, excellent guerilla fighters, and used to sparse living, the Montenegrins waged for centuries wars against Turks and all other Moslem neighbors. From the time of Peter the Great, imperial Russia, as protector of all Orthodox Slavs, subsidized Montenegro. One of the poorest countries in Europe, it depended on such aid as well as on plunder and raids against Moslems.

Until 1851 it was a theocratic state ruled by a prince-bishop from the Petrović family. One of the best-known was Petar II Petrović-Njegoš (ruled 1830–1851), the poet and philosopher; he wrote the epic *The Mountain Wreath* (Gorski Vijenac), one of the greatest works in South Slavic literature and dear to every Montenegrin wherever he may live. Montenegro's symbol is Mount Lovćen on whose top Njegoš is buried. In its vicinity is the little capital of Cetinje. Wherever a Montenegrin goes he carries with him the memory of Lovćen, his "holy mountain."

With constant warfare, Montenegro kept expanding at the expense of its neighbors. In 1878 the Congress of Berlin recognized its independence. The last ruler, and the most loyal ally of Russia, was Prince Nikola Petrović who in 1910 assumed title of king. In the Balkan Wars (1912–13) he led his people in the final struggle for liberation from Turks. The country's size was now increased to 5,600 square miles and some 290,000 inhabitants.

Among the first Montenegrin emigrants to America were those living in the region of Boka Kotorska, the Bay of Kotor, which was a part of Austrian-ruled southern Dalmatia. They accompanied their Croatian neighbors and employers to Louisiana and the West. In New Orleans in the South, in San Francisco and in other cities in the West, mixed with the Croatians were numerous Montenegrin pioneers. The natives called them "Slavonians." During and after the gold rush some Montenegrins joined Croatians and Serbs in San Joaquin Valley. In 1857 the Montenegrins founded, in San Francisco, a Slavonian-Russian-Greek Orthodox Church and Benevolent Society; its president was the Russian consul.

Nikola and Ilija Dabović were among the eminent Montenegrin settlers. Many of their relatives and clansmen lived in and around Jackson, Amador County. They prospered here as miners and merchants. With their Dalmatian friends they established several mining companies. In Jackson and Sutter Creek numerous Montenegrins settled along with the Serbs with whom they shared the same religion. In 1863, Nikola Bieladenovich, in partnership with two Dalmatians, founded the Illyrian Gold and Silver Mining Company in the San Domingo District of Calaveras County. A pioneer in Los Angeles was Ivan Lazarevich, who after a career as a gold miner during the 1850s came here, married an American woman, and raised a large family.

Rev. Sebastian Dabović, born in 1863 in San Francisco, and the son of Nikola Dabović, graduated from the Russian Theological Seminary in St. Petersburg, the capital of Russia. Ordained a priest in 1887, he returned to America and became the first missionary among the Montenegrins and Serbs. A saintly man and a devoted spiritual leader of his people, he was also a great patriot. He rushed with hundreds of volunteers to participate in the Balkan Wars and in World War I. He died in 1940 in the monastery Žića. What Baraga was for the Slovenians and Consag for the Croatians, Dabović was for the Montenegrins and Serbs.

Quite prominent was Stephen N. Mitrovich who came to Fresno, California in 1880 from most southern tip of Dalmatia (adjacent to Montenegro). Over the years he established a new industry: the growing and drying of figs, a new item in American markets. He too took part in the Balkan Wars and was decorated for bravery by King Nikola.

Events in the Old Country kept influencing the life of the Balkan immigrants in America. In June 1903, in Belgrade, the capital of Serbia, the army officers, in a bloody coup, overthrew the Obrenović dynasty, killing King Milan and his wife. They brought to the throne Peter Karageorgevich, who was son-in-law of the ruler of Montenegro. The new dynasty then tried by acts of violence to overthrow the Petrović dynasty in order to annex Montenegro to Serbia. These events caused a sharp division between the Montenegrins and Serbs in America. After 1903 the Montenegrins lived a more separated existence and to their societies and organizations they gave Montenegrin names.

After 1885 several thousand Montenegrins settled in Montana. In and around Butte, a lively and prosperous mining settlement, they formed a sizable colony, and banded together in a military fashion, a carry-over from the old country. When gold was discovered in Alaska many of them rushed there. As mountaineers used to harsh conditions, they didn't mind the cold climate. In other parts of the country, like Colorado, the Montenegrins left an unenviable reputation for low-grade living. However, this was observed also among other South Slavs who had come from very poor regions of the Balkans. Until the high tide of immigration preceding World War I, very few women were among the Montenegrin immigrants.

In 1906 the First Montenegrin Federation and the Serb Montenegrin Federation were established in Butte, Montana. On account of the political struggle between Montenegro and Serbia, bitter feuds arose between the Montenegrins and Serbs because the Serbian nationalists (encouraged by diplomatic representatives of Serbia) openly advocated the absorption of Montenegro by Serbia. Some joint Serbian-Montenegrin societies split and the Montenegrins founded separate organizations, which combined fraternal, political, and social functions.

During the long rule of Nikola Petrović (1860–1918)—whose one daughter became the queen of Italy and two others became Russian grand duchesses—under constant threat of an absorption by Serbia, the Montenegrins at home and in America definitely emerged as a separate nation. Most of the Montenegrins who immigrated came to America during Nikola's rule.

When in 1907 the United States counted some 27,000 as "Bulgarians, Servians and Montenegrins," more than 10 percent of these were Montenegrins. For a small country of some 290,000 inhabitants (in 1912), several thousand emigrants a year was a considerable drain of population. Among the "Dalmatians, Bosnians and Herzegovinians" (a puzzling category of our immigration authorities), quite a few were Montenegrins who lived in Austrian territory.

As early as 1905, Emily G. Balch, collecting information for her

Our Slavic Fellow Citizens, visiting Cetinje, found out that the authorities kept no statistics on emigrants. However, she found out from an Austrian agent in nearby Austrian-controlled Dalmatia that some 2,000 Montenegrins were leaving annually for the United States. A considerable number were going to Alaska where, in Douglas, a Montenegrin newspaper was printed.

Many Montenegrins headed for Pennsylvania, probably the best-known of all American states among all South Slavs. A large number went to Illinois, Minnesota, and parts of the West. Almost all of these immigrants were unskilled laborers eager to work at any kind of hard and dangerous jobs, many times jobs that Americans and other immigrants avoided.

Some joined the old settlers in the West where some Montenegrins had become wealthy and prosperous. Very few women were among them. They had to stay in the homeland to raise children, work on the land, and keep the ancestral hearth fires burning. *Ognjište,* or the hearth, was in all mountainous lands, stretching all the way from Trieste in the north to Scutari in the south, the symbol of a family's continuity. It had to be tended, it had to be kept burning for the present and future generations. The women of Montenegro were the patient guardians of these ancestral hearth fires.

The authorities in Cetinje were reluctant to issue passports to prospective emigrants, especially after they learned that in 1903 a group of 100 Montenegrins was rejected by immigration authorities at Ellis Island. The prospective emigrants were leaving by way of nearby Austrian-ruled Dalmatia. Many also left for America by way of Trieste after receiving necessary papers by Austrian agents.

In Montenegro every man regardless of his age was considered a soldier. Even those in America were considered soldiers on leave. In Butte, Montana and some other places where many Montenegrins lived, they marched in military fashion to and from work. In the period between 1904 and 1907 alone there were some 15,000 Montenegrins regarded by their country as soldiers on leave. On the eve of the Balkan Wars in 1912, well over 30,000 Montenegrins were residents in America; thousands of them returned home to fight in Balkan Wars. Hundreds of them perished in fighting the Turks.

Of the 11,543 "Bulgarian, Servian and Montenegrin" immigrants in 1906, fully 96 percent were listed as unskilled laborers. Some 80 percent of Montenegrins were completely illiterate because there were few elementary schools in Montenegro. Most of those that stayed in America learned to read and write. In America they worked hard performing mostly the most difficult and dangerous jobs. Virtually hundreds of them died in industrial accidents, especially in mines where death united many of the South Slavs.

Physically strong and possessed with natural intelligence, these mountaineers were in America diligent and vigorous workers, gaining respect from their American foremen and employers. Most of them came as temporary immigrants to spend here a few years in hard and hazardous labor, to save some dollars, and then to return to their stony and bleak mountains.

There were many reasons why they came. Theirs was one of the poorest countries in Europe; there was too little arable land where they lived under the most primitive conditions. The Montenegrin standard of living was the lowest in Europe. Before and after the turn of the century most of the men became tired of constant warfare either with the Turks or on many occasions between the clans where the blood feud was practiced. (Sometimes the blood feuds were carried over to America to the lawless towns of the West.) The inherited fear of feuding clans was stronger than the fear and hatred of the enemy, the Turk. And there was a great deal of dissatisfaction with the autocratic rule of the chieftains and the prince. They heard the fabulous stories from their Dalmatian neighbors about the life and high living standards of America and decided to leave.

As Edward A. Steiner and Louis Adamic observed in their writings, there was no more sturdy stock of Europe than the Montenegrin, "none more ready to turn from gun to the wood axe, from blood revenge to citizenship." They were described as tough guys, agile and hardy, fearless, diligent, proud people, impatient, ambitious, and naturally intelligent and inventive, despising life if it is separated from freedom. They worked hard and they—like other Slavs—had their "American Dream." They also participated in many labor struggles before and after World War I. In the winter and spring of 1913–14, among the strikers in Colorado who were finally suppressed by the National Guard in the infamous Ludlow Massacre, there were some Montenegrins who were the returned veterans of the Balkan Wars. To any Montenegrin any kind of existence in America was a vast improvement over the conditions he had left behind. But a price had to be paid, sometimes in blood.

Almost everywhere where Slavs struggled and labored the Montenegrins were present. However, after the Balkan Wars (1912–13) when Serbia openly embarked on a policy whose goal was a Greater Serbia and the elimination of Montenegro, the relations in America between the Montenegrins and Serbs turned from bad to worse. Already at the Serbian Congress in San Francisco, two years before the Balkan Wars, in June 1910, the Serbs vigorously denounced the king of Montenegro. Stephen N. Mitrovich (the pioneer of the fig industry), a great admirer of the king, sued the *Serbian Herald;* it was obliged to retract and apologize.

During World War I the relations between the American Serbs and

Montenegrins grew even worse. In late 1915 and early 1916, Montenegro was overrun by superior Austrian forces, and King Nikola fled the country for exile in France where a Montenegrin government in exile was formed. Before the country was overrun two of the king's representatives arrived in America and recruited several thousand Montenegrins for military service in the Balkans. As the Serbian representatives in America denounced King Nikola and advocated the absorption of Montenegro by Serbia at the war's end, the animosities between the diplomatic representatives of the two countries and both ethnic groups—Montenegrin and Serbian—increased steadily. Under strong Serbian pressure the Montenegrins in America became divided; while some were in favor of a union with the Serbian kingdom, others, like the group around *Crnogorski Glasnik* (The Montenegrin Messenger) in Detroit advocated a future South Slavic republic composed of equal partners. The activities of Montenegrin opponents of a royal Yugoslavia were hampered by agents of Serbia.

On May 6, 1918, in Rome, King Nikola of Montenegro handed the U.S. ambassador a document expressing the hope of his government that America, "the champion of liberty and Democracy," would help preserve the independence of his country which was mentioned in Point XI of President Wilson's Fourteen Points in January 1918. In August 1918 in New York the Montenegrin Committee for National Unification issued a memorandum signed by 126 leading Montenegrins repudiating King Nikola and demanding a future South Slavic state without an independent Montenegro. At the end of 1918 and early 1919, the Serbian troops occupied—after fierce resistance by thousands of Montenegrins—the centuries-old rocky asylum of freedom. Whole villages were razed. Thousands of civilians and fighting clansmen were killed. Only a few hundred managed to flee and make their way to America. Nikola's grandson Alexander Karageorgevich incorporated Montenegro. The old king died soon in exile in France, a brokenhearted man. A majority of the American Montenegrins mourned the death of their king and the loss of their state. The new political situation in the homeland created among the South Slavic immigrants, including the Montenegrins, lasting divisions, tensions, and feuds.

In 1921 with the creation of the Serbian Orthodox Diocese of the United States, under the jurisdiction of the Serbian Patriarch in Belgrade, all Orthodox Montenegrins became subject to it. By now the Socialist movements were strong among all South Slavs and many of them ceased their loyalty to their respective churches. With their fellow Socialists (especially the Bulgarians and Macedonians) the Montenegrins remained active politically, socially, and culturally during the 1920s–1930s period. Communism from Soviet Russia (the traditional protector of Montenegro) won over many Montenegrins. They became especially active in 1941, after Yugoslavia was overrun and partitioned by Germans, Bulgarians, Italians, and Hungarians. In July 1941, a group of nationalists, with Italian assistance, proclaimed an independent Montenegrin state. It was short-lived; it was crushed by Communist partisans who defeated the nationalist Chetniks. In a bitter civil war Montenegro and surrounding Balkan regions witnessed a wholesale butchery of thousands of innocent civilians. The news reported by the U.S. media about these events influenced the political activities in Montenegrin and other South Slavic settlements in America. The Montenegrins joined other South Slavs in pro-Soviet Communist front organizations that worked for the cause of a Communist Yugoslavia. Tito's National Liberation Front in the old country was victorious. In the newly established Socialist and federative Yugoslavia Montenegro was one of the six republics. The first 1946 Constitution recognized the Montenegrins as a separate and distinct nationality.

In New Orleans and in many places in the West these immigrants of several generations have achieved considerable success. After 1945 several thousands of their compatriots joined them either as "displaced persons" or, in later years, as immigrants from Yugoslavia. Savo Radulovich, who was during World War II in General Mark Clark's army, gained fame for his drawings and paintings of battlefront scenes. William Jovanovich, born in Colorado (his father was Montenegrin), at the age of thirty-four became the president of Harcourt, Brace and Co. In 1964 he published his *Now, Barabbas* where he also discusses the national identity of the Montenegrins. The last wife of Frank Lloyd Wright, America's greatest architect, was Olga J. Lazovich, whose father was the Supreme Court justice in Montenegro. After her husband's death in 1959, she established a very interesting commune in the West. The Montenegrins and their descendants are now in all walks of American life. The post–World War II immigration brought virtually thousands of skilled and professional people, a real "brain drain" from Yugoslavia.

The U.S. census of 1970 counted only 447,273 people whose country of origin was Yugoslavia. Of these probably 10 percent are of Montenegrin origin, and of some 4,000–5,000 yearly immigrants from Yugoslavia coming here during the past forty-odd years an estimated 10 percent are Montenegrins. They should be treated in the United States as a distinct nationality group. In the last census of 1981, the Yugoslav authorities counted 577,000 Montenegrins. While many Serbian scholars, in the homeland and abroad, regard the Montenegrins as Serbs, an increasing number of scholars in the Socialist Republic of Montenegro stress the existence of a separate Montenegrin nation based on historical, linguistic, and ethnical factors.

In the colorful mosaic of present-day America Montenegrins have earned a distinct and worthy place.

References
Oto Bihalji-Merin, ed., *Montenegro, Yugoslavia* (1961); Milovan Djilas, *Montenegro* (1962); George J. Prpic, *South Slavic Immigration in America* (1978); James W. Wiles, *The Mountain Wreath of P.P. Nyegosh, Prince Bishop of Montenegro, 1830–1851* (1930); William Jovanovich, *Now, Barabbas* (1964).

G.J.P.

MORGAN, THOMAS J. (1847–1912). Labor leader. Born into a poor working-class family in Birmingham, England, Morgan emigrated to the United States in 1869. He settled in Chicago and was employed as a machinist and brass finisher. His conversion to socialism came as a result of his bitter experiences during the panic of 1873. A few years later he became the leading figure in the Chicago Socialist Labor party.

Reference
Ralph W. Scharnau, "Thomas J. Morgan and the Chicago Socialist Movement, 1876–1901," Ph.D. dissertation, Northern Illinois University, 1970.

F.C.

MORMONS. The Church of Jesus Christ of Latter-Day Saints, better known as the Mormon Church, has been since its founding in upstate New York in 1830 a vigorous missionary church, intent on preaching the "Restored Gospel" to all nations before the great winding up prophesied in Revelations. In the nineteenth century, particularly, Mormonism preached and promoted "the gathering" of the faithful to America as the Land of Zion in preparation for the Second Coming. Conversion was tantamount to emigration, or at least the expectation of it. In their several removes westward across the United States the Mormons accommodated themselves to a succession of centers for the ingathering (at Independence, Missouri, at Nauvoo, Illinois, and finally, in 1847, in the Valley of the Great Salt Lake), proselytizing with evangelical fervor in the United States itself and in Canada and missions opened in Great Britain (in 1837) and northern Europe (Scandinavia in 1850). At the same time they marshalled the practical means for bringing their convert-emigrants on a massive scale to Zion.

Millennial expectations have abated and "the gathering" is no longer preached nor practiced, but the records of missionary and immigration activity are extraordinarily complete: "the gathering" has left a rich historical legacy engraved on Mormon memory and imagination and preserved in thousands of documents at the headquarters of the church. From the mission and emigration records assembled there, the names of Mormon convert-emigrants may be followed from the membership and minute books of mission congregations, with their notation "emigrated to America," to the emigration ledgers kept at mission headquarters (Copenhagen for Scandinavia, Liverpool for England), to the log of the journey kept by the clerk appointed in every shipboard company, to the passenger lists copied from the National Archives of vessels arriving in the United States, to the announcement in the *Deseret News* of the arrival of emigrant companies in Salt Lake City, and finally to their entry as "members of record" in one of the congregations in Zion. Mormon shipping lists, manuscript mission histories, a manuscript history of "church emigration" providing a description of each organized emigrant company to 1869, the records of mission congregations, and a growing collection of personal literature—immigrant letters, journals, and memoirs—may all be found in the Library-Archives Division of the Historical Department (formerly known as the Historian's Office) of the church, their use facilitated by both traditional card files and, increasingly, computerized indexes, guides, and registers, more fully described below.

Mormon historical activity is matched by a genealogical program yielding an international harvest of records of great interest and utility to the immigrant historian. Although large-scale immigration is over, the Mormons pursue another kind of gathering in their search for ancestors to complete family lines that they believe will exist in eternity and will give the unbaptized dead the opportunity to embrace the truth in the spirit world by performing gospel ordinances for them on earth by proxy. The "work for the dead" has given rise to a prodigious effort on the part of the Genealogical Society of the church to microfilm vital records around the world, as well as every conceivable document bearing on genealogy. Microfilms of land grants, deeds, probate records, marriage records, obituary and cemetery records, parish registers, military, naturalization, business, professional, and college records, personal papers, local histories, diaries, autobiographies, and correspondence, censuses, immigration, and ships passenger lists—everything of genealogical value—are finding their way from dozens of countries into the society's Granite Mountain Records Vault, a vast storage facility tunneled into the solid granite of the Wasatch Mountains east of Salt Lake City. The vault, equipped with sophisticated systems for processing, preserving, reproducing, and retrieving the film, is designed to keep "the world's genealogical information recorded through the ages . . . safe from the ravages of nature and the destructions of man."

Of these vast archives, Mulder writes:

> The devotion of the church to history and genealogy, twin fields of
> endeavor intimately related in Mormon thought and practice, finds

expression in the administrative structure and, almost symbolically, in the assignment of space in the new high-rise General Church Office Building at 50 East North Temple Street, across from Temple Square in Salt Lake City: the Historical Department and the Genealogical Department (synonymous with the Society) occupy opposing, symmetrical wings. They are private institutions with a philosophy of public service. Their specialized collections are open to qualified users without charge. *A Guide to the Historical Department* and a comparable *Genealogical Library Guide* quickly acquaint the visitor with the resources of each, their organization and location, and the regulations governing their availability and use. The research scholar will discover that the physical facilities and finding aids are superb and the staff professional.

References
William Mulder, "Mormon Sources for Immigration History," *Immigration History Newsletter* 10 (Nov. 1978): 1–7; William Mulder, *The Mormons in American History* (1981).

D.N.A.

MORSE, SAMUEL F[INLEY] B[REESE] (1791–1872). Inventor and artist. A founder of the National Academy of Design in 1825, Morse was involved in the development of the electric telegraph and codes, particularly at New York University where he taught painting and design. Morse was actively involved in the nativist and anti-Catholic agitation of the 1830s, and his *Imminent Dangers to the Free Institutions of the United States* (1835) is an attack on immigrants whom Morse characterized as "the ignorant and vicious . . . the outcast tenants of the poorhouses and prisons of Europe . . . exported by their governments to our loss and their gain."

References
E. L. Morse, *Letters and Journals of S. F. B. Morse* (1914; rpt. 1973); Carlton Mabee, *Samuel F. B. Morse* (1973).

F.C.

MOTHER EARTH. *See* Goldman, Emma.

MUEHLENBERG, HEINRICH MELCHIOR (1711–1787). Lutheran clergyman, recognized as the "Patriarch der lutherischen Kirche Amerikas." Born in Einbeck, he graduated in theology from Goettingen (1738), and was ordained in Leipzig (1739). He accepted a call from G. A. Francke to go to America and arrived in Philadelphia in 1742. Through his efforts German Lutherans held the first convention of the Evangelical Lutheran Ministerium of Pennsylvania in 1748. He is considered the founder of the Lutheran Church in America.

References
Journals (3 vols., 1942–1958); W. J. Mann, *Heinrich Melchior Mühlenberg* (1911).

D.N.A.

MUIR, JOHN (1838–1914). Naturalist, explorer. A Scottish-born conservationist who dedicated his life to preserving America's wilderness area, Muir was the author of *My First Summer in the Sierra* (1869); *Mountains of California* (1894); *Stickeen* (1909); *The Yosemite* (1912); and *Story of My Boyhood and Youth* (1913).

References
Michael P. Cohen, *The Pathless Way: John Muir and American Wilderness* (1984); Frederick Turner, *Rediscovering America: John Muir in His Time and Ours* (1987).

F.C.

MULTICULTURAL EDUCATION. A new recognition of American diversity and an awakened interest in the ethnic roots of its people brought about by the rise of the "new ethnicity" or "new pluralism" movement during the 1960s and 1970s has received widespread attention in recent years. The fact that pluralism rather than uniformity represents social reality in the United States and that the American educational system mirrors the intergroup relations that exist within the society has given rise to a new educational concept—that of multicultural education—as a need for educating America for this "new pluralism."

Multicultural education may be defined as the process of incorporating in the school's curriculum studies in ethnicity, culture, and values reflecting the pluralistic nature of American society as a means of enrichment and the fostering of acceptance or tolerance of ethnic or cultural groups leading to the equalization of American society in all its aspects. Accordingly, multicultural education views cultural differences more positively than schools have in the past with their assimilative curriculum which sought to eradicate these differences; but it is at the same time traditional both in its objectives and methods. It seeks to teach American pupils the contributions of ethnic groups to the ongoing development of American culture and the recognition that American society is culturally pluralistic, while at the same time stressing the needs for individuals to have positive ties to their backgrounds and, continuing the intergroup education tradition of the 1930s and 1940s, aims at building tolerance through mutual understanding. In short, multicultural education seeks to stress the objective of enhanced harmony through education, thereby depolarizing American society.

As such, multicultural education is related to the solution of a variety of social and economic problems in American society. Initially, it denotes human or intergroup relations and has as its primary objective the lessening of prejudice. Curriculum guides and teaching supplements include myths of prejudice, bigotry, and discrimination and the evils of stereotyping. Additionally, multicultural education is viewed by many curriculum designers as a means of bringing about an egalitarian social order by promoting equal educational opportunity, economic equity, and integration, thus providing for affective as well as cognitive results.

Multicultural education, then, is a study of ethnic groups, the ethnic experience, and the impact of ethnicity on American culture and society. The field spans the traditional boundaries of disciplines such as art, history, literature, psychology, sociology, linguistics, political science, cultural anthropology, music, and even theology. Some of the topics within the focus of multicultural education are immigration history and the immigrant experience; settlement patterns; the history, culture, and social patterns of individual groups; intra- and intergroup relations, and social and cultural change within a group and within society; values clarification; and questions of public policy related to cultural pluralism, ethnic studies, bilingualism/biculturalism, multiculturalism, nativism, immigration, and native land claims.

Basically, there are two approaches to teaching multicultural education: the separate course in the form of a unit, elective, or minicourse; or the incorporative approach. A separate approach is based in a self-contained body of knowledge about one or more ethnic cultures. An integrative strategy injects ethnic-related subject matter into established curricula. Most multicultural education is housed in the social studies curriculum.

A majority of school systems appear to use an historical approach to multicultural education. This has the advantage of placing the ethnic group's experience in perspective, seeing the evolution of its culture, and explaining present conditions by relating to the past. As a discipline, history can be truly integrative and interdisciplinary, for it deals with politics, economics, anthropology, and sociology in a time dimension.

The psychological dimension is often explored in the human relations approach, attempting to develop a youngster's sense of identity and build positive self-concepts. The program content points out the beauty of ethnic diversity and the positive values in each ethnic culture.

The socioeconomic treatment is "present" centered. It deals with expressions of ethnicity and culture in neighborhoods, organizational life, the business and occupational worlds, and politics. Materials produced for elementary and secondary schools relate to the multicultural dimensions of economics.

The examination of ethnic cultures and life-styles is important for understanding America's pluralistic and multicultural society. This is the humanities approach. Much of "American" culture is made up of contributions from many ethnic groups. For instance, American literature, since the founding of the Republic, has benefited from ethnic writers and is not solely "Yankee." In the arts, many fine creators and performers blend their artistic and cultural universals with their particular ethnic communal background.

Thus multicultural education values the concepts implied by cultural pluralism, multilingualism, cross-cultural studies, intercultural studies, and human relations, and includes the following features: (1) staffing patterns throughout institutional and organizational hierarchies that reflect the pluralistic nature of American society; (2) curricula that are appropriate, flexible, unbiased, and incorporate the contributions of all cultural and racial groups; (3) an affirmation of the languages of cultural groups as different rather than deficient; and (4) instructional materials that are free of bias, omissions, and stereotypes, that are inclusive rather supplementary, and that show individuals from different cultural and racial groups portraying the full range of occupational and social roles. Implicit in this statement is the demand for the evaluation of educational programs not only according to the content of the curricula and instructional materials, but also in relation to how successfully the experiences and materials help promote respect for all people.

Multicultural education is a negation of the "melting pot" doctrine that was viable at the turn of the century during the height of mass immigration and was reflected in public schools as an attempt to Americanize the immigrant and his offspring in conformity to the dominant Anglo-Saxon culture of the nation. It is, instead, an affirmation of multiculturism or cultural pluralism which gives each ethnic group the opportunity to develop and preserve its culture at the primary level of relationship, while participating fully and as an equal in the mainstream of American society on the secondary level of relationship.

Multicultural education received its first impetus from the civil rights or "Black Revolt" movement of the 1960s, which in addition to attempting to seek a fuller and equal share in American life for blacks was a complaint against invisibility in the public school curriculum. This complaint was echoed later by Spanish-language groups, American Indians, and Asian-Americans. Then the protest was picked up by white ethnic groups, who realized that their parents and grandparents had been relegated to "huddled masses" and "wretched refuse from teeming shores" in the gospel of American history. Everyone now wanted to be included.

The protest was fueled by a revisionist history of American public schooling which evolved at this time and which stressed that the school was not the "equalizer" of all people as Horace Mann once believed, but indeed served as an obstacle for some non–main-line children to upward social and economic mobility. This contributed to the rise of the "new ethnicity" or "new pluralism" movement which sought to correct this imbalance and which led to the development of "black studies," "Hispanic studies," "bilingual/bicultural" programs, and "white ethnic studies" in American schools. This new concept was given legitimization by the passage in 1967 of the Bilingual Education Act by Congress which was appended as Title VII of the Elementary and Secondary Education Act of 1965, and which provided federal funding for mounting bilingual/bicultural programs in the nation's schools. The movement was further strengthened by the prolific establishment throughout the country of organizations for promoting ethnicity in education such as the Illinois Consultation for Ethnicity in Education, which was founded in Chicago in 1968. Soon several states, influenced by such organizations, began to pass legislation mandating some form of ethnic accommodation.

On December 29, 1971, Massachusetts became the first state to have mandatory bilingual education for non–English-speaking students. The new law required every school system with twenty or more children of limited English-speaking ability to provide a transitional bilingual program. Children were to be taught regular lessons in their native tongue with a gradual transition to all classes in English as their proficiency increased. Similarly, New Jersey required that black history be part of the two-year American history curriculum, while in 1972 Michael J. Bakalis, state superintendent of public instruction in Illinois, established the Office of Ethnic Studies for the implementation of the teaching of ethnic studies that it mandated. Likewise, California legislated the "correct portrayal" of ethnic contributions, and Hawaii, perhaps the state most conscious and least shy of its diversity, called for a "more comprehensive program of ethnic studies" in 1972.

In the spring of 1972, in an effort to lend recognition to the ethnic pluralism of the United States as reflecting its historical origins and contemporary character, two hundred ethnic scholars and communal leaders met in Washington, D.C., and organized the National Assembly for Ethnic Studies. This viable group coordinated the efforts of such organizations as the National Center for Urban and Ethnic Affairs, the Institute of Pluralism and Group Identity, and others for the promotion and recognition, on the part of American society, of cultural pluralism.

Further legitimization was given to the multicultural education movement, especially with reference to teacher preparation when, in the fall of 1972, the American Association of Colleges for Teacher Education, representing eight hundred teacher-training institutions, formally adopted a multicultural statement that endorsed the concept of cultural pluralism in the nation's schools. The statement read in part:

> Multicultural education is education which values cultural pluralism. Multicultural education rejects the view that schools

should seek to melt away cultural differences or the view that schools should merely tolerate cultural pluralism. Instead multicultural education affirms that schools should be oriented toward the cultural enrichment of all children and youth through programs rooted in the preservation and extension of cultural alternatives. Multicultural education recognizes cultural diversity as a fact of life in American society, and it affirms that this cultural diversity is a valuable resource that should be preserved and extended. It affirms that major education institutions should strive to preserve and enhance cultural pluralism.

This statement was given meaningful implementation when, later, the National Council for the Accreditation of Teacher Education mandated multicultural criteria for the accreditation of teacher-training institutions in the United States.

The lobbying efforts of the National Assembly for Ethnic Studies and allied groups succeeded in 1974 in prompting Congress to implement the Ethnic Studies Heritage Act, which was passed in 1972 and was appended as Title IX of the Elementary and Secondary Education Act of 1965; this further legitimized multicultural education. The purpose of the act was "to afford students opportunities to know about the nature of their own heritage and to study the contributions of the cultural heritage of other ethnic groups of the nation." The act required the preparation of teachers and curriculum materials for schools by or in cooperation with ethnic groups. The passage of the act and its implementation by federal commitment and funding through federal agencies for the development of ethnic studies curricula represented official recognition by Congress of multicultural education. The national response to the act was immense, indicative of the widespread acceptance of multicultural education. Despite the brief one-month period available for the preparation of proposals, more than 1,000 plans were presented to the United States Office of Education for only forty-two grants. The federal appropriation in fiscal 1974 was a little more than $2 million, but eligible proposals sought over $83 million.

Finally, the White House Conference on Ethnicity and Education, held at the nation's capital in 1976, to which ethnic scholars and communal leaders were invited, provided further legitimization of the movement. The apogee of multicultural education was perhaps reached at this time, resulting in further implementation such as the publication of curriculum guidelines for the teaching of multiethnic education by the National Council for the Social Studies.

Since then, the multicultural education movement has slowed. The attrition of federal funds and charges, backed by empirical studies, that bilingual/bicultural education is not achieving its goal of bringing the linguistically and culturally different child into the mainstream of

American life, and attacks on both bilingual/bicultural and ethnic studies as fostering divisiveness in American society, have led to a reaction against multicultural education. Its permanence in the American educational enterprise remains a matter of conjecture.

References
James A. Banks, *Multiethnic Education* (1981); Henry Ferguson, *Manual for Multicultural Education* (1987); Margaret D. Pusch, ed., *Multicultural Education* (1987); Ned H. Seelye, *Teaching Culture: Strategies for Intercultural Communications* (1987); Edward C. Stewart, *American Cultural Patterns* (1987).

A.T.K.

MULTICULTURAL HISTORY SOCIETY OF ONTARIO (Toronto, Ontario, Canada). The Multicultural History Society of Ontario (MHSO) attempts to preserve, study, and celebrate Ontario's many heritages. With the support of the Ministry of Culture and Citizenship, over the last six years the MHSO has identified and gathered historical materials from more than sixty ethnocultural groups in the province. *Polyphony,* the journal of the society, appears twice a year and reflects the new multicultural learning made possible by better archival and library collections. Whether dedicated to the peoples of a single Ontario city, to one ethnic group, or to a theme or institution important for ethnic immigration studies, *Polyphony* is profusely illustrated and written for a variety of readers. In over a hundred pages of analysis, oral testimony, documentation, and photographs, it offers easy access to major issues and little-known facts about Ontario's many peoples. It has proven an excellent classroom tool for students, a useful reference book for libraries and, above all, a scholarly and readable means of bringing about a synthesis of individual family history, nearby history, immigrant history, and the larger history of Canada. The society publishes scholarly and popular volumes and manuals on immigration studies, ethnic group life, oral history, and local history. Recent publications range in subject matter from the diaries of a leader of Toronto's black community and those of a Mennonite farmer from Kitchener, to a volume of scholarly essays on Poles in North America and a bibliography of Ukrainian Canadian imprints available in greater Toronto. The society has also prepared heritage display panels about many ethnocultural groups, which are available on loan to schools, libraries, and community organizations. At the society's library, or from the collections given to the Archives of Ontario and to appropriate regional and ethnic archives throughout the province, interested students can work with a variety of ethnocultural sources. For example, the MHSO holds over 6,000 hours of oral interviews in almost fifty languages. There are as well extensive collections of the ethnic press, the minutes of organizations, private manuscripts, jubilee volumes, commemorative pamphlets, reference books, and many thousands of photographs. Seminars about multicultural studies, including workshops on the planning and preparation of heritage materials, collecting, and oral history projects, as well as tours of the society and lectures, are arranged for associate members.

F.C.

MUSEUM OF THE CITY OF NEW YORK (Fifth Avenue at 103rd Street, New York, New York 10029). A very rich collection of memorabilia, photographs, and other materials, particularly strong for the period 1880 through 1920. Includes the Jacob A. Riis Collection and the Byron collection, photographic archives rich for immigrant life in New York City. Many of the photographs of the Riis Collection have appeared in editions of Jacob Riis's books (*q.v.*). Many of the Byron photographs are reproduced in Grace M. Mayer, *Once Upon a City* (1958); Roger Whitehouse, *Sunshine and Shadow* (1974); John A. Kowenhoven, *The Columbia Historical Portrait of New York* (1953); and Oscar Handlin, *Statue of Liberty* (1971).

F.C.

MUTUALISTAS (mutual aid societies). *See* Mexicans.

NAACP (1909–). In response to the Springfield, Illinois riots of 1908, a small group of socialist activists met in New York City to discuss the plight of the black population. Among the initial participants of this body were William English Walling, Mary White Ovington, Charles Edward Russell, and Oswald Garrison Villard. These distinguished descendants of abolitionists were joined by black leaders like W. E. B. Du Bois, Ida B. Wells, and later James Weldon Johnson. Together, the group represented white liberals and black intellectuals who were frustrated with the accommodationist politics of Booker T. Washington, and were offended by the rising tide of racial hostility. The platform of the National Association for the Advancement of Colored People was a rejection of the existing status of race relations. From its inception, the NAACP dedicated itself to the full attainment of civil and political rights for all Afro-Americans.

Under the guidance of Joel Spingarn (1914–1935) the association vigorously attacked racial injustices. The NAACP supported the slogan "fight for democracy abroad to keep democracy at home" during World War I. It pressed the government on the role of the black troops and officers in the conflict, and encouraged the formation of an officer's training camp. In the 1920s it became involved in union activities and attempted to protect the rights of the black worker. Meanwhile, the scope of the association's civil liberties campaign increased in every decade.

In the 1930s, aided by a grant from the Garland Fund, the NAACP launched a massive legal campaign to gain equality for blacks. Through the efforts of Nathan Ross Margold, Charles Houston, and later Thurgood Marshall, the legal branch of the NAACP challenged inequality in education and the disenfranchisement of southern blacks. Their work culminated in the important *Brown* v. *Board of Education* case of 1954. This case overturned the concept of "separate but equal," and set the stage for the modern civil rights era.

After the Brown case the NAACP employed a more diverse strategy to improve racial conditions. Along with other civil rights organizations, the association attacked public and private institutions. Under the leadership of Roy Wilkens, Margaret Bush Wilson, and Benjamin Hooks, the NAACP remained the foremost advocate of Afro-American rights in the nation. Its major publication is: "The Crisis."

References
Minnie Finch, *The NAACP—Its Fight for Justice* (1981); Langston Hughes, *Fight for Freedom; The Story of the NAACP* (1962); Charles Flint Kellogg, *NAACP, A History of the National Association for the Advancement of Colored People* (1973); Mary White Ovington, *The Walls Came Tumbling Down* (1969); Barbara Joyce Ross, *J. E. Spingarn and the Rise of the NAACP* (1972).

L.W.

NAIMG, MIKHAIL. *See* Lebanese.

NAROD. *See* Czechs.

NARODEN GLAS. *See* Bulgarians.

NATHAN, MAUD (1862–1946). Reformer, philanthropist. After her marriage Maud Nathan gave much of her time to such genteel and philanthropic causes as the New York Exchange for Women's Work and the Hebrew Free School Association. As president of the National Consumers' League she worked with Josephine Shaw Lowell (*q.v.*) in the drive to make women aware of their power as consumers. She was active in the National Council of Jewish Women.

Reference
Maud Nathan, *Once Upon a Time and Today* (1933; rpt. 1975).

F.C.

NATIONAL ASSOCIATION OF ARAB AMERICANS. *See* Arabs.

NATIONAL CENTER FOR URBAN ETHNIC AFFAIRS (NCUEA). Founded in 1970 in Washington, D.C. by Monsignor Geno Baroni (1930–1984) (*q.v.*). The NCUEA has lobbied in behalf of old urban ethnic enclaves and has worked to help ethnic neighborhood groups in local political struggles. The NCUEA newsletter *Buildingblocks* maintains:

> Rightly nurtured, ethnicity is the bridge of community . . . not a code word of social divisiveness. . . . NCUEA will continue to aid the well launched neighborhood movement to organize transportation facilities, rebuild commercial areas, preserve and develop the particular character of the neighborhood, save and rebuild its stock of housing and get its share of services and resources from governing bodies.

Criticizing "narrow self-interest" and "selfish privatism," the NCUEA advocates political cooperation among groups, "the negotiation of ethnic alliances." "The urban ethnic working class," *Buildingblocks* concludes, "should champion the cause of cultural pluralism built on the most generous and unselfish impulses of ethnic values that have always sustained our people."

Reference
Buildingblocks (Washington, D.C.; NCUEA, 1970–).

J.A.K.

NATIONAL CHILD LABOR COMMITTEE. *See* Clopper, Edward N.

NATIONAL COMMISSION FOR MANPOWER POLICY, *Foreign Workers: Dimensions and Policies* (Special Report No. 34, National Commission for Manpower Policy, March 1979). Sets out a set of broad policy options with respect to the temporary importation of foreign labor to the United States, and evaluates the options.

F.C.

NATIONAL COMMISSION ON LAW OBSERVANCE AND ENFORCEMENT. *See* Immigrants and Crime.

NATIONAL CONSUMERS' LEAGUE. *See* Goldmark, Josephine.

NATIONAL COUNCIL OF JEWISH WOMEN. The National Council of Jewish Women was established in 1893, with Hannah G. Solomon as its first president, for the purposes of social work for Jews and immigrant support. In its first decade, the NCJW was deeply involved in training and education for social work, in Sabbath schools, in settlement houses, and in remedial work with juvenile courts. In 1903 the United States government asked the council's assistance in meeting the problems of immigrants, and a member of the council was sent to Ellis Island in 1904. The council also investigated labor conditions and cooperated in campaigns to improve housing for the immigrant poor. Council members were also prompt to help Jews during times of the most horrendous crises such as the Kishineff massacre of Russian Jews in April 1903. The council later supported efforts to bring the United States into the League of Nations. During the Depression years, it provided special free classes for some of the unemployed and actively participated in educational campaigns to encourage youngsters to remain in school. When another kind of threat emerged in Nazi Germany, the NCJW began to devote itself to aid for Jewish refugee children from Germany. It also undertook to develop educational materials that could be used to combat anti-Semitism. Since its inception the council has responded with support for social and humanitarian causes. Such activities have included social work; education for the unemployed; refugee aid; support for pregnant women; and the creation of child care centers.

Reference

Monroe Campbell, Jr. and Willem Wirtz, *The First Fifty Years: A History of the National Council of Jewish Women* (1943).

G.B.

NATIONAL FEDERATION OF SOCIAL SETTLEMENTS. *See* Woods, Robert A[rchery].

NATIONAL GERMAN-AMERICAN ALLIANCE. The alliance, "by far the largest organization of any racial group in American history," was incorporated on February 27, 1907 as an "educational and patriotic" society that supported representative government, the maintenance of civil and political rights, the protection and naturalization of German immigrants, the study of American history and institutions, the cultivation of German language and literature, and the perpetuation of German-American pioneers. It was a loose federation of some ten thousand clubs and possibly two million members. From 1914 to 1917, the alliance devoted its full energies to support American neutrality in the

European war. To the very last, the alliance strove to keep America out of the war. With the outbreak of hostilities between the United States and the Central Powers, the position of German-Americans deteriorated rapidly. Although "no act of disloyalty has been proved against the National German-American Alliance," it felt that its usefulness had ended, and on April 11, 1918, dissolved itself, allotting the $30,000 in its treasury to the American Red Cross.

Reference
Joseph P. O'Grady, ed., *The Immigrants' Influence on Wilson's Peace Policies* (1967).

F.C.

NATIONAL ITALIAN AMERICAN FOUNDATION (Washington, D.C.). Founded in 1976, the foundation serves as an advocate for Italian-American interests; it works with Italian-American congressional delegations on legislation of both special and national interests. It publishes a monthly newsletter and provides assistance to local groups seeking aid and information from federal agencies. Also, it conducts an extensive education and scholarship program and hosts meetings for visiting Italian government officials meeting with their U.S. counterparts. The NIAF monitors discrimination cases before various courts, and fights against media presentations depicting Italian-Americans in an adverse manner.

Reference
Ten Years of NIAF (National Italian American Foundation, 1986); *The Role of Americans of Italian Heritage in the 1980s* (1979).

F.C.

NATIONAL JEWISH IMMIGRATION COUNCIL. Founded in New York City in 1911 to coordinate the work of the organizations that dealt with the problems of Jewish immigrants.

Reference
Moses Richin, *The Promised City: New York's Jews* (1962; with new Preface, 1970).

F.C.

NATIONAL LEAGUE FOR THE PROTECTION OF COLORED WOMEN. *See* Kellor, Frances A.

NATIONAL SLOVAK SOCIETY. *See* Slovaks.

NATIONAL VIGILANCE COMMITTEE. *See* White Slave Trade.

NATIVISM. The nativist sentiment is one of ethnic prejudice, racism, and anti-immigration. Nativism is not new as a general term to mean suspiciousness of the outsider, the classification of newcomers to the land as dangerous, and the fear that they really owe their primary allegiance to something other than their new society. In America, particularly after the Civil War, nativism was a mixture of different antagonisms, some of which often melded with one another. The pre-1870s nativist heritage had already manifested itself in powerful anti-Catholic sentiments, partly expressing itself in the fear that Catholics if in political power would owe their first allegiance to the papacy. By the 1870s there was also a very strong feeling among many that the increased militancy among workers was due not to their desire to end their economic and social misery, but to foreign demagogues' importation of dangerous ideas. During the economic crises of the late 1870s and the 1880s waves of nativist hysteria swept through some part of the country. The Haymarket affair of 1886 greatly increased feelings of xenophobia and antiradicalism. The wildest stereotypes were used to describe the enemy. In newspapers, the immigrants were described as "long-haired, wild-eyed, bad-smelling, atheistic, reckless foreign wretches, who never did an honest day's work in their lives" and who threatened to cause "the destruction of our national edifice." By the 1890s there was widespread opposition to free immigration. By the early twentieth century, nativism had arrived at a point where in some respects it assumed the increasingly respectable mantle of racism as well. It was argued that the American nation had to be protected against being inundated by racial inferiors.

Reference

John Higham, *Strangers in the Land: Patterns of American Nativism 1860–1925* (1973 ed.).

G.B.

NATURALIZATION, old-new distinction, 1900. Guest (*infra*), on this distinction, states that

> The literature on American immigration frequently distinguishes between the assimilation of the old groups, primarily from Northern and Western Europe, and the new groups, primarily from Southern and Eastern Europe. This article analyzes old-new differences in naturalization, one possible measure of assimilation. Data described here indicate a clear difference in 1900 between the new and old groups in their rates of assimilation, but little difference in eventual degrees of naturalization among persons who have been in the United States for some period of time. It is suggested that some of the remaining differences may be a result of the social structures of the origin countries.

Reference

Avery M. Guest, "The Old-New Distinction and Naturalization: 1900," *International Migration Review* 14 (Winter 1980): 492–510.

F.C.

NATURALIZATION AND CITIZENSHIP, private organizations. Naturalization has special significance because in the process of becoming a citizen, the newcomer develops an identification with his new homeland. There is a great psychological difference between carrying an alien identification card and being able to say "I am an American citizen." Naturalization can be a significant step in integration. The importance of this has long been recognized by many public and private organizations. Blumenthal observes:

> This article is primarily concerned with the role of private organizations, although any discussion of naturalization must include the programs of the United States Immigration and Naturalization Service and the concerns of state and city Boards of Education. Also, there must be included the role of certain courts who have manifested an interest in the ceremonies dignifying the awarding of citizenship.

Reference

Sonia D. Blumenthal, "The Private Organizations in the Naturalization and Citizenship Process," *International Migration Review* 5 (Winter 1971): 448–462.

F.C.

NAUJIENOS. *See* Lithuanians.

NELSON, KNUT (1843–1923). Norwegian immigrant politician. Nelson's early years mirrored that of many Norwegians: emigration at age six with his family from Norway, settling in Chicago, and remigrating to Wisconsin. After serving in the Civil War, he studied law and served in the Wisconsin state assembly. In 1871, he moved to Alexandria, Minnesota, to farm and practice law. In 1882, he beat an American for the Republican nomination for the fifth Minnesota congressional seat by capitalizing on his ethnic background. In his subsequent political career (governor of Minnesota, 1893–95; U.S. senator, 1895–1923), Nelson transcended his ethnic base of power to include traditional Republicans. A conservative Republican, Nelson frequently found his positions at odds with many of his fellow Norwegian-Americans who supported radical and reform movements in the Midwest during the "Gilded Age" and the Progressive era.

Reference
Martin W. Odland, *The Life of Knute Nelson* (1926).

J.J.

NESTOR, AGNES (1880–1948). Labor leader. Nestor was elected president of the International Glove Workers Union in 1903, was a member of the executive board of the National Women's Trade Union League, and was active on behalf of immigrant women and children.

Reference
Agnes Nestor, *Woman's Labor Leader: An Autobiography* (1954).

F.C.

NETHERLANDS EMIGRATION SERVICE. *See* Dutch.

NEW AMSTERDAM. *See* Dutch.

NEW NETHERLANDS. *See* Dutch.

NEW ORLEANS: AS PORT OF ENTRY. *See* Immigrants in the Old South.

NEW YORK CALL. *See* Lilienthal, Meta.

NEW YORK CITY, Archdiocesan Survey, "Hispanics in New York." *See* [Hispanics]: In New York City, Archdiocesan Survey.

NEW YORK CITY, *Bilingual Education in New York City: A Compendium of Reports* (New York City Board of Education 1978). Gathered together in this compendium are three rare and otherwise unobtainable reports on educational programs for non–English-speaking students in New York City, delineating official responses over the course of a generation. Included are *A Program of Education for Puerto Ricans in New York City* (1947); *The Puerto Rican Pupils in the Public Schools of New York City* (1951); and *Bilingual Education in New York City* (1971). The 1947 report is the first official response to the educational needs of the growing number of non–English-speaking Puerto Rican students being encountered in the city's schools; it recommends the adaptation of "Grade C" classes, which were used in prior eras for immigrant children; the 1951 report, prepared under the auspices of the Mayor's Committee on Puerto Rican Affairs, is a detailed exposition of the need for bilingual resources and new community orientations;

and the 1971 report is an overview of basic information needed for the recruitment and training of bilingual teachers. Francesco Cordasco's introduction places the reports in historical perspective and relates them to current needs and practices.

F.C.

NEW YORK CITY, Board of Alms-House Governors. *See* Sanger, William W.

NEW YORK CITY, New York City Board of Estimate and Apportionment, Committee on School Inquiry, *Report of Committee on School Inquiry, Board of Estimate and Apportionment: City of New York* (3 vols.; New York: The Board of Estimate and Apportionment, 1911–13). Chaired by Professor Paul Hanus (1855–1941) of Harvard University, the *Report* dealt with the problem of massive truancy in the schools and other conditions in the New York City schools. See "Experts Criticize the Truancy System," *The New York Times* (Feb. 10, 1913), p. 7. Superintendent William H. Maxwell (*q.v.*) appended to the *Report* a summary of the "Improvements in the Public Schools of the City of New York, 1898–1911" (3:69–97), largely as a defense of criticisms contained in the report. The *Report* is an invaluable repository of materials on the immigrant child and the public schools.

References
"Hanus Experts," *Education* 33 (May 1913): 573; L. A. Cremin, *The Transformation of the School* (1961).

F.C.

NEW YORK CITY BUREAU OF CHILD HYGIENE. *See* Baker, S. Josephine.

NEW YORK CITY, City Vigilance League. *See* Tolman, William H.

NEW YORK CITY, course of study and syllabus: *English and Citizenship* (New York: Board of Education, 1922). Course of study for classes for foreign-born adults and evening elementary schools. The syllabus continued to be reprinted and used until the mid-1930s. Chase *infra:* "Public schools are agencies of the people organized as a government to form a more perfect union, insure domestic tranquility, provide for the common defense, promote the general welfare and secure the blessings of liberty to those now living and to their posterity." The syllabus includes a section on "American Manners, Customs, and Conduct."

NIAGARA MOVEMENT. *See* Afro-Americans.

NICARAGUANS. *See* Central Americans.

NIKANDER, JUHO KUSTAA (1855–1919). Pastor and professor. Nikander was born in Finland, educated at the University of Helsinki, and ordained in Porvoo. He emigrated in 1884 and began his work as an immigrant clergyman in Michigan's Upper Peninsula. He was one of the most important figures in the founding of the Suomi synod and was elected its first president. He was also instrumental in establishing Suomi College and both taught at the institution and served as its president.

Reference
Arthur Puotinen, *Finnish Radicals and Religion in Midwestern Mining Towns* (1979).

P.K.

NISEI. *See* Issei.

NOAH, MORDECAI M[ANUEL] (1785–1851). Community leader. Noah was long considered the most important American Jew of his time. A leader of the several-thousand-member Jewish community in New York, he was active in Congregation Shearith Israel and the director of innumerable Jewish organizations. He was equally involved in the general community. He edited several important New York newspapers, and filled a variety of political and government posts, including that of consul at Tunis; sheriff of New York; surveyor of the New York port; judge; chairman of the John Tyler Central Committee; and Grand Sachem of Tammany Hall. He was also a successful playwright, speaker, and author.

Reference
Jonathan D. Sarna, *Jacksonian Jew: The Two Worlds of Mordecai Noah* (1982).

F.C.

NOLI, FAN. *See* Albanians.

NONCITIZENSHIP. On November 19, 1973 the United States Supreme Court ruled that a rejection of an application for employment by a private employer because the applicant is an alien is not a violation of the Civil Rights Act of 1964. *Espinoza* v. *Farah Manufacturing Company, Inc.* (1973) and Section 703 of Title VII of the Civil Rights Act make it unlawful for an employer to refuse to hire an individual because of race, color, religion, sex, or national origin. The facts of the case are uncomplicated. The wife was a permanent resident alien, residing in Texas and married to a United States citizen. She applied for a job as a seamstress with the Farah Manufacturing Company and her application was rejected on the basis of a company policy prohibiting the employment of non-U.S. citizens. She contended in court that the Farah Manufacturing company had discriminated against her because of "national origin" in violation of the Civil Rights Act of 1964, under the above-cited definition. The district court, agreeing with her argument, held that refusal to hire her because of lack of U.S. citizenship constituted discrimination on the basis of national origin. The Court of Appeals reversed. The United States Supreme Court granted the writ of certiorari and affirmed the ruling of the Court of Appeals, with Justice Marshall speaking for the majority. The case was decided on the narrow ground of statutory construction—that is, an interpretation of the terminology "national origin." The majority pointed out that "the term national origin on its face referred to the country where a person was born, or more broadly, the country from which his or her ancestors came." The court went on to find that the term "national origin" was different than citizenship and, therefore, discrimination on the basis of citizenship was not discrimination on the basis of national origin, and the statute does not prohibit discrimination on the basis of citizenship.

Reference
Austin T. Fragomen, Jr., "U.S. Supreme Court's Decision on Non-Citizenship," *International Migration Review* 8 (Spring 1974): 77–78.

                                                                    F.C.

NORAID. *See* Irish Northern Aid.

NORKUNAS, MYKOLAS. *See* Lithuanians.

NORTEÑOS. *See* Mexicans, Norteños.

NORTH AMERICA CIVIC LEAGUE FOR IMMIGRANTS. *See* Progressive Reformers and the Immigrants.

THE NORTH AMERICAN ANTI-FASCIST ALLIANCE. Formed in 1924 by the Italian Chamber of Labor of New York, the Workers' Anti-Fascist Alliance of New York, the International Ladies' Garment Workers' Union, the International Workers of the World, the Socialists, the Communists, the Social Democrats, and the Republicans in exile. The alliance was organized for the purpose of combatting Fascist activities and propaganda in the United States and sought to help the cause of democracy in Italy by exposing the brutalities of Mussolini's Fascist regime.

The fact that the alliance became the first sanctuary of anti-Fascism in the world and was organized in the United States greatly disturbed Mussolini and his American supporters. Encouraged by the favorable press coverage that fascism received constantly in *The New York Times, The Literary Digest, Il Popolo, Il Corriere d'America, Il Carroccio, and Il Progresso Italo-Americano,* among others, Mussolini and his ambassador in Washington, Gelasio Caetani, tried to discredit the alliance by exerting constant pressure on State Department officials to expel or keep under surveillance those members who had been granted political asylum in the United States. To circumvent governmental harassment, the alliance restricted, until 1925, its activities to the labor movement where workers' support was strong and determined. By 1926, however, it had become evident that Mussolini's charisma and the myth of "Il Duce" had excited the imagination of many Americans and Italian-Americans. Thus, on August 26, 1926, the alliance issued a *Manifesto* with the objective of unmasking the true aims of fascism and of exposing Mussolini to international condemnation. It was published in the Italian-American newspaper *Il Nuovo Mondo* of New York and was addressed to "All workers of the United States, Canada, and Mexico; to all people of the world concerned about Italy's constitutional and civil liberties."

The *Manifesto* was an historic document of international importance. It was the earliest expression of an organized united front in the struggle against fascism. It pointed out that fascism had reduced the Italian people to the lowest form of slavery; that centuries of civilization had been destroyed and generations of democratic progress had been prostrated under the thumb of Benito Mussolini. Also, the document underlined that, even though the "fascistization" of Italy had been nearly completed by Mussolini, the irrevocable process of history was working to hurl fascism back to the abyss whence it had emerged. The universal quest for individual liberties, the human aspirations for a better and democratic life in Italy, would inevitable bring the downfall of fascism. Because the Italians were in no condition to stage a mass revolt against Mussolini and his Fascist cliques, it was the moral and political responsibility of the workers and the citizens of the United States, Canada, and Mexico to help, assist and support the Italians in their struggle for freedom and democracy. Finally, the document, in condemning the king of Italy, Victor Emmanuel III, for his acquiescence in the "fascistization" of Italy, proceeded in laying down the foundations of the Republic in Italy. The *Manifesto* was endorsed and signed by the following organizations, union leaders, and newspaper directors: Joseph Catalanotti, vice-president of the Amalgamated Workers of America; Joseph Altieri, secretary of the Veterans Association; "G. Pilati"; Arturo Giovannitti, secretary-general of the Italian Chamber of Labor; Michele Sale, president of the Club of Modern Culture;

Raffaele Rende, director of the newspaper *La Giustizia;* Enea Sormenti, director of *Il Lavoratore;* Carlo Tresca, director of *Il Martello;* Luigi Antonini, vice-president of the International Ladies' Garment Workers' Union and secretary-general of Local 89 of the ILGWU; Paul Graditi, secretary of the Italian Trade Union Progressive Center; Benito Mazzotti, director of *La Scopa;* and Frank Bellanca, director of *Il Lavoro* and *Il Nuovo Mondo.*

After the publication of the *Manifesto,* unfair Communist tactics caused the break-up of the North American Anti-Fascist Alliance. The Socialists charged that the Communists tried to capture the control of the alliance by controlling all other member organizations. In the meetings of the alliance, the Socialists, the Chamber of Labor, the trade unions, and others were outnumbered by Communist delegates who had infiltrated the alliance. The most prominent members of the alliance, Antonini, Bellanca, Artoni, Procopio, Valenti, and Romualdi, were systematically slandered in the Communist press. By the end of 1926, the North American Anti-Fascist Alliance was replaced by the International Anti-Fascist League for the Freedom of Italy. The league applied immediately for affiliation with the newly founded Anti-Fascist International with its headquarters in Vienna, Austria. The league appointed Eugene V. Debs as its honorary chairman and John Vaccaro as its secretary. The league declared that it had nothing to do with the Communists who advocated another form of dictatorship: "One could not be against the Black Shirts' dictatorship and at the same time approve, as the Communists did, the Bolshevist dictatorship in Russia" (*The New Leader,* Sept. 4, 1926).

Reference
The Manifesto of the North American Anti-Fascist Alliance (New York, August 26, 1926), edited and translated by Pellegrino Nazzaro in *Labor History* 13, no.3 (Summer 1972).

P.N.

NORTH AMERICAN BASQUE ORGANIZATIONS (NABO). *See* Basques.

NORTH AMERICAN GRUETLI-BUND. Founded in 1865 in Cincinnati and patterned after its Swiss prototype, the association aimed "to unite all Swiss support societies of North America" (Statutes of the Gruetli-Bund). By 1869 some member societies under the leadership of John Hitz (1828–1908) gave preponderance to the association's cultural rather than "benevolent" mission. It was to further "an active life of the mind, to nourish and nurture the love [for], and attachment to, the old fatherland, and to gain respect for the Swiss name" in the United

States (Statutes). Membership grew from 409 in 1865 to 3,620 in 1891, and then to 6,012 in 1915. The anti–German-language agitation of World War I and the cessation of large-scale immigration brought a precipitous decline. In 1938 the Bund was transformed into the North American Swiss Alliance, now basically a life insurance organization.

References
[Sigbert Meier], *Nordamerikanischer Schweizer-Bund 1865–1915* (1916); Leo Schelbert and Urspeter Schelbert, "Portrait of an Immigrant Society: The North-American *Grütli-Bund*, 1865–1915," *Yearbook of German American Studies* 18 (1983): 233–254.

L.S.

NORTH BENNET STREET INDUSTRIAL SCHOOL (Boston). Located in Boston's North End, long an immigrant neighborhood and since the turn of the century predominantly Italian. In 1879, when No. 39 North Bennet Street housed the Seamen's Friend Society, Mrs. L. E. Caswell rented space there for a sewing room for poor women; a laundry room was added soon after and the establishment was called the North Bennet Street Industrial Home. In June 1880 the home leased the entire building. It gradually added other activities: a cooking school, printing shop, kitchen garden, circulating library, cafe, and others. Probably in 1880, the home asked Pauline Agassiz (Mrs. Quincy A.) Shaw (1841–1917) to open a day nursery there, as she had elsewhere in Boston; she did so and evidently from then on took an active interest in the home, so that she has been regarded as the founder of the North Bennet Street Industrial School (NBSIS). In June 1884 the home's lease expired and Mrs. Shaw and others bought the building. During this time the name was changed to its present one. In April 1885 the school was incorporated and the building conveyed to it.

For several decades, beginning in 1885, the school had an arrangement with the Boston School Department under which it taught cooking, sewing, woodworking, and other vocational skills to public school pupils; eventually the public schools began teaching these courses themselves, and the school added other trades to its curriculum. NBSIS has also had after-school classes and both day and evening classes for older people, female and male. In addition, the school had classes in citizenship; in 1902 a settlement department (the Social Service House and Shaw House for Boys) was added, and a vocational guidance and placement department was begun in 1907. The school thus carried on a varied program in several adjacent buildings. The vocational training program has included industrial classes, a lunchroom, and various industries, notably lighting fixtures, lead garden ornaments, and homespun fabrics. The products of these industries, which flourished from the 1920s to the early 1950s, were sold at the school, at various exhibitions and shops, and at the Industrial Arts Shop, which was run by the school but was located on Beacon Hill, one of Boston's wealthier neighborhoods.

Even before a separate settlement department was established, the school was carrying on social service activities. In connection with the day nursery, school staff or volunteers visited the homes of nursery pupils and reported on conditions there, providing advice or arranging assistance when needed. The Social Service House and Shaw House sponsored numerous clubs and classes, for both children and adults; summer day camps and outings; pageants and plays, the Social Service Credit Union; and the Play School for Habit Training (1922–1946), an experimental day nursery for bright children with behavior problems. The school leased several sites for a summer camp, and in 1920 bought a farm in Boxford, Massachusetts, as a permanent camp; mothers with young children went there for one or two weeks, and older children by themselves.

The school had been affiliated with the Boston Council of Social Agencies; with the council's settlement subgroup, which was first called the Boston Social Union; and with their successor agencies. The trend from more or less informal sharing of information to joint fund raising and more and more centralized control of budgets and activities was accelerated by the Depression. NBSIS pioneered in developing the work relief program of the 1930s, in which unemployed persons did maintenance, repair, and other work at the school or at other social agencies. Later the school cooperated in the Greater Boston Community Survey of 1948–49. It also was an outspoken critic of conditions in the North End and active in improving them; the school participated in many North End organizations and projects, worked to get playgrounds built, and organized clean-up drives. The school has had extensive, long-term relations with three levels of government: city, state, and federal. The Boston School Department and the federal veterans' agencies are the most prominent in this category of outside connections, as both at different periods supported trade classes at the school.

The school has had a Board of Managers since its incorporation, and the board has always attracted numerous prominent Bostonians, may of them active well beyond attendance at meetings: serving as teachers, club leaders, or home visitors; organizing benefit performances; pricing antiques and managing the sales; chaperoning or hosting children's outings; serving on visiting committees; and advising on building or camp repairs, insurance, investments, and other financial matters. The records of the North Bennet Street Industrial School were given to the Schlesinger Library (Radcliffe College, Harvard University) by the school in 1968 and 1976.

F.C.

NORWEGIAN-AMERICAN HISTORICAL ASSOCIATION. The association was founded in 1925 by Norwegian-American leaders, scholars, and clergymen who believed that interest in the history of Norwegian immigration was endangered by World War I/1920s nativism and the apathy of younger Norwegian-Americans. In response, the association was designed to serve both the professional and lay historian. Headquartered at St. Olaf College in Northfield, Minnesota, the association maintains an archive of manuscripts and documents and a collection of historical works in the St. Olaf College library. To date, its extensive publications program has produced over six dozen books and monographs and thirty-one volumes of the journal *Norwegian-American Studies*.

Reference
Odd S. Lovoll and Kenneth O. Bjork, *The Norwegian-American Historical Association, 1925–1975* (1975).

J.J.

NORWEGIANS. Over 850,000 Norwegians immigrated to the United States since the 1820s. While they were a small proportion of America's immigrants (approximately 2 percent), the Norwegians were one of the first groups to arrive in substantial numbers in the nineteenth century and were instrumental in pioneering the Midwest and Pacific Northwest. Their rich institutional life in town and country reflects over 160 years of migration and interaction with American life.

Migration Trends. While records exist of Norwegian mariners in East Coast ports in the seventeenth and eighteenth centuries, organized emigration from Norway did not begin until 1825, when 52 emigrants left Stavanger for New York on the sloop *Restauration*. Migration to America was sparse in the following decade, when only a few hundred Norwegians left home each year. The annual rate leapt to over 1,000 in the 1850s, with some 8,000 crossing the Atlantic during the Norwegian agricultural recession of 1849–1850, and a pre–Civil War peak of 8,000 immigrants was reached in 1861. In all, 77,873 Norwegians settled in the United States between 1825 and 1865, over half of them after 1856.

The great era of mass migration from Norway between the Civil War and World War I can be divided into three waves. In the first (1865–1873), an average of 13,862 persons emigrated each year. This number was quickly surpassed in the second wave (1879–1893), when 250,000 migrated to the United States, a peak being reached, in 1882, of 28,804, a number that exceeded Norway's natural population increase. Even greater numbers arrived in the third wave (1893–1915). In the first decade and a half of the twentieth century alone, 214,985

Norwegians emigrated, the largest number of them between 1903 and 1907.

Following a brief recovery from World War I, Norwegian immigration fell off in the 1920s. It never filled its quota (2,377) allowed under the national origins restrictions (1924–1965), as migration was discouraged by the Depression and World War II. During the post–World War II period (1945–1960), immigration averaged 2,253 persons a year, a number that has declined steadily in each succeeding decade. In the 1970s and 1980s, fewer than 400 Norwegians have immigrated to the United States each year.

Reasons for Migrating. Patterns of migration from Norway to the United States reflect the interaction of economic and social trends in the two countries. Dramatic social change in early nineteenth-century Norway set the early migration into motion. Population rose as mortality rates fell in response to improved nutrition and medical practices. The rationalization of traditional agriculture brought a series of cycles of prosperity and recession into the countryside. The class most affected was not the rural poor, but the peasant landowning, or *bønde,* class. Larger families put great pressure on limited resources and endangered traditional ways of life. Marginal producers and younger sons fought their declining status by moving with their wives and children to nearby towns, to northern Norway, or to America.

Political and religious factors also influenced early migration. A political awakening of the *bønder* found fullest expression in the Eidsvold constitution (1814), in ideas compatable with the founding principles of the U.S. political system. In addition, Pietistic movements, most notably the Low Church movement of Hans Nilsen Hauge, reflected a *bønde* dissatisfaction with the state church leadership, a conflict believed to be nonexistent in the United States. Political and religious refugees were few among the Norwegians, however; on the whole, most emigrants left for economic reasons.

Conditions in the United States contrasted with those in early nineteenth-century Norway. At the same time that land became scarce in Norway, large tracts of the American Midwest were opened to settlement, creating a demand for agricultural workers and opportunities for land ownership. In addition, various individuals and agencies actively encouraged immigration. Norwegians learned of the new country in *amerikabrev,* "America letters" from friends, relatives, and neighbors who had previously emigrated. Many letters described conditions in the United States while offering practical advice for emigrants. Through letters and visits home, earlier emigrants encouraged others, setting into motion a chain of migrations of families and neighbors moving to specific destinations. Books by Norwegian settlers were widely read in Norway and serialized in Norwegian newspapers. In addition, states, railroads, and, later, steamship companies embarked on campaigns to attract Norwegians to the American heartland by advertising, publishing guidebooks, and sending agents to Scandinavia.

The mass migration of 1865–1915 was driven by economic motives. Farmers continued to dominate the stream as the flow of rural emigrants widened to include *husmenn,* or cotters, displaced by new technology and a more complex agricultural market economy. Other groups had been affected by the modest early industrialization in Norway. Sailors, maritime workers, and artisans left after their crafts had been altered radically by mechanization. In general, nascent Norwegian industrialization loosened the old bonds of society, cutting loose a numerous cohort of young workers who were attracted by the more extensive industrialism in the United States with its demand for skilled and unskilled laborers.

The migration of 1865–1915 was a labor migration of single young adults. Most were men (60 percent of the 308,270 who emigrated between 1880 and 1915). Two-thirds of those men were between the ages of fourteen and thirty, and a large majority of immigrants of both sexes were unmarried. Many were from towns and cities (nearly one-third in the 1880–1915 period compared with a mere one-tenth in the pre–Civil War era). While Norwegians continued to settled on American farms, an increasing number sought urban work, men in the factories and mills, women as domestic maids or seamstresses. Return migration was common; as many as one-fourth returned to Norway. The return rate was highest during recessions and depressions.

After World War I, differences between the two countries narrowed as Norwegian industrial development accelerated, land became scarcer in the United States, and the American industrial system matured. Many immigrants of the 1920s joined relatives on established farms in the Midwest or found employment in East Coast ports. The Depression of the 1930s tarnished America's attraction for Norwegians (32,000 Norwegians actually returned to Norway in the decade), while World War II made migration difficult and dangerous.

The composition of the postwar migration demonstrates the end of the great migration. In recent decades, Norwegian men and women have emigrated in near-equal numbers. The large number of engineers, physicians, and skilled workers among them indicates the closing of the long era of mass migration of Norwegian farmers and workers.

Patterns of Settlement. The immigrants of the sloop *Restauration* in 1825 settled in Kendall township, west of Rochester, New York. Soon after their arrival, they moved west to Illinois, setting into motion a pattern of rural settlement that moved steadily westward, decade by decade, throughout the nineteenth century.

Successive waves of Norwegian farmers took rural America in

stages. As one frontier settlement matured, it attracted newcomers from the homeland and became the "mother area" from which expeditions were dispatched to new unsettled areas further west which, once settled, became new "mother areas." Illinois represented a land of agricultural opportunity in the 1820s and 1830s, attracting Norwegians to the Fox River valley in the northeastern part of the state. By the end of the 1830s, offshoots of these first settlement cropped up in southern Wisconsin. Those who followed the Wisconsin pioneers, in turn, roamed north and west from the first settlements in Muskego and Koshkonong to the far reaches of the state by the Civil War.

The tide of Norwegian settlement crossed the Mississippi River into Minnesota and Iowa in the 1850s and 1860s, continued into the Dakotas in the 1870s and 1880s, and reached the Pacific Northwest by the 1890s. By the end of the century, Norwegian immigrants and their children comprised a significant proportion of the populations of the states of Wisconsin, Iowa, Minnesota, North Dakota, South Dakota, and Washington.

Norwegian America became increasingly urban after 1880. Three cities became major centers for Norwegians in their respective regions: Chicago for the Great Lakes states, Minneapolis for the upper Midwest and the Great Plains, and Seattle for the transplanted midwesterners in the Pacific Northwest. After the turn of the century, greater numbers of Norwegians made it no farther into the land than Brooklyn, the emerging center of Norwegian culture on the Atlantic coast. Pockets of Norwegians could also be found in Boston, Philadelphia, San Francisco, and other major cities on both coasts. Migration from farm to town stamped a Norwegian character on dozens of smaller cities and towns, such as Decorah, Iowa, and Stoughton, Wisconsin.

Institutional Life. Early immigrants tended to cluster together in rural settlements marked by a high concentration of immigrants from the same home region in Norway. Community life was strengthened by cooperation on community projects and intermarriage among settlement families.

The rural community's dominant formal institution was the immigrant Lutheran church. Doctrinal and organizational disputes created fourteen separate varieties of Norwegian-American Lutheranism in the nineteenth century, ranging from the High Church Norwegian synod to the antiecclesiastic Elling's Synod. Doctrinal disputes were largely resolved after the 1890s as synods merged, first with other Norwegian-American synods, and then with other ethnic and American Lutheran groups. While congregations and synods frequently disputed openly with one another, they all practiced a strict adherence to traditional Lutheranism and each congregation served as an agency of preservation of group identity.

The church defined the culture and social structure of the rural settlement. The minister was the social elite of the small community, and his home often served as a community center, library, and lodging for newcomers and visiting dignitaries. The church became a focus for immigrant life; the churchyard became the place to meet on Sunday to trade livestock, to catch up on gossip, and to hire farm help. The church sponsored a variety of clubs and organizations for both sexes and all ages, from youth groups and Sunday schools to Bible discussion groups and "ladies' aid" societies. Efforts to create parochial elementary schools were unsuccessful. After a long bitter fight in the mid-nine-teenth century, the ministry were unable to turn their immigrant par-ishioners away from American public education. Nonetheless, Nor-wegian-American synods were active in founding seminaries and colleges throughout the Midwest, including Augsburg College (Min-neapolis), St. Olaf College (Northfield, Minnesota), and Luther College (Decorah, Iowa).

Organizational life was more varied in American towns and cities. Urban Norwegian settlements often supported several Lutheran church-es in addition to ethnic Baptist and Methodist congregations. Church-sponsored clubs and societies had to compete for members and support with a wide variety of secular institutions. Often at first in collaboration with their Danish and Swedish neighbors, urban Norwegians founded temperance societies, singing societies, mutual aid clubs, brass bands, theater companies, rifle companies, trade organizations, labor unions, and other social clubs. Norwegians from specific rural districts in Nor-way gathered in *bygdelag* (*q.v.*), or regional societies.

The cities and towns also served as the settings for the celebration of ethnic holidays, such as Syttende Mai (17 May: Norwegian constitu-tion day) and Leiv Eirikssen Day (commemorating the Viking discovery of North America). The Sons of Norway (*q.v.*), a social and insurance organization founded among Minneapolis Norse in 1895, became the major Norwegian-American organization in the twentieth century. In 1906, during the peak years of Norwegian immigration to the United States, the Norwegian consulate counted 237 Norwegian ethnic organi-zations in the United States.

Newspapers and Political Life. In addition to churches and secular organizations, a variety of newspapers and magazines helped shape the Norwegian-Americans' group identity. Nearly 600 Norwegian-lan-guage periodicals were produced in the United States since 1847. Many were short-lived, lasting less than a year before going bankrupt or merging with a more successful publication. Immigrant papers reflected a rich spectrum of viewpoints and focuses: many were synod-sponsored religious organs; some were temperance papers; some promoted specif-ic clubs and organizations; a few were radical papers.

The immigrant press provided information about the United States as well as news from Norway and the Norwegian-American settlements. They also reflected and directed immigrant political involvement. Immigrants to the rural Midwest became involved in American public life early on. As Norwegians came to dominate a township, immigrants became officeholders at the local level, and many rose to county or state office. Norwegian names began to appear on state ballots in Minnesota and Wisconsin soon after the Civil War as state party officials openly courted ethnic voters.

Support for the Republican Party among nineteenth-century Norwegians in the Midwest was reflected in immigrant votes for Lincoln and participation in the Civil War. Many Norwegian immigrants were attracted to the GOP as a symbol of Protestantism, morality, Prohibition, and the "Free Soil" ideology. Nevertheless, significant numbers of Norwegians eschewed Republican politics for more progressive and radical movements in the late nineteenth and early twentieth centuries. Reform-minded Norwegians contributed to the rise of the Farm-Labor party in Minnesota and LaFollette's Progressive party in Wisconsin. Norwegians also played major roles in various Socialist parties and factions, the Farmers' Alliance, the People's party (Populists), and the Nonpartisan League of North Dakota. As a result, by the waning of mass Norwegian migration to the United States in the 1920s, immigrants and their children had been active in American public life along a broad spectrum of ideologies, parties, and organizations.

References

Theodore C. Blegen, *Norwegian Migration to America, 1825–1860* (1931); Theodore C. Blegen, *Norwegian Migration to America: The American Transition* (1940); Odd S. Lovoll, *The Promise of America: A History of the Norwegian-American People* (1984); Carlton C. Qualey, *Norwegian Settlement in the United States* (1938); Ingrid Semmingsen, *Norway to America: A History of the Migration* (1978).

J.J.

NOVOE RUSSKOE SLOVO. *See* Russians.

NUORTEVA, SANTERI (1881–1929). Radical organizer and journalist, government official. Nuorteva was a leading member of the social democratic movement in Finland and was elected to a seat in the Finnish parliament as a Socialist. Political repression forced him to emigrate to the United States, where he became an important organizer in immigrant radical circles. He served as the official representative of the Finnish People's Republic in the United States until he was forced to leave the country during the Red Scare period after World War I. Subsequently forced out of Canada and Great Britain, he ended up in the Soviet Union, where he worked in the Foreign Department and at an administrative position in Soviet Karelia.

Reference
Auvo Kostiainen, *Santeri Nuorteva: Kansäinvalinen Suomalainen* (1983).

P.K.

NURMI, MAIJU. *See Toveritar.*

O'CONNELL, DANIEL. *See* Irish.

O'CONNELL, DENIS J. (1849–1927). Catholic clergyman. One of the leaders of the liberal movements of American Catholicism in the late nineteenth century. Ordained in Rome in 1877, he was a favorite of James Gibbons, who became archbishop of Baltimore in that year and who appointed him a secretary of the Third Plenary Council of Baltimore in 1884 and then sent him to Rome to win Roman approval of the conciliar legislation. From 1885 to 1895 O'Connell was rector of the American College in Rome, in which capacity he also acted as agent for the American hierarchy and was on intimate terms with Pope Leo XIII and with other important Vatican officials. As the liberal movement took shape he became more and more the agent for the principal members of the Liberal party: Gibbons, then a cardinal; John Ireland, archbishop of St. Paul; and John J. Keane, successively bishop of Richmond, first rector of the Catholic University of America, and archbishop of Dubuque.

Reference
Gerald P. Fogarty, "Denis J. O'Connell: Americanist Agent to the Vatican, 1885–1903," Ph.D. dissertation, Yale University, 1969 (DA 30: 3396-A).

F.C.

O'HANLON, JOHN (1821–1905). Clergyman, author. O'Hanlon was born in Ireland in 1821, but before completing seminary training at Carlow College, he emigrated with his parents to Missouri, where he resumed his studies for the priesthood. After his ordination in 1847, O'Hanlon served as a priest in St. Louis for about six years. In 1853, he became seriously ill with bronchitis and returned to Ireland for his health, where he remained until his death in 1905. O'Hanlon wrote a number of books on historical and religious topics, but perhaps his most important writing was *The Irish Emigrant's Guide for the United States* (1851). This manual reflected O'Hanlon's anxiety concerning the fate of the hundreds of thousands of Irish refugees pouring into the United States technologically, culturally, and psychologically unprepared for their new existence. In his *Emigrant's Guide,* O'Hanlon instructed prospective emigrants on how to prepare for the journey and what to expect upon their arrival. He wanted them to stay close to their Catholic peasant cultural roots, which is why he recommended that they farm in the Midwest rather than settle in the cities of the East.

Reference
Edward J. Maguire, ed., *Rev. John O'Hanlon's The Irish Emigrant's Guide for the United States* (1976).

F.C.

OJETTI, UGO (1871–1946). Italian journalist, art critic. A correspondent for the Italian *Corriere della Sera,* Ojetti covered the Spanish-American War and traveled extensively in the United States in 1898–99; his observations were recorded in *L'America Vittoriosa* (1899), a far-ranging commentary on America at the close of the century. Ojetti was both fascinated and repelled by the immensity and frenetic activity of the United States. An example is his observation on a visit to the Library of Congress:

> Questo edificio immenso e lusuoso costruito ieri (1888–1897) con una spesa di trenta milioni, con un tesoro di quasi un milione di volumi e di quasi trecentomila stampe, ha nella vertiginosa celerità della sua creazione qualcosa di miracoloso che spaventa la nostra mente latina abituata alle lente secolari stratificazioni della scienza e dell'arte. Tutta la loro affannosa sete di sapere . . . si manifesta qui perspicuamente in tutta la sua frenetica esagerazione quasi puerile.

Reference
Giuseppe Massara, *Vigiatori Italiani in America, 1860–1970* (1976).

F.C.

OÑATE, JUAN DE. *See* Mexicans.

OPERATION WETBACK. The forced repatriation of perhaps as many as 1 million Mexican citizens from the United States in the summer of 1954. In addition to the 4.5 million workers contracted under the provisions of the bracero program, there were just as many if not more illegal workers, or wetbacks, who crossed the border in search of work. This "wetback invasion" was intolerable to many groups. Minority organizations such as the NAACP and the G.I. Forum believed that these workers depressed the wage structure and took jobs away from American citizens; labor unions shared these beliefs. Church and social welfare groups allied with liberal politicians and pointed out many instances of inhumane living and working conditions which employers forced upon the illegal entrants, and many who worked under contractual provisions of the international agreement. Growers and other employers, fearful that the chorus of criticisms might ultimately deprive them of cheap, plentiful braceros, agreed that something had to be done to check the increasing number of wetbacks in the Southwest. The report of the President's Commission on Migratory Labor in 1951 supported critics when it found proof of widespread abuse of workers and exacerbation of existing social ills. This imprimatur of the federal government then led to full coverage of the "invasion" by the print and electronic media. Negative stereotyping of the workers, now in the full glare of publicity, further heightened perceived dangers because most Americans "continued to blame the victims for their status in society." The Immigration and Naturalization Service's "Operation Wetback" mollified rising public concern, and provided at the same time the best political solution available.

Reference
Juan Ramon Garcia, *Operation Wetback: The Mass Deportation of Mexican Undocumented Workers in 1954* (1980).

F.C.

OPPORTUNITY SYSTEMS, INC. *See* Vietnamese Refugees, opportunity systems surveys.

ORDER OF SVITHIOD. *See* Swedes.

ORDER OF UNITED AMERICAN MECHANICS. *See* Junior Order of United American Mechanics.

O'REILLY, JOHN BOYLE (1844–1890). Journalist, poet, novelist. O'Reilly's roles as poet, novelist, and journalist gave him tremendous influence over Irish-American opinion. Born in County Meath, Ireland, O'Reilly served as a Fenian recruiting agent while a member of the British army. In 1866, the British government discovered that O'Reilly was a Fenian, tried him for treason, sentenced him to death, and then commuted his sentence and sent him to Australia as a political prisoner. In 1869, O'Reilly escaped, arrived in Philadelphia, moved to Boston, began his career as a journalist, and served as editor of the *Boston Pilot* (*q.v.*). He carried his hatred of Britain with him to America and continued to work for Irish nationalism but switched to the forces of constitutional rather than revolutionary nationalism. In addition to his role as nationalist advocate, O'Reilly functioned as defender of Irish and Catholic interests, social reformer, and champion of all religious, ethnic, and racial minorities. As a leader of Irish America, he encouraged ethnic cohesion, cultivated an intelligent Irish-American public opinion, and urged his coethnics to adapt to the American environment. His popularity among the leaders of Protestant Anglo-America benefited all Irish-Americans. McManamin concludes that O'Reilly, "honored and loved by the Catholic community, and esteemed by contemporaries of different religious and nationalistic backgrounds . . . did more than any other man of his generation to help bridge the gulf between Catholics and Protestants of New England."

Reference
Francis G. McManamin, *The American Years of John Boyle O'Reilly* (1976).

F.C.

ORGANIC ACT OF GUAM (1950). *See* Guamanians.

OTTOMAN EMPIRE. *See* Arabs.

OTTOMAN-MUSLIM SOCIETY. *See* Arabs.

OVINGTON, MARY WHITE. *See* NAACP.

OWENS, ALBERT A. *See* Americanization Movement.

OWEN, ROBERT. *See* English.

PACIFIC WEEKLY. *See* Koreans.

THE PADRONE SYSTEM. The origins of the padrone system are obscure. The system was not unique to the United States. Found among many immigrant groups, the padrone system became identified mostly with Italian immigrants. By the Civil War, padrones had earned an infamous reputation for indenturing Italian children. By the 1870s, the combined efforts of philanthropists, humanitarians, and governments on both sides of the Atlantic had put an end to the odious trade in children. Sensing the critical need for unskilled labor in the United States and encouraged by American businessmen, padrones turned their attention to tapping the great reservoir of unemployed peasants in Italy. They employed agents abroad to round up work forces and send them to America. They also sent representatives to Italy who would collect bands of workers in their home towns and bring them to the United States. Some padrones maintained agents in port cities in order to lure immigrants away from their destinations and to the padrones' areas. Steamship agents often cooperated with padrones in these ventures.

In effect, the padrone system was a mechanism for bringing immigrants to the United States and placing them in jobs throughout the country. Playing a vital role in stimulating and directing Italians to America, it enabled the vanguard of Italian immigration to establish a settlement pattern outside of the popular Northeast and helped American industry and agriculture to function effectively in an expanding economy.

Initially, padrones' clients were largely unskilled, highly mobile, and in need of basic human services. The system turned on the willingness of individuals to act as intermediaries in the delivery of services between immigrants and the host country. These padrones, as they came to be called, were responsible for advancing fares to immigrants or inducing prospects to spend their own money to come to America. They would then furnish food, clothing, shelter, a job, and whatever services the immigrants needed, all for a price. They often read letters to illiterate workers, wrote responses for them, banked their savings and/or transmitted money abroad, interpreted for them in legal matters, and the like. The system, largely unpoliced in the beginning, made possible plentiful abuses and the exploitation of human resources.

The Foran Act (Anti–Contract Labor Act) of 1885 was an early attempt to eliminate the padrone system, but it was easily violated by padrones whose personal relationship with immigrants was one of the cornerstones of the system. Numerous reform efforts to eliminate the padrone system and replace it with religious societies, philanthropic organizations, and state labor agencies also fell short. Aided by padrones, immigrants came. They filled the jobs that American industry desperately needed, especially in railroad and day labor work. As migrant farm workers, they roamed the country picking the ripening crops which would have otherwise been left to rot on the vines. Despite the abuses and the profits amassed by American businessmen and padrones, immigrants prospered and considered themselves much better off than had they remained in the Old Country. The system flourished as the principal distribution agency for Italian immigrants prior to World War I.

By then, this quasi-formal institution, whose main business was the recruitment and distribution of labor, had run its course. Societal and governmental pressures had taken their toll. Turning away from padrones, railroads, from 1906 on, had increasingly assumed direct responsibility for recruiting labor, paying wages, and regulating work camp conditions. Family members were turning to their own who, having preceded them and established themselves, were able to provide the kind of basic services which heretofore padrones had supplied.

The passing of the padrone system did not mean the end of padrones, nor of their service. Individual padrones continued to assist their compatriots whose needs had become increasingly varied and complex as they worked their way up in American society. Rather than seeking temporary pick and shovel work in some remote corner of America, more and more Italian immigrants were settling down and searching for better and permanent jobs. Italian-Americans wanted blue-collar jobs, white-collar work, and service jobs as policemen, firemen, teachers, and the like. Some sought to establish small businesses; most dreamed of owning their own home. With their economic and political clout, padrones made the attainment of these goals easier. They lent money directly to some aspiring Italian merchants and/or would-be homeowners. Others they recommended to American banks as respectable citizens who were good credit risks. Padrones had the clout to do that. They had grown with the Italian-American community. Business-minded, bilingual, passably articulate, ambitious, and energetic, they changed from brutish exploiters of children to labor hustlers and finally to legitimate businessmen, all the while adapting their talents to the changing scene. Padrones were usually the first in Italian communities to have political power, if not hold political office outright. Their strength came from their ability to represent a block of ethnic voters who were grateful to them for finding employment and obtaining mortgage money. Motivated partly by self-interest, padrones, like other immigrant leaders, pushed as vigorously for the education and Americanization of immigrants as they did for the preservation of Old World values that would be viable in the new environment. These things did not happen abruptly. The process took time and was often painful. But, as America advanced, so too did the ethnic broker and the ethnic community, hand in hand, gradually.

References

Charlotte Erickson, *American Industry and the European Immigrant 1860–1885* (1957); Victor R. Greene, *American Immigrant Leaders 1800–1910: Marginality and Identity* (1987); Robert F. Harney, "The Padrone and the Immigrant," *The Canadian Review of American Studies* 5 (1974), and "The Padrone System and Sojourners in the Canadian North, 1885–1920," in George E. Pozzetta, ed., *Pane e Lavoro: The Italian American Working Class,* proceedings of the Eleventh Annual Conference of the American Italian Historical Association, 1978 (1980); Luciano J. Iorizzo, *Italian Immigration and the Impact of the Padrone System* (1980), and, with Salvatore Mondello, *The Italian Americans* (1980); John Koren, "The Padrone System and Padrone Banks," *U.S. Department of Labor Bulletin,* no. 9 (1897); Humbert S. Nelli, "The Italian Padrone System in the United States," *Labor History* 5 (1964); F. J. Sheridan, "Italian, Slavic and Hungarian Unskilled Laborers in the United States," *U.S. Bureau of Labor Bulletin,* no. 72 (1907).

L.J.I.

PAISLEY WEAVERS. *See* Scots.

PALANDECH, JOHN R. *See* Serbs.

PALATINATE MENNONITES. *See* Mennonites.

PALESTINIANS. *See* Arabs.

PAN-SLAVISM. *See* Yugoslavs.

PAN-SLAVS. *See* Slavs.

PANAMANIANS. *See* Central Americans.

PANEL ON IMMIGRATION STATISTICS. *See* Immigration Statistics, National Research Council Report.

PANUNZIO, CONSTANTINE. *See* Immigrant Autobiographies.

PAPER SONS. *See* Chinese, paper sons.

PARK, ROBERT EZRA (1864–1944). Sociologist of the Chicago "School of Sociology." From 1914 until his death in 1944 Robert E. Park was one of the most eminent of American sociologists. He was one of the first to believe that public opinion could be measured. At the suggestion of Booker T. Washington, Park began to study the lives of southern blacks. This led him to believe that conflict leads to the formation of communities. From 1914 to 1929 he was with the Department of Sociology of the University of Chicago. From 1936 to 1944 he lectured at Fisk University. In the *Introduction to the Science of Sociology* (1921) he and co-author Ernest W. Burgess discussed their view that interaction assumes four forms: competition, conflict, accommodation, and assimilation. In his work *The Immigrant Press and Its Control* (1922) he argued that the press contributed to the eventual assimilation of newcomers. This position was quite different from that more commonly held, which argued that the foreign-language press represented a stubborn effort to maintain a separate culture and resist assimilation. In his work *Race and Culture* (1913–1944) he gave attention to the "marginal man," to one who moves in several different cultures and does not feel completely comfortable in any. For several decades Park contributed substantially to the literature on immigrants and their relationship to the new society, and cultural conflict and accommodation.

References
James T. Carey, *Sociology and Public Affairs. The Chicago School* (1975); Winifred Rauschenbusch, *Robert Ezra Park: Biography of a Sociologist* (1979).

G.B.

THE PASSAIC COUNTY, NEW JERSEY, HISTORICAL SOCIETY. The Passaic County Historical Society encourages an active public interest in the history of Passaic County by preserving the materials that interpret that history and making these available through exhibits, lectures, tours, and publications. Since 1924, the society has operated a museum in historic Lambert Castle, a structure owned by the Passaic County Parks Commission. The society maintains an important library and archives available to the amateur historian, professional scholar, and genealogical researcher with over 20,000 manuscripts, pamphlets, and maps. A superb collection of 80,000 domestic silk items represents an excellent overview of weaving and design techniques. The castle houses the society's fine and decorative arts collection and an unsurpassed collection of local history photographs. Lambert Castle was built between 1890 and 1893 for the Paterson silk magnate Catholina Lambert (1834–1923) and his family. The grandeur of the castle, which was further expanded by a 100-foot addition added in 1896, was the showcase of Lambert's famous art collection of paintings, statuary, and antiques. The castle was a center of social life among Paterson's industrial aristocracy who had made fortunes in silk, linen thread, machinery, and locomotives. Heavy debts forced Lambert to sell his collection in 1916. The castle was sold in 1925 and was used as a fresh air camp and hospital before the County Park Commission moved offices there and permitted the Passaic County Historical Society to operate a museum on the first floor. Current renovations will restore some of the original splendor of the castle and create a community room on the second floor. In addition to "The Silk Elite" component of "Life and Times in Silk City," there are period rooms and local history and art collections on display.

Reference
John A. Herbst and Catherine Keene, *Silk City: A Photographic Essay of Paterson, New Jersey* (1984).

F.C.

PASSAIC TEXTILE STRIKE (1926). A ten-month strike of 15,000 textile workers (largely immigrant) employed in the woolen and worsted mills of Passaic, New Jersey, that took place in 1926. The strike was under the leadership of members of the Communist party and attracted widespread public attention.

Reference
Morton Siegel, "The Passaic Textile Strike of 1926," Ph.D. dissertation, Columbia University, 1962 (DA 13:85).

F.C.

PASSENGER LISTS. An interest in genealogy largely stimulated in the 1930s called attention to the paucity of reference books in the field, particularly in immigration research, and the clear need for passenger lists. Lancour first issued a bibliography of passenger lists which in its 3rd edition (1963) recorded 262 sources, listed geographically.

Early lists by Strassburger and Rupp (mainly Germans to Pennsylvania) were important, but systematic and continuing research in genealogy and passenger lists was initiated by the Genealogical Publishing Company (Baltimore) in the 1950s and remains preeminent to the present time.

Lists had appeared frequently in the interval between Lancour and the 1980s, but the difficulty with these lists, published in books or in magazines, was that there was no published bibliography, and so it was necessary to check vast indexes and search for the name needed. From 1820 on the American Government demanded that every entrant should be listed and the records were kept in the National Archives, Washington. But immediately the researcher met with a difficulty; unless the name of the ship and the date of arrival were known, the National Archives could not help. Obviously hardly anyone knew this information, and researchers were at an impasse.

Filby remedied the deficiency with the publication of his *Passenger and Immigration Lists Index* (1981; annual Supp. ————.), and his *The Passenger and Immigration Lists Bibliography* (1981; 2nd ed., 1988). Other important works include Tepper, *Emigrants to Pennsylvania, 1641–1819; Immigrants to the Middle Colonies; New World Immigrants* (1975–1979); Boyer's *Ship Passenger Lists* . . . (1977– 1980); and Tepper, *American Passenger Arrival Records* . . . (1988).

In the early 1980s, the National Archives transferred the originals of the passenger lists (from 1820 on) to Temple University, Philadelphia, for research. In turn the records were transferred to the Balch Institute, Philadelphia, and under the guidance of Ira A. Glazier the lists are being transcribed to be merged with immigration records in other parts of the world. The Genealogical Publishing Company obtained transcripts of Irish immigrants, covering the years 1846–1851, a total of almost 700,000 immigrants. Scholarly Resources of Wilmington, Delaware has started a series, *Germans to America* which will cover the period 1850–1855, and will list 700,000 names. Other publishers are entering the field and the future is bright for genealogists and historians.

Recently the Ellis Island Restoration Commission decided to computerize the names of immigrants who passed through Ellis Island between 1892 and 1954, some 17,000,000 names, and expects to have the project completed by 1992, if funds allow.

The Filby compilation is not confined to passenger lists. Many naturalization lists may be considered passenger lists, since although the date of arrival is not known, all were immigrants. Similarly any list which mentions country of origin *inter alia,* has been used in the lists.

Thus there are thousands of names included which are not taken from passenger lists, but they can be regarded as such, and can be called "synthetic" or "inferential."

References

Carl Boyer, *Ship Passenger Lists* . . . (1977–1980); P. William Filby, *et al.*, *Passenger and Immigration Lists Index* (3 vols., 1981; *Supps.*, 1981 ————.); P. William Filby, *Passenger and Immigration Lists Bibliography* (1981; 2nd ed., 1988); *The Famine Immigrants* (7 vols., 1983–1987); *Germans to America* (1988 ————. 3 vols. to date); Harold Lancour, *Bibliography of Ship Passenger Lists, 1538–1825* (3rd ed., 1963); I. D. Rupp, *A Collection of Upwards of 30,000 Names of Immigrants* . . . (1931; rep. 1985); R. B. Strassburger, *Pennsylvania German Pioneers* . . . *1727–1808* (3 vols., 1934; rep. 1983); Michael Tepper, *Emigrants to Pennsylvania, 1641–1819* . . . (2 vols., 1975–1979); Michael Tepper, *American Passenger Arrival Records: A Guide* . . . (1988).

P.W.F.

PATRI, ANGELO (1876–1965). Educator; Italian immigrant school principal in New York City, with a strong commitment to assimilation. "Americanize the foreigner, nay, through the child let us fulfill our destiny and Americanize America." Autobiography: *A Schoolmaster of the Great City* (1917).

F.C.

PATRIOTIC ORDER SONS OF AMERICA. *See* Junior Order of United American Mechanics.

PAUL WILHELM, DUKE OF WURTTEMBERG (1797–1860). German nobleman; traveler; scientist. Author of *Erste Reise nach dem nördlichen Amerika in den Jahren 1822 bis 1824* (1835), a first-hand account of the American West, of the fur-trading Chouteaus, Robidoux, Papins, and Joshua Pilcher; of many French and American frontier types, and Indian tribes as widely disparate as the peaceful Osages and the powerful Pawnees and Arikaras of the Plains. At every stage, Duke Paul recorded not only the human beings he saw but also the vast array of plants and animals which only a scientist of his training could identify, sometimes for their first appearance in scientific description.

Reference

Paul Wilhelm, Duke of Württemberg, *Travels in North America, 1822–1824*, trans. W. Robert Nitske, ed. Savoie Lottinville (1973).

F.C.

PENSIONADO ACT OF 1903. *See* Filipinos, Pensionado Act of 1903.

PEREZ v. *BROWNELL* (356 U.S. 44). *See* Citizenship, determinations.

PERMANENT RESIDENT STATUS. On November 25, 1974 the United States Supreme Court in the case of *Saxbe* v. *Bustos* (43 L.W. 4017) held that permanent resident aliens residing abroad and commuting to work in the United States, on either a seasonal or daily basis, are entitled to maintain their status as permanent residents and may be admitted to the United States without further documentation, with the exception of evidence to show their status as permanent resident aliens of the United States. The Immigration and Naturalization Service has for a number of years permitted aliens who have their homes in Canada or Mexico the privilege of commuting daily to places of employment in the United States. Moreover, it has permitted aliens residing abroad to do so on a seasonal basis as well. The question before the Court was whether the practice of permitting aliens to reside abroad and to work in the United States either daily or seasonally conforms with the Immigration and Nationality Act. The essential question was whether or not alien commuters were immigrants who were "lawfully admitted for permanent residence" and were "returning from a temporary visit abroad" when they entered the United States and were, thus, "special immigrants" under the Immigration and Nationality Act. It had long been an administrative construction of the statute in the context of commuter aliens to permit such a practice. Mr. Justice Douglas delivered the opinion of the Court in the 5–4 decision.

Reference
Austin T. Fragomen, Jr., "Permanent Resident Status Redefined," *International Migration Review* 9 (Spring 1975): 63–68.

F.C.

PETROSINO, GIUSEPPE (1860–1909). Italian-American legendary New York City detective who fought the dreaded *La Mano Nera* (the Black Hand) (*q.v.*), whose terror (criminal violence, extortion, etc.) dominated the Italian-American communities of the first two decades of this century. Petrosino was murdered in Palermo, Sicily, in 1909 when he was on assignment to investigate the Italian criminal connections with the American Black Hand.

References
Arrigo Petacco, *Joe Petrosino* (1974); Thomas M. Pitkin and Francesco Cordasco, *The Black Hand* (1977).

T.M.P.

PHILADELPHIA MUMMERS PARADE. The early customs in the city of Philadelphia, at least those connected with mummery, resemble those found in Great Britain in connection with the Mummers' Play, the Plough Play, and the Sword Dance. These were always performed by the less well-to-do. The average parade participant was most certainly not one to keep a diary or leave any account of his social activities. The major source of information about this social order is from outsiders, people who did keep diaries; the public records, newspapers, and magazines; and the mummers themselves.

Reference
Charles E. Welch, "The Philadelphia Mummers Parade: A Study in History, Folklore, and Popular Tradition," Ph.D. dissertation, University of Pennsylvania, 1968.

F.C.

PHILADELPHIA ORPHAN SOCIETY. *See* Gratz, Rebecca.

PHILADELPHIA RIOTS OF 1844. The Philadelphia Riots of 1844, which pitted nativists against Irish Catholics, had roots in economic and social conflict as well as religious differences. A majority of the nativist rioters were skilled artisans in such trades as weaving, shoemaking, and ship carpentry. This preponderance of skilled workers among the rioters is to be attributed to the Depression of 1837–1843 and the fact that Irish Catholic immigrants often proved willing to work for employers in certain trades for less than the prevailing native wages.

Reference
Michael J. Feldberg, "The Philadelphia Riots of 1844: A Social History," Ph.D. dissertation, University of Rochester, 1970 (DA 31:3466-A).

F.C.

PICTURE BRIDES. *See* Koreans.

PIFER, ALAN. *See* Bilingual Education.

PINNOLA, REV. CIRO (d. 1946). *See* Italian-Albanians.

THE PITTSBURGH [PENNSYLVANIA] SURVEY. A massive survey of the city between 1904 and 1914, the first attempt made in the United States to examine thoroughly and at close range the conditions under which working people (largely immigrant) spent their lives in a modern industrial community. The *Survey* was sponsored by the Russell Sage Foundation and included a distinguished staff headed by Paul U. Kellogg (*q.v.*), Florence Kelley (*q.v.*), John R. Commons (*q.v.*), and

Robert A. Woods (*q.v.*). The Russell Sage Foundation, whose president was the ubiquitous Robert W. De Forest (*q.v.*), assumed the major share of the considerable costs of the venture. Field work, carried out in 1907 and 1908, was sufficiently near completion by November of the latter year to make possible an exhibition, patterned after the New York tenement house exhibition of 1900, to display the findings of the survey staff to the people of Pittsburgh. The findings were summed up at a joint session of the American Economic Association and the American Sociological Society in December 1908; and an abbreviated version of the *Survey* report appeared in special issues of *Charities and the Commons* in the winter of 1909.

The *Pittsburgh Survey* was the first attempt made in the United States to examine thoroughly and at close range the conditions under which working people spent their lives in a modern industrial community. The survey staff put the steel district under a microscope, and the facts revealed were far from pleasant. So far as the findings are susceptible of brief summary, they showed an incredible amount of overwork, reaching the extreme of a twelve-hour day and seven-day work week in the steel mills and railroad switchyards; wages that, though not lower than in other cities, were adjusted to the requirements of a single man rather than to the needs of a responsible head of a family; still lower wages for women, averaging about one-half to one-third of the earnings of men; an absentee capitalism with social and economic results similar to those produced by absentee landlordism; and the destruction of family life under the combined pressures of the extraordinary demands of work on men, women, and children, the prevalence of preventable diseases such as typhoid fever, and the cruelly high toll of industrial accidents.

The total picture that emerged from the laboriously compiled volumes of the survey was one of appalling waste resulting from social timidity and disinclination to interfere with the rites of moneymaking. In Pittsburgh, lives, health, strength, education, and even the industrial efficiency of workmen were treated as things of little worth. The important matters were output, time, cost, and profit. In comparison to these considerations human lives and happiness were relatively unimportant. "Make do, wear out, use up, replace, discard," applied no less to men and women than to other expendable items in the industrial process. It was easier and cheaper to do business that way, and it did not seem to matter much that this false economy imposed unnecessary hardship and suffering both on individual families and on the entire community.

The Pittsburgh survey was by far the most important of the prewar social investigations. It was discussed and studied not only in Pittsburgh but throughout the country. To its influence Jane Addams [*q.v.*] attributed "the veritable zeal for reform" that agitated the United States between 1909 and 1914. Supporters of nearly every good cause drew inspiration and ammunition from its pages; yet it was not a propagandistic or polemical work. It commanded respect because it was an outstanding piece of research—honest, informative, reliable. The facts it disclosed were their own best advocates. The survey findings, especially as they related to the waste of human resources, were taken to heart by a nation just awakening to the realization that conservation was as vital to its future as exploitation had been characteristic of its past. (Bremner, 154–155)

References
Paul U. Kellogg et al., *The Pittsburgh Survey*, 6 vols. (1909–1914); Robert H. Bremner, *From the Depths* (1964).

F.C.

PLATOON SCHOOL. *See* Wirt, William.

PLAYGROUND ASSOCIATION OF AMERICA. *See* Curtis, Henry Stoddard.

POLES. Exactly when and where the first Poles arrived in America remains uncertain, yet it is clear that there were Poles residing in the Jamestown colony as early as 1608. Probably employed as artisans making pitch, tar, and soap ash for glass production and export, they successfully won enfranchisement in 1619. We know, too, that there were Poles in the Dutch settlements of New Amsterdam, in Pennsylvania, and scattered throughout most of the other northern colonies. It appears that most of these early Polish settlers were craftsmen, traders, or professionals who were probably Protestant in their religious affiliation. It is also safe to conclude that these early migrations represented individual decisions prompted by personal or religious concerns rather than general political or economic conditions.

This situation began to change in the 1770s when Poland's powerful neighbors—Russia, Prussia, and Austria—conspired to divide Poland among them. During this period several Poles ventured to the New World to assist in the struggle for American independence. Chief among these were Casimir Pulaski and Thaddeus Kościuszko. Pulaski, the first commander-in-chief of United States cavalry forces, performed meritorious service at the Battle of Brandywine and was mortally wounded while leading an assault at Savannah, Georgia, in October 1779. Kościuszko served as an engineering officer, receiving considerable credit for the American victory at Saratoga and later designing and constructing the fortress at West Point (1778–1780).

The beginnings of permanent Polish migration to the United States can be traced to 1795 when the Third Partition of Poland erased that nation from the map of Europe. This resulted in a wave of political refugees who settled in neighboring European nations. Tens of thousands fought under the banners of Napoleon I in a vain attempt to restore Polish independence, but with this failure many veterans migrated to North America where they settled in the French-speaking areas around New Orleans, Mobile, and Charleston. These refugees were followed by small groups of political exiles who fled Europe following the unsuccessful Polish revolutions in 1830–31, 1846, 1848, and 1863, bringing the total number of Poles in America to about 8,000 by 1860.

For the most part, with the exception of a group of Silesian farmers who settled in Texas in 1854, Polish immigration prior to 1870 was comprised of political exiles who arrived individually or in small groups and settled within the established urban centers in the north. Indeed, there were sufficient numbers in New York City for the founding of the Polish Slavonian Literary Association in 1846, the formation of the radical, pro-Republican "Democratic Society of Polish Emigrés in America" in 1852, and the first Polish-language newspaper, *Echo z Polski,* in 1863.

Beginning in the 1870s the magnitude and composition of Polish immigration changed dramatically. The political exile gave way to the poor agricultural laborer seeking employment in America's growing industries. The census of 1910, which counted only immigrants and their immediate offspring, enumerated 937,884 people born in Poland and 725,924 with one or both parents born in Poland. At its peak in 1912, some 175,000 Poles arrived in the United States, forming fully 14.6 percent of the total immigration that year. Consisting largely of unskilled workers from the Austrian and Russian sections of partitioned Poland, with males outnumbering females by two to one, they settled primarily in the eastern and midwestern industrial cities where they quickly established ethnic enclaves complete with businesses, Polish-language newspapers, social organizations, and churches.

The Poles who came to America in this massive economic migration were by many standards a simple people, yet they were motivated by very clearly defined purposes. They came primarily for economic reasons, to make a better life for themselves and their families through employment in America's expanding mines and factories. Yet economic advantage was not their sole objective. Given Poland's sad history of oppression under the partitioning powers, her sons and daughters came to the New World in search of a land that would provide opportunity for a better life while at the same time guaranteeing them freedom and individual equality.

The America that the immigrants found met many of their hopes and expectations, but it presented them with an unexpected cultural shock as well. The crowded, hectic, often inhospitable surroundings of urban America were inconceivably different from those of the quiet, unharried life-style of rural Poland where most of the newcomers had previously lived. To survive in this urban environment the Poles reacted much the same as other immigrant groups by forming ethnic communities within the various cities where they settled. The initial focal point of these communities was the local church. In Poland, a century of occupation by foreign powers had taught the people to turn to the church and the Roman Catholic clergy as their link to Polish culture and heritage. Thus, it is not surprising that the immigrant in America, alone and overwhelmed by the enormity of the cities and the problems of urban life, turned to the Church for support. The Church provided a link of familiarity with the homeland, but more importantly it served as the focal point of Polish community life in America, providing cultural stability in a sea of instability, protection against outside influences, a source of education for both young and old, and a general group support system that allowed the immigrants to survive in their new surroundings.

Given the reliance of the immigrants on the Church, it is not surprising that the first successful attempt to create a national Polish organization began with the formation of what was to become the Polish Roman Catholic Union in 1872. Eventually becoming the second-largest Polish fraternal organization, the goals of the PRCU were to provide support for the faith and for Polish ethnic and national consciousness. Yet the rise of the PRCU did not succeed in encompassing all Polish-Americans. Many leaders argued that as a *Catholic* organization, the PRCU placed priority on issues of faith rather than Polish nationalism, and also that its religious affiliation excluded Poles who were not of that persuasion. Thus, in 1880 the Polish National Alliance was founded as a secular fraternal organization whose stated goals were (1) assisting in the restoration of an independent Poland and (2) providing assistance to Polish immigrants in the United States. Eventually, the PNA grew to become the largest Polish-American organization, but as its numbers began to increase it came into direct conflict with the PRCU which saw in it a threat to the propagation of the faith. Beginning in 1882, a bitter and often acrimonious rivalry developed between the PRCU and the PNA which split Polonia into two warring camps.

Nor was there always harmony within Catholic ranks. The Polish immigrant found that the Church, in America, wielded a foreign influence in the form of an American hierarchy dominated by Irish bishops. In Poland, religion and nationalism were inextricably interwoven; in America the immigrant found that "Polish" parishes were often led by priests who did not speak the language of the parishioners or share their traditions. Simultaneously, the Irish bishops actively pursued a course of "Americanization" which reminded the Poles all too much of Bismarck's enforced *Kulturkampf* which attempted to denationalize the Poles under German domination.

To the Polish immigrant of the 1880s the predominant values were those of *polskość* (Polishness) and *równouprawnienie* (equality). In America, the Church, as the single most important link with the Old Country and the focal point of the New World ethnic community, was also at once both the immigrant's succor and his antagonist. Gradually, issues such as the ownership of parish property, the teaching of Polish language and culture in parochial schools, and representation of Polish interests in the Church hierarchy led to significant disaffection among the faithful. By 1900 Poles constituted about 12 percent of all Catholics in America. On a numerical basis this should have dictated that there be eleven bishops and two archbishops of Polish background; but there were none, and that fact became the *cause célèbre* which led to the formation of the Polish National Catholic church in 1907, the only successful schismatic movement in American Catholic history.

Politically, the Poles supported the Republican party prior to the Civil War, and were advocates of the antislavery movement. Although many continued to favor the Republicans after the war, their support for labor unions drew some toward the Democratic party in opposition to factory owners. Polish political affiliation shifted dramatically to the Democrats when Woodrow Wilson included the independence of Poland among his "Fourteen Points." Reinforced by an overwhelming attachment to Franklin Roosevelt's "New Deal," it has been estimated that some 82 percent of Polish-Americans voted for John F. Kennedy in 1960, and that the alienation of Polish-American voters was a major cause for the defeat of Gerald Ford in 1976. In 1980 it was estimated that as many as 77 percent of all Polish-Americans are registered Democrats.

Today, most of the old Polish neighborhoods have disappeared except in the large urban centers of the Northeast, and there the Polish population is older, on average, than that of other groups. The third and fourth generations of Polonia have maintained many of the old Polish fraternal and cultural organizations, and Polish festivals and other activities keep alive the traditions and heritage of the past. But federal statistics indicate that the third and fourth generations have become suburbanites. By 1980 the mean income of Polish-Americans was above the national average, and information on home ownership, education, and other quality of life indices show Polish-Americans at or above the national average.

References
John J. Bukowczyk, *And My Children Did Not Know Me: A History of the Polish Americans* (1987); Victor Greene, *For God and Country: The Rise of Polish and Lithua-*

nian Ethnic Consciousness in America (1975); Anthony Kuzniewski, *Faith and Fatherland: The Polish Church War in Wisconsin, 1896–1918* (1980); Helena Znaniecki Lopata, *Polish Americans: Status Competition in an Ethnic Community* (1976); Frank Mocha, ed., *Poles in America: Bicentennial Essays* (1978); Donald Pienkos, *P.N.A.: Centennial History of the Polish National Alliance of the United States of North America* (1984); Frank Renkiewicz, ed., *The Polish Presence in Canada and America* (1982); Andrzez Brozek, *Polish Americans, 1854–1939* (1985).

J.S.P.

POLES, Association of Polish Journalists in America. Founded in Detroit in April 1929. The organization, designed to be professional and nonpolitical, had as its aim the inculcation of professional and responsible journalism among the members and the protection of "the good name of Poles and Poland." In the late 1930s, the association reorganized as the Association of Polish Journalists and Publishers. The decline of Polish journalism after World War II led to the association's gradual disbandment.

Reference
Eugene Obidinski, "The Polish American Press: Survival Through Adaptation," *Polish American Studies* 34 (Fall 1977): 42–46.

D.N.A.

POLES, *Dziennick Zwiazkowy. See* Americanization Movement.

POLES, Felician Sisters. Polish-American sisterhoods have played an important role in the American parochial school system. They staffed the Catholic schools the Polish immigrants founded to maintain Old World linguocultural values. By adapting their curriculum to the needs of the children and to the requirements of the local and state departments of education, the Felician Sisters served as agents of cultural transition. They provided for a gradual linguocultural transition whereby the Polish children were Americanized without the complete loss of ethnic identity.

Reference
Ellen M. Kuznicki, "An Ethnic School in American Education: A Study of the Origin, Development, and Merits of the Educational System of the Felician Sisters in the Polish American Catholic Schools of Western New York," Ph.D. dissertation, Kansas State University, 1973.

F.C.

POLES, *The Polish Peasant in Europe and America* (William I. Thomas and Florian Znaniecki; 5 vols., 1918–1920; rpt., ed. Eli Zareksky, 1984). A classic work which alleges a disintegration of the Polish family in America. See Herbert Blumer, "Critiques of Research in the Social Sciences: An Appraisal of Thomas and Znaniecki's *The Polish Peasant in Europe and America*" (New York: Social Science Research Council, Bulletin 44, 1939); and Konstantin Symmons-Symonolewicz, "The Polish-American Community—Half a Century After the Polish Peasant," *The Polish Review* 11 (Summer 1966): 67–73.

F.C.

"POLISH EMIGRÉS IN AMERICA." *See* Poles.

POLISH NATIONAL CATHOLIC CHURCH. A new American denomination created at the turn of the century by dissenting Roman Catholic immigrants from Poland, it is perhaps the only nationalist church to be formed in exile. It is probably the only immigrant-formed American denomination to establish a missionary branch back in the founders' homeland within the first generation. It is the only recognized American member of the Old Catholic Union of Utrecht. It had a relationship of "intercommunion" with the Protestant Episcopal church from 1946 until 1976, when the PNC church unilaterally severed it due to the ordination of women in the Episcopal church. The PNC church is the only church in the United States to have had such a relationship with the Episcopal church. In 1985, the Vatican recognized the validity of orders (ordination of priests) of the PNC church and a formal dialogue between the two separate religious denominations has begun. Apart from the Orthodox church, such recognition by the Vatican is unique in America.

The PNC church was organized by Rev. Franciszek Hodur, a Roman Catholic priest ordained in this country in 1893. The formal organization of the PNC church occurred in 1904 in Scranton, Pennsylvania. By tradition, however, the denomination dates its beginning from 1897 when the first religious service was held in the church edifice that would become its see, St. Stanislaus Cathedral in Scranton. Similar independent parishes and groups had already formed in other immigrant centers in America, such as Chicago, Buffalo, Cleveland, and Chicopee, Massachusetts. Elected a bishop in Scranton in 1904, Bishop Hodur traveled to Chicago in an effort to unite his group with that of Bishop Antoni Kozlowski of the Polish Catholic church. After the death of Bishop Kozlowski in 1907, Bishop Hodur was consecrated in Holland by the archbishop of Utrecht, the titular head of the Old Catholic denominations in Holland, Germany, and Switzerland. Bishop Hodur succeeded in uniting most of the Polish independent movement in America. He died in 1953.

The PNC church spread to Canada, Poland, and Brazil. At its peak, it had some 250 congregations. Among these were included not only Polish but also Italian, Lithuanian, Czech, Hungarian, and Slovak congregations. The Polish language began to replace the traditional Latin in the religious services in 1900. Other languages followed and English was accepted for use in the mass in 1958. In the United States, most services are now held in English.

Mandatory celibacy was abolished in 1921. The PNC church teaches that the Word of God is a sacrament together with the traditional seven of the Roman Catholic church. It has a democratic structure. The laity, men and women, are fully participant at almost every level of decision making.

Reference
Stephen Wlodarski, *The Origin and Growth of the Polish National Catholic Church* (1974).

T.L.Z.

POLISH ROMAN CATHOLIC UNION. *See* Poles.

POLYPHONY. See Multicultural History Society of Ontario.

POPE, GENEROSO (1891–1950). Generoso Pope was born April 1, 1891 in Arpaise, a small town in the province of Benevento, near Naples, Italy. He emigrated to the United States at the age of ten and settled in New York City with the equivalent of $4 in his pocket. As an Italian immigrant with but four years of schooling in Italy, Generoso Pope began a successful career in self-education and in various business enterprises. His first employment was as a water boy in a piano factory. Through dedication, perseverance, and commitment he progressed to become owner of Colonial Sand & Stone Co., Inc., and several Italian-American newspapers, which included *Il Progresso Italo-Americano, Il Bollettino della Sera, Il Corriere d'America,* and *Opinione,* a Philadelphia daily, all of which were subsequently merged with *Il Progresso.* He also became the owner of Radio Station WHOM which was to be known as the *Il Progresso* Station.

His very active and successful career earned Generoso Pope many honors from varied sources, including citations from the Italian and American governments for improving relationships between the United States and Italy.

Generoso Pope was deeply concerned about the well-being, both physically and culturally, of not only Americans of Italian origin, but also of all other Americans. With *Il Progresso,* he was involved in relieving human suffering in major disasters that struck Italy and the United States.

Pope launched many important and successful campaigns through *Il Progresso Italo-Americano* that tremendously benefited the Italian-

American communities. He conducted several campaigns to make the readers better acquainted with the history of America, with the duties of citizenship, and with the concepts of our democracy. He vigorously supported a campaign to combat juvenile delinquency and for years strove to bring into the homes of his readers ways and means to combat the peril among the youth of our communities. He directed several campaigns for the teaching of Italian in high schools and colleges, as well as a campaign for humanizing immigration and naturalization laws so that the sacredness of the home and family life could be preserved. Through *Il Progresso* and Radio Station WHOM he effectively urged readers and listeners and their friends and relatives to write the truth about America to their friends and relatives in Italy. He began the "letter-writing campaign" on January 19, 1948, and as a result, millions of letters praising the opportunities and freedom of America poured into Italy. He shared in the distinction of having done the most to help defeat the Communists in the elections held in Italy in April 1948. During World War II, he was chairman of the Committee for Americans of Italian Origin of the State of New York, which sold more than $400 million in bonds for the War Bond Drive. Finally, he campaigned vigorously to have Columbus Day declared a legal holiday.

When Pope purchased *Il Progresso* in 1928, there was only one Italian-American judge sitting on the bench. Through *Il Progresso,* he supported and fought for every qualified Italian-American running for office regardless of party affiliation, and also strongly recommended Italian-Americans for appointive offices. Many were elected and appointed through his efforts. He helped to break the ice that led to the successful rise of the Italian-Americans in America.

Pope also fought vigorously to combat antidefamation; any slur on Italians was quickly challenged by *Il Progresso* with scathing editorials and campaigns. He established and headed a committee whose membership included distinguished and influential leaders in business, government, politics, and religion. The committee sponsored the Columbus Day Parade and the Annual Columbus Banquet at the Waldorf Astoria in New York City. The proceeds of the banquet, which through the years amounted to over a million dollars, provided scholarships for deserving students in New York City public and parochial schools. The Pope family, several years ago, severed its relationship with the committee and is now awarding scholarships which are known as the Generoso Pope Memorial Scholarships. These scholarships are indicative of Pope's deep love for New York City and its inhabitants, especially youths with a compelling interest in attending college.

In 1916, Pope married Catherine Richichi and they had three sons. He died on April 28, 1950.

F.P.

PORTUGUESE. In this summary account of Portuguese immigration, the term "Portuguese" has a broader meaning than the one familiar to most readers. The reference is not only to that westernmost portion of (continental) Europe which adjoins Spain and is known as Portugal; it also includes the Azores, a group of nine islands about one-third of the way across the Atlantic from Europe to the United States. Discovered and settled by the Portuguese in the fifteenth century, the Azores are an integral part of Portugal in a political sense, although in 1976 they were granted a measure of regional autonomy. Additionally, Portugal in the broader sense includes the island of Madeira (plus tiny Porto Santo nearby), not far from Morocco off northwest Africa. Madeira, too, is considered an integral part of Portugal in a political sense, having been settled by the Portuguese during the fifteenth century; it attained regional autonomy at the same time as the Azores. Following official Portuguese terminology, we may distinguish between continental and insular Portugal, and therefore, with respect to Portuguese immigrants, between continentals and islanders. In earlier American immigration and population statistics, a distinction was usually made between "Portugal," intended to refer to mainland Portugal, and the Azores (also known as the Western Islands); Madeira sometimes shows up under the heading "Atlantic Islands" (which actually includes the Spanish Canary Islands). Actually, many immigrants listed under "Portugal" came from the Azores.

The picture is further complicated by the fact that accounts of Portuguese immigration have usually included people from the Cape Verde Islands, an archipelago off the westernmost tip of Africa, with a racially mixed population in which the African element predominates. These islands, also originally settled by the Portuguese, never attained the status of a full-fledged part of "Metropolitan Portugal," but remained a quasi-colonial "possession" until they were granted independence in 1975. (As regards language, Cape Verdeans usually speak a Portuguese-derived Creole, rather than standard Portuguese.)

Early Portuguese Settlement in North America (Up to the Civil War). Because of Portugal's early seafaring orientation and her closeness to Spain, some Portuguese were among the very first Europeans to explore North America, on their own or more often in Spanish service. Christopher Columbus himself picked up much of his nautical knowledge while living in Portugal. A few Portuguese seafarers reached Newfoundland by the turn of the fifteenth century; another, leading a Spanish expedition, sailed down the North American coast as far as Delaware in about 1525. A handful of Portuguese served under the Spaniard Hernando de Soto, reaching the Mississippi River in 1542; another handful, as members of Coronado's Spanish expedition about the same time, pushed northward from Mexico as far as Kansas; and

João Rodrigues Cabrillo, a Portuguese captain in Spanish service, set foot along San Diego Bay in 1542, and is now feted as the "discoverer of California."

Nothing is known of actual Portuguese settlement in North America before the second third of the seventeenth century. One document refers to a native of Lisbon who arrived in Maryland in 1634; another mentions the Portuguese wife of a Dutch ensign in New Amsterdam (New York) as of 1643. During the second half of the seventeenth century and through the eighteenth, hundreds of Jews of Portuguese or Spanish descent made their way to the American colonies, often via Holland or Dutch possessions. The first such group arrived in New Amsterdam in 1654, and soon spread out to Newport, Rhode Island. Lisbon-born Aaron Lopez, who settled in Newport in 1752, played a pioneering role in developing the New England whaling industry; he recruited part of his crews in the Azores, indirectly drawing the attention of some of those islanders to settlement in New England.

Apart from Jews of continental Portuguese birth or ancestry, scattered (Christian) Portuguese individuals are attested to have been present in southeastern New England by the late eighteenth century; by the early nineteenth we find a few in New York City, in Philadelphia, around New Orleans, and even in Los Angeles and Honolulu. Among these disparate early locations, southeastern New England alone was to attract a continuous stream of Portuguese immigration; it has remained its principal focus up to the present day.

Up to the Civil War days, the New England whale fisheries were the principal "vehicle" for Portuguese settlement in the East. Yankee ships roaming the Atlantic for whales would stop over in the Azores (following the example of Aaron Lopez) for provisions, and to replenish their crews. Soon the Cape Verde Islands also became such a stopover point. In both of these archipelagos, quite neglected by the Lisbon government, poverty more than anything else led young men to eagerly sign up on American whalers. (In the 1850s, a potato rot and a grape vine disease added to the usual hardships in the Azores.) A desire to evade military service was also a strong motive for emigration from those islands. Even beyond the Civil War period, almost all Portuguese settlers in the United States were of "insular" rather than of "continental" backgrounds. Starting about the middle of the century, Azorean women began to join their sailor husbands or fiancés in New Bedford, Boston, etc., coming over on sailboats. Eventually many of the men switched from seafaring to jobs in the developing textile and other industries. Census figures for Massachusetts show 855 natives of "Portugal" as of 1855, and 1,883 by 1865; smaller numbers were then living in Rhode Island and Connecticut.

Before we turn our attention to California as the second major area of Portuguese immigration, brief mention may be made of two episodes involving Louisiana and Illinois: In 1840, a few hundred contract laborers were brought from ''Portugal'' to Louisiana to work on the sugar plantations there; many of these later moved into New Orleans, or on to California. (Another less successful attempt to use Portuguese contract labor on the Louisiana plantations was to be made in the early 1870s). Also in the late 1840s, over a thousand Madeirans who had been converted to Protestantism by a Scotch missionary but had run into violent opposition by the dominant Catholic church decided to leave Madeira for Trinidad in the British West Indies, where there was an advertised need for plantation labor. However, unable to adapt to Trinidad's climate and work conditions, they soon moved on from that island to Illinois, where the American Protestant Society had promised to find them work. There they all settled around Springfield and Jacksonville (one of them becoming Abraham Lincoln's maid).

Many of the whaling ships carrying Azorean crew members did not confine themselves to Atlantic hunting grounds; while plying the Pacific they would visit the California coast (and occasionally Hawaii), as early as the 1780s and beyond the 1850s. Yet whaling was less of a factor in initiating Portuguese settlement on the West Coast than it was in New England. Instead, the gold rush of 1848–49 was the event that brought in the first small numbers of Portuguese, about 100 of them by 1850. By 1860, there were about 1,500 (most of them from the western Azores), chiefly along San Francisco Bay and in the San Joaquin Valley, where they soon turned to agricultural pursuits.

The First Period of Portuguese Mass Immigration (c. 1870–1921). Early United States immigration statistics, incomplete as they are, show the arrival of about 2,600 ''Portuguese'' during the forty-year period from 1820 to 1860. A similar number came during the single decade of 1861–1870. But the influx increased to some 14,000 during 1871–1880, and more thereafter (the peak decade being 1911–1920, with 89,732 official immigrants). In fact, we can fix the end of the Civil War as the start of Portuguese mass immigration (''mass'' being, of course, a relative term, but in any case implying the possibility of compact ethnic networks or neighborhoods with their own institutions). Putting it in terms of population rather than migration, the United States census counted a total of 4,477 ''Portuguese''-born residents as of 1860; 15,779 by 1880; 40,376 by 1900; and 106,437 by 1920 (always exclusive of Hawaii). Out of about 235,000 ''Portuguese'' immigrants admitted into the (continental) United States from 1870 through 1921, close to one-fourth came between 1870 and 1900, nearly three-fourths during 1901–1921.

As regards regional origins, roughly two-thirds of this total were from the Azores. Emigrants from continental Portugal (the vast majority of these going to Brazil) did not show up in the United States in appreciable numbers until after 1900; by 1921 they constituted about one-fourth of the total. Madeirans, also relative latecomers (except for the Louisiana and Illinois groups), and Cape Verdeans (coming in small numbers as early as the Azoreans), made up the rest.

For most of the period under consideration (c. 1870–1921), as well as before and after, southeastern Massachusetts and adjoining Rhode Island have constituted the principal and most compact area of Portuguese settlement; California was holding first place between c. 1870 and 1895. A third major settlement area opened up in 1878: Hawaii, then also known as the Sandwich Islands. Prior to that date, there had been a sporadic influx into the Hawaiian Kingdom of several hundred Portuguese, mostly Azorean and Cape Verdean "jumpers" from American whaling ships. After the Civil War, the growing West Coast market greatly stimulated the relatively young Hawaiian sugar industry. A search for suitable plantation labor led to Madeira and to São Miguel (the most populous of the Azores islands). Between 1878 and 1888, almost 12,000 of these islanders (entire families) were brought in on a contract basis. Some stayed on the plantations beyond the contract period; many others drifted into urban Honolulu or took up farming in other parts of Hawaii, or else moved to California. (There was also some migration from New England and California to Hawaii.) A few more shiploads of laborers from Madeira and São Miguel arrived between 1895 and 1909. Shortly after the fall of the Portuguese monarchy in 1910, labor recruitment shifted to the mainland of Portugal; but the almost 1,900 continentals brought in did not stick it out on the plantations for long. As a matter of fact, since 1913 there has been practically no more Portuguese immigration into Hawaii; the Portuguese stock has become heavily intermingled with the other ethnic groups.

In New England, the half-century prior to the throttling of immigration under the Quota Law saw the Portuguese immigrants and their American-born offspring become a major population element in such places as New Bedford, Fall River, Providence, and surrounding areas; also Taunton, Provincetown, Gloucester, and some sections of Greater Boston. Unskilled labor in the cotton industry became the economic mainstay of these immigrants. Relatively few of them found their livelihood in fishing and small-scale farming, which better fitted their Old Country backgrounds than factory work. In California, on the other hand, the majority of the Portuguese were able to establish themselves in agriculture, becoming a dominant element in the San Joaquin Valley's dairy production, and in fruit and vegetable gardening chiefly around San Francisco Bay; many of them moved toward middle-class status or even some wealth, sooner and to a greater extent than the Portuguese in the East were able to do.

Developments Under the Old Quota Law (1921–c. 1958). The literacy requirement for immigration as adopted in 1917 hit Portugal particularly hard because of the very high degree of illiteracy there. Moreover, under the Immigration Act of 1921 as revised in 1924 and 1929, the immigration quota for Portugal (including the Azores, Madeira, and Cape Verde Islands) was set at about 500 persons per year, although the restriction did not apply to children and spouses of United States citizens. Squeezing in while the gates were closing, some 19,000 Portuguese still managed to get admitted in 1921; but for 1922–1930 the average number of (quota and nonquota) arrivals per year dropped to little over a thousand. The total for the entire period from 1931 to 1958 fell to barely 20,000 (not counting a number of illegal entrants, of course).

Only a minor proportion of the roughly 50,000 Portuguese who immigrated from 1921 to 1958 (usually entering at Providence or New York) went on to California, and practically none to Hawaii. Thus the proportion of American born to foreign born, and de-ethnicization with it, grew most in Hawaii, and more in California than in the East. The period under consideration also brought a moderate extension of the eastern settlement area from southeastern into southwestern New England and into the New York–New Jersey metropolitan area (especially Newark, New Jersey). This was partly in connection with the gradual collapse of the New England cotton industry, which forced many Portuguese into some dislocation to enter other light industries or the service trades. In California, there was some shift from rural to urban, and from central to southern parts of the state. The proportion of continentals to islanders increased, but the latter retained majority status.

The New Portuguese Mass Immigration (1958 to the 1980s). The somewhat arbitrary choice of the year 1958 as the start of this latest period is due to the fact that in 1957–58 a series of earthquakes in the Azores left almost 25,000 inhabitants homeless, and that as a result of Portuguese-American pleadings Congress passed the so-called Azorean Refugee Act which permitted about 5,000 of the affected persons to enter the United States outside the regular quota. Although the new Immigration Act of 1965 eliminated the nationality quota system altogether, the (Azorean) Portuguese thus benefited from the postwar loosening of immigration restrictions a little earlier than other countries. Apart from the earthquake relief action, however, a true resumption of Portuguese mass immigration had to wait until 1966, with 8,713 arrivals that year, and 13,927 in 1967. As a matter of fact, for the ten-year period 1965–1974 the total number of Portuguese immigrants was about 120,000—far more than during any previous ten-year period. By 1967 Portugal had become one of the four leading sources of new immigration to the United States (after the United Kingdom, Italy, and Taiwan).

As regards regional origins of this new wave of immigration up to the present, the proportion of Azoreans and continentals was now roughly equal (with hardly any Madeirans or Cape Verdeans). The settlement pattern remained similar to the past: Massachusetts and Rhode Island still attracted at least half of the newcomers (because of existing social networks rather than good job opportunities). But there was an increase in the share of adjoining Connecticut and metropolitan New York–New Jersey (some 30 percent of the total), most of the rest trying their luck in California. Important differences between this new wave of Portuguese mass immigration and the earlier one include the fact that the newer immigrant is more literate, brings with him or her more of an urban background, and has more of a sense of nationality rather than village mentality.

Exact statistics leading into the 1980s are not at hand; but recent years have definitely seen a drop in the level of Portuguese immigration, compared to the 1970s.

References
Leo Pap, *The Portuguese in the United States: A Bibliography* (1976); Leo Pap, *The Portuguese Americans* (1981); Francis M. Rogers, *Americans of Portuguese Descent: A Lesson in Differentiation* (1974); Jerry R. Williams, *And Yet They Come: Portuguese Immigration from the Azores to the United States* (1982).

L.P.

POST, LOUIS FREELAND (1849–1928). Reformer and journalist involved in radical reconstruction in South Carolina, the Henry George single-tax movement, and various phases of Progressivism. Post's finest hour came in early 1920 during the Red Scare. Attorney general A. Mitchell Palmer and his men had rounded up thousands of alien radicals for deportation. Since the Labor Department had jurisdiction over deportation proceedings and since circumstances left Post as the highest-ranking officer in the department, it was up to Post to decide on the deportations. Post's perusal of the cases convinced him that Palmer and his young assistant, J. Edgar Hoover, had grossly overstepped the bounds of due process. Post's action was a key factor in bringing the excesses of the Red Scare into check.

Reference
Dominic L. Candeloro, "Louis Freeland Post: Carpetbagger, Singletaxer, Progressive," Ph.D. dissertation, University of Illinois, Urbana, 1970 (DA 31: 6509-A).

F.C.

PRÉVOST BROTHERS. *See* Swiss.

PREZZOLINI, GIUSEPPE (1882–1982). Italian journalist, educator. Prezzolini founded "La Voce" in 1908. Its credo was action and its

writers had an awareness of social and spiritual issues that enlisted the
support of the best minds of Italy. Its effect was felt in literature, music,
art, philosophy, and politics. Thus was Italian culture integrated into the
life of the nation. At the recommendation of Arthur Livingston, Prezzolini was invited to Columbia University in 1923 and soon won the
trust of its administrators. He was much appreciated by colleagues and
students. After the outbreak of World War II, he proudly became an
American citizen, and for another decade continued to teach, to study,
and to write at Columbia University. A tireless and intrepid exponent of
Italy's cultural legacy, Prezzolini made the Casa Italiana at Columbia
University (*q.v.*) a veritable beehive of scholarly and educational activity. He was a born educator. His writings, whether scholarly or
journalistic, are delightful because of his clear, precise, well-balanced
style. He had a great variety of interests and his pen ranges from
German mysticism to an erudite history of spaghetti, with biography,
criticism, philosophy, scholarship, reportage, religion, and psychology
filling the gap. Prezzolini was instrumental in bringing foreign liter-
atures to Italy, interpreting them to his audience, and then sharing with
the rest of the world the rich outpouring of Italian literature and cultural
achievements.

References
Prezzolini: un secolo di attività, ed. Margherita Marchione (1982); Giuseppe Prezzolini,
Come gli Americani scoprirono l'Italia (1933); Giuseppe Prezzolini, *I trapiantati* (1963).

M.M.

PROCLAMATION 3656. *See* Ellis Island.

PROGRESSIVE REFORMERS AND THE IMMIGRANTS. "In
politics, the immigrant was usually at odds with the reform aspirations
of the American Progressive," wrote Richard Hofstadter in *The Age of
Reform* in 1955. "Together with the native conservative and the politically indifferent," he continued, "the immigrants formed a potent mass
that limited the range and achievements of American Progressive."
Over the past quarter-century, there has been a significant outpouring of
scholarly literature on both the Progressive Era and on the political
behavior of immigrants and their immediate descendants which has, in
the main, modified the notion of an unbridgeable chasm between "reformer" and "immigrants."

Much of the difficulty in developing valid generalizations regarding the interaction between "Progressive" reform and immigrants lies
in the amorphous nature of both constructs. Regardless of claims to the
contrary made by contemporaries and historians, there never was anything like a single "Progressive movement" or a reasonably coherent
reform ideology deserving of the name "Progressive". Many of its

manifestations were mutually contradictory or of questionable "progressiveness." In short, the Progressive Era was characterized by a plethora of movements and proposals all claiming to be "progressive reforms." By the same token, there was clearly no such thing as a monolithic "immigrant" reaction to the era's variegated "reform" agitation. Every reform proposal, even those such as immigration restriction, Americanization, or the disenfranchisement of immigrants, created fissures among and within the various national groups, based upon such variables as religious values, socioeconomic status, length of U.S. residence, gender and age distribution, and commitment to retention of Old World beliefs and practices.

Recognizing the complexity and volatility of the situation, it seems feasible to assert that (1) only some types of native-stock reformers advocating certain proposals enjoyed much success at bridging the gap between themselves and some immigrant groups; (2) that many immigrants and their representatives played an influential and positive role in the enactment of labor and welfare laws, regulatory and tax reform, and democratization of the political process; and (3) that many of these same people constituted a vital segment of the opposition to structural political reform, to legislated cultural conformity, and, ultimately, to immigration restriction.

Perhaps chief among those native-born activists who succeeded in bridging the gap to immigrant America were the group of urban political leaders whom Melvin Holli has dubbed "social reformers." These were successful businessmen or professionals of old Protestant stock who emphasized socioeconomic reforms, opposed legislated conformity, defended ethnic and racial minorities from discrimination, dispensed patronage and recognition, and opposed such structural reforms as at-large and nonpartisan elections, the short ballot, and civil service.

Only slightly less successful were the residents of the social settlements that sprang up in the immigrant districts of the nation's largest cities in the 1890s. These "spearheads of reform" were managed by well-educated, religiously motivated men and women from affluent, native-stock Protestant backgrounds who endeavored "first to understand the peculiar customs and traditions of each group, and then to seek as much opportunity for them as possible." Settlement houses provided a wide range of services for the inhabitants of their neighborhoods, tried to build upon immigrant traditions and skills, and stressed their "contributions" through frequent festivals, pageants, literary, dramatic, musical, and dancing presentations, and arts and crafts fairs. Increasingly, they investigated working and housing conditions, and many became involved in unionization efforts and local politics, helping community leaders to run for office, lobby for ameliorative ordinances, and serve on city boards and commissions.

Closely related to the social settlement workers were social gospel clergymen, many of them proselytizing for converts, and organizations such as the American Association for Labor Legislation, the National Consumers' League, the Women's Trade Union League, and the National Child Labor Committee. Rejecting the elitism of many woman suffrage leaders, younger "social feminists" specifically recruited among the immigrant working class, stressing the vote as a means to better working and living conditions. A handful of "good government" associations, such as Chicago's Municipal Voters League, endorsed and supported immigrant-stock candidates in aldermanic races against organization war horses. Settlement residents and their allies were the driving force behind the Immigrant Protective League and the North America Civic League for Immigrants, and were the most influential lobbyists for state bureaus of immigration. Finally, they were largely responsible for the immigration plank in the 1912 platform of the Progressive party which denounced "the fatal policy of indifference and neglect which has left our enormous immigrant population to become the prey of chance and cupidity" and which pledged "the establishment of industrial standards" and governmental action "to encourage the distribution of immigrants away from the congested cities, to rigidly supervise all private agencies dealing with them and to promote their assimilation, education and advancement."

Yet, for all that, most native-stock reformers enjoyed only limited success in their efforts to involve immigrants in reformist activity. After studying the activities of sixty municipal activists for whom immigrants were the "main customers," John J. Carey found that they "largely failed to get the immigrant involved. The reformer's paternalistic posture was partly responsible for this defect in the reform structure in that the typical social betterment workers approved of only certain forms of democratic striving."

More noteworthy was the indigenous support given Progressive candidates and reforms by immigrant communities and their elected representatives. Immigrant wards provided much of the electoral support for social progressives at the municipal and state level. In a study of the relationship between Progressive reform and the foreign born in California, Oregon, Washington, Idaho, Montana, and Nevada, Leslie Wayne Koepplin investigated the participation of immigrants in reform organizations and politics, the attitude of the immigrant press toward reform, and voting on progressive issue referenda. He discovered that immigrants had their proportional share of reformers who operated in both the private and public sectors, that foreign-language newspapers backed many reform candidates and proposals, and that there was little to differentiate immigrant voters from native-born ones on most progressive referenda.

But it was in the industrial states of the Northeast and Midwest that immigrants and their children made their most significant contribution to the Progressive Era, practicing a brand of reformism that J. Joseph Huthmacher dubbed "urban liberalism." Operating primarily through the medium of the Democratic party, immigrant-stock legislators representing predominantly immigrant districts in New York, New Jersey, Massachusetts, Ohio, and Illinois provided much of the leadership and the voting strength that earned these states their "progressive" reputations. In Connecticut and Rhode Island, lawmakers of ethnic origins constituted the only truly progressive force in states controlled by rural-based, business-oriented Republican political machines. The great majority were the American born of immigrant parentage, were affiliated with the Democratic political machines of their state's largest cities, and had close ties with organized labor. They generally achieved power between 1911 and 1915, the high point of Progressive reform in their respective states, and played a role of primary importance in earning that record.

Urban liberalism was a major force everywhere that the immigrant-stock working class formed a significant portion of the population during the Progressive Era, and its general outlines strikingly similar. First and foremost was support for labor and welfare legislation. The regulation of the rates and service of public utilities was a common denominator, as was a taxation system based on the ability to pay. On political issues they generally favored any innovation that enhanced the influence of their constituents and that did not destroy the effectiveness of their political machines, whether primary elections, initiative, referendum, and recall; Home Rule; annual elections; and the popular election of U.S. senators. They normally opposed such innovations as civil service, the short ballot, at-large, nonpartisan local elections, and the city manager and commission forms of government because these curtailed their access and influence over municipal government. Finally, they usually constituted the vanguard of resistance to measures involving legislated conformity, such as Sunday blue laws, Americanization, immigration restriction, and Prohibition.

These positions on the major reform issues of the era clearly delineated the parameters of their interaction with native-stock, middle-class progressives. Cooperation was relatively easy to achieve on labor and welfare measures with social reformers, social gospelers, and settlement house workers, although the latter groups were less enthusiastic about the rise of organized labor. Cooperation on regulatory and taxation questions was also frequently the norm. Democratizing the political process was also a common goal, but structural political reform generally had a very divisive effect. But the issues that really set native-stock reformers and immigrants at odds were those that involved antagonistic cultural values. Prohibition and Sunday blue laws reflected a pietistic world view of a depraved human race that needed to be saved from itself, one that was anathema to Roman Catholics, Jews, Lutherans, Episcopalians, and Eastern Orthodox Christians. Americanization crusades made immigrants fight to retain cultural traits that might have eroded more quickly if they had not been threatened. Some prominent native, middle-class reformers sided with immigrants on these questions, but the majority yielded to the chauvinism of the times. The ultimate immigrant issue of the times was, of course, restriction, and here social reformers and settlement house residents were among those who battled side by side with immigrant organizations and representatives in opposition. They were joined, in curious combination, by urban political machines and by those businessmen who formed the National Liberal Immigration League. Still, most native middle-class reformers joined with organized labor, southern and western congressmen, and businessmen who feared the "radicalism" of newcomers.

References

John D. Buenker, *Urban Liberalism and Progressive Reform* (1973); John J. Carey, "Progressives and the Immigrant, 1885–1915," Ph.D. dissertation, University of Connecticut, 1968; J. Joseph Huthmacher, "Urban Liberalism and the Age of Reform," *Mississippi Valley Historical Review* 49 (1962): 231–41; Leslie W. Koepplin, "A Relationship of Reform: Immigrants and Progressives in the Far West," Ph.D. dissertation, University of California, 1971; Henry B. Leonard, "The Open Gates: The Protest Against the Movement to Restrict European Immigration, 1896–1924," Ph.D. dissertation, Northwestern University, 1968.

J.D.B.

PROLETAREC. *See* Slovenes.

PROSTITUTION. *See* Chicago Vice Commission; White Slave Trade.

PROSVETA **(Chicago).** *See* Molek, Mary.

PROTOCOL, THE (1910–1916). *See* International Ladies' Garment Workers' Union.

PUBLIC EDUCATION ASSOCIATION (New York City). Formed in 1895 by a group of concerned New Yorkers to improve the schools on New York City's Lower East Side, an impoverished neighborhood of immigrants living in sorely overcrowded tenements. The reforms advocated by PEA for that neighborhood proved to be beneficial for all the city's public school children. This principle has continued to apply as PEA continues to focus on children at risk: high school dropouts, children with handicapping conditions, and junior high school students whose educational needs are complicated by the changes of adolescence. As the looming teacher shortage disproportionately affects those children who are more difficult to educate, PEA has also focused its attention on teacher education and staff development.

Reference
Sol Cohen, *Progressives and Urban School Reform: The Public Education Association of New York City, 1895–1954* (1964).

F.C.

PUERTO RICAN FORUM (New York City). A major community action group whose *The Puerto Rican Community Development Project: Un Proyecto Puertorriqueño de Ayuda Mutua Para El Desarrollo de la Communidad: A proposal for a Self-Help Project to Develop the Community by Strengthening the Family, Opening Opportunities for Youth and Making Full Use of Education* (1964; rpt. 1975) was intended as a self-help project to develop the community by strengthening the family, opening opportunities for youth, and making full use of education. The proposal is a classic study of the Puerto Rican in New York, and a major source of data on the contemporary milieu in which the Puerto Rican is found. The proposal documents a number of postulates: that once they learn English, Puerto Ricans are not "making it"; that children born in New York City of Puerto Rican parents are not automatically becoming successful New Yorkers once they go through the city's school systems; that the fate of the Puerto Ricans will not be the same as that of other immigrant groups who came before —unless some lessons learned by past immigrations are applied and the significant differences are recognized and worked with. The proposal includes: a rationale for a culturally based project; a research proposal; programs; organization of programs with a project framework; and a succinct history of the Puerto Rican migration and its trends.

F.C.

THE PUERTO RICAN STUDY, 1953–1957: A REPORT ON THE EDUCATION AND ADJUSTMENT OF PUERTO RICAN PUPILS IN THE PUBLIC SCHOOLS OF THE CITY OF NEW YORK (New York City Board of Education, 1959). *The Puerto Rican Study* was, for its time, one of the most generously funded educational studies. The Fund for the Advancement of Education provided a grant-in-aid of a half-million dollars and "contributions equivalent in amounts authorized by the Board of Education made the study a vital operation in the school system" (Foreword). The study was not completed until 1957, and it was finally published in April 1959. It is, unquestionably, the fullest study ever made of the Puerto Rican educational experience on the mainland; and, in a broader sense, it remains one of the most comprehensive statements yet made, not only of the Puerto Rican school experience, but of the educational experience of the non–English-speaking minority child in the American school. As such it is an invaluable document in American educational historiography, with all of the contemporary relevancies to ethnicity, the minority child, the contexts of poverty, and the educational needs of the "disadvantaged" child. It is strange that, in the proliferating literature on the minority child and the schools, *The Puerto Rican Study* should have been neglected; its neglect may be due to its appearance before the advent of the Johnsonian antipoverty programs of the 1960s with their educational components, and to the inevitable fate of sponsored reports whose implementation and evaluation are seldom realized or avoided for a variety of reasons.

The Puerto Rican Study's objectives are clearly stated: In a narrow sense, *The Puerto Rican Study* was a four-year inquiry into the education and adjustment of Puerto Rican pupils in the public schools of the City of New York. In a broader sense, it was a major effort of the school authorities to establish on a sound basis a citywide program for the continuing improvement of the educational opportunities of all non–English-speaking pupils in the public schools.

While the study was focused on the public schools in New York City, it was planned and concluded in the belief that the findings might be useful to all schools, public and private, that are trying to serve children from a Spanish-language culture. As the study developed, it seemed apparent that it might have values, direct or indirect, wherever children are being taught English as a second language.

It sought answers to the following specific problems: (1) What are the most effective methods and materials for teaching English as a second language to newly arrived Puerto Rican pupils? (2) What are the most effective techniques whereby the school can promote a more rapid and more effective adjustment of Puerto Rican parents and children to the community and of the community to them?

As the study progressed, its staff developed two series of related curriculum bulletins—*Resource Units,* organized around themes and designed for all pupils, and a *Language Guide Series,* which provided the content and methods for adapting the instruction to the needs of the pupils learning English (the *Study* lists the *Units* and *Series*). The *Study* also furnished a detailed description of the Puerto Rican children; devised a scale to rate English-speaking ability; and constructed a detailed program for the in-service education of teachers.

Reference
The Puerto Rican Study . . . , with an Introductory Essay by Francesco Cordasco (1972).

F.C.

PUERTO RICANS. All Puerto Ricans are U.S. citizens by birth, making them unique among Hispanic subgroups. The population is further characterized by a pattern of circular migration that was encouraged, until recently, by cheap air fares. The ease of access has an often adverse impact on Puerto Ricans' socioeconomic status, as it militates against their establishing a firm foothold in either the mainland or the island economy and contributes to other problems of adjustment.

Migration to the Mainland. Puerto Ricans were living on the United States mainland more than 140 years ago, when the island was still a secure part of the Spanish colonial empire. During the 1830s, the founding members of a Spanish benevolent society in New York City included several Puerto Rican merchants. By the middle of the nineteenth century, Puerto Rico was engaged in more commerce with the United States than it was with Spain, and the sea route between San Juan and New York (as well as other mainland ports) was well traveled. In the late nineteenth century, the movement for independence from Spain was being planned in New York City by groups of Puerto Rican and Cuban patriots. A dozen years after the U.S. takeover of Puerto Rico in 1898, the Bureau of the Census noted 1,513 Puerto Ricans on the mainland. But large-scale Puerto Rican migration to the United States mainland is a post–World War II phenomenon.

In 1940 less than 70,000 Puerto Ricans lived on the U.S. mainland. Ten years later, the migrant community had more than quadrupled to 300,000 persons, and in the following decade the population nearly tripled, to 887,000. By 1970, persons of Puerto Rican birth or parentage living in the United States numbered at least 1.4 million, and the figure grew to 1.7 million by 1975.

New York City, the first home for millions of immigrants to this country, now became the new home for a massive influx of U.S. citizens from other areas: Puerto Ricans from the West Indies and blacks from the southern states. Between 1950 and 1970, the population size of New York City remained stable at 7.9 million, but the city's racial-ethnic composition changed. In those two decades, the Puerto Rican community grew from 3 percent to better than 10 percent of the city's population. In turn, the number of blacks and persons of other races (Asian-Americans, Native Americans, etc.) grew from 10 percent to 23 percent of the population. The city's white (non–Puerto Rican) population share dropped from 87 percent to 67 percent.

While data on the migration of Puerto Ricans between the mainland and the island are limited, crude estimates from airline passenger statistics suggest a decrease in Puerto Rican migration to the mainland from the 1960s to the 1970s, some of the net loss due to reverse migration occurring during the recession years 1970, 1971, and 1976. Indeed, the ebb and flow of Puerto Rican migration appears to depend to a great extent on the relative strengths of the mainland and island economies.

Reasons for Migration. Although economics is almost always a key factor in the movement of peoples from their native land, human motivation is never that simple or simplistic. Puerto Ricans fled neither political nor religious persecution, but life on the island for many young adults, particularly in rural areas, may have seemed intolerable. As is the case in many parts of the world, rural Puerto Rico offered a static environment, with few visible avenues for upward social mobility. In the years following World War II, the urban parts of the island began to modernize, offering access to modern homes, automobiles, and other lures of modern life. Television and radio (which became ubiquitous by the 1950s) tempted rural viewers with scenes of life elsewhere. Thousands of Puerto Ricans had served in World War II and later in Korea. They came home with tales of their travels throughout the world and on the U.S. mainland. In other cases, Puerto Rican rural laborers were recruited for seasonal work on U.S. farms and gained a taste of mainland life. Air travel between San Juan and New York was quick and economical (as recently as the early 1960s the round trip economy flight between San Juan and New York was less than $100 and it still remains relatively inexpensive). In many cases, migrants first moved from their rural homes to the island's cities, and then continued northward to the U.S. mainland.

The hardships endured by the earliest migrants became less harsh for the later arrivals, who found relatives and friends waiting, stores that sold familiar vegetables and fruits, and even Spanish-language newspapers and radio and television programs. Migration nourished itself, to the point where some made the three-hour flight to another world on a whim, or in reaction to some personal setback. If one can sum up the motivations, they could all be equated with the search for a better life.

The question of economics was, of course, ever present and probably decisive. Wage levels on the U.S. mainland were higher than those in Puerto Rico, and the opportunities for employment were more numerous and more varied.

Since the World War II, there have been three distinct trends in Puerto Rican migration, and all three have responded to job opportunities on the mainland and the island:

(1) In the 1950s, an average of 41,000 Puerto Ricans migrated to the United States each year. The U.S. economy was booming, and job recruiters came to the island in search of workers for the sweatshops in the needlework industry. During this period, Puerto Rico, unlike the mainland, offered few urban jobs, particularly in factories, that could serve as a social step upward in comparison to field labor. At the same time, thousands of Puerto Rican farm workers were afflicted by unemployment or had seasonal work (such as sugarcane cultivation) that left

them idle for several months of the year. This was the single biggest decade of Puerto Rican migration, as more than 400,000 persons (nearly 20 percent of the island's population) moved to the U.S. mainland.

(2) By the 1960s, life had changed in Puerto Rico. While the U.S. economy was still vigorous, the island itself had begun to industrialize; hundreds of new factories opened, offering jobs and the chance for a life of modest comfort in Puerto Rico. Although these opportunities blunted the migratory thrust somewhat, the new factories could absorb neither all of the young persons entering the labor force nor the farm workers idled by the shrinkage of agricultural jobs. During the decade, an average of 20,000 persons migrated to the United States each year.

(3) The U.S. economy began to turn sour in the early 1970s. Unemployment became widespread. Many factories closed in the New York City area. Despite the fact that Puerto Rico, too, was severely lashed by the recession of the 1970s (unemployment on the island soared to 19 percent by 1975), prospects for mainland jobs were so bleak that the migration flow was reversed. Since 1970 there has been a consistent trend of net return migration to the island each year. This is the first time that such a reverse migration trend has sustained itself over a prolonged period, except for the years 1931–34, when the United States was in the midst of the Great Depression.

It should be noted at this point that return migration to Puerto Rico is not just a phenomenon of the 1970s. There has *always* been constant return migration to Puerto Rico, but in previous years the number of migrants to the United States has almost invariably exceeded the number of return migrants. In 1965, for example, more than 22,000 persons moved back to Puerto Rico. In 1969–1970, nearly 129,000 persons returned. All of these persons had lived on the mainland for at least six months, and a third of them had lived there for more than six years.

With such constant back-and-forth movement, it is difficult to find a Puerto Rican adult on the island who has not spent at least some time in the United States. Some observers have perceived the two Puerto Rican communities (on the island and on the mainland) as two parts of the same organism, linked by a highway in the air. By 1980, the combined population of Puerto Ricans on the island and the U.S. mainland was in excess of 5.1 million, with 66 percent residing in Puerto Rico, some 20 percent in New York City, and the remainder living elsewhere on the U.S. mainland.

Estado Libre Asociado. The political status of Puerto Rico is a volatile issue among those who favor commonwealth status, statehood, or total independence. It is an issue that dominates Puerto Rican politics—on the island and the mainland. From 1898, at the conclusion of the Spanish-American War, to 1952, Puerto Rico was a territory of the United States. In 1952, it became an *estado libre asociado,* or commonwealth, which allows the island a measure of self-government while it remains part of the United States. Despite the fact that the new arrangement provided Puerto Ricans with a greater measure of self-government, many of the vestiges of colonialism that were present prior to the compact remain. For example, Puerto Ricans have no voting representation in Congress and cannot vote in U.S. presidential elections. However, the president can order Puerto Ricans into battle, as occurred in the Korean conflict, where one out of every forty-two Americans killed was a Puerto Rican. These and similar facts are cited by proponents of both statehood and independence. Supporters of commonwealth status recognize the shortcomings of the present situation but believe that they can be ameliorated gradually within the commonwealth framework.

It should also be noted that island residents do not pay federal income taxes, which permits the island to offer major tax advantages to qualifying firms. That allowed the famed Operation Bootstrap to attract new business into Puerto Rico and transform the island from a primarily agricultural society to an industrial one.

The history of Puerto Rican migration to the United States is similar to that of Mexican-Americans in a number of respects. Both flows included large numbers of unskilled laborers seeking work in the low-wage sector of the U.S. economy. Like Mexican-Americans, Puerto Ricans on the mainland are highly concentrated regionally; until recently, their migration has been directed primarily to New York City and its surrounding areas. Both groups have been victims of discrimination and prejudice. Reflecting the lateness of their large-scale arrival on the mainland, however, Puerto Ricans did not organize there in significant numbers until the late fifties, well behind the Mexican-American community in that respect. Another difference is that Puerto Ricans have always been concentrated primarily in central cities like New York, where their employment outlook has depended on the strength of the local manufacturing and service sectors. Their low wages in the secondary labor market of those sectors, the decline of manufacturing jobs in the Northeast, and the high cost of urban living have contributed much to the status of Puerto Ricans as the poorest of U.S. Hispanic groups.

References

Francesco Cordasco, *The Puerto Rican Community and Its Children on the Mainland* (1982); Francesco Cordasco, *The Puerto Rican Experience* (1975); Joseph P. Fitzpatrick, *Puerto Rican Americans: The Meaning of Migration to the Mainland* (1987); History Task Force, Centro de Estudios Puertorriqueños, *Labor Migration Under Capitalism: The Puerto Rican Experience* (1979); Manuel Maldonado-Dennis, *The Emigration Dialectic: Puerto Rico and the USA* (1980); Vilma Ortiz, "Changes in the Characteristics of Puerto Rican Migrants from 1955 to 1980," *International Migration Review* 20 (Fall 1986): 612–628; *The Status of Puerto Ricans in the United States* (National Congress for Puerto Rican Rights, 1985).

F.C.

PUERTO RICANS, Conference on Education of Puerto Rican children on the Mainland (October 18–21, 1970). An invitational conference held from October 18 through October 21, 1970 by the Commonwealth of Puerto Rico Department of Education. The participants, who included educators from both the island and the mainland, considered the following topics: the cultural background of the Puerto Rican child; the testing and placement of Spanish-speaking children; overcoming the language barrier of the Spanish-speaking child; recruiting and training teachers of English for Spanish-speaking children; preparing instructional materials; and the effective cooperation of Puerto Rican agencies.

Reference
José M. Gallardo, ed., *Proceedings of [the] Conference on Education of Puerto Rican Children on the Mainland* (1972; rpt. 1975).

F.C.

PUERTO RICANS, in Hawaii. After the Spanish-American War of 1898 and the new territorial status of Hawaii and Puerto Rico following annexation of both by the United States, Hawaiian sugar planters looked to Puerto Rico for a cheap labor supply. The migration of Puerto Rican workers (recruited by the Hawaiian Sugar Planters' Association) began in 1901 and continued for some years. Descendants of the elders who came to Hawaii may be found throughout the state. Some have left for other places, with a few going to their ancestral home, Puerto Rico. Many are a mixture of ethnic strains, as the percentage of interracial marriage has been high throughout the years. Statistically, they are difficult to identify, for population statistics over the years did not always identify them as a separate group. How those of mixed parentage have been counted is a complex process. The following table is based on the work of Robert C. Schmitt, Eleanor C. Nordyke, and the U.S. Bureau of Census.

Population Table of Puerto Ricans

Year	Number
1900–1901	5,200
1910	4,890
1920	5,602
1930	6,671
1940	8,296
1950	9,551
1960	Not available
1970	Not available
1980	19,351

The figures in the later years reflect a combination of contract laborers and their descendants, plus those persons who have come as individuals since the discontinuance of importation of contract laborers.

Reference
Blase Comacho Souza, "Trabajo y Tristeza—Work and Sorrow: The Puerto Ricans of Hawaii, 1900–1902," *Hawaiian Journal of History* 18 (1984): 156–173.

F.C.

PUERTO RICANS, Mayor's Committee on Puerto Rican Affairs.
See [New York City]: *Bilingual Education in New York City. . . .*

PULASKI, CASIMIR. *See* Poles.

PUPIN, MICHAEL. *See* Immigrant Autobiographies.

PURITANS. *See* English.

PURRY, JEAN PIERRE. *See* Swiss.

QUANDO CANTA IL GALLO. *See* Giovannitti, Arturo M.

QUILL, MICHAEL JOSEPH (1905–1966). Labor leader. Born in Kilgarvin, County Kerry, Ireland, Quill emigrated to the United States in 1926 and settled in New York. He was one of the founders of the Transport Workers of America (TWUA) and later became vice-president of the CIO. He fought with the revolutionary forces in Ireland during 1919–1923 and was reputed to have joined the IRA at fifteen years of age.

References
L. H. Whittemore, *Man Who Ran the Subways: The Story of Mike Quill* (1968); Shirley Quill, *Mike Quill Himself* (1985).

S.P.M.

QUINTILLIANO, LUIGI. *See* Bambace, Angela.

QUOTA IMMIGRATION ACT OF 1921. The first quota act passed by Congress in American history, signed into law by President Warren Harding on May 19, 1921. It limited the number of aliens coming to the United States as permanent residents to 3 percent of the number of foreign-born persons of that national origin who were enumerated in the 1910 census. The 1910 census was used mainly because during that year and the year preceding it the United States saw the greatest number of immigrants from England, Ireland, Scotland, and the Scandinavian countries.

Reference
Marion T. Bennett, *American Immigration Policies* (1963).

D.N.A.

RABBI ISAAC ELCHANAN THEOLOGICAL SEMINARY. *See* Yeshiva University; Bernard Revel.

RABINOVITCH, SHOLEM (1859–1916). Yiddish novelist, playwright, and short story writer. Pseudonym: Sholem Aleichem. Aleichem is credited with being one of the founders of contemporary Yiddish literature and of being the most widely read Yiddish writer in the world. His forte was his ability to describe the humor, life-style, and culture of eastern European Jews. Most of Aleichem's works have been translated into English and include *The Old Country* (1946); *Tevye's Daughters* (1949); *Adventures of Mottel, the Carpenter's Son* (1953); *The Tevye Stories and Others* (1959); and *The Adventures of Menahem-Mendel* (1969). Aleichem's "Tevye" stories are best known to Americans by their adaptation in the Broadway musical, "Fiddler on the Roof."

Reference
Encyclopedia of World Literature in the Twentieth Century (updated ed., 1967).

C.C.

RADNICKA BORBA. *See* Serbs.

"RAGTIME." *See* Jazz.

RAND CORPORATION STUDY. *See* Mexicans; Rand Corporation Study.

REBANE, HANS. *See* Estonians.

REFUGEE ACT OF 1980. Signed into law on March, 1980, by President Jimmy Carter after it was approved by both the House and the Senate on March 4, 1980. The Refugee Act of 1980, or Public Law 96-212, was enacted in response to increasing numbers of people seeking asylum from Vietnam, Kampuchea, and Cuba, and as a means of amending the Migration and Refugee Assistance Act of 1962. The act increased the number of refugees allowed to enter the United States from 17,400 to 50,000 annually, and the president was empowered to admit additional refugees in consultation with Congress. Among the law's other provisions were the creation of the Office of the U.S. Coordinator for Refugee Affairs and the Office of Refugee Resettlement, a new definition of refugee, and a federal program to assist refugees in their resettlement process. Some $200 million annually was authorized for special projects, programs, and refugee services.

Reference
Edward M. Kennedy, "Refugee Act of 1980," *International Migration Review* 15 (1981): 141–156.

D.N.A.

REFUGEE MOVEMENT, Overview. Jacobson (*infra*) states that

> while international migration has often furthered human rights, led to the enhancement of human dignity, relieved population pressures, helped in the development and enrichment of receiving nations and facilitated cultural interchange, hindrances to such international movement have just as often led to social injustice and the demeaning of various peoples at various points in history. In fact, to impede migratory movement is a violation of human rights which can lead to uncircumscribed human suffering such as that which existed during the Nazi hegemony over Europe, when escape routes were blocked.

Reference
Gaynor I. Jacobson, "The Refugee Movement: An Overview," *International Migration Review* 11 (Winter 1977): 514–523.

F.C.

REFUGEE POLICY. Congressional Research Service, *Summary of Hearings Held by the Senate Judiciary Subcommittee on Immigration and Refugee Policy, July 1981–1982* (Washington, D.C., 1983). The focus of the hearings was on the need for regaining control of the various forms of immigration. The hearings addressed five basic aspects of immigration: (1) legal permanent immigration, the subject of two days of hearings; (2) refugee admission and resettlement, considered in two hearings; (3) mass asylum and the related issues of adjudication, considered in three hearings; (4) illegal immigration, including work authorization, legalization, and temporary worker programs, considered in four hearings; and (5) nonimmigrants, the subject of two hearings.

F.C.

REFUGEES. Some two and a half million legal refugees have arrived in the United States since the end of World War II. The major groups have been from Eastern Europe following World War II; from Cuba, mostly during the 1960s; and from Vietnam, Cambodia, and Laos following the collapse of American-supported governments in those countries in 1975. In addition, there have been large numbers of other arrivals in the United States who meet many of the criteria of being refugees but have been denied that legal status by the U.S. government (particularly Salvadorans in recent years) or have been provided intermediate refugeelike legal statuses (particularly Cubans and Haitians in 1980). The experience of these refugees in the United States reflects not only the expulsive forces in their homelands that drive them out, and the inevitable difficulties in adjusting to a new country for which they are relatively unprepared, but also the complex and shifting legislative and programmatic context for refugee resettlement.

Legislative and Programmatic Developments. With modest exceptions (such as the waiving for religious refugees of the literacy requirements introduced in the Immigration Act of 1917), refugees as a distinct segment of U.S. immigration are a phenomenon of the post–World War II period. As early as December 1945, President Truman had created a special program for the acceptance of so-called "displaced persons" from Europe. Approximately 40,000 of these refugees, most originally from Germany and Poland, came to the United States under this program.

The Displaced Persons Act of 1948 (and its two amendments) provided for the acceptance by the end of 1951 of over 400,000 additional refugees. Again, Germany and Poland were the most frequent countries of birth, but there were also about 10,000 or more refugees each from Latvia, Lithuania, Estonia, Czechoslovakia, Hungary, and Yugoslavia. The refugees admitted under these laws were required to meet normal immigration requirements, including certification of the availability of employment and housing. Such certification was generally provided by voluntary agencies which have remained vitally involved in refugee resettlement ever since. The numbers of refugees admitted under these programs were to be taken out of subsequent quotas for the countries from which they came.

The admission of refugees during the 1950s retained the same general features, albeit with some modifications. The Immigration and Nationality Act of 1952 incorporated into statute the long-standing administrative practice of parole—this would later become a major mechanism for responding rapidly to refugee crises. The Refugee Relief Act of 1953 (as once amended), authorized the admission of over 200,000 additional refugees, again mostly those fleeing the new Communist governments of Eastern Europe. This act also provided that these admissions would be outside the existing national origins quotas, although it was not until 1957 that the existing "mortgages" on such quotas from the admission of refugees under the previous authority of the Displaced Persons Act of 1948 were revoked. In late 1956, it was the combination of remaining slots from the Refugee Relief Act and the parole authority under the Immigration and Nationality Act of 1952 that allowed President Eisenhower to authorize the entry of refugees from Hungary following the failed uprising there. The number of these Hungarian refugees eventually reached about 38,000.

The Hungarians were the last large group of refugees admitted from Eastern Europe. While modest numbers continued to be accepted from that region, the entry of refugees into the United States turned sharply in regional orientation with the rise to power of Fidel Castro in Cuba. The number of arrivals from Cuba also represented a sharp increase from the relatively small numbers during the latter 1950s: there would be about half a million Cubans entering during the 1960s, the great majority under the parole authority. With the Cubans, the basic structure of the resettlement program changed significantly. Faced with the disproportionate influx of large numbers of refugees into the Miami area, the federal government established the Cuban Refugee Emergency Center in that city in December 1960, beginning a policy of direct federal support for refugees. As later authorized by the Migration and Refugee Assistance Act of 1962, this program included funding for social services, cash and medical assistance, and educational assistance provided to refugees.

The issue of refugee entry into the United States was now complicated by a special federal program of postarrival assistance for Cuban refugees, with the voluntary agencies continuing their traditional responsibility for initial resettlement services provided to other groups of refugees; these different programmatic areas were under the jurisdiction of separate government agencies, raising concern about the organizational coherence of resettlement efforts. The Immigration and Nationality Act Amendments of 1965 addressed some of the unresolved issues in refugee admissions, including the need to provide for adjustment of legal status, but the numbers provided for refugees remained woefully inadequate. This situation remained much the same during the late 1960s and the very early 1970s, with steady numbers of Cuban arrivals (about 50,000 each year) and quite limited numbers of refugees from other countries. By the mid-1970s, even the number of Cuban arrivals had become very small. At this point came the fall of Saigon in April 1975.

Southeast Asian Refugees. The collapse of the Republic of Vietnam led to the largest single incidence of refugee resettlement that the

United States had witnessed. Within a period of weeks, about 130,000 refugees were brought into the American resettlement program, first through staging areas in the Pacific, then into resettlement camps in the continental United States. From there, the refugees were spread out across the country, sponsored by a variety of agencies, individuals, congregations, and other kinds of groups and organizations (including two states). As in previous refugee situations, initial resettlement efforts and a subsequent program of domestic assistance were authorized by special legislation establishing a program specifically for Indochinese refugees. Survey research over the next two years indicated that, at least in terms of the most elementary economic issues, the population was adjusting well, suggesting the relative success of a now-completed resettlement effort.

The events of the late 1970s, however, radically changed the situation. By 1978, increasing numbers of refugees escaping by boat from Vietnam were swelling temporary refugee camps in Southeast Asia. When the Vietnamese invaded Cambodia in December 1978, large numbers of Cambodian refugees moved into Thailand, and with the subsequent invasion of Vietnam by China two months later, there was heightened pressure on ethnic Chinese throughout Vietnam to leave. The plight of these refugees in turn helped focus attention on other Indochinese refugees who had already escaped but who remained in temporary asylum camps, particularly Laotians in Thailand. The net result was a sharp rise in the number of Southeast Asian refugees arriving in the United States: in 1978, the number of arrivals was only 20,000; this quadrupled to 81,000 in 1979, doubling to 167,000 in 1980, and declining to 132,000 in 1981. Declines to 72,000 in 1982 and 39,000 in 1983 brought the rate of arrivals toward the subsequently constant level of around 45,000—a level similar to that for Cuban refugees two decades earlier.

Within a decade, a sizable new segment of the Asian-American population was created. From about 20,000 persons prior to 1975, the overall Southeast Asian–origin population—including their children born in the United States—was probably close to one million by 1985, about the size of the long-resident Chinese- and Filipino-American populations, themselves the largest of the Asian-origin populations. In terms of specific nationality groups, the growth was no less impressive, with the Vietnamese probably the fourth or fifth largest segment of the overall Asian-American population (and likely to be the third by 1990), and with both Laotians and Cambodians among the ten largest segments.

This Southeast Asian refugee population is spread across the United States in ways both similar and dissimilar to the geographic distribution of other Asian-origin groups. Because of programmatic attempts to disperse the refugees, there are sizable numbers in many states, creating a broader geographic distribution than exists for the overall Asian-American population. In such states as Texas, Louisiana, Iowa, and Minnesota, for example, there is a significant refugee presence despite very limited numbers of Asian-Americans. In other cases, however, the refugee presence is consistent with long-established Asian-American population clusters. This is most notably the case in California where the state's percentage of the national total of Southeast Asian refugees rose from about 20 percent in 1976 to about 40 percent a decade later.

The Southeast Asian refugee population is a very diverse one. Within the three national origin groups, there are five major ethnic/language groups with distinct cultural and economic histories: these are the ethnic (lowland) Lao and the highland Hmong, both from Laos, in addition to Vietnamese, Khmer, and ethnic Chinese—the majority of the Chinese come from Vietnam but they are also a significant minority of those who come from Cambodia. There are also a variety of smaller populations. Even within the major ethnic divisions, however, lies additional diversity: great variations in educational level and occupational background; long-standing and culturally salient religious differences (especially between the Buddhists and Catholics, among the Vietnamese); and extensive political and ideological differences stemming from differing involvement in the events preceding the Communist takeovers. While the popular media have often focused on such diversity among the post-1978 arrivals, it was typical as well of 1975 arrivals, who varied from high government officials to rural farmers and fishers, from large families arriving together to single males arriving alone.

Despite such diversity, several common patterns emerge regarding the adjustment of Southeast Asian refugees to the United States. First, the extensive survey research on refugees' economic adjustment indicates strong improvement in their general economic situation with increased length of time in the United States. However, it is also clear that the initial economic situation of refugees is not a good one, and that many refugee households remain close to poverty, and may remain so for long periods of time. Second, Southeast Asian refugees have been very quick to utilize educational resources in the United States both for themselves and their children. Enrollment in language programs is very widespread, and even after several years in the United States, a large proportion of refugees are participating in some kind of education or training other than that for the English language. Third, despite increasing employment and broad use of educational resources, the first generation has experienced a severe drop in socioeconomic status and prospects. Particularly for those from the elite strata of society, conditions in the United States are unlikely to permit re-achievement of previous status. Fourth, it is clear that Southeast Asian refugees continue to suffer the social and psychological aftereffects not only of political loss, but also of the frequent horrors of exodus, and, for many, the conditions they endured after 1975 but before being able to leave—the holocaust in Cambodia is the most severe example.

Refugees in the 1980s. The massive influx of Southeast Asian refugees, while dominating U.S. refugee resettlement efforts, occurred in the context of several other important events. During the late 1970s, for example, there were also numerous refugee arrivals from the Soviet Union (about 90,000 during the second half of the decade), and concern for Soviet Jewish emigrés has remained strong in the U.S. refugee effort despite drastic declines in the number of those allowed to leave the Soviet Union. Another crucial event during the period was the enactment of the Refugee Act of 1980, legislation that served to bring together the efforts on behalf of different groups of refugees into one standard set of assistance programs. The Refugee Act also brought U.S. law into consistency with the United Nations definition of refugees as persons outside their country of origin and unwilling or unable to return "because of persecution or a well-founded fear of persecution on account of race, religion, nationality, membership in a particular social group, or political opinion." Nevertheless, those admitted to the United States as refugees after the passage of the act continued to be predominantly from Southeast Asia. Of non–Southeast Asian refugees, the only countries of origin with over a few hundred annual admissions during the early 1980s were the traditional Communist sources (Eastern Europe, Cuba), the more recently turned Communist countries (Afghanistan, Ethiopia), or the Middle East (Iran, Iraq).

No sooner had the Refugee Act become law, however, than the United States was faced with another refugee crisis. Crashing through the gates of the Peruvian embassy in Havana in the early spring of 1980, a group of asylum seekers began a chain of events that led the Cuban government to open the port of Mariel to all who wished to leave. By October, the number of Cubans who had reached Florida was about 125,000. The federal government declined to accord them the status of "refugee," ultimately designating them, and the approximately 25,000 Haitians who also arrived in Florida that year, as "Cuban/Haitian Entrants (Status Pending)." These "entrants" did, however, have access to the same services and assistance that legally designated refugees receive.

Definitional problems persisted in other areas as well. While the Refugee Act of 1980 had formalized the United States' use of the UN definition of refugees, the Immigration and Naturalization Service (INS) continued to use a more restrictive definition in dealing with asylum applicants—those already within the United States who claim the status of refugee. Instead of "well-founded fear," the criterion INS used was "clear probability" of persecution. Only in early 1987 did the Supreme Court rule that the INS was required to use the "well-founded fear" criterion (*INS* v. *Cardoza-Fonseca*) in its asylum determinations. Even with the previous standard, however, the ratio of asylum approvals had varied drastically depending on the applicant's country of origin. One of the lowest rates of approval was for asylum applicants from El Salvador, a point stressed by those involved in, or sympathetic to, the growing sanctuary movement.

References
Bruce Grant et al., *The Boat People: An "Age" Investigation* (1979); David W. Haines, ed., *Refugees in the United States: A Reference Handbook* (1985); Gail Paradise Kelly, *From Vietnam to America: A Chronicle of the Vietnamese Immigration to the United States* (1977); Barry N. Stein and Sylvano M. Tomasi, *Refugees Today* (special issue of *International Migration Review* [1981]); U.S. Committee for Refugees, *World Refugee Survey* (Washington, D.C.: Annual).

D.H.

REFUGEES, Church World Service Survey. With a high return rate of 65 percent, results showed that: (1) over time most refugees are finding jobs; (2) refugees' use of public assistance is significantly lower than is commonly believed; (3) over time most refugees are achieving self-sufficiency; and (4) CWS sponsors and congregations have contributed an estimated $135 million in cash, goods and services, and time over the past three and a half years.

Reference
Making It on Their Own: From Refugee Sponsoring to Self-Sufficiency, survey by Church World Service, Immigration and Refugee Program (1983).

F.C.

REFUGEES, Cuban refugee children. The experience of the Dade County Public School System, which accepted 11,000 Cuban (Mariel boatlift) children in just seven months. "Because they had spent all their lives in a regimented, economically stagnant communist society, the adaptation of the children of Mariel to democracy, free enterprise and a consumer society was a long journey from shock to integration," writes Silva. She shows how that journey was carried out with help from Dade County schools. Silva describes how the Dade County school system quickly devised a summer English immersion program that served 9,000 students, hired hundreds of bilingual teachers and other personnel for the fall, and opened several new facilities to be ready in the 1980–81 academic year for the massive influx.

Reference
H. Silva, *The Children of Mariel: Cuban Refugee Children in South Florida Schools* (1985).

F.C.

REFUGEES, global justice issue. The structural dimensions of the contemporary refugee problem. The thesis of the analysis is that the main refugee flows in the world today are the direct or indirect result of forces which lie outside the countries where the refugee originates. In most instances these forces are the extension of the conflict between the Soviet Union and the United States and the efforts by them to extend or maintain their areas of influence.

Reference
M. J. Schultheis, *Refugees: The Structures of a Global Justice Issue* (1983).

F.C.

REFUGEES, migration questions. The commission "Migrant Workers and Refugees," set up at the Geneva Congress of the WCL, has been entrusted with the survey of the problems arising from the migrations of workers in the world in general. The participation in this work of regional organizations affiliated to the WCL will offer the possibility of defining and establishing clearly what are the problems in the countries from which departure takes place and in the countries of arrival, and of furnishing the elements that will offer to the WCL the possibility of defining a trade union strategy that takes into account the historic and present reality of the migration phenomenon.

Reference
"The World Confederation of Labour and Migration Questions," *International Migration Review* 7 (1973): 289–321.

F.C.

REFUGEES, public attitudes toward refugees and immigrants. To improve the base of knowledge on public opinion regarding refugees, the U. S. Committee for Refugees undertook a telephone survey in February 1984 using a sample of 750 adults supplemented with one hundred blacks and one hundred Hispanics. The major findings: (1) contrary to the perception that the U.S. public is solidly antagonistic, there is substantial public sentiment to admit both refugees and immigrants; (2) most members of the public do not know the difference between refugees and other immigrants, the numbers in the various categories of people who come from elsewhere to live in the United States, or where they are coming from; (3) the more accurate knowledge a person has regarding refugee/immigrant issues, the more willing the person is likely to be to support a generous refugee/immigrant admissions policy; and (4) regardless of a person's attitudes concerning generous or restrictive admissions policy, the overwhelming majority of those interviewed considered the issue as one of moderate to low importance compared with other major national policy issues.

Reference
Kane, Parsons and Associates, Inc., *A Survey of Public Attitudes Towards Refugees and Immigrants. Report of Findings* (New York: American Council for Nationalities Service, 1984).

F.C.

REFUGEES, refugee resettlement. A two-axis model of refugee resettlement has been proposed that deals with volume of refugee intake and emphasizes economic or cultural adaptation. The resultant fourfold scheme yields three types of resettlement activities that can be sustained over a protracted period of time: large volume/primacy on economic adaptation; moderate volume/primacy on economic adaptation; moderate volume/primacy on cultural adaptation. Large volume/emphasis on cultural adaptation, however, is a type that is structurally unstable and in practice would modify into another form. The refugee resettlement practices of three major receiving countries, Canada, France, and the United States, reflect principles derived from the three stable types. France and Canada exemplify moderate intake with emphasis on economic adaptation, although Quebec uniquely demonstrates moderate intake/emphasis on cultural adaptation. Practices in the United States overwhelmingly correspond to large volume/emphasis on economic adaptation.

Reference
C. Michael Lanphier, "Refugee Resettlement: Models in Action," *International Migration Review* 17 (Spring 1983): 4–33.

F.C.

REFUGEES, research bibliography. On the difficulties presented by such research, Stein states:

> Refugee research extends across many disciplinary lines. The lack of an easy disciplinary fit combined with the common view that refugee problems are unique, atypical, and nonrecurring has produced both a scholarly neglect of refugee research possibilities and special research difficulties when one does undertake a project. Just a glance at the following bibliography will indicate a great diversity of scholarly journals, governmental documents and other

resources. The researcher needs clues on where to discover the basic materials and the few 'gems' required for a successful scholarly effort. A bibliography aids the researcher not only by listing previously unfound items but by giving an indication of where to look for more materials and ideas and an awareness of what has been and can be done.

Reference
Barry N. Stein, "Refugee Research Bibliography," *International Migration Review* 15 (Spring/Summer 1981): 331–393.

F.C.

REFUGEES, sanctuary. The sanctuary movement, which provides refuge chiefly to aliens from El Salvador and Guatemala, is seeking to have its policies vindicated, thus gaining political asylum for the thousands of aliens its members harbor. At issue is whether the refugees are in danger of political violence. The United States says most of theme are coming to the country for economic reasons: no Salvadoran human rights organization has reported a deportee's death since 1982.

Reference
Daniel Brock, "Movement Seeks Sanctuary for Itself as Well as Aliens," *Insight* 2 (Aug. 11, 1986): 18–20.

F.C.

REFUGEES, United States Committee for Refugees, *World Refugee Survey: 1985 in Review* (1986). A compendium of materials covering aspects of the refugee conditions such as: asylum, refugees, and the black community; Chadian refugees; Central American refugees; Vietnamese refugees in Thailand; refugee women; and emigration from Russia.

F.C.

REFUGEES, U.S. Congress, House and Senate, Subcommittee on Immigration and Refugee Policy, *Refugee Problems in Central America* (Washington, D.C.: U.S. Government Printing Office, 1984). The question of returning undocumented Salvadorans to El Salvador or providing them with safe haven in the United States has been the subject of debate both in Congress and in the media. The Immigration and Refugee Policy Subcommittee of the Committee on the Judiciary has monitored these humanitarian problems and the nation's response to the needs of refugees and displaced persons in Central America.

F.C.

REFUGEES, U.S. Congress, House and Senate, *U.S. Refugee Programs: Hearing Before the Committee on the Judiciary,* **U.S. Senate, 96th congress, 2d Session, April 17, 1980** (Washington, D.C.: U.S. Government Printing Office, 1980). The first formal "consultation" on the U.S. refugee programs required under the terms of the new refugee bill (The Refugee Act of 1980). The hearings contain the testimonies of government representatives as well as of refugee experts. The appendices include two reports to Congress and an overview of the world refugee situation by the State Department; two reports on the Indochinese Refuge Assistance Program by HEW; and the 1980 World Refugee Survey by the U.S. Committee for Refugees, Inc.

F.C.

REFUGEES, U.S. Congress, Senate, Committee on the Judiciary, "Caribbean Refugee Crisis: Cubans and Haitians" (Washington, D.C.: U.S. Government Printing Office, 1980). Reports on the hearings before the Committee on the Judiciary; includes opening statements by various persons, testimony by experts on the subject, prepared statements, and an appendix containing reports on human rights in Haiti.

F.C.

REFUGEES, United States Department of State, *Country Reports on the World Refugee Situation: Statistics,* **Report to the Congress for Fiscal Year 1985** (Washington, D.C., 1984). Based on figures provided to the Department of State by American embassies abroad. Embassies obtain the figures from foreign governments and representatives of the United Nations High Commissioner for Refugees and other international organizations, such as the United Nations Relief and Works Agency.

F.C.

REFUGEES, the unwanted. It is maintained that the appearance of masses of refugees is a recent phenomenon, a product of modern politics. Marrus's central theme (*infra*) is "the emergence of a new variety of collective alienation, one of the hallmarks of our time." The refugee is described as a person who has fled what he regards as intolerable conditions in his homeland, and the flight of tens or hundreds of thousands of people is part of the history of that homeland; but a special problem is created and a special history is engendered if these people, once they have gotten out, find that there is nowhere to go. It is this latter condition that is "the peculiar condition of the refugee of the 20th century."

Reference
Michael R. Marrus, *The Unwanted: European Refugees in the Twentieth Century* (1986).

F.C.

REINHOLD, HANS ANSGAR (1897–1968). Clergyman. The son of a prominent Hamburg Catholic, a veteran of over four years as a German soldier in World War I, a dedicated seamen's chaplain, one of the initial organizers of the International Apostolate of the Sea, and a priest forced to flee his homeland under Gestapo pressure in 1935, Hans Ansgar Reinhold came to America to spend the remainder of his life and to play a leadership role in the American Catholic liturgical movement. This study investigates Reinhold's vision as liturgical educator and popularizer within the American liturgical movement from 1936 until his death in 1968.

Reference
Joel P. Garner, "The Vision of a Liturgical Reformer: Hans Ansgar Reinhold, American Catholic Educator," Ph.D. dissertation, Columbia University, 1972.

RELOCATION CENTERS. Camps set up for persons of Japanese ancestry in the United States during World War II. After the Japanese attack on Pearl Harbor on December 7, 1941, President Franklin Roosevelt signed Executive Order 9066 on February 19, 1942, creating mechanisms for establishing camps for persons of Japanese ancestry in the United States. On the following day, Secretary of War Henry Lewis Stimson delegated responsibility for carrying out the executive order to General John Lesesne DeWitt, who issued Public Proclamation No. 1 on March 2, 1942, setting up Military Areas 1 and 2 on the West Coast.

In March 1942 President Roosevelt issued Executive Order 9102 creating the War Relocation Authority to supervise and control people evacuated from the West Coast. These evacuees were then transferred to relocation camps. Ten camps were established in different states, and approximately 112,000 persons of Japanese ancestry, including American citizens, were interned and detained in these camps. California had two centers, one at Manzanar with 10,000 evacuees and another at Tule Lake with a capacity for 16,000. Colorado had a camp established at Granada in Prowers County, with a capacity of 8,000 people. Arkansas had two centers, one at Rohwer and the other at Jerome. Each camp was able to detain 10,000 internees. Arizona also had two camps, one at Poston and the other at Gila River. Poston was built with a capacity for 20,000 detainees, and the Gila River camp was smaller with a capacity for 15,000 persons. Other camps were established at Heart Mountain, Wyoming, at Minidoka, Idaho, and at Topaz, Utah. Each of them was able to receive approximately 10,000 internees.

References
Lillian Baker, *The Concentration Camp Conspiracy: A Second Pearl Harbor* (1981);
Richard Conrat et al., *Executive Order 9066: The Internment of 110,000 Japanese Americans* (1972).

D.N.A.

REPATRIATION OF IMMIGRANTS. While the majority of immigrants who come to the United States do so permanently, there are immigrants who after a brief or lengthy stay in the United States choose to return to their homeland. The extent of remigration is not precisely known. Estimates of the total number or repatriates range from less than 10 percent of the total immigration to America in the years prior to 1860 to more than 50 percent in some years after 1900.

It was not until 1908 that departing aliens were officially recorded by the United States Office of Immigration and even then travel over international land borders was excluded so that Mexicans and Canadians were not counted. Since the passenger/immigrant distinction has not been constant over the years, repatriation statistics are inadequate and even more complex to use than other immigration data. Records do not tabulate how often one person arrived or departed nor do they distinguish permanent settlers from migrant workers. As with undocumented aliens today, it is extremely difficult to ascertain how long they stay in the United States and if they do indeed return home.

In 1910 the United States Commissioner of Immigration estimated that at least 30 percent of the people arriving stayed only temporarily. Statistics show that for every 100 immigrants to America between 1908 and 1924 approximately 38 repatriated. A table compiled from several government sources by Charles A. Price in Dirk Hoerder, ed., *Labor Migration in the Atlantic Economies* (1985) shows remigration figures from 1899 to 1952 as follows:

Period	Arrivals	Departures	Net Immigration	% Departures
1899–1924	17,636,083	6,095,019	11,541,054	34.6
1925–1943	2,294,943	914,605	1,480,388	38.2
1944–1952	1,396,923	169,351	1,227,572	12.1
Totals	21,427,949	7,178,975	14,248,974	33.5

Studies of repatriation show that it continued through three centuries of American settlement and involved all immigrant groups in varying numbers.

Repatriation in American History. Rowland Tappan Berthoff and Wilbur Shepperson studied America's first immigrants and repatriates—the British—in *British Immigrants in Industrial America* (1953) and *Emigration and Disenchantment* (1965). Shepperson estimated that substantial numbers of disappointed Englishmen left America in the eighteenth, nineteenth, and twentieth centuries. The authors were unable to denote any one, single explanation for the return movement. Many Englishmen were simply disappointed or disillusioned with life in America.

The United States' immigration data from the early 1900s tend to identify the "new immigrants" from southern, central, and eastern Europe between 1890 and 1930 as even more disappointed or dissatisfied with the new land than earlier immigrants. Their return movement was considerably larger than that of the pre-1890s or "old immigrants" (Scandinavians, English, Irish, German).

In fact, the time required to cross the ocean, the hardships of transatlantic travel, costs and settlement choices in the United States may have been factors discouraging a vast "return home" movement such as witnessed in the twentieth century. Steamships and an open immigration policy prompted more crossings among later immigrants which resulted in a higher degree of repatriation. Young men could come alone, take on industrial jobs in the cities, accumulate some savings, and return to their families after a temporary stay.

Theodore Saloutos, in *They Remember America* (1956), offered nostalgia, economic losses, the desire to fight for the Greek government, climate, and the impersonal American society as reasons for the Greeks' return home in the early decades of the twentieth century. Robert F. Foerster, in *The Italian Emigration of Our Times* (1919), concluded that large numbers of Italians, mostly unskilled males between sixteen and forty-five years of age, remained in the United States for fewer than five years and left in economic bad times.

Changes in United States immigration policy after 1924 muted the repatriation issue. While air transportation further eased travel time and costs, the difficulties encountered in obtaining entry to the United States made it less likely that large numbers of immigrants would leave.

Economics and Repatriation. It was the depression years of 1907–8 that drew attention to emigrating aliens. Economists attempted to explain the relationship between economic bad times and immigration. Some of their studies included repatriation and agreed that the number of arrivals into the United States increased in times of prosperity and fell off in times of depression. The converse was true for departures.

Harry Jerome, in *Migration and Business Cycles* (1926), noted that the arrival of hundreds of thousands of workers each year, especially during an up-swing in business, resulted in a surplus of workers which affected the economy through decreased labor costs. Repatriation, Jerome noted, sometimes mitigated the effects of cyclical variations in unemployment by withdrawing large numbers from the work force. As a safety valve, he argued, it was imperfect, since time necessarily elapsed between the decreased need for labor and the departure of workers.

With restrictive immigration quotas already in place during the Great Depression of the 1930s, repatriation gained support from those seeking to curb unemployment. Supporters wanted to ship unemployed Filipinos home. The United States Congress agreed to pay the passage of indigent Filipinos who voluntarily returned home. Faced with long lines of unemployed native-born workers and unwilling to grant relief to Mexican immigrants and their children, various local governments looked to repatriation as an answer.

In the years after World War II some immigrants chose to return to their homelands with their social security retirement benefits and pension plans. Their purchasing power improved tremendously in their native lands.

Impact of Repatriation. The impact of a sojourn is difficult to measure and mixed for the immigrant, the homeland, and the United States. For the majority of immigrants the original purpose of their migration was economic betterment, a search for work. Evidence of the employment/work motive behind the migration is found in the imbalance of sexes in the immigrant group's migration. In the nineteenth and twentieth centuries more men sought industrial work in the United States; in recent years as the nature of available work has changed there is an increase in the number of women immigrating. Some students of immigration view migration to the United States as an extension of the international seasonal migrations that were becoming common in Europe in the early twentieth century. This phenomenon has since spread to other parts of the world.

The technology of the factory and city offered jobs, but few ties, to the immigrants. They were paid in cash; their possessions were limited and portable. Immigrants have been known to transmit large amounts of money to their homelands. Their remittances add to the national income of their homeland and aid in alleviating an unfavorable balance of payments. Repatriates return with savings, improve their housing, and invest in land. Such investments have been viewed as conservative, in that repatriates tend to improve their own living standards and perhaps modernize some farm methods rather than investing in new business ventures at home or in the United States. Mobility studies have shown that repatriation delays upper social mobility for an immigrant group in the United States.

For the United States repatriation reduces immigration's demographic impact. It may also weaken the cultural influence of an immigrant group and American society upon each other. Remigration appears as the most distinguishing feature of immigration between 1890 and 1930. Returnees appear most prevalent among newer immigrant groups who may lack the "cultural toeholds" in American society available to arrivals from longtime immigrant sources.

For reasons already outlined a full discussion of the effects of repatriation is impossible. The back and forth movement of peoples continues, especially across the borders. As people return home with news of jobs, stories of success, and money in their pockets, others will be encourged to try the same.

References
Thomas Archdeacon, *Becoming American* (1983); Bernard Axelrod, "Historical Studies of Emigration from the United States," *International Migration Review* 6 (1972): 32–49; Dirk Hoerder, ed., *Labor Migration in the Atlantic Economies* (1985); *Historical Statistics of the United States Colonial Times to 1970*, 2 vols. (1975); David Reimers, *Still the Golden Door* (1985); Stephan Thernstrom, ed., *Harvard Encyclopedia of American Ethnic Groups* (1980).

F.K.

REPATRIATION, Italian. Cerase (*infra*) studied a group of Italians who migrated to the United States in the last fifty years or so and then returned to their mother country after some time in America. As such, his study is a contribution to an unwritten chapter in the history of Italian immigration to the United States. The returnees interviewed were made up of subgroups living in several areas throughout Italy. But this study of the returned migrants is relevant also to Italian history and was designed to test a general hypothesis connected to the Italian "southern question." This hypothesis relates Italian mass emigration to the United States to the peculiar way in which a liberal state was established in Italy in the nineteenth century and in which industrialization was brought about. It then states that the southern peasants, the protagonists of that emigration, although unwilling to tolerate any longer the state of misery to which they had been reduced, remained on the whole unaware of the economic laws that had produced that misery. To the extent that this is true, emigration, and more specifically the return, represented for them an individual act through which they expected to resolve the problem.

Reference
Francesco P. Cerase, "From Italy to the United States and Back: Returned Migrants, Conservative or Innovative?" Ph.D. dissertation, Columbia University, 1971.

F.C.

RETURN MIGRATION, European intercontinental emigration.
Gould discusses the differences between the terms "immigrant [or emigrant] alien" and "nonimmigrant [or nonemigrant] alien," and ex-

plains why these terms may cause the misrepresentation of the actual number of migrants who return home from the United States. He points out various reasons why U.S. immigrants decide to return to their homeland, emphasizes the distinction between gross and net migration, and offers an alternate method for figuring immigration and emigration rates. Italian emigration from 1876 to 1914 is highlighted.

Reference
J. D. Gould, "European Inter-Continental Emigration. The Road Home: Return Migration from the U.S.A.," *The Journal of European Economic History* 9 (Spring 1980): 41–111.

F.C.

REVEL, BERNARD (1885–1940). Jewish scholar, educator. President, after 1915, of the Rabbi Isaac Elchanan Theological Seminary of New York City, for which he labored devotedly to develop it as a liberal college committed to the training of enlightened rabbis and teachers for the Jewish community. *See* Yeshiva University.

Reference
Arnold Rothkoff, "Vision and Realization: Bernard Revel and His Era," Ph.D. dissertation, Yeshiva University, 1967 (DA 28: 605A).

F.C.

RHEE, SYNGMAN. *See* Koreans.

RICE, JOSEPH M[AYER] (1857–1934). Physician, social reformer. Author of *The Public School System of the United States* (1893; rpt. 1969), originally a series of articles appearing in *The Forum* (October 1892–June 1893) by this pediatrician interested in school reform. The articles reviewed visits to schools in thirty-six cities, calling for schools "absolutely divorced from politics in every sense of the word." This was the most influential first-hand appraisal of American public education in the period during the floodtide of European immigration. See also Rice's *Scientific Management in Education* (1914), which reports on systematic research into the quality of elementary school instruction.

Reference
Lawrence A. Cremin, *The Transformation of the School* (1961).

F.C.

RICHMAN, JULIA (1855–1912). Educator. Julia Richman successfully tilted at the windmills of the turn-of-the-century New York City public school system in the interests of the social as well as the intellectual needs of each individual child. Her career as teacher, principal, and district superintendent (1872–1912) and her involvement as an active participant in the concurrent social welfare movement coincided with the period during which New York City absorbed large numbers of eastern and southern European immigrants, and she concentrated her attention on the needs of these children. The correlates of poverty, such as malnutrition, unstable family and community life, mobility and its social and educational disruption, and language differences were of concern to Julia Richman then, as they concern us today among members of other immigrant groups. The pressure on children to leave school at the permissible age of fourteen, or even earlier, for available, and in the context of the times, desirable job opportunities added an additional dimension to her task.

Richman's special interest in the social welfare and educational needs of immigrant children led her to work toward institutional changes within the overcrowded school system. Her approach was to alter organizational structures to meet the needs of individual children without attempting to change the curricular patterns and academic standards of the traditional classroom. Among these organizational changes were the alteration of rigid promotional policies, which permitted individualized programs and progress from one grade to another throughout the school year. This controversial provision was especially important at the time so that able, motivated pupils could progress quickly before leaving school in order to work; it also provided a sensitive incentive system for other students discouraged by lack of progress through the grades.

Richman also instituted the homogeneous grouping of pupils, with frequent reevaluation and adjustment according to current performance, and special education programs for emotionally disturbed ("incorrigible"), retarded, newly arrived, overage, and truant children. Other services introduced or expanded under her guidance were eye examinations and free eyeglasses, school lunches, guidance services, and athletic programs, in which she took a particularly active interest. In all these innovations, her concern for the needs of the individual child, and her success in modifying the system to meet these individual needs, was clearly apparent; in her own words, "individual children cannot be cured . . . by giving a dose of medicine to the whole class."

References
Selma C. Berrol, "When Uptown Met Downtown: Julia Richman's Work in the Jewish Community of New York," *American Jewish History* 70 (1980): 35–51; Selma C. Berrol, "Superintendent Julia Richman: A Social Progressive in the Public Schools," *Elementary School Journal* 72 (1972): 402–411.

W.O.M.

RICHMOND, MARY E[LLEN] (1861–1928). Social worker; director of the Charity Organization Department, Russell Sage Foundation (*q.v.*). Richmond was very active in work among immigrant women, their children, and their families. Chief works: *Friendly Visits Among the Poor* (1899; rev. ed. 1914); *Social Diagnosis* (1917); *What Is Social Case Work?* (1922). Richmond was a decisive influence in the development of professional standards in social work.

Reference
Roy Lubove, *The Professional Altruist: The Emergence of Social Work as a Career* (1965).

F.C.

RIHANI, AMIN. *See* Lebanese.

RIHBANG, ABRAHAM MITRIE. *See* Lebanese.

RIIS, JACOB AUGUST (1849–1914). Journalist, social reformer. A Danish immigrant, he arrived in New York City penniless in 1870, lived in semipoverty for some seven years, and drifted almost haphazardly into newspaper work. By 1886, he was a seasoned reporter and had learned his craft out of police precincts for the *New York Tribune*, eking out of the crimes and accidents he reported a mosaic of human degradation, misfortune, and misery. In the ghettos of New York City's Lower East Side he recorded in hundreds of short, vivid pictures physical wretchedness, moral and spiritual degradation, and all the dynamics of the slum of his era: poignantly, sensationally, and in the crude journalistic idiom of the day. That he translated what he saw into a lifelong battle against the slum of the tenement districts and wrote a half-dozen books calling for social and economic reform is explained not only by an age imbued with humanitarian motive, but equally by his simple refusal to accept the horrors of a social pathology which he recorded in microscopic detail, and from which he recoiled.

The growth of industrialism in the United States after the Civil War, the growth of the cities with overcrowding in their slums, and the increasing European immigration brought in their wake terrible problems. By the late 1880s many American cities were haunted by the specter of a permanent pauper class. It was not crime or juvenile delinquency in the city slum, alone, that aroused serious concern. The wretchedness of life in the city tenements, the callous indifference of employers in their exploitation of the child and adult poor, the corruption of city officials, all help explain the ferment of social reform: the plans for economic reform, ranging from Henry George's single tax to the Socialist plea for public ownership; utopian fiction, of which Edward Bellamy's *Looking Backward* (1888) is representative; the founding of the American Federation of Labor (1886), and the dynamic tirrings of trade unionism; the settlement house movement; and a myriad of social work programs. The engagement with poverty was very real. By the end of the nineteenth century, America was on all fronts, philosophic, economic, and social, struggling with the dynamics of urban poverty, with urban blight, and with what a later age was euphemistically to call "the culturally deprived."

Jacob Riis was, then, part of a great movement for social reform. He was directly related to a number of organizations in New York City which were in the forefront of social welfare and reform, particularly with the work of the Charity Organization Society (*q.v.*) and that of the Children's Aid Society (*q.v.*). The first of these had been organized in 1882 by Josephine Shaw Lowell (*q.v.*) and was active in housing and legislative reform. The Children's Aid Society, founded as early as 1853, conducted a continuing battle against the slum and its deleterious effect on children, moving many children out of the city for short periods of time. It was out of these associations that Jacob Riis largely drew not the theoretic constructs of social reform but rather the idea of a concerted assault on the slum in the idiom and language of a journalistic reformer, and in this context that he published his first book, *How the Other Half Lives: Studies Among the Tenements of New York* (1890).

The ugly pictures Riis sketched in his vignettes of the slum and the tenement poor were not new; they had been done before, but what was new was the book's raucous cry for reform, the vividness of its description and its prescription for change. Riis described the "genesis of the tenements," and drew as a line of demarcation for his "The Other Half" the 37,316 tenement houses that harbored the poor. The quality of his writing sought a sharp delineation of the pauperism and the crime, the degradation and the vice, and all was pointed up in the sharp staccato of a reporter's penchant for statistics. *How the Other Half Lives* described the horrible conditions that Riis found in the tenements, and drew particular attention to the plight of neglected and abandoned children (he called vagabond children "street arabs"); it applauded the efforts of those agencies (e.g., The Society for the Prevention of Cruelty to Children) that were engaged in confronting the stark terror of a city in which nearly half a million people (in a population of a million and a half) were begging for food and in which one person of every ten who died was buried a pauper in Potter's Field.

For Riis the *bête noire* of this social pathology was the tenement, against which he offered no sophisticated theories for social reform. The only effective remedies were to be provided by law, by the remodeling of old houses, and by model housing built on new plans. The graphic quality of *How the Other Half Lives;* its muscular Christianity, cast in the mold of the nineteenth-century evangelism and individualism of Charles Kingsley; and the simplicity of its patterns of reform made the book an immediate success. In essence, it became the prototype of all of the books that Riis was to write against the tenement. The basic ingredients were always the same, and in holding up a mirror to his age, he awakened conscience and became a significant part of that age's reform. By 1900 (when Riis reviewed the history of the struggle in *The Ten Years' War*), significant gains had been achieved. The work of the Gilder Commission of 1894 outlawed the old rear tenements in the Tenement House Law of 1895. The notorious Mulberry Bend was demolished and replaced with Mulberry Bend Park. In 1900 the New York State Tenement Commission (*q.v.*) presented its report to the legislature, and the Tenement House Law of 1901 was enacted, representing in its provisions the first major advance in the fight against the tenement slum. According to this law all tenements built after 1901 had to provide for light and ventilation in all rooms as well as in public halls. Only 70 percent of the lot could be occupied by the building, which was also limited in height to one-half times the width of the street. No room of less than 70 square feet was to be permitted. Large courts, 12 feet wide, were provided in place of the small air shafts, and a 24-foot-wide court was to be in the center of the building. Nonfireproof buildings were limited to six stories, and fire escapes were forbidden in air shafts. Stairs and hallways were to be completely fireproof in buildings of five stories or more. In large measure, the law of 1901 was due to the efforts of Jacob Riis. In the New York City of today thousands of old-law tenements (built before the Law of 1901, and outside the purview of the law) still stand as grim evidence of the horrors against which Jacob Riis fought and won.

How instructive is Jacob Riis to our age, to its "Great Society," and to the contemporary patterns of social reform? Alongside much of the effort of our age his reforms may appear relatively small; the crusade he waged against the tenement could be regarded as but a minuscule part of what the Demonstration Cities and Metropolitan Development Act (1966) set out to provide in our cities in our time; and it might be cogently argued that Riis suffered all of the prejudices of his day and that in his books the immigrant tenement poor are at best crude caricatures, and that his concept of "Americanization" and his call for restrictive immigration were the harbingers of the isolationism and quotas of subsequent decades. Yet all of these misgivings would miss the point and deny us the full measure of the man. Jacob Riis was part of a reform age. With this age, he shared what we call "commitment": the restiveness of an age that saw trade unionism, humanitarian reformers, the churches, its creative literature, even the schools, jointly engaged in a massive assault against social ills, and with a buoyant optimism that prophesied inevitable change and melioration, the last phases of what the historian James Bury called the "idea of progress."

References
Francesco Cordasco, *Jacob Riis Revisited* (1968); James B. Lane, "Bridge to the Other Half: The Life and Urban Work of Jacob A. Riis," Ph.D. dissertation, University of Maryland, 1970 (DA 31: 4909-A); Jacob A. Riis, *The Making of an American* (1901); Louis Ware, *Jacob A. Riis* (1939); and see the edition of *How The Other Half Lives* (Dover Press, 1971) that includes 100 photographs (taken by Riis) from the Jacob A. Riis Collection of the Museum of the City of New York—since printers had not yet perfected the halftone process of reproducing photographs in 1890, Riis's photography included in *How the Other Half Lives* and in his other books were redrawn by artists.

F.C.

RIVINGTON STREET COLLEGE SETTLEMENT HOUSE (New York City). *See* Kellor, Frances A.

ROBICHAUD, LOUIS J. *See* Acadians.

ROCHESTER THEOLOGICAL SEMINARY. *See* Baptists and Immigrants.

ROCK SPRINGS MASSACRE. An attack on the Chinese quarter of a small coal-mining town, Rock Springs, Wyoming Territory, on September 2, 1885 by an armed mob of white men. The mob killed twenty-eight Chinese, wounded another fifteen, and drove the rest of the Chinese population into the surrounding hills. It is estimated that in the following weeks another fifty Chinese died of exposure and starvation.

Reference
Alexander Saxon, *The Indispensable Enemy* (1971).

D.N.A.

RØLVAAG, OLE E. (1876–1931). Norwegian-born novelist, teacher, essayist. Rølvaag was the best-known Norwegian-American novelist, primarily as the author of *Giants in the Earth*. Originally published in Norwegian, *Giants in the Earth* appeared in English in the United States in 1927 and sold 80,000 copies in its first year. Rølvaag's immigrant novels emphasized the psychological effects of migrating and settling in an often-hostile new American environment. In *Giants in the Earth,* a Norwegian couple struggles with the prairie, while in *Boat of Longing,* a young Norwegian becomes lost in the rough, seamy city of Minneapolis. Sequels to *Giants in the Earth* explore another major Rølvaag concern, the cultural conflict within the second generation. As teacher (St. Olaf College), essayist, and ethnic leader, Rølvaag struggled to preserve Norwegian identity in America. This crusade is revealed in *Omkring Faedrearven* (Concerning the Ancestral Heritage, 1922), as well as his participation in several ethnic organizations, including the founding of the Norwegian-American Historical Association (*q.v.*) in 1925.

Reference
Paul Reigstad, *Rølvaag: His Life and Art* (1972).

J.J.

ROMANIANS. Smaller, and indisputably less well known than some of the early mass migrations from Europe to the United States, Romanian immigration may be perhaps best characterized not only by the variegated and evolving nature of its constituent elements—chronological, areal, motivational—but as well by the more central questions of the ethnic and national origins of those we designate as "Romanians." In common with others in eastern and southeastern Europe under Austro-Hungarian suzerainty until 1918, immigrants from Bukovina or Transylvania, for example, were not officially counted as Romanians, but as Austrians or Hungarians. Further complicating the issue of ethnic, though not national, identity is the existence of other Balkan peoples sharing a cultural and linguistic kinship, e.g., the Istro-, Megleno-, and especially Macedo-Romanians, significant numbers of whom settled on the American eastern seaboard (e.g., Connecticut, Massachusetts) and who are today part of the Romanian-American experience. Add to this religious differences—not only Orthodox and Roman Catholicism, but also the "Uniates" or Byzantine rite Catholics, plus Baptists and a substantial number of Jewish Romanians, and we are presented with a picture that is far from uniform, and that becomes increasingly varied as we follow in time the socioeconomic backgrounds and political motivation of Romanian immigrants: in the years around the turn of the century up to World War I a largely peasant and politically disenfranchised class seeking short-term economic gain, but since World War II composed of individuals often with a high level of education and technical training, plus in a number of instances political and especially religious dissidents, all generally opposed to the contemporary political system in Romania. Especially notable figures of Romanian origin include Nobel Prize recipients: George Palade (1974, medicine) and Elie Wiesel (1986, peace), and the late historian of myths and religions, Mircea Eliade. Currently, some 2,000 Romanians are allowed to leave legally each year for the United States, to which may be added smaller numbers of defectors and refugees.

The First Years. Apart from reports of occasional early arrivals of Romanians in the United States—to pursue the 1849 gold rush, for example, or later to serve Union forces in the Civil War—the main wave of Romanian immigration commenced in the years just prior to 1900, mostly with peasants from south Transylvania (especially the Fagaras region), then, as has been noted, under Hungarian rule. (A parallel but distinct immigration of Bukovinans is observed for western Canada where the newcomers were offered homesteads, enabling them to continue living on the land.) While political repression played a role—Transylvanian Romanians were being subjected to "Magyarization," and in time would be obliged to serve the kaiser's army—the principal goal was economic, namely, the acquisition of a nest egg (specifically "one thousand dollars and the passage home") with which to return home one day to buy a plot of land, and an ox and a cow; hence a predominance of young males in a movement marked in its early years by its relative impermanence.

The Struggle. Life in the early days is well described in the literature—which is full as well of warnings about the pitfalls awaiting the naive immigrant—and often revolved about the boarding house and the tavern, themselves run by and catering to Romanians, thus providing a practical and social focus in a society not always accepting of eastern and southern Europeans. Contrary to our common conceptions of "success," it was often the case that those who were considered to have best managed things in America were those who went home, though in time, with the collectivization of agriculture and expropriation of property in post–World War II Romania, the irony of such a view would become obvious. Nor did early immigrants to America achieve an easy prosperity; some indeed ran afoul of the law, engaging, for example, in bootlegging during Prohibition. Still, most of the immigrants seem to have been driven by an uncommon steadfastness of purpose as the newcomers—fresh from the three-week trip in steerage from Bremen to New York City, and predominantly from an agricultural background—adapted to the exigencies of an industrial society, finding, for example, employment in the coal fields of West Virginia, and then, following the development of America, moving on to the steel mills of Cleveland and the auto works of Detroit, while others toiled in slaughterhouses, cement works, quarries, and so on.

Adaptation. Religious and fraternal organizations grew apace—for example, St. Mary's Romanian Orthodox Church (1904) and St. Helena's Greek Catholic Church (1905), both in Cleveland, plus social and mutual aid societies of which this is just a sampling: Albina (New Castle, Pennsylvania), Carpatina (Cleveland), Speranta (Chicago), Vulturul (Homestead, Pennsylvania), and especially the Union and League of Romanian Societies of America (which even today continues publishing the newspaper *America,* founded in 1905). In the meantime, the cyclical pattern of immigration return continued—still today one encounters in the villages of Transylvania individuals, elderly now, who spent their youth in America, an America long since gone, the America of Babe Ruth and the Charleston—until in time it subsided, through improvement in economic circumstances, the birth of a younger generation that felt American, and especially the advent of World War I which put a hold on any movement. Restrictive laws in the early 1920s largely stemmed Romanian immigration; gradually, marriage outside the Romanian circle became accepted, the Romanian-Americans entered the mainstream of American life.

Demographics. For reasons already noted, precise population figures for Romanians in the United States are hard to ascertain: according to the 1980 census some 315,258 Americans had at least one Romanian ancestor, i.e., 17 for every 10,000 Americans. The Romanian Orthodox and the Romanian Orthodox Missionary Episcopates (the latter under the jurisdiction of Bucharest) are both based in Michigan, which has the greatest number of Romanian-Americans, respectively in Jackson and Detroit, where they publish *Solia* and *Credinta.* Other publications with church backing include *Unirea* and *Luminatorul,* published respectively by the Romanian Catholic Exarchate of America and the Romanian Baptist Association of the United States. The past decade and a half has seen an increase in activities associated with Romanian culture, as in the establishment of the American Romanian Academy (1975), the Society for Romanian Studies (1971), the Romanian-American Heritage Center (Jackson), the Romanian Folk Art Museum (Evanston, Illinois), and the *American Romanian Review* (Cleveland, 1977).

References

Theodore Andrica, *Romanian Americans and Their Communities of Cleveland* (1977); Serban Andronescu, *Who's Who in Romanian America* (1976); Josef J. Barton, *Peasants and Strangers: Italians, Romanians, and Slovaks in an American City, 1890–1950* (1975); Gerald Bobango, *The Romanian Othodox Episcopate of America: The First Half-Century, 1929–1979* (1979); Christine A. Galitzi, *A Study of Assimilation Among the Romanians in the United States* (1929); Mary Leuca and Peter Georgeoff, *Romanian Americans in Lake County, Indiana: Resource Guide* (1977); Vladimir Wertsman, *The Romanians in America, 1748–1974: A Chronology and Fact Book* (1975).

C.M.C.

ROMANIANS, Romanian-American Heritage Center. Founded in 1978 with offices in Grass Lake, Michigan. A major repository of materials on Romanian immigration and ethnicity in the United States and Canada. Publishes a quarterly newsletter entitled *Information Bulletin* (1983–).

D.N.A.

ROOSEVELT, THEODORE (1858–1919). Politician, historian, twenty-sixth president of the United States. Roosevelt's complex attitude toward immigrants demonstrates his background and the political sensitivity of the "immigrant question" during the first years of the twentieth century. His writings celebrate the Anglo-Saxonism/Teutonism popular among other gentlemen-historians of his class and time. In political speeches, he often adopted an assimilationist stance, believing that white European immigrants could ultimately assimilate into a great "American race" built on a strong Anglo-Saxon base. The "Gentlemen's Agreement," a presidential policy to restrict Japanese immigration, revealed Roosevelt's pessimism concerning the ability of non-Europeans to "Americanize." As president (1901–1909), Roosevelt took an active interest in the several immigration bills before Congress. Fears of losing ethnic votes to the Democrats motivated him to pressure Senator Henry Cabot Lodge and other Republican restrictionists in Congress to curtail their drive for the literacy test restriction during his term. In deference to the rising political clout of the immigrants, Roosevelt named Oscar S. Straus secretary of commerce and labor, the first Jew to hold a cabinet position. Out of office and near the end of his life, Roosevelt's faith in the immigrants' ability to assimilate waned, and he increasingly wrote of his concerns of the "race suicide" of old-stock Anglo-Saxon Americans.

Reference
Thomas G. Dyer, *Theodore Roosevelt and the Idea of Race* (1980).

J.J.

ROSATI, JOSEPH (1789–1843). Catholic bishop. Rosati, born in Sora, Italy, on January 30, 1789, entered the Congregation of the Priests of the Mission in 1807. While a seminarian he gave much thought to serving God in the foreign missions. Therefore, when Bishop DuBourg went to Rome, in 1815, seeking laborers for the vast diocese of Louisiana, Rosati volunteered. He came to America in 1816 and was named superior of the diocesan seminar by Bishop DuBourg in 1818. During his term as administrator Rosati performed many creditable duties for the diocese. The explanation of these activities forms the core of this dissertation. Among his various achievements were a decisive blow to lay trusteeism in New Orleans, the clearing of the great debt of the diocese, obtaining needed priests, and the raising of a renewed interest in the question of a seminary for New Orleans.

References
The papers of Bishop Rosati at the Archdiocese of St. Louis Archives; Frederick J. Easterly, *The Life of the Rt. Rev. Joseph Rosati* (1974).

F.C.

ROSS, EDWARD A[LSWORTH] (1866–1951). Sociologist. A nativist and restrictionist, Ross taught at Stanford University and the University of Wisconsin, and analyzed collective behavior and social control with special interests in immigration and population. "His fascination with the immigration issue dates from his turbulent years at Stanford University, and his first polemic on the subject was an attack on the Oriental" (Higham, *Strangers in the Land*, 367). Chief writings: *Social Control* (1901); *Principles of Sociology* (1921); *Seventy Years of It* (autobiography, 1936).

Reference
Julius Weinberg, *Edward A. Ross* (1972).

D.N.A.

ROSSI, ADOLFO (1857–1921). Journalist, writer, Italian commissioner of emigration. Born in Lendinara, northern Italy, Rossi came to the United States at age twenty and worked in New York City at various jobs. In July 1881 he went by rail to Colorado and worked clearing forests and leveling the roadbed for tracks. A later job with a railroad required him to visit work camps throughout the West, which gave him the opportunity to observe the conditions of his fellow Italians. In 1882 he was called to New York to be the editor of the Italian daily *Il Progresso Italo-Americano*. In 1884 he returned to Italy and became a reporter for *La Tribuna* of Rome and *Il Corriere Della Sera* of Milan, covering national and international events. In 1892 he published an autobiographical book dealing with his American experience: *Un Italiano in America*, which became very popular and was reprinted six times. In 1902 Rossi was appointed royal commissioner of emigration, and traveled abroad investigating the conditions of Italian emigrants. He returned to the United States in 1904 and in 1906 when he established legal assistance and a placement office for Italian emigrants.

Reference
Adolfo Rossi, *Un Italiano in America* (1892).

R.U.P.

ROYAL COMMISSION ON BILINGUALISM AND BICULTURALISM. Canada established the Royal Commission on Bilingualism and Biculturalism in 1963; its publications constitute an invaluable repository of materials on the sociological, political, and educational challenges faced by modern states in dealing with the complex needs of language minorities. The findings of the commission include a vast assemblage of data of value to all societies dealing with the needs of ethnic minorities. Three reports selected from the commission's many publications constitute a compendious resource on all aspects of societal bilingualism and biculturalism. The *Preliminary Report* (1965) is a summary of the commission's deliberations with a conspectus of preliminary conclusions; [Book 1] *General Introduction: The Official Languages* (1967) is both a sociological and historical review of the origins, developments, and status of bilingualism and biculturalism in Canada; and [Book 2] *Education* (1967) is a comprehensive treatise on bilingual-bicultural practice in modern Canada with reference to established policy and objectives to be achieved.

F.C.

ROYAL HORTICULTURAL SOCIETY OF LONDON. *See* Douglas, David.

RUDDY, ANNA C[HRISTIAN] (d. 1946). (Christian McLeod, pseudonym) Settlement house worker. Ruddy came to East Harlem (New York City) from Canada in 1890 in the early days of Italian immigration. She devoted her life to working with Italian immigrant families, and particularly with the Italian immigrant young, learning Italian to be more effective. In 1901 Ruddy established "The Home Garden" as a meeting place for young Italians in East Harlem. In 1919, "The Home Garden" was renamed "Haarlem House," and in 1957 its name was changed to "La Guardia Memorial House." Ruddy's *The Heart of the Stranger: A Story of Little Italy* (1908), a series of fictional vignettes, is a distillation of her experiences among the Italian poor of East Harlem.

Reference
Leonard Covello, *The Heart Is the Teacher* (1958; rpt. 1970).

F.C.

RUSSELL, CHARLES EDWARD. *see* NAACP.

RUSSELL, LILLIAN (1861–1922). Singer and actress. An international celebrity, Russell was appointed by President William G. Harding (*q.v.*) in 1920 to make an investigation of the immigration problem in Europe, a task for which she had no demonstrable qualifications. Russell (as Lillian Russell Moore) submitted her report in 1922, recommending a five-year suspension of immigration. Quote: "The higher civilizations of past ages, history teaches us, succumbed to such foreign invasions as now threaten us." See *Congressional Record* 62 (1922): 5558, 5562.

F.C.

RUSSELL SAGE FOUNDATION (New York City). The Russell Sage Foundation is the principal American foundation devoted exclusively to research in the social sciences. Located in New York City, it is a research center, a funding source for studies by others, and an active member of the nation's social science community. The foundation is also a publisher, with its own imprint, producing a small number of books that derive primarily from the work of its grantees and resident scholars. One of the oldest private foundations in the United States, the foundation was established by Mrs. Margaret Olivia Sage in 1907 for "the improvement of social and living conditions in the United States." Before it turned exclusively to social science research following World War II, the Russell Sage Foundation played an active and pioneering role in dealing with problems of the poor immigrants and the elderly, in efforts to improve hospital and prison conditions, and in the development of social work as a profession. It was responsible for reforms in health care, city planning, consumer credit, labor legislation, the training of nurses, and social security programs.

Reference
[Russell Sage Foundation], *About the Russell Sage Foundation* (1986).

F.C.

RUSSIANS. Russians constitute one of the Slavic subgroups, along with Poles, Bohemians, Ukrainians, Slovaks, Bulgarians, Serbs, Croatians, Montenegrins, and Slovenians. Because of the complexity of the relationship between ethnicity and national boundaries, a considerable amount of confusion occurred in official statistics regarding levels of immigration of Russians, with a number of other Slavic ethnics as well as Finns and Jews frequently being classified as Russian. Thus, while the precise number of Russian immigrants is impossible to determine, it is probably the case that only 10 to 15 percent of those classified by immigration officials as Russian actually were. If accurate, this would suggest that the total Russian immigrant population prior to 1924 totaled between 100,000 and 150,000 persons.

The earliest Russian settlers arrived on the North American continent via the Bering Strait as early as the middle of the eighteenth century. They established hunting and trading colonies in Alaska and migrated as far south as present-day San Francisco. The first presence of Orthodox Christendom on the continent was established during this time. While the communities were small and male dominated, they continued to experience steady growth until the 1840s, and when a call was issued for colonists to return to Russia, and later, in 1867, when Alaska was sold to the United States. While many, in fact, returned, others remained behind, with a large enough number of the latter migrating to California that the Russian Orthodox Church in America was relocated in San Francisco. The Russian population grew in the early twentieth century with the arrival of relatively small numbers of members from several dissenting religious sects, including the Molokans, Old Believers, and Dukhobors.

Despite the longevity of the Russian presence in the United States, their numbers remained very small until the first two decades of the twentieth century. During this time perhaps as many as 90,000 Russians, primarily of peasant origin, arrived on the East Coast and chiefly settled in industrial states such as Illinois, Massachusetts, New Jersey, and New York. They entered the ranks of the unskilled working class, with heavy concentrations employed in mining, iron and steel manufacture, and meat packing. While certainly not leaders, it appears that a significant percentage of these workers were sympathetic toward and readily joined incipient labor unions and radical political organizations.

In many cities Russians initially located in close proximity to Russian Jews who frequently had arrived somewhat earlier. A symbiotic relationship emerged, with Jewish bankers and merchants providing services to the new arrivals. However, in a relatively short period of time Russian immigrants established their own ethnic institutions, including the Orthodox church and a variety of local and national fraternal organizations. In addition, Russian-language newspapers, such as *Novoe Russkoe Slovo* and *Russkii Golos,* met the needs of the immigrant community.

Since the immigrant population was male dominated, with only 10 to 15 percent of the total being female, the ethnic community confronted problems shared by a variety of other groups arriving during the same time period. In the Russian case, the scarcity of women in the community stimulated exogamous marriages. The pattern that developed was one in which Russians tended to marry women from other Slavic groups, with the Orthodox church serving to establish a powerful bond of commonality.

In the wake of the Bolshevik Revolution, Russian immigrants were among those frequently viewed with suspicion by U.S. government officials, and during the Red Scare era the repressive political climate forced many immigrants to attempt to downplay their ethnic attachments. At the same time, a new wave of migration brought anti-Soviet dissidents into the country. Included in this wave were Russians, Ukrainians, and Byelorussians, with the Russians constituting probably no more than 10,000 individuals. Many of these came from elite circles, be it from the ranks of the Orthodox clergy, the czar's officer corps, the aristocracy, or the conservative sector of the intelligentsia. Given their rightist political proclivities, it is not surprising that they came into conflict with the immigrant community that had arrived prior to the revolution.

This conflict manifested itself in various ways and often resulted in the establishment of organizational counterparts to those already in place. Perhaps most visibly, the conflict tore the Orthodox church apart as the conservative sector refused to affiliate with a church body that, in the Soviet Union, had reconciled itself to the new political powers. This split was further complicated by the debate over whether a distinctly Russian Orthodoxy was or was not preferable to a multiethnic church body. The ultimate consequence of these differences was the development of three distinct church bodies: the Orthodox Church in America, which is the largest body because it is multiethnic (with Russians constituting a small minority of the one million members); the 25,000-member Russian Orthodox church, which remains affiliated with the patriarchate in Moscow and contains many with histories of sympathy toward the Soviet regime; and the larger (approximately 55,000 member), anti-Soviet Russian Orthodox Church Outside Russia.

In part due to intraethnic conflict, but also because of the small size of the group and its geographical dispersal, the ethnic community has continued to erode during the past quarter of a century and the third and fourth generations have become increasingly assimilated into the larger culture.

References

Emily Balch, *Our Slavic Fellow Citizens* (1910); Jerome Davis, *The Russian Immigrant* (1922); Helen Kovach and Djuro Vrga, "The Russian Minority in America," in *Ethnic Groups in the City,* Otto Feinstein, ed. (1954); Joseph Roucek, "The Russians in the United States," *The Slavonic and East European Review* (1939); Archimandrite Serafim, *The Quest for Orthodoxy in America* (1973).

P.K.

RUTHENIANS. *See* Carpatho-Rusyns.

SACCO AND VANZETTI. During the Red Scare hysteria following World War I, two Italian immigrants personified to Americans the twin dangers of immigration and radicalism. Nicolà Sacco (1891–1927) and Bartoleomeo Vanzetti (1888–1927), both aliens, both avowed anarchists, had been draft dodgers during the war. Sacco worked in a shoe factory, while Vanzetti was a fish peddler. Both took active roles in Italian colony working-class organizations in the Boston area. In May 1920 the two men were accused of robbing and murdering the paymaster and his guard at the Rice & Hutchins shoe factory in South Braintree, Massachusetts, on April 15, 1920, and of unsuccessfully trying to rob a payroll truck in downtown Bridgewater, Massachusetts, on December 24, 1919. The prosecution obtained an indictment on September 14, 1920 in the South Braintree case. Authorities charged that a bullet taken from one of the slain men matched test bullets fired from a Colt .32 found on Sacco when he was arrested. The case against Vanzetti was much weaker and the prosecution first tried him for the earlier attempted robbery. This was a crucial decision, because in the trial, which took place in June 1920 in Plymouth, Massachusetts, Vanzetti made two serious mistakes. One was to entrust his defense to incompetents. He then compounded this mistake by deciding not to testify in his own behalf. Although the evidence against him appeared to be weak, Vanzetti was found guilty and sentenced to twelve to fifteen years in prison. Thus, Vanzetti was a convicted felon. His protestation of innocence in the South Braintree robbery therefore carried little weight.

On May 31, 1921, Sacco and Vanzetti stood trial in the South Braintree case in the superior court at Dedham, Massachusetts. On July 14 the jury found both men guilty of murder in the first degree. Their supporters believed that the decision reflected the defendants' foreign birth and political beliefs rather than the evidence. Judge Webster Thayer, a Boston patrician, supposedly was overheard referring to the "damned dagos," and publicly expressed his contempt for anarchism. Allegedly he boasted to a friend at a football game, "Did you see what I did with those anarchistic bastards the other day? I guess that will hold them for a while." During the trial Thayer also permitted the prosecuting attorney, Frederick Katzmann, to make the defendants' radicalism a cornerstone of his case.

While Katzmann effectively built the case for the prosecution, Fred H. Moore, chief counsel for the defense, complicated his clients' problems with his argumentative and emotional behavior. He was hard working; but his style caused friction with Judge Thayer, with whom he appeared to be in conflict during the entire trial. Moore was totally unfamiliar with the traditions of the Massachusetts bench and was not even a member of the state's bar. Himself a radical and the IWW's (Industrial Workers of the World) former general counsel, Moore used the trial at least as much to publicize his own beliefs as to develop and present a sound defense.

In 1948 the historian Edmund Morgan, an authority on the law of evidence, summarized the conduct of the trial: "Against a masterful and none too scrupulous prosecution was opposed a hopelessly mismanaged defense before a stupid trial judge." The case quickly assumed national and international significance. After numerous delays and despite the pleas of intellectuals, liberals, humanitarians, and other concerned Americans, Sacco and Vanzetti were executed on August 23, 1927. Even after the execution, the supporters of Sacco and Vanzetti agitated for their exoneration. In 1977, Massachusetts governor Michael Dukakis declared August 23 the fiftieth anniversary of the execution and stated that the trial had been unfair. The trial's integrity will undoubtedly continue to be debated.

References
Herbert B. Ehrmann, *The Case That Will Not Die: Commonwealth vs. Sacco and Vanzetti* (1969); Robert S. Feuerlicht, *Justice Crucified* (1977); Felix Frankfurter, *The Case of Sacco and Vanzetti: A Critical Analysis for Lawyers and Laymen* (1927); G. Louis Joughin and Edmund M. Morgan, *The Legacy of Sacco and Vanzetti* (1948); Katherine Anne Porter, *The Never-Ending Wrong* (1977); Francis Russell, *Tragedy in Dedham* (1971); Francis Russell, *Sacco and Vanzetti* (1986).

H.S.N.

SAGIC, DJORDJE. *See* Serbs.

ST. OLAF COLLEGE (Northfield, Minnesota). *See* Norwegians.

SAINT RAPHAEL SOCIETY FOR THE PROTECTION OF ITALIAN IMMIGRANTS. Italian mass migration to the Americas, which increased dramatically after 1887, confronted Italy and the host nations with both opportunities and problems. The latter included the rise of exploitative activities by immigrant recruiters in Italy and the usual resettlement problems. Two additional factors complicated the migration process, especially in the United States. The first was the emergence of the *padroni,* who provided the immigrants with services and jobs, but in exchange exploited them. The second involved the cultural identity of the immigrants, who brought with them a religious style that was repugnant to both the Protestant majority and the Catholic minority in America. These problems prompted Bishop Giovanni Battista Scalabrini (1839–1905) (*q.v.*) of Placenza, Italy, to establish in 1887 a missionary institute to recruit, train, and send missionaries to the Italian settlements in the Americas. At the same time he established an auxiliary lay emigrant society, with the Marchese Giovanni Battista Volpe Landi as president. Its aim was to protect and assist the emigrants at ports of embarkation, on board ship, at the ports of arrival, and in the places of settlement. The society developed branches in New York City (1891–1923) and Boston (1902–1907).

Reference
Edward C. Stibili, "The St. Raphael Society for the Protection of Italian Immigrants, 1887–1923," Ph.D. dissertation, Notre Dame University, 1977 (DA 38-1588-A).

F.C.

SAINT RAPHAELSVEREIN. *See* Germans.

SALATKA, CHARLES. *See* Lithuanians.

SALOUTOS, THEODORE (1910–1980). Immigration historian. Born in Milwaukee, Wisconsin of Greek immigrant parents in 1910, he was educated at the then Milwaukee State Teachers College (B.E.,

1933), and the University of Wisconsin, Madison (M.Ph. 1938, Ph.D. 1940). He taught in the public schools of Waukesha, Wisconsin; in the University of Wisconsin extension system; at Oberlin College; and, from 1945, at UCLA. He was a leading scholar in two separate subfields of U.S. history: the history of immigration and of agriculture. In the latter field his major publications include: *Agricultural Discontent in the Middle West, 1900–1939* (with his mentor, John D. Hicks); *Farmer Movements in the South, 1865–1933* (1960); and his presidential address to the Agricultural History Society, "The Professors and the Populists" (1966). A major work, *The American Farmer and the New Deal,* appeared in 1981.

As an immigration historian his chief works are the path-breaking *They Remember America* (1956), a significant study of the phenomenon of immigrants who repatriated, and the definitive *The Greeks in the United States* (1964). At his death he was at work on a project that united his subfields: a history of the Greeks in California agriculture.

References
Roger Daniels, "Theodore Saloutos, 1910–1980," *Immigration History Newsletter* 13 (May 1981): 13; Rudolph Vecoli, "Theodore Saloutos, 1910–1980: Scholar of Greeks in the United States," *Modern Greek Studies Yearbook* 1 (1985): 109–113.

D.N.A.

SALVADORANS. *See* Central Americans.

SALVADORANS: AS REFUGEES. *See* Refugees.

SALVADORANS, assistance. Mullaney seeks to frame the problem of displaced people in El Salvador by providing (1) an overview of the development of displaced populations in El Salvador and the conditions and problems they encounter; (2) an outline of the ways that the displaced are being helped by the governments of El Salvador and the United States, the churches and private voluntary organizations, including a discussion of why the aid is interpreted as a function of the political struggle; (3) a discussion of recent efforts to relocate large numbers of displaced people to more peaceful areas in the country; and (4) recommendations for future assistance.

Reference
J. Mullaney, *Aiding the Desplazados of El Salvador: The Complexity of Human Assistance* (U.S. Committee for Refugees, 1984).

F.C.

SAMOANS. As of 1970 approximately 15,000 to 20,000 Samoans were living in San Diego, Oceanside, the greater Los Angeles area, and the San Francisco Bay area. Traditionally, after the introduction of

Christianity to Samoa, churches became the most popular secondary social organization among Samoans. But in 1960 some 200 Samoans decided to organize the Samoan Civic Association in order to sponsor a number of community projects.

Reference
Joan Ablon, "The Social Organization of an Urban Samoan Community," in Emma Gee, ed., *Counterpoints* (1976).

D.N.A.

SANCTUARY MOVEMENT. *See* Central Americans.

SANGER, WILLIAM W. (d. 1894). Author of *The History of Prostitution: Its Extent, Causes, and Effects Throughout the World, Being an Official Report to the Board of Alms-House Governors of the City of New York* (1859; rpt., 1976). This official report of the Board of Alms-House Governors of the City of New York was compiled under the direction of the resident physician at Blackwell's Island. A massive survey, one-third devoted to New York City and based on interviews with 2,000 women (largely Irish immigrants) replying to the question, "What was the cause of your becoming a prostitute?" Its concern is with community safety, disease, female honor, crime and the callousness of wealth, the futility of punishment, the experience of regulation, and the hypocrisy of whispering.

F.C.

SANSEI. *See* Issei.

SANTERIA. A religion of African origin, brought to Cuba in the nineteenth century by enslaved men and women from what is now Nigeria, and brought to the United States by Cuban exiles from the revolution of 1959. While an essentially African way of worship, *santeria* has adapted to the Catholicism of colonial Cuba and to the pluralism of the United States.

Santeria centers on devotions to invisible spirits called *orishas* in the Afro-Cuban language Lucumi, and called *santos* in Spanish. This identification between African and Christian spirits has given rise to the Spanish word *santeria,* the way of the saints.

After nearly thirty years of development in cities of the United States, particularly New York and Miami, *santeria* attracts thousands of devotees from Cuban, Puerto Rican, Haitian, Dominican, and black and white North American backgrounds.

Reference
Joseph M. Murphy, *Santeria: An African Religion in America* (1987).

J.M.M.

SAVANNAH, GEORGIA: AS PORT OF ENTRY. *See* Immigrants in the Old South.

SCALABRINI, JOHN BAPTIST (1839–1905). Born in Fino Mornasco, Como (Italy), he was ordained a priest in 1863, became professor and rector of the minor seminary in Como until 1870, and was appointed pastor of St. Bartholomew in Como until 1875. In 1870 Scalabrini was consecrated bishop of Piacenza, where he remained until his death. Scalabrini was above all a pastor. On one hand, Scalabrini implemented the Tridentine Reformation in restructuring catechism and seminaries, clergy and liturgy, synods and pastoral visitations. On the other hand, Scalabrini was the precursor of new times. He dealt with courage and farsightedness with the major issues of his epoch: freedom of opinion in philosophical matters, the participation of Italian Catholics in politics after the unification of Italy, and working-class and social justice. However, Scalabrini is remembered especially for his activity in the field of migration. When mass immigration was met by indifference on the part of the state and by embarrassment on the part of the Church, Bishop Scalabrini emerged as the principal actor in developing a global approach for religious and social assistance to migrants, particularly in North and South America. He visited towns and countrysides left by emigrants; called a diocesan synod to conscientize the clergy; wrote extensively on emigration, on the conditions of emigrants, and on proposals for new immigration laws; lectured throughout Italy to arouse public opinion; organized the St. Raphael Society of lay people for assistance to migrants; founded the Congregation of the Missionaries of St. Charles–Scalabrinians for religious and social assistance to migrants; undertook two "pastoral visits" to the emigrants—in 1901 to the United States, and in 1904 to Brazil; and sent a memorandum to the Vatican secretariat of state outlining the plan for the pastoral care of migrants of all nationalities. In his writings, Scalabrini worked out a clear and complete theory on the immigration problem, its causes, effects, and the development of its various elements. He outlined directives for its solution, not only with respect to its religious aspects, but also its social, economic, legal, and political aspects. The contemporary sociologist Giuseppe Toniolo called Scalabrini the "Apostle of the Emigrants" with "an intuitive sense of the future." In 1987 Bishop Scalabrini was declared "venerable," which is the last step before being declared a saint by the Catholic church.

References

Marco Caliaro and Mario Francesconi, *John Baptist Scalabrini, Apostle to Emigrants* (1977); Mario Francesconi, *Giovanni Battista Scalabrini, Vescovo di Piacenza e degli Emigrati* (1985).

L.F.T.

SCALABRINIANS, Missionaries of St. Charles-Scalabrinians. A Catholic religious congregation founded by John Baptist Scalabrini (1839–1905), bishop of Piacenza, on November 18, 1887, with the approval of Leo XIII, as an apostolic institute of missionaries for the purpose of "providing for the care, especially the spiritual care, of the Italians who had emigrated, primarily to the Americas," who were then the most abandoned and least protected. Subsequently, the congregation extended its mission to Europe and into other countries where the care of migrants was urgent. As a result of pastoral needs, and corresponding to the spirit of Bishop Scalabrini who conceived a plan of action for the care of all migrants, the congregation began to work among migrants of different nationalities, for internal migrations, and for people of the sea: i.e., all those who are living outside their country or outside their social and cultural place of origin and, "because of real necessity," require a specific assistance.

The approximately eight hundred Scalabrinians are now working in nineteen countries in Europe, North and South America, Australia, and Asia. They staff parishes, seminaries, seamen's centers, diocesan offices for the pastoral care of migrants, and old people's homes. Since 1963 the Scalabrinian congregation's commitment to research, study, and strategy in the care of migrants took form in a series of Centers for Migration Studies. The centers are located in Rome, New York, Paris, Basel, Sydney, Caracas, São Paulo, Porto Allegre, and Buenos Aires, and form the "Federation of the Centers for Migration Studies J. B. Scalabrini." The centers work toward the total human promotion of migrants through documentation, research projects, symposia, and publications. Thus, for example, the *International Migration Review*, the quarterly journal that has developed into the leading scholarly journal in the field, is published by the Center for Migration Studies of New York.

References

Marco Caliaro, *La Pia Società dei Missionari di S. Carlo-Scalabriniani* (1956); Congregation of the Missionaries of St. Charles–Scalabrinians, *Rules of Life* (1981); Mario Francesconi, *Storia della Congregazione Scalabriniana*, vols. 1, 6 (1982); *Newsletter* of the Federation of the Centers for Migration Studies J. B. Scalabrini (New York: Center for Migration Studies, biannual).

L.F.T.

SCHIFF, JACOB H[ENRY] (1847–1920). Financier, philanthropist. A major figure in the amelioration of the plight of eastern European Jewish immigrants. His interventions in the cloakmakers' strikes of 1895 and 1910 demonstrate his concern for the immigrant workers. Schiff was the benefactor of several Jewish seminaries and contributor to countless non-Jewish charities including the Red Cross, hospitals, libraries, etc. He was one of the founders of the American Jewish Committee (*q.v.*) in 1906.

Reference
Moses Rischin, *The Promised City* (1962; rev. ed. 1970).

F.C.

SCHLATTER, MICHAEL. *See* Swiss.

SCHLEMIHL. The *schlemihl* is a Yiddish subspecies of the universal fool figure. A victim of endless misfortune, the *schlemihl* of Yiddish folk humor converts losses to verbal advantage and defeats into psychological victories. Yiddish storytellers, including Rabbi Nachman of Bratzlav, Mendele Mocher Sforim, Sholom Aleichem, and Isaac Bashevis Singer, created versions of the *schlemihl*-hero to explore the irony of a faith that could coexist with doubt. Though originally alien to America, Yiddish humor penetrated the general culture, particularly after World War II. American Jewish writers, like Saul Bellow and Bernard Malamud, used the *schlemihl* to explore the paradox of failure as success within a secular humanist culture.

Reference
Ruth R. Wisse, *The Schlemihl as Hero in Yiddish and American Fiction* (1971).

F.C.

SCHLESINGER, Arthur and Elizabeth Schlesinger Library on the History of Women in America, Radcliffe College. The Schlesinger Library's holdings have tripled since publication of the original catalogue in 1973, reflecting the dramatic growth in women's studies during the past decade. Included are some 18,000 bound books, more than 400 manuscript collections, and an extensive corpus of important photographs. Among the major subjects covered are education, employment, women's rights and suffrage, social welfare and reform, family and domestic history, and women's organizations. The library's collections in these and affiliated areas form an invaluable documentary history of American women (including immigrants) in the nineteenth and twentieth centuries.

Reference
Catalogs of the Books, Manuscripts, and Pictures of the Arthur and Elizabeth Schlesinger Library, 10 vols. (1983).

F.C.

SCHMUCKER, SAMUEL SIMON (1799–1873). Schmucker's own knowledge of his heritage provides an outline for an examination of four aspects of its development: German Lutheran Pietism and the men American Lutherans regarded as church "fathers"; the thought of a group of late-seventeenth-century radical Pietists who initially shaped his heritage in America; the religious thought and influence of Henry Melchior Muhlenberg (*q.v.*); and the work of three men who led the American church after Muhlenberg's death and who mediated the theological content and character of what had become a tradition to Schmucker.

Reference
James L. Haney, "The Religious Heritage and Education of Samuel Simon Schmucker: A Study in the Rise of American Lutheranism" Ph.D. dissertation, Yale University, 1968.

F.C.

SCHNEIDERMAN, ROSE (1882–1972). Labor activist. An immigrant from Russian Poland, Schneiderman was a labor activist throughout her adult life. In the mid-1890s, she found her first job in a New York department store. Oppressed by the long working hours and poor pay, she took a better job in a cap factory. Here she began a career in trade unionism and gained her first contact with radical activists. In 1903, with two co-workers, Schneiderman organized the first women's local of the Jewish Socialist United Cloth Hat and Cap Makers' Union. She emerged a local leader, a delegate to the New York Central Labor Union, and a militant agitator during a capmakers' strike in 1905. After 1907 the Women's Trade Union League became her organizational home.

Reference
Rose Schneiderman, *All for One*, with Lucy Goldwaite (1967).

F.C.

SCHOLTE, H. P. *See* Dutch.

SCHOOL SISTERS OF NOTRE DAME. The Congregation of the School Sisters of Notre Dame was founded in Germany in 1833, by Reverend Mother Teresa of Jesus Gerhardinger, for the education of youth. In 1847 the congregation established its first mission in the United States. As the congregation grew in America, a division of the territory into provinces became necessary. The Southern Province was formed in 1895, with the mother house, Sancta Maria in Ripa, at Saint Louis, Missouri.

Reference
Francis M. Sellmeyer, "The Southern Province of the School Sisters of Notre Dame, 1925–1965," Ph.D. dissertation, St. Louis University, 1967 (DA 28: 3125-A).

F.C.

SCHOOLHOUSE SOCIAL CENTERS. Social centers were established as "an agency of adjustment—an organizational response to the threat of instability, uncontrolled change, and the loss of traditional values faced by an immigrant industrial society.'' The following are representative works discussing the ''social center'': Irving King, *Education for Social Efficiency* (1913); Clarence A. Perry, *How to Start a Social Center* (1914); David Snedden, *Sociological Determination of Objectives in Education* (1921); and Edward J. Ward, *The Social Center* (1913).

Reference
Edward W. Stevens, Jr., ''Social Centers, Politics, and Social Efficiency in the Progressive Era,'' *History of Education Quarterly* 12 (Spring 1972): 16–33.

F.C.

SCHURZ, CARL (1829–1906). Political leader. Emigrated to the United States in 1852. Early support of the newly formed Republican Party, and of Abraham Lincoln's presidential candidacy in 1860, led to Schurz's appointment in 1861 as United States minister to Spain. After a distinguished military role in the Civil War (brigadier general of volunteers, 1862–1865), Schurz was an editor and journalist (New York *Tribune,* Detroit *Post,* St. Louis *Westliche Post* [a German-language daily]), United States senator (Missouri, 1869–1875), and served as United States Secretary of the Interior (1877–1881). Schurz exercised great influence through his extensive writings and speeches. His wife, Clara, introduced the ''kindergarden'' to the American schools.

References
Carl Schurz, *Reminiscences* (3 vols., 1907–1908); Joseph Schafer, *Carl Schurz* (1963); J. P. Terziani, *Carl Schurz* (1965).

D.N.A.

SCHUYLER, LOUISA LEE (1837–1926). Philanthropist, welfare work leader; active in responding to the needs of the immigrant poor. Schuyler was active in the [New York City] Children's Aid Society (*q.v.*) and the U.S. Sanitary Commission (Civil War). She helped organize the New York State Charities Aid Association (*q.v.*) in 1872, and was a major influence (as the leader of the Bellevue Hospital Visiting Committee) in securing the opening of the nurses' training school at Bellevue Hospital (New York City) in 1874, the first in the nation.

Reference
Edith Abbott, *Some American Pioneers in Social Welfare* (1937).

F.C.

SCHWENKFELD VON OSSIG, CASPAR (1489–1561). Schwenkfeld's pietism was elaborated as a result of his disappointment with the

Reformation. He felt that Luther had betrayed Protestantism by: (1) retaining unchanged the sacraments of baptism and the Lord's Supper; (2) accepting the coercive power of the State for the maintenance of the Lutheran Reform; and (3) overobjectifying Christian faith, thereby entering into a theology of biblical legalism and literalism contrary to the spirit of Christ. Schwenkfelders in Pennsylvania attempted to maintain a Christian nucleus without violating Schwenkfeld's theology, especially his warning against erecting an ecclesiastical superstructure.

Reference
Norman Dollin, ''The Schwenkfelders in Eighteenth Century America,'' Ph.D. dissertation, Columbia University, 1971.

F.C.

SCOTCH-IRISH. Because of the ambiguity of the words, the group described as ''Scotch-Irish'' is one of the most frequently misunderstood American immigrant elements. Put simply, the Scotch-Irish are people of Scottish background and ancestry who migrated to America from the northern parts of Ireland, where they and their forbears had resided for periods of as long as a century. The term most frequently denotes those who migrated to America in the eighteenth century. While other Americans of that era often simply called them ''Irish,'' the term ''Scotch-Irish'' was occasionally used. It came into more frequent use in the nineteenth century, when this mostly Protestant group found its necessary to distinguish themselves from the growing numbers of Catholic Irish immigrants.

The migration from Scotland to northern Ireland (and mostly to the northernmost province of Ulster) began in the first half of the seventeenth century with the policy of the early Stuart kings of England (who were the kings of Scotland as well) to use transplanted lowland Scottish Protestants to defend their claim to Irish domains against the native Irish. By 1640 perhaps 100,000 people of Scottish origin had taken up homes in Ulster; many were Presbyterians who left their native Scotland to escape religious persecution by the established Church of England. Migrations continued during the 1600s, and by 1715 about one-third of the 600,000 people in Ulster were Presbyterians of Scottish origin or descent. They predominated in areas around seaport cities such as Londonderry and Belfast. Most were tenants on the land and many traditionally engaged in the manufacture of woolen and linen goods.

A variety of circumstances combined to bring about the migration of large numbers of these people from northern Ireland to North America during the eighteenth century. Beginning in the late 1600s the English Parliament passed a series of mercantilist acts which restricted the agriculture and manufacture of Ireland in favor of the English commercial classes. Other measures limited the rights of religious dissenters such as the Presbyterians; the Test Act of 1703, for instance, required officeholders to take the sacraments in the established Church of England. Other pressures developed when the rents exacted by landlords for long-term leases in northern Ireland were raised drastically. Agricultural crises, beginning with a severe drought from 1714 to 1719, provided the final impetus for many to migrate to America.

Migration began in earnest in 1717, when about five thousand left Ulster, and continued through the middle decades of the 1700s until the time of the American Revolution. Estimates of those migrating during that period vary from 200,000 to 250,000. Peak periods of migration were in 1717–18, 1725–29, 1740–41, 1754–55, and 1771–75; these were generally also times of economic and agricultural depression in Ireland. The movement to America was encouraged by propaganda from promoters of settlement schemes and by those seeking indentured servants. The Scotch-Irish were one of the principal sources of indentured servants in eighteenth-century America.

The vast majority of Scotch-Irish migrants entered America through Philadelphia or other Delaware River ports. The tidewater South harbored the inhospitable institutions of slavery and the established Church of England; New England, though Calvinist, made the few Scotch-Irish Presbyterians who found their way there feel unwelcome. New York offered the unpleasing prospect of tenancy on great estates along the Hudson River. Pennsylvania, by contrast, had abundant fertile land and a reputation for religious toleration. The Scotch-Irish sought areas of the Pennsylvania back-country that had not been settled by the Germans who had arrived earlier; they thus gravitated to areas along and beyond the Susquehanna River. In such frontier areas the Scotch-Irish frequently squatted on vacant land without paying for it, to the wrath of Pennsylvania provincial authorities. From the Susquehanna region the path of settlement led in two different ways. One was westward through the mountains and valleys of Pennsylvania into regions still threatened in the mid-1700s by Indians. The other was southwestward through the Cumberland Valley and onward into the Shenandoah Valley of Virginia, which was first reached by Scotch-Irish settlers just after 1730. This stream of migration, which sometimes alternated settlement areas with Germans from Pennsylvania, eventually brought Scotch-Irish settlers into the back-country of the Carolinas, as well as into the mountainous regions of western Virginia. During and after the Revolution, these areas of Scotch-Irish settlement would be most favorably situated to begin the movement of population across the Appalachians and into Tennessee and Kentucky. Thus a great many of the frontiersmen who opened up the interior of the country in the early years of the Republic sprang from

Scotch-Irish background. They left their cultural mark in many ways upon the societies of the upland South and the lower Midwest.

In their Ulster homeland the Scotch-Irish had established a culture and identity that separated them both from the Catholic Irish around them and from the lowland Scottish environment from which they originally came. They maintained this separate identity in eighteenth-century America as well. Their Presbyterianism remained the principal vehicle of ethnic identity; in the far-flung and fluid environment of the frontier, there were few other institutions to bind them together. In time their religion was considerably influenced by the evangelism of both the First Great Awakening (in the 1740s) and the Second Great Awakening (just after 1800). Thus their descendants could be found not only in the Presbyterian denomination but among the Methodists, the Baptists, and the newer evangelical sects that formed in the American Midwest in the early nineteenth century.

While they remained in their homogeneous back-country settlements in the eighteenth century, the Scotch-Irish were able to wield some influence upon colonial politics. Their political positions often reflected their frontier location; they appealed for stronger defense against the Indians, more legislative representation, and less domination by eastern interests. In Pennsylvania, the Scotch-Irish were generally the strongest opposition against the Quaker party, which dominated legislative assemblies until 1756. Until the approach of the American Revolution, they generally sided with the proprietary party. At the time of the Revolution, the Scotch-Irish provided strong support to the radical movement in Pennsylvania advocating independence. Charles Thomson (1729–1824), who had come to America from Londonderry in 1739 as an indentured servant, was among the leaders of the independence movement in Pennsylvania and served as secretary of the Continental Congress during the Revolution.

Following the Revolution, migration from northern Ireland revived somewhat during the 1780s and 1790s, but declined during the period of the Napoleonic Wars. There was renewed migration after 1815, although the proportion of Protestants among the Irish emigrants began to decline and the Catholic Irish predominated beginning in the mid-1730s. The Protestants from Ulster who came to the United States in the post-Revolutionary era no longer sought the frontier areas as frequently; the majority went to eastern urban areas and took up working-class occupations such as the textile industry. As the Catholic migration increased, the conflict between Catholic and Protestant elements that had long existed in Ireland began to be renewed in American cities. Protestant Irish took an active role in anti-Catholic movements in the nineteenth century and were one of the principal elements in violence against Irish Catholics such as was manifested in the Philadelphia riots of 1844.

The nineteenth-century migrations to American cities did not maintain their strong sense of ethnic identity as long as had the eighteenth-century Scotch-Irish of the frontier. A Scotch-Irish Society was founded in 1889, but lasted only to 1901; other genealogical and historical groups were founded in the twentieth century, but these did not generally reflect strong ethnic consciousness among the mass of Scotch-Irish descendants.

References

R. J. Dickson, *Ulster Emigration to Colonial America, 1718–1775* (1966); Wayland F. Dunaway, *The Scotch-Irish of Colonial Pennsylvania* (1944); Henry J. Ford, *The Scotch-Irish in America* (1915); Maldwyn A. Jones, "Scotch-Irish," in *Harvard Encyclopedia of American Ethnic Groups*, ed. Stephan Thernstrom (1980); James G. Leyburn, *The Scotch-Irish: A Social History* (1941).

J.M.B.

SCOTS. Except for Norway and Ireland, no other European country has lost such a high proportion of its people through emigration as Scotland. But only a minority of Scotland's emigrants during the past two centuries have chosen America. Besides sizable contingents to Canada, Australia, and New Zealand, very large numbers crossed the border to England.

Immigration from Scotland to the United States differed in several respects from that from England. It began much later, retained its momentum for a much longer period, and from the mid-nineteenth century onward constituted a significantly larger proportion of the population. Scottish arrivals began to be appreciable only in the third quarter of the eighteenth century, did not assume mass proportions until a century later, and reached its peak only in the 1920s. Despite having only about one-eighth of the population of Great Britain, Scotland accounted for nearly one-quarter of total British emigration between 1853 and 1930.

In the seventeenth century Scotland, as a foreign country, was debarred from England's colonial trade. Hence Scots had only limited opportunities for reaching America. The arrival in Boston in 1652 of 272 Scottish Royalist prisoners, banished by Cromwell after the battle of Dunbar, represented the first considerable non-English element in the town. A further group of political prisoners was transported to Virginia in 1679 after the defeat of the Covenanter uprising at Bothwell Brig. In the 1680s several hundred Scots were settled in East New Jersey by its Scottish proprietors, and a smaller group founded Stuart's Town in southern Carolina. But only after the legislative union of England and Scotland in 1707 did Scottish immigration become continuous. Now that Scots were able to participate in trade with the colonies, many of them settled as merchants and factors in colonial seaports and larger numbers went as indentured servants to the tobacco colonies and New York. Some of those who became bound laborers emigrated involuntarily. They included some hundreds expelled for their part in the Jacobite rebellions of 1715 and 1745 and several thousand convicted felons transported between 1718 and 1775 along with their English counterparts, mainly to Virginia and Maryland.

Throughout the eighteenth century and the first half of the nineteenth, Scottish immigrants came disproportionately from the Highlands, the rocky, barren, densely populated, and chronically impoverished northern half of the country. What distinguished Highland immigration was its communal character. Highland communities began to be planted in the colonies as early as the 1730s; an Islay landowner brought hundreds of his tenants to settle on his land grant in northern New York and another Highland group established a frontier settlement on the Altamaha River in Georgia. In the decade or so after 1763 the Highland exodus accelerated strongly. Partly to blame were economic forces: a rapidly increasing population, a succession of cattle blights and crop failure, profiteering in rents, and evictions from crofts converted to sheep runs. But perhaps even more important was the destruction of the traditional cohesive social structure by the punitive laws that followed the 1745 rebellion. Led by their tacksmen, or intermediate landlords, for whom the end of the clan system meant a shattering loss of prestige, Highlanders flocked across the Atlantic. Between 20,000 and 25,000 left between 1763 and 1775. Many, especially from the Hebrides, went to Nova Scotia, Cape Breton, and Prince Edward Island. Others, encouraged by favorable reports from Highland soldiers who had settled in New York after the French and Indian Wars, congregated in the Mohawk and upper Hudson valleys. But the majority, responding to inducements offered by the North Carolina legislature, settled in the Cape Fear region.

Eighteenth-century emigration from Scotland was not, however, exclusively from the Highlands. An official emigration register for 1773–76 reveals that while the Highlands and the Hebrides accounted for nearly half the departures, almost all of Scotland was represented, with sizable contingents from the West Lowlands and the Borders. Whereas the Highland outflow consisted almost wholly of farmers and farm laborers, that from the relatively urbanized Lowlands had a comparatively high proportion of artisans, especially those who worked in the textile industry. The register also revealed that compared with English emigration a much lower proportion of Scots emigrants went out as indentured servants (18.4 percent as against 68.4 percent).

The problem of Highland distress, already acute by 1750, was greatly exacerbated in the ensuing century. The population increased phenomenally, and the development of large-scale sheep raising prompted the notorious Highland clearances and the consequent contraction of the already small area of arable land. Thus the heavy Highland emigration of the 1770s continued well into the nineteenth century, much of it from 1830 onward being financed by landlords who, having earlier opposed emigration, now saw it as the only remedy for the region's troubles. As late as 1841 the Highland, with no more than one-third of Scotland's population, accounted for 45 percent of its emigrants. Few Highlanders went to the United States after 1820; instead the tide turned decisively toward Canada and the Maritime Provinces.

Throughout the first half of the nineteenth century, Scottish immigration had a predominantly agricultural cast. This was largely a reflection of the scale of the Highland movement, but also of the fact that even in the Lowlands more of those leaving were from agricultural rather than industrial counties. The surplus of agricultural labor resulting from the consolidation of farms and the change from arable to pasture lands, together with the declining profitability of farming, explained the rural exodus. Periods of industrial depression, such as 1819–1820, 1826–27, and 1841–42, certainly stimulated the emigration of urban workers, particularly from the textile towns of Renfrewshire and Lanarkshire, where handloom weavers were suffering high rates of technological unemployment. But the numbers involved were never great, perhaps because unemployed Scottish weavers were too poor to emigrate without government help, and this was denied them.

The 1850s were a turning point in the history of Scottish emigration. Henceforth a growing majority of those leaving came from the Lowlands, and the bulk of them were urban workers rather than agriculturalists. Moreover, the United States now became an increasingly powerful magnet, the principal one, indeed, after 1870. In the 1880s and again between 1901 and 1911 more than 100,000 Scots arrived in the United States, and in the 1920s, when the movement reached all-time record levels and Scotland's population actually fell, it exceeded 200,000. Because of the inadequacy of immigration data it is impossible to be precise about the occupational characteristics of the immigrants. During the years 1850–1880 skilled industrial workers—especially those in textiles, mining, iron and steel, and shipbuilding—were fairly well represented. During the 1880s however, apart from miners and building trade workers, the outflow consisted less of skilled workers than of general laborers from the larger towns. Most of the immigrants of the 1880s were young unattached men and a sizable proportion were temporary or transient immigrants. This pattern may well have remained unchanged during the heavy immigration of the ensuing forty years. After 1930, however, immigration from Scotland, like that from the rest

of Europe, came to a virtual standstill, and when it revived after World
War II it was small by early twentieth-century standards and consisted
predominantly of skilled and professional people.

Distribution. Whereas Highland immigrants almost invariably settled in rural areas of the United States, Lowlanders were mainly to be
found in urban and industrialized states. In 1920 the Scottish born were
concentrated chiefly in New England and the mid-Atlantic states, but
they were also well represented in the Midwest (especially Ohio, Illinois, and Michigan) and the Pacific coast. The pattern of distribution
has changed little during the past half-century. The most visible groups
of Scotsmen, perhaps, were skilled artisans who headed for places
where they could follow their Old Country occupations. Thus Aber-
deenshire granite and stone workers clustered in the quarries of Maine,
Vermont, and Massachusetts; Paisley weavers and dressers were numerous in the textile and thread making centers of New England and the
mid-Atlantic states; and carpet weavers from Kilmarnock gave a pronounced Scottish flavor to the Connecticut carpet town of Thompson-
ville. Scottish skills contributed greatly to the development of Pennsylvania and Ohio coal mining and iron and steel manufacture, though the
most famous of all Scottish immigrants, the steelmaster and philanthropist Andrew Carnegie, had no previous industrial experience,
having arrived in America as a penniless boy of thirteen.

Adaptation and Identity. Like immigrants from other parts of
Great Britain, Scottish immigrants enjoyed a high standing in the
United States, were accepted as equals, and generally obtained better-
paid jobs than other groups. Yet Scots retained a strong sense of cultural
distinctiveness and were sensitive about suggestions that they were
merely British. To a far greater extent than English immigrants, therefore, they established separate social and cultural institutions so as to
preserve their distinctive heritage. Among Gaelic-speaking Highlanders
language was the main source of cohesion, and indeed Gaelic was still
widely spoken in the Cape Fear Highland settlements as late as the
1830s. For most English-speaking Scots religion provided a more dura-
ble bond. To be sure, Catholics and Episcopalians, who formed a substantial segment of the Scottish-born population, tended to lose their
separate identify in Irish and American parishes respectively. But the
more numerous Scottish Presbyterians did not usually feel at home in
the relatively lax American Presbyterian churches and, especially in
New England, insisted on building their own churches where their own
austere brand of Presbyterianism, which adhered strictly to the West-
minster Confession, might be practiced. The Scots also established their
own newspapers and periodicals, the best-known being *The Scottish-
American Journal,* which was published in New York from 1857 to
1919 and had at its peak a circulation of 15,000. During the middle third

of the nineteenth century Scots established hundreds of Caledonian clubs which staged traditional Highland games featuring not only track and field events but bagpipe and country-dancing contests. But the games became as popular with Americans as with Scots and the competitions were soon thrown open to all athletes, though in the process peculiarly Scottish events like caber-tossing were abandoned. The Scottish game of curling, a rudimentary form of ice hockey, was widely played in Scottish settlements but never attained wider popularity. Golf, on the other hand, introduced by Scots, who started the first American club at Yonkers, New York in 1887, rapidly became the sport of wealthy Americans. Likewise the largely unhistorical and commercially inspired cult of clans and tartans which developed in the late nineteenth century appealed not only to Scots but to many Americans who had no claim to Scottish ancestry.

References
Ian C. C. Graham, *Colonists from Scotland: Emigration to North America, 1707–1783* (1961); Eric Richards, *A History of the Highland Clearances*, vol. 2: *Emigration, Protest, Reasons* (1985); Bernard Bailyn, *Voyagers to the West: Emigration from Britain to America on the Eve of the Revolution* (1986); Malcolm Gray, "Scottish Emigration: The Social Impact of Agrarian Change in the Rural Lowlands, 1775–1875," *Perspectives in American History* 7 (1973): 95–176; Gordon Donaldson, *The Scots Overseas* (1966).

M.A.J.

SCOTTISH AMERICAN JOURNAL. *See* Scots.

SELECT COMMISSION ON IMMIGRATION AND REFUGEE POLICY (1978–1981). *See* U.S. Congress, House and Senate, Committee on the Judiciary.

SEPHARDIC JEWS. Sephardic Jews in the United States are a diverse group in language, national background, customs, and length of residence in the United States. Numbering as few as 100,000 according to some reports and as many as 250,000 according to others, Sephardim came to the United States in four periods of history. The first to arrive came in the early seventeenth century and traced their ancestry to Spain and Portugal. Among them were the Lopezes, the Gomezes, the Pereiras, and others who became extensively involved in commercial enterprises and came to have large interests in the shipping industry, fur trading, and real estate. They established the oldest synagogues in the United States, Shearith Israel in New York, Touro Synagogue in Newport, and Mikveh Israel in Philadelphia. Despite a history of some discrimination against them in official contexts such as voting and serving in the armed forces, they were active in colony—and later, American—life almost from the beginning. For example, they donated money to the building of Trinity Church in New York and served in Washington's army. Few in number, most of them eventually married Ashkenazi Jews, whose immigration quickly made them the more numerous Jewish population, and some intermarried with Christians. Today the Jews in the United States who are descendants of the Sephardim are included in studies of the twentieth-century immigrants, and especially in discussions of the interactions between the Sephardim and Ashkenazim in the early part of the century. The several hundred years of the Sephardim experience in the United States have been studied extensively by American historians; dozens of books exist, and there are numerous articles about them in the pages of the *Publications of the American Jewish Historical Society*.

Major Migrations to the United States. Between the early eighteenth and late nineteenth centuries, Sephardic Jews did not immigrate to the United States. Since the beginning of the twentieth century, however, Jews from the Levant, speakers of Ladino (Judeo-Spanish), Greek, and Arabic, have sought new homes in America during the great migration period of 1880–1924, after World War II, and since 1956. These Jews come from Salonika, Rhodes, Yanina, Kastoria, Monastir, and numerous Turkish towns, and from Aleppo, Damascus, Iran, Iraq, Egypt, Morocco, and Yemen. Those who migrated before 1924, between 30,000 and 50,000, were mostly of Ladino background, although there were a few thousand Greek- and Arabic-speaking immigrants. Although not all of these Jews trace their ancestry to Spain, current usage refers to the three language groups as Sephardic because the Sephardic influence in the Levant, beginning in the late fifteenth century, was so extensive that non-Sephardic groups often adapted their rituals and customs to the Sephardic mode.

In the Ottoman world Sephardim of all national backgrounds had been generally isolated from Moslem and Christian communities, and they had virtually no contact with Sephardim in other towns or with Ashkenazim. Like the non-Jews around them, they lived in a world characterized by high illiteracy, poverty, natural disasters, and the rule of opportunistic and ill-educated leaders. By themselves, these factors were sufficient to mobilize some of the Levantine Jews to seek new homes. However, the Young Turks' edict of 1908 that all national minorities would for the first time be conscripted into the service, the Balkan Wars, World War I, and a series of natural disasters all created an even more pressing need for the Jews to leave. Few at this time left because of persecution. In fact, some Jews from the largest Turkish cities—Salonika, Istanbul, Izmir—albeit a tiny minority, had prospered in the empire, become well educated, and joined the national movement for political change. Most of these never left the Levant, and those who did did so very reluctantly and fully intended to return. The poorer immigrants, those who were clearly searching for a better life in America, left their homes with strong regrets but with the intention of remaining in the new land.

After World War II the Sephardic populations of Salonika, Yanina, Rhodes, Monastir, and other formerly Turkish towns were decimated. Small numbers of survivors came to the United States, usually to be integrated into already existing Sephardic communities, but occasionally settled by HIAS (the Hebrew Sheltering and Immigrant Aid Society) in other areas; for example, thirty Greek-speaking families were settled in Baltimore, Maryland after 1946.

The most numerous Sephardic group in the United States, and once the smallest, is the Arabic speakers who have come in large numbers since 1956 and have retained a separate and essentially cohesive community, mostly in Brooklyn, New York.

Demographic Information. In the early twentieth century most Sephardim, whatever their linguistic or national background, settled in New York, on Manhattan's Lower East Side and in Brooklyn. However, small groups of Sephardim were relocated by the industrial Removal Office or traveled on their own to Indianapolis, Montgomery, Los Angeles, Seattle, Atlanta, and Rochester. Wherever they settled, Sephardim tried to maintain residential cohesiveness. Today, there are very few Ladino or Greek communities where the Sephardim continue to live closely as neighbors. Only the Arabic-speaking Jews of Brooklyn continue to live quite near one another in a several square block area where there are stores, synagogues, and social halls to meet their needs.

During the 1910s and 1920s Sephardic immigrants were generally single men under the age of thirty. The women who came were usually picture brides or sweethearts. During the earliest years of immigration those who came were usually poor, unskilled, and uneducated, although there was a handful of moneyed and educated businessmen among them. After World War I, the literacy rate among new immigrant males was relatively high, as many had been educated in the Alliance Israelite Universelle and other foreign schools.

For Sephardim, as well as other Jews, peddling was a most attractive occupation because as their own bosses they could be Sabbath and holiday observers if they chose to be. Others were shoemakers, tailors, carpenters, and painters. Some ran the shoeshine and candy concessions in theaters and hotels. On the West Coast many entered the flower, fruit and vegetable, and fish businesses. Arabic-speaking Jews were prominent in lingerie and lacemaking. By the mid-1920s there were a few lawyers, physicians, teachers, and accountants among Sephardim. On the whole, however, Sephardim were slow to enter the professions and to take advantage of higher education. This was especially true for women, who married early and often did not finish high school. Today

Sephardim are represented in every field and discipline. The more recent Syrian immigrants have become especially prominent as owners of a wide variety of well-known businesses selling consumer goods.

Institutions. Like other immigrants to the United States, Sephardic Jews established three major institutions: synagogues, mutual aid and burial societies, and newspapers. Like the Ashkenazi Jews they also attempted to create a unified and organized community.

Language, custom, variations in liturgy, and a history of separation into residential enclaves based on city of origin in Spain encouraged Sephardim to establish in the United States very small congregations based upon their country of origin. In the earliest days of their residence in America, they conducted religious services without a rabbi and met in small rented rooms. Shearith Israel in New York, which had a well-established and Americanized Sephardic and Ashkenazic congregation, did invite the immigrants to attend services in the synagogue; and the sisterhood of the synagogue established a settlement house on the Lower East Side for religious services, Hebrew education, and English classes. The sisterhood accomplished much good work, but misunderstandings and paternalism on the part of the American Jews often created rifts between the immigrants and the uptown Jews.

Mutual aid and burial societies and social groups were also organized along national lines, although by the mid-1920s Sephardim of various national backgrounds did join together as members of the many societies and even intermarried. Again, the exception to intermingling has been the Arabic-speaking group, which maintains its own institutions and generally eschews social and religious association with other Jews.

In the early twentieth century, the tremendous proliferation of small societies was disturbing to some Sephardic leaders who believed that a united community would better advance the needs of the entire group. United, they could pool resources, gain recognition from the larger Jewish community, and reach a wider range of immigrants with English classes, employment help, and other services. Through the late 1940s there were several attempts to organize a large communal organization; at their most successful these lasted a few years and ended because of disagreements among the various national groups.

Among the Sephardim, the Ladino speakers established a varied press. Many of the newspapers, *La Luz, La Bos del Pueblo, El Aguilar, La Epoca de New York,* had short lives. Poor immigrants were reluctant to spend a few pennies on a luxury item, and many of them could not read the papers. The longest-running paper of the immigrant period was Moise Gadol's *La America,* a paper that urged Sephardim to retain their centuries-old history and language while they became Americans, learned English, and became involved in Jewish as well as national issues. Gadol was one of the voices speaking for community organization. He was also a controversial figure who did not hesitate to argue quite publicly at meetings and in the press with all who disagreed with him. In 1922 *La Vara* appeared, and ran until 1948. This paper's editorials also urged the Sephardim to take advantage of the benefits America offered. Further, the editors included a satiric column, and by the early 1930s focused extensively on world affairs and included an English-language section. There is no longer an organized Sephardic press in America, although several social and cultural groups, most notably Los Amigos Sefardies in Oakland, California, publish newsletters.

Identity. When the Sephardic Jews from the Levant entered the United States in the early twentieth century, they encountered—most of them for the first time—a much larger Jewish population: nearly two and a half million eastern European Jews. Initially, the Sephardim, numbering at most fifty thousand, found that the Ashkenazim, largely ignorant of the Sephardim's very existence, could not believe Sephardim were Jewish since they didn't speak Yiddish. Calling them Italyeners or Turks, the eastern European Jews sometimes did not patronize Sephardi stores or permit their daughters to date Sephardi men. This lack of acceptance only strengthened the immigrant Sephardim's desire to cling to their Old World identities, maintaining separation in their coffee houses, synagogues, and communal organizations. They also kept an eye on the homeland, sending money to bring relatives or to aid them during the natural disasters that struck their towns of origin, and returning to find marriage partners.

In the Levant, Sephardim were not involved in any reforms of Judaic ritual; they have always been considered Orthodox. In reality, however, the level of observance among them both in the Levant and in the United States has varied a great deal. For many, Judaism has been an integral part of their daily lives; for others, it has been an expected part of community life; today there are significant numbers of Sephardim that are not affiliated with any synagogue. Many belong to Ashkenazi synagogues, and there are Sephardic synagogues that have a sizable Ashkenazi membership.

The national culture of the Sephardic Jews consists of folk tales and songs; stories of Spain; superstitions and medical practices; ways of socializing; gender roles; attitude towards education, work, family, and charity; language; foods; and religious customs, such as reciting prayers in Ladino or Greek or Arabic on Passover and other holidays and in the daily worship services. Immigrants rarely engaged in deliberate attempts to pass on these traditions to their children. They made more formal attempts to transmit religious culture by enrolling their children in Hebrew schools. Despite the absence of formal methods to transmit national culture, there were ample opportunities for children to be socialized into their parents' cultural patterns through observation and participation. Nonetheless, there were such strong forces pressing for Americanization in the early twentieth century that many second-generation Sephardim rejected their parents' language and customs and passed little on to their own children, the third generation. Again, the most ethnically coherent Sephardic community in the United States is the Arabic one, supported in its efforts to maintain an identity by large numbers of immigrants settling in Brooklyn after 1956 because of continuing political turmoil in the Middle East.

Fortunately, much Sephardic culture has been preserved by language, music, and religious scholars, and by lay people, who have studied and recorded Sephardic folk tales, music, and proverbs. Also, in the last twenty years, an increased number of third-generation Sephardim have displayed an interest in their culture, and this has led to the organization of Ladino and Sephardic music classes, Sephardic festivals, and cultural associations.

References

Albert Adatto, *Sephardim and the Seattle Sephardic Community,* master's thesis, University of Washington, 1939; Marc D. Angel, "Notes on the Early History of Seattle's Sephardic Community," *Western States Jewish Historical Quarterly* 7 (1974): 22–30; Marc D. Angel, *La America: The Sephardic Experience in the United States* (1982); Marc D. Angel, "'Progress'—Seattle's Sephardic Monthly, 1934–35," *The American Sephardi* (Fall 1971): 91–95; Marc D. Angel, "The Sephardim of the United States: An Exploratory Study," *American Jewish Yearbook* (1973): 77–138; Marc D. Angel, ed., *The Americanization of a Hispanic Group: The Sephardic Experience in America* (1981); David Barocas, *The History of the Broome and Allen Boys Association,* (1969); Jose Main Benardete, *Hispanic Culture and Character of the Sephardic Jews,* (1953); J. A. De Benyunes, "The Sephardic Jews of New York," *The America Hebrew* (Sept. 29, 1916): 718–719, 737; Sol Beton, *Sephardim and a History of Congregation or VeShalom,* (1981); Judith Endelman, *The Jewish Community of Indianapolis, 1849 to the Present* (1984); Lee Max Friedman, *Pilgrims in a New Land* (1948); Leon Huhner, *Jews in Colonial and Revolutionary Times* (1959); Jacob Rader Marcus, *Early American Jewry. The Jews of New York, New England and Canada, 1649–1794* (1951); Diane Matza, "A Bibliography of Materials on the National Background and Immigrant Experiences of the Sephardic Jews in the United States, 1880–1924," *The Immigration History Newsletter* 19, no. 1 (May 1987): 4–9; Dina Dahbany Miraglia, *An Analysis of Ethnic Identification Among Yemenite Jews in the Greater New York Area,* Ph.D. dissertation, Columbia University, 1983; Joseph M. Papo, *Sephardim in Twentieth Century America: In Search of Unity,* (1987); David de Sola Pool, "The Levantine Jews in the United States," *American Jewish Yearbook* 15 (1913–14): 207–220; Stuart Rosenberg, *The Jewish Community in Rochester, 1843–1925* (1954); Victor D. Sanua, "Contemporary Studies of Sephardic Jews in the United States," in A. D. Lavender, ed., *A Coat of Many Colors* (1977); Victor D. Sanua, "A Study of the Adjustment of Sephardi Jews in the New York Metropolitan Area," *Jewish Journal of Sociology* 9 (1967): 25–33; Morris U. Schappes, ed., *A Documentary History of the Jews in the United States, 1654–1875* (1950); John Schulter, "Washington's Moroccan Jews: A Community of Artisans," in A. D. Lavender, ed., *A Coat of Many Colors* (1977); Stephen Stern, *The Sephardic Jewish Community of Los Angeles* (1980); Joseph Sutton, *The Magic Carpet: Aleppo in Flatbush* (1979).

D.M.

SERBS. Unlike the Slovenians and Croatians, the Serbs are by mentality, location, and history a completely Balkan nation. They have traditionally long ties with the East. They accepted Christianity from the Byzantine Empire and after the eleventh century remained Eastern Orthodox. Their rulers had only occasional ties with the West. Their Orthodox church, headed by a patriarch, has existed—with some interruptions—for more than six centuries. They were influenced by Byzantine and later Ottoman cultures.

From the original area in Raša (between the Drina and Ibar rivers) their independent state expanded to reach its height under their greatest ruler, Czar Dušan (1331–1355). In June 1389 Serbia was crushed by the Turks at the field of Kosovo. Then, until 1878, Serbia existed under Turkish rule. Following a revolt in the beginning of the 1800s and subsequent existence as an autonomous principality, Serbia became completely independent in 1878 by the decision of the Congress of Berlin.

During the long Ottoman rule tens of thousands of Serbs, leaving from ancestral lands, settled in southern Hungary, Bosnia, Herzegovina, and Croatia. After 1878, when the Habsburgs occupied Bosnia-Herzegovina, and much earlier in Croatia and Hungary, many Serbs lived under Austrian rule. Even their patriarch resided in Austrian territory. Their Orthodox church, always close to the people, regarded everyone of Orthodox faith as a Serb even though many Orthodox people, especially in Croatian lands, were not of Serbian ethnic origin. Proud of their independent new state, with its capital in Belgrade, influenced by the extreme nationalism of their church, and supported by "Mother" Russia, the Serbs developed by the late 1800s and early 1900s a Great Serbian movement aimed at the absorption of all their South Slavic neighbors. In the Balkan Wars (1912–13) the Kingdom of Serbia, under the Karageorgevich dynasty, grew in size from 18,000 to 34,000 square miles, and its population from 2.9 million to 4.5 million. As allies of the Western powers in World War I, the Serbs were able at the end of 1918 to partly realize their old dreams. A kingdom of Serbs, Croats, and Slovenes was established against the will of the majority of the non-Serbian nationalities. The imposed union, torn by fierce antagonisms and strife, disintegrated in April 1941.

Before 1920 few Serbs immigrated to the United States from Serbia. Most of the people who were regarded as Serbs came from the Habsburg-ruled lands of Croatia proper, Dalmatia, Bosnia-Herzegovina, and southern Hungary. The first prominent Serbian pioneer, George Fisher (formerly Djordje Šagić), came from the Serbian diaspora in Hungary. He arrived in Philadelphia in 1815. After a colorful career in the East and South, he arrived in San Francisco in December 1851, and became judge of the county court. He died here in June 1873.

The Serbian Orthodox Church in America stems from the Slavonian-Russian-Greek-Orthodox Church and Benevolent Society that was incorporated on September 2, 1862 in San Francisco. Rev. Sebastian Dabovich, of Montenegrin origin, was born in the same city. After he was educated and ordained in St. Petersburg, Russia in 1887, Dabovich returned to America. In 1894 he established the first Serbian Orthodox church in this country in Jackson, California. In Chicago he established the headquarters of what became the Serbian Orthodox Church in the United States. He established other churches, schools, and cultural and national centers for his people. He also promoted the Orthodox church among the non-Serbian immigrants, translated the Orthodox liturgy into English, and for some time published a periodical entitled *Orthodoxy*. He participated in the Balkan Wars and in World War I. When the Serbian patriarchate finally organized the Serbian Orthodox Diocese in America, Dabovich was not named its bishop. Disappointed and ill, he died on November 30, 1940 in the Montenegrin homeland.

Many Serbs lived in Illinois and, after 1885, in Montana; quite a few lived alongside the Montenegrin and Croatian settlers in California. Pennsylvania, Ohio, and other industrial states attracted thousands of them. Among the earlier immigrants were: Mihajlo Pupin (a native of Idvor, Banat), who arrived in 1874; and Nikola Tesla, who came over from Croatia in 1884. Among the 18,548 immigrants classified by our immigration authorities as "Bulgarians, Servians [sic], and Montenegrins," who arrived here during the decade ending in June 1908, at least one-third were Serbs. Most of them settled in Pennsylvania to work in steel mills, mines, and other difficult and hazardous jobs. Because of its proximity to the Atlantic seaports (mostly New York), Pennsylvania was for many years a favorite destination for masses of all Slavic immigrants. By 1910 some ten thousand Serbs lived in Pennsylvania.

In 1903 some three hundred families and many single men established in Chicago the First Serbian Beneficial Federation, which in 1909 merged with the Serb Montenegrin Federation of Butte, Montana into the United Serb Federation, or "Harmony," at a meeting in Cleveland, Ohio. Because of the Old Country politics, "Harmony" split; after years of frictions several societies from all over the country founded, in Cleveland, the Serbian Beneficial Federation Unity. Out of several fraternal organizations, the Serbs formed, in Pittsburgh in 1929, the Serb National Federation (Srpski Narodni Savez) which on June 26, 1931 gathered for its first convention. The SNF is the largest Serbian fraternal organization today.

In 1907, according to Fr. Dabovich's estimates, there were between 150,000 and 200,000 Serbs in America. Of these a majority lived in the East, Midwest, and the West; smaller groups were scattered in many states and territories, including Alaska. Dabovich also mentioned Serbs in Canada; a great majority of these were Serbs from Croatian provinces, quite a few of whom, until the early 1900s, regarded themselves as Orthodox Croatians. Because of the similarity of Slavic languages, wherever Slavs labored and struggled, Serbs lived along with them.

The events in the Balkans—the Balkan Wars and World War I, to which thousands of Serbian volunteers rushed—caused more or less permanent frictions, animosities, and controversies between the American Serbs and the rest of the South Slavs. The assassination of Archduke Francis Ferdinand in June 1914 by a young Serbian nationalist, which triggered World War I, was enthusiastically applauded by a majority of Serbs and their newspapers. The most outspoken newspapers in advocating the cause of Serbia were *Srbobran* (The Serbian Defender), in New York, and *Srpski Glasnik* (The Serbian Messenger), in Chicago. The most active advocate of the Serbian cause was Professor Michael Pupin of Columbia University, who created a lot of ill feelings in the South Slav movement. He was supported by the Serbian Orthodox league "Srbobran," which had some seven thousand members. The Serbian legation in Washington encouraged Serbian political activities. The restoration of an independent Serbia was included in President Wilson's "Fourteen Points." The Serbian cause was victorious when on December 1, 1918 a kingdom of Serbs, Croats, and Slovenes was proclaimed by Belgrade.

The Socialist movement found many supporters among the Serbs. One of the oldest Socialist organs was *Radnicka Borba* (Workers' Struggle), in Cleveland; it was the organ of the South Slavic branch of the Socialist Labor party. For many years it owned a bookstore where, besides newspapers, it sold many pamphlets, books, and almanacs, all of them of Socialist orientation. The Socialists were opponents of monarchy in Yugoslavia; they promoted the education of the immigrants and were most active during the period between the two world wars. There were seven Socialist Serbian newspapers in 1939. John R. Palandech (who arrived in the United States in 1887 at the age of thirteen) was the best-known Serbian journalist; he was for many years the owner of a bookstore in Chicago, and was nicknamed "the Northcliffe of the foreign language newspapers." Leposava Djordjević was an active publisher in California.

According to U.S. census data there were, in 1916, twelve Serbian parishes with a membership of some 14,000 and eight Sunday schools. However, there were really twenty-eight Serbian parishes all over the country which in 1921 came under the jurisdiction of the newly organized Serbian Orthodox Diocese of the United States and Canada. By the 1930s it comprised some thirty-five churches with about 100,000 parishioners. Cathedrals were built in Milwaukee, Wisconsin and in Alhambra, California. Eight churches are dedicated to the Serbian national saint St. Sava. Millions of dollars have been spent for these churches and other buildings, testifying to the generosity of the faithful. The St. Sava Monastery and the see of the diocese are located in Libertyville, Illinois. The impressive St. Sava Church in Parma, Ohio was built and dedicated in 1967. Their Orthodox church in this country helped the Serbs to retain their national identity, and the church and the people are tightly knit together.

The Serbs are a very proud people, and nationalistic. The old settlers came as people of the soil, peasants for many generations who escaped poverty, conscription, and unsettled political conditions in the Balkans. Serbia before 1914 enjoyed a crude, popular democracy but was also plagued with violence and regicide. A typical Serb is from the Šumadija region, the cradle of the struggle for independence. The Serbs are extremely hospitable but at the same time remote and distrustful. They brought to America also their fierce love for freedom. Tradition was always their "spiritual food." As Pupin observed in his writings, they believed that "the noblest thing in this world is the struggle for right, justice, and freedom."

Like the rest of the South Slavs, the Serbs, too, got involved in radical movements culminating in the activities during 1941–45. Most of them, during the royal dictatorship in the 1930s, and even after 1941, were loyal royalists. The Serbian press denounced the writings of the Slovenian-born American writer Louis Adamic who in his books criticized the royal dictatorship and in the early 1940s started to promote the cause of a Communist-dominated Yugoslav republic.

On the eve of America's entry into World War II, a majority of Serbs were prospering in industry, various professions, business, and farming. Some were very wealthy truck farmers in the San Joaquin Valley of California. World War II, with the resulting industrial boom, brought even more prosperity to them. Thousands joined the armed forces and distinguished themselves on all fronts. In 1944 Lieutenant Mitchell Page (Milan Pejić) of the USMC was awarded the Congressional Medal of Honor for his heroic action at Guadalcanal.

The U.S. government supported the royal Yugoslav government-in-exile in London, which was headed by young King Peter, and lauded the activities of the nationalistic Chetnik movement under General Draža Mihajlović. After early 1943 Washington abandoned Mihajlović and started to support the Communist-dominated National Liberation movement under Josip Broz Tito. Many Serbs joined other South Slavs in pro-Tito and pro-Soviet activities. These were years of bitter controversies and feuds between all South Slavs. The Yugoslav ambassador in Washington, Konstantin Fotić (a Serb), the Serbian National Federation (with some 23,000 members), and its organ *Srbobran* remained staunch royalists and incessantly promoted the emotional feuds between the Serbs themselves and between them and especially the Croatians. These resulted in final divisions and animosities that have persisted to the 1980s. This was also partly due to the influx of postwar immigrants. First came hundreds of former royal officers who spent years in German prisoner-of-war camps; they were also joined by many former Chetniks who came as refugees and "displaced persons." After the 1960s, thousands of immigrants arrived directly from SFRY to join their families and closest relatives. The new generation that grew up under communism brought a wave of skilled and professional people whose contributions added to those already existing.

Among the old contributors the greatest was Nikola Tesla, who was partly of Serbian and Croatian origin. A genius in electrics, Tesla was by his many inventions one of the founders of modern industrial America, probably the greatest inventor that ever lived here. He died a forgotten man, in poverty, on January 7, 1943 at the age of eighty-seven. Only in recent years has he received proper recognition; he has been honored by a monument and a postal stamp. Michael Pupin (1855–1935) was a scientist and inventor in electronic engineering.

The Serbs also made their contribution in fine arts: John D. Brcin (born in 1899 in Gračac, Croatia) was a prominent sculptor; Vuk Vucinich was a painter and sculptor. Among noted singers were Danica Ilić, a soprano at the Metropolitan, and Mia Novich (Bosiljka Mijanović), a native of Chicago. Dr. Paul Radosavljevich was a noted professor of experimental education at New York University and author of several scholarly books. Among the dozens of educators is the historian Michael Boro Petrovich (of a Serbian father and Croatian mother) of the University of Wisconsin. Among writers is Stoyan Pribichevich, an author of several books who worked for a while for *Time* and *Fortune* as war correspondent.

The most successful postwar immigrant is Milan Panić who came in 1955 and established the International Chemical and Nuclear Corporation in Pasadena, California. During the 1970s it employed over 6,000 people, with sales of over $150 million. Helen Delich Bently, a longtime newspaper woman for the Baltimore *Sun,* was appointed in 1970 chairwoman of the Federal Maritime Commission.

The most important problem the American (and Canadian) Serbs have been facing since the early 1960s is the split within the organized church. By 1961 there were some seventy-three churches with approximately 200,000 Serbian Orthodox members, a remarkable record for an ethnic group that numbers probably some 400,000 people. The split occurred because a sizable number of the Serbian hierarchy and congregations refused to recognize the jurisdiction of the patriarch in

Belgrade who was under the control of the Communist government. Generally most of the old and American-born Serbs recognized the authority of the patriarch in Belgrade, while most of the postwar immigrants reject his authority and side with the separate diocese centered in Libertyville. The years-long emotional conflicts between the two feuding groups have involved long legal battles and even physical violence. A decision of the U.S. Supreme Court in June 1976 ended the bitter controversy, and the Serbian church remained widely and permanently split.

As a result of the immigrants' influx after the 1940s the life of the Serbian ethnic group has been revived and invigorated in many areas. There are about two dozen newspapers, some of them in Cyrillic and some in Latin (or mixed) script. In folklore, culture, social and political activities, and in religious life (in spite of the split in the church) the Serbs show great vitality. Thousands visit the homeland each year, while thousands of relatives, friends, and prominent singers and writers visit here. Because of their economic success it was possible for the Serbs, through the generosity and dedication of many individuals, to bring about a real renaissance of Serbian life in America.

References
Oto Bihalji-Merin, ed., *Serbia, Yugoslavia* (1961); Dusko Doder, *The Yugoslavs* (1978); J. M. Halpern, *A Serbian Village* (1958); Robert Gakovich and Milan Radovich, *The Serbs in the United States and Canada: A Comprehensive Bibliography* (1976); George J. Prpic, *South Slavic Immigration in America* (1978).

G.J.P.

SERBS, North American Society for Serbian Studies (NASSS). Founded and housed at the University of Illinois/Chicago. Publishes *Serbian Studies* (1980–), which deals with all aspects of Serbian cultural heritage and Serbian immigration to North America.

D.N.A.

SETTLEMENT HOUSE MOVEMENT. The settlement house movement began in London, England, with the establishment of Toynbee Hall in 1884. Its founder, Canon Samuel A. Barnett, believed that the complex industrial, urban world of his time was contributing to the widening gap between rich and poor and that existing institutions were not interested in meeting this problem of an alienated, slum society. Barnett proposed to connect "the centres of learning with the centres of industry." University men, "settling" or residing in the slums, would provide "education by permeation" and stimulate the underprivileged to aspire to higher goals. In this process the university men would fulfill an ethical and religious obligation to serve their fellow human beings. This concept of a university settlement was adopted by Stanton Coit when he founded the Neighborhood Guild in 1886 as the first settlement in New York as well as in the United States. Profile sketches of New York City settlement workers reveal a predominantly Protestant, college-educated group of men and women motivated by a need to fulfill religious and ethical obligations by serving the less fortunate members of the urban community. These settlement workers, of small town or rural background, were the first representatives of the middle class voluntarily to enter and live in the ghetto. Their purpose was to help improve the way of life of the slum residents whose condition, in this instance, was aggravated by their immigrant status. Settlement houses were the first to welcome the European immigrants without rejecting their Old World Culture.

Reference
Harry P. Kraus, *The Settlement House Movement in New York City, 1886–1914* (1980).

F.C.

SHARLIP, WILLIAM. *See* Americanization Movement.

SHAW, ADELE MARIE (d. 1937). Social reformer; critic of public school education and an advocate of immigrant education reform. See Shaw's "The True Character of New York Public Schools," *World's Work* 7 (Nov. 1903): 4204–4221, and *ibid.* 9 (1905): 5480–5485; "The Public Schools of a Boss-Ridden City," *World's Work* 7 (Feb. 1904): 4460–4466; "Common Sense Country Schools," *World's Work* 8 (June 1904): 4883–4894; and "The Spread of Vacation Schools," *World's Work* 8 (Oct. 1904): 5405–5414.

F.C.

SHAW, PAULINE AGASSIZ (1841–1917). *See* North Bennet Street Industrial School.

SHEPPARD-TOWNER ACT (1921). The Sheppard-Towner Maternity and Infancy Protection Act of 1921 was an important link in the 1920s between old Progressives and later New Dealers. It was also a product of the recent enfranchisement of women, who strongly supported the bill.

Reference
J. Stanley Lemons, "The Sheppard-Towner Act: Progressivism in the 1920s," *Journal of American History* 55 (1969): 776–786.

F.C.

SIEBERG, JACOB. *See* Latvians.

"SILK CITY" (Paterson, New Jersey). By the 1880s the juxtaposition of skilled labor and continuing migration from Europe, improved machinery, and the raw silk supply culminated in Paterson's earning the nickname "Silk City." Paterson was first in American silk production; but some of the very factors that contributed to its stellar position as the leading American silk manufacturer also led to its decline. Improved machinery did not require skilled labor; therefore, silk manufacturers, in an effort to cut production costs, sought locations where there was an abundant supply of cheap, tractable labor. Paterson workers, reacting to the effects of improving machinery upon their livelihood, climaxed a history of strikes with the silk strike of 1913. Rather than improving the lot of the workers, however, this strike only aggravated their plight, for it forced manufacturers to accelerate their exodus from the city.

References
Morris W. Garber, "The Silk Industry of Paterson, New Jersey, 1840–1913. Technology and the Origins, Development and Changes in an Industry," Ph.D. dissertation, Rutgers University, 1968 (DA 29: 1843-A); Anne H. Tripp, *The I.W.W. and the Paterson Silk Strike of 1913* (1987).

F.C.

SIMKHOVITCH, MARY KINGSBURY (b. 1867). Social reformer. Simkhovitch served as director of New York City's Greenwich House. In *The City Worker's World in America* (1917; rpt. 1971) Simkhovitch portrayed the urban immigrant environment at the start of the century; the pervasive influence of poverty on the one hand and opportunity on the other are skillfully traced, and she discusses the conditions in the workshop as well as in the home, the street, and the neighborhood club. How workers contend with rises in the cost of living, language problems, generation gaps, Americanization, and ethnic group competition are carefully spelled out. There are also sections on sickness, child labor, immigrant women, and the lung-blocks in the tenement neighborhoods.

F.C.

SIMPSON-MAZZOLI IMMIGRATION BILL, history.

It is said that Congress and the President have only dealt with immigration once in any generation: the post–World War I quotas, the post–World War II McCarran-Walter Act, and now Simpson-Mazzoli. Setting aside the question of whether immigration as a topic of legislation is in fact cyclical, and whether or not Simpson-Mazzoli was to be enacted and work as intended, it is unlikely legislation designed to deal with people coming to our shores will disappear from the political screen for another thirty years. Economists can debate how many immigrants we can afford to absorb and whether they help or hurt our nation. Demographers can debate population growth and the "push" and "pull" factors which send people from other nations to our country, but the issue will not go away. We can only hope that when future congressional and executive bodies are faced with immigration issues, they will deal with them constructively, as they have in Simpson-Mazzoli, so that we will never again see the day when nativism and racism become the basis of immigration policy. (Miller)

Reference
Harris N. Miller, "The Right Thing to Do: A History of Simpson-Mazzoli," in Nathan Glazer, ed., *Clamor at the Gates: The New American Immigration* (1985), pp. 49–71.

F.C.

SINCLAIR, UPTON (1878–1968). Novelist. Sinclair's literary works expressed his radical ideas of social justice. The prime purpose of his writing was to better human conditions, particularly those of the lowest working classes, who were mostly immigrants. *The Jungle* (1906) is his best known and most socially significant American novel, depicting the brutal working conditions of Chicago slaughterhouses. Sinclair, a literary radical from an upper-middle-class family, influenced American life more than any other novelist of his time by calling attention to the plight of the lowest working classes. All of his works depicted his hatred of capitalist wealth, corruption, and oppression. *The Jungle,* a story of a Lithuanian family that came to Chicago to achieve the American dream, portrayed a nightmare of struggle, poverty, and death. Other significant novels continuing the theme of wealth and corruption were *The Metropolis* (1908) and *The Moneychangers* (1908).

In 1914, disturbed by a mass killing of Italian striking and mine workers and their families in Ludlow, Colorado, he became involved in the labor and social problems of miners. Sinclair's involvement in labor led to his participation in electoral politics and his decline as a novelist. He was the unsuccessful Democratic candidate for governor of California in 1934. Between 1940 and 1953, Sinclair published novels whose central character was Larry Budd, and which depicted the historical struggle of socialism and communism against the oppression of capitalism and fascism. His chief works between 1917 and 1953 were *King Coal* (1917); *Oil* (1927); *They Call Me Carpenter* (1922); *Between Two Worlds* (1941); *Dragon Harvest* (1946); and *The Return of Larry Budd* (1953).

Reference
William H. Bloodworth, *Upton Sinclair* (1977).

C.C.

SINEY, JOHN (1931–1880). Labor leader. Siney was born in County Offaly, Ireland, and emigrated to the United States in 1863, settling in Schuylkill, Pennsylvania. He founded the Workingman's Benevolent Association (WBA) in 1868, the first miners union. He later chaired the 1873 convention that established the first national miners' union, the Miners National Association (MNA), and was elected president of the MNA three times. He was also active in the Greenback Labor Party of the 1870s.

Reference
E. Pinkowski, *John Siney: The Miners' Martyr* (1963).

S.P.M.

SINN FEIN PARTY. *See* Irish.

SLAVE TRADE. *See* Afro-Americans.

SLAVONIANS. *See* Slavs.

SLAVS. "Slav" is a term used to denote peoples of southern and eastern Europe who speak languages that are related and, in some instances, mutually comprehensible. Linguists have grouped these peoples as East Slavs (Russians, Ukrainians, Byelorussians, Carpatho-Rusyns, and Cossacks); West Slavs (Poles, Czechs, Slovaks, and Lusatian Sorbs); and South Slavs (Serbs, Croats, Slovenes, Bulgarians, and Macedonians). Today the East Slavs live in the Soviet Union; the West Slavs have two independent states (Poland and Czechoslovakia), while the Lusatian Sorbs are part of East Germany; and the South Slavs also live in two independent states: Yugoslavia (Serbs, Croats, Slovenes, and Macedonians) and Bulgaria.

All of these groups migrated to the United States in varying numbers in the nineteenth and twentieth centuries and, because at that time many of them did not have their own states, they were often known by their region of origin, by the foreign states in which they lived, or by what their neighbors called them. Thus, Czechs were originally called Bohemians in the United States (after their ancient kingdom); Slovaks were originally referred to as Hungarians or "Hunkies" (they came from the Kingdom of Hungary), but the Pan-Slavs among them called themselves "Slavic," "Slavish," or "Slavonians" to stress a dreamed-for but nonexistent Slavic unity; Lusatian Sorbs were named "Wends" and Slovenians "Windisch" by their German neighbors; and Croatians from the region of Dalmatia were initially known as Dalmatians. Only after these groups discovered their true identities in the United States did they begin to call themselves by their proper names. Many, however, missed the boat of nationalism and to this day continue to use the ancient (and erroneous) designations and, thus, confound the Bureau of the Census which, since 1980, has been trying to get an accurate count of America's many ethnic groups, among them the Slavs.

References
Francis Dvornik, *The Slavs in European History and Civilization* (1962); Emily Greene Balch, *Our Slavic Citizens* (1910).

M.M.S.

SLIPUAS, JONAS. *See* Lithuanians.

SLOVAK v AMERIKE. *See* Slovaks.

SLOVAKS. Although they are the second-largest Slavic group in the United States (after the Poles), the Slovaks remain largely unknown. The vast majority came in search of work before World War I but smaller numbers appeared later as well. They settled in the industrial Northeast and Midwest and helped build America's heavy industry.

Migration to the U.S.A. The first Slovaks appeared in the United States in the 1840s, although large numbers did not come until the 1870s. After the Civil War, when the United States began to industrialize in earnest, the captains of industry needed cheap labor and found it in eastern Europe, where millions of people had only recently been freed from serfdom. The Slovaks, who at that time lived in northern Hungary, responded to advertisements by agents of American railroads, coal mines, and steel mills to come to the United States to work for up to $1.50 per day. While native-born Americans considered that to be a very low wage, Slovak peasants who could make only fifteen to thirty cents a day (if they could find work at all) on the landlords' estates regarded it as a handsome salary. The trickle who had come in the 1870s turned into a deluge in the 1880s and 1890s, and peaked in 1905 when 50,000 crossed the ocean. By 1914 650,000 had made the journey and about 500,000 (one-fifth of the Slovak nation) chose to stay permanently.

Initially only young and male Slovaks came to the United States in the expectation that, once they had made their "fortunes," they would return home. Indeed, many of them did return to the Old Country, often several times, but the majority (80 percent) finally got so used to American life that they decided to stay for good. They then sent for their wives or girlfriends and settled down to a better life in the New World.

After World War I three more waves of Slovaks came to the United States, but never in the same numbers as before. Just prior to the 1924 Immigration Act, which severely restricted arrivals from eastern and southern Europe, several thousand Slovak women arrived to join their husbands or sweethearts in America. This time the Slovaks were coming from the newly created Republic of Czechoslovakia (founded in 1918 on the ruins of Austria-Hungary). The new state did not satisfy all Slovaks and several thousand more fled after World War II, either because they did not wish to live with their neighbors, the Czechs, or else because they were fleeing the Communist takeover of the country in 1948. A final (and continuing) trickle of Slovaks from Czechoslovakia began in 1968 when the Soviet Union invaded to prevent the liberalization of that country's government.

Most Slovaks settled in America's industrial heartland. Half ended up in Pennsylvania, chiefly in the anthracite coal mine region of Scranton–Wilkes-Barre or else in the steel mill and bituminous mining region of Pittsburgh. Large numbers also settled in New York City, in northern New Jersey, in Ohio (particularly in Cleveland), in Michigan (especially Detroit), and in the Chicago area.

Institutions. In the United States Slovaks created three kinds of institutions that would define their communities—fraternal-benefit societies, parish churches, and a newspaper press. The fraternals came first because, in the late nineteenth century, there were virtually no social services in this country. If an immigrant fell ill, suffered an accident, or died, no one paid him or his family any compensation. Therefore, Slovaks established more than forty fraternal-benefit societies in the 1880s which provided their members with insurance and a rudimentary social welfare system. Some of these local lodges federated into the National Slovak Society with headquarters in Pittsburgh in 1890; into the First Catholic Slovak Union, with headquarters in Cleveland, also in 1890; or into another half-dozen nationwide Slovak fraternals.

While the fraternals took care of some of the material needs of their members, the Slovaks also had spiritual needs. Therefore, Slovaks of all denominations (Roman Catholics, Lutherans, Greek Catholics, and Reformed) began to establish their own parish churches in the United States starting in 1884. By the 1930s they had over 300 parish churches in their principal areas of settlement. Most were founded by fraternal-benefit societies and for many years the latter were also their chief sources of support.

Since Slovak immigrants were naturally curious about news from home, they established a very vigorous newspaper press. It encompassed a wide variety of periodicals, ranging from dailies to weeklies, monthlies, and quarterlies, and represented all shades of opinion, from the far left to the far right. While the independent, commercial press had the largest number of titles, the fraternal press (especially the weeklies) has had the longest life. In 1935 American Slovaks published 51 newspapers (this was the peak year), and altogether between 1885, when the first Slovak periodical appeared, and 1985 they have published over 220 different titles. After World War II the Slovak-American press started a slow decline and today there are fewer than two dozen periodicals catering to Slovak-Americans, and only one—*Slovak v Amerike* (founded in 1889)—appears exclusively in the Slovak language.

Identity. Because other groups have ruled over the Slovaks for over a millennium, the latter have always had problems of identity. Until 1918 the Slovaks were part of the Kingdom of Hungary, and the ruling Magyars of that state tried to forcibly assimilate the Slovaks. Some went along with this policy, while others resisted. Furthermore, local dialects, which can be grouped into eastern, central, and western Slovak, divided the people even more, and continued to do so in the United States. The Reformation of the seventeenth century also splintered the Slovaks into Roman Catholics (about 80 percent), Lutherans (about 15 percent), Greek Catholics (3 percent), and Calvinists or Reformed (2 percent). In the nineteenth century Slovak Lutherans, who used the Old Czech Bible, chafed more under Hungarian rule than the Catholics, and were the leading Slovak nationalists. In the twentieth century, after Czechoslovakia was created, most Lutherans were satisfied, but the Roman Catholics were not. The latter accused the Czechs and Slovak Lutherans of trying to create a new ethnic group that would be called "Czechoslovak." To complicate matters even more, Americans originally referred to Slovaks as Hungarians, "Huns," and "Hunkies" because they had come from Hungary. Later, the Slovaks were called Slavs, Slavish, Slavic, or Slavonian, because certain American Slovaks liked to stress their ties with other Slavic groups. Finally, after Czechoslovakia was created in 1918 many Americans followed the lead of certain Czech and Slovak leaders and began to refer to all the people who originated on Czechoslovak territory as Czechoslovaks. It is not surprising, therefore, that only 776,806 Americans of Slovak descent properly identified themselves in the 1980 federal census. Their true number is somewhere between 1 and 2 million but, because of the reasons outlined above, we may never discover precisely how many there are.

References

Thomas Bell, *Out of This Furnace* (1941); Vasil S. Koban, *The Sorrows of Marienka* (1979); Ewa Morawska, *For Bread with Butter: Life-Worlds of East Central Europeans in Johnstown, Pennsylvania, 1890–1940* (1985); M. Mark Stolarik, *Growing Up on the South Side: Three Generations of Slovaks in Bethlehem, Pennsylvania, 1880–1976* (1985), and *Immigration and Urbanization: The Slovak Experience, 1870–1918* (1988).

M.M.S.

SLOVENES. Slovenes (Slovenians) are a predominantly Roman Catholic South Slavic people. In both language and culture they are distinct

from the other principal groups of South Slavs, the Croats and the
Serbs. Their ancestral homeland lies in the northwestern part of Yugoslavia, a nation in which the majority of Slovenes have formed a constituent part since its formation in 1918. Historically, however, the Slovenes lived in subordination to the Austrian Habsburgs in the provinces
of Carniola, Carinthia, Styria, and Istria, and in the area around Trieste.
A smaller, secondary body of Slovenes lived a detached and isolated
existence in the Prekmurye region of southwestern Hungary.

The Slovenes are a small people, numbering fewer than 3 million
persons worldwide. Perhaps 300,000 individuals of Slovene extraction
reside in the United States. Slovenes have been characteristically migratory, and many of their number had migrated to German and non-
Slovene Habsburg provinces to work as artisans and miners before the
onset of large-scale emigration to the United States. A number of Slovene priests emigrated to the United States in the early nineteenth century
to engage in missionary work, but emigration on a significant scale
began in the 1880s and ended by 1914. A subsidiary migration followed
in the years 1919–1923, and another group, primarily political refugees
from the Tito regime in Yugoslavia, relocated in the United States in the
late 1940s and early 1950s.

Immigrants in the 1880–1914 period displayed a preference for
employment in the mining industry or engaged in services fundamental
to life in mining towns, especially the grocery business and saloon
keeping. Hence, early Slovene settlers normally lived in isolated communities. Calumet, Michigan, a copper-mining town in the Upper Peninsula, attracted the earliest significant population of Slovene miners,
followed in turn by the Minnesota Iron Range communities of Eveleth,
Hibbing, and Virginia, the Montana towns of Butte and Anaconda, and
the coal-mining area of southeastern Kansas. Others settled in the coal
and steel centers of Pennsylvania, and large Slovene colonies developed
in Johnstown, Steelton, and Pittsburgh.

More diversified industrial opportunities attracted Slovenes to the
Chicago-Joliet area of Illinois and especially, in the 1890s, to Cleve-
land. By 1900 the Ohio city had emerged as the "capital" of Slovenian
America, the center of the cultural, religious, and institutional life of the
ethnic group. Since 1900 the locus of Slovenian America has been
Cleveland's St. Clair Avenue.

Slovene immigrants exhibited the cultural traits common to all
Slavic groups. A considerable number terminated their relationship with
Roman Catholicism and established a freethinking movement, but this
tendency was not as pronounced among the Slovenes as it was among
the Czechs. Like other Slavs the Slovenes displayed an intense mate-
rialism, reflected essentially in an obsession with property ownership
and with the creation of mutual benefit societies. The consolidation of

these self-help organizations eventually led to the formation of fraternal insurance institutions of considerable size, each of which represented a Catholic or a secularist exclusiveness. The largest of these institutions were the Grand Carniolan Slovenian Catholic Union of U.S.A., founded in 1894 and currently known as the American Slovenian Catholic Union, and the secular Slovene National Benefit Society and Slovene Mutual Benefit Association, currently named the American Mutual Life Association. The secular organizations date, respectively, from 1904 and 1914. Approximately half of Slovene-Americans retain membership in one or more of the fraternals, a participation rate unequaled among other Slavic groups.

While immigrants of the pre-1914 period were frequently illiterate, the Slovenes nevertheless developed a substantial press in America. Commencing with *Amerikanski Slovenec* (American Slovene), founded in 1891 in Chicago, Slovenes created seventy-five newspapers and periodicals by 1920. Many were short-lived, but more than forty survived until the 1920s. The Slovene-American press was typical of Slavic groups. Some papers represented the Catholic interest, while others emanated from the fraternals, women's organizations, or ideological elements in the community. One of the longest lived was *Proletarec* (Proletarian), a Socialist paper which appeared from 1906 to 1952. The attrition implicit in acculturation and generational change gradually afflicted the Slovene-language press, and of the few papers that survived into the 1980s only one appeared more frequently than on a weekly basis.

Like other Slavic groups, moreover, political consciousness and political participation developed slowly among the Slovenes. Before 1930 the Socialists, operating through the Slovene section of the Yugoslav Socialist Federation, were clearly the best organized and most aggressive. Mainstream Slovene-Americans, of course, identified with the Democratic party, and eventually contributed such notable public servants as Frank J. Lausche, successively major of Cleveland, governor of Ohio, and United States senator; and John Blatnik, who from 1948 to 1975 represented the Democratic–farm labor stronghold of Duluth and the Minnesota Iron Range in the House of Representatives and became influential in the inner councils of the party.

The preservation of ethnic identity has been rather pronounced among Slovene-Americans, a testament to the influence of the Catholic parishes and the fraternal organizations. Diminution of ethnic conscious has, of course, occurred in the second and third generation, and competence in the Slovenian language is no longer widespread. Yet the maintenance of Slovene distinctiveness appears to be a significant concern, and two organizations, the Cleveland-based Society for Slovenian Studies and the Slovenian Research Center of America at nearby Kent State

University, have been established to perpetuate Slovene-American culture.

References
Gerald G. Govorchin, *Americans From Yugoslavia* (1961); Ivan Molek, *Slovene Immigration History, 1900–1950: Autobiographical Sketches* (1979); Ewa Morawska, *For Bread with Butter: The Life-Worlds of East Central Europeans in Johnstown, Pennsylvania, 1890–1940* (1985); Marie Prieland, *From Slovenia to America: Recollections and Collections* (1968); George J. Prpic, *South Slavic Immigration to America* (1978).

K.D.B.

SMITH, VENTURE. *See* Immigrant Autobiographies.

SOCIETÀ NAZIONALE DANTE ALIGHIERI. Founded in Italy by secular and private auspices to maintain *Italianità* among transplanted Italians. During the period of great migrations, the society made continuing efforts to sponsor Italian language and culture abroad. In the United States, it made a special effort to support schools for immigrant children, but its success was very limited due to a complex set of factors, chief of which was the disinterest of Italian immigrants.

Reference
Napoleone Colajanni, *La Dante e Gli Emigranti Analfabeti* (1904).

F.C.

SOCIÉTÉ NATIONALE DES ACADIENS. *See* Acadians.

SOCIETY FOR GERMAN-AMERICAN STUDIES. Established in 1968 and registered in the state of Ohio as a nonprofit organization, the society is a professional association of individuals and institutions interested and involved in the field of German-American studies. The purposes of the society are to engage in and promote interest in the study of the history, linguistics, folklore, genealogy, literature, theater, music, and other creative art forms of the German element in the Americas; to publish, produce, and present research findings and educational materials of the same as a public service; to assist researchers, teachers, and students; and to improve cross-cultural relations between German-speaking countries and the Americas. The society endeavors to realize its purposes by means of its quarterly newsletter, its annual yearbook, and its annual meeting and other symposia. Annual meetings of the society are held in various parts of the country. Recent meetings have been held in Kansas, Missouri, Texas, Minnesota, Pennsylvania, Wisconsin, and Nebraska. Meetings were also held in Ohio (1986), Kansas (1987), and Pennsylvania (1988).

F.C.

**SOCIETY FOR THE PREVENTION OF CRUELTY TO CHIL-
DREN.** *See* Riis, Jacob A.

SOCIETY FOR THE PROPAGATION OF THE GOSPEL. *See*
Afro-Americans.

**SOCIETY FOR THE PROTECTION OF GERMAN IMMI-
GRANTS IN TEXAS.** *See* Von Herff, Ferdinand.

**SOCIETY FOR THE PROTECTION OF ITALIAN IMMI-
GRANTS** (aka The Society for Italian Immigrants). Founded in 1901,
the society was a major agency for the guidance and direction of Italian
immigrants and was jointly supported by American, Italian, and Italian-
American philanthropists. Gino C. Speranza (*q.v.*) served as secretary of
the society. At Ellis Island (*q.v.*) the society maintained representatives
to assist newcomers, and its Labor Bureau helped to find work for
immigrants outside New York City. Under Speranza's dynamic leadership, the society became an investigatory agency for the reporting of
immigrant labor abuse. The society's influence declined after World War
I. The [Annual] *Reports* (1902–1919) of the society are available in the
New York [City] Public Library.

F.C.

SOKOL. *See* Czechs.

SOLIA. *See* Romanians.

SONS OF ITALY. Organized in 1905, the Order Sons of Italy in
America (OSIA) soon became the largest Italian fraternal organization
in the United States. For over eight decades the order has played a
crucial role in the social, cultural, and political life of Italian-Americans. OSIA has provided a national voice and direction on Italian-
American issues, and its leadership has constituted an ethnic elite including prominent businessmen and politicians.

The founder of the Sons of Italy, Dr. Vincenzo Sellaro, was born
in Sicily and graduated from the medical school at the University of
Naples before coming to the United States in 1897. Recognizing the
need to unite the multitude of Italian mutual aid societies into a single
federation, Sellaro called together a small group of professionals in
New York City and founded the Sons of Italy. The new group adopted
the nomenclature and organizational scheme of American fraternal
groups, using a structure of national, state, and local lodges. Under its
emblem, the golden lion, and its slogan of "Liberty, Equality and
Fraternity," OSIA grew in the New York area.

The order soon mushroomed as lodges were organized in New Jersey, Connecticut, and other neighboring states. During the decade 1910–1919 OSIA initiated over 960 lodges and spread to additional states. Many of the lodges were preexisting local mutual aid societies which were drawn to the order during the World War I years. By the mid 1920s the order boasted 300,000 members and 1,500 local lodges in thirty states and two Canadian provinces. Early in its history OSIA offered women complete parity and many of its local lodges had either an all-female or combination male and female membership. Women have been present on the National or Supreme Council since 1931, and three women were elected as state lodge presidents during the past quarter-century.

OSIA provided mutual assistance in times of sickness and death, and has also sponsored an impressive array of cultural, social, economic, and political programs. An OSIA representative assisted immigrants at Ellis Island in the 1910 era, and since 1914 the order has maintained the Garibaldi-Meucci Museum on Staten Island. The grand lodges of Pennsylvania and New Jersey erected orphanages in the early 1920s. During World War I the families of members serving in the U.S. military received subsidies from the organization. OSIA encouraged its members to join AFL unions and actively supported the Paterson textile strikers in 1913.

The organization's prosperous growth did face a number of severe challenges. In 1908 a dissident faction formed the Independent Order Sons of Italy, which grew to over 500 lodges by 1926. In 1928 a group of 20 lodges in western Pennsylvania split off from OSIA and formed the Italian Sons and Daughters of America, which is still functioning as a separate fraternal organization. However, the most divisive schism occurred in 1925 in the Grand Lodge of New York, the order's largest state organization. Led by Fiorello LaGuardia and New York State Senator Salvatore Cotillo, a large faction of the membership, upset by the Supreme Venerable's close relations with Mussolini's Italy, left the order. The ensuing legal and polemical struggle caused a nationwide division in OSIA. This breach was finally healed in 1943 when the dissident group, the Sons of Italy Grand Lodge Inc., rejoined the order. Although prior to World War II the organization was split by the question of how to balance the spirit of ethnic nationalism with the assimilationist demands of the new country, the order rallied unanimously behind the United States when war came.

OSIA has served as a cultural and political bridge between Italy and the United States since its earliest days. It has mobilized assistance for the victims of natural disasters and war in Italy. Following both world wars the order sought to influence U.S. policy with respect to peace treaties and territorial disputes. Cultural and student exchanges between the two countries have been an area of OSIA activity for many years. The order has taken a strong interest in immigration and naturalization issues, lobbying vigorously against immigration restriction in the 1920s and for liberalization in the 1950s and 1960s.

The order has served as an agent for activating the Italian-American community on particular issues and as a lobby in Washington, the state capitals, and city halls. It has gained the attention of the White House ever since Woodrow Wilson appointed the Supreme Venerable to an advisory committee during World War I. President Carter addressed the organization's national convention in 1979. OSIA has been an active proponent of the advancement of Italian-Americans in the public and private sectors, and has been an active opponent of defamation of Italian-Americans in the media.

The order has sponsored a variety of programs throughout its history: banks, savings and loan associations, charities, senior citizens' housing, newspapers, citizenship classes, foundations, Columbus Day celebrations, language courses, student scholarships, and recreational programs. It has encouraged both the maintenance of the Italian culture and language and assimilation into American social and political life. As the second generation came of age after World War I, OSIA increasingly stressed American-style activities such as sports, and organized 400 junior lodges to hold the young people.

Throughout its eighty-year history, OSIA has founded 3,050 local lodges in forty-three states, the District of Columbia, Guam, Bermuda, and the provinces of Ontario and Quebec in Canada. Grand lodges have been formed in twenty states and two Canadian provinces having the greatest concentration of local lodges and members. The Order Sons of Italy in America has been both a mirror that has reflected the full scope of Italian-American life as well and a catalyst that has affected the status and participation of Italian immigrants and their descendants in American society. Today, with 91,000 members in 850 local lodges, OSIA remains the largest Italian fraternal group in North America.

The story of OSIA not only contributes to our understanding of the Italian-American experience, but also helps clarify the larger issues of ethnicity, community, and politics in pluralistic America. While two histories of the order have been published (Baldo Aquilano, *L'Ordine Figli d'Italia in America,* New York, 1925; and Ernest Biagi, *The Purple Astor,* Philadelphia, 1961), there is no scholarly history of OSIA. To make such a history possible OSIA and the Immigration History Research Center (IHRC) have joined efforts to identify, collect, and preserve the order's records, which have existed in locations scattered throughout the United States and Canada. The three-year (1985–88) Sons of Italy Archives Project will culminate in the formation of the permanent OSIA Archives at the IHRC which will provide scholars with a core collection of surviving records. In addition to primary records and photographs, the Archives Project has compiled data on most of the 3,050 lodges and the 3,000 men and women who have held national or state offices in the order since 1905. The project will also produce a catalogue describing all known OSIA records, both at the IHRC and other sites throughout North America.

References
Baldo Aquilano, *L'Ordine Figli d'Italia in America* (1925); Salvatore Benanti, *La Secessione della "Sons of Italy Grand Lodge"* (1926); Ernest Biagi, *The Purple Astor* (1961); Robert Ferrari, *Days Pleasant and Unpleasant in the Order Sons of Italy in America* (1926); OSIA Archives, fifty-four manuscript collections and fifteen newspaper collections at the IHRC.

J.A.

SONS OF ITALY IN AMERICA, Grand Lodge of the State of New York. The order was first organized in New York State during 1905. It has since spread throughout the United States, Canada, and Bermuda. Its growth has continued and new lodges are daily being developed, chartered, and initiated into the order. The composition of the order is made up of the local lodges that are located throughout the territory that it covers. The lodges in turn come under the guidance and direction of a grand lodge of a state or group of states. The Order Sons of Italy in America, while seeking to preserve and disseminate the rich cultural heritage of our forbears, encourages and creates the involvement by its members through their lodges in all civic, charitable, patriotic, and youth activities—to the end that they contribute to a greater America. Through its social, cultural, and interlodge relationships, it brings together the united effort of its members in worthwhile community affairs that contribute to the betterment of our municipalities, states, and nation. Individual and collective goals or campaigns are initiated so that funds are made available for scholarships, aid to the needy, and for other local and national causes. To be eligible for membership, one must have been born in Italy, or be a descendant or a spouse of one of Italian lineage, or one who has been adopted by persons of Italian descent, or a spouse of said adopted. The order is nonsectarian, nonprofit, and nonpartisan. It respects the rights of its members to be affiliated with the religious and political entities of their choice. The order publishes the *OSIA News,* a monthly national newspaper, relating the activities of the local and grand lodges throughout the United States, Canada, and Bermuda. It also publishes the *Golden Lion,* with up-to-the-minute news of local lodge activities in New York City.

F.C.

SONS OF NORWAY. Norwegian fraternal and insurance organization. The first lodge was organized in Minneapolis in 1895. Its purpose
was to provide mutual aid, insurance, and social opportunities for Norwegians during the depression of the 1890s. Based loosely on American
fraternal lodges, the Sons of Norway instituted secret rituals and ceremonies which often attracted the opposition of the Norwegian Lutheran
clergy. In 1900, a Supreme Lodge was established. Lodges appeared on
the West Coast (Seattle) by 1903, and on the East Coast (Brooklyn) by
1910. By 1914 the Sons of Norway had emerged as the largest secular
Norwegian-American organization, with over 12,000 members. A sister organization, the Daughters of Norway, was begun in 1897 and
merged with the Sons of Norway in 1950. In the mid-1980s, the Sons of
Norway claimed 100,000 members in 350 lodges. In addition to insurance, the organization offered its members auxiliary organizations and
has encouraged the preservation of Norwegian culture in American
through publications, language classes, and tours of Norway.

Reference
Carl G. O. Hansen, *History of Sons of Norway* (1945).

J.J.

SORBS. *See* Wends.

SOUTH END HOUSE (Boston). *See* Woods, Robert A[rchey].

SOUTH SLAVS. *See* Slavs.

SOUTHERN CHRISTIAN LEADERSHIP CONFERENCE. *See*
King, Martin Luther, Jr.

SOVIET KARELIA. *See* Finns.

SPANIARDS. The migration of Iberian peoples to the Americas represents a centuries-old process, stretching back, in fact, to the initial
voyages of Columbus. Therefore, the story of the Portuguese and Spanish division and many times brutal colonization of the New World is
part of the historical legend of Western man. The Iberian culture, political and legal institutions, language, and religion were transported and
implanted in an area that would incorporate all of South America and a
sizable section of the North American continent, including large regions
within the present-day western and southern United States. This was to
be the historical configuration of a major part of the New World between the fifteenth and nineteenth centuries. Even the political revolu-

tions that swept through the Spanish dominions in the 1820s and finally reached Portuguese Brazil in 1889, though Brazil was nominally independent after 1822, could not offset the years of cultural domination of the respective mother countries.

This situation still remains largely the case after over a century of Latin American political independence. In terms of the continued impact of the Spanish people upon the continental United States, there has been a long hiatus separating (particularly Spain's) early and significant involvement in American history from the Spaniards' later historical role. Recent Spanish population movements have simply been statistically unimportant in comparison to the earlier period. This is not to imply that immigration from Spain ceased entirely between the years of American independence and the large wave of European migrations so common to the fabric of American life in the late nineteenth century. What this does mean, however, is that throughout this period and into the twentieth century Spanish immigration was small in numbers when contrasted with the movements of many other European countries. For instance, during the 146-year period between 1820 and 1965, 297,363 Portuguese and 196,972 Spanish immigrants came to the United States. These numbers are in sharp contrast to the 6,845,239 Germans, 5,041,268 Italians, 4,704,251 Irish, 465,200 Poles, 506,479 Greeks, 709,359 French, and 356,389 Danes who came to America during the same period.

As with most complex social phenomena, there are a variety of reasons that explain the relatively minor immigrant role of the Spanish in American history. Perhaps the principal factor in this process has been the maintenance by Spain of tightly administered overseas colonies, particularly in Africa, which have provided a logical outlet for surplus populations. In this case we can see an active government policy that oversaw and encouraged migration in a direction that was ostensibly engineered to best benefit the mother country. Another plausible explanation for the relative paucity of Spanish immigrants to the United States has been a determined preference, when migrating from parent countries, to move to former Latin American colonies. Here the immigrants found a recognizable culture and a familiar language which fortunately forged a conducive atmosphere for adaptation. Once more the centuries-old ties between Spain and these New World territories paid definite human dividends by providing suitable homes for an excess population. In addition to these factors, the continued agricultural orientation of the economy of Spain well into the nineteenth and twentieth centuries worked to preserve the traditional aspects of its society, even in the face of political instability. In practice this meant that the customary population displacement generally associated with industrialism did not create a large potential reservoir for emigration.

Thus, Spain differed in its historical situation when compared to many other European nations. The revival of American nativism in the late nineteenth century, which culminated in the literacy test of 1917 and the even more decisive quota legislation of the 1920s, also worked to put a further damper on the remaining Spanish immigration. From the 1924 legislation on, then, the increasing though still comparatively minor Spanish immigration, by fiat, was reduced to an unobtrusive trickle. However, even in the face of these numerous qualifications, Spanish people did come to the United States in the thousands, with the largest migration occurring in the 1911–1920 period when 68,611 Spanish came to the United States. Though this decade represented the largest influx to American shores, the historical roots of the Spanish can be traced back to the very beginning of the European presence on the North American continent.

The Spanish have had even a smaller proportional role in the immigrant process in America than the Portuguese. Nevertheless, their impact has been a sizable and lasting one. State names like Colorado, Florida, Nevada, and California are Spanish in origin. This situation stems from the early Spanish exploration into the American Southwest, such as when in 1598 Juan de Onate and a band of 136 men pushed their way north of the Rio Grande. Thus, much of the American Southwest is dotted with Spanish place names and other historical and architectural remnants of Spain's long rule in North America. The American language itself has not been immune from this Spanish influence. Spanish words such as guerrilla, grenade, armada, flotilla, commodore, embargo, cargo, alfalfa, cigar, gala, sierra, siesta, sombrero, tornado, barbeque, and countless others have been brought into common English usage. In fact, considerable portions of Arizona, Texas, and New Mexico have maintained a bilingual environment. There has been, however, a mistaken tendency to group all Spanish-speaking peoples together as one immigrant group. This, of course, has worked to obscure Spain's unique immigrant role; the Spanish have been confused with the Mexicans, Puerto-Ricans, Cubans, and other Latin Americans who have migrated to this country in large numbers.

When the Spanish immigrants are separated from other Spanish-speaking groups, it may be seen that they compose three basic groups: seafaring people from the coastal cities of northwestern Spain; those from the Basque provinces; and those from central and southern Spain. As could be expected, those from the first group have generally settled in coastal cities; for the most part the second group went to the western states, particularly to Idaho; much of the third group, from central and southwestern Spain, settled first in the Hawaiian Islands and then migrated to the greater San Francisco area. It was in this settlement pattern that Spanish-Americans located and proceeded to enrich American life with their customs, ethnic celebrations, and artistry. Spanish contributions to America, both culturally and in terms of raw labor, are legendary. The Basque element has built a well-respected reputation for itself in sheepherding in the Northwest. During World War I a large number of the unskilled workers in munitions plants were from Spain. Their political consciousness during the Spanish Civil War, as reflected in the Los Angeles publication *El Anti-fascista,* worked to circulate the dangers of the approaching political change. In addition, the large Spanish press has helped encourage the preservation of the Spanish language in America, and, in doing so, has furthered a more cosmopolitan image for the United States. On an individual basis, many Spanish-Americans have bettered life in America. For example, in 1859 Jose Francisco de Navarro built the first American seagoing iron steamship, the *Matanzas,* and in 1878 he constructed the first elevated railway in New York City. Later he was to become one of the organizers of the Equitable Life Insurance Company. More recently, Spanish writers like J. Alvarez del Vayo have catalogued the pains of political exiles. In sum, the Spanish immigrant experience in the United States offers the willing researcher, particularly in the later period, an open and surprisingly little explored field for study. *See* Basques; Canary Islanders.

References
L. H. Gann and Peter Duignan, *The Hispanics in the United States* (1986); John Higham, "Current Trends in the Study of Ethnicity in the United States," *Journal of Ethnic History* 2 (Fall 1982): 5–15

                                                                        D.N.A.

SPANISH-AMERICANS, residential segregation. Massey measures residential segregation among Spanish-Americans, whites, and blacks in the twenty-nine largest urbanized areas of the United States. The relative proportions of Spanish who live in central cities and the relative number of Spanish who are foreign stock are both highly related, across urbanized areas, to variations in the level of Spanish-white segregation.

Reference
Douglas S. Massey, "Residential Segregation of Spanish Americans in United States Urbanized Areas," *Demography* 16 (Nov. 1979): 553–563.

                                                                        F.C.

SPANISH-SPEAKING CHILDREN IN AMERICAN SCHOOLS. Cordasco (*infra*), on this subject, states that the

> latest Census Bureau figures report about 10.8 million persons of Spanish origin in the United States, comprising nearly 5.2 percent of the nation's population. Persons of Mexican origin make up more than half of the Spanish group, with some 6.5 million per-

sons; Puerto Ricans are next with more than 1.5 million, followed by Cubans with 689,000; and, there are some 2 million other persons of Latin American origin. The N/E child's educational problem begins with a rejection of his language, reaffirmed in the rejection of his culture and heritage of which his language is an extension. And it often results in his effective exclusion from the processes of education.

Reference

Francesco Cordasco, "Spanish-Speaking Children in American Schools," *International Migration Review* 9 (Fall 1975): 379–382.

F.C.

SPARGO, JOHN (1876–1966). Social reformer, Socialist. Spargo was an English immigrant, active in the Socialist party; with Samuel Gompers (*q.v.*) he organized the American Alliance for Labor and Democracy in 1917. He was also active in the settlement house movement. Chief works: *The Bitter Cry of the Children* (1906), which included an introduction by Robert Hunter (*q.v.*); *Applied Socialism* (1912); and *The Psychology of Bolshevism* (1919).

Reference

John Spargo, *The Bitter Cry of the Children,* with an Introduction by Walter I. Trattner (1968).

F.C.

SPERANTA. *See* Romanians.

SPERANZA, GINO CHARLES (1872–1927). Lawyer. Speranza served as the first secretary of the Society for the Protection of Italian Immigrants (*q.v.*), founded in New York City in 1901 by the social reformer Sarah Wool Moore (*q.v.*). He married the American heiress Florence Colgate, and was an ardent advocate of Italian immigrants, and a prolific pamphleteer and contributor to periodicals espousing immigrant problems and immigration reform. Toward the end of his life, Speranza became an ardent restrictionist and a spokesman for assimilation. In *Race or Nation: A Conflict of Divided Loyalties* (1925) his assimilationist and restrictionist tendencies are conceptualized. Speranza's papers and letters (largely unworked) are in the Manuscript Division, New York [City] Public Library.

Reference

Gino C[harles] Speranza, *The Diary of Gino Speranza, Italy, 1915–1919,* 2 vols., ed. Florence Colgate Speranza (1941).

F.C.

SPINGARN, JOEL. *See* NAACP.

SPRAVEDLNOST. *See* Czechs.

SROBRAN. See Serbs.

SRPSKI NARODNI SAVEZ. *See* Serbs.

STANIUKYNAS, ANTANAS. *See* Lithuanians.

STATUE OF LIBERTY. A statue of enormous size on Liberty Island in Upper New York Bay commanding the entrance to New York City. Originally known as "Liberty Enlightening the World," it was initially proposed by the French historian Édouard Laboulaye in 1865 to commemorate the French alliance with the American Colonies during the American War of Independence. A Franco-American Union (founded in 1875) raised funds, and the statue was designed by the French sculptor F. A. Bartholdi as a woman with an uplifted arm holding a torch. The statue, using Bartholdi's 9-foot model, was constructed of copper sheets. It was shipped to New York City in 1885, where it was assembled and dedicated in 1886. The base of the statue is an eleven-pointed star. A 150-foot pedestal, American funded, is made of concrete faced with granite. An elevator runs to the top of the pedestal, with steps within the statue leading to the crown. The statue became a national monument in 1924, and an American Museum of Immigration was established there. In 1965, Ellis Island (*q.v.*) was named part of the Statue of Liberty National Monument. In 1982, Secretary of the Interior James Watt announced the creation of the Statue of Liberty/Ellis Island Centennial Commission. The Centennial of the Statue of Liberty was celebrated in a four-day extravaganza in July 1986, with President Ronald Reagan, French President François Mitterand, and many other dignitaries in attendance. As of July 1987, the Centennial Commission (largely through the efforts of its chairperson, Lee Iacocca, president of the Chrysler Corporation) had raised $230 million, more than half of which was spent restoring the statue.

References
August C. Bolino, *The Ellis Island Source Book* (1985); Ann Novotny, *Strangers at the Door* (1971); Harlan D. Unrau, *Statue of Liberty/Ellis Island* (1984).

F.C.

STAUB, PETER. *See* Swiss.

"STEAMER CLASSES." *See* [New York City]: Department of Education, Board of Superintendents.

STEFFENS, LINCOLN (1886–1936). Journalist reformer; held editorial positions on major magazines (1902–1922), e.g., *McClure's, American, Everybody's,* and turned their pages over to the exposure of municipal corruption, immigrant poverty and exploitation, and a wider range of social ills. Chief works: *The Shame of the Cities* (1904); *Struggle for Self-Government* (1906); and *Upbuilders* (1909). His *Autobiography* (1931) is a valuable source for the social history of his time. Steffens, a partisan of the Soviet Union from 1917 to his death, increasingly came to believe in violent social upheaval for the correction of social ills.

Reference
Justin Kaplan, *Lincoln Steffens* (1974).

F.C.

STELLA ALBANESE. *See* Italian-Albanians.

STELLA, ANTONIO (1868–1927). Stella was a physician specializing in pulmonary ailments who worked primarily among New York City's Italian immigrant poor. He was active in medical and civic affairs. He is the author of *Some Aspects of Italian Immigration to the United States* (1924; rpt. 1975), which includes a preface by Nicholas Murray Butler (1862–1947), president of Columbia University from 1902 to 1945. Stella also wrote *The Effects of Urban Congestion on Italian Women and Children* (1908), observing that "the vast number of returning [Italian immigrant] consumptives—both men and women—has taken such proportions of late that the Italian government is considering special measures of quarantine both on board the ships and the point of debarkation."

F.C.

STEVNE. *See* Bygdelag.

STODDARD, THEODORE LOTHROP (1883–1950). Author, lawyer, publicist of nativism, and supporter of Madison Grant (*q.v.*) and other racial theorists. Stoddard believed that the immigration of inferior white races would mongrelize the Nordic into "a walking chaos so consumed by his jarring heredities that he is quite worthless." Chief writings: *The Rising Tide of Color Against White Supremacy* (1920), for which Madison Grant wrote an introduction; *The Revolt Against Civilization: The Menace of the Under Man* (1922); *Racial Realities in Europe* (1924); and *Clashing Tides of Colour* (1935). Stoddard was repelled by German Nazism, for which see his *Into the Darkness: Nazi Germany Today* (1940).

F.C.

STREET ARABS. *See* Riis, Jacob A.

STROSSMAYER, JOSIP JURAJ. *See* Yugoslavs.

STUDENT NONVIOLENT COORDINATING COMMITTEE. *See* Afro-Americans.

SUOMI COLLEGE. Members of the Finnish Evangelical Lutheran church (Suomi Synod) founded this educational institution in 1896, motivated by a combination of religious, nationalistic, and cultural concerns. It was located in Hancock, Michigan, and it was designed to provide immigrants and their children with educational opportunities; its theological seminary was intended to supply the church with pastors, thereby ending their dependence on the Finnish state church. During the period from its founding until the end of World War I, it was primarily an ethnic institution. The period between 1920 and 1950 marked growing Americanization. When the Suomi Synod merged with other Lutheran bodies to form the Lutheran Church in America in 1963, the seminary was closed. Today the institution is a junior college with an enrollment of approximately 600 students.

Reference
Douglas Ollila, Jr., *The Formative Period of the Finnish Evangelical Lutheran Church in America or Suomi Synod* (1963).

                                                                    P.K.

SUPPIGER, JOSEPH (d. 1857). Traveler; author of a journal on a voyage to the United States in 1831. First published in Switzerland in 1833, the greater part of the journal consists of notes kept by Suppiger during the migration to the United States in 1831 of eleven Swiss Germans under the leadership of the physician Kaspar Koepfli. The balance is made up of letters to Switzerland by members of the group about their experiences during the first year of their settlement in the environs of Highland, Illinois. Suppiger's journal traces the group's movement through France to Le Havre, across the ocean to New York, up the Hudson, and west by canal, lake, and river to St. Louis. Compared to Tocqueville's (*q.v.*) philosophical *Democracy in America*, written in the same period, the journal records the concrete experiences of the immigrants. Suppiger writes of travel conditions, meals, lodgings, and costs, as well as of the exasperating practices of European customs officials and ship owners. The account is spiced with comments on national characteristics and on human nature generally. The immigrants, in their letters, stress the advantages of their new home over what they had known in the Old World and their admiration of the energy of the settlers of the West. This is an immensely informative account, useful to those interested in social and immigration history.

Reference
Joseph Suppiger, *Journey to New Switzerland: Travel Account of the Koepfli and Suppiger Family to St. Louis on the Mississippi and the Founding of New Switzerland in the State of Illinois,* by Joseph Suppiger, Salomon Koepfli, and Jasper Koepfli, trans. Raymond J. Spahn, ed. John C. Abbott (1986).

F.C.

SURVIVANCE, LA. *See* French.

SUTHERLAND, EDWIN H. *See* Immigrants and Crime.

SUTTER, JOHANN AUGUST. *See* Swiss.

SVERDRUP, GEORG (1848–1907). Theologian. Educated in theology in Norway, Sverdrup came to the United States as a professor of theology at Augsburg Seminary in Minneapolis in 1874. At that time the Norwegian Lutherans in America were divided into several parties. Sverdrup soon became the foremost leader of what might be called an "Americanization" emphasis or thrust. He defended the American "free church" system, and, outstandingly, he pressed for the public schools as over against the parochial school system advocated by other Norwegian Lutheran leaders.

Reference
James S. Hamre, "Georg Sverdrup's Concept of the Role and Calling of the Norwegian-American Lutherans: An Annotated Translation of Selected Writings," Ph.D. dissertation, University of Iowa, 1967.

F.C.

SVOBODA. *See* Ukrainians.

SVORNOST. *See* Czechs.

SWEDES. Swedish mass immigration to the United States began around 1845, and lasted until 1930, when some 1.3 million Swedes had arrived on American shores, making Sweden the largest sending country in Scandinavia and the eighth-largest sending country over all to the United States between 1820 and 1950. Initially the Swedes settled in agricultural areas, primarily in the Midwest, but at the end of the mass immigration era, they were urbanized and largely employed in American industries. The Swedish presence in North America dates back to 1638, when a mercantile company in Sweden established the colony

New Sweden along the Delaware River, which existed until 1654 when it was ceded to the Dutch. The colony's population never exceeded 400, and its impact on subsequent American history was rather limited. The Church of Sweden did, however, maintain a salaried pastor in the area until the early years of the nineteenth century.

Reasons for the Migration. Mass emigration from Sweden was one aspect of the transformation and modernization of Swedish society from an agrarian-rural to an industrial-urban country. From the middle of the eighteenth century, Sweden experienced a tremendous population growth as the country went through the so-called "demographic transition." During the course of a century the population doubled, and stood at 3.5 million in 1850. In 1900 it had reached 5.1 million. Since Sweden essentially was an agricultural country (in 1850 80 percent of the population was economically dependent on the agricultural sector), the population increase meant that the pressure on the available land increased greatly, leading to parcellization, overpopulation, and the rapid growth of a landless agricultural proletariat. This resulted in a migration from the countryside, and besides internal migration to cities and expanding areas in the country, North America quickly emerged as a place where landless young people could find better economic opportunities.

Although Swedish immigrants to the United States kept coming throughout the entire period 1845 to 1930, certain peaks and lows can be observed. These variations were responses to specific conditions in Sweden and the United States. In Sweden, crop failures and the subsequent famines in 1868 and 1869, a recession in the lumber industry beginning in 1879, and the agricultural crisis in the late 1880s were important such factors, and in the United States the recessions in the American economy (such as the Panic of 1893) played a similar role. Still, once great numbers of Swedes were established in the United States, to a great extent Swedish immigration became self-sustaining. Communication channels were established between the United States and Sweden through letters, word of mouth, and newspaper accounts, leading to the creation of numerous migration links between particular sending and receiving areas in both countries. Once these links had been established, this tradition of emigration ensured that the rate of emigration remained high, even when opportunities improved in Sweden or recessions hit in the United States.

Religious and political factors were rarely direct causes of emigration. Some notable exceptions include the exodus of some 1,500 followers of the charismatic religious leader Erik Jansson, who in 1846, following bitter conflicts with ecclesiastical and secular authorities in Sweden, established the utopian colony Bishop Hill on the prairies in Henry Country, Illinois; and a number of labor leaders who left the country following some strikes in the first decade of the twentieth century.

Chronology and Composition of Immigration. The period from 1845 to 1860 can be characterized as the pioneer phase of Swedish mass immigration to America. Some 15,000 persons left Sweden during this time and settled in rural areas in Illinois, Iowa, and Minnesota, establishing these states as receiving areas for future Swedish immigrants. During this period, most Swedes came in families and were typically skilled craftsmen and landowning farmers. A number of well-known group emigrations took place during this phase, including the Peter Cassel settlement in Iowa, S. M. Swenson's group emigration to Texas, and the already mentioned colony in Bishop Hill, Illinois.

Following the end of the American Civil War, Swedish mass immigration to the United States began. The immigration was particularly high between 1868 and 1873 (103,000) and 1880 and 1893 (475,000), the peak of Swedish immigration occurring in 1887 with 46,000 immigrants, and during the first decade of the twentieth century (214,000). World War I put a halt to the influx of Swedes, but the migration resumed in the 1920s (90,000) with a peak in 1923, the year before the American quota laws went into effect.

During these peak periods of mass immigration, fewer families and more single persons left Sweden for the United States. Typically, they were sons and daughters of landowning farmers, farm hands, apprentices, and members of the agricultural proletariat, who had been left landless by the population growth and who were particularly badly hit by the agricultural crisis of the 1860s and 1880s. As industrialization and urbanization gained momentum in Sweden during the last decades of the nineteenth century, beginning around 1890 and continuing until the close of the mass immigration era, more and more unskilled laborers from urban areas left Sweden for the United States. It has been estimated that prior to 1890 the relationship between agriculture and industry was 3.5 to 1, that between 1890 and 1914 it was 1:1, and that after World War I, more immigrants had an industrial background than an agricultural one.

Settlement Patterns in the United States. The American Midwest was the most common destination for the Swedish immigrants. Many migration links had been established with places in the Midwest during the early years of Swedish immigration, which meant that in 1880, the U.S. census recorded more than 75 percent of the almost 200,000 Swedish born as living there. It was the availability of land, particularly after the adoption of the Homestead Act of 1862, that attracted great numbers of Swedes to the Midwest, where they settled as farmers, primarily in Minnesota and Illinois, but also in Iowa, Kansas, Nebraska, and the Dakotas.

In the last decades of the nineteenth century, there was a shift away from the Midwest, and major Swedish settlements appeared in the eastern and western states as well. In 1910, 59 percent of the Swedish born lived in the Midwest, 24 percent in the East, and 10 percent in the West. In the East, many Swedes settled in New York, Massachusetts, and Connecticut, and in the West California and Washington became the most attractive areas.

This geographical shift was coincided with a greater tendency for Swedish immigrants to settle in urban milieus. As the land available grew scarcer (the Bureau of the Census had declared the frontier closed in 1890), Swedish immigrants became a part of the overall urbanization process in the United States. In 1890, one-third of the Swedish immigrants lived in American cities, and when the Swedish-born population in the United States reached its maximum in 1910, almost two-thirds were urbanites. The largest Swedish urban settlement was in Chicago, which in 1910 counted 10 percent of all first- and second-generation Swedish-Americans, making it the second-largest Swedish city in the world—second only to Stockholm. Other major urban settlements included Minneapolis; New York City; Seattle; Jamestown, New York; Worcester, Massachusetts; and Rockford and Moline, Illinois.

The urbanization of the Swedes in America also meant that they found new occupations. More and more of the Swedish immigrants got jobs in American industries, and by 1900 there were more Swedes active in industry than in agriculture. The growing American service sector also attracted many urban Swedes, and Swedish single women frequently found work as domestics.

The Creation of a "Swedish-America." During the latter part of the nineteenth century, a Swedish ethnic community in the United States was established, often referred to as "Swedish America." It reached its peak during the first decades of the twentieth century, with a period of decline setting in after the Depression. "Swedish America" was made up of a number of ethnic institutions serving various needs of the immigrants and promoting a Swedish ethnicity. The immigrant church was the first of these institutions and it has been estimated that in 1920 25 percent, or some 350,000 persons, of the Swedish immigrants and their children belonged to a Swedish-American denomination. The Lutheran Augustana Synod, founded in 1860 by a number of ministers from the Lutheran state church in Sweden, was the largest church body among the Swedish-Americans, as well as the single largest Swedish-American organization in general with a membership of 290,000 in 1920. Other Swedish-American churches include the Swedish Mission Covenant church, the Swedish Baptist church, and the Swedish Methodist church.

The Swedish-American churches did not just fulfill the religious needs of their members; through their many other activities they assisted the immigrants in adjusting to the new life in the United States. One example of this is the educational institutions started by Swedish-American churches, serving both as theological seminaries and regular colleges. The leading Augustana Synod school was Augustana College in Rock Island, Illinois; the Mission Covenant church founded North Park College in Chicago, and the Swedish Baptists started Bethel Seminary and College in St. Paul, Minnesota.

A great number of secular organizations were started by the Swedish immigrants as well. During the 1890s several mutual aid societies were established, which quickly attracted a significant membership, particularly in the urban areas. The largest of these societies include the Independent Order of Svithiod, the Order of Vikings, the Vasa Order of America, and the Scandinavian Fraternity of America. At the close of Swedish mass immigration to the United States, the Vasa Order counted over 72,000 members in 438 lodges. In addition to these "orders," a great number of social, cultural, and musical organizations for Swedish immigrants could be found all over the United States.

Since most Swedish immigrants were literate, a market was quickly established for Swedish-language publications in the United States. Around 1,500 Swedish-language periodicals of different kinds were started between 1851 and 1910, mostly newspapers. Most of them were short-lived, and only about a dozen achieved a national circulation. In 1915, the Swedish-language press had a total circulation of 650,000 copies, after which a period of decline set in. Today, three Swedish-language newspapers remain in the United States.

A substantial body of Swedish-American literature was also a part of "Swedish America." A dictionary from 1897 lists over 300 active authors publishing in Swedish in the United States. A number of publishing companies existed, the largest being the Augustana Book Concern, which between 1911 and 1915 published 140 Swedish titles with a total circulation of 840,000 copies.

After the Immigration. Following the close of Swedish mass immigration after 1930, the Swedes and their children moved towards becoming a part of "mainstream America." This was achieved through of a process of both cultural and structural assimilation, where the use of the Swedish language dropped drastically beyond the second generation, intermarriage became quite common (although at least initially, mostly with other white, northern and western European groups), and the support for the Swedish ethnic institutions dwindled.

A renewed interest in Swedish ethnicity did occur in the 1960s and 1970s. Consequently some old organizations became more active and attracted a new membership and new ones were started. For the most part, however, this interest was of an historical nature and Swedish ethnicity in the United States today is largely symbolic, concerned with geneaology and the preservation of certain traditions and foods.

References
H. Arnold Barton, *Letters from the Promised Land: Swedes in America 1840–1914* (1975); Ulf Beijbom, *Swedes in Chicago: A Social and Demographic Study of the 1844–*

1888 Immigration (1971); Sture Lindmark, *Swedish America 1914–1932: Studies in Ethnicity with Emphasis on Illinois and Minnesota* (1971); Harald Runblom and Dag Blanck, eds., *Scandinavia Overseas: Patterns of Cultural Transformation in North America and Australia* (1986); Harald Runblom and Hans Norman, eds., *From Sweden to America: A History of the Migration* (1976); George Stephenson, *The Religious Aspects of Swedish Immigration: A Study of Immigrant Churches* (1932); *Swedish Pioneer Historical Quarterly* (1950–1981); *Swedish-American Historical Quarterly* (1982–).

D.B.

SWEDES, Evangelical Free and Covenant traditions. Hale breaks new ground in interpreting the transatlantic roots of conservative Protestantism in the Evangelical Free church and the Swedish Mission Covenant church in America. He analyzes the Pietism, revivalism, and scriptural emphasis of various nonconformist groups in Sweden, Norway, and Denmark and their reactions to the evangelistic techniques popularized by Dwight L. Moody and Charles G. Finney, nineteenth-century British and American millenarianism, and German "higher criticism" of the Bible. Two divergent types of Protestantism developed among these Nordic free churchmen in both the Old World and the New—one springing from Pietistic Lutheranism in Sweden, the other strongly influenced by revivalistic and millenarian currents of British and American origin. Migration, travel, and cooperation with non-Scandinavian Christians nurtured transatlantic religious continuities. This study of cultural diffusion illuminates several Scandinavian "segments of the intricate mosaic of conservative Protestantism in America."

Reference
Frederick Hale, *Trans-Atlantic Conservative Protestantism in the Evangelical Free and Mission Covenant Traditions* (1979).

F.C.

SWINTON, JOHN (1830–1901). Journalist and reformer born in Salton, Scotland. In 1843 his family emigrated to Montreal, and in 1849 to New York City. Having been a printer's apprentice while in Montreal, Swinton worked, from 1857 to 1860, as a printer for the *Lawrence* [Kansas] *Republican,* a free-soil weekly. Back in New York in 1860, he became a member of the editorial staff of the *New York Times.* Swinton left the paper in 1869, and for the next five years he was variously employed. In 1875 he joined the editorial board of the *Sun,* where he was employed until 1883 and again from 1892 to 1897. The high point of his career came during the years 1883 to 1887, when he published his own weekly, *John Swinton's Paper.* Swinton's significance was as a journalist and speaker, in giving public expression to problems and proposals of interest to laborers of America, and in urging workers (both urban and rural) to join together in independent united political action.

Reference

Marc Ross, "John Swinton, Journalist and Reformer: The Active Years, 1857–1887," Ph.D. dissertation, New York University, 1969 (DA 30:2638-A).

F.C.

SWISS. Between 1600 and 1980 some 400,000 people from Switzerland are estimated to have stayed at least for some time in what is now the domain of the United States. Estimates count some 25,000 of them before 1776, about the same number for the years 1780 to 1820, some 265,000 for the next one hundred years, and about 85,000 since the quota system was instituted. Many did not stay permanently, however, but moved elsewhere or returned to Switzerland. Between 1925 and 1935, for instance, 13,660 were admitted to the United States and 5,614 (that is, nearly 40 percent), departed from that nation.

Swiss at Home and Abroad. Switzerland is a small European nation, bordered by France, West Germany, Lichtenstein, Austria, and Italy. Its area covers 15,943 square miles and was inhabited in 1700 by 1.2, in 1800 by 1.68, in 1900 by 3.315, and in 1980 by 6.366 million people. Swiss national history dates back to 1291 when the forest cantons Uri, Schwyz, and Unterwalden formed an "oath-association" (*Eidgenossenschaft*) to preserve their regional autonomy and the control of the mountain passes that for centuries formed a vital link between northern Europe and the Mediterranean world. By 1513 the Swiss Confederacy had grown to thirteen member states, called cantons, and remained fairly stable as to territory and internal structure until 1789. During the following decades the Confederacy was transformed from a league of states to a federal state which today numbers twenty-six cantons.

The nation comprises four indigenous language groups: German (about two-thirds), French (about one-fifth), Italian (below one-tenth), and Romansh (about one percent); these are further divided into a variety of local dialects, the main mode of communication in everyday life. A good half of Swiss belong to the German Reformed persuasion and nearly half are Roman Catholic. After 1525 small groups of "Swiss Brethren and Sisters," known in the United States as (Swiss) Mennonites and Amish, emerged. After 1848 the Mormon mission was quite successful in the Bernese and St. Gallen region, and small Jewish communities are attested to have existed since the thirteenth century. Economically the nation shifted in the later nineteenth century from an agrarian to a highly industrialized state with a market economy heavily engaged in international trade and finance.

Throughout the past four centuries, many Swiss went at least temporarily abroad and many foreign born resided in Switzerland. In the sixteenth century some 50,000 to 100,000 Swiss served abroad as soldiers or craftsmen; in the seventeenth century 250,000 to 300,000, and about 350,000 in the eighteenth century did so. For the years 1798 to 1914 W. Bickel, *Bevölkerungsgeschichte der Schweiz* (1947), offers the following estimates: From 1798 to 1850 about 50,000 foreign born entered Switzerland and about 100,000 Swiss went abroad; from 1850 to 1914 some 410,000 Swiss left home and 409,000 foreign born resided in Switzerland who hailed mainly from neighboring countries. In 1880, for instance, of the 211,000 foreign born in Switzerland 45.1 percent came from Germany, 27.8 from France, and 19.5 from Italy. Of the 234,000 Swiss abroad in 1880, 38 percent resided in the United States, 29 percent in France, 13 percent in Germany, and 5 percent each in Italy and Argentina; small contingents of Swiss were to be found in nearly every corner of the globe.

As to migratory context, two levels must be distinguished. On the personal level social forces such as strife between spouses, parents and children, in-laws, neighbors, or villagers predominated. Some sought quick riches in the expectation of speedy return; others hoped to hold on to their accustomed craft in lands abroad. Careers in commerce, the military, or the missions attracted others. On the systemic level, entrenched migratory traditions, participation in white expansion into territories overseas, and transnational networks of economic activity provided the most important contexts.

Swiss in British North America. The first known Swiss to have set foot on North American soil was the Bernese Diebold von Erlach (1541–1565), member of a French Huguenot expedition attempting to gain a permanent foothold on the southern North American coast. He perished in the ensuing conflict with the Spaniards who founded St. Augustine, Florida, as a protective measure in 1665. In 1607 some "Switzers" served as craftsmen in Jamestown where a William Henry Volday [Walder ?] incurred the wrath of Captain John Smith (1579–1631). In 1687 the French Swiss Jean François Gignilliat of Vevey, the ancestor of a large southern family, received some 3,000 acres from the South Carolina proprietors "to encourage more of the Swisse nation" to settle there. Some Swiss were also among the settlers of Germantown, founded in 1683, and shortly after 1700 a Franz Louis Michel searched Maryland and Pennsylvania for mines and a suitable place for settlement.

In 1710 Christoph von Graffenried (1661–1743) from Yverdon, Canton Bern, led a group of Swiss and Palatines to North Carolina; they were part of the 1709 exodus of some 13,000 people intent on settling in British domains. At the confluence of the Neuse and Trent rivers,

Graffenried founded New Bern, but returned home in 1713. His grandson Tscharner, born in 1691 in Virginia, became the progenitor of a large southern family.

In the 1690s the religious movement known as Pietism brought dissension to the Swiss churches of the Reformed persuasion. Several ministers lost their posts, among them Samuel Güldin (1664–1745), who went in 1710 to Pennsylvania. In the same year a first group of Swiss (Mennonite) Brethren and Sisters settled at Connestoga along the Pequea Creek where they bought a tract of some 10,000 acres. During the next four decades some 4,000 Swiss Brethren and Sisters followed and moved southward and westward. They lived on individual farms and formed congregations of some twenty to thirty families. Their religiously based way of life preserved many features of their Swiss and Palatine origin.

Several thousand Swiss Reformed moved to Pennsylvania, Virginia, and the Carolinas. They were joined by ministers, among whom Michael Schlatter (1716–1790) was the most prominent. In the 1730s Jean Pierre Purry (1675–1736) of Neuchâtel conducted an effective emigration campaign and founded Purryburg some twenty miles upriver from Savannah, Georgia. He brought some 450 people to South Carolina and induced about as many to move to other areas of the North American coast.

Many Swiss settled as craftsmen or businessmen in cities like Philadelphia and Charleston. Noteworthy among them are Jeremiah Theus (1719–1774), a successful portrait painter in Charleston, and Johann Joachim Züblin (1724–1781), a Swiss Reformed preacher from St. Gallen, who as John J. Zubly was actively involved in the revolutionary agitation. Henri Bouquet (1725–1791); the brothers Jacques (1725–1776), Augustin (1723–1786), and Marc (1736–1781) Prévost; and Frédéric Haldimand (1725–1791) were high-ranking officers in the British colonial forces.

During the revolutionary crisis Swiss immigrants and their descendants followed the general pattern. Some remained loyal to the British Crown, others stayed aloof, and still others fought with the rebel forces. The Reformed minister Abraham Blumer (1736–1822), for instance, supported the Revolution. Michael Schlatter first joined the British forces, whereas his sons fought on the rebel side; he then refused to serve any further. John J. Zubly, in contrast, although he had been severely critical of British policies, remained loyal to the Crown, was tried in Georgia, and lost a good part of his property. Although the initial immigrants differed quite widely in their response to the new land, their descendants blended easily into colonial culture and, the Mennonites excepted, became indistinguishable from the general population.

After the 1750s, Swiss group immigration had largely ceased, but single families or individuals arrived steadily throughout the next decades. In 1780 the Genevan Albert Gallatin (1761–1849) arrived in Maine, then taught briefly at Harvard, and finally settled in Pennsylvania. He actively participated in politics and from 1801 to 1808 served as secretary of the treasury in the Jefferson and Madison administrations. He also had a distinguished career as a diplomat and scholar.

Swiss in the United States, 1820 to 1920. During the nineteenth century the United States was transformed from a coastal nation to one of continental size. The conquered territories were mainly resettled by descendants of the colonial population, but to a minor degree also by people from abroad. The Swiss participated in that migratory movement. Between 1820 and 1920 about 220,000 arrived in the expanding United States. Most Swiss going abroad, however, went to European countries. In 1850, for instance, 63.4 percent of the 72,500 Swiss abroad had stayed in Europe, 28 percent had moved to countries in the Americas, the rest to other parts of the world. In 1880, the proportion of the 234,000 Swiss abroad shifted to 51.1 percent for Europe and 46.1 for the Americas; in 1928 the proportion moved back to 72.9 and 23.9 percent, respectively.

The majority of Swiss dispersed widely in the newly opened areas for white settlement or went to the rapidly growing urban centers. Yet a series of initially quite homogeneous Swiss settlements did emerge. One of the first was Vevay, Indiana, on the Ohio; it was founded in 1803 by Jean Jacques Dufour (1767–1827), who had decided in his youth to introduce viticulture into the United States. Although success was moderate, by 1810 the settlement produced some 2,400 gallons of wine that "connoisseurs thought to be better than the claret of Bordeaux." In 1831 members of the Köpfli and Suppiger families established Highland, Illinois, some sixty miles east of St. Louis on the Looking Glass Prairie. By 1870 some 1,500 Swiss had settled in the region, among them the Bandelier family. Adolph Bandelier (1840–1914) became a leading anthropologist of the Southwest whose works are still valued today. Wisconsin attracted some 8,000 Swiss. They centered in Sauk County; in Alma, Buffalo County; and in Green County, especially Monroe and New Glarus. In 1845, 119 Swiss arrived from the Glarus Valley of Switzerland to found a New Glarus. By 1860 the inhabitants cultivated over 10,000 acres, had established 149 farms, and numbered 960 people. In the 1870s dairying replaced wheat growing. In the mid-twentieth century New Glarus became increasingly conscious of its roots. An "Historical Village" and festivals celebrating William Tell and Heidi yearly attract numerous visitors to the area.

After 1817 descendants of Swiss Mennonites moved westward into the midwestern territories, joined by coreligionists directly from

Switzerland. Predominantly Swiss foundations were Sonnenberg (1817) and Chippewa (1825) in Ohio, Berne (1838) in Indiana, and Madison Township (1849) in Iowa. In the second half of the nineteenth century the movement continued to the farmlands of Missouri, Kansas, and Oregon; the main settlements were Whitewater (1883) in Butler County, Kansas; Tipton (1886) in Morgan and Moniteau Counties, Missouri; and Silverton and Salem in Oregon. Like their eighteenth-century counterparts, these settlements were not compact villages, but consisted of family farms forming Swiss Mennonite congregations. The impact of the American environment transformed several of them; English replaced German, a trained clergy the lay ministry, and town living the farming way of life.

In the 1880s a "réveil"—that is, awakening—occurred among the Reformed churches of French-speaking Switzerland. Some of the awakened became "Open" or "Plymouth Brethren," and several families moved to the environs of Knoxville, Tennessee, where they continued to practice their evangelical faith for some generations.

Several secular Swiss settlements emerged in the second half of the nineteenth century. Tell City on the Ohio in southern Indiana was started in 1857 as a business venture. In the later 1860s West Virginia actively recruited European immigrants to settle its mountainous regions. In 1869 Helvetia was founded, followed by Alpena, West Huttonsville, Cotton Hill, Kendalia, and New St. Gallen. Also in 1869 Peter Staub (1827–1904) founded Grütli in Grundy County, Tennessee; by 1886 the settlement counted 330 Swiss among its 400 inhabitants. In 1881 two Swiss entrepreneurs promoted the founding of Bernstadt, Kentucky; by the end of the decade over a thousand Swiss had settled in the region that included also East Bernstadt, Grünheim, and Crab Orchard in Lincoln County.

In 1839 Johann August Sutter (1803–1880) established a vast plantation called Helvetia on California's Mexican frontier. The discovery of gold on his property in 1849 attracted some 300,000 people from all over the world to California who hoped for quick riches in the exploration of gold mines. Two-thirds of Sutter's land claims were declared invalid by the United States government, which had annexed the West Coast to its own domain after the war against Mexico. After 1850 California also attracted many Italian Swiss, mostly single men in search of work who returned home after some years. By the end of the century, however, family migration predominated and the majority became permanent immigrants engaged in grape growing, dairying, and cattle raising. They concentrated in the coastal region of Marin County and in the Central Valley's Stanislaus County. Others settled in cities like San Francisco and Sacramento.

In the second half of the nineteenth century the Mormon mission induced about a thousand Swiss to settle in Utah; they centered in Midway, Wasatch County; Santa Clara, Washington County; Providence, Cache County; and in Bern and Geneva of Bear Lake County, Idaho. These immigrants had large families, especially during the phase of plural marriages, and their descendants took an active part in recruiting further compatriots to their New Zion.

The immigration of Swiss Catholics led to the founding of monasteries and convents. In 1852 the Benedictine monastery of Einsiedeln, Switzerland, founded St. Meinrad, Indiana, which developed into an educational and pastoral center for German-speaking Catholics who settled in that region. It also became the nucleus of the Swiss Benedictine, today called Pan-Benedictine, congregation. The Swiss Benedictine monastery of Engelberg supported the founding of Conception, Missouri, and of Mount Angel in Oregon. From these foundations further monasteries were established. Benedictine sisters followed the example of the monks; Anselma Felber (1843–1883) founded the convent at Conception, Missouri, which later moved to Clyde as the Benedictine Convent of Perpetual Adoration; Gertrud Lenpi (1825–1904), from the same Swiss Benedictine Convent of Maria Rickenbach, Canton Nidwalden, founded a convent in Maryville which then was moved to Yankton, South Dakota. Franz von Sales Brunner (1795–1859) introduced the Order of the Precious Blood into Ohio, and a first Capuchin Friary was founded in Milwaukee in 1859.

A good number of Swiss immigrants moved to urban centers. In 1870, for instance, 2,902 Swiss lived in St. Louis, Missouri; 2,844 in New York City; and 1,791 in Philadelphia. In 1890 New York counted 6,355 Swiss, Chicago 2,262, St. Louis 2,209, and San Francisco 1,696. Other concentrations of urban Swiss were in Paterson, New Jersey; Cleveland, Ohio; Pittsburgh, Pennsylvania; Portland, Oregon; and Milwaukee, Wisconsin. In these centers Swiss immigrants created a variety of organizations that were largely adaptations of institutions from their home country. Before the Civil War, for instance, the New York City Swiss had a Benevolent Society, a Helvetia Rifle Club, a Society for the Benefit of the Sick, a Helvetia Lodge, and a Helvetia Men's Choir. These were designed to assist those in need, to create social cohesion, and to preserve Swiss traditions. In the second half of the nineteenth century the North American Grütli-Bund, which in 1915 counted six thousand members, strove for Swiss-American unity on the national level. The democratic and culturally pluralist orientation of the Swiss made them easily blend into mainstream American society where they did not meet obstacles that derived from their ethnicity.

Some nineteenth-century Swiss achieved national renown. Among them were Louis Agassiz (1807–1873), a natural scientist noted for his anti-Darwinian stand; the Guggenheims of Philadelphia, who had come from Lengnau, Canton Aargan, in 1847; Martin Henni (1805–1881), who became the first Catholic archibishop of Milwaukee; and Philip Schaff (1819–1893), after 1870 a leading ecumenical Protestant theologian.

Swiss in the United States Since 1920. By 1920 the United States had reached its present territorial size and had joined the world powers. Immigration became regulated by the quota system, set for Swiss at 3,752 per year in 1921, and by 1929 reduced to 1,707. The new arrivals were mainly professionals, often connected with large international firms such as Nestlé, Ciba-Geigy, Hoffmann-LaRoche, and Holderbank. With the advent of air travel these newcomers cross the Atlantic often, and many do not settle permanently in the United States. They are the counterpart of Americans in Switzerland.

Many twentieth-century Swiss had remarkable careers in the United States. Among them are Othmar Ammann (1879–1965), the designer and builder of famous suspension bridges in the New York City environs; William Lescaze (1896–1969), a designer of early skyscrapers; Adolph Meyer (1866–1950), who dominated American psychiatry up to 1940; Ernest Bloch (1880–1957), the creator of modern Jewish music; Mary Sandoz (1901–1966), a noted novelist and historian of the Nebraska plains; and William Wyler (1902–1981), a producer of acclaimed films and documentaries.

Today the Swiss-American group is composed of four major strands. First, descendants of eighteenth-century immigrants have, if at all, mainly a genealogical interest in their origin. Second, descendants of Swiss Anabaptist groups, that is, about two-thirds of all American Mennonites, view their ancestors as formulators and prototypes of their persuasions who lived their faith under adverse Swiss conditions. The third group, the offspring of nineteenth- and twentieth-century immigrants, are often fully assimilated already in the second generation, but preserve ties with their country of origin by frequent visits and by active participation in Swiss-American societies. A fourth group consists of recent newcomers who adhere to an updated version of Swissness and are often quite active in strengthening the bonds with the past.

References
Giorgio Cheda, *L'emigrazione ticinese in California* (1981), two of five projected volumes; Delbert L. Grätz, *Bernese Anabaptists and Their American Descendants* (1953); Leo Schelbert, "On Becoming an Emigrant: A Structural View of Eighteenth and Nineteenth Century Swiss Data," *Perspectives in American History* 7 (1973): 440–495; Leo Schelbert, "Swiss Migration to the Territory of the United States: A Historiographical Introduction," *The Immigration History Newsletter* 14 (Nov. 1982): 1–5; Swiss American Historical Society, ed., *Prominent Americans of Swiss Origin* (1932).

L.S.

SWISS AMERICAN HISTORICAL SOCIETY. Founded in Chicago in 1927, the organization aims "to institute, conduct, and encourage historical research" and "to serve as a meeting ground" for people interested in relations between Switzerland and the United States. In 1932 the society published *Prominent Americans of Swiss Origin*, and in 1940 *The Swiss in the United States*. In the same year the headquarters of the organization moved to Madison, Wisconsin, but interest in its activities declined among the Swiss. In 1949 the first volume of *The Swiss Record* was published, and in 1950 the second and last, by the efforts of Alfred Senn, professor at the University of Pennsylvania. Then the society became dormant, until it was reactivated in 1963, especially by the efforts of Dr. Lukas F. Burckhardt, cultural counselor of the Embassy of Switzerland, and Heinz K. Meier, professor of history at Old Dominion University in Norfolk, Virginia. Since 1964 the society issues a *Newsletter* three times a year, holds an annual and regional meetings, and furthers publications of Swiss-American interest. Among recent works are Heinz K. Meier, ed., *Memoirs of a Swiss Officer* (1972); Paul A. Nielson, *Swiss Genealogical Research* (1979); Carol Williams, *The Switzers. A Novel* (1981); and Hedwig Rappolt, ed., *An American Apprenticeship* (1986).

Reference
Heinz K. Meier, *The Swiss American Historical Society 1927–1977* (1977).

L.S.

SWISS SOUTH GERMAN MENNONITES. *See* Mennonites.

SYNDICALISM. Syndicalism refers to a revolutionary political philosophy that emerged among radical labor unions in France during the 1890s. It was influenced by several intellectual sources, including Proudhon, Marx, Bakunin, and Sorel. While there is a lack of consensus about the definition of syndicalism, there is general agreement that it can be viewed as an anticapitalist doctrine which argued that the proletarian class struggle should be confined to the economic sphere, with the principal weapons being the boycott, sabotage, mass demonstrations, and the strike, especially the general strike. The eschewal of political action was, in part motivated by an antipathy toward parliamentary socialism due to its dampening of revolutionary fervor. It also meant that syndicalists sought to prevent class conflict from getting enmeshed in nationalism and militarism.

The most important American variant of syndicalism was the Industrial Workers of the World (IWW), frequently known as the "Wobblies." Founded in 1905, the IWW would prove to be the most militant labor organization in the country for the next two decades, playing a key role in numerous important battles in labor history, including the strikes at Lawrence, Paterson, and the Mesabi Range in 1916. Like their French counterparts, the IWW refused to affiliate with political parties. However, its advocacy of industrial unionism, which was a challenge to the craft unionism of the American Federation of Labor (AFL), suggested its endorsement of dual unions. This was in contrast to the French syndicalists' tactic of "boring-from-within" existing unions.

Emerging at the period of peak emigration of workers from eastern and southern Europe, organizing activities focused on attracting ethnic groups from these regions. Since most of these immigrants were unskilled, the AFL expended little effort in organizing them. The IWW met with varied results in unionizing efforts, but with considerable success among Italians and a group that was proportionally overrepresented in the organization, Finns. The significance of the IWW for Finnish radicals can be attested by the fact that an institution they created, the Work People's College, would ultimately become the official school of the IWW. The union worked very hard to overcome ethnic boundaries that tended to divide European-origin workers. Furthermore, it sought to organize blacks and, in stark contradistinction to the xenophobic AFL, Asians.

The IWW's hostility to World War I and its reputation (largely undeserved) for violence led to a campaign of repression during the Red Scare era, culminating in the trial of the "Chicago 166." Combined with the attraction of Bolshevism for American radicals during the 1920s, the Wobblies were a spent force by the advent of the Depression.

References
Melvyn Dubofsky, *We Shall Be All: A History of the Industrial Workers of the World* (1969); Philip S. Foner, *History of the Labor Movement in the United States*, vol. 4 (1965); Peter Kivisto, *Immigrant Socialists in the United States: The Case of Finns and the Left* (1984).

P.K.

SYRIAN WORLD. *See* Lebanese.

SYRIANS. *See* Arabs.

SYTTENDE MAI. *See* Norwegians.

SZABADSAG. *See* Hungarians.

SZOLD, HENRIETTA (1860–1945). Jewish leader active in the American Zionist movement; founded Hadassah (*q.v.*) in 1926.

Reference
Marvin Lowenthal, *Henrietta Szold: Life and Letters* (1942).

F.C.

TALBOT, WINTHROP (d. 1937). Educator; a major advocate of the Americanization of immigrants and immigrant children. Chief works: *Adult Literacy* (1916); *Americanization* (1917); *Teaching English to Aliens* (1918); *Home Lessons in English* (1928); also, "A Public School in the Slums That Does Its Job," *The World's Work* 18 (1909): 11567–11572.

Reference
Robert A. Carlson, *Quest for Conformity: Americanization Through Education* (1975).

F.C.

TAMIMENT LIBRARY (New York University, Bobst Library). A rich collection of books, periodicals, pamphlets, manuscripts, and miscellanea illustrating the history of American labor, and radical movements from the mid-nineteenth century to the present. The library holds important materials on the immigrant in American labor history.

F.C.

TAYLOR, GRAHAM (1857–1938). Theologian, social reformer. Taylor was an important figure in the "social gospel" movement which brought the churches into battle against urban social ills. Of his *Religion in Social Action* (1913), Jane Addams said: "The author lived for twenty years at the Chicago Commons, a social settlement which he founded in one of those shifting city districts in which people of a score of nationalities are drawn from all parts of the world in response to industrial opportunities . . . that too often exploit them but seldom unite them. . . . This book will doubtless be of value to men and women of all faiths who are eager that the current of their religion should pour itself into broader channels of social purpose" (Introduction). Chief work: *Chicago Commons Through Forty Years* (1936).

F.C.

TAYLOR GRAZING ACT (1934). *See* Basques.

TEACHERS COLLEGE (Columbia University). Founded in 1887, chartered in 1892, and affiliated with Columbia University since 1893. Teachers College exerted great influence in educational planning for immigrant children.

Reference
Lawrence A. Cremin, David A. Shannon, and Mary E. Townsend, *A History of Teachers College, Columbia University* (1954).

F.C.

TEMPORARY FOREIGN WORKERS, policies. A special report of the National Commission for Manpower Policy illuminates the policy issues regarding H-2s (temporary foreign workers mostly other than high-level professionals), providing a factual record of the H-2 program, a structural background on conceptual framework, a survey of the policy options that are available and the relevant criteria, and an evaluation of the most feasible options in terms of their comparative benefits and costs. The report evaluates not only how well these options meet the "needs for workers" and the problems of "absorbing foreign workers," but also distinguishes short-term adjustments from long-term development.

A second report on immigration problems (1) summarizes the dimensions of immigration, both legal and illegal, into the United States in recent years, from all countries and particularly from Mexico; (2) reviews the forces underlying and sustaining the emigration of Mexicans and their inflows into the United States; (3) indicates the major impacts—benefits and costs—of migration; (4) outlines the range of alternative approaches for dealing with the migration; (5) sketches U.S. experience with TFW programs, specifically the "H-2 visa" operation; (6) proposes a revised and enlarged treatment of H-2 visas as a new LVFW (limited visa foreign workers) program; and (7) assesses the advantages and disadvantages of this LVFW program in comparison with alternative lines of action, and in the context of alleged rights and duties on the individual, national, and international levels.

References
E. P. Reubens, *Temporary Admission of Foreign Workers: Dimensions and Policies,* special report of the National Commission for Manpower Policy, Special Report No. 34 (1979); also, E. P. Reubens, *Immigration Problems, Limited-Visa Problems, and Other Options* (1980).

F.C.

TEMPORARY WORKER PROGRAMS, U.S. Congress, House and Senate, Committee on the Judiciary, *Temporary Worker Programs: Background and Issues.* A report prepared at the request of Senator E. M. Kennedy for the use of the Select Commission on Immigration and Refugee Policy by the Congressional Research Service of the Library of Congress, 96th Congress, 2d Session, February 1980 (Washington, D.C., 1980). This report reviews U.S. and European experience with selected temporary programs, identifies the problems that have arisen under these various programs and the lessons that may apply to any future attempt to control the illegal flow of alien workers by means of an expanded legal program. It contains an annotated bibliography on alien labor programs and alien labor, 1975–79.

F.C.

TENEMENT HOUSE PROBLEM (1903). *See* De Forest, Robert W[eeks].

TERMAN, LEWIS M[ADISON] (1877–1956). Psychologist. Terman was a major theoretician of intelligence measurement who felt that his studies "gave considerable support to Sir Francis Galton's theory as to the hereditary nature of genius." Terman devised the Stanford revision of the Binet scale in 1916, the most important of the revisions and scoring methods extensively used on immigrant children. Chief work: *The Measurement of Intelligence* (1916). See also Terman's *The Hygiene of the School Child* (1914), "devoted to the physical defects of school children."

Reference
Stephen Jay Gould, *The Mismeasure of Man* (1981).

F.C.

TESLA, NIKOLA. *See* Croatians.

TEXAS SCHOOL CASE. *See* Illegal Aliens.

TEXAS WENDISH HERITAGE SOCIETY. *See* Wends.

THAYER, WEBSTER. *See* Sacco and Vanzetti.

THEUS, JEREMIAH. *See* Swiss.

THOMAS, NORMAN MATTOON (1884–1968). Pacifist, socialist leader. Thomas was a graduate of Princeton (1905) and Union Theological Seminary (1911), and served as pastor of several Presbyterian churches in New York City with service in settlement house work which brought him into direct contact with immigrants. He served as coordinator of the Presbyterian immigrant ministry in New York City and supervised programs involving three Italian immigrant congregations. Thomas formally left the ministry in 1931. Chief works: *Human Exploitation* (1934); *Appeal to the Nations* (1947); *Great Dissenters* (1961); and *Socialism Reexamined* (1963).

References
B. K. Johnpoll, *Norman Thomas* (1970); M. B. Seidler, *Norman Thomas* (2d ed., 1967).

F.C.

THOMAS, WILLIAM I[SAAC] (1863–1947). Sociologist; leading exponent of psychological sociology. Adjustive behavior is the central concern of his sociological theory, principally illustrated in his study (with Florian Znaniecki [*q.v.*]) of *The Polish Peasant in Europe and America* (5 vols., 1918–1920; ed. Eli Zaretsky, 1984) which alleged a disintegration of the Polish family in America. *See* K. Symmons-Symonolewicz, "The Polish American Community—Half a Century After the Polish Peasant," *The Polish Review* 11 (Summer 1966): 67–73.

F.C.

THOMPSON, FRANK V[ICTOR] (b. 1874). School administrator. Thompson was Boston's superintendent of schools. His *The Schooling of the Immigrant* (1920) was part of the "Americanization Studies: The Acculturation of Immigrant Groups Into American Society" (*q.v.*) commissioned by the Carnegie Corporation. His *Schooling of the Immigrant* deals with school administration, the teaching of English, schooling in citizenship, and the training of teachers for the Americanization of the immigrant.

F.C.

THOMSON, CHARLES (1729–1824). Politician and revolutionary. Born in County Derry, Ireland. Thomson came to the United States as an indentured servant at age ten. He was one of Washington's generals in the revolution and served as secretary of state for the Continental Congress. He contributed to the drafting of and signed the Declaration of Independence; he also designed the Great Seal of the United States.

S.P.M.

THORNDIKE, EDWARD L[EE] (1874–1949). Psychologist. Thorndike spent 1899 through 1941 at Columbia University's Teachers College, appointed originally as an instructor in genetic psychology. His research and work in educational psychology were largely in methods to test and measure children's intelligence. Thorndike was influenced by the work of eugenicists, and was harsh in his judgments of immigrants and the learning capacities of immigrant children. In his *The Elimination of Pupils from School* (1907) he concluded: "I estimate that the general tendency of American cities of 25,000 and over is, or was at about 1900, to keep in school out of 100 entering pupils 90 till grade 4; 81 till grade 5; 68 till grade 6; 54 till grade 7; 40 till the last grammar grade (usually the eighth, but sometimes the ninth and rarely the seventh); 27 till the first high school grade; 17 till the second; 12 till the third; and 8 till the fourth." The attrition was, in Thorndike's view, due to the large number of immigrant children. Chief works: *Educational*

Psychology (1903); *Mental and Social Measurements* (1904); *Animal Intelligence* (1911); *Human Nature and Social Order* (1940).

Reference
G. M. Joncich, *Edward Lee Thorndike* (1968).

F.C.

TOCQUEVILLE, ALEXIS DE (1805–1859). French politician, traveler. Prominent in French politics during and after the Revolution of 1848, and briefly French minister of foreign affairs in 1849. His travel in the United States was the basis of his *De la démocratie en Amérique* (2 vols., 1835; translated as *Democracy in America*, 4 vols., 1835–1840), an attestation of de Tocqueville's belief in political democracy and social equality. His analysis of the American experience was intended to serve as the basis for lessons Europe could learn from American challenges and successes.

References
Marvin Zetterbaum, *Alexis de Tocqueville* (1967); S. I. Drescher, *De Tocqueville* (1968); André Jardin, *Alexis de Tocqueville* (1985).

F.C.

TOLMAN, WILLIAM H[OWE] (1861–1932). Social reformer. Involved in a wide range of activities to improve the condition of the poor and the immigrants. A member of the [New York City] City Vigilance League for which he prepared *The Handbook of Sociological Information* (1894), his *The Better New York* (1904) was a handbook to the "many-handed philanthropies, as various as human needs" of New York City presented in a series of vignettes and informational digests on all of the charitable and philanthropic efforts in New York City at the turn of the century. Other works: *Municipal Reform Movements in the United States* (1896); *Industrial Betterment* (1900); *Social Engineering* (1909); *Hygiene for the Worker* (1912); and *Alcoholism in Industry* (1913).

F.C.

TONGHOE. *See* Koreans.

TONGJANG. *See* Koreans.

TOVERITAR. Newspaper, part of the Socialist Finnish-American labor movement, founded in 1909, and edited by women and devoted primarily to women's issues. Its early editors, particularly Selma Jokela McCone, managed to keep the newspaper alive and to make it responsive to its female readers. With McCone's management, the *Toveritar* achieved a circulation of 5,000 in 1915 and became a women's newspaper, with household tips, advice columns, a children's department, and the usual literary and political articles. *Toveritar*'s subsequent editors, Maiju Nurmi and Helmi Mattson, brought the newspaper through the wartime censorship of radical periodicals into the 1920s.

Reference

Hilja J. Karvonen, "Three Proponents of Women's Rights in the Finnish-American Labor Movement from 1910–1930: Selma Jokela McCone, Maiju Nurmi and Helmi Mattson," in *For the Common Good: Finnish Immigrants and the Radical Response to Industrial America* (Superior, Wisconsin: Tyomies Society, 1977), pp. 195–216.

F.C.

TRANSATLANTIC CROSSINGS. What is invariably described as the plight of the immigrants depended, during their crossings at least, on the technological sophistication of the vessels accommodating them. For our purposes, we can divide the immigrants' shipboard experience into three categories: steerage under canvas, steerage under steam, and finally and briefly, steerage on the superships.

Under sail, immigrants were subjected to weeks of damp, claustrophobic and an often seemingly interminable life between decks. Sailing schedules were irregular, and "coffin brigs"—christened thus with a realistic sense of morbidity—left port only when their cargo holds were full; human cargo awaited the master's or owner's pleasure. But whereas goods could wait loaded on board, immigrants could not, and funds for their journey might well be exhausted because of dilatory departures and resultant gouging by unscrupulous doss-house owners near the piers. At sea, sailing ships were at the mercy of contrary winds and weather. Crossings might extend for unforeseen weeks. Since immigrants brought their own rations, additional sea days could reduce them to near-starvation. Conscientious owners gave their masters jurisdiction to issue lifesaving supplementary company rations if necessary; hence the origin of the captain's dinner, originally a matter of survival rather than celebration.

With the arrival of steam in the mid-nineteenth century, schedules were fixed. Vessels left for America on advertised dates. Paddle steamers reduced crossing time: in the 1840s, Cunard's steam packets reached Halifax in a record-breaking fourteen days. But, typically, that kind of super-service was restricted to what were called cabin passengers (prosperous voyagers) and Her Majesty's mails. Immigrants could never profit from the relative brevity and luxury of only a fortnight's crossing to America.

But in the latter half of the century, the immigrant flow grew apace

with America's westward expansion. Advancing steam technology produced larger and faster hulls, requiring more passengers to fill their
holds. Owners of British, Dutch, French, German, Scandinavian, and
Italian steam tonnage entered into a fierce, competitive battle for the
immigrant dollar.

The agreeable aspect of the traffic was its high profitability. Cheap
fares reflected negligible costs per passenger. Fed and housed mini-
mally, immigrants were packed into large berthing compartments. The
earliest pejorative "steerage," given originally to the after 'tween
decks, became common usage for inferior accommodation anywhere in
the hull. Although the companies had, by then, assumed responsibility
for victuals, steerage cuisine scarcely tantalized. Immigrants ate on
trestle tables at the foot of multiple berths in bleak, utilitarian compartments walled with the ship's naked steel. They slept on straw palliasses,
"donkeys' breakfasts" that, the last sea day, were hurled overboard by
overworked berthing stewards. Few company servants were assigned to
the steerage; on White Star tonnage in the 1870s, a forbidding factotum
known as the Steerage Matron kept unmarried sexes ruthlessly segregated. Overall, it says something of even those later immigrant quarters
that cattle could be—and were—accommodated within them on empty
eastbound crossings.

The third, final, and briefest immigrant phase occurred just prior to
1914, resulting from a combination of mega-ships—in excess of 50,000
tons—and shrewd marketing. The way was led by Albert Ballin, head
of Germany's Hamburg-Amerika Linie or HAPAG, situated in a prime
geographical location to capitalize on Slavik immigrants anxious to
reach America. Ballin foresaw, accurately, that a fair shake for his
humblest clients would pay enormous dividends. Moreover, it was not
lost on him that sequential, familial crossings typified the immigrant
tide: sons or nephews reaching America first would be followed by
siblings, parents, cousins, and grandparents, all of whom might book
on recommended tonnage.

Ballin upgraded his immigrant space radically. He called it "Third
Class," banishing "Steerage" from HAPAG's lexicon. Starting with
the *Imperator* of 1912, he had his naval architects subdivide conventional berthing compartments into hundreds of four-berth rooms: mirac-
ulously, immigrants were transformed, *faute de mieux,* into cabin passengers. These were admittedly modest quarters, low in the ship and
many without portholes. But they were marked improvements over
previous conditions, a Third Class approximating the Second Class of a
previous decade. Down the passage were proper baths, stewardesses,
and a dining saloon; though this latter's tables were covered with
oilcloth rather than linen, there was now a rudimentary menu.

Ballin's other pioneering preoccupation was the health of his Third

Class passenger load, a reflection less of humanity than practicality. United States Public Health officials at Ellis Island were empowered to bar entry to any unwell immigrants: trachoma, venereal disease, consumption, or lunacy occasioned automatic refusal of entry. Worse, those refused immigrants had to be returned to their port of embarkation at the shipping company's expense. This provision of the law had the effect of mandating embarkation health inspections by the companies themselves to ensure that only fit immigrants were carried. Ballin designed and built immigrant villages on the banks of the Elbe where westbound clients could be accommodated and examined in sanitary and supervised surroundings.

But the new age was over almost before it began. Ballin's enlightened and profitable approach ended with the outbreak of World War I. After it was over, the Immigration Restriction Acts of the 1920s reduced the flow to a trickle. Ballin's *Imperator*-class trio of ships was seized by the Allies, and his immigrant quarters, upgraded only slightly, accommodated eastbound American tourists instead.

References
Frank A. Bowen, *A Century of Atlantic Travel, 1830–1930* (1930); Laurence Dunn, *North Atlantic Liners 1899–1913* (1961); Rhoda Hoff, *America's Immigrants* (1967); E. Huldermann, *Bernhard Albert Ballin* (1922); John Maxtone-Graham, *The Only Way to Cross* (1972); Ann Novotny, *Strangers at the Door* (1971); Robert Louis Stevenson, *The Amateur Emigrant* (1911); Philip Taylor, *The Distant Magnet: European Immigration to the United States* (1972).

J.M.G.

TRANSPORT WORKERS OF AMERICA (TWUA). *See* Quill, Michael Joseph.

TRANSPORTED FELONS. *See* English.

TREATY OF CHEMULPO. *See* Koreans.

TREATY OF GUADALUPE HIDALGO. *See* Mexicans.

TRESCA, CARLO (1879–1943). Journalist, revolutionary activist. Tresca migrated to the United States in 1904, and founded the anarchist newspaper *Il Martello* (The Hammer), serving as editor for thirty years. From the 1920s until he was shot to death in 1943, Tresca was an unrelenting foe of both Communists and Fascists. He played a leading role in labor unrest and strikes (in which immigrant workers were preponderantly represented) in Paterson, New Jersey; Lawrence, Massachusetts; Pittsburgh, Pennsylvania; and elsewhere.

Reference
Frank Rosengarten, *The Italian Anti-Fascist Press* (1968); Dorothy Gallagher, *All the Right Enemies: The Life and Murder of Carlo Tresca* (1988).

F.C.

THE TRIANGLE FIRE. A tragic loft fire in New York City on March 25, 1911, which claimed the lives of 148 immigrant women (Italian and Jewish, largely) shirtwaist trade workers. A fictionalized treatment is James Oppenheimer's *The Nine-Tenths* (1911).

Reference
Leon Stein, *The Triangle Fire* (1962).

F.C.

TROLLOPE, FRANCES (1780–1863). Writer. Trollope visited America in 1827–1830 and an account of her travels was published as *Domestic Manners of the Americans* in 1832, enjoying tremendous popularity in England, rivaled only by Charles Dickens's *American Notes* (1842); both were generally hostile to the evolving (largely immigrant) new America. Despite its deprecatory tone, Trollope's *Domestic Manners* is a valuable contemporary register of early nineteenth-century American life with sharply etched vignettes of the immigrant experience in the new society.

References
James Pope Hennessy, *Frances Trollope* (1972); and earlier biographies by F. E. Trollope (1895) and A. O. J. Cockshut (1955).

D.N.A.

TUCKERMAN, JOSEPH (1778–1840). Unitarian clergyman who conducted a mission to the poor (overwhelmingly immigrant) in Boston. Tuckerman's Boston experience was emulated in other growing cities in the Jacksonian period, and his message, sensitive to the plight of the needy, helped to awaken middle- and upper-class Americans to the problem. Chief work: *On the Elevation of the Poor* (1830).

F.C.

"TURKEY IN ASIA." *See* Arabs.

TURKISH CULTURAL ALLIANCE. *See* Turks.

TURKS. The Turks are a very small immigrant group in the United States. The 1980 U.S. census reported 64,691 persons citing Turkish ancestry, with 39,117, or 60.5 percent, claiming single ancestry. They are concentrated in the Northeast, with the largest concentration in New York City. Other cities throughout the country with significant population concentrations include Chicago, Los Angeles, Houston, and Washington, D.C.

Turks arrived in the United States in two distinct periods: during the period of mass migration between 1880 and 1924, and since the 1950s. Regarding the former cohort, much remains unknown about them. It is estimated that approximately 22,000 Turks arrived during this time, though they proved to be "birds of passage," with more than three-fourths of them returning home, in part due to the encouragement and financial incentives provided by the Turkish government. This was an overwhelmingly young male group, composed chiefly of unskilled workers. The illiteracy rate of 75 percent was among the highest of all immigrant groups. During their generally brief tenures in the United States, they found employment as manual laborers. There is evidence from Labor Department sources around the turn of the century to indicate that, like Italians, Greeks, and a number of other ethnic groups, Turkish workers were often involved in a padrone or "bossism" system.

Unlike other Middle Easterners, notably the Syrians, the Turks were mainly Moslem rather than Christian. This served to accentuate their outsider status. These immigrants did not manage to establish religious institutions. For that matter, an ethnic community did not emerge, due to group size, lack of economic resources, reemigration, and probably (though this has not been documented) nativist hostility. As a consequence, there are few historical traces of this migrant group.

Furthermore, there is a marked discontinuity with the more recent migration. While unskilled workers have continued to emigrate from Turkey during the post–World War II period, they have not migrated to North America. Rather, they have come to be an important sector of the "guest worker" population in Western Europe, particularly in West Germany. However, Turkey has also experienced a "brain drain." While Western Europe is the major recipient of migrating professional white-collar workers, several thousand have settled in the United States, especially after the reform of immigration laws in 1965 lifted the quotas established four decades earlier.

These immigrants tend to be secular and intent on assimilating into the mainstream of American social life, though some have been slow to become U.S. citizens. They have not created many ethnic institutions nor have they established an ethnic press. Of the twenty-two Turkish organizations listed in a directory of ethnic organizations, most are local enterprises, with New York City containing the largest number of them. The oldest, the Turkish Cultural Alliance of Flushing, New York, was founded in 1933. All the rest are no older than 1957. The emphases of these organizations reflects a newly arrived group relatively at home in the United States, but not intent on forgetting the homeland. Thus, the organizations stress cultural exchange and travel. However, there is impressionistic evidence to indicate that the second generation has placed a higher premium on being American than their parents.

References
Leonard Dinnerstein et al., *Natives and Strangers* (1979); John Koren, ''The Padrone System and Padrone Ranks'' (1897); Bernard Lewis, *The Emergence of Modern Turkey* (1969); Eliot Mears, *Modern Turkey* (1924); U.S. Bureau of the Census, ''Ancestry of the Population by State: 1980'' (1983).

P.K.

TURNER, GEORGE KIBBE. *See* White Slave Trade.

TUSKEGEE INSTITUTE. *See* Afro-Americans.

UHRO-RUSYNS. *See* Carpatho-Rusyns.

UJ ELORE. *See* Hungarians.

UKRAINIANS. Ukrainians are one of the most well-organized and active ethnic groups in the United States. There are today about 730,000 Americans who identify themselves as being of Ukrainian heritage.

Ukrainian immigrants began coming in significant numbers to the United States in the 1880s. For the most part, they left what was then the Austro-Hungarian Empire (in particular the provinces of Galicia and Bukovina), that is, lands that are today in the western part of the Ukrainian S.S.R. and far southeastern Poland. It is impossible to determine the exact number of Ukrainians who arrived in the United States, especially during the early decades, because they were classified either by the country they came from (Austria, Poland, Romania, Russia, Soviet Union) or used names other than Ukrainian to describe themselves (Ruthenians, Russians, Austrians, etc.).

The Ukrainian migration process can be seen to have occurred in four phases or waves. The first and largest took place from the 1880s until the outbreak of World War I in 1914; the second was during the interwar years, 1919–1939, mostly from what was then eastern Poland; the third included displaced persons (DPs) who arrived between 1945 and 1952, mostly from camps in the American zone of Germany; and the most recent fourth phase was connected exclusively with Poland and its political instability during the 1980s.

The motivation for leaving the Ukrainian homeland has varied depending on the phase. Before World War I, the approximately 250,000 who left for the United States did so for economic reasons. The underdeveloped agrarian countryside of Austria's province of eastern Galicia was unable to support a population that was increasing steadily during the third quarter of the nineteenth century. The potential wealth that could be gained in America's growing industrial economy attracted Ukrainians, of whom many came to stay permanently, while others simply wanted to work for a period of a few years and then return home.

Those Ukrainians who came during the second phase, most especially during the early 1920s before the imposition of American restrictions on immigration from eastern and southern Europe, were motivated in part by the continuing underdeveloped economy of their Galician and Bukovinian homelands (then respectively in Poland and Romania) and in part by the political upheavals of the immediate postwar years when Ukrainians fought and lost a war with Poland in an attempt to obtain independence. The third wave arrived exclusively for political reasons. As a result of the Nazi German occupation of virtually all Ukrainian lands in Poland and the Soviet Union during World War II, hundreds of thousands were shipped to Germany as forced laborers. Then during the last years of the war, numerous others fled the advancing Red Army, not wanting to live under Soviet rule, which as a result of the world conflict expanded westward, incorporating virtually all Ukrainian inhabited territory within the boundaries of the Ukrainian S.S.R. After spending several years in DP camps in Germany and other parts of Western Europe, these Ukrainian political refugees were admitted to the United States.

The fourth and smallest wave of Ukrainians consists of a few thousand people from various parts of Poland, who fled that country during the 1980s, seeking in the United States both greater economic opportunities and political freedom than they were able to find in post–World War II Communist-ruled Poland.

The settlement patterns established by the first wave of Ukrainians before 1914 have been more or less maintained by the group to this day. As farmers or unskilled laborers, the early Ukrainian immigrants worked in the coal mines of eastern Pennsylvania and the mills and factories of metropolitan areas like New York City (including northern New Jersey), Philadelphia, Camden, Chicago, Detroit, Pittsburgh, and Cleveland. Although the percentage of skilled workers and professionals increased substantially during the post–World War II wave of DPs, they were drawn to the areas where Ukrainians had lived already.

To be sure, economic mobility (the Ukrainian-American family median income was 12 percent above the national average in 1970) has prompted Ukrainians to move increasingly from the old inner-city neighborhoods to the suburbs. Nonetheless, they have remained concentrated with one exception in the same states as their predecessors who came during the early decades of this century. In 1980, 61.1

percent lived in Pennsylvania, New York, New Jersey, Michigan, and Ohio, the newest exception being California (in fourth place) with another 6.8 percent whose presence reflects a general American migration trend toward that Pacific coast state.

Ukrainian-Americans maintain their cohesiveness through a wide variety of organizations which directly or indirectly are concerned with the fate of the European homeland. Before 1918, Ukrainians had no distinct political entity to call their own. Since that time, a Ukrainian Soviet Socialist Republic has existed within the framework (after 1923) of the Soviet Union, but the vast majority of Ukrainian-Americans do not consider it a Ukrainian state, and therefore Ukrainian cultural and political independence are still goals to be attained in the future. In the meantime, Ukrainians in the United States (together with their brethren in neighboring Canada) strive to preserve what they consider traditional Ukrainian values that are not permitted to function in the Soviet Union and neighboring Communist-ruled lands where Ukrainians live.

Among the most important of those values for the early immigrants as the church. Ukrainians are in the main Eastern Christians, belonging to either the Greek Catholic or Orthodox religion, known in the United States as the Ukrainian Catholic and Ukrainian Orthodox churches. Both Ukrainian Catholics and Orthodox derive their spiritual roots from the Orthodoxy of the Greco-Byzantine Empire. However, whereas the Orthodox still recognize as their ultimate spiritual head the Greek ecumenical patriarch of Constantinople, the Ukrainian Catholics recognize the pope in Rome. The relationship to Rome dates from 1596, at which time Ukrainian Catholics were allowed to retain certain "Orthodox" traditions, such as a married clergy, a liturgy in Church Slavonic instead of Latin, and use of the Julian instead of Gregorian calendar.

In the years before 1914, the vast majority of Ukrainian immigrants were Greek Catholics (the exception being the Orthodox from Bukovina). The attempts by Greek Catholics to establish churches that would preserve their traditional customs were opposed by the American Catholic hierarchy. Eventually, the Greek Catholics received their own bishop (1907) and the Ukrainian Catholics their own distinct church structure in 1924 (which today has a metropolitan see in Philadelphia and three bishops), but this proved to be at the expense of many of their traditions (including a married clergy), which they were forced to abandon.

Nonetheless, the situation of the Ukrainian Catholic church in the United States is healthy compared to the homeland, where it was outlawed by the Soviet government in 1946, surviving today only unofficially and at great risk as a persecuted underground church. The fate of the Ukrainian Orthodox church at home is not much better. It, too, was outlawed by the Soviet government already in the 1930s. Since then, the only Orthodox parishes allowed in the Soviet Ukraine are those which belong to the Russian Orthodox church. Thus, the Ukrainian Orthodox church in the United States (of which there are two major jurisdictions with metropolitan sees in South Bound Brook, New Jersey and New York City) considers itself the last body to preserve distinctly Ukrainian Orthodox religious traditions.

In order to keep the specifically Ukrainian Christian faith alive, the American structures maintain parishes throughout the country, which include an estimated (1980) 265,000 members among the Ukrainian Catholics and 120,000 among the two largest Ukrainian Orthodox churches. Beyond these dry and somewhat unrepresentative statistics is the fact that in many ways it is the numerous Ukrainian parishes spread throughout the country which provide the mortar that holds the Ukrainian-American community together. This occurs regardless of actual membership or faith, because it is at the church and its related halls that the familial and life-cycle events take place, whether baptisms, weddings, deaths, or other anniversaries.

Most of the Catholic and Orthodox parishes use the Ukrainian language in their services and attempt to keep the religious aspect of the Ukrainian heritage alive by building or maintaining Eastern-style architecture in their church structures; by sponsoring newspapers, publications, youth groups, and other organizations; and by holding commemorative events, among the largest of which will be connected with the millennium of Christianity in Rus'-Ukraine to be celebrated in 1988.

Ukrainian-Americans have also established a wide variety of secular organizations. The earliest of these were fraternal brotherhoods designed primarily to provide insurance and other benefits to workers who had little or no coverage against accidents on the job or unemployment that may have occurred because of layoffs or strikes. The oldest and largest of these fraternals is the Ukrainian National Association, founded in 1894 in Jersey City, New Jersey. This association has through the years not only served as an important fraternal insurance agency, it has also helped to keep an awareness of the Ukrainian heritage and the fate of the homeland alive through numerous publications and in particular the daily Ukrainian-language newspaper *Svoboda* (Jersey City, New Jersey, 1894–present) and the English-language *Ukrainian Weekly* (Jersey City, New Jersey, 1933–present).

In more recent decades, most especially since World War II, the new Ukrainian-American organizational structures that have been established are concerned primarily with educational, scholarly, cultural, and political matters. Ukrainian-language elementary schools, begun as early as 1893, still function in the form of Ukrainian Catholic day schools and Saturday cultural schools. At the more advanced level, the last two decades have also witnessed the establishment of courses in Ukrainian subjects (primarily language, literature, and history) at several American universities, including three professorial chairs and a research institute (1973) at Harvard University.

More traditional are a whole host of scholarly institutions, literary societies, journals, scouting groups (Plast), and professional organizations (artists, engineers, doctors, and lawyers) which were brought from the homeland where they were banned by the Soviet regime and then reconstructed in the United States. Several political organizations were brought under a loose coalition known as the Ukrainian Congress Committee of America, which since its establishment in 1940 has attempted to represent Ukrainian interests vis-à-vis the American government and other world organizations. With the exception of a very small group of pro-Soviet Ukrainian-Americans, the vast majority of the group and its religious and secular structures are demonstrably anti-Soviet and they work in whatever way possible to change what is considered "Russian imperialist domination" of the Ukrainian homeland.

In recent years, the Ukrainian-American community has been led primarily by the post–World War II DP wave of immigrants and their sons and daughters. A large percentage are university-trained professionals whose concern with their ancestral heritage is no longer limited to family- and church-oriented concerns. Rather, this generation hopes to have things Ukrainian recognized in the larger arena of the mass media and American political circles. Hence, among the most recent projects and organizations have been the Ukrainian Helsinki Accord Watch Committee and the U.S. Congressional Commission on the Ukrainian Famine of the 1930s.

The struggle for recognition in the larger American scene for a relatively unknown Slavic group and stateless people has not been an easy one, and it has been complicated by the view (widespread in certain circles) that Ukrainians are anti-Semitic Nazi collaborationists. Thus, in the last decade alone, much of the energies of the group have been directed to combating negative publicity aroused toward them in widely viewed American television programs like "Holocaust" and "Sobibor," or in the trial in Israel for war crimes against the deported Ukrainian-American immigrant John Demanjuk (1986–1987). Clearly, however, Ukrainian-American society remains a vibrant phenomenon, and the negative as well as positive attention it has received in recent decades is an indication that it is a force to be reckoned with in the social fabric of the United States.

References
Wasyl Halich, *Ukrainians in the United States* (1937; 1970); Myron Kuropas, *The Ukrainian Americans: Roots and Aspirations* (1987); Paul R. Magocsi, "Ukrainians," in *Harvard Encyclopedia of American Ethnic Groups* (1980), pp. 997–1009; Aleksander Sokolyszyn and Vladimir Wertsman, *Ukrainians in Canada and the United States: A*

Guide to Information Resources (1981); Oleh Wolowyna, ed., *Ethnicity and National Identity: Demographic and Socioeconomic Characteristics of Persons with Ukrainian Mother Tongue in the United States* (1987).

P.R.M.

UNDOCUMENTED ALIENS IN THE NEW YORK METROPOLI-TAN AREA: AN EXPLORATION INTO THEIR SOCIETY AND LABOR MARKET INCORPORATION (1986). This final report of a five-year project conducted under the auspices of the Center for Migration Studies probes many aspects of the undocumented alien population. Unique for its examination of unapprehended, undocumented aliens, this text also presents new data on the much-contested questions of rates of payment of taxes and utilization of the social infrastructure by undocumented aliens. Voluntary agency personnel, legislators, policy-makers, research analysts, and academicians will find *Undocumented Aliens* valuable for its critical review of literature on undocumented immigration and the methodologies used in this field, its 363-question interview schedule, and its summary of the policy implications of the research study.

F.C.

UNIATES (Byzantine rite Catholics). *See* Romanians.

UNION AND LEAGUE OF ROMANIAN SOCIETIES. *See* Romanians.

UNION OF AMERICAN HEBREW CONGREGATIONS. *See* Gamoran, Emanuel.

UNIREA. *See* Romanians.

UNITED NATIONS RELIEF AND WORKS AGENCY. *See* Refugees.

UNITED NEGRO IMPROVEMENT ASSOCIATION. The United Negro Improvement Association was founded by Marcus Garvey in Jamaica in 1914 and its headquarters were moved by him to New York City in 1916. The UNIA was the base on which Garvey strove to develop a new sense of black pride and black separatism. Its philosophy was in sharp contrast to that of the National Association for the Advancement of Colored People, founded in 1909, which worked to create an integrated society in America. The UNIA attracted large numbers of blacks who had recently migrated from the rural South and felt alienated in northern urban society. It established a variety of black men's and women's organizations which gave the migrants a sense of belonging and worth. It sponsored the creation of chains of black-owned businesses, including a daily paper and the Black Star Steamship Line. Black Americans were urged to take a leading role in freeing Africa from white colonialism; but the creation of such black nations did not occur for another quarter-century. The UNIA got into legal and financial problems because of mismanagement of the steamship line, and Garvey, after a short time in prison, was deported. The American branch of the organization crumbled away very quickly without his dynamic leadership, and many felt that this proved the weakness of its philosophy. But the Black Power ideology revived with new vigor, and there are indirect connections between the UNIA and the later Black Muslim movement; Malcolm X's father had worked for Garvey, just to cite one example. The Black Power leaders of the 1960s looked to Garvey as a trail blazer.

References
J. H. Clarke, ed., *Marcus Garvey* (1974); Robert A. Hill, ed., *The Marcus Garvey and the United Negro Improvement Association Papers*, 5 vols. (1987); Edmund Cronon, *Black Moses: The Story of Marcus Garvey and the Universal Negro Improvement Association* (1955).

N.C.

UNITED STATES CATHOLIC MISCELLANY. *See* England, John.

U.S. CHILDREN'S BUREAU. The Children's Bureau was established by an act of Congress in 1912 and charged with responsibility to "investigate and report . . . upon all matters pertaining to the welfare of children and child life among all classes of our people. . . ." Under the brilliant leadership of Julia Lathrop (*q.v.*), Grace Abbott (*q.v.*), Katharine Lenroot, and Martha Eliot, the bureau was the most important federal agency promoting the health and welfare of children and young people. It was a major influence in promoting the welfare of immigrant children.

Reference
Robert H. Bremner, ed., *The United States Children's Bureau, 1912–1972* (1974).

F.C.

UNITED STATES COMMITTEE FOR REFUGEES. *See* Refugees.

U.S. CONGRESS, House and Senate, Committees on the Judiciary, Select Commission on Immigration and Refugee Policy. In

1978, Congress established a Select Commission on Immigration and Refugee Policy to make a major study of immigration and recommend changes; the sixteen-member commission (including congressional representatives and senators, cabinet officials, and presidential appointees) was chaired by Father Theodore Hesburgh, president of Notre Dame University, and its work directed by Professor Lawrence Fuchs of Brandeis University. The commission's *Report* was submitted to Congress in March 1981; its recommendations were that the basic immigration system be kept intact, with more flexibility, adjustments in preferences, and increases in immigration to assist in easing backlogs in certain nations. Its recommendations on illegal (undocumented) aliens proved very controversial, but it became the basis for immigration reform legislation pending in Congress. Its contents are: Foreword; Executive Summary; Introduction; Section 1, International Issues; Section 2, Undocumented/Illegal Aliens; Section 3, The Admission of Immigrations; Section 4, Phasing in New Programs Recommended by the Select Commission; Section 5, Refugee and Mass First Asylum Issues; Section 6, Nonimmigrant Aliens; Section 7, Administrative Issues; Section 8, Legal Issues; Section 9, Language Requirement for Naturalization; Section 10, Treatment of U.S. Territories Under U.S. Immigration and Nationality Laws; Appendix A, Recommendations and Votes; Appendix B, Supplemental Statements of Commissioners; Appendix C, Action Required on Recommendations; Appendix D, Evolution of Key Provisions Relating to Immigration; Appendix E, The Role of the Federal Government in Immigration and Refugee Policy; Appendix F, The U.S. Refugee Program; Appendix G, Research Contracts and Papers Prepared for the Select Commission; Appendix H, Select Commission Briefing and Background Papers; Appendix I, Dates and Sites of Regional Hearings Held by the Select Commission; Appendix J., Select Commission Consultations and Participants. *See* Immigration Reform and Control Act of 1986.

Reference

U.S. Congress, Committee on the Judiciary, U.S. Select Commission on Immigration and Refugee Policy, *U.S. Immigration Policy and the National Interest* (1981), with six volumes of appendices.

F.C.

U.S. CONGRESS, *U.S. Immigration Policy and the National Interest.* "Staff Report" of the Select Commission on Immigration and Refugee Policy (April 30, 1981), and supplement to the Final Report and Recommendations of the Select Commission (*q.v.*). Provides a background to the commission's major recommendations and strategies and the procedures for implementing some of them. An introduction outlines the human dimensions of the world migration. Four succeeding chapters explicate the underlying principles of immigration reform—international cooperation, the open society, and the rule of law—which formed the basis for most of the commission's recommendations. Two other sections spell out the background to some of the important recommendations made by the select commission dealing with the number of immigrants and refugees to be admitted, the criteria for their selection, and the enforcement of immigration policy—and the strategies for implementing those recommendations. The last section consists of an extensive bibliography. Nine appendices accompany the staff report. The first seven contain compilations of papers that came to the attention of the commission, either through research it undertook or contracted for, testimony received at public hearings, papers submitted at consultations conducted by the commission, or in requested agency research. Several summaries of papers published elsewhere have been included because of their importance. Other appendices contain additional information on public affairs activities and summaries of select commission votes.

F.C.

U.S. DEPARTMENT OF LABOR. *Seven Years Later: The Experience of the 1970 Cohort of Immigrants in the United States* (1979). Gives answers to questions about the labor force characteristics of recent immigrants and what happened to them in the labor market. An analysis of the 1970 cohort is set in a legal, demographic, and historical context. The report concludes with a series of recommendations regarding immigration, employment, and training policies.

F.C.

THE U.S. IMMIGRATION AND NATURALIZATION SERVICE. Efforts to regulate immigration into the United States are almost as old as the nation itself, but the attempts to develop a policy that was definably federal, and to establish an agency responsible for its implementation and enforcement, did not emerge until the last years of the Civil War.

The authority to regulate immigration was originally based on the concept of national sovereignty rather than on any specific constitutional grant of power to Congress. Until the early nineteenth century, the individual states as well as the federal government enacted similar immigration and naturalization laws, but with the exception of the infamous Alien and Sedition Act of 1798, the federal government maintained a stance that was, by and large, noninterventionist.

From 1819 to 1860, the main objectives of federal immigration legislation were to improve conditions for steerage passengers and to provide Congress with statistical information on all immigrants arriving in the United States. Not until 1864 was any law passed to set up a federal bureau charged with the supervision of immigration. In that year, Congress appropriated the sum of $25,000 for the appointment of a commissioner of immigration and a staff of five to assist immigrants in their transportation and settlement problems.

Measures to encourage immigration stimulated, among other things, the importation of contract labor. In response to its perceived evils, Congress began to consider ways of limiting such immigration, but its initial efforts in this regard came in 1875 with the passage of an act restricting the entrance of criminals and prostitutes.

The next year saw a Supreme Court decision declaring that immigration laws passed by the states were unconstitutional, thus finally asserting that the power and responsibility to enact laws on immigration resided uniquely in Congress. But it took that body until 1882 to write the first effective immigration law, and even then it delegated implementation powers to the states. The legislation of the 1880s set the pattern for what was to follow. Now prohibitory in nature, immigration laws were designed to exclude certain classes of aliens. At the beginning, it was those judged to be politically, emotionally, or economically undesirable, and then, under the guise of eliminating the exploitative conditions of contract labor, the Chinese Exclusion Act was passed. Toward the end of the nineteenth century and because of the rapid increase in immigration, Congress conducted several studies that concluded that the divided authority for supervising immigration was permitting widespread violations of the various laws. The resulting Immigration Laws of 1891 gave the federal government sole enforcement responsibility. Further, the law established a centrally organized Bureau of Immigration under the Treasury Department and codified all the existing laws. Thus, it took more than 100 years after its founding for the United States to evolve a policy and a system for the regulation of immigration that could be said to be truly national.

Shortly thereafter, the Bureau of Immigration was transferred to the newly created Department of Commerce. The administrative changes, along with an increase in budget and staff, however, scarcely prepared it for the tremendous spurt in immigration in the two decades prior to World War I. Major concerns included the need to delineate between the customs and immigration functions, the desire to achieve a more even dispersement of aliens throughout the country, improved border control, and systemization of the naturalization process. The establishment of the Naturalization Division constituted an important step forward, but even that measure created its own jurisdictional difficulties. Organizational arrangements were constantly in flux, and in 1913 the bureau was transferred to the new Department of Labor. In the meantime, legislation, such as the 1907 act, was enacted with the purpose of stemming the flow of immigration, primarily by enlarging the categories of immigrants assumed to be undesirable. The annual reports of the bureau clearly identified people of Mediterranean and Slavic stock as being difficult to assimilate into the American mainstream and therefore to be admitted in curtailed numbers. It was the report of the Dillingham Commission in 1911 that first suggested a national origins quota system that would limit immigrants of southern and eastern European origin. Yet despite growing sentiment against certain classes of aliens, that feature was not incorporated into the Immigration Act of 1917. World War I had brought immigration from Europe virtually to a halt and the broadened powers of the bureau were mainly directed toward protecting national security by increasing surveillance over all points of entry into the United States. To this end, the passport system was instituted. By the end of the war, the scope and responsibilities and the size of the bureau had expanded to the degree where it had taken on a quasi-judicial function with organizational and personnel needs appropriate to that role.

The surge in immigration by people fleeing the turmoil of postwar Europe revived nativist views and fears of competition from cheap labor. By 1921 Congress was ready to accept the proposals of the Dillingham Commission, and a quota system was established. It was renewed in 1924, but areas such as Mexico, which was looked to for a steady supply of cheap agricultural and construction labor, were exempt from the restrictions. Furthermore, thousands of other aliens found ways to enter illegally across some border or at some port in spite of having been denied entry by the Bureau of Immigration. As a consequence of the quota system, the watchdog activities of the bureau increased. For the next several years the bureau and its agents were preoccupied with keeping out those aliens the United States did not want and deporting those who still managed to enter. That the agents and field workers were overworked and underpaid did not deter the bureau from asking for additional powers to collect more data relative to the whereabouts of aliens and to tighten naturalization procedures.

In 1933, by executive order, the present Immigration and Naturalization Service was created. Not until then were the concerns for bringing greater uniformity to the naturalization process addressed. At the same time the INS was forced to turn its attention to the problem of the growing number of people seeking safe haven from the religious and political persecution of the Nazi regime in Germany and Austria. Reconciling the tragic dimensions of the problems with the need to maintain its adherence to existing legislation seemed to confound the INS, which momentarily came down on the side of the law.

In the history of the INS and its predecessors, perhaps the most significant development, next to the introduction and implementation of the quota system, was the transfer, in 1940, of the INS from the Department of Labor to the Department of Justice. While the apprehension and prosecution of individuals who had entered the United States illegally or had obtained naturalization fraudulently had long been a function of the agency, combatting subversion and threats to national security became its foremost objective. These concerns were capped by the Alien Registration Act of 1940, which provided for the registration and fingerprinting of all aliens. As the United States became more involved in World War II, new restrictions on the movement of aliens were imposed and the INS stepped up border surveillance. The INS arrested and detained thousands of aliens suspected of being sympathetic to the cause of the Axis powers. It was also again engaged in dealing with the problem of a labor shortage, and again reacted to the problem by admitting large numbers of immigrants from Mexico and the Caribbean.

Little time was lost by the INS after the end of the war in readjusting its focus and concerns. Prosecuting illegal aliens remained a constant and, ironically, the INS was now deporting many of the Mexicans who had come across the border during the war to become part of the labor force. But Congress had also made it possible for the INS to lower the barrier still further against Asian immigrants and to extend a warm welcome to victims of World War II, described as displaced persons.

The new attitudes were short-lived, however, and the viewpoint that prevailed in the 1950s was motivated once more by a fear of subversion—this time from people suspected of being in sympathy with Communist ideologies. The Internal Security Act of 1958 provided the basis for the INS to vigorously revive its investigative activities intended to safeguard the security of the United States. Passed after a comprehensive study by the Senate of immigration legislation, the Immigration and Naturalization Act of 1952 (popularly known as the McCarran-Walter Act) clearly exemplified not only the mood of the period but also the ambivalent course of direction that U.S. immigration policy had taken for nearly the past century. While on the one hand it guaranteed due process to individuals caught up in the legal complexities of the immigration laws, it substantially reasserted its faith in the quota system.

New laws did not resolve old concerns of the INS, and the McCarran-Walter Act was no exception. If its provisions were complex, so was their implementation. The alien registration system and the issuance of visas were new burdens to be borne in the interest of maintaining the security of U.S. borders, but in the end, the basic objective of the INS remained unchanged—excluding or deporting illegal aliens, admitting legal aliens, and preparing them for naturalization.

Whenever major policy changes were adopted, they invariably reflected widespread popular sentiment. In some instances a commission's recommendation was followed by swift legislative action. In the case of the repeal of the quota system, a set of recommendations issued during Harry Truman's administration was not embodied into the law of the land until the administration of Lyndon Johnson. In 1965, amendments to the Immigration and Naturalization Act of 1952 abolished the use of national and ethnic criteria, and a series of categories based largely on compassionate considerations were developed to take their place. America opened its doors to those with special skills, but ranked family reunification among the most important qualifications.

Since it would have been impractical to allocate an admissions quota to refugees, a policy was usually improvised to fit a particular situation. For the most part, however, no such policy was necessary since the discretionary powers of the attorney general allowed him to waive the established formula and admit specified groups of refugees. It was under this special dispensation that, between 1965 and 1980, Cubans, Indochinese, and Haitians were permitted to enter the United States. Though the decisions were made by the State Department, the responsibility for carrying them out fell to the INS. The haste with which the Cubans and Haitians had to be processed and the lack of clear direction as to their status created difficulties which led to criticism of the INS services.

The amendments of 1965 generated new activities for the INS each year, corresponding to the increased volume of people entering and departing from the United States. Inspection systems had to be devised to facilitate the huge flow of traffic passing through the international airports and to accommodate the many different categories of resident and nonresident aliens, not to mention the American traveler.

Demands made upon INS personnel at the airports competed with the need to control traffic across the Mexican border. Inadequate staff forced choices that resulted in fewer border cards being issued to visitors from Mexico. To combat the ever more serious problem of illegal border crossings, the INS resorted to aircraft reconnaissance and electronic fences, and conducted periodic sweeps of areas within the United States. More criticism was heaped upon the INS for its apparent failure to solve the problem. Nor did the INS escape censure for its allegedly poor management practices. Aside from suggestions for computerization of its records and accounting system, congressional studies over the years expressed dissatisfaction with the overall efficiency of the agency, pointing out that many of its functions were duplicated by other governmental bureaus such as the State Department, the Treasury Department, and the Bureau of Customs. Divided responsibility for controlling the drug traffic across the borders was a special target of criticism.

Some of these recommendations were incorporated into a Reorganization Plan, adopted in 1973, but up to and through the Carter administration, efforts to reduce paperwork, set priorities, increase efficiency, and ensure fair and impartial treatment for everyone including undocumented aliens were met with less than the degree of success desired. The particular provisions of each reorganization plan were met with objections by one affected group or another. As for the issue of undocumented aliens, that was to await action by a subsequent administration.

References
S. D. Masonz, *History of the Immigration and Naturalization Service* (1980).

P.S.C.

UNITED STATES IMMIGRATION COMMISSION, *Report of the Immigration Commission* (41 vols.; Washington: Government Printing Office, 1911), vols. 29–33: *The Children of Immigrants in Schools.* Republished with an introductory essay by Francesco Cordasco, 1970. The five-volume report is a vast repository of data on immigrant children (analyses of backgrounds, nativity, school progress, home environments, etc.). In all, 2,036,376 school children are included (in both public and parochial schools in thirty-seven cities). Data on 32,882 students in higher education and 49,067 public school teachers are also presented. "The purpose of the investigation was to determine as far as possible to what extent immigrant children are availing themselves of educational facilities and what progress they make in school work."

F.C.

UNITED STATES IMMIGRATION COMMISSION, *Report of the Immigration Commission* (61st Congress, 2d and 3d Sessions) (41 vols.; Washington: Government Printing Office, 1911), vols. 1–2: *Abstracts.* These volumes include a statistical review of immigration; emigration conditions in Europe; dictionary of races and peoples; immigrants in industries; immigrants in cities; occupations of immigrants; the fecundity of immigrant women; the children of immigrants in schools; immigrants as charity seekers; immigration and crime; steerage conditions; the bodily form of descendants of immigrants; federal immigration legislation; state immigration and alien laws; and other countries; and statements and recommendations. *The Index of Reports of the Immigration Commission* (S. Doc. No. 785, 61st Congress, 3d Session) was never published. The *Report* was restrictionist in its basic recommendations; the chairman of the commission was Senator (Massachusetts) William P. Dillingham (*q.v.*). The *Report* is summarized in Jeremiah W. Jenks and W. Jett Lauck, *The Immigration Problem: A Study of Immigration Conditions and Needs* (1912; 6th ed., 1926). Isaac A.

Hourwich, *Immigration and Labor: The Economic Aspects of European Immigration to the United States* (1912; 2d ed., 1922), subsidized by the American Jewish Committee, was a statistical attack on the commission's report. *See* Immigration Restriction.

F.C.

UNITED STATES OFFICE OF EDUCATION, *Bulletin Series.* These were published irregularly by the United States Office of Education beginning in 1906, and numbered some 1,400 by 1966 when they were discontinued. For the period 1908 through 1920 they are an invaluable archive which both defines and delineates the official attitudes toward the immigrant and his progeny. Edward L. Thorndike's *The Elimination of Pupils from School* (1908) is a detailed conspectus of the process of elimination and attrition that engulfed the immigrant child; the abstracts of papers read at a conference on the *Education of the Immigrant* (1913) supply a register of official views on all aspects of what was viewed as an intractable problem; *State Americanization* (1919) is part of that movement which enlisted all forces in the assimilation of the immigrant; and *The Problem of Adult Education in Passaic, New Jersey* (1920) is a stark delineation of industrialism and the immigrant poor, for whom education was to be the instrument of "social communication."

References
Bibliography of the Publications of the United States Office of Education, with an Introductory Note by Francesco Cordasco (1971); *Education Literature, 1907–1932,* edited with an Introduction by Malcolm C. Hamilton (1979).

F.C.

UNITED STATES–PUERTO RICO COMMISSION ON THE STATUS OF PUERTO RICO (1964). The commission was convened in 1964 and chaired by the late Senator Jacob Javits (R–New York) to "study all factors . . . which may have a bearing on the present and future relationships between the United States and Puerto Rico." Its *Report,* published in 1966, includes a summary of the legal-constitutional, economic, and sociocultural factors that relate to the status of Puerto Rico; the history and organization of the commission; and the commission's conclusions and recommendations. The *Report* also includes an extensive bibliography.

The *Selected Background Studies* (published in 1966) were prepared for the commission's use during its deliberations and include: (1) The Puerto Rican Political Movement in the 19th Century; (2) Historical Survey of the Puerto Rico Status Question, 1898–1965; (3) Significant Factors in the Development of Education in Puerto Rico; (4) Unionism and Politics in Puerto Rico; (5) Puerto Rico: An Essay in the Definition of a National Culture; (6) The U.S. and the Dilemmas of Political Control; (7) Selected Trends and Issues in Contemporary Federal and Regional Relations; (8) The Netherlands, French and British Areas of the Caribbean; (9) Toward a Balance Sheet of Puerto Rican Migration; (10) Inventory of Government Documents: part 1, Departments, Agencies, and Instrumentalities of the Executive Branch of the Commonwealth of Puerto Rico; part 2, Federal Agencies with Offices in Puerto Rico. Together, the *Selected Background Studies* constitute one of the major informational sources on modern Puerto Rico.

F.C.

U.S. SELECT COMMISSION ON WESTERN HEMISPHERE IMMIGRATION (1965). In 1965, the U.S. Congress approved the establishment of a Select Commission on Western Hemisphere Immigration, composed of five presidential appointees, five senators, and five representatives. The commission studied such vital hemispheric and national issues as demographic, technological, and economic trends; unemployment; immigration; security; and inter-American relations. The commission's *Report* (1968) contains not only majority recommendations, but also minority positions on immigration ceilings and Cuban refugees. Significant are the 170 pages of research appendices laden with data, graphs, statistics, laws, syntheses, and future projections, which make this one of the most valuable single published sources available on Latin American immigration into the United States.

F.C.

UNITED STATES v. *BHAGAT SING THIND. See* Asian Indians.

UNITED STATES v. *BRIGNONI-PONCE. See* Aliens, Constitutional Rights.

UNITED STATES v. *GUE LIM* (1900). *See* Chinese.

UNITED STATES v. *WONG KIM ARK* (1898). *See* Chinese.

VANKA, MAXO. *See* Croatians.

VAN KLEEK, MARY (b. 1883). Social reformer; headed the Committee on Women's Work sponsored by the Russell Sage Foundation (*q.v.*) and founded in 1910. Van Kleek conducted a series of inquiries into women's work in bookbinding, artificial flower making, and the millinery trade. Most of the workers were immigrant women. "In these studies, [Van Kleek] conclusively proved the fallacy of the pin money theory and demonstrated that in case after case wages adjusted to the supposedly meager needs of the girl who 'lived at home' were a major cause of poverty and an important factor in perpetuating it" (Bremner). Chief works: *Women in the Bookbinding Trades* (1913); *Artificial Flower Makers* (1913); *A Seasonal Trade: A Study of the Millinery Trade in New York* (1917). In 1916, the Committee on Women's Work expanded its inquiries to include the work of men as well as women and was renamed the Division of Industrial Studies.

Reference
Robert H. Bremner, *From the Depths* (1956).

F.C.

VAN RAALTE, A. C. *See* Dutch.

VAN VORST, BESSIE (d. 1927). Social reformer. With her sister, Marie Van Vorst, she was author of *The Woman Who Toils, Being the Experiences of Two Ladies as Factory Girls* (1903), which reports their experiences among largely immigrant women workers in a Pittsburgh factory, a New York shirt factory, a Chicago theatrical costume factory, a Lynn, Massachusetts shoe factory, and a southern cotton mill.

Reference
Robert H. Bremner, *From the Depths* (1956).

F.C.

VASA ORDER OF AMERICA. *See* Swedes.

VEILLER, LAWRENCE T[URNURE] (d. 1943). Social reformer; served as secretary of the Tenement House Committee established by the Charity Organization Society of New York (*q.v.*) in 1898. Veiller arranged the famous tenement house exhibition in 1900 sponsored by the Tenement House Committee. The exhibits included over a thousand photographs, detailed maps of immigrant slum districts, numerous statistical tables and charts, and papier-mâché representations of tenement blocks. The exhibition was a notable success, and much of its material was included in the massive two-volume *The Tenement House Problem* (1903), co-edited by Robert W. De Forest (*q.v.*) and Veiller, which proved the most thorough and constructive examination made to date in any American city, but "also the most effective in securing remedial action." Veiller was also author of *Tenement House Legislation in New York, 1852–1900* (1900) [prepared for the Tenement House Commission], an indispensable register of legislative efforts in urban tenement reform. Lubove: "Veiller, America's first professional housing reform-er, not only changed the course of New York City's housing develop-ment, but influenced the housing history of states and cities throughout the nation in the two decades after 1900."

Reference
Roy Lubove, *The Progressives and the Slums: Tenement House Reform in New York City, 1890–1917* (1962).

F.C.

"VESTIBULE CLASSES." *See* New York City . . . *A Syllabus for Teaching English to "Grade C" Classes.*

VIENBE LIETUVNINKV. *See* Lithuanians.

VIERECK, LOUIS (1851–1922). Journalist, educator, popularizer of German culture in America. Viereck was one of the outstanding German-Americans of the late nineteenth and early twentieth century who sought to publicize the German contribution to American society. He belonged to a generation of German immigrants who came here after having participated in working for the working class in Germany and who continued to labor for the downtrodden in America. He was responsible for running two newspapers in the United States: the *Der deutsche Vorkämpfer* (1907–1910) and *Rundschau zweier Welten* (1911–12). In 1901 he saw the publication of *German Instruction in American Schools,* a historical overview of the role of the German language and German literature in American schooling on every level. In this book, as in many of his other writings, he sought to bring home the message that the German contribution to American education had been substantial since the colonial period and, if anything, had become more significant with the passage of time. He reminded readers that German immigrants had contributed the idea of the kindergarten, of the university seminar, and the study for the Ph.D. Viereck saw it as one of his tasks to combat the common prejudice that the Germans were boors who spent much of their time drinking. Viereck was one of the important bridge builders between American and German culture at the turn of the century.

Reference
George Bernstein, "Introduction" to Louis Viereck, *German Instruction in American Schools* (1978; original edition, 1901).

G.B.

VIETNAMESE. There are more than 700,000 persons of Vietnamese ancestry in the United States today, which makes them the fourth-largest group of Asian-Americans, following the Chinese, Filipinos, and Japanese. The 1990 census of population may well find them in third place. About three-quarters of them are refugees who have entered since 1975; another 50,000 are immigrants who left under the Orderly Departure Program established by Vietnam in 1980 in response to world pressure over the outpouring of refugees; the rest are American-born children of the refugees and immigrants. Before the fall of the South Vietnamese government which led to the exodus, only a small number of Vietnamese had come to the United States as students or as spouses of Americans. Thus, unlike other newcomers from Asia, the "first wave" of Vietnamese refugees found no established communities of their coethnics to greet them upon their arrival.

The reason that the bulk of the refugees who have escaped from Vietnam, Laos, and Kampuchea (Cambodia) have ended up in the United States is that the American government feels some responsibility for the consequences of its role in the war in those countries. The United States first became involved in Vietnam during the last days of French colonial rule. The Geneva Accords that ended hostilities between the Vietnamese and the French partitioned the country at the seventeenth parallel, pending a political settlement through a nationwide election, which was never held. As the French withdrew, President Dwight D. Eisenhower sent a personal envoy to assure newly installed Prime Minister Ngo Dinh Diem that he had America's support, which came in the form of U.S. $100 million in aid. Starting in 1955, the United States began sending aid to the Saigon government and training the South Vietnamese army.

Sporadic Communist insurgent activities began in 1957 in South Vietnam. Five years later, the United States increased the number of U.S. advisors posted there from 700 to 12,000. In August 1964, the North Vietnamese shelled the American destroyer *Maddox* in the Gulf of Tonkin. Within five days, Congress passed a resolution that gave President Lyndon B. Johnson extraordinary powers to act as he saw fit in Vietnam.

In February 1965, the United States began the first of many bombing raids on North Vietnam, and in March, the first American combat troops landed in South Vietnam. From then on, the war escalated. By the end of 1967, there were half a million American troops in the country. But when Communist forces captured several cities in central Vietnam during Tet (the lunar New Year) in 1968, the belief that the United States could win the war by the massive use of the most sophisticated and destructive weapons of modern warfare was shaken.

National security advisor (later secretary of state) Henry Kissinger began negotiating secretly with the North Vietnamese in early 1970. After protracted talks, the United States and North Vietnam signed a cease-fire agreement in late January 1973, over the opposition of South

Vietnamese President Nguyen Van Thieu, who had not been a party to the talks. American troops began withdrawing from Vietnam at the end of March. However, the civil war between north and south continued.

By March 1975, when Thieu's troops abandoned the highlands of central Vietnam, observers around the world thought that the fall of the Saigon government was imminent. On March 18, President Gerald Ford authorized the "parole" of 130,000 refugees into the United States and created the Interagency Task Force, with representatives from twelve agencies, to oversee the resettlement of the refugees so admitted. President Thieu left his country on April 25, 1975, as Americans, their Vietnamese dependents, and selected Vietnamese government and military personnel who were deemed "high risk" individuals were evacuated under chaotic conditions. South Vietnam surrendered on April 30. The last batch of evacuees were lifted out by helicopters the day before.

The "First Wave," 1975–79. Although Clark Air Force Base in the Philippines (which the United States still controls) was the most logical place to which to take the evacuees, in the end it was not used because Philippine president Ferdinand Marcos announced that Vietnamese refugees would not be welcome in his country. So, as a humanitarian gesture, Governor Ricardo Bordallo of Guam offered his hospitality, and the entire military population on Guam (about 10,000 persons) worked around the clock to clear 1,200 acres. In three days they built a tent city that could house 50,000 refugees at any one time. The first planeload landed two hours after orders were given to receive them. Troops in passing ships, civilians, and whoever else would volunteer—an additional 10,000 individuals—all pitched in to help. A massive logistical airlift brought supplies from other bases in the Pacific and from the continental United States.

Smaller numbers of evacuees were also taken to Thailand, the Philippines, Wake Island, and Hawaii. Of the 130,000 refugees evacuated, 95 percent were Vietnamese and the rest were Kampucheans, whose government had fallen (in less dramatic fashion) to the Khmer Rouge on April 17, 1975. Virtually no Laotian refugees came in the first batch because they were initially not granted parole status and had to be reviewed on a case-by-case basis. By August 1975, the ceiling of 130,000 refugees authorized for admission had already been exceeded by 1,000 persons, but the flow continued.

After being processed by the Immigration and Naturalization Service in Guam, the refugees were flown to four receiving centers in the United States: Camp Pendleton in southern California, Fort Chaffee in Arkansas, Fort Indiantown Gap in Pennsylvania, and Elgin Air Force Base in Florida. As soon as they arrived they were screened for security clearance and were given medical examinations and identification numbers. They also had to register with one of the nine voluntary agencies (dubbed "volags") which had contracted with the federal government to resettle them.

The volags, which received a grant of $500 for each refugee they aided, were the United States Catholic Conference, the Lutheran Immigration and Refugee Service, the International Rescue Committee, the United Hebrew Immigrant Aid Society, the World Church Service, the Tolstoy Foundation, the American Fund for Czechoslovak Refugees, the American Council for Nationalities Services, and Travelers' Aid–International Social Services. Since about 40 percent of the refugees were Catholics, the United States Catholic Conference played a major role in the resettlement process. Some tension developed between the Interagency Task Force which allowed the volags a maximum of forty-five days to find the refugees sponsors, and the professional staff of the organizations who wanted to do a more careful and protracted job of placing their clients.

Getting a sponsor was one of four ways refugees were allowed to leave the centers. Sponsors promised to provide food, clothing, and shelter until the refugees could fend for themselves. They also agreed to help the latter find employment, to enroll their children in school, and otherwise to ease their traumatic entry into American society. Almost 60 percent of the sponsors were families, 25 percent were churches and other organizations, and the rest were individuals.

Refugees could also leave the reception centers if they had at least $4,000 per household member to insure their self-sufficiency, if they arranged for resettlement in a third country, or if they requested repatriation to Vietnam. The vast majority (121,610 out of the initial 130,000) departed with a sponsor; only a few had sufficient cash to leave under their own auspices; some 1,500 persons were repatriated from Guam to Vietnam in October 1975 (but the requests for repatriation of those who had already reached the mainland were ignored); and a small number joined relatives who had resettled in other countries, mostly in France. All of the reception centers were closed by the end of December 1975.

The resettlement was financed under the terms spelled out in the Indochina Migration and Refugee Assistance Act of 1975. The federal government was to reimburse state governments for the cash assistance and the medical and social services that the refugees received. The Department of Health, Education, and Welfare (now the Department of Health and Human Services) also gave grants to public or nonprofit private agencies to provide English instruction, employment counseling, and mental health services to the refugees. When the 1975 act expired in 1977, a continuing resolution extended it for another year, but Congress did not allocate an appropriation until March 1978, thus disrupting services in many states for more than half a year.

Federal policy focused on finding gainful employment for the refugees as quickly as possible and on minimizing the burden on any single locality. Since many of the "first wave" refugees came from the elite stratum of their society—two-thirds had white-collar occupations, and two-fifths of those had professional, technical, or managerial backgrounds—they secured jobs rather speedily, although a large number suffered significant downward occupational mobility. As early as August 1975—that is, barely four months after their arrival—two-thirds of the men and half of the women had found employment. Two and a half years after their arrival, 95 percent of the men and more than 90 percent of the women who desired employment were working. However, many of the jobs were entry-level, minimum-wage positions, so quite a number of individuals held multiple jobs or worked overtime. Others continued to depend on public assistance, but households receiving cash assistance had declined from 44 percent in 1975 to only 19 percent two and a half years later.

The attempt to disperse the refugees did not turn out as policymakers had intended. Due to the importance of the extended family among Vietnamese, many refugees made determined efforts to reunite scattered family members and friends through secondary migration. California has been the favorite destination of a large number of secondary migrants. While the state received only 21 percent of the "first wave" refugees and between 25 to 30 percent of the "second wave," as a result of secondary migration, over 40 percent of all refugees from Vietnam, Kampuchea, and Laos now reside in California. Texas, the state with the second-largest number, is home to only about 10 percent. Vietnamese are drawn to California not only by the sizable Asian population in the state, but also by its warm climate and relatively generous public assistance programs.

The refugees have encountered considerable hostility in some localities. A number of incidents flared up in public housing projects, but refugee fishermen have perhaps met the most systematic opposition to their attempts to earn a living. White fishermen along the Gulf of Mexico and in Monterey Bay (California) have accused them of unfair competition and of not abiding by existing rules and regulations. Although tensions have subsided, the newcomers and the local fishermen still coexist today under an uneasy truce.

The Second Wave, 1979–present. The refugees who have arrived since 1979 have been much more heterogeneous than the "first wave" and can be divided into the "boat people" from Vietnam and the "land people" from Kampuchea and Laos. On the whole, they have been poorer, less educated, and more ethnically diverse—consisting mainly of Sino-Vietnamese, Kampucheans, lowland Lao, and Hmong—with a far smaller percentage of Catholics and many more Buddhists.

The post-1975 outflow of refugees from Vietnam reflects the fact that the Vietnamese government has alienated many people who had initially rejoiced over a Communist victory in the south. Even a few high-ranking members of the Vietcong have escaped, feeling betrayed by Hanoi, which made little effort to include them in the national government after the war ended. The family members of officials, civil servants, and soldiers of the former South Vietnamese government who have been sent to "re-education" camps, from which few have returned, have no love for the new government either. Severe economic hardships resulting from an ecology devastated by war, crop failures, a trade embargo by the United States, and the high cost of maintaining a large standing army (used to invade Kampuchea in late 1978 and to occupy it since then, as well as to fight a border war against China in early 1979), have all made life rather grim.

Chinese living in Vietnam, in particular, who had controlled retail trade in the country for centuries, were branded as undesirable "bourgeois" influences. As controls over them tightened, hundreds of thousands tried to escape. Over a quarter-million Sino-Vietnamese have been taken in by the People's Republic of China, while another estimated quarter-million have left in hastily equipped and grossly overcrowded small boats unfit for sailing on open seas. The plight of these so-called "boat people" captured the attention of the world, as they ran out of food, water, and fuel, were preyed upon by Thai pirates, and even after sighting shore were forbidden to land by authorities in neighboring Malaysia, Indonesia, and the Philippines. Some estimates place the loss of lives at 50 percent or more.

In the face of the massive outflow of both boat and land refugees, the United States committed itself in early 1979 to accepting 7,000 refugees a month. Later the same year, President Jimmy Carter doubled the number. Annual arrivals jumped from 20,400 in 1978, to 80,700 in 1979, to 166,700 in 1980. To deal with the situation, an international conference was convened at Geneva in 1979, during which the "first asylum" nations in Southeast Asia agreed not to turn refugees away if "second asylum" countries such as Australia, the United States, Canada, and France agreed to accept them for resettlement.

Also during 1979, Congress debated a bill concerning refugees. The 1980 Refugee Act adopted the United Nations definition of "refugee" and systematized procedures for admitting such persons; allowed refugees to acquire permanent resident alien status after one year's "conditional" stay in the country; and gave Congress, rather than the executive branch (through its parole authority), jurisdiction over refugee policy. From a 1981 figure of 132,500 entering refugees, the number has dropped, and now about 50,000 refugees from Vietnam, Kampuchea, and Laos are entering per year. Slightly over 50 percent come from Vietnam, 40 percent from Kampuchea, and the rest from Laos. Approximately another 5,000 persons from those countries (90 percent of them from Vietnam) now enter each year as bona fide immigrants.

The "second wave" refugees and immigrants have not done as well as the "first wave" in terms of achieving self-sufficiency. The 1980 Refugee Act provides special domestic resettlement assistance for eighteen months, with a three-year limitation on reimbursement for cash and medical payments. After that, refugees are treated the same way as other Americans by state and local public assistance programs. A 1983 study found that 37 percent of those who had been in the country for four years were receiving cash assistance while 64 percent of those who had been here for one year were doing so.

Contemporary Developments. Most of the studies done of the refugees so far have been either surveys documenting statistically measurable characteristics (particularly demographic and employment data) or clinical analyses probing the mental health aspects of refugee adaptation. Very little is known about the social and political organization of the communities that have emerged, except that like other immigrants, the Vietnamese have also formed many organizations that cater to their social, economic, and political needs. Hundreds of mutual assistance associations across the country, about 100 Buddhist temples (all, except one being built in East Palo Alto, California, housed in ordinary residential buildings or storefronts), some two dozen Catholic "personal parishes" (formerly called "national churches," which are based on ethnicity rather than geography), and a Vietnamese Presbyterian church (in Santa Ana, California) provide focal points for social, cultural, and spiritual activities. Groups such as the National United Front for the Liberation of Vietnam and the Vietnamese Organization to Exterminate Communism and Restore the Nation serve as channels for expressing the refugees' and immigrants' political concerns.

The public catches glimpses of the internal organization of Vietnamese-American communities only through occasional newspaper coverage or through its members' own interaction with Vietnamese. Journalists have focused on several topics: the superb academic performance of Vietnamese students such as Hoang Nhu Tran, valedictorian of the class of 1987 of the U.S. Air Force Academy and winner of a Rhodes Scholarship and future attendance at Harvard Medical School; the emergence of Vietnamese entrepreneurs who are revitalizing downtown areas in many cities, making them into "Little Saigons"; the increasing number of youth gangs and the rise of criminal activities; the murder of several individuals allegedly for political reasons; and the growth of religious organizations.

One recent train of events illustrates both the tension between the refugees/immigrants and the larger society and the internal cleavages within the communities the former have established. In San Jose, California, where about 70,000 Vietnamese now live and among whom there are some 7,000 Catholics, a feud has been raging since mid-1976 between a group of Vietnamese Catholics led by Thien Cong Tran, president of the Vietnamese Catholic Council, and Bai An Tran, a leader of the Committee for the Defense of Justice and Peace, and Bishop Pierre DuMaine of the Diocese of San Jose. Although five churches in the greater San Jose area now offer mass in Vietnamese, the two Trans and their followers wanted the Vietnamese mission at Our Lady Queen of Martyrs Church to be made into a personal parish, but the bishop said that cannot happen until they can financially support themselves in full. But the bishop's opponents considered his reticence to be an indication of his desire to assimilate them. They charged that when he replaced the popular Rev. Joseph Ting Van Nguyen with the Rev. Paul Luu Dinh Duong (who had not supported the request for a personal parish), he was in fact making sure that no personal parish would ever materialize.

The conflict escalated when the opponents of the bishop bodily barred the Rev. Duong from entering the church, which they then occupied. The bishop, for his part, locked the tabernacle and withdrew the two associate pastors from the mission, which meant that no mass could be said on the premises. He also excommunicated the two leaders, while the lawyer for the diocese obtained an injunction from the court ordering the occupiers to leave. The latter filed a countersuit against the diocese, claiming title to the church, arguing that they had not only contributed the downpayment but had also been making the monthly mortgage payments for the building. But church authorities said that making such payments does not give the group title to the property. The conflict spread when Vietnamese who supported the bishop formed their own organization, various individuals received threats, and disruptive behavior occurred during services at several other churches.

Even a mediator appointed by the pope failed to settle the controversy, which has both divided the Vietnamese community and roused considerable anti-Vietnamese sentiment. Although an accord was reached in May 1987, tensions have not yet subsided. Rumors spread that someone would immolate himself during the visit of Pope John Paul II to California in September; however, no such thing happened. The sore point involves the Rev. Duong, whom the bishop's critics continue to oppose for complex reasons that some observers think are related to regional antagonisms among the Vietnamese and others believe reflect a real struggle for power.

There is merit to the latter theory because the Catholic church in

Vietnam (like the Buddhist hierarchy there) had in fact been a power base in pre-1975 politics. Back in Vietnam, after many long years, a Vietnamese had finally been named archbishop, so being told now that they cannot have a church of their own—the daily administration of which they would control—seemed like a setback to the autonomy that many Vietnamese Catholics had acquired and dearly cherished. Moreover, the Vietnamese protestors are well aware that there is plenty of precedence in the history of American Catholicism for their request: the first "national church" was created by German immigrants in the late eighteenth century, while Catholics of Polish, Italian, and Portuguese ancestry in the United States have all successfully set up their own churches. For the Vietnamese, the church has assumed a special significance since the fall of the Saigon government. As Thien Cong Tran said, "To us who had to give up our country because we could not live under a communist regime, a personal parish is like an oasis in the desert." Seen in this light, the fierce battle that has raged becomes understandable. In a real sense, these developments mark the transformation of refugees into immigrants, who—like many other immigrants before them—are struggling to find a place for themselves in American society. In this instance, religion, rather than electoral politics, is providing the first arena for action.

References
Linda W. Gordon, "Southeast Asian Refugee Migration to the United States," in James T. Fawcett and Benjamin V. Carino, eds., *Pacific Bridges: The New Immigration from Asia and the Pacific Islands* (1987); Gail P. Kelly, *From Vietnam to America: A Chronicle of the Vietnamese Immigration Into the United States* (1977); Darrel Montero, *Vietnamese Americans: Patterns of Resettlement and Socioeconomic Adaptation in the United States* (1979); Paul J. Strand and Woodrow Jones, Jr., *Indochinese Refugees in America: Problems of Adaptation and Assimilation* (1985); U.S. Department of State, *Report of the Indochinese Refugee Panel* (1986).

S.C.

VIETNAMESE REFUGEES, family and community. Haines focuses on the maintenance, extent, and structure of family and community ties among Vietnamese refugees in the United States. The findings from a series of field efforts in northern Virginia indicate the continuing and pervasive importance of both family and community. The family, in particular, extends well beyond the boundaries of the household and is capable of furnishing significant amounts of emotional and practical support.

Reference
David W. Haines, "Family and Community Among Vietnamese Refugees," *International Migration Review* 15 (Spring/Summer 1981): 310–319.

F.C.

VIETNAMESE REFUGEES, opportunity systems surveys. Montero (*infra*) presents data, from the surveys of the refugees conducted by Opportunity Systems, Inc. (OSI) for HEW, about the resettlement and adaptation of the Vietnamese refugees to life in the United States. He includes a brief history of Vietnam, but the central objective is to analyze and document the background characteristics of the refugees and their progress in adjusting, economically and socially, to their new life during their first three years in America. A second objective is to develop a theory of spontaneous international migration (SIM), analyzing the Vietnamese experience in a broader sociohistorical context. The relatively brief text is supplemented by 125 pages of tables from the OSI surveys.

Reference
Daniel Montero, *Vietnamese Americans: Patterns of Resettlement and Socioeconomic Adaptation in the United States* (1979).

F.C.

VIETNAMESE REFUGEES, research. The article (*infra*) was written with two objectives: first, to describe some of the critical methodological problems encountered in research with Vietnamese refugees in San Diego, California, about which few studies have been conducted previous to their arrival in 1975; second, to discuss the policy implications of research beset with these difficulties, some of which are unique to studies of refugee populations per se, while others are common to research on small ethnic minorities in general. This article focuses on four major issues: the quality of refugee studies; the purpose and functions of such research; the ethical dilemmas of studying refugees; and public policy implications of refugee research. Recommendations are offered to resolve some of these issues which would call for policy changes both in the ways refugee research are conducted, and in the training of researchers themselves.

Reference
Elena S. H. Yu and William T. Liu, "Methodological Problems and Policy Implications in Vietnamese Refugee Research," *International Migration Review* 20 (Summer 1986): 483–501.

F.C.

VILLARD, OSWALD GARRISON. *See* NAACP.

VILMIS. *See* Lithuanians.

VINELAND [NEW JERSEY] TRAINING SCHOOL FOR FEEBLE-MINDED GIRLS AND BOYS. *See* Goddard, Henry H.

VIRGIN ISLANDS. *See* Danes.

VIRGIN ISLANDS, alien legalization program. North (*infra*) states:

> The United States Congress, as this is written [1983], is contemplat-
> ing an immigration reform package along the lines of the Simpson-
> Mazzoli bills, which passed the Senate, but not the House, last year.
> One of the principal elements of that package is a proposed legaliza-
> tion program (or amnesty) for many aliens currently in the nation
> but out of legal status. Meanwhile in a totally separate action, the
> Congress last year passed the Virgin Islands Nonimmigrant Alien
> Adjustment Act of 1982 (Public Law 97-271), a small-scale legal-
> ization program. It is my belief that, although the Virgin Islands
> program is tiny and specialized, it can be regarded as a trial run for
> alien legalization on the Mainland. In both instances, there is a body
> of aliens with historical grounds for disliking the Immigration and
> Naturalization Service (INS); in both the Government has decided
> to change the basic rules of the immigration game retroactively, and
> to provide a substantial benefit for an alien population; and in both
> INS is working with (or contemplating working with) voluntary
> agencies. Further, the medical screening that accompanies the Vir-
> gin Islands program is likely to be duplicated on the Mainland.
> There are, of course, substantial differences, but the similarities are
> such that we decided to examine the administration of Public Law
> 97-271 hoping to learn some lessons for the Mainland.

Reference
David S. North, *The Virgin Islands Alien Legalization Program: Lessons for the Mainland* (1983).

F.C.

VISITING NURSE MOVEMENT. The emergence and development
of visiting nursing in pre–World War I America is to be understood in
the context of the social forces and factors that influenced the practice of
visiting nursing. In the latter part of the nineteenth and the early twentieth century, New York City was coping with the problems of inadequate housing, inadequate facilities for the care of the sick poor, and a
population that was growing rapidly from immigration. Visiting nursing
began as a response to the health needs of the people of New York City.
These health needs were not being met by the medical profession, as
they extended beyond the scope of medical practice, and they were not
being met by philanthropic workers, who lacked the necessary skills to
cope with varied medical and social problems. Finally, the health needs
were not being met by institutional care, as approximately 90 percent of
the sick poor remained at home during illness.

Reference
Gloria G. B. Caliandro, "The Visiting Nurse Movement in the Borough of Manhattan, New York City, 1877–1917," Ph.D. dissertation, Columbia University, 1970 (DA 32:1680-B).

F.C.

VLADECK, B[ARUCH] CHARNEY (1886–1938). Socialist, Jewish labor leader. Born in 1886 in Dukor, Lithuania, a tiny, predominantly Jewish town, Vladeck migrated in 1908 to the United States, where after World War I he emerged as a spokesman for the Jewish labor movement of New York City. He was an opponent of the Communist wing of the Socialist party. Vladeck was for many years associated with the New York City *Jewish Daily Forward* (*q.v.*), as manager of its Philadelphia edition, and after 1916 as editor of the New York City *Forward*.

Reference
Franklin L. Jones, "The Early Life and Career of B. Charney Vladeck, 1886–1921. The Emergence of an Immigrant Spokesman," Ph.D. dissertation, New York University, 1972 (DA 33: 698-A).

F.C.

VOLPE LANDI, JOHN BAPTIST, MARQUIS (1841–1918). From Piacenza, Italy; a prominent Catholic layman and social activist. He became Bishop John Baptist Scalabrini's right hand for all initiatives dealing with lay people working for migrants. He was appointed, by Bishop Scalabrini, president of the Diocesan Committee of the Opera dei Congressi, which was in 1881 the strongest organizing force for Italian Catholics in a field that was at once religious, social, and political. Marquis Volpe Landi was one of the pioneers of the Opera dei Congressi and of social action on behalf of the poor. He was active in the Benevolent Society for aid to migrants, which had been proposed by Bishop Scalabrini and approved by Leo XIII on June 26, 1887. The society was composed of both the church-affiliated and the laity and was to assist the spiritual and material needs of the Italians on both their departure and their arrival. In 1894 the Benevolent Society was renamed the St. Raphael Society because its beginning and structure were similar to the German society of the same name, founded in Magdeburg in 1871 and approved by Leo XIII in 1878. Marquis Volpe Landi became the first president of the St. Raphael Society, which was organized with a central committee in Piacenza and local committees in the ports of embarkation and debarkation, as well as in those Italian cities that contributed the most or evidenced the greatest awareness of the migrant phenomenon. Father Pietro Bandini of Forli (1853–1917) founded the St. Raphael Society in New York.

Marquis Volpe Landi was also Scalabrini's valued collaborator in his contacts with the government to promote the new Italian immigration laws of 1901, which included many changes suggested by the memorandum to Foreign Minister Visconti-Venosta, written by Scalabrini with the cooperation of Volpe Landi and Father Pietro Maldotti. Marquis Volpe Landi wrote with Peter Paul Cahensly the "Lucern Memorandum" to the Vatican on April 16, 1891, requesting priests and bishops of the same nationality of the immigrants.

References
Giovanni Baltista Volpe Landi, "Emigrazione: sue cause, suoi bisogni, suoi provvedimenti," *Atti del I Congresso Catholico Italiano degli studiosi di Scienze Sociali* (Genova, Oct. 8–11) 1 (1893): 236–238; G. B. Volpe Landi, "Il problema dell'emigrazione," *Revista Internazionale di scienze sociali e discipline ausiliarie* 13 (1897): 500–520; G. B. Volpe Landi and Pietro Maldotti, *Società di Patronato per gli Emigranti, Relazione . . . il Ministro degli Esteri* (1896).

L.F.T.

VON GRAFFENRIED, CHRISTOPH. *See* Swiss.

VON HERFF, FERDINAND (1820–1912). Physician; led a group of German immigrants in 1847 to establish a commune in Texas. The ill-fated commune venture, called Bettina, was sponsored by the Mainzer Adelsverein, the Society for the Protection of German Immigrants in Texas. Members of the commune did not cooperate among themselves, and within a year the commune failed. Herff used his experience in Texas to formulate plans for the emigration of 20,000 Germans to Texas, a venture he described in a treatise on the incremental transplantation of the German proletariat to Texas by a heavily financed national organization. This grandiose scheme called for a controlled economy, directed production and distribution, and curtailed personal liberty designed so that the lower classes could rise by their own efforts to become decent and worthy citizens of their new fatherland. The plan was never implemented, but Herff and his family returned to Texas in 1849.

References
Henry B. Dielmann, "Dr. Ferdinand Herff, Pioneer Physician and Surgeon," *Southwestern Historical Quarterly* 57 (1954): 268–284; Arthur L. Finck, "A Translation and Edition of Ferdinand Herff's *Die Geregelte Auswanderung des deutschen Proletariats . . . auf Texas*," Ph.D. dissertation, University of Texas, 1949.

D.N.A.

VON ZINZENDORF, NICHOLAS LOUIS. *See* Danes.

VUCINICH, VUK. *See* Serbs.

VULTURUL. *See* Romanians.

WALD, LILLIAN (1867–1940). Social reformer; a leader in nursing who was active in health and social work among immigrants in New York City's Lower East Side. Wald founded the Henry Street (New York City) Settlement House, whose visiting nurse services were pioneering efforts. Chief works: *The House on Henry Street* (1915); *Windows on Henry Street* (1934). The Lillian Wald papers are in the New York Public Library.

References
Doris Groshen Daniels, "Lillian Wald: The Progressive Woman and Feminism," Ph.D. dissertation, City University of New York, 1977; Sally Rogow, *Lillian Wald* (1966).

F.C.

WALLING, WILLIAM ENGLISH. *See* NAACP.

WALTHER, CARL FERDINAND WILHELM (1811–1887). Lutheran clergyman. Walther emigrated to America in 1839, and settled in Missouri where he served in Perry County as pastor. With others he founded a school at Altenburg in 1839, which moved in 1850 to St. Louis and became the Concordia Theological Seminary. Pastor in St. Louis after 1841, Walther became professor of theology in Concordia Seminary in 1850. As early as 1844, he had begun the publication of *Der Lutheraner,* and he organized the Missouri Synod where he served as president in 1847–1850 and 1864–1878. Walther stressed the importance of parochial education and emphasized that youth should be instructed in Lutheranism in the German language. He is considered the greatest Lutheran clergyman in nineteenth-century America.

D.N.A.

WAR BRIDES ACT OF 1945. Passed during the first session of the 79th Congress, introduced by Representative Samuel Dickstein of New York; it allowed alien wives, children, and husbands of the members of the U.S. armed forces to come as nonquota immigrants, and eliminated provisions concerning mental and physical defectives. The bill was signed into law on December 28, 1945.

D.N.A.

WARD, ROBERT DE COURCY (1867–1931). Educator, climatologist. Taught at Harvard University from 1890. Ward was active in the Immigration Restriction League (*q.v.*) with Prescott F. Hall (*q.v.*)

which was "determined to mount a counteroffensive against the strange invaders who seemed so grave a threat to their class, their region, their country, and their race" (Higham, 102).

Reference
John Higham, *Strangers in the Land: Patterns of American Nativism, 1860–1925* (1965).

F.C.

WARE, CAROLINE (b. 1908). Social worker, specialist on community development; taught at Vassar College, Sarah Lawrence, American University, University of Puerto Rico, and Howard University School of Social Work. Ware was a consultant on community development to the Organization of American States, and a contributor to the UNESCO-sponsored *History of Mankind*. Ware's classic *Greenwich Village, 1920–1930* (1935; new Preface, 1965)

> examines a sample of America's past population of immigrants who had come at the rate of a million persons a year in the peak years before World War I, at a time when they were striving to find a place in American urban life. . . . It catches the older, American-born children of this mass migration just as they were coming of age, facing the rejection of depression and joblessness, and thereafter the trauma of war.

F.C.

WARNER, AMOS GRISWOLD (1861–1900). Sociologist who taught economics at Nebraska and Stanford universities. Warner's *American Charities: A Study in Philanthropy and Economics* (1894; rpt. 1971) was a standard text of the period on poverty and charity that emphasized hereditary weakness. It is important for understanding attitudes toward poverty and the immigrant child and family.

F.C.

WASHINGTON, BOOKER T. *See* Afro-Americans.

WEINSTEIN, GREGORY (1864–1931). Essayist, social reformer. Weinstein is author of *The Ardent Eighties* (with a Foreword by Lillian Wald, 1928), an intimate portrayal of life in the urban minority subcommunity and of the world of work in late nineteenth century urban America; it contains biographical and critical accounts of social reformers, e.g., Stanton Coit, Henry George, Felix Adler, Lillian Wald, and Josephine Shaw Lowell.

F.C.

WELCH ACT. *See* Filipino Depatriation Act of 1935.

WELSH. The Celtic people in the mountainous country of Cymru, or Wales, migrated in three directions after 1790: eastward to the manufacturing centers of England; southward to the coal fields and steel towns in South Wales, a booming area until 1920; and westward to North America, the last being the smallest flow of emigrants. One can spot a handful of Welsh in the first settlements of Virginia and Massachusetts, but the largest concentration sprang up near Philadelphia, because the Quakers led by William Penn recruited Welsh Quakers and Baptists. These newcomers left their impact and nomenclature—Bryn Mawr, Haverford, Llanerch—but they had lost most of their identity by the time of the Revolution. Estimates based on the census of 1790 assign 4.3 percent of the nation's population to the Welsh, a figure lower in total and in proportion to those for the English, Scots, and Irish.

Emigration and Settlement. The United States census bureau recorded only 94,894 Welsh immigrants between 1820 and 1976, a total considerably less than the true figure because officials often lumped the Welsh in with the English. Four out of five immigrants arrived after 1880, the influx peaking in 1890 at approximately 100,000. Thirty years later estimates of Welsh stock (immigrants and their children) exceeded 250,000.

Five states—Pennsylvania, Ohio, New York, Illinois, Wisconsin—attracted the great majority of Welsh families. Almost half of the Welsh born, in 1900, had settled in Pennsylvania because the coal mine operators around Scranton and Wilkes-Barre and the managers of steel mills in Pittsburgh and nearby towns hired and even recruited skilled miners, puddlers, and rollers. Families from rural Wales often bought farms in the Appalachian uplands, and their butter sold at premium prices. Oneida County in central New York, Cambria in Pennsylvania, and Paddy's Run and the Welsh Hills in Ohio had small settlements by the opening years of the nineteenth century. By the 1840s Welsh families had discovered the fertile land of Wisconsin, and after the Civil War the prairie states, notably Iowa, Kansas, and Minnesota, had Welsh enclaves. Converts to Mormonism settled in Utah, and almost every mining town in the western mountains had its Welsh contingent.

Adjustment and Assimilation. Adjustment to American society came more easily for the Welsh than for most immigrants if only because they were British, and thus members of the dominant group. Furthermore, they were evangelical Protestants: Presbyterians (Calvinist Methodists in Wales), Congregationalists, Baptists, and Methodists (Wesleyans in Wales). In fact they matched American denominational patterns more closely than the Scots (Church of Scotland) and the English (mainly Church of England). Moreover, a series of revivals had swept Wales after 1735 paralleling the colonial Great Awakening. Subsequently, the events leading to the Revolutionary War, the wartime upheaval, and the political debates thereafter led to a decline in religious activity in America, whereas revivalism and the spread of Sunday Schools continued to dominate Welsh life. In 1818 Hugh Jones, who had settled in Utica, complained that "there is no difference between work days and Sundays here." After 1825 the Finney revivals swept through the northern states and Welsh immigrants joined hands with American reformers, crusading for temperance and limits on slavery expansion.

Most immigrants arrived with sufficient skills to secure a comfortable living, although recessions and strikes brought hard times to many communities. During the great strikes of the 1870s some miners led the fight for better wages, but they had as much antagonism toward Irish and Slavic miners as for the capitalists. The Protestant work ethic remained strong among the Welsh, who identified closely with the republican ideal of individualism and civic virtue represented by such figures as Benjamin Franklin. Essentially egalitarian in nature, community life in Wales encouraged and recognized individuals of talent, whether preachers, musicians, or poets. The Welsh peasants distrusted the landed gentry and the coal operators of South Wales, who preferred to associate with English aristocrats and industrial magnates.

Old-stock Americans in the northern states generally favored the Republican party after its emergence in 1855–56. The Welsh joined this party in overwhelming numbers partly because the Democratic party catered to the Catholic Irish, the opponents of Prohibition, and the defenders of slavery. Republican leaders cultivated the Welsh vote, sizable in Pennsylvania, by nominating Welsh-Americans in local races. In 1916 Charles Evans Hughes, the son of a Baptist minister, ran for president on the Republican ticket and later became chief justice of the United States. "Puddler Jim" Davis was appointed secretary of labor by President Calvin Coolidge, a post that was also offered to John Llewelyn Lewis, the leader of the United Mine Workers Union, 1920–1960. Although supporters of the Labor party and socialism captured the majority of parliamentary seats, their American cousins became staunch conservatives.

Loyalty to their language was the major barrier to rapid assimilation for immigrants. Professor Rowland Berthoff observed: "of all the British-Americans they were the most anxious to preserve the culture—particularly the language—of their fatherland." Isolated and homogeneous communities such as Remsen in Oneida County, the slate villages on the New York–Vermont border, and the Blue Earth district of Minnesota retained the language for two or even three generations. The Hyde Park area of Scranton and the Corn Hill section of Utica had enough Welsh families to maintain the Welsh language well after the immigrant generation. The constant loss of young people was more than offset by the influx of immigrants. Once the flow of immigrants slowed in the 1920s and ended during the years of the Great Depression, almost all churches found it necessary to drop the Welsh language.

Communal solidarity led to a high rate of in-marriage in Welsh settlements. For example, in Utica's Moriah Presbyterian Church during the period between 1909 and 1931, 46 out of a total of 160 marriages involved a non-Welsh partner. Between 1932 and 1954 out of 165 marriages, 128 involved a non-Welsh partner. Thereafter only 6 percent married persons of Welsh descent. This trend was also observed in Columbus, Ohio, and Minneapolis.

Culture. The *eisteddfod,* a festival in which individuals vied with each other for prizes in singing, writing, and reciting, reached America in the 1850s. At first the emphasis was on excellence in writing poems, stories, and essays. Gradually sponsors added recitations, orations, and especially vocal music. Members of the audience evaluated the various performances and eagerly awaited the detailed adjudication of experts such as Dr. Daniel Protheroe, a distinguished composer in Chicago. The *eisteddfod* flourished in the period between 1875 and World War I. Choirs of more than one hundred voices traveled long distances to compete for handsome prizes such as those offered at the Chicago World's Fair of 1893. The success of this institution led to the formation of a National Eisteddfod Association in 1923, and for the next decade various centers conducted festivals. The decline of immigration and the depressed times in the 1930s saw most communities give up this festival, and only a handful survived after World War II.

The *Gymanfa Ganu* or singing assembly developed somewhat later than the *eisteddfod* and in the twentieth century became the most popular institution in Welsh-American circles. Even third-generation individuals and persons of no Welsh blood enjoyed singing *Cwm Rhondda* and other hymns in four-part harmony. At first churches of one denomination would meet together, but later the meetings became ecumenical. A *gymanfa* at Niagara Falls in 1929 attracted more than two thousand participants and its success led to the formation of a national association, which has sponsored an annual festival on Labor Day weekend. Thousands have journeyed to Los Angeles, Toronto, Columbus (1986), and St. Paul (1987). Conductors have discovered that they must use the English words for most hymns.

Publications sprang up to strengthen denominational loyalties and to give individuals in widely scattered communities information about relatives and news of the Old Country. In 1938 *Cyfaill o'r Hen Wlad* (Friend of the Old Country) printed its first number for the Presbyterians (Calvinist Methodists), and this monthly survived until 1933. The Congregationalists and the Baptists also had monthlies published in Oneida County. In 1860 *Y Drych* (The Mirror) moved from New York City to Utica, its home for almost a century before it shifted its base to Wisconsin. The *Cambrian* (1880–1920) began in Cincinnati but moved to Utica. Published in English, it served individuals interested in Welsh history and institutions. The Welsh collection at the Utica Public Library has most of the one hundred or so books published in Welsh in Oneida County.

The ethnic revival that touched many groups besides blacks after the 1960s had considerable impact upon Welsh-Americans. In 1975 *Ninnau* (We Ourselves) appeared as a rival to *Y Drych;* both contain news about new groups of Welsh-Americans in various centers. Welsh-Americans, however, have little knowledge of current trends in Wales, whether in rugby, the Labor party, or the nationalist movement. They view Wales with nostalgia; and a few place decals on their car bumpers: Thank God, I'm Welsh.

References

Alan Conway, ed., *The Welsh in America* (1961); Arthur H. Dodd, *The Character of Early Welsh Emigration to the United States* (1957); David Maldwyn Ellis, "The Assimilation of the Welsh in Central New York," *New York History* 53 (July 1972): 299–333; Edward George Hartmann, *Americans from Wales* (1967); R. Brinsley Jones, ed., *Anatomy of Wales* (1972).

D.M.E.

WENDS. The Wends [Sorbs] are part of the Slavonic people, but because of their small number and their failure to establish a political unit, they are comparatively unknown. Since the time of recorded history they have occupied the area between the Elbe and Oder rivers in eastern Europe. As a result of contact and conflict with the Germanic people, the Sorbian area was restricted so that at the present time they live in a region of Lusatia, southeast of Berlin, around the two major towns of Bautzen and Cottbus.

At the time of migration, in the nineteenth century, these people were called Wends, a German term given to Slavs in general. While "Wends" has remained as the name used in North America and Australia, the preferred term in Lusatia is "Sorb," which is derived from *Srbi,* a term from their own language. Their language is divided into two dialects, Upper Sorbian, spoken in southern Lusatia, and resembling Czech, and Lower Sorbian, spoken in northern Lusatia, resembling Polish. Although some Sorbs remained Roman Catholic, most became Lutheran in 1530, after the Council of Augsburg.

Both religious and economic motives were influential causes for migration. Some Sorbs, living in Prussia, objected to the attempt of the Prussian rulers to force a union of Lutherans and Calvinists into a single state church. Saxon Wends, on the other hand, objected to the rationalism of the Saxon church which encouraged laxity in religious life Jan Kilian was the pastor who spoke out against both tendencies and was the spiritual leader of the Wends who migrated to Texas. Economic factors resulting from population growth, the failure of the potato crop and wheat harvests, and widespread poverty influenced others to migrate. Beginning in the late 1840s, groups of Sorbs left for Australia Canada, South Africa, and the United States.

The major migration to the United States took place in 1854 when more than 500 Wends traveled to Liverpool and there transferred to a ship bound for Galveston to pick up more cotton for the English mills. A few Wends had migrated earlier as part of the German migration to Texas, and more followed in the three decades after the Civil War.

Most of the Wends became farmers, and the 1854 migrants purchased land near what became Serbin, in Lee County. From that base, Wends expanded to other communities in Lee and neighboring counties and also to the Rio Grande Valley and northward to Vernon. Many in succeeding generations sought employment in cities such as Houston, Austin, and Port Arthur.

Although the Wendish language was used in church and school until 1920, many Wends knew German in Europe and the remainder learned it in Texas. Even though the Wends have maintained their ethnic identity to the present day, they first changed to German as a common language. Then, as a result of World War I and II and also because of the decline of rural isolation, German gave way to English. Wendish continues as a third language for a few residents, while German is widely used among the older people. In 1971 the Texas Wendish Heritage Society was formed to help preserve the tradition and in 1987 the foundation was laid in Serbin for a new building to house the Wendish museum.

References
Anne Blasig, *The Wends of Texas* (1954); George R. Nielsen, *In Search of a Home: The Wends (Sorbs) on the Australian and Texas Frontier* (1977); Gerald Stone, *The Smallest Slavonic Nation: The Sorbs of Lusatia* (1972).

G.R.N.

WEST INDIAN IMMIGRANTS. Immigration from the West Indies to the United States was quite limited until the twentieth century. While many of the slaves who were brought to the United States from Africa spent several months in the West Indies for "seasoning," they were not there long enough to qualify as West Indian immigrants. One of the earliest free blacks to immigrate from the islands was Prince Hall, who came to Boston shortly before the Revolution. He founded the African

odge as a self-help organization for Afro-Americans. In so doing he
established a leadership role which has been followed by many of his
successors.

In the twentieth century, West Indians found themselves living in
an economically depressed region, and many, who believed that emigration was the only avenue to personal advancement, left for the more
affluent, industrialized nations of Europe and America. The 1924 immigration act established quotas stifling the influx of immigrants from
southern and eastern Europe, but it failed to control the flow of immigrants from America's neighbors in the Western Hemisphere. Besides
the economic stimulus, political oppression in Cuba and Haiti provided
further incentive for immigration into the States. These groups, however, will be given fuller treatment in separate articles. This discussion
will focus on those coming from the British West Indies. Many of them
maintained their British citizenship for a long time; they seemed to hope
that it would be some protection against American racism. It was also a
way to try to hold on to some sense of uniqueness. Because they had
been members of the Church of England, they now adopted the American Episcopal church. Most black Episcopalians have a British West
Indian heritage.

The Bureau of the Census calculates that about 1 percent of American blacks are of West Indian origin. Early in the century most settled in
New York City, and perhaps as much as 15 percent of the population of
Harlem were from the Caribbean. Recently, they have also settled in
urban centers in the Southeast and West. Early in the century, their
literacy rate was higher than for most incoming groups. Many started
small businesses and became property owners. They were also prominent in political and cultural leadership activities.

Scholars have long debated why West Indian immigrants usually
are better than the average of Afro-Americans. Certainly, they too had
suffered the brunt of both slavery and racism. Nevertheless, in America, they tended to stick together and to outperform other blacks. First,
the act of immigrating was a selective factor in itself, appealing to those
who were more motivated and discontented. Second, although slavery
in the West Indies was very harsh, it may not have created as much
dependency. Because whites were fewer in number, slaves had to be
taught many skills if work was to be done. Masters also provided plots
of land for the slaves to grow crops and feed themselves. Slaves in the
United States were seldom taught any craft, and the master provided
them with their food and clothing. West Indian slaves even had some
experience in marketing their own produce and having money of their
own. Finally, slavery in the Indies was ended a whole generation
sooner. After its termination, because of the much higher proportion of
blacks, they were needed in a larger range of employment. Not that

racism was so much less, but their numbers meant that they could not b
limited to jobs at the very bottom. These differences may account fo
their entrepreneurial activities in the United States.

Besides involvement in business, West Indians became promine
in community affairs, politics, and the arts. Undoubtedly, the bes
known political leader was Marcus Garvey, who came from Jamaica i
1916 and brought the United Negro Improvement Association with hir
he was deported a decade later, however. Malcolm X, who was th
charismatic spokesman for the Black Muslims in the 1950s and earl
1960s, also had a West Indian heritage—his mother came from Gre
nada and his father had worked for Garvey. Shirley Chisholm's paren
came from Barbados; she became a political leader in New York Cit
politics and was also a congresswoman. Stokely Carmichael was bor
in Trinidad and came to the States as a youth. He was a leader in bot
the Student Nonviolent Coordinating Committee and in the Black Pa
thers during the 1950s and 1960s. However, he became disillusione
with America and moved to Africa. Perhaps the most famous We
Indian immigrant in the arts was Claude McKay. He came from Jamaic
to study agriculture but soon changed to writing, and is best known as
poet; has also written several novels, and he was one of the inspirers c
the Negro Renaissance during the 1920s. Although the singer Harr
Belafonte was born in the States, as a child his parents took him wit
them back to Jamaica. After only five years they returned to America
and he went on to be well known as a singer of West Indian–styl
music, reaching the peak of his popularity in the 1950s and 1960s.

References
R. W. Palmer, "A Decade of West Indian Migration to the United States," *Social an
Economic Studies* 23 (1974): 571–587; Lennox Raphael, "West Indians and Afro-Amer
cans," *Freedom Ways* (Summer 1964): 438–445; Thomas Sowell, *American Ethn
Groups* (1978).

N.C

WEST INDIANS, beliefs and values. Glantz compares the attitud
toward work and the American legal system of English-speaking Wes
Indians who arrived in New York in 1971–72 with those of American
born blacks. West Indians are generally more optimistic about thei
chances, see the police as fairer, and are convinced that hard wor
rather than violence will pay off.

Reference
Oscar Glantz, "Native Sons and Immigrants: Some Beliefs and Values of American Bor
and West Indian Blacks at Brooklyn College," *Ethnicity* 5 (1978): 189–202.

F.C

WEST SLAVS. *See* Slavs.

WESTERN BOHEMIAN FRATERNAL ASSOCIATION. *See* Czechs.

WESTERN FEDERATION OF MINERS. *See* Irish.

WHEATON, HARRISON H[YLAS] (b. 1884). Educator; specialist in immigrant education. See his "Recent Progress in the Education of Immigrants," *Annual Report* 1 (U.S. Commissioner of Education) (1914): 425–454; "Survey of Adult Immigrant Education," *Immigrants in America Review* 1 (June 1915): 42–71; "United States Bureau of Education and the Immigrant," *Annals of the American Academy of Political and Social Science* 67 (Sept. 1916): 273–283; "Education of Immigrants," *Annual Report* 1 (U.S. Commissioner of Education) (1916): 425–454.

F.C.

WHITE SLAVE TRADE AND THE IMMIGRANTS. In its encyclopedic study of immigration, the Immigration Commission (*q.v.*), convened by the United States Congress in 1907 (and whose *Reports* constituted 41 volumes) did not neglect the white slave trade and the immigrants. In its report on "Importation and Harboring of Women for Immoral Purposes," the commission observed:

> The importation and harboring of alien women and girls for immoral purposes and the practice of prostitution by them—the so-called "white slave traffic"—is the most pitiful and the most revolting phase of the immigration question. It is in violation of the immigration law and of the agreement of 1904 between the United States and other powers for the repression of the trade in white women.

This business had assumed such large proportions and was exerting so evil an influence upon our country that the Immigration Commission felt compelled to make it the subject of a thorough investigation. Since the subject is especially liable to sensational exploitation, the Commission's report is primarily a statement of undeniable facts calculated to form a basis of reasonable legislative and administrative action to lessen its evils.

There is little question that prostitution was a vexing problem to the immigration authorities who administered the offices through which millions of immigrants entered the New World. The commission, of course, was restrictionist in its views, and prostitution was seen as peculiarly European accommodation against which the United State had to protect itself:

> Owing to the difference between the European and American views regarding prostitution, cooperation for the suppression of the white slave traffic can be expected from most of the European nations only along certain lines. Most European countries are rigid in their regulations regarding the procuring for purposes of prostitution of minor girls or of any women by means of fraud and deceit. Women who are of age, however, and who enter the business of their own accord are not interfered with. From continental countries where the conditions exist practically no cooperation could be expected to prevent the sailing of professional prostitutes to the United States. They probably would cooperate to prevent the seduction of minors or the fraudulent or forcible exportation of their women. In the main, however, the United States Government must rely upon its own officials for the prevention of this traffic.

However xenophobic the view (although there is ample documen tation available to illustrate the continuing concern of emigrating na tions), the commission's report on the white slave trade proved "liabl to exploitation." The New York afternoon papers on November 21 1902, carried the story of large-scale vice raids in Philadelphia that ha revealed the existence of an international ring trafficking in young girls It was said that the ring had its headquarters in Germany, with branche in Philadelphia and New York, and that its business was to supply girl for "disorderly houses" in those two cities, in Baltimore, Chicago, an elsewhere. According to reports, the raids had been made at the instanc of the German consul in Philadelphia on advice from his ambassador i Washington. Most of the girls picked up in the raids were said to b Jewish, and Rabbi Joseph Krauskopf of the Keneseth Israel Synagogue who had taken part in the preliminary investigation, was interviewin them. Representatives of the Protestant Episcopal church and of th Baron de Hirsch colony in Woodbine, New Jersey, were assisting him It quickly developed that there were French, Italian, and other girl among those picked up and taken to City Hall for examination and trial The girls were recruited over much of Europe under a variety of fals promises, it was reported, and were shipped through the Port of Nev York and sold into absolute slavery.

The whole problem of immigration, which was rising to floo proportions in these years, was discussed at great length in a conferenc held at Madison Square Garden in New York in December 1905, unde the auspices of the National Civic Federation. There was much re strictionist sentiment expressed by delegates who came from fort ates, but white slavery was not once mentioned in the accounts of the conference, nor in the resolutions adopted at its close. Nevertheless, Commissioner Robert Watchorn, who had succeeded Williams at Ellis Island, a few weeks later expressed concern at the traffic. New York City was now the center of the white slave traffic of the world, he told newsmen. "Many Hebrews, Italians and Frenchmen come over here to earn a living in a criminal way, sending back for young women," he said. "The women are well drilled on the other side and when they get here know enough to say that the men who meet them are relatives, sometimes their brothers."

As the great Jewish immigration from eastern Europe developed, a new contingent of alien prostitutes appeared. Like every other major migration, this one contained its criminal element. Jewish gamblers, thieves, and procurers quickly adapted themselves to the corrupt political system that controlled the Lower East Side, where Jews and Italians were displacing the older Irish and German elements, and formed alliances with the Irish politicians who dominated Tammany Hall.

The great wave of Italian immigration followed and accompanied the Jewish. Italian colonies appeared in different parts of New York City, but the greatest concentration developed alongside that of the Jews on the Lower East Side. More often even than was the case with the Jews, Italian immigrants were men coming alone. They furnished much of the unskilled labor force on widely dispersed construction projects, and tended to return to the district during slack seasons. They formed a booming market for female companionship. Abetted by local Tammany chiefs, Italian pimps set out to satisfy it. Writing in about 1900 for the U.S. Industrial Commission, Kate H. Claghorn reviewed the situation that had developed on the Lower East Side in recent years. Living in crowded tenements, Hebrews and Italians alike were thrown in with "the corrupt remnants of Irish immigration." The Bowery, with the Italians on one side and the Hebrews on the other, was "the focal line" of the evil influences that had developed under the existing administration. "Until within a very few years," Miss Claghorn stated, "the Italian laboring population in New York was notably free from glaring vice and intemperance. There were few or no disorderly resorts for Italians, and such practice as the importation of Italian women for immoral purposes was unknown." Under existing conditions in the city, however, "positive inducements having been given for the extension of vice of all kinds, many disorderly resorts have been opened in their most crowded quarters, and it is said that many Italian girls from Naples and other cities have been imported to fill them."

As a new immigration law began to shape up in 1906, including a number of additional restrictions, the only provision relating to prostitution at first was one proposed by Commissioner Watchorn of Ellis

Island. This broadened the exclusion of prostitutes by extending it
"women or girls coming to the United States for the purpose of pro
titution, or for any other immoral purpose." This was directed primari
against female procurers and house madams, but was later applied
private mistresses as well. An amendment extending to three years t
period during which alien prostitutes, procurers, and criminals might
deported was later agreed to without debate. The problem of forei
prostitution was recognized and the bars against it were being raise
but there was no suggestion of a crusade on the subject. There was
reference to the white slave trade by name. The annual report of t
commissioner-general of immigration made no mention of foreign pro
titutes and procurers as a special problem, though its tabulations show
a slight increase in rejections of these classes. As the immigration b
moved to passage in the following session of Congress, debate center
mainly on a proposed literacy test, Japanese exclusion, and other ma
ters, but the language on the subject of alien prostitution was strengt
ened. Penalties were added to apply to anyone who should hold
attempt to hold an alien prostitute or should "keep, maintain, contr
support or harbor" her within three years after she entered the Unit
States. The problem was recognized, but there was no great alarm

The white slave trade was not yet a matter of great national co
cern, but events were rapidly shaping up to make it such. Willia
Coote, whose fervid warnings and appeals throughout Europe had be
largely responsible for the international congresses of 1902 and 190
had made several attempts "to focus the attention of the Americ
people on the Suppression of the White Slave Traffic," and to urge t
formation in the United States of a national vigilance committee alor
the lines of the British organization that he headed. In 1906 a group
social workers and reformers concerned with the problem of prostit
tion, generally referred to as "the social evil," began forming such
organization. They invited him to visit the United States and help the
guaranteeing his expenses. Coote was a zealot and had no doubt
direct inspiration from God in his work. He accepted the call as '
remarkable intervention of Providence," arriving early in the followi
year. In New York, Washington, Philadelphia, Baltimore, and Bosto
he met with private groups and held public meetings, and "was able
arouse much interest in the hearts and minds of the people," as
recorded later. There were numerous organizations in the United State
some of long standing, generally sympathetic to his views, and it w
not long before a National Vigilance Committee appeared, soon fo
lowed by vigilance committees in many states. These organizatio
made war on sexual vice in general, the term "white slavery" bein
quickly expanded to cover the whole field. It was equated with comme
cialized vice and applied to the strictly domestic traffic as well as to t

nternational, but the tendency was to blame foreigners for both. These ommittees and their allies sponsored most of the repressive legislation n the subject that proliferated on the state statute books in the years that ollowed, and they soon made themselves felt at the national level.

More important than Coote's missionary work in stimulating this ort of activity was a sensational exposé of vice conditions in Chicago. Vhile the muckraking periodicals that flourished in the early twentieth entury had devoted a good bit of attention to political corruption in the ities and in the national government, it was not until 1907 that any of hem took up the subject of vice dramatically. In the April issue of *McClure's Magazine* appeared George Kibbe Turner's "The City of Chicago," and probably the most notable crusade of the Progressive eriod was launched. Turner, who was on the magazine's staff, set out o describe the seamy side of life in the nation's second city, starting vith the liquor traffic. Next he turned to "the second great business of lissipation—prostitution." He estimated that there were at least 10,000 professional prostitutes in the city, and that the revenues from the busi-ness in 1906 amounted to over $20,000,000. The women were badly xploited and received only a small share of their earnings. English-speaking girls were recruited by professional pimps from among the ow-paid employees of the department stores and factories. "The argest regular business in furnishing women, however," Turner de-lared, "is done by a company of men, largely composed of Russian ews, who supply women of that nationality to the trade. These men iave a sort of loosely organized association extending through the large ities of the country, their chief centers being New York, Boston, Chicago, and New Orleans."

The Immigration Commission had begun its study of the white lave trade in New York and other American cities in November 1907, collecting most of its data in the following year. The commission was omewhat critical of the immigration authorities, but more sympathetic o their problems. Close examination of the ships' manifests stored at Ellis Island had revealed that in the past, women who had given ad-dresses at well-known disreputable houses in New York and other cities iad been allowed to land. Most of these had come in the second cabin; procurers knew that they would escape the close scrutiny given to teerage immigrants, but were reluctant to spend money for first-class passage and knew that their women might be conspicuous in the first cabin. Much greater care was now being taken by the immigration inspectors, the commission noted, but it was often extremely difficult to prove the illegal entrance of either prostitutes or procurers.

The belief that a vast international organization controlled the white slave trade had become widespread since Coote's evangelizing visit to the United States. Even well-informed social workers sometimes

accepted it. Frances Kellor (*q.v.*), writing for the *Atlantic Monthly* earl
in 1908, demanded greater protection for immigrant girls who, she said
received adequate protection from the wiles of procurers only when the
were actually passing through Ellis Island. Action was called for at bot
state and national levels. The new immigration law was helpful as far a
it went, but "Unfortunately the government does not realize the powe
of the strongly intrenched syndicate, with its many agents abroad an
distributed in the various cities, with large financial backing, whic
imports immigrant girls and sells them from city to city, and has no
provided adequate machinery to reach this all-powerful combine." Thi
belief ran parallel in time to the popular acceptance of the existence of
vast Black Hand (*q.v.*) criminal organization among Italians. Both add
ed to the growing hostility to the so-called "new" immigration, es
pecially the Jews and the Italians. Together, in their day, they provide
what Thomas Beer called "the demonic shape essential to America
journalism."

The commission had found that while many innocent foreign girl
were brought into the country, most of those imported were alread
professionals, lured by the promise of vastly improved earnings. Th
traffic was quite extensive, several thousands of women being importe
annually. Many of them came through the Port of New York, but larg
numbers were now coming through Canada. The business was "strictl
foreign commerce for profit." The earnings of the women might b
large, but they were badly exploited by their pimps and usually by thei
house madams. They were often diseased, and were having a ruinou
effect on American home life. Only a small proportion of the wome
were discovered and barred from the country, but "the greater care c
the immigration officials" was producing improved results, especiall
in New York. There was not only importation but also extensive domes
tic recruiting of prostitutes, especially among ignorant foreign girl
already landed in the United States. Thousands of young men, "usuall
those of foreign birth or the immediate sons of foreigners," were en
gaged in this, "the most accursed business ever devised by man," an
"a disgrace to American civilization."

The principal groups importing women, the commission ha
found, were French and Jewish. The French, as a rule, imported wome
of their own nationality: "The Jews often import or harbor Russian
Austrian, Hungarian, Polish, or German women, usually doubtless c
their own race." There had been much talk of a great monopoly traf
ficking in women from country to country, but the commission ha
been unable to learn of any such corporation and did not believe in it
existence. Men engaged in the business had a large acquaintance wit
each other, however, and there was cooperation and some organizatio
among them. Two organizations of importers, one French, the othe

Jewish, had been identified. They kept their women in brutal subjection amounting to actual slavery, at times resorting to murder to maintain discipline. Apparently they hated each other, but their members would join forces against the common enemy, the law. Both the French and the Jews in the business operated through loose associations in many cities of the United States, and there seemed also to be "a number of Italian pimps scattered throughout the country who are apparently vicious and criminal," with women of various nationalities under their control.

Meanwhile, the Immigration Service, using the 1910 legislation removing the time limit on deportation, had been actively and systematically combing the country for foreign prostitutes and procurers. This went on year after year, with the help of the Department of Justice and local authorities. In the spring of 1914, the *Times* reported the passage through Buffalo of two cars filled with men and women on their way to Ellis Island for deportation. "Among the forty-five women," it was learned, were "hardened residents of the underworlds of a dozen great cities, as well as many young girls from Russia, Spain, and Italy. The men represent cadets, procurers, and agents for the White Slave traffic." The train had started from San Francisco, picking up undesirables along the way. Federal marshals and Chicago detectives were in charge of the prisoners. This shipment of deportees was only one of many. In the fiscal year 1914, the commissioner-general reported "392 immoral women, 154 procurers, 155 persons supported by the proceeds of prostitution," and a good number of criminals as having been deported. Almost as many of these classes had been debarred from entry at the ports. There had also been 44 prosecutions of importers of immoral women on evidence obtained by immigration agents, with 29 convictions. But the commissioner-general believed that this activity was only "scratching the surface," so far as the sexually immoral classes were concerned. He urged a larger appropriation to expand the work.

In 1913, the Immigration Bureau published, as the first of a number of studies, a detailed report on commercialized prostitution in New York City, showing that vice was flourishing. There were not quite so many elegant parlor houses as there had been before the 1907 raids, but they still existed in numbers. Prostitution was also practiced openly in hotels, including some of the better ones, in houses of assignation, tenements, and massage parlors. Thanks to the work of the Committee of Fourteen, the Raines Law hotel had almost disappeared, but prostitutes were found in the back rooms of hundreds of saloons. Prostitutes and their pimps solicited openly on the streets. The business was highly commercialized, and the names and addresses of over 500 men engaged in it had been collected. "The majority are foreigners," the report said, and they often moved their operations from city to city in the United States, or to other countries as far as South America and South Africa. These were men with a substantial stake in the business. There were also probably several thousand pimps with only one or two girls working for them. Estimates of the number of prostitutes in New York ranged from 25,000 to 100,000. Nearly 15,000 of them had been counted in Manhattan alone. A large proportion of their customers were out-of-town visitors. The murder of the gambler Herman Rosenthal, in the middle of July 1912, and the subsequent investigation of the police department, it was noted, had alarmed many of the bigger operators, and a number of houses had since been closed; they were no longer sure of protection.

The white slave traffic, in the original and narrow sense of an international trade in young girls, ceased to be a serious problem as far as the United States was concerned. Recruiting for the profession was overwhelmingly domestic. But meanwhile, prevailing poverty in war-stricken Europe, together with the loss of manpower during the war, provided ample material for such a traffic, and there were other markets for it. The League of Nations became concerned about it and conducted a three-year, worldwide investigation with money and experts supplied by the Rockefellers. Its report, published late in 1927, found the traffic still flourishing in many lands, but gave the United States a relatively clean bill of health. Except for some continued smuggling of Chinese girls to the Pacific coast, "the United States was found to be hard to enter, and still harder to use as a base of operations." Many of the chief operators in New York City, the league reported, had gone into the bootlegging business or even into "something respectable."

References
Francesco Cordasco and Thomas M. Pitken, *The White Slave Trade and the Immigrants* (1981); Egal Feldman, "Prostitution, the Alien Woman and the Progressive Imagination, 1910–1915," *American Quarterly* 19 (Summer 1967): 192–206.

F.C.

WHITERUTHENIAN-AMERICAN   NATIONAL   ASSOCIA-TION. *See* Byelorussians.

WICKERSHAM, GEORGE W. *See* Immigrants and Crime.

WILLIAMS, LOUIS L[AVAL] (b. 1859). Physician. Williams served as a chief medical officer at Ellis Island. In his view, "The day is not far distant when the intending immigrant must present a clean bill of health, physically and mentally, and a clean bill of character as well, through agencies to be devised by the scientist and statesman of the future" ("The Medical Examination of Mentally Defective Aliens,"

American Journal of Insanity 71 [Oct. 1914]: 257–268). See also James
W. May, *Mental Diseases* (1922), a standard medical text of the period,
particularly chapter 9, Immigration and Mental Diseases, in which Dr.
May purports to show how differing racial characteristics seem to call
forth differing mental diseases. His survey of New York State hospitals
admissions for mental disorders (for 1916 through 1920) show the
"three highest races in the following order: Irish, German, Hebrew."
For a dissenting view, see A. J. Rosenoff, *Manual of Psychiatry*
1920).

F.C.

WINTHER, SOPHUS KEITH. *See* Immigrant Novel.

WIRT, WILLIAM A[LBERT] (1874–1938). Educator. William Wirt
had a greater impact upon public education's Americanization of immigrant children than any other local educator during the first three decades of the twentieth century. Wirt grew up in rural Indiana, studied at
DePauw University and at the University of Chicago, taught school,
served as school superintendent in Bluffton, Indiana; then, in 1907 until
his death in 1938, he supervised the school system of Gary, Indiana—a
new industrial city that U.S. Steel built in 1906. This new city was
populated in great part by immigrants.

Gary's problems reflected those of other industrial immigrant centers. In this period of massive immigration, school construction nationally, and in Gary, did not keep up with demographic changes.
Moreover, immigrant children and the children of immigrants presented
other, more complex, issues for educators: language barriers, diverse
cultural patterns, and among some nationalities poorly educated parents
who were hostile to the demands education placed on their children.

Wirt designed a comprehensive educational system to overcome
problems created by scarce resources and the non-American heritages of
school children. He called it the "Work-Study-Play Plan," but nationally it was more commonly called the "Platoon School Plan," or
simply the "Gary Plan." Its popularity partially rested on its efficiency.
Students in each school were divided into two platoons. While half of
the students occupied the existing classrooms, the other half used other
school and community facilities, virtually doubling school capacity.
The purpose was not simply to save money, but to use a wide range of
resources to prepare students for life in America and to Americanize
their lives. To do this Wirt designed the schools as comprehensive
institutions to serve as instruments of immigrant socialization.

In addition to standard academic subjects, the schools promulgated
the attitudes and ideas that Wirt considered truly American: thrift, util-

izing branches of the local banks which were housed in the schools study and leisure skills, using the school libraries; rudiments of civic life through student government and by making field trips to local government agencies; American roles through home economics classes acceptable American dance, music, and art, in the classrooms and auditoriums; patriotic, free enterprise attitudes and conservative religious views, advocated by the local Protestant clergy and usually taught for one hour per day in local churches; the flaws, backwardness, and shortcomings of immigrant cultures, advanced in many facets of school life and perpetuated by the teachers and administrators; and, perhaps most significant, occupational skills and subservient worker attitudes desired by American industry. It is not surprising that the schools had first-class forges, foundries, and machine shops in this steel-based city.

Some saw Wirt's approach as a progressive attempt to prepare children for social reality; others deemed it an elitist vehicle for creating docile, hard-working, law-abiding, patriotic, semi-skilled steelworkers. Irrespective of its critics, the Gary system flourished. In 1912, hundreds of articles appeared in education journals and popular magazines discussing the program. Supporters even published their own journal, *The Platoon School*. By the end of the 1920s, two hundred cities had adopted the plan, and portions of the program filtered into other school systems throughout the country.

References
Ronald D. Cohen, *The Paradox of Progressive Education: The Gary Plan and Urban Schooling* (1976); Raymond Mohl and Neil Betten, *Steel City: Urban and Ethnic Patterns in Gary, Indiana, 1906–1950* (1986).

N.B

WIRTH, LOUIS (1897–1952). Sociologist. One of the founders of the American Council on Race Relations. Author of *The Ghetto* (1928), a classic study of immigrant Jews in Chicago. In "The Ghetto, A Reevaluation," *Social Forces* 37 (March 1959): 255–262, Amitai Etzioni uses Wirth's *Ghetto* to explore the shift of ethnicity from a basis in the ecological community to a reference group concept.

References
Albert J. Reiss, ed., *Louis Wirth on Cities and Social Life* (1964); Roger A. Salerno, *Louis Wirth: A Bio-bibliography* (1987).

B.L

WOMAN'S AMERICAN BAPTIST HOME MISSION SOCIETY. *See* Baptists and Immigrants.

WOMEN AND CHILDREN WAGE-EARNERS, U.S. Congress Senate, *Report on the Condition of Women and Children Wage-Earners* *in the United States,* 61st Congress, 2d Session, Senate Doc. Nos. 86–104 (Washington, D.C.: U.S. Government Printing Office, 1912), 19 vols. An invaluable repository of data on the "industrial, social, moral, educational, and physical condition" of women and children. The report was begun in 1907. The nineteen volumes are titled as follows: vol. 1: The Cotton Textile Industry; vol. 2: Men's Ready-Made Clothing Industry; vol. 3: The Glass Industry; vol. 4: The Silk Industry; vol. 5: Wage-Earning Women in Stores and Factories; vol. 6: The Beginning of Child Labor Legislation, prepared by Elizabeth L. Otey; vol. 7: Conditions Under Which Children Leave School to Go to Work; vol. 8: Juvenile Delinquency and Its Relation to Employment; vol. 9: History of Women in Industry in the United States, prepared by Helen L. Sumner; vol. 10: History of Women in Trade Unions, prepared by John B. Andrews and W. D. P. Bliss; vol. 11: Employment of Women in Metal Trades, prepared by Lucian W. Chaney; vol. 12: Employment of Women in Laundries, prepared by Charles P. Neill; vol. 13: Infant Mortality and Its Relation to the Employment of Mothers; vol. 14: Causes of Death Among Women and Child Cottonmill Operatives, prepared by Arthur R. Perry; vol. 15: Relation Between Occupation and Criminality of Women, prepared by Mary Conyngton; vol. 16: Family Budgets of Typical Cottonmill Workers, prepared by Wood F. Worcester and Daisy W. Worcester; vol. 17: Hookworm Disease Among Cottonmill Operators, prepared by Charles W. Styles; vol. 18: Employment of Women and Children in Selected Industries; and vol. 19: Labor Laws and Factory Conditions.

F.C.

WOMEN IMMIGRANTS, occupational prestige. Sullivan analyzes the occupational prestige of women workers born in Cuba or Mexico who were at least twenty-five years of age at the time of their immigration to the United States. The dependent variable is NORC prestige scores; independent variables are age, U.S. experience, southern residence, weeks worked, and schooling. Predicted prestige scores, controlled for social class, narrow the prestige score gap between Cuban and Mexican women, but increase the gap between immigrant men and women. The data suggest that the social mobility process for female immigrants differs from the process for males, perhaps because cultural barriers to "pink collar" jobs of nominally higher status restrict women's mobility.

Reference

Theresa A. Sullivan, "The Occupational Prestige of Women Immigrants: A Comparison of Cubans and Mexicans," *International Migration Review* 18 (Winter 1984): 1045–1062.

F.C.

WOMEN'S TRADE UNION LEAGUE OF NEW YORK. Trade unionism, reformism, feminism. In 1903 a group of settlement house residents and social reformers founded the Women's Trade Union League of New York. Their goals were to improve the working conditions of the city's women wage earners and improve their position in the labor movement. The leaders of the league saw themselves as both trade unionists and feminists. From 1903 through 1913 they were responsible for a popular campaign which drew thousands of women into new unions for hat trimmers, milliners, and clerks, among others, but growth was limited to a few industries. As well, the league dealt mainly with young Italian and Jewish immigrant women, and in time the language and social and cultural differences between them and the members of the league proved to be insurmountable. The league changed its emphasis, turning to political and legislative work. Between 1920 and 1955 it became an increasingly poor social welfare group which struggled for women's protective legislation. Although it declined as a force to be reckoned with in New York life, it had performed the useful service of educating many women to become effective union organizers, speakers, business agents, and negotiators.

Reference
Nancy Schrom Dye, *As Equals and as Sisters. Feminism, the Labor Movement, and the Women's Trade Union League of New York* (1980).

G.B.

WOODS, ROBERT A[RCHEY] (1865–1925). Social reformer, settlement house movement pioneer. Woods founded (1891) South End House, Boston, which he headed until his death. He was a leader in the development of the National Federation of Social Settlements, which he served as secretary from 1911 to 1923, and as president, 1924 to 1925. Woods's *The Poor in Great Cities: Their Problems and What Is Doing to Solve Them* (1895; rpt. 1970) cast new light on the transformation of American attitudes toward the poor, and this noted collection of essays contains some of the earliest and freshest reactions of Progressive reformers to poverty. The scope is wide, ranging from descriptions of the immigrant poor in Chicago and Boston to developments in Naples and London, from tenements to the fresh air fund, from settlement houses to boys' clubs. Other works include (with Albert J. Kennedy) *Handbook of Settlements* (1911; rpt., 1974). Compiled at the height of the settlement house movement, this book offers the most comprehensive listing available of settlement houses throughout the United States. It also enumerates the activities of each settlement house. An important reference, it illustrates the size and scope of the settlement house movement and leads to a realization of the enormous influence Progressive era reformers had on the neighborhoods of the nation. Also with Albert J.

Kennedy, *The Settlement Horizon: A Natural Estimate* (1922; rpt., 1974) is a comprehensive account of the work of the settlement houses from their inception in England in the 1880s through to 1922. *The Neighborhood in Nation-Building: The Running Comments of Thirty Years at South End House* (1923; rpt. 1974) includes articles and addresses written and delivered over a period of thirty years, and deals chiefly with the methods and results in city settlements, especially with those of South End House, and is a record of the milestones in Woods's career. In *The University Settlement Idea* (1892) Woods had argued that a college or university has an obligation to work for social improvement, and that recreational, health, educational, and infant welfare services ought to be provided for the community.

Reference
E. H. Woods, *Robert Archey Woods* (1929).

F.C.

WOOLF, MICHAEL ANGELO (1837–1899). Artist. Many of his pictures of slum life and children were affectionate portrayals and bore little resemblence to the ''dangerous classes'' of Charles Loring Brace (*q.v.*). Chief work: *Sketches of Lowly Life in a Great City* (ed. Joseph Henius, 1899), which contains a collection of Woolf's early drawings and a biographical sketch of the artist.

F.C.

WORKINGMAN'S BENEVOLENT ASSOCIATION. *See* Siney, John.

WORLD CONFEDERATION OF LABOUR. *See* [Refugees]: Migration Questions.

WRIGHT, CARROLL D[AVIDSON] (1840–1909). Public official, social economist; first commissioner, U.S. Bureau of Labor, 1885–1905; president of the American Statistical Association, 1897–1909; and first president of Clark University, 1902–1909. Compiled during his tenure as commissioner of labor, Wright's *Annual Reports* offer valuable data on wages, standards of living, and sanitary conditions in factories for the working immigrant poor. *Annual Reports* published under Wright's direction include *Industrial Depressions* (1886); *Working Women in Large Cities* (1888); *Strikes and Lockouts* (1894); *Trade and Technical Education* (1902); and *Convict Labor* (1905). A *Seventh Special Report* was entitled *The Slums of Baltimore, Chicago, New York, and Philadelphia* (1894; rpt., 1970) and was addressed to the growing concerns over urban slums and poverty. His *The Working Girls of Boston* (1889; rpt. 1971) is an actual case study which fully outlines the working situations of girls (largely the immigrant Irish) in Boston, detailing their occupations, income, and financial difficulties, and consequently destroying the widely held view that loose behavior is characteristic of working women. For example, he found that of the 39,000 women employed in Boston in 1880, some 20,000 were in occupations other than domestic service, and of those, 69 percent lived at home.

Reference
James Leiby, *Carroll Wright and Labor Reform* (1960); Horace G. Wadlin, *Carroll D. Wright: A Memorial* (1911).

F.C.

WRIGHT, RICHARD. *See* Afro-Americans.

YARBOROUGH, [SENATOR] RALPH. *See* Bilingual Education.

YELLOW PERIL. A catch-phrase used mainly against Japanese and Chinese in the United States to signify Orientals as a great menace to Western civilization.

Reference
William F. Wu, *The Yellow Peril: Chinese Americans in American Fiction, 1850–1940* (1982).

D.N.A.

YEMENIS. *See* Arabs.

YESHIVA ETZ CHAIM. *See* Yeshiva University.

YESHIVA UNIVERSITY (New York City). The university began in the Rabbi Isaac Elchanan Theological Seminary, and developed under the leadership of Dr. Bernard Revel, its first president, into a complete system of Jewish education from elementary school through ordination. The seminary, which was incorporated early in 1897 by eastern European immigrants, later absorbed the Yeshiva Etz Chaim, an elementary school founded in 1885, and was the mother institution from which have sprung the fifteen schools that make up the university today.

Reference
Gilbert Klaperman, *The Beginnings of Yeshiva University, the First Jewish University in America* (1955).

F.C.

YEZIERSKA, ANZIA (1885–1970). Novelist and short story writer. In her *Hungry Hearts* (1920), which made her a celebrity, Anzia

Yezierska described the effect of the tensions between the values of the Old World and those of the new on the poor, immigrant Jewish woman, who was struggling to achieve the American Dream. The film rights to *Hungry Hearts* were bought by Samuel Goldwyn. Soon after, Yezierska was dubbed "Queen of the Ghetto." Her unique contribution was the depiction of the Jewish immigrant experience from the view of the Jewish immigrant woman. Yezierska knew her heroine well. Born in a mud hut on the Russian-Polish border, Yezierska came to New York at the age of fifteen, worked in a sweatshop, and studied English at night. Yezierska also studied at Columbia University, and her literary career was launched in 1915 with a short story in *Forum* called "A Free Vacation House," a story of a Jewish immigrant mother and children on charity.

Yezierska was married twice and later developed a romantic, stormy relationship with John Dewey, who frequently appeared in her works as the prototype of the WASP mentor and scholar.

Chief works: *Salome of the Tenements* (1923); *Children of Loneliness* (1923); *Bread Givers* (1925); *Arrogant Beggar* (1927); *All I Could Never Be* (1932); and *Red Ribbon on a White Horse* (1950).

Reference
Carol B. Schoen, *Anzia Yezierska* (1982).

C.C.

YICK WO v. HOPKINS (1888). *See* Chinese.

YIVO INSTITUTE FOR JEWISH RESEARCH. The YIVO (acronym for "Yidisher Visenshaftlikher Institut") Institute is the principal world organization conducting research in Yiddish; it was founded in Berlin in 1925 at a conference (August 7–12, 1925) of Jewish scholars:

> The original proposal for a Yiddish academic institute by Nahum Shtif and published in the pamphlet *Di Organizatsye fun der Yidisher Visenshaft* (The Organization of Yiddish Scholarship, 1925), was twofold: that Jews participate in scholarly research in their own language, and that the results of world scholarship be made available to those Jews unfamiliar with languages other than Yiddish. Noting the achievements of various scholars during the preceding decade in new areas of Jewish research, Shtif proposed the coordination of the planning, conduct, and dissemination of such research, so that individual scholars might have a common platform, and the Jewish community, authoritative, informative material for its deliberations and development. The founding conference selected Vilna, as the center. Subsidiary branches functioned in Berlin, Warsaw, and New York. Friends of YIVO were also active in Argentina, Austria, Brazil, Chile, England, Estonia,

France, Latvia, Rumania, and Palestine. YIVO's Vilna period reached its peak at the 10th anniversary conference (1935), which was attended by leading scholars from most of the important Yiddish-speaking communities. When Vilna was occupied by the Nazis, the American branch, earlier known as Amopteyl (Amerikanishe Opteylung) took over the central direction (1940). (*Encyclopedia Judaica*)

Unique among American institutions, the YIVO Institute for Jewish Research is a center of study, research, and publishing dedicated to the Eastern European Jewish cultural heritage and to the impact of Eastern European Jewish immigrants, and their descendants, on American life. In 1940, YIVO moved to New York from its first home in Vilna, in the wake of the Nazi invasion of Poland. Here in New York, YIVO carries on its mission—to rescue and restore, preserve and study the documentary treasures of European and American Jewish culture. To its current location on Fifth Avenue's Museum Mile come scholars, students, musicians, film makers, and lay people from all over the world, drawn to YIVO's unique library, archives, courses, and public events.

YIVO's multilingual library of 300,000 volumes includes the world's largest collection of Yiddish books and rare volumes of Judaica dating from the sixteenth century. The archives, which include numerous items dramatically rescued from the ravages of Nazi destruction, consist of 22,000,000 pieces, organized in more than 1,100 collections. Together the library and archives constitute major resources for research in the areas of Eastern European Jewish history and settlement of Jews in the United States; and Yiddish language, linguistics, literature, folklore, and ethnography. Both the library and archives are open to the public, free of charge.

YIVO also conducts a formal program of graduate study at its Max Weinreich Center for Advanced Jewish Studies, whose courses are recognized for credit at universities in this country and abroad. The Max Weinreich Center complements the programs of degree-granting institutions of higher learning by providing essential opportunities for graduate training and postdoctoral specialization in the fields of Yiddish and Eastern European Jewish Studies. The center received its charter in 1968 and is supported by its parent organization, the YIVO Institute for Jewish Research. In addition to its scholarly services, YIVO serves the community at large through its publications, public lectures, and conferences, through its information services, and through photographic and documentary exhibitions.

References
S. Liptzin, *YIVO Way* (1943), *YIVO in America* (1945); E. Sapir, *The Work of the Yiddish*

Scientific Institute (1933); and *YIVO. Its Meaning and Significance* (1958), and *The Maturing of Yiddish Literature* (1970).

D.A.

YOUNG MEN'S HEBREW ASSOCIATION. *See* Educational Alliance.

YOUNG MEN'S ITALIAN EDUCATIONAL LEAGUE. *See* Covello, Leonard.

YUGOSLAV SOCIALIST FEDERATION. *See* Molek, Mary.

YUGOSLAVS. Most Americans, including the federal authorities, scholars, and historians of immigration call all immigrants from Yugoslavia Yugoslavs. Inevitably, this causes confusion among the Americans, and emotional reaction on the part of immigrants. Unfortunately, too few Americans are acquainted with the history, ethnography, and geography of all Slavic peoples, especially those in the Balkans.

"Yugoslav" (*Jugoslaven*) means in all South Slavic languages (Slovenian, Croatian, Serbian, and Bulgarian) "a Slav from the South." "Yugoslavia" (*Jugoslavija*) means literally "the country of the South Slavs." All those using the term "Yugoslav" are not aware of the fact that the Socialist Federal Republic of Yugoslavia is not inhabited by a single nation or people, but is rather a multinational state composed of several Slavic and non-Slavic nationalities and national minorities.

The "Yugoslav Idea" developed in Croatia (now western and central parts of Yugoslavia). It advocated solidarity of *all* South Slavs: the Slovenes (commonly referred to in the United States as Slovenians), Croatians, Montenegrins, Serbs, Macedonians, and Bulgarians. Influenced by Romanticism and partly by Russian-sponsored Pan-Slavism, it implied that all these peoples stretching from the Alps to the Black Sea (an area of approximately 150,000 square miles) are basically the same people speaking dialects of a common Slavic language. The Yugoslav movement advocated a South Slavic confederation of equal partners and was strongly influenced by two eminent Croatians: Ljudevit Gaj (1809–1868), the leader of the Croatian national renaissance starting in the 1830s; and Bishop Josip Juraj Strossmayer (1815–1905), who was one of the founders of modern Croatia. Even the idea of Pan-Slavism has its roots in Croatia. One of its forefathers was Rev. Juraj Križanić (1617–1683). Pan-Slavism was later embraced by the Russians and utilized for their expansionist and imperialist designs. Officially it sponsored the solidarity of all Slavs under Russian leadership.

"Yugoslavism" like "Pan-Slavism" was based on idealistic and unrealistic concepts about the unity of all Slavs. In modern history, with the rise of nationalism (influenced among the South Slavs by the ideas of the French Revolution and the existence of the Napoleonic Illyrian Provinces, 1806–1813), a majority of Slavs (North and South), especially their educated people, rejected these ideas as utopian and contrary to their national interests. There were too many differences among them. There was the Russian oppression of the Ukrainians, Byelorussians, and Poles to consider; and there were differences in religions; an ever-rising linguistic difference; different alphabets (all Orthodox Slavs use the Cyrillic, while all Catholic Slavs use the Latin alphabet); an historical division into two spheres of culture and civilization (Latin or Roman, and Byzantine and Near Eastern); and the territorial partition lasting for centuries under various powers (the Austrian, Russian, and Ottoman empires). All of these have been regarded as final obstacles to the unity of Slavs. Instead, all the Slavic nations, including all South Slavs, have established in this century their movements toward independent and sovereign states for each nationality. This goal was partly achieved by some Slavs in 1918 at the ruins of the Habsburg and Romanov empires.

The first South Slavic state was founded in December of 1918; it was officially called the Kingdom of Serbs, Croats, and Slovenes. Instead of a union of equal partners, existing together in a democratic federal state, it proved to be a centralistic state dominated by Serbs who tried to impose on other nationalities a Great Serbia. In January 1929, King Alexander, who started to rule as a dictator, introduced the new name for the state—Yugoslavia. The Belgrade government did not even recognize the existence of Macedonians (historically, ethnically, and linguistically a western branch of the Bulgarians), or for that matter of the Montenegrins. Their country was forcibly incorporated after 1918. Royal Yugoslavia fell apart in April 1941, after it was invaded by Germans, Italians, Bulgarians, and Hungarians.

The new Communist Yugoslavia under the leadership of Josip Broz-Tito—and with the help of Western Allies and Soviet troops— was established in May 1945. In November 1945 it became a Socialist Federal Republic, a harsh police state, under the dictatorship of the Communist party and the control of its secret police. Having liquidated virtually hundreds of thousands of its opponents (most of them Croatian) it proclaimed as official slogan: "Brotherhood and Unity." The new regime and its first constitution (based on Soviet example) recognized in principle the existence of: Serbs, Slovenes, Croatians, Montenegrins, and Macedonians. The country became divided into six republics: Serbia (with the autonomous regions of Vojvodina and Kosovo), Slovenia, Croatia, Bosnia-Herzegovina, Montenegro, and

Macedonia. The regime claimed that the nationalities question was successfully resolved. Various minorities were also recognized.

There were several constitutions, in 1953, 1963, and 1974, gradually giving more power to the individual republics in matters of economy, cultural development, and party politics. Since 1974 the SFRY is legally a confederation where "the states" have even the right of secession. However, in reality any stirrings or movements toward "separatism" are suppressed by the government in Belgrade. Dissatisfied by political and economic conditions, over a million people (60 percent Croatian) have emigrated to foreign countries since the late 1940s. The authorities permitted them to leave. After Tito's death in May 1980, the economic situation has deteriorated drastically.

By the official census taken in 1971, out of total population of 20,806,000, only 408,000 people declared themselves as Yugoslavs. A unique feature in the census was the designation of all Muslims in Bosnia-Herzegovina (who are of Croatian origin) as a new Muslim nationality. (Muslim Albanians or Macedonians may be counted as Albanians or Macedonians.) The new and most recent census of March 1981 counted a total population of 22,411,000; among these were 1,215,000 regarded as Yugoslavs. This census and the number of Yugoslavs it reports have provoked a heated controversy on part of various circles in Slovenia, Croatia, and Serbia; it is well known from history that all Balkan censuses present documents of dubious nature.

The critics of the item "Yugoslav" in the census intimate that such a category is unrealistic, and that the attempts to force many to declare themselves as such reflect a centralistic and unitaristic policy denying the existence of separate and distinct nationalities that are recognized by the 1974 Constitution. However, even if the number of "Yugoslavs" is correct, it implies that in Yugoslavia only about 6 percent of the population regards itself as Yugoslav.

The U.S. Immigration and Naturalization Service perpetuates the confusion regarding the term "Yugoslav." Traditionally, the INS has counted all immigrants according to the country of their birth. In the case of immigrants from Yugoslavia the INS lumps them all together as "Yugoslavs" regardless of their ethnic origin. "Yugoslav immigrants" embraces all South Slavic nationalities *and* members of the strong Albanian "minority" (there are today more than 2.5 million Albanians—and they are not Slavs—more than, for instance, Slovenians), in addition to Hungarians, Romanians, Romi (Gypsies), Turks, and others. The American Albanians and Macedonians fiercely resist being called Yugoslavs. The older generations of Croatians, Slovenians, Serbs, and Montenegrins—and their descendants—usually don't mind being called "Yugoslav."

A great majority of the fraternal organizations, the largest being the Croatian Fraternal Union, use the name of their respective nationality. A great majority of the more than 150,000 immigrants that have arrived here after World War II reject being named "Yugoslav" and insist on their proper ethnic names. This is especially evident among the Croatian immigrants. The intensely nationalistic younger generations (who paradoxically brought their nationalism from a Communist state) insist on being called Croatian. Indirectly these trends were facilitated by the rising ethnic pride that has developed in America during the past twenty years.

Many thousands of South Slavs and Albanians in the United States regard Yugoslavia as a country of oppression and political and economic suffering from which they escaped to choose freedom and prosperity in America. They feel that they have a right to declare their nationality according to their conviction.

G.J.P.

ZAKRZEWSKA, MARIE E[LIZABETH] (1829–1902). Physician. Having overcome the numerous obstacles faced by women venturing into medicine, Zakrzewska became a doctor and carried her personal crusade into the big city where ignorance and poverty battered immigrant women and children into sickness and early death. She strove successfully to found hospitals for women and children in Boston and New York. Marie Zakrzewska was the first resident physician of the New York Infirmary for Women and Children.

References
Agnes C. Vietor, *A Woman's Quest: The Life of Marie E. Zakrzewska* (1924; rpt. 1976); *Marie Elizabeth Zakrzewska, 1829–1902. A Memoir* (1903).

F.C.

ZANGWILL, ISRAEL (1864–1926). English author. A prominent Zionist, Zangwill wrote *Children of the Ghetto* (1892) and *Dreamers of the Ghetto* (1898), a series of biographical studies. His *The Melting Pot* (1914), as a drama, had wide influence in America in its advocacy of assimilation.

Reference
Joseph Leftwich, *Israel Zangwill* 1957).

B.L.

ZEBRIS, JUOZAS. *See* Lithuanians.

ZIZHUI HUI. *See* Angel Island.

ZNANIECKI, FLORIAN (1882–1958). Sociologist, major representative of the analytical trend in American sociology. Author (with William I. Thomas [*q.v.*]) of *The Polish Peasant in Europe and America* (5 vols., 1918–1920; ed. Eli Zaretsky, 1984). Znaniecki's theoretical system may be best understood as an unfolding of the postulate of "universal cultural order," itself of particular interest in the study of immigrant socialization in the United States.

F.C.

ZÜBLIN, JOHANN JOACHIM. *See* Swiss.

ZUBLY, JOHN J. *See* Swiss.

Appendix

AMERICAN IMMIGRATION:
A HANDLIST OF
SELECTED BIBLIOGRAPHIES AND
REFERENCE WORKS

Allen, James P., and Eugene J. Turner, eds. *We the People: An Atlas of America's Ethnic Diversity.* New York: Macmillan, 1987.

American Council for Nationalities Service. *The Ethnic Press in the United States: Lists of Foreign Language, Nationality and Ethnic Newspapers and Periodicals in the United States.* New York: 1974.

Arndt, Karl J. R., and May E. Olson, eds. *German-American Newspapers and Periodicals, 1732–1955: History and Bibliography.* Heidelberg: Quelle and Meyer, 1961.

[Asian American Studies]. University of California/Davis. *Asians in America: A Selected Annotated Bibliography. An Expansion and Revision.* Davis: University of California, Asian American Studies, 1983.

Baden, Anne L. *Immigration in the United States: A Selected List of Recent References.* Washington, D.C.: Library of Congress, 1943.

Balch Institute. *The Balch Institute Historical Reading Lists. Nos. 1–31.* Philadelphia, 1974–1976. (Brief commentaries and bibliographies on European-American ethnic groups.)

Balys, Jonas. *Lithuania and Lithuanians: A Selected Bibliography.* New York: Praeger, 1961.

Barton, H. Arnold. "Swedish-American Historiography." *Immigration History Newsletter* 15 (May 1983): 1–5.

Barton, Josef J. *An Annotated Guide to the Ethnic Experience in the United States.* Cambridge, Mass.: Press of the Langdon Associates, 1976.

Beers, Henry P. *The French in North America: A Bibliographical Guide to French Archives, Reproductions, and Research Missions.* Baton Rouge: Louisiana State University Press, 1957.

Bengelsdorf, Winnie. *Ethnic Studies in Higher Education: State of Art and Bibliography.* Washington, D.C.: American Association of State Colleges and Universities, 1972. Reprint, New York: Arno, 1978.

Brana-Shute, Rosemary. *A Bibliography of Caribbean Migration and Caribbean Immigrant Communities.* Gainesville, Fla.: University of Florida Center for Latin American Studies, 1983.

Briani, V. *Italian Immigrants Abroad: A Bibliography on the Italian Experience Outside Italy in Europe, the Americas, Australia, and Africa.* Edited and with a supplementary Bibliography by Francesco Cordasco. Detroit: Blaine Ethridge, 1979.

Brickman, William W. *The Jewish Community in America. An Annotated and Classified Bibliographical Guide.* New York: Burt Franklin, 1976.

Brozek, Andrizej. "Historiography of Polish Emigration to North America." *Immigration History Newsletter* 18 (May 1986): 1–4.

Buenker, John D., and Nicholas C. Burckel. *Immigration and Ethnicity: A Guide to Information Sources.* Detroit: Gale Research Co., 1977.

Catsumbis, Michael N. *A Bibliographical Guide to Materials on Greeks in the United States, 1890–1968.* New York: Center for Migration Studies, 1970.

Chan, Sucheng. "Asians in California: A Selected Bibliography on Chinese, Japanese, Korean, Filipino, Asian Indian, and Vietnamese Immigrants and their Descendants." *Immigration History Newsletter* 18 (Nov. 1986): 1–12.

_____. "Selected Bibliography on the Chinese in the United States, 1850–1920." *Immigration History Newsletter* 16 (Nov. 1984): 7–15.

Chartier, Armand B. *A Selected and Thematic Checklist of Publications Relating to Franco-Americans.* Kingston: Department of Languages, University of Rhode Island, 1975.

Choi, Kyung-Hee. *Korean-Americans: An Annotated Bibliography.* Berkeley: University of California, 1983.

Clarke, Robert L. *Afro-American History: Sources for Research.* Washington, D.C.: Howard University Press, 1981.

Cohen, D. *Multi-Ethnic Media: Selected Bibliographies in Print.* Chicago: American Library Association, 1975.

Cordasco, Francesco, ed. *A Bibliography of American Immigration History. The George Washington University Project Studies.* Fairfield, N.J.: Augustus M. Kelley, 1978.

_____. "Bilingual Education in American Schools: A Bibliographical Essay." *Immigration History Newsletter* 14 (May 1982): 1–8.

_____ *Immigrant Children in American Schools: A Classified Anno-*

tated Bibliography with Selected Source Documents. Fairfield, N.J.: Augustus M. Kelley, 1976.

———. *The Immigrant Woman in North America: An Annotated Bibliography of Selected References*. Metuchen, N.J.: Scarecrow Press, 1985.

———. *The Italian American Experience: An Annotated and Classified Bibliographical Guide. With Selected Publications of the Casa Italiana Educational Bureau*. New York: Burt Franklin, 1974.

———. *Italian Americans: A Guide to Informational Sources*. Detroit: Gale Research Co., 1978.

———. *Italian Mass Emigration: The Exodus of a Latin People. A Bibliographical Guide to the "Bollettino dell'Emigrazione," 1902–1927*. Totowa, N.J.: Rowman and Littlefield, 1980.

———. *Italians in the United States: A Bibliography of Reports, Texts, Critical Studies, and Related Materials*. New York: Oriole Editions, 1972.

———. *The New American Immigration: Evolving Patterns of Legal and Illegal Emigration. A Bibliography of Selected References*. New York: Garland Publishing, 1987.

———. *Puerto Ricans on the Mainland: A Bibliography of Reports, Texts, Critical Studies and Related Materials*. Totowa, N.J.: Rowman and Littlefield, 1972.

———, and David N. Alloway. *American Ethnic Groups: The European Heritage. A Bibliography of Doctoral Dissertations Completed at American Universities*. Metuchen, N.J.: Scarecrow Press, 1981.

Cuddy, Dennis L., ed. *Contemporary American Immigration: Interpretive Essays*. Vol. 1 (European); Vol. 2. (Non-European). Boston: Twayne Publishers, 1982.

Deodene, Frank, comp. *The Origins of Ethnicity: Immigrants in America, Including the Immigrant in Fiction*. Chatham, N.J.: Chatham Bookseller [c. 1978]. (A catalogue of 623 items.)

Diodati, C. M., et al. *Writings on Italian Americans: Bicentennial Bibliography*. New York: Italian American Center for Urban Affairs, 1975.

Doezema, Linda P. *Dutch Americans: A Guide to Information Sources*. Detroit: Gale Research Co., 1979.

Eager, Alan R. *A Guide to Irish Bibliographic Materials*. London: Library Association, 1964.

Erickson, E. *Swedish-American Periodicals: A Selective and Descriptive Bibliography*. New York: Arno, 1979.

Eterovich, Adam S. *A Guide and Bibliography to Research on Yugoslavs in the United States and Canada*. San Francisco: R and E Research Associates, 1975.

———, ed. *Jugoslav Immigrant Bibliography*. San Francisco: R and E Research Associates, 1968.

Fishman, Joshua A., ed. *Language Loyalty in the United States.* The Hague: Mouton, 1966; rpt., New York: Arno Press, 1978.

Funchion, Michael F. "Irish-America: An Essay on the Literature." *Immigration History Newsletter* 17 (Nov. 1985): 1–8.

Gakovich, Robert P., and Milan M. Radovich. *Serbs in the United States and Canada: A Comprehensive Bibliography.* St. Paul, Minn.: Immigration History Research Center, 1976.

Georges, R. A., and S. Stern. *American and Canadian Immigrant and Ethnic Folklore: An Annotated Bibliography.* New York: Garland Publishing, 1982.

Glanz, Rudolf. *The German Jew in America: An Annotated Bibliography Including Books, Pamphlets and Articles of Special Interest.* New York: Ktav, 1969.

Glazier, Ira and Luigi de Rosa. *Migration Across the Nations: Population Mobility in Historical Contexts.* New York: Holmes and Meier, 1986.

Greene, Amy Blanche, and Frederic A. Gould. *Handbook-Bibliography on Foreign Language Groups in the United States and Canada.* New York: Council of Women for Home Missions, 1925.

Greene, Victor R. *American Immigrant Leaders, 1800–1910: Marginality and Identity.* Baltimore: Johns Hopkins University Press, 1987.

———. "Recording the Slavic American Past: Polish, Czech, and Slovak American Historiography, 1890–1975." *Immigration History Newsletter* 7 (Nov. 1975): 6–11.

Gregorovich, Andrew. *Canadian Ethnic Groups Bibliography: A Selected Bibliography of Ethno-Cultural Groups in Canada and the Province of Ontario.* Toronto: Department of the Provincial Secretary and Citizenship of Ontario, 1972.

Groennings, Sven. *Scandinavia in Social Science Literature: An English Language Bibliography.* Bloomington: Indiana University Press, 1970.

Haines, David W., ed. *Refugees in the United States: A Reference Handbook.* New York: Greenwood Press, 1985.

Hellwig, David J. "Afro-American Views of Immigrants, 1830–1930: A Historiographical-Bibliographical Essay." *Immigration History Newsletter* 13 (Nov. 1981): 1–7.

Herman, Judith M. *White Ethnic America: A Selected Bibliography.* New York: American Jewish Committee, 1969.

Herrera, Diane, ed. *Puerto Ricans and Other Minority Groups in the Continental United States: An Annotated Bibliography.* With a new Foreword and Supplemental Bibliography by Francesco Cordasco. Detroit: Blaine-Ethridge, 1979.

Hofstetter, Richard R., ed. *United States Immigration Policy.* Durham, N.C.: Duke University Press, 1984.

Hoglund, A. William. *Immigrants and Their Children in the United States: A Bibliography of Doctoral Dissertations, 1885–1982.* New York: Garland Publishing, 1986.

Horecky, Paul. *East Central and Southeast Europe: A Handbook of Library and Archival Resources in North America.* Santa Barbara, Calif.: American Bibliographical Center, 1975.

Hutchinson, Edward P. *Legislative History of American Immigration Policy, 1798–1965.* Philadelphia: University of Pennsylvania Press, 1981.

Ichioka, Jyji. *A Buried Past: An Annotated Bibliography of the Japanese-American Research Project Collection.* Berkeley: University of California Press, 1974.

Ichioka, Yuji. "Recent Japanese Scholarship on the Origins and Causes of Japanese Immigration." *Immigration History Newsletter* 15 (Nov. 1983): 2–7.

Inglehart, Babette F., and Anthony R. Mangione. *The Image of Pluralism in American Literature: An Annotated Bibliography on the American Experience of European Ethnic Groups.* New York: Institute on Pluralism and Group Identity of the American Jewish Committee, 1974.

————. *Multi-Ethnic Literature: An Annotated Bibliography on European Ethnic Group Life in America.* New York: American Jewish Committee, Institute of Human Relations, 1974.

[Institute for Research in History.] *Ethnic and Immigration Groups: The United States, Canada and England.* New York: Haworth Press, 1983.

Jaffe, A. J., Ruth M. Cullen, and Thomas D. Boswell. *The Changing Demography of Spanish Americans.* New York: Academic Press, 1980.

Janeway, William Ralph. *Bibliography of Immigration in the United States, 1900–1930.* Columbus, Ohio: Hedrick, 1934. Rpt., San Francisco: R and E Research Associates, 1972.

Jenswold, John R. "The Missing Dimension: The Historiography of Urban Norwegian Immigrants." *Immigration History Newsletter* 18 (May 1986): 4–7.

Jerabek, Esther. *Czechs and Slovaks in North America: A Bibliography.* New York: Czechoslovak National Council of America, 1976.

Juliani, Richard N. *Immigration and Ethnicity.* (Balch Institute Historical Reading Lists, No. 1.) Philadelphia: Balch Institute, 1974.

Kantautas, Adam, and Filomena Kantautas. *A Lithuanian Bibliography: A Checklist of Books and Articles Held by the Major Libraries of Canada and the United States.* Edmonton: University of Alberta Press, 1975. *Supplement,* 1979.

Kelly, Gail P. *From Vietnam to America: A Chronicle of the Viet-*

namese Immigration to the United States. Boulder, Colo.: Westview Press, 1977.

Keresztesi, Michael, and Gary R. Cocozzoli. *German-American History and Life: A Guide to Information Sources.* Detroit: Gale Research Co., 1980.

Kim, Hyung-Chan, ed. *Dictionary of Asian American History.* New York: Greenwood Press, 1986.

Koivukangas, O., and S. Toivonen. *Suomen Iürrtolais uuden ja Maasamuuton Bibliografia: A Bibliography on Finnish Emigration and Internal Migration.* Turku, Finland: Migration Institute, 1978.

Kolehmainen, John I. *The Finns in America: A Bibliographical Guide to Their History.* Hancock, Mich.: Finnish American Historical Library, Suomi College, 1947.

Kolm, Richard. *Bibliography of Ethnicity and Ethnic Groups.* Rockville, Md.: National Institute of Mental Health, Center for Studies of Metropolitan Problems, 1973.

Kuehl, Warren F. *Dissertations in History: An Index to Dissertations Completed in History Departments of United States and Canadian Universities, 1873–1960.* Lexington: University of Kentucky Press, 1965.

Levine, Gene N., and Robert C. Rhodes. *The Japanese American Community.* New York: Praeger, 1981.

Long, J. *The German-Russians: A Bibliography.* Santa Barbara, Calif.: American Bibliographical Center, 1978.

MacCorkle, Lyn. *Cubans in the United States: A Bibliography for Research in the Social and Behavioral Sciences.* New York: Greenwood Press, 1984.

Magocsi, Paul R. *Our People: Carpatho-Rusyns and Their Descendants in North America.* Toronto: Multicultural History Society of Ontario, 1984.

Matza, Diana. "A Bibliography of Materials on the National Background and Immigrant Experiences of the Sephardic Jews in the United States." *Immigration History Newsletter* 19 (May 1987): 4–9.

Melendy, H. Brett. *Asians in America: Filipinos, Koreans, and East Indians.* Boston: Twayne Publishers, 1977.

Metress, Seamus P. *The Irish-American Experience: A Guide to the Literature.* Washington, D.C.: University Press of America, 1981.

Meyen, Emil. *Bibliography on German Settlements in Colonial North America.* Leipzig: Otto Harrassowitz, 1937.

Miller, Randall M. "Immigrants in the Old South." *Immigration History Newsletter* 10 (Nov. 1978): 8–14.

Miller, Sally M. *The Ethnic Press in the United States: A Historical Analysis and Handbook.* New York: Greenwood Press, 1987.

Miller, Wayne C., ed. *Comprehensive Bibliography for the Study of American Minorities*. 3 vols. New York: New York University Press, 1976. (See review: F. Cordasco, *Contemporary Sociology* 6 [Sept. 1977]: 594–595.) *Annual Supplements:* 1976 (1985); 1977 (1986); 1978 (1987).

Mohl, Raymond A. "Cubans in Miami: A Preliminary Bibliography." *Immigration History Newsletter* 16 (May 1984): 1–10.

———. "The New Haitian Immigration: A Preliminary Bibliography." *Immigration History Newsletter* 17 (May 1985): 1–8.

Mortensen, E. *Danish-American Life and Letters: A Bibliography*. Des Moines, Iowa: Committee on Publications of the Danish Evangelical Lutheran Church in America, 1945. Rpt., New York: Arno, 1979.

Mulder, William. "Mormon Sources for Immigration History." *Immigration History Newsletter* 10 (Nov. 1978): 1–8.

Myroniuk, Halya, and Christine Worobec, eds. *Ukrainians in North America: A Select Bibliography*. Toronto: Multicultural History Society of Ontario, 1983.

Pap, Leo. *The Portuguese in the United States: A Bibliography*. New York: Center for Migration Studies, 1976.

Park, Robert E. *The Immigrant Press and Its Control*. New York: Harper and Brothers, 1922. Reprinted with a new Introduction by Read Lewis, Montclair, N.J.: Patterson Smith, 1971.

Pochmann, Henry A., and Arthur R. Schultz, eds. *Bibliography of German Culture in America to 1940*. Madison: University of Wisconsin Press, 1953.

Prpic, George J. *Croatia and Croatians: An Annotated and Selected Bibliography in English*. Cleveland: John Carroll University, 1972.

———. *South Slavic Immigration in America*. Boston: Twayne Publishers, 1978.

Pula, James S., and M. N. Pula. *An Index to Polish American Studies, 1944–1973*. Chicago: Polish American Historical Association, 1977.

Rischin, Moses. *An Inventory of American Jewish History*. Cambridge, Mass.: Harvard University Press, 1954. (Also, the author's "Since 1954: A Bicentennial Look at the Resources of American Jewish History." *Immigration History Newsletter* 7 [Nov. 1975]: 1–6.)

Robet-Petitat, C. "Bibliographie sur les femmes immigrantes." *Migrants-Formation* 32–33 (March 1979): 149–154.

Rose, Peter I. *Working with Refugees*. New York: Center for Migration Studies, 1986.

Rose, Walter R. *A Bibliography of the Irish in the United States*. Afton, N.Y.: Tristram Shandy, 1969.

Roucek, Joseph S., and Patricia N. Pinkham. *American Slavs: A Bibliography*. New York: Bureau of Intercultural Education, 1944.

Russo, Pietro. *The Italian American Periodical Press, 1836–1980*. New York: Center for Migration Studies, forthcoming.

Saito, Shiro. *Filipinos Overseas: A Bibliography*. New York: Center for Migration Studies, 1977.

Schelbert, Leo. "Swiss Migration to the Territory of the United States: A Historiographical Introduction." *Immigration History Newsletter* 14 (Nov. 1982): 1–5.

Silverman, Jason H. "Writing Southern Ethnic History: An Historiographical Investigation." *Immigration History Newsletter* 19 (May 1987): 1–4.

Simon, Rita J. *Public Opinion and the Immigrant: Print Media Coverage, 1880–1980*. Lexington, Mass.: Lexington Books, 1985.

Singerman, Robert. "The American-Jewish Press, 1823–1983: A Bibliographic Survey of Research and Studies." *American Jewish History* 73 (June 1984): 422–444.

Social Science Education Consortium. *Materials and Human Resources for Teaching Ethnic Studies: An Annotated Bibliography*. Boulder, Colo.: 1975.

Sorrell, Richard S. "The Historiography of French Canadians." *Immigration History Newsletter* 11 (May 1979): 1–6.

Stein, Barry N. "Refugee Research Bibliography." *International Migration Review* 15 (Spring/Summer 1981): 331–393.

Swierenga, Robert P. "Dutch Immigration Historiography." *Immigration History Newsletter* 11 (Nov. 1979): 1–9.

Taravella, Louis, and Graziano Tassello. *Les Femmes Migrantes: Bibliographie Internationale, 1965–1982*. Roma: Centro Studi Emigrazione, 1983.

Thernstrom, Stephan, ed. *Harvard Encyclopedia of American Ethnic Groups*. Cambridge, Mass.: Harvard University Press, 1980.

Tolzmann, Don H. *German-Americana: A Bibliography*. Metuchen, N.J.: Scarecrow Press, 1975.

Tomasi, Lydio F., ed. *Defense of the Alien*. Vols. 1–8. New York: Center for Migration Studies, 1978–1985. (*Proceedings* of the Annual National Legal Conference on Immigration and Refugee Policy sponsored by the Center for Migration Studies.)

Tomasi, Silvano M., and Edward C. Stibili. *Italian Americans and Religion: An Annotated Bibliography*. New York: Center for Migration Studies, 1978.

Vivó, Paquita. *The Puerto Ricans: An Annotated Bibliography*. New York: R. R. Bowker, 1973.

Vlachas, Evangelos. *An Annotated Bibliography of Greek Migration*. Athens: Social Sciences Centre, 1966.

Vollmar, Edward R. *The Catholic Church in America: An Historical Bibliography*. 2d ed. New York: Scarecrow Press, 1963.

Wasserman, Paul, and Jean Morgan. *Ethnic Information Sources of the United States*. 2d ed. Detroit: Gale Research Co., 1984.

Weed, Perry L. *Ethnicity and American Group Life: A Bibliography*. New York: Institute of Human Relations, 1972.

Wertsman, Vladimir. *Romanians in the United States: A Guide to Information Sources*. Detroit: Gale Research Co., 1980.

White, Joseph M. "Historiography of Catholic Immigrants and Religion." *Immigration History Newsletter* 14 (Nov. 1982): 5–11.

Wolkovich-Valkavicius, William. "Toward a Historiography of Lithuanian Immigrants to the United States." *Immigration History Newsletter* 15 (Nov. 1983): 7–10.

Wynar, Lubomyr R. *Encyclopedic Directory of Ethnic Newspapers and Periodicals in the United States*. 2d ed. Littleton, Colo.: Libraries Unlimited, 1976.

_____. *Encyclopedic Directory of Ethnic Organizations in the United States*. Littleton, Colo.: Libraries Unlimited, 1975.

_____. *Guide to the American Ethnic Press: Slavic and East European Newspapers and Periodicals*. Kent, Ohio: Center for the Study of Ethnic Publications, Kent State University, 1987.

_____, and Lois Buttlar. *Guide to Ethnic Museums, Libraries and Archives in the United States*. Preliminary edition. Kent, Ohio: Program for the Study of Ethnic Publications, Kent State University: School of Library Science, 1978.

Zurawski, Joseph W. *Polish American History and Culture: A Classified Bibliography*. Chicago: Polish Museum of America, 1975.